Revolutionary Ideas

Revolutionary Ideas

AN INTELLECTUAL HISTORY
OF THE FRENCH REVOLUTION
FROM *THE RIGHTS OF MAN*
TO ROBESPIERRE

Jonathan Israel

Princeton University Press
Oxford & Princeton

Copyright © 2014 by Princeton University Press
Published by Princeton University Press, 41 William Street, Princeton,
New Jersey 08540
In the United Kingdom: Princeton University Press, 6 Oxford Street,
Woodstock, Oxfordshire OX20 1TW

press.princeton.edu

Frontispiece: The unity and indivisibility of the Republic, 1793. Image
courtesy Bibliothèque nationale de France.

Jacket illustration: Allegorical emblem of Republic Fasces topped by Cap of
Liberty and ribbands with legend, "Liberty, Fraternity, Egality, or Death."
French Revolution 1789, contemporary popular colored print. Courtesy
Image Asset Management Ltd. / Superstock.

LIBRARY OF CONGRESS CATALOGING-IN-PUBLICATION DATA
Israel, Jonathan.
Revolutionary ideas : an intellectual history of the French Revolution from
the Rights of Man to Robespierre / Jonathan Israel.
pages cm
Includes bibliographical references and index.
ISBN 978-0-691-15172-4 (hardcover : alk. paper) 1. France—History—
Revolution, 1789-1799—Causes. 2. France—History—Revolution,
1789-1799—Historiography. 3. France—Intellectual life—18th century. 4.
Revolutionaries—France—History—18th century. I. Title.
DC147.8.I87 2014
944.04—dc23
2013018208

British Library Cataloging-in-Publication Data is available

This book has been composed in Garamond Pro and Pastonchi

Printed on acid-free paper ∞

Printed in the United States of America

1 3 5 7 9 10 8 6 4 2

Contents

Figures

Acknowledgments

In writing any work of scholarship, one incurs a large number of debts. For vigorously debating the themes of this book with me, I would like especially to thank Peter Campbell, Aurelian Craiutu, David Bell, Jeremy Popkin, Ouzi Elyada, Harvey Chisick, Steven Lukes, Nadia Urbinati, David Bates, Pasquale Pasquino, Bill Doyle, Helena Rosenblatt, Bill Sewell, and Keith Michael Baker. For unflagging and invaluable help with the bibliography, finding eighteenth-century texts, obtaining the illustrations, and checking details, my thanks are due especially to Maria Tuya, Terrie Bramley, and Sarah Rich. I was hugely helped at the last stage also by my copy editor at Princeton University Press, Cathy Slovensky. In addition, a special debt of gratitude is owed by me to the library staff at the Institute for Advanced Study, Princeton, and to the Institute itself for being supportive in every respect and in every way an optimal place to reflect on historical research and debate, and to think and write to the best of one's ability.

Finally, for immense and unstinting assistance throughout with editing, checking, and helping to finalize the text (as well as putting up uncomplainingly with my endless talk about the Revolution and its personalities in recent years), it is a particular pleasure to add that I owe a very great deal, more than I can possibly say, to my wife, Annette Munt.

Revolutionary Ideas

Prologue

On November 18, 1792, more than one hundred British, Americans, and Irish in Paris gathered at White's Hotel, also known as the British Club, to celebrate the achievements of the French Revolution. While in general British opinion, encouraged by the London government and most clergy, remained intensely hostile to the Revolution, much of the intellectual and literary elite of Britain, the United States, and Ireland was immensely, even ecstatically, enthusiastic about those achievements and determined to align with the Revolution. Although the later renowned feminist Mary Wollstonecraft only arrived at White's shortly afterward—and Coleridge, during the 1790s, another fervent supporter of the new revolutionary ideology, was absent—those attending formed an impressive group. Present were Tom Paine, author of the *Rights of Man* (1791); the American radical and poet Joel Barlow; several other poets, including Helen Maria Williams, Robert Merry, and possibly Wordsworth;[1] the Unitarian minister and democrat David Williams, author of the *Letters on Political Liberty* (1782); a former member of Parliament for Colchester, Sir Robert Smyth; the Scots colonel John Oswald; the American colonel Eleazar Oswald; and the Irish lord Edward Fitzgerald. It was a sharp reminder that, leaving aside Gibbon and Edmund Burke, distinguished and politically aware British, American, and Irish intellectuals, poets, and authors, like their German and Dutch counterparts at that time, mostly endorsed and applauded the Revolution.

The president of the British Club in Paris at the time was John Hurford Stone (1763–1818), a former London coal merchant originally from Somerset, and a friend of such leading British democratic reformers as Joseph Priestley and Richard Price (both great enthusiasts for the French Revolution). Hurford Stone had settled in Paris where he owned a chemical works and a printing press with which he produced materialist and antitheological texts, including those of Paine and Barlow. He was a close ally of both Paine and Barlow, the latter a Yale graduate, some editions of whose vast American epic, *The Vision of Columbus*, were published on Stone's press in Paris. Paine and Barlow believed the American Revolution had not gone far enough and that far more was needed if democracy and emancipation were to be genuinely achieved in the United States. Both men, like Stone and the others, were not only directly involved in French Revolution politics but at that stage hoped that the United States and Britain, as well as Continental Europe—indeed, the entire world—would learn and borrow much from the French Revolution.[2]

The high point of the daylong banquet on 18 November 1792, to which delegations from several other nations were also invited, was sixteen toasts: the first, to the French Republic embodying the Rights of Man (here the trumpets of the German band played the famous revolutionary tune "Ça Ira"); the second, to the armies of France ("may the example of her citizen soldiers be followed by all enslaved nations until all tyranny and all tyrants are destroyed"; the German band played the recently composed "Marseillaise," soon to be proclaimed the Republic's official national anthem); the third, to the achievements of the French National Convention; and the fourth, to the coming constitutional Convention of Britain and Ireland. Here came a hint of the club's subversive intent, as it agreed not just that Ireland had been unjustly "enslaved" by England but that Britain too needed a democratic revolution akin to that in France.

The fifth toast was raised to the perpetual union of the peoples of Britain, France, America, and the Netherlands: "may these soon bring other emancipated nations into their democratic alliance"; the sixth, to the prompt abolition in Britain of "all hereditary titles and feudal distinctions." This toast was proposed by Sir Robert Smyth (1744–1802), former MP for Colchester, and Lord Edward Fitzgerald (1763–98), a dashing Irish noble and friend of Paine who held the rank of major in the British army and later became a principal plotter in the United Irishmen Conspiracy of 1796–98. Fitzgerald's and Smyth's total repudiation of aristocracy was greeted with outrage in England when reported in the papers soon afterward, leading to the former being cashiered from the British army and the latter being firmly ostracized.[3] On the eve of the Irish uprising of 1798 (which was vigorously suppressed amid terrible slaughter), Fitzgerald was killed in a fray with British officers who broke into his Dublin lodgings to arrest him.

The seventh toast was "To the ladies of Britain and Ireland" and especially those distinguished by their writings supporting the French Revolution, notably Charlotte Smith, authoress of *Desmond* (1792),[4] a recently published pro-Revolution novel, and Helen Maria Williams. Half Scottish and half Welsh, Williams was Hurford Stone's lover and with him presided over the Paris British Club, in effect a salon where British and American radicals like Paine, Barlow, and Eleazar Oswald conferred and met with members of the Brissot circle, their French allies, who then constituted the republican leadership of the Revolution. In Paris since July 1790, Williams had become internationally known for her volumes of poems and essays, *Letters from France* (1790). These made her, after Paine, possibly the single most important writer in English supporting the Revolution. For this she was virulently denounced in Britain as an unashamed agitator and democrat who also violated conventional female propriety.

Like the French feminist Olympe de Gouges, Helen Maria Williams (1762–1827) was strongly committed to democracy and black emancipation, as well as women's rights. Like Olympe de Gouges, Mary Wollstonecraft, and other outstanding feminists of the Revolution such as Etta Palm d'Aelders—and indeed nearly all the principled, high-minded, and aware writers, intellectuals, and commentators in France, Germany, Holland, and Britain—she was passionately opposed to Robespierre and his herald, Marat. Like Paine, Barlow, Hurford Stone, Coleridge, and Wordsworth, she viewed Robespierre not as the culmination but as the undoing and ruin of the Revolution. This attitude landed her (as well as Paine and Palm) in prison during the Terror, and led to Olympe de Gouges, the most outspoken of those demanding woman's liberation (and denouncing Robespierre as a scoundrel), being guillotined. This seventh toast constituted an inherent part of the feminist movement established by these remarkable women. So did the eighth toast: "to the women of France," especially those bearing arms to defend liberty's cause, such as Mademoiselles Anselme and Fernig, female officers in the entourage of the commander of the revolutionary army in Belgium who later attempted to form a female army contingent called the "Fernig corps." Few men at the time took the idea of women's army units seriously, but John Oswald, Scots officer, editor, and apostle for vegetarianism, strongly advocated the use of women's contingents and made other innovative suggestions as to precisely how to form the world's first democratic army.

Toasted next were the heralds and champions of the Rights of Man, who, via their writings, formed the Revolution's avant-garde, formulating and propagating its essential principles. These were listed as "Condorcet, Brissot, Sieyès, Carra, Kersaint, Louvet, Gorsas, Audouin, etc. . . ."[5] Condorcet, among the principal revolutionary leaders, was also one of the most radical philosophes and, like Sieyès and Brissot, a vigorous exponent of human rights, republican constitutional theory, black emancipation, women's rights, and educational reform. The authentic Revolution, this ninth toast proclaimed, the revolution based on democracy and human rights, was principally the work of this mix of philosophes and radical-minded newspaper editors. To leaders of the British Club, the true revolution, that precious to all humanity, stood in stark contrast to the populist authoritarianism of Marat and Robespierre embodied in the Jacobin faction known as the Montagne, which (except for John Oswald) they rejected unreservedly. For opposing the Montagne, Brissot, Gorsas, Kersaint, and Carra, among the Revolution's preeminent journalists and orators, were all guillotined during the Terror, while Condorcet was proscribed and hounded to death. Louvet, among the Montagne's fiercest detractors, only narrowly survived.

The tenth toast was to the French revolutionary generals, the eleventh to the local democratic clubs active throughout France, and also in Belgium, Britain, the French-occupied Rhineland, and Ireland, and the twelfth, proposed by Hurford Stone (also imprisoned during the Terror), was to Tom Paine and "his novel method of making good books known to the public" via royal prohibitions and prosecution of authors, an allusion to the British government's fierce suppression of Paine's writings, especially his internationally famous *The Rights of Man* (1791). Toast thirteen was to all other "Patriots of England" who by their speeches and writings spread the principles of the French and "the General Revolution"—Priestley, Price, Sheridan, Barlow, Thomas Cooper (leader of the radical reform society of Manchester), Tooke, and Mackintosh. Number fourteen eagerly anticipated the "dissolution of the German empire" and its replacement with democratic republics that would enable Germany's inhabitants to live in freedom. Toast fifteen, on a more humorous note, expressed the wish that the republican tunes of the Légion Germanique might soon become the favorite marching music of the British army.

Finally, on an unreservedly serious note, number sixteen was to *la paix universelle* (perpetual peace).[6] Although most outside observers, then as now, deemed the idea of perpetual peace among peoples a hopelessly utopian mirage, sheer nonsense, this concept had become a central theme of radical thought since the 1770s. Diderot, Raynal, d'Holbach, Cerisier, Paine, and others—and lately, with special emphasis, also Volney in his *Les Ruines* (1791)—argued that if the majority of people ever ceased to be the prey of ruling elites and vested interests; if government was no longer controlled by kings, aristocrats, or narrow oligarchies but genuinely pursued the interest of society as a whole; if all nations became representative democracies; if (non-Rousseauist) *volonté générale* became actual and universal, then there would be no more wars. It was an appealing argument.[7]

CHAPTER 1

Introduction

French Society in 1789

Historians working on the French Revolution have a problem. All of our attempts to find an explanation in terms of social groups or classes, or particular segments of society becoming powerfully activated, have fallen short. As one expert aptly expressed it: "the truth is we have no agreed general theory of why the French Revolution came about and what it was—and no prospect of one."[1] This gaping, causal void is certainly not due to lack of investigation into the Revolution's background and origins. If class conflict in the Marxist sense has been jettisoned, other ways of attributing the Revolution to social change have been explored with unrelenting rigor. Of course, every historian agrees society was slowly changing and that along with the steady expansion of trade and the cities, and the apparatus of the state and armed forces, more (and more professional) lawyers, engineers, administrators, officers, medical staff, architects, and naval personnel were increasingly infusing and diversifying the existing order.[2] Yet, no major, new socioeconomic pressures of a kind apt to cause sudden, dramatic change have been identified. The result, even some keen revisionists admit, is a "somewhat painful void."[3]

Most historians today claim there was not one big cause but instead numerous small contributory impulses. One historian, stressing the absence of any identifiable overriding cause, likened the Revolution's origins to a "multi-coloured tapestry of interwoven causal factors."[4] Social and economic historians embracing the "new social interpretation" identify a variety of difficulties that might have rendered eighteenth-century French society, at least in some respects, more fraught and vulnerable than earlier. Yet these factors, all marginal when taken individually, hardly suffice to fill the explanatory gap left by the collapse of every general argument, such as the Marxist thesis of class struggle or the once widely held view that impoverishment and falling real wages created a severe subsistence crisis with deteriorating living standards for most. The latter contention, if correct, would assuredly provide a concrete, compelling argumentation, a comprehensive explanation of why a generalized revolt occurred and possibly why so many major changes were subsequently introduced. There would be a clear logic to accepting that the Revolution was a response to misery and deprivation caused by receding living standards. But the evidence shows that no such crisis occurred. Per capita income in France actually grew over the eighteenth century as towns expanded, along with commerce and industry, shipping, and overseas trade. Agriculture prospered. What then moved the French urban affluent, and the urban poor and peasants, usually considered the main active agents of the Revolution?

"The Revolution," affirms our present academic consensus, "had many origins."[5] Losing all prospect of a compelling narrative in terms of social groups and mechanisms, social and economic historians have in recent years focused on the unbalanced character of the general expansion. France's population grew from around twenty-one to twenty-eight million between 1700 and 1800, an increase of roughly one-third. But the accompanying growth in activity and prosperity in the towns outstripped that in the countryside, where 80 percent of the population dwelled. Consequently, agricultural output only just, and only erratically, kept pace. Narrow surpluses in some years alternated with mild or severe shortages in others. Lack of food and intermittent price surges were, of course, nothing new, but they were undoubtedly relevant to shaping the Revolution at crucial moments.[6]

As elsewhere in Europe, the main French cities grew impressively during the eighteenth century, expanding by between a third and a half, with Bordeaux more than doubling to 111,000. Paris swelled by a third, reaching around 650,000.[7] Small towns often increased by more than half. Until 1789, the crafts flourished, especially those producing luxury goods for the wealthy and for export. Real wages rose overall. Nevertheless, most townsfolk remained poor and unskilled and, for many laborers and artisans, combined demographic pressure and uneven economic growth caused real wages to fluctuate during the 1770s and 1780s, with a downward tendency affecting some by perhaps around 10 or 12 percent. Expansion, as frequently happens, occasioned fresh collisions of interest with certain groups losing ground.[8] Some resentment may have been caused by the tax burden on the slowly expanding agricultural sector, taxes on land and food output growing somewhat as a proportion of the whole. The burden on the commerce and crafts generating most of France's growth correspondingly fell slightly. But the imbalance was marginal and developed against a background of prior heavy fiscal over-emphasis on trade and towns so that this change could be viewed more as a corrective than a tangible grievance.[9] If agricultural output represented around two-thirds of the French economy in 1788, land and agriculture still accounted for only 56 percent of royal revenues.

What the "new social interpretation" plainly demonstrates is that there was no major crisis troubling late eighteenth-century French society of the kind apt to generate serious destabilizing discontent across society. Certainly, there was extensive poverty and misery but within an entirely familiar and traditional format. There was a growing affluent urban bourgeoisie, slowly expanding in size, wealth, and ambition, that entered into increasing competition with the privileged elites for government posts, prerogatives, and honors, but both the nobility and these upwardly mobile strands of the bourgeoisie remained politically, socially, culturally, religiously, and, in general outlook, intensely conservative.[10] For the rest, the "new social interpretation" yields only a few relatively minor tensions affecting particular groups. The economic gap between aristocratic bishops and parish curates widened. With the general economic expansion, demand for and ability to pay for ennoblement, dignities, and high office outstripped the rise in prosperity, causing the fortunes of poorer noble families to deteriorate relative to recently ennobled newcomers and possibly a degree of frustration and resentment among the uppermost strata of the mercantile and professional classes, although this is hard to document. In any case, the overall impact of such factors on the Revolution cannot have been great.[11]

The nobility, broadly defined, had long comprised five or six distinct elite strata all continually jostling for power, influence, and advantage. There were the court and higher military nobility, recently ennobled wealthy bourgeois (the *annoblis*), municipal oligarchies, the episcopate, the often quite poor rural gentry, and the noblesse de robe, or urban judicial aristocracy staffing the country's regional high courts (*parlements*). But none of these fissures presented anything at all new. Claiming "multiple, overlapping origins of the French Revolution" may initially sound promising but proves inadequate when all the factors identified are too long-standing, slow-moving, marginal, and insufficiently specific to apply convincingly to the actual political clashes, crises, and debates driving the Revolution. In any case, how economic and other material factors could directly cause such a dramatic shift, as the

Revolution rapidly entailed, to democracy, freedom of thought, expression, and the press, human rights, secularism, sexual liberation, gender and racial emancipation, individual liberty, and equality before the law, no one can really say. "The prime defect of the revisionist accounts," as one historian relevantly remarked, "has been their failure to offer a plausible alternative to the Marxist version."[12]

At most, the "new social explanation" authorizes us to claim that "what pushed the Revolution forward was the willingness of disenfranchised robe nobles, alienated parish priests, and ambitious professionals to challenge the old order."[13] But such an explanation, even if possessing a considerable background validity as it does, cannot easily be applied to the revolutionary process itself since none of these groups figured prominently among the revolutionary leadership. By and large, as we shall see, the principal organizers, spokesmen, and publicists of the factions that forged the great changes of the Revolution in legislation, institutions, and practices prior to Robespierre's coup d'état in June 1793 were not robe nobles, parish priests, or ambitious professionals. There was never a greater or more rapid transformation in the shape, values, and politics of any society. We can only know for sure that a given factor directly contributed to this vast vortex of change when the evidence of the primary sources proves particular grievances or tensions motivated, inspired, or induced key groups or individuals to initiate the actual transformation of institutions, laws, and culture constituting the Revolution.

Only one major, tangible, material factor directly linked causally to the revolutionary foreground can be pointed to: the royal financial crisis of 1787–89. In terms of timing, the political revolution unquestionably began with the French Crown's chronic financial difficulties of the mid- and later 1780s and the ensuing attempts at fiscal reform. In 1787, faced by overwhelming deficits made worse by feverish speculation in French government bonds on the international market, Louis XVI was forced into political moves that eventually triggered the revolutionary process. From the Crown's (and soon also the aristocracy's) standpoint, matters spun out of control under the energetic reforming minister Charles-Alexandre de Calonne (1734–1802), a high official and robe noble of the *parlement* of Douai, who by trying to tackle the deficits destabilized first the monarchy and then the country. "O my dear Calonne!" mocked one of the most republican-minded of the young revolutionaries of the years 1788–89, Camille Desmoulins, later Danton's right-hand man.[14] But even fully allowing for the gravity of the financial crisis and Calonne's errors, neither the subsequent breakdown of government nor, still less, the vast revolutionary process that followed are really explained by it.

How and why Calonne's abortive reform program, designed to remodel the ancien régime monarchy on the basis of new taxes, including a universal land tax, while fully accommodating the existing elites, turned into a broad-based campaign to emasculate the Crown, suppress all the country's pre-1789 institutions and obliterate nobility, clergy, and the noblesse de robe (judicial aristocracy), has never been adequately explained, and cannot be in terms of financial factors or the wider economic context. About this there is a remarkable consensus. Even those stressing the financial crisis most concur that in itself the king's financial predicament does little to dispel what some historians, in evident frustration, have called the "mystery" of the Revolution's origins and subsequent course.[15] "Why did an apparently traditional fiscal crisis engender the massive transformation of an entire social order?"[16]

Today scholars abandoning economic interest—class, class struggle, and economically defined social groups—as the key to unraveling the Revolution often seek a more sociocultural form of explanation, basing their interpretation on changes in cultural context, identifying elaborate networks and changing patterns of human relationships, and especially examining "fields of discourse," along with their attached ceremonies and symbols. This intense preoccupation with "discourse" has proved extremely valuable in providing background, and assumes several forms. One useful approach invokes "an enlarged and renovated public sphere of sociability and debate" that created a wider arena of action for "professionals."[17] This line of investigation builds on what we know of the expansion of elites in pre-1789 France and locates the Revolution's chief motor in a mix of lawyers, medical men, and other professionals closely tied through their occupations to the urban market and other social groups. There was, undeniably, a strikingly high proportion of lawyers, more than three hundred in the National Assembly in 1789 and subsequently.

But however helpful such research is, it does no more than enrich the background: there is little sign lawyers played a particularly significant role in forging the democratic Revolution prior to Robespierre's takeover. Rather, as one would perhaps expect, lawyers and other professionals mostly preferred to stick to existing norms and were conspicuously absent among the orators, publicists, editors, and political leaders dominating the committees and shaping revolutionary legislation before 1793. If focusing on "professionals" tells us little about the main actors in the Revolution, even more unhelpful is focusing on the attitudes of entrepreneurs and men of business. In the capital, as in the great ports—Bordeaux, Nantes, Marseilles, and Saint-Malo—merchants and bankers mostly avoided involvement with the Revolution, remaining as politically neutral as possible. Thus, a wide variety of different social groups subscribed to pro-Revolution newspapers from 1789, but the subscription lists show that the proportion of their regular readership consisting of businessmen was strikingly low compared to other groups, virtually negligible.[18]

Admittedly, for historians subscribing to a brand of "revisionism," popular in the 1980s and 1990s, our apparent inability to find a "major cause" scarcely matters. Perhaps great new developments in history do not have "big" causes. Some argue that the English Revolution of the seventeenth century demonstrates that great changes can follow from relatively small and insignificant causes. Arguably, the true interpretation of the French Revolution is precisely that there is no overarching, grand interpretation, a suggestion that strongly appeals to some philosophers as well as historians.[19] But the French Revolution was a rupture with the past so complete and dramatic, the scale of the departure from ancien régime society, culture, and politics so total and far-reaching, the transformation so foundational for subsequent Western and eventually also non-Western developments in the nineteenth and twentieth centuries, that arguing there was no major social structural cause—only a tableau of, in themselves, relatively minor ones—is not just unconvincing, it is not even remotely plausible.

The reconstitution of the legal, religious, educational, cultural, and political foundations of French society, along with the general emancipation of all minorities and the abolition of slavery, were interlinked, simultaneous, and comprehensive. The Revolution denied the validity of ideas, customs, institutions, or laws inherited from the past absolutely and totally. Furthermore, this undeviating repudiation and discrediting of all previously accepted values, moral codes, laws, and practices transpired with astounding speed between 1788 and 1793, despite being opposed or uncomprehendingly regarded by most of the population and even most of the National Assembly. Indeed, the transformation occured despite a lack of popular support for many key changes, such as giving equal rights to Protestants, civil divorce, suppressing the old regional high courts or parlements, emancipation of the Jews, ending the slave trade, and abolishing the old provinces—Brittany, Normandy, Provence, Alsace, and Languedoc—with their separate identities and privileges.

A reexamination of the actual leadership of the Revolution seems called for as a way to build on the emerging sociocultural approach, and, especially, more effectively integrate social history with intellectual history. This present study attempts to establish new empirical findings by quarrying the main primary sources, above all, the amazingly detailed record of the debates in the successive French national assemblies that spoke for the Revolution, the corpus known as the *Archives Parlementaires*. Consulted together with other key records of decisions and debates, such as the discussions in the Paris city government and records of the meetings of the Jacobin Club, much of it verbatim, the debates in the legislature provide a solid basis for reconsideration. Additional light emerges from the extraordinarily rich contemporary newspaper coverage for the years down to 1793, and then again from 1795 to 1800. All this material takes on a new significance once the socioeconomic assumptions that steered research for so long are set aside, and the sociocultural approach is combined with the lessons of intellectual history.

The Revolution's preoccupation with laying down fundamental new guidelines not only helps define its significance but also delimits its beginning and end. The Revolution was above all a process of emancipation, democratization, and fundamental renewal on the basis of human rights—ruthlessly interrupted in 1793–94 and progressively aborted in 1799–1804. The epoch-making egalitarian, libertarian, and democratic ideals of 1789 were rendered moribund, at least in terms of immediately forseeable possibilities, politics, and international relations, when the Life Consulate, embodied in the Constitution of the Year X, assigned unlimited dictatorial powers to Napoleon on 3 August 1802. This finally terminated the tumultuous search for fundamental new criteria and categories that had previously gripped France for fourteen years. Breaking with the Revolution, Napoleon first imposed a qualified amnesty allowing émigré nobles living outside France to return and, in April 1802, a comprehensive amnesty, permitting all but members of the royal family and the most committed counterrevolutionaries to reintegrate.

Freedom of the press and expression, even if sorely dented between 1789 and 1799 at times, was not finally suppressed until 1799–1800. Until 1799, press freedom always remained an intensely live issue and immediate possibility, and much of the time it was a reality. The universal principle of equality embraced in competing ways by all ruling factions between 1789 and 1799 was only finally discarded as the basis of citizenship and men's rights with the new Constitution of 1799. This also discarded the Declaration of the Rights of Man, which in successive formulations had been fundamental to the Revolution throughout the momentous years from 1789 to 1799. Linked to this, black slavery, abolished by the Revolution in principle in 1794, was reintroduced by Napoleon in 1802. The Napoleonic regime fell back on a quasi-hierarchical vision of society, fostering a new ruling elite comprised of a mix of recently elevated notables and rehabilitated old nobles. Likewise, from 1802, most revolutionary innovations in marriage and family law were canceled. Under the new civil code of 1804, woman's legal subordination to her husband within marriage and subordination to paternal authority before marriage were reaffirmed. The 1804 code replaced the Revolution's incipient gender equality with an openly discriminatory double standard for processing adultery suits, applications for divorce, and property rights.[20] However, the circumstances driving these setbacks to basic human rights—the postrevolutionary regime's unrelenting authoritarianism, Napoleon's overweening personal authority, and rejection of the legislature's supremacy over the executive and the judicial arm—all commenced with the new Constitution of 1799. Effectively, this marked the end of the Revolution.

That the Revolution ended with Napoleon's rise to dictatorial power is also reflected by developments in religion. Before 1788, church and state in France, as everywhere in Europe, were closely intertwined. During the Revolution this pattern was fundamentally transformed in stages. Stripped of all political and legislative authority, the Church also suffered expropriation of its lands and revenues by the state. A comprehensive religious toleration prevailed (except under the Terror during 1793–94) and Catholicism was no longer the authorized, public church. The state as such, and in intention also public education, became essentially secular. However, this bitter struggle between revolution and religious authority ceased after 1800, and at Easter 1802 Napoleon, as First Consul, formally ended the rift between France and the papacy by restoring the old episcopate and recognizing its power to appoint and control the lower clergy and exercise an unhindered spiritual authority over French Catholics and much of primary education.

Contemporary Interpretations

Thus, both the "new social interpretation" and the sociocultural approach enrich our understanding of the Revolution's social background without identifying any single dramatic factor that can be highlighted. A basket of gradual and relatively minor economic, social, and cultural factors, such as those identified by the new socioeconomic and sociocultural methods, certainly provides valuable background but cannot explain why French society, politics, and institutions came to be transformed suddenly and dramatically in every way, why all precedent and tradition were systematically uprooted. Far more exceptional and specific factors *must* be adduced to account for the overthrow of this vast edifice of conservative thought, practice, and ancien régime institutions. Between 1788 and 1820, the most common explanation of the French Revolution both in France and outside was, overwhelmingly, that it originated in "philosophy." Contemporaries recognized that discontent and social frustration fueled the unrest once the body politic was plunged into turmoil and instability, helping make the Revolution possible, but also clearly understood that social tensions by no means determined its character, course, and outcome. The people's exasperation merely helped *l'esprit philosophique*, as Jacques Necker (1732–1804), Louis XVI's chief minister in 1789, called it, to assume command of the discontent and convert it to its own purposes. This was the general view, so commonplace in fact that its cultural implications urgently need to be explored. The question is: Was this assumption prevailing throughout the revolutionary era actually correct?[21]

Not only did radically new concepts "capture" the unrest, but from the summer of 1788, l'esprit philosophique, held Necker, daily extended its conquests, exploiting old grievances and causing "all the insurrections against received ideas and commonly accepted truths." The institutions and laws that had previously been accepted by practically everyone came to be challenged, scorned, and overthrown, not by the people or France's elites but by an unrepresentative fringe. During the decades preceding the Revolution, explained Necker—who despite exalting "virtue" and wanting to help mold a happier and better society had also earlier attacked l'esprit philosophique in his book *De l'importance des opinions religieuses* (1788)—l'esprit philosophique first corrupted all sense of duty by assailing religion and then broke all constraints by wrongly reworking the principles of morality and politics, substituting an exaggerated notion of liberty for the wisdom of limits and fomenting the confusion spread by the idea of "equality" in place of the traditional hierarchical conception of society headed by aristocracy, which obliterated the "prudentes gradations" composing the social order.[22]

Admittedly, strikingly few philosophes or enlighteners figured in the Estates-General of 1789. Most committed "Enlightenment" candidates in the 1789 elections were unable to get elected. Condorcet, soon among the foremost architects of the Revolution, failed to be elected as a deputy.[23] Sieyès only just scraped in. The Royal Academy astronomer Jean-Sylvain Bailly (1736–93) *was* elected, but his election was highly exceptional, he explained, since "a great disfavor [prevailed] in the electoral assembly for the men of letters and *académiciens*." Though more esprit philosophique would have helped the Estates, in Bailly's opinion, most of the college of electors, being merchants and lawyers, displayed a marked antipathy to philosophes. (Condorcet was almost as suspicious of the lawyers and merchants as he was of the nobility.) At Lyon, too, records one of the Revolution's great personalities, Mme. Roland, the "commercially minded" showed great aversion to philosophy and those ardent for the Revolution. Only about ten members out of the twelve hundred Estates-General deputies of 1789 could be described, like Mirabeau and Sieyès, as philosophes in the Enlightenment sense. But this acute paucity of intellectuals in the Estates of 1789 makes it all the more extraordinary and astounding that precisely this group, both inside and outside the Estates, could so swiftly come to dominate the revolutionary leadership in the National Assembly and its guiding committees, as well as (initially) the Paris municipality and practically all of the influential pro-Revolution papers.[24]

"Before it was made into law," affirmed Pierre-Louis Roederer (1754–1835), a prominent revolutionary leader from Lorraine, the "Revolution was made in men's minds and habits."[25] How and why? Because the great revolutionary principles and enactments—abolition of aristocracy and eventually the use of all aristocratic titles, equality before the law, democracy, press freedom, equality of all cults and their separation from the state, the Rights of Man (1789), civil divorce (1792), the suppression of monarchy (1792), and the abolition of slavery (1794)—were all manifestly saturated in Enlightenment language, debates, and philosophical categories. A "revolution of ideas" was necessary before there could be a revolution of fact, agreed Dominique Joseph Garat (1749–1833), a revolutionary leader from the southwest, and did actually occur from the 1740s down to 1789. It paved the way for the "revolution of events" and was its motor and shaping force.[26]

Like virtually all major participants, Camille Desmoulins (1760–94), son of a Picard local official and one of Danton's closest advisers, held that "the people" certainly played a large part but needed to be led, identifying "ce siècle de lumières" (this century of Enlightenment)—the "most beautiful monument that philosophy and patriotism had bequeathed to humanity"—as the Revolution's true inspiration. "Philosophy," he believed, was the chief agent of the Revolution.[27] In the years immediately before the Revolution, discerning observers stressed, the general intellectual context was dramatically transformed by a torrent of new philosophy. Often the particular revolutionary ideas disseminated on the eve of 1788 seemed too familiar and too obvious to require detailed explanation. "Today with Rousseau, Price, Helvétius 'entre les mains de tout le monde' [in everyone's hands],"commented Brissot in 1786, there was no longer any need to explain to readers the main themes of their writings.[28]

Of course, the vast majority had not read any philosophes and were hardly equipped to do so. But most people participating in the great mass movements of the Revolution were less the agent of revolution, suggested Desmoulins, than the Revolution's prime obstacle. In his seminal pamphlet *La France libre* (1789), he claims that the nobility and clergy held their dominant position in pre-1789 French ancien régime society not because they had forcibly conquered this right and appropriated their privileges but because the ancien régime social order had long endured with the "consent" of the vast majority.[29] He and the rest of the democratic revolutionary leadership of 1788–89, like the radical philosophes earlier, considered this broad, popular acquiescence a gigantic edifice of ignorance and superstition, an obstruction to be cleared away as fast as possible. Opponents of the Revolution, and nearly all merchants, lawyers, and other professionals, abhorred Desmoulins's irreverent republican standpoint. Yet, strikingly, whatever their views, nearly everyone agreed that *la philosophie* was the principal factor undermining the foundations of French society and the legitimacy of its moral code and religion, and shaping the new order. The people had been on the right path before, held those opposing the Revolution, but in their simplicity were now disastrously misled by a handful of republican militants like Desmoulins, inspired by la philosophie.

Virtually all highly educated observers identified the Revolution's chief cause as *cette grande révolution morale* (this great moral revolution), as it was called by Pierre-Louis Ginguené (1748–1816), an ardent Rousseauist republican imprisoned during the Terror.[30] Father Claude Fauchet (1744–93), among those most eager to combine revolutionary ideology with Catholicism (until guillotined in 1793), considered France in the 1780s to be split between two vast cultural forces—solid tradition and religion on one side (the France of the great majority) and la philosophie on the other. In his view, France in 1789 really comprised two nations: those bending to ecclesiastical authority and the confessional and those inspired by the *Encyclopédie*. One side admired political economy and Rousseau's *Social Contract*, the other monarchy, bishops, and consecrated authority. This both caused and shaped the Revolution. Fauchet did his best to rise above this division, rebuking both sides. A sincere Catholic of a most unusual kind, he believed that religion teaches men the deepest truths. It was divine Providence that brought the French people to the threshold of liberty in 1788. But Christians must accept, he added, that Christianity does not demonstrate the correct way to organize society and politics in accordance with liberty, equality, and truth. Providence prepared the ground but "philosophy was the actual instrument of Providence in bringing about this marvel" that "filled our minds with ideas of liberty, inflamed hearts and enlivened courage."[31]

Among the best-known antiphilosophes, the ex-Jesuit Luxembourgois, François-Xavier de Feller (1735–1802), dubbed this world conspiracy, as he saw it, "l'empire du philosophisme." *Philosophisme*, he explained, was a mighty construct begun in the 1740s by a group of extraordinary writers who managed to impress sections of all classes with their wit and sarcasm, devising a whole new language and way of thinking, and by cunning dexterity and obscure use of terms made their ruinous ideas seem "sublime" to many. The "conspiracy" commenced with Diderot, who turned the *Encyclopédie* into an engine of subversion and impiety. All the chief conspirators were, like Diderot and d'Alembert, atheistic "parasites" who lounged in cafés, insinuating, flattering, and mocking their way to domination of the salons and academies, and who eventually conquered positions of great power. Among their chief weapons, suggested Feller, was their appeal to women, especially young, pretty women susceptible to fine phrases, elegant turns of speech, witticisms, and subtle and less-than-subtle erotic suggestion.[32]

But the claim that philosophisme as such caused the Revolution remains too vague to serve as a useful explanatory tool. The philosophie that most writers, including the Counter-Enlightenment antiphilosophes, considered the Revolution's prime cause embraced virtually the entire Enlightenment. But ascribing the Revolution to an undifferentiated *philosophie moderne* undermined their case by being too sweeping and too general. They failed to focus on the particular current embodying the main revolutionary tendency. This was pointed out by various contemporary observers, often political and Enlightenment moderates like the young revolutionary leader Antoine-Pierre-Joseph-Marie Barnave (1761–93) and the celebrated legal reformer Jean-Étienne Portalis (1745–1807). L'esprit philosophique was the Revolution's principal cause, agreed Barnave and Portalis, but it was not Enlightenment philosophy generally, only a certain kind of philosophy, that was responsible. The real agent was the radical current that rejected Locke and Montesquieu, which was promoted by Denis Diderot (1713–84), Claude-Adrien Helvétius (1715–71), and Paul-Henri-Thiry, Baron d'Holbach (1723–89).[33] Portalis, like the journalist Jacques Mallet du Pan (1749–1800), believed thoroughgoing legal and penal reform in Europe could have been accomplished by the moderate Enlightenment, by kings and courts, without any revolution and without adopting the radical systems Mallet dubbed *la philosophie de Paris,* which they all deemed the root of the Revolution.[34]

Exactly this same insistence on the need to distinguish between moderate and materialist-revolutionary philosophy recurs in another well-known late eighteenth-century writer, Jean-François de La Harpe (1739–1803). La Harpe first ardently supported and then later, after the Terror, equally fervently repudiated the Revolution. What exactly is the philosophy that caused the Revolution, asked La Harpe in 1797? A Parisian-born foundling of unknown parentage and recognized philosophe in his own right, La Harpe's perspective is of particular relevance here. Applauded by Portalis among others for disavowing the Revolution and the philosophy that caused it,[35] La Harpe, originally a disciple of Voltaire, had known several leading philosophes personally. His principal work rejecting philosophique and Revolution principles, the two-volume *Philosophie du Dix-Huitième Siècle,* was mostly composed in 1797 while the Revolution was still in full swing. Voltaire, he argued, was the first to emancipate the human mind and render philosophique reason popular with readers. But Voltaire was marginal in terms of the philosophy that caused the Revolution. It is in his long chapter on Diderot that La Harpe chiefly develops his critique of the *secte philosophique.* Here he sought to uncover the intellectual and psychological causes of what he, like the apologists he had once combated, now considered a revolutionary catastrophe.

Primarily responsible, argued La Harpe, were those propagating the doctrines of Diderot, including in one crucial respect Rousseau. For despite the great quarrel that shattered their former friendship, from 1757, the two great thinkers nurtured one particularly subversive political doctrine that Rousseau derived from Diderot, namely, that all the ills and crimes of the world arise not from innate defects of human nature (which both saw as fundamentally good) but from the "radical viciousness" Diderot was the first to see in all existing institutions, systems of government, morality, and society. This was a truly monstrous tenet, held La Harpe after 1794, an absurdity, destroying "all social order among all nations." It stemmed not just from the implacable aversion to all existing authority common to Diderot and Rousseau but also from their fervent conviction that their insights supplied a basis for giving the world an entirely new set of moral rules and laws. There is a direct line, contended La Harpe, connecting Diderot to the Revolution's most socially uncompromising initiatives, including the conspiracy of Babeuf and his followers, crushed by the Directory in 1797.[36]

These two fundamentally opposing tendencies within the Enlightenment, one accepting and the other rejecting the prevailing social and political order, must be the essential starting-point for any valid account of the Revolution. The revolutionary philosophical tendency, acknowledged political leaders belonging to the *parti de philosophie* like Mirabeau, Sieyès, Brissot, Condorcet, Volney, Ginguené, Roederer, and Desmoulins, had absorbed the contributions of many different writers—d'Argenson, Voltaire, Montesquieu, Mably, Diderot, Rousseau, Helvétius, d'Holbach, and Raynal. Brissot also deeply admired the subversive roles of Bayle and Boulanger. Revolutionary leaders construing the Revolution as they did often commented on the various contributions. Thus, Voltaire mattered chiefly for his peerless literary skill and relentless ridiculing of old, established prejudices, for the rest being a friend of kings and aristocrats. Brissot was especially caustic about Voltaire, whom he rightly judged no friend of the people.[37] Montesquieu seasoned the collective philosophical recipe with "salt and energy," commented Roederer; but this great man, being "unfortunate enough" to be a nobleman and *parlementaire* himself, also fell into *des erreurs* regarding social status and "corporations."[38] Rousseau taught readers to think about "les droits des hommes" (the rights of man). A key role in the 1770s and 1780s was afterward widely and correctly ascribed to the subversive group referred to collectively as Raynal, who, unlike the others, directly attacked social oppression and tyranny "armé d'une plume de fer" (armed with a fiery pen).[39] Many also warmly praised Mably's contribution.

Most of the Enlightenment in France and Europe generally was moderate and therefore, in La Harpe's opinion in 1797, good. Only a fringe was sweepingly subversive religiously and politically. Whereas Fontenelle, Montesquieu, Buffon, d'Alembert, and Condillac were true philosophers deservedly exonerated of responsibility for the great catastrophe that engulfed France and Europe, those responsible were the "false philosophers and *sophistes*," the worst, in his opinion, being Diderot, Raynal, Rousseau, Voltaire, and Helvétius. These were the Revolution's true "artisans," the "first and most powerful movers of the frightful *bouleversement*."[40] To Helvétius, whose materialism had, in his view, attracted attention for all the wrong reasons, he dedicated a separate refutation. La Harpe, like Portalis, saw la philosophie moderne as a complex, cumulative corpus of ideas and attitudes reaching back many decades, gradually distilling within itself all the *extravagances* of which the human mind is capable: "By a necessary consequence, the revolution that [subversive philosophy] has caused in our century nurtured all the crimes and ills to which the human species is susceptible."[41]

Whereas the Revolution's supporters conceived la philosophie moderne as the path to universal emancipation and happiness, after 1794 La Harpe located the secte philosophique's revolutionary potential in its having evolved under oppression into an effective bandwagon for attracting all the vain, grudging, and resentful spirits opposing the existing order. Radical Enlightenment, he recognized, was not just the intellectual cauldron of the Revolution but, equally, its principal social and cultural factor, for it was primarily this package of interlinked concepts that channeled, organized, armed, and mobilized the great mass of endemic, long-standing, popular disgruntlement, frustration, resentment, and ambition.[42]

What was Rousseau's role in this revolution of the mind? On the one hand, he was the ubiquitous inspirer of the age. As one perceptive author put it, "every party of the Revolution made some claim on the heritage of Rousseau."[43] An immense variety of participants of varying stripes adored Rousseau, from the celebrated court portraitist Elisabeth Vigée Le Brun (who detested the Revolution) and Fauchet the Catholic revolutionary to Robespierre and Saint-Just, the men who wrecked the Revolution of 1788–93. Rousseau was the surpassing hero simultaneously of the Left and Right, a status no other ideologue ever achieved. Nevertheless, major leaders of the Revolution prior to 1793 remained mostly rather guarded and critical in their assessments of his admittedly massive contribution and some, like Condorcet, barely referred to Rousseau at all. Shortly after the Bastille's fall in July 1789, Mirabeau, who like most radical revolutionaries disparaged Montesquieu in his paper, the *Courrier de Provence,* exalted Rousseau for his central role in preparing the Revolution: never should one speak of liberty and the Revolution without paying homage to this immortal "vengeur de la nature humaine."[44] Among Rousseau's "truths" pronounced truly philosophique by Mirabeau was his doctrine that the social system benefits men only if they all own something and no one possesses too much, a notion dear to Fauchet and many revolutionaries.[45] Yet, there was also a continuous tension between the Rousseauist claim that men should be primarily guided by moral instinct and "feeling," "le sens moral," and the Radical Enlightenment's allegiance to "reason" alone.[46]

Furthermore, the democratic republicans who made the Revolution of 1789–93, or as Mme. Roland expressed it, the "wise men" showing the people the way who "helped them recover their rights" until pushed aside by more ambitious characters who "flatter and delude the people and turn them against their true defenders," objected to major strands of Rousseau's political thought. It was impossible for the republican democrats to embrace Rousseau's stern strictures regarding "representation," his claim that "sovereignty cannot be represented," and extremely difficult to accept his view that republics can be viable only in small countries, that popular piety should be respected (not attacked), and that a measure of book censorship is needed. Very many, like Brissot, disliked Rousseau's aversion to cosmopolitanism, universalism, and the pursuit of universal peace, and like d'Holbach especially despised his veneration of the Spartan martial spirit and the narrow chauvinism his thought appeared to encourage.[47]

This friction between the cosmopolitanism of the parti de philosophie, later taken to its furthest extreme by ideologues like Gorani, Proly, and Cloots, and the narrow patriotism and xenophobia of Robespierre, Saint-Just, and their populist faction, lay at the root of the ceaseless battle waged unremittingly within the Jacobins and throughout the Revolution between the Revolution of Reason and the Revolution of the Will, a tension that needs to be emphasized more than it has been by historians. The uncompromising antilibertarianism, anti-intellectualism, and chauvinism of Robespierre' s Revolution justified itself in large part by appealing to emotional, sentimental aspects of Rousseau, whereas opposing Robespierre's ideology inevitably meant questioning much of Rousseau from the critical perspectives of Diderot, d'Holbach, Helvétius, Naigeon, and Condorcet.[48] Hostility to the secte philosophique during Robespierre's ascendancy intensified, together with rejection of atheism as unpatriotic and contrary to virtue and the ordinary.[49] The institutionalized Rousseauism of the post-1793 (*Robespierriste*) Jacobins was the militant opposite of the Radical Enlightenment guardedness toward Rousseau of Mirabeau, Sieyès, Brissot, Cloots, Volney, Condorcet, and the revolutionary leadership of 1788–93 generally. Here was a clash between two antagonistic, ideological streams pervading the struggle for control of the Revolution's course and direction.

Robespierre identified "atheism"as a defining feature of the radical ideology, republican and democratic, of the parti de philosophie that he overwhelmed. But why did the question of atheism play such a pivotal role in the fight between the Revolution of Reason and the Revolution of the Will, as well as in the battle between Revolution and Counter-Enlightenment? In 1789, after all, the vast majority everywhere in the Western world regarded atheism as "madness," as Desmoulins expressed it, believing it obvious the cosmos was created by God. But what chiefly distinguished the democratic philosophique standpoint from how most men thought, explained Desmoulins, was not their questioning God's existence as such, or the issue of whether or not God created the world, but rather the question of whether and how, if divine Providence exists, it governs the world. The real issue segregating most of society, including Robespierre, from the parti de philosophie that made the Revolution of 1788–93 was whether God is an authority to whom men can appeal. For God offers no sign. He does not show himself. It is in vain, held Desmoulins, that men ask which cult is the most pleasing to him; his natural power revealed in earthquakes, floods, and other calamities wrecks churches no less than mosques or synagogues. Since he manifests the most perfect indifference to which religion men choose and his providence does nothing for Christians or Muslims in preference to others, why not, asked Desmoulins, replace the "dismal" cult the French revered for so many centuries, a faith supportive of the Inquisition, kings, monks, and self-mortification, with a religion of joy, like that of the ancient Greeks, a cult friendly to pleasure, women, and liberty?[50]

Morally and politically, it was urgent that the French should make this substitution, for "the most devout of our kings were the worst." Mirabeau and other philosophes, contended Desmoulins, had wholly disproved claims that monarchical government is the best form of government. Louis XIV was certainly venerated by a horde of flatterers, but in the "eyes of reason" he was a despot, contemptible egoist, bad parent, and abysmal friend and husband. Cruel and vindictive, this "Jesuit king" who loved war was an insane persecutor who used his dragoons forcibly to convert millions of "heretics." To combat tyranny one must combat religious authority together with all conventional notions. If the nobility and clergy resisted the critiques and attacks on monarchy, faith, and hereditary privilege, the rest of society did too. The Revolution had to fight them all.[51]

In 1789, Desmoulins justified imposing Revolution principles on a largely uncomprehending and partly unwilling people, and remaking France's institutions and laws, repudiating all previously accepted laws, on the grounds of *la volonté générale* (the general will). This was a principle locating sovereignty in the people as a whole, defined by what best serves the majority according to "reason" and what people would want if prejudices did not prevent them from actually wanting it,[52] a new principle in political thought devised by a specific group of philosophes beginning in France with Diderot and his circle in the 1740s. These were the thinkers who were rejecting modérantisme, relativism, traditionalism, and enthusiasm for the British model, taught by Montesquieu, Voltaire, and Hume. Society was not created for the misery of the majority or happiness of the few, typically asserts the tract *Vérités philosophiques et patriotiques* (late 1788) by the Norman lawyer Jacques Guillaume Thouret (1746–94); rather, everyone's will is subject to the volonté générale, the common will working for each individual's happiness subsumed within that of all in general.

Deriving from a complex interplay reaching back, underground, over many decades, volonté générale, originally introduced by Diderot, had been vigorously adopted in his sense by d'Holbach, Helvétius, Condorcet, and Volney but adapted to mean something rather different by Rousseau.[53] Intimately entwined with the greatest innovation in political thought of the eighteenth century—the doctrine that sovereignty lies in the people—the term is mostly used in early Revolution debates in its more general, non-Rousseauist sense. Thus, the pending Estates-General, proclaimed Thouret (one of the few lawyers among the revolutionary leadership), must be an assembly based on the volonté générale, meaning the needs and desires of the whole nation with every individual's interest being treated equally. Neither God nor the Church nor any prophet or tradition decreed this. It is stipulated rather by that "eternal reason that regulates the universe," an "eternal reason" that predicted the coming *révolution*.[54] Sieyès, among the Revolution's chief promoters of the doctrine of volonté générale, was especially unsympathetic to Rousseau's inflexion of the concept, most obviously in his views on representation and direct democracy.[55]

Hence, the democratic republican publicists of 1788–93 were summarizers, not innovators. It was not his purpose to say anything new, explained Desmoulins in *La France libre*. An ardent disciple of Rousseau as a young man, Desmoulins, like most key revolutionary leaders, became more critical later. His aim was to expand on the useful things already demonstrated, fanning a fire "happily relit by the flame of philosophy." And what exactly had la philosophie demonstrated? It had proved, averred Desmoulins, that the nobility are the worst of pests, that all the laws of every country needed rewriting, that the monarchical is not the best but the worst form of government, that monks are useless, and that religion is in need of fundamental reform.[56] Kings had turned France into a land of despotism, but even the most downtrodden people produce a few republican-minded souls for whom love of liberty outweighs all existing institutions. Despite the ignorance and prejudice inculcated by religion, "the lies of orators and poets," the eternal eulogies of kingship pronounced by priests, publicists, and "all our books," by 1788 he himself burned with republican ardor impelling him toward liberty. What society needed was not just a republic but a democratic republic: "je me déclare donc hautement pour la démocratie."[57] By displaying ingenuity and constancy in his writings, agreed the long-standing republican Brissot in 1782, the philosophe can conquer "l'opinion publique," and "l'opinion publique" would before long "prove stronger than kings and command the entire universe." The true esprit philosophique, he asserted in 1782, "necessarily brings also *l'esprit républicain*."[58]

Most Frenchmen during the early Revolution assuredly had little thought of rejecting monarchy or embracing revolution. But the "radical" wing of the revolutionary leadership—in sharp contrast to Robespierre and his allies—was already uncompromisingly republican by 1788. To Desmoulins, fighting "error" and "slavery" with philosophy meant replacing the existing legal framework with enlightened laws and an Enlightenment morality, the true sources, as he saw it, of man's future happiness and prosperity. In another early revolutionary democratic pamphlet, *Réflexions d'un philosophe Breton*, of 20 December 1788, by a minor noble and former mayor of Quimper, Augustin Le Goazre de Kervélégan (1748–1825), the "philosopher" summons the Bretons to recover "their rights" by shattering the "humiliating chains" of slavery, whereby nobility and clergy had always oppressed the Third Estate. These "rapacious" orders are here denounced by philosophy, not for overstepping precedent or infringing some privilege but for appropriating "all the advantages of society" for themselves.[59]

Such views explain the highly exceptional cultural and political character of the Revolution—its undeviating resolve to set aside all existing precedents and models. To the revolutionary leadership reorganizing the body politic and society more broadly, there were no grounds for consulting, much less emulating, any earlier or still existing model. "We shall surpass these English," affirmed Kervélégan, "who are so proud of their constitution and so used to insulting our abasement." In fact, the French would eradicate all hereditary nobility, venality of office, purchasing of noble titles for money, hereditary privilege, monopolies, arbitrary arrests, seigneurial jurisdiction, and illicit decrees. There would be no more Richelieus or Catherine de Medicis. The revolutionaries would establish liberty of commerce, liberty of conscience, liberty to write, liberty of expression. The Revolution would extinguish the parlements with their decrees, prohibitions, and lording it over the public. Once the Revolution gathered momentum, the parlementaire elite of France would perish, its influence and very name eradicated. France's laws would henceforth be identical for everyone and the system of police spies and secret reports abolished.[60] The Bastille will be raised to the ground, predicted Kervélégan, and a "National Assembly" put in its place, a "temple of liberty" subordinate to the nation and stripped of all hereditary trappings, that in the future would remain permanently in session and decide all questions of peace and war. Desmoulins, echoing Mirabeau, envisaged completely transforming the magistracy, priesthood, army, and state finances on principles national in character and destined solely for national purposes.[61] Moreover, this Revolution about to begin, admonished Desmoulins in 1789, would unquestionably succeed. "Sublime effet de la philosophie," no power on earth, he predicted (wrongly), could resist the revolution that had won the minds of those, like himself, eager to lead the people. To him, la philosophie had accomplished its task. The most crucial part of the revolution was effectively over. Even before anything had yet been formalized or accomplished, there was already a vital sense in which "la France est libre."[62]

By 1788, emerging Third Estate leaders already proclaimed equality the overriding moral and legal principle in legitimately determining relations among men. To them, the Crown was irrelevant, the clergy's authority usurped, and nobility illicit. Their plans were molded not by social class or experience, nor profession or economic interest, but a comprehensive, interlocking system of principles rooted in la philosophie, which, according to Mirabeau, Sieyès, Volney, Condorcet, and Brissot, was solidly anchored in empiricism and science.[63] By 1788, this republican and near-republican core had long rejected the division of a future national assembly into three orders—nobility, clergy, and Third Estate—along with everything Montesquieu recommended concerning division of powers and emulating Britain. They were uniformly disdainful of "institutions aristocratiques."[64] Society would be reordered on the basis of equality. All men should enjoy the same "rights." The law should be remade on the basis of philosophique principles because "reason" and equity are the sole criteria of moral and social legitimacy.

To them, equality was the key to establishing basic human rights and reconstituting politics, institutions, social relations, marriage, education, and the law on their proper basis. For the Revolution's innumerable opponents, by contrast, whether Counter-Enlightenment ideologues or "moderate" enlighteners, equality was an artificial and illicit concept. Opponents viewed their doctrine as derived from a false philosophy rooted in irreligion, fanaticism, and Freemasonry, or, as Burke, Gibbon, and Portalis preferred, in unwisely adopted "abstract propositions."[65] What made it necessary to proclaim the Rights of Man, harnassing the power of the state to the principle of human rights, held Roederer, was inequality of means and wealth in society. Unless one accepts government by vested interests at the expense of the weak that oppresses the majority and enriches the strong, government must intervene to help the deprived, watch over the whole citizenry, and guarantee to all "le plenitude de leurs droits" (plenitude of their rights).[66] Only in light of the "revolution that occurred before 1789"—the "revolution in concepts"—does it emerge clearly why the Revolution was not just a political but also a "financial, military, civil, moral and religious revolution."[67]

The Paris librarian and bookbinder Louis-Marie Prudhomme (1752–1830) expressly set out with his illustrated Sunday paper, the Révolutions de Paris, launched in July 1789, to forge a new society based

on a "Declaration of the Rights of Man," guided principally by "la philosophie."[68] While oppression was ubiquitous and the ultimate cause
of all revolutions, nowhere had there been any real revolution prior to
1788, held Prudhomme. Such a revolution requires "les lumières de la
raison," la philosophie moderne, to forge the awareness, analysis, plans,
media, knowledge, and conditions without which real revolution in the
new sense, disseminated by the *philosophes-révolutionnaires*, is not possible. Doubtless, some peoples, like the Dutch and English, partially recovered "their rights" through revolt "before the reign of philosophy."
But this Prudhomme deemed sustainable only in a hesitant, vengeful,
and incomplete manner, where not guided by "la pacifique opération de
la philosophie." The more philosophy guides, the less violent and more
complete the revolution will be. It is earnestly to be hoped, he added,
that la philosophie will overawe passion, hatred, and resentment during
the revolution now commencing.[69] Here, Prudhomme, Desmoulins,
Kervélégan, La Harpe, and many others were to be gravely disappointed.

Authentic revolution of the kind these writers envisaged needs not
only to be made but also consolidated. If philosophy alone enables men
to understand the human condition sufficiently to accomplish genuine
revolution, likewise philosophy alone can prevent men from immediately sliding back under slavery. Without philosophy mankind cannot
devise adequate, well-designed constitutions or correctly formulate "les
droits sacrés de l'humanité," or counter the risk of rural disorder and
"le despotisme du peuple."[70] There is no such thing as a successful fight
against credulity and religious bigotry, contended Prudhomme, not directed by la philosophie. "O mes concitoyens!," urged his journal, "do
not forget that ignorance is the mother of error"; banish ignorance and
your liberty is safe.[71] Here was an ideology bound to convert the clash
between la philosophie and its foes into a long and bitter struggle.

Those Roederer termed "les disciples de la philosophie moderne" in
the end failed to consolidate the revolution they forged and, for a time,
from the summer of 1793 to late 1794, were ousted by the Montagnards, the populist bloc derisively given this name originally because
they sat on the highest benches, on the Left, in the Assembly. According to this faction, the people's will and common man's sentiments were
the Revolution's sole legitimate guide. This interruption, especially the
ten-month Terror (September 1793–July 1794), followed a prolonged
power struggle. It produced a complete reordering of the Revolution's
basic values, in fact, the undoing of the Revolution. During these
months, democracy, freedom of thought and expression, and the Rights

of Man were jettisoned, freedom of the press aborted, individual liberty annulled, and terror exalted. But this catastrophic upset and trampling of human rights proved relatively brief and was then largely reversed again between 1795 and 1799.

Nevertheless, this bloody aberration, relatively short-lived though it was, posed (and still poses) a question that from 1795, in turn, became an ideological battlefield. Was the Terror inherent in the revolutionary principles of 1789 and hence also the outcome of la philosophie? This was the undeviating claim of all antiphilosophes, ultraroyalists, constitutional monarchists, and disillusioned former revolutionaries like La Harpe. These were all eager to link philosophisme, republicanism, materialism, and atheism to moral perversity. But were they right to attribute the Terror to the secte philosophique? A thorough sifting of the evidence suggests that they were wrong. Many of the philosophe-révolutionnaires responsible for the revolution of 1788–93 were ruthlessly guillotined by Robespierre. The survivors adamantly denied that the Revolution had immolated itself. They explained the doctrine of Robespierre and his allies as the outcome of a completely different and antagonistic ideology. If Marxist accounts of the Revolution as the outcome of class struggle today look flawed, François Furet's widely respected thesis ascribing innate totalitarian leanings and an embedded latent illiberalism to the Revolution in its origins and basic principles needs rejecting just as comprehensively.

Among the strangest misconceptions plaguing accounts of the French Revolution nowadays is the still-predominant consensus that the "break between the Revolution and Christianity"—especially the Catholic Church—was "non-essential, contingent and explicable only in terms of the subsequent vicissitudes of the Revolution itself." The break was supposedly not inherent in the context of 1789. In fact, all the evidence demonstrates the opposite. The impulse to (nonviolent) revolutionary de-Christianization was basic to the outlook of the philosophique leadership who made the Revolution before, as well as in, 1789.[72] There are also other widely accepted, striking, and utterly unfounded myths. Among the revolutionary leadership "in the summer of 1789," reaffirmed one leading scholar recently, "virtually no one challenged the principle of monarchy," a statement for which he assumed it suffices to invoke the general consensus.[73] There is, indeed, a wide consensus among historians about this. But no close observer took this view at the time—quite the contrary. When Jean-Louis Carra (1742–93), among the principal National Convention deputies, Jacobin activists, and Parisian newspaper editors, remarked in a pamphlet of June 1793 that he was a "republican" who had roundly rejected monarchy in 1789 and who had done so also long before 1789, he was merely echoing a standpoint not just widespread but general among the French revolutionary vanguard (but not, of course, Robespierre and the populist faction).[74] It would seem that historians' prevailing consensus here once again rests on nothing more than the long-standing failure to give sufficient weight to the Revolution's intellectual history and hence is likewise in urgent need of revision.

The Left revolutionary leadership in 1789 both rejected Christianity (whether from a deist or atheist-materialist standpoint) *and* as a bloc abjured the principle of monarchy, either wholly, like Carra, Brissot, and Desmoulins, or, as with Mirabeau and Sieyès, in the main. In 1789, Carra's and Desmoulins's republican stance was shared, we shall see, throughout the revolutionary democratic vanguard—by Condorcet, Kersaint, Dusaulx, Mandar, Lanthenas, Gorsas, Brissot, Pétion, Chamfort, Volney, Pierre-François Robert, Bonneville, Paine (who joined the French revolutionary leadership in the autumn of 1792), and the playwright Marie-Joseph Chénier. The philosophique revolutionary leadership as a group (unlike authoritarian populists such as Marat, Robespierre, Saint-Just, or Hébert) was overwhelmingly republican from the outset. In short, key general assumptions about the French Revolution, everywhere frequently repeated and long accepted by both philosophers and historians, turn out to be fundamentally incorrect, leaving us with an uncommonly urgent need for some very sweeping and drastic revision.

CHAPTER 2

Revolution of the Press

(1788–90)

By 1787, the French Crown was on the verge of collapse. Financially ruined by the ballooning of an immense state debt, the monarchy's prestige lay shattered by defeat in Europe and vast colonial losses. France had lost Canada and nearly all her outposts in India. At this point the monarchy found itself without the resources to support the status it had consistently enjoyed for centuries in international, maritime, and colonial affairs. Worsted by Britain in the Americas, Asia, and Africa, since 1750, the French Crown had also been humiliated in European great power rivalry, most recently in the Dutch political crisis of 1787 when, "by virtue of the right of brigands," as the Milanese radical philosophe, Giuseppe Gorani (1740–1819), expressed it, Prussia's new king, spurred by the British prime minister Pitt, invaded the United Provinces. Crushing the Dutch democratic revolution (whose leaders were allied to France), Prussia had restored the House of Orange, a firm ally of Britain and Prussia. Most European rulers celebrated the defeat of democratic ideas in the United Provinces. But the triumph of Anglo-Prussian influence in the Netherlands represented a major international setback for France, implying unsuspected weakness.[1]

The Versailles court, paralyzed by spiraling debts and unable to finance the upkeep of its armies, fortresses, and navy, saw no solution to its difficulties other than to reorganize and rationalize the state in the only way apt to furnish new resources. This involved persuading the privileged elites, who owned most of the wealth, to surrender some of their immunities and exemptions and contribute more to state revenues. Discussion followed as to how the monarchy's fiscal, legal, and administrative apparatus could be reformed, the process marking the commencement of the ancien régime's breakdown. The elites proved willing enough to exchange their privileges and immunities for an altered role in the monarchy, provided they remained privileged and shared more directly in the exercise of royal power. Indeed, by 1788, the weakened monarchy was distinctly at risk of being reconstituted as an aristocratic republic, with the king reduced to a mere figurehead. Initially, the three main elites—nobles, clergy, and parlementaires—seemed well placed to preside. France's domestic situation was volatile. Bread prices were high and the urban and rural population restless. But this was nothing new. Popular disaffection, experience suggested, could mostly be shepherded wherever the elites wished. Superficially, little seemed to threaten France's traditional elites or the complex, long-standing, but apparently mendable institutional framework some of them aspired to refashion.

In 1786, the royal Controller-General, Calonne, aired his plans for reorganizing the state finances, administration, and local government, and establishing new mechanisms of consultation between court and provinces. Opposition came principally from the Parlement de Paris, France's chief regional high court, a body with a long record of obstructing royal fiscal and political initiatives. To outflank parlementaire opposition, Calonne advised the king to convene an Assembly of Notables representing all classes of society but dominated by the nobility and higher clergy. His scheme failed. Despite alarm at the vastness of the royal debt, estimated at 113 million livres, this assembly rejected Calonne's plans. Confidently recalcitrant nobles, parlementaires, and clergy opposing the royal will received ample backing from below, as had often occurred in the past.

In April 1787, Louis replaced Calonne with another experienced man of state affairs, Étienne-Charles de Loménie de Brienne (1727–94), archbishop of Toulouse. Predictably, since nothing else suggested itself, the archbishop, altering a few details, reintroduced basically the same reform package as his predecessor. But judicial and aristocratic obstruction proved unrelenting. The regional parlements were highly experienced in such confrontations and readily mobilized support, not just among the nobility and clergy but also in the streets of regional capitals, as they had for centuries. Politically, the Crown was continually frustrated. At this point, nobility, clergy, and parlementaires, spurred by the Paris Parlement, urged a convening of the Estates-General (which had not met since 1614) as a way through the impasse. This body was expected to be dominated by the privileged orders, and to sanction the privileged elites' capture of France's fiscal machinery and administration.[2] Revealingly, where the hierarchical traditions of the provincial estates, local parlements, and noble precedence persisted most (in provinces like Brittany, Béarn, Navarre, and the Dauphiné), popular opposition to the Crown was fiercest. But however useful for stiffening the elites' demands, popular unrest remained perennially volatile, shifting, and readily manipulated. Since newspapers and pamphlets had in the past always been muzzled by royal censorship, few imagined the press might emerge as a powerful counterweight presenting an alternative agenda and principles.

At Rennes and Grenoble, the provincial capitals of Brittany and the Dauphiné, massive demonstrations erupted, in the latter case expressly championing privilege, the old constitution, and the parlements against royal authority. In the Dauphiné, government efforts at fiscal reform in 1787–88 had the effect of pitting the privileged—the nobility and parlementaires—together with the Third Estate against the Crown. On 7 June 1788 a particularly violent tumult occurred in Grenoble—the so-called Day of the Tiles. This commotion in support of the existing order, and of the parlement and provincial estates, was partly the work of angry peasants crowding into the city from nearby villages for the usual market day trading; it left several dead in the streets. Support for nobles and magistrates opposing royal initiatives also characterized the disturbances in Béarn, where peasants again figured prominently. The people spontaneously rebelled on hearing royal officials were attempting to intimidate parlementaires resisting royal demands.[3] The united cry everywhere was no consent to new taxes or procedures prior to the convening of the Estates-General.

While resentment against seigneurial dues was also fairly widespread in parts of the French countryside, including the Dauphiné, Lorraine, Navarre, the Basque Country, and Normandy, little of this was either new or very virulent.[4] Nevertheless, during the years 1787–88, there were several early warning signs potentially disturbing for both urban and rural elites. For one thing, town dwellers had come upon a new and independent way of learning about current affairs from the growing mass of topical and often stridently expressed pamphlets. The impact of these pamphlets, noticeable already in 1787—in which year 217 appeared—by late 1788 had grown in unprecedented fashion. In 1788, 819 were published, and in 1789 the equivalent figure was no less than 3,305.[5] They were becoming the chief means of fomenting resistance to the Crown. Still more disturbing, even if confined to just a few regions, was the socially divisive effect of royal efforts at fiscal reform, most obviously in Provence and in Brittany, where it pitted the Third Estate against the Crown *and* the privileged. Indications that friction between nobility and the Third could become acute were discernible also in Béarn, Navarre, and some other regions.[6]

The difficulties encountered on all sides left the king little option but to yield to the demands for convening the Estates-General. With both the privileged and the people demanding respect for precedent, existing laws, and parlements, in August the convening of the Estates-General was announced for 1 May 1789. For nine months, preparations for this great gathering dominated politics in Paris and the provinces alike. Initially, discussion of old precedents and charters predominated. But during the summer of 1788, the struggle between Crown and privileged elites changed into a battle between elites demanding the Estates-General's traditional format, ensuring nobility and clergy together commanded twice the Third Estate's voting power, and a group of wholly unrepresentative newcomers to the scene. The latter, mostly literary men and intellectuals, wanted privilege curbed and the Third Estate's representation doubled to ensure formal parity of voting power with the privileged orders (which actually meant overall superiority as a minority of clergy and nobility backed the Third's demands).

Here in embryo, in the drive to overturn nobility and privilege, a revolution was implied. All kinds of local clubs and reading societies that had flourished in recent years, sometimes decades (albeit until 1788 strictly nonpolitical),[7] together with new ones set up at this time, joined the agitation for the "doubling" of Third Estate representation. Among the new associations was the Club of Thirty, established in Paris by Mirabeau, Sieyès, Clavière, Hérault de Séchelles, and Chamfort. Nicolas Chamfort (1741–94), the illegitimate but highly educated son of a grocer, was a brilliant aphorist and *littérateur* (intellectual) who featured prominently among those organizing contacts between provincial clubs and Paris. Accustomed to refined drawing rooms and literature, he now concentrated on the Paris streets, especially the Palais-Royal district, helping to stir opinion in the city center. Among those openly voicing republican ideas, and unrepresentative like the others of any economic interest, Chamfort was an intellectual prominent in calling for the Third to take the lead.[8] The Palais-Royal, located on the north bank close to the Louvre, was to play a peculiarly formative role in ensuing developments, Mallet du Pan dubbing it the "vestibule" of the Revolution. Surrounded by arcades filled with cafés, such as the Café de Chartres, Café de Conti, and Grotte Flamande, bookshops, restaurants, and entertainment locales attracting visitors of all types, the site was already Paris's chief venue for political debate. Bequeathed in 1780 to the son of the Duc d'Orléans, the district was open to the public yet remained a private domain relatively free from police supervision. By 1788, it was notorious for lively café debate, prostitution, and the furtive vending of forbidden texts and obscene prints. It was the place, remarked Desmoulins, who developed into a skilled agitator here, where all of France digested the subversive brochures that "changed everybody— even soldiers—into *philosophes*."[9]

But the chief opinion-shaping instrument wielded by the Third Estate's aspiring leadership, even more than the cafés, clubs, and reading societies, was the press. The past promised nobility, clergy, and parlementaires an easy ascendancy. Bourgeoisie, peasants, and artisans seemingly offered no obstacle. But by late 1788, as preparations for the Estates-General progressed, the primacy of rank and tradition in shaping opinion no longer went unchallenged. Indeed, opinion suddenly became extremely difficult for the elites to control as others began directing gatherings and demonstrations. The demand for "doubling" the Third Estate's representation rapidly caught on. As the struggle intensified, an unprecedented wave of militant antiaristocratic and anticlerical discourse, denouncing privilege, nobility, clerical influence, and the parlements, began affecting the course of events.

In 1788 a "revolution in political culture" occurred, especially in the language of politics, which proved decisive for shaping the Revolution.[10] The political initiative was seized from the privileged elites by an extremely hostile, largely unrepresentative group lacking professional or economic ties. This occurred principally owing to the royal censorship's progressive collapse and the press's newfound capacity to shape opinion. At the same time, social disorder, especially endemic peasant violence, became more widespread, particularly in rural Provence.[11] The Revolution commenced, explained Jean-Paul Rabaut Saint-Étienne (1743–93), a Protestant pastor from Nîmes and one of its early leaders, not with the meeting of the Estates-General in 1789, as most people later assumed, but during the months preceding its convening, when "a great number of writers" set to work influencing elements of the Third Estate, diffusing texts and reminding the people of their "rights."[12]

The "new political culture" first invaded the large cities via speeches and pamphlets. In Marseille, the philosophe Guillaume-Thomas Raynal (1713–96) helped direct the initial uproar and spate of radical speeches in person; working with Honoré-Gabriel Riqueti, Comte de Mirabeau

(1749–91), one of the champions of press freedom, he "directed the first steps of the Marseillais in the astonishing Revolution" that followed.[13] This escalating ideological assault on the ancien régime was concerted not by professionals or lawyers but by a handful of discontented nobles, littérateurs, renegade priests, and journalists, a group completely heterogeneous, socially and by education. What counted were neither numbers nor social background but rather their striking ideological cohesion and ability to sway their audience. They seized the urban public's attention, deploying an entirely new revolutionary rhetoric of equality, democracy, and volonté générale.

This budding intellectual leadership was uniformly republican in tendency and eager to weaken the Church, even if, for the moment, little was said openly about republicanism or religion. The key subversive pamphlets expressed not political pragmatism deriving from experience, or anything drawn from precedent, charters, the law, parlements, or Jansenism (detested by all the philosophes), but a fully developed, elaborate ideology employing a wholly fresh terminology devised since the 1750s and widely propagated only since the censorship's collapse. If the principal radical pamphleteers of 1788–89 were not all overt republicans and democrats, even the intellectual vanguard's least militant voices were astoundingly ambitious, aiming for the root and branch transformation of society. Joseph (Giuseppe) Cérutti (1738–92) is especially interesting here, being less polemical and aggressive than Desmoulins, Volney, Chamfort, or Mirabeau. A Turin-born former Jesuit professor at Lyon who admired d'Holbach, Cérutti abhorred violence. Firmly among the revolutionary vanguard, in 1788 he refrained publicly from embracing democracy or republicanism (though he too was already privately a republican). Nevertheless, his *Mémoire pour le peuple françois* (1788) figured among the foremost subversive pamphlets assailing the privileged orders and traditional format of the Estates, doing so, though, while imploring the Third not to force "a revolution" that was realizing itself anyway. "*La Philosophie* has worked for you: don't make her repent." Violence had forged more chains than it had broken. The people should not combat the "old order" violently but instead patiently wait for enlightenment and the logic of events to transform everything, led by the soon-to-emerge representative legislature bound, he thought, shortly to supplant the Estates.[14]

Envisaging the complete overthrow of the existing order and its religious sanction in 1788–89 was not just implausible but altogether impossible without being, like Cérutti, saturated in the philosophical writings of Helvétius, Mably, Price, Raynal, d'Holbach, Rousseau, and other such writers familiar only to a small minority. Where else in 1788 would one find the notion that "a revolution" was essential in order to fundamentally transform every single aspect of society, politics, and institutions, and that unbeknown to most this process had already begun? Everyone thinking in these uncompromising terms—Mirabeau, Sieyès, Brissot, Volney, Chamfort, Prudhomme, Mercier, Desmoulins, Pétion, Roederer, and Cérutti—belonged to this unrepresentative fringe category. Emmanuel Sieyès (1748–1836), son of a postal official (another renegade priest), possessed little worldly experience; in fact, he had spent his entire life immersed in books. The three resounding tracts he published between November 1788 and January 1789, before the Estates-General convened, nevertheless exerted a vast impact. Especially the first, *Essai sur les privilèges*, and last, *Qu'est-ce que le Tiers-État?* (January 1789), both partly products of group discussion at the Parisian Club of Thirty, vigorously propagated the phrases and philosophique terminology of the wider 1788 philosophique press campaign. They helped forge the rhetoric of the entire early Revolution and, like the other major tracts, were not broadly *Rousseauiste* in character, though he uses some of Rousseau's phrases. The concepts Sieyès's 1788–89 tracts were based on relied on a range of recent thinkers, a systematically materialist epistemology and metaphysics that he had continually refined since the early 1770s and turned into an instrument for attacking social hierarchy. As early as 1773, Sieyès avowed that his aim was to "seat *la philosophie* on the throne" by changing how the common people think. His materialism underpinned his guiding idea that "liberty in general" is what most favors the pursuit of individual happiness in society, the chief foes of liberty being the particular "liberties" of privilege, charters, and special rights, the status that existing society accorded nobles and clergy.[15]

The astounding press ferment of 1788 spread across France. In Brittany, the contest between the seven to eight hundred nobles controlling the provincial Estates and the Third's spokesmen over whether the Breton delegations to the Estates-General should accept "equality in repartition of taxes," and the cutting back of the noblesse de robe's privileges, quickly turned vitriolic. Against the journalists, the Parlement de Rennes, "perhaps the most ignorant of the thirteen [judicial] senates of France," according to one journal, lent the privileged orders unstinting support.[16] At stake was the primacy of privilege, charters, ennobled magistracy, clergy, and tradition, the very principle of a society of ranks. Especially prominent in stirring opposition at Rennes was Volney's five-pamphlet series, *La Sentinelle du peuple*, commencing on 10 November 1788 with a blistering attack on the nobility's self-interested scheming. At a time when friction between defenders of the old order and "young patriots" at Rennes was turning violent, causing ugly clashes in the streets, in late January 1789 Volney openly summoned the Third to reject all the claims of the *privilégiés*.[17]

Constantin-François Volney (1757–1820), son of an ennobled family of local notables from Mayenne, had, like Sieyès and most of the others, no experience in politics and was steeped only in books. An energetic young orientalist and zealous disciple of Helvétius and d'Holbach, a materialist and atheist belonging to the intellectual circle around Madame Helvétius (and disdainful of Rousseau), he propagated Radical Enlightenment in the most uncompromising terms. With newspapers as his tool, he helped fashion Breton dissatisfaction into an effective force. His very first issue denounced the Breton Estates as "des États illégales et abusives" and called for superfluous ecclesiastical properties to revert to the nation. In subsequent issues, Volney openly incited the Bretons to defy both nobility and clergy by refusing to permit voting by orders in the Estates-General. The "public interest" is that of the people, and Bretons must ensure they are not the last to move "in the Revolution now encompassing the whole of France."[18] Where "moderates" in the debates of 1788 typically invoked Montesquieu and eulogized the British constitution, by December 1788 Volney further manifested his radicalism by publicly mocking Britain, where a king supposedly held an entire people in the balance. He admonished his countrymen to ignore existing models since "tous les hommes naissent égaux." He likened the Breton nobility to a sickly old aristocratic lady, needing much medicine and intensive nursing from underlings (the clergy and parlementaires) to prop her up, her imminent demise being sure to transform everything for the better.[19]

Another prominent non-Rousseauiste voice proclaiming and advocating revolution was that of Chamfort, a member of Mirabeau's entourage, brooding, sour, and fiercely hostile to aristocracy. Envious of those possessing by birth what he lacked (but also scorning the people's "ignorance"), he made no secret of the fact that were he and his friends to prevail, they would go "much further than any popular mandate entitled them to do." Some candidates for the Estates-General, cuttingly remarked a literary acquaintance, Marmontel, seemed to have their own ideas about what needed changing. "Bon!" retorted Chamfort, "la nation sait-elle ce qu'elle veut?" A big flock seeking pasture, the people could be led to want what they had never imagined. Shepherds with good dogs would herd them wherever they wished. "In tracing our new path we have every reason to want to make a clean sweep."[20] The people, as yet, knew nothing about it, but republicanism, eliminating nobility, and weakening religious authority were already entirely fundamental to the Revolution as it was evolving in his mind and those of his circle.

The revolutionary leadership's emerging discourse was increasingly characterized by the totality of the rupture with the past that it demanded. Already in 1788, many key commentators refused to concede any legitimacy or constitutional standing to the Estates-General as historically defined, demanding sweeping reforms before acknowledging its legitimacy.[21] Their platform was the electoral districts and assemblies authorized by the Crown throughout the country to organize the election of representatives. But what was voiced was not popular opinion. Numerous pamphlets of 1788 claimed to be "popular," pamphleteers frequently posing as artisans, townsmen, "serfs," or peasants. Strictly speaking, though, all this was bogus, as the pamphlets were invariably the work of highly educated polemicists.[22] Little evidence survives as to how the uneducated common people really thought. Nonetheless, these pamphlets, deliberately addressing the lower orders, circulating in town and country, succeeded in some degree in arousing artisans and peasantry against both Crown and aristocratic policies, including in the Dauphiné and Brittany.[23] In the capital, sixty electoral districts were formed over the winter and entrusted with choosing the "assembly of electors" that would then select Paris's representatives to the Estates. In these district assemblies, popular opinion was allegedly the key, but who was shaping opinion? Historians have often claimed such pamphlets ultimately served the needs of the educated and affluent bourgeoisie.[24] But key writers like Mirabeau, Sieyès, Carra, Cérutti, Pétion, and Desmoulins made no explicit appeal to any particular group and lacked ties with every major economic bloc.

The new electoral system was introduced by the Crown itself when the Assembly of Notables reconvened in November 1788, in preparation for the elections for the Estates-General. The Crown proposed "doubling" the Third Estate's representation and making each delegate the representative of an equivalent number of voters, hoping thereby to counterbalance the formerly overweening influence of the privileged and play off the Third against the nobility and clergy. But ministers had no wish to end separate voting by orders or to weaken privilege as such. They desired France to remain a society of orders politically and socially, with nobility and clergy able to overrule the Third. Over the next months the Crown pursued what royal ministers judged a responsible, even-handed strategy designed to minimize friction and enhance the Third's status while retaining safeguards to ensure the continued ordering of society into ranks.

Delegates to the Estates-General in the past had been expressly mandated to support or oppose particular proposals, and in 1788–89 too, before the Estates convened, matters proceeded along traditional lines. Delegates were deemed to represent particular orders in specific localities, not individuals or citizens. *Cahiers de doléances* expressing local opinion in the parishes were drawn up in all localities to direct the delegates. This conformed to precedent and under more normal circumstances could only reinforce the elites' predominance, as these gatherings were chaired and notarized by nobles, notables, and lawyers, with nobles and clergy also holding separate meetings. This time matters proceeded rather differently, though, due to the tide of oppositional rhetoric surging up from the clubs, literary societies, and increasingly unfettered press, backed by growing popular unrest following the disastrous grain harvest of 1788. In a number of places, highly articulate and literate "Patriot" committees, dominated by club members, editors, and literary men, supervised the elections for Third Estate representatives, ensuring the election of some delegates who were militantly antagonistic to the system of orders and the preeminence of "aristocrats" and priests. Infiltrating the electoral committees and selection of the Third's representatives, radical thought for the first time penetrated the political arena.

The Revolution's second phase commenced in late April 1789 when the Third's newly elected six hundred deputies—half of the Estates-General's total of 1,200 delegates—duly gathered at Versailles, refusing the royal agenda and procedural directions. Not only these twelve hundred gathered for the political drama—so did a sizable body of eager, unelected commentators, journalists, and independent observers, many ambitious but unsuccessful candidates in the elections, including Chamfort, Ginguené, Brissot, the mathematician Gilbert Romme (who had spent five years in Russia tutoring the sons of aristocrats), and a discharged schoolmaster soon to win renown, Antoine-Joseph Gorsas (1752–93).[25] Chamfort, not elected but eager to participate nevertheless did so, like his Breton journalist friend Ginguené, by providing close support for Mirabeau. At this point, Sabatier noted, in both Estates-General and at court, a new and divisive discourse arose—adopted earlier in the 1780s in Switzerland and Holland and now pushed hard by this tiny and unrepresentative but highly articulate, intellectualized, nonprofessional clique following Mirabeau and Sieyès—that labeled the two principal, opposed blocs in the Estates-General *aristocrates* and *démocrates*.[26]

The Third's deputies, historians often note, included no peasants, artisans, or laborers. But while peasantry and workingmen *were* indeed missing, it is equally striking that the Third, as constituted at Versailles in 1789, included practically no businessmen, bankers, entrepreneurs, or other members of major occupation groups characteristic of "bourgeois" upper-middle-class life either. Edmund Burke, closely observing from London, was quite appalled by the Third's composition. What horrified him was the striking lack of monied men, big landowners, and high-ranking churchmen. If the Third Estate was to emulate British practice and the House of Commons, then it must represent possession of land, money, and position, the very attributes the budding revolutionary leadership in Paris conspicuously lacked. Burke did notice the high proportion of lawyers in the Assembly, but, like most modern historians, failed to perceive the near absence of professionals and lawyers from among the leading cliques of orators, pamphleteers, and reformers.[27]

In terms of bacgound, the revolutionary leadership represented no established social categories. It consisted predominantly of editors, journalists, writers, tutors, librarians, renegade priests, and renegade nobles turned littérateurs. Among the foremost were Mirabeau, Sieyès, Bailly, Volney, and Barnave—a renegade parlementaire from the Dauphiné, a spellbinding orator, and, like Rabaut, doubly unrepresentative in being a Protestant as well as an intellectual.[28] Mirabeau was a philosophe, historian, and political commentator with numerous publications to his name; rejected by his own order, the nobility, he was elected at Aix-en-Provence by the Third. These "philosophes du Tiers" as opponents derisively called them, representing no professions or social groups, confidently assumed the lead. They took the offensive from the start, adopting a deliberately provocative rhetoric, precluding all possibility of preserving privileges for the nobility and clergy, and repudiating the very title "Third Estate"—a designation, however well entrenched in constitutional law, scorned by them as redolent of "slaves," "helots," and "negroes." In fact, they repudiated the entire abasing terminology of the past, prohibiting the term "orders" from their chamber's deliberations. By redefining the nobility and clergy as "classes privilégiés" instead of "higher orders," they ruled out special status a priori for any and every social class.

Equally, they rejected curbs on press freedom. Among the "rights" constantly aired in early 1788–89 was freedom of thought and the notion that "every people has the inviolable right," as Brissot put it, agreeing with "le sage Mably," to pass its own laws and "is only great, virtuous, and happy when it does so."[29] Jacques-Pierre Brissot (1754–93), soon to emerge as a key revolutionary leader, was the son of a pious restaurant owner (who virtually disowned him on account of his impious views), a veteran writer, legal reformer, and antiestablishment polemicist briefly imprisoned in the Bastille in 1784 for subversive writings. In Brissot's eyes, anyone preventing the man of the people enlightening himself, or a slave ridding himself of his chains, is an enemy of the human race. As "the American Revolution gave birth to ours," he expected the new "revolution" to encompass all of Europe. Spain, Germany, and other countries would become conscious of the feudal chains weighing them down "en nous voyant libres and heureux." Haughty Britain too would blush on seeing the nation she called her rival acquiring a better constitutional framework without the deficiencies of her "constitution défectueuse."[30] If one wished to instruct the people, one must not just permit but positively encourage the publication of political gazettes.[31]

Long aspiring to be a philosophe, Brissot knew all the philosophes and how to deploy their ideas as effective propaganda. His particular favorites early on were Rousseau and Montesquieu, but his debt to Rousseau has sometimes been rather exaggerated. Certainly, he admired Rousseau greatly, but he also disagreed with him on numerous points, especially representation, patriotism, and censorship. Liberty he called the first of basic rights because "liberty is nothing other than the right, in man, to develop his faculties for his well-being." Writing and printing are the most apt means of perfecting humanity's faculties. Every man possesses, by nature, the right to think, write, and print independently whatever he considers necessary for his welfare and that of others. Every human obstacle to freedom of expression "is therefore a violation of natural right, a crime." No such restriction should mar any constitution "since every constitution should defend men's natural rights and not infringe them."[32]

The French desired a constitution, affirmed Brissot at this time, that would be fully "l'expression de la volonté universelle."[33] How was it to be secured? Through liberty of the press. He had argued unceasingly since the early 1780s that a free press alone would enable reading and debating clubs to organize and express la volonté générale. Only a publishing revolution could transform France from a backward monarchy into a representative democracy equipped to promote its citizenry's best interests and protect their rights.[34] From July 1789 Brissot turned his newly established newspaper into a major vehicle of revolutionary ferment.[35] What an enormous distance the French had traversed since 1787, he commented in June 1789. Who would have guessed in 1787 that by 1789 the French would be vigorously demanding "une constitution libre"? But prior to the Bastille's fall, it was only his particular small group—the philosophique vanguard of revolutionary publicists, orators, and spokesmen—who thought in terms of giving France a wholly new constitution, not anyone else, including the great majority of the deputies to the Estates-General.

Who had "enlightened" the French people sufficiently for this first crucial step to be taken, asked this quintessential representative of antireligious and antiaristocratic radical Enlightenment thought, and how had they done it? The Revolution's first phase was indubitably achieved by the press—thus far, mainly books and pamphlets—and if these books "that so few are able to read" produced such an effect, averred Brissot, what will happen when the press is truly liberated, "when the papers, above all papers everyone reads, will be free"? Before the Revolution the Crown was much more vigilant, Tocqueville observed later, in censoring newspapers than it was books. In early 1789, royal licensing of newspapers was the last lingering part of the royal censorship still operative.[36] But once this too was neutralized, "the light," today concentrated among "la classe aisée" (the leisured class), will reach all men's minds.[37] In the *Journal de Paris* and other conservative organs, Brissot was rightly identified as a particularly dangerous and incendiary writer, an undisguised enemy of ecclesiastics and sovereign rulers, "un Apôtre du républicanisme."[38] By June 1789, the belief that France stood poised to embrace a new constitution based on natural rights and fundamentally change its laws permeated Brissot's circle, an ambitious group of like-minded, would-be politicians who had failed to win election to the Estates, including Condorcet, the Genevan republican exile Clavière, and the physician Lanthenas. Among this avowed revolutionary clique, it was already customary to refer to *la Révolution* with a capital "R" and label the pre-1789 order "the *ancien régime* and to think of the imminent Revolution as universal in its significance."[39]

Brissot and his circle joined the campaign headed by Mirabeau, Sieyès, Gorsas, Chénier, Chamfort, Cérutti, Mercier, Beaumarchais, and
other pro-Revolution littérateurs pursuing a thoroughgoing revolution
of the press, theater, and culture generally. Brissot aimed to become a
revolutionary leader, realizing that he could through his writing. His
newspaper would especially spread "les lumières" (enlightenment)
among all classes of the population by utilizing his earlier research on the
laws and constitutions of Britain and the United States, and the social
effects of these, to benefit France. Both Britain and the United States
supposedly already enjoyed the vast advantage of press liberty. But the
Americans had improved on England's press freedom, he thought, by
preserving their gazettes from the heavy stamp duties the British press
incurred.[40] Briefly, in early 1789, French licensed papers with royal and
parlementaire backing could still obstruct the unlicensed papers that
were beginning to appear, for example, by obtaining a royal ban, in May
1789, after just one issue, on Brissot's paper.[41] He resumed publishing
Le Patriote français, soon among the foremost pro-Revolution papers,
only on 28 July. His efforts as a journalist were aided by several future
allies in revolutionary politics, notably Lanthenas and Clavière. From
July 1789, *Le Patriote français* appeared regularly, figuring prominently
throughout—until suppressed by Jacobin populists in June 1793. From
July 1789, its declared mission was to "prepare a nation to receive a free
constitution."[42]

Royal press censorship in France disintegrated completely with the
storming of the Bastille in July 1789.[43] Although the first major pro-
Revolution journals, Mirabeau's *Courrier de Provence* and Brissot's *Patriote français*, had begun tentatively slightly earlier, most revolutionary
journals emerged following the Bastille's fall, an occurrence that an-
nounces still bigger, "happy revolutions," exclaimed Gorsas on 15 July,
and so important that it would be remembered "for ever."[44] Among the
principal papers was the *Révolutions de Paris*, commencing on 18 July,
edited by Louis-Marie Prudhomme and perhaps the single most successful early Revolution paper, with the librarian philosophe Sylvain
Maréchal contributing regularly from late 1790.[45] The *Journal de Perlet*, edited by a Genevan, Charles Perlet (1766–1828), also penetrated
widely (until suppressed after the coup of Fructidor in 1797), first appearing on 1 August 1789. It was followed by Louise Kéralio's *Journal
d'état et du citoyen* and many other remarkable papers. Gorsas's journal, originally entitled *Le Courrier de Versailles à Paris*, though likewise

commencing earlier, only appeared regularly from July. Gorsas, eager to help perfect the happiness of the people from whose ranks he himself came, labeled all opposition to the Left republican literary vanguard "despotisme aristocratique."

Gorsas reviled aristocracy. Yet, typical of this unrepresentative fringe, he also disdained what he considered the ignorance and prejudiced outlook of the ordinary man. Witness to many ugly street scenes, Gorsas unsparingly recorded firsthand the people's unfortunate tendency to irrationality and brutal violence.[46] After the spreading disorder of mid- and late July began to include anti-Semitic disturbances in early August in Alsace and Lorraine, during October his paper, among the most attentive to the confused flurry of events across France, vehemently deplored the unreasoning "hatred of the people," the pillaging of Jewish homes in Lixheim, Lorraine, and nineteen villages in Alsace, and the potential threat this and the unrest more generally posed to the Revolution. Due to ingrained ignorance and credulity, he warned, urging the Assembly to take measures to protect them: "great danger surrounded in particular the Jews in Lorraine and Alsace."[47]

The Revolution first considered the question of Jewish emancipation in the autumn of 1789, but it was by no means the Revolution itself that first introduced the idea of integrating Jews fully into society and allowing them to live free of restriction where they wanted. (Under ancien régime French law, Jewish residence was confined to Alsace-Lorraine, Avignon, Bordeaux, and Bayonne.) Rather, this idea was first developed and powerfully publicized during the years immediately before the Revolution, most vigorously by Mirabeau, Brissot, and another key revolutionary journalist, Anacharsis Cloots (1755–94), who all condemned Christian anti-Jewish prejudice before 1789. The idea was also promoted by a prize competition announced by the Société Royale des Sciences et des Arts of Metz in 1787 that asked whether it was possible to render the Jews "happier and more useful in France." Three texts were "crowned" winners by the academy, all urging comprehensive Jewish emancipation and integration. These were by the Jewish savant Zalkind Hourwitz (1738–1812), a Polish Jew employed from 1789 on the staff of the Bibliothèque du Roi (from 1792 the Bibliothèque Nationale), the Abbé Grégoire, and Claude Thierry, an *avocat* of the parlement of Nancy.[48]

By 1787 the revolution in educated French minds regarding the Jews had already occurred, contended Thierry, and philosophy had effected it by scorning all theological arguments against the Jews. Though Mirabeau was the philosophe to whom most credit was due for effecting this sea change in educated opinion, acknowledged Thierry, he claimed to have reached the same conclusions independently. Thierry stands out not just for urging Jewish emancipation unreservedly, but insisting, like Cloots, that the entire responsibility and guilt for the oppression of the Jews in Europe since the first Christian centuries lay with the churches and with the common people in their ignorance.[49] His tone shows Thierry fully conscious of the revolutionary character of what he was saying and how difficult this was for the vast majority to accept. Continually attacking traditional prejudice, Thierry maintained that successful Jewish emancipation and integration required an end to separate Jewish education based on religious authority. It required the state to introduce a secular, universal education under which Christian and Jewish children, mingling together, would jointly overcome obstacles created by the prejudices of centuries and equally imbibe enlightenment, morality, and civic values.[50]

The July 1789 revolution in publishing and public debate not only generated a huge number of new journals of every complexion but also transformed the status and role of the publicist and journalist, the pro-Revolution press quickly and massively proliferating. From 25 August 1789 appeared one of the most influential and best edited revolutionary journals, *La Chronique de Paris*, to which Condorcet, Rabaut Saint-Étienne, and Jean-François Ducos (1765–93), philosophe and friend of Raynal, all regularly contributed. Shortly afterward, François-Jean Baudouin (1759–1838) established the *Journal des débats et des décrets*, and on 3 October 1789, Jean-Louis Carra (1743–93), librarian and *érudit*, steeped in radical philosophy since the early 1770s and a would-be philosophe himself,[51] initiated his widely selling *Annales patriotiques et littéraires*. Jean-Pierre Audouin began the *Journal universel*, destined to last five years, on 23 November.[52] All these hailed freedom of the press as a basic human right and overriding principle. Hostile commentators, of whom there were many, complained already during the Estates-General's opening days that the press had suddenly gained an excessive sway. In particular, Mirabeau's *Courrier de Provence* and Gorsas's *Courrier* were denounced for appropriating an undue influence with their detailed reporting and (according to some) slanting of what transpired at Versailles and their relaying this swiftly to the capital. Their commentary, assailing nobility, clergy, parlementaires, and court, Gorsas admitted in his paper, helped shape the way political news was understood and received in Paris.

With the Estates-General commencing in April 1789, a satirical pamphlet appeared that attacked the coterie of self-proclaimed "experts" who were advising the nation how to organize its affairs. The French, it complained, had been plunged into profoundly unsettling anxiety and alarm by la philosophie. The "incomparable geniuses" suddenly presiding over the Estates and all France appeared impressive to some but "were really just a batch of pretentious, babbling journalists." Mirabeau, Gorsas, Beaumarchais (author of the *Marriage of Figaro*), and the librarian Carra, the last styled a "little lieutenant of Mirabeau," were the "geniuses of France" derided here by name. These presumptuous upstarts, the people must realize, utilized their undeserved influence not just to make the press a powerful tool but also themselves unduly powerful political agents. The pamphlet proved more accurately prophetic than its author could possibly have imagined.[53]

Not only successful papers emerged during the opening weeks of revolutionary ferment, however, but also short-lived failures, which were, in fact, the majority. More than 515 papers appeared in Paris alone, it is estimated, between May 1789 and October 1791, 54 percent of which lasted less than a month. Nor did only prorevolutionary papers appear. There was an equally striking surge of right-wing, anti-Revolution journals that likewise figured prominently from then until 1793, like *L'Ami du Roi* of the Abbé Royou, the *Gazette de Paris* of Bernabé Durozoy (1745–92), the *Journal politique national des États-Généraux et de la Révolution de 1789* by the antiphilosophe Sabatier, and *Le Mercure de France* (1789–92) of Mallet du Pan, a prominent Swiss ideologue and later intermediary between Paris royalists and the émigrés abroad.[54]

The editors of several of these were also profoundly influenced by the Enlightenment—only in their case not the Radical Enlightenment. Despite being an unrelenting royalist, Durozoy, a mediocre poet, wrote favorably of Protestants, Jews, and divorce, and even recommended the marriage of priests. Mallet du Pan, whose *Mercure* achieved great popularity (its circulation during 1789 reached more than eleven thousand),[55] was a deist detested by liberal monarchists and republicans alike who had known and admired Voltaire, and became a fervent disciple of Burke. Originating from a republic (Geneva) but scion of the antidemocratic patriciate, Mallet made his living by incessantly denouncing equality and democracy and seeking to mobilize popular sentiment against the Revolution.[56] He expressly repudiated the thought of Helvétius, Raynal, and Diderot, and reviled Condorcet, his abhorrence of democracy closely linked to his antiphilosophisme.[57] More liberal monarchist in tone was *Le Journal de la Société de 1789,* edited by Pierre Samuel Dupont de Nemours (1739–1817), Claude-Emmanuel de Pastoret (1756–1840), an important figure in the Revolution, and André Chénier (1762–94), an eminent poet steeped in la philosophie, later executed in the Terror.

Thomas-Marie Royou (1743–92), a Breton and, before the Revolution, teacher at the famous college Louis-le-Grand in Paris, had known Diderot but detested his legacy. Although his *L'Ami du Roi,* founded in May 1790, appeared for less than two years (1790–92), it too was widely read with substantial distribution also outside Paris, circulating in Provence, Bordeaux, and the Bourgogne, besides Brittany and the north, selling especially well to conservative-minded women, clergy, and army officers. The paper's circulation figures climbed steadily to more than five thousand, placing it among the foremost journals of the early Revolution.[58] Royou has been called the "Marat" of French royalism, but unlike Marat, he abjured violence, dreading civil war more than anything. He was an antidemocratic and antirepublican extremist only in principle, always relentlessly hostile to la philosophie. Politically, he stood closer to rightist constitutional *monarchiens* like Mounier than the ultraroyalists. His paper's principal promoter was Anne-Françoise Fréron, Royou's sister and widow of Élie Fréron (1718–76), sworn enemy of Diderot, the critic whose journal, the *Année Littéraire,* had for decades conducted a bitter crusade against the philosophes and *Encyclopédie.*[59] In the autumn of 1790, rivalry between royalist editors briefly led to Paris actually having three dailies entitled *L'Ami du Roi,* all invoking Fréron's Counter-Enlightenment. "Never had the king so many friends," joked Royou's publisher.[60]

The Revolution's leaders, complained royalists, were just a minute, wholly unrepresentative group, embodying no established segment of society, just "des philosophes" and "démi-philosophes." The authority and privileges of king, nobility, clergy, and parlements were being challenged by men uttering philosophique rhetoric, possessing no standing in ancien régime terms, who were rendered momentary masters of the country by a wave of vague, inarticulate discontent. Admittedly, there was also a rival, more moderate revolutionary creed that rejected la philosophie and urged France to emulate Britain and the United States. The constitutional monarchist Nicolas Bergasse (1750–1832), in his *Lettre de M. Bergasse sur les États-Generaux* of 12 February 1789, for example, implored readers to weigh the advantages of the British

parliamentary system and consider the United States "where the equality of men is the first of political dogmas" and the legislature in all
states "composed of two chambers." Bergasse considered two chambers
indispensable for genuine mixed government, with an upper house mediating as an "independent voice" between monarch (or president) and
Commons.[61] But precisely this summons to forget philosophy and follow Britain, sublime to some, failed to predominate before the Estates-
General met, or during its meetings, or later. All this amounted to an
extraordinary, unheard-of situation. This strange, upstart revolutionary
clique pushing for fundamental reforms would soon find that breaking
all the bonds of the past, as they proposed, is impossible except in "un
monde de philosophes." These philosophes, admonished Sabatier, ignoring society's need for dependence and subordination, and forgetting
about envy, greed, duplicity, and villainy, would eventually discover that
they could not possibly succeed.[62]

How exactly did the *philosophe-revolutionnaires* of 1789 achieve their
ascendancy with substantial popular support, given that most ordinary folk did not read their books and would scarcely have understood
had they tried?[63] It was actually the ephemeral press, cheap tracts, and
pamphlets—not books—that first powered philosophy's breakthrough.
Popular response to the events of 1789, noted Sabatier, Mounier, and
other observers, was chiefly shaped by pamphlets, posters, and papers—
short, cheap texts easily consumed by the public, presenting summa-
ries and excerpts supplied by heirs of the philosophes. Such extracts
the people "a fort bien saisis" (perfectly grasped).[64] One pamphlet, of
March 1789, urged Raynal to be more specific in providing political
guidance "since it is certain you prophesied the great event we are witnessing. You showed the nation the justice of its rights, and by instilling
hope of seeing these recovered, inspired the courage, force and means of
a happy revolution that your work has prepared."[65] Sabatier cites a "disgusting" paraphrase of lines from Rousseau's *Contrat Social*, featured in
Carra's tract *L'Orateur des États Généraux* of late April 1789, a brochure
he notes that penetrated "incredibly among the common people," swaying many who were completely incapable of reading the *Contrat Social*
itself.[66] It was via printed discourses and tracts, explained Desmoulins
in *La France libre*, that the revolutionary leadership began liberating
the nation, a task that was chiefly educative and involved repelling the
"pastors" who had lorded it over the "vile troupes of slaves" the French
had been hitherto. This 1788–89 campaign to spur the people against
despotism was headed, averred Desmoulins, by "Raynal, Sieyès, Chape-

lier, Target, Mounier, Rabaut, Barnave, Volney and Mirabeau," the last someone who "has contributed more than anyone to emancipate us."[67]

That a full-scale revolution was under way even before the Estates-General convened in late April 1789 was not obvious to most, but it was to Mirabeau, Gorsas, Brissot, Carra, and other publicists emerging as the Revolution's opinion makers. Carra, ally of Brissot and Mirabeau, had, like them, published widely before 1788, since the 1770s adhered to radical ideas. He had expounded his prerevolutionary views in *La Raison, ou le prophète philosophe*, a book banned in 1773, then reissued at Bouillon in a revised version, and again suppressed in 1782. Its argument was the "système de la raison" rooted in a materialism drawn from d'Holbach's *Système de la nature* (1770).[68] Attracted to the idea that all living creatures emerged from inanimate matter and that humanity's history is a slow evolution from brute animal sensibility toward clear consciousness and mastery of language driven by the progress of "universal reason," he envisaged society as progressing via the advance of reason toward Man's eventual emancipation from "ignorance and imposture." Carra defines reason as the "harmony resulting from the convergence of images all the human senses communicate to our brains"; only vulgar minds construed "reason" as an attribute of an immortal spiritual entity (the soul) separate from the body.[69] Though, like Brissot, he knew England, spoke English, and admired the American Revolution, Anglo-American influences remained marginal to Carra's ideological makeup. His political message was unwaveringly blunt: as the sole function of existing laws was to oppress the weak on behalf of vested interests, the nation, not the king, must be acknowledged as "first and true sovereign" and royal ministers set aside as "apologistes" of "despotisme." The principle of orders must be repudiated and the nation restored to "all its rights and functions."[70] Existing law being just an organized system of injustice, completely new laws, "simple, just and general" were required, conceived on the basis of equality of rights and obligations, framing the "universal society" of the future in accord with the "principles of universal reason."[71]

Universal wretchedness for Carra, as for Diderot, D'Holbach, and the *Histoire philosophique*, stemmed directly from man's inability to understand his situation; this, and popular deference for religious authority, enabled ruthless and rapacious men to set themselves up as kings, nobles, and priests who then exploited the rest like a herd of pack animals. Tyrants easily subjugate men steeped in superstition, especially with "ridiculous myths" about gods who reward and punish, and a paradise where "this earth's wretched souls will find peace and happiness after death."[72] Every people, held Carra, forms part of "la société universelle" and equally needs emancipation.[73] With laws affecting everyone equally, society evens the balance between its members, preventing the strongest and cleverest from exploiting the less advantaged. The prime agent of human progress powering emancipation and revolution, and securing these "advantages" for everyone, is the advance of reason, or "la vraie philosophie."[74]

"What caused the Revolution?," asked Rabaut Saint-Étienne, a Protestant preacher now an Estates deputy. Its origin lay in ideas circulating beforehand containing "all the germs of the Revolution" expressed in the writings of those philosophes who most powerfully assailed the *préjugés* of the age, a school of "hommes supérieures" whose writings diffused "a mass of useful truths" on all sides. Voltaire started the process by fighting for liberty of expression. Those following him went further but were persecuted by king, Church, and parlements. Yet, through their efforts, "the truth" permeated every part of the kingdom, including "houses of all kinds," until finally, by 1788, France's "inquisition" of thought, worn out by its burgeoning task, ground to a halt. Widely circulated pamphlets, he rightly surmised, made possible by the de facto press liberty (except for newspapers) gained by 1788, were the first major step of the Revolution.[75] These "heroes of thought" then generated a "multitude de disciples," forming a new kind of reading public, a bench of critical opinion that finally assumed the role of a collective tribunal, judging kings and ministers and examining more general questions of government. Such a large, informed sector was unknown to the ancients because they lacked printing.[76] The *Encyclopédie* especially laid the basis for public discussion of politics, economics, and state finances by bringing all sciences together in a single compilation. Rousseau exerted a huge impact. Raynal denounced all "les tyrannies," unmasking every hypocrisy, the *Histoire philosophique*, the most widely read work of the later Enlightenment, making contemporaries share his "indignation contre les tyrans."[77] Finally, the great agitation of 1788 arose, shaped especially by the pamphlets of the philosophes' disciples, the ideas of Mably, Rousseau, and Raynal pervading every debate. In 1788, claimed Rabaut, Paris became the "foyer" of Enlightenment discourse. Paris was indeed the Revolution's foyer, agreed the constitutional monarchist Mounier, an active power obliging some revolutionary leaders like Barnave, Bailly, and Rabaut himself to step well beyond the limited positions their instinctive moderation originally recommended to them.[78]

Diderot's disciple Naigeon similarly highlighted this process of intellectual subversion before and during 1788. Ardent for the Revolution of reason and the Rights of Man,[79] he later fiercely rejected the populism of Marat and Robespierre, which, in his view, perverted the Revolution's core values. The ancien régime's collapse, held Naigeon in 1790, resulted from a process irreversible once diffusion of new revolutionary ideas penetrated beyond a certain point, touching all social classes.[80] Intellectually, by 1790, the "gothic building" of the ancien régime lay in ruins. But the Revolution would remain incomplete, he admonished, while freedom of thought, expression, and the press were not fully formalized and religious authority was not drastically curtailed. Laws needed changing so that it no longer mattered whether a man was a Christian, Jew, deist, or idolater, and the "true faithful" were simply the "good citizens."[81] Only by liquidating royal, ecclesiastical, and aristocratic power could government establish mankind's rights on the basis of "justice envers tous," without which no governmental authority can be truly legitimate.[82]

These dogged campaigners for press freedom spoke of basic human rights. In his memoir of June 1789 on press freedom to the Estates, Brissot proclaimed liberty of the press "un droit naturel à l'homme."[83] He also raised the issue of liberty from theater censorship, totally lacking even in Britain, he notes, where the stage was strictly licensed by the Crown. Theater freedom mattered more for renewing "liberty" than people think, since the theater exerts a great influence "sur l'esprit public," a point he would develop further, he adds, were not a writer of energy and talent already doing so. He was speaking of the poet Chénier's brother, the playwright Marie-Joseph Chénier (1762–1811), among the Revolution's principal champions of free expression and free theater.[84] By July 1789 the question was not whether or not France should possess freedom of expression and of the press but rather whether this freedom needed limits. Should there be "liberté illimité de la presse" without legal responsibility for calumny or inciting violence? This posed a dilemma, for aside from the principle itself, there lingered much anxiety concerning its real cultural effects. Many assumed that the campaign to bring philosophy to the people would fail. It was in the people's name that press freedom and the other new rights were justified, and yet, not one-hundredth part of the people actually read, while only one-thousandth part read with sufficient discernment and knowledge, admonished the writer, veteran republican and future deputy Louis-Sebastien Mercier (1740–1814), to separate truth from falsehood. The ordinary man, being ignorant, judges politicians' reputations by ostensible probity and popular reputation rather than talent or knowledge—with predictably disastrous results.[85]

Experience soon revealed the drawbacks of full freedom of expression. It was highly dangerous, concluded some, to permit unlimited freedom. For this enabled ill-wishers to continually denounce the best, most knowledgeable, and virtuous as "scoundrels" and "traitors" who conspired with *aristocratisme* and monarchism. Unrestricted press freedom, lamented Desmoulins (who later with Danton, in 1793–94, tried to curb the Terror),[86] called into existence a new species of political deceiver, *le calomniateur* despot, who systematically defamed rivals, forging a new kind of tyranny—*le despotisme populacier*—built on organized ignorance. The "whole art of the vile rascals" blighting the Revolution by discrediting men of principle, he came to believe, lay in mimicking popular parlance and expression while disseminating views designed to cheat the multitude. It was certainly with barely camouflaged lies and distortion that populism eventually overpowered the Revolution, aborting the first modern democracy.

CHAPTER 3

From Estates-General to National Assembly

(APRIL–JUNE 1789)

In April and early May 1789, more than 1,000 delegates for the Estates-General, elected in local assemblies all across France—the number eventually rose to 1,200—converged on Versailles, bringing instructions from their particular localities. Only around 800 (about half representing the Third), had actually arrived, though, in time for the opening. The day before, on 4 May, a vast ceremonial procession headed by the king and queen, and the princes of blood, followed by around 800 delegates, had proceeded from the church of Notre-Dame to the church of Saint Louis. On 5 May, the elaborately choreographed inauguration ceremony itself passed off smoothly, except that when the king gave permission for the nobility to resume wearing their hats in his presence, some of the Third did so too, causing momentary confusion, consternation, and outcries. Otherwise, the occasion was resplendent and focused on the glittering figures of the king and queen. Never had the monarchy looked more imposing. The king delivered a solemn discourse outlining the financial predicament of the realm. Paris's scheduled thirty-nine deputies, however, were among the many who missed it. The capital's "primary assemblies" had convened in the city's larger churches where 11,706 voters had elected 407 "electors." But these assemblies had a great deal to discuss and had not yet finalized their delegate selection.[1]

Once begun, the Estates-General promptly stalled. The 400 or so members of the Third present, swayed by the antiaristocratic publicity of recent months, demanded a joint procedure that subjected delegates for the three orders to approval by all and refused to permit the higher orders to verify their deputies' credentials separately. This procedural revolt was tentative but resolute. As days and then weeks passed, the Third refused to budge. "The classes that live by abuse," complained Volney, deputy for Angers, three days after the opening on 8 May, already impatient with most of his colleagues' timidity, were "determined to permit no real change." Self-interested calculation was the explanation for their unbending insistence on precedent. The obduracy of the *privilégiés* and hesitancy of the Third's response filled "all Paris with false rumor and calumny." Comprehensive change was required. All outmoded formulae should be discarded, formal minutes kept, more formality in speaking adopted, and less freedom to interrupt permitted. All "metaphysical" veneration for the past should be delegitimized. Nothing should deter their introducing political terms never employed before in the Estates-General, such as "constitution," "chamber," and "deputies."[2]

Even stronger than Volney's and Mirabeau's summons to the Estates was a detailed, full-length plan issued shortly before the Estates-General opened, published by a close observer outside the Estates, namely, Brissot. This was his *Plan de conduite pour les députés du peuple aux États-Généraux* of April 1789, a key text that uncompromisingly asserted the principle of equality and demanded that the deputies stand firm against all the privileged classes, not just the nobility and higher clergy but also the high judiciary and the haute bourgeoisie. Brissot insists here, more so, perhaps, than any writer had before, on France's need to adopt an entirely new constitution, including a carefully formulated Declaration of the Rights of Man as the foundation of a "free constitution" based on equality. He even lists what he considered the seven foremost of these, one of which was that all Frenchmen are born equal and are equal in rights and cannot be subjected to any law not assented to by them "or by their representatives in the Estates-General."[3] His text also cited the names of those deputies Brissot thought could be relied on to lead the legislature to unrestricted independence, control of the nation's finances, and the legislature's right to convene independently of the Crown every year and fight both Crown and privilégiés unremittingly. These key personages cited by him in April 1789, constituting the effective leadership of the Revolution, were Mirabeau, Volney, Sieyès, Bergasse, Rabaut de Saint-Étienne, Mounier, and Lafayette. Among writers most apt to second their efforts, he identified Condorcet, Cérutti, Target, and his own comrade, Clavière.[4] He praised but also disagreed with Sieyès, criticizing his exalting representative democracy without allowing for a measure of direct democracy to offset it.[5]

By seeming too diffident, the Third meanwhile risked being accused of betraying the people's trust. This feeling of urgency, spurred by a public expecting tangible progress, intensified through June, as did the Paris electoral assemblies' impatience. Nor was it left only to radical tracts to prod the Third's timid majority. Those prominent earlier in the Paris electoral districts (or sections), prolonged their active role by appropriating the right to serve as a political pressure-group petitioning the Estates-General on the capital's behalf. Though supposed only to finalize the capital's list of deputies, Paris's general assembly of "electors" continued meeting while the main drama unfolded at Versailles, and where May's hesitant noncooperation became open revolt in June. After weeks of disputing the verification of credentials, the obdurate Third were joined by contingents of clerical and noble defectors. Then, contrary to all precedent and quite illegally, on 17 June the resulting enlarged Third proclaimed itself the "National Assembly," which prompted still more lower clergy and a third of the nobility's delegates to come over. The latter joined the fifty-eight "nobles," including Mirabeau and Volney, already elected to represent the Third Estate.[6] "We shall know I think within a day or two," reported Jefferson, the American ambassador in Paris, to Madison the next day, "whether the government will risk a bankruptcy and civil war rather than see all distinction of orders done away with which is what the Commons will push for."[7]

This declaration of 17 June 1789, as has often been noted, took onlookers by surprise and constituted a stunning revolutionary act in itself, signifying not just rejection of noble and ecclesiastical privilege but also France's entire existing institutional structure. Most nobles and higher clergy simply refused to acknowledge the new body. Yet, the privileged orders, initially given no lead by the court, offered only passive resistance. Then, on 20 June 1789, royal troops did appear, and the Assembly deputies, on arriving at the meeting hall "as usual, found the doors shut and guarded," reported Jefferson, "and a proclamation posted up for holding a *séance royale*, on the 22nd, and a suspension of their meetings until then."[8] The Crown, seemingly, would now make a stand. Convening instead in the nearby royal tennis court and urged on by the astronomer Bailly, the deputies collectively took the famous Tennis Court Oath, immortalized later in a stirring painting by the Revolution's greatest artist, Jacques-Louis David (1748–1825), vowing "never to separate" until the constitution was satisfactorily recast (figure 1).

Louis XVI, surrounded by nobles and ecclesiastics, offered a long, detailed, and, in traditional terms, perfectly reasonable compromise

Figure 1. Jacques-Louis David (1748–1825), *The Tennis Court Oath, Versailles, 20th June 1789*, 1791 (pen washed with bistre with highlights of white on paper). Chateau de Versailles, France / The Bridgeman Art Library.

on 23 June, which he read out to the gathering in person. The Crown conceded many points outright—abolition of privileged fiscal immunities, ending arbitrary arrest under lettres de cachet, and abolishing rural forced labor on roads and bridges under the corvée.[9] The king also agreed to negotiate on other points, inviting "the Estates," for example, to propose how to reconcile "liberty of the press with the respect due to religion, morality and the honor of citizens."[10] But he rejected outright several of the Third's key demands staunchly opposed by the Notables, in particular, refusing to abolish voting by orders in "the Estates-General" or to liquidate honorary privileges. The orders should remain separate entities with separate rights and, in part, separate functions. Thus, the "particular consent of the clergy would remain necessary for all resolutions concerning religion." Louis also vigorously reaffirmed his sole sovereignty and control over police powers and the military.[11]

The Third, prompted by Mirabeau's stirring oratory, seconded by Barnave, Pétion, Buzot, and Sieyès, rejected separate orders and insisted on their unilaterally declared title of "Assemblée Nationale," refusing the royal compromise.[12] More clergy joined them. But still, most nobility and a majority of the First Estate, 132 churchmen, stubbornly resisted. Tension rose. Then, dramatically, on 27 June, the brewing storm was dispelled, but with the court—not the Third—backing down. This was at least partly because, as Jefferson noted, the unrest was visibly spreading to the king's French troops, some of whom "began to quit their barracks, to assemble in squads, to declare that they would defend the life of the king, but would not cut the throats of their fellow citizens," leaving onlookers in "no doubt on which side they would be in case of a rupture."[13] Hesitantly, Louis opted to acknowledge the new body, "inviting" the recalcitrant noblesse and rump of rejectionist clergy to rejoin the rest of what he too now designated the "National Assembly."[14] With Bailly as "president," this new body opened its first session on 30 June.[15] Sovereignty had been partially transferred to the people. The Revolution was truly under way.

Meanwhile, there was a considerable ferment in the Paris electoral districts. Having chosen Brissot as an "elector," the district assembly of Des Filles Saint-Thomas section was persuaded by him, at a meeting on 21 April, of the need for a correspondence committee connecting the Paris electoral assemblies with their deputies at Versailles. This committee should function until the already discussed and projected future Declaration of Rights was obtained. Support for this strategy proved forthcoming also from other districts, notably Carme Déchaussés, where the recently elected president was Nicolas Bonneville (1760–1828), friend of Tom Paine and professional writer and translator. Bonneville vigorously supported Brissot's proposal that the Paris assembly reconstitute itself as the mouthpiece of Paris to pressure the National Assembly.[16] The council of 407 Paris electors, meeting in the town hall, not only sifted the capital's petitions and cahiers of grievances for their deputies to the Estates but resumed conferring as a general assembly of the capital's electors in June, and on 12 July constituted a provisional city government, the forerunner of the revolutionary Commune.[17] It was in these circles that pressure for a constitution and a declaration of rights first gained momentum and that several foremost publicists of the 1788 pamphlet controversies, having failed to be elected as Estates-General deputies, reemerged as leaders of this assembly and of the Revolution more generally.

In this way, the assembly of Paris electors promoted radical principles, prodding the National Assembly from outside. It considered itself the voice of the citizenry's will and the capital's deputies at Versailles to be bound by its instructions. The Declaration of the Rights of Man, to which some Paris primary assemblies had been committed since April, was designated to include full freedom of thought, freedom of expression, and freedom of the press. The Paris assembly of electors was backed by the city's local "sections," clubs, and reading societies, as well as the press, throughout France. It thus formed a pyramidal platform of opinion capable of stiffening the radical clique at Versailles, serving as an invaluable reinforcement for Mirabeau's and Sieyès's bid to lead the National Assembly despite the philosophe-révolutionnaires' miniscule numbers there and the antipathy of the merchants and lawyers.[18]

By 9 July, the National Assembly's newly formed constitutional committee had embraced the Paris radicals' initiative, agreeing that France needed a new constitution and that it "should begin," Jefferson informed Paine, "by a Declaration of the natural and imprescriptible rights of man."[19] At this point, one of the liberal members of the Assembly noblesse, Marie-Joseph-Paul, Marquis de Lafayette (1757–1834), hero of the American Revolution and friend of Jefferson, aiming to seize the initiative with Jefferson's help, drew up a draft list of basic rights in thirteen carefully crafted articles.[20] Paris, meanwhile, became very tense. The Assembly's defiance of court, nobility, and clergy was bolstered by the groundswell of support in the Paris streets and cafés. Transmitting this support through the assembly of electors proved crucial. The leaders of opinion there—Brissot, Bonneville, Carra, Desmoulins, Gorsas, and Condorcet—were principally, in Sabatier's words, "philosophes," a mix of intellectuals and literary people. Those supporting them, echoing the revolutionary leaders and passing on the word in the streets, he designated "demi-philosophes." These demi-philosophe street agitators dominated the Palais-Royal, the locale that in turn steered opinion in Paris. These "esprits extrêmes" were now so implacably fired up against noble birth and priesthood that the very word "noblesse" drove them into a fury capable, complained Sabatier, of precipitating a "saint Barthélémi philosophique."[21]

Deferring to the king's wishes, the National Assembly remained at Versailles. But no one knew for sure whether king and court really acquiesced in the changes adopted thus far or were merely playing for time, stalling while preparing a grand countercoup. If the much-rumored royal "conspiracy" really existed (in Jefferson's view, the king probably had no intention of bombarding Paris and suppressing the National Assembly by force),[22] it was very poorly executed. But the danger seemed real enough at the time. Several minor disturbances occurred, and on 8 July the Versailles Assembly convened in an emergency session. There were now 35,000 royal troops with artillery positioned between Versailles and Paris, announced Mirabeau, with another 20,000 expected shortly. On 10 July, the Assembly voted to send a deputation of six nobles, six clergy, and twelve of the Third to read an address, penned by Mirabeau, to the king. The bringing up of these forces, they protested respectfully, directly contradicted Louis's stated desire to calm the country, and prejudiced the Assembly's liberty and honor.[23]

Everyone knew of the disturbances daily unsettling Paris, replied Louis, turmoil under the very eyes of court and Estates. He judged it necessary to use the means at his disposal to maintain order in the capital and its environs. The sole purpose of the troops, he urged the deputation to assure the Assembly, was to prevent further unrest: "only ill-intentioned persons could mislead my peoples about the true motives of the precautionary measures I am taking."[24] As more royal regiments moved up, some newspapers and verbal reports reaching the Palais-Royal from Versailles deliberately fomented the impression that a full-scale counterrevolution by military force was imminent. Especially dismaying to Parisians was the king's dismissal of the popular reforming minister, Necker, on 11 July, a move that greatly aggravated the crisis and was deemed proof of "the aristocracy's perfidious intentions" and of the parlements wanting "the great project of our regeneration aborted."[25] "The mobs immediately shut up all the play houses," reported Jefferson, "the foreign troops were advanced into the city. Engagements took place between some of them and the people."[26] Amid unprecedented ferment, the Paris electoral districts and assembly gathered to debate the crisis while a "dangerous tumult" surged also at Rouen (where German dragoons were deployed) and at Versailles, where the streets were disturbed by both mob demonstrations and friction between the Swiss and French Guards.

Necker's dismissal heightened the tension between king and Assembly and simultaneously deepened the split emerging in the Assembly between constitutional monarchists and the Left. The small but vociferous core of crypto-republicans and virtual republicans sought to curtail royal authority as much as possible, rendering ministers responsible to the legislature, while an increasingly vocal center right, headed by the Anglophile monarchist, Jean-Joseph Mounier (1756–1806), wanted the king to retain an unrestricted choice of his ministers and the right to dismiss them at will. With the Third divided, serious unrest ensued on 11 July and continued for four days. Fear and uncertainty, sharpened by the grain shortage, did most to provoke the turmoil, resulting at Rouen—France's sixth city, with some 70,000 inhabitants—in spontaneous pillaging of shops and grain stores and leaving several killed and wounded.[27] In Paris, by contrast, the rioting assumed a distinctly more organized format with virtually no pillaging or pilfering. "There was a severity of honesty observed," noted Jefferson, "of which no example has been known." Popular anger and frustration in the capital was channeled by republican agitators and subversives—most conspicuously by Bonneville, Desmoulins, and Théophile Mandar, an expert in English republican thought. Desmoulins and Mandar—both able orators thoroughly steeped in philosophy, along with others—delivered rabble-rousing speeches in the Palais-Royal cafés, exhorting action and a call to arms.[28]

On the evening of 12 July, Desmoulins, having earlier that day been at Versailles, delivered a particularly inflammatory speech at the Palais-Royal Café de Foy, assuring the crowds that a court plot certainly existed to suppress the Revolution by using the king's foreign regiments to massacre everyone who defied the royal will.[29] At this point, Desmoulins had already written (though not yet published) his fervently republican pamphlet *La France libre*. As a cheering crowd swirled around him, he famously leaped onto a table and summoned the people to save themselves and the Revolution by resorting to arms. That evening, there was a dangerous confrontation on the Champs-Élysées, where units of Swiss and German dragoons were encamped. Armed rioters began a noisy demonstration, to which the troops responded by firing blanks into the air.[30] The mob, led by veterans like Mandar (formerly a soldier), secured arms by breaking into the civic arms store. An alarming situation turned into a catastrophe for the Crown when the demonstrators were joined by hundreds of deserting troops of the Garde Française (the French palace guard). For days, the city remained gripped by an extraordinary turmoil. An immediate consequence was the dissolution of the old city council and transfer of control to a steering committee of the assembly of electors presided over by Brissot, Bonneville, Carra, Fauchet, and other leaders of the Parisian assembly. Accusing the court of conspiring against the National Assembly, these representatives assumed responsibility for restoring order and grain supplies. Having secured control of Paris, it was this emergency committee, following detailed deliberations on 11 and 12 July, that created a new Paris civic militia called the National Guard. This freshly formed militia was then ordered to mount day and night patrols to prevent uncontrolled disorder and crime.

On 13 July, informed that an immense crowd had gathered at the Palais-Royal, including numerous armed men, the National Assembly met again in emergency session. The crowds reportedly intended to confront the troops encamped on the Champs-Élysées. Another deputation, this time twenty commoners, ten nobles, and ten ecclesiastics, including four bishops, besought the king to withdraw his troops, suggesting that it might be best if the National Assembly transferred to Paris. The king doubly refused: he would remain judge of where and when to deploy armed force; the Assembly would remain at Versailles.[31] On 14 July, crowds of artisans, shopkeepers, and journeymen, many from the poor Saint-Antoine district of Paris,[32] protesting against the "conspiracy" at court, spent the morning standing about in confused indecision. Many wanted to march on Versailles, chief focus of their resentment, but suddenly the crowds moved off toward the Bastille instead. The project of capturing this "monument of *despotisme*" and releasing the prisoners had seized their collective imagination and, as if directed by Providence (some said)—and in uncannily orderly fashion—the people marched to the Bastille in one body with Bonneville and Fauchet among the electors in the lead.[33] At the Bastille, Bonneville in particular tried to convince the garrison to surrender peacefully. The governor, the Marquis de Launay, refused. As the crowds pressed forward, the 150 defenders lining the walls under the royal white banner opened fire with cannon and muskets. The well-armed besiegers, headed by defecting French guards, responded by using cannon to breach the walls. After five hours of bombardment, they succeeded. Storming the fortress, the mob massacred everyone who refused to surrender, including de Launay, who fired on the insurgents to the last. Twenty or thirty were killed. The fortress stormed, a liberty hat was hoisted to vast applause, the prisoners in the cells were released, and the cannon removed to the town hall. The Bastille was handed over to the new city militia, and order was restored throughout the capital.

Afterward, a vast throng of armed citizens gathered in the city center, especially around the Palais-Royal. Trenches were dug and barriers thrown up around a ring of streets to prevent cavalry incursions from breaking through. Word crossed Paris that the Prince de Condé would shortly appear, commanding 40,000 troops intent on massacring enough citizens, perhaps 100,000, to end the insurrection then and there. Masses of carts were used to block all entrances to the city, which were heavily manned. The entire capital was lit up as never before in a blaze of illumination and celebration. Hardly anyone slept that night, since everyone expected an imminent attack.[34] The crowds in the streets were simultaneously fearful and exhilarated, as were the philosophe-révolutionnaires who had brought matters to this point. Over subsequent days, persistent rumor alleged a court plan for multiple thrusts into the city from four or five directions at once, with Condé advancing through the Faubourg Saint-Martin and the Maréchal de Broglio via the Place de Louis XV (today Place de la Concorde). But the court, deeply dismayed, simply caved in again. After the king had twice publicly refused to withdraw his regiments, stiffened by advisors intent on reimposing his authority, the encamped troops were quietly withdrawn, creating an unprecedented situation.

If the court was stunned, Paris was euphoric. As news of the Bastille's fall swept the city, a group of revolutionary intellectuals immersed in café discussion, including Jefferson, Volney, and Louis-Marie de La Réveillière-Lépeaux (1753–1824), a vehemently republican, anti-Catholic botanist-philosophe, broke into excited laughter and shouts of joy with much stamping of feet and jigging around tables. Jefferson, since June an enthusiastic sympathizer, ventured: "Eh bien! oui, Messieurs, you are delighted by this triumph. But you must contend with the nobles and priests, and until you have dealt with them you will never have liberty."[35] Realizing the Bastille's storming was a decisive event affording them the psychological and potentially political upper hand, Mirabeau's following, like the Paris assembly of electors' steering group, became inebriated figuratively and literally. Later that day, Volney attended another gathering of intellectuals at Helvétius's mansion in nearby Auteuil-Passy. Present besides himself, Sieyès, and Madame Helvétius (who resented the royal court's hounding of her philosophe husband) were Garat, Chamfort, and Pierre-Jean-Georges Cabanis (1757–1808), a young medical man close to Condorcet, a republican-materialist philosophe who was shortly to join Mirabeau's team of researchers and speech writers. Earlier on 14 July, Cabanis had stood nearby watching the storming of the Bastille. Fervent for la philosophie moderne, he was close, not just to Condorcet and Mirabeau but several other deputies "des plus violens." He and his circle not only exulted over the Bastille but also the recent peasant risings and attacks on noble property, including in the Bas-Limousin (Cabanis's native region) where serious disorder had erupted.

These ardent *réformateurs*, long embracing philosophically radical positions, were motivated according to the moderate philosophe Morellet, who knew them intimately, by dangerous passions and *l'ambition démocratique*. The worst among them, in his view, were Sieyès, Volney, and Chamfort.[36] Cabanis, Garat, and Mme. Helvétius were also totally convinced, he later recalled, that Louis and the court had plotted to bludgeon the capital into submission. Over this, the Helvétius salon, like all of France's intellectual bodies, not excepting the Académie Française itself, irrevocably split. Despite differences, until July 1789, enlightened opinion had remained broadly united. Liberty, toleration, "horror of despotism and superstition," and "le désire de voir reformer les abus" (the desire to see abuses reformed), had, after all, long been common ground among enlighteners, moderate and radical.[37] All this changed from 14 July as emotions ran high, opinion polarized, and questions of social hierarchy, monarchy, and religious faith became unavoidable. Diderot's disciples, Deleyre and Naigeon (with whom Morellet had clashed in the past), figured among the "most zealous partisans" of equality and the Revolution.[38] Conservatives like Morellet, Marmontel, and Suard, by contrast, defended their aristocratic preferences and now opposed the Revolution. But abjuring the Revolution inevitably meant breaking also with the Helvétius salon, with their former friends, now mostly declared democrats and republicans, and withdrawing into a brooding silence.[39] Instead of staying neutral, as Morellet implored, Mme. Helvétius aligned with Volney, Garat, Cabanis, Chamfort, Sieyès, and Mirabeau.[40] The Bastille's storming thus dramatically widened the rift between the rival Enlightenment wings—radical and moderate—in their respective views about politics and reform.

On the evening of 15 July, another group of revolutionaries staged a remarkable piece of political theater. A crowd, led by Georges Danton (1759–94), wound its way to the Bastille. Of humble background from a small town in the Champagne, a hundred miles from Paris, and a recently qualified junior lawyer, Danton had emerged through the sheer force of his personality—hearty, hot-tempered, and boisterous—as leader of one of the liveliest of the capital's circles of committed revolutionaries. Marching from the Cordeliers district, one of the precincts most stirred by Desmoulins and Mandar in recent days, starting from the Café Procope, where Danton and his comrades had spent the day conferring and drinking, the crowd sought to demonstrate that the royal fortress had come under the people's sovereignty. The officer in charge, just installed by Lafayette, the head of the National Guard, was summoned and subjected to a citizen's arrest. The procession then escorted this officer to the city hall where, however, Paris's freshly appointed mayor, Bailly, frowning on Danton's antics, released him and sent him back to his post.[41]

The Cordeliers district, in the heart of Left Bank Paris, later to give its name to one of the foremost revolutionary clubs, was a particular

Figure 2. *The Storming of the Bastille, Paris, 14 July 1789.* Image courtesy Bibliothèque nationale de France.

hub of political ferment. A mixed, partly working-class district, skilled artisans supplied most of the club's membership, infusing it with some vigorous social discontent. But what shaped the Cordeliers precinct as a revolutionary spearhead was less the local artisans and their grievances than its leading figures—Danton, Desmoulins, Fabre d'Églantine, Mandar, Maréchal, Manuel, Prudhomme, Marat, and Pierre-François Robert (1762–1826), a prominent revolutionary journalist and author of another principal republican tract of 1789, *Le Républicanisme adapté à la France.* Aside from Danton himself, a brilliant orator but no intellectual, these were all highly literate and accomplished writers, editors, or publishers. Above all, what lent the Cordeliers its republican stamp, remarks Desmoulins, was the intensely literary Café Procope, in 1789, as in past decades, a constant focus of ardent philosophical debate.[42]

During the summer of 1789, after the Bastille's fall, a tussle for power developed in Paris between three rival political factions. One was headed by the astronomer Bailly, Condorcet's rival for primacy within the Academy of Sciences and secretary of the council of electors, who was appointed mayor with the approval of the crowds on 15 July by the Paris electors' assembly.[43] A long-standing critic of the ancien régime, Bailly, unlike Desmoulins, Carra, Condorcet, Robert, Bonneville, Brissot, and Mandar, was no republican democrat, however, but a constitutional monarchist, if more liberal than Mounier.[44] Son of the keeper of the king's pictures, former protégé of the renowned biologist Buffon, he was an eminent scholar and the first academician since Fontenelle to belong simultaneously (from 1784) to all three principal royal academies—the Académie Française, the Académie des Inscriptions, and the Académie des Sciences. A well-meaning man, resented by Mesmer enthusiasts for his part in the Académie des Sciences' condemnation of Mesmerism as "superstition,"[45] Bailly enjoyed a splendid reputation as an Enlightenment leader, or at least did until Catherine the Great discovered that he had become a revolutionary. Incensed, having earlier approved bestowal on him of an honorific medal depicting herself as the glorious sponsor of the sciences, she canceled the award.

Bailly was backed by Lafayette as well as, initially, by Gorsas and several pro-Revolution papers. Opposition to his leadership emanated partly from the almost openly republican democratic faction in the municipality headed by Brissot, Condorcet, and Bonneville. But confronting both Bailly and the Brissot faction was a third bloc—those inner Paris districts, like the Cordeliers, loudly voicing claims of "popular sovereignty." Everyone agreed that a new municipal constitution for Paris was required. Accordingly, Bailly convened a civic convention consisting of three representatives from each of the city's sixty districts, hence, a council of 180. At its first meeting on 25 July 1789, this new communal assembly empowered a committee of sixteen to deliberate articles for the projected new Paris municipal constitution, asking Brissot to draw up the plan for the committee to review, since he had already published more on constitutions and legal reform than practically anyone and had firsthand knowledge of England and the United States.[46]

As a legal theorist and social reformer, Brissot was especially indebted to Beccaria, Helvétius, and Rousseau. Besides having (like Mirabeau) personally witnessed the Geneva revolution of 1782, he was prominent in the Franco-British-American antislavery movement and, again like Mirabeau, a long-standing spokesman for another special cause—Jewish emancipation. His *Plan de municipalité* proposed organizing the new city government on three levels: a broad-based general assembly comprising five representatives from each electoral district, hence, three hundred delegates; an executive city council comprising sixty delegates chosen by the communal assembly; and, finally, the executive proper, consisting of the mayor and the National Guard commander, which carried out the executive council's orders. Representative democracy, of which Brissot, Condorcet, and Bonneville were committed advocates, was combined here with a well-defined executive and policy-making machinery. To prevent excessive direct democracy and demagoguery, Brissot's scheme denied the electoral districts the right to impose binding instructions mandating their representatives in the communal assembly. The city districts were declared to be the chief focus of the democratic process at specified election times but not otherwise.[47] Brissot located final authority to make overriding decisions in the assembly of three hundred. It was a plan that affirmed representative democracy, but also included an element of direct democracy.

Clashing directly with this concept, several inner-city primary assemblies, notably the Cordeliers, opposed both the mayor and the communal council and urged the primacy of the districts. If Bailly was checked by Brissot's constitutional commission, Brissot antagonized several inner precincts by trying to impose representative democracy on them.[48] Brissot and his allies did not reject direct democracy, popular petitions, and representations as such. Like Carra, Brissot willingly accepted Rousseau's doctrine that people's assemblies, when properly constituted, override the authority of any representative.[49] What he rejected was excessive subordination of the people's representatives to local assemblies and an uncritical enthusiasm for Rousseau. Here, in a nutshell, was the germ of the later split between the Revolution's three main factions: constitutional monarchism, core Revolution democratic republicanism, and unbending Rousseauist populism.

Within days, enthusiasts were recommending that 14 July should become a national festival.[50] On 17 July, a thoroughly chastened and downcast king entered Paris in person with a small entourage of officers. In an extraordinary ceremony, interpreted by most as one of "contrition," he participated in a deeply symbolic official consecration of the Bastille's storming, representing the event as a liberation from "despotism."[51] Inevitably, such a ceremony marked a considerable, decisive curtailment of royal prestige. Publicly reconciling himself to the Paris insurrection, the king approved replacement of royal troops with the new city militia and Bailly's appointment as mayor, while the latter cheerfully welcomed and applauded the monarch as "the father of the Revolution" and the people's liberation, and pinned a tricolor cockade to his hat. The crowds were euphoric. There was tremendous jubilation. Most revolutionaries nevertheless still deeply distrusted Louis.

Newspaper accounts of the Bastille's fall circulated everywhere. Within days, cheap prints visually depicting the event were on sale in the streets.[52] In Bordeaux, massive crowds, summoned by wall posters, gathered in the Jardin Publique to celebrate, hear speeches, and yell support, with large numbers donning tricolor emblems. In Bordeaux and other cities, municipal government was now dramatically broadened, taken over, as in Paris, by the assemblies of electors, with local branches of the National Guard being established.[53] Disturbingly, though, in several provinces the Bastille's fall was followed, from 20 July, by more than two weeks of chaotic rural unrest, attacks on noble châteaus, and, in places, extensive murder and pillage. In Brittany, more than forty châteaus were sacked and two burned down. Dozens more were attacked in Alsace and the Franche-Comté. By early August, according to the Venetian envoy, nearly fifty noble châteaus had been attacked in the Dauphiné, and several torched.[54] The National Assembly repeatedly expressed outrage and dismay at the anarchic conditions. But having become the voice of the people, noted one observer, the Revolution had no means of controlling the people.[55]

Widespread peasant violence in turn precipitated a wave of emigration (the first of several) of nobles from the countryside. Some of the most illustrious families—the Condés, Contis, Polignac, and Bretuil—fled from the environs of Paris, vowing to organize armed repression to defeat the Revolution from without.[56] This combination of rural savagery with the July unrest in Paris and Rouen, withdrawal of troops, and emergence of a more vigorous and confident revolutionary press all acted as levers operating a basic shift of social and political power from aristocracy and parlements to Third Estate opinion-formers and the dominant cliques in the Paris communal assembly and National Assembly. At the same time, urban employment and economic circumstances generally deteriorated, especially in Paris where conditions grew worse as the months passed due to the flight of hundreds of nobles and other wealthy families, and the consequent redundancy of thousands of domestics, cooks, coachmen, tailors, and servants. The luxury trades, servicing aristocratic households, the city's chief industry, ground almost to a standstill. Distress, shortages, and high food prices in turn intensified the strange mix of euphoria and disgruntlement gripping the city.

Under the combined pressure of Revolution and shortages, many former practices and fixed boundaries crumbled away, losing all meaning. The psychological impact of the Bastille's fall and its aftermath had, as is well known, a lasting influence on the course of the Revolution and cultural life of the nation. The entire press, literary, and cultural

scene split asunder. Five days after the storming of the Bastille, the Paris
theater world erupted with its own revolutionary drama. The noted
young playwright, Marie-Joseph Chénier, another republican zealot
later loathed by Robespierre, appealed to the Comédie-Française's actors to stage his newly completed antimonarchical and anti-Catholic
play *Charles IX*. Designed to inspire hatred of "les préjugés, le fanaticisme et la tyrannie," it represented a new kind of political drama recounting a "national tragedy," the Saint Bartholomew's Day massacres
of 1572. The Revolution had invaded the world of the theater, but most
actors, accustomed to aristocratic audiences and royal censorship rather
than deferring to dissident playwrights, refused to represent a French
monarch onstage as a despot, criminal, and perjurer. Chénier countered
with a publicity campaign demanding his *Charles IX* be performed for
the public good, even loudly interrupting an evening performance of
another play at the Théâtre-Français.

As the furor escalated, the actors found themselves in a weak position because the republican papers, notably Prudhomme's *Révolutions
de Paris* and Brissot's *Patriote français*, unstintingly backed Chénier.
Chief among Chénier's aims was the complete liquidation of the ancien régime censorship by eliminating its last effective strand—theater
censorship.[57] It was the philosophes who taught him and his generation
to think, explained Chénier in his best-known pamphlet (already written but not released until late August), leading them, as if by the hand,
toward the truth: "eux seuls ont préparé la Révolution qui commence"
(they alone have prepared the Revolution now commencing).[58] He
lists philosophy's principal heroes as "Voltaire, Montesquieu, Rousseau,
d'Alembert, Diderot, Mably, Raynal and Helvétius."[59] They had served
society during their lives and now "from the tomb" inspired the Revolution, including the upheaval transforming the theater. How, asks Chénier, did "la philosophie moderne" evolve before 1789 from the writings
of the philosophes into a formidable force reordering all of society?
Through their writings, their example, and society's mounting persecution of them. He particularly stressed the unwitting contribution of the
bishops, who for years fought from the pulpit, issuing pastoral circulars
denouncing la philosophie and its "doctrine abominable" as the source
of all misfortune. The episcopate's campaign had been amply seconded
by what he called the "tyrannie continuelle" of the parlements opposing
philosophy in every way. If philosophy in recent decades had pervaded
France, entered the royal council, and entrenched itself in aristocratic
homes, and if men had finally become reasonable in many respects, the

Revolution and France's citizens owed it all to those hounded before 1788, not just by the Crown but by all branches of authority.[60]

The *Charles IX* furor was a major cultural revolutionary episode with implications extending far beyond freedom of expression. At stake was the social function of culture itself. During the summer of 1789, those resisting *Charles IX* at the same time often accepted freedom of the press as such.[61] At issue was the right to stage material that was topical and indeed divisive—politically, religiously, and socially. In eighteenth-century England, the press was (partially) free, assuredly, but the theater remained rigidly controlled, and more tightly than ever since Walpole's time.[62] Freedom of the theater existed nowhere, and never had, but promised to be a major extension of liberty, opening up a vast new thought-world to innumerable city-dwellers not fully literate. Theater culture stands apart from the world of print by being experienced collectively in an atmosphere of heightened emotion in which the semiliterate fully participate. There can be no true freedom of expression, contended Chénier, where theater is aligned behind conventional thinking. Theater only reflects the people's will where free from the strict conventions to which historically it has been subjected. Hence, the stage, held Chénier, La Harpe, and other stalwarts of the 1789 theater controversy, could be a more potent agent of change than even reading.[63] Equally, the "antitheatricalism" of Chénier's opponents played on the seemingly acute danger of unchaining previously restrained popular emotion.

The newly reformed municipality under Mayor Bailly had to intervene. Both sides in the public dispute accepted that society had entered a new era of freedom, and that the theater represented a potent agent of inspiration and reeducation. In terms of freedom of expression and the much-discussed but not-yet-proclaimed Declaration of the Rights of Man, Chénier might have seemed justified. But Bailly and the antirepublican opposition arguably held the more logical position. France was a monarchy, they pointed out, that had always proclaimed Catholicism the state church: any play purposely aiming to render monarchy and Catholicism odious was therefore contrary to public order and the public interest. Undeniably, *Charles IX* not only dramatized the undesirable consequences of "tyranny" and "fanaticism" but actually equated monarchy with tyranny, and Catholicism with fanaticism, declaring the Saint Bartholomew's Day massacre a crime committed by king and court.[64] Bailly opposed staging *Charles IX*, sharply distinguishing, like British ministers, between liberty of thought and the press and freedom of theater, because in the theater people experience spectacles collectively and, as he put it, "s'électrisent" (mutually electrify each other), becoming potentially disruptive of public order and good morals.[65] Several critics, like Quatremère de Quincy, agreed that the multitude was unpredictable and easily steered in the wrong direction by unpatriotic writers.[66]

Backed by the mayor, the actors briefly regained the initiative. But the republicans mobilized support in the Paris sections against Bailly, in part by buying up large quantities of tickets and packing performances with supporters.[67] On 19 August 1789, demonstrators disrupted a performance at the Comédie-Française, calling out from the pit for *Charles IX*. There was no official permission for this, the actors protested, to which the demonstrators replied: "no more permissions!" As the republicans gained ground in Paris municipal politics, so did Chénier, La Harpe, and other republican theater men in the capital's theater wars. Finally, on 4 November 1789, with the theater's name officially changed from Comédie-Française to Théâtre de la Nation, the play was staged against the actors' wishes. On opening night, both Danton, who had attended some rehearsals, and Mirabeau figured among the audience, endorsing the play's message. As the curtain rose, Danton, despite his huge girth, leaped onto the stage to direct the applause. Staged for several months over the winter of 1789–90, *Charles IX* was indeed a landmark in theater history, inaugurating an era characterized (until Robespierre's coup) by an entirely new close alignment of the stage with philosophy.[68]

The events of the summer of 1789 thus had a most remarkable outcome. Leadership of the Revolution had fallen into the hands of a small, unrepresentative clique. Those leading the Revolution inspired by la philosophie remained, moreover, remarkably confident that they knew where and how to lead. Officially, France remained a monarchy with Catholicism its public religion. But behind the scenes, the republican-minded Left among the leadership was already bent on eliminating every last vestige of genuine monarchy, allowing no aristocratic strand in the new constitution, and very drastically curtailing religious authority. Theoretically, Mirabeau and Sieyès were constitutional monarchists, but only minimally. A materialist philosophe since at least 1770, Sieyès was a hardened ideologue who wholly excluded faith, theology, metaphysics, spirituality, and miracles from his thought, which the curious but persistent notion of aligning him with Locke has tended to obscure.[69] His notes on philosophy, the "Grand Cahier métaphysique" of the 1770s, explores Helvétius, Condillac, and Bonnet on evidence and mental processes, and displays familiarity also with many other Enlightenment thinkers, including Leibniz and Wolff. Already in the 1770s, Sieyès was much preoccupied with the ideal of "le bonheur général" (the general happiness) of society, rejecting all social privilege outright.[70]

Sieyès's central doctrine, linking him closely to Helvétius, d'Holbach, and Diderot, is that man's principal goal and all his activity "carries him to seek his happiness." "True social order" is where the individual's interests are treated equally, and equality of the right to protection and assistance becomes the supreme interest and collective good of all.[71] Hobbes's conception of sovereignty as transferable is altogether abjured by Sieyès. This, along with his undeviating rejection of Montesquieu's relativism and respect for privilege, and Rousseau's strictures against representation, shaped his political thought. Loathing nobility and privilege, Sieyès also refused to eulogize the unanimity of views and austere discipline venerated by the authoritarian populists, including the pristine "virtue" of ancient Sparta and Rome so lauded by Mably and Rousseau. To him, these were models entangled in slavery and irrelevant to the true revolutionary project. As has sometimes been noted, there are therefore striking affinities between his general approach and late seventeenth-century one-substance democratic thought, as is hardly surprising given his long immersion in radical ideas.[72]

A small, unrepresentative group of philosophes, journalists, librarians, and pamphleteers, with Sieyès and Mirabeau at their head, had stirringly taken the lead. Furthermore, it was already evident, as the great Welshman and Enlightenment political thinker Richard Price expressed it on 3 August 1789, writing to Jefferson, that "this was one of the most important revolutions that have ever taken place in the world. A Revolution that must astonish Europe; that shakes the foundations of despotic power; and that probably will be the commencement of a general reformation in the governments of the world which hitherto have been little better than usurpations on the rights of mankind, impediments to the progress of human improvement, and contrivances for enabling a few grandees to suppress and enslave the rest of mankind."[73]

CHAPTER 4

The Rights of Man

SUMMER AND AUTUMN 1789

From the Bastille to the King's Return to Paris
(July–October 1789)

Politically and psychologically, the king had lost much ground. After July 1789, he was never trusted again. Obliged to acquiesce in the Revolution, he could at the same time barely conceal his distaste for the unprecedented changes occurring around him. He abhorred the "metaphysical and philosophical government" with its slogans, symbols, and uniforms, along with the far-reaching constitutional proposals, so injurious to his prestige and authority, formulated by a bunch of ideologues he seemed powerless to check.[1] Three crucial sets of decrees dominated developments during the late summer of 1789: the abolition of feudal privileges of 4 August, the 26 August Declaration of Rights, and curtailment of the royal veto in September.

Resounding initiatives, all proposed within a few weeks of the Bastille's fall, these were plainly not the work of rioting peasants or hungry or unemployed artisans. But neither were they promoted in the slightest degree by business, finance, or lawyers. The parlements, the country's chief repositories of legal expertise, were abhorred by all democratic revolutionary leaders due to their prominent role in the royal censorship and long campaign since the 1750s against the *Encyclopédie* and la philosophie, and hence purposely excluded from the revolutionary process altogether. That a small steering group of the Assembly could prod the rest into accepting that neither parlements nor any past or existing body, institution, charter, law, or precedent possessed any validity was something unparalleled in history and left foreign envoys aghast. Bad laws had corrupted society, affirmed Sieyès, among the "most resolutely philosophical of the major political actors of the French Revolution," and continually conspired "contre la multitude."[2] Morals and the laws were all wrongly constituted, concurred Mirabeau, Roederer, and the pro-Revolution press. Yet it was one thing for Sieyès, Mirabeau, Brissot, Pétion, or Volney to pronounce every privilege by definition an affront to the rights of the "non-privilégiés" composing the majority, but quite another for the Assembly to agree that liquidating all privileges is required by reason and must ensue without delay.[3]

A small fragment of the Assembly, the parti de philosophie achieved a temporary ascendancy over its proceedings by speeches, publications, forming committees, and dominating the debating clubs and reading societies both in Paris and provincial centers.[4] Most Frenchmen witnessed the Revolution in action, locally, observed Rabaut, in the primary assemblies, political clubs, politicized cafés, and reading circles, all divided into vying factions for or against the new ideas.[5] Paris abounded in "hommes instruits" who understood the new republican, egalitarian, and democratic concepts, and explained them to those for whom all this was new. These then, in turn, passed on the word to the great mass of the uninstructed. It was a strange, wholly unprecedented form of power wielded through speeches, pamphlets, the theater, and the press, a phenomenon that the royal government remained if not completely blind to, broadly unable to cope with. When not holding forth in the cafés and parks, the revolutionary leadership of 1789 was to be seen haranguing the Paris city government (Commune) and editing the revolutionary press.

The mounting rural and urban unrest was all wind in their sails. On 4 August 1789, an Assembly majority, including many nobles and clergy, thoroughly panicked by the attacks on aristocratic châteaus in the provinces, the wave of peasant violence known as "La Grande Peur" (20 July–11 August), agreed to abolish serfdom and feudal dues, and suppress all provincial privileges forever, albeit certain long-standing feudal "rights" in the countryside survived as money payments deemed a form of property that could only be liquidated by purchase. Among the privileges abolished outright were favored access to military, diplomatic and civil posts, hunting "rights," and special status before the law. For the first time in recorded history, all citizens, without distinction of birth, became eligible for all posts, positions, and dignities. The entire system of status, exemptions, and special fiscal privileges, including ecclesiastical immunities, ended.

Sieyès's overriding principle (drawn from Diderot), that all privileges are by nature "injustes, odieux, et contradictoires à la fin suprême de toute société politique" (unjust, odious, and contradicting the supreme end of all political society),[6] infused every aspect of the early Revolution. In the next few days, it was further agreed to end venality of judicial offices, all vestiges of seigneurial jurisdiction, and to abolish the ecclesiastical tithe.[7] The ancient privileges of the guilds and guild masters were abrogated also. Taking advantage of the intimidated state of the more conservative representatives, the Assembly's philosophique clique, headed by Mirabeau and those surrounding Barnave pushed these momentous edicts through.[8] Barnave, a brilliant orator from the Dauphiné, though later a confirmed constitutional monarchist and centrist, during 1789 spoke in the Assembly more like an "ardent friend of liberty," as republicans put it, than an ally of the court. Rather farcically in the circumstances, the Assembly, prompted by Trophime-Gérard Lally-Tollendal (1751–1830), a royalist eager to salvage whatever possible from the wreck of monarchical authority, awarded Louis the title of "Restaurateur de la Liberté française," while the archbishop of Paris ordered a special *Te Deum,* thanking the divinity for abolishing feudalism.[9]

The abolition of "feudalism," recorded Bailly, transpired in an instant. In hours, the Assembly accomplished more for the people than the wisest, most enlightened rulers had in centuries.[10] It marked a stunning change. Centuries of law, tradition, and theology had proclaimed inequality of condition the mutual dependence of men, "a design marked out by Providence to which all men must submit," as the antiphilosophe Chaudon, one of the chief Catholic apologists of the age, explained the matter. According to religious authority, it is only in spiritual status and matters of faith that men are equal, not worldly condition. Those who rejected this, challenging custom and aristocratic, ecclesiastical, and parlementaire "rights," privilege, and social hegemony, were few and exclusively disciples of the philosophes.[11] Nothing, remarked Brissot, better proves that government draws its power from public opinion than the Revolution's dramatic course. Philosophy swayed the public and no one could arrest its course.[12]

Ending tithes without compensation, however, complicated matters for Sieyès. Condemning privilege more vehemently than anyone, he termed the ancien régime "l'empire de l'aristocratie," "feudal" superstition that "still abuses most minds."[13] He was personally irreligious, like virtually all the major revolutionary leaders except Grégoire, Lamourette, and Fauchet, and wanted religious authority drastically curtailed. But he targeted the nobility without comparably denigrating ecclesiastical privilege, indeed opposed abolishing tithes without compensation, considering this unjustified despoliation of property. This provoked criticism, some deputies construing his reluctance as that of a priest unwilling to set his own group's special interest aside. He remained prominent, but, after August, this uncharismatic, unlovable, isolated figure never enjoyed quite the same profound respect in the Assembly as he had earlier.[14] This only enhanced Mirabeau's ascendancy as he further broadened the attack on privilege.

As a political leader, Mirabeau operated in a very different fashion from Sieyès. Where Sieyès worked mostly alone, Mirabeau headed a large and impressive team constituting the mostly egalitarian, republican core of the revolutionary leadership until April 1791 and, simultaneously, the regular headquarters of radical Enlightenment attitudes, ideology, journalism, and propaganda. Where Sieyès was largely unknown before the Revolution, by 1787 Mirabeau already possessed a wide-ranging international reputation, or rather two reputations—one enviable, the other less so. The latter was his fame as a rakish, disorderly, conspiratorial, renegade aristocrat, indebted and corrupt in lifestyle and habits, with an unscrupulous love of luxury and fine living. His positive reputation was as a veteran reformist publicist who had long been busy broadcasting his wide-ranging critique of existing society and institutions, even if many of his publications were collaborative enterprises written with the help—and often in large part by—those with whom he associated, a whole phalanx that since 1785 prominently included Brissot and Clavière.[15] Mirabeau stood out among those publicly supporting Geneva exiles after 1782 and condemning the Anglo-Prussian suppression of the Dutch democratic movement in 1787. He maintained high-level contacts in Paris, Berlin, London, Geneva, Amsterdam, and Brussels all at the same time. Helped by several leading German enlighteners, he had published the best-known and most important critique of the Prussian monarchy of the age, *De la monarchie prussienne sous Frédéric le Grand* (6 vols., "Londres," 1788). He had written memorably on Jewish emancipation, the French prison system, and infamous royal lettres de cachet, education, the American Revolution—warning against incipient tendencies toward informal "aristocracy" in the United States[16]—and on a host of other topics. If the remarkable quantity of his publications impressed, equally striking was the consistency and comprehensiveness of his antimonarchical, antiaristocratic, enlightened stance.

In short, during the 1780s, Mirabeau had emerged not just in France but across Europe as the author who had, and was best known to have, continually attacked absolutism, royal courts, aristocratic predominance and privilege, financial speculation, anti-Jewish prejudice, Prussian militarism, British imperialism, the British constitution, British law, the Dutch stadtholderate, and the conservative "aristocratic" tendency, led by John Adams and to a degree George Washington, in the American Revolution. He had attacked all these more incisively, effectively, and unsparingly than anyone else. He had done so by skillfully coordinating his team to amplify the effect, developing a versatile, well-oiled, political-ideological machine. Around him congregated a whole faction, partly in and partly outside the National Assembly, linked for a time to the Society of 1789 and noticeably more radical than the group around Lafayette. Strongly backed by key journalists like Brissot and Desmoulins, and supported by his paid assistants, the Genevan revolutionaries Étienne Dumont and Jacques-Antoine Duroveray, this was a bloc with which Sieyès and Talleyrand regularly associated, and which included, among others, Volney, Roederer, Cabanis, and Chamfort.[17]

Aided by his outstanding oratory and formidable coterie of philosophique advisers, Mirabeau's continual seizure of the initiative in Assembly debates and effective propagation of radical ideas rendered him the nearest thing to the Revolution's leading figure down to 1791. This confirms once again that little about the revolutionary leadership itself, down to early 1791, can be correctly understood without heavily stressing this confident and forceful intellectual background. The Assembly had settled accounts with "priestly aristocrats," "judicial aristocrats," and "noble aristocrats" but not yet with the sitting oligarchies controlling the city councils and dominating the towns, contended Mirabeau in a fiery speech on 13 August 1789. It was time to deal with "l'aristocratie municipale." To eradicate "la corruption de l'aristocratie et du despotisme" from local government, held Mirabeau, city councils needed to be enlarged, made elective and accountable, and staffed with men of talent and experience. Comprehensive change here was as essential as extinguishing other forms of "aristocracy" from national politics and public life. The resulting decree fixed the same ratio of municipal officers to the population in all French towns, stipulating that all town council deputies must represent constituencies of equivalent size. Urban wards were allocated their own primary assemblies to sound out local opinion.[18]

Substituting elected mayors and officers representing the population's wishes, on the model of Paris, for hereditary oligarchies that had long controlled town government assemblies was no simple matter.

How this should be accomplished even in Paris remained in dispute for months. During late August and September, efforts by the Right to recoup lost ground and lend the Revolution a more monarchical and hierarchical shape resumed. Brissot's forty-eight-point plan was shelved by the Paris assembly. By ordering new elections to choose a fresh communal assembly charged with revising the city constitution, Bailly hoped to bend the new body in a more oligarchic direction, if not marginalize the democratic tendency altogether. Brissot and his allies, however, succeeded in ensuring that all men older than twenty-five who paid taxes were admitted to vote. Democratic elections followed, held through July, August, and September 1789, to Bailly's consternation, resulting in Brissot, Condorcet, La Harpe, Beaumarchais, Bonneville, and Fauchet—all the most republican and democratic candidates and those most resistant to his constitutional royalist views—being re-elected and presiding over the new communal council.[19]

Even more momentous than eliminating urban oligarchy was the Declaration of the Rights of Man and the Citizen. Like other key edicts of 1789, it emerged from arduous debate among a small steering group of leading spokesmen, especially, but not only, the Assembly's constitutional committee of eight (Mounier, Sieyès, Bergasse, Le Chapelier, Lally-Tollendal, Clermont-Tonnère, Talleyrand, and the archbishop of Bordeaux), the more radical figures vigorously backed by Prudhomme's *Révolutions de Paris*, Mirabeau's *Courrier,* and Brissot's *Patriote français.* Saturated in the revolutionary terminology of the democratic Enlightenment, these organs proclaimed the Rights of Man to be established by la philosophie, not anyone's laws or charters, or any religion, and hence, "éternels, inaliénables, imprescriptibles."[20] Lawyers, businessmen, and professionals, once again, played little or rather no part.[21] The debate was led principally by Sieyès, Mounier, Lafayette, and Mirabeau, with Brissot—although outside the Assembly—called in by the committee to advise,[22] and Rabaut, Volney, and Condorcet, now the Paris municipality's envoy to the Versailles Assembly, also prominently participating.[23]

The revolutionary leadership proclaiming basic human rights did not derive the doctrine (as has been claimed) from the "natural right" theories of Grotius, Pufendorf, Barbeyrac, and their disciples. Rather, late seventeenth- and early eighteenth-century natural right theories, indeed the whole corpus of natural law, was scorned by them because natural lawyers from Grotius down to Barbeyrac understood natural law to derive from the divine will and divine Providence and thus

pronounced monarchy, aristocracy, and slavery all "natural" compo-
nents of society. Carra had earlier dismissed the entire tradition of natural law theory in 1773 for its essential theological slant and failure to
make equality the fundamental principle of natural right.[24] In 1789,
all the Assembly leaders of a philosophique disposition, that is, most
of those who counted in this debate, eschewed traditional natural law
theories.

Condorcet, having long advocated the need for a philosophical "declaration of the inalienable rights" of man, had had his own first draft
printed back in February 1789.[25] Soon other draft versions proliferated, generating what soon became a tangled, heated debate revolving around the question: What does it mean to declare men naturally
free and equal? Many deputies were averse to all the philosophy, some
greatly disliking the idea of enacting any such set of principles before
the future constitution itself was agreed on and, even more, to insert-
ing such a document in the preface to the constitution.[26] Other critics
wanted affirmations of the Decalogue, religion, and piety prominently
placed in the preface. Volney early on scandalized the Assembly's entire
conservative majority by proposing an incisive and uncompromising
formulation that averred a Declaration of Rights necessary because the
people's liberty, property, security, and fiscal contributions had, under
French kings, been continually "violated" owing to ignorance and the
executive power's oppressive instincts.[27] The committee labored long
and hard, and faced major divisions within itself.

The Declaration slowly emerged, then, from prolonged debate amid
serious disagreement between moderates and radicals, with numerous
revisions hammered out in committee. The American Declaration of
1776 had set a crucial example, granted Mirabeau, but he also insisted
on what he saw as crucial defects. Ignorance and "error" being the chief
reasons why basic human rights had been trampled for so long, one
needed to go beyond the American Declaration and secure a universal justification of human rights, a "declaration raisonée," something
more abstract and philosophical, invoking "plus hautement la raison."
The American Declaration had not, after all, issued from extensive public or legislative debate but instead been penned behind closed doors
by a small committee. In an enlightened age, it befitted France to proceed further and more broadly, presenting humankind with a universal
model, "un code de raison et sagesse" (a code of reason and wisdom),
that would be admired and imitated by other nations.[28] Condorcet was
equally dissatisfied with the American Declaration and also formulated

objections to seven different American state constitutions, criticizing Virginia's Declaration of Rights (1776) for enacting a public obligation to support religion and churches, which, he believed, no democratic republic should do.[29]

Sieyès, whose original draft met with some support but also fierce objections, initially led the campaign for human rights based on fundamental principles. Mirabeau expressly endorsed Sieyès's political, theoretical principles. All public authority and powers without exception, maintained both theorists, are an "émanation de la volonté générale."[30] Their reasoning rested on the distinctly un-Hobbesian doctrine that men do not surrender their natural liberty and "rights" when establishing society, but rather secure them on an equal basis, protecting the weak from the strong and precluding all institutionalized subordination.[31] Mirabeau objected only that the declaration needed to be shorter and more readily comprehensible.[32] A people shaped by antisocial institutions cannot immediately adjust to "des principes philosophiques" in all their fullness.[33] Claiming the law cannot be other than the "expression de la volonté générale," expressed by representatives chosen for a "short time" by the citizenry,[34] Sieyès's draft proved theoretically acceptable likewise to Brissot and Prudhomme's *Révolutions de Paris*, and for the most part to Rabaut, though they too judged it "trop métaphysique," too much of a "thèse philosophique," and beyond most people.[35] Their criticism prompted Sieyès's second, shorter version formulated at the beginning of August.[36] The emphasis in Sieyès, Mirabeau, Brissot, and all the radical faction on "ignorance" as the main reason why the people had hitherto possessed no grasp of their rights derived broadly from the Radical Enlightenment standpoint, if also (but far more tangentially) from the physiocratic tradition.[37]

Numerous deputies opposed their principles. To the exasperation of the majority, who preferred to avoid "abstract" rights, the debate occupied the Assembly for a whole month, the process clogged in disputes over words and "metaphysical" battles that turned the chamber into what one irritated observer called a Sorbonne philosophy class. An indignant Jean-Paul Marat, both at the time and later, condemned these "speculations métaphysiques" in his paper *L'Ami du peuple* and urged more direct democracy and that everything be brought to the level of the ordinary person. Malouet was disgusted by the "metaphysics" and wanted no declaration;[38] Lally-Tollendal, a disciple of Voltaire, wanted all "metaphysical ideas" jettisoned and urged the Assembly to base the declaration on the "wise" English Bill of Rights of 1688, that is,

(a)

(b)

(c)

(d)

Figure 3. (a) Bust of Mirabeau, (b) Sieyès, (c) Brissot, (d) Condorcet. (a) J. A. Houdon (1741–1828), marble bust portrait of Honoré-Gabriel Riqueti, Count of Mirabeau. Preserved in the Museum of the Castles of Versailles and Trianon, Versaille. 1908 © Alinari Archives / The Image Works. (b) Jacques-Louis David (1748–1825), *Emmanuel Joseph Sieyès*, 1817, oil on canvas. Fogg Art Museum, Harvard University Art Museums, USA / Bequest of Grenville L. Winthrop / The Bridgeman Art Library. (c) Portrait of Jacques-Pierre Brissot, known as of Warville, 1784. © Roger-Viollet / The Image Works. (d) Portrait of Marie Jean Antoine Nicolas de Caritat, Marquis de Condorcet, engraving. © Photo12 - Elk-Opid / The Image Works.

on experience and social hierarchy rather than la philosophie. He and Mounier conceded the need for some concessions to ideas of equality and democracy but believed abstract rights could be broadly withstood, and aristocracy in some form—or at least informal aristocracy—upheld, as in Britain and the United States, by establishing strong, positive "liberties" that safeguarded property and the principle of mixed government and curtailed the democratic tendency.[39]

With more than twenty different submissions considered down to mid-August, for weeks the main contest remained between Sieyès and Mounier.[40] But for most deputies, adopting the "old constitution" as the base, as Lally-Tollendal, Malouet, and Mounier urged, and their preference for "separation of powers," had the irremediable drawback of dragging in "ancient rights and liberties," creating what one democratic révolutionnaire, Villette, scornfully called "un équilibre chimérique" more monarchical and aristocratic than democratic.[41] Defeated, Mounier and Lally-Tollendal fell back on Lafayette's brief, non-philosophique, American-style draft, a text later dismissed by Robespierre as "rather banal" and definitely inferior to the other drafts.[42] Before long, Lafayette too was beaten. From mid-August, the debate entered a new stage. A fresh Committee of Five was formed (from which the authors of all twenty main drafts were excluded), comprising Mirabeau, Démeunier, the bishop of Langres, and two lawyers, to select and weld the best elements into a final draft.[43] This change enabled Mirabeau, assisted by his regular editorial team, Duroveray, Clavière, and Dumont—backed by Brissot and Volney—to regain the initiative, and he presented his own proposed, revised text in nineteen articles (against seventeen in the final version) on 17 August.[44]

Characteristic of Mirabeau was his identifying ignorance and "contempt for the natural, inalienable and sacred rights of men" as the root cause of the misfortunes of peoples. "Every political body," reads his second article, "receives its existence from a social contract, explicit or tacit, by which each individual puts in common his person and faculties under the supreme direction of the *volonté générale*, and at the same time that body receives each individual as an [equal] portion."[45] Both legislative and executive powers of government exist solely for the advantage of those governed and not to serve the advantage of those that govern. The principles of monarchy, aristocracy, and ecclesiastical authority must all be denied in favor of volonté générale, Article VI affirming "law is the expression of the general will." Philosophy, commentators agreed, won most clashes but not all, being defeated specifically on Articles X and XI regarding freedom of expression and religion, clauses provoking many angry exchanges in the Assembly, especially between the clergy and those Brissot called followers of a "philosophy of gentleness and toleration." The moderates, conservatives, and clergy regrouped around the formulation of one of the thirty "bureaux" into which the Assembly was divided during the intervals between plenary sessions to facilitate detailed business—the Sixth Bureau. Although no important leader, orator, or thinker of the Revolution belonged to this Sixth Bureau, a group of about forty deputies chaired by the bishop of Nancy, the very conservatism and antiphilosophique character of its recommendations led to these figuring prominently during the debate's final phase.

The Sixth Bureau's effort to stop the philosophes was a draft declaration of twenty-four articles that were pressed very insistently, but in the end largely, though not entirely, rejected. Its declaration contained four principal conservative points that the Left moved to block: first, Article VI introduced the principle of the "inequality of means" as inherent in nature, claiming that natural inequality counterbalances "equality of rights"; second, Articles VIII, IX, and X broadly offset natural rights with natural "duties" (*devoirs*); third, Articles XVI and XVII proclaimed the maintenance of religion indispensable and something that demanded respect for the "public cult"; fourth, freedom of thought and conscience should apply only insofar as these do not "trouble" the publicly established religion of the state. None of these provisions survived intact.[46]

Nevertheless, Mirabeau, Sieyès, and the radical leadership failed to secure unqualified freedom of expression or recognition of the liberty and equality of all religious cults.[47] The final version of Article XI adopted Mirabeau's clause, including "free communication of ideas and opinions among the most precious rights of man" but also qualified it by adding the proviso (likewise in Article X) that the individual "accepts responsibility for any abuse of this liberty set by the law."[48] Everyone knew what this meant. Mirabeau recorded his "pain" that instead of fully eradicating intolerance, the Assembly had, as it were, placed its "germ" in reserve, keeping open the possibility of restoring the Church's authority at some later point. And this in a declaration of human rights! This compromise, he noted, flagrantly contradicted Article III, which averred that no one may "exercise authority not expressly emanating from the nation."[49] The philosophique leadership also partly lost the clash over press freedom; they had to concede the continued banning of obscene and "mauvais livres."[50]

Backing Mirabeau and his team in these encounters, Brissot's *Patriote français* vigorously endorsed Mirabeau's draft.[51] The denouement was now close. In the crucial vote on 19 August, 620 deputies voted for Mirabeau's formulation, 220 for Sieyès's second draft, and, despite Lally-Tollendal's pleas to cut the metaphysics, only 45 for Lafayette's.[52] Finalized on 26 August, the Rights of Man and the Citizen envisaged society's renewal on a completely fresh basis, not one supposedly inherent in the nation's legal past (as with the American Declaration).[53] Where the American Declaration declares natural rights inherent in British constitutional liberties, the French Declaration invokes rights enshrined in laws yet to be made. The Assembly, Mirabeau, Condorcet, and Volney felt, had in some degree "disfigured" the outcome by qualifying freedom of thought and the press.[54] Even so, the result was a stunning success for Mirabeau, Sieyès, Volney, Brissot, Condorcet, Destutt de Tracy, Pétion, Rabaut, and, generally, the radical bloc. For the first time in history, equality, individual liberty, the right to equal protection by the state, and freedom of thought and expression were enshrined as basic principles declared inherent in all just and rational societies. The bedrock of democratic modernity was in place. The rights the French adopted for themselves were proclaimed universal rights belonging equally to all of whatever nation, station, faith, or ethnicity. It was undeniably Mirabeau and, outside the Assembly, also Brissot, observed Carra, who eclipsed everyone else in securing the Declaration, the new revolutionary creed: "the nation owes each a fine civic crown."[55] Of course, most contemporaries had little inkling of the republican, democratic, and Radical Enlightenment motivation that shaped this result.

American independence "opened our eyes about the true destiny of peoples," their "natural rights, and the equality of everyone's rights," acknowledged Carra in October, confident the entire world would be transformed by the principle of human rights based on equality. To Carra, the force of "des idées philosophiques" loomed irresistibly: "rois de l'Europe—voyez comme l'empire de la raison étend son influence de toutes parts."[56] Already, "the plains of Mexico and mountains of Chile echo to the exciting call to liberty." The small principality of Liège "emulated the thirty-two provinces of France," encouraging the insurgent Brabant Patriots to follow. As for English oppression in India, that would have to end soon. For the same reasons, the Declaration was immediately attacked by the royalist and Catholic press, as well as in Rome and across Europe, though its principles were not formally condemned by Pope Pius VI until 1791.[57] Not only ultraroyalist and

Catholic opinion but also most moderate Enlightenment "centrist" liberal opinion rejected basic human rights as formulated by the French Revolution. Portalis, like most lawyers, considered the enactment disastrous, believing it contradicted every tradition of French law and was a device for fomenting despotism based on "idées bien exagérées de liberté et d'égalité."[58]

Among the first to denounce these revolutionary new principles abroad were the prestigious German moderate enlighteners August Ludwig von Schlözer (1735–1809) and Justus Möser (1720–94), the latter in the *Berlinische Monatsschrift*. Their attacks opened a deep split within German thought.[59] Disciples of Montesquieu, Voltaire, and Hume uniformly rejected equality and human rights, as they rejected la philosophie moderne and the Revolution. Men are only truly equal, insisted Möser, in a Christian sense, spiritually. Nowhere should Christians consider men equal in worldly status or civil rights. Several commentators, including the liberal theologian Johann August Eberhard (1739–1809), in his *Philosophisches Magazin*, disagreed.[60] A vigorous reply to Möser, "Gibt es wirklich Rechte der Menschheit?" (Are there really Human Rights?), appeared in Eberhard's *Philosophisches Magazin,* penned by the Spinozist Carl von Knoblauch (1756–94).[61] "The great inequality of force [among men] and consequent insecurity among the weak this creates," explained Knoblauch, reiterating a key Spinozist argument, "drives people to form a state whose force, resulting from the uniting of many individual capacities and interests, then becomes a purposely directed power," providing security and stability for all and "protecting the weak against the usurpations of the strong."[62] "Equality" not only exists, he berated Möser, but is a universal principle, the best of all political and legal doctrines. What does not exist are "rights" conceived as concessions or decreed as gifts and privileges by rulers, lawyers, or priests. Equal human rights exist everywhere, proclaimed Knoblauch, universally.

Building a New Constitution

One of the Declaration's goals was to set guidelines for the forthcoming French Constitution, ensuring that it derived from philosophique principles and not existing practices, laws, or charters. Nothing at all should survive of a society of orders. In reaction, the group most opposed to the republican vanguard, the "English bloc," or *parti anglais,* led by Mounier and Lally-Tollendal, advocated constitutional monarchy organized on bicameral lines with a royal veto over legislation and a monarch equipped with real powers, able to choose his ministers. Throughout September 1789, these two leaders remained in a strong position, the first "a serious dry politician" loathing "abstract propositions," according to the great historian Edward Gibbon (who agreeably dined with both Mounier and Lally-Tollendal at Lausanne later that year, after they fled revolutionary France), the second, Lally-Tollendal, "an amiable man of the world and a poet."[63] Regularly invoking Montesquieu, the thinker most often criticized by Sieyès, this group wanted to retain as much monarchy and aristocracy as they could in the new constitution. Other "moderates" included Nicolas Bergasse (1750–1832), celebrated foe of la philosophie moderne, scorned by Cloots as an admirer of Mesmer and ardent Rousseauiste.[64] The struggle between the parti anglais and the "party of philosophy," as Roederer called it, culminated in clashes over the royal veto and bicameralism.

Bicameralism was urged by Mounier, Lally-Tollendal, and Bergasse, the last having advocated a two-chamber system since before the Estates-General's convening, though he preferred a nonaristocratic upper chamber while Mounier wanted something like Britain's House of Lords, which formally embodied aristocratic preeminence in society. Even if at first glance such a hereditary aristocratic chamber shocks "les notions philosophiques," held Mounier, France should definitely emulate Britain.[65] The Assembly deferred too much to the "impractical notions" of the philosophes, he insisted, and too little for the once immensely admired British model. A few decades before, everyone had admired Britain unreservedly: the French should revert to political wisdom based on experience.[66] Unlike Brissot, Volney, and Mirabeau, Mounier also eulogized the American state constitutions. The sensible Americans, after all, had followed British practice—except in Pennsylvania, the only formally democratic state at that point in the United States, but one which then had a single-chamber legislature. Mounier scorned the Pennsylvania democratic model as based on "abstraites et métaphysiques" ideas.[67]

Continually stressing British superiority and American good sense and "experience," Mounier aimed at mixed government—a balance of powers between executive, legislature, and judiciary.[68] But he stood little chance of succeeding, as his ideas involved returning much status and authority, now already lost, to the Crown and nobility.[69] Backed though he was by moderate Enlightenment opinion abroad, including

Schlözer at Göttingen and Gibbon at Lausanne, Mounier's conservative monarchiens were thoroughly routed in the French Assembly.[70] Adulation of Britain, Sieyès had repeatedly asserted in his tracts of 1788, was a crass state of mind appealing to an ignorant majority who liked waffling about "experience" and who disdained "la philosophie," disdain that in reality served only the interests of a corrupt and rapacious nobility. The legislature alone should embody the will of the nation, the executive's task being to carry out, not obstruct, the people's will.[71] Britain's constitution, a product of contingency and circumstance, fell far short of the "véritable ordre politique." Condorcet, on the other hand, did favor a bicameral arrangement, but only provided the upper house did not resemble the London House of Lords and consisted of "hommes éclairés" distinguished by their intellectual abilities and allowed only a limited veto over the main Assembly's resolutions.[72] On 10 September 1789, the Assembly followed Sieyès and Mirabeau by voting 849 to 89 to reject Mounier's proposals and adopt only one chamber in the new legislature.[73]

As for the unlimited royal veto over legislation that monarchiens favored, this too stood little chance of succeeding. Where they wanted an absolute royal veto to entrench monarchy, radicals wanted either a diminished vetoing power or no veto at all. Lafayette, Barnave, and soon a majority of Assembly deputies, including Mirabeau, believed the only way to unite the Assembly and "give the king a due influence" was to opt for a "sanction limité" or suspensive—that is, temporary—veto. A temporary royal veto, urged Mirabeau, would not clash with la volonté générale but enhance and protect it. Those more republican than him disagreed and certainly won the publicity battle in Paris. On 15 September, the "suspensive veto" passed nevertheless by 673 votes to 352, with Sieyès and Rabaut among the considerable minority, around 143 deputies, wanting no veto.[74] As the prolonged veto debate shows, all the philosophe-révolutionnaires were more or less solid republicans from the outset, insisting that the National Assembly possess all the power, authority, responsibility, and prestige of government. But Mirabeau and Sieyès were de facto not doctrinaire republicans, and both aimed to keep the monarch as a figurehead while rendering him virtually powerless in practice.[75] The veto debate was the first "constitutional" controversy in which Paris actively intervened and tried to reverse the Assembly's decision. Working with Brissot as leader of the Parisian republican faction and editor of the *Patriote français*, Sieyès continued to fight the temporary veto.[76] The republicans, especially around the

Palais-Royal, mobilized some solid support. Brissot and his allies, Prud-homme's *Révolutions de Paris* recounts, orchestrated public pressure against those championing the royal *veto suspensif*, especially Barnave and his faction, but also Mirabeau.[77] Advancing the Revolution, held Brissot, Carra, Gorsas, Chénier, Villette, and other key publicists out-side the Assembly, required wielding la philosophie like an external battering ram, and harnessing all the possibilities offered by liberty of thought, speech, the press, theater, clubs, and to gather, petition, and demonstrate.

"Progress of knowledge" working on *la raison publique* would even-tually teach men what was lacking for the true good of society, and such enlightenment, held Condorcet, would become the "legislator of all men." The philosophie moderne shaping the Revolution derived, he thought, from a cumulative inheritance generated by many Enlighten-ment writers, some deserving more recognition than they had received. Boulanger in his *Despotisme orientale*, had been "no less inspired" and provided just as many innovative insights as Voltaire, Rousseau, and other better-known philosophes.[78] In the same issue of the *Chronique de Paris* of 22 September 1789, he also stressed the "necessity" of the forthcoming constitution being ratified by the citizenry, urging the need for representative bodies of rural communities to counterbalance the towns. Democracy must emancipate the rural population too, en-suring the voice of the whole country was heard. Legal safeguards must prevent the formation of a new oppressive landowning elite.[79]

The theme of an accumulated democratic Enlightenment featured again in the *Chronique de Paris* in October, in a review of a recently published two-volume collection of Mably and Condillac extracts. The overthrow of the Bastille and "our servitude," of which "we have had the happiness to be the witnesses," was the joint achievement of many heroic thinkers who consciously prepared the overthrow of oppression. "Gloire à ces écrivains immortels!" It was "essential their principles should become those of everyone" and their ideas circulate and form "l'esprit publique." This applied both to France's youth, who needed education, and to "those classes of society previously permitted to suf-fer but not to enlighten themselves."[80] In 1789–90, the Revolution's democratic republican publicists judged legislation good or bad not on the basis of precedent, experience, interest, or religion but according to whether it was, as Carra liked to say, "vraiment philosophique." Ev-eryone had to adjust to this to an extent. Pro-Revolution clergy now openly proclaimed, like the Abbé Fauchet in his *Second Discours sur la Liberté française*, delivered at the church of Sainte Marguerite, Faubourg Saint-Antoine, on 31 August 1789, that the sole true religion is religion "united" with la philosophie.[81]

But what if the people were persuaded to follow different leaders? Marat, with his bracing, widely read paper, *L'Ami du peuple*, which commenced in September 1789, sounded a shrill new note of illiberal extremism extraneous to the proceedings thus far. Denouncing the "criminal project" of "les classes privilégiés" with unparalleled vehemence, Marat demanded the elimination of the "aristocratic party" from the Assembly.[82] Marat might be right, granted those opposing the *veto suspensif*, to assail the "corrupt faction" of monarchiens trying to mislead the Assembly, but he was mistaken in employing such violent and intemperate language. Foes of liberty should be denounced "avec modération." This, retorted Marat, was like putting a soldier on trial for fighting his hardest against perfidious enemies.[83] In his issue of 28 September 1789, he extended his assault to the bankers and financiers "who build their fortunes on the ruin of others."[84] Bailly figured among those he denounced for styling themselves "bons patriotes" while actually seeking influence and pensions at court.[85] By labeling the current revolutionary leadership disloyal to their proclaimed egalitarian principles, Marat inaugurated what became the standard technique of populist authoritarians tarring their opponents.

Marat's setting himself up as public censor—aggressive verbal assaults, rhetoric of secret intrigue, and incessant calls for unsparing punishment and purges—provoked angry demands for his journal to be shut down.[86] These failed, thanks to the vigilance of Brissot and other stalwart defenders of freedom of the press. In the years 1789–92, as Mme. de Staël later observed, French society was "allowed, freely and unequivocally, the liberty of the press."[87] But the problem of how to check plebeian anger deliberately stirred by virulently divisive journalism, inciting the unruly against political rivals, proved irresolvable. Slowly, support grew for Marat's contention that it is not philosophy but the people's will, direct popular sovereignty, that constitutes the true criterion of legitimacy. "Public opinion alone . . . can make laws," insisted sympathizers later prominent in the Jacobin Club.[88] Marat's tireless insistence on "morality," "virtue," and the ordinary man's feelings created a powerful underlying tension that would eventually derail the Revolution of Reason.

Proclaiming an overriding popular sovereignty, Marat was the first systematic critic, from a populist standpoint, of the principle of representation espoused by the "party of philosophy." If his temperament and readership contributed to his dogmatism, militancy, and anti-intellectualism, so did his long-standing fervor for his compatriot, the "sublime Rousseau."[89] If scholars often note how far Sieyès and Mirabeau diverge from Rousseau on questions of representation and popular sovereignty, attention must also be fixed on the clash between what were soon the two main rival revolutionary factions over Rousseau's critique of representative democracy.[90] The people's representatives must defer to the popular will, contended Marat, replacing "la philosophie" with unrelenting stress on popular sovereignty, ordinary men's feelings, and "virtue," like Danton and Robespierre later. With Marat's *L'Ami du peuple*, intolerance of dissent and a harshly dictatorial tendency first emerged.[91] The main Brissotin charges against Marat during the power struggles of 1792–93 were precisely the incitement to violence and urging the populace to take the law into their own hands.

Marat's supporters professed to be more authentic egalitarians than the current leadership, most of whom—like Sieyès, Mirabeau, Brissot, Volney, Bailly, Barnave, Roederer, Carra, Gorsas, and Desmoulins—more or less openly disdained the multitude's ignorance and addiction to "superstition." It was Marat's subordination of reason to popular will and the common man's feelings that especially separated his and his allies' Revolution of the Will from the Radical Enlightenment's Revolution of Reason. The materialism of Helvétius, Diderot, d'Holbach, Condorcet, and Sieyès was wholly incompatible with Marat's cult of "virtue" and the popular will; their philosophy prioritized science, knowledge, and understanding, while his stressed the common man's instinct. For Marat, intellectual understanding counts for less than the ordinary man's will; where reason remains fixed, the popular will remains free. His opponents' materialism struck Marat as useless for explaining the passions, quest for "glory," and power of sentiment. Helvétius, in his estimation, failed entirely to render the passions and reason contrary principles.[92]

Tension between court and Assembly intensified once more in the autumn of 1789, principally because the king loathed and hesitated to assent to the August edicts. As economic distress, food prices, and political uncertainty mounted, a critical turning point was reached. To aggravate matters further, the arrival at Versailles, from Douai, in late September, of the 1,050 men of the prestigious Flanders regiment fed fresh rumors that the "parti aristocratique" planned a *contre-révolution* using the military. Reports circulated, notably in Gorsas's paper on 3

October,[93] recounting scenes of royal troops cheering, stamping, and yelling "Vive le roi!" at Versailles, and trampling tricolor cockades underfoot. This instantly inflamed opinion around the Palais-Royal. On 5 October, groups of demonstrators, gathering first in Paris's public gardens and squares and then before the city hall, and eventually constituting a crowd of some thirty thousand mostly female citizens, led by the market women of Les Halles carrying homemade pikes and other makeshift weapons, set off in a long and angry procession to Versailles. This mass of hungry women chiefly demanded bread, but some also backed the aspirations of Louis-Philippe, the flamboyant Duc d'Orléans (1747–93), a prince descended from the younger brother, Monsieur, of Louis XIV and a great enthusiast for British constitutional monarchy and Freemasonry (as well as horse-racing and other pastimes), and one of the richest men in France. Louis-Philippe hoped to head the liberal monarchist Revolution.

On reaching Versailles many hours later, toward evening, the unruly mob bivouacked around the palace gates for the night. Lafayette had followed the crowds with a force of the National Guard. On reaching the palace, Lafayette conferred at length with the king, who had ordered his guards on no account to fire on the women or anyone else. Lafayette assured the monarch that he had been unable to prevent the crowds marching on Versailles but would now firmly take charge of the situation and ensure the royal family's and the palace's safety. Despite these assurances, early the next day, crowds assailed the palace guards, killing several, including a brother of Villette, and then invaded the entire palace, causing pandemonium though only slight damage. The extraordinarily unpopular queen, Marie Antoinette, was lucky to escape by a secret passage to the king's apartments unscathed. The crowds also swamped the Assembly's meeting hall.[94]

Order was belatedly restored by the National Guard. Later on 6 October, the royal family was escorted to Paris by Lafayette and his men, a seven-hour procession accompanied by an immense and growing crowd amounting perhaps to sixty thousand. Welcoming the dazed, utterly traumatized royal family in the capital, Bailly delivered a rousing speech, setting the municipality's seal on a momentous day that marked the end of the French court at Versailles and the virtual end of traditional monarchy in France. Whether or not Louis himself had really contemplated a military coup, some of those close to him assuredly had, and their intrigues continued. But the events of 5 and 6 October effectively ended all direct royal resistance to the Assembly's proceedings, forcing the king to accept the temporary royal veto and the end of privilege. Louis and Marie Antoinette, installed in the Louvre, were now virtual "hostages," living the next tumultuous months in an isolation not far removed from custody. The king gave up his favorite activity, hunting, and both king and queen became semirecluses largely confined to the Tuileries where the rituals and ceremonies of Versailles were reconstituted but on a much-diminished scale.

Whether or not Louis personally had been playing a double game earlier, now that he was stripped of nearly all his authority, he certainly did so from 6 October 1789 onward, in public acquiescing in his role as the servant of the people and the Revolution, while secretly writing to fellow monarchs, as he did to the Spanish king on 12 October, assuring him that he rejected entirely the destruction of "royal authority" in which he had been forced to acquiesce against his will.[95] No one failed to discern the momentousness of what had occurred. In a panic, a fresh wave of courtiers and grandees departed, as did a considerable number of rightist deputies defecting from the Assembly and as also did the celebrated court portraitist Elisabeth Vigée Le Brun (1755–1842), who fled with her daughter by carriage to Italy, where she stayed until 1792 before venturing farther.[96] To an appalled Gibbon, observing developments from Lausanne, the situation looked catastrophic:

> their king brought a captive to Paris after his palace had been stained with the blood of his guards; the nobles in exile, the clergy plundered in a way which strikes at the root of all property; the capital an independent republic; the union of the provinces dissolved; the flames of discord kindled by the worst of men (in that light I consider Mirabeau); and the honestest of the Assembly, a set of wild visionaries (like our Dr Price) who gravely debate, and dream about the establishment of pure and perfect democracy of five-and-twenty millions, the virtues of the golden age, and the primitive rights and equality of mankind, which would lead, in fair reasoning, to an equal partition of lands and money.[97]

He was right on two counts: the situation had changed dramatically, and it was the "set of wild visionaries" allied to Price who had brought it about, even if elements of the Paris populace now acted as their watchdogs.[98] The march on Versailles, this second "access of revolution," commented the *Chronique de Paris* two days afterward, would doubtless "hasten the work of the Assembly" by undoing the "intrigues of the majority of deputies" (supporting Crown, aristocracy, and ecclesiastical authority). It would enable "the 150 or so deputies" who, according to the *Chronique*, regularly supported the philosophique leadership, the "généreuse minorité" (often helped by the Fayettiste faction and Orléanistes) to "feel more secure."[99] The court's transfer from Versailles to the capital, moreover, was immediately followed by the National Assembly's, the latter taking up new quarters in the Tuileries close to the royal family. Thus, Paris consolidated its grip on the Revolution while intensifying economic distress continued to afflict and exasperate the poor. "These *philosophes* who are not even able to read," sneered the Venetian envoy, deriding Paris's artisans for their growing plight, as well as their mouthing democratic slogans, "have not yet learnt that philosophy has always been poor."[100]

Brissot and Condorcet, their position within the joint assembly of Paris sections (now reduced to forty-eight) much enhanced, were asked to compose two crucial municipal addresses, the first welcoming the National Assembly to Paris, the second assuring France's provinces and municipalities that Louis had freely chosen to transfer to the capital. Brissot personally spoke on behalf of the Paris delegation in the Assembly, and afterward both addresses were printed and distributed around the country. The king and Assembly, Brissot and Condorcet assured their countrymen, would be treated with fitting deference and kept perfectly secure, but about the popular insurrection that produced this result Brissot and Condorcet said as little as possible. They and the Paris Commune chose not to explicitly condone it but stressed rather the responsible conduct of the National Guard and city authorities in restoring order and organizing the transfer from Versailles.[101]

Nevertheless, no one could be in any doubt as to what had actually happened. Even if it was partly true, as Lafayette's supporters claimed, that the insurgent women had been stirred up by Orléanist agents, nothing could conceal the fact that the urban lower orders had now categorically joined the insurgent rural peasantry as a major force in the Revolution—and not just the men but, even more strikingly, the womenfolk. Not only did the revolutionary popular press as such begin to emerge as a distinct impulse within the Revolution during the autumn of 1789, but, unsurprisingly, so did a new kind of big-city *presse populaire* that appealed directly to the market women and laundresses, the illiterate female presence teeming around the capital's central markets, as well as the poor Paris suburbs or faubourgs of Saint-Antoine and Saint-Marcel. Reflecting the volatile and angry but also hesitant, unaware, and uncertain character of the revolutionary popular voice—

constantly pulled as it was in divergent directions—the popular press directed at women emerged in late 1789, dividing into rival streams respectively backing the Orléaniste and Lafayette factions, competing for what later became the liberal monarchist center ground, though until early 1791 the Fayettistes in the poor faubourgs remained broadly allied to the democrats belonging to the organizations of the Cercle Social and Amis de la Vérité.[102] Gradually, through 1790 and especially 1791, the *presse populaire* directed at lower-class women came to reflect the basic three-way split dividing the Revolution as a whole, becoming more and more internally divided. Largely defecting from the liberal monarchist centrist factions that attracted most popular female support in October 1789, urban plebeian womanhood, like every other section of the population, fragmented into three competing tendencies supporting the three main rival ideological blocs.[103] The populist journalists more and more intensely contested the political orientation of the now seemingly crucial typical illiterate market woman. Her being pulled relentlessly in three contradictory directions did not prevent her being metamorphosed into the legendary "Mother Duchesne" figure— the presiding motherly market lady selling old hats, swearing continually and tolerating no nonsense, who iconically represented lower-class female rectitude.

One series of Mother Duchesne gazettes, designed to be read aloud to groups of illiterate women gathering to discuss political affairs in the streets, appeared in late 1790, edited by the Abbé Buée. This Mother Duchesne portrayed the "wise," upright, and savvy market woman as someone who conforms finally to the views of the clergy, always prioritizing religion and faith above revolutionary ideals and refusing to defer to their "foolish" menfolk who were more vigorously supporting the Revolution. This tendency was then countered by a Left radical series of Mother Duchesne gazettes, the *Lettres bougrement patriotiques de la Mère Duchêne*, which summoned women to fight alongside their men for revolutionary ideals, doing so as equals, vigorously and independently, and always thinking for themselves.[104] The radical appeal to illiterate women was then in turn countered by a third series of Mother Duchesne newssheets opposing both the radicals and the center, insisting that the veritable woman of the people, the genuinely upright and admirable ordinary woman, invariably accepts her husband's views and adopts a strictly subordinate role, women being subordinate to men in everything concerning public affairs and politics. The latter, strongly Rousseauiste impulse, powerfully affirming gender inequality, was the tendency that aligned with the Montagne and, from late 1791, energetically supported Marat and Robespierre in their war against the democratic republican radicals who directed the early stages of the Revolution and had chiefly benefited from the women's march of 5 October 1789.[105]

The move of both court and Assembly to Paris was bound to result in increasing popular intimidation of that part (the majority) of the Assembly comprising liberal aristocrats, clergy, conservative lawyers, pragmatists, and monarchiens. They had striven, albeit thus far ineffectually, to withstand the universalist, egalitarian constitutional proposals of Sieyès, Mirabeau, and the steering group. At this point, Mounier, Lally-Tollendal, and the archbishop of Paris, feeling they had irretrievably lost their fight for a conservative outcome, withdrew from the Assembly altogether.[106] Resigning from the Comité de Constitution, Bergasse too retired; one of the relatively few monarchiens to survive the Terror, he later reemerged as an ultraconservative.[107] Lally-Tollendal departed for Switzerland, where he produced a political memoir justifying his efforts to rescue Crown and aristocracy that was witheringly reviewed in the *Chronique de Paris* the following March.[108] "Mounier who was looked on as the chief of the discontented," reported the secretary of the United States embassy, William Short, to Jefferson, now back in America, "and who, it was supposed, meant to excite a fermentation in Dauphiné, has lost his influence there."[109] Before long, he too left for Switzerland, where he also resumed the struggle by writing.

In his *Considérations sur les gouvernements et principalement sur celui qui convient à la France* (Paris, 1789), Mounier renewed his call to the Assembly to discard principles emanating from antimonarchical philosophes who disagreed with the "wise Montesquieu." Settling in Geneva, he commenced his new life by putting on a public lecture course on natural right, where he scathingly attacked the Revolution and rejected Sieyès's and Mirabeau's principle of popular sovereignty. All the fashionable ladies and gentlemen of Geneva reportedly attended. The antiaristocratic philosophes may have been justified in attacking popular préjugés, but their obsession with ignorance and error had led them to overstep bounds they ought to have respected. Prioritizing ideas over experience, they erred deplorably, introducing "d'erreurs méprisables" and emulating Plato in creating republics that could never exist outside their heads. The great danger was that their philosophy would usher in "la tyrannie démocratique." Every properly organized society must be led by men of rank. Mixed monarchy on the British model was the answer, an upper chamber composed of peers and political bishops providing genuine social hierarchy balanced by real monarchical authority.[110] Britain, objected his opponents, was less perfect than he maintained. But English pride in their constitution and belief in its superiority, Mounier retorted, even if blinding them to its defects, was admirable, for it ensured that the sensible British followed experience and received notions, rejecting la philosophie.[111] Mounier's defense of rank and aristocracy was enthusiastically received at Geneva, resounding also in Berne and all the "aristocratic cantons of Switzerland."[112] Geneva remained a crucial ideological battleground, pitting the views of the democratic revolutionary leadership in France, Belgium, and Switzerland against the moderate Anglophile Enlightenment and the many French aristocratic émigrés who sought refuge in its environs. This intensifying ideological warfare also fed into the bitter contest, raging since 1782, between "aristocrats" and "democrats" vying for control of the Genevan republic itself. In Geneva, commented the *Chronique de Paris*, you see fought out in miniature most of the great debates presently engaging the forces of liberty.[113]

The constitutional monarchists found themselves obliged to regroup. After Mounier's and Lally-Tollendal's departure, there still remained in the Assembly a sizable centrist residue or party of modérantisme. Indeed, together with the recalcitrant, ultrarightist bloc, conservatives composed a firm majority potentially rallying behind Crown, aristocracy, and Church, but the disagreements between these blocs, as well as between the strict *constitutionnels* and the liberal monarchists backing Barnave, remained deep, bitter, and obdurate.[114] As the struggle on the Assembly floor resumed, the designations "Right" and "Left" came to be regularly employed to label the factions in the hall. Republicans and democrats gravitated to the left, monarchists and most clergy to the right. It was at this point that one of the deputies' clubs repairing from Versailles, the Club Breton (so-called because it had originally consisted of delegates from that province), resumed in Paris in the former convent of the Jacobins. It became the debating home of a large part of the Assembly, some two hundred deputies, Barnave among them, initially mostly representing the center ground.[115]

The National Assembly remained divided into the four main blocs, characterized by Jefferson on 19 September. First, as before, there were the aristocrats, comprising the nobility, high clergy, and parlementaires who wanted executive power vested in the Crown and not the representative body. Now led by Pierre-Victor Malouet (1740–1814), a former intendant of Toulon, and the Abbé Maury, the legislature's doughtiest monarchist during 1791–92, this group wanted a France run not by a National Assembly acknowledging a monarchical figurehead, such as Barnave proposed, but a reformed, more efficient, centralized monarchy with a weak representative body. Second, and very different, were the "moderate royalists who wished for a constitution nearly similar to that of England." These men were oblivious to the complaints of British democrats, like Price and Priestley, that the English constitution was corrupt and undemocratic and that the British, as Price put it, "are duped by the forms of liberty." Third was the flamboyantly liberal monarchist Orléanist faction. Last, there were the "republicans, who are willing to let their first magistracy [i.e., the Crown] be hereditary," explained Jefferson, "but [intend] to make it very subordinate to the legislature, and to have that legislature consist of a single chamber."[116]

Despite consistently being a relatively small minority of deputies, the revolutionary Left dominated the Assembly's proceedings and standing committees and undeviatingly pursued their course, thanks to sentiment in the streets, the liberal rhetoric and ambitions of the Orléanistes and Fayettistes, and the profound divisions debilitating the Right.[117] Among conservatives, the Paris mob were intensely resented for behaving like obedient "watchdogs" shepherded by the Assembly's most radical faction—upstart publicists, journalists, and self-proclaimed shapers of opinion acting against Crown, Church, parlementaires, and nobles.[118] Their most robust support emanated from the cafés and journals. Outside the capital, this inevitably encouraged murmuring about "Paris" exerting undue influence. Such protests were dismissed by the prorevolutionary press as an insidious ploy to stir up jealousy against Paris in the provinces. Meanwhile, there was no slackening in the pace of fundamental change.

In late October, the Assembly decreed that no "distinction by orders" was permitted any longer in meetings of municipalities or other public gatherings anywhere in France, being wholly "contraire aux principes établis par l'Assemblée Nationale."[119] During November, the Assembly moved on to examine schemes to abolish the particular privileges and procedures—as well as physical boundaries—of France's historic provinces, such as Normandy, Brittany, Dauphiné, Languedoc, and Provence, as these were of very different sizes, traditions, and rank, and, hence, unsuitable for a new order rooted in philosophical reason. To replace them, the Assembly proposed "departments" of equivalent size and status, though initially there was disagreement as to whether these should be equal in population or area. As with the other great revolutionary changes, this one had been projected long before, especially by Sieyès and Condorcet, borrowing partly from Turgot. Suppression of historic provincial identities and privileges, urged Mirabeau, Rabaut, Thouret, and Condorcet, would underpin the emerging new constitution by securing that "equality of influence that belongs essentially to every individual."[120]

The final arrangement, aiming to ensure that elected "representatives" represented equal numbers of people, was a deft compromise devised by Barnave between the two principal criteria: population and territory. Henceforth, France would comprise more than eighty departments of roughly comparable geographical size, but to ensure that the number of representatives was fixed in proportion to population, each department was further divided into either three or four electoral districts.[121] The committee implementing this ingenious plan proceeded briskly. By 12 November, Rabaut announced the boundaries of the first forty new departments.[122] More outlying regions took longer to delimit, but this too was accomplished within weeks. "This great and magnificent work," commented the bookseller Nicolas Ruault in January 1790, was principally due to the Abbé Sieyès and Marquis de Condorcet, the latter having placed himself alongside the Patriots. Aristocrats deride this philosophe with a weak voice and quiet manner, he added, as "le mouton enragé" (the enraged sheep).[123]

Equally vital to the philosophique agenda was reforming France's antiquated judicial machinery. Dispensing justice should no longer be the preserve of an entrenched elite. The Revolution and the people, averred the *Chronique de Paris* in December 1789, have no more committed or embittered enemy than the parlements.[124] Eliminating the existing judicial elite, projected in August 1789, proceeded in stages until finalized in March 1790.[125] At Bordeaux, the *palais* of the parlement was bolted and sealed by the municipality on 30 September. Paine's ally, the American radical Barlow, later described France's pre-1790 "judiciary nobility" as a "set of men who purchase the privilege of being the professional enemies of the people, of selling their decisions to the rich, and distributing individual oppression; hence the source of those draconian codes of criminal jurisprudence which enshrine the idol property in a bloody sanctuary, and teach the modern European, that his life is of less value than the shoes on his feet."[126] Among the Revolution's finest achievements, concluded Naigeon later, was the complete extirpation of the regional high courts, or parlements, and with them of the so-called noblesse de robe.[127]

Defense of the parlements became a rallying point in the Assemblée Nationale for numerous deputies. As the dismantlement of France's ancient institutional structure accelerated, several parlements—those of Rouen, Rennes, Toulouse, and Metz, along with the provincial estates of Languedoc, Dauphiné, and the Cambrésis—stubbornly contested the legality of the enactments destroying the parlements' powers, citing numerous historic charters, constitutions, and privileges. In November, the Assembly replied by suspending the parlements' functions indefinitely, and before long decided on their complete abolition. The Assemblée, protested the Right, was despoiling the parlementaires of their professional status and competence, in fact, their property, their families having purchased their elevation to the noblesse de robe. Previously, parlements had often succeeded in obstructing royal intentions whenever they objected to new laws and in mobilizing popular support for their obstructionism. But this time, when they strove to block the uprooting of France's existing laws and institutions, few came to their assistance.[128] The only Frenchmen supporting the parlements, the newssheets sent to the villages assured the peasantry, were the same officials who opposed dismantling feudal dues, church tithes, the corvée, and gabelle, namely, the magistrates, intendants, and officers of the *capitaineries*.[129]

These outmoded corporations, the parlements, commented republicans unsympathetically, endeavored to "perpetuate the abuses of the *ancien régime*." The people deserted them. The contrast with neighboring Belgium was nothing less than astounding. Over the winter of 1789–90, the Belgian Revolution took what, to the French revolutionaries, was a highly perplexing turn. The Brabant urban and judicial elites, equivalents of the French urban oligarchies and parlementaires, successfully mobilized the people against the local democrats, called Vonckists after their leader, Jean-François Vonck (1743–92), allied to the Left republican leadership in Paris. The Belgian common man rallied behind the judicial elite and violently assailed the democrats. How could the Belgians, asked the pro-Revolution journals in Paris, allow themselves to be so outrageously misled? The answer was that Emperor Joseph II had tried to reform the Southern Netherlands' judicial system and curtail church property, revenues, and privileges by imperial decree. This, to Condorcet and the *Chronique de Paris* editors, was putting the cart before the horse. Fundamental social and legal realities were not transformed by royal edicts, they held, but by la philosophie gradually shifting attitudes and preparing the people for great changes. Public opinion cannot be prematurely dragooned as Joseph sought to do. Being "faite dans les idées" (made in ideas), the French Revolution would prove sturdier than the Belgian and also (one of the Revolution's resoundingly incorrect predictions) less violent since France, unlike ignorant Belgium, embraced la philosophie and rejected traditional thinking.[130] The French Revolution, the *Chronique* confidently assumed, would be "a gentle one," unlike that in Flanders and Brabant, where developments were marred in November and December 1789 by widespread violence.

Along with the parlements, the entire ancien régime legal and administrative system, lettres de cachet, venality of office, the remaining feudal courts, and local juridical procedures specific to particular localities, often of great antiquity, were liquidated. On 14 November, the Assembly abolished the system of royal intendants, the pivot since Louis XIV's time of French royal provincial administration.[131] This once-powerful administrative elite, now cashiered, was replaced as originally projected by the reforming minister Turgot in the 1770s, with a new standardized administration operating on an equivalent basis throughout France, consisting of departmental councils, municipalities, and rural districts. The new courts and their jurisdictions corresponded to the projected electoral districts like the jurisdictions of their presiding judges, functionaries henceforth elected by the "active citizens" of their districts. Standardizing French administration in this way rendered it easier to introduce equality of treatment in electoral and representative functions, fiscal matters, and judicial administration.

Meanwhile, the Parisian assembly's republican vanguard simultaneously battled constitutional monarchists, and the populists of some crowded inner-city districts. On 2 November 1789, Condorcet was elected first president of the reorganized Paris general assembly. Populist opposition to Brissot's circle was confined at this time to just a few sections and centered on the group controlling the Cordeliers district, now renamed the Théâtre-National section. This Left Bank constituency, the "principal foyer" of disaffection, as Bailly put it, extended from the Sorbonne to the Luxembourg Gardens, and with its numerous bookshops and printing works was an area where la philosophie rubbed shoulders with skilled artisans. The Théâtre-National was Marat's headquarters and also that of the political machine headed by Danton and his group of locally based littérateurs and journalists.[132] At this stage, Danton's circle clearly dominated what later became known as the Cordeliers Club, soon the foremost political club in Paris after the Jacobins. In 1789–90, the leadership of this club—apart from Danton himself, an impressive and often inspiring speaker and a revolutionary genius unique (like the Cordeliers itself) in stressing and exemplifying the need to unite the intellectuals and the masses—did not differ greatly in character from the wider phalanx of republican révolutionnaires heading the Revolution.[133]

Danton's chief publicist, Desmoulins, the mordantly irreverent editor of the *Révolutions de France et de Brabant* and member of the Cercle Social forum, was an enthusiast for Latin classics, steeped in Cicero, Tacitus, and Livy, and an ardent exponent of a universalist democratic republicanism rooted in materialism and antiprovidential philosophy. Early in the Revolution he admired Mirabeau above all and, after March 1790, remained among the most reluctant of the democratic republicans to accept that Mirabeau had clawed back his earlier radicalism and been bought by the court.[134] In addition, the club featured several other notable political theorists, such as Pierre-François Robert and the club's secretary, Théophile Mandar (1754–1823), author of a 1788 tract on emancipation of the blacks. In 1790, Mandar, who knew English, published a translation of Marchamont Nedham's republican tract *The Excellence of a Free State* (1656), replete with footnotes citing Rousseau, Montesquieu, Mably, Condillac, and Raynal. Thanks to the French, Mandar assured readers, their century of "enlightenment and philosophy" would ensure the "triumph of man over tyranny and despotism," and secure liberty for future societies.[135] To make it fit his purposes, Mandar was not above manipulating Nedham's text to render it more democratic than it really was. Another key member of Danton's circle was Philippe Fabre d'Églantine (1755–94), a dramatist from Carcassone who later helped compose the new revolutionary calendar. The success of his comedy *Philinthe* (1790) briefly placed him among the best-known stage writers of the revolutionary era.

Outside Danton's circle, and scorned by Danton, but central to the feuding between the primary assemblies and the Paris general council, an unavoidable local presence, was Marat. Fiery journalist and orator, Marat expressed the disgruntlement of the Paris poor more aggressively than Danton or indeed anyone else. His usual strategy was to accuse the Commune's general council, Brissot's assembly of three hundred, of aspiring to become a new civic aristocracy of "tyrants" oppressing the people. To curb the Commune's power, the Théâtre-National section primary assembly, with Danton just elected section "president," passed motions on 11 and 12 November 1789, imposing on their five representatives in the general council binding instructions not to be departed from even when a large majority of the governing council supported a different point of view. In this way, the section leaders sought to discipline, or recall, their delegates whenever their section assembly saw fit.[136]

Here was a direct challenge to Brissot's and Condorcet's system of "representative democracy," a challenge going to the heart of the revolutionary dispute concerning the true character of democracy. Sovereignty resides in the people, populists and Brissotins agreed. Every section had the right to comment on and approve or disapprove of Commune assembly decisions, as well as petition their representatives. The bone of contention concerned rather the limits of popular sovereignty and whether localities could justifiably impose binding decisions and principles on delegates to a representative assembly to obstruct majority votes. Hence, the quarrel concerned the nature of representation itself.

CHAPTER 5

Democratizing the Revolution

The Failure of Liberal Monarchism

Over the winter of 1789–90, the National Assembly's constitutional committee, an impressive panel of political and legal theorists headed by Sieyès and Mirabeau, labored to complete a constitution combining the radicalism of the Rights of Man with strands of restraining "moderation." By mid-1790, the Assembly's constitutional committee had effectively completed its work. France was now a fully articulated constitutional monarchy comprising eighty-three departments with sovereignty theoretically vested in the people, but with the nation actually represented by both legislature and king. That France was and should remain a monarchy most did not question. However, the pathbreaking Constitution, with its eventually 195 articles, was not yet finalized, since the king withheld formal assent.

Mirabeau and Sieyès were grandly but justifiably designated by many the "pères de la constitution" (of 1791).[1] They had created what the vast majority conceived of as a reformed monarchy but was in fact nearer to being a republic. Under the not yet formally completed but already operative Constitution, only the legislature could initiate legislation and appoint royal ministers. The Assembly controlled the purse strings, the king's limited financial resources being allocated by the legislature via a civil list. A permanent body of 745 deputies, the projected legislature would wield virtually all the power, its mandate renewed by elections every two years. A royal veto existed but was confined to one sitting, hence, two years. Assembly deputies, unlike British MPs, could not become royal ministers directly but only three years after leaving the Assembly. Elections for the Assembly, along with local elections for mayors and judges, were to assume a uniform character across France. All officeholders were now elected by urban "sections" or rural electoral districts. The first municipal elections under the new system were held in the early summer of 1790. Paris henceforth comprised forty-eight sections, Lyon and Marseille each thirty-two, Bordeaux twenty-eight, and Toulouse fifteen. Each section assembly was simultaneously a representative body for the locality, forum for debate, and key part of the electoral process.

For the first time in Europe's history, a constitutional monarchy emerged that blended a minimum of royal authority with a powerful republican tendency and equality on the basis of the Rights of Man. But was not this, objected Necker, a gigantic contradiction gnawing at the Revolution's very foundation? The Assembly proclaimed France "a monarchy" but repudiated all rank, hierarchy, and privilege. Yet, how can a monarchy promulgate equality, a fundamental democratic republican principle? How can a monarch preside over a "constitution démocratique"? Refusing all social gradations, the Revolution grafted monarchy onto democracy, blithely unaware that something so incoherent philosophically could work only by embracing mixed government based, like Britain's, on an unchallenged domination of society by aristocracy and rank. Eliminating privilege undermined the entire edifice, held Necker, rendering popular favor, flattering the people, the sole route to power. The basest of all motives, winning influence through flattery, thus fused perversely with the Revolution's core principles of equality and volonté générale.[2]

The catastrophe of France's post-1789 instability, held Necker, commenced with the Rights of Man and became irreversible with the 19 June 1790 abolition of all remaining status, titles, and distinctions. Not realizing the danger, the people complacently acquiesced in the glaring contradiction between a monarchical constitution and the Revolution's unyielding, officially stated egalitarian goals. Yet, there was little real need, he argued, to hazard what he rightly saw as an unsustainably destabilizing contradiction since very few desired to abolish titles, extinguish primogeniture, or deprive the Church of its special status. Tragically, he maintained, it was not popular sentiment that drove the Revolution but the views of an unrepresentative fringe, denying and suppressing rank and tradition altogether. The Club Monarchique was no less irritated by the marginal, unrepresentative character of republican opponents progressively subverting the emerging constitution and doing so with right seemingly on their side, owing to their ability to continually invoke equality and the Rights of Man as the Revolution's core principles.

The edict of 18 June 1790 prohibited use of any title of nobility whether of prince, duke, count, marquis, baron, or any other designation of status, together with the public display of any coats of arms and liveries in public documents, meetings, and reports. This ban on the use of noble titles, protested the outraged royalist press, ultra and constitutional, was incompatible with any kind of monarchy. No other people had ever attempted the like.[3] Among its antiaristocratic provisions, the June 1790 decree ordered the demolition of all public monuments infringing the "liberty" of either the French or other peoples. If the night of 4 August 1789 eliminated "the prejudices and errors of ten centuries," that of 19 June 1790 crowned the edifice, putting the seal on the revolutionary achievement. However, there was a clear difference between these two hugely memorable legislative landmarks. On 4 August 1789, everyone was either swept up in the frenzy or too scared to resist. On 19 June 1790, by contrast, suppressing hereditary titles and coats of arms, even if logically just the completion of what went before, provoked a famously long and furious quarrel at the end of which that solid "old oak" Montesquieu, as one observer put it, was "torn up by the roots."[4]

During 1790, conservative sentiment indeed suffered one symbolic reverse after another. In an article published in episcopal Liège in January 1792, the antiphilosophe Feller explained this process as le philosophisme overreaching and consuming itself. A ceaseless, creeping subversion, constantly encroaching on Crown and Church, progressing since its slow, clandestine origins more than fifty years before, now finally descended unsparingly on its chief agent: high society. For it was via the aristocracy, especially *femmes de qualité*, that philosophisme had originally been diffused in France, and it was the nobility that philosophisme now assailed and overwhelmed.[5]

A few days after the June 1790 edict, with Montesquieu, the foremost philosophical champion of aristocracy, moderate Enlightenment conservatism, and British constitutional "moderation" metaphorically toppled, the celebrated bust of Rousseau by the sculptor Jean-Antoine Houdon (1746–1828) was installed in the Assembly hall. Rousseau was unquestionably worthy to stand alongside Washington and Franklin, onlookers were assured by the speakers during the impressive inaugural ceremony, but as the busts of the latter already graced the Left, or what republicans called the chamber's "patriotic" side, leaving insufficient room for "Rousseau," the bust of the man many considered Liberty's foremost champion had to be placed on the conservative side, as if silently glowering on the "enemies of liberty and equality," as republicans designated the Right.

The Revolution was threatened by challenges both within and without. The greatest challenge facing Mirabeau and Sieyès was that of how to organize political representation. Hostile to Montesquieu's relativism and suspicious of Rousseau, both "fathers of the constitution" were likewise incisive, long-standing critics of the British and American constitutions. They rejected division of powers, together with all notion of balancing the monarch or quasi-monarch (the American president) against the nobility and Commons. There exists just one volonté générale, they contended, and this requires a single legislature controlling a subordinate executive and dependent judiciary. If the legislature truly represents the sovereign, it must remain in permanent session, supervising the state finances and, broadly, all policy, controlling every branch of government. Elections were central to the functioning of the new representative system. But how should the electorate be constituted that elects the nation's representatives?

In October 1789, an Assembly majority had defined those entitled to vote as the "active citizens"—adult males older than twenty-five who paid the equivalent of three days' unskilled labor in taxes—a category proposed by Sieyès. But differentiating the adult male population into "active" and "inactive" citizens, distinguishing between those with a certain level of resources from the impoverished, seemed highly problematic to many. Since the new Constitution's raison d'être was upholding equality and the Rights of Man, it was wholly unclear how restricting the suffrage to "active citizens" classified by financial status could be justified.[6] Sieyès, compounding his anti-Rousseauism, attempted to distinguish between *droits passifs*, passive rights held by everyone, the benefits for which society exists, and "droits actifs," active political rights attached to those who select the nation's representatives. In Sieyès's political philosophy everyone possessed the right to liberty and the security afforded by *droits passifs*, but only some men the right to participate in constituting representative public authority.[7] Excluded from active rights under the new Constitution were, besides women, children, and foreigners, adult men lacking sufficient means to contribute to the costs of the public establishment.

The central doctrine of Sieyès's *Préliminaire de la Constitution française* of July 1789, expounding his ideas for the emerging constitution, is entirely un-Rousseauist (and un-Hobbesian): man's transfer from the state of nature to the social state, "far from diminishing individual liberty, extends it and guarantees its use"—a thesis plainly derived from the clandestine tradition of the radical philosophes. Hence, men enhance their moral and physical capabilities on entering the social state, transcending dangers to which they were previously exposed. Liberty flourishes solely in the social state, and even then only under carefully prepared conditions. For if less menaced by intruders and marauders than in the state of nature, the individual is exposed now to abuse of power by vested interests and government. Correctly defining and guaranteeing human rights by means of a viable constitution is therefore indispensable, the sole means to preclude abuse and exploitation, ensuring government for the well-being of the majority and in the interest of all.[8] In a properly constituted social order, the law can have no other object than the "intérêt commun." In both Sieyès's and Mirabeau's minds, this encompassed all aspects of social life. Besides security and justice, the state must also acknowledge the "rights" of those citizens lacking the means to satisfy their basic needs, argued Sieyès on the constitutional committee, and hence play a socioeconomic support role. If the revolutionary leadership really intended to abolish privilege and reorganize society on the basis of equality, then it must devise a progressive tax system, taking more from the wealthy than in the past, to fund new systems of social welfare.

The National Assembly was split between monarchists and republicans, the former constituting the great majority in theory but divided and the latter holding the initiative politically but precariously, creating a rift the solution to which, most deputies supposed, was a spirit of moderation and less emphasis on equality and democracy. To bridge Left and Right and stabilize the country, Mirabeau, Sieyès, and other leading deputies resorted to the Club de 89, a society of prominent figures in and outside the Assembly sworn to uphold the Declaration of Rights and other great legislative acts of 1789 while also upholding limited monarchy and the Constitution. Formed by Mirabeau, Sieyès, Talleyrand, Chamfort, and Lafayette in April 1790, the Club or Société de 1789 had as its explicit goal to reconcile liberal monarchists with the Assembly's small but active minority of democratic republicans so as to ensure a large and stable leading bloc dominating the Assembly. Besides Mirabeau and Sieyès, the club accommodated many on the Left, including Volney, Ginguené, and Marie-Joseph Chénier. But despite the obvious logic and good sense of trying to stabilize the Revolution by forging a strong center, the club's plea for a merger of radical egalitarianism and political moderation proved unsustainable and encountered insuperable difficulties.

The unresolved split could for a time be camouflaged with rhetoric and pomp. To celebrate the first anniversary of the Estates-General's transformation into the Assemblée Nationale, on 17 June 1790—the day before the elimination of all noble titles—the Club de 1789 arranged a sumptuous banquet, attended by 190 club members. But fine dining to fanfares and marches played by sixty musicians could not remove the double conundrum that some members sought to liquidate, others to preserve—the influence of Crown, court, aristocracy, and Church. Some wished to halt the Revolution where it now stood, others to advance it further. Many of the club's more distinguished members began drifting away once they realized that a genuine compromise between center and Left was impossible. This was the signal for the factions in the Assembly to regroup and for the liberal monarchist center to aspire to dominate the Revolution. By mid-1790, the National Assembly's center began to look preponderant while the Left appeared to be fragmenting and growing weaker.

As the Club de 89 disintegrated, its "moderate" core sought to dominate the National Assembly, many joining the more conservative Club Monarchique, which adroitly circumvented the difficulties undermining the Club de 89 by repudiating Mirabeau and Sieyès and leaving the democrats out in the cold.[9] Presided over by three prominent deputies—the Abbé Maury, Malouet, and Stanislas, Comte de Clermont-Tonnerre (1757–92), a cultivated army officer, among the chief noble movers of the abolition of feudal rights of 4 August 1789—the Club Monarchique allied the Assembly's Right to remnants of the Société de 89 and of another expired, more conservative centrist group, the Club des Impartiaux, formed by a number of Assembly deputies under Malouet in October 1789.[10] The Abbé Jean-Siffrein Maury (1746–1817), a bitingly ironic, brilliant Assembly orator, among the few able to withstand Mirabeau and who enjoyed humiliating less eloquent opponents, blended strict constitutional monarchism and veneration for royalty and aristocracy with a fierce zeal to uphold Catholicism as France's public religion. Meanwhile, Mirabeau's incomparable standing at home (among friends of the Revolution) and abroad also came under assault, from the spring of 1790 on, from Marat and other populists accusing him of treachery in collusion with the court and (with greater justification) profiting financially from his mediating role. Sieyès too found himself in a weakened position, increasingly isolated on the Assembly's constitutional committee.

But if republicans and the liberal monarchists led by Barnave, Bailly, Lafayette, and the brothers Alexandre and Charles de Lameth failed to combine and establish a stable hegemony in 1790, before long it emerged that no alignment between Maury's constitutional Right and the liberal monarchists could attain a stable ascendancy either. There were some points where the Assembly's Right and center could agree. Both opposed republicanism and democracy, and wanted a restricted electorate. Where republicans like Jérôme Pétion (1756–94), among the Assembly's foremost democrats, dismissed Britain's constitution as "toute vicieuse" and needing thoroughgoing reform itself, Maury shared Mounier's and the liberal monarchists' enthusiasm for Britain, Parliament, and British "good sense."[11] But Maury and Malouet expounded a monarchical constitutionalism far more genuinely monarchist, legitimist, and pro-Church than the positions of Barnave and the Lameths, let alone Mirabeau or Sieyès. It was the king who had sanctioned the National Assembly, insisted Maury, and the nation that "imperiously declared none of our decrees should be implemented without the free assent of the king."[12] Maury and his following refused to accept the overriding power of the Assembly. The Assembly could not unilaterally change the Constitution or detract from royal or ecclesiastical authority any more than Britain's Parliament could. If they did, the deputies "would no longer be the guardians of the national rights but tyrants over your fellow citizens." Rousseau in "his too famous *Contrat Social*," Maury reminded his centrist as well as republican adversaries, argues that the "people's deputies are not and cannot be its representatives being mere *commissaires*, unauthorized to conclude anything definitively." His critics continually invoked Rousseau, complained Maury, but were not respecting his political theory at all. "Every law the people itself have not ratified is void, not a law."[13]

The Club Monarchique's membership cards, styling its members *Amis de la constitution monarchique*, and its journal, the *Journal monarchique*, looked respectable enough. Officially, this club's membership, many of whom were nobles and prelates, championed a strict reading of the Constitution. Their political strategy pivoted on the hope that they could carry the people with them, not an unrealistic expectation, remarked Cérutti in August 1790, given that most Frenchmen, being politically naive, were perfectly content to extol royal ministers and submissively follow the Right despite its obvious aim of seeking the advantage of the Crown, aristocracy, Church, and the old judicial order rather than that of the majority of the nation. Believing that the ancien régime had been sufficiently revolutionized and transformed, and applauding the liberal monarchists' assurances, the great majority failed to realize how the new arrangements in fact cheated the people. To complete the Revolution, a full-scale war on prejudice was required, waged by "a great nation enlightened with all the enlightenment of philosophy."[14]

The Club Monarchique urged strict adherence to the Constitution. In doing so, according to Gorsas and Fréron, in December 1790, the club's primary goal was actually to mobilize popular prejudice against "republicanism." Both Maury's conservatives and the liberal monarchists were right in claiming that republicanism largely lacked popular support. Nevertheless, republicans remained heavily preponderant among the most articulate and literate, especially the intellectual fringe that engineered the Rights of Man and controlled the prorevolutionary press and Paris cafés. To defeat the democratic objectives of the republican press, the Club Monarchique appealed to the traditional values of the people, aiming to divide the capital and sap the Revolution's momentum.[15] Two hard-hitting pamphlets, *Les secrets révélés par l'Anti-Carra-co-Gorsas*, and *Pourquoi Mesdames sont elles parties?*, issuing from the Club Monarchique in late 1790 (possibly by the same writer), highlighted the widening rift between the Assembly's center and Right and the democratic republican Left. The "disgusting absurdities" propagated by about a dozen "republican" journalists, argued these tracts, were the evil principally responsible for subverting the Constitution, misleading the public, and blighting the economy. Republican journalists, of whom Gorsas and Carra were pronounced the worst, were shamelessly corrupting Paris and the entire social order.

In the last four months, contended these pamphlets, more than two hundred families possessing annual incomes surpassing 20,000 livres had emigrated.[16] Society's most select and wealthiest, all deluged in "revolting calumnies" concocted by these egalitarians, were leaving in droves, among them members of the royal family, including the monarch's two unmarried aunts, Marie-Adelaide and Victoire-Louise, aged, respectively, fifty-eight and fifty-nine, who departed for Rome on 18 February 1791. (This was the event that first gave rise to popular rumors that the king himself was likely to depart soon.) In fact, less than 10 percent of France's nobility, modern research shows, had become émigrés by 1791. Nevertheless, these included many of the richest aristocrats and courtiers, and even this modest proportion amounted to between 25,000 and 30,000 people, a total only slightly exceeded by the number of clergy fleeing abroad. The overall number of émigrés of all kinds, more than 150,000, or around half of 1 percent of France's total population, undoubtedly did entail a damaging depletion of national capital.[17]

By late 1790, the three main impulses represented in the National Assembly and the Revolution more broadly—Maury's, Cazalès's, and

Malouet's conservative constitutional monarchism, Barnave's liberal centrist monarchism, and philosophique democratic republicanism—all firmly blocked one another. Despite the relative stability of 1790, the effort to convert the Rights of Man into reality and renew society on the basis of equality inevitably descended into bitter strife and political paralysis, the deep splits within the Revolution being far from the only divisive factor. The moderate monarchical Constitution's vulnerability sprang partly from rifts within the Revolution, but equally from the fact that monarchism more generally, both inside France and even more in exile, was predominantly not constitutional monarchist but ultraroyalist. If most French monarchists, including the royalist press, rejected Barnave's center outright, most émigrés and many within also looked with suspicion on Maury's conservative bloc. Ultraroyalists despised the National Assembly and considered the king the Revolution's prisoner, not its patron. Equally, ecclesiastical resistance to the Revolution from late 1789 veered largely toward nonconstitutional monarchism. The unbreakable deadlock in the country thus stemmed from the broad political and social support for each main rival faction within the National Assembly, compounded by the stubborn tenacity of extraconstitutional conservatism.

Despite official adherence of king and court to the Revolution, by early 1790 the *parti anti-révolutionnaire*—ultraroyalist and proaristocratic—had become widely active as an organized force throughout France and around her borders. Numerous small towns, the Montpellier city council reminded the Assembly on 31 July 1790, were now heavily infiltrated by counterrevolutionary agitators and propagandists, and required help from the main cities to curb disorder and stay under revolutionary control.[18] Ultraroyalist repudiation of constitutional monarchy was underpinned by the claim that whatever Louis had agreed to was invalid, as he was really just the revolutionaries' captive. Unable to compromise politically, Malouet constitutional monarchists and Barnave centrists and ultraroyalists were just as hopelessly divided over religion. Universal toleration and freedom of thought were strongly promoted by the center and (officially) acceptable to the constitutional Right but were overwhelmingly rejected by ultraroyalism.

Even without the economic malaise gripping the country, a constitution exalting equality while incorporating monarchy and a restricted suffrage made little sense. Widening the divisions still further, the "common interest" based on equality trumpeted by the republicans was intended to reshape the whole social economic and cultural context, not just politics. Education illustrated the difficulty. Many Frenchmen were illiterate and most no more than semiliterate. Educating the people was in no way inherent in liberal monarchism and still less in the two divergent conservative royalist currents. But it was basic to the democratic republicanism of Brissot, Condorcet, Bonneville, Fauchet, Desmoulins, Vergniaud, Carra, Gorsas, Volney, Manuel, Lanthenas (translator of Paine's *Rights of Man* into French), and other key ideologues dominating the Left, and hence central to the Revolution's core values. Society needs an educational system suited to forming free men, as Condorcet put it in October 1791, to "advance the progress of reason, and perfect the human race," without which democracy and human happiness are impossible. Only thus can the harmful effects of popular notions, privilege, and religious authority be remedied.[19]

Here was a doctrine deriving directly from the revolutionary ideology of Diderot, d'Holbach, Helvétius, Raynal, and other collaborators on the *Histoire philosophique*: "wise of the earth, philosophers of all the nations, it is for you alone to make the laws, by indicating to other citizens what is needed, by enlightening your brothers."[20] Sieyès went part of the way with this reasoning: "nothing is more appropriate for perfecting the human race in both the moral and physical spheres," he concurred, "than a good system of public education and instruction."[21] But educating the people was an essentially republican concept. Such schemes could only intensify the Revolution's central dilemma, since they clashed with tradition and religious authority, and most Assembly deputies disliked all such ideas. At the same time, while absolute equality of political rights for "active citizens" (the voting electorate) remained "un principe fondamental" for Mirabeau and Sieyès, and all privilege was ruled out as inadmissible, adult males were nonetheless divided by the Constitution into voters eligible for office and ineligible "passive citizens" lacking political rights. This implied to those who thought like Sieyès that there was no need to extend publicly supported education to the latter.

The unsustainability of the centrist monarchical Constitution, insoluble character of the divisions in the Assembly and widening rifts dividing French society in 1790, were highlighted by disagreement over the status of religious authority and the place of religion in the nation's life. Undoubtedly, Catholic authority and overall preeminence in society and culture was perfectly acceptable to the vast majority of Frenchmen in town, country, and even, though here more tentatively, the National Assembly. The problem was that church authority on a traditional basis was entirely unacceptable to many centrists (and the Protestants), as well as the entire republican clique forging the Revolution. Defeated in the Assembly in December 1789, pleas to salvage Catholic primacy were advanced again on 12 April 1790, amid a tense atmosphere, by a much-respected Catholic deputy, the mystic Carthusian Dom Christophe-Antoine Gerle (1736–ca. 1801), among the first ecclesiastics to merge with the Third in 1789. Supported by Maury, his motion was robustly opposed by Barnave besides Mirabeau, the republicans, and the entire pro-Revolution press, provoking the worst-tempered battle between the Right and the philosophique revolutionary tendency witnessed thus far. An impassioned two-day debate failed to obtain any privileged status for the Church whatsoever, the Catholic bloc losing the final vote by 400 to 495, with many deputies absent or abstaining.[22] On leaving the Assembly afterward, Maury was yelled at by a furious crowd and chased through the streets. Notwithstanding the vote, insisted a minority printed protest on 19 April, signed by more than 300 indignant deputies (more sympathized but preferred not to sign), Catholicism remained France's sole authorized religion. This protestation elicited an ominously powerful wave of sympathy around the country, with supportive letters pouring in from all over France.[23]

Deepening the divisions further, both the constitutional and extra-constitutional Right fused their political and religious rejectionism with an economic ideology well tailored to sway the masses. Unemployment had risen dramatically, proclaimed the royalist press, and the ateliers and workshops of Paris had fallen silent. At Lyon, estimated the Gazette de Paris, the Revolution had left 40,000 workers without recourse or basic sustenance, while at Rennes the population had supposedly slumped from 71,000 in 1751 to only 33,000 by early 1791.[24] The Revolution was a catastrophe for artisans and the poor no less than it was for the aristocracy, held the pamphlet État actuel de la France of January 1790, by Comte Antoine-François Ferrand (1751–1825), a former royal minister soon to join the émigrés on the Rhine. "The artisan cannot live without the resources the luxury trades furnish him"; possessing no land or rents he must live from his labor. The revolutionaries had mobilized the populace against society's high-status consumers, but the people made their living from the consumption of the rich. By multiplying needs, luxury trades enhanced the incomes of those laboring to satisfy those needs. But now whole towns and cities had withered under the collapse of the luxury trades and flight of the émigrés.[25]

By supporting the Revolution, the laboring class had grievously erred, wrecking their own livelihoods, and worse would follow, admonished Ferrand, because the goal of the most subversive and ambitious element in the Assembly, just as Mounier had warned, was undoubtedly to turn France into "a republic." Admittedly, for the moment the Revolution's leaders paid lip service to monarchy. But whatever they professed, they had been de facto "regicides" since at least October 1789. In reality, the revolutionary leadership were out-and-out "republicans," imprisoning the king, stifling the royal veto, and banishing the aristocracy. The catastrophe facing France was thus a double one, in Ferrand's view, economic and political (he said nothing about religion), the seeds of which he traced to Montesquieu's *L'Esprit des Lois*, the work that had first seduced the nobility into curbing royal authority.[26] Ferrand's argument was broadly right, even though he ignored the effects of the Church's loss of property, tithes, and other revenues, which in some places was no less devastating than the flight of the nobility. The municipality of Riez in the Basses-Alpes, for example, appealed to the Assembly in July 1790 regarding the loss of its bishopric, cathedral chapter, religious houses, and seminary, which together spelled the virtual destruction of the town's trade; the town assembly pleaded for something, at least a district court, to alleviate the "despair of the people."[27] Though not Douai's only industries, Church and parlement were so vital to the local economy that with its theology schools, high court, law college, medical college, monasteries, and ecclesiastical establishment all decimated by October 1791, the town reportedly resembled "a desert."[28]

Open conflict between the now five main rival blocs vying for control of France—ultraroyalist, conservative constitutional royalist, liberal centrist, authoritarian populist, and democratic republican—erupted first in places traditionally plagued by religious strife, like Nîmes, Montauban, Uzès, and Strasbourg. In 1789 Nîmes was home to approximately 40,000 Catholics and 13,000 Reformed (Calvinists), though the latter were a much more prosperous community, long dominant in commerce and the professions. Unsurprisingly, the religious orders, on the point of being dissolved, the Capuchins especially, stirred local Catholic resentment as a way of resisting the Revolution. Nîmes Protestants opposed demands that their numbers on the new Commune council be proportionate to their numbers in the community, historical precedent giving them half the council seats and the right to choose the mayor. Despite being trounced in the municipal elections on 28 March 1790, when they won scarcely any seats, they still tried to dominate the local National Guard and, as at Montauban, preside over the revolutionary club, or Friends of the Constitution—organizations increasingly used by them as instruments of local political control.

Destruction of ecclesiastical privilege, and the Assembly's refusal to acknowledge Catholicism as the state religion, rendered it easy to convince the illiterate that the Revolution was basically a Protestant, Jewish, and Masonic "conspiracy." On 20 April 1790, a crowd of Nîmois, infuriated by the failure of Dom Gerle's motion, gathered at the Church of the White Penitents to draw up a petition demanding Catholicism be acknowledged as the sole religion of the state. Exhorted by local theologians and the lawyer François Froment, chief spokesman of local ultraroyalism, they demanded a halt to church reforms and restoration of the king's executive powers. Royalism, like religion, noted observers, prevails most strongly among the most ignorant. The petition gathered five thousand signatures and was published locally. White cockades appeared. The local revolutionary club responded by denouncing the Nîmes "fanatics" to the Paris Assembly. Attempts to remove white cockades provoked the first armed clashes on 2 and 3 May 1790, leaving one dead and several wounded. Later that month similar events followed also in Montauban and Uzès.[29]

A fraternal ceremony of reconciliation on 4 May in Nîmes' main square, with National Guard of both faiths swearing oaths of eternal respect, sealed by a nightlong civic party, calmed passions fleetingly. But the very next day a fresh demonstration by women, furious that religion was not being respected, erupted at the Capuchins, where the order's confiscated property was being inventoried. Pending municipal elections, scheduled for early June, contributed to the friction. Finally, on 13 June, a full-scale battle erupted in the streets, starting with stone-throwing at Protestant dragoons, leading to firing, and then general tumult. Martial law was declared. On 14 June, Protestant armed men from neighboring rural districts invaded the town, avid to support their coreligionists. The battle culminated in an assault, amid much firing, on the Capuchins, the slaughter of five monks, and pillaging of the monastery, followed by the storming of the locality held by Froment's adherents, several of whom, including Froment, were killed.[30]

The clashes at Nîmes, Montauban, and Uzès shocked opinion throughout France. Reports that "Protestants" were slaughtering Catholics, sacking monasteries, and trampling the "holiest objects underfoot" circulated widely. Catholic troublemakers bent on tumult and murder, reported the prorevolutionary press, had declared the Assembly "suspect" in religion and outraged wearers of the revolutionary cockade. Some suggested the perpetrators' rights as "active citizens" should be abrogated. A huge row erupted in the Assembly. Nîmes

Catholics, countered Malouet, had done nothing more than hold meetings, exercising their constitutional right to freedom of opinion and to submit petitions.[31] A pamphlet, cast in the form of a dialogue between four worthy market women, reporting the exchanges between Right and Left in the Assembly at this point, described the conflict as a fight between the "good" and "bad angels." The "good angels," striving for everyone to be equal and "happy," for the good of the nation, were Mirabeau, Barnave, Lafayette, Rabaut, Pétion, and Grégoire. France's "bad angels," royalist "evil oppressors" seeking to ensure "poor people should be always down-trodden," were Maury, Malouet, Cazalès, Duval-d'Eprémesnil, and another antidemocrat, Count François-Henri Virieu-Pupetières (1754–93), a Dauphiné deputy and founder of the Club des Impartiaux.[32]

That the Left fought for "everyone to be equal and happy" certainly meant something to artisans and the rural peasantry. In August 1789, the Assembly had proclaimed the feudal regime at an end, a staggering change in a Europe dominated by nobility for centuries. But if the peasants rejoiced, their gains, it quickly transpired, were less than initially supposed. If the revolutionary press deemed feudal rights and perquisites "nothing but usurpations founded on violence," in practice these remained a vast and perplexing legal tangle vitiating rural lives. The 4 August 1789 decree abolished outright, without compensation, all forms of *servitude personnelle* (vestiges of serfdom lingering mainly in Burgundy and the Franche-Comté), rights of *péage* for transport and moving flocks of sheep and herds of cattle along paths belonging to lords, dues on the sale of products and animals, on use of lords' mills, olive oil and wine presses, "protection" rights, hunting rights on non-noble land, and all ancient claims to precedence in selling products at certain times of the year. However, other "rights" remained valid until the "owner" was bought out, at least in theory, as the peasants, in many areas, simply refused to pay them. The August 1789 decree recognized many rural dues as vested in land ownership, as property, including most heavier obligations like harvest dues (*champart, terrage*) and seigniorial dues on land sales (*lods et ventes*). These, peasants either had to continue to pay or purchase from the supposedly rightful owners, or resist.[33]

Ending such obligations without compensation, held the Assembly's majority, would violate the "sacred right of property."[34] Justice having been administered for centuries by nobles, surviving charters frequently listed as property rights exactions that seemed to many wholly contrary "au droit naturel des hommes."[35] But since nearly all "documentary evidence" supporting such obligations were thoroughly vague in origin, ample scope remained for lawyers massaging matters in the landowners' favor. The Assembly's principal lawyers, François-Denis Tronchet (1726–1806) and Philippe Auguste Merlin de Douai (1754–1838), presiding over the committees implementing the 4 August decrees, deliberately consolidated property rights where they could to minimize abolition without compensation. For a time, tenancy and sharecropping arrangements were construed as freely entered into and hence subsumed within ownership of particular farms. Shoring up the interests of aristocratic landowners became far harder, though, after the 25 February and 9 and 15 March 1790 edicts on land tenure ratified by the king soon afterward.[36] Tackling points left unresolved in the 4 August 1789 decree, these measures slowed the recouping efforts on behalf of the nobility. More, but by no means all, vestiges of the "feudal regime" and forms of *péage* were abolished outright, and "toutes les distinctions honorifiques, de supériorité et puissance résultants du régime feudal" were definitively abolished. Additionally, despite tenacious resistance in the Assembly, rights of inheritance under primogeniture enabling large estates to be passed on intact, a pillar of the aristocratic system, was formally abolished.[37]

Right and Left unrelentingly attacked each other for betraying the Constitution, the nation, and the poor. Measured by loyalty to the Constitution, objected conservative and centrist royalist writers, crypto-republicans like Brissot, Gorsas, Carra, Pétion, Condorcet, Volney, and Cérutti, acted and spoke anticonstitutionally more flagrantly than the Assembly's monarchists. Gorsas, in the twentieth issue of his *Courrier*, even had the impertinence to openly deride monarchy, calling the king an "imbecile." However, it was not just ideological rhetoric that destabilized France in 1790 but also the real underlying incompatibility of the rival social and political blocs. According to supporters, the Club Monarchique heroically resisted the raging torrent of antiaristocratic and antimonarchical discourse. Far from fanatical priests and émigrés threatening France with civil war, as the "republicans" alleged—another example of their "insolence"—it was actually these anticonstitutional "vile pamphleteers" themselves who were poisoning society with their criminal democratic attitudes and practices. The only solution, held the author of *Pourquoi Mesdames*, was to mobilize the people and thoroughly crush democracy, "civisme jacobin," and "philosophy."[38]

Thus, a wide range of opinion on both the Right *and* Left rejected the liberal monarchist Constitution both in theory and in practice. From their oratory and activities, it was hard to know whether even the Club

Monarchique genuinely supported the Constitution. Behind the scenes many of its members undoubtedly aligned with the aristocratic extra-constitutional and counterrevolutionary Right. Accordingly, it increasingly failed to attract authentic moderates. By late 1790, the club was deeply embroiled in the Paris sections, implicated in riots and fights, as well as accused of distributing bread at below current prices in the shops to "seduce the people" into "the poison of aristocracy."[39] Several Paris sections, after legally convoking their assemblies with the required fifty "citoyens actifs" present, submitted petitions to the Assembly alleging that the Club Monarchique deliberately provoked disturbances, including a major street brawl in Paris, on 24 January 1791.[40] For this reason, as well as the disagreement over religion, centrist constitutional monarchists, opposing ultraroyalism, turned increasingly against the club. Barnave, particularly angered by its opposition to ecclesiastical reform, delivered a scathing denunciation of the club (and the Right generally) in the Assembly on 25 January 1791, designating the Club Monarchique an organization wholly inimical to the public interest and subversive of the law.[41]

Elimination of rank was followed by that of court pensions and gratifications. In a long debate during the summer of 1790, the Assembly sought to separate the civil list, over which the king retained discretionary powers, from the main body of state pensions, to eliminate rank and royal favor as factors in determining pension levels. On 16 July, the chairman of the Comité de Pensions, Armand-Gaston Camus (1740–1804), librarian, archivist, and republican, proposed abolishing all existing pensions but leaving current, without interruption, small grants of 600 livres or less for nonofficer military veterans. Existing officers' pensions would be reinstated only after claims and qualifications had been reexamined, titles discounted, pensions deemed invalid canceled, and those set too high lowered. Except for cases of severe injury or infirmity, no one in state civil or military service would henceforth be eligible for a royal pension, recommended the committee, until after thirty years of service or reaching fifty years of age, with a fixed general maximum of 6,000 livres yearly, no exceptions allowed.[42] Happy to draw the "hatred of all the vampires of the court," Camus expressed satisfaction at this outcome, though he felt concern at leaving some worthy retired army officers, previously enjoying higher pensions, penniless until these could be reviewed.

Numerous nobles were crossed off the list or had their pensions drastically curtailed. The Assembly proposed to replace social status with merit and service. Another key principle governing the pension reform legislation was that the Assembly itself should henceforth be the sole authority assigning grants from the public purse, even if these were still paid in the king's name. Less straighforward than military pensions was the question of distinguished scientists and savants. Among *pension-naires* proposed for exemption from the mass of canceled court pensions was the great geometer Joseph-Louis Lagrange (1736–1813), founder of the Turin Academy of Sciences. Lagrange had later directed Frederick the Great's Berlin Royal Academy for many years, contributing more than sixty mathematical and astronomical papers. Invited to Paris after Frederick's death, he had been installed in the Louvre with a 6,000 livres pension. Impressed, the committee also presented a more general case for subsidizing scientists, writers, and artists. Some might challenge the principle that revolutionary France should subsidize the sciences and arts, commented the deist philosophe La Réveillère-Lépeaux, but the Assembly would surely not fail to acknowledge savants as "benefactors of the human race who through their efforts and genius increase the sum of enlightenment." The Assembly agreed. Determined to suppress court pensions, the Assembly, in highly non-Rousseauiste mode, simultaneously endeavored to "protect in every way savants, artists and literary men and establishments that primarily serve the progress of the sciences and arts."[43]

Eligible scientists, artists, and littérateurs were split into three classes to receive large, medium, and small pensions, levels determined by the importance of their work and length of service. Unlike military and administrative pensions, savants' pensions were no longer payable automatically on a yearly basis, as this would encourage unnecessary prolongation of research, but in a staged fashion, only research or artworks actually accomplished being rewarded.[44] Special attention was given to those traveling long distances, often at great risk to their health and finances, to enlighten men by studying nature, discovering new plants, finding products beneficial to humans, or perfecting the arts. Under the new rules, grumbled some deputies, senior army officers would "scarcely receive more than artists," but dissent was muted. At least one deputy complained that the proposed pensions were inadequate, reflecting "a shameful parsimony"; he also criticized the procedure for applying for grants from the departmental councils as demeaning. "Picture to yourself the Abbé Mably, Raynal, Montesquieu, Pingré, Poivre, La Peyrousse, Buffon, Morveaux, Bailly, Lalande, Petit, Louis, Le Brun, Girardon, Pajoux, etc. etc. queuing up with their *mémoires* of expenses."[45]

Instituting Equality

"The age of ignorance is over," proclaimed the *Chronique de Paris*, assuring readers that it was to la philosophie that France owed the Revolution, and men generally owed their ability to discern with "sentiments plus doux et plus humains" than in the past.[46] Yet nothing was clearer than that the Revolution's core principles clashed fundamentally with many deputies' preferences and the unequal suffrage. For those who most insistently attacked Sieyès's doctrine of *droits actifs*—Brissot, Bonneville, Carra, and Fauchet, as well as Condorcet—this strand of the Constitution inadmissibly clashed with liberty and the Rights of Man. All men are "égaux en droits [equal in rights]," proclaimed Condorcet, leaving no room for financial status in defining citizenship rights. The Cordeliers group of republicans—Desmoulins, Robert, Mandar, and James Rutledge (1742–94), a Franco-Irish writer from Dunkirk—felt likewise.

Even if it were advantageous (which Condorcet denied) to restrict the vote to the financially independent and hence less liable to be corrupted, confining officeholding to those of a given educational level, the enactment still made no sense, as the thresholds were set too low to provide any such safeguard. A false principle that unjustly deprived many of their equal right to participate and hold office, it had to be overturned. Despite Bailly's opposition, the Paris Commune led by Brissot and himself, announced Condorcet in an open letter in the democratic paper *La Bouche de fer*, intended to present the National Assembly with weighty arguments against it.[47]

This democratic view permeated radical circles, especially the republican journalists, progressive Paris salons, Cordeliers Club, and the Cercle Social, or Amis de la Vérité. The last, founded in early 1790, but a political club only since October, was an organization originating in the continuing battle over democracy within the Paris city assembly. Established by Fauchet, Bonneville, Condorcet, Lanthenas, and other Paris Commune republican democrats as a tool for reeducating the public, the Cercle's founders sought ways to bridge the gap between Commune and city sections, and especially to enlighten the people. Following publication of his republican journal, *Tribun du peuple*, Bonneville had emerged in 1789 as "president" of his Paris electoral district. Poet, littérateur, translator of Shakespeare, and specialist on Lessing and German theater, long steeped in la philosophie and initially allied with Sieyès, Bonneville was an unyielding republican stalwart who even before the convening of the Estates-General had advocated a complete recasting of France's political institutions and laws.

The Cercle, representing an essentially new democratic republican approach to propagating the Enlightenment and steering the Revolution, aimed to attach the Assembly more closely to the people, the provinces to Paris, and France to advanced philosophique circles at home and abroad. Enlightened ideas combined with "excellent works," proclaimed this body, would "defeat hypocrisy, charlatanism, and tyranny for ever."[48] The Cercle Social's unbending opposition to the liberal monarchist center, to Bailly, Sieyès, and those seeking to exclude the multitude from the political process, was, of course, viewed unfavorably by most Assembly deputies, as well as by the court.[49] But the organization rapidly gained widespread support in Paris and beyond. Its bookstore, housed in the Cercle's offices, advertised works by Condorcet, Brissot, Bonneville, Mercier, Athanase Auger, Tom Paine, and François Lanthenas (1739–1816). Lanthenas figured in the Cercle's publicity among that select body of "upright men whose conduct accords marvelously with his principles" and who, through his writings and speeches, had rendered the Revolution signal services.[50] A medical man close to Mme. Roland, who regularly contributed to Brissot's *Patriote français*, yet another indefatigable theorist of democratic revolution, Lanthenas, like Condorcet, Brissot, and Bonneville, labored to bridge the gap between philosophique principles and the masses.[51] Author of a text on the evils of primogeniture, he also published more generally on human rights and the "principles of universal morality." In his text on press freedom, *De la liberté indéfinie de la presse* (1791), he emphasized the wide gap between Britain's limited, controlled press freedom so admired by France's constitutional monarchists and the radical, unrestricted press freedom now prevailing in France.[52]

Emancipating the people by reeducating them meant disseminating radical ideas, including social concepts that had little immediate connection with popular concerns and needs. In the view of the republican leadership, everything "de plus philosophique" concerning the origin of societies, kinds of government, laws, religion, and moral principles needed to become more familiar. To sustain the momentum, the main revolutionary journals regularly carried references to and extracts from philosophes "of the first order" like Mably, Condillac, Boulanger, Raynal, Diderot, Paine, and d'Holbach, besides Rousseau and Voltaire.[53] Informed the Besançon civic guard had established a reading room at their own expense to help them better comprehend their interests and duties as citizens, the *Chronique de Paris* called for this example to be universally emulated.[54] Many key radical proposals—reform of the marriage laws, emancipating women legally and politically, dissolution of religious orders, integrating "free blacks" and Jews, abolishing slavery—lay so far beyond the bounds of received thinking that they met with incomprehension and a broadly unsympathetic response. Black emancipation was a cause Brissot, Condorcet, and Lanthenas had identified with well before 1789. Anacharsis Cloots was also fervent for black emancipation.[55] They tried to mobilize mass support for the Amis des Noirs, the abolitionist association they presided over, as a way of defeating the opposition to equal rights for free blacks, and ending slavery.

Civil marriage and civil divorce, together with abolishing the dowry system, regular topics of public debate since the summer of 1789, were another particular sphere of Cercle Social effort. The Revolution would have "une grande influence" on the lives of women, announced the *Chronique de Paris*. Several of the Revolution's most outstanding women, Sophie Condorcet (1758–1822; Condorcet's wife), Olympe de Gouges (1748–93), and the Dutch exile Etta Palm d'Aelders (1743–99), participated prominently in the Cercle's work. Through the Cercle's efforts, civil marriage, divorce, equality within marriage, a national education system for girls, and legal majority at twenty-five became stock themes among the revolutionary vanguard. Sophie Condorcet, Adam Smith's future translator, a strikingly beautiful woman nicknamed "la belle Grouchette" after her maiden name (Grouchy), became a prominent figure in her own right among the Revolution's democratic leadership. She and Condorcet, for whom she became a true *collaboratrice*, had married, with Lafayette present, in December 1786. Their salon, which met in their apartments on the Quai Conti in the Hotel des Monnaies, became a principal gathering point in Paris for all the "troupe philosophique" subsequently leading the Revolution. Despite her aristocratic background and provincial convent education, twenty months since arriving in Paris in 1784 sufficed to convert her into a well-read, ardent republican, burning with zeal for la philosophie and revolutionary equality. With a keen interest in the United States as well as France, she exerted a powerful influence over the entire philosophique sect, including her husband, albeit contributing in a quieter, more modest way than Mme. Roland, and without seeking to upstage her husband. Like her close male associates, she was a convinced atheist. She was in some ways an even more philosophique presence than her sister revolutionaries, Mesdames Roland, Palm d'Aelders, and Gouges.

Prior to 1789, Sophie's salon had featured Adam Smith, Jefferson, Morellet, Suard, Beaumarchais, Lafayette, Ginguené, and David Williams (1738–1816), the former Unitarian turned deist, and briefly, during 1789–92, democratic radical. During the early Revolution, her salon was a regular focal point for the Revolution's leading republicans: her husband, Brissot, Garat, Ginguené, Chamfort, Volney, Chénier, Paine, Cloots, the materialist Cabanis, who later married Sophie's sister, Charlotte de Grouchy (1768–1844), and Claude Fauriel (1772–1844), professor of literature, critic, historian, and philosopher, the scholar who, after 1794, became her lover.[56] She often urged Condorcet on to even more uncompromisingly democratic positions than he was inclined to anyway, and, along with Gouges and Palm, lent a major impulse to the birth of modern feminism.[57] Since women have the same moral and intellectual capacities as men, anything but equality for women, argued Sophie Condorcet, is by definition incompatible with the Rights of Man and discriminatory. After the Terror, and Condorcet's death, she remained steadfastly loyal to his philosophique legacy. Her salon resumed both in Paris and her summer residence, the suburban château of La Villette, where she continued defending the Revolution's core principles. Her salon also remained a focus of philosophique criticism and quiet opposition after the death of Mme. Helvétius in 1800 and Napoleon's consolidation of power.[58]

Plans for reforming the marriage laws, ending the dowry system, and introducing civil divorce had been nurtured by the radical philosophes for decades.[59] "Philosophy," explained Brissot in his *Lettres philosophiques sur Saint Paul* (1783), requires every enlightened nation to adopt a comprehensive divorce law because an enlightened society refuses to chain together "irrévocablement" husbands and wives who make each other unhappy.[60] Before the 1780s, only Diderot, d'Holbach, and a few others urged such a reform, but by 1789 the concept was being broadcast widely, especially by Mirabeau, Brissot, and Condorcet.[61] The obvious injustice of laws that reduced women "to the condition of slaves" and compelled a mistreated wife to remain under her husband's tyranny (unless she could prove her life was in danger) must end and a more rational marriage system instituted.[62] But little progress was made initially despite legal removal of the obstacle of religious vows and sacraments, which were nowhere, the Cercle reminded readers, explicitly endorsed in the emerging Constitution.[63] Mirabeau was the first to propose civil divorce in the Assembly, noted an abused wife writing to the *Chronique de Paris* on 22 January 1792. During the early Revolution, little attention was paid to female victims whom "our barbaric laws still oblige to live under their husbands' cruel domination." Tyrannized by her father and married off at thirteen to a drunken gambler who abused her dreadfully, this lady longed for the liberation civil divorce alone could bring. Legal divorce would already be available, she lamented, had not Mirabeau's death "aborted all the good he wanted to do."[64]

From January 1790, the Condorcet circle initiated several motions in the Assembly to improve the lot of women.[65] Condorcet designated indissolubility of marriage as a blight on society and prime cause of prostitution, bastardy, wife-beating, and emotional misery.[66] France's marriage laws must be reformed, urged the Cercle, especially by instituting a comprehensive divorce law according women equal rights with men in seeking divorce.[67] The 1791 Constitution did make marriage a civil contract but failed to equalize marriage rights or provide for divorce. Philosophically, the case for seeing divorce as essential to human freedom is unanswerable, commented the *Chronique de Paris*, reviewing the forty-page text *La necessité du divorce* by the writer Cailly on 6 January 1791; yet civil divorce and treating men and women equally continued to be opposed by most of the general public and most of the legislature.[68] Support for civil divorce, it should be noted, invariably went hand in hand with republican views and antagonism to religious authority.[69] "Divorce is forbidden by the Christian religion," the Abbé Royou reminded his readers on 25 February 1792, celebrating the repulse in the Assembly of the draft divorce law supported by Cercle leaders and democratic journalists. No one in France advocated divorce, declared Royou (with only scant exaggeration), aside from philosophes, *déistes*, Protestants, and Jews.[70]

Condorcet's arguments for woman's political emancipation appeared first in his article of July 1790, *Sur l'admission des femmes aux droits de la cité*. Women may be unequal in physical strength but are men's equals in intellect and moral stature, even if this becomes evident only when we disregard the "inequality with which the sexes are treated by the laws, institutions, custom, and prejudice."[71] Only stupidity and barbarism could sustain a code as "impertinent as that contemporary society applied to women," Charles-Michel du Plessis, Marquis de Villette (1736–93), an ex-noble who had formally renounced his former noble status concurred in the *Chronique de Paris* that same month. He had no wish to waste his time on "fools and the ignorant," he added: he knew perfectly well most of the public took no interest in women's rights; his goal was to persuade men of discernment and understanding—philosophes. Reason, morality, and the progress of the sciences and arts had all transformed women no less than men. Was any contradiction more "revolting" than that great sovereigns like Catherine II and Maria Theresa, acknowledged by Europe's powers, would be excluded from "our political assemblies" and organizations? For many centuries women had been subjected to senseless "feudal servitude"; "our legislators" should now accord the twelve million females in France "the rights they possess from nature." Villette especially championed women's right to attend the primary assemblies and participate in their decisions.[72]

"Woman, be a *citoyenne*!" within the French Revolution hence remained exclusively the call of la philosophie and republican philosophisme. It was not promoted by liberal monarchism, Marat's populism, or any other revolutionary political, cultural, or social movement. Backed by Condorcet, Bonneville, Brissot, Villette, and the Revolution's leading women—Gouges, Palm, and Sophie Condorcet—an argued, developed, politically organized feminism that conquered a narrow but real enclave in the public sphere was forged for the first time in human history. As a public persona, Sophie Condorcet was undoubtedly eclipsed by Mme. Roland, Palm d'Aelders, and the fiery Gouges. Angered by the Assembly's refusal to consider women's rights, Gouges, before 1789 a high-class *courtisane* and then dramatist, published her famous *Declaration of the Rights of Women* in September 1791. To highlight her satirical intent, she composed it in the same number of articles, seventeen, as in the Declaration of the Rights of Man. Her first four articles proclaimed:

(I)   Woman is born free and lives equal to man in her rights. Social distinctions can be based only on the common good.

(II) The purpose of any political association is the conservation of the natural and imprescriptible rights of woman and man; these rights are liberty, property, security, and especially the right to resist oppression.

(III) The principle of sovereignty rests essentially in the nation, which is nothing but the union of woman and man. No body or individual can exercise authority that does not derive expressly from the nation.

(IV) Liberty and justice consist in restoring all that belongs to any, to all. Thus, the only limits on the exercise of the natural rights of woman are perpetual male tyranny. These boundaries are to be reformed by the laws of nature and reason.

The first gathering of the Cercle's "women's circle" who established their own *directoire*, meeting at the offices of the Cercle in the Paris Théâtre-Français section, occurred in March 1791. In her inaugural speech as their first "president," Etta Palm d'Aelders, an emancipated lady from Groningen (close to Brissot and Carra) who had lived in Paris since 1774 and was the translator of Mirabeau and Condorcet into Dutch, expressed the hope that their group would secure concrete advantages for women. Earlier, in December 1790, she had delivered an acerbic discourse on how French law discriminated against the female population, which was later printed by the Cercle Social.[73] "Our holy Revolution," proclaimed Palm d'Aelders "we owe to the progress of philosophy"; but now a second revolution must be wrought by la philosophie, this time in social practice, so that discrimination against women, condemned by *la vraie philosophie*, "gives way to a gentle, just and natural order."[74]

Palm d'Aelders spoke optimistically of the future, lauding the Cercle Social "the first organization in France to admit women to political meetings."[75] The March 1791 meeting agreed to establish a full-fledged society with local branches, admission cards, and a vetting system for excluding undesirable types, so as to ensure the women's circle consisted only of "excellentes patriotes."[76] Each Paris section needed its own locally affiliated *société patriotique de citoyennes* that met weekly and was sustained by a small entry fee. These women's section associations would spread enlightenment, assist the destitute, run nurseries for children of unmarried women and vagrant girls, and help guard society against "the people's enemies," namely, aristocrats, royalists, and theologians.[77] Charity schools, presently entrusted to ignorant beings "nourished on prejudices of all kinds," should also come under their supervision.

The fight was on in Paris, and soon also provincial centers like Caen and Bordeaux, where local patriotic societies likewise set up women's circles. Etta Palm continued delivering speeches defending women's rights. Many of these speeches were subsequently printed by the Cercle. To develop a sound moral sense in women, society must provide education equal to that for men, not impose unequal restrictions and penalties. The law, urged Palm d'Aelders, should protect women and men equally and promote equality within marriage. She especially deplored the Assembly's new police code, with its Article XIII, which stipulated that adultery charges could be brought only by husbands against wives, and that women convicted of adultery, unlike men, could be imprisoned. She excoriated all the highly unequal laws concerning adultery and the one-sided arrangements for matrimonial settlements, labeling the corpus of supposedly revolutionary marriage law approved by the Assembly's constitutional committee an affront to human rights that rendered women men's slaves.[78] "Moderate" monarchist papers, like the *Gazette universelle*, vilified her as an extremist democrat, *contre-révolutionnaire*, prostitute, and agent of the Prussian court in "criminal correspondance with the nation's enemies."[79] A hard-hitting retort by Palm d'Aelders, carried by the *Bouche de fer*, accused the Assembly of abasing women with barbaric rules indubitably formulated by a constitutional committee that consulted "theologians instead of *philosophes*."[80]

Scorn, noted Villette, was the usual response among both sexes to the Cercle's campaign on behalf of women. Palm d'Aelders, protested many, seemed not to consider sexual chastity something that should be imposed upon women. But here the clash was complicated by the ongoing conflict between radical thought and populist Rousseauisme. Not a few, including Ginguené, extolled Rousseau's *Lettre à d'Alembert* for censoring everything impinging on woman's virtue, everything worldly, and philosophique detrimental to woman's special charm.[81] Robert's ardently Rousseauiste wife, Louise Kéralio-Robert, a prominent political journalist collaborating with him on the *Mercure national*, furiously attacked Palm d'Aelders and her feminist cohort. The Cercle should concentrate on improving morals, not establishing women's political clubs or seeking woman's emancipation. Instead of convening a "crowd of idle and curious women," the Cercle should follow Jean-Jacques in exhorting women to chastity, staying at home, and concerning themselves with children and serving their husbands, not with meetings and enlightenment.[82]

The marriage laws were eventually further reformed, and civil divorce was secured on 20 September 1792, when the legislature finally mustered sufficient votes, at Brissot's urging, to institute civil divorce in law, with incompatibility of temperament firmly included among grounds for ending marriages.[83] But most of the Cercle's women's rights program was not accomplished. Opposition arose on all sides. The philosophes had acquired their ability to influence society, warned Feller, in no small part by appealing to young and pretty women. If the philosophisme behind the Revolution advanced further, women would become "the instruments of their power," endorsing their arrogance, *tolérantisme*, and freeing the passions, dissolving the very fabric of society.[84] Opposition stemmed not least from among Faubourg Saint-Antoine workingmen, chief focus of Marat's authoritarian populism. On returning from a hard day's work, they wanted their dinner, complained the men, not to find their wives had gone out to political meetings.[85] Putting women in their place became a goal of Rousseauist populist authoritarianism, no less than of the Counter-Enlightenment war on philosophisme. As authoritarian populism gained ground in 1793, women's emancipation inexorably receded. During the Robespierriste repression (1793–94), Chaumette, a leading proponent of the drive to confine women to the home, denounced Olympe de Gouges as the very epitome of the revolutionary virago, a dangerous man-woman and sexually immoral creature.[86] Most of the agenda of woman's emancipation projected by Condorcet and the Cercle, Robespierriste reaction ensured, remained a distant ideal.[87]

The secte philosophique fought to emancipate blacks, Jews, and women. They likewise strove to alleviate the plight of the "illegitimately" born and the social stigma condemning pregnancy and births out of wedlock. Villette, an ex-marquis of notoriously homosexual proclivities, published an open letter in the *Chronique de Paris* in August 1790 demanding justice and humanity also for "these unfortunates called natural children." Laws were urgently needed to rescue the illegitimate from the demeaning abasement to which for centuries theologians had condemned them. Existing laws curtailed their inheritance rights and unjustly disallowed their legacies. Church law excluded them from the priesthood. As a bastard, the great académicien d'Alembert was unable to leave a final testament or receive a proper funeral. "Prejudice scarcely allows the illegitimate to exist." It was an issue taken up by the Cercle repeatedly. It was the Assembly's duty, contended Villette, to acknowledge the illegitimate as full "citizens" enjoying equal rights.[88]

The Cercle tried to connect Enlightenment and popular attitudes by encouraging people to submit their views to the leadership via the *Bouche de fer* (the journal's title alluded to the famous lion's mouth, providing Venetian citizens a means to communicate anonymously with the republic's ruling council). Appearing sporadically at first, *La Bouche de fer* came out regularly from October 1790 on, aspiring to be the staple vehicle of the "bons citoyens." But from the outset, it found itself entangled with the militant demagogues of the poor faubourgs, especially Marat. In principle, the Cercle, like the Société de 89, acknowledged the people as "sovereign" and "soul" of the Assembly, and their representatives as heralds of the volonté générale. The Cercle's goal, urged Bonneville, was "to give the people's voice its full force and scope to censure."[89] Yet while everyone had a right to discuss and help form public opinion, the Cercle assumed the people could not "by itself exercise either the legislative or the executive power."[90] The people's views should be freely expressed but also channeled, refined, and guided by philosophes presiding over a free press and the now-transformed educational and political spheres.

Republicans defended freedom of speech even in the case of their staunchest enemies. An indictment of Marat for sedition, instigated in January 1790 by Bailly and others denouncing his violent tone, was backed by much of the Assembly. Month after month in his *L'Ami du peuple*, Marat vilified the regime and revolutionary leadership, urging the populace to rise, break open the arsenals, and arrest all royal ministers and their underlings, and thoroughly purge the city government and National Guard. Chopping off five or six hundred heads was the right way to prevent the "privileged orders" from reestablishing despotism. Malouet and especially Maury—who over many months found himself the target of a vitriolic press campaign originally inspired by Desmoulins, who derided him unrelentingly and accused him of vindictiveness, corruption, loving luxury, and continually consorting with prostitutes—responded by denouncing Desmoulins, Marat, and others for propagating calumnies and demanded that the *colporteurs* selling revolutionary papers and pamphlets in the streets be curbed.[91] A sixty-seven-page "project" composed by the Comité de Constitution, including Sieyès, submitted to the Assembly on 20 January, recommending limits on press freedom where abusers spread calumny and incited violence, and attaching appropriate penalties, met with a sharply divided response.[92] Malouet exhorted the Assembly to proceed against "writers inciting the people to bloodshed and disobedience to the laws." Applauded from the Right, his harangue was pilloried by Pétion and the Left. If Marat's and Desmoulins's papers needed suppressing, objected one deputy, then so did the *Gazette de Paris*, *Actes des apôtres*, and other royalist papers.[93]

The *Chronique de Paris* vehemently condemned Sieyès's attempt to bridle Marat and Desmoulins, urging unrestricted press freedom and warning of "dire consequences" should this be compromised.[94] When magistrates ordered Marat's arrest for sedition in March 1790, and Lafayette was sent to arrest him, the Cercle came to the aid of the populists, as did Danton, Desmoulins, and the Cordeliers committee, all equally eager to champion the Rights of Man, and despite having their own difficulties with Marat. The Cercle and Cordeliers encouraged the fugitive to go underground in their ward, obstruction that resulted in Danton too being arraigned for sedition. The Commune's general council, a body where Brissot and Condorcet for the moment remained prominent, directly clashing with Bailly, thereupon sprang to Danton's defense.

A Crypto-Republican Revolution

Understandably, the first anniversary of the Bastille's fall, though lavishly celebrated with splendid illuminations and firework displays, was far from being the harmonious occasion many historians have claimed it to have been. Rather, despite the hype, it reflected deep and irresolvable splits that increasingly menaced the Republic and the Revolution's future. The Bastille's ruins, the Assembly decreed, should be surrounded by a grill and preserved as they were, without adornment, as a national monument, at the center of which would be erected an obelisk inscribed with the Rights of Man. Preceded by an unprecedented ferment in the theaters, the anniversary was accompanied by much sarcastic comment on its (patently false) message of admirably harmonious collaboration of monarch and a jubilant people. The main point of the pompous festivities arranged by Bailly and the *fripons* around him, suggested Marat, was to distract the citizenry from the tense political situation and the "universal misery" caused by the shortage of work and collapse of manufacturing, and long months of "famine" that was their lot.[95]

On 11 July 1790, three days before the anniversary of the Bastille's fall, the Americans in Paris appeared in the Assembly, headed by John Paul Jones (1747–92), the United States' heroic naval commander during the Revolutionary War, to pay homage to the Revolution and eulogize the much-acclaimed *patriotisme* of Louis XVI.[96] On 14 July itself, the Assembly took the day off to attend the ceremonies marking the anniversary; the main parade, commencing at the Porte Saint-Antoine, took eight hours to wend its way across the city through the dense mass of humanity to the Champs de Mars. For the occasion, the Place de la Bastille was turned into an open-air stage festooned with garlands and revolutionary insignia. A large bust of Rousseau, bedecked with a civic crown, was carried in triumph several times around the ruins by the pupils of the Academy of Painting, escorted with quasi-religious solemnity by a National Guard contingent and crowds of citizens singing a specially composed hymn summoning all to invoke the "holy name of Rousseau, this sublime name."[97] Rousseau may not have been the chief intellectual inspiration of Condorcet, Mirabeau, Sieyès, Cérutti, Volney, Brissot, or the revolutionary vanguard, but he was unquestionably the unrivaled chief teacher and prophet venerated by revolutionary popular culture.

The culminating ceremony, held in the presence of king, court, and the whole Assembly, with National Guard commander Lafayette assigning himself the central role, was watched by an immense crowd, the king, and various other dignitaries publicly swearing to uphold the Constitution to the accompaniment of salvos of ceremonial artillery. Afterward, there were "magnificent illuminations" and much partying and dancing.[98] For showing the king exaggerated respect on this occasion, as well as hogging center stage for himself, Desmoulins's paper heaped insults on Lafayette. Others, too, including Robespierre, derided Lafayette's posturing. Immediately after the 14 July celebrations, Marat and Desmoulins were again formally charged by Malouet and the Club Monarchique with subverting the Constitution. Desmoulins was plainly trying to render royalty an object of contempt, styling Louis a king "with his hands tied behind his back, following [the 14 July triumphal parade] in humiliation."[99] Plainly, these men wanted no king or monarchical government and were depicting monarchists as foes of the people. Certain papers continually invoked the danger of counterrevolution. But was it not "counterrevolutionary" to try to overthrow king, Constitution, and the law? Malouet produced a fresh draft decree, pronouncing all who "in their writings incite the people to insurrection against the law, to bloodshed and the overthrow of the Constitution" guilty of a criminal offense. "Authors, printers and street-vendors of writings inciting such insurrection" must be punished.[100] Again the Cercle and the Cordeliers sprang to Marat's and Desmoulins's defense.[101]

The "truest friends of liberty," as Lanthenas called them, responded by forming a defensive alliance, the Amis de la Liberté Indéfinie de la Presse. The priceless freedoms gained in 1789, contended republican democrats, were won essentially by press freedom, and this liberty was also the sole means to defend freedom generally.[102] "Moderates" fighting to curtail press freedom cited British practice to justify the proposed restrictions. But the vagueness of their press freedom and strength of their libel laws, objected republicans, rendered the British approach "détestable" to any people aspiring to be free.[103] Lanthenas extolled unlimited freedom of the press as the guardian and sole infallible safeguard of the volonté générale. Volonté générale was the engine serving society's true interests and object of all free and understanding "private wills," but was genuinely expressed only where reason was the sole evaluating criterion.[104]

Lanthenas's thesis relied wholly on reason's power to subdue ignorance. Dispensing with libel laws left no other recourse than to shrug off malicious insults, calumny, and ill-grounded criticism. Let royalist journalists like Mallet du Pan, Royou, Rivarol, and so on "vomit their lies, *sophismes* and insults against the people" and against la philosophie. Let their presses and bookshops be respected and their infamous trade faithfully served by the national postal service. Let us take all measures to ensure the triumph of the *bons principes* supporting humanity's rights and interests through a national campaign of public instruction.[105] Full, unrestricted freedom of the press thus became inextricably linked to the task of reeducating the population and teaching children to develop an independent and sound critical judgment. Needed above all was free public schooling that inculcated knowledge of the Constitution, civics, and the rudiments of science, geography, and history, where *la morale universelle* and *la politique naturelle* (his employing d'Holbach's book titles was no accident) infuse what is taught.[106] Only education of this sort can enable the people to judge correctly.

Aside from the main festivities in Paris, smaller reenactments of the taking of the Bastille, using papier-mâché models of the fortress, were staged in the Paris outskirts by the best-known of the Bastille's "conquerors," Pierre-François Palloy, "the Patriot." Such playacting set the pattern for open-air reenactments around the country, ritual commemorations in which a model Bastille was "stormed" and an old man symbolically laden with chains "liberated" to thunderous crowd applause.[107] The papers, eager to enhance the image of the Revolution as a world event, also reported banquets marking the anniversary held in foreign metropolises. There was clearly real enthusiasm in certain circles in Britain, Germany, and Holland. In London and Amsterdam, in Stuttgart, at Schiller's old school, the Hohe Karlsschule, students mounted a lively celebration, and also at Hamburg, where "worthy men participated in the happiness of twenty-five million humans who had recovered their liberty."

At Hamburg, Georg Heinrich Sieveking organized a grand all-day festival and banquet for eighty guests on his property at nearby Harvestehude. Those present included Reimarus's son, Johann Albert Heinrich Reimarus (1729–1814); his famous unmarried sister, Lessing's and Mendelssohn's friend, Elise Reimarus (1735–1805); the poetess Caroline Rudolphi; the former leader of the Illuminati in Protestant Germany, Knigge, among the foremost supporters of the French Revolution outside France; and the poet Friedrich Gottlieb Klopstock (1724–1803). The banquet, accompanied by live music, a women's choir, discharge of ceremonial cannon, and two revolutionary odes by Klopstock, lasted all day, the participants successively toasting the "happiness of France," the glorious 14 July, the French National Assembly, Bailly, Lafayette, Mirabeau, and Klopstock. The men, sporting tricolor cockades, and the women, wearing white dresses with tricolor sashes and hats with tricolor cockades, drank also to "prompt consequences" and an end to princely *Despotismus* in Germany.[108]

The Paris theater world also stoked the fierce ideological furor of July 1790. As the first anniversary of the Bastille approached, the actors were besieged with demands for performances of Voltaire's *Brutus* (1731) and *The Death of Caesar* (1735); Antoine-Marin Lemierre's *Guillaume Tell* (1766), a play revived with success, earlier, in 1786; *Barneveld*, also by Lemierre; and especially Chénier's *Charles IX*. In recent months, all such requests had been rejected by royal ministers and theater directorates due to the overtly republican slant audiences would inevitably place on their content. Boycotting them all, the former Comédie-Française, since November 1789 renamed the Théâtre de la Nation, performed what La Harpe and another playwright, Palissot, called "the most insignificant pieces" they could find, all breathing the spirit of "servitude" and "adulation."[109] Comédie-Française actors, who despite the change in the name of the theater still styled themselves "Comediens français ordinaires du roi," mostly, reports La Harpe, backed the *parti anti-révolutionnaire*. With a blatantly biased choice of plays, they tried to foment adulation of kings and nobles among the least sophisticated, "nothing being easier than to mislead ordinary folk and seduce their minds" by manipulating emotions in ways they fail to understand. Resistance collapsed, though, amid a growing commotion in the French theater world in July.

Pressure to stage republican material eventually proved irresistible. The Théâtre de la Nation agreed to stage its first ever performance of *Barnevelt*, a drama about Oldenbarnevelt's downfall in 1618. The premiere took place on 30 June 1790, its more obviously republican moments eliciting embarrassingly lively applause from the audience. A spectator, defiantly expressing monarchical indignation by hissing

loudly, was hounded from the theater.[110] Predictably, *Charles IX*, performed thirty-four times in the autumn of 1789, was loudly demanded
and provoked a still greater furor. Like the rest of society, the actors were
hopelessly split, most resisting the pressure to stage the play. A minority, led by the radical François-Joseph Talma (1763–1826), the most
renowned tragic actor of the revolutionary era, and his leading lady,
Mme. Vestris, wished to perform it. Requests flowed especially from
volunteer soldiers (*fédérés*) from the provinces sent to participate in the
14 July marches and celebrations. Those from Marseille demanded the
play with particular fervor and enlisted Mirabeau to help secure it. A
disturbance calling for the play, openly encouraged by Talma, occurred
at the theater on 22 July. Opposing efforts to enlist Bailly to ban the play
and arrest Talma as an *incendiaire* failed. Chénier mobilized additional
support in the Cordeliers section.[111] Noting Mirabeau's intervention,
Danton's interest, and the fédérés' enthusiasm, Bailly wisely permitted
the performance but took care to post armed guards around the theater.
The play was finally staged on 23 July, with Danton present. Trouble ensued afterward when Talma, now publicly allied to Mirabeau, Danton,
and Chénier, so antagonized fellow actors that they ejected him from
the theater and permanently boycotted him.

The French theater world was plunged into ferment, one side adhering to a "moderate" course, the other proclaiming the theater "the
modern school of liberty." When Voltaire's *Brutus* was repeated on 17
November, the audience, relating events onstage to events in the country, immediately split into opposed factions, one side yelling "Vive le
roi!," the other "Vive le roi, vive la Nation!" During a performance of
La Liberté conquise at the Théâtre de la Nation, at the moment the Bastille's assailants proclaim their oath to "conquer or die," the audience
rose to their feet as one, the men lifting their hats on the ends of their
canes and shaking them in the air, the women holding aloft their hands
and throwing up handkerchiefs, thoroughly stirring all present. During
another performance of this play, "the brave Arné"—the grenadier who
overpowered the Bastille's governor and then clambered up the Bastille's highest turret to raise his hat high into the air on his bayonet—
was spotted. The audience spontaneously demanded he be crowned
with a liberty cap. As Arné was "crowned," enthusiastic market women
sang an uplifting chorus in the hero's honor.[112]

The Paris Opera became equally polarized. *Iphigénie en Aulide* by
Gluck, first performed at the Paris Opera in 1774, produced an unruly
incident in December 1790, with *patriotes* occupying the parterre in

force, and monarchists predominating higher up, in the more expensive seats. When the aria "let us celebrate our queen" was sung, aristocrats in the boxes thunderously applauded while the parterre stamped, hissed, and jeered. In response, Antoinettistes hurled down apples, provoking *Patriotes* to try to climb up to the boxes with little "martinets" for whipping fine ladies sporting the white cockade, only to be repelled by the National Guard posted to keep order.[113]

At a meeting on 27 September 1790, Théâtre de la Nation actors expressed resentment at being called "réfractaires" and "authors of counterrevolution" by hostile audiences. Unable either to secure court permission to perform *Charles IX* or persuade audiences the play was forbidden, the actors requested a civic directive requiring performances of *Charles IX* on specified days as a way of evading recrimination for staging "republican plays."[114] When the autumn season of *Charles IX* eventually opened, Mirabeau was spotted among the audience and given a rousing ovation.[115] On 18 December 1790, with tension between Assembly and Church escalating, the Théâtre de la Nation premiered *Jean Calas*, based on Voltaire's most famous public campaign against bigotry, by the Left republican playwright Jean-Louis Laya (1761–1833), a play reportedly "applauded universally," in which the judges' "fanaticism" and ecclesiastical intolerance were fiercely pilloried.[116]

As the revolutionary leadership of 1789 split, especially over restricted suffrage, respecting the royal veto, and press freedom, the democratic republican Left appeared to be in danger of being politically marginalized, pinned to the defensive. The municipal elections of August 1790 were a particular setback: Bailly was reelected mayor, with 12,000 out of 14,000 votes, and a new communal assembly was chosen, composed overwhelmingly of moderates.[117] Brissot, Bonneville, Fauchet, and Garran-Coulon lost their prominent positions in the Commune, and from October 1790, Brissot no longer played a role there at all. But as the *Chronique de Paris* and other revolutionary journals pointed out, this outcome was principally due to the new financial qualifications for "active" citizenry, which had the effect of disadvantaging known republicans and democrats and securing their rejection by the more affluent. The results were not a reflection of sentiment more generally in Paris or the press. Republicans responded by redoubling their efforts to cultivate the Palais-Royal and the streets. From late 1790, the democratic Left took to opposing the Commune as well as the mayor by mobilizing support among the wider public outside the official political sphere.

This shift in revolutionary politics during late 1790 also reflected a regrouping of the political factions in the National Assembly with Sieyès, Barnave, Lafayette, and Bailly now leaning more and more toward the center, Mirabeau (in secret contact with the court since March 1790 and abandoning his earlier radicalism) becoming isolated, and those to the Left for the moment a reduced minority. Former allies parted company. Already in July, Desmoulins bitterly mocked and rebuked Sieyès in his paper for becoming too deferential toward the king, reminding him of the vast applause in early 1789 for his famous pamphlet *Qu'est-ce que le Tiers* and its huge impact on the Café Procope, the engine room of the Revolution. Was it possible that this same hero of 1789 now proposed penalties for those writing irreverently about kings?[118] The most outspoken opposition journalists (whether democrats or populists)— Desmoulins, Marat, and Fréron—increasingly had batches of their papers seized and saw the colporteurs peddling them molested.[119] In October, the Cercle Social converted its organ, the *Bouche de fer*, into a regular journal designed, under Bonneville's and Cérutti's editorship, to secure a wide readership. It was at this point that its directoire, now joined by Cloots and Lamourette, adopted the technique of holding mass debates at the Palais-Royal. The alliance between the presiding radical clique in the Cordeliers and the Cercle grew closer.

The first meeting of the Cercle's new club, the Confédération des Amis de la Vérité, took place on 13 October 1790 before an audience of more than four thousand crowded into a circus building adjoining the Palais-Royal.[120] A second mass meeting on 22 October was attended by a still larger throng. The Cercle, the only Paris club organizing its membership on the basis of subscriptions to a journal, the *Bouche de fer*, steadily recruited more orators and journalists, including Desmoulins, Cloots, and Mercier. Its journal ensured the club both a huge membership and enviable national outreach. With a membership roll oscillating between three and six thousand, by a loose definition it was in fact the largest political club of the early Revolution. From the autumn of 1790, large, undogmatic, and broadly accommodating, the Cercle at this stage attacked neither monarchy nor religion explicitly. Outwardly compatible with a minimalized monarchism, a lively religious dimension was also provided, especially by Lamourette and Claude Fauchet, who strove, not without some success at first, to bridge the gap between Catholicism and radical thought, assuring listeners at every turn that Jesus was a lover of liberty, equality, and human rights, and a great foe of despotism and privilege.

The philosophique fringe now found themselves effectively in opposition to an expanded Assembly centrist bloc and moderate Paris Commune. They responded by equipping themselves to propel a radicalization of the Revolution from below. The Revolution, and all the people's gains, had been achieved by la philosophie, a complete mystery to most; to explain this, the Cercle neglected no opportunity to trumpet philosophy as the Revolution's guiding spirit. The demise of Benjamin Franklin—whose death on 17 April had been marked in Paris in July 1790 with a grand commemoration, including a famous banquet at the Café Procope—signaled the start of a veritable cult of the great man. Several cafés and clubs in Paris dedicated hecatombs with funerary busts and solemn epitaphs commemorating the lofty American. The Cercle converted Franklin into a public symbol and perennial teacher of international republicanism—virtuous, austere, public-spirited, and wise. Franklin was the figure who enabled revolutionary orators to praise philosophy and its capacity to ameliorate the world without offending religion, as eulogizing Voltaire was bound to do. The high point of the July festivities was a speech by Fauchet before the Commune and twelve leading deputies, including Mirabeau, Sieyès, and Dr. Guillotin.[121] Fauchet hailed Franklin, "claimed by two worlds," as a benefactor of the human race, one of those enlightened men who in recent decades had changed the world. At the same time, he fiercely denounced the "ridiculous etiquette" of monarchical courts, which for centuries had deemed only the demise of royalty and great aristocratic personages worthy of public mourning.[122] Lavish public commemorations celebrating true benefactors of mankind, stripped of all courtly "hypocritical mournings" and posturing, would henceforth typify the new revolutionary era. The Revolution should in the future designate for public homage exclusively "les heroes de l'humanité [humanity's heroes]," true benefactors of the human race, like Franklin.[123]

But the Franklin cult, like the wider philosophique message pervading the Cercle and Cordeliers leadership, was bound to look menacing to anyone opposing republican principles and deepened the Revolution's divisions. Claiming that the Cercle and (authentic) Jacobins shared the same antiaristocratic and democratic doctrine, Desmoulins vigorously rebutted a speech attacking the Cercle, delivered in the (still predominantly "moderate") Jacobin Club in December 1790 by the novelist and Rousseau admirer Pierre Choderlos de Laclos (1741–1803), a former army officer and fortifications expert who had emerged as a leader of the Orléanist faction.[124] If Desmoulins had also befriended another

Rousseau admirer and stalwart defender of constitutional monarchy in the Jacobins, namely, Robespierre, intellectually he remained closer to Left republicans like Bonneville and Brissot.[125]

The involvement of both Commune and National Assembly in the Franklin commemoration owed much to Fauchet, who greatly valued the discretion of "ce grand homme," utter religious skeptic though he was. Fauchet too was a republican and representative of Radical Enlightenment, an ardent reformer and foe of aristocracy. A thoroughgoing democrat, he was among the most prominent advocates of the principle of having bishops and priests elected by the whole people instead of chosen by the court. Fervent disciple of Rousseau (while disagreeing on certain political points), he viewed Rousseau's books as the key to the reconciliation of religion and la philosophie he so tirelessly sought. As a member of the Cercle's directorate and its *procureur-général*, he delivered a long series of public lectures in the Cercle's name, invoking Rousseau as the society's true guiding intellectual light. He believed his demand that the land should be apportioned in a more equal fashion among the peasantry was supported by both Scripture and Rousseau. But in a speech on October 1790, and thereafter increasingly, Fauchet also denounced the "atheism" and irreligion of the philosophes, dismissing Voltaire for his aristocratic connections, personal wealth, and alleged unoriginality, and, despite his eloquence and wit, a generally malign influence.

Christianity is *la liberté universelle* and the people's true guide, held Fauchet, and any philosophe who denied this was not an authentic philosophe but rather, like Julian the Apostate, a ridiculous sophist.[126] Among those annoyed by these sallies and his insistence that "true Christianity is the only veritable fount of liberty and *volonté générale*," were Bonneville, Desmoulins, Cloots, and the antitheological social reformer Villette. A noble landowner wounded at the battle of Minden in 1759, Villette had often stayed at Voltaire's mansion at Ferney. It was in Villette's house in Paris that Voltaire had lodged during his last days in 1778, and died (and where his body was embalmed). Villette had no patience at all for Christian values. Since joining the Cercle's directoire in October 1790, the declared atheist Anacharsis Cloots had also been disturbed by the "mystical" and Christian atmosphere infusing some Cercle meetings. To him, the Gospel and Koran, like the Zend Avesta and Hindu scriptures, were sources only of trouble, confusion, and error. In late March 1791, Cloots and Fauchet publicly quarreled in Cercle meetings over two vital points: Fauchet's negative campaign against irreligious philosophes and his supposedly demanding that wealth and the land be systematically and equally divided among the people, a proposition Cloots pronounced excessive and "dangerous."

Fauchet, who believed property pertains "to need, not luxury," felt obliged to reassure his colleagues in Cercle meetings that what he wanted was that every man should have his own domain on which to exist on earth, that the poor man be assured of his bread, and that the multitude not be at the mercy of the rich, things they all agreed on. Nowhere had he maintained that the way to "assure a sufficient and free existence to all men" necessitates an "equal distribution of the land." Such a plan would indeed be "an apple of discord that would destroy the human race." He urged only what Rousseau demanded, namely, that all the poor should have something and no wealthy person have too much.[127] Besides ridiculously rating Voltaire above Rousseau as "a reasoner," Cloots, in his opinion, had a mistaken conception of la philosophie, wanting no religion at all.[128] Fauchet was the Revolution's foremost representative of Christian Radical Enlightenment. Most of the Cercle's directors and leading lights expounded materialism, atheism, and hostility to organized religion. But for the moment, there was enough common ground to bridge the gap. The leadership all agreed that they sought an enlightened philosophique "democracy," a term Fauchet frequently used; they all wanted the whole population to be "enlightened," however vast this task. They were all without exception crypto-republicans.

To engage with the illiterate peasantry, the Cercle launched a successful paper specifically addressed to the villages, La Feuille villageoise, designed to be read aloud to peasant gatherings by village curates and schoolmasters. Its circulation rose to perhaps fifteen thousand during 1791.[129] The education needed for participation in politics, announced the first issue of La Feuille villageoise in October 1790, had thus far mostly been confined to the towns "where good books had gradually enlightened minds and prepared the Revolution," from which, however, the peasantry "reaped the first advantages." It was through reading that the courageous men "you have charged to represent you and defend your rights were cultivated: through reading you yourselves will learn to know and defend your rights."[130] The ancien régime rested on "prejudice," "superstition," and "ignorance." Without ignorance there can be no kings, aristocrats, parlementaires, or other privileged elite oppressing the peasantry. However, without la philosophie, ignorance and prejudice cannot be eradicated. Some claimed ignorance was the peasant's natural portion. But peasants too must make judgments, and, hence, comprehend politics and the Constitution, and this can happen only via reading. If the people failed to become "enlightened," the Rights of Man, the new revolutionary order, and the Constitution would not survive, and the Revolution would indubitably perish. The great Franklin had pursued philosophy with such energy, explained *La Feuille villageoise*, that "like Newton, Leibniz, Voltaire, and other illustrious *philosophes*," he kept his special vision to the last. He began his career as a printer: printing and la philosophie—the one aiding the other—"have been of greater service to the human race than all other arts put together."[131]

France's peasantry needed to know why and how their revolutionary leadership was so deeply split. All those designated "aristocrats," explained *La Feuille villageoise* on 11 November, "were *privilégiés* in our *ancien régime* and aspired still to re-introduce that régime and recover the privileges that they lost."[132] Dialogues featuring villagers appeared regularly in this journal, continually reminding the peasantry that it was the new philosophique ideas that had made the Revolution and freed them from feudalism, which alone, with liberty of the press, could protect their newly won rights. When the "peasant" in these dialogues inquired why the Rights of Man only came to light as recently as 1789, he learned that human rights were discovered so late because, earlier, most people could not read. "The people could not educate itself on its own, and so it let itself be deceived by others." To the peasants' question, "What is the greatest service villagers can render their children?," the paper answered: teach them to read and to examine everything they are told before believing it, for the peasants have long been deceived at their cost.[133]

Peasants were also taught basic international and world politics. How should peasants understand the struggle in India between the British and princes, like the son of Hyder Ali, who opposed the East India Company and was supported by the French and Dutch? Eventually, explained *La Feuille villageoise*, the Revolution would overthrow the colonial regime, like the ancien régime in France, and the English in India would be "exterminated." Should Frenchmen rejoice over the death of these exploiters? No, the English "are our brothers; but so are the Indians and we should wish that the oppressors, the English, be punished and the oppressed, the Indians, become 'independent.'"[134] But neither French peasants nor India's oppressed would enjoy freedom, peace, and happiness without reading, a free press, and the reign of la philosophie.

CHAPTER 6

Deadlock

(NOVEMBER 1790–JULY 1791)

The Unviability of the 1791 Monarchical Constitution

Could constitutional monarchism consolidate in a land infused with so powerful a *philosophique* republican undercurrent? The Revolution's first Constitution, though not officially finalized until September 1791, was already substantially in place by the summer of 1790. Its eventually 208 articles opened with a ringing declaration that there no longer existed in France any nobility, hereditary distinctions, division of society into orders, titles, feudal regime, servile dues, or religious vows or obligations contrary to natural rights. It was certainly a comprehensively liberal monarchist Constitution that firmly anchored some fundamental human rights, ensured the primacy of the legislature, and attached an elaborate constitutional apparatus to monarchy. It guaranteed freedom of thought, freedom of conscience, and freedom of expression. But for multiple reasons, there was little chance that it could last long or form the basis of a stable polity.[1]

In the first place, it compelled the radical-minded republican leaders in the press, clubs, Paris Commune, and the Assembly, who had forged the great legislative enactments of 1789, to steer a tortuous, contested course hardly likely to be viable for long. They felt obliged to conform outwardly to a Constitution they did not believe in, able neither uninhibitedly to avow their republican goals nor disavow the Constitution's assertion of monarchical principles and antidemocratic tendency. A leading Assembly radical who admitted profound reservations about the Constitution was Jérôme Pétion de Villeneuve (1753–94), a deputy for Chartres, whose *Avis aux français* ranked among the prime assaults on the ancien régime of 1788. Pétion, affable and honorable but hesitant, published his political profession of faith in the *Mercure na-*

tional, one of the papers overtly propagating republican ideas, on 24 April 1791. That he entertained such reservations had lately been revealed to the public by the Belgian republican publicist, François Robert, the *Mercure's* editor. Pétion acknowledged, albeit guardedly, three fundamental objections to the 1791 Constitution. First, the king, in his view, should have no role in legislation at all, and hence, no veto. Second, the Constitution should be democratic, according all citizens, without distinction, both the vote and eligibility for office; this meant France's suffrage limitations should be abolished. Third, the nation's finances should be not just mainly but wholly under the legislature's control, with the king wielding no influence whatsoever over the appointment or activities of deputies, ministers, military commanders, or other officeholders. At some future point, the *bons citoyens* must, in the people's interest, eliminate royal executive power and democratize suffrage. Meanwhile, he and his colleagues respected the Constitution and the law, if only provisionally.[2]

Pétion, like his colleague François-Nicolas Buzot (1760–94), a declared foe of Bailly, figured among the Assembly's ablest orators and critics of the liberal monarchist center. His underlying stance was one of outright democratic republicanism, but he stopped short of publicly endorsing overtly republican views like those propagated by such leading journalists as Gorsas, Carra, Robert, and Desmoulins, who were, he acknowledged, attacking the Constitution and breaking the law. In addition, outspoken, impatient republicans like these were, he admonished, frightening France's vast majority, especially the artisans, laborers, and peasants, most of whom had not the slightest idea what *républicanisme* was.[3] Readers, he warned, needed to guard against harsh, simplistic terminology classifying *républicanisme* and monarchy in black-and-white terms. The best government is not one that carries a particular label but one that yields the highest sum of happiness and security (*la plus grande somme de bonheur, de sûreté*) and is safest from bad administration. Pétion perceived the risk of a damaging rift over republicanism. A major destabilizing factor in 1790, then, was that republicanism pervaded the Revolution's Left political and press leadership (though rejected by Robespierre and the Jacobins) while there was only very limited support for republicanism among the population. Most members of what was to become the largest and most important political club, the Jacobins, at this time remained forthrightly both centrist and monarchist.

Pétion's dilemma was equally that of Brissot, Condorcet, Bonneville, Cérutti, Desmoulins, Lanthenas, and a long list of other democratic republicans, in fact, all those forming the authentic backbone of the democratic Revolution. Left republican radicalism completely dominated the thought and practice of the main revolutionary press, the Cordeliers and other radical clubs, and the Cercle Social, and remained a substantial contingent in the Paris Communal council. If, after October 1790, Brissot himself no longer occupied a place on the Paris Commune committees, several of his allies did. Prominent among these was Louis-Pierre Manuel (1751–93), a former teacher and bookseller's assistant, imprisoned briefly in the Bastille when still young, for his subversive *Essais historiques* (1783). Manuel was yet another leading revolutionary who was convinced that the path had been cleared by la philosophie prior to 1788, and that France was now ridding herself of the legacy of centuries of oppression. La philosophie drove the Revolution by establishing the people's rights, proving that existing laws derived from "prejudice" and "ignorance," and that laws "made by nature and reason are lacking." The pens of Rousseau, Mably, and Raynal, claimed Manuel, had contributed more to the Revolution than the swords of the revolutionary militias. "The nobility cited charters, titles and privilege" in 1789, but in vain. The principle of equality introduced by philosophy taught the people that they possessed natural rights and that these rights should ground the new order.[4]

During 1790 and early 1791, the republican leadership sought to make the best of the constitutional monarchy they were stuck with while safeguarding basic freedoms, rights, and equality. These men were resolved to ensure that, as the *Chronique de Paris* expressed it, France acquired a "constitution worthy of a free people." They would be "vigilant and courageous sentinels," denouncing old and new abuses, pursuing foes of the public good, uncovering plots, and unmasking "false patriots," of whom there seemed to be a vast number.[5] They hoped to attain their goals by propagating Enlightenment ideas among the public. A nation is only free, held Condorcet and his editorial colleagues, "when it is enlightened, as prejudices are additional fetters." It was both essential and, he and his allies believed, also inevitable that "'la philosophie,' like the sun, should cast its light everywhere." Before 1789, the two greatest enemies of human freedom and well-being—ignorance and superstition—had domineered, blocking reason's progress. But now that liberty of thought and the press prevailed, nothing could prevent the swift advance through society—and soon the entire world—of the Rights of Man. Provided their authors and titles were well publicized, the "good books" that earlier planted "the seeds of the Revolution," held the *Chronique* (those of Boulanger, Diderot, Raynal, d'Holbach, Helvétius, Paine, Price, and Priestley) "will govern both kings and peoples."[6]

Philosophique republicans like Pétion, Manuel, Brissot, and Condorcet were the backbone of the democratic, egalitarian Revolution but had so far all along remained a small minority in the legislature. Most National Assembly deputies remained convinced and resolute defenders of monarchy, and for the moment so did the Paris Commune. But this large majority was irretrievably divided between conservative monarchists anxious to defend king and Church, and (to a lesser degree) the parlements and "moderate" constitutionalists seeking to subject the court effectively to the legislature, weaken religious authority drastically, and pursue and marginalize the old aristocracy. The first category more or less openly opposed the Revolution's essential principles while the second claimed to support them but were regarded by republicans (with considerable justification, it turned out) as "enemies secrets du bonheur public." The rift dividing these two numerically dominant blocs was not just irreparable but extremely bitter. In December 1790, Barnave proposed a decree that ex-patriots failing to return within a month to reside under French laws, including the king's relatives, should lose all pensions and gratifications received from the Crown. Maury and Cazalès furiously opposed this attempt to strip the fugitive princes and principal émigrés of their court sinecures and gratifications, pronouncing it an outrageous affront to royalty and aristocracy, and a blatant violation of the sacred right of property.

The liberal monarchist center led by Barnave and the Lameths aspired to capture the Revolution and dominate the legislature. Their tactical position was considerably strengthened in March 1790 when a faction including Lafayette (who earlier had assured republican allies that he too was a republican) and another leading deputy, Isaac René Le Chapelier (1754–94), from Rennes, prominent in the Estates-General of 1789 and later on the constitutional committee, moved rightward and joined them in combating the parti de philosophie.[7] Yet, the center suffered several—in fact four—major structural weaknesses that rendered these men not just unlikely to succeed in their aims in the medium term, but actually the weakest of the major blocs vying for control of the country. First, the moderates (*modérés*) had most of the pro-Revolution press against them; second, they had less capacity to mobilize support in the streets than their rivals both of the Right and Left; third, there was never any true alliance or trust between them and the royal court; and finally, their vehement anticlericalism guaranteed unceasing strife with the Church and hence with conservatism more generally. Speaking in the Assembly on 7 June 1790, Alexandre de Lameth (1760–1829), who like Lafayette had fought in the American War of Independence and had earlier claimed to be a republican, labeled the "so-called Catholics" of Nîmes "fanatics" guilty of treason, berating them especially for claiming the king, since his transfer to Paris, was no longer "a free agent." The king, insisted Lameth, had come in person to ratify the Assembly's main decisions. Louis had fully participated in the great enactments, and publicly proclaimed himself "le chef de la Révolution."[8]

Besides changes to the Constitution, there were, of course, many other changes to institutions, society, and the laws the republicans aspired to bring about. But for most Frenchmen, the ancien régime had by no means disappeared beyond recall, and there was considerable nostalgia for it. The widely selling ultraroyalist press continually reminded Parisians that their capital had been more imposing, prosperous, pious, and orderly before the Revolution. Until 1788, Paris's once-tidy public squares and gardens had never echoed to the cries of demonstrators or "audacious *colporteurs*" vending "infamous" brochures. The royal police had ensured there were no disturbances or disrespectful behavior toward nobles or churchmen. By contrast, churches were now daily violated and priests and friars openly derided in the streets and theaters. Since 1788, in the view of many, Paris had become depraved morally, politically, and socially. But this could be reversed. If the people would rise in arms to destroy philosophy and the revolutionaries, and restore monarchy and religion, better days would return and great benefits accrue.[9]

The counterrevolutionary ultraroyalism that seethed in late 1790, especially in once-preeminent regional and judicial centers, was everywhere stronger in society than liberal monarchism. The Assembly's edict of 6 September 1790 suppressing the parlements, appropriating their buildings and archives, and quashing the old subsidiary law courts, intensified economic recession and émigré exodus alike. At Aix and Pau, the ceremonies of closure passed off without incident, with sullen crowds looking on silently. But the Parlement of Toulouse refused to give in quietly, issuing two edicts on 25 and 26 September 1790 vowing to withstand the onslaught on law and the monarchy, and calling on all loyal people to support them.[10] Such defiance by "infames sycophantes" outraged both the radical and left center deputies, Mirabeau terming it a "crime manifeste." Parlementaires signing these treasonable edicts were accused of *lèse-nation*, treason against the nation; the only deputy who spoke in their defense, a lawyer, Madier, was soon obliged to flee the country.[11] Suppression of the parlements was fully enforced but left the former judicial capitals awash with resentful ex-magistrates, advocates, and officials stripped of their former status, besides former domestics, coachmen, and artisans whose livelihoods depended on the conspicuous consumption of the elites of sword, robe, and host.

But the powerful upsurge of loyalist and pronoble sentiment in France during late 1790 was by no means confined to former regional capitals with parlements. Its impact was general and accompanied by a renewed wave of fear or "grand peur" from December 1790 to June 1791, causing pamphlets, newspapers, and the cries of the colporteurs alike to resound obsessively with talk of conspiracy, plots, and Counter-Revolution.[12] Caen, where unrest was chronic and the booksellers' boutiques supposedly overflowed with brochures decrying the Assembly's deputies as madmen avid to "dethrone their king," teemed, reports Gorsas, with nobles, gravitating from the surrounding region of Lower Normandy, who uttered "insolent declamations against the Constitution" and preached sedition and civil war.[13] Dialogues between fictitious former "servants" exchanged claim and counterclaim. A republican pamphlet of late 1790 defending freedom of expression featured two former lackeys, one berating the "clique infernale" of Maury, Malhouet, and Duval d'Eprémesnil as malicious stalwarts inexplicably allowed by a supine Assembly to defame the Revolution and its legislation; his better-informed friend, "Bon-Coeur," explaining that the Constitution obliges the Assembly to tolerate all opinions, since every Assembly deputy had an equal right to voice his views, good or bad.[14]

Lyon, though not the seat of a former parlement, was another major focus of royalist subversion. The main pillar of the city's economy, the silk industry, was gripped by recession. Redundancy, misery, and high food prices converted the city into a turbulent hub of unrest. Rioting erupted in mid-July 1790 when workers demonstrated against the Assembly's new sales taxes, ferment the republican press attributed chiefly to "incendiary writings" disseminated by royalists. Working people's despair, anxieties, unawareness, and volatility became more and more evident. On 27 July, a major disturbance occurred when two thousand "workers" filled the Place Bellecour, marched on the town hall, mobbed the mayor, and seized the arsenal. The mayor mobilized the National Guard. Firing broke out in the city center, several workers were killed or wounded, and many were arrested before order was restored.[15] The chief difficulty at Lyon, explained one deputy, was that the city's mostly illiterate textile workforce, though "naturally good," were unfortunately gullible and "easily misled by those aiming to sow confusion and disorder."[16]

Exploiting the collective panic were a group of nobles who met in one another's houses—D'Escars, Quillengle de Poujelon, and Terasse. They mobilized working people's disgruntlement by employing agents lower down the social scale to ply the city sections, disseminating Royou's *L'Ami du Roi*, *La nouvelle lanterne magique*, Durozoy's *Gazette de Paris*, and printed circulars issued by bishops, all passionately denouncing the Revolution.[17] Lyon reactionaries, suggested the republican press, finding it was easy to sway the faithful, unlettered masses, were planning a Saint Bartholomew's Day massacre of Patriotes. "Brigands" had been smuggled into the city to lead the massacre and money distributed among the poor. Nearby, across the Piedmontese frontier at Chambéry, the princes of Artois and Condé were preparing to invade with their aristocratic armed bands the moment the people rose in their blind fury. Workingmen's frustration had turned Lyon into the capital and arsenal of the Counter-Revolution. At length, however, in December 1790, the aristocratic conspiracy was unmasked, and D'Escars and his accomplices arrested.[18]

Another chronic trouble-spot, despite the lack of nobles and parlementaires, was the city of Toulon, where the elite mainly comprised merchants and officials. With its large, illiterate, and poorly paid force of dock laborers, Toulon, from late 1790, simultaneously became a focus of both panic and militant pro- and counterrevolutionary sentiment. Culminating in August 1791, its streets resounded to brutal clashes. With their simplistic rhetoric and intolerance of dissent, both proletarian currents—populist and royalist working-class reactionary—fed on the class rift, more sharply defined there than elsewhere, with the merchant class mostly backing Barnave's liberal, constitutional monarchism. Untypical though it was, the Toulon ferment of 1790–91 mirrored the wider situation in France in one major respect: a powerfully resurgent ultraroyalist Right and pro-Revolution militancy pulverized the weak constitutional monarchist center.[19]

Aix-en-Provence, former provincial capital and seat of a parlement, provided a still more dramatic scenario. After the parlement ceased functioning, noted Gorsas in December 1790, Aix, where seemingly most people opposed the Revolution,[20] positively seethed with unrest, stoked by "the *fanaticisme* of priests" who daily concerted with a horde of lawyers, parlementaires, and disaffected nobles, sowing discord among the people. They allegedly saturated the town with the "hypocritical and incendiary productions of priests avid for blood."[21] Aix's counterrevolutionary club, Des Amis du Roi, was headed by a lawyer named Pascalis, who was furious at how Mirabeau and his supporters had electrified Provence in January 1789 by assailing the parlementaires, nobles, and ecclesiastics. Pascalis championed privilege, nobility, and the "liberties" of Provence unreservedly.[22] The club's public activities—disseminating royalist papers, mocking the Assembly, exhorting citizens to sport the white cockade and exalt the king—were not (so far) illegal as such. By the autumn of 1790, despite National Guard contingents arriving from Marseille, Aix royalists felt sufficiently buoyant to gather in cafés and openly jeer tricolor-bearing passersby. Rioting ensued in December 1790 after a Jacobin deputation, passing some nobles lounging at a café, were taunted and attacked. The royalists were eventually routed but only with the aid of yet more volunteers from Marseille who provoked further violence: some four hundred men guarding the town prison were thrust aside, the prison gates smashed, and, in an excess of Patriot zeal, Pascalis and another counterrevolutionary, both recently locked up for provoking an earlier commotion, dragged out and lynched from nearby lampposts.[23]

Revolutionary violence of this sort was welcomed by Marat, who demanded more hangings of "traitors and scoundrels." He construed the Assembly's failure to crack down harshly at Aix as fresh evidence that the Assembly, apart from his favorite deputy, Robespierre, had "prostituted" itself to the court and betrayed the people. He accused Mirabeau of plotting contre-révolution in collusion with the Lameth brothers. In the Assembly, only Robespierre, he maintained, was worthy, reliable, upright, and irreproachable, a true paragon of revolutionary integrity and *civisme*.[24] By this time, Maximilien Robespierre (1758–94) had already won an outstanding reputation as a critic of ministers, denouncer of aristocratic intrigue, and censor of corrupt practices, as well as a stalwart opponent of the royal veto and the distinction between active and passive citizens. Having lost his mother at six and been left by his father (an Arras lawyer) in the care of a grandmother and aunts, he had been educated in Paris. Even at school, he had shown an adroitness and gift for clever rhetoric, which was to become his principal political tool. In 1789, as one of the leading lawyers of Arras, he had been elected an Estates-General deputy. Passionate devotee of Rousseau, he especially admired the great Genevan's idealization of ordinary people. At this stage of the Revolution, Robespierre was also a leading advocate of unlimited freedom of the press, stressing especially its value as a safeguard against corruption.[25] He closely collaborated at this time with several deputies, notably Pétion and Buzot, later to be among his foremost enemies.

Where Maury and Malouet defended royalist agitators in the disturbed regional centers on grounds of freedom of expression and assembly, dismissing talk of "conspiracy" as "imaginaire," Barnave and the Lameths accused the Right, both the ultraloyalists and Maury's strict constitutionalists (whose loyalty to the Constitution many doubted) of launching a concerted effort, linked to the émigrés encamped around France's borders, to mobilize the people against the Revolution. By late 1790, the Revolution's predicament was worsening and within the existing framework obviously irresolvable: there was no way the modérés could collaborate with the Catholic-royalist majority. The bloc with the largest number of votes in the Assembly formed a solidly liberal monarchist entity but one unsustainably fragile in terms of press resources and popular support, unable to cope with the multiple challenges from right and left. Wholly at odds with the republican tendency, it had no prospect of a rapprochement with Maury's faction.

Far from compelling an early resolution, the chief effect of the Assembly's irresolvable rifts was to reproduce these in cities all across France. The impressive growth in the number of local Jacobin societies affiliated with the parent society in Paris certainly reflected a rising interest in the issues of the day. But it also meant that the splits continually plaguing the Jacobins from late 1790 to September 1792 were replicated everywhere. The Jacobin Club at Toulouse, a city where nobles and parlementaires were numerous and highly disgruntled, was founded in May 1790. In February 1791, enthused *La Feuille villageoise*, it began holding meetings before mass audiences amid continual applause. This showed, claimed *La Feuille villageoise*, that "la philosophie, c'est à dire le bon sens mieux instruit," was making rapid progress among Toulouse's population of 68,000, who reportedly now blushed to think how they were formerly "abused" and submerged in ignorance and prejudice by clergy and nobles. Philosophical truth, "like the light," was bringing a properly connected sequence of ideas into the minds of those who for so long failed to understand their own situation. But was it? Toulouse Jacobins, like those elsewhere, were hopelessly split between modérés and democrats. Jacobins were detested by conservatives, both Maury strict constitutionalists and the ultraroyalists; but everywhere their clubs strove to accommodate all three factions of the center and Left, constitutional monarchists like Barnave and authoritarian populists who were not yet republicans like Marat and Robespierre, as well as republicans like Pétion, Manuel, Brissot, and Carra. Was this a feasible project?[26]

Divergent "Fathers of the Revolution"

For a democratic outcome, the first priority was to liquidate the distinction between "active" and "inactive" citizens. But constitutional monarchists, Sieyès among them, robustly defended the distinction. In an Assembly debate early in 1791, a bill restricting National Guard membership to "active citizens" was moved but vigorously opposed by Pétion, Robespierre, and Buzot, one of the few practicing lawyers among the radical leadership. The centrists had the votes to overrule objections, but this could not make any more palatable a principle disliked by many outside, as well as within, the legislature. Mme. Roland, who was present, was distressed to realize such a restriction meant thousands of textile workers in her native Lyon were automatically debarred from the militia. Soon to emerge among the Revolution's foremost figures for her impressive personality, eloquence, and rare ability to gather around her the most serious, insightful, and highly motivated revolutionary spirits,[27] through the spring of 1791, she, like Pétion, felt continually aggrieved and disillusioned by the undemocratic monarchical course onto which revolutionary "moderation," presided over by Barnave, had unsteadily lurched.

Inevitably, much of the ensuing struggle revolved around conflicting claims as to who were the Revolution's inspirers and what was their authentic message. On 2 April 1791 Mirabeau died. That evening, all the theaters of Paris closed in mourning.[28] His death prompted immediate adoption of earlier proposals to formalize veneration of those who inspired the Revolution. A grandiose plan, presented by the Paris Commune, was accepted by the Assembly two days later: the still incomplete church of Sainte-Geneviève, among the capital's largest buildings, now renamed the Panthéon, would be converted into a magnificent mausoleum to receive the remains of the Revolution's principal authors and heroes and those earlier "great men" who laid the Revolution's foundations, in particular Descartes, Voltaire, and Rousseau.[29] The Enlightenment was invariably viewed by everyone, right, left, and center, as the Revolution's chief foundation. The question was what precisely did this designation mean? The Assembly alone, it was decreed, could confer the honor of entombment in the Panthéon, and no one could be designated for it until after their death.

Installing the first "great man" in the Panthéon was a truly historic event. Never before had so many attended any funeral. The obsequies of past kings hardly compared to such colossal solemnity. According to Fréron, more than 400,000 people joined the procession that filed for hours along the boulevards. Practically all 1,200 deputies of the Assembly (who had voted to appear collectively) walked with the coffin, with only Maury, Cazalès, and a few other hard-core royalists pointedly absent. All royal ministers joined the cortege except one (who was ill), followed by the presidents and committees of all forty-eight Parisian sections, 12,000 troops, and a deputation of 4,000 citizens dressed in special black gowns. Mirabeau was interred under the resounding inscription: "Aux grands hommes, la Patrie reconnaissante."[30] The funerary oration was delivered by Cérutti, who proclaimed Mirabeau's greatness as a revolutionary and philosophique constitutionalist. Insurrections against tyranny in the past had mostly failed because people seeking to rebel remained steeped in credulity. A successful revolution without the people's outlook being transformed is impossible. The men who prepared the people and fathered the Revolution were "Montesquieu, Voltaire, Mably, Rousseau, Fénelon, and the wise school of the *Encyclopédie*," as well as the *économistes* and Necker. Mirabeau's greatness consisted in his absorbing their thought and applying it. He fought despotism with his counsel, aristocracy with eloquence, anarchy with audacity, and superstition with la philosophie. The outraged royalist and foreign press could only protest that Mirabeau was in no way "great."[31]

Mirabeau's interment in the Panthéon resounded throughout France. Gorsas received more than thirty reports of ceremonies honoring Mirabeau at Toulouse, Lyon, Rennes, Nantes, Bayeux, and elsewhere.[32] The event also initiated revolutionary street-name changing. Removing the plaque from the street where Mirabeau had lived, a crowd renamed it "Rue de Mirabeau." Preoccupation with street names rapidly caught on.[33] Villette shortly afterward effaced the sign "Quai de Théatins" on the corner of his opulent mansion (where Voltaire had died), on the Seine's south bank, replacing it with Quai de Voltaire, the name it bears today. He also summoned the inhabitants of the Rue Platrière (where Rousseau had inhabited third-floor lodgings) to remove that "paltry name" and rename the street "Rue de Jean-Jacques Rousseau."[34] The

Commune approved the last change in May. Name-changing fervor so gripped the Café Procope at this point that its habitués publicized a startling proposal for renaming the city's sewers and waste runoffs. It would be appropriate to designate the sewers after leading royalist writers, the Rue de Tournoi to be called Égout Mallet du Pan, those of Saint-André des Arts the Égout Abbé Royou, those of Ponceau the Égout Abbé Maury, of Montmartre the Égout de Monarchiens, and those under Pont Saint Michel the Égout Gautier.[35]

Voltaire, after his death on 30 May 1778, had not been given an honorific public burial. Crown and Church had not allowed it. To rectify this slight for the thirteenth anniversary of his demise on 30 May 1791, the Assembly, overruling those questioning whether Voltaire had actually been a "friend of the people," voted entombment in the Panthéon with equivalent splendor to Mirabeau's. Had not Voltaire assailed *le fanatisme* on every side, denounced the "idolatrous errors" of France's ancient institutions, been the "libérateur de la pensée"? The whole nation, supposedly, had been "insulted" by the snub to his memory in 1778. Among chief promoters of the campaign to project Voltaire as a major progenitor of the Revolution was the vastly successful and affluent playwright Beaumarchais, who had spent a fortune since 1779 editing and printing the first comprehensive edition of Voltaire's collected writings, complete sets being available since 1787 (the duodecimo version comprising sixty-seven volumes).[36] Besides *panthéonisation*, a public statue of Voltaire should be erected, proposed an Assembly deputy who also protested at the dilatoriness of steps to erect Rousseau's statue, commissioned earlier. At this, another deputy proposed Montesquieu's remains should also grace the Panthéon while a third urged Mably.[37]

But no amount of hype surrounding Mirabeau, Voltaire, and Rousseau could paper over the cracks within the Revolution. In the Assembly, the minority of 150 or so radical deputies (called the "factious" opposition by the center) relied for their political clout on the Paris sections, press, and clubs. They had far fewer votes in the legislature than monarchy's defenders but were resolved to deploy their strength in the press, Paris cafés, and streets. The war between the factions thus inevitably developed into a wider political struggle. The capital's numerous local political clubs set up a *comité central*, meeting in the regular assembly hall of the Cordeliers, to coordinate efforts to steer the Revolution in a radical direction. A veritable war of placards began, not least in the Tuileries section, where the royal family resided and the Assembly met. By early 1791, democrats continually put up political *affiches* (posters), often daily news bulletins deriding the centrist leadership, while groups of men backing the center, frequently in National Guard uniform, toured the streets tearing them down, and confiscating "incendiary papers" from colporteurs, tearing these up on the spot. A meeting of the Tuileries section assembly, with more than a hundred in attendance (as required under the Constitution), denounced removal of posters as a violation of Articles V, VI, VIII, IX, X, and XI of the Declaration of Rights, and a clear sign that liberty of expression and the Constitution were being subverted. The section forbade anyone, even in uniform, to remove posters in their precinct, or to seize journals from street vendors without their authorization.[38]

The struggle between the "moderate" center and revolutionary Left steadily intensified. Through the spring of 1791, the air of Paris was replete with rumors that the king designed to flee the country. Privately, Louis had always abhorred the Revolution. But by early 1791 this had become obvious, due to his piety and attachment to the conservative clergy, which rendered his relationship to constitutional monarchism ever more fraught and placed his alignment with the Revolution, despite Barnave's protestations, increasingly in doubt. A late-evening royal excursion, supposedly to Saint-Cloud, on 18 April, commonly deemed an attempt (which it may not have been) to abandon Paris, was prevented by suspicious crowds gathering around the palace entrances. After a tense two hours, Mayor Bailly arrived and smoothed things over, but with the royal family humiliatingly obliged to leave their carriages and return to the palace.[39]

Tension between the Assembly's radical fraternity and the dominant centrist bloc under Barnave, the Lameths, Bailly, and Lafayette was aggravated by renewed efforts to curb liberty of the press and the Assembly's constitutional committee's decision to propose a ban on collective petitions from political clubs and organizations. On 10 May 1791, despite vigorous opposing speeches by Pétion and Robespierre, the liberal monarchists passed the law restricting petitioning.[40] The measure, presented by Le Chapelier, confined the right to petition to individual "active citizens," forbidding clubs and sections, as well as "inactive" citizens, from either petitioning or affixing posters in the streets. The measure was plainly designed to emasculate the clubs, especially in Paris, where there were now around thirty, according to Robert in a journal article on 9 May.[41] Under the 1791 Constitution, the legislature was strictly representative, not mandated by the people, a principle dear to Sieyès and the center. Legally, the people had no right either to criticize or petition through any organizations or local assemblies. But denial of the right to petition amounted to denial of the volonté générale, retorted republicans and populists. The ban affronted both the Rousseauistes' popular sovereignty ideology and the Cercle Social's representative democracy seeking to bridge the gap between people and Assembly.[42] Given the financial qualifications for active citizenry, the ban meant that the poor were altogether excluded from expressing their views politically. The Lameths, Barnave, Lafayette, and Le Chapelier had begun a concerted campaign to exclude the wider public from the political process.

Another measure passed by the center in the early summer of 1791 was "Le Chapelier's Law," an enactment responding to a petition from the Paris master carpenters requesting changes in the way their craft was organized. It dissolved all craft organizations and corporations. Later, in the nineteenth century, Le Chapelier's law became a notorious device of manufacturers for preventing the formation of craft unions. In 1791, by contrast, most supporters of the measure viewed it more as a way of ending the restrictive role of traditional craft corporations and of widening economic freedom.[43] It was much less this than the irksome restrictions on petitioning and collective political expression that antagonized and outraged the Cordeliers and other Paris section assemblies at the time, and was broadly attacked by the capital's pro-Revolution press.[44] Outside Paris, vociferous support for the Cordeliers stemmed especially from the radical sections of Marseille, which on 5 May dispatched a fierce denunciation of the "scheming against liberty" by Lafayette and others.[45]

The right to gather and petition became a rallying cry of the Cercle, the Cordeliers, Robespierre, and the revolutionary press. Banning collective petitioning was wholly incompatible with the Declaration of Rights, held the democrats, and clear evidence of retreat from the principles of 1789. At a joint meeting of the Cercle and the Cordeliers on 20 May, there was thunderous applause for speeches attacking the Assembly's restrictive measures. The Cordeliers disseminated a remarkable printed address to all the "sociétés patriotiques" of France, and "generally all men who profess and cherish liberty." The Constitution and liberties achieved by the Revolution were being overthrown by "insolent satraps" who exploited the people's ignorance and propagated arrogant, erroneous principles destructive of the true foundations of the "bonheur général." Propagators of false principles, secret abettors of right-wing papers like *L'Ami du Roi* and the *Gazette de Paris*, were publicly insulting patriotic societies like the Cordeliers. Where the clubs championed the Rights of Man, centrist tools of "abominable tyranny," feigning patriotism, insidiously deceived "les citoyens simples et peu instruits" (simple and uneducated citizens). But all was not lost as these same citizens would eventually spot the deception and punish the "vile detractors of their true friends." Even if the people's recognition of the liberal monarchists as deceivers proved slow, the republicans "faithful to our principles and oaths . . . shall perish rather than bend the knee to the idol" and abandon the fight. "Join us, brothers and friends!" All of France's *sociétés patriotiques* were urged to send delegates to forge a common pact.[46]

The proposition that any legislature unchecked by criticism and petitions from organized groups degenerates into rampant tyranny formed common ground between republicans and populists at this stage. A committee drawn from all the democratic clubs asked Bonneville to compose a general petition to the Assembly, demanding acknowledgment of the right of all to participate in the political process. Their petition also demanded abolition of financial qualifications for active citizenship. There were only 80,000 "active citizens" in Paris, noted Bonneville, a capital where, on 14 July 1789, more than 300,000 armed men rose to topple tyranny. "Compare and judge!"[47] Ignored by the Assembly, the petition appeared in the *Bouche de fer* and resounded widely on walls and in the streets. Tension between the rival blocs intensified further when the Assembly, collaborating with the Paris city government, announced the closure of a network of public workshops providing employment for the redundant. This happened at a time of yet further economic deterioration in Paris's poor quarters. The Cercle Social, through its branch, the Point Central des Arts et Métiers, had for some time argued that it was part of the government's responsibility to support the unemployed and provide work. The Point Central (an initiative to help distressed laborers), and the Cercle, accordingly, now also organized a mass petition demanding the Assembly provide employment by commissioning canals, clearing marshes, improving navigability of rivers, and generally assisting the unemployed to dispense with charity from "rich aristocrats and hypocritical priests." This petition urged outright confiscation of the property of aristocrats who had fled the country to oppose the Revolution, the proceeds to support the poor.[48]

To force the Assembly to abandon its "aristocratic" course, the clubs followed the Cercle Social in seeking to mobilize larger numbers of the

capital's poor. They strove to generate a spreading political consciousness. Marxist scholars have often claimed Brissot stood for class interests
allied to the bourgeoisie. Yet, in an article in the *Patriote français* on 15
June 1791 entitled "Whom shall we elect?," afterward reprinted in Desmoulins's paper and others, Brissot clearly specified the different social
groups whose presence he thought chiefly desirable in politics and the
National Assembly. Whether delegates were bourgeois or laborers, rural
or urban, big property-owners or small property-owners, he contended,
mattered less than their intellectual level and principles—and especially whether or not they were genuinely "enlightened." In particular,
he recommended more rural representatives and ordinary city dwellers
to check the influence of the "capitalists, bankers, *commerçants*"—
increasing rural representation requiring the propagation of enlightenment from the cities. If his circle upheld property rights, they also
sought to remove extreme inequalities.[49] In Brissot's estimation, the
Assembly's best delegates were simply the best educated—mostly prac-
titioners of medicine and law. Artisans, he agreed, loved liberty and
sought to defend it but were unreliable because they lacked literacy, enlightenment, and independence of judgment. Despite being cosmopolitan in outlook and sometimes useful, big merchants should, however,
be regarded with greater suspicion since they care only for their own
interest and generally operate to society's detriment. Worst of all were
bankers, according to Brissot. These should be generally shunned and
excluded from the legislature as an entirely antisocial group.[50]

Brissot, Condorcet, Pétion, Carra, and their allies were not the party
of "the capitalists." The evidence produced by scholars to show that they
disdained the lower classes proves only that they disdained ignorance
and superstition.[51] Nevertheless, it is true that Marat's populists were at
greater pains than the republicans to pack the clubs and section assemblies with workingmen. The populists did so, moreover, worrying less
about workers' ignorance than applauding their ordinariness, simplicity, and "civic spirit." This viewpoint was strongly affirmed by the former Capuchin monk François Chabot (1759–94), a vehement foe of
Brissot and Condorcet. Among the Revolution's foremost demagogues,
for Chabot, the "popular" was always the true measure of revolutionary legitimacy. Adopting Marat's use of unrestrained language, he subsequently edited the *Journal populaire*, or *Catéchisme des sans-culottes*,
propagating militant sansculotte views. He also favored purges and violent measures while, like Marat, abhorring intellectual pretensions.[52] As
it happened, Chabot later proved dishonest, self-seeking, dissolute, and

ambitious. Briefly, though, he was hugely successful and tireless in eulogizing ordinariness and Marat.

In the ideologically highly charged spring of 1791, a soon-notorious open letter from Raynal, rejecting the Revolution's core principles, read to the Assembly on 31 May 1791, intensified the furor over the Revolution's true credentials. A renowned exponent of "idées philosophiques" through the 1770s and 1780s, in 1789 Raynal had been urged to join Mirabeau in representing Marseille in the Estates-General.[53] He was actually elected but resigned, pleading old age. During 1788–89, he was regularly extolled alongside Rousseau and Mably as one of the "pères de la Révolution," as Manuel called him, and as a denouncer of absolutism and noble oppression.[54] In a pamphlet of mid-1789 purporting to be a "conversation" between Raynal and Linguet, "Raynal" repeats phrases condemning monarchy, today known to have been penned by Diderot.[55] The *Dictionary of Atheists* (1800), by the Jacobin *érudit* Maréchal, later attributed to Raynal the maxim "it is philosophy that should be the divinity on earth."[56] The *Parlement* of Paris's various pre-1789 edicts suppressing the *Histoire philosophique des Deux Indes* were annulled on 15 August 1790 by the Assembly, who declared the ban "contrary to the inalienable rights of Man." The king found himself obliged to rehabilitate Raynal—a philosophe under royal prohibition for nearly twenty years—and acknowledge him as an "active citizen."

Raynal's sensational 1791 missive repudiating "his old errors," as Malouet put it, was preceded by two earlier such open letters, the first, of December 1789, according to Brissot a "diatribe perfide" against the people, read to the deputies on 5 January 1790 but ignored,[57] and another, of September 1790. These, though disconcerting, received a muted response owing to doubts whether they really were by Raynal. There, as in his 1791 missive, Raynal endorses popular sovereignty, universal toleration, equal and proportional taxation, and equality before the criminal law, but rejects civil equality and democracy.[58] But all doubt ended with Raynal's unequivocal open letter to the Assembly of May 1791, encouraged by and composed in collusion with Malouet.[59] Visiting Paris after a long absence, now nearing eighty, Raynal submitted it in person two days prior to publication. Asked whether they wished to hear it read, the deputies cried "yes, yes," but the democrats, listening with keen expectation, were astounded by its contents. By 1790, Raynal had become estranged from the Revolution due to the country's increasingly anarchic state, infractions of individual liberty, and the intrusive role of the clubs. The king, who was his people's first friend, was being insulted while real power accrued to the clubs "where ignorant and vulgar men expatiate on all political questions." "I have long contemplated the ideas you are applying, but at a time when they were rejected by all authorities, groups and prejudices and represented only the allure of a consoling wish." In the 1770s Raynal and his friends had not needed to consider the risks and dangers of applying philosophique principles the Assembly now confronted. Raynal refused all responsibility for the consequences of a false, recklessly democratic understanding of his principles. The "bold conceptions of *la philosophie* were not meant by us to be the measure of legislation."[60]

Cheers from the Right mixed with dismay on the Left. "Bah! Malouet and his people say the same every day." "Apparently, we are now restoring despotism," protested some. At Raynal's remark that the Declaration of Rights was acceptable apart from certain "metaphysical abstractions" apt for anarchy, a radical deputy interjected, "it is Malouet who wrote this letter"; another yelled, "this is a calumny against the Abbé Raynal who is incapable of writing anything like this, even at eighty."[61] The *Histoire philosophique*'s unparalleled impact since the 1770s ensured Raynal's "shameful apostasy," as Brissot called it, vast notoriety. It was promptly reprinted and condemned in Brissot's *Patriote français* and elsewhere, and anatomized in the press for weeks. This octogenarian who accused the Left of irresponsibility was denounced for "hypocrisy," betrayal of philosophy, and helping prepare "a new revolution serving the criminal designs of enemies of the *patrie*." Robespierre dismissed it as calumny against the people. A Provençal deputy, André-Louis Esprit de Sinéty, acknowledged Raynal's role in initiating the Revolution in Marseille but deplored his cold indifference during the twenty-five months since. Why did he not speak when his words would have counted? "Pourquoi a-t-il gardé jusqu'à ce jour le plus profond silence?"[62] The Right countered by applauding Raynal's epistle as the finest instrument available for discrediting republicanism among the reading public.[63]

Chénier and Cloots both published pieces denouncing Raynal's epistle, the latter dismissing him in the *Chronique de Paris* as an impostor, turncoat, and mediocrity who stole the honors rightfully due to Diderot, d'Holbach, Naigeon, and Pechméja. He was without talent, a police spy. Everything valuable in the *Histoire philosophique* was really the work of "Pechméja, Diderot, Dubreuil, Naigeon, Selback, etc."[64] Such flagrant betrayal was unsurprising, held the anonymous *T.G. Raynal démasqué, ou lettres sur la vie et les ouvrages de cet écriv-*

ain (1791), for it was not Raynal who wrote the *Histoire philosophique* but Diderot, Deleyre, Pechméja, Guibert, Kniphausen, d'Holbach, and Diderot's classicist assistant, La Grange, the translator of Lucretius.[65] Raynal must be senile. Others concentrated on vilifying the "perfidious" schemers who had captured a frail old man, aiming to bring him to his grave covered in opprobrium. The public was being subjected to an infamous deception, organized by Malouet and his friends, of which Raynal was the first victim.[66] An undated polemical print of 1791 depicts Maury, Royou, and Malouet lamenting that their ploy to detach Raynal from the Revolution had failed to trick the Marseille populace. A bust of Raynal is depicted being carried into the city's madhouse with an attached banner reading: "admiration for the *Histoire des Deux Indes*, contempt for the *Letter to the Assembly*!"[67]

Diderot, several commentators reminded the public, figured among the Revolution's foremost hidden hands. Naigeon, a zealous révolutionnaire during 1788–93,[68] recalled that "mon intime ami" Diderot was the bravest of the philosophes and most resolute in combating "la superstition." His own task in the Revolution was to complete Diderot's labors by editing his papers.[69] Everyone invoked Rousseau, Voltaire, Mably, Raynal, Montesquieu, and Helvétius as precursors of the Revolution, but in his *Philosophie ancienne et moderne* (Paris 1791), Naigeon lent Diderot (like La Harpe later) still greater prominence. Montesquieu, Helvétius, d'Alembert, and Buffon had mumbled, mincing their words through fear of the theologians. Now one could be open about Diderot's achievement, the new revolutionary order "so desired and so unexpected," identifying "la superstition" as the worst of human weaknesses, could, thanks to liberty of the press, at last overpower reason's enemies.[70] The public mostly remained unaware of Diderot's crucial contribution because he had had to oppose authority chiefly through anonymous clandestine publications and multiauthored compilations like the *Encyclopédie* and the *Histoire philosophique*. But his ideas were basic to the Revolution's core values and remained relevant for resolving political difficulties "auxquels la Révolution a donné lieu."[71]

Rousseau's influence needed opposing, argued Naigeon, and here was one area where Diderot remained especially useful. Citing a passage where Diderot contradicts Rousseau's conception of popular sovereignty, Naigeon urged that a democratic executive must properly respect the citizenry's demands but be able to withstand popular pressure where appropriate. He considered Diderot to have been the first to demonstrate the need to mix direct with representative democracy.

Under Diderot's suggested rules, petitions signed by more than a specified number of citizens must be considered by the legislature; petitions
failing to meet that threshhold could be ignored. The Revolution, held
Naigeon, needed a genuine balance between an executive arm not permitted to become overly confident of its power and the dangerous ca-
prices of a volatile people. It needed to steer judiciously between direct
democracy and pure representative democracy without degenerating
into crass demagoguery. Popular opinion may often prove shifting and
ill-considered, Diderot had emphasized, yet it remains the opinion
of the people: "quelque fou soit le peuple, il est toujours le maître."[72]
But "the master" must be helped to preside in an orderly, controlled
fashion.

Reflecting pro-Revolution opinion generally, the largest Parisian political club, the Jacobins, remained hopelessly divided throughout the
spring of 1791, like the Assembly itself. The Jacobins were paralyzed by
three main splits: between constitutional monarchists, the most influential of its streams for the moment; democratic radicals; and Marat's
authoritarian populists. The last were greatly buoyed by the emerging
popular press. By early 1791, Marat was strongly backed by middle-
class journalists like himself, such as Jacques-René Hébert (1757–94)
and Jean-Charles Jumel (1751–1823), who likewise appealed to the
illiterate and barely literate in the streets. Hébert was a well-educated
and ambitious journalist from Alençon, from January 1791, a force in
the Cordeliers, though not associated with either its Dantonist or republican wings. Like Marat, these men consistently declined to clearly
take sides in the growing conflict between the liberal monarchists and
"democrats," preferring instead to build up their own excitable, panicky,
illiterate, and volatile following by using sensation, theatrical exaggeration, and rumor-mongering as their chief instruments.[73] In addition,
there remained the split within the Cercle's leadership between philosophique republicans who admitted the primacy of "reason" alone versus
Christianizing Rousseauistes like Fauchet. This quarrel pitted Fauchet
against Bonneville, Brissot, Cloots, Desmoulins, Villette, and Condorcet. The theology of the revolutionary priests—Fauchet, Grégoire,
and Lamourette—though ardent and sincere, seemed a "dangerous"
intellectual puzzle to the materialists and, amid the escalating struggle
with the center and Right, threatened to become a further considerable
complication. In the *Bouche de fer* issue for 1 April, Bonneville intensified the controversy by reviewing Desmoulins's recent *Éloge non funèbre
de Jésus et du Christianisme,* where the latter denied all possibility of

miracles, highlighting what he deemed Christianity's abuse of man and thousands of "crimes" over the centuries. The same *Bouche de fer* issue also contained a discourse of Fauchet invoking divine Providence and Rousseau.

Where Bonneville praised Desmoulins's critique of Christianity, albeit suggesting he had confused the abuses of "a disfigured religion with its true principles," Fauchet assailed Desmoulins for blatant impiety. Afterward Fauchet got into an unfortunate quarrel about the same issues with Bonneville, Cloots, and Villette. Bringing the matter up at a Cercle gathering, he rebuked both "Brother Camille [Desmoulins] and Bonneville."[74] Fauchet seemed to have "forgotten" the Cercle's rule, answered Bonneville in the *Bouche de fer*, that no "religious sect" should be "favored" in any of its speeches. It was official policy of the Cercle not to associate with Christianity. Cloots published an open letter to Fauchet, dated 4 April, accusing him of preaching that without religion society would consist only of "lying *philosophes*, aristocratic brigands, soulless peoples and endless crime." Cloots rejected Fauchet's claim that religion is indispensable to society and the basis of morality, holding that the true moral basis of the laws is the common interest, which has nothing to do with religion. Even if religion were the moral base, it would not follow that a civic cult and priesthood are society's essential guides. The Constitution acknowledged only individual religion and freedom of conscience, not any state cult or superiority of one cult over another. Cloots had "de-baptised" himself to be logically consistent; he invited Fauchet to "de-baptize" too for the same reason.[75]

Fauchet's impassioned religious inspiration, aggressive manner, and repeated attacks on philosophique atheism made a rupture inevitable, the ideological rift further intensifying the Cercle leadership's emphasis on philosophique "reason."[76] In the Jacobins it was reported that the Cercle consisted of "dangerous men" resolved to redistribute wealth forcibly. Fauchet replied, likewise in the *Bouche de fer*, denying that he and his supporters were *incendiaires* avid to plunge the country into anarchy to redistribute land and wealth. Cloots and other Jacobins, he accused, misrepresented his views. The true basis of *la morale universelle*, those eager to reconstruct society on the principles of equity and justice agreed, was that it is "in nature itself that one finds the fundamental basis of all rights and duties." But as God is the supreme spirit infusing nature, only a "misérable philosophie" believes it can "form a *patrie* without religion, and institute a nation without conscience." Man has a deep religious instinct that "only the pride of false geniuses or baseness of depraved souls can deny."[77] His Catholic Radical Enlightenment, believed Fauchet, was the true philosophy of the Revolution.

Fauchet's mid-April harangue to the Cercle denounced those who denied that religion is the Revolution's moral base as "the most dangerous adversaries of the public interest, who will ruin the Revolution by provoking a reaction against it among all those patriots who are religious."[78] Pronouncing la philosophie and Christianity entirely compatible, Fauchet resigned from the Cercle in high dudgeon, a serious blow since he was their best orator. Trapped between the warring factions and marginalized, he afterward set up his own journal, the *Journal des Amis*, dedicated to the proper "instruction of the people," still convinced all humankind would one day be free with all thrones overthrown, that the "age of reason" was dawning, that "le bonheur naîtra de l'alliance des Lumières et de la vertu." From here on, Fauchet remained irretrievably estranged from the republican Jacobins, as well as the moderates and Robespierrisme. Robespierre and the authoritarian populists, though, he considered infinitely worse than the republican materialists and atheists. Robespierre talked constantly about "the people," but he and his followers, contended Fauchet, were just a bunch of "anarchistes," foes of the people, and Robespierre's principles the "last phase of night," the last gasp of nonenlightenment.[79]

The rift between Catholic radical reform and philosophique republicanism proved as deep and permanent as the split between revolutionary left radicalism and the popular press. The *Bouche de fer* headed its 14 April issue with a quote from Fauchet's own first discourse to the Cercle: "et si l'Évangile s'écarte de la raison, il faut y ramener l'Évangile" (if the Gospel departs from reason, it must be brought back to it).[80] This schism, however, was not the reason for the Cercle Social's abrupt disappearance as a mass movement following its last gathering on 21 July 1791, or the lapsing of the *Bouche de fer*. The Cercle ceased as a mass movement owing, rather, to the dramatic intensification of the political crisis in June, following the king's flight to Varennes.[81]

The Flight to Varennes (June 1791)

The country was shaken to its foundations by the news of the king's attempt, on 21 June 1791, to flee his realm. Until June, Louis XVI, characteristically, remained in two minds: loathing the Revolution privately while resisting pleas from advisors, family, and supporters to flee abroad and lead an international counterrevolution backed by the papacy, to defeat the Revolution and extinguish its principles. It was Louis's religious sensibilities, and sense of guilt for approving Church reforms the papacy condemned, that finally persuaded him to risk life, family, and all he possessed—indeed, the monarchy itself—by repudiating the 1791 Constitution and liberal monarchism, and seeking to join the émigrés.

Louis resorted to flight only after long hesitation. But his bid to escape hardly came as a surprise. Rumor and republican journalists had been predicting such an attempt for months.[82] Nevertheless, the psychological shock, especially in small towns and the countryside, was considerable. Even in Paris, most had not suspected until now that, privately, the king wholly rejected the Revolution and its principles. Then, suddenly, the matter was beyond doubt. Louis left behind a manifesto at the Tuileries, dated 20 June, deploring the erosion of monarchy and breakdown of order, the discomfort of the Tuileries, persecution of those most attached to himself and the royal family, and the humiliating way he had been treated since July 1789. Another reason for his repudiating the Revolution was the continual appearance of seditious writings disparaging and defaming himself and his family. Since his palace was "a prison," he abjured categorically the constitutional commitments he had entered into under duress.[83] The flight to Varennes thus marked a total break. It was a disastrous setback for constitutional monarchism, though this did not prevent Marat, Hébert, and the populist press from accusing Bailly, Cazalès, and the others of the "black band of conspirators" of complicity in the plot.

News of the king's flight generated great apprehension. Should it succeed, it signified inevitable foreign intervention and civil war. While the immediate threat eased with news of the royal family's interception at Varennes, the country nevertheless faced a dire predicament, for Louis's repudiation of the Constitution and Rights of Man was now public knowledge, plunging the National Assembly into turmoil. Constitutional monarchists found themselves tied to a sullen prisoner king and court who resented and opposed them secretly, abetted by much of the army's officer corps and clergy. However one construed it, constitutional monarchism was severely wounded and ultraroyalism encouraged. The king's attempt to flee transformed the entire French political situation by bringing the "moderate" Revolution's and the Constitution's underlying illogicality and incoherence fully to the surface. For the first time, Varennes also provoked a few elements of the public to swing behind the republican goals of the intellectual fringe leading the revolutionary Left. Among the flight's chief political and psychological effects was a growing realization that the cultural-ideological (and soon actual) war between France and Europe's monarchies, a struggle in which the king's brothers openly—and the king and court covertly—supported the coalition of France's enemies striving to restore monarchy, aristocracy, and ecclesiastical authority, must divide the nation and all Europe.

The king's "treason" outraged numerous citizens, causing many who had only the vaguest notion of what republicanism was to support the democrats. But equally important was the fresh impetus it imparted to the thus far broadly monarchist populists who decried the corruption and betrayal of the center. The only way to prevent the people from falling off a precipice, thundered Marat and others of Robespierre's partisans, was to name a "dictateur suprême" to assume control of the country and liquidate the "traitors." Like Marat, Hébert, and Jumel, the editors of the rival *Père Duchesne* papers, took advantage of the general atmosphere of panic, feverish rumor, and thirst for sensation, always presenting themselves as the guardians and sentinels of the *bons patriotes*, a simplistic revolutionary vision dividing everyone and everything between the forces of good and evil, between the good people and malign conspirators avid to betray and sacrifice the common folk to perfidious Counter-Revolution, aristocracy, and before long also royalty.[84] Their title referred to a much-loved, popular, burlesque, pipe-smoking, iconographic figure, the gruffly outspoken "Father Duchesne," who adored Marat and stoutly defended the bons patriotes, uttering only the most simplistic phrases, and continually swearing.

Over the past year, this formula had transformed both Hébert's and Jumel's journals into two of the most read (and feared) in France. By March 1791, their rival *Père Duchesne* papers appeared daily and were on sale everywhere in Paris—in the streets, cheap taverns, and at market stalls.[85] Prior to the flight to Varennes, Marat's paper made no move to denigrate the king or monarchy as such, and (unlike Jumel) Hébert did not do so before April 1791. But these papers were less concerned with concepts like monarchism, republicanism, or democracy than building popular paranoia for mass collective action. Continually appealing to the least educated, Marat's and Hébert's creed was a polarizing populist chauvinism, a kind of protofascism, in Marat's case continually calling for a dictatorship of the most uncompromising kind to rescue "the people." What was needed, urged Marat, was a personal dictatorship, preferably Robespierre's. In Robespierre, Marat recognized a towering leader as steely, unbending, and uncompromisingly Manichaean as he himself, someone who divided all mankind into the good and the evil, oppressed and oppressors, ceaselessly attacking corruption in high places and eulogizing "the people." Meanwhile, both Barnave and the democrats underestimated Robespierre, Marat, and the popular press, hardly recognizing as yet the challenge they would soon face.[86]

The impact of Louis's flight was immense. On the day he fled, the Assembly closed the borders and declared itself in permanent session. The whole country was placed in a state of emergency. The National Guard stood at arms. The king was suspended from all his constitutional functions, the Assembly decreeing its decrees valid without royal approval.[87] Three "commissioners," including Barnave and Pétion, were dispatched to escort Louis back to Paris. Other than the royal family itself, everyone implicated in the royal flight was arrested. Loyalty oaths to defend liberty were exacted from military commanders and high functionaries; peasants spontaneously formed armed groups (sometimes again attacking local châteaus). Executive and military authority was transferred to a council of ministers meeting in rooms adjoining the Assembly. Once back in the Tuileries, the king and queen were guarded not by their own guards as previously but by the National Guard. While suspending Louis from his constitutional functions, the Assembly at the same time ignored the demands of the Cordeliers and Cercle, and a small minority of Jacobins, to depose the king.

Until 21 June, neither Cercle nor Cordeliers, while attacking the distinction between "active" and "inactive" citizens and denouncing the "English system" of mixed government and a restricted electorate,[88] had ever called openly for abolition of the monarchy as such. This now abruptly changed, opening a wider gap than ever between republicans and the Assembly's "moderate" leadership, which announced plans to restore all the forms of constitutional monarchy, after an interval, when safe to do so, reinstating Louis in his previous functions. Logically, it was easier to defend the principle of constitutional monarchy than Louis's conduct. To justify outright reversion to the status quo ante, Barnave and his allies introduced the rather desperate fiction that Louis was entirely "innocent" of any attempt to flee, and had not in fact repudiated the Constitution. Officially, Louis had been "kidnapped" by the Marquis de Bouillé and other conspirators, although the entire Assembly knew this was untrue. To ease public acceptance of this flagrant falsehood, several "guilty" plotters were imprisoned in the Abbey Saint-Germain.[89]

Most of the Assembly backed the ploy, some swayed by fear of provoking Prussia, Austria, and Britain into war, others by fear of democracy or straightforward preference for constitutional monarchy. But nothing could mitigate the divisive effect. The collision between "moderation" and democratic republicanism became a public, open, and dangerous rift, bound to inflame and destabilize the country, armed forces, and National Guard. The princely courts of Europe were unhappy that Louis's "evasion" had miscarried. The French royalist press briefly fell silent, then resumed publication.[90] Among ultraroyalists, there was utter dismay over Louis's being "dragged back" and the "inscrutability of divine providence," as the *Gazette de Paris* put it, which precipitated a fresh wave of emigration of nobles and officers. On the night of 24 to 25 June, all the higher officers of the strategically key maritime border garrison of Dunkirk deserted to nearby Austrian territory.[91] But it was liberal, constitutional monarchism as a concept that was politically most damaged. The manifesto issued on 6 July at Verona in Italy by the new emperor, summoning Europe's monarchies and all loyal Frenchmen to join in rescuing "his most Christian Majesty" and suppressing the Revolution, only highlighted the country's besieged, deeply divided state. Psychologically, France was already at war with Europe.

Yet, what was most amazing, noted the Venetian ambassador, was the spirit of concord and resolve manifesting itself in Paris behind the Revolution.[92] So electrified were the Cordeliers and Cercle by the king's flight that they, too, over the next weeks, remained in "permanent session." The struggle was on for the people's support and the backing of the cafés and streets. If the center lost prestige through the flight, both Right and Left gained. The *Bouche de fer* began appearing as a daily paper, the very first issue publicizing a fact that astounded many readers: privately, every one of this journal's editors had been a republican in principle since before 1789. Since 1789, the Cercle leadership had "respected" the monarchical Constitution while always hoping an eventual republican outcome would follow, owing to "the progress of enlightenment and *la philosophie*."[93] The Cordeliers began publishing their own popular antimonarchical newssheet, the *Journal du Club des Cordeliers*. On hearing of the king's flight, Condorcet and Sophie Condorcet plunged into frenetic activity, convening a group they called the Société des Républicains, figuring Brissot, Bonneville, Lanthenas, and Tom Paine, likewise all convinced republicans since before 1789.

Louis was denounced for "desertion" and the Assembly for base collusion and permitting the king excessive power under the Constitution and an excessive civil list.[94] Cercle, Cordeliers, and some provincial Jacobin clubs also agitated for a popular referendum to pronounce on the monarchy's future. As Pétion commented in the *Chronique de Paris* later in July, here was a national crisis on an unprecedented scale. Discussed in the clubs, streets, town squares, and gatherings, the people participated directly and emotions became heated.[95] Yet, if it sharpened the split between between Left and Right, reenergizing revolutionary republicanism while discrediting constitutional monarchism, the flight to Varennes was disastrous for the deeply split Jacobins too. Far from leading the Revolution, this club became increasingly divided in ensuing weeks. Their dominant bloc remained loyal to the Assembly liberal monarchist leadership. Most Jacobins for the moment reaffirmed their "moderate" course, albeit agreeing with the Left republicans about the probability of war with Austria and Prussia.[96] A vocal Jacobin republican minority leaned, however, toward the Cordeliers and Cercle. Carra, very active in the Jacobins at the time, figured prominently among opponents of exonerating the king. Keeping the crown on Louis's head without submitting the matter to the nation in a referendum, through the primary assemblies, was considered an outrage by Carra. His paper proclaimed kings the idols of fools and scoundrels.[97] On 11 July, Carra delivered a strongly republican speech at the Jacobins, openly calling for dethronement and suggesting there should be a transition stage prior to a fully republican constitution, with the Dauphin made temporary king in place of "Louis-le-faux."[98]

Besides Jacobin moderates and republicans, there was a middle group under Robespierre critical of both king and Assembly that resolutely distanced itself from republicanism and firm constitutional commitments. Robespierre, Brissot, and Pétion had been conversing at Mme. Roland's when news of the king's interception at Varennes arrived. Disagreeing with the others and unwilling to renounce constitutional monarchy, a dismayed Robespierre at once grasped the precariousness of his populist-monarchist strategy.[99] For the moment, his group found itself particularly awkwardly placed. He repudiated the preposterous talk of a "kidnap" but remained loyal nevertheless to the principle of monarchy, now openly scorned and repudiated by the Cercle, Cordeliers, some section assemblies, and the more radical element among the Jacobins. The Cercle's and Cordeliers's obvious aim, from which Robespierre pointedly disassociated himself, was to foment a popular republican movement on the streets. On 1 July, posting republican proclamations all over Paris clandestinely during the night, the Cercle's leadership publicly called for deposition of the king and a new republican order based on universal suffrage.[100] The Société's stated goal was to enlighten the public regarding the meaning of the term "republic," focusing their critique on monarchy's defects as such.

If there were still relatively few out-and-out republicans as yet in the Assembly, Paris Commune, or the Jacobins, many found it impossible any longer to view Barnave, the Lameths, and Assembly leadership as anything but a discredited power-hungry clique. Liberal monarchism, the party of the "aristocrats" as republicans called them, still possessed the advantage, though, of posing as the party of legality, constitutionality, and "patriotism" while remaining the king's advisers. Aided by the widespread aversion to la philosophie moderne among lawyers, the commercially minded, and the public generally, modérantisme now launched an all-out intellectual campaign deploying Montesquieu, moderate Enlightenment, and the British model. Republicanism was impracticable, the people were assured, resembling a turbulent sea continually agitated by storms, easy prey to conquest by an aspiring Sulla, Cromwell, or other great scoundrel. With such rhetoric, observed Carra, Barnave rallied most Jacobins and all the ignorant and unaware.[101] Yet not everyone bowed to such arguments or embraced Robespierre's populist monarchism. Carra, Brissot, and the republicans vigorously rebutted Alexandre and Charles de Lameth's repeated invoking of Rousseau to try to persuade the public that the republican form was unsuited to large states like France.[102] The rift paralyzing the Jacobins, meanwhile, became nationwide.

Calls for a republic were heard most loudly outside the Jacobins, in the main pro-Revolution papers. Brissot published his democratic republican profession of faith, calling for an end to the monarchy, as early as 5 July. If most provincial Jacobin clubs stood by the constitutional monarchists, or else Robespierre, rejecting republicanism, eighty-three at least demanded either suspension or dethronement of Louis personally, including Angers, Arras, Bordeaux, Le Mans, Lyon, Orléans, Rennes, and Toulouse. The Club National of Bordeaux's declaration was circulated with considerable impact throughout the southwest.[103] Moreover, full-fledged antimonarchism and republicanism now pervaded not only the Revolution's Left intellectual leadership as before but was obviously winning recruits in cities all over France, including among mainstream Jacobins.[104] At Dôle, in the night of 3 to 4 July, dissidents effaced the words "royal" and "king" from every public inscription and sign in the town, prompting outraged complaints from the Assembly's monarchiens. Some local Jacobin clubs not only broke ranks with the majority and with Robespierre, but actively joined the Cordeliers and the Cercle in demanding that monarchy be ended, calling for the establishment of a republic, including that at Noyon and the currently dominant bloc among the Jacobins at Marseille, where a leading spokesman, Moyse Bayle, published an openly republican tract on 2 August.[105]

Despite Robespierre's distinctly more conservative stance,[106] much of the populist bloc now abruptly abandoned constitutional monarchism, a trend that eventually forced Robespierre, however tentatively, to end his resistance to republican ideology. Thus, Georges Couthon (1753–94), coauthor of Clermont's petition demanding dethronement, read to the Paris Jacobin Club on 24 June, lawyer and leading provincial Jacobin and later among Robespierre's closest aides, though not previously attracted to republican ideas, felt so disgusted by the king's defection he too now opted for republicanism.[107] Of the populist papers, the crassest apart from Marat's and most given to expletives was Hébert's *Le Père Duchesne*. Unlike his sworn foe, Desmoulins, but like Robespierre, Hébert continually praised popular, ordinary notions, and hence, until April, also the mystique of kingship. The flight to Varennes, though, profoundly shocked his audience, leading him uninhibitedly to denounce the king: "What are we going to do with this fat pig," he demanded, referring to "Louis le traitre" and Marie Antoinette "his whore."[108]

In his *Annales patriotiques*, Carra lauded the calm, orderly attitude of the Paris populace and its open revulsion against the king's behavior. At a massed rally on 24 June, a reported thirty thousand men, women, and children, including many members of the Cordeliers and republican Jacobins, gathered in Paris to endorse, and present to the Assembly, a petition composed by Brissot asserting that on particularly fundamental issues the people had the right to express their view and "direct" their delegates, in accordance with the volonté générale. The petition demanded that the Assembly make no decision concerning Louis's fate until the country's eighty-three departments had been consulted. A Cordeliers delegation, headed by Mandar, vice president of the Paris Temple section, presented this petition on 29 June. The Assembly angrily dismissed it. The Cordeliers had it printed and circulated among all the patriotic clubs and posted up on street corners around Paris, though many were soon torn down.[109]

Organized opposition to Assembly policy and the monarchy undoubtedly became a full-scale popular and plebeian movement at this point, one orchestrated not by Robespierre or the populist leadership but the radical intellectuals who forged the Revolution.[110] Those gathering at the Cordeliers and Cercle refused to be "the dupes of charlatanisme" and the designs of Lafayette, Barnave, and the Lameths.[111] A resounding speech at the Jacobins by Brissot on 10 July defended républicanisme and ridiculed majority Jacobin objections to republican ideas as self-contradictory prejudice and ignorance: by denying modern republican principles, deputies were rejecting the representative system at the heart of the Constitution, a constitution already virtually republican. The current battle was less a fight between monarchy and republicanism, the creed of all genuine patriots, he contended, than true friends of the Constitution and friends of royal influence, patronage, and pensions, cronies of the "civil list."[112] The argument for the king's inviolability, adduced by the reduced but still large centrist Jacobin majority, he termed "la monstruosité la plus révoltante" and directly contradictory to the Constitution. If the Rights of Man render all equal before the law, sovereignty of the nation acknowledges no citizen to be above the rest.

A temporary respite from the turmoil convulsing the Assembly, Paris Commune, and Jacobins was the long-planned triumphal procession of Voltaire's remains through Paris to the Panthéon. On the same day as Brissot's speech at the Jacobins, 10 July 1791, the papers announced the arrival of Voltaire's coffin from Ferney and formal reception by the mayor. The magnificent planned ceremony would proceed the next day. Here was a rousing, unifying revolutionary event around which, exceptionally, center and Left could equally rally. Voltaire's role in preparing the Revolution was everywhere unrelentingly proclaimed. Here, at least, the center could connect with the Revolution's authentic origins and the public. Among the greatest writers of his age, Voltaire had begun the revolt against intolerance and prejudice, and introduced vast changes in thought and literature; in particular, remarked Fréron, he composed dramas like *Brutus* and *La Mort de Caesar*, powerfully contributing to the drive against despotism.[113]

Voltaire's portrait was on sale everywhere. Despite the "pious rage of enemies of *la philosophie*," a performance entitled the *Arrivé de Voltaire à Romilly* was staged at the Théâtre de Molière shortly before the commemoration, while the equally anticlerical *Chevalier de la Barre* played at the Théâtre Italien. Outside the Théâtre de la Nation, columns were inscribed in gold with the titles of all Voltaire's plays. Catholic outrage only enhanced the myth of revolutionary unity, of center and Left united around Voltaire. A recent petition composed by devout Catholics, with multiple copies affixed to street corners, in public places, and cafés, had been gathering signatures. But by summoning the people to demonstrate their loathing of Voltaire, it helped solidify his status as an icon of revolutionary anticlericalism who no one on the Left any longer expressed reservations about. Brissot's objection that Voltaire "was no friend of the people" was forgotten. Heaps of Catholic protest posters were smeared over with mud, torn to shreds, or burned. Every care was taken, reported Carra, to ensure "no foe of the human race, king or queen, aristocrat or fanatical priest, should disturb this historic public festivity."[114]

On 11 July, commencing at the Place de la Bastille, where Voltaire's coffin, sufficiently well guarded to have fended off a night attack by unknown assailants, rested on a purple and white bed among the fortress ruins, his remains were conveyed amid astounding pomp, directed by the supreme revolutionary impresario, the artist David, to lie at Mirabeau's side.[115] Despite the rain, it was a great event, the first time, apart from Mirabeau's funeral, that anyone other than a monarch or saint had ever been publicly exalted on such a scale, let alone celebrated for writings, drama, and political achievements.[116] Preceded by a detachment of cavalry, the cortege was accompanied by trumpeters, followed by a battalion of military cadets, and then delegations from the clubs carrying banners styling Voltaire a true hero of liberty. A phalanx of women wearing antique costumes had to be abandoned due to the rain, but the cortege did include a deputation of actors and managers from the theaters, a float displaying copies of all Voltaire's works (donated by Beaumarchais), and delegations from the academies followed by younger *gens de lettres* (writers) bearing busts of Voltaire, besides smaller medallions of Mirabeau, Rousseau, and Franklin. Next came two or three hundred "victors of the Bastille" carrying a model of the stronghold to highlight the main theme of the celebration—Voltaire, foe of *despotisme,* as well as flayer of "lying preachers," as it was put in Chénier's poem celebrating the event, the hero who "prepared the ruin of all forms of tyranny." One device on a float read, "poete, philosophe, historien; il a fait prendre un gran essor à l'esprit humain" and prepared the French for freedom.[117] The sarcophagus itself was accompanied by twelve Assembly deputies, bands of musicians, and a Commune delegation, with yet more cavalry bringing up the rear.

No one could fail to notice that Voltaire's triumph on 11 July contrasted dramatically with the furtive, forced return of the humiliated

Figure 4. The transfer of Voltaire's remains to the Panthéon, Paris, 10 July 1791. Image courtesy Bibliothèque nationale de France.

monarch three weeks before. As the procession proceeded through the most prestigious boulevards along the Seine, passing the Tuileries (where king and court took care not to appear), crossing the river via the Pont Royal, it paused before Villette's residence where, from the balcony, Villette and Condorcet watched with members of the Calas family, then resumed along the newly renamed Quai de Voltaire past the Comédie Française, finally reaching the Panthéon where it lay in state for three days.[118] Many buildings the cortege passed, including the opera, were festooned with garlands. All Catholic Europe heard the news with stunned outrage. The mighty church of Saint-Geneviève in Paris has become the shrine of the "carcasses" of Mirabeau and Voltaire, scoffed Feller, the new "divinities" of the Parisian rabble daily manipulated by fanatical "débauchées," that is, the "devôts de la philosophie."[119]

By July 1791, Mirabeau and Voltaire had been magnificently pantheonized, but Rousseau, then as now considered by most the Revolution's foremost inspirer, had not. How could Rousseau be omitted from the great philosophique triumvirate? The artist Baudon, then preparing elaborate portrait engravings of all three titans—Mirabeau, Voltaire, and Rousseau—confidently expected these three to grace buildings and offices throughout the eighty-three departments of France.[120] However, Rousseau was not a unifier of center and Left to the same extent as Voltaire. In some respects, he was more divisive than a unifier.[121] A deputation of writers, artists, and others presented the Assembly with a formal petition demanding Rouseau's *panthéonisation* on 27 August 1791, their petition bearing no less than 311 signatures, including those of Chamfort, Clavière, Lanthenas, Roland, Mercier, Gorsas, Duroveray, Perlet, and Fanny Beauharnais.[122] If Voltaire had deservedly been installed for crushing fanaticism "under the feet of philosophy," clearing away *débris* from where "you have raised the edifice of our liberty," how could the Revolution fail to discharge its debt to Rousseau, "le premier fondateur de la constitution française"? First to establish "equality of rights among men" and "sovereignty of the people," the "idées-mères" from which the Revolution arose, Rousseau accomplished this under the eyes of despotism itself. If some of his teaching did not conform to the Assembly's monarchist principles, his thesis that republican forms suit only small states and hence was inappropriate for France surely did. Much of the Constitution stemmed from Rousseau's ideas.[123]

The complaint that the Revolution had *panthéonised* Mirabeau and Voltaire but not Rousseau was composed by Chamfort's friend, Pierre-Louis Ginguené (1748–1816), future member of the Convention's committee of public instruction. Besides Rousseau's *panthéonisation*, it demanded a state pension for his widow and implementation of the December 1790 decree authorizing a public statue for central Paris honoring the *Contrat Social*'s and *Émile*'s author under the rubric "La nation française libre, à J.J.Rousseau."[124] The difficulty, granted Ginguené, was that opinion about Rousseau's contribution remained seriously divided. In Paris cafés, the habitués disagreed about Diderot's claim that the inspiration of the *Discourse on Inequality* originally came from him: Had he lied or told the truth? Were the philosophes right to say Rousseau, over whom so many enthused, was an "homme à paradoxes" whose moral thought is a ridiculous distortion?[125] There was no denying their century's great debt to Diderot and the *Encyclopédie*. Yet, having closely studied the dispute between Rousseau and the philosophes, and reread all Voltaire's works, Ginguené felt that responsibility for the unhappy rift lay mainly with the philosophes. Despite defending Calas and "all the oppressed," Voltaire hardly compared with Jean-Jacques as a foe of oppression.[126]

Diderot and Voltaire had unjustly persecuted the man of "virtue," as had the "good and honest M. d'Holbach, eulogized in December

1789 by Cérutti in the *Journal de Paris*," a figure influential among many revolutionary leaders. Ginguené had known d'Holbach and his "intimate circle" personally. He agreed with "everything [d'Holbach's] friends stated honorable to his memory." Yet d'Holbach had a penchant for "banter, a tendency to jeer," and the battle between Rousseau and the *coterie d'Holbachique*, as Cérutti's eulogy admitted, involved much personal rancor.[127] The feud had focused in part on the status of "the ordinary." Rousseau's "war" on the philosophes was retaliation against their "philosophie anti-Théresienne," their scorning his humble companion, Thérèse.[128] And precisely their "aristocratic disdain" for the ordinary rendered the philosophes inferior to Rousseau, who taught men to "penetrate behind the mask of false social convention, and see man as he truly is, fostering contempt for vain titles and illusions of grandeur, fomenting that preference for simple tastes, natural sentiment, virtue and liberty permeating all his publications and inspiring the Revolution."[129] Pantheonization, besides violating Rousseau's last testament, answered Charles de Lameth, would infringe the property rights of the landowner on whose land he was presently entombed and who had sheltered him in his last days. In his last testament, Rousseau stipulated that he should not be buried in the city he loathed (Paris), preferring rural solitude. His resting-place, near Montmorency, corresponded to his wishes. A final decision was deferred.[130] Rousseau's pantheonization was again petitioned for, on 4 September, and again deferred.[131]

The most dramatic contrast offered by Voltaire's pantheonization, however, was with the 14 July celebrations held three days later, on the second anniversary of the Bastille's storming. Another huge procession wound its way from the Place de la Bastille through the Paris boulevards, this time to the Champ de Mars. But where the first anniversary in July 1790 had been a genuinely festive occasion presided over by Louis, Mirabeau, Talleyrand, and Lafayette, disturbed only by rain, the second anniversary was extremely tense and fraught, an event from which both king and queen were pointedly absent. The looming presence of Lafayette on his white charger, commanding the National Guard, failed to deter sporadic cries from a generally disgruntled crowd denouncing the king. At Bordeaux, ten thousand women citizens marched in ranks like soldiers on the Champ de Mars, wearing tricolor cockades and proclaiming undying allegiance to the Constitution. Yet the efforts to present monarch and monarchy as presiding harmoniously over France's liberation from oppression, in contrast to the previous year, carried little conviction.[132]

The National Assembly's constitutional committee, ignoring the proposal made three days before by Pétion and Robespierre that the decrees awarding Louis XVI the title of "restaurateur de la patrie" be rescinded, chose to announce its findings, absolving Louis XVI of any offense, precisely on 14 July with the Paris crowds absent on the Champ de Mars. Louis was absolved from all blame, but criminal proceedings would be initiated against Bouillé for attempting "to kidnap" the monarch. When rumors swept the city, around two in the afternoon on 14 July, that the Assembly was using the absence of most of the capital's populace to exonerate the king, an irate, yelling crowd streamed back until halted by the guards.[133] This was a crucial moment. For the first time the Assembly clashed openly with a considerable section of opinion in the streets.[134]

On 15 July, the political crisis intensified. Barnave stepped onto the podium and delivered a decisive speech, warmly applauded "by the great majority of the Assembly," refuting Buzot, the young Norman deputy figuring prominently among the republicans who had just affirmed that all France had lost confidence in the king.[135] Barnave did not attempt to justify Louis's actions but instead vigorously defended the principle of monarchy, insisting a republic could not be viable in a large, thickly settled "old society" like France. Though he was as steeped in la philosophie as the republicans, and like Condorcet had developed an antiprovidentialist, materialist conception of history, he firmly rejected republicanism and democracy.[136] Republicanism might work in the United States—where there was land for everyone, no foreign enemies nearby, and no external threats—but in France a republic would mean instability and chaos. Long an admirer of Montesquieu, he accepted that the Revolution and his own early role in it had been chiefly initiated by the philosophes. Revolutions are consolidated, though, not by "metaphysical principles" but by the people. What the common people cared about were tangible things, not principles, and if the Revolution was not concluded now, the next stage, unfortunately, would be a general assault on property.[137] There were too many destitute and envious for any other outcome. It was time to end the Revolution, stop the disorder and affirm the "inviolability of the king" within constitutional limits.[138] Barnave's plea for stability, property, and monarchy proved effective. Inside the Assembly, he swayed a large majority. The "moderates" wanted monarchy and some of its trappings but remained unwilling to defend ecclesiastical authority. To the antiphilosophe Feller, the liberal monarchists seemed an illogical lot trapped in contradiction, a "political sect tending equally to overthrow the old and the new order of things," a shrewd enough description.[139]

The Constitution must be adhered to, affirmed Barnave, concluding the debate the next day with another powerful speech, and the Assembly must uphold its authority and France's stability.[140] Replying, the Cordeliers and Cercle convened another mass gathering that day, lasting for several hours. Encouraged by a raucous crowd, a string of republican orators, including the radical printer who published the *Journal du Club des Cordeliers*, Antoine-François Momoro (1756–94), one of the Cordeliers's best speakers, demanded Louis's dethronement and a republic. A direct challenge to the Assembly's authority, the republican movement was bound to result in a major confrontation. The gathering adopted a mass petition demanding the king's trial before a National Convention convened for the purpose. Crowds seethed in the streets around the Jacobins, the Palais-Royal, and the Tuileries. A crowd of reportedly four thousand invaded the Jacobins in an attempt to enlist support there.[141] Posters acclaiming the king were torn down; the affiches posted up all demanded his trial.

The Jacobins, the only political club with mass support that also provided a regular platform for Assembly deputies, remained utterly divided. In fact, they split four ways. The dominant faction backed Barnave, the Lameths, and Lafayette, intent on upholding monarchy and retaining Louis XVI; a second group spoke of deposing Louis but retaining the monarchy, substituting for the present incumbent the self-proclaimed constitutional monarchist Louis-Philippe d'Orléans. A third group, the populist faction, nervous lest the Jacobins, Robespierre's essential platform, disintegrate, sought a middle path; they deplored the king's conduct and urged his trial but stopped short of calling for an end to monarchy. Finally, there were the democratic radicals, who urged a republic. Where the Jacobins could partially unite was by combining groups two to four, to censure the Assembly's constitutional monarchist majority.[142] Three Jacobin streams, headed by Brissot, Pétion, Danton, and Robespierre, in this way briefly converged to hammer out a compromise resolution demanding Louis's trial and judgment before an elected National Convention. Nothing further should be done without consulting the people.

A large crowd of some twelve thousand citizens gathered on the Champ de Mars on 15 July and approved a petition calling for Louis's trial. Many signed and joined the march toward the Assembly, delegated to present their text to those deputies—Pétion, Grégoire, and

Robespierre—who had delivered speeches in the legislature condemning the declaration of the king's "inviolability."[143] Their petition inveighed against the king for perjuring himself, abandoning his post, and exposing France to "the horrors of civil war," while accusing the Assembly of "proceeding without consulting the people." The people's "delegates cannot do anything," held the petitioners, "except through and by us." The people would reject the Assembly's resolutions unless these conformed to their will. Should the deputies "who dared to advise such a thing" refuse to consult the eighty-three departments, the citizenry would disavow them as "traitres à la patrie." Afterward even Pétion described this as a "shocking irregularity."[144] The marchers were halted by guards outside the Tuileries. Emerging from the Assembly hall, Robespierre and Pétion explained that the demonstrators were too late to prevent passage of the edict that had angered them; the vote was over.[145]

Charles Lameth, president of the Assembly, sent the delegation a formal reply, contradicting their assertion of direct democracy: the crowd represented only the will of a handful of individuals, not that of France. Under the Constitution, the Assembly alone represented the people's will. The Assembly would not defer to theirs but act according to its own will. Petitioning collectively was illegal, their action insurrectionary. Worse, they were permitting a handful of schemers to manipulate them, turning Paris—a city of intrigue—into the foe of all France.[146] No sooner was the exoneration decree published than the city became very tense. The theaters around the Palais-Royal were closed.[147] The Lameths and Barnave were right that the crowds were defying the Assembly and violating the law and Constitution. The problem was that the Constitution itself was an unsustainable fudge, an undemocratic and oligarchic contradiction, not genuinely based on the Rights of Man or popular sovereignty.

Barnave had persuaded the Assembly to exonerate the king, using the fiction purporting that Louis had been "kidnapped" by conspirators. Now the Assembly needed to quell the noisy opposition in the streets. On 16 July, another mass rally convened on the Champ de Mars, where a Jacobin compromise resolution was read out by Danton. Its deliberate obscuring of the issue of whether or not a republic should be declared so exasperated the radicals and Cordeliers present, as well as Bonneville and the Cercle, however, that Danton had to return to the Jacobins and plead for some radicalizing of its content. A much tougher formulation, amended by Bonneville, appeared in the *Bouche de fer*, declaring that the Paris petitioners rejected Louis and any candidate for the throne unless a majority of the nation first voted for monarchy to continue. Meanwhile, even the less radical joint stance of the three Jacobin anti-Barnave streams proved unacceptable to the liberal monarchist leadership. On the evening of 16 July, Barnave, Lafayette, the Lameths, Bailly, and their supporters stormed out of the Jacobins, seceding from the club. The defectors were joined by nearly every single Jacobin deputy in the Assembly except Robespierre and Pétion, numbering altogether more than two hundred deputies.

This finalized the break between the Assembly and the clubs. Infiltrated by suspect persons, the Jacobins had abandoned their original mission, declared Barnave and the Lameths: instead of championing the laws, they were now undermining them. The two hundred defectors transferred to the convent of the Feuillants where they established a rival club, the Amis de la Constitution, henceforth dubbed the "Feuillants."[148] The Jacobins, provincial clubs were informed, had been invaded by extraneous elements, including foreigners like Paine and Cloots, who were seeking to undermine the Constitution and the Assembly's decrees. They were eroding freedom of expression by labeling everyone who disagreed with them as "traitors." Affiliated societies were urged to switch their correspondence to the Feuillants, and many did.[149] So massive and destabilizing was the defection that it briefly paralyzed both the Paris Jacobins and many provincial offshoots.[150] Some Jacobins, Pétion acknowledged, had used intemperate language, but this did not justify mass defection. Far from motivated by authentic Jacobin principles, the Feuillant schism was "the fruit of intrigue"; those in power realized they had lost control of the club.[151]

The Jacobin schism of 16 July 1791 marked the start of a powerful moderate, liberal monarchist reaction against the Left *and* against the Revolution's core values. Repudiating the Jacobins, and attempting to curtail freedom of expression, the Feuillants labeled everyone wanting Louis brought to trial as rebels against the Constitution and "republicans." They moved swiftly to curb the demonstrations in the streets, reinforcing the Paris city government's authority with new police powers to restrict crowd movements and repress disturbance. Over the next days several members of the Cordeliers were arrested, some for posting up petitions demanding an end to monarchy.[152] The democratic press retaliated by accusing the Feuillants of adopting a divisive strategy that was bound to fail. The Jacobin rump, the three groups forming the "strict observance Jacobins," justifying their opposition to royal "inviolability" and hailed by the pro-Revolution press for resisting the "brigands," issued a general circular urging affiliate clubs to defy the Feuillants. However, dominated by Robespierre's populism, they still claimed not to be opposed to monarchy as such. Briefly, both chief stands of strict observance Jacobins—populists supporting Robespierre and Brissotin republicans—seemed to have become allies fighting the Feuillant "impostors" together. This rapidly proved a delusion.

CHAPTER 7

War with the Church

(1788–92)

"At the beginning of the Revolution, no apparent contradiction between the Revolution and religion" existed, it has been argued, and from the standpoint of popular culture and society overall this is broadly true.[1] But this contention needs qualifying. From the perspective of the Revolution's Left republican leadership, if not the populace, it was absolutely certain from the outset that the Revolution, given its priorities, would confront the Church as an authority, autonomous institution, value system, and set of doctrines.

Full freedom of thought, conscience, and expression, and the Rights of Man, were central to the Revolution but condemned by ecclesiastical authority. Even for Cérutti, mildest of the philosophique pamphleteers of 1788, la philosophie was inevitably at "war" with a too "opulent church" because the clergy, despite their unrivaled preeminence in society and resources, neither adequately supported the poor nor assisted the bankrupt French state. Rather, the clergy unhesitatingly defended what to the Left revolutionary leadership seemed barbaric, unjustified privileges, antisocial attitudes, and immunities. "If in the centuries of ignorance [the clergy] held sway over the ignorant, today when the brightest light enlightens the nations, they must," held Cérutti, "yield to justice and virtue, becoming priests of the *patrie*, as they are priests of religion." The Church's personnel, property, revenues, and rents had to be made to serve the people to a far greater extent than in the past.[2]

No part of French society enjoyed greater autonomy before 1789, commented Tocqueville later, or more special privileges than the Church. No other slice of society, apart from the army and navy, so completely reflected the social hierarchy; practically all archbishops and bishops were aristocrats.[3] Hence, it was central to the leading révolutionnaires' vision of the Revolution and democracy that the Church should be deprived of its autonomy, immunities, independent resources, privileged status, and solidly aristocratic leadership.[4] Nor was this all. There was also a more directly political aspect. A haven of privilege, immunities, and autonomy, the Church had for decades combated la philosophie moderne, and now offered France's elites their best hope of mobilizing substantial backing among the common people for the ancien régime and conservatism in their fight against equality and democracy. In effect, the Church's authority, doctrines, and preaching were conservatism's most formidable weapon against the Revolution. "Nobility," exclaimed the *Gazette de Paris* on 15 January 1791, "never forget this sublime idea: the clergy alone, through their heroic resistance, can rescue you from the Revolution."[5] The Catholic Church, the "most powerful organization inside the kingdom," did indeed lead the crusade against the Revolution, and especially against the philosophique revolutionary leadership's ideology.

Equally, everyone steeped in the writings of Diderot, d'Holbach, Raynal, and Helvétius took it as axiomatic that a close alliance had long existed between the "two classes of civil and sacred tyrants" against the interests of the majority. The thesis that clergy, kings, and nobility collaborate to keep the people ignorant and unaware, first powerfully formulated by Meslier and Boulanger with their theories of how and why priests, nobles, and kings mutually support each other, pervaded the thought-world of Mirabeau, Brissot, Condorcet, Sieyès, Bonneville, Chamfort, Volney, Cérutti, Desmoulins, and journalists like Carra and Gorsas. Ignorance and church authority were deemed indispensable to kings if they were to succeed in misleading the people and getting them to submit to notions and institutions essentially detrimental to their own interests. Only through religion can kings blind men sufficiently to acquiesce in their own exploitation, abasement, and misery. "Les tyrants civils et sacrés des peuples," affirmed Volney in his most important book (and commentary on the Revolution), published in 1791, "formèrent une ligue générale," to exploit and oppress the vast multitude of the deluded.[6]

The papacy and ecclesiastical hierarchy repudiated the Revolution's core values altogether. Outright conflict between Revolution and Church was wholly certain from the outset.[7] If Robespierre consistently remained more moderate on this point (as on some others), and far more willing to defend religion and popular piety than his philosophique opponents,[8] this in no way alters the fact that the philosophique clique that forged the Revolution of 1788–93 always intended to assail the Church as a property-owner, educator, social force, and moral, political, and cultural influence. The mounting, multifaceted assault on the Church, as Archbishop Puységur of Bourges noted in September 1789, followed directly from this "audacious and culpable philosophy which, in its fury, attacked heaven only to see things on earth overthrown."[9]

Conflict arose first over toleration, a central plank of the Enlightenment. A few clergy accepted comprehensive toleration for all churches, but most repudiated the principle. Leading royalist editors like Royou not only championed monarchy, nobility, and ecclesiastical authority, and excoriated philosophes, but rejected even a qualified formal toleration.[10] Protestants appeared in the 1789 Estates-General following a royal provision of January 1789 that extended the franchise to them, a change enabling Rabaut Saint-Étienne, Barnave, and thirteen other Protestants to be elected Estates-General deputies. These had then, for their own reasons, vigorously supported both general toleration and proposals to weaken the dominant Church. Protestant support for the Revolution, however, only intensified Catholic resistance. For months, from the summer of 1789, the clergy obstructed the comprehensive toleration urged by Mirabeau and the philosophique vanguard, but were finally defeated with a decree passed on Christmas Eve 1789, that for the first time in history in any country stipulated fully equal legal and political rights for minority churches.

Under this landmark decree, Calvinists, Lutherans, and other Protestants were placed on an equal footing with Catholics: henceforth, any Christian (and by implication non-Christian), every citizen swearing allegiance to the Constitution, became eligible to hold office irrespective of religion or ethnicity.[11] The only legitimate creed in France now was "le patriotisme éclairé." Even a "Negro, Turk, or idolater," sneered the Venetian envoy, or "Salé corsairs, can become representatives of the nation or cabinet ministers of France!"[12] Opening up all professions, offices, and political functions to non-Catholics was decidedly a sensational step, even if the measure still (illogically) expressly excluded Jews. Furthermore, given the Declaration of Rights, how long could opponents defend the age-old principle that non-Christians, especially Jews, should be excluded from society?[13]

Proposals to emancipate the Jewish population, insistent from October onward, encountered vehement opposition led by Maury and Bishop Lafare of Nancy. Religious toleration, conceded Maury, might possibly be extended also to the Jews, but not rights of citizenship. Political rights for Protestants were one thing, but the Jews constituted a separate nation addicted to commerce and impervious to the responsibilities of citizenship, set apart from society for seventeen centuries. In Poland, Jewish "opulence" arose from the "sweat of Christian slaves." Refusing Fontenelle's thesis that the fathers' sins should not be visited on the sons, he cited Voltaire's anti-Semitism to "prove" the Enlightenment too recognized Jewish "perversity." Besides, argued Maury, popular sentiment must be heeded. Ordinary people detested the Jews, and granting them citizenship would only make them more hated. In Nancy, declared the bishop, there was talk of Jews trying to appropriate the best parts of town for themseves; there was a constant threat of popular violence against them.[14] Yet the Assembly would contradict its own principles, noted the Venetian envoy, if it attempted to exclude Jews from the Rights of Man.[15] After an ill-tempered debate on 28 January 1790, the more affluent and integrated but small Sephardic community, and those Jews domiciled (for many centuries) at Avignon, were emancipated by 374 votes to 224, the main proposer being Mirabeau's only ally among the old episcopate, the ambitious and cynical bishop of Autun, Charles-Maurice de Talleyrand (1754–1838).[16]

However, dividing Jews into two categories—Sephardim possessing full citizenship rights and a Yiddish-speaking Ashkenazic community in Alsace-Lorraine remaining excluded—was unsustainable, making no sense to anyone. It is a "monstrosity" in logic, concurred the Venetian envoy, defying all common sense: "a Jew of Bordeaux will enjoy the Rights of Man, but not a Jew of Lorraine or Alsace."[17] Even so, so great was the reluctance of the Assembly majority, it took until September 1791 before the Ashkenazic community finally received equality of rights.[18] Last among France's religious blocs rescued by the parti de philosophie from the disabilities imposed by the Church for centuries were the Anabaptists, who possessed a network of congregations in Alsace, on the upper Marne, and in the Vosges. Appearing before the Convention on 9 August 1793, an Anabaptist delegation, acclaiming the Revolution, received citizenship and exemption from bearing arms.[19]

Toleration soon gave way to monasticism, and then church property, as the principal battlegrounds. The Rights of Man proclaimed not just freedom of thought and expression but individual liberty of lifestyle. On 28 October 1789, the Assembly ended government recognition of all religious vows in France. Exacting vows of celibacy, poverty, and submission infringed individuals' natural rights and could no longer legitimately be imposed by any authority or organization. But the fight over this was nothing compared to the war over church property. The 4 August legislation abolishing feudal rights had also envisaged suppressing the tithe, but did so without clarifying whether this would be with or without compensation. To most Frenchmen, this whole furor was a puzzling development, as the Revolution had made a point of guaranteeing property rights, and in the rural and urban cahiers of 1789, few among the provincial laity had questioned the Church's right to its property.[20] But on 10 October 1789, less than a week after the women's march on Versailles, Talleyrand (virtually the only ecclesiastic in the Assembly proposing such a policy),[21] collaborating with Mirabeau, stunned the legislature by advocating a general confiscation and sale of church lands, benefices, and nonecclesiastical buildings, together with suppression of the tithe, all without compensation. To the episcopate, this was a catastrophic, breathtakingly vast, and cynical betrayal.

Philosophique demands for a general confiscation of church property provoked total uproar, with many (especially senior) churchmen protesting that religion and ecclesiastical authority were being annihilated. Religion and church dogma, replied the revolutionary leadership, were being left untouched; the clergy were merely being asked to reform their external organization for their own good. The Church, averred Charles Lameth in February 1790 (with unintended irony), was no more threatened by the Assembly's plans than royalty.[22] The October motion on church property lacked popular support but perfectly illustrated Chamfort's thesis that the people would be led by "the shepherds" where they had no idea they were going.[23] As yet, though, there was little attempt to interfere with doctrine or the clergy's pastoral or educational roles. Thus far, curtailing the Church remained essentially economic and institutional. Even so, these early measures clearly also menaced the clergy's general status, power, and independence, and more was certain to follow.

Were lands, benefices, and endowments donated over the centuries genuine church property? Ecclesiastical endowments had been made to support the clergy, help sustain the cult, education, and poor relief, functions society needed but could now better provide outside the Church. The change, from society's point of view, would eliminate much waste and corruption. Hitherto, prelates had led an aristocratic existence. Bishops, vicars general, cathedral canons, priors, and abbots all dwelt in splendid luxury at the expense of others, a system socially and morally insidious and indefensible. Crown and lay donations to the Church really belonged to the people, maintained Mirabeau and his allies (on this issue, especially Thouret and Volney). Volney, prominent among Mirabeau's entourage over the winter of 1789–90, had loudly and publicly insisted since at least 1788 that church property belonged to the nation. Confiscation and sale of ecclesiastical property, he hoped, would convert thousands of presently impoverished peasant laborers and wage-earners into small property owners.[24]

The Church was rapidly worsted in this battle. Chamfort contributed behind the scenes, publishing article after article urging the Revolution's need to weaken church authority.[25] Together with Talleyrand, the leaders of this philosophique anti-Church campaign ceaselessly plied the distinction between property of individuals and property belonging to institutional bodies performing a social role. Church property, they claimed, belonged to a different category from other property because it had been donated by parishioners and held in trust for poor relief, education, and other social purposes. Such claims made it appear initially that ecclesiastical authority and religion as such were not in dispute, thereby enabling the revolutionaries to win over some lower clergy.

Preserving endowed benefices in ecclesiastical hands, moreover, would have the serious disadvantage, argued Mirabeau, of leaving intact the old method of choosing bishops and other higher clergy, and hence perpetuating ancien régime "corruption." This argument also appealed to some lower clergy who rarely benefited from those assets. For the Assembly to acknowledge that lands and revenues possessed by the Church were its rightful property effectively meant respecting "and consolidating the distinction of orders."

Led by Maury, the clergy's representatives in the Assembly resisted this "spoliation" of "our property" as best they could. Few clergy agreed with Fauchet and Lamourette that a Church without property would be spiritually better off, wealth being the "root of depravity."[26] (Even the Abbé Grégoire opposed the clergy's transformation into salaried officials of the state.) But many lower clergy were swayed by Talleyrand's assurance that the proceeds from the planned sale of church lands would be used for paying curés' salaries, a key clause of the confiscation decree guaranteeing that no curé would subsequently receive less than 1,200 livres annually.[27] Exploiting the friction between higher and lower clergy helped push the hierarchy onto the defensive. The bishops retaliated by denouncing philosophique ideas as the worst of the evils afflicting the land.[28] Rousseau would in no way have condoned Mirabeau's attacks on the Church, protested conservative clergy. Rousseau maintained that "religion" is always the basis for a country's laws. Eager to demonstrate that the revolutionary leadership publicly pretended to venerate Rousseau while actually disregarding the people's new hero, Maury highlighted Rousseau's scorn for the irreligious inclinations of his philosophe foes.

Terminating the Church's financial independence, on 2 November 1789, the Assembly voted by 568 to 346 with forty abstentions, on a motion of Talleyrand, to place all church property "at the disposition of the nation" with a view to paying the clergy salaries and supporting their social functions.[29] The revolutionary leadership, backed by the Paris cafés and streets, could in the prevailing atmosphere of late 1789, the substantial voting margin in favor proved, fairly easily pressure most deputies into following their lead. Just prior to this pivotal vote, noted the Venetian envoy, Chénier's *Charles IX* opened on the Paris stage, a play vilifying the Church and evoking the Saint Bartholomew's Day massacre with the obvious aim of channeling opinion behind the revolutionary leadership. The Assembly's leaders, concluded some clergy, consisted not of Catholics but "Protestants and unbelievers."[30] On 5 February 1790, the Assembly voted for all ecclesiastical benefices and pensions to be inventoried and for registration of property belonging to regular orders to begin.[31] Disputes over how confiscation should proceed persisted for months. But by 14 May, the Assembly had fixed the terms of sale for ecclesiastical land, and from June, an immense quantity of farms, pasturage, and forests, as well as urban properties, was unloaded onto the market.[32] Though critical of the ham-fisted way a vast mass of church property was suddenly dumped on the open market, thoroughly depressing land prices, Condorcet otherwise concurred with Mirabeau and Volney, being no less keen to confiscate for social purposes.[33]

The next step was dissolution of the monasteries. Although "the great question" whether religious orders were useful or not had been decided by the philosophes and "la raison" long before, suggested Mirabeau's *Courrier de Provence*, in September 1789, opposition remained intense.[34] Where the "bons esprits" saw truth and justification in abolishing contemplative orders, noted the *Chronique de Paris*, the pious perceived only impiety and blasphemy.[35] Ostensibly, conservatives controlled the Assembly's *comité ecclésiastique*, which included two bishops and seven other members who preferred bishops to philosophes. But it was not easy to block the anticlerical offensive since, once again, the "bons esprits" proved better placed to exert pressure.[36] This was shown in a series of stormy debates between December 1789 and March 1790. On 17 December, Jean-Baptiste Treilhard (1742–1810), a former *avocat* of the Paris parlement and now president of the *comité ecclésiastique*, recommended full dissolution of those orders under vows of strict seclusion, as these served no social function and merely enabled monks to live at the expense of others.[37] After a tumultuous debate, in which Barnave (a Protestant) claimed that religious orders contradicted the liberty, equality, and rights of men,[38] the Assembly rejected a compromise to spare at least one monastic house in each town, despite Abbé Gregoire's plea that the "destruction absolue" of the orders was "impolitique," and that scholarship, agriculture, and the cult would suffer.

On 13 February 1790, the Assembly declared all monastic establishments not devoted to educational or charitable work contrary to society's interests, abolishing them "for ever."[39] To determine which monasteries should be spared as socially useful, questionnaires requiring details of their governance, rules of life, and goals, and the identities and ages of all occupants were circulated to all France's monastic establishments, male and female, in early March.[40] As the country's laws no longer recognized "monastic solemn vows either for the one or the other sex," everyone wishing to leave monastic houses or nunneries was free to do so. Nuns refusing to relinquish their vows could remain in the convents where they were; monks and friars adhering to vows had to recongregate in monastic houses deemed charitable (of whatever order), still counting at least fifteen members.[41] Thus, in each region a few houses designated "charitable" absorbed residues from larger batches of monastic houses now dissolved. Most regular clergy made little protest and simply vacated their premises, many emigrating, or abandoning monastic life for good. Indiscriminate commingling of orders in surviving monasteries, moreover, quickly persuaded some who had not initially chosen to forsake their vows to reenter secular life after all. Monks and friars departing voluntarily received pensions of between 700 and 1,200 livres, though sequestration began immediately but promised pensions only from January 1791. Here and there, defiant stalwarts remained a solid majority in control of their monasteries. At Saint-Germain-des-Près, the great abbey in central Paris, thirty-seven out of forty-seven monks refused to leave.

Most ecclesiastical deputies continued attending the Assembly's meetings over the winter of 1789–90 and into the spring, preferring to resist from within the Assembly for as long as possible.[42] France's battered episcopate, despite the affronts to which, from October 1789, it was continually subjected, made no move yet to openly repudiate the Revolution. By April 1790, though, those clergy still attending sessions were nearing the point of absolute rupture. On 11 April, they formally protested at the anticlerical tone of much of the debate, threatening to boycott the Assembly's sessions. Some walked out. On 12 April, the mystic Carthusian Dom Gerle introduced his unsuccessful motion, prepared with other clerics, proclaiming Catholicism France's sole publicly acknowledged religion. Some lower clergy still hoped the alliance of Revolution and clergy of June 1789 would somehow surmount all obstacles. But there was scant likelihood of this. Doubtless relatively few Frenchmen rejoiced at the monasteries' dissolution, but precisely these considered dissolution a mere preliminary preceding still more drastic action directed against the Church. Among the fiercest anti-Church tracts at this juncture was the *Catéchisme du curé Meslier*—penned by the militantly egalitarian atheist republican philosophe of the Cordeliers, Sylvain Maréchal (1750–1803)—which revived the irreligious communism and atheism of Jean Meslier (1664–1729) and plainly intended to spread his anti-Christian message far and wide.[43]

Meanwhile, deteriorating relations with the papacy, and the strife in the papal enclaves of Avignon and Comtat Venaissin, as well as Pius VI's condemnation of the Declaration of Rights at Rome on 29 March 1790 (even if thus far only in secret consistory), aggravated the general position. By the spring of 1790, revolutionaries had won control of the Avignon city council and were agitating for annexation to France, a development from which local Protestants, Jews, deists, and nonbelievers stood to gain. The pope's supporters fought back by instigating popular riots in Avignon on 10 June 1790, physically attacking revolutionaries, Protestants, and Jews, to which the insurgents responded by proclaiming the enclave's annexation to France. This was furiously resisted in the Comtat and precipitated a miniature civil war that lasted an entire year.

However, the principal battle, the culminating struggle, was fought over the Assembly's proposals for a comprehensive restructuring of the Church designed to subordinate it firmly to the interests and "general will" of the nation, ending the Church's autonomy and aristocratic dominance of the episcopate and drastically curtailing the hierarchy. Church activities in future should be confined to administering the cult, pastoral care, primary education, and charity. The key legislation was framed and advanced by a group of radical revolutionaries, including Mirabeau, Treilhard, Lanjuinais, and Camus, a "fervent Jansenist," according to Malouet, and certainly an erudite expert in church history and canon law (as well as the later founder of the Archives Nationales),[44] but actually an uncompromising republican and foe of aristocracy with a vehemently erastian and antipapalist attitude, detested by practically all clergy.[45] These men worked together with a handful of radical reforming clergy, notably Lamourette, Fauchet, and Grégoire, and a few Jansenists. The enactment amounted to a fundamental reorganization of the Church's institutional structure. To justify the many changes, the reformers claimed not to be transforming the Church itself but restoring its long-lost authentic apostolic character, rendering it again poor, propertyless, and the "servant" of the people, embodying, as Fauchet put it, *la liberté universelle*. The large revenues and aristocratic pomp of the episcopate, which Treilhard did not hesitate to label "corruption," and the bishops' ingrained "despotisme," were heavily stressed. Jesus Christ established no hierarchy among the apostles, claimed one pamphlet, but rather placed them all on the same level. The apostles' successors had been appointed "bishops" by the people, not a corrupt court (i.e., the papacy). Supposedly, the Civil Constitution of the Clergy "far from advancing anything contrary to religion is, in fact, in perfect agreement with Gospel doctrine."[46]

The Assembly's Ecclesiastical Committee, doubled in size in order to swamp the ecclesiastics with nonecclesiastics, presented its proposed Civil Constitution of the Clergy on 29 May 1790.[47] There were four main aspects to this key decree: reform of the episcopate, reform of the parish system, instituting the election of both parish priests and bishops, and finally ending jurisdictional appeals to Rome.[48] Under the edict's terms, the episcopate was drastically diminished in size, resources, and competence. Diocesan boundaries were redrawn so that there were now only eighty-three dioceses corresponding exactly to each *departement* in France, thereby ending the age-old inequality between dioceses. The result was that fifty-two sees disappeared outright, reducing the number of French bishops from 135 to 83 (subsequently 85). At the same time, surviving bishops had their incomes drastically reduced, afterward receiving relatively modest salaries of only 20,000 livres for those residing in towns of more than 20,000 inhabitants and 12,000 livres for smaller centers—barely more than double that of curés of large parishes.[49] The rank of "archbishop" disappeared altogether, horrifying the entire upper hierarchy. The ten most senior prelates, now designated "metropolitans," were henceforth those of Paris, Rouen, Reims, Lyon, Besançon, Aix-en-Provence, Toulouse, Bordeaux, Bourges, and Rennes.

Parish boundaries were redrawn, rendering the parishes likewise equal in territory and population, with the consequence that hundreds disappeared. The number of curés in both town and country fell precipitately, especially in towns with populations of less than ten thousand, where there was now just one curé.[50] In Paris, under one-third of former parishes (eleven) were eliminated.[51] In smaller centers, though, the proportion was considerably higher, often comprising the majority. Parishes in Arras dropped from eleven to four, in Auxerre from twelve to four.[52] To end the old patronage system for episcopal appointments, cathedral chapters and vicars general, with their extensive aristocratic establishments, were also all suppressed. Henceforth, every bishop must previously have served for fifteen years as a curé in an ordinary parish and be "elected" by the citizenry. Fauchet stongly supported election of *pasteurs* and bishops by the people, seeing no other way to extirpate everything "aristocratic" and hierarchical and effectively subject the Church to the "public voice," la volonté générale. Bishops would be elected in departmental assemblies, curés in local ones, without those standing being allowed to solicit Vatican or any external endorsement.[53] Curés and bishops would be elected, moreover, not by Catholic congregations alone but by all "active citizens" enfranchised to vote, Protestants and Jews included, a democratic principle intended to render all clergy public servants.

These measures entailed noble exclusion from the episcopate and massive diminution of the higher clergy generally. All clergy would now be salaried officials of the state and could be only curés or bishops. That every public official in a free state "doit être salarié" (should be salaried), commented Mirabeau's *Courrier de Provence* in September 1790, was a revolutionary principle many found hard to comprehend. Under the ancien régime, the notion "le salaire déshonore" had prevailed. A salaried position implied public service, a status dishonorable for nobles and senior churchmen. But in revolutionary France, no position could any longer be hereditary, hierarchical, or nonsalaried; judges were now salaried and dismissible, elected in four classes according to the population of the jurisdiction served. Similar rules must apply to all public ministers, bishops and curés included.[54] Every public servant must be salaried, in society's service and subject to dismissal.

King, clergy, and much of the Assembly were aghast at the Ecclesiastical Committee's swinging plans.[55] An immense portion of the ecclesiastical sector was simply abolished, including cathedral chapters, canons, choir schools, and, in part, the study and practice of sacred music.[56] Admittedly, some ecclesiastics, influenced by pre-1789 Jansenist arguments, supported extensive reform, and a few, like Fauchet, had proposed election of bishops and priests, and other sweeping changes, already before 1789.[57] But none, apart from the cynical Talleyrand, could accept the philosophique principle that there is no such thing as a spiritual sphere beyond the secular authority's competence, or that changes should be imposed without consultation with the clergy and their consent. In the Assembly, ecclesiastical resistance was appreciably weakened, though, by a growing and (for the clergy) awkward rift between hard-line conservatives refusing any concession and a more flexible liberal bloc anxious to compromise where possible. The conservatives had mostly walked out by early June. Further prolonged and exhausting debate, lasting more than six weeks, ended in final and total ecclesiastical defeat on 12 July 1790. The Civil Constitution of the Clergy passed decisively, but over the vehement opposition of 290 conservative deputies.

Deemed excessive by many, this drastic measure hardly sufficed for some. In mid-September, several deputies, headed by Alexandre de Beauharnais (1760–94), a veteran of the American Revolution and among the first nobles to join the Third in 1789, whose wife, Josephine, later married Napoleon, proposed abolishing the traditional "costume" of those monks belonging to the still-permitted orders as an undesirable vestige of the past. Hard-liners also urged a prohibition on wearing ecclesiastical dress of any sort while the cult was being celebrated, so that clergy should no longer stand out from other citizens—a most sensible proposal, remarked the *Courrier de Provence*, that should be extended to all public officials.[58] "True friends of the moral regeneration of France," reported the *Chronique de Paris*, "also hoped the Assembly would now allow priests to marry," even though much lingering prejudice would need to be expunged and many "philosophical truths" asserted before this could happen. Such a reform, protested opponents, would require papal approval. No, answered Mirabeau's supporters, the Assembly, guided by "the empire of reason, nature and the nation"—not some authority outside France—should determine whether the right to marry can be denied to any citizen.[59]

That the rift between Revolution and clergy was completely unbridgeable already prior to the Civil Constitution of the Clergy is illustrated by a collective petition to the Assembly on 17 July 1790 by 105 curés of the Nantes region. Social order, properly maintained, they insisted, is inseparable from keeping the spiritual and worldly powers apart. God commanded his Church to be built on "an altogether different basis from that of the governments of this world." If ecclesiastical hierarchy could be transformed by human command, then it is not di-

vinely instituted "and we have been deceived." Neither the people, nor
their representatives, can claim an authority higher than the Church's.
The reformers professed to be reviving the *formes primitives* and integrity of the original Church. But research into early texts proves bishops
were never elected by the people. According the right to choose their
pasteurs to the people contradicts canon law and is wholly invalid unless endorsed by the Holy See. The veritable chain of authority, established by Saint Peter, was being ruptured, creating a schism estranging
the Church, the path of salvation, from the Revolution. Willingly, they
conceded to Caesar what is Caesar's, but spiritual matters transcend the
wishes of men: usurping spiritual authority violates *la volonté suprême*.
A national church council must be convened to devise a more canonical
and acceptable reform plan than that announced.

Humiliation and impoverishment were being inflicted on the priesthood by "a too accredited philosophy." The petitioners renounced all
desire to stir up popular resistance, or oppose "losing our property, since
Christianity teaches us to make sacrifices." But freedom of thought and
unrestricted religious toleration were impermissible.[60] The Revolution,
rejecting "unity of cult in the French monarchy," permitted a "monstrous variety of cults," something indefensible and wrong. Protestants
had devastated France during the Wars of Religion when they were permitted no freedom at all. What will happen when their audacity enjoys
unlimited freedom? Hatred and strife will erupt everywhere. For all the
odious *libelles infâmes* continually "vomited on" the clergy, the Assembly itself was responsible. The Revolution sought to force opinions on
the clergy contrary to the Rights of Man, menacing them with losing
their salaries if they resisted, imposing the "terrible choice of violating
our consciences or dying of hunger." Without status and dignity, what
service can clergy render religion?

Clergy win their parishioners' respect, contended the Assembly,
through "virtue alone." Yet the apostles *were* "virtuous" but incurred
thereby only insults, imprisonment, and execution. The world's conversion to Christianity resulted from astounding miracles, "not virtue."
Without miracles what can today's clergy hope for from the people?[61]
The petitioners abhorred the revolutionaries' "proud indifference for
eternal truths" and "thoughtless license of arbitrary beliefs," making
"reason our idol." Religion alone makes men free. The alternative is "un
pyrrhonisme inextricable." When a man fears nothing beyond what his
own reason reveals, possesses no other brake than nature, men's reciprocal rights have little force. That all men are by nature brothers may be a

principle of la philosophie but only religion can persuade the people of this. Religion consecrates fraternity's precepts; without religion fraternity lacks force. The Assembly cultivated a *culte adultère*, a total reorganization vitiating a spiritual power based on principles wholly different from those governing the worldly sphere.

No other revolutionary measure cost the king such soul-searching as approving the Civil Constitution of the Clergy. Though highly reluctant to do so, on 24 August 1790, Louis provisionally sanctioned the measure, officially requesting the pope's endorsement despite (or perhaps because of) prior papal rejection (so far only private). Royal assent greatly dismayed those hoping Louis would lead the Church's crusade against the Revolution. But with or without the monarch, the clergy's opposition continued. A key protest was the *Exposition of Principles* by Archbishop Boisgelin of Aix on 30 October, endorsed by thirty bishops and ninety-eight other clerical Assembly deputies. Though diplomatically worded, this text rejected all talk of abolishing bishoprics and other reforms without papal approval as lacking canonical validity. Approved eventually by 119 prelates, the manifesto summoned France's clergy to oppose the Revolution, albeit solely via passive resistance.[62] Only after further long hesitation, as the king himself admitted, did he formally ratify the Civil Constitution on 27 December, feeling he had no alternative. Hugely applauded in the Assembly with rousing cries of "Vive le roi!" his belated assent plunged the antirevolutionary deputies into "despair." By deferring his definitive assent for months, Louis had undoubtedly sought to encourage priests and monks to resist, bind them closer to the royal cause, and mobilize "all the enemies of liberty," as Marat bluntly put it, "and all feeble minds, the pious and imbéciles."[63] The king would never have sanctioned such a measure, protested the ultraroyalist press, were he really a free agent. It is contrary to Christian tradition for the Church to be subordinate to the state, held the *Gazette de Paris*, and a fundamental principle of all Christian values and society, that religious authority presides over society. Religion should receive the state in its bosom, not vice versa. Only diffusion of pernicious republican ideas (backed by Protestantism) could possibly have produced such an outcome.[64]

A revolution in religion commenced. Suppressing cathedral chapters, a considerable undertaking in itself, began at Notre Dame in Paris with immediate effect. Dozens of canons lost their positions and incomes. Within days, all precious metal objects not strictly required for celebrating Mass were removed from the cathedral and all other Paris churches.[65] Meanwhile, on 27 November, the Assembly had promulgated a supplementary decree, moved by the fierce anticlerical Nicolas-Louis François de Neufchâteau (1756–1828), poet, playwright, and member of four academies, requiring all clergy exercising public functions in France to swear allegiance to the Constitution, in accord with provisions in the Constitution of the Clergy.[66] All ecclesiastics had to swear loyalty to the nation, law, and king, and to uphold the Constitution. Except those who were Assembly deputies who took the oath there, curés and bishops had to take these oaths on Sunday, after mass, in their parish churches or cathedrals with the local town councils present, on dates agreed upon with municipal officials and publicly announced beforehand. Clergy refusing or subsequently retracting would be "rebels against the law," forfeiting their positions, salaries, pensions, and rights as "active citizens." Nonjurors would also lose their eligibility for other public office. This edict caused further outrage, but again, the clergy found it hard to resist effectively. On 27 November, Barnave, as "president" of the Assembly, distributed so many president's "white cards," admitting "paid idlers" specially "recruited" by Jacobins to deride the clergy, held the ultraroyalist press, that holders of opposition "red cards" could find scarcely any seats. Packing the galleries created an intimidating atmosphere, which contributed to the Right's defeat. The decree on oaths passed, albeit with the king prevaricating as to whether to assent.[67]

The next day, Abbé Grégoire, appearing in the Assembly and leading sixty other curés, took the new oath, swearing to "maintain with all my power the French Constitution and especially the decrees relative to the Constitution of the Clergy." There was nothing in the Civil Constitution, affirmed Grégoire, that contradicted Catholic doctrine.[68] But most clergy disagreed, since the oath's wording failed to mention either spiritual supremacy or the papacy. An alternative "serment civique" was proposed in the Assembly on 2 January by the bishop of Clermont, a leading opponent on the Assembly's Ecclesiastical Committee (and vehement foe of Jewish emancipation). Under his proposed formula, ecclesiastics would swear to uphold both the Constitution and the Constitution of the Clergy "excepting those points depending fundamentally on the spiritual authority." This prompted a tumultuous debate in the Assembly on 3 and 4 January 1791. The Assembly must stipulate that the reforms would not infringe the Church's "spiritual authority," demanded the Right, led by Cazalès. "Impossible," retorted Mirabeau, since what the clergy calls "spiritual" the Assembly terms

"temporal."[69] Consequently, apart from Talleyrand and another prelate, the remaining forty-four prelates in the Assembly all refused the
oath. A far larger proportion of the lower clergy in the Assembly fell
into line, swayed partly by Grégoire, but most refused, joining the bishops in a mass walkout. Altogether, only one-third of the clergy in the
Assembly, eighty-nine allowing for several agonized retractions in subsequent days, acquiesced. These then became the leadership of the new
"constitutional" Church.[70]

Rejecting the bishops' protests, on 4 January 1791, the Assembly
ruled that the positions of all "ecclesiastical functionaries" refusing the
sermon civique would be declared vacant and their places and salaries
transferred to clergy who *were* willing to swear. This was a decisive moment, for most of the old episcopate and much of the priesthood were
now breaking permanently with the Revolution. The bishops' compromise formula was rejected outright just as firmly by the center under
Barnave and Charles Lameth, it should be noted, as by the democratic
republicans. For both center and Left, acknowledging any authority as
overriding the Constitution was simply inadmissible. Only seven out of
France's 135 bishops complied, among them Louis XVI's former chief
minister, Cardinal Loménie de Brienne, archbishop (now reduced to
bishop) of Sens who, however, had been a friend of the philosophes
and was a notorious nonbeliever.[71] With all "ecclesiastical functionaries" in the now twenty-four Paris parishes required to take the oath on
Sundays 9 and 16 January 1791, tension in the capital remained acute
for weeks. According to the journal *Le Creuset*, published by the Cordeliers firebrand, James Rutledge, there was no religious motive behind
the nonjuring clergy's resistance, only worldly calculation.[72] On 9 January, the churches were packed. To prevent disturbance, infantry and
cavalry detachments were stationed outside all the main churches. Surrounding streets were patrolled from six in the morning. Twenty-eight
of the fifty-two curates in Paris, a bare majority, swore allegiance initially, though some afterward retracted, placing the nonjurors slightly
in the majority.[73]

Both jurors and nonjurors were applauded and inveighed against,
though most Parisians, reportedly, wanted the curates to swear. The
Paris theaters at this juncture staged deliberately provocative plays like
Calas, ou le fanatisme, the *Rigueurs du cloître*, and *L'Autodafé, ou le tribunal de l'Inquisition*. These performances were frequently watched by
audiences provided with free tickets. In this way, an already considerable popular antichurch constituency was extended. Emotions ran high,

but in parishes where the curate refused the oath, he was allowed to explain his objections and protected from demonstrators. At the large Church of the Madeleine, nearly all the attached clergy refused, declaring colleagues acquiescing to be "false priests."[74] At one point, bent on smashing the presses of *L'Ami du Roi*, a hostile crowd gathered to assail the Abbé Royou's home but was prevented by the National Guard. On 27 January, the republican-led Paris assembly of "electeurs" was summoned for 30 January to decide how to replace curates refusing the oath.[75]

Altogether, the number of ecclesiastics in France refusing the oath was probably correctly estimated by Malouet in July 1791 at between 20,000 and 30,000, or slightly under half the 60,000 or so ecclesiastics in France.[76] Of a total of 23,093 priests, in forty-two departments, comprising around half the area of France, 13,118 took the oath while 9,975 refused. While overall approximately 55 percent of preaching clergy in France took the oath, the picture varied markedly from region to region.[77] At Bordeaux, more than half the clergy acquiesced, while at Limoges only five out of twenty-three priests did so, and at Rennes only one.[78] In the Paris basin outside the capital, and in the Dauphiné, jurors slightly predominated, while in Paris itself, nonjurors were a slight majority. Among professors and directors of the Paris seminaries, all but two refused. Besides Alsace-Lorraine, Brittany, and the West, nonjuring clergy heavily dominated in Artois and French Flanders, the high incidence here reflecting the already prevailing antagonism toward the Revolution rife among the less educated in these areas.[79] In Provence, by contrast, some 80 percent of the clergy complied, and in Basses-Alpes and Loiret more than 90 percent. However, in May 1791, the balance shifted back somewhat against the *constitutionnels* due to the pope's explicit condemnation, which prompted many reluctant jurors to retract, a reversal vigorously encouraged by Royou and the ultraroyalist press.[80] Approximately 10 percent of clergy who had sworn the oath retracted again following the pope's intervention.

While the bishops of Blois, Chartres, and Besançon backed the Assembly, accepting the new diocesan and parish boundaries and the oath, most sitting bishops, including those of Soissons, Quimper, and Amiens, condemned the Civil Constitution outright. Bishop Machault of Amiens had publicly repudiated the Rights of Man since August and, since October, boycotted the Assembly.[81] The first two new constitutional bishops were inaugurated in Paris on 24 February.[82] In the eyes of the revolutionary leadership, bishops should no longer be figures of splendor and rank but candidates of merit and talent, a respected elite embodying popular sovereignty and the Rights of Man. "Where the former bishop of Rouen was the product of the nobility and the court," explained *La Feuille villageoise*, "the new one is a product of liberty and virtue."[83] These 1791 episcopal elections were undeniably real contests, and the gap between the old and new bishops reflected a striking contrast of social background and qualifications, despite some vigorous canvassing. In the contest for the new bishop of Lyon (Rhone-et-Loire), in March, Mirabeau and the Paris Jacobins urged the affiliated Lyon club to broadcast the merits of their ally, Adrien Lamourette (1742–94).[84] Like Fauchet in Calvados and Grégoire in Loir-et-Cher, Lamourette cut an impressive figure among those elected to the new episcopate. Fauchet's election to the diocese of Calvados, after a fierce contest against two other worthy contenders, caused a "véritable scandale" among the devout. Compared to this apostle of "fanaticisme révolutionnaire" and "soiler of religion with impious doctrine" whose "seditious and blasphemous harangues" maintained that Jesus Christ had been crucified by "the aristocrats," the Jacobin Club, according to Royou's *Ami du Roi*, was an academy of wise men.[85]

The old aristocratic episcopate either emigrated or was expelled. By late April 1791, some sixty new "constitutional bishops" had been installed, each election memorably celebrated with considerable pomp. The new bishop of Troyes was inaugurated on 16 April before vast crowds, departmental National Guard contingents, and deputations from regional administrative bodies, besides local Jacobin clubs.[86] Most new bishops elected during these months *were* indeed well-qualified, conscientious men, drawn from parish clergy or teaching orders, whose upward mobility had been blocked before 1789 by the prevailing aristocratic system.[87] However, the position of the new constitutional episcopate was seriously weakened by Pius VI's Brief *Quod aliquantum* on 10 March 1791, which condemned the constitutional bishops and fulminated against the Revolution in every respect. The further papal condemnation on 13 April and conclusive Brief *Caritas quae* on 4 May removed any lingering doubt: the pope repudiated the French church reforms unreservedly, proclaiming the Civil Constitution of the Clergy altogether "schismatic and heretical." Lay bodies could not pronounce on spiritual matters. Only the nonjuring, anticonstitutional episcopate was recognized by the pope. All elections of "constitutional bishops," past and future, were declared annulled. Priests complying with the imposed oath of loyalty must retract within forty days or face suspension by the Vatican. The previously in camera papal condemnation of the Rights of Man on 29 March 1790 was finally published.

In remoter provinces, oath-swearing and transfers of dioceses and parishes dragged on for months amid mounting resistance. In the far southwest, the bishops of Tarbes, Dax, and Bayonne all departed during May 1791, the last setting up a focus of opposition in Spanish Pamplona.[88] In the Var department, though most clergy eventually complied, all four bishops, those of Toulon, Fréjus, Grasse, and Vence, refused and departed for Italy.[89] Likewise in Corsica where the bishoprics were reduced from five to one (Bastia), no prelate would take the oath. The new constitutional bishop, Ignace-François Guasco, elected by 105 out of 215 electeurs on 8 May, was previously provost of Bastia cathedral. His installation provoked some of the ugliest rioting resulting from the Civil Constitution of the Clergy witnessed anywhere in France, culminating on 2 and 3 June 1791 in the sacking of the bishop's palace. In response, Corsica's presiding revolutionary hero, Pascal Paoli (1725–1807), ordered a heavy-handed repression known as the *cocagna di Bastia*. Paoli could not, however, prevent Guasco from being subsequently firmly boycotted as a "détestable schismatique" by most of the island's womenfolk. Later, stranded by Paoli's defection from the Revolution, on 23 December 1794, a beaten and dejected Guasco underwent the humiliation of public retraction and implored the pope's forgiveness.[90]

With the royalist insurrections of late 1790 at Aix, Lyon, and Toulon, religious strife spread across France. The Revolution had made France a "véritable république," observed the *Chronique de Paris* in July 1791,[91] engulfing the country in a struggle pitting ultraroyalists against anticlerical liberal monarchists, and both these against republicans and authoritarian populists; and in this vast, complex, and escalating ideological conflict, religion inevitably played a central part. The first of the Assembly's special commissions to recalcitrant regions, to accelerate implementation of revolutionary decrees, was commissioned in January 1791 to stabilize Alsace, one of the most agitated border areas. Three commissaires, including the young judge Hérault de Sechelles, later a prominent figure in the Revolution, were assigned broad powers in both Alsatian departments (Haut and Bas-Rhin) to deal with a dire situation. At that point, numerous officers from Alsatian garrisons were defecting, and Strasbourg's many refractory priests were deliberately fomenting Catholic resistance to the Civil Constitution of the Clergy. Rioting in Strasbourg on 3 January, partly aimed against Protestants, followed rumors that holy relics were being removed from one of the city's most venerated chapels.[92] The commissaires' arrival in Colmar on 3 February, a town where most people reportedly opposed the Revolution, precipitated a furious popular outbreak that was dispersed only with difficulty.[93]

To add to the commissaires' difficulties, Cardinal Louis de Rohan, the former archbishop of Strasbourg, strongly backed by the Strasbourg cathedral chapter canons (all princes of the German Empire and even richer and more aristocratic than the canons of other regional capitals) colluded with the émigré armed force under the princes of the blood encamped across the Rhine.[94] The cardinal-archbishop had officially been dispossessed of his former extensive jurisdiction and "rights" either side of the Rhine, but devout Catholics remained unshakably loyal to him despite his immense revenues and princely status, luxurious lifestyle, uninhibited gambling, and overt incitement of Catholic resistance to the Revolution.[95] Against Rohan's wishes, the commissaires aimed to enforce the constitutional oath and ensure orderly elections and the inauguration of the resulting two new bishops of the departments of Haut and Bas-Rhin, though most Alsatian priests remained loyal to Rohan and refused to acknowledge the new prelates. Nonjurors did not scruple to mobilize popular bigotry against Protestants, Jews, and Anabaptists as a way of opposing the Revolution.[96] On 26 March, there was a riot inside Strasbourg cathedral, beginning with a violent quarrel in the sacristy between a former curate, loyal to Rohan, and his replacement, installed by the new constitutional bishop, François-Alfred Brendel, who had assumed office the day before. Rohan had issued a circular commanding Catholics not to obey the "schismatic" bishop elected by Strasbourg's primary assembly, a "vicious and scandalous election" in which local Lutherans participated. Refractory clergy, dominant in the seminary and local monasteries as well as the cathedral chapter, helped Rohan retain his authority from a distance and generally incite "fanaticisme."[97] By late May 1791, the situation in Alsace had scarcely improved. Services conducted by constitutional clergy were widely boycotted in favor of refractory clergy. The opposition of those believing they "are defending religion when they are merely being blindly subservient to refractory ecclesiastics" remained so extensive the departmental directoire in Strasbourg requested five thousand National Guard militia from the interior of France to help secure the lesser Alsatian towns, especially Colmar, where the bons citoyens were losing out to Catholic militants.[98]

In terms of tradition, canon law, and papal authority, the recalcitrant parish clergy were justified. In February 1791, the *Feuille villageoise* published the views of a village priest—styled by Cérutti an *ignorant* and fanatic—who had refused the *sermon civique*. But from a purely Catholic standpoint, the priest was surely correct. The quarrel concerned the very existence and status of separate spiritual authority. The republican press pursued its quarrel with the réfractoires throughout France, denouncing "fanaticism" and broadcasting the sermons of pro-Revolution priests, assuring Catholics the Church's true traditions and teachings *were* being respected. In its issue of 10 February 1791, *La Feuille villageoise* printed the sermon of the curé of Aujargues, reminding parishioners that Jesus urged submission to worldly powers and that "our dogmas are still what they have always been," the mysteries the same "mysteries" as before: "our faith has suffered no infringement; the belief of our fathers remains our belief today."[99] The difficulty with this insistent message was that it was untrue.

Furthermore, constitutional clergy and réfractoires alike found themselves in an extremely weak position from which to defend the Church's remaining interests, because centrist liberal monarchists and democratic republicans, despite disagreeing about virtually everything else, largely converged on church affairs. Over the winter of 1790–91, the Assembly, dominated by "moderates" led by Barnave and the Lameths, goaded a reluctant monarch into embracing their secular, liberal monarchist ideology while the Church further fragmented politically and theologically: jurors opposed nonjurors, the latter comprising approximately 45 percent of the total French clergy.[100] The constitutional clergy in turn divided between a small faction backing Fauchet, Lamourette, and Grégoire, aligned with the Left republican democrats, while the rest backed the constitutional royalist moderates. Yet by embracing the Civil Constitution, jurors at the same time opened the door wider to the new radical Christian ideology propagated by Fauchet, Grégoire, and Lamourette, who equated Christianity with democracy. Those on the Left, viewing the Civil Constitution as just a half measure, often openly cast doubt on the loyalty of the constitutional clergy. "What we know of their morality and past conduct, through so many unfortunate experiences," affirmed the *Chronique de Paris*, induced hard-core republicans to consider the loyalty to the Revolution of practically all the Catholic and Protestant clergy as distinctly dubious.[101]

A particular worry to Condorcet and his colleagues were the *sophismes adroits* and "maximes les plus inconstitutionelles" inculcated into the thousands of theology students attending France's 140 seminaries. With their job prospects massively curtailed, their instructors exhorted them to fight la philosophie moderne and its secularizing doctrines, and oppose the *parti révolutonnaire*, however they could, openly or behind the scenes. After the pope's pronouncements, "priestly fanaticism and vindictiveness" were, by June 1791, causing widespread turbulence, not just in Alsace-Lorraine, Provence, Artois, and Corsica but to an extent everywhere, most worryingly in Normandy, Brittany, and the Vendée region.[102] Doubtless, uncooperative churchmen deemed themselves the wronged party and not as rebels subverting the state. But it was difficult for the revolutionary leadership not to consider them outright "rebels." In and around Nantes, by December 1791, local clergy, it was reported to the Assembly, were actively fomenting discord, ostracizing elected constitutional clergy, dissuading men from joining the National Guard, and encouraging defiance of the law.[103]

For several months, from January 1791, the battle "over the oath" and inauguration of constitutional clergy was undoubtedly the issue that most agitated French communities at the provincial and village level. Open opposition to the church reforms further intensified the revolutionary leadership's anticlerical sentiments and profoundly dismayed pro-Revolution priests like Lamourette, who was convinced the papacy had made a fatal mistake.[104] Before being ousted, Bishop Sebastien-Michel of Vannes in Brittany, like other soon-ejected bishops of neighboring dioceses, in February 1791 commanded the clergy to denounce the reforms in their sermons. The Assembly's proceedings, local peasants were assured, would blight their crops and cause sterility throughout the land. Sacraments administered by civil clergy were null and void and, worse, sacrilegious, and would cause the sick to die. As for the newly elected "bishops," these were heretical; the only correct response was to boycott the churches, cemeteries, and confessionals, and fight.[105] Numerous nonviolent—and soon also violent—demonstrations ensued, especially by infuriated women expressing pro-réfractoire sentiment. When the leading revolutionary figure at Montpellier, the mayor Jean-Jacques Durand, proceeded to install the new constitutional curés, he was stoned by furious women and injured.[106] When the curate of a church in Troyes convened a meeting to explain his opposition to the Civil Constitution in March 1791, an official enforcing the law was driven off by an irate female mob screaming support for religion.[107]

No one failed to notice the Revolution's growing blanket hostility to the faith of the majority. The revolutionary press professed not to be anti-Catholic. Officially, it lambasted only recalcitrant clergy, accusing nonjurors of shamelessly fanning popular fanaticism, ignorance, and superstition, including anti-Protestantism and anti-Semitism.[108] But its comments were often indiscriminately hostile. Citing the backlash against Joseph II's 1780 toleration decree, granting religious toleration to the Hapsburg Empire's Protestants and Jews, *La Feuille villageois* denounced not just Austria's conservative bishops but all bishops, alleging that "the episcopacy is the most dreadful aristocracy and most odious privileged elite that has ever existed."[109] Even a paper intended for simple, uneducated villagers regularly slipped into comprehensively anti-Catholic rhetoric. Refractory clergy responded in kind. The legislature claimed to honor Christ's name, but how was it composed? It was evidently stocked chiefly with atheists and irreligious men—Freemasons, skeptics, Protestants like Barnave and Rabaut, and an unspecified leader who was "a Jew."

The Revolution could scarcely avoid acting to weaken the episcopate as a social force and suppress obstreperous remnants of the cathedral chapters, monasteries, and seminaries. A supplementary ecclesiastical reform edict on 7 June 1791 engineered a huge further fall in ecclesiastical employment: the Assembly ruled that each cathedral, the ecclesiastical hub of every department, could have no other regular paid parish priest than the bishop himself.[110] At the same time, all the Revolution's leading figures acknowledged the need to harmonize the Civil Constitution of the Clergy with freedom of thought, belief, and expression. Some advocated a gentle approach, others more forceful methods. Sieyès publicly criticized the Civil Constitution and the way it was implemented, deploring use of coercive methods and the onset of a persecuting attitude contrary to the spirit of freedom of conscience.[111] The Assembly agreed to adhere to the policy of toleration and not act against refractory priests celebrating mass and preaching within existing Catholic churches or establishing separate congregations. Over the next two years, the principle that "prêtres non-assermentés," refractory priests, remained "citizens" enjoying all the rights of citizens, "provided they remained subject to the law," was broadly respected. (Organized persecution did not commence until after June 1793.) In the Revolution's early years, refusing the oath incurred only loss of salary, exclusion from the public Church, and the obligation not to publicly condemn the Assembly, reforms, or constitutional clergy.[112] An Assembly decree of July 1791 reaffirmed the rights and freedom of the *prêtres non-assermentés*, except that, like former monks forsaking their vows and reentering private life, they must not reside within thirty leagues of any border (because of the security risk). If residing closer to a border, they had to move inland and notify the municipalities where they had previously been of their new locations.[113]

In his Brief *Quod aliquantum* of 10 March 1791, Pope Pius VI comprehensively condemned the philosophical principles underpinning the Rights of Man, religious toleration, freedom of expression and the press, and the Civil Constitution of the Clergy, accusing the National Assembly of "heresy" and perpetrating "schism."[114] The idea that men enjoy an "absolute liberty" regarding their religious views and freedom to think independently about faith and morality rather than submit to ecclesiastical guidance and authority, and the constraints imposed by Original Sin, the pope declared a "monstrosity." The Brief *Caritas* of 13 April further condemned the principles of elections and democracy applied to the Church.[115] The Revolution's measures amounted to changing the universal discipline of the Church, overthrowing the hierarchical order that lay at its heart and transforming the character of the episcopate. Loménie de Brienne, who renounced his cardinal's hat in March 1791, was declared an apostate by the papacy the following September. The departure of the papal nuncio from Paris in late May 1791 marked the final rupture in relations between the papacy and the Revolution and also, if only privately at first, between Louis XVI and the Revolution. It was a break not healed until Napoleon's concordat with the Church in 1801.

CHAPTER 8

The Feuillant Revolution

(July 1791–April 1792)

The Feuillant coup of July and August 1791 was the constitutional royalists' last and most vigorous attempt to capture the Revolution. A heavy reverse for the Left, the episode began with an ugly incident on 17 July 1791 when some six thousand people convened on the Champs de Mars to sign a petition. Acting against the advice of Robespierre and most Jacobins, with the latter still profoundly divided and weakened, the petitioners urged the Assembly to withdraw their exoneration of the king. Their radical, forthright petition demanded France become a democratic republic, republicanism being "the masterpiece of human reason." Never would they recognize Louis XVI as rightful monarch, they swore, unless his kingship was first endorsed by the nation's voters. Orchestrated by the Cordeliers and Cercle Social, the crowd comprised mainly Cordeliers, Dantonistes, and "Brissot" Jacobins with some Hébertistes, Orléanists, and mere curious onlookers.[1]

The scene was peaceful enough initially until four thousand men of the Paris *National Guard* arrived under Lafayette, accompanied by Mayor Bailly, brandishing a red flag proclaiming martial law. Lafayette commanded the crowd to disperse, all such gatherings being banned. The largely unarmed crowd greeted this with shouts of "à bas le drapeau; à bas les bayonnettes!," provoking scuffles and then stone-throwing.[2] The militia responded by firing first blanks, and then live volleys, converting the affray into a hideous massacre. Bailly afterward admitted to eleven or twelve killed, but far more were "impitoyable-ment massacrés," insisted the Cordeliers newssheet, besides fifty bullet-ridden wounded left strewn over the field. Soon, wildly exaggerated reports circulated that claimed there were four hundred dead.[3] Foreign agents had paid troublemakers to "mislead" the crowds and stoke the unrest, Bailly assured the Assembly. Most deputies applauded him, several expressly condemning Brissot and Danton. Barnave congratulated the National Guard on its "courage" and "fidelité," he and his colleagues believing that with this show of severity they had finally quashed "le parti républicain."[4]

Placards denouncing the radical democrats as "des factieux" inundated Paris. If their tactics were deplorable, Lafayette and Bailly were at any rate right that most Frenchmen preferred monarchy and a moderate course, rejecting the republicanism of the crowd-mobilizing Cordeliers and Cercle. Monarchical sentiment prevailed too at the divided Jacobins, especially among Robespierre's followers, despite a powerful speech by Brissot arguing that the Dutch and English revolutions of the sixteenth and seventeenth centuries foundered precisely through vainly attempting to overthrow monarchical despotism without eradicating monarchy.[5] In the Jacobins, Robespierre, while vehemently critical of the Feuillants, defended the existing Constitution, assailing Brissot, Condorcet, Paine, and Carra for laboring distinctions between "monarchy" and "republic," which signified little to him and nothing to ordinary people. The term "republic" was divisive, savoring of an unappealing intellectual dogma, inducing distraction and causing unnecessary loss of life. Robespierre squarely attributed the Champs de Mars massacre to what, to him, was Brissot's overblown republican zeal and intellectualism. Robespierre frowned on the efforts to promote republican ideology,[6] but had not yet acquired that unchallenged grip over the club, later to be the springboard of his power. Outraged republicans blamed the once republican-minded Lafayette and berated the Assembly as "l'assemblée anti-nationale." The Champs de Mars' name, proposed the *Journal du Club des Cordeliers*, should be changed to "Saint Barthélemy des Patriotes."[7]

With Robespierre's Jacobins rejecting republicanism, the moment for a general crackdown by Barnave, the Lameths, and their allies was adroitly chosen. Planned or not, "this bloody catastrophe," as Desmoulins called the massacre, triggered an organized repression, sustained for many weeks, aimed at crushing support for democratic republican equality. The moderates went all out to neutralize "Brissot, Carra, Bonneville, Fréron, Desmoulins, [and] Danton," and for a time, recorded Desmoulins bitterly, succeeded in convincing Assembly and public alike that these were "dangerous agitators." Committed republicans were appalled to find that the Assembly contained so many "charlatans" and "tartuffes" ready to betray the Revolution's basic principles. After 17 July, those still publicly championing the people's cause in the Assembly found themselves diminished to a tiny rump, the rest proving an abject "mass of nobles, priests, intriguers, preachers of counter-revolution and imbeciles."[8] To add insult to injury, the repression proceeded under Lafayette, who earlier, as Condorcet's and Paine's associate, had joined them in denouncing the "vile individuals" with whom he now collaborated, assuring Desmoulins, Paine, and others "a hundred times" that he too was a "republican." "Oh, Mirabeau where are you? Why had I never believed you," exclaimed Desmoulins, "when you assured me the Lameths were just clever, ambitious scoundrels ready to betray liberty at the first opportunity?" Seeing the ungrateful masses turn "against their most illustrious champions," those cherishing the "sacred flame of patriotism and sublime passion of liberty" in their hearts could only "grind their teeth" at their fellow citizens' baseness.[9]

Prussia and England, admonished Barnave, actively sought to destabilize the Revolution by distributing cash to troublemakers. Suspects accused of instigating "sedition" included a Prussian Jew named "Ephraim" who supposedly disbursed funds among the unruliest.[10] Several Cordeliers members were arrested. The police searched for Danton, Desmoulins, Robert, and his wife, Louise Kéralio, among others. Danton fled to England where he remained for several weeks. Desmoulins, rumored to be in Marseille, hid in Paris.[11] Although the red flag of martial law was removed from before the Paris town hall on 7 August, repression continued for weeks after that. Additional suspects were arrested on 9 and 10 August, including Momoro and Etta Palm, the latter denounced by the *Gazette universelle* as the daughter of a Groningen innkeeper, very free with her favors, who pretended to fight for *la liberté démocratique* but who was actually a paid agent of the stadtholder.[12] Posters proclaiming republicanism, most notably Condorcet's and Paine's newssheet *Le Républicain*, were everywhere ripped down. So grim was the atmosphere, the Cordeliers closed their doors. Both its public and committee meetings lapsed.

For a time, much of the republican revolutionary press ceased publication. Desmoulins's journal vanished from the scene, as did that of Lanthenas. *Le Républicain* appeared for the last time on 23 July, six days after the "massacre." The *Journal du Club des Cordeliers*, launched on 28 June, ended on 10 August, having appeared in only ten issues, its bitter penultimate issue on 25 July. On 28 July, the Cercle suspended the *Bouche de fer*.[13] Especially dismaying to Desmoulins, Sophie Condorcet, and others was the seeming fickleness of the masses. Paris street posters from which people had earlier garnered shreds of "bonne doctrine," now shamelessly regurgitated the same ludicrous rigmarole about "subversion," "foreign agents," and "anarchy" emitted by the Feuillant press. From 17 July, the public backed the moderates, adopting their rhetoric so completely, complained Desmoulins, one would suppose counterrevolution had conquered every mind. He encountered a crowd near the Théâtre de la Nation yelling at passers-by "Vive le roi!"—presumably paid to do so. With this, the philosophical observer could recognize the common mass in the streets for what they were—"sans caractère, imbecile, inconstant comme l'onde," unworthy of the courageous men braving a thousand perils to enlighten them.[14] "Pétion, Robespierre, Buzot, Brissot, Danton and all the writers previously deemed *Patriotes*," the people passively accepted, had, like Palm, been "bribed" by foreign governments.[15] A fitting constitution, Desmoulins realized more than ever, can only emerge "in the light of la philosophie," the sole means to rescue men from "the depths of slavery and incomprehension for which they seemed born."[16]

That the Revolution of the democratic republicans, the Rights of Man, and a free press faced virtual extinction appeared all too likely during late July and August 1791. The Feuillants seemed to have conquered the court, the Assembly, royal ministries, the Paris Commune, the National Guard, and the army.[17] There remained, estimated Desmoulins, only twelve to twenty stalwarts in the Assembly who publicly defended basic rights and democracy, leaving the moderates virtually a free hand to pervert the principles of 1789. Sieyès, totally isolated on the Assembly's constitutional committee, remained stolidly silent throughout the summer.[18] Desmoulins could not fathom how the few remaining "upright deputies" did not resign in protest.[19] Barnave, Bailly, Lafayette, and the Lameths looked poised to fortify constitutional monarchy and marginalize the voice of the streets and the clubs, rendering the legislature as absolute as the British Parliament.

Yet, despite everything, Desmoulins could not believe the masses had definitively abandoned the ideals of 1789. "No, I cannot believe this frightful apathy, in which some vile schemers have plunged us, can last." The Revolution cannot have been permanently reversed by modérantisme. The "torrents of light a free press has cast on society" cannot have been altogether expended "sans profit pour le genre humain."[20] He was right. Looking deeper, the Feuillant ascendancy, beset from Left and Right, was more fragile than appeared superficially. July's repressive measures violated the Rights of Man, but they could not continue indefinitely and dismayed dozens of provincial "Jacobin" clubs. This was reflected in the Feuillants' failure to carry most provincial Jacobin clubs more than partially with them. They succeeded in causing widespread hesitation and some defection from the Jacobins in most French towns. Many provincial Jacobin clubs, or "Friends of the Constitution," had sprung up during the past two years, and now not only divided but dropped drastically in membership for the remainder of 1791. Some were paralyzed for months by the Feuillant walkout. But a number resisted vociferously. A petition to the Assembly, signed by the Clermont-Ferrand Jacobins and read on 30 July, demanded the immediate lifting of the 15 July emergency restrictions and warned that their future compliance with the Assembly was strictly provisional. The *pétionnaires* praised those "courageous" leaders—Pétion, Robespierre, Grégoire, Buzot, and Camus—who, together with other deputies embracing the "unalterable principles of justice and liberty," opposed the "liberticide" measures of the "moderates."[21] Toward the end of the summer, the Feuillants lost momentum with a marked drift back to the Jacobins, replete with profuse apologies for having been "misled." A missive from the Beaune Jacobins dated 31 August congratulated the Paris club on welcoming back all "true friends of the Constitution" into their midst: briefly "seduced" by the Feuillants, "a factious horde" everywhere causing damage, Beaune's Patriots now rejoiced at being received back.[22]

Equally bad for them, the Feuillants failed to sway the Assembly's Right. No less than 290 conservative Assembly deputies, according to Royou's nephew, Stanislas Fréron (1765–1802), who edited the important *L'Orateur du peuple*, openly scorned the Constitution in favor of ultraroyalism and denied the principle of popular sovereignty and their own titles as "representatives of the people." These "slaves of a perjurer and tyrant" detested the upstart Barnave and the Lameths.[23] Monarchist papers, labeling the king's attempted escape "a flight" and stressing Louis's repudiation of the Constitution, challenged the Feuillants no less than philosophique republicanism or sansculotte populism. In recent months, claimed Carra, *L'Ami du Roi* had inundated France with "over 20,000 copies daily," distributed free, particularly in small towns and the countryside where reactionaries thought it easiest to sway the uneducated.[24] Royou also went into hiding. Raiding *L'Ami du Roi*'s offices, the National Guard seized its papers and interrupted publication for two weeks. Madame Fréron was detained for a week and intensively interrogated about links with émigrés and refractory clergy.[25] Orders were issued for Suleau's arrest and that of another leading royalist journalist.[26]

If the Feuillant center ground possessed a well-tried, formidable ideology in Montesquieu, moderation and veneration of the British and American models, this faction proved simply too narrow in its appeal, and too powerfully besieged from Right and Left, to succeed. While Right, Left, and center wrestled to steer the Revolution, within the clubs the fight between republicanism and populism raged with ever greater intensity. Condorcet, together with Brissot, Paine, and a younger editor, Achille du Chastellet, had brought out *Le Républicain*'s first issue in early July (before the "massacre"), claiming the king, by deserting his post, had effectively abdicated. The nation could never trust a man who violates his oath, fraudulently obtains a false passport, and disguises the monarch's person under a domestic's attire. Had Louis's flight been directed by others? What did it matter whether he "is an imbecile or a hypocrite," idiot or scoundrel, he was equally unworthy of the "fonctions de la royauté."[27] Very different from oligarchic republics like the United Provinces, Venice, and Genoa, Paine eulogized genuine republicanism as government by representatives based on popular sovereignty and the Rights of Man.[28] Saving the thirty millions it cost annually to keep the king in splendor would provide means to reduce taxation and curb the political corruption threatening the Constitution. Their efforts to publicly promote republicanism were checked, though, by the sheer difficulty of disseminating the Revolution's core values effectively and widely enough.

Condorcet later recalled (in particular to Joseph Lakanal) that his and Paine's public "debate" with Sieyès in July in *Le Républicain*, over whether a republic or constitutional monarchy was preferable, was a bogus exchange, concocted between the three of them to create a public sensation. Sieyès had supposedly advanced arguments for constitutional monarchy in *Le Moniteur* in a deliberately halfhearted manner, which enabled Paine and Condorcet to demolish them for the public's benefit. Certainly, Sieyès scorned Barnave's thesis that the executive power needed reinforcement as a check to the legislature, a reversion to Montesquieu and the British (and United States) systems wholly contrary to his ideas.[29] His was a virtual republicanism. Yet there remained some difference between his stance and the more forthright democratic republicanism of the Brissot faction. Wary of formal republics, Sieyès still preferred to retain a monarchical figurehead. Under monarchy, he argued, echoing Montesquieu, individual liberty flourishes more than in a republic.[30]

Opposing Barnave on one side and Robespierre on the other, Condorcet, Brissot, Carra, Cérutti, Paine, and the others strove to enlighten men about républicanisme, stressing the vices, abuses, and structural deficiencies of royalty, which only "prejudice" and "ignorance" stubbornly defended. Had conventional thinking been eradicated earlier, contended the second issue of *Le Républicain* on 10 July, the king's flight would have inspired general jubilation, not consternation, but reason had unfortunately not yet sufficiently penetrated. So much "superstition" surrounded the Estates-General's opening in May 1789 that liberty's "true friends" had virtually despaired of such a nation of "idolaters." The republican-minded had persevered for more than two years "to open the nation's eyes" sufficiently for them "to see that the monarch could conspire against the monarchy itself," as finally had happened.[31] Yet even now the majority remained deaf to the republican message. The people had reverted to "idolatry," remarked the *Chronique de Paris*, describing the "adoration" of 6 September when crowds surrounded the Tuileries endlessly shouting "Vive le roi!" So limitless was popular "superstition" that to most people, Louis, with "his great virtues," had made sufficient amends for "his flight."[32]

Barnave responded vigorously to the republican challenge, attacking la philosophie and the republican journalists almost daily, noted the *Chronique de Paris*, publicly disdaining their "metaphysical ideas" and dismissing Brissot as a "philosophical bigot," no better than the religious bigots.[33] On the question of republicanism, furthermore, he received Robespierre's tacit support, besides that of the Right. Malouet violently denounced *Le Républicain* as flagrant subversion of the Constitution (which it was). But if *Le Républicain* was unconstitutional, retorted Carra and the democrats, why did Malouet not condemn the *Mercure politique*, Royou's *Ami du Roi,* and other "royalist poison"? These "infamous journals" continually vilified the Rights of Man, preaching subservience to king and pope instead of elected representatives. Deputies, supposedly sworn to uphold the Constitution, like Maury, Cazalès, and the ex-bishop of Clermont, noted Carra, regularly contributed to such anticonstitutional royalist papers.[34]

Insisting they alone correctly represented the Revolution's principles, the Feuillants strove to consolidate their hegemony, plastering their foes with accusations of foreign plots and street protests arranged by paid "agents." Paris seethed with reports of suspicious foreigners who perverted public opinion, Pétion and Brissot having supposedly sold their souls to foreign powers for cash.[35] Such incessant "conspiracy" rhetoric, protested Brissot, was designed to mire everyone aiding the people against the true "enemies of the Constitution."[36] Exploiting every popular prejudice, Feuillants also spent heavily, printing and posting up in the streets at night a daily newssheet, *Le Chant du Coq*, which poured vituperation on Brissot, Pétion, and other radical leaders, though Feuillant efforts to harnass Marat's technique were blunted by undaunted democrats tearing the posters down or adding the letters "uin" in ink, altering its title to "Chant du Coquin."[37]

Virulent political-ideological rivalry inevitably also seeped into the theaters whenever they staged anything of a serious nature. Consequently, they met with pressure from the Left to do so, and from the center not to. One commentator, disgusted by this Feuillant stratagem, was the fervently Rousseauiste, antifeminist journalist Louise-Félicité Kéralio-Robert (1757–1821). She had already scornfully derided Feuillant notions of "liberté des théâtres" in an article in the *Mercure national* on 22 April 1791. When the Assembly proclaimed liberty of the theater, it had wanted to multiply France's "schools of patriotism" and cultivate "virtue." Yet, under the Feuillants, establishments dignified with the name of "theater" offered only light entertainment, comedies, and comic operas, spectacles crammed with frivolity and love affairs featuring "actresses utterly without shame." It was not because the people were tired of public affairs that they imbibed mainly "immoral spectacles," but because staging "such rubbish," scheming theater managers expected, would deflect theatergoers from public affairs. According to Jean-Jacques, censorship belonged exclusively to the people. If the people were sovereign, they must direct the theater with a firm hand, mobilizing the patriotic press to eliminate insignificant and "immoral plays" and compelling the staging of patriotic dramas. The people must unflinchingly counter the "poisoned cup of corruption" their foes used to lure them into neglecting their most essential interests. Fervent Rousseauistes, like Mme. Kéralio-Robert, supported the sansculottiste drive for uncompromising popular censorship.[38]

Nevertheless, politicization of the theaters gradually advanced. In late July 1791, the director of the Paris Théâtre de Molière, following audience protests, promised to stage only "plays that fortify the public spirit and love of liberty."[39] Disturbances at Marseille in October 1791 obliged *comédiens*, supposedly infused with *incivisme*, not to perform plays "unworthy of a free people," nor forget "what they owe to a Constitution that has lifted them from ignominy."[40] A riot at the Paris Théâtre du Vaudeville in late February 1792 revived the earlier furor surrounding Chénier's *Charles IX*. A one-act farce entitled *L'Auteur d'un moment*, by François Léger, satirized Chénier under the name "Damis," represented as an untalented, inordinately vain author who won undeserved success by manipulating "the credulous public" by using "friends" and the journals.[41] The Parisian public, the play suggested, was undiscriminating and easily led by the nose. Set in a garden adorned with statues of Corneille, Racine, Voltaire, Montesquieu, and d'Alembert, the farce revolved around Damis imagining a bust of himself being installed beside these great figures. But he had made a ludicrous error. At the close, the bust carried onstage by four damsels dressed in white, accompanied by a choir chanting the author's praises, is Rousseau.[42] A Feuillant attempt to disabuse theatergoers of Chénier's talent, it rebounded on the Vaudeville. On 24 February, the audience rioted, occupied the theater, and burned copies of the play, forcing the theater director to remove the piece from the repertoire.

France's liberal monarchist Constitution, long ready in outline, was finalized only on 2 September 1791. Sponsored by the Feuillants and backed by Robespierre, the Constitution was vigorously criticized, not only by the republicans and ultraroyalist Right but also by the Assembly's strict constitutionalists under Malouet and Maury. The legislature, objected Malouet, had solemnly promised on 9 July 1789 to frame the new constitution "in concert with the king." Instead, they had excluded Louis from their deliberations, stripping France's monarch of most of his authority, and now brutally confronted him with the simple, straightforward choice of acceptance or rejection.[43] The Assembly should opt for a genuine constitutional monarchism, not this emasculated, bogus monarchism. The center deputies and Left shouted Malouet down. To present the Constitution to the king, the Assembly sent an imposing delegation of sixty, headed by Barnave, Alexandre Lameth, Sieyès, Pétion, Rabaut, and four bishops.[44] If there was much opposition, public enthusiasm, at any rate, seemed distinctly encouraging.

On 14 September, the king appeared in person to accept the Constitution, following a last angry exchange in the chamber with Malouet urging the whole legislature to stand during the king's speech as a mark of deference to the monarch. Malouet could greet the king on his knees if he wished, retorted one deputy, but he would not. Louis entered and read his acceptance speech, standing at the podium, only belatedly noticing everyone else was seated. Stopping, covered in confusion, he then also sat to finish his speech. Royal assent was the signal for jubilant festivities throughout France. To a rousing chorus of "Vive le roi!," the whole Assembly accompanied Louis triumphantly back to the Tuileries.[45] Bells were rung throughout the capital. Public illuminations lit up the Tuileries and Champs-Élysées.[46] The Paris theaters put on special performances, some gratis, to celebrate the occasion. All the towns of France erupted in celebration. The people looked entirely reconciled to constitutional monarchy even if the Constitution's festive inauguration itself subtly reflected the continuing tension between Feuillant strategy and authentic loyalism. When the news reached Rouen, reported Helen Maria Williams, lodging there at the time, "cannons were immediately fired, the bells of all the churches rung, and the people displayed their joy by crowding the streets with bonfires, at the distance of every eight or ten yards." Strangers stopped and congratulated one another in the streets, which resounded with cries of exultation, among which the sounds of "Vive le Roi des François," however, were almost lost amid those of "Vive la nation." "C'est la nation qui triomphe. C'est la constitution qui triomphe."[47]

The Constitution accepted, the democratic republican Left, despite their considerable reservations, promised to abide by it. "We have fought as long as possible," declared the *Chronique de Paris* on 6 September, "to prevent certain features that have been included in the Constitution, but now it is finalized we should remember its deficiencies only when an opportunity arises to revise it. It is still a great achievement with freedoms based on the Rights of Man, a landmark in mankind's history, 'la plus belle constitution connue' among those so far existing, that one would be happiest living under."[48] If radicals had hoped to minimize the "civil list" to prevent its functioning as an instrument of corruption (as in Britain) for manipulating legislature, ministries, judiciary, and military command, most people entertained few such worries. Much stress was laid, by Feuillants especially, on the need to forget former divisions and extend a general amnesty over past misdeeds. The word "royal" reappeared in numerous public place-names and on buildings from which it had been effaced in late June and July, including the Académie Royale de Musique and the royal lottery. As befitted modérantisme, though, in other instances, including the Jardin du Roi and the Bibliothèque du Roi, former usage lapsed, these remaining the Jardin National and the Bibliothèque Nationale.

Many ambiguities remained. What, for example, was the proper form for receiving the king in the Assembly? There could be no Assembly deliberation in the monarch's presence, stipulated the Constitution, since he constituted a different category of "representative of the nation" than the deputies. Hitherto, the Assembly had adhered to ancien régime procedure, the king occupying the largest chair before any deputy could sit. But the new rule, held the Left, should be that deputies seat themselves and don hats simultaneously with the king, the latter seated in a chair resembling that of the Assembly's weekly "president," to symbolize equality. Hérault des Séchelles, a notorious trimmer, so antirepublican (at this stage) that he even refused to dine with Lafayette, having abandoned the Jacobins, condemned this radical suggestion as unconstitutional and insulting to the monarch's august status. Among the most opportunist, as well as learned, of the deputies, Hérault, assuming the Feuillants had won a solid ascendancy, clashed in the Assembly over this with the republicans and won the ensuing vote. On 7 October, the king was duly received following the old etiquette and seated in an oversized chair.[49]

The people's jubilation was real. Hérault des Séchelles's calculations looked realistic. Montesquieu had not yet been torn up by the roots after all. But the Feuillants lacked the means to consolidate a solid preponderance. They could offset neither the soon-reviving republican press onslaught to their Left nor Catholic fervor to their Right—nor manage the growing confusion and frustration of the people—except by means of an outright repression, which, under the newly proclaimed Constitution, now had to be lifted. Finalizing the Constitution did not remove either its basic contradictions or the swelling mass of republican literature pointing these out. If most Frenchmen preferred monarchy, monarchist support remained hopelessly divided between four distinct and incompatible blocs—Barnave liberal constitutionalists, Malouet strict constitutionalists wanting government by the monarch, ultraroyalists, and Robespierre authoritarian populists. Barnave, the Lameths, and Lafayette championed an authentically moderate monarchical constitutionalism but one lacking genuine royal and aristocratic elements, at war with the aristocracy and Church, backed by an unreliable Assembly majority and purely ephemeral wave of popular support. If helped by the vacillating, divided state of popular opinion initially, their Feuillant revolution became increasingly fraught and embattled, as angry scenes and demonstrations in streets, cafés, and theaters all over the country constantly reminded onlookers. Almost anything staged that seemed to allude to "democracy, the captivity of the king and the new revolutionary order" exacerbated the nation's divisions. Theater crowds split, audiences partly yelling, "Vive le roi!," partly chanting, "Vive la nation!"[50]

A harmonious system of mixed government based on no clear principles worked splendidly in Britain in the 1790s. But there, most people willingly deferred to the long-standing aristocratic and monarchical norms of ancien régime society. Indeed, by 1791, British public opinion had worked itself into a veritable frenzy of loyalism and "king and Church" fervor, readily joining in the hounding of democrats and trials of radical reformers. English reformers and democrats were almost all supporters of the French Revolution, but by supporting democracy, they clashed directly with Parliament, found themselves ostracized by polite society, and fiercely denounced by nine-tenths of the people. In quantity, English conservative publications overwhelmingly outweighed radical literature.[51] Nothing like this kind of deference and ideological solidarity existed in France. Rather, ideological bankruptcy contributed both to the narrowness of Feuillant support and the Feuillants' repeated but fumbling attempts to curtail freedom of the press, theater, and expression.

With the new Constitution operative, the emergency restrictions on expression and press liberty had to be lifted. If, during July and August, Brissot, Condorcet, Desmoulins, Paine, and the others found themselves relatively isolated in opposing restoration of the king's powers, and constitutional monarchy,[52] much of the Assembly, it turned out, was only briefly swayed by Barnave, the Lameths, and Lafayette. Fatally for modérantisme, during the autumn of 1791 the embattled space between the Left's democratic republicanism and the Right's ultraroyalism rapidly began to disintegrate.[53] By abandoning "the Revolution" to align with the court, the Feuillants simply ensured that many prominent figures, initially siding with them but taking the Revolution's core principles seriously, fairly soon entertained second thoughts. Roederer figured among those who joined the Feuillants briefly but quickly reverted to the Jacobins. The Cordeliers resumed their meetings and their attacks, and most of the newspapers that had suspended operations recommenced publication, disparaging the regime with redoubled energy.

The Cercle Social, however, never resumed, and its journal, the *Bouche de fer*, never reappeared. This was because by the autumn of 1791 the partly depleted but also now no longer centrist-dominated ranks of the Jacobin Club, with ties across the whole of France, alluringly beckoned. A club conveniently self-purged of monarchists and moderates by the Feuillant defection, and hence much closer than before to the *sociétés populaires*, especially after opening its regular meetings fully to the public in October 1791, the Jacobins offered a wider, more regular platform than the old Cercle for reaching the public, influencing proceedings in the Assembly and organizing beyond Paris.[54] Filling the gap left by the departing Feuillants, from the late summer of

1791, however, loomed two rival impulses. On the one hand, Brissot, Carra, Cloots, Condorcet, and other key Cercle figures renewed their efforts to concert a broad, democratic counteroffensive; opposing them was the antirepublican, populist phalanx led by Robespierre and Marat, which was equally striving to fill the vacuum. While populist elements gained ground in both the Jacobin and Cordelier clubs, in his speeches during the summer of 1791, Robespierre continued to reiterate that the republican system was unsuitable for France.[55]

The mounting conflict between democratic republicans supporting Brissot, Condorcet, and Bonneville, on one side, and populist authoritarians adulating Marat and Robespierre, on the other, is usually presented by historians as one between "moderates" and radicals. This is mainly because for the most part, Marat's and Robespierre's supporters stemmed from lower social strata, especially shopkeepers and artisans, and used harsher and more uncompromising language than the republicans, more frequently demanding economic measures favoring the poor and punishing the rich. But in terms of the philosophique values of 1789, and eagerness to champion freedom of press, individual liberty, and racial and gender equality, it was the Brissotin Jacobins, not the Maratiste or Robespierre Jacobins, who were France's democratic radicals and republicans. The populist factions, in fact, were not really republican or democratic at all but, rather, unrelentingly authoritarian, in Marat's case expressly aiming at dictatorship and stringent censorship, a group not just ready to accept but actually demand abandonment of basic freedoms.[56] This did not seem especially off-putting at first. In classical republicanism, and in Machiavelli—as well as Rousseau—"the dictator" is powerfully projected in much the same terms as the Roman Republic had envisaged, that is, the dictator is the all-powerful leader who steps in with the support of the plebs when dire peril threatens and the normal procedures of the republic need to be interrupted; he is a leader who is given emergency powers to be used only to restore the suspended Constitution. Dictatorship was not conceived of as replacing or overriding the Constitution. Insisting on the need for a dictator in 1791–92 did not therefore necessarily meet with the widespread revulsion and negative response it would elicit later and normally has in the West following the rise of full-blown fascism in the early twentieth century.

In book 4 of the *Social Contract* Rousseau admonishes that "only the greatest dangers can counterbalance the risk of disturbing the public order" and that one should "never suspend the sacred power of the laws except when the salvation of the *patrie* is at stake," warning that the "dictatorship" he expressly sanctions as a necessary tool in certain circumstances should be rigorously delimited by being instituted only for the briefest duration. However, Rousseau also firmly insisted that when dire peril looms, it is essential to embrace "dictatorship," entrusting supreme power to the "worthiest person," in order to save the patrie. Harping on Robespierre's alleged "incorruptability" in 1791–92 was thus directly linked to Marat's tireless reiteration that the gravest peril surrounded the nation. In this way, the cult of the supreme leader adroitly exploited the doctrine of dictatorship expounded by Rousseau, as well as the unawareness of the least educated.[57] Authoritarian populists venerating Rousseau, unlike Left republicans, continually urged undivided unity, their goal being to eliminate dissent and repress political foes. Marat's and Robespierre's supporters, noted Royou in October, were increasingly refining what he saw as their favorite ploy—passing off their own opinions as "the will of the people" and the volonté générale by organizing street petitions and addresses backed by crowds carefully recruited and paid for the purpose. This "ridiculous charade," instead of reflecting, proved a highly effective means of dragooning popular opinion in the capital.[58] The growing weight of orchestrated, organized populism also left those to the Left voicing genuinely republican sentiments increasingly vulnerable to Robespierre's charge that they were elitists disseminating ideas alien to ordinary folk.[59]

While the evidence of the provincial clubs and their factional splits does confirm that Marat's admirers derived predominantly from a lower social stratum and tended to be less educated than Brissotins, it also shows that the sansculotte elements providing the populist campaign's muscle formed a considerably narrower social base than the democratic Jacobins who were championing basic freedoms. Local splits between philosophique republicans and populist authoritarians in the provinces during late 1791 and 1792 reveal that the sansculottes, as a regularly active, politicized social segment, were actually a strikingly small minority. This was partly because the poorer, less literate classes were generally less interested in and able to follow politics than the more literate, and partly because only modest numbers could be mobilized by the dragooning organizational methods employed by the Robespierristes. In Bordeaux, the socially humbler Club National was undoubtedly staunch in supporting Marat's and Robespierre's cult of the leader throughout 1791–93, but was also much smaller than the Récollets, a club led by town notables but accommodating a wide spectrum of

(a)

(b)

(c)

(d)

Figure 5. (a) Robespierre, (b) Pétion, (c) Danton, (d) Marat.
(a) Portrait of Maximilien de Robespierre. © Musée Carnavalet / Roger-Viollet / The Image Works. (b) French school, portrait of Jérôme Pétion de Villeneuve, 18th century, pastel and charcoal. Musée Carnavalet, Paris. © Roger-Viollet / The Image Works. (c) Constance-Marie Charpentier (1767–1849), *Georges Danton (1759–1794)*, oil on canvas. Musée Carnavalet, Paris. © Musée Carnavalet / Roger-Viollet / The Image Works. (d) Joseph Boze (1744–1826), *Jean-Paul Marat (1743–1793), French Politician*, oil on canvas. © Musée Carnavalet / Roger-Viollet / The Image Works.

Bordeaux society with a sizable membership, in December 1791, of 1,533.[60] At Libourne, near Bordeaux, there were likewise two societies of Friends of the Constitution, the Club National, affiliated with the Bordeaux club of that name, fervently Maratiste but tiny, with just a score of active members in 1793, and Libourne's principal club, led by men of standing, admittedly, but also more broadly based, numbering in the hundreds.[61]

In Nantes, one of France's foremost commercial centers, with a population of some sixty thousand, there were again two clubs, a dominant Club Mirabeau, which included all the "enlightened" men of the city, and a more plebeian but also much narrower society. The Club Mirabeau's leaders, significantly, were professionals, not merchants, Nantes merchants, like those elsewhere, evincing scant enthusiasm for the Revolution or its principles. Although at Nantes the old mercantile elite were not swept aside to the same extent as at Saint-Malo, business remained politically inactive, preferring to defend commercial interests by avoiding association with political and social reformers.[62] The top hundred or so great merchants and slave-dealers, and leading civic office-holders, many of whom were ennobled under the ancien régime during 1788–90, had in fact identified with France's "aristocracy" rather than the bourgeoisie proper. During 1791–92, they remained neutral as far as possible while also fiercely resisting Brissot's and Condorcet's endeavors on behalf of black emancipation.

Angers likewise featured two societies of Friends of the Constitution, an "eastern" and a "western," with a clear division along class lines, the western club comprising mainly artisans and shopkeepers. The eastern Jacobin club was more affluent and educated, yet also larger and more diverse, until after June 1793 when the western club became the organ of the militant sansculottes and the eastern club was suppressed. At Aix-en-Provence, formerly the capital of Provence, the situation was similar, only here the influence of Marseille, chief focus of populism in the Midi, registered strongly, and the originally larger club eventually disintegrated, its remnants absorbed into the popular club, the Antipolitiques. The Marseille club gained special importance owing to its ability to dominate lesser clubs over a large region. Unlike other main centers, Marseille featured only one revolutionary club throughout, but this fragmented early on and was captured in stages during 1792–93 by a minority group resembling those dominating the artisan clubs elsewhere. Like Lyon and Toulon, Marseille was the scene of growing class tensions during 1792–93 and a deliberate whipping up of resentment of the affluent among the poor by certain club leaders. At Rennes, a single revolutionary club suffered a triangular split in the summer of 1791 between Feuillants controlling the club until 1793, vigorously championing modérantisme while battling rival Brissotin and Montagnard factions, but, as elsewhere, the Brissotins were the larger of these two, and, during 1792, the more important bloc.

The fact that some clubs drew their membership predominantly from the lower classes during the Revolution does not mean, then, that they were left-leaning or reflected the opinion of a large slice of society; it usually signified, rather, that they were given to an aggressive cult of the leader of an emphatically authoritarian kind. Everywhere in France the most plebeian and least literate were the readiest to support both counterenlightenment ultraroyalism and the (in some ways not dissimilar) antilibertarian collective consensus political culture of Marat and Robespierre. Uncompromising stress on unity and the ordinary man's sentiments, chauvinism and anti-intellectualism, became devices for crushing dissent and building dictatorship; Montagnard populism resembled less a libertarian, emancipating movement than an early form of modern fascism. However, during late 1791 and early 1792, this tendency within the Revolution was not yet sufficiently powerful to bid for dominance. The political weakness of plebeian Jacobinism was reflected for the moment in both its limited popular support and the equally conspicuous fact that no major editors, pamphleteers, and journalists of the kind supporting the Revolution's core values would align with them.

Barnave and his colleagues relied especially on a harmonious working relationship with the king, his ministry, and the court, continually urging Louis to publicly display loyalty to the Constitution. With much of the old aristocracy gone, the Feuillants needed the newly arisen wealthy landowners and property-owners, and those with privileged status as "active citizens," to rally on behalf of moderation, money, and monarchy. But despite being held under a restricted suffrage of which they were the sole champions, in the autumn national elections for the new legislature, the Feuillants performed relatively poorly, swaying few beyond the affluent bourgeoisie. When the new legislature convened in October 1791, moderates were dismayed to find they lacked sufficient votes to dominate the legislature effectively. Barnave, Bailly, and the Lameths themselves were excluded from the new body as ex-constituants, owing to a self-denying ordinance of the previous legislature. They now wielded their dwindling influence largely indirectly through the Feuillant Club and secret contacts with the court, especially the queen. During early 1792, well-founded suspicion that the Feuillant leadership was actually in league with the court, and conspiring against the Revolution, scheming to revive aristocracy (to an extent criticized even by Lafayette), further discredited the Feuillants in the public's eyes.[63]

Overall, the September 1791 elections greatly strengthened the republican Left in the legislature and sharply polarized the Assembly into Left and Right factions, to the horrified indignation of others beside the Feuillants. The new Assembly shocked all sensible people, protested *L'Ami du Roi*, revealing a disgusting "enthusiasme" for philosophy. Among the new Assembly, hardly anyone of genuine social rank remained. How could a legislature with no dukes, bishops, or parlementaires, and scarcely any high bourgeoisie, genuinely uphold monarchy, position, and wealth? The reality, observed *L'Ami du Roi*, was that France was now utterly divided by the Revolution into two separate warring parts: on one side stood all the solid bourgeois, traditionalists, nobility, clergy, royalists, and lovers of order and peace who wanted monarchy, religion, and the old order and broadly boycotted the Feuillants; on the other, still more hostile to the Feuillants, surged what Royou termed the *horde philosophique*—"all the men of letters, bankrupts, criminals, atheists, deists and Protestants."[64] To ultraroyalists, the Feuillants were reprehensible but those principally responsible for the country's appalling plight were indubitably the vile "impostors deceiving the people with the hope of a happy future"—the democrats.

On 1 October 1791 the inaugural meeting of the new legislature, known as the Assemblée Législative, was attended by 434 deputies. When the rest arrived, of a total of 767, all newcomers to the legislature, only around 170 deputies (22%) aligned firmly with the Feuillants, affording a slight edge over the roughly 150 (20%) deputies designated "Jacobins," the rest forming a floating, vacillating center with another hundred or so deputies favoring the Right. The 150 Jacobins included many now-prominent national figures renowned for their role in press battles, mass rallies, and Paris politics, including Condorcet, Vergniaud, Guadet, Chabot, Fauchet, Lamourette, and Brissot, the last elected for the department of Paris, winning his seat with a considerable majority over rivals.[65] Money and court influence could doubtless lure some additional deputies into the Feuillant camp. By early 1792, the pro-Jacobin bloc had contracted somewhat, and Feuillant allegiance swelled to around a quarter. But Feuillant primacy remained conspicuously vulnerable to the frequent shifts of mood among the large floating "centre."[66]

To secure legislation after October, the Feuillants could afford to ignore Marat and the populists but had to work with Brissot and the republican faction, which by late 1791 had consequently acquired a firm toehold on power.[67] A major further success for the Brissotins and setback for the Feuillants were the Paris municipal elections of November 1791. A triumph for the Left, a whole new set of civic officers replaced those previously espousing constitutional monarchism. Pétion replaced Bailly as mayor; Louis-Pierre Manuel became city procurator, and Roederer procureur-général of the department. Democratic republicanism, instead of being routed by a thumping majority, was daily winning new triumphs. These results enhanced the weight of the municipality and major clubs, rendering them, even more than the Assembly's anti-Feuillant contingent, watchdogs of the democratic cause. So decisive a shift in Paris induced several key Assembly centrist deputies to abandon their previous ties with the Feuillants. A sure sign the Feuillants were losing their grip were the gyrations of trimmers like Hérault de Séchelles, who now abandoned monarchism and Montesquieu with no less alacrity than he had adopted them just weeks earlier. On 2 December 1791 he too secured readmission to the Jacobins.

In the French Revolution, Left republicanism predominated in the prorevolutionary press and key Paris cafés throughout. Now it dominated in the press, cafés, and (again) in the Paris municipality, and loomed strongly also in the legislature and the Jacobins. Democratic republicanism more than ever infused and defined the essential values, conscience, and principles of the Revolution. But could la philosophie moderne mobilize the people? Failing to control legislature, press, provincial clubs, or the Paris municipality, the only recourse left to the Feuillants in their efforts to renew their ascendancy was to try to emasculate the press and clubs. A measure proposed by Le Chapelier on 29 September 1791, which renewed aspects of the July restrictions, forbade the clubs to appear collectively in public ceremonies or to interfere with the work of government. Additional clauses designed to prevent the clubs from printing their debates and interacting so flagrantly contradicted the Constitution and the Rights of Man, and were so vehemently inveighed against by Brissot and the Jacobins that they had to be dropped.[68] Le Chapelier became a particular hate figure among the Jacobins and Cordeliers, who responded by appealing to the public. From 14 October 1791, when the Jacobin Club held its first ordinary meeting fully open to the public, populists and the Left both disseminated their ideologies more widely. During late 1791 and early 1792, the Jacobins provided a collective, joint platform for Brissot, Carra, Lanthenas, and others associated with the Cercle Social (now an offshoot of the regrouped Jacobins), and the Brissotin Paris Commune, as well as Danton, Marat, sansculottisme, and Robespierre.

With the new Constitution and legislature inaugurated, the door was opened wide to debate, republican criticism, and schemes for renewal. The *Chronique de Paris* issue for 18 September approvingly reviewed Volney's chief work, *Les ruines, ou meditations sur les révolutions des empires*, a major text begun ten years before but only published in August 1791. A materialist meditation on the tendency of governments to prey on their own populations, in the tradition of Diderot, d'Holbach, and Raynal, the book stressed the *perversité de gouvernements* and analyzed the processes by which men are tyrannized over, misled, and abased. Volney also discussed how the dismal cycle of oppression and superstition might be broken and emancipation achieved, inaugurating "a century of astonishment for vulgar minds," fright for tyrants, and hope for everyone.[69]

The Cercle, no longer a forum for meetings, continued as a publicity machine. It established yet another journal designed to promote the Left's ideals nationally, the *Chronique du mois*, in November 1791, which appeared also in German translation. This journal's goal was to demonstrate how human science and knowledge little by little, thanks to printing, could transform and ameliorate the human race "en général," driving what Bonneville called Man's "marche universelle à la perfection sociale." Spreading democratic republican ideas abroad, explained Lanthenas, another of the editors, would enable the French to assist all peoples eager for liberty, eventually to realize that "perpetual and universal peace [la paix perpetuelle et universelle] so desired and yet so far off," proclaimed by Raynal and for which so many illustrious men (Diderot, d'Holbach, etc.) had striven.[70] Edited by Bonneville, Lanthenas, and a dozen others, including the Scots republican John Oswald (ca. 1760–93), in Germany this remarkable periodical was dubbed the "journal of the fourteen editors." Son of an Edinburgh coffeehouse owner, Oswald, secretary to "the British Club" in Paris until its near dissolution in February 1793, was a former Indian army officer who had traveled widely among the Kurds and Turkomans, detested high-society cravats and wigs, and supported vegetarianism and Irish independence from Britain. A declared atheist, he believed people were becoming more enlightened, and the more enlightened they became, the more they would collaborate.[71]

While the sociétés populaires diffused a destabilizing "exaggeration of principles" derived from la philosophie, which underminded the Constitution, complained a Feuillant journalist in May 1792, hardly any papers defended the Constitution "in all its purity."[72] In fact, even the best Feuillant papers, such as the *Gazette universelle*, edited by Antoine-Marie Cerisier (1749–1828), who seemed to Brissot and Carra to have abandoned his own earlier radicalism (derived from the philosophes), failed to make much impact despite a huge ministry subsidy and artificially boosted print-run .[73] Their media campaign faltering, the Feuillants again tried to overawe their detractors by muzzling liberty of the press. In May 1792 a prominent liberal monarchist, Comte Jacques-Claude Beugnot (d. 1835), urged suppression of Marat's paper, a recent issue of which summoned the troops to massacre all their generals. He also urged the legislature to prohibit Prudhomme's *Révolutions de Paris*, Fréron's republican *Orateur du peuple*, and all "contemptible authors" attacking the Constitution, including those of the royalist *Gazette de Paris*, *Mercure politique* (Mallet du Pan), and *Journal Général de France* (Louis-Abel, Abbé de Fontenay). Right and Left, held the Feuillants, were all propagating the same "poison" under sundry ideological labels, instilling contempt for and inciting violence against the Constitution. Royalist and populist authors were accused of inciting civil war in collusion with provincial aristocratic papers like the *Mercure anglais* of Rouen, the *Journal de Lyon* edited by Carrier, and "all the papers that infect the south."[74]

Over the winter of 1791–92, most Frenchmen were less concerned with the regime's growing instability than more pressing problems. The disappointing harvest of 1791 caused a substantial rise in the bread price, which by September was already spreading alarm and distress.[75] Equally, owing to clawing back of the August 1789 abolition of feudal rights encouraged by the Feuillants, the countryside remained plunged in endemic unrest. Action was urged to make state loans available to poor tenants to help buy out seigneurial dues still protected by the law and eliminate harvest obligations, the triage, and other seigneurial "rights." On 27 October 1791, the Assembly appointed a fresh committee to examine landowners' claims and charters, but until March 1792 this body simply continued its predecessor's policy. Marat's *L'Ami du peuple* and the populist press contrasted the growing hardship besetting the poor and low-paid with luridly depicted scenes of corruption and excess in high places. The royalist opposition also highlighted the growth of poverty. More than three-quarters of France's inhabitants, exclaimed Royou in February 1792, were sunk in deprivation, misery, and fatigue, most, in his opinion, regretting the Revolution and longing for the ancien régime to return. The dreadful "night" afflicting France for three years would soon end, he predicted, thanks to the mounting distress. Royalism would triumph with the aid of economic hardship: "thus will the reign of *philosophisme* pass [ainsi le règne du philosophisme va passer]."[76]

Adverse conditions in the countryside weakened the procourt, pro-landowner "moderation" espoused by the Feuillant leadership. Liquidating all remaining remnants of feudal dues was urged by both the populists and the Jacobin Brissotin philosophique faction. On 11 April 1792, an Assembly majority admitted that in 1789–90 the Revolution "had only cut off the branches of the feudal tree leaving its trunk intact."[77] Joining forces, democrats and populists finally overcame the obduracy and legalistic procedures encouraged earlier. The burden of providing documentary proof that dues were not property rights inherent in ancient grants of land was transferred from the tenant to the landowner, who now had to provide documentation proving "rights" were his property—a crucial shift. A further decree of 18 June 1792 comprehensively canceled seigneurial rights to collect dues on land sales.[78] After the Brissotins finally gained full control of the Assembly in August, seigneurialism was finally eradicated. On 25 August 1792, all remaining dues and perquisites, water rights, dues on water mills, and rights of passage by waterways were abolished without compensation in perpetuity.[79]

With the Feuillants fatally weakened, the real question now was who would triumph in the three-cornered contest to inherit their mantle, the horde philosophique, the populists, or what Royou saw as France's solid majority of all classes preferring order, tradition, and religion. Over the winter of 1791–92, populist authoritarianism did not yet appear to be in the running for control of the Revolution. To Royou, it seemed as certain that ultraroyalism and religion must triumph as that the democrats and already-receding Feuillants must fail.[80] The horde philosophique would assuredly be beaten back. For decades, the philosophes had vaunted their wisdom, promising readers that with la philosophie on the throne, all people would be happy. In 1789, God had permitted la philosophie its brief triumph, surmised *L'Ami du Roi*, doubtless so as to undeceive mankind about this wretched dream, thereby ridding mankind permanently of an illicit, deceptive hope. Already the people were abundantly disillusioned, witnessing the effects of the flight of the nobles and the rich. The only way to revive employment, wages, and fortunes was to repair the appalling injustice done to "the orders," the nobility, clergy, and parlementaires. Catholics must rise and overwhelm the Revolution.[81]

Democratic republicans, of course, had every reason to dread the twin Counter-Enlightenment onslaughts of ultraroyalism and Marat-iste authoritarianism. "We are far from having toppled the throne of prejudice," lamented Lanthenas in April 1792. "With regard to emanci-pating peoples from error and lies, what has really been achieved since that memorable day, the 14 July? 'L'instruction publique,' which should be the first of our concerns, has been the last thing we have been oc-cupied with."[82] Children's education remained vital, but still more so, held Lanthenas, was that of the adult population. If men's rights are to triumph, genuine Patriots must "unite, laboring in town and country at public instruction, something so necessary and so neglected." Under the ancien régime, education sought to inculcate as little genuine knowledge as possible while fostering every error "with the aid of which aristocracy and despotism maintain themselves." Britain, instead of per-fecting her constitution, had lapsed back into the "mire of aristocracy" after 1688, for no other reason than that the English failed to become enlightened. Ethics and politics are vital spheres of awareness since the "universal regeneration of Man" involves creating a society "where the only cult is that of truth." The Revolution's true tool was the sociétés populaires, the sole instrument able to prevent "the aristocracy of the rich" from consolidating its grip.[83]

The election results of the autumn of 1791 blighted the prospects of all who had vested their hopes in "moderation" and liberal monarchism. Unable to provide either stability or economic normalcy, the Feuillants equally failed to secure genuine collaboration with the court due to their policies on émigrés and religion, while Brissot and Clavière seized the initiative in the Assembly by encouraging the king to go to war with Prussia and Austria. Once the outbreak of war looked certain toward the end of 1791, it was a foregone conclusion that the Brissotins would eventually enter the revolutionary government, sharing power with the Feuillants and the king's advisers. Meanwhile, the divisions within the regime only widened. Brissot's motion, put forward early in the new As-sembly on 9 November 1791, stipulating that all émigrés holding offices or commands who failed to return to France by 1 January 1792 would be deemed "traitors" and their property would be subject to confisca-tion, markedly aggravated the feuding between Feuillants and the Right, and also between the king and the Assembly. Brissot, who proposed the measure with precisely this objective in mind, advocated stringent action against émigré princes, aristocrats, army officers, priests, and other functionaries who had gone abroad purposely to fight the Revolution, and leniency for misled "simples citoyens" who fled without taking up arms against the Revolution.[84] Condorcet seconded his call for firm measures against the émigrés, who represented a formidable political and military threat and were actively mobilizing opinion against the Revolution in Switzerland, Britain, and Italy, as well as on the Rhine, in the Low Countries, and at Vienna.

Brissotins benefited too from the fragmented, ramshackle revolutionary regime's need to adopt tougher measures against the refractory clergy. The political oath of allegiance to be exacted from priests under the edict of 29 November 1791—blacklisting nonjurors, stripping them of their pensions, and where involved in active subversion, imprisoning them—was rebuffed by the king as well as the ultraroyalist and strict constitutionalist Right. Caught in a maze of contradiction, Louis vetoed the measure against émigrés on 12 November and nonjuring clergy on 19 December, while nevertheless increasingly depending on the Brissotins for his war policy. The Revolution had reached a critical juncture. In March 1792, three "Brissotin" figures, including Jean-Marie Roland (1754–93), an official from Lyon who exercised a considerable influence over the Brissotin faction through his wife's famous salon, and now as interior minister, were brought into the royal ministry. But the long-standing royal vetoes eventually created complete deadlock, paralyzing the Assembly and leading to months of chronic political crisis through early 1792. So grave were the obstacles, by early 1792 the constitutional monarchy had for most intent and purposes ceased functioning. Blocked by the court's lack of confidence in him and sidelined by Brissot's maneuvers, Barnave, seeing the ruin of his schemes, retired from the active political scene in January 1792 and returned to the Dauphiné.

Barnave abandoned his political role and ambitions. He had rejected democracy throughout and, in his speeches, had come to reject philosophisme, continually calling for moderation, but as his writings of this period show, he retained an acute sense of the logic of revolutionary momentum and how economic and social forces combine with attitudes and philosophic awareness to reshape political institutions. No one understood better that it was the expansion of the towns and commerce that had undermined the old aristocracy of the land and created a new political milieu. He wanted his constitutional monarchy to be based on "the new rich," the men of commerce, banking, and industry. But he also understood that there is no such thing as an automatic logic of social forces, and that the final outcome depended on people's ability to conceptualize and respond to their circumstances, needs, capacities, and rights. He and his faction, he knew, could not succeed without mobilizing stronger support and politically defeating the *parti républicain*, whose arguments he had failed to counter.[85]

Meanwhile, in spring 1792, rapprochement between Louis and the Brissotins proved, inevitably perhaps, unhappy, strained, and brief. Military defeat heightened popular suspicion of Louis and still more the queen and court. On 15 May, a Brissotin deputy, Maximin Isnard (d. 1830), revealed that France's military plans had been betrayed to Vienna by individuals inside the Tuileries. Despite the loyalty of most of Paris's population to "liberty and the Constitution," declared Pétion, the new mayor, on 29 May, in a general report on the state of the capital, royalist intrigue and conspiracy were rife among dangerous insurgent elements and a mounting threat. Repeated clashes over the royal veto, and Louis's obduracy in blocking the Assembly's decrees relating to émigrés and nonjuring priests, were followed by reports that the royal guard at the Tuileries, a newly recruited force guaranteed by the Constitution and paid from the civil list, had been illegally composed and deliberately screened to exclude Patriots and include only royalists.[86] In response, on 29 May, the Assembly ordered most of the several thousand men of the royal guard to be disbanded.

That a new major constitutional crisis was brewing, if obvious since November 1791, looked particularly threatening by late spring 1792 due to the military setbacks suffered during early 1792. However one looked at it, the 1791 Constitution was simply unworkable in the circumstances. Like his policy on émigrés and réfractoires, disbanding the palace guard perfectly fitted Brissot's strategy of marginalizing court, aristocracy, and Church, and steering the country toward republicanism. But disbanding most of the guard also convinced the king that, far from accommodating and softening the Brissotins, as he had hoped, his ministry was sliding under Brissot's thumb. As the military situation deteriorated further, yet another key measure was vetoed by Louis. This was the summoning of 20,000 National Guard militia, or *fédérés,* from the provinces to Paris, to facilitate dispatch of more regular troops to the frontier and secure the capital against reactionary elements plotting counterrevolution (including the disbanded royal guard). An emergency measure passed by the legislature on 8 June, the summoning of these 20,000 National Guard militia or fédérés from the provinces to Paris was equally firmly opposed by Lafayette and Robespierre. In theory there was room for pragmatic cooperation between Feuillants, Brissotin Jacobins, and populists, against court and Crown, on fédérés, no less than émigrés and refractory priests. But in practice all cooperation was blocked by the intense jealousy souring relations between the factions and Robespierre's suspicion that the fédérés would simply strengthen the Brissotin hand.

At Marseille, a key ally of Brissot, Charles-Jean-Marie Barbaroux (1767–94), successful lawyer and scholar from a wealthy family aligned with Vergniaud and Mme. Roland, persuaded the mayor, Jean-Raymond Mourraille, to immediately dispatch a column of six hundred armed men, under his command, to reinforce the democratic Revolution in the capital.[87] On 10 June the Brissotin interior minister, Roland, urged on by his politically ambitious wife, Manon-Jeanne, Mme. Roland (1754–93), twenty years his junior, challenged the king with a remarkable fourteen-page letter composed together with (or largely by) her. Their missive stressed the seriousness of the months-long political deadlock since November 1791 and claimed it was caused by men wrecking the Constitution for the sake of misplaced notions of monarchy, religion, and nobility. Use of the royal veto to block the Assembly's emergency measures was turning the "bons citoyens" against the king, and turning the Crown into the abettor of "conspirators against the people." Blind to his real interests, Louis was being misled by malicious advisers and rendering France prey to populist *démagoguistes*. It might be hard to accept curtailment of the royal prerogatives, but the monarch must now make a fateful choice: either he assented to the vetoed edicts regarding nonjuring clergy and the fédérés, making the sacrifices demanded by "la philosophie," or else remain aligned with the selfish, vested interests oppressing the people.[88]

The king was furious to be faced with such an ultimatum. Under the 1791 Constitution, the ministers were responsible to the Crown rather than the legislature. Roland, an unusually honest minister (as even enemies acknowledged), and long a republican, was dismissed three days later, as were Clavière and the third republican minister, Servan, soon afterward (both likewise insisting on the summoning of the fédérés). They were replaced by Feuillants (but now without Barnave), who resumed their failed and hopeless bid to capture the Revolution. With this, Louis finally and irretrievably broke with the Revolution.[89]

CHAPTER 9

The "General Revolution" Begins

(1791–92)

The French Revolution represented an alarmingly disruptive force in international relations from the outset. Since the new French constitutional monarchy, from the summer of 1789, broadly repudiated the principles and precedents on which monarchical Europe based its alliances, treaties, and established procedures for resolving disputes, and professed to be guided in international relations, as in domestic affairs, by the principles of the Rights of Man, friction between revolutionary France and Europe's monarchical courts was inevitably acute. Equally apt to generate friction, the far-reaching European reform programs of the 1770s and 1780s inspired by Enlightenment ideals were everywhere abandoned or reversed by princes and oligarchies from mid-1789, in Germany, Italy, Spain, and the Low Countries alike. This left a widespread legacy of bitterness among enlightened reformers everywhere, often jolting long-standing "moderates" into a defiant stance, which, in turn, translated into pro-French political subversion and support for extending the General Revolution.[1] A vast European war over the Revolution's principles, claims, and actions was thus always a probability before it actually commenced.

From 1789 onward, activists championing democracy and the Rights of Man in Germany, as in Switzerland, Italy, and the Low Countries, were automatic allies of the Revolution, declared enemies of the "Royalisten, Aristokraten und den Priviligierten," as one of them, the Mainz elector's former body physician and professor of medicine, Georg Wedekind (1761–1839), put it. "Defenders of freedom and equality" believing "justice permits me to do whatever does not harm my equal," averred Wedekind, in his 1793 Kommentar on human rights, battled the forces of conservatism like "defenders of toleration" fought intolerance.[2] Prominent German conservatives, like the Hanover enlightened bureaucrat August Wilhelm Rehberg (1757–1836), warned princes that while the new French Constitution might claim to be "monarchical," the radical group responsible for the egalitarian legislation of 1789 were actually 'republicans' wishing to wipe the slate of the political past entirely clean, four principal pamphleteers of 1788, Sieyès, Brissot, Pétion, and Kersaint, being entirely republican in orientation.[3] Brissot, he noted, was obviously a democrat who sought to balance representative against direct democracy already in 1788.[4] The armed conflict into which the international struggle between the Revolution and Europe's princes descended in 1792, was therefore, generally perceived by the sharpest, best informed (surely rightly) as not just inescapable but fundamentally a conflict between monarchy, aristocracy, and religion versus republicanism, democracy, and philosophy.

If diplomatic relations with neighboring European powers steadily deteriorated, there was one foreign potentate the Revolution antagonized at every step—the papacy. For besides questions of church reform and human rights, the papacy was a territorial power in France, as well as central Italy, that possessed two neighboring principalities in the Midi—Avignon and the Comtat Venassin—which the Vatican had every intention of retaining. In the villages and main town of the Comtat, Carpentras, most people remained loyal to Church and pope. But serious strife erupted in Avignon, a city where pro-Revolution sentiment and desire for union with France had gained ground. In August 1790, a virtual miniature civil war broke out. Avignon also posed a thorny problem for relations with ancien régime Europe more generally. The Revolution proclaimed the Rights of Man, promising not to perpetrate unjustified aggression against any neighbor. What justification could there be for dispossessing the pope of a territory uninterruptedly held since the fourteenth century? But while conservative Catholics championed the pope's historic rights, the Left refused to acknowledge them at all. Pétion initiated the campaign to annex Avignon in the Assembly, in November 1790, by claiming the "social contract" is not between ruler and ruled, as most supposed but, as Rousseau taught, between all individuals uniting together to create the social state. By vesting sovereignty in the people, the Revolution, by definition, subordinated the pope's rights and those of rulers everywhere to the people. The *Journal de Paris* agreed, albeit correcting him on one point: it was not Rousseau or Locke (where this idea is not found) who invented this quintessentially modern idea but Hobbes. Hobbes had discovered this pivotal doctrine so destructive of court culture but then failed to make any proper use of it.[5]

Ideology pointed to a prolonged European war, and so did factional interests. By late 1791, most groups within the French political arena were actively angling for war between France and her monarchical neighbors. Some moderate royalists, Lafayette and Dumouriez, most of all, hoped that widening the revolutionary conflict would tilt the domestic struggle advantageously from their standpoint, and enhance their own roles as military leaders.[6] Ultraroyalists and Louis XVI's intimate advisers desired war, deeming this the likeliest way to release king, court, and themselves from the Revolution's tightening grip. War allured all those hoping aristocracy, parlements, and Church would regain their privileges and hegemony over society. Nobody doubted that most aristocratic émigrés wanted war, seeing this as the only way to regain their lands and status. Equally, most Jacobins—though not Robespierre and his circle—saw advantages in launching a European war.[7] After the Feuillant secession, although most Jacobins were not yet republicans, they *were* mostly convinced that war with Austria, Prussia, and the Rhenish states was inevitable or probable and should not be shied away from.[8] France was surrounded by a wall of denunciation and threats. Prussia, Austria, and Britain, not to mention Holland, the Swiss oligarchies, and the Italian states, spared no effort to meddle in the volatile course of events in France.

From October 1791, Brissot publicly urged an ideological war of peoples against princes, or what the *Gazette de Paris* dubbed a "guerre universelle à tous les souverains," partly as a way of undermining the Feuillants, partly to discredit the king, and partly to end France's isolation and aid the republicans and democrats of Germany, Italy, Belgium, Holland, and Switzerland. Louis had vetoed Brissot's measure against the émigrés.[9] The king's obstructionism must lapse once war loomed. But republican ambition stretched even further. According to the royalist writer Mallet du Pan, Brissot's war policy was designed "to gain the opportunity at the first reverse, to accuse the king of collusion with the enemy and force him from the throne."[10] Admittedly, Robespierre and his supporters opposed the talk of war. But at this point they remained a small minority of the Jacobins and had great difficulty convincing others Europe's rulers were not, in fact, planning war. Few believed that Europe's rulers looked on "unmoved," as Royou's *L'Ami du Roi* sarcastically put it, at the "'volcano' vomiting its lava across France."[11] Danton was among those who expressly stated in the Jacobins that war was inevitable. At the same time, for tactical reasons, he and Desmoulins adopted a calculating middle position between Brissot and Robespierre.[12]

In short, the vast international conflict commencing in 1792 was welcomed by most of the French factions for diverse and multiple reasons. The French Revolution, one must constantly bear in mind, was not primarily a "national" occurrence rooted in French society and culture but part of a wider democratic, egalitarian, and libertarian upsurge in all Western Europe, in no way separate from the revolutionary wave engulfing France's immediate neighbors. During the spring and summer of 1790 both Flanders and Brabant, including Brussels, were deeply split between *aristocrates* and *démocrates,* with the latter increasingly adopting the rhetoric and attitudes of the French revolutionaries.[13] In December 1790, as the Austrian forces advanced on Brussels, *La Feuille villageoise* tried to explain the precipitate collapse of the Brabant Revolution to French villagers. Hendrik Van der Noot (1731–1827), the lawyer leading the conservative coalition dominating the Brabant Revolution, urged Belgians to accept the compromise Joseph II's successor as emperor, Leopold, was offering. Belgians submitted to the emperor in exchange for Leopold's agreeing unconditionally to restore the "constitution ancienne," the old South Netherlands constitution of the fifteenth and sixteenth century that guaranteed the ascendancy of the nobility, clergy, and city magistracies.[14] Since the Flemish-Brabantine ancien régime had always favored the "tyranny of the bishops and monks," according to *La Feuille villageoise*, these groups readily jettisoned the Revolution on hearing that privilege, rank, and the old order would be restored.

Against the reactionaries, the Vonckists, "les démocrates" led by Jean-François Vonck (1743–92), tried to rescue the Belgian Revolution under the noses of the returning Austrians. The Vonckists fought to join France in ushering in an age of democratic freedom and equality, or what the antiphilosophe Feller termed "un anarchie parfait," but were crushed by Van der Noot's conservative counterrevolution. Most but not all Belgian popular sentiment came out against the Revolution. South Netherlanders, observed Feller, preferred religion, royalty, and aristocracy to democratic revolutionary values.[15] How could this be explained to the French peasantry? "A revolution led by monks and nobles," the *Feuille villageoise* assured the villages, must end in "slavery." Yet, such "slavery" imposed by mobilizing "credulity and fanaticism" could not possibly last. With la philosophie and la liberté française powerfully entrenched on Belgium's borders, "our good books will little by little chase out both superstition and the monks."[16]

Whether ordinary folk support revolution or counterrevolution, argued *La Feuille villageoise*, is chiefly a matter of whether enlightenment or superstition predominates. Currently, enlightened reform was being abruptly reversed by princely governments and replaced with "credulity." In July 1789, the elector of Mainz, Archbishop Friedrich Karl von Erthal, discarding his earlier scheme to project himself as an enlightened reformer, disavowed reform and repudiated the Enlightenment.[17] The archbishop-electors of Cologne and Trier followed his example, denouncing Enlightenment and revolution and harboring thousands of aristocratic émigrés on their territory, close to France's borders, permitting them to organize armed contingents and actively plan intervention. In December 1789, together with the electors of Cologne and Trier, Friedrich Karl issued a joint patent warning all subjects of the Rhenish electorates and German ecclesiastical states not to demand "rights and liberties" like the French.[18] But there was no way they could prevent Mirabeau, in particular, from gaining an immense reputation in Germany.[19]

Throughout Western Europe beyond France, censorship grew much stricter from 1789 and soon amounted to a concerted repression of radical *philosophisme* in academic and general society. Rehberg warned the princes that it was the brochures and pamphlets of 1788 that had started the Revolution and first introduced the republicanism, the idea of a Declaration of Rights, and the democratic notions driving it.[20] The democratic republicanism threatening to overturn the old order, he further observed, sprang directly from the surge of materialism, atheism, and "moralischen Egoismus" impelled by Diderot, Helvétius, and d'Holbach since the 1770s in Germany as well as France.[21] Those states where enlightened reigning princes had left their subjects relatively free from censorship, like Brunswick-Wolfenbüttel, where the sole explicitly pro-Revolution journal in Germany, the *Braunschweigisches Journal philosophischen, philologischen und pädagogischen Inhalts*, was published, came under pressure to tighten up.[22] To this the small principalities bowed, some quicker, others, like Brunswick, more reluctantly. The *Braunschweigisches Journal* was edited by Joachim Heinrich Campe, the best-known German sympathizer with the Revolution at the time, but an admirer of Sieyès, Mirabeau, and Lafayette, and a liberal monarchist, not a republican.[23]

Persecuting the enlightened constituency in the German secular and ecclesiastical states was effective up to a point, but came at a price. If the Aufklärung of the 1780s was still predominantly "moderate" and deferential to princes, it included a vigorous, radical undercurrent whose

intellectual leaders now faced fierce persecution and state-organized vilification. Even Aufklärer (enlighteners) previously committed to reform
in collaboration with princely authority, perceiving the path to acceptance and reform blocked, became politically and psychologically more
disposed to embrace radical ideas and strategies, and, consequently, the
Revolution. In November 1791, Anton Dorsch (1758–1819), a Kantian philosophy professor and leader of the Mainz Illuminati, fled to
Strasbourg where he was appointed a professor of philosophy, and,
swearing allegiance to the French Constitution, became active among
local Jacobins. Like the Swabian Jacobin journalist and law professor,
Christoph Friedrich Cotta (1758–1838), expelled from Stuttgart a few
weeks earlier, Dorsch plotted political sedition from Strasbourg in the
Rhineland.[24] Among other subversive activities, Cotta edited the Jacobin *Strasburgische Politische Journal*.[25]

Democratic sentiment represented a formidable threat to the existing order everywhere in the German-speaking world, as it did in Italy
and the Low Countries.[26] Radical thinkers and writers, including the
poet Hölderlin, who had links with former Illuminati and wrote several
hymns to Freedom in the autumn of 1791,[27] regularly pilloried former
"enlightened" German rulers and writers who had once supported "the
cause of reason" against "superstition" but now opposed the Revolution in every way. Hamburg-Altona, Berlin, Kiel, Halle, Mainz, Stuttgart, and Aachen were all known foci of radical intellectual ferment.
Such sentiment surged especially among the reading societies, student
groups, professoriate, and former cells of the suppressed secret societies, the Deutsche Union and the Illuminati, before long all seething
with sympathizers with the French republican Left. Some of these figures, including Wedekind, were certainly republican-minded, and some
felt so strongly about the need to assist the progress of the Revolution
across Western and Central Europe that when the French armies began
their advance, they dispatched reports on the state of local defenses and
strongholds to the French commanders.[28] The fact that the backbone
of German prorevolutionary sentiment consisted of professors, scholars, students, and writers contributed to the widely expressed contempt
for such subversive thinking among the German courts and most of the
population.

In December 1791, Volney, scornful of Catherine the Great's rejection of Enlightenment reform, returned the honorific medal she had bestowed on him in January 1788. He addressed a sensational letter to her
agent in Germany, the Baron Friedrich Melchior Grimm (1723–1807),

Diderot's former friend who had, since the early 1780s, rejected the political part of Diderot's radical legacy. Volney decried what he hoped would prove only a temporary alliance of the empress with the "rebels" (i.e., Louis XVI's brothers and aunts, aristocratic émigrés, and exiled French bishops) and the Counter-Enlightenment courts opposing revolutionary France. His tirade against German and Russian court conservatism prompted a ferocious retort in an anonymous pamphlet that appeared shortly afterward at Coblenz, styling Volney and his friends a "lodge" of madmen and Mme. Helvétius, whose dead husband's book had been a major inspiration to the German Illuminati, an "espèce de folle de la moderne démocratie."[29] Germany was suffused with ideological war, a struggle waged on every side, leaving the post-1789 Aufklärung dramatically polarized.

By December 1791, the much-contemplated outbreak of war seemed imminent. On one level, acting as the absolutist monarch he was at heart, Louis sent secret messages to Berlin and Vienna appealing for a general coalition of European powers to invade France and destroy the Revolution.[30] In his capacity as a constitutional monarch, on the other hand, working with his official minsters, he issued stern warnings aimed at deterring the small Rhenish principalities from assisting the émigré military effort. The French Assembly's ultimatum of November 1791, prompted by Brissot, demanding the electors expel the émigré princes' armed contingents from their territories, was a logical reaction to the electors' undisguised zeal for bolstering reactionary royalism, religion, and social hierarchy in France. But threatening the Rhenish ecclesiastical states with unpleasant consequences should they fail to expel all armed French émigrés by 15 January 1792 carried an obvious risk. A fresh French ultimatum in December 1791 obliged the archbishop-elector of Mainz to ask Louis-Joseph, Prince de Condé (1736–1818), commanding the main émigré force there, to depart forthwith. The elector of Trier, though furious about the ultimatum and that his diocesan rights and revenues in Alsace-Lorraine had been annulled, felt obliged to follow suit. But behind the ecclesiastical princes stood Prussia, Austria, and Britain, and these conservative powers were by no means willing to allow, and could not afford to see, the small states of Western Europe become submssive to the requirements of the French revolutionary state.

On 21 December 1791, the Viennese court threatened war in their turn, if the ultimatum to the Rhenish electorates was not promptly withdrawn. Given the hostility to the Revolution emanating from

Vienna, Berlin, The Hague, Rome, Turin, Naples, and Madrid, there was every reason to expect a broad anti-French coalition to rapidly co-alesce. With the Feuillant leadership deeply split over the advisibility of war, and war seemingly immanent, Brissot's strategy had already paid handsome dividends. Desiring war but blocked by the Feuillants, Louis XVI, spurred on by relatives and advisers, halfheartedly adopted an extremely risky strategy. On 10 March 1792, he dismissed his Feuillant ministers and, seeing little alternative, brought in the republicans Roland and Clavière, doubtless hoping republican Jacobins in office would discard their oppositional attitude (which they did not);[31] Louis turned also to Dumouriez, a leading general likewise eager for war, whose military experience derived from the 1760s conflict in Corsica. With Austria refusing any guarantee of peaceful intentions and mobilizing her forces, Louis stuck to his ultimatum.

With both the French court and principal German courts refusing to back down, the revolutionary Left in Paris, assuming conflict could not be prevented anyhow, also believed it could be managed to their advantage. Condorcet afterward wrote that he hated war but voted for Brissot's policy in this instance, convinced it was necessary to wage such a war to make the public see the truth about the French court's nefarious designs and to consolidate the Revolution.[32] His and Brissot's republican campaign of June–July 1791 had failed dismally; an aggressive strategy toward the émigrés and a European war promised to be a more successful way of promoting the republican bloc's fortunes and swinging most of the Jacobin Club behind them. While there was no majority for repudiating monarchy and the Constitution, there was a large majority favoring war, which was a sure means of turning the tables on the Feuillants and bound to split that faction wide open. Some Feuillants sought to avoid war at all costs, believing their plans for constitutional monarchy could work only in the context of peace, while Lafayette and Dumouriez unequivocally sought war.[33] Second, not only would the struggle render Louis XVI's duplicity and treachery as plain as daylight,[34] it would shatter all trust between Feuillants and king and eradicate the aristocracy from their remaining positions of power, ultimately enabling the Assembly to democratize the army, National Guard, Constitution, and hence the entire country.

In addition, argued Brissot in a speech to the Convention on 29 December, Austria and Prussia faced so many internal difficulties they could not wage a sustained conflict effectively. Austria had already displayed both her weakness and her vulnerability to Belgian revolt during the earlier strife in Belgium. France had all the potentates of Europe against her, but she had the people on her side. The Hungarians were restless. "Poland is now bound with a common interest with France" and would be a source of trouble to Russia, Prussia, and Austria alike.[35] As for France's domestic position, war would end uncertainty, compel waverers to take sides, unmask opponents as traitors, and finally discredit the domestic reputations of the émigrés and refractory clergy. It was logical to expect supporters of the 1791 Constitution to split away from a French court seeking émigré and foreign support to overthrow that Constitution on behalf of the old aristocratic order. Brissot's policy was designed to prize Feuillant modérantisme away from conservative monarchism and discredit and defeat both. It was a means of preparing the way for republicanism.[36]

If always a gamble, war could also be expected to enhance the revolutionary élan and cohesion of the National Assembly. Since the Revolution every Frenchman had become a soldier, declared Brissot, which meant that there were six million of them.[37] Equally important for Left republicans, war would reignite the half-suppressed revolutions of Geneva, Aachen, and Liège, and destabilize Zurich (where pervasive resentment against the ruling oligarchy was palpable),[38] as well as the Rhineland and the Low Countries, spreading the "General Revolution" across monarchical, aristocratic Europe. Most Jacobins agreed. There were loud objections, however, from the Montagne—the Jacobin minority opposing Brissot, which acquired that name from their preference for sitting on the Assembly hall's most elevated benches. Montagnards realized that whether such a war strengthened republicanism or weakened it to monarchy's advantage, it would not work to their advantage. To Brissot and his colleagues, Marat's and Robespierre's priority seemed to be to build on the current instability within France to extend their own following and power.

The vehement public quarrel between Brissot and Robespierre over the advisability of war did not mark the start of their differences (as has often been claimed), for those reached back to the summer of 1791 and originated in the rift over republicanism of June and July 1791. But it was the issue over which Robespierre could most effectively and widely sow suspicion concerning Brissot's motives, since the court also wanted war.[39] In different circumstances, held Robespierre, in a well-judged, effective reply on 2 January 1792, he would wish, no less than Brissot, to assist Brabant, aid the Liégeois, and break the chains oppressing the Dutch. But the conflict was manifestly being planned and fomented by the "domestic enemies of our liberty"—king, court, Dumouriez, and Lafayette. All the trumpets of the nobility, émigrés, ministers, and court intriguers plotted war, and the mere fact that they all wanted it was grounds enough not to get into it. A European war would assist court, nobles, modérés, and royal ministers, corrupt men ideally placed to lodge their own nominees in command of France's armies. How could such a struggle serve the people, or liberty? Brissot admitted the modérés wanted an "aristocratic constitution" on the British model, and yet urged the Jacobins to embrace their projects! Why distract the public's attention from their most formidable enemies, those within, to confront a less immediately urgent peril at such a dangerous time?[40]

With those Jacobins supporting Marat and Robespierre opposing war, in March and April 1792, Louis and the Left republicans briefly joined hands, each with a view less to helping than undermining the other. Unlike Louis, the Feuillants, or Robespierre, Brissotins viewed the coming struggle as an integral component of the fight against "tyrants" everywhere, against what Condorcet termed "l'hypocrisie des prêtres" and the foolish pride of the "noblesse héréditaire."[41] Armed conflict, prognosticated Brissot, would interrupt communication between the Revolution's internal and external foes, and render it easier to crush internal enemies by unmasking them as traitors collaborating with the foreign enemy. But such a war, countered Robespierre, scorning Brissot's arguments, and those Condorcet added in his speech in the legislature immediately following Brissot on 29 December 1791,[42] would merely provide fresh opportunities for aristocratic subversion of public opinion aided by émigrés and foreign courts. Condorcet and Brissot sought to consolidate and internationalize the Revolution using the army as an instrument to bolster revolutionary ideology around France's borders. Cordorcet claimed her ability to wage war on kings would show Europe that France was united with one national will by "l'amour de la liberté." But it was likelier, insisted Robespierre, that the army, in its frontier camps, would become isolated from sources of libertarian principles, enabling officers to foment the old blind obedience, discipline, and ancien régime military ethic.[43]

The Feuillants remained badly split, deprived for the moment of their brief political ascendancy. Demonstrating treasonable conduct on the part of Louis XVI's court and army officers would perhaps have enabled Brissot and his three ministerial colleagues—Roland, Servan, and Clavière—to wreck Feuillant hegemony permanently and replace the 1791 liberal monarchical constitution with a republican one. But

Robespierre, determined to block Brissot's strategy, far preferred to retain the existing Constitution than see a full-fledged republic intro-duced.[44] At this time, Robespierre regularly dismissed the label "repub-lican" as chiefly useful to conspiring royalists who vilified Patriots in the eyes of a nation uneducated in the refinements of political thought, enabling them to label all Jacobins disloyal. Above all, Robespierre ex-ploited Brissot's principal difficulty, namely, that for the moment, he and Roland professed to have confidence in a court and generals that they actually vastly distrusted.

On 20 April 1792, the king appeared before a cheering, still predom-inantly moderate Assembly that mostly had no desire to change the mo-narchical Constitution but was entirely willing to confront France's foes abroad. France, he announced, was now officially at war with Austria and her allies. With some justification, Louis's relatives expected the armed conflict to strengthen monarchism irrespective of whether the fighting went well or badly. If the Austro-Prussian forces swept aside the ragged, half-disintegrated shambles of the French revolutionary army from which many noble officers were deserting, then the war would provide opportunities to persuade more to defect, and for conservative social forces finally to prevail and restore the old order. If the French military gamble went well, contrary to expectations, Louis's standing as a consti-tutional monarch in France and within the Revolution would soar and Dumouriez, a declared constitutional monarchist, would help bring the army and national resources under royal control. Either way the Feuil-lants and republicans would lose, but the king would gain.

With war declared, the French launched a spring offensive into the Low Countries that ground to an immediate and humiliating halt, suf-fering reverses at Mons and Tournai. After proclaiming a universal ideo-logical conflict with great fanfares in the press, the fiasco, much to the jubilation of the émigrés, seriously damaged the democratic republicans' prestige in France and among the republicans of the Low Countries and Germany.[45] The Belgian populace showed no inclination to rise. Much to Brissot's discomfiture, Robespierre could now deride Brissotin Jacobins and monarch bracketed together. Over the ensuing months, the Jacobins remained deeply divided, while the Cordeliers sided with Robespierre. The feuding was not in essence a personality clash, though it was that too, but a profound ideological rift. One unfortunate casu-alty was Condorcet's long-considered, carefully deliberated report on education reform, possibly his second-most important contribution to the Revolution (after the February 1793 democratic Constitution), a report completed in April 1792, but then, owing to the war crisis, shelved indefinitely. By April and May 1792, the sparring between Robespierre and the Brissot circle in the Jacobins had evolved into a bitter, unedifying slanging match with Robespierre and Marat continually accusing Brissot of colluding secretly with Dumouriez, Lafayette, and other aristocratic intriguers, terming Dumouriez "l'instrument et le protecteur" of the Brissotins. (In fact, Dumouriez equally detested Montagnards and Brissot Jacobins.)[46] The royalist Mallet du Pan, while deeming both Jacobin factions unscrupulous, noted that the Brissotins were "plus habiles" than the Montagnards but "moins féroces";[47] this was to prove their undoing.

Their ideological differences rent the Jacobins asunder. Their split had a polarizing effect, the Left republicans becoming more overtly cosmopolitan and the Montagnards more narrowly chauvinistic. The Cercle Social and fourteen *Chronique du mois* editors expounded a particularly ambitious theory of international relations and war, rooted in their philosophique perspective. Since all men possess the same rights, no one can deprive one people of these without violating the Rights of Man generally. Denying the natural rights of the French or Germans, for example, inevitably entails betraying whatever nation the oppressor belongs to. No agreement between two nations can deprive any part of either citizenry of the imprescriptible right to obey only laws freely embraced by themselves. Thus, the Holy Roman (i.e., German) Empire, being a land of princes and ecclesiastics, resting on dynastic inheritance and privileges, long recognized "by the troup of sophists aristocratic Machiavelisme has on its pay-roll," merited prompt dissolution with French revolutionary help into a confederation of republics, or into a single united republic, with all the princes ejected. The National Assembly's cause in its fight with the German princes was, to Condorcet and his colleagues, that of the German as much as the French nation. The German princes' unjust war against France was equally an unjust war of oppression against the populace of their own states.[48]

Condorcet fully backed Brissot in these vicious polemics because he too was convinced of the looming danger that court subversion and aristocratic intrigue would otherwise swing a Feuillant-dominated Assembly against the Revolution.[49] France's Revolution might well collapse, like that of Brabant, under the heel of nobles and hostile clergy.[50] Condorcet attributed the fact that the American Revolution had succeeded and helped foment a powerful democratic tendency in Europe, Britain, and Ireland in large part to the heroic effort and struggle against the British Crown (and German princes) to gain American Independence. The fighting had steeled the American Revolution, transformed the Americans into a nation, and led Europeans to study and weigh the principles proclaimed by the American insurgents. The new war against tyranny would similarly mobilize opinion against monarchs and despotism everywhere.[51] Brissot, Condorcet, Carra, Gorsas, Roederer, and their foreign associates Cloots, Gorani, and Paine, all believed the Revolution could ultimately succeed only by defeating the combined internal and external menace—French royalism *and* the European powers linked by the armed émigrés. The Jacobin majority backing Brissot (for the moment) had a reliable ally in the thousands of prominent Dutch, Belgian, Swiss, Italian, and German Patriots who had fled to France since 1787 and formed an expatriot republican vanguard, mostly democrat. Even those several Dutch political refugees in France supporting French constitutional monarchism in preference to democracy, and preferring Feuillants to the Jacobins, like Assembly deputy Jean-Antoine d'Averhoudt (1756–92), still supported the war of liberation and demanded an "heureuse révolution" in Holland, closely linking the Belgian and Dutch refugees' interests with those of France.[52]

Brissot responded to his critics at the Jacobins yet again on 25 April 1792 by designating Robespierre one of those dangerous individuals who flatter the people "pour le subjuguer," tyrannizing over opinion in the name of liberty, casting suspicion over virtue, and maligning opponents without justification. Where are your qualifications, he demanded, for "audaciously" assailing Condorcet? Have you, like him, launched courageous attacks over thirty years on fanaticism and "despotisme parlementaire et ministeriel," allied to Voltaire, d'Alembert, and Diderot? What services have you rendered "à la patrie, à la liberté, à la philosophie?," he asked the man who had undoubtedly played less part in the great revolutionary *journées* than any other major revolutionary leader.[53] Interrupted by howls of protest from the Montagne, Brissot eulogized Condorcet as a philosophe, journalist, and Jacobin. Robespierre had savaged Condorcet, whose revolutionary career "has been nothing but a series of sacrifices for the people: a philosophe, he became a politician; an académicien, he became a journalist; a noble, he became a Jacobin."[54]

The next day, Condorcet published an article in the *Chronique de Paris* accusing Robespierre and his friends of undermining the Revolution by deliberately agitating the people with continual attacks on "the true friends of liberty." Guadet too publicly assailed Robespierre, in particular, for encouraging Marat's *L'Ami du peuple*, the paper that most praised him in repeatedly calling for a "dictator" and recommending that this supposedly urgently needed *dictateur* must be none other than the incomparable, "incorruptible" Robespierre.[55] His pen was not rented out to anyone, retorted Marat, and he had hardly ever engaged in direct personal contact with Robespierre. Pétion was lambasted by Marat for siding with Brissot rather than Robespierre and joining their "ridiculous farce" of claiming la philosophie as prime agent of the Revolution. The Jacobins would never resolve their present quarrels, avowed Marat, until they had expelled the Brissot clique from their midst, ejecting the scoundrels casting aspersions on Robespierre, men aspiring to direct the Revolution while, under the mask of patriotism, insidiously betraying it, in league with the court.[56]

Robespierre further defended his position at the Jacobins on 27 April. Brissot and Condorcet absurdly assailed him for upholding Jean-Jacques's finest principle that only the people are "good, just and magnanimous" and that "tyranny is the exclusive attribute of those who disdain them." Had not Condorcet originally been groomed as a philosophe by Voltaire and d'Alembert, two of Rousseau's greatest foes? If the academiciens and mathematicians Brissot eulogized combated the priesthood, they also courted kings (a charge true of Voltaire and d'Alembert, but not of Diderot and Condorcet). "Who is unaware," demanded Robespierre, pointing to the bust of Rousseau nearby, "of the ferocity with which these men persecuted Jean-Jacques," despising the "virtue and genius for liberty of he whose sacred image I see here?"[57] The rift between Montagne and Brissotins ran so deep by April 1792 that it overshadowed the entire subsequent course of the French and General Revolution. "The divisions among the Jacobins are the subject of all conversation in the capital," observed Marat, ridiculing Brissot's efforts to cast Condorcet as a "grand homme" and Robespierre as an ambitious upstart who employed paid hacks to pack the Assembly's galleries and rig elections.[58]

When Louis XVI abruptly changed course, dismissing Roland, Sevan, and Clavière in mid-June and reverting to the Feuillants, the switch further increased suspicion of royal intentions and how the war was being waged. Movements of troops became the focus of obsessive scrutiny. That Dumouriez, dismissed as a minister but retained as a general, now directed military operations in the north (while continually blaming France's setbacks on the Jacobins) was a particular cause for anxiety in the Assembly and Jacobins. Robespierre and his allies redoubled their accusations. Was there a hidden league to rally the army against the Revolution between the king, Feuillants, Dumouriez, and the once-republican Lafayette, an alliance encompassing also the Brissotins who had, after all, earlier helped make Dumouriez war minister?

In mid-July 1792, the Prussians and Austrians commenced their joint invasion of France. The lesser princes participated, the archbishop-elector of Mainz contributing two thousand troops to the invading army. Princes and émigrés, the entire European antirevolutionary coalition backed by Britain and the papacy, were on the march. Prussia brought redoubled pressure to bear on Germany's small states to vilify and persecute writers like Campe, Klopstock, Cramer, and Mauvillon, who openly supported the Revolution.[59] On 25 July, the allied commander, the Duke of Brunswick, issued a ferociously belligerent manifesto designed to spread panic in France, as it did. The Hapsburg emperor and Prussian king were jointly invading to end anarchy and restore throne and altar in France. The invaders intended to reverse the Revolution in every respect and stabilize politics throughout the Rhine Valley, the Low Countries, and Switzerland. Anyone resisting the Austro-Prussian forces or threatening the French royal family would receive the most exemplary punishment. In late August, the Prussians overran much of Lorraine. By 2 September the allied army had passed Verdun and directly threatened Paris.

CHAPTER 10

The Revolutionary Summer of 1792

The Journée of 10 August

On 10 June, the Rolands challenged the king with their remarkable fourteen-page letter, stressing the seriousness of the political deadlock. If the king was outraged, most of the legislature were appalled by his action in dismissing Roland and the two other Brissotin ministers and aligned with the democrats, ordering Roland's letter to be printed and nationally distributed. Critics of royal policy turned to the forty-eight Paris sections, instigating renewed agitation against the court and especially Lafayette, whose arrest and impeachment republican deputies now vociferously demanded. On 19 June 1792, Brissot, the Rolands, the Cordeliers leaders, and others—but not Robespierre or the authoritarian populists—made preparations for a major demonstration the next day. At odds with the Brissotin Jacobins, Robespierre and his populist Jacobins subsequently pointedly disassociated themselves from this insurrection, claiming the Brissotins "provoked it solely to force Louis XVI to recall their ministers."[1]

Massing on the pretext of commemorating the Tennis Court Oath anniversary, the 20 June demonstrators tried to intimidate Louis into canceling his vetoes and restoring the dismissed Brissotin ministers, hoping by this means to dislodge Lafayette and the remaining Feuillants and put the Brissotins in power. The Commune, under Pétion, cooperating with the plans, marches, and planting a liberty tree in the Tuileries gardens, made no objection to marchers carrying pikes, scythes, and other makeshift weapons. Brissot, Pétion, Desmoulins, Manuel, Danton, Vergniaud, and most other radical leaders were implicated in this business, as were Condorcet, Chamfort, and Ginguiné.[2] In principle, most of these men disliked such direct mass action and disapproved of using mass intimidation. But they had little alternative if they were adequately to counter Lafayette and "l'hypocrite Feullantisme." Only through insurrection could they defeat the politics of the court, refractory priests, generals, and counterrevolutionary nobles. Thus, "on 20 June 1792," as one leading democratic journalist, the librarian, journalist, and divorce campaigner, Jean-Baptiste Louvet (1760–97), expressed it, "the men of '89 reawakened."

A large, orderly, and peaceful but resolute rising occurred. Crowds amounting to more than 10,000 (some claimed 50,000) sansculottes, including many women, some armed with clubs and pikes and carrying banners inscribed "Liberté, Egalité," marched from the city's poorer eastern quarters.[3] Congregating at the town hall, and afterward around the Assembly, they heard petitions read out. Then, chanting "Vivent les patriotes, vivent les sans-culottes, à bas le veto!," they invaded the Tuileries gardens and palace, their vanguard holding up the Rights of Man inscribed on two tablets. In the lead was Louis Legendre (1752–97), an uneduated former sailor and butcher, now a Cordeliers leader among the sansculottes' most vigorous orators, carrying a petition Danton helped compose. Lacking clear orders, the recently purged and reformed royal guard hesitated and fell back, allowing the entire palace to be inundated with noisy protesters.

The king found himself obliged to receive a vast crowd in his rooms, where he remained pinned to a corner for nearly four hours during which he affected a convincing enough show of bonhomie, nodding agreeably, donning a red liberty bonnet, drinking a toast to the nation's health, listening to petitions exhorting him to abide by the Constitution, and studying the wording of the Rights of Man thrust under his nose.[4] The royalist, Durozoy, blamed the king's humiliation on the inertia of the capital's six or seven hundred thousand inhabitants who continually allowed themselves to be manipulated. How could the people tamely permit a relatively modest crowd of just seven or eight thousand people (according to his estimate), composed of the vilest element of all classes, to occupy the royal palace shepherded by the "sect of Pétionistes and Brissotins"? There could be no doubt as to who the "faction regicide" trying to intimidate the court into acting against the émigrés and refractory priests were. They were led by "republicans, Pétionistes, novateurs, Brissotins, philosophistes." How could the Parisian majority permit what might yet degenerate into a Saint Bartholomew's Day massacre of the *royalistes*?[5]

The crowds were eventually persuaded to depart by the mayor, Pétion, among those with the most credit with the sansculottes. Dispersal took hours, though, as the demonstrators filled all the palace rooms, galleries, and gardens, and even occupied the roof. Not until ten in the evening was Paris calm. The demonstrators dispersed willingly enough, however, supposing Louis had assented to their wishes. But the very next day, he reacted in a manner showing they had entirely misread his response. Far from yielding, a furious monarch demanded the Assembly take prompt measures to ensure the "inviolability and constitutional liberty of the hereditary representative of the nation" and royal family, and severely punish the insurrectionists. He confirmed his dismissal of the Brissotin ministers. Lafayette, then at the front, returned immediately to Paris. The Tuileries gardens were closed to the public, the royal guard was again considerably strengthened, and no one was allowed into the compound any longer without a special identity card. Eleven thousand of these were issued but only, noted Carra, to the king's "faithful slaves." Louis XVI took a huge gamble on 20 June 1793, staking his entire prestige and future, and that of the Bourbon dynasty and the monarchy itself, on the ability of the conservative forces around him to rally and overcome the philosophistes and their (temporary) sansculotte allies.

The 20 June rising showed for all to see that France's constitutional monarchy had broken down. The king, Lafayette, and the moderates went all out to reverse the creeping Brissotin Revolution. Allied to the court and wildly applauded by the majority of the legislature, Lafayette, wearing his general's uniform, harangued the Assembly on 28 June. He intended to restore order with an unyielding hand. He wanted the Assembly's public galleries closed, the Jacobin Club suppressed, and the instigators of the 20 June rising severely punished. Mass petitions from Rouen, the Pas de Calais, and elsewhere were read out, hailing Lafayette as France's savior and demanding dissolution of the sociétés populaires. Was the Revolution about to be captured by a different "dictator" than that which Marat had called for, by Lafayette, the hero of American liberation, the "nouveau Cromwell," as the republican press called him, the man who formerly assured friends he was a "republican," but now faced the democrats as commander of the Republic's largest army, threatening to suppress them by force? Inevitably, Lafayette faced a hail of criticism from much of the Assembly. He himself had been a founder, he was reminded, of the very Jacobins he wanted closed. Had not Mirabeau dubbed the public galleries the "safeguard of public opinion"? Condorcet, like Paine, once a close friend, berated him for breaking with them and, worse, with the people.[6]

Lafayette and the court were stridently denounced by the populists and Brissotins alike. Brissot openly advocated republicanism but also urged the Assembly not to be precipitate in dethroning the king. Dethronement should follow only after mature reflection and consultation with the primary assemblies. Representative democratic republicanism, he contended, must be tempered by a measure of direct democracy. Should the Assembly depose Louis without first ensuring it truly spoke for the nation, it would afterward surely (and rightly) be blamed.[7] Pierre-Victurnien Vergniaud (1753–93), prominent in organizing the 20 June rising, ranked among the Assembly's best orators and typified what Mme. Roland (who disliked him for his intellectual arrogance) called "the philosopher's egotism."[8] Prior to attending Assembly sessions, he routinely conferred with Brissot and Condorcet, determining political strategy over lunch at an apartment in the Place Vendôme, political lunches frequented also by Roederer, Gensonné, Guadet, and Brissot's most long-standing and closest political ally, the Genevan republican economist Étienne Clavière.[9]

Even a suddenly alarmed Robespierre briefly felt obliged to close ranks with the Left democrats he so abhorred, to block Lafayette.[10] Yet while acknowledging the danger of a "new Cromwell," and likewise demanding his arrest, he persisted in rejecting Brissot's republican principles. So great was his antipathy to Brissot, recorded Mme. Roland, that he automatically opposed him on every question, whether monarchy, religion, war, colonies, or representation, tirelessly reiterating Rousseau's strictures against "gouvernement réprésentatif absolu."[11] Robespierre was assuredly no "moderate" like that "political sect conventionally termed 'moderates'" upon which he too poured vituperation, but with his rather threadbare ideology neither was he a radical theorist or innovator. For the present, he adhered to the existing monarchical Constitution. Through June and early July, Robespierre issued his newly established (but little-read) paper, Le Défenseur de la Constitution, begun in April as a redoubt of authoritarian populist moderation and the existing Constitution, scorning Brissot and Cordorcet for their academic republicanism. Only from late July 1792—Roederer says August 1792—did he waver on this point and cease to be a "defender of royalty."[12] Incessantly complaining of being maligned by his democratic adversaries, and denouncing Brissotin talk of "republicanism" and disdain for the common people, he grew profoundly ambivalent on this question.

"Sovereignty of the people" was proclaimed by the Assembly but not promoted as Robespierre aspired to do.[13] Designated in the republican press a "tribun ambitieux et dangéreux," aiming to fullfil Rousseau's (and Marat's) doctrine of "necessary dictatorship," his speeches were pervaded by an almost Manichaean dualism, stressing the purity, disinterestedness, generosity, and moderation of ordinary folk and corrupt character of those seeking to raise themselves above them. Prominent among the latter, in his worldview, were the "writers" and intellectuals he saw as betraying the people: they too were "aristocrats" of a kind.[14] The "people alone is good and just, and magnanimous," ran Robespierre's interminable refrain. If Brissot and Condorcet preferred philosophes, he aligned with "des hommes simples et purs," ordinary folk.[15] This cosmic drama was then crucially mirrored in the antagonism between the philosophes (whose heirs he identified with his own chief enemies, Condorcet and Brissot) and "the sublime Jean-Jacques," fervently venerated by both Marat and Robespierre.[16] If Robespierre later proved reluctant to install Rousseau's remains in the Panthéon, this was because, to him, it was an edifice mired with the remains of Mirabeau and Voltaire, a monument "debased." Mixing Rousseau with philosophes seemed to him sacrilege—"quel décadence de l'esprit public!"[17] He disclaimed all responsibility for the vituperation heaped on Brissot by his allies Collot d'Herbois, Chabot, and others. It was Brissot, he maintained, who was the veritable aggressor, a wild republican answerable for the Champ de Mars massacre, since his rash petition demanding abolition of monarchy had overly excited the crowd, provoking the slaughter.[18]

How was the political crisis to be resolved? Most Assembly deputies spurned all thought of a fresh insurrection. Could a change of heart among the deputies themselves save the Revolution? A famous scene of reconciliation occurred on 7 July 1792 when Lamourette, constitutional bishop of Lyon, delivered a rousing speech in the legislature urging reconciliation. He knew an infallible means to end factional strife: no quarrel in the world is truly irreparable except that between the malicious and the well intentioned. The Assembly majority accused the Left of wanting a republic; Feuillant moderates were accused of designing mixed government, nobility, and a two-chamber legislature.[19] "Messieurs," he pleaded, "the rift can be healed!" The answer lay in heartfelt reciprocal oaths, simultaneously abjuring republicanism and "two chambers." Superb! In a frenzy of collective transport, everyone rose, wildly applauding, tears streaming down faces, stepping forward mutually to embrace, avowing reconciliation. This unforgettable moment was dubbed the "kiss of Lamourette."[20]

Yet, the clasping of hands lasted not even a single day. On 21 June, the king had accused Pétion of not doing all in his power, as mayor of Paris, to prevent the "scandale" of the 20 June rising.[21] On 7 July, egged on by the court, the Feuillant departmental directoire announced Pétion's dismissal and that of Manuel from their posts at the Paris Commune for failing to take proper steps against the 20 June insurrection. This immediately provoked fresh demonstrations. The Assembly was bombarded with addresses from around the country, rebuking the court and demanding reinstatement of the *procureur-syndic* and extremely popular mayor.[22] In the Paris sections, so reviled were the Feuillant departmental authorities that of three hundred Paris *afficheurs* employed to post up official notices in the streets and public places, not one, reportedly, could be found willing to post up the regime's explanation of Pétion's and Manuel's removal. In any case, the move proved overly confident. Within a week, an Assembly majority rescinded their dismissal, causing the jubilant Paris crowds to "deliver themselves over," as one foe of the Brissotin democrats, the Cordeliers firebrand Chaumette, sourly expressed it, "to the excesses of idolatry." Detesting "Brissot et toute sa académie," Pierre-Gaspard Chaumette (1763–94), a failed medical student among the most ardent republicans, atheists, and demagogues of the Cordeliers, closely analyzed the Brissotins' sway in the streets. For now, the people "adored" Pétion as earlier they had Necker, Mirabeau, Barnave, and Lafayette. But the people lurched continually, first one way, then another. Soon enough they would again repent their "blind and stupid mania" and abandon their new champions. He and his friends groaned at hearing cries of "Vive Pétion! Pétion ou la mort!" yelled on every side and seeing this absurd slogan crayoned on hats. He accused Pétion of posturing initially as the friend of the poor against the rich, but later of tiring of "this class" aspiring to climb from its wretchedness.[23] Unlike Robespierre but like Cloots, Chaumette represented a dogmatic strand of philosophique republicanism opportunistically aligned with the populists, partly driven by personal enmity. He vigorously championed "the people" in the abstract while actually disdaining them.

The invasion of France, meanwhile, gathered momentum with many armed émigrés advancing with the Prussians. The Prussian king, Friedrich Wilhelm, had perhaps miscalculated in supposing the revolutionaries would collapse quickly, as earlier in Holland in 1787, but there seemed every prospect that reaction and the European powers would shortly overwhelm the revolutionary challenge. On 11 July, the Jacobins won an emergency vote in the wavering Assembly, declaring the nation in danger and drafting all Parisians with pikes or pistols into the National Guard. With this they democratized that key entity, ending its previous bias in favor of royalism and modérantisme. This confirmed once again that Brissot was right in claiming that the European war would shatter the monarchy and open the way for the republicans. Just weeks after reigniting the struggle, the Feuillants had signally failed to establish either a solid ascendancy or to curb the ferment in the streets. War forced the Revolution to depend on the people, and, as Brissot had predicted, this rapidly undermined both court and Feuillants. During the 14 July 1792 festivities marking the third anniversary of the Bastille, the last occasion when the royal family participated in public ceremonies as France's royalty, hostility to monarch and court was palpable. Order was kept on the Champ de Mars by a guard of six thousand men. But this could not hide the tension, even if the "celebration" passed off without serious incident. Some shouted, "Vive le roi"! but "Vive la nation!" preponderated. "Quatorze juillet," enthused the ecstatic longstanding republican Mandar, "je te salue! sois à jamais l'époque de la liberté de ma patrie!" How fascinating for the philosophique observer, remarked Chaumette, to see how disciplined yet unmistakably sullen the crowds were.

On 25 July, the Brissotins in the legislature presented the king with a fresh ultimatum, repeating Roland's original demand that he must now choose between the people and counterrevolution. Undoubtedly, Brissot would have preferred to intimidate king and Feuillants in the Assembly's name. But the Left's demands, drafted by Condorcet as president of the Assembly's emergency Committee of Twenty-One, were in the end rejected by the Assembly majority. Equally, the republicans' efforts to impeach Lafayette in the Assembly (here with Robespierre's support) provoked only protracted, furious wrangling that dragged on until 8 August, when a bare majority finally dismissed the charges against the general. Thus, the Legislative Assembly by hairbreadth refused to repudiate the Feuillants or Lafayette, and "the party of liberty," as Condorcet expressed it, "acted from day to day, forced to follow the impulse of its enlightenment, acquiescing in developments the rest of the Assembly's dithering left it no means of preventing." Failure to rally enough of the Assembly against the court and Feuillants had grave consequences. The republicans had now exhausted every legal channel. It was difficult to condone insurrection when the people had representatives elected to act in a considered and lawful fashion, and with foreign armies invading the country. On behalf of the Committee of Twenty-One, which afterward authorized its printing, Condorcet composed an address to the French people explaining popular sovereignty, its exercise under representative government, and the need for orderly acceptance of its procedures. The tragedy was that the threat of armed insurrection the Left had counted on to intimidate the king, had, owing to Feuillant tenacity and deadlock in the Assembly, now instead to be directed against the Assembly itself.[24]

For both democrats and populists, renewed popular insurrection offered the sole feasible solution. Deposing the king and ending the monarchy, Brissot, Condorcet, and their colleagues became convinced, was the only way for the Revolution to survive and the revolutionary war against Europe's kings to be prosecuted more vigorously. On 17 July a deputation of fédérés entered the Assembly, reiterating the call for impeachment of treasonable ministers and Louis's suspension. The arrival of more fédérés on 30 July, the force from Marseille chanting the recently composed but already famous marching anthem, the "Marseillaise," inexorably raised the pressure. The balance of forces had visibly shifted against modérantisme and royalism. On arriving, the Marseille volunteers, led by Barbaroux, effaced the name "Lafayette" from the street carrying that name and thronged around the Palais-Royal, continuously singing their new war song, yelling "Aux armes citoyens!" and waving their hats and sabres in the air "even during performances."[25] On 3 August Mayor Pétion delivered an impassioned speech in the Assembly on behalf of "the true sovereign"—the people. Since the Revolution's outset, the king had shown only aversion to the nation and their interests, and a stubborn predilection for nobles and priests. Frenchmen had every reason to dethrone their disloyal monarch. The people made the Revolution and the Constitution, and their rights were now directly threatened by the monarch, court, priests, and "the intriguers." Yet, who had the nation placed over their armies and security? The king and nobles! This had created a dire predicament requiring immediate resolution by breaking the court's independent power and dislodging the residual court elite. Manifestly, either this corrupt tyranny or the Revolution must triumph.[26]

Amid the unprecedented clamor and excitement, Paris seethed with rumor: the king—a thousand times a traitor and perjurer in Carra's words—was again conspiring to flee with the royal family.[27] Preparations began in the Paris sections for a new—and this time decisive—confrontation plotted by Brissot's adherents, Dantonists, the

Cordeliers, and Barbaroux's fédérés. On 30 July a declaration drawn up
in the Cordeliers district, repudiating all distinction between "active"
and "passive" citizens, pronouncing the patrie in danger, and summoning "all citizens" to arms, had been posted up across the Théâtre-Français
section, signed by Danton as section president, Chaumette as vice president, and Momoro as secretary. The balance of forces had shifted. But
was this the will of the people? Parisians, bourgeoisie, and artisans were
bitterly rebuked by the royalist *Gazette de Paris* for their inertia and
for permitting themselves to be manipulated by a small, "vile populace"
drawn from all classes who were agitating for the king's removal, orchestrated by Brissot, Condorcet, and Pétion. Allegedly, a mere 4,000
"muddled simpletons," recruited into the capital's forty-eight section
assemblies, were being ruthlessly orchestrated to manipulate 700,000
spineless Parisians.[28] By early August, so demoralized were some Assembly deputies of the center and Right that they began boycotting
meetings and likewise to contemplate fleeing the capital. With republican journalists and orators—but not Robespierre—openly demanding
Louis's dethronement, royalist journalists urged Prussia and Austria to
hasten their advance and rescue France's monarchy and nobility before
all was lost.[29] Trying to halt the drift to a republican outcome, nobles
and army officers congregated in the capital and were increasingly in
evidence, venturing out from the Tuileries and other locations. Over
several days and nights clashes in the streets turned central Paris into a
no-man's-land, disputed by rival armed camps, royalist and democrat.

All the Paris section assemblies, several demanding dismissal of the
"executive power," others demurring, went into permanent session in a
frantic climax of debate and local wrangling. The Mauconseil section,
after its 31 July meeting, reported in letters to other section assemblies
and sociétés populaires that with the required number of more than six
hundred of their section members present, they had agreed the nation
could only surmount the "dangerous crisis in which it now finds itself"
by repudiating the present Constitution, since this no longer expressed
la volonté générale. All Paris sections together, urged Mauconseil, must
announce that "Louis XVI is no longer king of the French."[30] Marseille too was plunged into extreme ferment. A notably uncompromising republican speech was delivered there on 2 August by Moise Bayle,
procureur-général syndic of the department of Bouches-du-Rhône, to
which the city belonged. Representative government, held Bayle, should
be in essence "la pure démocratie." The king did not represent the supreme will of the nation, and the people should now choose between

executive power, like that exercised by Louis Capet (i.e., the king), and one elected by, and accountable only to, the people. No executive power should possess a veto over the national legislature's decrees. "Kings are the curse of the earth."[31]

As the German armies advanced, a missive from the Palatinate's clandestine Society of the Rights of Man at Mannheim, dated 2 August 1792, was read to the Assembly on 9 August. Mannheim Jacobins applauded the French for their revolutionary courage and ardor while bitterly deploring the fatal rift in their midst threatening to wreck the Revolution by burying democratic principles under a deluge of acrimony and strife. They summoned the Assembly's deputies to stop their bickering, end the stormy "convulsions" marring their debates, and "save France!" With France's destiny in their hands and all Europe mobilizing against them, the French would lose their liberty and decimate the hopes of all freedom lovers in France, Germany, and everywhere if they failed to rally at the eleventh hour. If the Revolution was doomed, at least the Assembly should afford mankind the consolation of knowing they had done everything possible to repel the monster of monarchical despotism menacing them all with annihilation. Europe's princes detested Feuillant constitutional monarchists no less than Jacobins, and, if victorious, would decimate all the revolutionary factions with equal fury, trampling liberty underfoot. Only moments remained if they were to save liberty and the Revolution. Was there any lovelier destiny on earth? Be the saviors of France and all Europe, the Mannheim society urged, "et faire triompher la philosophie."[32]

"Faire triompher la philosophie," Robespierre's and Marat's aversion notwithstanding, was indeed the essence of the Jacobin revolution of August 1792. "Among enlightened men attached to the public good," exclaimed Condorcet in the *Chronique de Paris* on 5 August, "it is no longer Louis XVI's treason (sufficiently demonstrated by his entire conduct), nor his deposition," as the appropriate punishment, that "divides opinion, but rather the consequences of such a measure at a moment when the enemy is at the gates." Insurrection, he averred, like Diderot and d'Holbach before him, "is the last resort of oppressed peoples."[33] If the Assembly fragmented, so did most Paris sections. Throughout the sweltering evening of 9 August, the furious struggle in the section assemblies intensified with insurrectionist democrats battling waverers and government supporters. In section Roi-de-Sicile, corresponding to what today is the Marais district on the Seine's Right Bank, the conservative section president and his supporters withstood the insurrectionists.[34]

In the Lombards section, where the Left republican Louvet presided, anti-Robespierre Jacobins, backed by Condorcet and the *Chronique de Paris*, gained the upper hand.[35] Elsewhere, Robespierristes predominated. But nowhere was there any clear-cut class or sociological differentiation lending a social base to republican insurrectionism: most Parisians remained both confused and inactive. While representatives from at least twenty-eight Paris sections participated in mobilizing the insurrection of 10 August, the basic impulse emanated from tightly organized committees concentrated in a few sections, chiefly on the Left Bank, especially the Cordeliers, where Danton, Chaumette, and Desmoulins presided, the Lombards, and Mauconseil, as well as among the fédérés, particularly the Marseillais contingent under Barbaroux.[36]

The highly disciplined and coordinated uprising, led by politicized commissaires of the democratic sections, commenced during the night of 9 August at three or four different locations—the Cordeliers; the barracks of the Marseillais, where Carra prominently participated; the Faubourg Saint-Antoine, where the Alsatian officer, François-Joseph Westermann (d. 1794), a friend of Danton, commanded with Antoine-Joseph Santerre (1752–1809), another veteran of the faubourgs; and the Faubourg Saint-Marceau, where furious locals eager to smash the busts of Lafayette and Bailly were aroused by Claude Fournier *l'Américain*, military veteran and long-standing rabble-rouser.[37] Beginning in the early hours with alarm bells pealing, the new insurrection first engineered a coup in the Commune. "Commissaires" named by the insurrectionary sections converged, dissolved the old Commune, and formed a new city government to lead the uprising.[38] Early on 10 August 1792, a few hours after the coup at the city hall, crowds of sansculottes led by the Marseillais initiated the second stage. At daybreak, contingents of armed men from the sections, with Desmoulins figuring prominently, marched in a swelling column via the Pont Royal toward the royal palace. Robespierre, by contrast, remained out of sight throughout the next twenty-four hours, inactive and wholly uninvolved, as in previous insurrections (though Marat and Danton were also not conspicuous).[39]

The crowds surged forward. But in directing this rising, what counted was the cadre of professional revolutionaries, a totally unrepresentative (as well as mostly non-Parisian) clique of mob organizers and section leaders. As Durozoy put it, they were all "republicans, Pétionistes, *novateurs*, Brissotins, and *philosophistes*," the veteran "secte régicide."[40] Initially, armed troops of royalist contre-révolutionnaires also roamed the streets. In fact, elements at court and of the Feuillants attempted a preemptive military strike to restore the monarchy's authority. Paris's royalist journalists, Suleau, Suard, and Rivarol, with many of their editorial and printing staff, rushed to arms to help defend the king.[41] A royalist group headed by Lafayette tried to effect the king's escape from Paris. But as the huge scale of the rising materialized, few royalists remained in arms in the streets; most, like the journalist Durozoy, hid, or, like Lafayette and Malouet, fled. The Feuillant club's premises were ransacked. Several prominent monarchiens were killed, including Clermont-Tonnerre and Suleau, editor of the royalist *Journal de Suleau* (1791–92), who, having declined Desmoulins's offer to shelter him in his apartment, was caught near the wrecked Feuillant club, beheaded, and had his head affixed to a pike.

A moderately large and noisy but organized mass of approximately twenty thousand, chanting the "Marseillaise," surrounded and then entered the palace grounds, fairly peaceably at first. A coolheaded plan of Roederer to extricate the royal family and usher Louis, Marie Antoinette, and their children in among the deputies helped the Brissotins control a key strand of the drama. Many aristocrats and courtiers around the palace disappeared, while others donned the uniform of the Swiss and joined the guards. The waiting massed Swiss, after initially offering the crowds signs of an amicable reception in the main courtyard, suddenly delivered a withering fusillade, downing some four hundred *patriotes* and initially driving the invaders back. But their volleys so infuriated the demonstrators, especially the Marseille and Brest volunteers, that these launched a full-scale assault, employing cannon. There was an immense amount of firing in and around the Tuileries, some musket balls hitting the walls of the adjoining Assembly building. Finally, after a bitter fight, the insurgents stormed the palace and overwhelmed the guards, the battle ending in the massacre of those who had tried to slaughter the Patriots, around six hundred Swiss and courtiers. Those not shot dead were hacked to death with knives, hatchets, and pikes. Only a handful of Swiss survived, helped by Louvet, Brissot, and others to hide in the Assembly's corridors.

By the late afternoon of 10 August the insurgents controlled the capital, having lost some ninety killed and around 300 wounded. Jacobins and Cordeliers, some carrying banners inscribed "Patrie, Liberté, Égalité," held the city hall, all the capital's sections, and the entire palace grounds. Blood and corpses lay strewn throughout the Tuileries courtyard, on the staircases, and in the galleries, chapel, and gardens. The adjoining barracks of the Swiss guards were ablaze. Strikingly, there was practically no pillaging of the staggering quantity of valuables, jewelery, and art found scattered everywhere within the palace, most of these items being brought into the Assembly corridors and rooms by honest plebeians for safekeeping.[42]

The 10 August uprising was promptly sanctioned politically by the Assembly, now emptied of Feuillants and spurred by the Commune. In the late morning, with the fighting at the Tuileries continuing, an Assembly commission of twelve prepared a sensational emergency decree suspending the king from his constitutional duties, dissolving the ministry, and announcing there would shortly be elections for a new National Convention. A fresh executive ministry would be elected by the legislature that very day. The king was suspended "until the National Convention has pronounced on the measures it believes should be adopted to assure the people's sovereignty and the reign of liberty and equality." Placards were posted up in the streets on Assembly orders, summoning all citizens in the name of the nation, liberty, and equality to respect the Rights of Man and the liberty of others, an initial warning to the démagoguistes.[43] At the same time, the Assembly's sweeping law of 9 November 1791 proscribing aristocratic émigrés in arms against the Revolution, vetoed by the king and inoperative until now, was implemented with immediate effect.

The king and royal family were to remain the people's "hostages," guaranteeing there was no further treachery and that those vile "conspirators," the Feuillants, could no longer undermine the "tranquilité publique" through intrigues with the king. Later, on 10 August, the Assembly proclaimed that France's internal troubles since 1789 were due to the nation being continually betrayed by "the executive power," especially a monarch feigning to uphold the Constitution while actually constantly scheming to subvert it. Louis had conspired with the aristocracy "contre la liberté publique" and hence lost all legitimacy. His "continual acts of counter-revolution" necessitated a new constitution, the chief task of the National Convention about to be elected. The royal family, meanwhile, would remain among the Assembly until calm was restored and subsequently be lodged, Brissot intended, under citizen guard in the Luxembourg. Louis was to be detained for as long as the European powers remained in arms fighting on his behalf, the queen and their family also remaining "pour la nation des otages de rigueur." All court pensions were stopped forthwith, with a much-reduced provision of 100,000 francs monthly assigned for the royal family's upkeep.

Figure 6. French School, *Attack on the Tuileries, 10th August 1792*, 18th century, colored engraving. Bibliothèque Nationale, Paris, France / Giraudon / The Bridgeman Art Library.

A delegation of twelve informed the king of his family's indefinite detention and reduced status and upkeep.[44]

More important still, universal male suffrage was proclaimed the fundamental principle of the Revolution. For the first time anywhere in the modern transatlantic world, democracy was adopted as the basis of political legitimacy, a great landmark. All male citizens older than twenty-one, after swearing a civic oath to maintain everything in "the new French constitution that does not depart from the two basic principles of the Revolution, liberty and equality, or in any way infringe the Rights of Man," would be entitled to vote.[45] To ensure the elections' integrity, each departmental primary assembly would send observers to follow proceedings in the others. Several additional revolutionary principles were also clarified on that day or soon afterward. At Brissot's suggestion, before proceeding to elect the new ministry, the Assembly announced that the outgoing ministry "did not have the confidence of the nation," and that formal accusations would be propounded in the people's name.[46] Organizing the Assembly's proceedings was vested, from 12 August, in a new steering committee of twenty-five chaired by Brissot. Proclaiming its own primacy as the voice of the "true sovereign," on 13 August, the Assembly issued an official account of the dethronement, composed by Condorcet, deliberately minimizing the role of popular intervention in the outcome.

To replace the Feuillant executive arm, a new executive of six ministers—of the interior, war, public finances, justice, naval affairs, and foreign affairs—would be elected by the legislature. Voting began immediately. For the first time ever, every minister, commencing with the interior minister, was chosen by the Assembly alone. Each deputy named two candidates (in a loud voice), after which a list was compiled recording how many votes each candidate had received. Then, knowing how much support each candidate had, every deputy would name one on the agreed list for each ministry. Roland triumphantly secured the interior ministry, Danton justice, Clavière finances, Servan army administration, Lebrun foreign affairs, and the mathematician and academician Gaspard Monge (1746–1818) naval affairs. One of the world's chief experts on cannon design as well as geometry, Monge was put forward on Condorcet's recommendation.[47] Pierre Lebrun-Tondu (1754–93), also an eminent mathematician close to Brissot, Carra, and Roland, was yet another prominent editor and intellectual gracing the revolutionary leadership. Prominent in the Liège Revolution of 1787, he had been a leader of the Belgian Revolution's democratic fringe. Danton joined the executive with Brissot's support, the latter hoping in this way to render his then still friendly relations with him a feature of the new power structure.[48] Predictably, not a single Robespierriste or, apart from Danton, populist candidate, was chosen for any ministry or for the Assembly's new steering group. Several sections, including Quatre-Nations, Luxembourg, Arsenal, and Faubourg-Montmartre, asked Pétion to stay on as Paris mayor. But he resigned, preferring to stand for election to the forthcoming Convention and join Brissot's steering committee, in effect becoming part of France's new democratic government.

Even more remarkable than the efficiency and incisiveness of the rising in the capital was the 10 August revolution's swift success in securing concurrence in the country. Lafayette's efforts over the next few days to mobilize forces under his command in the north and bring the Ardennes department over to the king failed dismally,[49] as did his ally Baron Philippe Frédéric Dietrich's attempt to raise Strasbourg. At Marseille, where the mayor, Mourraille, patron of Barbaroux, favored a radical course, the republicans at once won the backing of the section assemblies; Feuillant opponents found themselves arrested. At Avignon too, republican and pro-Jacobin sentiment easily triumphed. The electoral assembly there, meeting on 2 September, chose as their Convention deputies Barbaroux, Omer, Granet, and Bayle, all strongly committed republicans set on ending the monarchy.[50] Town governments that resisted were rapidly replaced. On 22 August, a column of radical Marseillais marched on the departmental capital at Aix-en-Provence, ransacked the city hall, and arrested many administrative officers and staff, along with other suspects, transferring the departmental administration to Marseille, which now dominated the Revolution throughout Provence.[51]

What explains the astonishing solidarity of the August 1792 revolution? By this point, both Feuillants and modérantisme were widely discredited. It was not just the usurpations of particular individuals, many realized through reading and debates, that accounted for France's ills. The moderate constitutionalist structure was illogical, unworkable, and urgently needed changing. Intellectually, observed Lanthenas, the most aware had fully grasped beforehand the need to break the monarchical and modérantiste grip. A key feature of the 10 August rising, he noted, was that practically no one of any reading, judgment, and discernment was any longer willing to support the Crown, aristocracy, and clergy.[52] Meanwhile, Robespierre stayed altogether out of the picture until it was all over, authoritarian populism not yet strong enough to challenge the mix of Brissotins and Left populists who had engineered the insurrection. The French Republic came about suddenly, in a moment, on a basis of surprising consensus without significant resistance in the Assembly, thanks less to the deputies, or indeed, as Prudhomme emphasized, the people, than a band of "courageous writers who had fearlessly proclaimed and developed republican principles" beforehand.[53] It is therefore altogether untrue, as has often been maintained, that on 10 August the people "went further than the Assembly" and "forced its hand."[54] On the contrary, the people played only a passive part: the Assembly's democratic republican wing, concerting with the leadership of certain Paris sections, planned, organized, and engineered a "popular" rising that took charge and consolidated its grip over the Revolution, while the vast majority looked on mostly inactively and uncomprehendingly.

Consolidating the Democratic Revolution

Embracing democracy and freedom of expression and to petition, the legislature, at the urging of the Assembly's committee of public welfare (*secours publics*), also declared for a more interventionist social conscience than in the past. The numbers of poor, it was acknowledged, had considerably increased due to the departure of so many noble émigrés. The nation's responsibility was to ensure a tenable balance between the needs and means of the destitute. Declaring the "poor man's right to public assistance" a guiding principle of democracy and the Revolution, the Assembly began by authorizing a national subsidy for civic hospitals. Hospitals were required to submit certified lists of the revenues they had possessed in 1789 and subsequent losses to their incomes through confiscation of ecclesiastical endowments and benefices.[55] Plans were drawn up for the treasury to transfer a bloc grant to the interior ministry intended to cover the cost of all the hospitals over the next year.

Louis and his family, now truly prisoners, were transferred from the Tuileries on 13 August, not to the sedate Luxembourg, as Brissot proposed, but—at Commune insistence—to the dour Temple instead. On the way, records Gorsas, the royal carriage stopped to view the shattered fragments of the famous seventeen-meter-high equestrian statue of Louis XIV sculpted by François Girardon, inaugurated in 1699 and dominating the Place Vendôme (until now called the Place Louis-le-Grand). The monument had been overthrown and shattered by the crowds on 10 August, and the Commune was considering replacing its pitiable fragments with a pyramid, commemorating the citizens who died in the attack on the Tuileries.[56] Everywhere, the monarchy's end was reflected in the Revolution's changed symbolism. Over the next few days, mountains of statues, busts, portraits, coats of arms, emblems, and inscriptions glorifying monarchs, grandees, courtiers, aristocrats, and cardinals disappeared from sight across France.[57] The names of royal towns, gardens, and palaces at Fontainebleau, Saint-Germain, Saint-Denis, and Choisy-le-Roi were all changed, while the capital's great aristocratic palaces became the headquarters of revolutionary committees and sociétés populaires. Versailles became virtually depopulated within months, its famous gardens sadly degenerating into wretched ruins.

Relentless street-name changing spread to all France's cities, countless local designations redolent of royalty and aristocracy being effaced. No Paris section any longer retained the words "king" or "royal" in its name. On 13 August, section Louis-le-Grand changed its name to Mail; on 21

August, Roi-de-Sicile became Droits-de-l'Homme.[58] The Rue d'Artois, named (since 1770) after the king's brother, the Comte d'Artois, one of the émigré leaders striving to topple the Revolution, became the Rue de Cérutti after the philosophe-révolutionnaire who died the previous February. The section Henri IV was renamed Pont Neuf. Although the "virtues" of Henri IV had previously kept the well-known statue of that monarch beside the bridge in place, it was now removed; in its place was installed a pedestal with tablets proclaiming the Rights of Man.[59] On 17 January 1793, the Paris Commune even ruled that the medieval stone kings adorning the facade of Notre Dame cathedral, and the medallion portrait of Louis XV in the cathedral curate's courtyard with its "blasphemous" inscription "Pietas augusta," should be removed, along with the marble statue of Louis XIV in the Academy of Surgery. All these, the city works department was directed, in consultation with the "commission des arts," were to be stored away unseen.[60]

After the initial euphoria came swift disappointment. The revolutionaries failed to stabilize and consolidate the democratic revolution that now ensued, chiefly because two rival and quite distinct entities— the Brissotin-dominated Assembly and the populist Paris Commune, where Robespierre's men now largely displaced the previous Pétion circle—presented themselves as the authentic voice of the 10 August insurrection. Those who most forcefully appropriated the title of being the true authors of the rising were the factions of Marat and Robespierre, even though, as Pétion expressed it, "the men who attribute to themselves the glory of this *journée* are those to whom it belongs the least."[61] The people, disorientated and divided enough already, found themselves confronted with two strenuously competing accounts of the insurrection and conflicting claims as to what constituted its criteria of legitimacy. The legislature, despite a long speech by Mandar on 17 August eulogizing popular insurrection as the basis of democratic principles, not unnaturally preferred to play down the role of insurgency, emphasizing rather the centrality of constitutional principle.[62] According to the now Brissotin-dominated Assembly, only the future democratically elected new Convention would possess the authority to formalize Louis's dethronement, decide whether to try him for treason, and end the monarchy. Robespierre, Saint-Just, and the now Montagnard-dominated Paris Commune, by contrast, preferred to proceed without more ado to dethrone Louis, sentence him to death for treason—deeming him to have been judged by the people on 10 August—and reorganize the country.[63]

Canvassing and campaigning in the primary and electoral assemblies for the National Convention proceeded throughout late August and early September. In the Théâtre-Français section, the former "citoyens passifs" in theory increased those entitled to vote from 2,617 to 4,294 adult males. But, as before, only a few—under 10 percent—actually attended meetings and voted.[64] These being the first elections in history ever carried out on a universal suffrage basis, the Left republican press went all out to convince the electorate of their special importance, how much the future would be shaped by them, and, as Louvet's *La Sentinelle* stressed, the need for deputies of proven talents and enlightened attitudes to be elected. However, the poorest citizenry were not just urged to vote: in Paris especially they were shepherded a particular way, in favor of the Montagne, with citizens known for Brissotin, as well as "moderate" or royalist sympathies, being firmly discouraged from voting. Those illiterates and barely literate who voted did so rigorously ushered and canvassed by section bosses—in Théâtre-Français, especially the affluent printer Momoro—who were hardly humble men themselves. The outcome was not healthy democratic debate and still less class solidarity but assiduously managed ideological consensus. From August 1792 onward, both the Cordeliers and Jacobins functioned more as ideological vetting machines than debating clubs.

In preparing the elections for the National Convention, Brissotins stressed the, to them, overriding importance of filling the legislature with distinguished men of outstanding talent and revolutionary principle. In this connection, on 24 August, the Assembly adopted the proposal of a delegation led by Marie-Joseph Chénier, with Condorcet's support, urging that France's pending National Convention should be the "congress of the entire world" with regard to the great principles of human happiness and democracy. To promote this ideal, the Assembly should offer honorary citizenship and the right to participate in the Republic's politics and debates to all of humanity's most eminent "apostles of liberty" and foreign benefactors. Since France's Convention was about to forge the world's first democratic constitution based on the Rights of Man, everyone who had helped advance "la raison humaine et préparé les voies de la liberté" in the world, should be recruited as public "allies" of democratic France in her struggle against kings, nobles, and "superstition." Just as the Roman Empire enlisted vassal "kings" as allies, the Republic must adopt all the "philosophes courageux" known for combating tyranny and bigotry and declare these "benefactors of humanity" prized honorary citizens. Particularly honored should be writers whose texts had materially assisted the American and French Revolutions.[65]

Among those proposed by Chénier were Paine, "the immortal author" of *Common Sense* and the *Rights of Man*, Madison of the *Federalist*, and Joseph Priestley, whose victimization at the hands of the Birmingham "King and Church" mob had "covered him with glory," along with Wilberforce, Robertson, Makintosh (for refuting Burke), and the Dutchman Willem Bolts (1735–1808), author of the *Histoire philosophique et politique de Bengale*,[66] "persecuted" by the English East India Company for claiming India's poor and exploited "were not destined by nature to groan eternally under the yoke of oppression."[67] Other nominees were the Milanese radical Gorani, "illustrious through the persecution and hatred" of the Austrian Hapsburgs, inveterate foes of the "bonheur des hommes"; the Swiss school reformer Pestalozzi; and another Dutchman (and uncle of Cloots), Cornelis de Pauw, "flail of all prejudices in his writings on Greeks, Chinese and [Native] Americans." Germany, bent under "the triple yoke" of monarchical, military, and "feudal" tyranny, should be honored through those "esprits généreux" who had achieved self-emancipation despite public servitude, though only one such writer was initially named—Joachim Heinrich Campe (1746–1818). A leading school reformer who had visited Paris in August 1789, together with his later famous pupil, the Aufklärer Wilhelm von Humboldt, to witness the Revolution's initial stages, Campe edited the former *Braunschweigisches Journal*, now transferred (under Prussian pressure) to Danish Altona and renamed the *Schleswigsches Journal*.[68] Denouncing the principle of aristocracy and severely criticizing Montesquieu, Campe and his circle defended "French liberty" and the Rights of Man, propagating in Germany the "immortal principles that will break the chains of all the peoples of the world." For leading Polish opposition to the tyrannical empress Catherine "on the banks of the Vistula," General Malakowski was proposed. By such means could "fraternité universelle," the aim of philosophers and purpose of the social order, be realized.[69]

Chénier's list was debated in the Assembly and expanded, with some names deleted in favor of others. Reflecting Brissot's own background, those afterward receiving honorary citizenship were in fact mostly British and American—Paine, Priestley, Bentham, Wilberforce, Clarkson, Mackintosh, David Williams, Hamilton, Washington, and Madison. But Continental Europeans figured prominently too, namely, Gorani, Cloots, Pestalozzi, Schiller, Klopstock, and another Polish liberator,

Tadeusz Kościuszko, friend of Jefferson, devotee of the *Histoire philosophique,* and advocate of black emancipation, replacing Malakowski. Receiving his letter of invitation to become an honorary French citizen, signed by Roland, Klopstock promptly accepted with pleasure, albeit admonishing Roland that the Revolution must punish those guilty of atrocities (like the September killings in Paris) perpetrated in its name.[70] Though curiously bereft of Belgian Vonckists and leading Dutch Patriots like Pieter Vreede or Gerrit Paape, who had collaborated with Mirabeau in 1787, as well as German democrats like Forster, Dorsch, and Knigge, an impressive enlightened global coterie was in this way officially mobilized behind the Revolution (although several of these, like Washington and Pestalozzi, were not in fact enthusiasts for democracy or the Revolution). The resulting decree of 26 August 1792, moved by Marguerite-Élie Guadet (1758–94), yet another powerful orator and one of Robespierre's most vehement Brissotin foes, marked the high tide of the Revolution's internationalism.

Unrelenting antagonism between the competing Jacobin blocs vying for control of the Revolution—Left democrat and authoritarian populist—was highly obtrusive from the outset, even before the elections for the National Convention. Where Montagnards wanted as much direct popular influence in the forthcoming elections as possible, to maximize the Paris Commune's role and that of the inner sections, Brissotins sought to prevent primary assemblies being captured by cabals of populist "electors." With their stress on talent and experience, Brissotins wanted members of the previous legislative assemblies to be eligible for the new legislature, whereas Robespierre opposed this, aiming to reduce the Brissotin clique as much as possible. Where one side wanted to minimize the role of the Paris municipality in the country's transformation from constitutional monarchy to republic, the other sought to maximize it. When, on 15 August, a delegation from the Commune, headed by Robespierre, demanded all those taken prisoner by the demonstrators on 10 August, together with a list of other "conspirators," should be tried by judges elected by the Parisian sections, this was immediately opposed by the Assembly. The prisoners of 10 August, explained Condorcet in the *Chronique de Paris,* belonged to the whole nation and should be judged constitutionally in its name. Robespierre's demand was fundamentally undemocratic and wrong. The Commune nevertheless arrogated to itself sweeping judicial powers over "suspects."[71]

From 10 August 1792 onward, Montagnard populism was openly at war with Brissotin representative democracy. This marked a most troubling start to the world's first modern democracy. The elections themselves, held in late August and early September, were a long, drawn-out, complex process. Across France, the turnout, as has often been noted, was low. But this was due less to indifference than the arduousness of the procedure. If illiteracy and remoteness hindered many, village and small-town citizens eager to vote had to travel at their own expense to each canton's main place to register with the local primary assembly, establish their credentials often over legal objections used to block votes, and then wait while electoral officials were sworn in and other complex procedures followed. The worst obstacle, though, was the marked tendency, especially in Paris, for primary assemblies to be dominated by cabals of local activists that frequently deterred and disgusted the well intentioned. Although turnout in the departments was commonly under 10 percent and sometimes under six, in some departments it was considerably higher. The vote reached 23 percent in the Pas de Calais, where broad and militant Catholic sentiment was balanced by substantial republican support.[72]

Meanwhile, somber fear and suspicion gripped the capital. The continuing Prussian advance, fall of Longwy, and siege of Verdun, and Lafayette's defection to the Austrians on 17 August 1792—taking many officers with him—spread panic throughout the northeast. The Paris Commune proclaimed a state of emergency, including a general curfew from 29 to 31 August. Between 10 August and the end of the month, an additional 520 individuals, around half of them refractory priests, were arrested on accusations of counterrevolutionary activity.[73] Among those arrested was the royalist journalist Durozoy, seized on 13 August. Robespierre and Marat were later accused by Pétion and others of deliberately fanning this hysteria by inflating talk of betrayal and the number of arrests to unsettle the populace and extend their sway. By 27 and 28 August, wild rumors of plots, spiriting away the king, and releasing all the political prisoners filled the streets and, in turn, provoked talk of breaking into the prisons and slaughtering the interned "counterrevolutionaries" before they could escape. All this, coinciding with the open breach between Assembly and Commune, proved decisive for the Revolution's subsequent history. The Commune decided to arrest Brissot's coeditor at the *Patriote français*, Girey-Dupré, for denouncing the despotic, heavy-handed manner in which the populist section committees carried out searches of homes and individuals. Girey went into hiding. Robespierre addressed the Commune general council defending the house searches, including Girey's arrest, and furiously berated Brissot, Condorcet, and Roland.[74] The Assembly replied on 30 August by quashing the Commune's arrest order as contrary to liberty of the press. A decree formulated by Guadet was issued, dissolving the "provisional general council" of the Commune and instructing each Paris section to appoint two citizens within twenty-four hours to form a new provisional general council until fresh municipal elections could be held.[75] This, of course, was ignored by the Commune and most sections.

Commune and Assembly were now at swords drawn, with Robespierre and his following resolved to work no longer with the democratic republicans. The principal power struggle of the French Revolution had begun. Already earlier, Robespierre's journal had proclaimed that it was not the philosophes, "Condorcet's teachers," the persecutors of Jean-Jacques, who had discovered the true revolutionary path, but plain, ordinary men inspired by "la nature."[76] The balance palpably changed in the wake of the 10 August insurrection. The Montagnards had now captured control over many inner Paris electoral assemblies, though they also still faced stiff opposition in others, notably Lombards, Pont-Neuf, Croix-Rouge, Champs-Élysées, and Louvre. Known for its vigor in opposing aristocracy, the Lombards section, under its president Louvet, fiercely resisted Robespierre's "tyrannie démagogique," declaring the Commune's general council "the usurper" of the sections' rights. Withdrawing their representatives from the council, the Lombards urged other anti-Robespierre sections to follow its lead. The Montagnard section bosses retaliated by pouring vituperation on Louvet and organizing a noisy march on the Lombards section to demonstrate "the people's anger" against this impudent critic of "the Incorruptible." Local feuding in the capital between Robespierre activists and Left republican intellectuals, with the Marseille volunteers often siding with the latter, continued unabated for months and from Paris spread throughout France.[77] Because they had challenged him in his and Marat's Parisian fiefdom, Robespierre bore a special grudge henceforth against Louvet, Girey, Pétion, and Guadet, as well as Brissot and Condorcet, both of whom he ceaselessly vilified.

Robespierre's bid to exclude members of the previous Assembly having failed, Jacobins associated with the former Cercle Social recommended numerous distinguished candidates of all stripes to Paris's voters, including various outgoing deputies. Working through the press, especially Louvet's paper posted up as an affiche in the streets, they urged the election of Pétion, Sieyès, Robespierre, Rabaut, Garat, Buzot, and Grégoire, besides journalists, authors, and local section politicians like Bonneville, Chamfort, Cloots, Carra, Chénier, Collot d'Herbois, Billaud-Varenne, Gorsas, Danton, Chaumette, Fabre, Lanthenas, Manuel, Poullenot, commandant of the Guard in the Lombards, Tallien, and Robert.[78] Robespierre, though, had entirely different ideas. These were all prominent names but by no means all acceptable to him and his populist section bosses. At the Jacobins, it was disputed whether Sieyès and Rabaut should be on the list at all. Considered by some a proponent of "two chambers," a damning charge, Sieyès was defended by others. Rabaut was a Feuillant, objected some, others denied it.[79] Although they disagreed with Sieyès in principle, Brissotins defended his right to stand. In inner Paris, the electoral process was especially closely scrutinized by Jacobin and Cordeliers committees controlled by subordinates of Robespierre, Danton, and Hébert. This involved systematic exclusion of numerous prominent names, especially anybody unsympathetic to Marat and Robespierre. Among those firmly blacklisted were Carra, Gorsas, Louvet, Condorcet, Pétion, and Brissot.[80]

The election process in Paris was interrupted (and influenced) from 2 September by extremely ugly and sinister developments linked to the escalating struggle between the Revolution's two rival factions, occurrences that were to stain the Revolution's reputation permanently. The Paris Commune held an all-night meeting on 30 August at which Robespierre for the first time publicly denounced Brissot, Condorcet, Roland, Guadet, Louvet, and Girey-Dupré as "enemies of the people." The Commune led the revolution of 10 August and was authorized by "the people" to exact vengeance in the people's name on all the Brissotin miscreants defying "the people's voice." Exploiting the momentum flowing from the panic and confusion generated by the developing Prussian invasion, on 2 September Robespierre publicly accused Brissot before the Paris Commune of betraying France to the Prussian commander, "Brunswick."[81] That night, the Commune's Comité de Surveillance ordered a search of Brissot's house and papers. Three commissaires ransacked Brissot's effects but without finding anything incriminating.[82] The Commune's vigilance committee, at Marat's prompting (having himself joined it earlier that day), on 2 and 3 September nevertheless launched an unsuccessful attempt to apprehend the "traitor" Brissot and remove Roland from his ministry. Orders were issued for the arrest of Brissot, Roland, and other deputies accused of "treason." Danton and

Pétion came personally to the town hall, confronted Robespierre, and had the arrest orders rescinded.[83]

The thwarted coup d'état went no further in the end than searches of the houses of the Brissotins,[84] though efforts to tar Brissot and Roland as traitors, planning to flee to England, resumed on 4 September, albeit again countermanded by Danton.[85] By this time, though, the coup had triggered the supposedly spontaneous "popular" disturbances, commencing on the evening of 2 September, that resulted in gruesome organized assaults on the many hundreds of prisoners the Commune and sections had herded into the prisons since 10 August. These numerous political prisoners had deliberately been turned into the object of hysteria and the focus of mounting recrimination between legislature and Commune. Prefaced by talk of finishing with the traitors, the operation was initially encouraged by Carra and Gorsas, as well as Marat and others.[86] Months of exhorting the people to liquidate counterrevolutionaries, aristocrats, rebel priests, and traitors had their fatal effect. The horror began with twenty-four refractory priests being conveyed on four carriages to the Abbey of Saint Germain-des-Prés prison, where they were set upon and butchered in the streets. That night, groups of sansculottes, yelling for the blood of counterrevolutionaries, broke into the prisons, dragging out and executing the political captives crowded within, a horrific nighttime reckoning that converted into reality Marat's and Hébert's ceaseless verbal violence. The scenes were witnessed by small, sullen crowds more inclined to applaud occasional acquittals pronounced by the makeshift juries and benches of judges than the summary executions.

Although afterward Marat, Robespierre, and Danton always insisted on the massacre's spontaneous, "popular" character, its being the work of "the people," Pétion, a helpless eyewitness, Girey, Roland, and other Brissotins, and also the German Jacobins Oelsner and Lux, more accurately labeled the 2–5 September atrocities a systematic, planned conspiracy, methodically perpetrated by just a few dozen people.[87] Prison guards were pushed aside, as was a commission of twelve sent by the Assembly, in an effort to stop the disorder. The perpetrators, recorded Mercier, possibly numbering as few as 300 at each prison, meted out summary "justice" on the spot, both in central Paris and the outlying prisons in Faubourg Saint-Marceau. Peremptory interrogations by makeshift sansculotte committees, backed by armed bands (some reportedly paid by the Commune),[88] prefaced the systematic massacre of the political internees, those "sentenced" to death identified simply

Figure 7. Jean-Louis Prieur the Young (1759–1795), *Journées de Septembre, massacre des prisonniers de l'Abbaye, nuit du 2 au 3 Septembre 1792*, drawing. Musée Carnavalet, Paris. © Musée Carnavalet / Roger-Viollet / The Image Works.

as "nobles," "refractory priests," "Swiss Guards," or "murderers." Altogether, those slaughtered totaled between 1,090 and 1,400, of whom around 223, or about 16 percent, were clergy and another 6 percent Swiss or other royal guards.[89] At the Carmelite Convent, 115 priests were hacked to death, including the ex-archbishop of Arles and bishops of Beauvais and Saintes. More than half the male captives in the Paris prisons were massacred by these gangs and around 8 percent of the women, including thirty-five prostitutes wholly unconnected to the Revolution.[90]

While little documentary evidence survives proving the premeditated complicity of leading Montagnard politicians, and the subsequent widespread talk of their complicity may have been overstated, the atrocities were too organized and the proceedings at the various locations too much of a pattern to have resulted just from spontaneous "popular justice." At the Conciergerie where around 300, the largest batch, were slaughtered, at the Abbey, the Châtelet, where around 220 died, at La Force, and elsewhere (except the Temple where the royal

family was confined), the outbreaks all happened in the same methodical fashion. Billaud-Varenne may not have literally paid cutthroats to
dispatch listed victims at twenty-four livres each,[91] but lesser Commune
officials were physically present at the larger prisons, acting as makeshift
"judges" working from prisoner lists and notes. Sansculotte leaders, recorded Mandar, whose book *Des Insurrections* appeared a few months
later (discreetly pointing to Robespierre's guilt without naming him),
became veritable local "dictateurs," dragging out victims and pronouncing death sentences with unrelenting ferocity.[92] Among those directly
complicit were the Hébertiste Jean-Antoine Rossignol (1759–1802)
at La Force; Stanislas Maillard (1763–94), who had led the march on
Versailles in October 1789, now a Commune official; a "judge" at the
Abbey; and Étienne-Jean Panis (1757–1833), prominent in the house
searches (including that of Brissot's house) and a member of the Commune's vigilance committee who presided at the Châtelet.[93]

Marat and the Commune's vigilance committee, on which Billaud-
Varenne also sat, issued a sinister circular on 3 September to the departments, in the Commune's name, a text apparently printed on Marat's
own press, summoning them to follow Paris's example and slaughter
their interned political prisoners.[94] Attributing responsibility to the
Montagne, especially the Commune's vigilance committee, afterward
regularly infused Brissotin polemic against the Montagnards. The taint
of complicity, however, spread far. Danton, outraged but worried about
compromising his favorable standing among the sansculottes in the
section assemblies, signally failed to take the vigorous action Manuel,
Mandar, and others urged to stop the atrocities.[95] Robespierre, after agitating the people with ceaseless talk of treachery, did nothing at all to
restrain the gangs' fury (apart from visiting the Temple prison to ensure security around the royal family).[96] The slaughter continued until 6
September. "All principles" were sacrificed on the night of 2 September
1792 and subsequent days, lamented Mandar, on the pretext of saving
the country from the enemy. Silence was imposed on the sacred voice
of justice and the cry of humanity. Among the few who made strenu-
ous efforts to halt the atrocities, Mandar rushed to Danton when these
began, pleading for immediate action. He found Danton gathered with
Pétion, Robespierre, Desmoulins, Fabre d'Églantine, Manuel, and the
presidents of the forty-eight sections, partly distracted by news just arrived of Verdun's fall and the latest Prussian advance. Manuel, Brissot,
Fauchet, Mandar, Pétion, and other leading revolutionaries tried to halt
the killing. Pétion's deputy, Louis-Pierre Manuel, visited the Abbey

twice with a Commune deputation, endeavoring to stop the violence. But the bands rebuffed him.[97] The National Guard inexplicably remained inactive.

Brissot's and Girey's *Patriote français* was the only major paper to denounce the atrocities immediately and unreservedly. The rest of the pro-Revolution press did so only belatedly.[98] Robespierre's claim that the killings stemmed from "un mouvement populaire" and were not due to any organized sedition executed by elected officials, was thus initially shared also by non-Montagnards who construed the slaughter as an unfortunate but "necessary" act of popular justice. Prudhomme, Maréchal, Gorsas, Carra, and other anti-Robespierriste journalists admitted as much publicly after later substantially changing their initial view. Looking back in 1797, Prudhomme, as a former front-rank newspaper editor at the time, publicly apologized for and bitterly repented of having whitewashed the horrors of September 1792. He had been grievously at fault, together with Carra and Gorsas, in pronouncing the killings a necessary "act of justice," rough justice executed by an angry, frustrated populace, against the Revolution's enemies, whom lax magistrates were examining too slowly.[99] By contrast, the Dantonist republican theorist Pierre-François Robert (1762–1826) remained adamant that the killing, though terrible, was indeed *nécessaire,* and that those who subsequently changed their tune were "Girondins" who perfidiously defamed Paris and the Revolution.[100]

The inclination to excuse the killings as a frantic, panicky response to the dire circumstances of September 1792 did not, however, alter the fact that the slaughter *was* instigated by one side in the political struggle and subsequently came under the formidable protective curtain of Robespierre's political fiefdom. There can be no serious doubt that the September massacres were closely linked to an organized conspiracy, part of a quest for power, both condoned and organized by authoritarian, antidemocratic elements within the Commune. From October 1792 onward, the prison atrocities were regularly and combatively endorsed only by Marat's and Robespierre's adherents.[101] "The good" and the defensible in Robespierre's discourse were defined exclusively by the *populaire,* even when no genuine popular movement was involved and the outcome was a horrific mass crime.

While the prison massacres continued, so did the process of "electing" Paris's deputies for the Convention. First in his own section, Vendôme, and then in most sections, Robespierre organized an extremely stringent vetting procedure. Candidates were nominated by the section assemblies' *électeurs* and then the candidates proposed were discussed in the assemblies prior to voting, with the Jacobins supervising the process. The sections accepted Robespierre's proposal that broad categories of candidates would be declared "anti-civique" and disqualified as unsuitable via a double screening procedure both beforehand and after the voting. Officially, those deleted before voting began belonged to the Club Monarchique and Feuillants, but even if provisionally elected, in practice those disqualified included also all Brissotins. On 5 September, Robespierre himself triumphantly emerged as the first of Paris's new deputies "elected." Desmoulins was voted in next, but the third "winner," Armand, Comte de Kersaint (1741–93), who also won a considerable vote, was immediately disqualified as a Brissotin (rather than as a noble), as were others afterward.[102]

Like so much in his career, Robespierre's unabashed vote-rigging and manipulation of the electoral assemblies was, of course, angrily denounced by his opponents, Carra labeling it a "scandalous empire." "Almost always at the moment despotism is overthrown," held Louvet, "*agitateurs* appear fomenting anarchy to oppress and tyrannize in their turn."[103] Brissot and Pétion formally protested to the Commune. The sections, complained Brissot, were being obliged by the "charlatans manipulating the people by proclaiming popular sovereignty" to vet their choice of candidates rigorously prior to and subsequent to voting. Although the virulent feuding between Left republicans and démagoguistes had been obvious to seasoned observers for months, on the eve of these historic and crucial elections, most Parisians understood little of this. The fierce vilification of the still widely popular Pétion by self-styled Patriots, a campaign denounced by *La Sentinelle* as a "horrible manoeuvre," seemed incomprehensible to most people.[104]

The vote-rigging was relentless. In a speech before the Paris electoral assembly on 9 September, Robespierre directed the "electeurs" to prefer Marat to the English philosopher Joseph Priestley, a candidate proposed by Brissot and Condorcet. "I know there exists a coalition of *philosophes*," complained Robespierre, "I know that Messieurs Condorcet and Brissot seek to put *philosophes* in the Convention. But what need have we of these men who have done nothing but write books?" What was needed were pure, ordinary men, Patriots fighting despotism and thoroughly identifying with the people and understanding their needs.[105] What could be meaner, more dishonest, or ridiculous, retorted Louvet, than claiming, without mentioning Priestley's heroic commitment to democracy and free expression, his science and philosophy, or the riot that demolished his home and laboratory in Birmingham, that the odious Marat, loathsomely hailed at the Jacobins by Chabot as a great man, was a worthier candidate than the Englishman?[106] Priestley's candidacy was backed by *La Sentinelle*, as were the candidacies of Bentham and the Manchester radical Cooper.[107] The *Patriote français* urged Parisians to elect Sieyès, Condorcet, Kersaint, Dusaulx, Chamfort, Lanthenas, Louvet, and Gorsas, as well as Priestley, Bentham, and David Williams.[108] But in Paris Robespierre's insistence on "ordinary" men triumphed, and all Brissotin candidates were excluded.

The republican press repeatedly warned Parisians of the danger they incurred with their apathy and failure to attend section assemblies in adequate numbers. Dwindling attendances rendered chicanery and manipulation easy. The Paris electoral council, explained Pétion, worked from a fixed list adhered to "exactement," ensuring only Marat's and Robespierre's partisans were elected. The point of the manipulation was to remove from Paris's representation in the national legislature every independent-minded figure likely to back the republican democrats. Brissot, Pétion, Sieyès, Condorcet, Bonneville, Villette, Guadet, Paine, Priestley, and other prominent Left republicans accordingly all failed to secure Convention seats for Paris. Not one of the "excellent republicans" proposed by Brissotins was adopted. In the new legislature, all twenty-four deputies representing the capital firmly aligned with the Montagne, no less than fourteen, including Billaud-Varenne, Hébert, Chaumette, Fréron, Ronsin, Vincent, Legendre, Danton, Marat, and Desmoulins—all residents of just one section, the Cordeliers-controlled Théatre-Français, the most fertile in instigating insurrection. Sixteen of the new Paris deputies were simultaneously members also of the new Paris city council, with only Pétion and Manuel remaining from the former Commune.[109] The resulting Montagnard team representing Paris in the legislature, or what Prudhomme termed "députation exécrable," exuded unremitting consensus directed from the city hall.

Vote-rigging could not, however, prevent the distinguished candidates rejected in Paris from securing election as Convention deputies elsewhere, and most did.[110] Debarred in Paris, Sieyès was elected by three departments far from the capital; Pétion and Brissot were adopted by Eure et Loire, Cloots and Villette by L'Oise, Lanthenas by Haute-Loire and Rhône-et-Loire.[111] Gorsas was elected by two departments, Priestley two, Paine by three, Condorcet five, and Carra, rejected in Paris but famous throughout France due to his paper, by no less than eight departments.[112] What the manipulation did achieve was a formidable

Parisian bloc in the Assembly, firmly under Robespierre's thumb. It also generated a wholly artificial ostensible rift between "Paris" and the "Gironde," loudly trumpeted by the Montagne but actually nothing of the kind. This bogus split between Paris and distant provinces worked well for the Montagne in publicity terms but had little to do with reality on the ground. Ironically, several of those around Brissot and Pétion (who both came from nearby Chartres, and had lived mostly in Paris), were, like Louvet, more authentically Parisian than Robespierre (who was from Arras), Marat (who was Swiss), or Billaud-Varenne (raised in La Rochelle). Among leading démagoguistes, only Collot d'Herbois could plausibly be termed "Parisian."[113]

The National Convention comprised 750 deputies, ninety-six of whom had sat in the 1789 Assembly and 190 in that of 1791–92. Assembly seating arrangements underwent a notable shift. Until now, the left side had been associated with democratic, republican, and radical viewpoints. But with the developing quarrel about which faction truly represented the people's interests, the Montagne occupied the Left while the Brissotins moved their seats to sit opposite and confront their opponents, enabling the Montagnards to label Brissot, Vergniaud, Buzot, and others who moved at this juncture "the Right." As the struggle developed, though, the democratic faction (with more justification) reversed the perspective for viewing the hall, designating themselves "the Left," which philosophically and constitutionally they were, being the more democratic and republican grouping. Hence, "the Left" in journals like Louvet's *La Sentinelle* are the Brissotins while Marat's and Robespierre's populist faction, demanding undivided authority, became the new "Right," replacing the Feuillants.[114] From the quarrel as to who genuinely represented the Left arose a confusion of terms that typified the ensuing struggle for the Revolution during 1792–93. Nearly all the real intellect and talent in the Assembly, Levasseur and honest Montagnards admitted, lay on what the Brissotins called "the Left" with the philosophistes.[115] Montagnards hoped to compensate for what they lacked in intellectual standing with solid zeal and unquestioning loyalty to their "glorious" leaders, Marat and Robespierre.

Democratically elected, the Convention possessed greater stature and authority than any previous legislature had enjoyed. The new Assembly congregated on 20 September amid extraordinary euphoria, coinciding as it did with the repulse of the Prussian invasion with the decisive victory at Valmy. The legislature's first act, following a long celebratory opening session amid frantic applause, was to declare the

thirteen-hundred-year-old French monarchy at an end. Year I of the Republic, it decreed, would begin on 22 September. France thus became a
formal republic in September 1792, adopting a stringently antimonarchical and antiaristocratic rhetoric and profile in visual imagery while
simultaneously launching a barrage of political propaganda closely
linked to the intensifying war with practically all of Europe. French officers, deserting at this point by the same token, privately declared war
on the Republic, joining with the émigrés already abroad in waging a
universal struggle of democracy versus rank, religion, and monarchy.

CHAPTER 11

Republicans Divided

(SEPTEMBER 1792–MARCH 1793)

From August 1792 until June 1793, for the first time in world history, declared democratic republicans held the reins controlling government, albeit precariously. More firmly, they also dominated the pro-Revolution newspapers and public ceremonies shaping public opinion and debate. Until 1789, royalty, aristocracy, and the high clergy had alone shaped French society's international and public image. Now, for a time, the core values of a republican Revolution determined the styles, emblems, and architectural facades, and fixed the forms and themes of the new society, determining policy in education, science, and the arts, and correctness in the renaming of buildings, streets, squares, palaces, law courts, naval vessels, barracks, and gardens.

From the summer of 1792 until Robespierre's coup (June 1793), the Left republicans proclaimed democracy, universalism, and equality anchored in reason and Enlightenment—mankind's new secular creed—and created France's new public imagery of great men and worthy accomplishment. To help project this postmonarchical, postaristocratic, and postecclesiastical world, a vast quantity of busts, portraits, and fine engravings of France's publicly acclaimed "grands hommes" was mass-produced to be exhibited in homes, offices, and public buildings, displayed in public ceremonies, and advertised in the papers. It was a gallery of the nation's heroes, with all military commanders, aristocrats, and royalty duly purged. In the autumn of 1792, the main series of advertised engravings presenting the Republic's grands hommes (until democratic values were discarded in the summer of 1793 and Marat had to be added) were Mirabeau, Voltaire, Rousseau, Mably, Montesquieu, Montaigne, Linnaeus, Buffon, Fénelon, Helvétius, Diderot, and Raynal, with the projected addition of Descartes. Never before had science, literature, and philosophy exercised such hegemony over officially inspired representation of what is admirable, instructive, and worthy in human life and achievement, and what should be publicly celebrated.[1]

Cultural transformation began immediately. Furiously applauded, the Paris procurator, Louis-Pierre Manuel, informed the Commune's general council meeting on 21 September 1792 that the National Convention had voted to abolish the monarchy and the royal succession forever. Just minutes later, as a subsequent point of business, the Commune accepted his proposal that a central Paris street, the Rue Sainte-Anne, should be renamed the Rue d'Helvétius, since Helvétius's works were among those that had introduced "the Revolution" into men's minds and because this "philosophe had consistently pleaded the cause of the people." In this way, as La Harpe later noted disapprovingly, the Revolution consecrated Helvétius as *un sage révolutionnaire*, a revolutionary thinker.[2] The transformation in imagery and compulsive renaming accompanied a renewed surge of revolutionary enactments, a grandiose program of fundamental social and institutional reform intensively debated and cast into legislation during the autumn of 1792. The first and most crucial priority was the new Constitution, the world's first modern democratic constitution. Fundamental new approaches to marriage, gender relations, taxation, pensions, education, organizing the armed forces, and regulating family law followed closely behind. Civil divorce and the right of immediate remarriage, thus far successfully resisted by clergy, king, and Feuillants, finally became law during the very last session of the old legislature on 20 September 1792. There was little opposition in the Assembly, but once promulgated, the world's first modern divorce law provoked considerable disapproval in the country, not only among conservatives but with much of town and rural society deploring what was deemed its sanctioning of license and undue personal freedom for women.[3]

The vital principle of steeply graduated taxation, creating tax bands to be imposed on surplus landed and inherited wealth, was established for the first time by an edict of March 1793.[4] No less essential, thorough reform of the country's inheritance laws was promulgated under decrees of 25 October and 14 November 1792, and 4 January and 7 March 1793. Composed by a group led by a passionately anti-Montagnard legal expert from Montpellier, Jean-Jacques Régis de Cambacérès (1753–1824), these equalized the rights of male and female direct descendants, including the illegitimate; drastically curtailed the ability of the wealthy to dispose of possessions unequally or according to preference through wills and codicils; and ended bequeathing of large estates intact (primogeniture) wherever more than one direct descendant existed.

But if the Revolution was to remain securely on track as an enlightened democratic republican revolutionary program, there was also an urgent need, stressed Lanthenas, to hold fast to and amplify its core principles, and this meant carefully distinguishing between genuinely instructing the people, indispensable if the Revolution was to succeed, and manipulating popular passions and prejudices in the style of Marat and Robespierre.[5] The latter, Lanthenas believed, were steadily perverting popular sentiment for political ends, a tendency exceedingly prejudicial, dangerous, and inimical to the Revolution. They were not just manipulating popular disgruntlement in the streets but channeling it to create a new kind of "theology." Robespierre's philosophique detractors, including Condorcet in the *Chronique de Paris* on 8 November, viewed him as literally a "chef de secte," a preacher attended by his *dévots*.[6] Asked by colleagues at this point to draft an appeal to the nation reaffirming the principles of representative democracy, Condorcet wrote his *Adresse de l'Assemblée nationale aux français*, explaining what he too considered the greatest peril confronting the Revolution—the advance of prejudices and a new form of tyranny. But it was not easy to project this message widely and vigorously enough. In the upshot, it was Maratisme and the Robespierristes that persuaded some sansculottes and some of France's activist illiterate and barely literate. This was the tragedy of the Revolution.

Despite awareness of the Montagne's obvious complicity in the September massacres, and Brissotin control of the journals, the Left republicans inexorably if slowly lost ground. The "true republicans," recounted Mercier later, toppled the Lameths and expelled the Feuillants from the Jacobins. But, subsequently, it was the turn of the "true republicans" to be ejected, as the club's majority shifted behind Robespierre, Marat, and Hébert.[7] Opposition to Robespierre and Marat, observed Mercier, was led by men who acquired their revolutionary values through study, philosophy, and literary activities. Because their revolution was rooted in la philosophie, they established the tolerance, "inclinations paisibles," and regard for the Rights of Man that eventually caused their own downfall. The Brissotins eventually lost the struggle for the Revolution and for France, he explained, because they did not believe you must "immolate human victims on the altar of liberty," because they were less ruthless and dishonest than their rivals. Men's misfortunes, they supposed, stem more from error than depravity, but in this regard they were fatally mistaken.[8]

So poisoned were relations between the factions by wrangling over the September prison massacres, there seemed to be no way to dissipate the bad feeling that powerfully erupted in a furious debate in the National Assembly, now split irretrievably along Brissotin-Montagnard lines, on 24 and 25 September. On that occasion, the veteran Breton naval official and foe of the Montagne, Kersaint, recently debarred from the Paris elections, stressed the danger posed by a certain powerful bloc extending its grip over Paris and urged the need to neutralize it by stationing a force of volunteer National Guard from other departments near the capital. Complete uproar ensued. Deputies aligned with the Paris Commune considered this a political declaration of war.[9]

Revolutionary democratic republicanism was overwhelmed first, after a bitter fight, in the Paris Commune and the Jacobin Club. From the defection of the Feuillants in July 1791 until August 1792, as Mercier noted, the radical Left predominated at the Paris Jacobins. But from August 1792, their ascendancy eroded as Marat and Robespierre decisively gained ground. During the autumn, as the feuding between the rival blocs vying for control of the Republic was further embittered by the political and psychological aftermath of the September massacres, the coalition of Robespierre, Marat, Hébert, Billaud-Varenne, Chabot, Collot d'Herbois, Couthon, and Jean-Lambert Tallien, a notary's clerk before the Revolution and now a key manager of the Lombards section, began widening its grip over inner Paris sections and consolidating its hold over the Commune and Jacobins.

The festering rift within the Jacobins had been obvious for months. But from September 1792 onward, revulsion over the ghastly slaughter widened the split both in the Convention and the Jacobins, fueling bitter recrimination and helping spread the feuding to sociétés populaires throughout France. This process led to the gradual forcing out of the Left democrats from the Paris club. There were signs of this already earlier. In March 1792, noted the astronomer Jérôme Lalande (1732–1807), Condorcet ceased attending the Jacobins "where Robespierre was preparing the ground for despotism."[10] But after the September massacres, leading Brissotins were one by one virulently denounced and systematically excised from the Jacobins' membership rolls. Continually exalting the *tout populaire*, and vilifying Brissot, Pétion, Guadet, Vergniaud, and Condorcet as "ambitious aristocrats," Robespierre's followers won over the galleries.[11]

Brissot's expulsion followed several articles in his *Patriote français* of September 1792, berating the group of "anarchic, demagogic deputies" who now dominated the Commune and had caused the Convention to become hopelessly divided between opposing factions, his opponents controlling the Jacobins despite comprising under a third of the Assembly. This faction was playing a ruthless disruptive, counterproductive, and anarchic role, endangering the Revolution.[12] Chabot and Collot d'Herbois retaliated by accusing Brissot (and Roland) of conspiring to besmirch the reputations of Robespierre and Marat in the club and among the public. Accorded opportunities to appear in person to explain his press attacks on the Montagne's leaders, Brissot declined. Following an official letter of warning, composed by Desmoulins, he was expelled from the Jacobins by majority vote on 12 October 1792. Members intending to speak in Brissot's favor were prevented from doing so, a clear sign the era of genuine debate was over. Afterward, the Club circulated a letter of justification, dated 15 October, to provincial affiliate societies, repeating Desmoulins's earlier charge that Brissot had colluded with Lafayette and defended him after the July 1791 Champ de Mars massacre, and advocated war without having adequately prepared the country.[13]

Brissot replied with a pamphlet entitled *À tous les républicains de France, sur la Société des Jacobins de Paris*, dated 24 October 1792, publicly attributing his expulsion to "perfidious men" who were out to level all knowledge, virtue, and talent by applying the principle of equality in the crassest fashion. Lafayette, he admitted, had systematically tricked and deceived him. He had wrongly believed Lafayette's assurances that he was a "republican," but had since broken with him altogether. Despite Desmoulins's role in rendering him a victim of conspiracy charges, it was Robespierre who led those designating Brissot as a traitor working with Lafayette. Yet, far from being a paragon of revolutionary virtue, Robespierre had not even been a republican either before July 1791 or after the king's flight to Varennes, when Condorcet, Bonneville, and Brissot had prepared and directed the Revolution's turn toward republicanism.[14] Robespierre, furthermore, had been absent on 20 June and 10 August 1792, and, indeed, was nowhere to be seen during any of the Revolution's major journées.

Reaction to Brissot's expulsion was everywhere mixed. Cherbourg, Périgueux, the Bordeaux Club of Recollects, and the "eastern club" of Angers backed Brissot, the last publishing a missive threatening to sever relations with the Paris Jacobins if Robespierre and Marat were not sent packing. Brissot urged the provincial clubs to respect the Convention's rulings but boycott directives from the Jacobins. Indeed, he urged provincial Jacobin clubs to disaffiliate. The whole principle of affiliation he now dismissed as an unhealthy device of subordination to the capital. Backed by Gorsas's paper in particular, Brissot and his allies succeeded in persuading Chartres, Meaux, Nantes, Béziers, and eventually Caen and some other societies to break with the Paris Jacobins. But his expulsion also greatly weakened the voice of the remaining Leftist republicans who were fighting within the Jacobins. Before long, during October and November, Roland and Lanthenas were similarly expelled, as was Louvet, while Carra, earlier among the Jacobins' most active members, also began boycotting the club.[15]

At the Paris Jacobins, Robespierre now held sway unchallenged, and over the next months addressed the club more frequently than anyone else, partly denouncing the court and Lafayette but chiefly, observed Louvet, declaiming "without pause and without restraint" against la philosophie and the philosophes, against the genuine republicans, and all those "known for their virtues and talent."[16] His speech at the Jacobins on 28 October 1792, shortly after the appearance of Brissot's pamphlet, for example, was extremely clever in its way of depicting his Brissotin political rivals. "More criminal in their methods than all the factions that preceded them," their hearts full of the poison of hatred and defiance, they had turned calumny into an art. No one was more skilled than the Girondins at defaming Paris and the true defenders of the Revolution. How do they dishonor liberty? They refer to the political clubs as a source of "anarchy," revolutionary insurrections as "troubles" and "désordres," opposition to tyrannical decrees aimed at reducing most of the people to the status of helots as "déclamations extravagantes." In this way, Brissot and his friends refined the art of using odious words to disguise their ambition and "aristocratic" intrigues under the guise of honorable labels.[17]

With his acolytes carefully distributed around the hall, Robespierre's method of orchestrating debates was daily to pack the galleries with seven or eight hundred sansculottes, paid for the day, trained to cheer together, applaud, hiss, or stamp following given signals. Robespierre turned the club into a well-oiled machine attuned to his autocratic will.[18] The uninterrupted applause greeting his speeches was no longer applause in any ordinary sense but a ritual response, "un enthousiasme réligieux," holy fury ready to rip apart any dissenter. If a non-Robespierriste deputy objected to his pronouncements at the Jacobins, an infallible mechanism for wrecking every such attempt was now firmly in place. It began with gentle murmuring, worked up to loud interjections, and culminated in thunderous stamping, hissing, and denunciation. If a critic evinced only mild republican inclinations, he would be shouted down as a Feuillant; if he praised "the Left wing of the Assembly, he was an *intriguant*." If he disputed the outrageous calumny heaped on the Left republicans, he was a traitor. If he implied the people should not idolize anyone, he was an enemy of the people.[19] By such methods were Condorcet, Brissot, Roland, Guadet, and Louvet hounded out. Robespierre professed to idolize only what was *tout populaire*, but he alone classified what was *populaire* and how the views of ordinary man should be channeled. This step-by-step expulsion of Brissotins from the Jacobins eventually isolated the democratic republicans from the streets and section assemblies, turning the Revolution's intellectual powerhouse, its circles of leading deputies, and the key salons—those of Mme. Roland, Sophie Condorcet, and Mme. de Helvéius—and finally even the Convention and press, into a segregated world beyond, rejected, besieged, and aloof.

Yet, for the moment, Louis XVI's dethronement resounded as a triumph for both sansculottes and democratic republicans. The main question in the autumn of 1792 was how the irreparable rift polarizing the country's politics could be prevented from becoming a paralyzing deadlock. The new Paris Commune had consolidated its grip too far for its ascendancy over many Paris sections and the Jacobin Club to be further contested. Tension in the capital indeed reached such a point that "certain deputies" now felt unsafe there, Barbaroux and Vergniaud being especially at risk, reported the press, owing to their forthright denunciations of Marat over the September massacres.[20] Honest Montagnards like the surgeon René Levasseur (1747–1834), a deputy from Le Mans, genuinely regretted needing to fight such obviously sincere and gifted republican democrats as Barbaroux, Vergniaud, or Louvet. What lay behind this struggle? To Levasseur, the tragedy arose from Brissot's and his colleagues' selfish pursuit of personal feuds against the only two absolutely irreproachable and indispensable revolutionary leaders, Robespierre and Marat.[21] It was this robust egalitarian's absolute, unquestioning trust in these leaders that fatally misled him and convinced him that the Brissotins had to be overcome.

Most aware commentators close at hand, like Mercier or Bishop Fauchet, viewed matters rather differently. The radical Christian bishop Fauchet of Calvados, having bitterly quarreled with both factions, nevertheless entertained no doubt that the "Girondins" were more honest, as well as more eloquent and talented, than the Robespierristes. He opposed Brissot as well as Bonneville and Cloots, but insofar as Brissot "conspired," it was only, he believed, to advance "la liberté, la raison et la philosophie." The most essential difference between Brissotins and Montagnards, he maintained, was that the Brissotins were sincere republicans while the Robespierristes were predominantly ambitious hypocrites manipulating the most ignorant part of the population, albeit Marat, at least, was no hypocrite. Rather, he all too openly said what he meant: "cut off two hundred thousand heads" and impose "Robespierre's dictatorship!"[22]

Of course, the Montagne were inspired by more than just appetite for power. There were two other powerful currents, one of which was Robespierre's "theology" mixed with a debased form of philosophy. The Revolution began well, recounted Mercier years later, but in the summer of 1793, it was diverted by ambitious upstarts. Some of these were obvious rascals, but they were mixed with dangerously fanatical types like "Collot d'Herbois, Billaud-Varenne, Lequinio, Babeuf, [and] Antonelle," who deemed themselves philosophes and, like the main bloc of the revolutionary leadership, extracted their ideas from books of "modern philosophy," but more superficially and differently, perverting the core concepts into "émanations contagieuses." "True republicans" were right to insist that ignorance is the basis of barbarism but forgot that "un demi-savoir," half knowing, is even worse, producing instead of genuine philosophes a breed of intolerant "theologians," usurpers emanating error, exaggeration, and extravagance, disastrously embraced as the truth by the ignorant.[23]

Equally integral to the clash that wrecked the Revolution was a powerful socioeconomic factor. This was emphasized, among others, by the older Marc-Antoine Jullien (1744–1821), "Jullien de la Drôme," father of the Marc-Antoine Jullien (1775–1848) who was one of Robespierre's most ardent acolytes. Elected a Convention deputy in September 1792, the older Jullien also backed Robespierre. In a letter of the following December, he warned his son against too obviously parading his zeal for equality. The "great vice of our social system," something probably irresolvable, is "the monstrous inequality of fortunes." The rich understand the resentment this causes but will not tolerate a genuinely democratic republic, knowing sooner or later this will deprive them of some of their wealth. "That is the rock on which the modern philosophy founders. It has indeed established equality of rights, but it wants to uphold that prodigious inequality of fortunes, putting the poor at the mercy of the rich, and making the rich arbiters of the poor man's rights, by withholding the right to subsistence."[24] Yet, while la philosophie moderne as developed by Diderot, d'Holbach, Helvétius, and Condorcet certainly declined to promote wealth redistribution over everything else, and was accused by militant egalitarians of nurturing *principes anti-populaires*,[25] neither did it sanction gross inequality of wealth. Rather, it undertook to counter inequality while also rejecting draconian recipes. The real stumbling block was that radical ideas placed political and legal reform, basic freedoms, human rights, education, and public instruction alongside reducing economic inequality, rejecting extralegal means, tyranny, and social violence as ways to achieve wealth redistribution. This created the possibility to mobilize sansculotte resentment against the Left republicans who forged and directed the Revolution. By promising more draconian recipes and giving greater priority, at least rhetorically, to economic leveling, the Montagne were able to wrest power from the democrats.

Yet, most Montagnards, stressed the older Jullien, unlike him and his son, were not strongly committed to the cause of economic equality. The career of Jean-Marie Collot d'Herbois (1750–96) well illustrates the paucity of most of the populist authoritarians' political culture. A flamboyant comedy actor, after 1789 he abandoned the theater and became active in the Revolution. A long-standing Jacobin, in the autumn of 1792 he emerged, with the ex-Capuchin Chabot, as a leader of the campaign in Paris to denounce Brissot, whom he fiercely resented, following an earlier personal quarrel. Collot d'Herbois, the man who during the Terror put Lyon to the sack—and who in late 1793 directed the repression of the French theater world—perfectly illustrated the narrowness, intolerance, and brutality of the "Revolution of the Will" and its ability to sway the galleries with half-baked concepts ruthlessly applied.[26]

Many years afterward, an old Montagnard approached Mercier saying, "Hé! Philosophe, what should we have done?" The opposite," retorted Mercier, "to what you did."[27] The philosophes always intended a revolution in "les mœurs"—men's attitudes, habits, morality, and way of life. Most Montagnards, on the other hand, according to Mercier, characterized principally by ignorance and lack of enlightenment, desired (unlike the Julliens) only a revolution in government to concentrate power within their own hands, which they eventually achieved, though not until June 1793. Meanwhile, was there any way to resolve the crisis in such a manner as to preserve the Revolution's core values?

While Danton's group retained some standing with the Paris sansculottes and could act as a bridge to the Left republicans, the Revolution's democratic freedoms could perhaps still be defended in the Paris sections, Commune, and Jacobins, and the budding dictatorship averted. Ideologically, Dantonistes, and Desmoulins especially, tended to side with the democrats committed to upholding freedom of expression. Desmoulins constantly invoked the Rights of Man and freedom of the press in his speeches and articles, inspired less by Rousseau (of whom he became increasingly critical at this time) than a range of radical republican thinkers.[28]

Republicanism is one thing, admonished Jean-Baptiste Louvet de Couvret (1760–97) in his affiche paper of 29 September 1792, the doctrine of the *tartuffes* and sycophants of the Montagne something entirely different. The Montagne was simply a new kind of despotism claiming to be backed by the common people. In fact, nobody spoke more of their devotion to the people and the "public happiness" than these "hypocrites," whose bloodied hands propagated only strife, hatred, oppression, and death. Louvet, a former bookseller's agent who, in April 1792, had campaigned for a law to fix authors' rights over their writings to prevent "brigands" from producing pirated editions,[29] now ranked among the most outspoken Left republicans fighting the Montagnard challenge in Paris. He labeled the perpetrators of the September horrors sycophants of "the decimvirs, Mariuses and Sullas" (i.e., Robespierre and Marat). The daggers had to be wrested from the hands of such *missionaires de despotisme* while there was yet time.[30] To achieve this, Parisians must stand together against those usurping their name, and so must the philosophes: for the philosophes, the Montagne "have sworn an undying hatred; they wish to snuff out the light that they flee and fear."[31]

The Revolution was divided by a schism philosophical, moral, ideological, and personal, but contrary to what has often been claimed, the rift was in no way geographical. Superficially dominant, but by no means swaying the majority or uncontested in Paris, the Montagne's great weakness was a general lack of support throughout provincial France, with the partial exceptions of Lyon, Strasbourg, and Marseille. Although there was also much opposition to the Montagne in Marseille, the Jacobin faction there, headed by Moise Bayle and Granet, had for the moment defeated Barbaroux's followers.[32] Broadly, the effect of the expulsions from the Paris Jacobins was to spread the growing ideological rift everywhere across France.

Mandar wrestled with the country's predicament in his remarkable treatise on popular insurrection, completed under the shadow of the September massacres and published (with some hesitation) in January 1793. His sole concern, he claimed, was the well-being and *bonheur* of the people. All republicans agreed that sovereignty lies in the people and that the sole purpose of the state is the people's welfare.[33] No matter what titles the state and its representatives award themselves, where laws are not made for the people's benefit, subjects remain "slaves." It is via popular insurrections that tyranny is overthrown and a people frees itself to become great, happy, and powerful, "libre en un mot." The Dutch and Swiss owed their splendid republican traditions to popular insurrection undertaken with courage and resolve. Admirable also was the Neapolitan revolt of 1647–48 led by Masaniello. But it was especially the American Revolution that had given the French a "great and instructive lesson," for it demonstrated that while popular insurrection opens the way to liberty, it is also dangerous.[34]

Mandar peppered his text with quotes from Montesquieu, Rousseau, Helvétius, Gibbon, Paine, Rabaut, Cérutti, Mirabeau, Bonneville, Nedham, and the Dunkirk writer James Rutledge.[35] Mandar's most essential doctrine, though, was rooted in Diderot and the *Histoire philosophique*: his principal point was that revolutionary gains are prone to be rapidly negated by popular ignorance.[36] Had not Cromwell ruined the English Revolution by exploiting the people's naïveté? Had not Maurice of Nassau overthrown Oldenbarnevelt, wrecking the Dutch Republic by mobilizing Calvinist bigotry—that is, exploiting ordinary men's ignorance? Were not the Dutch today, despite Johan de Witt's efforts, again utterly abject under the House of Orange's despotic sway, owing to ordinary prejudice and error? Mandar (like Diderot and Mirabeau before him) urged the Dutch to rise again, only this time with more awareness, discarding the old constitution, reversing the "odious revolution" that had chained them down for sixty months (i.e., since the Dutch democratic movement's overthrow in 1787), expelling the Orangists, and breaking their stadtholder's "slavish alliance" with Britain and Prussia.[37]

Popular insurrections are indispensable to the fight for freedom but are equally a menace driven by passion, "tempests" lurching all too readily to excess, undermining the very principles that drive them and the liberty that is their goal. Unfortunately, the French had not yet grasped this. All popular insurrection fights oppression but is readily diverted by vested interests and intruders to become an instrument of tyranny.

It was the people's ignorance and strange submission to "superstition," contended Mandar, that accustomed them to willingly allow the wealth accruing from their own labor to be appropriated by kings, nobles, and Church, and their young men to be recruited into armies wholly dedicated to the "superstition of royal ambition"![38] The July and October 1789 risings grounded the Revolution and its core values, but only because the Revolution's course followed a mature system of revolutionary thought perfected by those "immortal geniuses"—"the prophetic Mably," the "wise Condillac," Boulanger, Raynal, Voltaire, Helvétius, and Diderot. These sages had generated "un atmosphère croissant de lumières et de sagesse," solidly anchoring the Revolution in true enlightenment and dissipating the darkness of ignorance. The Revolution was the fruit of a sudden, general upsurge of understanding: "en un moment l'explosion a été général." It occurred chiefly in France, but not only, and belonged to everyone everywhere, including England, where it was insistently proclaimed by "T. Paine, J. Courtenay" and "J. Priestley."[39]

When organizing insurrection, revolutionary leaders must, of course, secure key targets—arsenals of weapons, the national treasury, prisons, guard-posts, and granaries. But these must be held by reliable soldier-citizens, "citoyens vertueux," something impossible without first cultivating "good citizenship" by inculcating justice and understanding, and instituting checks to constrain the people's natural fury and irrationality. Brutalized by tyranny, ignorant minds acquire a more elevated character only slowly, by degrees. Had not Rousseau shown, in the dedication of his discourse on inequality to the Genevan Republic, that a people long subjected to tyranny, and abject from ignominious labor, becomes "une stupide populace," to be managed with wisdom, tact, and care if it is to breathe the air of liberty?[40] But where Rousseau locates this higher character in virtue, nature, and proud courage, Mandar, like the Left republican leadership, emphasized rather Enlightenment and understanding. Only when the citizenry combines "vertus civiques" and an intrepid spirit in defense of liberty and humanity, justice, and obedience to the law, disdaining superstition, hatred, and vengeance, can despotism be overthrown securely and legitimately.[41] Pétion, the former mayor of Paris (famous for his speeches urging black emancipation), in Mandar's opinion provided an outstanding role model of such integrity and civic virtue (a judgment shared by Mme. Roland). The true criteria for evaluating officeholders, Mandar agreed with Pétion, are equality and justice, and pursuit of "le plus grand bonheur de tous et l'harmonie sociale."[42]

Public education and information was an arena where republican Left and populist authoritarianism clashed unceasingly. Education is the source of everything good, held Pétion, and ignorance the source of everything bad. It was essential to instruct the artisan class and dispel the thickening cloud obscuring laboring men's grasp of what was happening. When addressing the laboring classes, revolutionary leaders should never resort to authority or force but employ *la raison* and explain things. Teaching the people meant, above all, inculcating virtue and binding men to the public interest. To delay instructing the laboring class meant hindering the making of the Constitution, damaging its progress, and subjecting it to perpetual shocks. Failure here meant kindling the cruelest of all wars, civil war—"la guerre intestine."[43]

On 29 October, Roland, whose reinstatement at the interior ministry had been widely applauded outside Paris, launched a tirade in the Convention, denouncing the Paris Commune's illegal and insidious activities. He boldly challenged Robespierre directly, his ringing accusations leaving the latter momentarily taken aback. Danton leaped to Robespierre's defense and, in one of his toweringly impressive speeches, reminded the Assembly of the danger of a festering, permanent split. Vague charges of wrongdoing damaged the Convention's reputation. If anyone had concrete proof of misconduct, this needed examining. But let the Convention cease being a forum for unsubstantiated charges. Danton knew as well as any that Roland's accusations were well-founded and was deeply distrustful of Robespierre himself. But he also knew that his own standing with the sansculottes and the Convention depended on maintaining unity within the now greatly narrowed Jacobins and Commune. He relied on his own supporters to keep Robespierre in check.[44]

Danton's intervention prompted Louvet, editor of *La Sentinelle*, to rise. A hard-core republican and since August editor for Brissot, Guadet, and Condorcet of the *Journal des débats*, a paper whose circulation he tripled in a short time, aided by his clever, literary-minded mistress, Mme. Cholet, Louvet radiated in the thick of Paris's extremely bitter local politics. An eager Jacobin for eighteen months, he idolized the Revolution and detested tyranny. With Danton challenging accusers to present concrete accusations, Louvet delivered a withering philippic, his so-called Robespierride seconded by Guadet, Roland, and Gensonné, and afterward backed also by Barbaroux, Buzot, and Lanjuinais. He pronounced Robespierre an aspiring "dictator," not just complicit in the September massacres but exploiting every form of dishonesty known to man, guilty of presiding over the shameless rigging of the recent elections in Paris while presenting himself as the most "virtuous" of citizens. He recounted how gangs of illiterate Parisians, specially recruited from the streets and directed by trusted agents, had been dragooned into cheering certain deputies and decrying authentic republicans. Acolytes drummed into the multitude that "Robespierre was the only virtuous man in France" and that the people's destiny must be entrusted to him. Inordinately fond of flattery, Robespierre ceaselessly flattered the people, invoking popular sovereignty while never forgetting to add that he alone represented the people. It was the same contemptible ruse dictators from Caesar to Cromwell, and from Sulla to Machiavelli, always employed.[45] Nothing on earth was so preposterous as Robespierre's vaunted incorruptibility. "Robespierre," he declaimed, "I accuse you of tyrannizing over the electoral assembly of Paris using every form of intrigue and intimidation."[46]

Louvet's speech had a stunning effect. Briefly, the Montagne was silent and the Assembly wavered. But Pétion, Vergniaud, and other key allies were reluctant to press home the attack. The Assembly gave Robespierre a week to reply, and on 5 November he responded, haranguing the Assembly for two hours with the public galleries packed with noisy supporters. Denying involvement in vote-rigging and the September killings, he derided Louvet's charge that he practiced "low populist flattery" (*populacière flagornerie*). Where was the evidence? Crucially misled, the Convention allowed the charges to lapse on a point of order. Louvet afterward maintained that they could have broken the Montagne on the day of his impassioned speech had Brissot, Vergniaud, Condorcet, Gensonné, and Pétion not wrongly and fatally calculated that saving Robespierre—while supposedly leaving him too discredited to remain a threat—was a preferable course. The failure to break Robespierre while there remained some chance of doing so indeed proved a fatal miscalculation. The Montagne, of course, were outraged by the attempt to defame Robespierre. On 29 October, the names of Louvet, Roland, Lanthenas, and Girey-Dupré were added to the growing list of "enemies of the people" ritually expunged from the Jacobins' membership rolls.[47]

Delay in bringing Louis XVI to trial greatly exacerbated a political arena near to total deadlock. A Convention majority, claimed the Brissotin journals, wanted the final outcome of Louis XVI's trial to be determined by the people. The Montagne denied those advocating a popular referendum were "the majority." The Convention seethed with disagreement and this needed explaining to the nation. Among the first publications justifying the Montagne's unyielding obstructionism nationally was Cloots's *Ni Marat, ni Roland*, a pamphlet of November 1792. A deputy since September, Cloots despised Marat and was assuredly no friend of Robespierre, scorning both his crude Rousseauisme and his character. If Robespierre passed among the populace as "incorruptible," "in my eyes," remarks Cloots, in his *République universelle* (1793), he "is the most vicious and corrupt of bipeds; his *paralogismes* would lead us to ruin, anarchy and slavery." In fact, contended Cloots, Robespierre was not a revolutionary at all but just a shrewd, aspiring dictator and dishonest conspirator.[48] Why then did Cloots align with the Montagne? Until November 1792, Cloots frequented the Roland salon, but after dining there several times quarreled with the Rolands over their efforts to foment provincial indignation "against Paris" and the Jacobins. Cloots charged them with waging a vendetta against Paris and making political capital out of the September massacres, a "tragic necessity that had saved the Revolution." He also rejected Condorcet's incorporating elements of local autonomy into the new Constitution, instead preferring undeviating centralization. In his pamphlet, he urged Roland to read *The Federalist*, the American debate detailing the disadvantages of entrenched state rights from a republican standpoint. Discussed at the Jacobins on 18 November, his pamphlet met with mixed reaction due to its unflattering remarks about Marat, but, warming to Cloots's denunciation of the Brissotins as pernicious "federalists," the club voted to reprint and distribute it nationally.[49]

Cloots subordinated everything to his ideal of a *république universelle* under French tutelage.[50] Where Brissot opposed territorial annexations, believing France should remain within her natural borders bounded by the Rhine, Alps, and Pyrenees, surrounding herself, through war, with "républiques fédératives," Cloots urged annexation and a greater France. Cloots deemed Brissot, whom he had met only recently (at a dinner where Paine was also present), a shifty mediocrity, substantiating this by citing Brissot's alleged twisting of Paine's remarks on annexation. But it was Cloots, retorted Brissot in a printed reply, who misrepresented Paine (who spoke little French). Since Cloots possessed scant English, Brissot alone, as translator, could report the exchange accurately. Paine had agreed with Brissot that Cloots's ideal was a chimera. Denying they were "federalists," the Rolands replied to Cloots in a tract (anonymously penned by Mme. Roland) appearing in Brissot's *Patriote français*, entitled "Mon mot aux gens de bien, sur Clootz," afterward reprinted in the

Chronique de Paris, a paper Cloots himself had formerly been a prime contributor to but was debarred from since siding with the Montagne. Cloots, complained the Rolands, was assisting crass demagogues and publicly justifying the killings of 2 and 3 September, a slaughter that was "la honte de l'humanité" (the shame of humanity), which Roland had done everything possible to stop.[51]

While Brissot, Condorcet, the Rolands, and Paine shared Cloots's universalism up to a point, especially his idea that the spread of democratic republicanism was the path to *la paix universelle*, the "orateur du genre-humain" was, to them, dogmatic and unrealistic. Prudhomme, editor of the *Révolutions de Paris*, in an article entitled "D'un petit pamphlet qui fit grand bruit," reproached Cloots for having further poisoned the political atmosphere. What was needed was calm and mature judgment.[52] Unfortunately, Cloots, renowned throughout Europe as a champion of the Revolution, had descended from his pedestal as lofty legislator into a scandalously bellicose arena where there were already too many "political gladiators." Prudhomme, an independent backing Brissot in the main, also criticized "le sage Roland," though, for replying publicly to one violent diatribe with another equally seething with invective.[53]

In Paris, the battle between those championing the Revolution's core values and those urging populist dictatorship raged deep within the sections. In January 1793, some disaffected provincial fedérés formally complained to the Assembly that a mere fifty or sixty "factious spirits," claiming to represent "the will of the sovereign," the people, had organized a vicious, informal "tyrannie" over *certain* inner Paris sections. One section controlled by this gang of "conspirators" openly called for a dictator, or "defender of the Republic," as the Robespierristes called their leader, all the *ignorants* there being shepherded behind this slogan and demanding a "committee of surveillance" to compel unity and crush dissent.[54] But the Robespierristes' vote-rigging, foot stamping, shouting down, and paying hired bullies to intimidate opponents, however effective in some inner-city sections, did not yet stretch to all the city's inner sections and still less to the more outlying ones. The populists also failed to secure Pétion's successor as mayor, their candidate, the city's public prosecutor, Lallier, gaining only 2,491 qualified votes. He was defeated by the physician Nicolas Chambon de Montaux (d. 1826) who won 3,630 votes, with another 4,132 going to other candidates.[55]

An incisive critic of the surveillance methods and *listes de proscription* used by the Robespierristes in the Paris inner sections was Voltaire's disciple Villette. Appealing "to his brothers the Parisians," in the *Chronique de Paris* on 27 December 1792, he decried Robespierriste public vilification of dissenting club members and signatories of petitions. Most "bons Parisiens," deterred from resisting by brutal intimidation, unfortunately remained inert before the looming menace of dictatorship. Given the prevalence of bullying and chicanery in the sections, it was hardly surprising that whole crowds stood by inactively during the atrocities of 2 and 3 September. Outraged by these observations, several sections denounced Villette to the Commune. Orders were issued for his arrest. But Left republicans still exerted enough clout during the winter of 1792–93 for revolutionary integrity in this case precariously to prevail. Villette's detention was countermanded by officials declaring it a flagrant infringement of liberty of expression. Villette thereupon published an open letter, on 1 January 1793, to the mayor, complaining of being treated as a "bad citizen" by Panthéon section populist leaders for publicly deploring the Commune's repression of dissent. Public proscription of "bad citizens" was a perfidious evil impressing only the most ignorant. "Who has given you the right," he demanded, "to make your *compatriotes* targets for the fury and ignorance of those you mislead?" Section bosses denounced Villette as a modérantiste fomenting "civil war" between Paris and the provinces. But it was the Montagnard faction, Villette assured readers, not their detractors, who had introduced into popular parlance in the first place the ridiculously bogus notion that the Brissotins were "enemies of Paris."[56]

On the last day of 1792, a Champs-Élysées section delegate decried "the principles" and behavior of some inner-city sections in the Convention, especially the practice of labeling residents "bad citizens" if they opposed the creeping tyranny. Intimidation bolstered by affiches and the populist press had compressed local power into unscrupulous hands manipulating the sections in a thoroughly Machiavellian manner.[57] Other section deputations, including one from the poorest faubourgs, Saint-Antoine and Saint-Marceau, complained of being daily bombarded with the rhetoric of "conspiracy."[58] Most inner-city sections, if not the sansculotte masses as such, were by now thoroughly overawed by the Montagne. For the moment there seemed no way to halt the bullying. Whenever he cried "conspiracy," Marat was thunderously applauded from the Convention galleries. In his speech of 31 December, he claimed to have infallible evidence that "the Roland faction" was persecuting "le patriote" Jean-Nicolas Pache (1746–1821), former deputy of Roland, a wealthy and notoriously dishonest Swiss (and former antidemocratic reactionary) who had invested extensively in nationalized church property and who, after quarreling with the Brissotins, had become an acolyte of Marat and Robespierre. To advance their "criminal schemes" the Rolands, aided by Dumouriez, plotting on behalf of a claimant to the throne, Philippe d'Orléans, had sought to destroy the "honest" Pache. Alleging they were unsafe in Paris, the perfidious Rolands wanted to summon provincial volunteer units to overawe the capital. Every good patriot must support Pache, declared Marat, and all France should flock behind the "true *patriotes*" of Paris.[59]

A tremendous onslaught, led by Marat, Chabot, and Hébert (editor of the *Père Duchesne*), was unleashed in the popular press. Who would believe that Brissot, whose election to the Convention had been greeted with jubilation by the sansculottes, would so soon "trample on the people," becoming their sworn enemy? Who would believe Manuel, formerly the sansculottes' friend, would become a vile Brissotin? When Buzot battled Cazalès in the Assembly, he was splendid; who would think he was really "a wolf disguised in sheep's clothing with the deceitful soul of a Barnave?" According to Marat, Buzot particularly declaimed against and insulted Paris.[60] And what of Pétion, whom every true patriot had reckoned the "pearl of men," who loved the people and was loved by them? If ordinary folk are betrayed even by Pétion, who could one trust? Brissotins were subverting the Republic, trying to disillusion the people sufficiently to get them to call for the return of the ancien régime. Not daring to proclaim themselves aristocrates and royalistes, they may have resembled Patriots on 10 August 1792, but these "corrupt *contre-révolutionnaires*" were really dissembling royalists. The people must show their mettle, counter their perfidy, and deal with the "traitors" once and for all.[61]

The delay in trying "the drunkard Capet" (Louis XVI) was part of a conspiracy, contended Hébert, to save Louis, something many readers were persuaded to believe. Brissotins wanted "Capet" exonerated and his son enthroned, as they aspired to rule as regents during the new king's boyhood and thereby "fatten themselves on the blood of the people."[62] The monarchy is overthrown: "Shall we allow another 'tyranny' to rise in its place?" Today, Mme. Roland is the person who leads all France by the strings, manipulating men as dextrously as ever the Pompadour and Du Barry did at court.[63] "Brissot is her equerry, Louvet her chamberlain, Buzot her grand chancellor, Fauchet her chaplain, Barbaroux her captain of the guards, Guadet her cupbearer, and Lanthenas her master of ceremonies." Stretched on her sofa, surrounded by her "beaux esprits," this "new queen" presides over her salon, impudently pronouncing on politics and war while emulating the debauched lewdness of Marie Antoinette.[64] This was the new "court," disposing of everything in both Convention and departments. Thirsting for money and advantages for themselves, these "jean-foutres" should, in Hébert's opinion, have all been liquidated on 10 August. It is not on the frontiers that Hébert exhorted his readers to seek the enemy: "it is among us." A new revolution was needed. "The moment to strike will come." The people must express their justified fury and end the chicaneries of these *coquins*. The new year, predicted *Le Père Duchesne* in January 1793, would be the last for these *jean-foutres*, Brissotins, and Rolandistes.[65] The prediction proved accurate.

On 30 December, a delegation from the Paris section sansculottes condemned Manuel's *patriotisme équivoque* before the Convention. Manuel's actions outrageously contradicted his principles. A defender of press freedom, he had ordered pamphlet stalls and paper-vendors cleared from the Convention hall's environs, chasing away "the people," banishing publications whose "surveillance" of him and his Brissotin friends he disliked.[66] An architect of the nation's new cult of republican grandeur and "great men," Manuel had persuaded the Convention to transfer the Tuileries and its gardens, together with the Place de la Révolution and the Champs-Élysées, from the Commune to the interior ministry as national assets, and rename the Tuileries palace and gardens the Château and Jardin National. This was resented by Paris sansculottes, as well as the Commune, because the boutiques and market stalls that had "transformed it into a kind of market" were compulsorily removed from the new "national garden."[67] At the Cordeliers on 2 January 1793, a unanimous vote expelled Manuel from the club.[68] Under a hail of denunciation for disdaining the people, Manuel resigned his administrative functions and a few weeks later also left the Convention.

Over the winter of 1792–93, signs of crisis abounded in the streets, section assemblies, public places, cafés, and theaters. Numerous municipalities and local patriotic societies deplored the ceaseless feuding. An address from the *conseil général* of Finisterre (Western Brittany) was read in the Convention on 6 January: Finisterre demanded a republic united and indivisible, based on liberty, equality, and the people's happiness, not harassed by "a vile faction" paid by some shadowy paymaster or foreign despots. France's greatest foes were not the princes waging war on the country but those unsettling the Convention: "les Marat, les Robespierre, les Danton, les Chabot, les Bazire, les Merlin," and their accomplices. "Voilà, les anarchistes!" They were "the true counter-revolutionaries." If the Convention believed it lacked the means to stop them, it should turn to the sovereign, appeal to France's primary assemblies! Finisterre claimed to represent the majority view embodying the common good, expressing the hopes of provincial France, and those of "the major part of the Parisians whose voice is stifled at this time under the knife of a bunch of petty tyrants." This scandalous "aristocratic piece," retorted Marat, leaping to the podium, should be returned to Mme. Roland's boudoir, whence it had undoubtedly come.[69]

As always, the theater was a particular focus of ideological struggle. A sensationally controversial play staged at the Théâtre-Français in January 1793 was *L'Ami des Lois* by Jean-Louis Laya, a Voltaire admirer and enthusiast for the Revolution, and author of *Voltaire aux Français sur leur constitution* (1789). Two other plays by Laya, *Le Danger des Opinions* and *Jean Calas*, both ridiculing religious intolerance, had previously been successfully staged. Laya's new piece—according to *Le Père Duchesne*, a disgraceful travesty concocted in Mme. Roland's boudoir but praised by the pro-Brissot *Gazette nationale* as excellent for enlightening Parisians about their "true interests"—actually dared put "Robespierre" onstage. This five-act satire, played by some of the best-known actors of the day, also featured "Marat" under the ludicrous name of "Duricrane." From the day of its premiere, 2 January 1793, it caused a massive furor.[70]

Laya's Robespierre and Marat were paragons of hypocrisy and villainy, building their tyranny through devious machinations designed to mobilize the most ignorant and gullible against the true revolutionaries. Among the latter was the play's hero, Forlis, an enlightened aristocrat who loves his fellow citizens and always champions the Revolution's true principles but is trapped by his unscrupulous demagogic foes. The hugely popular "true defenders of the people" villify Forlis while dishonestly claiming to have eclipsed everyone in braving Lafayette's bayonets to defend liberty and equality. Robespierre appears under the name "Nomophage" (Eater of the Law) and is a complete "tartufe de civisme," hypocrite, and egoistic impostor who continually flatters the crassest elements while spouting about virtue, though invoking it only for his own profit. Ordinary people are so uncomprehending, Duricrane persuades Nomophage, they can easily be persuaded to liquidate those who champion their true interests. Finally, though, the people prove to be less gullible than Nomophage supposes. In the denouement, he is thwarted and sent to prison.

On opening night, three weeks before the execution of Louis XVI (who read the play in his cell for diversion), tremendous excitement gripped the theater. The play should be performed everywhere, not just in Paris, recommended the *Gazette nationale*. Furiously denounced at the Jacobins and the Commune by Chaumette and Santerre, on 10 January, Montagnard deputies besieged the Convention, condemning the play as *contre-révolutionnaire*, a charge denied by Louis-Pierre Manuel, who invoked "la liberté de la presse," and the Bordeaux deputy Jean-François Ducos, a follower of Diderot, Raynal, and the *encyclopédistes*. Two Paris sections, those of La Cité and Reunion, petitioned the Commune, denouncing the scandalous license of theater directors staging plays filled with blatant "incivisme" designed to corrupt the public spirit.[71] Laya responded by asking the Convention to allow him to dedicate his play to the legislature. After its initial performances received thunderous applause, the Commune became more anxious than ever to suppress the play. A score of deputies "on the right," as the Left republicans called the Montagne, led by the prominent deputy Claude-Antoine Prieur-Duvernois (called de la Côte d'Or; 1763–1832), denounced it as "aristocratic." "Incendiary plays" were being staged in Paris, vile "manoeuvres de l'aristocracie," complained a delegation of fédérés before the Paris Commune on 11 January. If the Convention refused to stop Laya's piece, they would force it off the stage, "exercising their rights."

The Commune unilaterally voted to ban the play on 12 January. Pétion's successor as mayor, Nicolas Chambon de Montaux, among the foremost physicians and experts on pregnancy of the era, appeared at the theater as the fifth performance was about to begin, escorted by police and populists yelling, "À bas *L'Ami des Lois!*"[72] The mayor produced a city council order declaring the play banned as "inflammatory" and aimed at misleading the people by casting intolerable aspersions on citizens of known "patriotisme." The "immense crowd" that had gathered was so determined to resist the municipal ban that they began shouting and stamping for the performance to proceed, obliging the police to retreat. Laya was at the Convention, Chambon was told, with an audience deputation requesting the overturning of the Commune's ban. After four perfectly peaceful performances, the "false counterfeiters of patriotism," as Laya termed them, were trying to suppress his patriotic play in open defiance of the Convention. Vergniaud, presiding at the Convention, had to deal with "violentes interruptions et murmures" as Prieur, Duhem, Delbret, and other Montagnards insisted the ban must be upheld, while Lehardy and other Left republicans deplored the "cabale abominable" trying to suppress the play. Although the Montagne succeeded in preventing Laya from addressing the Convention—he planned to ask whether the deputies had forgotten that even the despicable "despots of Versailles" watched performances of *Brutus*, *Le Mort de Caesar*, and *Guillaulme Tell*—he obtained the president, Vergniaud's confirmation that there was no law authorizing municipalities to ban plays, and that the performance could proceed.[73]

On the next two evenings, the play was again staged before enthusiastic audiences. Most people in Paris, Laya demonstrated, did not support the populist authoritarians controlling the Commune, a message potentially so damaging to Robespierre that the populist press now summoned "the people" to take matters into their own hands and enforce the ban. All the "people's enemies, all the *coquins* in Paris," wrote Hébert, were "gathering nightly to applaud the *Amis des Lois*." The sanscullottes should use force to prevent the theater from being used to "corrupt public opinion."[74] Only dramas like *Brutus* and the *Death of Caesar*, denouncing tyranny, should be staged. On 14 January, the Commune ordered all theaters to close that evening. The Convention, seeing no justification for closing the theaters, overturned this too. Theater managers were commanded by the Commune to ensure that plays apt to cause disturbance were *not* performed. Bancal de Issarts and Pétion then asked the Convention to countermand this order likewise, as the Commune "has no right to instruct theater directors which plays they should stage," its intervention being a "flagrant violation of freedom of thought and writing." Even forbidding plays that could cause disturbance infringes liberty, affirmed Pétion, "as one does not know how far to extend the prohibition."[75]

The Commune had a problem. Municipal officials sent to stop *L'Ami des Lois* on 15 January were insulted by the crowds. General Santerre, commandant of the Paris National Guard, arriving with a militia force to enforce the ban, was also jeered. Santerre tried to address the audience but was drowned out with cries of "Down with the beggars [gueux] of 2 September!" "À bas les assassins!" Those in the audience were all "aristocrates," retorted a furious Santerre. Hundreds of people, some armed with sticks, continued chanting and demanding the play, the incident triggering another furious row in the Convention. The commotion amply demonstrated the wisdom of the Commune's ban on plays likely to cause disturbance, insisted populist deputies. No authority could be permitted to overstep the law, answered Guadet, Pétion, and Lehardy.[76] When Voltaire first staged *Mahomet* and *Le Fanatisme*, observed

Lehardy, every bigot in France cried out in protest, but still these plays were performed. Now, the most abominable tartuffes of civisme howled in anger, the Convention must ensure nothing was done to protect the vanity of hypocrites aiming to suppress freedom of thought and subvert the law.[77] Danton's attempt to shrug the whole thing off by reminding the Convention they had more important matters to worry about than comedies was countered by Pétion assuring the Convention that it was not just a play that was involved but rather the issue of whether municipalities could suppress freedom of expression. It was by citing danger of public disturbance that the ancien régime had curtailed liberty.[78]

More trouble gripped the theater world soon afterward, in late January. A production of Suzannah and the Elders, entitled *La Chaste Suzanne*, appeared to allude to Robespierriste demands for a *comité de surveillance* to counter subversion. Marat and Robespierre were now so closely identified with surveillance of individuals' private activities, conflating private and public life and enforcing a repressive sexual code, that the right to privacy and personal liberty appeared to be directly threatened. The spying Elders in this piece were ridiculed as immoral intruders ruthlessly using surveillance to accuse the virtuous Suzannah of adultery. Several evenings running, groups of populist rowdies forced their way into the Vaudeville theater, menacing the performers who were satirizing Robespierriste surveillance. Finally, furious populists climbed onto the stage, threatening to beat the actors mercilessly and turn the theater into a "bloody hospital" full of injured if the play was not stopped immediately. This time, ominously, the play remained banned as apt to corrupt "republican morals."[79]

Hébert urged the poor of the faubourgs to descend on the Saint-Germain district and teach actors and audiences a lesson: "it is for you to censure their plays." Admittedly, the workingmen his paper addressed did not attend theaters. They preferred to drink when their work was done; theaters, Hébert presumed, were mostly attended by idlers with time to kill. "However, my friends, be on your guard!" With a light farce one can cause more harm than one might think. The theater is a rallying-point for the people's "enemies," who are trying to damage the reputations of Marat and the "incorruptible Robespierre," "our Revolution's greatest hero, the man who never falters in defending the people's rights."[80] Those planning Robespierre's destruction accuse him of wanting to be "a dictator!" Robespierre—who never ceases to combat tyrants and rouse citizens to abase all seeking to elevate themselves above the rest![81] The Commune sought to muzzle the Paris theater, and despite renewed trouble on 4 February with crowds again demanding *L'Ami des Lois*, succeeded eventually in forcing both *Suzanne* and Laya's *L'Ami des Lois* off the stage.

More ominous still, over the winter of 1792–93, were the Montagne's repeated denunciations of the main Left republican papers, especially those of Brissot, Condorcet, Gorsas, Louvet, Perlet, and Carra. Brissotin publications allegedly propagated only "perversité," encouraging antipathy to Paris in the provinces. Speaking at the Jacobins on 30 December 1792, Chabot, editor of the *Journal populaire, ou catéchisme des sans-culottes*, inveighed against Carra, since August 1792 a key ally of Brissot and Roland, designating him one of the worst of the "journalistes perfides" corrupting patriotism, morals, and proper civic spirit.[82] Nominated director of the Bibliothèque Nationale—part of his "reward" for treachery, suggested Jacobin critics—Carra responded by plunging into an extremely vituperative public feud with Chabot, Marat, and Hébert, each side accusing the other of purveying lies and "perfidious commentaries." Carra's paper, along with Gorsas's *Courrier* and the *Patriote français*, now edited by Girey-Dupré, heaped scorn on the Commune by questioning the republican credentials of the "true Jacobins" before the provincial clubs and city administrations.

It was far harder for populists to bully the press than the clubs or stage. Republican papers, noted Mercier in December,[83] formed a largely solid front against Robespierre and Marat. Only the crassest newssheets backed Robespierre's populism. The main pro-Revolution papers unreservedly condemned the Montagnards as foes of the Revolution's core principles—sovereignty of the people, freedom of thought and expression, liberty of the press, and the principle of representative democracy. For a time, this assured the Brissotins a definite advantage, especially outside Paris. Roland was later accused by Desmoulins of being the first republican leader to massively infringe upon liberty of the press by abusing his position as minister of the interior to block the passage of Montagnard newssheets and reports to provincial centers, thereby ensuring that one-sided Brissotin accounts misinformed vast numbers, contributing to unnecessary strife, especially in southern France.[84] The mayor of Montpellier, Durand, later assured the Convention that the "writings of the *parti Brissot*" were the only ones reaching Montpellier, so that all the journals people read there exalted the patriotism and principles exclusively of that bloc.[85]

Pro-Montagnard papers mostly avoided discussion of the Revolution's core principles, preferring to summon the people to punish, coerce, boycott, and suppress. Clubs around the country backing the Montagne often opted to shun journals linked to the Brissotins. However, this was as yet hard to do effectively because there was no legal basis for sweeping repression, and because there was little at all intellectually respectable with which to replace Left republican papers.[86] The virulence of Marat's, Chabot's, and Hébert's denunciations worked admirably among the semiliterate but mostly proved counterproductive among the better educated, eliciting more revulsion than support. In May 1792, Robespierre had established his own paper, the *Défenseur de la Constitution*, to broadcast a more elevated antiphilosophique message, but this was distinctly uninspiring and little read. Except in a few large cities where the sansculottes held sway, notably Marseille, Lyon, and Strasbourg, in the provinces Brissotins mostly commanded more support than the Robespierristes and took the credit, in the autumn of 1792, for the fervently hoped-for turnaround in the fortunes of war.

Since late 1792, Robespierre had broken successively with Brissot, Buzot, Carra, and, finally, Mme. Roland and Pétion. To offset his growing preponderance in Paris, Brissot and Condorcet sporadically courted Danton, who remained popular in the poorer Paris sections and was likewise increasingly wary of Robespierre. Danton and Robespierre, recalled Louvet later, both secretly planned to supplant the other when circumstances were ripe.[87] Danton might have helped prevent the tragic downward spiral into murderous strife and retrieve the Revolution's core ideology from its debasement by Marat and Robespierre, as Desmoulins and his closest supporters hoped he would, even as late as the spring of 1794. Several times he offered to collaborate with Brissot, with whom he was on friendly terms. This never sufficiently materialized, partly due to the feud between Danton and Roland, and especially the latter's wife (who loathed the Cordeliers leader, strongly suspecting him of complicity in the September massacres), but also due to Danton's nervousness about jeopardizing his sansculotte base.[88] Mme. Roland considered Danton to be another Marat, a demagogue inflaming the plebs for nefarious purposes. But her influence on relations between the Brissotins and Dantonistes proved as unfortunate as her lingering respect for Robespierre, whom she persisted in taking at face value, misled in part by their common ardor for Rousseau, though she did notice that in small-group discusssion, Robespierre's behavior was "extraordinary": "he spoke little, sneered a great deal, and threw out sarcastic

asides, but never gave a straight opinion." She believed she was advising a sensible, trustworthy "friend" when telling him that although she
agreed government is for the people, and the people are naturally good,
he should be more conscious that in their ignorance, the people are easily misled by calculating opportunists.[89]

The Montagne did everything possible to block legislation they disliked, which meant everything proposed by Left republicans. The latter stood not just for individual emancipation and basic human rights
but also for balancing representative democracy with a carefully ad-
umbrated admixture of direct democracy. In principle, the new draft
constitution, presented to the Convention by Condorcet and his
constitutional committee in February 1793, was a remarkable breakthrough, for it assigned all adult men the right to vote for the first time.
But the Brissotins' February 1793 draft constitution was immediately
rejected by the Montagnards as "antipopular" and weighted in favor of
the better educated. It was voted down and a new constitutional committee was appointed to revise it. Nominally, Marat and Robespierre
stood for Rousseauiste direct democracy but actually promoted a collective vision emphasizing conformity with "the people's will," which
was envisaged as a monolithic entity fixed by the people's leaders from
which no dissent was permitted. Provincial Jacobin clubs supporting
the Montagnards endorsed their rejection of the new constitution,
Lyon suggesting that further discussion of its terms be put off until the
country was at peace.

A useful tool for undoing the values of 1789 was the discrediting of
Mirabeau's legacy. There had been greater geniuses and more perfect
orators, remarked Garat, but no one put eloquence to work more powerfully to convert into political action and laws "les hautes pensées de
la Philosophie," and this, the best of all talents, Mirabeau employed "in
the revolution of a country used to being the model for all Europe."[90]
Brissot agreed, styling Mirabeau a great man and a lover of liberty.[91] So
did Desmoulins. But Marat and Robespierre saw only his secret deal-
ings with Louis XVI over the winter of 1789–90, revealed by the soon-
notorious *armoire de fer*, the casket of secret royal papers found hidden
in the ransacked palace on 20 November. Populists pronounced Mirabeau's conduct "treason" and his philosophy worthless. On 5 December
1792 at the Jacobins, Robespierre publicly denounced the dead philosophe, inciting those present to pull down Mirabeau's bust together
with that of Helvétius, busts that had hitherto presided over their meetings. He declared Helvétius a philosophe whose presence should not

be tolerated in their hall, since he was a complete unbeliever in religion and foe of Jean-Jacques. Both busts were smashed and trampled to dust underfoot.[92] This was the signal for Jacobin clubs across France to topple Mirabeau and philosophy, and intensify their offensive against Brissotin intellectualism. Busts of Mirabeau were torn down in the "clubs populaires" of Dijon, Langres, Châtillon-en-Seine, and other places. Mirabeau "is not a great man any more" sneered Feller's journal, "what true *philosophe* would not make salutary reflections on the course of fleeting reputations to which certain madmen sacrifice honor, virtue and religion!"[93]

Roland's resignation from the Interior Ministry in February 1793, undermined by Danton (now at the peak of his influence), proved a turning point. The Convention's large, wavering middle ground had since September 1792 mostly leaned toward Brissot's side. After Roland's withdrawal, the middle ground increasingly leaned the other way. As tension mounted, more and more warnings were heard—like Laya's, Villette's, Lalande's, and Pétion's—concerning Robespierre's real character. On 6 November, Olympe de Gouges placarded central Paris with her *Pronostic sur Maximilien Robespierre*, mocking his claims to be a man of simplicity and virtue, incorruptible, a "modèle des philosophes." "Toi philosophe? You, the friend of your co-citizens, of peace and order? I will cite this maxim for you: 'quand un méchant fait le bien, il prepare de grands maux' [when a wicked man acts as a good one, he is preparing great mischief]." All true philosophes were infinitely superior to Robespierre, whose understanding of virtue Olympe considered abysmal. She herself had a far more genuinely republican soul than the man from Arras. "Do you know the vastness of the distance between you and Cato? It is that separating Marat from Mirabeau, the *maringouin* [flying insect] from the eagle, and the eagle from the sun."[94]

Pétion, who knew him better than most, described Robespierre at this time as extremely mistrustful, perceiving intrigues and plots everywhere, "imperious in his opinions, listening only to himself, intolerant of objections, never pardoning those who wounded his vanity, never admitting mistakes, denouncing irresponsibly while taking offence at the slightest criticism of himself, always glorifying his own achievements and speaking of himself unrestrainedly, and assuming everyone was chiefly preoccupied with and persecuting him." No one courted and flattered the people more assiduously than this man, "always thirsting for applause." One might consider this judgment harsh. But Pétion here actually misses several of his former ally's principal traits, unlike the German Jacobin Oelsner, who also knew Robespierre socially and stressed Robespierre's "theological" dimension, his extreme dogmatism and tendency to believe he alone possessed "virtue" and true insight. Like Louvet, Condorcet, and Cloots, Oelsner emphasized Robespierre's preaching, extreme intolerance, fixation with martyrdom, and quasi-religious zeal for virtue.[95]

Suppressing liberty of thought, expression, and the press had become a Montagnard priority, as was further demonstrated in early January by a clash over the imprisonment of two royalist editors, Gautier and Lafarge, by the Comité de Sûreté Générale. This was a key committee of the Convention, created on 2 October 1792 and, since January, under Jacobin control. On 10 August rioters had smashed the royalist presses, but no journalists were arrested for their writings, and during the autumn Gautier, editor of the *Journal de la cour*, and his deputy Lafarge resumed their efforts to "corrupt opinion" and denigrate the Revolution. Two articles particularly provoked Montagnard ire, one denying the Convention had the right to judge Louis XVI, urging the people to rise up, the other pointing out that, after more than three months, the Convention had still not revealed the names of perpetrators of the September atrocities, proving murder was now a tool of the Revolution. The imprisonment of Gautier and Lafarge at the Abbey, under an arrest order signed by Chabot, Tallien, and three others, and the arrest of another journalist who had published an attack on the Comité in the *Tableau politique de Paris*, initiated a fresh stage in the quarrel about press liberty. Royalists accused Tallien, Chabot, and Bazire of complicity in the September massacres, and now Chabot and Tallien were signing their critics' arrest warrant![96] In late January 1793 Buzot concerted an organized campaign against the Comité for flagrant misconduct in this case. The Comité, Buzot pointed out, was controlled by Chabot, Bazire, and other "men of blood, disposing imperiously of the lives, honour and fortunes of citizens like the Council of Ten at Venice." They have only to say "stab that one" and a citizen is stabbed. The Comité was an obvious instrument of tyranny. He demanded its abolition. The Montagne, swaying the uncommitted center, successfully warded off Buzot's motion and kept the royalist dissident journalists in prison.[97]

Most crucial of all, by January 1793, was the wrangling over the *appel au public* or popular referendum, to decide the king's fate. The continuing battle between the rival republican wings occurred against a background of vigorous royalist agitation. Moyse Bayle, leading the Marseille populists, warned of a disturbing upsurge of "aristocratic insolence" there, which he blamed on the Brissotins. A Rouen delegation on 13 January claimed Brissotin advocacy of the appel au peuple, with Normandy teeming with refractory priests and aristocrats seeking to "poison" the people with royalist propaganda, was a recipe for civil war. Disturbances had erupted in Rouen three days before, following an open-air meeting of some two thousand royalists addressed by a former magistrate of the Rouen parlement, Georges Dumont, and the posting up of his harangue all over Rouen by enthusiastic groups yelling, "Vive le roi et au diable la République!" The crowds had even hurled down the liberty tree before being chased away by rival crowds of "bons citoyens."[98]

The "appeal to the people" to decide whether Louis should be executed became central to the culminating political struggle of the Revolution. The Convention had voted for a formal trial, rendering the process a constitutional procedure rather than a crude act of vengeance. Nation and Convention should join in whatever judgment was reached. But if found guilty, should he be executed? Besides principle, many worried lest executing the king make him a martyr for the pious. Consequently, many deputies, including Danton and most Brissotins, wavered, many preferring either perpetual imprisonment or permanent banishment. Even before 10 August 1792, Montagnards argued that the appel au public was merely a ploy to forestall just retribution, there being enough modérés and royalistes for such a referendum to trigger civil strife, and perhaps save the king's life. Louis had sufficiently incriminated himself, contended Robespierre, to deserve death without trial. The appel au peuple was denounced in August 1792 by section bosses like Léonard Bourdon (1754–1807), the notoriously unscrupulous president of the Gravilliers section, as a "fatal abuse" and clear "evidence" of modérantisme.[99] But what greater hypocrisy is there, objected Pétion, than claiming to venerate the people's voice and then insisting, like Bourdon, that the nation's preference should not be consulted, as it might differ from that of the Montagne! If the people willed the king should not be executed, what right had the Montagne to negate the people's will? In theory, Robespierristes proclaimed direct democracy and popular sovereignty. But while eager to use the rhetoric of direct democracy to combat the democrats, what they meant by "the people's will" was simply their leadership's undisputed right to define that will. Only Brissotins took the doctrine of volonté générale seriously, albeit mostly refusing to define it as Rousseau had. "It is not for any individual, or minority to diverge from the *volonté générale*," affirmed Pétion, "or there is no more society."[100]

Antoine-Louis de Saint-Just (1768–94), soon to emerge as the Montagne's chief theorist and Robespierre's right-hand man, in his maiden speech in the Convention, on 13 November, maintained (discarding his earlier royalism) that kingship, like all tyranny, contradicts nature: the Convention would be justified in executing Louis not as a citizen but as an "enemy" to be liquidated without appeal.[101] Hardly any deputies agreed with the unfamiliar and strange doctrine expounded by Saint-Just, entirely outside the main line of revolutionary thought, that "the sovereignty of nature is above the sovereignty of the people," the people having no right either to dispense with or mitigate the sentence passed on the king. Saint-Just's doctrine that "la souveraineté de la nature est au-dessus de la souveraineté du peuple," that peoples have no right to pardon tyrants,[102] conformed to the ideas of a few others, like Jean-Baptiste Milhaud (1766–1833), a military man and harsh disciplinarian, later esteemed by Bonaparte, who also held that "the sovereignty of nature is above the sovereignty of the people," as he expressed it during the appel debate.[103] But this so flagrantly contradicted the fact that their own influence derived from the section assemblies that it was hardly a useful or appropriate concept for the Montagne to propagate.

The Montagne accused the Brissotins of menacing France with civil war. But it was the Montagnards, replied their opponents, "who pervert all ideas of morality," and with "specious discourse, hypocritical, base and self-interested flattery" drive the people to deplorable excesses, and foment civil war. Jacobin leaders vaunt their virtue. One calls himself the *Ami du peuple*, the other the *Incorruptible*. Yet, Marat and Robespierre accuse their opponents of "betrayal," knowing perfectly well there is no truth in such accusations. So instinctive are deceit and murder to these men, they daily violate every basic human right and revolutionary principle, popular sovereignty most of all, flattering the people's prejudices and pampering their credulity, simply to deceive them. There were also, admittedly, Montagnards of good faith. These must now awake, admonished Gensonné, and rescue popular sovereignty before it was too late, otherwise they will just be the base instruments of impostors and deceivers. "It is time to tear aside the veil," declared Gensonné on 2 January, "and show all Europe we will not be the passive instrument of a faction usurping the people's rights, but rather wish to remain the faithful organ of the national will. Just as there are 'charlatans' in medicine, so liberty too produces vile hypocrites, bogus cults, *cafards*, and false *dévôts*. 'On les reconnait à leur haine pour la philosophie et les lumières [They are recognized by their hatred for philosophy and Enlightenment].'"[104]

By maintaining that Louis's fate should not be submitted to the people, held Vergniaud, Montagnards implied that France consisted mostly of "intriguers, aristocrats, Feuillants, *modérés* and *contre-révolutionnaires*." They consider virtue the distinguishing mark of that minority, convinced that the "majority must be coerced through *La Terreur*," a perverse lie, an atrocity. Outside Paris, respect for the rule of law and obedience to the volonté générale prevailed; the people understood that both individual and public liberty require such submission. Once the primary assemblies and departments pronounce their view, few try to undermine the result. That the Constitution must be submitted to the will of the nation, everyone, section leaders included, agrees, so why not Louis's fate? Yet, those recommending a referendum and respect for popular sovereignty, the Montagne "label royalists, conspirators against liberty," allies of Lameth, Lafayette, and the Feuillants, despite knowing perfectly well they are nothing of the kind.[105]

The debate over the appel au peuple dragged on for weeks, enabling many deputies to expand on why they supported or rejected a referendum. Brissot, Pétion, Vergniaud, Barbaroux, Fauchet, Louvet, Buzot, Garran-Coulon, and Gorsas declared unequivocally in favor of the referendum. Kingship could not be said to have been finally eradicated constitutionally, argued Gorsas, until the people pronounced its end. It was an insult to the nation to suggest the appel meant civil war.[106] But when the decisive vote came in the Convention, the Montagnards won easily. The appeal to the people was rejected, not because the Montagne commanded a majority in the Convention (which they did not) but because the center and some Brissotins feared nobility and priesthood were indeed sufficiently strong to exploit the opportunity. Around one-quarter of the Convention's 170 or so Brissotin deputies voted against the referendum.[107] The Dantoniste Philippeaux, having himself earlier proposed the referendum to the Comité de Legislation, now changed his mind, saying he had been persuaded the referendum would destroy, not consolidate, popular sovereignty.[108] Desmoulins and Fabre d'Églantine, by contrast, rejected the appel out of hand, urging the king's immediate execution, the latter repeatedly citing Rousseau to prove volonté générale is never adequately manifested in primary assemblies.[109]

Rejecting the referendum, Montagnards also repudiated the doctrine that popular sovereignty is expressed in votes and referenda. What Condorcet and his friends (including Paine) offered was a full-blown representative, democratic culture, with elections and assemblies on different levels and just one legislative chamber at the apex, with an executive managed by the legislature. Montagnards, by contrast, with their very different ideology, preferred a strong executive and weak legislature, with less say for departments and municipalities. They propounded a more abstract view of popular sovereignty. But it was not this that enabled them to win the argument but rather invoking the likelihood of civil war. Closing the debate on 15 January, the Convention president announced that of 707 deputies present and voting, 424 rejected the appel as against with 283 in favor, a majority of 141.[110] Losing this vote over the referendum placed the democratic republicans in a most awkward position, for this reverse obliged them to qualify their assent to the king's execution in ways that supplied further pretexts for styling them modérantistes, crypto-royalists, and counterrevolutionaries.

Without a referendum, most of the Brissotin leadership hesitated to declare the death penalty legitimate; only Carra pronounced "our Revolution the product of the progress of reason" and urged prompt execution.[111] Manuel and Villette proposed imprisonment until the war ended and, like Kersaint and Garran-Coulon, "perpetual banishment" thereafter.[112] Manuel, opposing kings while the Constitution was monarchical, sneered Le Père Duchesne, now says "if we do not preserve Louis alive we shall soon have instead 'king Marat' or 'king Robespierre.'"[113] Pierre Daunou preferred permanent detention. Paine and Condorcet too rejected the death penalty, the latter suggesting the Convention should first pass sentence and then suspend it until the new Constitution was finalized; when the referendum was held asking the people to endorse the new Constitution, the king's fate and other questions could be put to the primary assemblies at the same time.[114] Pétion, Vergniaud, Guadet, and Gensonné all still supported the death sentence in principle but now wanted implementation postponed indefinitely. Louvet advised execution but only after endorsement of the new Constitution by referendum. Brissot had all along deemed Louis "guilty of treason," he explained on 16 January, and deserving of execution, but implementing this sentence without consulting the people, he also thought, must create "de terribles inconvénients." The real solution—submitting the matter to the nation's judgment—the Assembly had resolved to dispense with. Whoever the evil genius behind this was, "he had prepared incalculable misfortunes for France."[115]

With the appel dismissed, and no referendum, the Convention overwhelmingly found France's monarch guilty of treason. The resolution to execute him, however, passed only narrowly, by 387 to 334 votes, rendering his fate a fraught issue for weeks. While among the Brissotins only Buzot and Barbaroux voted unequivocally for death, all that faction was obliged to acquiesce, noted Hébert, in what they could not prevent.[116] Louis XVI was guillotined on 21 January 1793, with an immense crowd looking on, in the former Place Louis XV, now renamed Place de Révolution (figure 8). Culturally and psychologically, this was a crucial landmark. But the January drama over the king's fate actually made little difference to the basic rift determining the Revolution's course, as the real divide separating the revolutionary Left from the authoritarian populists was scarcely affected by it.

Economic hardship also contributed to the Brissotin ascendancy's gradual crumbling from January onward. With war burdens and exactions weighing heavily, a grave subsistence crisis developed in the main cities over the winter. The Brissotin regime's approach was to combine economic freedom and free trade with aiding society's weakest. Brissotins preferred not to infringe upon the basic principle of economic freedom by imposing sweeping price controls, or taking the draconian measures against hoarders and speculators urged by Marat and Hébert. The government attempted to assist particular groups with special needs. Under a decree of late December 1792, public assistance was made available to those wounded, and the wives, children, and elderly relatives of those killed, fighting at the front or participating in the 10 August insurrection. Everyone eligible for help under its terms was required to inscribe his name on official lists kept by the municipal sections and smaller municipalities. The wounded applying for aid had to submit certificates from physicians or other health functionaries providing details of their wounds, copies of their marriage certificates, and the birth certificates of their children, which enabled the sections to determine the sums each should receive from the public purse.[117] But it was all too little.

In response to soaring prices, a peaceful mass demonstration by Parisian women demanding cheaper food and soap (essential to laundresses) occurred on 24 February 1793. This was followed by ugly rioting on 25 and 26 February, marked by assaults on food stores. A striking feature of this commotion was that shops belonging to known Jacobin supporters were spared while others, not owned by Jacobins, both small and large suppliers, were indiscriminately pillaged. Many grocers were ruined in the riots. But ordinary sansculottes were not those principally involved. Rather, the disturbances were fomented by organized gangs deliberately inciting violence. According to a shopkeepers' delegation that

Figure 8. Execution of Louis XVI, Paris, 21 January 1793, in the Place de la Révolution (formerly the Place Louis XV, renamed in 1795 Place de la Concorde). Image courtesy Bibliothèque nationale de France.

afterward appealed to the Convention, presenting a detailed statistical table of cost prices verified by noninterested parties, the crisis stemmed not from hoarding or profiteering but from surges beyond their control in the basic prices of flour, sugar, soap, and other key items.[118] An angry row ensued in the Convention between sympathizers, who argued that the grocers should be indemnified, and Montagnards, who demanded they be made to restitute "what they gained since the start of the Revolution by selling food too dearly." The Montagnard stance elicited lively applause from the galleries but was condemned by Buzot, Boyer-Fonfrède, and other Brissotin deputies. Little doubt remained, retorted Buzot, provoking much indignant yelling from the galleries, that the rioters wrecking the shops had been incited to do so. The Convention could not condone organized violence perpetrated by "brigands," nor allow the "morality of the people" to be "corrupted."[119]

Renewed rioting erupted on 9 and 10 March, this time in response to military defeat in Belgium. On 9 March, Marat's *L'Ami du peuple* violently denounced the "great treason of the generals," especially

Dumouriez and Miranda.[120] At the Jacobins, Hébert likewise demanded the heads of the generals and ministers responsible. Armed bands of insurgents and Enragés, a few thousand strong, endeavoring (not very successfully) to provoke a wider insurrection and pouring abuse on Brissot, Pétion, Gorsas, Barbaroux, Vergniaud, and Roland, roamed the Paris streets, some yelling their undying veneration for the "great Marat" and their resolve to kill the "traitors" responsible for the military disaster. Several section bosses adroitly exploited the military reverses to inflate "the people's" demand for a special tribunal révolutionnaire to execute "traitors" and "conspirators." A tiny club of extremists, the Défenseurs de la République Une et Indivisible, headed by Hébert, Fournier, and several others of the unruliest sansculotte leaders—impatient with Robespierre's preference for methods ostensibly legal—directed the most militant sections to call out the sansculottes and assail the print-shops "where the papers of Brissot, Gorsas and others of that nature are printed."[121] On the evening of 9 March, a troop of two to three hundred ruffians invaded the print-shops of Gorsas and Condorcet's *Chronique de Paris*, smashing the presses, destroying the type, and wrecking much else. As armed rioters broke in, Gorsas, pistol in hand, escaped via a back window. Condorcet's paper was now permanently disabled. Prudhomme and his friends, grabbing weapons, managed to drive off the gang before they could wreck his print-shop.[122] This episode, about which Louvet published a damning account on 3 May, marked a major step toward both demolishing the revolutionary press and forcibly suppressing press freedom as such.

There was serious trouble also at Bordeaux. On 8 March, a furious crowd, mainly women, marched on Bordeaux's majestic riverside city hall from the city center, smashing windows and throwing stones at the National Guard. A deliberately instigated, organized disturbance, eyewitnesses attested spotting male Jacobins, disguised as women, directing the crowd. The Guard halted the mob by firing in the air, albeit killing one protester.[123] But however deadlocked the Convention and the whole country was, the 10 March journée proved that those demonstrating in the streets at this point comprised only a few unrepresentative and disparate groups orchestrated by disparate but highly organized political cliques. The two journées were scarcely a manifestation of popular sentiment in any genuine sense. In any case, helped by rain, the crowds were relatively easily dispersed.[124] In Paris, a recently arrived battalion of four hundred volunteers from Brest, lodged in a suburb and mobilized by Goazre de Kervélégan, a Left republican deputy from Finisterre, quickly suppressed the main anti-Brissotin ferment.[125]

Only four section assemblies—Mauconseil, Bonne-Nouvelle, Lom-bards, and Théatre-Français—openly joined the attempted coup by labeling the Brissotins as traitors responsible for the Belgian debacle. Blaming the defeats on the Brissotins, not bread shortage, was clearly the demonstrations' chief theme, even though these two chaotic days were the work of a typical mix of unruly elements—resentful and im-poverished sansculottes, groups of disgruntled and angry soldiers and féderés embittered against their commanders, and gangs aiming to channel protest into targeted attacks on Brissotins. To evade the mobs, Left republican leaders kept away from both the Assembly and their homes, gathering, under Louvet's lead, in locations unknown to the ri-oters. Consequently, none were caught. The Commune, Jacobins, and National Guard made no overt move, and the disturbances rapidly pe-tered out.

The three most important features of the March 1793 riots are the very small number of people involved, the riots' prearranged, manipula-tive character, and the growing tension they revealed—evident already in the February riots—between Marat's followers and Enragé elements that resented the manipulation aimed at channeling sansculotte dis-content and protest behind Marat, Robespierre, and Billaud-Varenne. The unrest proved for all to see that the main body of hard-core sanscu-lotte activists was far from being firmly behind the Montagne and that there was a bitter struggle for the loyalty of the poor faubourgs. Anti-Montagnard posters had appeared denouncing Marat and Hébert, one signed by "Harrington," urging "all republicans" to "unite with the wor-thy industrious people and the bourgeois" and wage "implacable war on the brigands seducing the ignorant" (into demanding the Brissotins' arrest).[126]

The sansculotte group actively involved in the 9 and 10 March dis-turbances, called the Défenseurs de la République Une et Indivisible, a bunch of rowdies fond of publicly burning Brissotin literature, dis-rupting "unpatriotic" theater performances, and ejecting "undesirables" from Palais-Royal cafés, had among their leaders the notorious Claude Fournier *l'Américain* (1745–1825). Once a rum distiller in Saint-Domingue (hence his nickname), Fournier had been a leading agita-tor in all the great Parisian movements since July 1789, and was the street boss for whom Gracchus Babeuf, the future conspirator, was at this point acting as deputy. On 8 March Marat, angered by Fournier's unwillingness to respect the Jacobin leadership, had launched a vitri-olic attack on him in the Convention and, backed by Billaud-Varenne, tried to get him arrested. A leading rabble-rouser, Fournier retaliated by denouncing his rival in the streets and afterward publishing a vitriolic printed attack on Marat, dated 14 March, that may have been penned by Babeuf. This pamphlet depicts Marat as utterly base and false, no "friend of the people," someone condoning harassment of the "best patriots" like Fournier, and, unlike him (but like Robespierre), nowhere to be seen during the storming of the Bastille, the 5 October march on Versailles, the 17 July Champs de Mars journée, the 20 June 1792, or the 10 August insurrection. Marat and Fournier mutually accused the other of complicity in the September massacres.[127]

The justice minister, Garat, a Condorcet disciple, reporting afterward to the Convention, blamed the March disturbances, quite rightly, not on the sansculottes or the poor but a mere twenty to thirty "dangerous men" belonging, like Fournier, the Polish agitator Lazowski, and Babeuf, to small extremist popular societies, especially the Cordeliers splinter group, the Défenseurs de la République. Among several personages afterward arrested in this connection was Jean-François Varlet (1764-1832), a fiery Enragé street orator, prominent in the 10 August uprising, who deemed the Paris Commune no less "infected with aristocracy" than the Brissotins, and who, like most revolutionary leaders of whatever stripe, had no high opinion of Robespierre. Also detained was Lazowski, a street leader earlier active in Bordeaux who had commanded the assailants' artillery at the Tuileries on 10 August. Accused of breaking in to Gorsas's print-shop, Lazowski was a great favorite of the sansculottes of the faubourgs (despite not being of plebeian origin and having only lately discarded his love of elegant dressing). He, however, proved much more palatable than Fournier to the Montagnard leadership. When Vergniaud demanded his imprisonment, later in March, Lazowski was defended in the Convention by Robespierre in person.[128] When some weeks later Lazowski mysteriously died at home, seemingly from an illness, the Brissotins were promptly accused of poisoning him. Keen to profit politically from the death of this renowned sansculotte leader, the Commune bestowed on him a splendid, triumphal funeral to which the section assemblies were directed to send large contingents of mourners. Building on a wave of popular emotion, Robespierre extolled Lazowski as a "grand homme," a hero of the people, and a model revolutionary, at the Jacobins, and warmly supported the Commune's (apparently serious) suggestion that Lazowski be interred in the Panthéon.[129]

Subversive factions in Paris, Bordeaux, Lyon, and Marseille had demonstrated their capacity to launch targeted attacks on Brissotins and their supporters. In the Convention, during the bitter recrimination following the March riots, Montagnards loudly demanded that the Comité de Sûreté Générale's powers be strengthened. Pouring vituperation on Brissot, Gorsas, Guadet, and Gensonné, Montagnard populist deputies like Didier Thirion (1763–1816), a former priest and close ally of Marat, Jacques Garnier (1755–1818), a former small-town mayor and violent if incoherent loudmouth, Sylvain Lejeune (1758–1827), small-town lawyer and violent persecutor, Benoît Monestier (1745–1820), another ex-priest, and others loudly hailed the demonstrators and eulogized the sansculottes.[130] But there was little sign the authoritarian populists enjoyed genuine mass support or had an effective mechanism in place for mobilizing large-scale mob frustration. Neither had they shown much capacity to shepherd the sansculottes effectively or even control the Jacobins' provincial affiliate societies. If the Jacobins refused to back street initiatives departing from the agenda set by Marat and Robespierre, by no means all provincial Jacobin clubs supported the main Jacobin-concerted effort to undermine and overthrow the democratic republican regime. Some local societies, including Bayeux, Dieppe, and Amiens, vehemently condemned the "partisans of Robespierre and Marat," calling for the arrest of Marat, Robespierre, and Danton as the way to stabilize France and the Revolution.[131] The confused March commotion subsided, to be followed by weeks of uneasy quiet, the cafés continually seething with talk of finishing with the traitors.

CHAPTER 12

The "General Revolution" from Valmy to the Fall of Mainz

(1792–93)

The French National Convention assembled on 20 September 1792. By this time revolutionary confidence was reviving, indeed bordered on euphoria following the great victory over the Prussians and lesser princes (accompanied by Goethe) at Valmy, a battle fought that very day with massed artillery salvoes in the Champagne-Ardennes hills northeast of Paris, in which the Prussians were badly mauled. Previously disdaining the French, the Prussian commanders—Goethe informed Herder in Weimar on 27 September—now took the enemy more seriously.[1] Both Prussians and Austrians found themselves obliged ignominiously to retreat. On 29 September the Prussians evacuated Verdun. Enraged by Louis XVI's dethronement and the proclamation of the Republic in September, the reactionary Prussian king, Friedrich Wilhelm, could only fulminate and vow unrelenting war on the Revolution until absolute monarchy and aristocracy *were* restored.

The Republic replied with a propaganda barrage culminating in its famous decree of Fraternity and Help for oppressed foreign peoples of 19 November (afterward rescinded by the Montagne) threatening all Europe's rulers with the loss of their thrones. Left republican journalists jubilantly proclaimed their project of expanding the Revolution into a General Revolution transforming the world. None enthused over this prospect more than Anacharsis Cloots, a Prussian subject of Dutch background based in Paris where, since 1790, he had emerged among the leading journalists and ideologues. Cloots spoke repeatedly in the Assembly, demanding a democratic constitution also for Prussia since the "Bible of liberty," the code of happiness, was meant for all nations.

Dubbed the "orator of the human race," he thought nothing of publicly denouncing Prussia's monarch, the Hapsburg emperor, Catherine
the Great, and the Turkish sultan as worthless, villainous despots who
crushed their subjects underfoot. Less loudly (for now), this dogmatic
materialist also reviled revealed religion. In addition, during the autumn
of 1792, he helped form a unit, the Légion Germanique, modeled on
the existing Belgian and Dutch revolutionary legions fighting alongside
the French: serving under German officers, often Prussian and Austrian
deserters, this unit was sworn to promote the fight for republican liberty in Germany.[2] For more than five months, from September 1792,
the democratic republican war of general liberation verged on success.
The French overran Savoy in September, captured Nice on 29 September, Speyer on 30 September, and Worms on 4 October—the day
Friedrich Karl's court evacuated Mainz—and then Mainz itself on 21
October. Together with Dumouriez's triumph in storming the Austrian
lines at the battle of Jemappes, near Mons in Belgium, on 6 November,
a victory forcing open the road to Brussels, these victories transformed
the European situation and intoxicated all France. In full retreat in the
Southern Netherlands, the Austrians abandoned Namur to the revolutionaries on 15 November, Ypres on the 18th, and Antwerp on the 19th.
On 19 November, France's National Convention proclaimed "fraternity and assistance" to all peoples aspiring to achieve their liberty by
hurling off the oppressive yoke of Europe's princes. On 28 November,
the revolutionary army entered Liège amid cheering crowds, the prince-
bishop hastily evacuating just hours before.

The 1792 autumn offensive was marred, however, by the Austro-
Prussian success in retaining Luxemburg, Trier, and Coblenz, a wedge
of territory blocking all communication between the revolutionary
armies under Dumouriez (in Belgium) and Custine (Rhineland).[3] The
offensive also raised the thorny question of France's future relationship
to the "liberated" areas. Brissot and Condorcet opposed annexations
in principle, clashing first with Cloots (president of the Convention's
diplomatic committee), Grégoire, and other committee members, over
the desirability or otherwise of annexing the Savoy region of Piedmont,
as France's eighty-fourth department. This French-speaking region,
contended Cloots in his address to the Savoyard people on 3 October
1792, and in the *Chronique de Paris* and his pamphlet *Ni Marat, ni
Roland* (November 1792), was naturally part of France and had merely
experienced a "long esclavage" from which Savoyards were now happily
emerging.[4] In and around Savoy's capital, Chambéry, there was indeed

extensive support for union with France. Brissot rapidly lost this argument. On 27 November, the Convention proclaimed Savoy's annexation, renaming the duchy the department of Mont Blanc.

Key foreign exponents of the General Revolution, such as Cloots, Gorani, Paine, Barlow, Godwin, Proly, Dorsch, Wedekind, Cramer, Forster, Klopstock, Knigge, Hölderlin, and Fichte, were convinced that pen and press were no less vital than the sword for furthering the Revolution. These ideologues helped direct France's political and propaganda offensives in the Low Countries, Germany, Italy, and Switzerland, generating an ardent revolutionary universalism and high hopes for a general transformation of society for the better.[5] As the war and political struggle within France intensified, all these figures became deeply embattled in the wider European conflict. The American revolutionary Barlow was asked to visit Savoy and help steer the Savoyards toward liberty and equality, a task he commenced at Chambéry in December by publishing an open *Lettre addressée aux habitants du Piémont*. Patriotic societies and primary assemblies were set up.[6] By March 1793, two deputies had been elected as Mont Blanc's representatives and assumed their seats in the Paris Convention.

There was a pressing need for an "Anacharsis Cloots" in their city, the "brothers" at Geneva had assured the *Chronique de Paris* earlier in August 1791. The Geneva democrats wanted an "orateur du genre humain" like Cloots leading their fight against the oligarchy oppressing their republic, they explained, someone who would issue "briefs," "bulls," and "excommunications" "like the Pope from Rome" and denounce all the "Raynals" trafficking in the rhetoric of liberty, the hypocritcal oligarchs who scorned Rousseau and tyrannized over Geneva and its democrats, These *oppresseurs* had indeed violated every freedom, replied Cloots, but he disagreed with one aspect of the democrats' "missive patriotique": they overrated Rousseau, whose errors "are just as dangerous as his genius is sublime." If Geneva's democrats embraced Rousseau's ideal of small, independent republics rather than Cloots's "systeme régénerateur de la république unique"—a single, large republic based on Paris— the Genevan Revolution would be lost. Genevan democrats should acknowledge France's National Convention as the "corps constituant du genre-humain" and Paris as headquarters of a new universal republic of which all free peoples formed "sections."[7]

The French would rescue the Genevans from patrician arrogance and, equally, promised Cloots, on 10 December 1792, in his *Anacharsis Cloots aux habitans des Bouches-du-Rhin*, the Belgians from Hapsburg and the Dutch from Orangist and Anglo-Prussian "tyranny." "La démocratie représentative" would soon replace the detestable "aristo-cratic" constitutions of the Austrian Netherlands (Belgium) and the United Provinces, and the liberated Belgians and Dutch, enlightened by the same flame of philosophy, would march in unison with the French.[8] It was a message greeted with some enthusiasm in the Dutch cities and Liège, but much less so in Brussels and Antwerp. In Belgium, France would eliminate Austrian imperial authority, the Convention's executive council declared on 16 November, and open the Scheldt estuary to shipping of all nations, thus revoking the Scheldt restrictions enforced by the Dutch since 1572. This not only invoked revolutionary scorn for archaic legal provisions and historic treaties upholding privileges and special advantages of any kind, but offered concrete benefits to Antwerp (at the expense of Amsterdam's position in maritime trade), and in other circumstances might have bolstered support in Belgium.

Despite considering most Belgians "abjectly subservient" to Catholicism, Cloots predicted (wrongly) that they would adopt "the religion of the Rights of Man" (*la religion des droits de l'homme*). Belgians would fight Britain and "other enemies of the human race" together with friends of "la liberté" and "universal equality" everywhere. Unfortunately, in the Rhineland too, the great majority opposed the Revolution. On occupying Mainz, a city of around twenty-five thousand, fiercely loyal to its archbishop-elector, the French troops encountered a conspicuously sullen reception.[9] Nevertheless, the French enjoyed some support. They were noticeably better received in and around Speyer and Worms on arriving in the autumn of 1792 than in much of Belgium.[10] In rural areas on the Left Bank of the Rhine, west and south of Mainz, there were definite pockets of support, as also in Heidelberg and Mannheim, where organized revolutionary clubs were established well before the French invasion. Even at Mainz, jubilation reigned among the small fringe of highly educated intellectuals and secularists attracted to republican ideals and abhorring ecclesiastical sway.

Headed by Wedekind, Professor Dorsch, who returned in early November, and Georg Forster (1754–94), the Mainz University librarian, the Mainz Jacobins were a small but dedicated group originating in the local reading society.[11] Briefly, they held the initiative with the tacit moral backing of the many quietly disgruntled under the elector, including the city's substantial Jewish population, hitherto systematically discriminated against and squeezed into a small ghetto, but now emancipated by the Revolution. Wedekind, Dorsch, and Forster chiefly vested their hopes of mobilizing more local support for Freiheit und Gleichheit and molding a new democratic rights-based society in the Rhineland, in freedom of press and expression. Organizing their supporters through the Jacobin Gesellschaft der Freunde der Freiheit und Gleichheit (Society of Friends of Liberty and Equality), set up by twenty founding members within days of the city's falling to the French and following the founding of a similar organization in Worms, their first general meeting registered an attendance of around two hundred. Adopting the same club regulations that applied in Strasbourg, Mainz Jacobins began meeting regularly in a hall of the archepiscopal palace, ironically previously used for electing the German emperors, as if "purging that hall" of everything impure that despotism had deposited there.[12]

Backed by the French commander, the liberal monarchist Adam Philippe Custine (1740–93), and the latter's German secretary, Georg Wilhelm Böhmer (1761–1839), a former professor at the Worms gymnasium, Wedekind, Dorsch, Forster, and yet another key radical professor, the mathematician Matthias Metternich (1747–1825), dominated the purged city government and regional administration. At the same time, they launched a tremendous propaganda barrage addressed to all Germany. During the ten-month span the area remained in republican hands (from October 1792 to July 1793), Mainz democrats published more than 120 pamphlets, speeches, and other pro-Revolution texts in German. Forster threw himself feverishly into the work of propagating Republikanismus and establishing a genuinely democratic republican movement in collaboration with the French, though he soon became deeply disillusioned with the prejudiced, unresponsive attitude of most Mainz burghers and Rhineland peasants who bent their ears, it seemed to him, mainly to the reactionary admonitions of the Catholic clergy.[13] One of Europe's leading ethnologists and anthropologists, he was much struck by how the French officers and men sat together at meals and treated one another as comrades, something never witnessed in European armies before.

Local Jacobins had only a narrow base of support. But they remained convinced the Revolution resulted from mass enlightenment, that such enlightenment follows the printing press, and that their propaganda offensive could decisively mobilize opinion behind the General Revolution.[14] Several regular pro-Revolution journals, most notably the *Neue Mainzer Zeitung* and the weekly *Der Patriot*, commencing in November 1792, featured translations of speeches by prominent pro-Revolution cosmopolitans like Cloots, Proly, and Gorani, as well as material contributed by editors Wedekind and Forster, indefatigably explaining the new doctrine of Human Rights. They strove to expound and win support for *representative Demokratie* and demonstrate to the Rhineland's Protestant and Jewish religious minorities that the revolutionary ideal of freedom of thought and the press was a manifest improvement on the more grudging princely system of *Toleranz*.[15] However, signs of support among Protestants and Jews only intensified the Catholic majority's estrangement. For centuries, princes, nobles, and priests, held Forster, had exploited the people; now the people must learn to comprehend their circumstances and end the oppression that abased them. National hatreds, Mainz democrats concurred, would disappear with the advance of popular Aufklärung. The new Universal-Konstitution and the new Universal-Republik of the future would provide the basis for a collective good, a beneficent universalism nurturing a new and higher ideal of humanity.[16] *Der Patriot* attributed revolutionary ideals exclusively to the Aufklärung, the march of reason, and the obvious reluctance of most German scholars to embrace democratic principles to the painful dilemma in which they found themselves—being stuck in the service of princely rulers. A majority of Mainz professors and students had fled over the Rhine following the archbishop-elector and his court, but only because, held Wedekind, few had the necessary means to offset the loss of their university or administrative positions and salaries, and hence be independent intellectually and politically.[17]

The climax of the efforts to sway the Rhinelanders was a grand civic ceremony on 13 January 1793 at Mainz, a jamboree with brass bands, speeches by Forster and Custine, and the erection of a liberty tree adorned with a red liberty cap and the caption "Peace to the People, War to the Tyrants." The crowds listened listlessly and noncommittally, but they listened. Forster explained their deference to Kaiser und Reich and their refusal to support the Revolution in terms of the limited horizons of the typical Mainz burgher. But their docility also facilitated rapid assimilation of the new order at a certain level, and a more-or-less general acquiescence in the new arrangements, slogans, and principles. There was scarcely any armed resistance. While Rhinelanders predominantly stayed loyal to prince and Church, outright opposition to the French presence and ideological offensive for liberty and equality in the occupied regions of Germany was rare. No doubt those joining the Mainz Jacobins did so often for reasons not especially high-minded. Nevertheless, at its peak the club boasted 492 members and unquestionably included a hard core of highly motivated reformers.[18]

Pro-Revolution propaganda emanating from Mainz, Liège, and other centers formed part of a wider appeal to Europe's peoples launched by Condorcet, Cloots, Paine, Gorani, Barlow, Proly, and other renowned champions of the General Revolution. Germany was particularly in need of reform, but it was also necessary to democratize the existing constitutions of Britain and Sweden (as well as the 1791 French monarchical Constitution), these constitutional monarchies being highly defective, only *demi-libres*. Doubtless no worthwhile reforms could be expected from absolute rulers or courts, or for that matter, the ordinary people. But Condorcet confidently predicted, in his undated address *Aux Germains*, the "irresistible force of reason, the inevitable influence of Enlightenment progress triumphing equally over princely perfidy and the errors and feebleness [of understanding] of the multitude." In Germany, he thought, especially Imperial Free Cities like Frankfurt, Hamburg, and Augsburg possessed "des hommes éclairés [enlightened men]. Will compatriots of Copernicus, Kepler, Bekker and Leibniz refuse to march with us under the banner of reason? Germans, the destiny of humanity is decided; but that of the present generation lies in your hands." Toppling kings and princes would, he thought, prove relatively easy.[19]

In his *Adresse aux Bataves*, Condorcet summoned the Dutch to remember that it was they and the English who had taken the lead, in advance of other peoples, in former centuries, not just in science and knowledge but also the quest for freedom. The Dutch began the great task of "enlightening your enslaved neighbors about the true interests and the sacred rights of humanity,"[20] but they had stopped at a certain point and now needed a truly free constitution to perfect their enlightenment. "Those wanting men to remain superstitious, do not wish to see them free, and if freedom of thought necessarily leads to a free constitution, one can equally say a free constitution necessarily leads to liberty of thought." In his address to the Spaniards, one finds the same appeal to Enlightenment values as the decisive factor as in his addresses to the Dutch and Germans. Spain had long been downtrodden by Hapsburgs and Bourbons. Since in Spain the Church was even more repressive than the Crown, Enlightenment's task would prove harder than elsewhere. But Spaniards would eventually conquer both Crown and Church, helped by the French, and this would accelerate both their own and the general Enlightenment from which all humanity must benefit. Enlightenment overcomes received notions and generates revolution, and this is also the sole means to consolidate revolution. "A revolution that advances beyond the people's ideas risks being thrust backwards before long." A handful can initiate a revolution but they must powerfully disseminate democratic Enlightenment: trying to end oppression without enlightening the people is fruitless and in vain.[21]

The unfolding struggle was a war against Austria, Prussia, Piedmont, and the Rhine electorates, but equally against Dutch Orangists, the papacy, and Genevan "aristocrats," Belgian ecclesiastical and secular aristocracy, and, of course, British domination of Ireland, Holland, and India. The purpose of advancing on Holland, for Condorcet, Brissot, Cloots, Paine, Gorani, and other propagandists of the General Revolution, was to overthrow the stadtholderate and the country's old constitution. Only by this means could Holland's "slavish" subservience to Britain cease, and a democratic republic under the universal Rights of Man be instituted. But first the Revolution had to eject the Austrians from the Southern Netherlands, where there was a limited initial wave of support, and from the prince-bishopric of Liège. The revolutionary army advancing on Brussels in November 1792 included around twenty-five hundred armed Belgian exiles and democrats eager to liberate their homeland. As they entered Brussels in triumph, the people, erecting liberty trees in the city's squares, yelled out in Dutch (Brussels was then Dutch-speaking): "Viva the French! Viva our Liberators!" On 16 November, a giant liberty tree was hauled up in Brussels' Grande Place, opposite the town hall, to the crowd's applause. A Jacobin Société des Amis de la Liberté et d'Égalité was founded, its first meeting gathering in the Hotel de Galles, with a "Citizen Balza," fresh from establishing a similar society in Mons, elected "president."[22]

However, when Dumouriez's 15 and 17 December proclamations were read out, urging Belgians to exercise their rights, and especially when the crowds heard the sixth article, which required citizens to swear an oath to maintain "liberty and equality" and accept all basic constitutional laws proposed by the French National Convention, a vehement reaction began. The cry went up: "No equality! No new laws! We want our Estates, we want our old constitution and nothing else!" Fierce declarations acclaiming the Three Orders of Brabant and demanding Catholicism as the country's sole faith resounded in the primary assemblies. All twenty-one Brussels sections refused the required oath. Mass rejection of the democratic program, echoing the rhetoric of H. J. Van der Hoop, a writer recently imprisoned by the French as an "aristocratic pamphleteer and agitator," and the Catholic Counter-Enlightenment apologists Van Eupen and the Abbé Tongerloo, was all the more striking, commented eyewitnesses, in that few nobles, magistrates, or high bourgeois attended section assemblies. It was the common people, artisans, laborers, and peasants who abjured the General Revolution. The Vandernotistes triumphed yet again.[23]

Most Belgians, retorted local Jacobin *clubbistes*, were simply blinded by error and prejudice, together with the self-interested propaganda of the Belgian Estates and lies of French émigrés, "traitors" serving the interests of their former sovereign. The existing Belgian constitution did not even remotely embody the "sovereignty of the people" but only that of the nobility, judicial elites, and higher clergy. It was manifestly a legal device supporting rank and privilege. It was not French occupation per se that Belgians abhorred, explained the antirevolutionary journals. Ordinary Belgians were as indifferent to the presence of the French as to the Austrians. What enraged them were the "principes démocratiques de la République françoise," in particular, the Revolution's disdain for clergy and religion.[24] Brabanters remained deeply attached to their existing constitution, laws, and religion, noted Feller's *Journal historique et littéraire* (now appearing just out of French reach at Maastricht). Many were appalled by French behavior. A petition from the Mechelen (Malines) cathedral chapter to Dumouriez in February reproached the general for impounding the cathedral archives, placing sentries inside as well as outside the cathedral, and seizing ritual objects, crosses, flagons, and silverware. In contrast to the Rhineland, street assaults on democrats and French soldiers regularly occurred by night and day.[25]

Rejected in Brabant, the Brissotin ideal of a democratic Belgian republic protected by France enjoyed some support, though, in Flanders and Belgian Limburg as well as Liège. Jacobin clubs sprang up in various places, and by December 1792, democratic principles were being expounded against the Vandernotistes, nobles, and clergy.[26] Although Vonck himself died at Lille on 1 December 1792, Vonckisme, even if a distinctly minority movement, remained a force, especially at Ghent, where the reactionary summons of the Bruxellois and Montois was rejected and support for the French National Convention affirmed. In the Flemish cities, unlike Brussels, Mons, and Antwerp, crowds removed the insignia and coats of arms of the counts of Flanders and Austria. Whereas at Brussels by late December, the French "libérateurs" were being openly insulted and the occasional sentry murdered, in Ghent the mood remained predominantly pro-Revolution.

The French were astonished by the virulence of the backlash in Brabant. On 29 December, the day fixed for the newly established Brussels sections to choose their electors, there was uproar in the city. All the Brussels sections had unanimously rejected every French proposal, swearing unwavering allegiance to their "constitution, priests and estates" under the leadership of Van der Noot, Van Eupen, and Van der Hoop. The few courageous clubbistes speaking in favor of "democratic principles" were insulted, assaulted, and chased through the streets. Yet, even in Brussels, the Amis de la Liberté gained a few recruits, including artisans and laborers. At the meeting of the Brussels Amis de la Liberté on 5 January, the Brussels central market "fish boys" appeared. Having learned more about the Revolution, they explained, they had changed their minds, no longer wishing to be deceived "by priests and monks." Having discovered the new order released them from the ancient grip of the master fish-vendors, whose guild now lost its hold over the fish market, and under the new dispensation the fish boys could sell fish themselves; they had decided to enter "with joy and confidence into the temple of liberty and stand with the defenders of the Rights of Man."[27]

It was abundantly clear to the Belgian clubbistes that local "fanatisme aristo-théocratique" would not hesitate to take up arms in alliance with the Hapsburg Crown, Dutch Orangists, Britain, and the papacy against the Revolution.[28] According to the French pro-Revolution press, money, promises, menaces, pamphlets, sermons, secret meetings, everything was brought to bear to inject error into the minds of *les simples*.[29] Uneducated and barely educated Belgians were fanatically averse to the clubs and the "friends of liberty." But it scarcely worried the Feuillant monarchist Dumouriez that the clubs attracted scant support in Belgium. He preferred the 1791 French monarchical Constitution to republicanism and scorned the growing role the sociétés patriotiques had arrogated for themselves in France. The clubs, held the Brissotins, would provide a platform of opinion supporting the Revolution. Dumouriez, though, had no wish for the sociétés to play a political role in Belgium or France. The sole aim of the sociétés patriotiques, stated a proclamation he issued from Brussels on 11 March 1793, was to advance the "instruction des peuples" through propagating revolutionary principles. Such clubs become "dangerous," he maintained, when tempted to meddle in political matters. Before long, he forbade the Belgian and Liège clubs to concern themselves with public affairs at all; a strict prohibition was posted up in Dutch and French in all the occupied towns that made club presidents and secretaries responsible for their good conduct.[30]

In the prince-bishopric of Liège, where the French émigré military leaders, the Comte de Provence, and the Comte d'Artois had recently established their headquarters, and which the (now-ousted) prince-bishop had converted into a Counter-Enlightenment bastion, demo-cratic fervor predominated. Many people detested ecclesiastical sway. There was jubilation when the French émigrés pulled out. A liberty tree was erected before the town hall and arrangements made to establish sections, primary assemblies, and democratic elections.[31] On 30 No-vember, Liège's Société des Amis de la Liberté et d'Égalité, suppressed early in 1791, reopened as a Jacobin affiliate club in the former Jesuit church amid lively applause. Evacuating Liège together, the Austrians and émigrés alike behaved despicably, wreaking vengeance on this rebel-lious populace, besides carrying off the finest church treasures "for safe-keeping." If the French revolutionaries behaved only somewhat better, their priorities were different. For religion, they showed no respect whatsoever, protested Feller, profaning even the loveliest churches, pil-laging and turning them into arsenals, stores for all kinds of supplies, "and stables full of dung."[32] In early February, the *Neue Mainzer Zei-tung* reported that all eight sections of the city of Liège had voted in favor of merging the principality with the French Republic.[33]

The émigrés disbanded by Louis XVI's brothers (whose financial resources were now depleted), and thoroughly demoralized, mostly scattered—some to Dutch territory, others to Düsseldorf or nearby Aachen—until the latter too was overrun by the French shortly after-ward. The Paris Convention approved a financial indemnity to com-pensate both Liège and Aachen citizens pillaged by the enemy. At Aachen, a focus of political turbulence since 1786–87, and where a new republican and semidemocratic constitution had been drawn up in April 1790,[34] a local Jacobin club, the Klub der Freiheit, Gleichheit, und Bruderliebe, was founded on 8 January 1793. Like French Jacobins (and other German Jakobiner), Aachen Jacobins were sharply divided, however, between a radical republican wing and a prevailing liberal monarchism more in tune with the empire's traditions and the ethos of the princely courts.[35] Where Campe, editor of the leading prorevo-lutionary paper in German, the *Schlewigsches Journal*, published at Al-tona, admired Sieyès and the 1791 Constitution, and, like Klopstock deemed the Revolution compatible with conventional religion (albeit thoroughly approving of the Civil Constitution of the Clergy),[36] more radical German Jacobins like Forster, Wedekind, Dorsch, Metternich, Cramer, and brothers Johann and Franz Dautzenberg (the former

a professor, the latter editor of Aachen's now openly prorevolutionary paper, the *Aachener Zuschauer*) rejected all princes—monarchy in
principle—and advocated democratic republican values and the drastic curtailment of religious authority. Most Aachen citizens, observed
Christian Wilhelm Dohm (1751–1820), the deist, republican, and
enlightener chiefly responsible for the 1790 Constitution, a friend of
Wedekind, and chief advocate of Jewish emancipation in Germany, resented seeing Protestants and Jews made equal to Catholics and refused
to separate from the German Empire.[37]

At Aachen the crucial question was whether to keep the compromise, liberal 1790 Constitution, chiefly framed by the Prussian envoy
Dohm, and remain part of the German Empire, retaining numerous
religious and constitutional forms from the past, or opt for a complete
break. By February 1793, the Aachen club had been taken over by the
republicans, led by the Dautzenberg brothers, but this estranged the
club from mainstream Aachen opinion.[38] Dohm had assured the philosopher Jacobi, back in 1781, that he did not consider his "echt re-
publikanischen Grundsätze" to conflict with his loyalty to the Prussian
state, at least as it functioned in its reforming mode under Frederick the
Great (r. 1740–86); rather, he believed Frederick's Prussia represented
the best kind of monarchy available.[39] But the split between the two
varieties of German Jacobins disunited and gravely weakened the pro-
Revolution camp in Aachen, Jacobi—who disapproved of both Dohm's
Deismus and his republican preferences—reported to Goethe on 24
January, especially by embittering both the Catholics and Lutherans,
the two largest religious communities.[40] Aachen citizens felt affronted
by the liberty caps placed on images of Catholic saints and the statue of
Charlemagne in front of the town hall. Aachen's Jakobiner soon came
to be considered basically a club of foreigners, Calvinists, and Jews (several of whom joined).[41]

The French émigré princes withdrew to nearby Prussian territory,
basing themselves at Hamm, where, with the Prussian king's permission, they established their new headquarters and, in January 1793,
received the news of Louis XVI's execution. There they issued their
proclamation recognizing Louis's son, the boy prince imprisoned with
his mother at the Temple in Paris, as Louis XVII,[42] and named the
Comte de Provence, Louis-Stanislas (1755–1824) regent (though only
Catherine the Great officially recognized him as such) and acknowledged leader of the émigré diaspora fighting democracy together with
Prussia, Austria, and Britain. Strikingly, the princes' joint proclamation

made no concession to constitutionalism whatever. The future king Louis XVIII, Louis-Stanislas, promised only to mete out severe punishment to those responsible for dispossessing France's royal family, nobles, parlementaires, and Church of their status and revenues, and to return to all these elites their privileges and lands and rebuild royal authority on the basis of absolutism. Until November 1793, Louis-Stanislas continued to preside over the émigrés' counterrevolution from Prussian territory.

On 8 January 1793, provisional representatives of Brussels, Antwerp, Mechelen, Louvain, and Namur convened in the Belgian capital to draw up a manifesto rejecting the French decree proclaiming the Revolution's universal principles and laws, and the Rights of Man, valid in Belgium. The people rejected equality, republicanism, and French interference. Dumouriez's declaration of November 1792, they reminded the Paris legislature, promised no intervention in their affairs or constitution, provided Belgians "establish the sovereignty of the people." These words had thoroughly enthused Belgians, a people always against tyranny, with optimism. Had they not welcomed the French as "de généreux libérateurs"? How great then was their disillusionment on hearing of the Convention's 15 December edict imposing principles directly violating "la souveraineté du peuple Belgique."[43] It was for Belgians to determine their civil and political institutions and shape their laws. The eyes of all Europe were fixed on Paris: a foreign authority violating "the sacred rights of a sovereign people," declared the Brussels manifesto, the Republic would no longer be seen as a revolutionary power but *un pouvour tyrannique*.[44]

Catholic theologians took the lead in urging magistrates and officeholders to refuse oaths to uphold equality, liberty, and popular sovereignty. Such oaths were understood by the revolutionaries in a sense totally unacceptable to Church and princes alike. To uphold the "sovereignty of the nation" in the manner implied by the revolutionaries meant acknowledging that no individual or institution exercises authority not emanating from the nation. Such oaths were a conceptual dismantling of monarchy, nobility, custom, and "our Estates and ancient constitutions," amounting to outright rebellion against throne and altar. The oaths subverted religious authority something wholly impermissible. Any magistrates acknowledging such principles would be endorsing heresy, apostasy, incredulity, and the emblems and principles of *impies*, libertines, "sworn enemies of Jesus Christ."[45] Embracing "equality" as defined by clubbiste revolutionaries made subjects equal to their king, vassals to their lord, parishioners to their priest—abolishing all rank and religion.

Democratic zeal for the Revolution flourished most at Geneva, where, by November 1792, there was a real likelihood of a democratic uprising. More and more Swiss, observed Edward Gibbon (1737–94), among the most reactionary figures of the conservative Enlightenment, fearful he might soon have to flee his Lausanne home and abandon his beloved "library to the mercy of the democrats," were becoming "infected with the French disease, the wild theories of equal and boundless freedom." Democratic ideas had already "embittered and divided the society of Lausanne" and could easily overwhelm Geneva.[46] The Genevan oligarchy were distinctly apprehensive, knowing how interested French republicans were in their republic and that Clavière, one of the democrat leaders expelled after the patrician triumph in 1782 was one of Brissot's closest allies. To forestall the threat, the patriciate summoned three thousand auxiliary troops from the neighboring conservative oligarchy of Berne.

Because of the territory's proximity to Geneva, the French seizure of Savoy particularly worried foes of the Revolution in Switzerland. There was scarcely any Savoyard resistance to the occupying French army encamped across Lake Geneva, noted a perturbed Gibbon, surveying the Savoyard coastline through his telescope. Unable to ascertain "whether the mass of the people" there was "pleased or displeased with the change," it disturbed him that there was no discernible resistance to the annexation and that "my noble scenery is clouded by the democratical aspect of twelve leagues of the opposite coast, which every morning obtrude themselves on my view." All reports suggested the revolutionary army encamped there, like that in the Rhineland, offered an unprecedented spectacle with "the officers (scarcely a gentleman among them) without servants, or horses, or baggage," actually mixing "with the common men, yet maintaining a rough kind of discipline over them."[47]

Widely predicted even before 1789, Geneva's renewed democratic revolution erupted in December 1792, "sooner than I expected," remarked Gibbon. Hardly had the French promised not to invade, causing the Bernese to withdraw their troops, than, on 28 December 1792, Geneva's democrats, the Égaliseurs, rose, seized the city gates, disarmed the garrison, and overthrew the ruling oligarchy. "Citizens of the best families and fortunes" not imprisoned, Jacques Necker and his family among them, immediately fled with the many émigrés lodged in Geneva to neighboring Swiss cantons that were still under patrician oligarchies. Sovereignty reverted to the people under a decree enacted by the Grand Conseil on 12 December. Privilege and oligarchy were abolished and citizenship assigned to the entire citizenry, or, as Gibbon noted, they gave "the rights of citizens to all the rabble of the town and country."[48] Three weeks sufficed to erase every trace of Geneva's ancien régime. The democrats annulled all Geneva's political edicts of the past century, including the ban on Rousseau and his books. To ensure an orderly transfer of power, on 28 December, the insurrectionists instituted a provisional Comité de Sûreté Générale (of thirteen leading citizens) that announced a complete revision of the republic's laws and constitution by a "national assembly" of forty, shortly to be elected. "Theory always proceeds far in advance of practice," reported one enthusiast to the Paris *Gazette nationale*: "les vrais principes sont dans les livres." The French had implemented what the philosophes had conceived and "Geneva having received the lessons earlier, now finally followed the example."[49]

Genevans "are all for a pure and absolute democracy," wrote Gibbon to the Lady Sheffield on 1 January 1793, "but some wish to remain a small independent state, whilst others aspire to become a part of the republic of France; and as the latter, though less numerous, are more violent and absurd than their adversaries, it is highly probable that they will succeed."[50] "The new constitution of Geneva," he added in early February 1793, is "slowly forming, without much noise or any bloodshed; and the patriots, who have stayed in hopes of guiding and restraining the multitude, flatter themselves that they shall be able at least to prevent their mad countrymen from giving themselves to the French, the only mischief that would be absolutely irretrievable. The revolution of Geneva is of less consequence to us [in Lausanne], however, than that of Savoy; but our fate will depend on the general event rather than on these particular causes."[51] By early February, Gibbon felt slightly calmer as "all spirit of opposition is quelled in the Canton of Berne" and the Helvetic Confederation's neutrality (despite its refusal to recognize the French Republic) seemed more assured. Even so, it upset him that news of Louis XVI's execution in January 1793 was "received [in Switzerland] with less horror than I could have wished." So insecure were the French noble émigrés living in Lausanne that they "do not wear black, nor do even the Neckars [*sic*]." As a consequence, Gibbon too felt constrained from "going into mourning."[52] (In Mainz, Forster, Metternich, and Böhmer approved the execution unreservedly; other German Jacobins disapproved, some from a liberal monarchist standpoint, others, including Cramer and Oelsner, from a Brissotin republican standpoint.)[53]

The French occupation of Nice and Savoy, and developments in Corsica, were suggestive of what the Revolution might signify for Italy. Corsica remained broadly untouched by the Revolution's early stages. The former Genoese island brought under French rule in 1768 had been declared an integral part of France by the National Assembly on 29 September 1789, and, on the island, in an elaborate ceremony with local elites participating on 30 November. In the National Assembly, Corsica was represented by four deputies—a noble, a clergyman, and two Third Estate delegates. The 1791 Constitution was received calmly enough. But after the singing, artillery saluts, *Te Deums,* and declarations, little actually changed. Corsica's ancien régime continued intact with the local aristocracy and clergy holding sway, aided by the peasantry's poverty, illiteracy, and abased condition, and their knowing little French.[54] Since the capital Bastia's ten or twelve thousand inhabitants "lived from abuse," as one observer put it, and derived their employment from serving the aristocracy and clergy, they felt little inclination to do other than support the existing order. To the inhabitants' great joy, the hero of their revolt against Genoa, General Pascal Paoli, after twenty-one years of exile, returned to the island in glory on 17 July 1790. Everyone crowded into Bastia for a glimpse of him.

By late 1791, little had been done to end noble privilege, reform the legal system, eliminate the old entrenched town oligarchies of Bastia and Ajaccio, or take over church properties and revenues. Everything remained under "des ligues aristocatiques." With originally five bishoprics, numerous clergy, and ten to twelve thousand nobles, magistrates, and officials, Corsica remained a heavily traditional society, dominated by men who had discreetly opposed the Revolution since its inception. National Assembly decrees were not even published on the island, let alone implemented. The military garrison habitually still wore the royalist white cockade instead of the tricolor.[55] While the Corsican revolutionaries' hopes focused on the towering figure of Paoli, most Corsicans, directed by the clergy, rural and urban, joined the nobles and Church in opposing the Revolution.[56] Among the island's few active agents of revolution were the Bonaparte family and Christophe Salicetti (1757–1809), a Bastia-born lawyer (much esteemed by Napoleon), one of Corsica's Estates-General delegates instrumental in arranging Paoli's return.

Among those sharing Condorcet's and Brissot's view that the Revolution's core values must be exported and internationalized to be consolidated was Volney, who was commissioned by the Assembly in late 1791 to be its envoy, working with local revolutionary elements to dismantle the Corsican ancien régime. Corsica struck Volney, on his arrival, as deplorably feudal and corrupt. He could see no way of countering the ignorance and "blindness" of the people and implementing the Revolution's legislation since, to his bitter disappointment, there was not even a bookshop on the island, or any regular arrangement for receiving French journals propagating enlightened ideas. He tried to advance the Revolution in the only way practicable—proclaiming freedom of the press and helping establish the island's first revolutionary journal, the *Giornale patriotico di Corsica*, which commenced publication on 3 April 1790 and was edited by a renegade Pisan noble, Philippe Buonarroti (1761–1837). It was the only revolutionary paper in Italian during the early 1790s.

The Corsican revolutionary faction led by Salicetti and Buonarroti faced obstacles of every kind. The first serious trouble followed the announcement that four of Corsica's five bishoprics would be quashed and that there were plans for drastically reducing the size of the island's senior and lower clergy. The entire ecclesiastical establishment was outraged, though popular opposition was constrained for the moment (until 1793) due to Paoli's temporary loyalty to the Revolution.[57] Paoli wanted the Corsican clergy to accept the constitutional oath, and most lower clergy did so. Paoli chose to work with Ignace François Guasco, the man elected (with Paoli's aid) as the island's sole constitutional bishop. The refractory friars and priests replied by engineering a furious riot in Bastia on 3 June 1791, with the crowd, mostly women, averring unswerving loyalty to their faith, storming the constitutional bishop's palace and ransacking the two patriotic clubs, as well as the Freemasons lodge.[58] Denounced as an "atheist," Buonarroti was chased through the streets. Paoli cracked down hard, arresting sixteen friars and monks for sedition. But he also deported Buonarroti to Tuscany, where he was imprisoned for a time (before later returning to Corsica).

Volney's political scheme, to revolutionize the island in alliance with Paoli, came to nothing, as Paoli increasingly proved he was interested only in extending his personal power and family's influence, at bottom caring little for the Revolution.[59] Volney's economic plan to stimulate the production of coffee, cotton, sugar, and indigo, which would enable its inhabitants to prosper while Corsica's cash crops compensated France for her losses in the Caribbean, especially on Saint-Domingue, equally foundered. By early 1793, a serious rift had developed, with

Paoli turning against the Revolution, publicly proclaiming his admiration for Britain. Led by the clergy, at least fourth-fifths of Corsicans, reports suggested, backed the growing counterrevolutionary movement, with Paoli soon seeking to detach Corsica permanently from France.[60] By early 1793, the revolutionary party led by Buonarroti, the Convention's *commissaire observateur*, had been driven from much of the island by a victorious Paoli leading the clergy, nobles, and common people.[61] Volney's local reputation was wrecked by Paoli's denouncing him too as a "heretic." In February 1794, Paoli signed a treaty converting Corsica into a protectorate of the British Empire while a British expeditionary force occupied the island's main ports. For the moment, monarchy, aristocracy, and clergy had triumphed in Corsica.

The French military triumphs of late 1792 plunged all Germany into consternation while simultaneously exciting the country's republicans and democrats. A liberty tree appeared one night in October, in the main square of the Westphalian town of Paderborn. At the court of Hanover, in November, an order was issued forbidding all officers to discuss politics.[62] In Prussia, where in December, a member of the Berlin Royal Academy of Sciences, Professor Borelly, was expelled for publicly praising the Revolution and another professor thrown into irons at Magdeburg, there was an unremitting crackdown.[63] The Prussian king became obsessively vigilant to suppress every sign of atheist-materialist philosophy and the egalitarian, pro-Revolution democratic fringe penetrating further, but undoubtedly it did, especially in several university towns and academic contexts.[64] The chief organizer of the Deutsche Union, Carl Friedrich Bahrdt (1740–92), already in prison at Magdeburg for writing against the Prussian censorship, died behind bars in 1792. But Bahrdt's disciples and sympathizers abounded, especially in the university world. Egalitarian secret societies, the Illuminati and the Deutsche Union, strongly infiltrated by the materialism of Helvétius, Raynal, d'Holbach, and Diderot, and surviving under repression since the 1770s, penetrated particularly among sections of the academic community and the publishing world.

Among the best documented examples of this subversion, curiously, was a Protestant seminary at Tübingen in Württemberg, where Hegel and Hölderlin were then students. The director himself remarked that most of his students were at this time sympathetic to the Revolution, while the duke complained the place had become "äusserst demokratisch." In July 1793, Hölderlin communicated to his brother his deep sympathy for Brissot and joy at the assassination of the "schändliche Tyrann" Marat.[65] The young Hegel likewise passionately embraced the ideals of the Revolution. The tendency of both Hegel and Hölderlin to link the Revolution "with moral and spiritual renewal," and a future era of beauty and freedom, derived partly from their simultaneous immersion during the early 1790s in Spinozism and the texts of the great German Spinoza controversy of the 1780s.[66] Among the foremost participants defending Spinozism and Lessing in that controversy was the Leipzig professor Karl Heinrich Heydenreich (1764–1801), who was also, from 1788, among the leading Kryptodemokraten of the Deutsche Union in Leipzig.[67] Almost without exception, the German pro-Revolution writers and intellectuals condemned Robespierre and Marat.[68]

German princely repression was sustained, systematic, and broadly effective, except in Schleswig-Holstein where the Danish Crown held sway and the press was freer than elsewhere. But if reactionary forces generally predominated, princely repression in Germany also exerted a strong cultural-psychological contrary effect, intensifying the deep estrangement of the "enlightened"' reform-minded. Besides Dorsch, Cotta, Wedekind, Forster, and the Dautzenbergs, those most obviously under suspicion included the former Illuminati leader Adolph Freiherr Knigge (1752–96) and, at Kiel, a professor of Greek, the orientalist and translator of Tom Paine into German, Carl Friedrich Cramer (1752–1807).[69] Knigge and his publisher were threatened with dire consequences if they did not cease threatening religion, morals, and the social order.[70] Cramer's efforts, especially publishing his German version of Paine's *Rights of Man* and other subversive works in Copenhagen, and radicalizing students, were deeply resented, but with Kiel being under Danish jurisdiction, it was not until May 1794 that Prussian pressure secured his dismissal from his university chair. Another courageous rebel was a young professor at Jena, deeply preoccupied with Kant's philosophy, Johann Gottlieb Fichte (1762–1814). Already a marked man for the Spinozistic tone of his *Kritik aller Offenbarung* (Critique of All Revelation; 1792), Fichte emerged in 1793 as a leading voice of pro-Revolution opinion. Although an early draft of his *Zurückforderung der Denkfreiheit von den Fürsten Europens die sie bisher unterdrückten* (Reclaiming Freedom of Thought from Europe's Princes which they have until now suppressed; 1793), originally penned in 1792, was distinctly conciliatory in tone, his final version was a vehement demand that "freedom of thought" be returned to the people. Powerfully renewing Bahrdt's attack on the princes and their censorship, Fichte deplored the entire German "system of patronage and tutelage."[71]

Fichte's *Zurückforderung* was followed by his refutation of the *Investigations on the French Revolution* (1793) by the Hanoverian conservative official, August Wilhelm Rehberg (1757–1836). This was entitled *Beitrag zur Berichtigung des Urtheile des Publikums über die französische Revolution* (Contribution to rectifying the Public's Judgement of the French Revolution). For both the Humean Rehberg and Fichte, the crucial issue was how to assess the the Revolution's basic significance for humanity and locate it correctly in the context of philosophy. The Revolution was valid and "important for all mankind," contended Fichte in his two-hundred-page retort to Rehberg, its essential principles, especially the concept of volonté générale, which he claimed Rehberg had misrepresented, and its attack on privilege and elites being broadly justified. Every people has the right to change its constitution. Fichte dismissed Rehberg, and other prominent conservative ideologues like Schlötzer, as superficial Sophisten.[72] Despite his visceral hatred of the Jews, Fichte at this stage combined his defense of the French Revolution with a general plea for universal toleration.

The upheaval of the General Revolution, surging over Europe in late 1792 politically, militarily, and as a wave of emotion and propaganda, also touched Swedish shores. Sweden too became tense as the authorities forbade the newspapers to discuss the French Revolution and banned the Swedish translation of Paine's *Rights of Man* that appeared in Stockholm that year. The radical poet and Spinozist, Thomas Thorild (1759–1808)—"Sweden's Tom Paine" and "chief martyr for freedom," as Cramer called him—caused a public scandal in Stockholm on 21 December 1792 with his tract *The Liberty of Reason presented to the Swedish Regent and Nation*, which assailed the monarchical Constitution, princely oppression, and the clergy.[73] The people's happiness, he declared, means rejecting monarchy and adopting republican and democratic government. By the point the authorities seized the remaining stock of this "incendiary text" and arrested its author, several thousand copies had been distributed. When Thorild appeared in court on 8 January, a noisy crowd forced their way in, demanding to witness the proceedings. "Every time the accused opened his mouth to defend himself," the crowd cheered. When he was taken away, a near riot commenced, the crowd outside in the street shouting, "Long live Thorild! Long live Liberty!" Troops were deployed in inner Stockholm to silence the "badly intentioned." The capital's military garrison was reinforced and guard patrols doubled. Inns and taverns were ordered to close at nine in the evening. Two manufacturers, accused of fomenting the Thorild demonstration, were imprisoned. Thorild was afterward deported to Germany. Condemning the sedition, the municipality and magistrates hastened to assure the Crown of their unshakable loyalty to monarchy, nobility, constitution, and religion.[74]

On 1 February 1793, after weeks of deteriorating relations between Britain and France, the French Convention declared war on Britain and the United Provinces. For months, Dumouriez had been preparing the "liberation" of the United Provinces, a liberation keenly desired by many in Amsterdam, Utrecht, and Rotterdam. A published manifesto was printed in large quantity, in French and Dutch, at Antwerp with the help of the Dutch Patriot Comité Revolutionair, which also raised loans, using their own credit, to expand Dumouriez's limited cash resources.[75] "Prussian tyranny," declared Dumouriez, had dragged the Dutch back under the yoke of monarchical despotism in 1787, suppressing all hope of liberty and driving many Patriots abroad until the most astonishing revolution known to history (i.e., the French) changed the situation. The French were now invading as the "ally of the Dutch" and "irreconcilable enemies of the House of Orange." Is not the Prince of Orange "at this moment surrendering your foremost colonies, the Cape of Good Hope, the island of Ceylon and all your commerce in the Indies to the only nation whose ceaseless rivalry you need fear [i.e., Britain]? I enter your homeland [surrounded] by the generous martyrs of the revolution of 1787. Their perseverance and sacrifices, and the revolutionary committee they have formed to direct the initial stages of your revolution entirely merit your confidence and mine."[76]

As the manifesto indicated, Dumouriez deliberately surrounded himself with Dutch revolutionaries. Scorning Dumouriez's manifesto as full of "absurdities," Feller's *Journal historique* predicted that the planned new Dutch Patriot rising of 1793 would not amount to much. Britain and Prussia exerted greater leverage in Holland than they had before 1787. The pastoral instructions issued by the papal nuncio and vicar apostolic of the United Provinces, Monseigneur Brancadoro, of 11 February, were very clear. Catholics formed a sizable, tolerated minority in the United Provinces, and Catholics had provided a major component of support for the Dutch Patriot movement during 1780–87. In towns with sizable Catholic minorities, like Utrecht and Amersfoort, there remained, Feller granted, some risk to conservatism from a "coalition of *la secte philosophique* with Jansenism," such as had disastrously occurred "with the forging of the [French] Civil Constitution of the Clergy." But this peril was now considerably lessened: Dutch Catholics were being continually commanded by their clergy in the pope's name to support the stadtholder, Britain, and Prussia, and combat "le fanatisme démocratique."[77]

The Dutch Comité Revolutionair organized Dumouriez's intelligence service and encouraged men to desert from the Prince of Orange's army, issuing two pamphlets for this purpose. The committee clearly commanded a strong following in Holland, especially in Amsterdam, Haarlem, Dordrecht, and in Zeeland. Generally, Patriot support in the United Provinces was judged to outweigh support for Orangism.[78] For its supporters, the invasion began promisingly. Dumouriez's Venezuelan deputy, Francisco de Miranda (1750–1816), a friend of Brissot and Pétion (but abhorred by Cloots), accompanied by two members of the Dutch revolutionary committee (representing the sovereignty of the Dutch people), in early February captured Roermond, besieged Maastricht, and took several major forts between. Miranda directed only the military side, the political task of revolutionizing the captured Dutch areas being the responsibility of the revolutionary committee. The Batavian Revolution's first liberty trees were erected in mid-February at Deurne, Eindhoven, and Helmond.

The main invasion, commanded by Dumouriez personally, commenced on 17 February, the French accompanied by the "Batavian legion" under Lieutenant Colonel Herman Willem Daendels (d. 1818), or three legions as it soon became, totaling fifteen hundred men, including many long-exiled Dutch refugees recruited in France and Belgium. These, Dumouriez later recalled, performed "excellent service."[79] The invasion received a notably warm welcome from the local population. Breda and Geertruidenberg were quickly taken, bringing much of the States of Brabant under revolutionary control. Oaths to uphold freedom and equality were exacted from magistrates and municipal officeholders. Coats of arms of the House of Orange and other symbols and insignia of the old order vanished from buildings, church pews, organs, and shop signs. The House of Orange's largest and best-known coat of arms were removed from the great church of Breda and hacked to pieces in the town's main square. At Breda, municipal elections were held and a new municipality installed under the Patriot leader Bernadus Blok (1756–1818), previously a prominent figure among the Dutch exiles in France.[80]

In February 1793, it was possible to believe all Western Europe was on the verge of being democratized, secularized, and emancipated. In the Rhineland, elections were planned for 24 February 1793, for local primary assemblies to choose new municipal governments in Mainz, Worms, Speyer, and smaller places, from which representatives would be selected to constitute the projected new Rheinisch-Deutsche Nationalkonvent (Rhineland National Convention) with the capital at Mainz. All adult male residents older than twenty-one (except servants and foreigners) were eligible to vote, but only after swearing an oath to Freedom and Equality and abjuring forever all special "liberties" and historic privileges.[81] A deputation of five French National Convention representatives, headed by Grégoire and Merlin de Thionville, arrived to supervise. In the towns and countryside of the French-occupied Rhineland, local authorities all received directives from the clergy and the elector's officials across the Rhine to boycott these elections. As in Belgium, the Catholic clergy directed magistrates and citizenry to refuse loyalty oaths and all other formulae implying repudiation of princely and ecclesiastical authority. In retaliation, many clergy, "privileged," and officeholders were expelled by the French; others departed voluntarily.[82] At Speyer, nearly everyone refused the oath and practically all the clergy fled.[83] Those who remained were in no mood to cooperate. Altogether, only a few hundred voters turned out, though even this counted as a success after nearby Frankfurt's capture by the Prussians on 2 December.

It was the military defeats of March 1793, a month of unmitigated disaster for the French, that aborted the resumed Dutch democratic revolution (for the moment) and ensured the prompt collapse of the Rheinisch-Deutsche Freistaat (German Rhenish Free State), as well as Jacobin Belgium. With powerful coalition forces deploying for a massive counteroffensive, the Austrian commander, the Archduke Charles, issued a ringing manifesto on 1 March condemning what the allies considered the Revolution's perfidious principles. The German, Dutch, Belgian, and Swiss revolutionaries, no less than their French counterparts, were a sect "equally the enemy of religion, morality and all social order."[84] On 2 March, Miranda was forced to abandon the siege of Maastricht to avoid being cut off by the Prussian advance farther south. Simultaneously, the French and local Patriots evacuated Liège. On 18 March, Dumouriez's army was crushed in the Battle of Neerwinden and, a few days later, again at Aldenhoven. The revolutionaries' and clubbistes' retreat became a rout. Within days, the French, together with the Dutch legionaries (many of whom now deserted), evacuated virtually all the territory they had occupied.

A strategic disaster, the sudden French military collapse was an even greater psychological, cultural, and ideological setback. Dumouriez blamed the Paris Convention for "oppressing" the Southern Netherlands, contrary to his promises of November 1792. Marat blamed Dumouriez and Brissot in a blistering attack published on 20 March that caused a considerable stir in the Assembly. Marat did not hesitate to label Dumouriez as one of the "faction Brissotine," which, according to him, falsely styled themselves "Jacobins" and had deliberately installed Dumouriez alongside Roland and Clavière to betray the Revolution. Dumouriez's ban on the Belgian sociétés populaires participating in political affairs, alleged Marat, proved him an "enemy of liberty," as did his supposed sympathy for émigrés, his telling local nobles he was "their protector," and wasting the lives of his troops. According to Marat, Dumouriez aspired to become "sovereign" of a united Belgium and Holland.[85]

The French were astounded by the immense crowds shouting, "Vive l'empereur! Vive l'archiduc Charles!" and thronging the streets to greet the victorious Austrians as they swept first into Antwerp and then Louvain and Brussels. The people definitely welcomed the Austrians with greater ardor than they had the revolutionaries the previous November. Following the departure of the last French troops on 24 March, the liberty tree on the Grande Place in Brussels was hauled down and burned and the houses of local sansculotte leaders pillaged. Officials implicated in the revolutionary regime mostly responded with alacrity to the emperor's offer of amnesty and defected, disavowing every link to the Revolution. Those who refused hurriedly departed.[86] Of the Belgian deputies elected to represent Belgium in the Paris Convention, only three or four remained loyal to the Revolution's ideology. The departure of the French garrison from Mons on 26 March was likewise preceded by evacuation of the entire local Jacobin clubbiste set. Scarcely were they gone than the Mons liberty tree was seized from the towns' central square, together with that in the clubbistes' hall, and publicly burned, along with the hall's liberty insignia, podium, and galleries.[87] Omitted from the imperial amnesty due to the tenacity there of pro-Revolution sentiment, Liège incurred special retribution. Liégeois who had collaborated were proscribed, thousands being forced into exile or imprisoned. A special court was erected to try those chiefly implicated. Every law promulgated in the prince-bishopric since November 1792 was annulled, every official employed by the prince-bishop before 27 November 1792 reinstated.[88]

Outraged at being vilified by the Montagne, Dumouriez contemplated using the beaten remnants of his army to stage a coup and overthrow the Paris clubs. At Tournai on 28 March, he met with the Convention's three commissaries to the army—citizens Pierre-Joseph Proly (1752–94), Pierre-Ulric Dubuisson (1748–94), playwright and author of a history of the American Revolution, and the Jewish merchant Pereyra, representatives involved with supplying the troops, besides supervising Dumouriez's political activity. A Belgian baron and natural son of the Austrian minister Kaunitz, Proly edited the republican journal *Le Cosmopolite*, which aligned with the Left republicans in Paris, as well as the wider international pro-Revolution literary fraternity. In their secret talks, Dumouriez tried to persuade them of the need for "a moderate [i.e., monarchical] course" on the basis of the principles of 1789. All three commissaries rebuffed him, remaining loyal to the Revolution's republican democratic principles.[89]

The French troops in the Rhineland stood their ground with reportedly hardly any desertions. Responding to a further surge of resistance fomented by clergy, Custine rounded up and deported more priests and "privileged" across the river. The property of those expelled was "put in the hand of the nation," that is, confiscated. The traditionalism, piety, anti-Semitism, and notorious xenophobia of the Mainz burghers, and the likelihood Mainz would soon revert to the elector's control, all depleted the Rhineland Revolution of popular backing and helped boost support for Kaiser und Reich. Reviled by the Catholic clergy, the club was increasingly monopolized by Protestants from elsewhere in Germany, such as Forster, Böhmer, Wedekind (from Göttingen), and Cotta. Meetings of the Mainz Jacobin club began to be beset with hissing, whistling, and stamping from unsympathetic listeners.

Following elections (with a low turnout) in 270 communities on the Rhenish west bank from Landau to Bingen, a confirmed favorable result was declared in 130 of these. Despite the unfavorable circumstances, more than a hundred deputies were duly elected by the Rhenish municipalities and, on 17 March 1793, the day before the heavy defeat at Neerwinden, with the first sixty-five representatives present (rising to around a hundred by 22 March), the Nationalconvent der freien Deutschen, or Convention-nationale, as the French called it, the Rhenish-German National Convention, was inaugurated in Mainz, in the presence of Merlin de Thionville, who represented the French Convention. On 18 March

1793, this congress declared the Rhineland Republic an independent and indivisible state based on liberty, equality, and popular sovereignty, and issued a carefully crafted decree welded from drafts submitted by four of its formidable phalanx of professors—Dorsch, Wedekind, Metternich, and Forster. Proclaiming the Rhineland an independent republic free of princes and aristocracy, the assembly formally dispossessed the elector of Mainz and other Left Bank Rhenish princes, lords, and ecclesiastical authorities of their jurisdiction and lands within its boundaries, forbidding them to return to the new entity under pain of death.[90] Sovereignty on the Rhenish Left Bank from Landau to Bingen, encompassing Mainz, Speyer, and Worms, resided in the people alone. The edict was printed in thirty thousand copies, the republic's towns and communities being asked to adopt it amid public celebrations, and in Mainz, at least, they did. The turnout for the elections was dismally low but this did not prevent a considerable, jubilant crowd from attending the inauguration celebrations in Mainz's market square. With the Rhineland Republic's new tricolor flag flying and accompanied by the French garrison's military band, an impressive crowd, standing before the liberty tree, joined in the singing of republican hymns, roaring out "Es lebe die Freiheit! Es lebe das Volk! Es lebe die Republik!"[91]

The Mainz Convention elected Andreas Joseph Hofmann (1753–1849), yet another professor, president, and Forster vice president. Delegates were divided, though, between Dorsch's followers, the Dorschianer, who wanted the occupied Left Bank formally integrated into the French Republic, and a more popular grouping, Hofmann's followers, two-thirds of the Rhenish Jacobins, who preferred a nominal French protectorate over an essentially independent daughter republic.[92] Dorsch and Forster, whom Hofmann accused of being too close to the French, by this stage felt deeply estranged, owing to corrupt collusion between the raucous Hofmann, who was much implicated in the deportations of clergy and officeholders across the Rhine, and the French Montagnard commissioner, Antoine-Christophe Merlin de Thionville (1762–1833), a Metz lawyer and Jacobin allied to the even more corrupt populist deputies, Chabot and Bazire. "A Revolution that needs only scoundrels," Forster wrote to his wife, "does not need me."[93] But with the Prussian and Austrian forces approaching, there was little time to argue the point. The Rhenish republican legislature held its last meeting on 30 March 1793. On 31 March, the Prussians occupied Worms, demolished the liberty tree, and dissolved the local Jacobin club; the houses of leading Klubisten were pillaged.[94]

In practice, no alternative remained but to propose union with France. A delegation of three—Forster, another academic, Adam Lux (1765–93), and a merchant—set off on 24 March for Paris to request annexation of the liberated Rhineland's fast-diminishing remnant to the French Republic. Their request was submitted by Forster to the Convention the very day he arrived, 30 March, and accepted. But by then most of the "liberated" Rhineland had been overrun by Prussian forces. The surviving sliver enjoyed only a brief existence. Forster and Lux, their return cut off by the siege of Mainz, remained as the protectorate-republic's representatives in Paris, where they were joined at the end of March by Dorsch.[95] Wedekind fled to Strasbourg. In both Paris and Strasbourg, practically all the German expatriot colony, or Revolutionsfreunde, sided with the Brissotins against Robespierre from July 1793, with only Forster trying to stay more or less neutral; virtually all accepted the Brissotin, not the Montagnard, view of the September massacres.[96] On 19 July, Forster again appeared in the name of the Rhenish Republic before the Convention, this time to endorse the French democratic Constitution of June 1793.[97] The Revolution in Germany and the Low Countries (but not Switzerland) had collapsed, but something of the ideal survived, and the Austrians and Prussians were still defied by several centers of stubborn resistance. In particular, Mainz held out, though that could not disguise the fact that France stood on the verge of total defeat.

The Pitt government in Britain chose March 1793, the month of France's military collapse, to commit all its power and resources to overthrowing the Revolution, entering into alliances with Spain, Sardinia, Portugal, Naples, and Russia, and intensifying the repression of radicals at home. British cash, diplomacy, influence, and naval power surrounded the Revolution on every side, backed in England by overwhelming popular and elite support. While some British writers and reformers still supported the Revolution, conservative, proaristocratic views heavily predominated at home. Edmund Burke could not understand anyone wanting anything less than an all-out drive to obliterate the Revolution and its enactments.[98] Repression was the order of the day. This was reflected in Paine's conviction for sedition in absentia, in December 1792, and the proceedings against the Unitarian William Frend, an ally of Priestley who was agitating for mild reforms in Cambridge and against the "ecclesiastical tyranny" practiced by the university. Frend's pamphlet *Peace and Union* (February 1793), gently pleading for Britain's withdrawal from the war against France, though only mildly critical of the British establishment and the currently aggressively intolerant mood in England, struck a chord among progressive students, including the young Coleridge. "Frend for ever!" was chalked subversively on Cambridge college walls. The master and fellows of his college passed resolutions condemning Frend for "disturbing the harmony of society," "prejudicing the clergy in the eyes of the laity," and undermining the standing of the established Church.[99] Ignominiously expelled from Jesus College, Frend's books were thrown out into the street.

By April 1793, the democratic republican vision of a new European order lay in ruins, and reactionary opinion could confidently expect the immanent extinction of democratic constitutional systems. Europe appeared to be on the verge of a general reversion to absolutism, British mixed government, and restored ecclesiastical authority. The "wise elector of Saxony" seemed to be amply justified in designating the French Constitution of 1789 a *galimathias* (monstrosity), based on what conservatives viewed as "la déclaration anti-sociale" of the Rights of Man. Constitutional monarchy on the French model of 1791 was something altogether pernicious, argued Feller, since it rendered the king merely the *sanctionateur* of the legislature's decrees. In truth, the 1791 Constitution was not really monarchical at all but republican, and by permitting all confessions equality of status "persecutes Christianity, requiring its office-holders to take iniquitous oaths that no officials or priests should embrace." Dumouriez was perverse enough to want to build on France's hideous "constitution monarchico-républicaine," but Europeans generally should now eschew constitutionalism altogether and comprehensively espouse monarchy, nobility, and religion.[100]

In Paris, the mood was dismal. Those backing Brissot, Pétion, Paine, and Condorcet in the desperate struggle raging in Paris, including the foreign republicans, were thrown into deep consternation by the shattering reverses and their ruthless exploitation by Marat and Robespierre. Among those denounced for criminal negligence, incompetence, and suspected espionage on behalf of Britain was General Francisco de Miranda, a friend of Pétion through whose influence he had become a French revolutionary general.[101] Democratic republican ideologues rallied to defend him during a heated public debate lasting five days, with Pétion, Guadet, Barlow, and Paine among those robustly defending his integrity.[102] Yet, despite it all, Herder wrote to Klopstock from Weimar, commiserating with him over the setbacks in May 1793, neither Robespierre nor Marat could prevent the fight for what was valuable in the

Revolution, continuing: "Hoffnung bringt Geduld, und Geduld Hoffnung."[103] The disastrous defeats notwithstanding, the vision of a new democratic republican Europe precariously survived in Germany, the Low Countries, and Italy alike, defended by a tiny band of ideologues thrown back on Paris, all decried and reviled throughout Europe, as well as by most in France and in the French National Convention.

CHAPTER 13

The World's First Democratic Constitution

(1793)

Following the journée of 10 August 1792, the National Assembly, shorn of its monarchist bloc, agreed that France should become a democratic republic based on universal male suffrage, and that the Constitution once drafted would be submitted to the people via a referendum. By late March 1793, besieged by Prussia, Austria, and Britain without and by royalists and zealous Catholics within, the Revolution appeared to be on the verge on collapse. Yet optimism had not altogether vanished. The democratic Constitution, complete in draft and under intensive discussion, was seen by many as a kind of savior. The new Constitution, republican and democratic, most of the Convention fervently believed, was "the true and only means," as one deputy put it, "to end both the exterior struggle and France's interior troubles."[1] The world's first democratic republic based on equality, human rights, and freedom of expression could and would be established and stabilized.

Superficially, forging the new Constitution did not seem to involve any considerable disagreement about what democracy is and how to establish it.[2] On the surface, the Convention's constitutional committee, the Convention majority, and the pro-Revolution press were agreed regarding the main principles. The Constitution would combine elements of representative and direct democracy, and there would be no division of powers. According to Condorcet, the deputy assigned the principal role in drawing up the Constitution by the Convention, the people possess the right to elect and, under certain circumstances, dismiss their representatives, besides effect changes in the law through criticism, debate, and referenda. Seemingly, the entire republican camp concurred.

In their constitutional thinking, both Brissotins and the Montagne aimed to combine elements of direct and representative democracy. But the seeming convergence of principle was altogether superficial. Closer inspection of their rival political cultures reveals sharply antagonistic interpretations of the key concepts—representation, people, popular sovereignty, elections, rights, and volonté générale, disagreement sufficient to produce massively divergent outcomes.

The Convention appointed its committee to draft the Constitution on 11 October 1792 while the Brissotins still firmly presided over the legislature. Human rights, equality, and the sovereignty of the people would be its guiding principles. In the new Constiution there would be no religious or aristocratic component of any kind. Executive and judiciary, in sharp contrast to the United States Constitution, would remain wholly subordinate to the legislature. Given the importance and complexity of the task, few disputed that the Convention's constitutional commission should consist of France's best and most philosophique theorists. It comprised nine members, six of whom were Left republicans—Condorcet, Brissot, Paine, Pétion, Vergniaud, and Gensonné; the remainder consisted of Sieyès, the principal intellectual link with the discarded Constitution of 1791, and two Montagnards, Danton and Barère.[3]

Sieyès, for his part, advocated a strictly representative system without any admixture of direct democracy, as in 1791. This was unacceptable to Brissotins and Montagnards alike. Major theorist though he was, Sieyès consequently played little part in the Revolution's culminating constitutional deliberations.[4] During the great 1793 constitutional debate, he remained largely isolated, albeit his ardent constitutionalism and "respect for individual liberty" aligned him closer to the democratic Left than the Montagne.[5] Bertrand Barère (1755–1841), a former advocate of the Parlement of Toulouse and deputy in the 1789 Estates-General, esteemed by and very helpful to Robespierre, was an able organizer, writer, and speaker, later a prime mover of the Terror. But he alone among the nine served Robespierre's ambitions and preferences, and he had no way of promoting the Montagne's authoritarian populism on the constitutional commission on his own.[6]

Condorcet's task was to establish "a real institutional foundation for the general will."[7] Committed to the idea of volonté générale but differently from Rousseau, wanting it guided not by the unified will but the *raison collective* of the collective body of the citizenry, he refused to accept either that there is a single will or that society needs to be a battlefield of conflicting interests but believed it possible to devise a system in which decisions are based on the real interest that unites people in a society.[8] He and his colleagues, moreover, felt they were "not called to prepare a code of laws just for France," but "the entire human race," an intensely radical and un-Rousseauist doctrine redolent of the universalism of Diderot, d'Holbach, Helvétius, and the *Histoire philosophique*.[9] With monarchy, the civil list, division of powers, and restricted suffrage all roundly rejected, and the 1791 Constitution dismissed as "monstrueuse,"[10] the broad contours were clear. The Republic would be a democracy with *all* adult men, servants included, possessing the vote. Elections for both legislature and executive would occur via a two-stage electoral system with primary assemblies electing a preliminary list of candidates, all the winning candidates voted by the primary assemblies in each department, numbering three times the number of offices to be filled, then being collated and announced by the departmental authorities, after which the lists would be sent back to the primary assemblies where the voters would vote again, registering their preferences among this authenticated candidate list.[11]

The draft constitution presented to the Convention on 15 February 1793, based on Condorcet's ideas, was by far the most democratic devised during the French Revolution or anywhere before the twentieth century, a great landmark in world history.[12] Condorcet and his commission rejected not just the 1791 Constitution's monarchical character and limited suffrage but also its allocating excessive power to representatives. To balance people and representatives, a truly democratic constitution must, they argued, provide for frequent and regular elections with carefully defined powers of recall. They strove to reconcile representation with "the general will" by ensuring that the law (and hence individual submission to the volonté générale) always and fully conserved all five ingredients indispensable to republican democracy as defined by Condorcet and his colleagues, namely, sovereignty of the people, equality of status, individual liberty, freedom of expression, and government for the common good, defined as what is best for society when everyone's interests are treated equally under the criterion of "reason" alone. In Cordorcet's and their vision, the national legislature controlled the executive and remained in permanent session, observed by galleries open to the public. Half its membership was to be renewed after a year, along with half the municipal and departmental administrations. Each deputy in the legislature would thus sit for a two-year term unless deselected after one, or reelected.

Rooted in an intellectual culture reaching back less to Rousseau than to Diderot, d'Holbach, Helvétius, Boulanger, Mably, and Raynal, the Constitution of February 1793 marked the culmination of the Radical Enlightenment tendency. French revolutionary republicanism at its peak expressly sought a judicious middle path between the Scylla of direct democracy and Charybdis of pure representative democracy. "We shall not have achieved anything in overthrowing the throne," admonished Barthélémy Albouys (1750–95), an anti-Montagnard deputy for the department of Lot, proudly designating himself a "Jacobin," "if we permit a band of fresh tyrants to usurp the people's authority in the people's name," on the foundation of error. He deemed pure, direct democracy the closest thing to anarchy, but pure representative democracy seemed equally vicious, the nearest thing to despotism being "la pure représentation: évitons ces deux écueils."[13] A middle path was essential, as was a viable balance between center and regions. To achieve this, Condorcet intended to institutionalize local opinion. Primary assemblies in town and country, his commission proposed, should comprise roughly six hundred citizens, each locally resident for at least six months. These primary assemblies would not just organize the electoral process but channel debate and criticism, enabling those that collected sufficient votes to register protests and, when they wished, attempt to change opinion beyond their boundaries, potentially modifying laws. The primary assemblies were therefore empowered to debate the legislature's proceedings and submit petitions, enabling the people to accept, refuse, or initiate legal changes.[14]

Those resisting the looming dictatorship of the Montagnard clique controlling the Paris inner sections fought the battle now under way on a theoretical level by further elaborating the principles of volonté générale and popular sovereignty. Condorcet's and the democratic republicans' general will was emphatically not Rousseau's particularist general will but something universal, unalterable, and designed to safeguard all men's basic rights and freedoms. Admittedly, not all opponents of the Montagne were as explicit about this as Department Du Nord deputy François Poultier Delmotte (1753–1826) or Jean Debry (1760–1844), another staunch adversary of Robespierre both before and after 2 June, who defined volonté générale as participation of all in the *force publique,* understood as a system of rights allowing the majority no right to mistreat, impoverish, or intimidate minorities.[15] Poultier Delmotte wanted it in the Constitution "that the allegedly general will voted by the majority cannot bind the minority when it evidently violates the

Rights of Man. The minority always remains free to remind the majority of their true sovereign—*la raison universelle*—the sovereign that dictated those rights."[16]

Poultier Delmotte, among the Convention's most colorful personalities, once a priest and later a soldier, was too independent-minded to align with any faction. A revolutionary journalist and littérateur who had written one book on Condillac's epistemology and another on the Polish partitions, he saw the history of revolutions as a story of how easily the people are deceived by impostors. Ambitious men directing "the sovereign's will" in ways conducive to their own sway substitute their own private will for that of those they dupe. The majority's will itself can involve unjustly subjecting the weakest to the strongest and hence become a gateway to a new tyranny. Volonté générale untreated, taken in its Rousseauiste sense, facilitates subjection to tyranny and oppression, blighting everyone's rights. "Let us assert, then, that reason is the only veritable sovereign among men; and that to reason alone belongs the right to make laws. Laws not dictated by reason are never obligatory, even when sanctioned by the majority." "Let us begin, then," he urged his colleagues, "by recognizing this great truth: that among men there exists no other legitimate sovereign on earth than *la raison universelle* and that this truth constitutes the most fundamental principle on which we base the majestic edifice of our Constitution."[17] Here was the true language of encyclopedism, Diderot, d'Holbach, Raynal, and Radical Enlightenment.

The constitutional commission agreed at the outset (not all the Convention did) to immerse itself in the best enlightened political theory available internationally, discarding all existing models at every stage. Their broadly agreed principles meant the existing British constitutional model was altogether ruled out beforehand, as were the American federal and state constitutions. Besides failing to declare the well-being of the majority the goal of society, and government, the American constructions all suffered from what Condorcet and his colleagues considered the obvious defects of an excessively strong presidency reminiscent of monarchy, senates not democratically elected, and a largely independent legal authority in the Supreme Court supervising a body of law with British case law (thoroughly scorned by Brissot, Condorcet, Clavière, and most revolutionary commentators) as its foundation. To them, the American Constitution was not based on volonté générale at all but on guaranteeing property, inherited privilege, and informal aristocracy, roughly on the British model.

French constitutional drafts in 1793 mostly rendered both executive and judiciary constitutionally subordinate to a legislature empowered to elect and control the executive's members. What strife-torn France needed, the Convention agreed, was not any foreign model but a means of preventing splits within the legislature producing legislative paralysis. The solution, some deputies believed, lay in investing in the people an overriding power, "une censure sevère," revoking the mandate of representatives who lost their confidence.[18] The commission aimed both to protect individual liberty and direct the improvement and well-being of society.[19] Since Condorcet's, Paine's, and Brissot's democracy pivots on the idea of the volonté générale seeking the well-being of all, the Constitution needed to be both democratic electorally while formally acknowledging society's obligation to counter economic inequality, albeit pursuing this goal by lawful and equitable means, especially progressive taxation and government grants to bodies assisting impoverished invalids, abandoned children, and "every man whose work is insufficient to support his subsistence."[20]

As the commission grappled with their text during late 1792 and early 1793, heaps of theoretical treatises and proposed draft articles, indeed entire suggested draft constitutions, were submitted and circulated among the committee, Convention, and sometimes the eighty-four departments. Most participants in the debate showed considerably more enthusiasm for Rousseau than did Condorcet. But Rousseauist political thought remained deeply problematic from a democratic standpoint, and few insisted on Rousseauism to the point of questioning the representative principle itself. Among those who did was Charles Lambert, representing Côte d'Or. "Rousseau who will always be, in legislation as in politics, our polar star," he declared on 10 June 1793, shortly after Robespierre's coup had brought the Montagne to power, during the debate's last stage, proved a "véritable démocratie" must reject "representative government."[21] Whenever the people's representatives "betray its confidence, when the people feel mistaken in their choice, or those chosen are corrupted, whenever the national representation endangers instead of safeguards, the people must save the public interest themselves with no other recourse than their own energy." France's difficulties could be solved by an explicit, readily mobilized "révocabilité des représentants du peuple soit individuellement soit collectivement." Not only must the people be empowered to direct and, when desired, cashier its representative body, replacing it at any time, it must "sit in judgment on every representative suspected of having prevaricated in his functions." Rousseauism of this kind meant sanctioning lesser insurrections besides the great "insurrections générales," such as 14 July 1789 or 10 August 1792. If all Convention members acknowledged the legitimacy of *insurrection générale* against oppression, the legitimacy of lesser insurrections remained questionable. It was precisely to avoid the perils of *insurrections partielles*, argued Robespierristes, that revocability of representatives wherever any suspicion arises is indispensable.[22]

Besides Rousseau, other sources of inspiration offered pathways to counter the radical republicanism of Condorcet, Brissot, and the democratic leadership. One recommendation, inspired by the seventeenth-century English republican James Harrington (1611–77), who advocated an elitest gentry republicanism, now brushed up and given a democratic gloss, was that of James Rutledge (1743–94), whose journal *Le Creuset* during 1791 had praised Robespierre while pouring vituperation on Bailly, aristocracy, and the Club Monarchique. This grandson of an Irish Jacobite and son of a Dunkirk banker had originally idolized the Cordeliers, dubbing it the *sentinelle* of the Revolution,[23] but in November 1791, his circle had provoked a furor over a projected public territorial bank, attacking Brissot and Pétion so vehemently that he and around twenty supporters were ejected. (These included Chaumette who, however, later withdrew from the splinter group, complaining of its proneness to intrigue.) Rutledge's political philosophy included a feature strongly appealing to some "true Jacobins." Following Harrington, Rutledge advocated using lots to choose both legislative representatives and the electors who would appoint them and the magistrates. Their method would circumvent Condorcet's and Brissot's doctrine that the people's representatives should be men of superior merit and education, rendering them representative in the sense of being selected from, and like, ordinary people—a crucial distinction. Harrington's republicanism modified could be used to ensure the primacy of the ordinary, removing the emphasis on merit, knowledge, and experience.

A notable foreign commentary was presented on 29 April 1793 by Brissot's friend David Williams, the British Unitarian who came to Paris after being chosen as an honorary French citizen in September 1792, hoping to assist the Comité de Constitution. He judged the doctrine of volonté générale as truly philosophique but only when applied with unremitting precision.[24] Among other things, this should include the right of women to vote and be active citizens, to have equal access to education, and constitute half the members of juries dealing with cases involving both sexes. It was strange, he remarked, that in Britain the concept of equality was generally rejected, while in France it possessed great weight but was so inconsistently applied. A Declaration of Rights, like that proposed, couched in the new language of republicanism would hardly be of much use among a population unused to hearing such language, he stressed, without a prior campaign of public education to render its ideas more familiar. Rousseau's brilliant imagination had induced the French to waste much time and effort on illusory notions of volonté générale, providing too few bonds and platforms for debate at intermediate levels.

Even if the people had the leisure and opportunity to make political judgments, they would still be too swayed by local and individual interests to reason adequately in relation to the whole. There was an absolute need for more layers and balance. "The works of Helvétius and the *Système de la nature* [d'Holbach] and the *Systeme social* [d'Holbach]," Williams (like Condorcet's and Brissot's circle generally) had no doubt, were "much more correct and masterly" than Rousseau's. Had the "authors of these writings applied themselves to draw up a political constitution, they would have greatly abridged the work of our contemporaries." But while endorsing the radical agenda partly, Williams simultaneously obscured matters in a way that sharply diminished his relevance. Unlike Condorcet and Gensonné, he did not consider "reason" the exclusive criterion for judging constitutions and deplored how little attention was being accorded to the past, seeing in particular a need to accommodate Anglo-Saxon notions of representation. The Convention should supplement its abstract ideas by studying Tacitus, Julius Caesar, Selden, Spelman, "the Saxon chronicle," Hotman's Franco-Gallia, and the Anglo-Saxon laws edited by David Wilkins.[25]

For Condorcet, Diderot, and d'Holbach, the central problem of politics was how to prevent the majority from being preyed upon by governments captured by vested interests. This remained the chief problem of politics throughout the Revolution. But in the context of early 1793, this preoccupation assumed a new form: how to prevent popular sovereignty and the doctrine of equality from becoming instruments of intimidation used to mobilize popular anger and prejudice behind dictatorship and tyranny.[26] Paris was besieged by flatterers, false "friends," and self-proclaimed *protecteurs* who enveloped themselves in the sovereignty of the nation while plunging the country into catastrophic political crisis, lamented Jean-Pierre Picqué (1750–1839), a deputy for the Hautes-Pyrénées, among the many expecting the Constitution to become the means to save France. Consider, urged Picqué, how easily errors are made in so complex an undertaking as forging a constitution. Only recently had Montesquieu's writings afforded some grasp of the moral and social factors governing the rise and decadence of states. How many Englishmen predicted "the rebels" who founded the United States and their new federal constitution would fail?[27] Had not Mably misconstrued the politics of Sweden where government in recent years had gone from bad to worse? An independent, thoughtful observer who never spoke in the Convention, Picqué abhorred the Montagne. Ordinary people would eventually learn to spot the insidious "sophisms of the intriguers," the "apostles of anarchy" now blighting all virtue and promoting vice. He was greatly encouraged by the Marseille popular rising against the Montagne in late May. Perhaps the "crazed demagogues" herding the public with paid hands, thugs, and dupes could be stopped after all.[28] The answer to populist demagoguery and the "seducers" is to educate the people and advance the power of reason sufficiently to enable everyone to use philosophique arguments to defeat popular prejudices.[29]

Among the Convention minority attracted to the view that the sole legitimate kind of government is *gouvernement populaire* was François de Montgilbert (1747–ca. 1814), author of an unusually detailed set of Montagnard recommendations. The philosophes, in his opinion, exhibited excessive intellect, sophistication, and vanity. "Les philosophes ont trop d'esprit." Their writings show that "while it is easy to discuss government," one only gets to the heart of the matter through considering nature and the people's solid common sense, the simplicity dictated by "nature." The Convention should not "gather from [the philosophes'] works a few sparse notions, brilliant conjectures and comparisons to adorn our discourse." Virtue, not talent or intellect, is the decisive quality in a democratic assembly's deputies. A genuine republican constitution must forge one morality, pure and enlightened, rendering men happy by uniting them closely through the bonds of equality and fraternity. The best insights on government were indeed those of Rousseau, though he was not infallible, warned Montgilbert, just the best guide.[30] He proposed a national legislature of five hundred deputies not checked by other arms of government, or regional or primary assemblies, but tightly subordinate to an abstract and uniform sovereignty designated "the people." Leaders specially entrusted with the people's confidence, should, with the people, carefully scrutinize the operations of government.[31]

Robespierristes aimed to maximize the people's notional authority over their representatives, and this cornerstone of populist authoritarianism, in turn, relied on the idea that volonté générale cannot be represented, so that the legislature's deputies must be rigidly mandated and readily recalled. For this reason, Rousseau's thought was fundamental to the structure of Montagnard Jacobinism in a way that it never was for democratic republicanism. The challenge facing Condorcet was how to temper representation with direct democracy without surrendering to Montagnard rhetoric and dictatorship, or to Rousseau. Condorcet's principle that the "law must conform to the actual will of the majority" meant that both mandating and revoking representatives needed to be complex electoral procedures carefully supervised.[32] Accordingly, from September 1792 until June 1793, as long as the Left republicans shaped the Revolution's course, one heard more criticism than praise of "the immortal Jean-Jacques," repudiation not just of his claim that republics were for small, not large, nations, and views on censorship and religion, but equally of his ideas on representation and revocability. His detractors, and indeed some enthusiastic Rousseauists too, like Fauchet and Billaud-Varenne in his *Élements du républicanisme*, also rejected Rousseau's emphatic insistence on natural man as an essentially solitary being freest when outside society.[33]

Considering the difficulties, Condorcet's constitutional committee worked rapidly and efficiently. By early February 1793, the fruit of their endeavors was ready for presentation to the Convention. The draft submitted was signed by all nine members of the commission except Danton (who refused) and read over two sessions (15 and 16 February). Condorcet, speaking in the Comité de Constitution's name, opened the proceedings on 15 February. Marat's *L'Ami du peuple* that same day taunted Pétion for not having been seen for two weeks and Vergniaud, Guadet, Brissot, Gensonné, Barbaroux, and Salles for being little noticed either. "Where are they, then, these leaders of the infamous band of enemies of the people and supporters of royalisme? They lurked in obscure taverns," he suggested, "conspiring against the patrie with emissaries of generals, corrupt ministers, declared foes of liberty and secret agents of hostile powers."[34] "The friend of the multitude is not always the friend of the people," replied Brissot, in the *Chronique du mois*, and those like Marat and Robespierre, "stealing the name of the people," were overawing the multitude to control society. If, formerly, popular superstition venerated kings, today it venerates certain individuals "who direct the opinion of the multitude." "The *philosophes* are not any

less hated by these new tyrants than by the old ones, because they unmask them with the same courage as before. Nor is the multitude any
less the foe of the *philosophes* today than they were before."[35]

If the multitude, seduced by the court, denounced the philosophes
before 1789, today, invested with the sovereignty that really belongs to
all the people, the "multitude denounces the people's true friends in the
people's name." Until the multitude "s'éclaire" (becomes enlightened)
or else this intrigue was defeated, the minority would tyrannize over
the majority. The situation was dire because the *dénonciateurs* and the
people's flatterers were deliberately exploiting their poverty and inciting them against the rich, labeling the latter "aristocrates" and foes of
the people. But the rich were at fault too, because they wanted the sea
to become calm after a vast tempest without the necessary conditions
being in place. The Republic could be rescued only by citizens willing
to locate sovereignty "in the entire people" and "ascertain means to curb
the influence of the rich."[36]

Condorcet began with a general statement that democracy and a just
society stem from the principles of equality and submission of the individual will to la volonté générale, and that Enlightenment alone had
brought the people to correct ideas about society, liberty, and government.[37] He rejected federalism outright, specifying what he believed
were its deficiencies in the United States. He proposed a powerful
single-chamber legislature balanced by public criticism and suggestions, expressed via vigorous primary assemblies in an orderly fashion
through formal procedures of censure, approval, and petition.[38] To
scrutinize and adjudicate the legislature's conduct, and channel opinion
from the primary assemblies, there was also to be a constitutional court,
a *conseil d'agents nationaux*.[39] After Condorcet's exposition of general
principles, the newly revised Declaration of the Rights of Man in thirty-
five articles was read out by Armand Gensonné (1758–93), a famously
upright deputy from Bordeaux and the second-most active of the commission after Condorcet. It was a fuller version of the 1789 Declaration,
many of the 1789 articles being retained with the wording only slightly
altered. The additional articles were mainly intended to reinforce individual and collective liberty and build on the principle of equality.

The new Declaration significantly widened the framework provided
by its predecessor. The 1789 Declaration does not expressly stipulate
press and theater freedom, nor fully guarantee liberty of religious practice and belief. By contrast, the new Declaration's Article IV reads:
"Every man is free to manifest his thought and his opinions," Article V

that "liberty of the press and all other means of publishing one's ideas may not be interrupted, suspended or limited," and Article VI that "every citizen is free in the exercise of his cult." Article VIII declares not only are men equal before the law, but that the law must protect all, discipline society's members, and respect their economic freedom equally. Article XVII incorporates Beccaria's principle that the penal code must be both "proportionate" to the crimes it punishes "and useful to society." Unlike any article in the 1789 version, Article XXVII explicitly affirms that sovereignty resides in the whole people with each citizen possessing an equal right to participate in its exercise.[40]

Where the new French Declaration diverged most markedly perhaps from 1789, and also from the United States Constitution, was in stressing and expanding the right to "sûreté" (security). The 1789 Declaration merely cites "security" with liberty, property, and the right to resist oppression among the Rights of Man. The Condorcet draft explains "security" in Article X as the protection society affords every citizen in conserving his person, goods, and rights, and a minimum level of subsistence. Financial assistance to the needy, stipulated Article XXIV, is therefore "a sacred debt of society; it is for the law to determine its extent and application." Otherwise, everyone is free to trade, labor, or hire out his labor, as he wishes, state Articles XIX and XX, except that no one can sell themselves—one's person is not an alienable property.

Agreement about the new broader Rights of Man was swiftly attained in late April 1793, "happily suggesting a rapprochement between men of sharply differing opinions," commented the *Journal de Perlet*. The consensus reached offered a "happy augury for the Constitution to follow that all Frenchmen await with such impatience."[41] The revised Declaration, though not faultless, reportedly manifested greater coherence and more "véritable philosophie" than the 1789 text. The subsequently amended Montagnard version of June 1793 altered some phrases and contained a few additional elements. In particular, it included a reference to being proclaimed "in the presence of the Supreme Being," an interpolation over which Montagnards and Brissotins had clashed in April and was now added at Robespierre's insistence, against the wishes of his intellectually more radical opponents.[42] But twenty-three of the thirty-five articles remained essentially unchanged, as did Condorcet's characteristic balancing of individual liberty and social harmony based on progressive taxation and compulsory elementary education.[43]

Gensonné then declaimed the actual articles of the draft constitution.[44] With its elaborate provisions at local, departmental, and national level for reporting, criticizing, and censuring the legislature and council of ministers, its assuring the right to protest and petition, and commitment to progressive taxation, the text embodied the democratic Revolution's quintessence. All men older than twenty-one residing in France uninterruptedly for a year beforehand, unless medically certified as mad or stripped of citizen's rights as a punishment (like some refractory clergy), received the vote. All male citizens older than twenty-five became eligible for office. Primary assemblies, the cornerstone, were to consist of more than 450 and no more than 900 local adult male residents for more than a year and have elected standing committees to supervise.[45] Several draft articles provided checks clearly designed to discourage vote-rigging, intimidation, and vote-buying. A vital component of Condorcet's direct democracy (afterward deleted by the Montagne from the new Constitution's final version approved in June), was the choosing of the national executive council—seven ministers and a secretary comprising the government's executive arm—not by the legislature but by the people directly through the primary assemblies.[46] The seven ministers were designated for war, foreign affairs, naval affairs, treasury, agriculture, trade and manufactures, and most remarkably, *secours publics* (public assistance), including public works, organizations, and the arts.

To equalize their status and deter an aspiring "Cromwell," this executive would be chaired in turn by each minister, changing every fifteen days. No minister, in or out of office, could be criminally prosecuted for conduct in office, other than by the legislature, a key safeguard, though censure could be initiated by primary assemblies. Condorcet's constitution also afforded a mechanism whereby the volonté générale could rebuke or censure the legislature—a bench of public reviewers charged with safeguarding liberty by scrutinizing the assembly's proceedings and convening the primary assemblies where appropriate.[47] Condorcet's draft, protested Marat, assigned no role to the (vetted and sifted) sociétés populaires, confining the electoral process and all right to petition and protest to communities. How can "virtue" and "the people" impose their will unerringly, eliminating dissent with the clubs emasculated?[48]

"All those whose vanity, ambition and avidity require disorder," predicted Condorcet in his preliminary discourse, "all those amounting to nothing without faction and trouble, would unite to block the Constitution." He was swiftly proved correct. The Convention had the text printed and distributed in multiple copies to all deputies, six copies each, with the eighty-four departments receiving sufficient copies for distribution through their councils to all the municipalities, sociétés populaires, and districts of France.[49] The Montagne's reaction in both Assembly and the Jacobins was vituperative. Rejected out of hand by Marat, *L'Ami du peuple* scorned the commission's work as unworthy of discussion, an "essai monstrueux" composed by "a criminal faction," confused, ungrounded, and redolent of the "crass ignorance of a patrician."[50] Robespierre and Danton refused to endorse it. Robespierre, for his part, summoned "the people" (that is, Commune and sections) to ensure the legislature remained under their tight control, "to put their *mandataires* [representatives] in a position where they could not possibly damage liberty."[51] In an article published in February 1793, Condorcet charged Robespierre with deliberately blocking the Constitution and sowing dissension in the country, championing the "popular cause" out of self-interest, and manipulating the people using the pretext of high food prices to impose the will of a few major cities on the rest of France.[52] Robespierre and his followers too claimed to be democrats. But their "democracy" was not the combination of direct and indirect democracy involving regular consultation with primary assemblies, petitions, and referenda most deputies envisaged and some militant Montagnards ardently desired. Robespierre preferred a view of volonté générale anchored in Rousseau that envisaged the will of the people as indivisible and collective, a unitary abstract with an unchallengeable executive (in effect, Robespierre and his aides). For purposes of swaying popular opinion, he combined this with what Condorcet called the "absurde doctrine" that every popular gathering is invested with a share of sovereignty.[53]

Representatives at every level of deliberation, from city sections and local primary assemblies to the Convention, according to Robespierre and Saint-Just, needed to be rigorously subordinated to "the people" conceived as a unitary bloc, able to revoke measures and recall representatives whenever these betrayed "the people's confidence." Robespierre's methods in the Paris sections—rigorous vetting and scrutiny of candidate lists beforehand, vote-rigging, stifling dissent, and unquestioned direction from above—revealed clearly enough what democracy meant to him. The people would follow willingly, experience in the Paris sections suggested, where vigorously dragooned and with everything justified in their name. His was a theoretical construct backed by a highly efficient organization. To Condorcet, Brissot, and their allies, it seemed that Robespierre opposed France's democratic Constitution of February 1793 because it would promote genuine democracy and social welfare, guided by true talent, and win popular esteem, blocking the way to "charlatanisme, intrigue," and "l'hypcrisie politique."[54]

Explaining why he rejected Condorcet's constitution as a basis for further discussion in the Convention on 24 April, Saint-Just dismissed it as too "intellectual."[55] The notoriously ignorant Couthon invoked its "immenses défauts." For an entire month, the most vocal *anti-constitutionnaires*—Couthon, Tallien, Fabre, Thuriot, and Chabot—"like pygmies around Hercules," as the *Patriote français* put it, heaped "vague and immaterial criticism" on Condorcet's constitution as "un project aristocratique et liberticide."[56] Even Barère thought the virulence with which Robespierre's followers denounced the Condorcet constitution rather shameful. Aside from Saint-Just, who assumed greater prominence at this point, the *anti-constitutionnaires* produced few real arguments and refused to discuss the draft point by point. Their style was to arouse public hostility through scornful, harsh denunciation. Those backing the Montagne, observed the *Patriote français*, do not read and were little given to logic, but responded to condemnation and calumny. Many were persuaded that Condorcet *was* an "aristocrate, contre-révolutionnaire."[57] Among grounds used to discredit Condorcet's work was a relatively minor discrepancy between what was read out in the Assembly and subsequently printed, additional matter regarding procedures prior to the legislature's voting, swiftly deleted by majority vote. Should interrogating the printer prove the Comité de Constitution deliberately smuggled it in, interjected the younger Jullien, the commission should be declared to have betrayed the Convention's confidence.[58]

Despite three weeks of uninterrupted debate from mid-April to early May, the deadlock proved irresolvable while the tension remained acute. When Marat remarked the "braves sans-culottes" were insufficiently educated to suspect the dark, perfidious intrigues pervading the Comité de Constitution's endeavors, he was interrupted by the radical Breton jurist Jean-Denis Lanjuinais (1753–1827), famed for his acerbic interventions: "Marat's objections are assuredly the finest eulogy the Constitution could receive." "Censure him [Lanjuinais]! Send him to the Abbaye!" yelled the Montagne. On 16 February, a Convention majority accepted Montagnard demands for delay during April and May, to enable the entire Convention to participate in the constitutional debate and permit dozens of alternative drafts and projects various deputies had proposed to be printed at public expense, circulated, and discussed.[59] "It is from the Montagne that the Constitution will emerge," held Marat, "and despite this puerile, perfidious essay [of Condorcet] the expectation of the people will not be disappointed."[60]

This wider debate opened with Robespierre, Marat, and Saint-Just repudiating the Brissotin draft constitution altogether. Presenting his own proposed alternative on 24 April, Saint-Just dismissed Condorcet's work as "weak," self-contradictory, and insufficiently democratic, creating a legislature that was no true *représentation générale* but *fédérative* and an executive that was *réprésentatif* but should not be.[61] Condorcet's constitution resembled Athens during the sad last days of her independence, "voting without democracy and decreeing the loss of its liberty." Particularly reprehensible, held Saint-Just, was the Constitution's avoidance of Rousseau and its defining the "general will" from an intellectual standpoint rather than as a doctrine that was essentially "popular."[62] "Liberty is not found in books." Liberty does not lie in intellectual categories but in the heart—it impels the spirit. Direct election by the people rendered Condorcet's proposed ministers "representatives" of the sovereign in flagrant disregard of Rousseau and would place every means of "corruption" in the ministry's hands.[63] The Convention must follow Rousseau who "wrote with his heart" and not "from philosophy," never suspecting that in "establishing the volonté générale for the principle of the laws, it could, as in Condorcet's constitution, become a principle antagonistic to itself."

According to Saint-Just, more coherence and centralization was required with the primary assemblies being largely eliminated. Volonté générale was a collective will, one and undivided, not requiring elaborate electoral and consultative processes. Nothing less than defining volonté générale as the people's spontaneous, active will was acceptable.[64] While he too advocated universal male suffrage and equal eligibility for office, rather than a large national assembly annually reelected, he recommended a smaller body of 340 members (roughly five per department) more readily brought to converge.[65] To ensure the candidate rota was truly "populaire," Saint-Just recommended a single-stage, undivided national election by the whole electorate, every citizen in the country, he suggested, voting for a single candidate. All the votes cast in France would then be counted, those registering the most votes being elected. But this was technically not feasible at the time. Saint-Just's scheme was certainly much simpler but not practicable.[66]

In the Rousseauiste ideal of a unitary populace, Robespierre and Saint-Just found a higher authority not subject to questioning in the Assembly or to active criticism from below. Such an abstract would turn the legislature into what it shortly was to become—a passive mouth-piece of "the will of the nation."[67] Instead of directly elected by the electorate, ministers should be chosen by Assembly committees, hence, by the dominant faction's leaders. Invoking "the people" as an abstract to erase the people's rights and subvert democracy was thus implicit in Saint-Just's and Robespierre's stated doctrines from the outset. Indispensable to Robespierre and Saint-Just was the distinction between the indivisible "absolute rights of the people" and exercise of such rights through an electoral procedure based on primary assemblies.[68] If all deputies acknowledged the people as the only legitimate sovereign, behind this phrase loomed vastly different conceptions, as was emphasized by Albouys in his *Principes constitutionelles présentées à la Convention nationale* of early May. "Oh sacred name of the people! To what point have I not seen you profaned and degraded!" The people is the source of all legitimacy; and yet those invoking "the people" most loudly, even maintaining they are "the people," are the "men of 2 and 3 September, that is, a horde of brigands," including truly abominable types, capable of monstrous ferocity. The first three articles of the new constitution, advised Albouys, should read: "(1) the people is the sole legitimate sovereign; (2) the people is the universality of its citizens; (3) every other association, or gathering, arrogating to itself the title of 'people' is guilty of usurping that sovereignty."[69]

Concentrating on what was practicable, Condorcet had left aside his own preference for advancing women's rights. But besides his circle and David Williams, there remained also other outstanding partisans of women's rights in the Assembly, including Gilbert Romme and Pierre Guyomar (1757–1826). Guyomar was a deputy for Côtes-du-Nord who, during the spring of 1793, figured among Condorcet's staunchest defenders against Robespierrisme. A thoroughgoing democrat, egalitarian, and one of the substantial phalanx of advanced French political thinkers embracing republicanism before 1789, Guyomar on 29 April reminded the Convention that he had published two political tracts in 1779 entitled *Citoyen de l'univers* and *l'Antinoble*. Braving the ridicule heaped on him then, he had persisted in expounding his republican views all those years without believing the democratic republic for which he yearned could ever become reality. Rooted prejudice and custom would doubtless move the Convention to refuse equal rights to women; yet, like Condorcet, Romme, and Williams, Guyomar vowed to fight "this prejudice" as wholly contrary to the *cosmopolitanisme*, equality, and liberty he and they professed. Is the alleged difference between the sexes better grounded than claiming the color of the blacks validates slavery? If the difference between black and white fails to justify exclusion from sovereignty, so does that between the sexes. La philosophie had made all males one grand family and sought to unite blacks and whites. Reunion of diversely colored males of the species in the same primary assemblies will prove for all time the imbecility and depravity of men, and the stunning triumph of the philosophes over prejudice. "Republicans! Let us free women from a slavery that flays humanity just as we are breaking the chains that hold down our neighbors." In Condorcet's plan, Guyomar, like other sincere democrats, esteemed especially the centrality of the primary assemblies.[70]

A distinct Montagnard disadvantage was that relatively few of their deputies, apart from Robespierre himself, Saint-Just, Barère, and Billaud-Varenne, were intellectually equipped to debate complex constitutional issues. Even after April, most interventions still supported the Brissotins. On a purely theoretical level, Robespierre's and Saint-Just's ideology, though representative of a distinct variant within revolutionary republican theory, remained that of a tiny unrepresentative minority. With its uncompromising insistence on Rousseau, their approach was not just directly contrary to the Revolution's core values but opposed to all the major currents of democratic ideology in the Convention, not just Brissotin ideas but also those of the Dantonistes, independent republicans like Poultier Delmotte and antiauthoritarian street populists like Roux, Fournier, and Varlet. Nevertheless, Robespierre could expect the approval of the many deputies disliking the radical democratic tendency, the support of all the populists wanting consensus without dissent, of Jacobin priests disliking Condorcet's militant secularism and everyone wary of broad consultation and direct democracy.

Robespierre and Saint-Just were also assured of the support of all disliking the democrats' emphasis on philosophy. Among the relatively few Montagnard submissions were *Quelques idées préliminaires soumises à l'examen de ses collègues* by Jean-Pierre Audouin (1760–1840), deputy from Seine-et-Oise and editor of the *Journal universel*. Typically, his contribution was far less radical than Condorcet's, scarcely attempting to link democracy with universal rights and maximize "freedom" in Condorcet's democratic sense. With aristocracy on the march and "despotisme" (the European monarchs) battering on the Republic's doors, France required a constitution "vraiment républicaine," urged Audouin, but by this, it turned out, he meant "vraiment populaire," that is, with the people exercising direct sovereignty over the legislature through the executive.[71]

Condorcet's approach alienated all foes of radical ideas, just as Rousseauism attracted them. Seconding Mably's warning against the dangers of excessive, direct democracy, and employing his expertise in ancient history, the educationalist Antoine-Hubert Wandelaincourt (1731–1819), for example, constitutional bishop and a deputy of the Haute-Marne, published an interesting set of *Observations sur le plan de Constitution* in May 1793. The people of ancient Athens, he warned, "obeyed all the caprice and passions of the intriguers who knew the art of gaining their confidence." But when it came to choosing, Wandelaincourt was less concerned to block the intriguers than ensure the emerging constitution accorded with divine intentions. He agreed with Rousseau that "every legislator should by means of the laws summon the citizen to virtue." For Wandelaincourt, like Fauchet, Rousseau's thought connected the new revolutionary creed with religion. Every society, Rousseau's *Social Contract* proved, deems it necessary for public tranquillity that the divine will lend the sovereign authority a sacred and inviolable character. The *philosophes modernes* excluded religion and religious authority from the Republic's political life. In his eyes, that made them worse than the Montagne. He dismissed them as *philosophes d'un jour*, ignorant of politics' true principles. What could be more absurd than a philosophisme claiming the people make foolish choices through ignorance and fanaticism, that religious prejudice governs the world, and then refusing to incorporate religion into the Constitution! Only a Constitution proclaiming religion can defeat superstition by eliminating intolerance, "monarchical morality," and unconcern for men's worldly condition. Without religion, "our Constitution" will be "as feeble as mud."[72]

The new committee appointed in April to redo Condorcet's work was a mixed Commission of Six, not elected but co-opted by the Convention's newly established Comité de Salut Public. Its members were Mercier, Valazé, Barère, Lanjuinais, Romme, and the staunch republican Jean Debry. Four were Brissotins with Barère again the lone supporter of Robespierre, though the sixth member, Romme, high-minded mathematician, partisan of women's rights, and admirer of Condorcet though he was, also dissented from the rest of the committee.[73] Robespierristes had no more footing in the new committee than in Condorcet's. Debry, another advocate of the right to petition and need to balance direct and representative democracy, presented his own draft constitution on 26 April.[74] From mid-April to the end of May, three days per week were allocated for debating the articles and rival formulations. On 29 April, Lanjuinais presented an interim report on behalf of the Comité de Six. History proved that in all known societies, tyrannical aristocracies of one kind or another had constructed edifices of oppression. Every past legislator had been complicit in slavery in one form or another. Shameful caste distinctions degraded the entire East. The English excluded everyone who was not a substantial property-owner and taxpayer from the political process. The United States proclaimed liberty, yet, there, too, equality and political rights remained highly defective. The status of citizen attaches to the person not the property. Servants should receive political rights precisely as Condorcet argued. Condorcet's direct election of the executive's ministers via the primary assemblies should be retained.[75]

Most proposals submitted to the Convention in April and May 1793 emanated from the "Girondin" side and frequently reflected this bloc's anger against what Alain Bohan (1750–1814), a deputy for Finisterre and judge by profession whose *Observations sur la Constitution du peuple français* appeared shortly after Robespierre's coup of 2 June 1793, called the "anarchistes," the "false friends of the people who ceaselessly mislead, agitate and drive the people to its perdition."[76] Bohan shared one preoccupation with Robespierre and Saint-Just, though, from which nearly all other participants were free—a militant if simplistic notion of "natural right." "Natural right" chiefly impressed ardent deists venerating Rousseau like Bohan, Robespierre, and Saint-Just. To some philosophes and legislators, it was madness to believe in God's existence or that divine Providence governs the universe, and that we have an immortal soul. But unless one truly believes these things, insisted Bohan, natural right, and hence, natural law, has no sanction, no authority: it amounts to nothing since, according to them, there exists no "législateur suprême qui commande à tous les hommes, à tous les peuples." For the monist philosophes, "the state of nature is no longer that primitive society, established by God himself, where all men are subject to a common law demonstrating their rights and duties always to be in perfect union." Bohan considered God, immortality of the soul, and natural law the indispensable triad for differentiating between vice and virtue, and justice and injustice. Only under "the Supreme Being's auspices," legislators must assure their co-citizens, "can we proclaim men's rights and ground our Constitution."[77]

The text of Marc-François Bonguyod (1751–1805), a deputy for the Jura, entitled *Réflexions sur l'organisation des assemblées primaires*, passionately anti-Robespierriste, focused on cleansing the electoral process at the local level and eradicating the vote-rigging and prior exclusion of candidates in which the Paris section bosses specialized.[78] Among the bitterest adversaries of Robespierre (and Pache) in the Convention was Jean-François Baraillon (1743–1816), a physician from the department of Creuse who submitted a full-length draft constitution in sixty-four articles. Like other drafts, his demanded France's fundamental laws must be republican, based on equality of rights and eligibility, and "purement démocratique." Persuaded that democracy was also the path to "perpetual peace," he wanted the Constitution to make a strong stand against militarism and expansionism, urging inclusion of clauses stipulating that the Republic would never invade or annex the territory of others. His article fifty read: "the Republic will have no diplomacy except to sign treaties of peace, alliance or commerce, the basis of which will be 'la plus exacte reciprocité.'"[79] So vital was universal education, the Constitution itself should lay down that there must be public schools providing education to all free of charge in every rural locality and city section. The entire body of scientific and scholarly expertise should be sponsored, regulated, and supported by the public and the legislature. Baraillon's article forty-two read: "all the men famous for their knowledge and their talents will be reunited in one society which, under the name of Société encyclopédique de France, will strive to advance the sciences, fine arts, and work ceaselessly to expand the mass of human knowledge and perfect it." As for public celebrations, he suggested, these should celebrate only peacemaking and the triumph of justice, liberty, and *saine raison* elsewhere in the world.

A key figure in the April debates who, after the Terror, was destined to play a leading role in reviving the Revolution's core values, and discredit Montagnard ideology, was Pierre-Claude-François Daunou (1761–1840), from Boulogne, a former philosophy professor and constitutional priest strongly committed to public education and advancing the sciences. Daunou, observed Lanjuinais, was among the ablest participants in the constitutional debate. He agreed with Condorcet that among the more comprehensive rights secured by the new Declaration of Rights should be the right to petition and to hold meetings peaceably. Like Condorcet, Lanjuinais, and Brissot, Daunou sought a carefully calculated balance between representative and direct democracy, and judicious balance also between guaranteeing property rights and countering wealth inequality.[80] Like Brissot and Condorcet, Daunou aspired effectively to remedy the "enorme et monstrueuse" disproportion of fortunes in France by dividing large holdings, expanding the number of property owners, and ensuring low incomes suffice at least for subsistence.[81]

A central Montagnard aspiration never achieved was to tie the sansculottes solidly to their faction. Chabot's *Projet d'acte constitutive*, for example, prioritized food price subsidies and the idea that the bread price and other basic foodstuffs—the sole goods of necessity for everyone—should be tightly regulated and equal for all. Levies on the rich were needed to ensure food price stability at moderate levels.[82] Ironically (considering what was to come), Chabot also urged abolition of the death penalty as "contrary to the principles of nature and society."[83] If he scorned the intellectualism of the philosophes,[84] still more uncompromisingly "populaire" was the rural *dirigisme* of the priest Jacques-Marie Coupé (1737–1809), representing the department of the Oise. Jacobin curé, fervent egalitarian, and disciple of Mably (even more than Rousseau), Coupé wanted to see the legislature closely bound by the electorate and under vigorous popular surveillance.[85] The best constitution derives from the pure elements of natural principles. Political life should be grounded on the sentiments of the common man and ordinary common sense and nothing else. Ordinary people reject "cet art philosophique de gouverner" of Condorcet and the Brissotins. Officeholders should be *hommes ordinaires*, des sansculottes. The need to prevent the ordinary man from being duped by Condorcet's *charlatanisme académique* was, to him, the first rule of politics. The February draft constitution stemmed from philosophisme and was an outrage, a scandal. Where was the "natural right"? Where the empire of the ordinary? Coupé wanted it inscribed in the Constitution: "the law of equality rejects eminent personalities and wants only ordinary men."[86]

Another Montagnard assault on la philosophie and the *beaux esprits* "duping" ordinary folk was mounted by Didier Thirion (1763–1816), disciple of Marat and rhetoric teacher expert at swaying crowds. Deputies elected to the new legislature should be elected by the people and as close to ordinary people in thinking and attitudes as possible. Every influence alien to the people, foreign or intellectual, should be disowned. The Convention must reject "beaux génies, les illustres orateurs, les talents académiques." He attributed the divisions wrecking the Convention to an election process thus far insufficiently *populaire*. Condorcet's constitution was defective also in according too much electoral influence to primary assemblies and the departments. Aggressively populist, Thirion, like Chabot, Coupé, and Robespierre, was also antifeminist and, at bottom, antidemocrat, exalting only a collectivity defined by virtue capable of overriding all dissent and subsuming all localities in one united entity, legitimized at every turn by the "ordinaire."[87]

"The people is good but its delegates are corruptible," intoned Robespierre in person on 10 May, reiterating that much was wrong, and that it is virtue and popular sovereignty that must be "safeguarded against vice and the despotism of the government." Governmental corruption originates in excessive power over, and excessive independence from, the true sovereign, "the people." Public opinion alone should judge those who govern; it is not for governments to domineer over opinion. Above all, the Constitution must subject officeholders to a real and effective dependence on the sovereign. "The public crimes of magistrates" should be no less rigorously punished than private crimes.[88] He fully shared Rousseau's doubts and reservations about representation. Where for Condorcet republican politics means maximizing "social freedom," a fusing of individual freedom and political freedom fixed by the Constitution, for Robespierre it meant imposing the popular will forcefully on all government, executive, judiciary, legislature, departmental councils, and primary assemblies alike.[89]

Among the more substantial Montagnard contributions was Billaud-Varenne's *Élements du républicanisme*. This text fiercely derides Voltaire's defense of social hierarchy and his claim that artisan and laborer are born to be poor. Why had all the world's peoples prior to 1789 been "martyred" and exploited by the very laws and regimes under which they dwelt? "Everywhere the multitude is sacrificed to a few privileged individuals. Advantages, benefits and comfortable living were reserved for a proud handful. Education, refinement and expertise were the preserve of the rich; ignorance and misery the eternal lot of the majority." Billaud-Varenne's fervent Rousseauism inspired a Manichaean split between true "citizens" infused with social duties, who saw everything in terms of the public interest and investing "their own happiness and glory in securing the happiness of their country" and the depraved selfishness of those refusing to do so. Good men predominate only where popular sovereignty triumphs and virtue is venerated. "Individuals isolated within themselves, working solely for their own interest," seek to break "l'équilibre de l'égalité" and build their own personal well-being by usurping that of others.[90]

Billaud-Varenne's social program diverged from that of Brissot, Condorcet, Daunou, and others seeking to incorporate into the Constitution the state's duty to counteract excessive wealth inequality, and provide subsistence and reasonable bread prices, in ends as well as in method with his preoccupation with price-fixing and imposing forced loans. If his and Montgilbert's insistence on including the "right to subsistence," and considering this the most basic of all rights, was shared by much of the chamber,[91] countering wealth inequality in Billaud-Varenne was infused with a strong preference for rural simplicity and agriculture over commerce and industry. For Billaud-Varenne, Jullien, and Chaumette, unlike Brissot or Daunou, condemning wealth inequality was tied also to a fierce tirade against luxury and "epicureanism" in favor of austerity and lifestyle equality. Both rival blocs identified *le capitaliste* as antisocial, selfish, and damaging, apt to subvert government in his own interest. Billaud-Varenne assailed *capitalistes* as "proud vampires" who exploited those they employed while scandalously pillaging the public purse. But Montagnards like Billaud-Varenne also thought in terms of imposing new egalitarian lifestyle norms through education and public instruction. The duty of the Revolution, in his eyes, was to bring men back to their supposed (by Rousseau) primordial, virtuous essence, to their essential "disposition irrésistible" to cultivate virtue.[92]

Virtue, not philosophisme, held Robespierre, Saint-Just, and Billaud-Varenne, must be society's guide. A true republic based on equality and popular sovereignty stems not from enlightenment but from the struggle between virtue and selfishness. Cato the Censor Billaud-Varenne proclaimed mankind's supreme role model. Appointed to the republic's highest offices, he adhered to a simple lifestyle and manners. What most differentiated "true Jacobin" egalitarian ideology in its most cogent form, as expressed by Billaud-Varenne, from Brissotin philosophique principles was the idea that to create a viable republic, behavior—indeed, human nature itself—must be remade using a combination of coercive measures and rigorous education. To fortify French patriotisme and esprit public, "vast and majestic amphitheatres" should be built so that the people could appear en masse in national celebrations and festivities as a single body, elevating each other with displays of noble zeal for the public cause.[93] Billaud-Varenne, like Rousseau, summoned women to return to the tasks proper to them: cultivating modesty above everything and assisting the return to simplicity, equality, and nature. Segregating the sexes, abjuring alluring fashions and the erotic, eulogizing only tender mothers and loyal wives would reinforce society's march to simplicity.[94]

The French constitutional debate of 1792–93 proved the Revolution in its republican phase was a battleground between two passionately held and implacably opposed ideologies, at bottom so different
and incompatible that no way existed to reconcile them. Exalting the
Rights of Man, ostensibly common to all the Convention theorists of
1793, actually masked a vast cauldron of disagreement. The planned
popular referendum, to ask the people to abjure monarchy "for
ever," should also urge the people, suggested Jean-Baptiste Harmand
(1751–1816), to reject every form of government incompatible with
popular sovereignty. Their *république démocratique* should be exclusively based on the Rights of Man, that is, espousing human rights,
including satisfying men's economic needs, on the ground of reason
alone.[95] Both the Constitution and the Revolution itself were directly
threatened by this deadlock in the Convention and the country. Intense
anger and exasperation accumulated on both sides. The constitutional
quarrel could be resolved only when the deadlock was broken.

Once this happened, with the Montagne's forcible seizure of power
on 2 June 1793, the ensuing changes unsurprisingly proved fairly extensive both rhetorically and in substance, though a recognizable residue
of Condorcet's work still remained. The amended June Constitution
was still recognizably Condorcet's in numerous respects but adjusted
to render it less democratic, less favorable to individual liberty, and
fully equipped to curtail the roles of the electorate, primary assemblies, departmental councils, and legislature.[96] Outlining the principles
by which he had revised the Constitution, on 10 June the chairman
of the new Montagnard committee of five (altogether excluding the
Brissotins)—Hérault de Sechelles, Couthon, and Saint-Just, plus two
little-known figures—Hérault explained that his committee's goal was
to achieve a volonté générale not fragmented, divided, or subject to
dissent. He would have adopted Saint-Just's proposal for a nonstaged,
single, nationwide election of deputies to the legislature had this been
practicable.

Where Condorcet's constitution invokes reason alone, omitting all
mention of any supernatural sanction, the amended Rights of Man affirms these in the "presence of the Supreme Being,"[97] a notable concession to Rousseauist deism and to the Convention's Christian
egalitarians. The primary assemblies would still gather each year to select
the electors for each departmental district to choose the Assembly deputies, judges, and bishops, but they lost most of their powers to debate,
criticize, and petition. Where Condorcet's constitution protected the
people's right to consider, criticize, and amend legislation, Hérault's

revisions restricted the right to debate and criticize the legislature's enactments from below. Public functionaries, explained Hérault, would now be elected indirectly by small bodies of chosen "electeurs" rather than the primary assemblies; everyone knew this was a device more amenable to management from above than Condorcet's open voting in primary assemblies.[98] Where Condorcet's constitution lent a voice to the departmental councils, as well as the primary assemblies, this too was canceled. To weaken the legislature, the new executive council of twenty-four supervising the ministry would now not come under the control of the legislature but be chosen from nominations compiled by the primary assemblies' benches of electors, a mechanism plainly devised, held Brissotin critics, by "brigands" depriving the legislature of direct oversight and power over ministers and their ministries.[99]

Robespierre, Marat, and Saint-Just sought to curtail scope for democratic expression from communities and districts from below while introducing an efficient mechanism for recalling individual deputies through the communes (that Condorcet had blocked) so as to weaken the legislature as well. Saint-Just had all along sought to ensure that when an Assembly member was accused by a commune, he must justify himself or resign, and wherever a deputy lost the confidence of most deputies, he must be tried. Hérault tried to limit the scope for infringing individual rights by the Assembly with his independent national grand jury, or constitutional court, erected to adjudicate possible violations of human rights. But deferring to Robespierre (and Chabot), the Convention removed this safeguard "destined to revenge the oppressed citizen for the vexations and wrongdoing caused either by the legislature or the cabinet of ministers," reducing the grand jury instead into a means of surveillance of the legislature.[100]

Final revisions, following the Montagnard seizure of power on 2 June, were debated between 10 and 24 June when the Constitution was pronounced complete. The Assembly's remaining Left republicans, led by Ducos and Boyer-Fonfrède, fought to render particular articles more democratic while Robespierre and his allies battled to render them less so.[101] Several deputies, most vocally, Ducos, attempted to retrieve Condorcet's provisions for the primary assemblies. The primary assemblies were to meet once a year automatically, on 1 May, to conduct elections. To convene an extraordinary session of a primary assembly, a petition from one fifth of the citizens with a right to vote was proposed; binding decisions would require half plus one of the active citizenry present at the meeting. It was Robespierre in person who scotched this, claiming that Condorcet's principle undermined government, establishing the kind of democracy that overthrows instead of defends the people's rights. On 14 June, he criticized amended Article XII in Hérault's draft, which stipulated (while diluting the equivalent provision in Condorcet's draft) that the primary assemblies could still assemble for extraordinary meetings whenever a majority plus one of their voters composing it so desired. "This article is hardly at all *populaire*," objected Robespierre, but rather an "excès de démocratie." Declared foe of representative democracy, Robespierre turned out to be equally opposed to direct democracy, insistently depleting it in the name of virtue, the people, and Rousseau. If it gave any scope to the primary assemblies, the Constitution would create a wholly undesirable *démocratie pure*.[102]

Besides reducing the influence of primary assemblies and departments over national decision making and powerfully strengthening the executive, another key difference between Condorcet's draft and the amended Constitution adopted in June, was the Montagne's canceling direct suffrage for higher offices in deference to a Montagnard "principle" Hérault could scarcely ignore. While deputies were still to be selected by democratic elections, ministers and executive committees would now be chosen only indirectly, by committees of the deputies.[103] In this debate, Robespierre unreservedly backed the antidemocratic, populist reasoning of Chabot: if the executive council is to be fully subordinate to the people, then it must not be elected by the people. The Convention duly obeyed, voting for the executive not to be selected directly by the electorate but behind closed doors, indirectly, by a restricted committee of Assembly "électeurs."[104]

Hérault appeared before the Convention for the final reading on 24 June. A majority of the Convention had decreed that this was definitely the last reading and that the new Constitution would be presented without delay to the people. A commotion occurred when a deputy named Guyet-Laprade, for Lot-et-Garonne, interjected that unresolved points remained. He was shouted down, several Montagnard voices adding that the protester should be locked up in the Abbaye. At this, a courageous band of protesting Brissotin deputies rose to their feet: "Let's all go, all go to prison, the Convention no longer exists!"

In late June, the new regime presented the Constitution to the people, thereby adopting an elaborate moral fig leaf conferring legality and constitutionality on the coup of 2 June. This, more than anything, impressed the primary assemblies and communes to which the text of the new Constitution was sent. The primary assemblies were asked to endorse the Constitution without comment and without having a chance to digest its contents, and especially without listening to the arguments of Brissotin objectors. It received a broadly positive reception. Many who opposed the coup d'état of 2 June, and arrests of the Brissotin leadership, understandably hesitated to join the armed rebellion against the usurping clique, as they were unwilling to provoke civil war amid the Revolution's life-and-death struggle with Europe's monarchies, and were tempted to assume such a drastic remedy was in any case unnecessary. For here, finally, was the so-greatly-longed-for Constitution, the new democratic machinery and affirmation of basic human rights, surely a sufficient antidote! They were to be bitterly disillusioned.

The Constitution was the new regime's most effective weapon in winning sufficient support and legitimacy to govern. When a delegation from the société populaire of Soissons arrived on 25 June to endorse the 2 June coup, they applauded the "courage that you have shown in removing from the Constitution's bosom those perfidious representatives of the people who by their clamour retarded your work." Soissons wished to be a model of republican solidarity and "virtue fighting for liberty," dissenting from the departmental administration of Aisne (supporting the Brissotin rebellion sanctioned by the Aisne deputies, Condorcet and Debry). Soissons, the delegation assured the Assembly, would oppose everyone attempting to march on Paris to reverse the coup, their town viewing with contempt the "liberticide writings of the Condorcets, Jean Debry, etc."[105]

Yet, despite all this, the revised 1793 Constitution remained a remarkable achievement. Article 124 declared that the new Declaration of the Rights of Man, with its ringing first article proclaiming "the goal of society the common happiness" together with the entire text of the Constitution, should be inscribed on special tablets to be displayed in the Convention hall and in public places. Condorcet's constitution, even though somewhat disfigured, nonetheless recognizably survived in a document of surpassing importance in world history, even though the text so long contested and finally adopted on 24 June was only legally in force for three months before being suspended indefinitely on 10 October 1793. It remained the first modern democratic constitution and the first constitution ever, as Condorcet had stressed, not imposed by an aristocracy on the basis of the myth of an existing particular constitution, like the Bill of Rights and English Constitution of 1689. It was the first ever constitution established by "reason" in the name of the people as a whole.[106] Under its Article IV, "every man born and domiciled in

France" older than twenty-one and every foreigner older than twenty-one living and working in France for more than a year, or married to a Frenchwoman or who has adopted a French child or supports any elderly person, was admitted to the full rights of citizenship.[107]

It was also the first (male) democratic Constitution in world history without any hint of theocratic power. Population, each individual treated as equal in his interests, was the exclusive basis of representation in the national legislature, each deputy notionally representing forty thousand people. Article IX of the new Declaration of Rights, "that the law should protect public and individual liberty from oppression by those who govern" was itself a massive advance in the development of mankind. Large quantities of printed copies, it was agreed, following the final reading, should be dispatched to all towns and judicial bodies in France with ten copies for each deputy in preparation for the referendum.[108] Outside the Convention a ceremonial cannon was fired as a signal to begin the general rejoicing: the Constitution was finished at last. Through July and August 1793, celebration of the finalization of the world's first democratic constitution filled all France with new hope. When the votes cast in the referendum were counted, 1,714,266 voters were found to have endorsed the Constitution with only around 12,000 against.[109]

As for the Constitution's chief author, Condorcet, he had to go straight into hiding. Denounced in the Convention on 8 July 1793 by Chabot, speaking for the Comité de Sûreté Générale, he was charged with penning a clandestinely published tract, *Aux citoyens français sur la nouvelle constitution*, published in late June. It criticized the newly approved Constitution, terming it "undemocratic" and, a feature that particularly outraged Chabot, apt to produce "a new tyrant in place of the king." Condorcet was accused also of persisting in circulating copies of his February draft constitution, claiming it was better than that approved by the Convention. The Montagne controlling the now-purged legislature pronounced Condorcet guilty of a capital crime and ordered his arrest pending trial for betraying the people.[110]

CHAPTER 14

Education

SECURING THE REVOLUTION

Prior to 1789, the Enlightenment had comparatively little impact on primary and secondary schooling in France. Well before 1789, however, Enlightenment discourse had convinced many that it was necessary to move away from school teaching based on the catechism and Catholic doctrine, and had forcefully propagated the idea, associated especially with Diderot, the encyclopédistes, and Helvétius, that education can play a decisive role in changing the moral profile and character of society. Unsurprisingly, a close link existed at all stages during the Revolution between Enlightenment reform ideas and proposals propagated in the decades from the 1740s to 1788 and the post-1789 revolutionary transformation of education, first in theory and then gradually in reality.

Only when there were no more adults unable to read, write, and do basic arithmetic, affirmed Condorcet, like Turgot, Mercier, d'Holbach, and other philosophes of the previous generation, would society consist of independent individuals no longer reliant on others to perform the elementary transactions of their everyday lives. The attempt to introduce compulsory universal primary schooling under exclusively secular state supervision, and revolutionize secondary and higher education, were among the boldest, most significant undertakings of the democratic republican Revolution of 1788–93. From early on, conflicting approaches to these challenges marked out key differences between the basic social and cultural goals of the rival factions battling for control of the Revolution. Hence, the political disputes and ideological clashes surrounding educational issues during these years constitute an important indicator to the character and nature of the Revolution overall. That a large proportion of the democratic republican revolutionary vanguard were former tutors, librarians, journalists, and literary men was of itself a potent factor for educational reform.

Constitutional monarchists, centrists defending a restricted suffrage, authoritarian populists, and Left democrats all developed their own distinctive positions on education policy, and their divergent stances reflected the wider differences separating these competing antagonistic blocs. Thus, Sieyès's preference during the years 1789–92 for restricting the franchise, and his distinction between "active" and "passive" citizenship, excluding part of the adult population from the electorate, was tied to his assumption that much of society would remain uneducated.[1] By contrast, commitment to democracy in Condorcet, Brissot, Daunou, Lanthenas, Lakanal, Romme, and Lanjuinais directly shaped their collective summons for free and universal primary schooling, and a transformed secondary education, as preconditions for aware, meaningful, and involved participation and the citizenship of all.

Literacy rates in France had gradually risen since the seventeenth century and at a basic level were relatively high by the 1780s, at least in the cities. In Paris, approximately two-thirds of salaried workers could read at an elementary level and literacy rates for women of this class were only slightly lower. In the villages, literacy rates were markedly lower, albeit with a noticeable tendency for reading ability to be more widespread in the rural northeast and Alsace and lower in the south and west. But if most urban adult men and women could sign lists and read at an elementary level, only a small fraction were capable of absorbing to any extent or examining seriously the vast body of ephemeral literature available from 1787–88 in the poor quarters of the towns and countryside, the cheap pamphlets, extracts, and *feuilles volantes* constituting the bulk of the revolutionary reading material they were apt to encounter.[2]

Before 1789, French towns and villages possessed an elaborate, long-established network of schools supported by donations, endowments, and municipal grants but with both elementary and secondary schooling overwhelmingly directed toward religious instruction. Most teachers both in town and countryside were priests or under priestly supervision. What the populace imbibed from the printed material at hand in schools, often *catéchismes*, was Catholic piety and doctrine (or alternatively, in places, Protestant teaching), a school culture slanting popular attitudes in directions that republicans and philosophes, but also the centrist faction led by Barnave and the brothers de Lameth, viewed negatively. The first fundamental change in French education on the ground followed an Assembly decree, of March 1791, requiring the *maîtres d'école*, France's schoolmasters, to take the civic oath swearing fealty to the National Assembly and, where applicable, the Civil Constitution of the Clergy. French education hence first became a bitter, and soon ferocious, ideological battlefield during 1791 on the initiative of the liberal monarchists, no less than the democrats.

The revolutionaries of 1789 needed little persuading that schooling should become more secular, broadly available, and differently organized. Rousseau's masterpiece *Émile* (1762), the book where he chiefly expounds his educational ideas, focusing on private individual tuition, sharply separating education for boys and girls, and powerfully advocating a shift away from book learning and reading,[3] had appeared regularly in new editions from 1762 down to the years immediately after his death in 1778. Since around 1782 there had been few new editions. But with the onset of the Revolution in 1789 ensued a veritable explosion of fresh editions and greater differentiation in their format and cost, evidence confirming that this key work was being even more widely read than earlier. No one could discuss, reflect on, or write about education during the French Revolution without having Rousseau's *Émile* in mind.[4]

Yet, while Rousseau helped put educational reform very much in the air, his book made no plea for "public education," and conflicting reactions to his arguments only accentuated the sharp divergence of approaches under consideration among the revolutionaries. In fact, Rousseau had relatively little direct impact, except rhetorically, on the debate prior to June 1793 and at first his call to make schooling less academic and book-oriented exerted scant appeal.[5] The main emphasis among the revolutionaries was on the need for public education and on preparing good citizens. "Nothing is more suited to perfect the human species both morally and physically," proclaimed Sieyès, "than a good system of public education and instruction."[6] Yet it was no part of Sieyès's revolutionary constitutional monarchism between 1788 and 1792 to demand free and universal public education as a preparation for democracy, even though he too deemed it the duty of a well-ordered state to minimize the number of adults unfitted for "active citizenship" to the smallest proportion feasible, in particular by widening access to and raising the quality of education.

Mirabeau drafted the first extended reflections on the changes needed by a Revolution aiming to replace religious doctrine in the schools with the "cult of liberty, the cult of the law" during the months before his death (in April 1791). These were further elaborated and published shortly afterward by his disciple Cabanis. Mirabeau was actually the first revolutionary leader to publicly expound the un-Rousseauist thesis, central to the Revolution, that without a fundamentally transformed system of "public education," the new political order and constitution would not survive but soon be supplanted by what he called "anarchy and despotism." To equip men to enjoy their rights and generate an authentic volonté générale from all the private wills of men, the state must take direct charge of the schools and replace religious authority, theology and "sectarian superstition" with exaltation of the new civil values as its basis. Mirabeau clearly established the revolutionary principles that teachers as a group must never be permitted to oppose "la morale publique," must be uniformly placed under the departmental and civic authorities, that the general guidelines should be those stipulated by the philosophes, and that merit and ability were the qualities that should be chiefly rewarded in teachers.

"The present Revolution is the work of writers and of philosophy. Should the nation," admonished Mirabeau, "not respect its benefactors?"[7] Opponents of the Revolution were already disparaging it as a barbaric revolution "of Goths and Vandals." "Philosophes, littérateurs, savants, artists, the nation should honor and recompense them all." Teaching in the universities and colleges must switch from being Latin-based to being conducted in French, the roles of theology and law severely curtailed, and more emphasis put on professional training in administration, medicine, surgery, and pharmacy, with separate medical colleges entrusted with issuing qualifications for all practicing the medical professions. Standards of training for various other professions too, including notaries and bakers, must be fixed, regulated, and upheld by public authority.[8] All this was indubitably revolutionary. Mirabeau did not, however, call for free, obligatory, or universal primary schooling, or place the principle of equality at the forefront of the debate; indeed, he expressly rejected free primary education and endorsed Rousseau's principle that teaching for girls and boys should be separate, in different schools and fundamentally different.[9]

Universal secular education, building equality, and providing equality of opportunity in the early years of the Revolution was pursued as an ideal only by the democratic republicans. A nationally uniform school system, conceded Condorcet in the first of a series of discourses on education that he published in the *Bibliothèque de l'Homme Public* between 1790 and 1792, cannot prevent the social predominance of those "whom nature especially favors" in terms of ability and intellect.

However, a balanced, meaningful equality of rights, he argued, requires only that natural advantages should not create a legalized, institutionalized subordination of the less gifted and that everyone should be educated sufficiently to make the main decisions in their lives without being directed by others. Besides possessing literacy and arithmetic, this meant acquiring the ability to sift information, "reason" correctly, grasp "truths" when these are adequately expounded, spot errors, and develop an independent, critical judgment without which the citizen is ill-equipped to avoid the snares the malicious and devious set for them, or "repel the errors" with which elements of society "wish to render them victims." The more a nation expands the numbers of those elevated by the Enlightenment, the more the nobility, priesthood, and bureaucracy are swamped by well-educated commoners, the more society may "hope to obtain and keep good laws, a wise administration and a truly free constitution."[10]

Condorcet's chief point was that a "free constitution and society in which all classes of society enjoy the same rights cannot survive where the ignorance of part of the citizenry prevents them knowing its nature and limits, obliges them to pronounce on matters of which they have no knowledge, and to choose when they are unable to judge." Such a constitution would surely "destroy itself after a few stormy upheavals and degenerate into a form of government that merely preserves order amidst a people ignorant and corrupt."[11] Here was a doctrine frequently reiterated through the 1790s: "an ignorant people," as Lanthenas expressed it in April 1792, "lapses back very easily into slavery, a dreadful truth proved by all that has impaired the Revolution, restricted liberty and endangers liberty today."[12]

Closely connected to this claim was the idea, dear to all republicans, that "l'instruction publique," besides educating children and youth, necessarily also involved reeducating adults and especially artisans and manual laborers. For tyranny cannot easily reestablish itself without restoring ignorance first: in fact, affirmed Lanthenas (another of the reformers conscious that the Revolution was in the main disregarding Rousseau's views on education), echoing Diderot, Helvétius, and d'Holbach, weakening liberty and equality goes hand in hand with instilling superstition, prejudice, and error.[13] According to Pierre-Claude-François Daunou, "grand vicaire" of the constitutional bishop of Pas-de-Calais before becoming a Convention deputy and who, with Condorcet and Lakanal, was one of the Revolution's three foremost educational reformers, adult instruction should consist of three main elements: public lectures and conferences to promote secular morality, what he called "l'éducation morale" (as well as teach agriculture and commerce); public libraries established in all parts of the Republic containing not only books but also natural history exhibits and antiquities; and, third, the fixed national festivals commemorating great revolutionary events and seasons of the year.[14]

A free society provides education for all its citizens, held Condorcet (doubly contradicting Rousseau), identical for men and women. All valid education in a democratic state should aim to teach "truths" on the basis of proofs and demonstrations, and how could the differences between the sexes possibly imply any difference between the truths being taught or the manner of demonstrating them? A separate or lower level of schooling for women, such as Rousseau's admirers advocated, must inevitably institutionalize inequality, not only between husband and wife but between brother and sister and son and mother, causing undesirable effects within the family. What authority can "maternal tenderness" exert over sons where the mother's ignorance renders her an object of disdain or ridicule in her sons' eyes? Women possess identical rights to men and thus the same right of access to enlightenment, which alone enables women, as it does men, to exercise their independence and rights.[15]

Since boys and girls require the same schooling, contended Condorcet, they should be taught together by the same teachers, male or female. Women are perfectly capable of teaching at any level, including from university chairs, a claim Condorcet substantiated by citing the example of two women virtual professors who had taught sciences at Bologna University. Grouping boys and girls together in the same schools, besides, was the only practicable approach at the primary level, as it would be difficult to establish two schools in each village or find enough teachers to school the sexes separately. Familiarity between the sexes was no bad thing, added Condorcet, as it would restrain latent tendencies toward homosexuality.[16] Subsequently, though, in his report to the Assembly of April 1792, he bowed to the majority view, discarding the call to teach boys and girls together (except in villages where there were sufficient population and resources for only one school). Even so, he adhered to his un-Rousseauist principle that what is taught should be broadly the same for boys and girls.[17]

"Friends of equality and liberty" must ensure the state provides public instruction that renders "reason" itself populaire. Otherwise, held Condorcet, the revolutionaries would quickly forfeit the fruits of their efforts. Even the best-framed laws cannot render an *ignorant* equal to an educated person or emancipate individuals sunk in credulity and prejudice. The more the laws respect men's rights, personal independence, and natural equality, the more potentially they also ease the path for the "terrible tyranny" that cunning can exercise over ignorance when the *ignorant* becomes simultaneously the agent and victim of the devious. In a land with a free constitution where "a troop of audacious hypocrites" creates a network of affiliated societies in a hundred other towns, recruiting uneducated accomplices and fomenting herdlike acceptance, they can easily propagate everywhere the same false opinions that infuse the main organization. A people devoid of education would be consigned hand and foot to the "phantoms of belief and snares of calumny." Such an organization easily gathers under its banners every scoundrel, dishonorable talent, and ambitious mediocrity, and understands that it can capture power by dominating the uneducated mass through seduction and "terror." Under the "mask of liberty," the uneducated and ignorant would themselves become the agents as well as the victims of a shameful and ferocious tyranny.[18] Inequality of education is one of the main sources of "tyranny" counted among Condorcet's favorite maxims, implying the need to instill into the population through education a whole new attitude toward morality, authority, social status, and the state.

During the early Revolution, it was not only in the National Assembly that education policy was debated. Not yet a deputy, Condorcet published his views in the journals. Daunou first seized the public's attention between October 1789 and January 1790 through his *Lettres sur l'éducation* appearing in the *Journal Encyclopédique*. The Cercle Social did much to promote awareness in France of the vital importance of the debate about l'instruction publique, creating its own national education committee meeting weekly working alongside the Cercle's directoire and submitting recommendations as to how primary, secondary, and higher education should be reformed. Headed by Cérutti, the Piedmontese ex-Jesuit journalist ally of Mirabeau, it included the future Montagnard Joseph-Marie Lequinio (1740–1814) and Athanase Auger (1734–92), an educational and legal reformer especially eager for the new primary schools to inculcate civics, the new morality, and the rights and duties of the citizen.

If the Cercle strove to bring the Enlightenment to the masses in the cities,[19] Cérutti and Lequinio, as the *Feuille villageoise*'s editors, endeavored to bring la philosophie to the peasantry. An early issue of *La Feuille villageoise* of October 1790, explaining the Declaration of Rights of Man to villagers, insisted that rights, and the other key truths about society and politics the peasantry must imbibe, possess no basis in religion but derive from philosophy. A philosophe is a "man courageous enough to say and write all the truths useful to men," writers whose books the parlements burned and whom they persecuted and banished "or worse," as philosophes expound those indispensable truths ancien régime authorities did not wish ordinary folk to discover or learn about.[20]

The Legislative Assembly set up its twenty-four-member national Comité d'Instruction Publique in October 1791, and by the autumn of that year boldly ambitious plans were being aired. This committee, chaired by Condorcet, was charged with drawing up a comprehensive plan for reforming all stages of education. Until late 1791, relying on the constitutionalist clergy and those religious teaching orders still functioning to operate the schools seemed the only practicable method to transform the schools, given the lack of nonclerical village schoolmasters to provide an alternative in the countryside. But gradually the perspective changed. The ideas of Mirabeau, Talleyrand, Cérutti, Garat, Auger, Daunou, Cabanis, Lakanal, and especially Condorcet himself, slowly coalesced into a detailed plan for the reform of public instruction presented to the National Assembly in its mature form by Condorcet on behalf of the Comité d'Instruction Publique in April 1792.[21]

The guiding doctrine of the Revolution's education theorists was that a democratic republic requires its citizens to be educated to understand and fulfill the requirements of their own liberty, their civic responsibilities, and duties, as well as contribute to the advancement of the nation's prosperity and their own fulfillment and happiness as individuals. What is taught must therefore be unreservedly based on Enlightenment and science. Children from poor families must be given the opportunity to develop their talents on as equal a footing as possible with the help of society.[22] Universal education—that is, education of all citizens—is essential to society, and hence the responsibility of society. Primary schooling must be universal, compulsory and free, and administered by the state. Condorcet's report was printed, discussed, and widely applauded but as yet not acted on.

Condorcet distinguished four levels of education: primary, secondary, tertiary (the level of what he called the "instituts"), and higher education in what he called the "lycées." The entire system was to be supervised by a national "society" or academy of sciences and arts. Secondary schooling was for the children of families that were able to forego their offspring's work for longer than the rural poor, especially children intended for work outside agricultural labor. Despite the marked disequilibrium between the urban and rural contexts his plan introduced, secondary teaching too, insisted Condorcet, must be universal in character and based on the principle of equality. Every town with four thousand inhabitants or more should have a secondary school equipped with a small library and a cabinet with meteorological instruments, a natural history display, and models of machines. In these schools, children from ten to thirteen would principally be taught mathematics, natural history, moral sciences, history, geography, politics, chemistry, and physics.[23] The traditional orientation toward Latin, Greek, and theology would cease. Condorcet apparently did not think it desirable to teach Latin and Greek, or classical literature and rhetoric, at any level. This fitted with the wider Enlightenment preoccupation, reaching back to d'Alembert's article on "colleges" in the *Encyclopédie*, with countering the emphasis on rhetoric in Jesuit and other pre-Enlightenment education and replacing rhetorical persuasion and eloquence with "reason," genuine argument, and demonstration.[24]

Condorcet's scheme envisaged primary education from six to ten, providing levels of literacy and awareness sufficient to enable citizens to follow politics, vote, sit on juries, and hold local office of the kind that any citizen would be expected to undertake. Every village or community counting four hundred inhabitants or more should have its own primary school and teacher. Besides reading, writing, and arithmetic, children would learn about the Constitution and the rudiments of philosophique morality and be taught about local agriculture and products. Human rights and basic (nonreligious) morality should also be taught to further strengthen awareness of political realities. On Sundays, the schools would feature public debates with adults present who would discuss social and political issues with the teacher and children.[25] No people can enjoy an assured stable liberty, insisted Condorcet, if teaching the political sciences is not generally adopted in and outside the schools, and if the enthusiasm that teaching politics arouses in citizens' minds "is not directed by reason, if it can be aroused by what is not the truth."[26]

Universal, secular education effectively became a state goal, given high priority by the Revolution only after the republican triumph of 10 August 1792. But clearing the way ideologically still left many practical obstacles: How would the new secular schools, teachers, and schoolbooks be paid for? While Article XIII of the 1789 Declaration of the Rights of Man and the Citizen required that taxation should be apportioned equitably among the citizenry according to capacity to pay, it remained vague about what taxation was for. As head of the National Assembly's constitutional committee, Condorcet presented his expanded affirmation of the Rights of Man on 15 February 1793. Article XXII of the 1793 Declaration, more forthright than that of 1789, stipulated that "no contribution may be introduced," except to support public needs on the basis of "utilité générale." This opened the door to Condorcet's costly schemes, as did Article XXIII (with which the Montagne concurred, but Sieyès disliked) that elementary schooling is the concern of all, and owed by society to all its members equally.[27]

Though supposed not to challenge the private religious views of parents and families, the task of "public education," it was agreed, was to teach civics, morality, and the public sphere without conceding any role to religion. It was thus primarily the philosophique principles of the revolutionary leadership, originating in Mirabeau and Condorcet especially, that led to reconsideration of the exempt status granted the regular clergy's teaching orders under the 1789–90 legislation. On 4 and 18 August 1792, the Legislative Assembly forbade members of the orders to concern themselves further with public education, and in effect suppressed the remaining religious orders.[28]

Although Brissotins and Montagnards plainly intended different things under the heading of education, they mostly agreed that free, uniform, and universal primary schooling was indispensable to a society based on liberty and equality. All children in every canton of every department should have access to primary schools not only to learn arithmetic, reading, and writing, and to speak "correctly," but also learn the Rights of Man and the principles of the Revolution, Constitution, and government of France. Almost all the revolutionaries proved hostile to encouraging or teaching in local dialects, patois, and regional languages, such as Provencal, Breton, Flemish, and Basque. All children should be taught a common, centralized French language, study elementary geography and the history of the world's peoples by epochs, and imbibe secular morality detached from religion "without which neither liberty nor happiness on earth," as the Montagnard Montgilbert put it, "can exist for men."[29]

The essential function of the public elementary schools, the Brissotins envisaged, was to equalize opportunity, establish the hegemony of talent, and ensure equality between social classes, as well as (potentially) between men and women. Higher education was to provide a modernized curriculum and serve the whole of society and not simply the gifted, with advanced education organized to produce the individuals of superior talents needed to staff the administration, magistracies, and higher political councils of the Republic, as well as its seats of learning, schools, and institutes. It was precisely a major function of primary education, argued Concorcet, to enable the mass of the citizenry to recognize those enlightened men to whom they could best and most safely entrust their interests, and of secondary and tertiary education to supply the stream of talent the people need to enshrine and protect their rights and safeguard their happiness. In this connection Condorcet stressed the need for special provisions for youths of superior talents lacking means to pay for higher education.[30]

Condorcet and his colleagues thought that the teaching of every discipline at all levels of schooling needed to be revolutionized. Society must acquire a wholly new conception of, for example, history (*une histoire toute nouvelle*). Instead of being about kings and military exploits, and still less religion, history should be about the "rights of men and the vicissitudes to which these have everywhere been subjected, and the knowledge and enjoyment of these rights." History should be a study where the wisdom and prosperity of nations is judged according to their ranking regarding men's rights, the advance and retreat of social inequality, the historical process that constitutes "almost the sole source" and measure of the well-being and misery of civilized men.[31]

The system envisaged in 1791–93 was intended to accomplish a wide spectrum of effects but along divergent lines depending on whether one's ideological preferences were democratic republican or Montagnard.[32] Brissotin plans for educational reforms faced stiff opposition from the Montagne, who detected an affront to equality in Condorcet's ideas, disliked his emphasis on developing talent through secondary and higher education, and had reservations about his proposal to strip religion out of education and replace it entirely with philosophy, science, and mathematics. Much of the Convention, either out of principle or because of the war emergency, was reluctant to approve his sweeping recommendations, and objected to erasing religion from education, at any rate, as drastically as Condorcet proposed. "Some philosophes," recalled Levasseur later, "sought to minimize religious instruction in the name of toleration. Many Montagnards, filled with hatred of priests, agreed." Robespierre and Danton, though, he recorded, did not but rather resisted, preferring to retain conventional religion in education. It was not only the war and the Republic's difficult financial situation that impeded the progress of the democratic Left's educational plans but also objections to their aims.[33]

If primary and in principle secondary schooling was for everyone, tertiary education for children from thirteen to seventeen in the institutes, and higher education for youth from seventeen to twenty-one, Condorcet's fourth stage, were intended for those with the talent and the ability to benefit from such opportunities. If the Montagne was deeply suspicious of this program, Brissotins and Montagnards could agree at least on the need to shut down the old university system, dominated by theology and law. The universities' theology faculties had already been closed down during 1791. The universities were then comprehensively dismantled in 1792–93, the Sorbonne closing altogether in April 1792 and the endowments of its colleges being sold off; the other ancient universities—Toulouse, Montpellier, Caen, and others— were suppressed in particular during the summer and autumn of 1793.

Meanwhile, the old system of primary schools was in ruins. All leading figures in the revolutionary government, including Sieyès, understood the urgency of introducing a comprehensive new public system to replace them. From February 1793 when Sieyès rejoined the National Convention's Committee of Public Instruction, he began collaborating more closely with Condorcet, Lakanal, and Daunou, and, in May, became the committee's president. On 8 March 1793, the Convention issued an edict appropriating all surviving school endowments in an attempt to find the resources needed to implement far-reaching reform plans. On 30 May 1793 one elementary school was decreed along the lines recommended by Condorcet for each village with more than four hundred inhabitants. But efforts to put the plans into practice were dramatically interrupted by the journée of 2 June 1793, ending the Brissotin ascendancy and causing fundamental changes in revolutionary school policy.

On 26 June 1793, the latest version of the education committee's general reform of the school system was presented to the Convention by Joseph Lakanal (1762–1845), a philosophy professor and Voltairean deist close to Condorcet who was later, in 1816, exiled from France as a regicide (he migrated to the United States, where he eventually became first president of the University of Louisiana). A philosophe and educator, he was also a prominent egalitarian and pioneer of methods of imposing progressive taxation, a specialist at devising tax forms that impinge on the rich. The situation was urgent, Lakanal stressed, as the old system of education had broken down, but nothing substantial had yet replaced it on the ground, so that in most places youth was practically "abandoned to itself."[34]

For both Brissotin and Montagnard Jacobins, public instruction involved far more than just school education. Both sets of reform plans envisaged a permanent system of public festivals and celebrations at the departmental and local level to commemorate the Revolution's great events and principles, the seasons of the year, and other natural events. The Convention also considered establishing "national theaters" in each electoral district to accommodate large gatherings, debates, and celebrations, as well as drama, music, and dance. Where in the past the Church provided opportunities for local communities to convene in festivity, mourning, processions, and morally uplifting communal events, under the new order "public education" was rooted in the new festivals and the electoral districts forming the basis of France's projected representative democracy.[35]

Brissotins and Montagnards disagreed about the character and form of primary and secondary education and, even more, over Condorcet's and Lakanal's institutes, afterward dubbed *écoles centrales*, designed to replace ancien régime higher education. The latter issue also inevitably raised the wider question of the status of science, scholarship, and advanced research in society, including the question of how to reform the old royal academies, not least the Académie Française. Almost from the outset, the latter's forty members had been sharply divided in their views on the Revolution. As the Revolution itself became more fragmented, the split deepened. While Suard, Marmontel, and other Academy conservatives rejected the Revolution and its aims, pro-Revolution academicians, headed by Condorcet, Chamfort, and La Harpe, urged revolutionary principles and a program of far-reaching reform.

To the revolutionaries, the Académie Française in its existing format and the other academies, national and provincial, represented an unacceptable vestige of monarchical culture and patronage, uncritical, stilted, and top-heavy with ceremonies, eulogies, and court flattery. Mirabeau, backed by Condorcet and Chamfort, had initiated moves in the Assembly to integrate the academies into the projected new vision of national research. Royal patronage and deference to Church and aristocracy were to be eliminated from the administration, practices, and culture of the nation's advanced scholarship and science, and the role of the academies, including those of the arts and architecture, revised to fit the Revolution's core goals. But here a rift developed between reformers and those advocating the academies' abolition. This eventually became an aspect of the conflict between Brissotins and the Montagne, albeit on this issue Chamfort sided with the Montagne. Already among the project papers circulating in April 1791, around the time of Mirabeau's death, was a vehement attack on the royal academies penned by Chamfort that was far too acerbic for Condorcet, who planned to reform, not destroy, the academies. The Académie Française must be suppressed, insisted Chamfort, since its entire way of proceeding was a survival from the ancien régime; its pre-1789 leadership, d'Alembert especially, had been excessively meek under royal authority (though Chamfort himself, Morellet later pointed out, had for years accepted this uncomplainingly).

Prospects for the academies deteriorated sharply with the Montagnard victory of June 1793. Where Condorcet and his colleagues sought to remodel the ancien régime royal academies so as to embody the Enlightenment and serve as a national network or "society" of research, debate, and consultation organizing and directing the nation's intellectual and cultural life, and the entire national system of primary, secondary, and higher education, Marat and Robespierre were against anything of the sort. The Brissotins had wanted the old structure of privilege based on royal favor and status replaced by a new system of merit and honors built on autonomous, self-selecting intellectual distinction and excellence alone. Lavoisier and other leading scientists and educationalists, including Lakanal (who alone remained on the committee) after June 1793, continued to champion this strategy. But science and scholarly research now lost their former high priority for the regime. In fact, Marat and Robespierre stepped up the attack on the academies as refuges of elitism, prerogative, charlatanism, and imposture, as privileged, irrelevant, and detrimental.

Marat and Robespierre particularly disliked Condorcet's, Danou's, and Lakanal's idea that the academies should be consolidated under a new institute or super academy, a national society or directorate of the sciences, humanities, and social sciences. For this was clearly designed to create a kind of senate of philosophes and scientists, largely independent of the Convention and the Jacobins in thinking, policy, and appointments, empowered to preside over the entire educational and scholarly sector.[36] Where Condorcet's vision meant enthroning the Enlightenment in a supervisory position, directing the educational system and ultimately the entire nation in esprit public via la philosophie, Marat and Robespierre intended a comprehensive dictatorship in the name of equality. Condorcet's Enlightenment vision was a scheme educational, moral, and scientific, and ultimately also political, nurturing a democratic republicanism in which the people's attitudes and responses would be refined and elevated so as to become receptive to the ideals of the expounders of philosophy and social science. This the Montagne wholeheartedly rejected, though Romme, one of their main spokesmen in educational affairs, strove valiantly to combine Condorcet's and the Montagne's divergent positions.[37]

Cutting back scholarship and learning was inherent in the Montagne's approach and its agenda, and this led to its plan, enthusiastically urged by Marat, to extinguish the academies, including the art and military academies, altogether. For his part, the painter Jacques-Louis David loudly denounced the academies' influence in the arts, depicting them as a patronage mechanism inherently elitist and alien to ordinary men. Accordingly, the Convention abolished all the academies, national and provincial, on 8 August 1793, including, soon afterward, the military academies.[38] The Académie Française, hallowed sanctuary of literary, intellectual, and linguistic studies, founded by Richelieu in 1635, held its last meeting on 5 August. When Chamfort heard the news of the academies' dissolution, he was at Malesherbes's residence at Fontainebleau discussing the implications of a change so shocking to some, defending it before the former minister and the philosophe Delisle de Sale.

During the summer of 1793, the Committee of Public Instruction, led by Lakanal and Grégoire, fought a rearguard action to salvage some elements of state support for scholarship and science. The Academy of Sciences at least should be spared, they urged, given its intrinsic usefulness to military technology, saltpeter production, and advancing chemistry and the war effort. The academy also supervised the commission, occupied since 1791 with overhauling France's system of weights and measures according to universal metric criteria, preparing a new system likely to be adopted everywhere. Despite help from friends, Lavoisier's attempt to rescue the inner core of the Academy of Sciences' activities via a private Free and Fraternal Society for the Advancement of the Sciences was firmly blocked. The Jacobin leadership was adamant. When his society attempted to continue their activities, the ex-academicians found the Academy's rooms, archives, and equipment all sealed and bolted against them.[39] Montagnard attitudes toward science, scholarship, and research proved even more Counter-Enlightenment in character than their aims in elementary and secondary education.

When the finalized general education reform plan based on the ideas of Mirabeau, Sieyès, Condorcet, and Lakanal came before the Convention on 15 July 1793, it was Robespierre himself who rose to block it. He spoke in favor of the rival, more populist scheme formulated by the "true Jacobin" Louis-Michel Lepeletier (1760–93) prior to the latter's assassination by a former royal guard in January 1793 (figure 9). Lepeletier's and Robespierre's objective was to regenerate society on a Rousseauiste basis and "create a new people."[40] Universal elementary education, Montagnards concurred, should be the basis of public instruction. But Lepeletier, Robespierre, and even more emphatically Saint-Just, all uncompromising Rousseauists, wanted boarding schools separating children from their parents for long periods—boys from five to twelve (or later) and girls from five to eleven—to enable society to more fully mold their development, morals, and outlook. In every respect, Robespierre and Saint-Just wanted more emphasis on surveillance, physical exercise, and group activities.[41] The most essential difference between the rival philosophies as regards primary education was that Robespierre's was less concerned with fashioning enlightened, independently thinking individuals accustomed to evaluating proofs, less preoccupied with what he called *l'instruction*, than instilling virtue, raising children in a collective fashion, feeding them on frugal but healthy meals, and dressing them uniformly, moral formation he termed *l'éducation*.

In short, Montagnard education was not for knowledge, judgment, or critical appraisal, and least of all intended to teach civics, independent thinking, and political consciousness, as in Condorcet, Lakanal, and Daunou, but rather intended for mass indoctrination and Spartan behavioral and moral molding. Few of those passing through the Montagnard primary school system were intended to proceed to secondary and higher education. More Rousseauist than Mirabeau's, Condorcet's, Sieyès's, Daunou's, or Lakanal's conceptions, Robespierriste education chiefly stressed primary schooling, viewing the nation's children as pliable material to be fashioned by the Montagne to produce a disciplined new nation reminiscent of the ancient Spartans, hardened by gymnastics, consensus-oriented, and geared for discipline, austerity, and uniformity.[42] This wide gap between education for Enlightenment and schooling for virtue and collective action, between republican Left and authoritarian populism, between the educational vision of the Revolution of 1788–93 and that of 1793–94, of course, directly mirrored the wider ideological rift separating the vying political blocs. Unlike Condorcet's plan of teaching morality without any religion, Robespierre's

Figure 9. The "Exposition" in the Place des Piques (today the Place Vendôme) of the corpse of Michel Lepeletier prior to his pantheonization on 24 January 1793. Image courtesy Bibliothèque nationale de France.

plan envisaged that children would be strongly imbued with "natural religion."

Another striking difference was the emphatic reversal of Condorcet's scheme for joint primary education of girls and boys. Since character formation rather than enlightenment was now the goal, separating the sexes acquired a central place in Montagnard school policy. Throughout his writings, Rousseau's concern when discussing girls and women, as Mercier, Mirabeau, and Cabanis emphasized, was that females had their own separate role in society and should become imbued with fitting modesty and good morals.[43] While both boys and girls would learn to read, write, and do arithmetic, and sing patriotic hymns, they would otherwise largely be taught different things, boys learning carpentry, surveying, and arduous gymnastics while girls were destined to "spin, sew and bleach."[44]

Montagnard populist and democratic republican school policies were thus not just different but inherently antagonistic. The former was really a form of organized ignorance, the other designed above all to conquer popular ignorance. Cercle Social intellectuals saw themselves as the teachers of the masses, not just of an elite;[45] Montagnard publicists utterly scorned such teachers. If most of the Convention showed little enthusiasm for the scheme to take children from their parents to educate them in boarding schools, there was robust support for a Rousseauist switch from education as promoting knowledge of philosophy, the sciences and arts to education as character formation, de-emphasizing the philosophique goals of learning and judgment. Rousseauism fused with anti-intellectualism typified Montagnard thinking and also pervaded the attitudes of other foes of the Enlightenment. A member of the Convention's education committee who loudly rejected Robespierre's politics but agreed with his Counter-Enlightenment stance was Michel-Edme Petit (1739–95), one of the deputies who attempted to indict Marat in April 1793. It was not philosophy, insisted Petit, but inculcating belief in God and immortality of the soul, together with Rousseau's deism and love of nature, that were necessary for an adequate esprit public. Of all forms of aristocracy, "the most pernicious for republicans," he agreed with the Montagne, in an impassioned speech in the Convention on 1 October 1793, "is that of science [i.e., learning] and the arts."[46]

Petit's address was a fiery exhortation against Condorcet, la philosophie, and "all the plans for education" in the Revolution thus far. An ardent adherent of Rousseau's educational antiphilosophisme, he abominated the approach of the philosophe reformers, and especially their doctrine that "nothing concerning religious cults will be taught in the primary schools."[47] "Despite all the efforts of the Bayles, Mirabeaus, Helvétius, d'Alemberts, Boulangers, Frérets, Diderots and all modern imitators of Epicurus and Lucretius, the sublime idea of a God who rewards and punishes remains in all sound minds and all upright hearts triumphing over the obscure errors and brilliant sophisms of which egoism and crime are always in need."[48] Besides, the stress on history, geography, social sciences, and all academic disciplines was quite wrong, in his estimation, being of scant use to those destined for artisan, mechanical, or laboring occupations. The educational system should focus on vocational skills and tasks essential to ordinary, everyday life. La philosophie should yield to "the ordinary" and the God of Rousseau, giving the religion of the people a central place in primary education. If the education reformers succeeded in prioritizing academic learning, sciences, and arts, they would ruin France's children, preparing them for leisure and enjoyment instead of manual labor, for luxury instead of austerity. Primary education should be to prepare children for a life of work, austere morals, and "simplicity."[49]

The primary school system envisaged by the Convention's education commission came haltingly into existence in 1793 but only in the most skeletal fashion. Lakanal personally took charge of a pilot scheme in the Dordogne in the southwest in October 1793. Each of Bergerac's four sections acquired an elementary school at that point installed in a confiscated émigré residence. Partitions and benches were furnished. The teachers, men and women recruited from the local société populaire to ensure that they had the right Jacobin and de-Christianizing credentials and attitudes, were paid equally, receiving the relatively high salary of 1,200 livres each, placing them on the same level as constitutional curés. To provide for this, a common municipal educational fund was established to which the town's poor contributed little, and most funds were exacted from the affluent.[50] Religion disappeared from the curriculum; family influences over the forming of children's attitudes were curtailed. The republican quest to revolutionize elementary education then continued, albeit with the scope and length of primary education considerably reduced, under a package of decrees promulgated on 19 December 1793 proclaiming elementary education free, general, and obligatory in France.[51] Municipalities were summoned to find premises and teachers, and pay their salaries. The Convention and its committees would supply the basic guidance and the textbooks. Close supervision at the local level would be via the municipalities and revolutionary committees. Marseille was among those cities where by late 1793 the municipality was actively taking concrete steps toward standardizing, secularizing, and expanding primary schooling.[52]

The Condorcet-Lakanal system of free, standardized, and secular universal primary education with teacher's salaries paid by the Republic thus haltingly evolved into reality in late 1793, if in a degraded version. It was rapidly undermined within months, however, by the collapse of the Republic's printed money and consequent rapid reduction of teachers' salaries to unsustainably low levels.[53] From the ambitious perspective of the plans of 1791–93, the primary school reform program of

1793–94 could be judged to have been a catastrophic failure.[54] Many or most of the thousands of new primary schools hoped for failed to materialize. But measured in terms of the difficulties the Revolution faced, the Revolution in education was far from an unmitigated failure even in 1793–94, and its achievements went much further subsequently. In most departments of France, a substantial proportion of the planned primary schools eventually came into existence possessing a very different character from the primary schools of the past.

After Thermidor, the Conventions's Comité d'Instruction Publique was drastically changed. Consisting henceforth of sixteen members chaired by Lakanal, it introduced a series of key reforms in the autumn of 1794. Especially important was the Lakanal law of 17 November 1794 (27 Brumaire of the Year III), which included the words "ignorance and barbarism will not have the triumphs they promised themselves!" The changes marked the complete overturning of Montagnard insistence on character formation and equality of attainment as the central principles of children's schooling while especially repudiating Marat's and Robespierre's views on Enlightenment, adult education, and higher education.[55] It also reintroduced an element of choice for parents, allowing the continuance of private religious schools where approved by local authorities. Primary schools were now to be maintained at the rate of one for every thousand inhabitants, to be divided into boys' and girls' sections. Departments were advised as to how many schools and teachers each of their districts was to maintain. Teachers were to be recruited and paid by departmental and civic authorities at nationally fixed rates, 1,200 livres remaining the level for most teachers.

The attempt to place the entire cost of the education reforms on the public purse at a time of such difficulties and exigency greatly hindered realization of the plans especially for universal, free, and compulsory primary education. Administrative difficulties and serious disequilibriums between town and country, and between different districts, abounded. After the advent of the Constitution of 1795, which authorized the functioning of private religious schools, triggering a proliferation of what republicans called "écoles anti-républicaines," especially during the years 1795–97, rival private Catholic schools cut into the numbers of teachers available for the public schools and their ability to function. The revised education law framed by Daunou and adopted by the legislature on 25 and 26 October 1795 was hurriedly framed, encouraged the reemergence of private schools, and notably failed to boost provision of teachers in public primary schools or their supervision by the state. Daunou, even earlier in 1793, always displayed considerably less enthusiasm than Condorcet, Lakanal, or Romme for measures prioritizing teachers paid and supervised by the state over private teachers.[56] Nevertheless, a substantial minority of the planned schools were functioning within two years of the Lakanal decree.[57]

More impressive were developments in tertiary and higher education. Although it took time, the network of écoles centrales (the realization of Condorcet's lycées) eventually became the Revolution's most concrete educational legacy. In the proposed draft law on secondary and tertiary education of December 1794, the écoles centrales differed little from Condorcet's earlier instituts and, like the latter, also came under the supervision of the planned Institut National des Sciences and des Arts, except that Lakanal added plans, inspired partly by Adam Smith, to teach commerce and agriculture as well as the sciences and academic subjects. Comprehensive formal suppression of secondary and higher education colleges in France and their replacement by the écoles centrales, one in each departmental capital, on the lines recommended by Condorcet and Lakanal began in earnest with the Convention's decree of 25 February 1795.[58] Financial exigency and the pressures of war certainly caused delays, as did the difficulties created by the wide gap left by the Daunou law between the educational levels attained by the top year in the primary schools and the high starting level required by the écoles centrales. Yet, remarkable progress was achieved.

The ideological basis of the Revolution's écoles centrales, established in recently conquered Belgium and the Rhineland, as well as in France proper between 1794 and 1797, was the uncompromising secularism and scientific academicism of the Radical Enlightenment and in no way the populist egalitarianism Robespierre and the Montagne had urged. Following Condorcet's concept, seconded by Lakanal, each department capital's école central, in theory staffed by thirteen "professors," was equipped with a public library, public botanical garden, a cabinet of natural history, and a laboratory for scientific experiments.[59] Philosophy teaching in these schools was saturated in democratic republican ideology exhorting both teachers and students to demolish what government instructions called the "yoke of prejudice and fanaticism." The output of schoolbooks supplied from Paris for this new sector formed a whole new dimension of publishing encouraged in particular by Condorcet's ally François de Neufchâteau. It consisted of editions and abridgements of Buffon, Daubenton, Bonnet, Linnaeus, Rousseau, Mably, Raynal, d'Alembert, and d'Holbach. D'Holbach's *Politique naturelle* was purposely used in teaching social studies and politics throughout the system, including, for example, in the Mons école central set up in 1798.[60] The importance assigned in these schools to the *Encyclopédie*, and to the ideas of Diderot, d'Holbach, Helvétius, and Condorcet, on the reciprocal interaction of all the various branches of human learning and science was striking.[61]

Often established in buildings formerly housing convents or monasteries, in Mons the old convent of the Ursulines, by late 1797 a majority of French departments had écoles centrales already operative, sixty-eight reportedly by June of that year. There were by then three of these institutions in Paris, although a total of five were planned for the capital. By 1802, the year in which Napoleon suppressed the entire system of écoles centrales as being too emphatically revolutionary, democratic, and secular in character, there were no less than ninety-five of these establishments functioning in places as diverse as Ajaccio, Cologne, Mainz, Maastricht, Antwerp, Liège, and Brussels, as well as in all the departmental capitals of France proper. Nothing more clearly revealed the Montagne's defeat and the true face of the "real French Revolution." The Revolution's flagship achievement in the educational sphere, the écoles centrales were truly Condorcet's posthumous revenge on the Montagne.

CHAPTER 15

Black Emancipation

"We are trying to save millions of men from ignominy and death," wrote Condorcet in 1788, in a text condemning the slave trade, "to enlighten those in power about their true interests and restore to a whole section of the world the sacred rights given to them by nature."[1] The advent of black liberation in the Caribbean during the years 1788–94 confirms that la philosophie moderne was not only the primary shaping impulse of the French Revolution but the primary spur to black emancipation in the late eighteenth-century Caribbean world. The social revolution that ensued during the years 1792–97 was not merely concerned with abolishing slavery as such, like the Christian abolitionist movements in England and Pennsylvania, but formed a broader, more comprehensive emancipationist movement seeking to integrate the entire black population—"free blacks" and slaves—into society, legally, economically, educationally, and also politically.

The movement for black emancipation in its broad philosophique sense was thus unique to the French context, having no parallel in Britain or the United States. Offspring of the Radical Enlightenment, it emerged as a political factor for the first time in 1788–90. The organization the republican democrats founded to work toward black emancipation, the Société des Amis des Noirs was inaugurated in Paris on 19 February 1788. By early 1789, it had 141 signed-up members headed by Brissot, Clavière, Mirabeau, Condorcet, Carra, Lafayette, Bergasse, Grégoire, Pétion, Volney, Cerisier, and Raynal, though the latter soon broke with it.[2] Besides this group there were several key advocates of black emancipation, notably the philosophe Antoine Destutt de Tracy (1754–1836), active in the National Assembly, who were not members of the Amis des Noirs.

The Declaration of the Rights of Man was a manifesto entirely incompatible with all ancien régime notions of social, racial, and religious hierarchy, and of itself imparted a vigorous impulse to revolutionary esprit as a reforming force in all social contexts. The implications for women, religious minorities, the illegitimate, ethnic minorities, and homosexuals, as well as free blacks and black slaves, were bound to be far-reaching. The very first meeting of the Société des Amis des Noirs, after the Bastille's fall on 23 August 1789, with Condorcet presiding, issued a public statement calling for an immediate end to the slave trade between Africa and the New World, and for existing slaves in the Americas to be treated better. The Société's manifesto, stressing the implications of the Declaration of Rights, echoed widely in the French Caribbean and was reissued in Canada by the *Gazette de Montréal*, a paper edited by Fleury Mesplet (1734–94), a radical-minded pro-Revolution printer (originally from Lyon). Officially, there were then only around three hundred black slaves in Canada. But the French landowners there were already flatly against the ideas of the revolutionary philosophes, knowing these involved a thoroughgoing attack on privilege, noble status, and social hierarchy. The French Canadian clergy were equally hostile, seeing religion under threat. Landowners and clergy closed ranks with the British administration. Canada, the British authorities were assured, detested the principles of 1789 and would stand unshakably firm with Britain against the Revolution.[3]

From August 1789 ensued a fiercely contested, widely publicized transatlantic debate focused on the French National Assembly, with antiemancipationist and antiegalitarian arguments being assiduously promoted by the colonial and slaving commercial interest in Nantes and Bordeaux. The Société was accused of planning to disrupt the colonies and colonial trade. As yet, there could be no immediate end to slavery itself, responded Brissot, Condorcet, and the Société, because the slaves were not yet sufficiently "mature" to adjust to freedom and equality in an orderly fashion. But while the slaves had first to be prepared, abolition must be urged, justified, and planned at once to win over public opinion and create the conditions for emancipation.[4] Ending slavery, they explained, was not just a matter of legal emancipation but of absorbing former slaves into society in a nonviolent, meaningful, and durable manner. Their resulting press campaign impacted powerfully through the pages of the republican papers, Brissot's *Patriote française*, Mirabeau's *Courrier*, the *Chronique de Paris*, Prudhomme's *Révolutions de Paris,* and other papers. "Humanity demands, commands, that slavery be softened first and abolished soon," explained the main paper reporting revolutionary developments to the French peasantry, the *Feuille villageoise*, in January 1791. "But this great change, humanity also requires, must be carefully prepared to avoid civil war and safeguard France's commerce."[5]

Brissot and Condorcet agreed that France's colonies were essential to the country's overseas trade and must be preserved from chaos and economic ruin. Between 1770 and 1790, sugar, indigo, tobacco, coffee, and other cash crop exports from Saint-Domingue, Cayenne, Martinique, Guadeloupe, and the other French colonies rose to a value of 217 million livres, or nine million pounds sterling, approaching double the figure for Britain's Caribbean exports (five million).[6] The total area cultivated using slaves in the French colonies was now also considerably larger than the plantation area cultivated in the British Caribbean. Reflecting this expansion, the slave population of the French Caribbean colonies grew during these two decades from approximately 379,000 to 650,000. Meanwhile, answering to the high mortality rate, the slave trade, indispensable to maintaining levels of black labor in all the plantation economies, burgeoned. In 1790, only about half the slaves on Saint-Domingue were locally born "Creoles," the remainder having been transported from Africa on the slave ships. To avoid devastating the colonies, the Société maintained, it needed to proceed in planned stages, publicizing the black cause first, then legally suppressing the slave trade, something that, of itself, would end the practicability of slavery as the legal-economic basis of Caribbean plantation agriculture. Abolishing the slave trade would render the slave population a rapidly shrinking, inadequate labor force while simultaneously forcing slave-owners to treat their surviving slaves better, and improving the status of poor "free blacks." Only with these goals achieved could slavery itself be dismantled. Abolition, however, Brissot, Condorcet, Lanthenas, and their circle regularly stressed, would not be enough. The culminating phase was to educate and integrate both former slaves and those who were already legally free into society.[7]

The clashes in the revolutionary press and the National Assembly were fierce. Revolutionary propaganda was vigorously countered by the slaving interest and the Caribbean planters. The declarations issued by Condorcet, as the Société's president, in December 1789, were answered by Caribbean planters claiming the Société's ideals were impracticable and reckless, apt to plunge the colonies into fearful disruption, pillage, and strife. Initially, the democratic republicans made little concrete progress, as most deputies (some 15 percent of whom themselves owned properties in the colonies) were monarchists and modérés who were in varying degrees hostile to the Société and its egalitarian aims. By March 1790, some aristocratic émigrés reportedly drew more satisfaction from the wrangling over black emancipation than virtually any other current quarrel of the Revolution. Should the democrats indeed attempt to emancipate the blacks, they would surely open up an unbridgeable rift in the National Assembly, causing the colonies to secede and Bordeaux and Nantes to revolt. The consequent civil war and collapse of the Revolution could be expected to mean the triumph of monarchy, colonial trade, and the landed interest in both France and the colonies.[8]

The General Revolution in the Caribbean thus began with a war of words, an international battle of values and concepts centering on Paris with both the press and the arts enlisted by the philosophe-révolutionnaires to help shift public perceptions. The author of a novel entitled *Le Nègre comme il y a peu de blancs*, judged "mediocre" in the *Chronique de Paris* in October 1789, was nevertheless praised for helping change the way Frenchmen viewed blacks, especially by restoring "their virtues" in white eyes and hence fostering "love and esteem" for them. These excellent aims, noted the *Chronique*, echoed what "des philosophes éloquens et sensibles" had continually written in defense of the blacks in recent decades.[9] A play entitled *Les Esclaves* (reviewed in January 1790), which presented an imaginary conspiracy of blacks and Indians to expel the English from Barbados and emancipate all the non-whites together, was also pronounced "mediocre" literature but full of admirable ideas manifestly inspired by "Raynal" and the *Histoire philosophique*. The Paris stage, aided by freedom of the theater, could help propel "la réformation publique" and gradually weaken the defenders of the old order and "corruption."[10]

But the opposing pro-planter, colonial lobby also won notable successes in the world of the arts, press, and the theater. In January 1790, Olympe de Gouges's abolitionist drama, *Zamore et Mirza*, after three reasonably successful performances on 28 and 31 December 1789, and 2 January 1790, suddenly disappeared from the Comédie-Française's repertoire. This play, originally written in 1784 but not staged until the Revolution, now renamed *L'Esclavage des nègres*, centers on two fugitive slaves condemned to death for murdering a tyrannical slave-owner. It was forced off the stage by shouting and audience disruption, assisted by the actors' palpable reluctance to perform it, following a vigorous drive to discredit Gouges by the Club Massiac, a focus of monarchist sentiment and chief haven of procolonial money and influence.[11]

Disgusted by the intensity of conservative sentiment, this courageous female writer, who before any other French dramatist boldly presented slavery, divorce, and illegitimacy onstage, retorted by expressing her loathing of race prejudice and injustice in her terse *Réflexions sur les hommes nègres*, calling on France's "philosophes bons et sensibles" to fight together to rescue the Revolution from the "destructive efforts of our common enemies."[12]

Urging the slave trade's immediate end, on 1 February 1790 the Amis des Noirs submitted a fresh petition to the Assembly, signed by Brissot. The Assembly must suppress the slave trade, a "vile commerce" that totally contradicted the Revolution's principles, and especially the Declaration of the Rights of Man. Among other beneficial effects for Africa, Europe, and the Americas alike, French Caribbean slave-owners, once prevented from replenishing their stock of slaves, would be forced to better feed, house, and treat their blacks.[13] At the same time, the Assembly must move to secure for the free blacks and mulattoes of Martinique, Guadeloupe, Saint-Domingue, and Cayenne (French Guiana) rights equal to those of the whites, including political representation with their own deputies in the National Assembly.[14] Already, from late August and through the autumn of 1789, a small group of mulattoes in Paris, around thirty initially, under their leader, Julien Raimond (1744–1801), an educated and eloquent mulatto afterward suspected by royalists of colluding with Brissot and Condorcet to excite black insurgency against the white slave-owners in Saint-Domingue, were encouraged by the Assembly's republican deputies to organize. Mirabeau, Grégoire, and, outside the Assembly, Brissot and Condorcet, exhorted them loudly to invoke the *droits de l'humanité*.[15]

Through 1790–91, black emancipation remained one of the foremost and most passionately promoted causes of the Revolution but continued to be obdurately opposed by modérantisme, liberal monarchism, and the colonial interest. If the Société de 1789, founded by Mirabeau, included such advocates of black emancipation as Condorcet, Brissot, Carra, and Lavoisier, it also included allies of the Club Massiac and the colonial status quo, such as Moreau de Saint-Méry, Bailly, and Le Chapelier.[16] Unfamiliar with the actual Caribbean, Brissot, Condorcet, and their organization were continually accused by moderates of being led by the "devouring zeal of their *philosophie théorique*" to embrace disastrously impractical policies.[17] A particularly violent antiemancipationist pamphlet, entitled *Découverte d'une conspiration contre les interêts de la France*, squarely blamed recent disturbances in

Martinique and Guadeloupe on the Société des Amis des Noirs, its author predicting not just Caribbean mayhem, should they succeed, but the complete collapse of France's dyeing, textile, and luxury industries and merchant marine. The revolutionaries of the Société are here depicted as a diabolical "conspiracy" concocted by the British to secure "la destruction de la France." Attempting to free the French Caribbean blacks would allegedly blight all French prosperity, fortunes, and hopes, the Caribbean being the cornerstone of the French Atlantic economy.

Without her colonies, France would be deprived of 1,500 ships and the employment of those whose professions and crafts depended on colonial trade, estimated by this tract at five million people. Should the "conspiracy" succeed, France's commerce and industries would disintegrate and her entire consumption of sugar, coffee, cotton, tobacco, and indigo would in future need to be purchased from Britain. This violently antiphilosophique tract urged readers to consult a recent text entitled *Essai sur les Illuminés* "proving" that behind the Amis des Noirs lurked a clandestine sect, the Illuminati, whose speciality was proclaiming ideals that looked pure and uplifting but really constituted an insidious plot to annihilate empire, religion, and authority. Mascarading "under the veil of humanity and liberty," and the "modest and specious title of Société des Amis des Noirs," the Illuminati sought to plunge the "entire universe into combustion." Who were these "criminal visionaries, conspiring against the human race," this "horrible société" spreading revolution everywhere except England? Three in particular were denounced, two of whom, Duroveray and Clavière, were actually not French but Genevans, banished from Geneva in 1782 for democratic conspiracy. But the principal culprit was certainly Brissot, "son of a Chartres confectionist," who, like the others, had sojourned in England and even been "recommended" to the prime minister, Pitt, by that dangerous philosophical dogmatist Price.

Not content with sending emissaries to the colonies to incite blacks to massacre the whites, the Amis des Noirs relentlessly strove to abolish the vital slave trade. They also incited the effrontery of the Paris mulattoes, ex-slaves mostly banished by their masters for insolent intractability, and encouraged them to petition the Assembly to be declared "the equals of the whites in the Caribbean." The pamphlet concludes with a table listing the Paris Société's approximately one hundred registered members, among them five foreign associates, including William Short, secretary of the United States Embassy, and eight corresponding members outside Paris. Besides the "odious" Brissot, this tract noted the prominence in the Société of Condorcet, Sieyès, Mirabeau, Alexandre de Lameth, the Marquis de Saint-Lambert, Lavoisier the chemist, and the educationalist Lanthenas.[18]

A prompt reply, entitled "*Il est encores des Aristocrates . . .*" styled the Amis des Noirs as a small opinion-forming group inspired by the highest motives that neither worked for Britain nor threatened anyone. Their latest open meeting was attended by only around two hundred people.[19] The "infamous author" of the *Découverte d'une conspiration* apparently believed flaying the friends of liberty demonstrated "patriotism." If the French nobility were a disreputable bunch, the Caribbean planters were a thousand times worse, being a group who mercilessly oppressed their slaves, discriminated against "free blacks," and deceived the public. Only whites owning at least twenty-five blacks were admitted to the island assemblies. They treated both their slaves and the free blacks, estimated by some at well over twenty thousand, like animals. The free blacks, argued this tract, were just as numerous as the whites in the French colonies, yet they were not admitted to positions of responsibility or dignity, even though often braver, cleverer, and more useful to the patrie than the mostly indolent whites. Opposition to Les Amis des Noirs was nothing but a "vile pillar" of the most "horrible aristocratie."[20]

Between May and September 1791 ensued a fierce five-month debate in the National Assembly over whether the Assembly's colonial committee should be permitted, as Barnave and his associates wanted, to relegate all matters relating to the status and conditions of the free blacks in the colonies to the white-dominated colonial assemblies. In May 1791, owing to the efforts of the Société, the Brissotins, and the mulatto circle around Raimond, the National Assembly provisionally agreed that free blacks in the colonies should be given voting rights where they met the property qualifications. But the colonial assemblies flatly refused to accept this.[21] The calculated effect of Barnave's and the "moderate" royalist policies was to exclude the blacks from their political rights under the Declaration, from every public office, from expressing their views, and from every opportunity for upward mobility. Grégoire, Pétion, and Destutt de Tracy led the philosophique denunciation of the schemes of Barnave and the friends of the white planters in the Assembly. The free blacks of Saint-Domingue, declared Destutt de Tracy in his major speech on the subject of 23 September 1791, if released "by us from oppression, will be our natural allies; it is neither just nor *politique* to abandon them."[22]

To justify landed oligarchy and slavery in the Assembly, and bolster their strong monarchist preferences, white planters' spokesmen regularly employed Montesquieu's relativism of climate and conditions as a counterrationale to radical claims that slavery was unjustifiable. Montesquieu was by no means a defender of slavery as such but, typically of the moderate Enlightenment, he did defend the necessity of black slavery in certain practical circumstances. Montesquieu was not an abolitionist because he believed the practicalities stood in the way. Especially, Montesquieu's statement in book 7 of part 3 of the *L'Esprit des Lois* that "there are countries where the heat debilitates the body, and so weakens resolve that men are not brought to arduous labour except through fear of punishment: there black slavery seems less shocking to our reason" proved useful to the colonists' apologists. Among those who most utilized Montesquieu in this manner was Médéric-Louis Moreau de Saint-Méry (1750–1819), lawyer, leader of the Club Massiac, and author of several books on the Caribbean who served as an energetic deputy for Martinique in the Assembly.[23]

In the Caribbean, where whites could not easily work the fields, slavery, argued the planters' representatives, was "natural" and indispensable. Meanwhile, if the Caribbean revolution began as a cultural war in Paris, it quickly translated into rising tension punctuated by disturbances in the colonies. Certainly, the National Assembly's Comité des Colonies, formed in March 1790, was dominated by constitutional monarchists and friends of the white colonists, for the moment ensuring the planters a solid hegemony. The white colonial assembly meeting at Cap-Français, the main town of Saint-Domingue, France's foremost Caribbean colony, stubbornly rejected all concessions to the "free blacks," *gens de couleurs*—mulattoes who were in some cases substantial property owners and owners of slaves themselves—slaves, and the Assembly's Left democrats alike. There was practically no support among whites or blacks in the Caribbean for the radical philosophique tendency or republicanism. Several new, staunchly monarchist newspapers appeared in Saint-Domingue's towns. But how solid in reality was a white planter ascendancy underpinned by modérantisme, royalism, Locke, and Montesquieu in the French revolutionary context of 1790–91? It was impossible, even on the most conservative reading of the August 1789 enactments and the Rights of Man, to prevent growing friction between the Revolution's core values and Caribbean reality. A grand banquet organized at Port-Royal (today Fort-de-France) on Martinique, on 28 September 1789, to celebrate adoption of the tricolor cockade as the Revolution's symbol, was scandalously disrupted by white officers attempting, against the governor's orders, to prevent free blacks from participating.[24] White resistance to black emancipation in the French Caribbean held firm for three years (1789–92), but did so only because liberal monarchists retained the upper hand during that period in France. Supporters of white hegemony in the Caribbean faced a much stronger challenge once the Feuillant revolution in France, and with it constitutional monarchism, Montesquieu's prestige, and modérantisme, faltered.

Black emancipation remained massively controversial through the early Revolution but, until 1792, Brissot, Condorcet, and the Left republicans possessed insufficient clout in the Assembly to foment more than a general tension and restlessness throughout the greater Caribbean. While modérantisme and constitutional monarchy remained dominant, the white colonists' interests suffered no head-on legislative attack. They were aided by the fact that free blacks in the colonies were deeply divided among themselves, most of the wealthier fringe of *gens de couleur* supporting the "aristocrates" owning the plantations. Moderates and monarchists could not, though, prevent a spreading insurgency among a minority of free blacks. A first rising on Saint-Domingue, near Cap-Français, involving a few hundred free blacks demanding equality of rights, erupted in October 1790. Among its leaders was Vincent Ogé (1757–91), a wealthy quadroon (one-quarter black) who knew and admired Lafayette and was cultivated by Brissot, had spent years in Bordeaux and then Paris but found himself refused admission to the Club Massiac and the white planter elite in France. Resentment and self-aggrandizing ambition inspired him to foment insurrection on Saint-Domingue after arriving back there from France in October 1790. The rising was quickly crushed by the colonial authorities. Captured, Ogé was publicly displayed in Cap-Français's main square and, as a deterrent to the rest of the mixed bloods and free blacks, horrifically broken on the wheel and executed.[25] But this was no deterrent, argued Brissot's *Patriote français*: rather, it showed that the National Assembly should concede the "[propertied] mulattoes what they are demanding and what is just, the rights of active citizens [under the 1791 Constitution]."[26]

A new and larger insurgency in Saint-Domingue followed in August 1791, while in November 1791, clashes between whites and free blacks spread to Port-au-Prince, leading to a conflagration on 21 November that burned down most of the town. Each side blamed the unrest on the other. White colonists and the Club Massiac, led by Malouet, attributed the disaster and the wider black unrest in the Caribbean to the activities and propaganda of the Brissotin republicans; the revolutionary democrats blamed it on the blinkered, reactionary, and uncompromising attitude of the white colonists encouraged by Malouet, Barnave, and both the liberal and strict constitutional monarchists.[27] A sure sign of the depth of change wrought by the Revolution culturally and psychologically by late 1791 was the dramatic expansion and arming of the white militias and progressive tightening of security measures in all the French colonies. In April 1792, Saint-Domingue's colonial assembly permanently closed its visitors' gallery to hinder awareness of the radically novel terms in which Caribbean affairs were being discussed in the French press and Assembly.[28]

Developing in stages, the Caribbean Revolution reached a crucial turning point with the Paris Assembly's edict of 4 April 1792, a law partly ensuing from the free black (and slave) insurrection of August 1791 in northern Saint-Domingue, and partly from the Brissot circle's ideological campaign.[29] Introduced by Brissot amid a fresh flurry of antislavery rhetoric, the measure simultaneously formed part of the parti de philosophie's struggle against the Feuillants and Brissot's war strategy in Europe. The aim of this legislation was to end the white colonists' previously extensive autonomy so as to overcome French white Caribbean conservatism and monarchism. Charging the colonists with violating basic human rights, this crucial decree dissolved the old colonial assemblies. Full equality of persons among the free population, white and black, was proclaimed. Brissot's strategy was to reassert France's grip over her colonies by ending the racial hierarchy sanctioned by the ancien régime and comprehensively emancipating the free blacks. Shelving the slavery question temporarily, the Brissotins sought to win over the French Caribbean free blacks, converting them into supporters of the democratic republican Revolution.[30] The decree reached the outraged and deeply disconcerted colonial assemblies of Martinique, Guadeloupe, and Saint-Domingue during May and June 1792.

The Brissotin republican tendency in Paris opted for a high-risk strategy and thereby became the principal agent of the Caribbean revolution. Following the downfall of monarchy and the Feuillants in August 1792—and closure of the principal colonial lobby in Paris, the Club Massiac, and seizure of its papers—the Caribbean revolution proper began with the dispatch to Saint-Domingue of 6,000 troops (bringing 30,000 rifles), to assert the now fully republican Assembly's authority. With the troops arrived a civil commission chosen by the new republican

ministry, on Brissot's recommendation, headed by Léger-Felicité Sonthonax (1763–1813) and Étienne Polverel (d. 1796), the historian of
the Navarrese constitution. A hard-core republican ideologue of only
twenty-nine, supporter of universal education and vehement foe of the
Catholic Church (and indeed all churchmen), Sonthonax was closely
allied to the Brissot faction and firmly presided over this powerful commission mandated to transform France's entire posture in the Caribbean
(where he had never set foot before). Sonthonax fully shared Brissot's
enthusiasm for emancipating the mulattoes of the French Caribbean
and recruiting them as allies of the democratic Revolution. Writing in
the *Révolutions de Paris* in September 1790, he had predicted the European reactionary powers would not long be able to resist the "cries
of philosophy and principles of universal liberty" spreading among the
nations.[31]

Disgusted with the hypocrisy and reactionary views of the colony's
whites during the first months of his ascendancy on Saint-Domingue,
Sonthonax antagonized them in every way. Lacking specific orders regarding slavery, he vigorously implemented his instructions concerning
"free blacks," and especially the April law, reconstituting the colony's assembly on a new and democratic basis so as to equitably represent both
free blacks and poor whites.[32] The wealthy whites on the island opposed
him in every way they could, some conspiring with exiled monarchist
Malouet, who was now in London (and all of whose fortune was in the
form of property and slaves on the island) to bring Saint-Domingue
under British control.[33]

The achievement of Sonthonax and Polverel in establishing a functioning revolutionary government in Saint-Domingue, and enlisting
the previously mostly royalist "free blacks" to their cause, was no mean
feat given the isolated, embattled circumstances in which they operated.
They failed to end the slave revolt in the northern hills. But in a way
this helped, as Saint-Domingue's whites remained too alarmed by the
continuing insurgency to effectively fight the democratic revolutionary regime. For the moment, the commissaires kept the larger part of
France's most productive colony firmly under French control. By contrast, a smaller force of three thousand revolutionary troops dispatched
to Martinique was repulsed by the white colonists, now unambigu-
ously aligned with royalisme, counterrevolution, and Britain. Beside
the white planters and wealthier free blacks, Sonthonax and Polverel
faced stubborn resistance from the substantial body of white sailors
in Saint-Domingue's ports. Subject to harsh discipline on both naval

and commercial vessels, and largely illiterate, this disgruntled element proved peculiarly receptive to the fiercely reactionary monarchism and racial superiority complex rife among white colonists. Simultaneously managing their recalcitrance and black insurgency, while confronting Britain and Spain, now at war with France, was no easy task. To complicate matters further, before long the commissioners also came under fire in France from the Montagne as well as the monarchists. Robespierriste Montagnard authoritarian populism (like Rousseau himself) invariably showed less concern for ending slavery and for black emancipation (and noticeably more sympathy for the white planters) than the Left republicans proclaiming the Revolution's democratic principles.

With the Brissotin-Montagnard struggle intensifying in France, Sonthonax and Polverel pressed on with their Caribbean revolution. Dissolving the colonial assembly in October 1792, they replaced it initially with an interim commission of twelve, comprising six whites and six blacks selected by them and headed by Pierre Pinchinat and Charles Guillaume Castaing. Castaing, among Cap-Français's leading propertied men of color, aligned especially closely with Sonthonax. The commissioners also established a local mixed-race political club at Cap-Français affiliated to the (pre-1793 Brissotin) Jacobins. Several white royalist officers were purged. White resentment intensified. A dangerous turning point was reached on 2 December 1792 when Sonthonax summoned a force of several hundred mulatto and free black National Guards to face down a white militia unit encamped on the Champ de Mars outside the town, who refused officers of mixed race. Confrontation between blacks and "foes of equality and the law of 4 April," as the *Patriote français* put it, produced an armed clash that only narrowly avoided becoming a pitched battle. No slaves were involved, but the outbreak of shooting appalled the whites of nearby Cap-Français. According to a letter to Raimond from his brother, the shooting resulted in the deaths of thirty whites and six free blacks.[34] Worse bloodshed was prevented owing to the intervention of Pinchinat, a mulatto resented by whites as a leading advocate of black pride and ambition. He was eloquent, literate, and able to write. Pinchinat swayed the free black militia sufficiently to secure a general disengagement.

A less satisfactory outcome followed the next outbreak, the journée of 20 June 1793. Despite the commission's readiness to improve the lot of Saint-Domingue's free blacks, numerous grounds for friction remained, not just white opposition but also the prevailing lack of understanding for revolutionary principles among both free blacks and slaves.

Blacks were mostly puzzled or alienated by republican discourse and intensely disliked the white democrats' overt irreligion. Priests remained influential in the insurgent districts. Most blacks showed a clear preference for old-fashioned royalism and traditional Catholicism, repugning republican ideas, which to Sonthonax only confirmed that without la philosophie humans are blind to their own real interests. Blacks found difficulty in grasping the abstract principles of republican liberty and equality, he reported to Paris, preferring to assume it was "their king" who wanted to free them but that his royal will was being frustrated by evil councillors and the slave-owners.[35] The slaves seemed even more fervent for monarchy and religion than the free blacks.

During early 1793, an uneasy calm prevailed and the previously sporadic killing of whites in black-held interior areas subsided as Sonthomax and his free black allies widened the sphere of revolutionary control. If Sonthonax showed considerable sympathy for both free blacks and slaves, he displayed none whatsoever for the tenacious insurgency against the Revolution, which to him was utter madness fed by religion and royalism. Meanwhile, the white oligarchy of the colony's other main town, Port-au-Prince, openly defied the revolutionary regime and, in April 1793, had to be blockaded with the aid of local free blacks and finally bombarded into submission. As the town fell, hundreds of royalist, counterrevolutionary whites fled into the interior; others were caught and imprisoned. Jacmel was similarly reduced with black help. But with the commissioners and their troops operating in the northern interior and then the south, the situation in Cap-Français too began to deteriorate. The chief agents of subversion there, as at Port-au-Prince and Jacmel, were neither free blacks nor slaves but recalcitrant whites defending the colonists' supremacy and the old colonial assembly. The mood among Sonthomax's Cap-Français opponents, often white refugees from the black insurgency in the interior, or monarchist seamen and merchants whose activities were now heavily disrupted by the maritime war with Britain, became increasingly aggressive. A deteriorating situation exploded into a full-scale crisis on 20 June, when the Cap-Français sailors mutinied and set siege to the commission's headquarters, the governor's house. Units of free black militia rallied to the commission's defense. Serious fighting erupted, plunging the entire town into chaos.

At the height of the fighting, and entirely on their own initiative, initially solely as a local emergency measure, Sonthonax and Polverel offered local slaves their freedom if they would fight for the Revolution.

This was the origin of the famous printed edict of 21 June 1793 releasing Cap-Français's slaves from bondage in exchange for their supporting the embattled Brissotin regime. Many slaves responded with alacrity, rushing armed into the streets. The shooting and killing spread. Fires started. Numerous houses were pillaged. Finally, like Port-au-Prince earlier, the entire town was consumed by flames and reduced to ashes. While many mulattoes and blacks assisted fleeing or wounded whites, others cut their throats. Besides several thousand blacks, well over a thousand whites were butchered in this horrific episode. Whites who escaped did so mostly by reaching the vessels in the harbor, often bringing (usually) female slaves with them. The survivors were evacuated to New York and other North American ports.

The outcome of a sudden emergency, the 21 June emancipation decree nevertheless constitutes a veritable landmark in human history. Over the next four months, the emancipation process dramatically broadened under pressure especially from the blacks, the northern province receiving its own local decree, citing the Declaration of Rights, on 29 August.[36] By October 1793, all former slaves in Saint-Domingue were legally free. Officially, the colony had been transformed into a different world. However, of itself this failed to rally the black insurgency in the interior to the Revolution. Toussaint-Louverture (1743–1803), a former slave taught to read, who during the summer of 1793 emerged as the foremost black insurgent leader in the hills, rather than allying with the republicans construed "liberty" to mean independence from French control and playing the Spaniards, who occupied the larger eastern part of the island, against the French.[37] Toussaint-Louverture assured the Spanish authorities that in exchange for their support, and allowing black rebel commanders to operate on their own, they would faithfully align with religion and monarchy against the Revolution. Failing to persuade most blacks, the revolutionaries had to simultaneously fight Spain and Britain, both powers being determined to overwhelm the Caribbean revolution. Both invaded different parts of Saint-Domingue and other French colonies. On 18 February 1793, the British captured Tobago from the French. The British also recruited hundreds of French émigrés for action in the Caribbean as well as France.[38]

Sensational rumors circulated in the Caribbean (and the United States) that the new masters in Paris, the Montagne, repudiated Sonthonax and Polverel, their actions, policies, and authority. With the Brissotin overthrow in France, in June 1793, the victorious Jacobins did not hesitate to cancel the Brissotin commissioners' edicts and counteract their policies. As Robespierre's dictatorship was consolidated in France, the white antiemancipationist camp began recovering lost ground.[39] As with the social status of women, populist authoritarians, unlike the Brissotin leadership, showed little interest in black emancipation. Their ideological concerns not only contrasted dramatically with those of their Brissotin foes but, we have seen, from an Enlightenment and democratic viewpoint, were less sweeping, radical, and universal. Momoro's press had recently published a pamphlet concerning slavery by an author who readily conceded that it was the philosophes that had changed people's perceptions of the black race but also accused Brissot, Condorcet, and the Amis des Noirs of moving too far, too fast toward abolition. When representatives of Bordeaux's commerce point out the disadvantages to France of abolishing the slave trade and slavery, complained this tract, entitled *Coup-d'oeil sur la question de la traite et de l'esclavage des Noirs*, the Amis des Noirs simply answered, "froidement que la traite et la servitude sont une violation des droits de l'homme."[40] Under "natural law," argued Montagnards, abolition of black slavery was not really a "patriotic" goal.[41] "Le pacte social" is with the nation, not with humanity in general. To "prove" its argument that nation and patriotism matter more than universal human rights, the tract chiefly appeals to "nature," following Rousseau and Robespierre. Genuine, unqualified patriotisme cannot flourish "except by abandoning a part of the affection that attaches us to the entire human race."[42] Besides disliking Brissotin universalism, it suited the Montagne to blame the turmoil in Saint-Domingue and Martinique on Brissot and his allies. Thus, some leading authoritarian populists close to Robespierre, most notably the lawyer Jean-Pierre-André Amar (1755–1816), the official compiling the Convention's indictment against Brissot, vigorously sided with the white colonist lobby against the emancipationists. In a speech at the Convention on 18 November, Robespierre himself accused the Brissotins of being in league with Britain and deliberately arming Saint-Domingue's slaves to destroy France's colonies; Robespierre, too, like Collot d'Herbois (but also Camille Desmoulins), was at best ambiguous with regard to emancipating the slaves.[43]

The head of the mulatto emancipationist group in Paris, Julien Raimond, was drawn into angry encounters with Montagnard and procolonist opponents at meetings of the Convention's colonial committee and persisted in backing Brissot and Sonthonax long after it was safe to do so. Raimond was arrested on 27 September 1793. In January 1794, when Sonthonax dispatched Jean-Baptiste Belley (ca. 1746–1805), the commander of the "free blacks" who had led the defense of Government House during the Cap-Français fighting of 20–21 June and been seriously wounded fighting for the Revolution, together with two other representatives (one white), to France to submit petitions to the Convention requesting endorsement of the emancipation decrees and recognition of the revolutionary mixed-race regime on Saint-Domingue, they met with a distinctly frosty reception. The two Saint-Domingue delegates other than Belley were imprisoned also.

In September 1793, Belley, a freed former slave born in Senegal, became the first black deputy in the French National Assembly, another landmark in world history. During 1793–94, Belley battled tenaciously on behalf of black rights but faced considerable opposition.[44] The impressive portrait of him, placed alongside a bust of Raynal (see figure 10), painted later, in 1797, by the revolutionary artist Anne-Louis Girodet (1767–1824), who consciously sought to make France's first black deputy look formidable and yet "beautiful," became the most celebrated picture linking the Revolution with black emancipation. A disciple of David, Girodet was an ardent republican already famous in his own right, in 1793, for his defiantly republican behavior in papal Rome where he was then living as a student at the French Academy. The provocative sensationalism of the Belley portrait, and what later became his wider, more general challenge to David's neoclassicism, prompting some modern art historians to label Girodet a "herald of romanticism," eventually led to a bitter quarrel with David, who once later described Girodet as a "lunatic." An explosive personality, he sought to employ art to liberate emotion from neoclassicism's straitjacket, mankind from prejudice, and blacks from slavery.

Amicable relations between the white colonists and the Robespierriste faction based on populist patriotisme and common aversion to Brissotins did not last, though, beyond the end of 1793. By January 1794, with the Martinique whites openly colluding with the British, and those of Saint-Domingue virtually in open alliance with Britain and Spain, colonist collusion with monarchy, aristocracy, and clergy became too overt even for the Montagne to stomach. With most of the French Caribbean either in revolt or British hands, the Robespierriste Convention in Paris saw little alternative but to disregard Amar and the white colonial lobby and, if somewhat halfheartedly, embrace Brissotin general emancipation of the slaves and blacks after all. This transition was largely pushed through by Danton, who launched into another of his rousing speeches. It was his circle who in effect engineered the

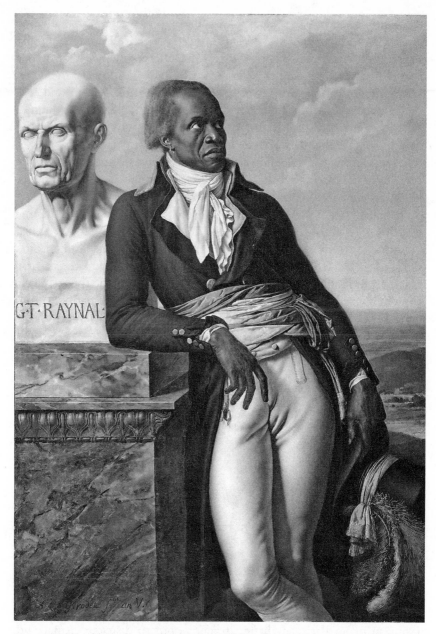

Figure 10. The black deputy Jean-Baptiste Belley (ca. 1746–1805) beside the bust of Raynal. Anne Louis Girodet de Roussy-Trioson (1767–1824), portrait of Jean-Baptiste Belley, 1797, oil on canvas. Inv. MV4616. Photo: Gérard Blot. Château de Versailles et de Trianon, Versailles, France. © RMN–Grand Palais / Art Resource, NY.

world's first general edict of emancipation of the slaves, dated 4 February 1794.[45]

The Montagne embraced black emancipation in early 1794, but not to the extent of dropping pursuit of the Caribbean Brissotins. By the time the orders recalling the commissaires who had freed the slaves reached Saint-Domingue, however, the Haitian Revolution proper was in motion. On Saint-Domingue, ironically, the battered remnant of Sonthonax's authority was temporarily resuscitated in May 1794 by none other than Toussaint-Louverture, who now entertained second thoughts about the wisdom of combating the Revolution allied to Spain and Britain, reactionary powers obviously intent on restoring slavery. Especially after the arrival of more Spanish troops from Cuba and Puerto Rico, he realized that religion or no religion, fighting France was simply not in his interest. Performing a sudden volte-face, he publicly disavowed the "enemies of the Republic and the human race," throwing his lot and four thousand men behind Sonthonax.[46] In May 1794, Toussaint-Louverture had apparently not yet studied the February 1794 emancipation decree. He knew about it, and the earlier Saint-Domingue emancipation decrees, only in vague terms. But as he himself reports in a surviving letter, he *had* studied their wording by June 1794 when he proclaimed the February decree happy news "for all the friends of humanity," and expressed a sudden interest in the progress of French arms in Europe.[47] Recurrent use of universalist Brissotin revolutionary language in his letters to French commanders, a style originating in the *Histoire philosophique*, has prompted the suggestion that he might have read parts of the *Histoire philosophique*. This point remains uncertain but, in any case, Toussaint-Louverture regularly employed Brissotin universalist rhetoric drawn from la philosophie moderne from the summer of 1794.[48]

The decree of February 1794, however significant in the abstract, had little immediate effect since the Saint-Domingue slaves had already been freed, and the British prevented implementation on the other major French islands by occupying Martinique in March and Sainte-Lucie and Guadeloupe in April 1794. Formal abolition followed directly only in Cayenne (French Guiana) where it was proclaimed amid fanfares on 14 June 1794, a few weeks before Robespierre's downfall. Remarkably, there was little resistance or protest. Under the terms of the emancipation decree, the newly created "citizens" were obliged to register with their nearest municipality to obtain certificates of citizenship and draw up contracts with their former owners, choosing whether to work henceforth for wages or on a sharecropping basis. Under regulations imposed by the colonial assembly, Cayenne's freed slaves were not supposed to move from where they had been previously domiciled to seek a new home or employment without the consent of proprietor and municipality. In effect, they were not entirely freed and did not always much benefit.[49] But they were no longer slaves.

Montagnard pursuit of the Brissotins was unrelenting. In June 1794, peremptory orders were dispatched from Paris for the seizure of Sonthonax and Povérel above every other priority. Eventually, the two principal agents of the Revolution on Saint-Domingue were captured by pro-Robespierre forces at Jacmel and returned to France where they were imprisoned. The emancipators of Saint-Domingue's free blacks and slaves were saved from the guillotine only because they had evaded the Montagne for so long. Shortly after their return, a week after Thermidor, the two Brissotin commissaires were released.

The French began recovering lost ground in the Caribbean after Thermidor, in the late summer of 1794. A leader of the La Rochelle Jacobin Club, appointed civil commissioner for Guadaloupe with responsibility to emancipate the slaves, Victor Hugues (1762–1826), a tradesman with previous experience in Saint-Domingue, arrived in the Caribbean with a small fleet and 1,200 troops. Facing far superior British forces, he succeeded in reoccupying part of Guadaloupe and waging a tenacious mini–revolutionary war from this enclave with black support. By October 1794, Hugues had beaten the 3,000-strong British army with their allies, the royalist plantation-owners helped by some local free blacks; the British commander was obliged to surrender his remaining troops, thirty-eight cannon, some free blacks, and 800 counterrevolutionary émigrés before sailing away. Several French noble émigrés were executed on Guadeloupe using a guillotine Hugues had specially brought from France. Guadaloupe's slaves were all freed under the 1794 emancipation edict; however, this same Hugues was later instrumental, from 1800, as governor of French Guiana under Napoleon, in the process of re-enslaving the freed slaves of the French Caribbean.[50]

The Caribbean Revolution, much underestimated and ignored, even by French writers, in the nineteenth and early twentieth centuries because it challenged European imperial sway and primarily assisted blacks, in fact rapidly developed into an event of profound global significance. Having liberated the slaves and crushed royalism in Guadeloupe, Hugues proceeded to organize a highly effective privateer fleet financed partly by the Republic and partly by private investors. Over the next four years, this fleet captured considerable numbers of British, Spanish, and American vessels. Hugues also dispatched expeditions that succeeded in bringing the whole Franco-Dutch island of Saint Martin under French rule (from 1795 until 1801) and seizing the Dutch island of Saint Eustatius. The struggle spread to the former French islands of Grenada and Saint Vincent, occupied by Britain since the 1760s, where French republican propaganda and standards inscribed "Liberté, Égalité ou la Mort" helped inspire insurrections of slaves and free blacks, led on Grenada by a legendary mulatto landowner, Julien Fédon.[51] During 1795, the Revolution also regained lost ground on Saint-Domingue and came close to conquering the key Dutch island of Curaçao, as well as establishing a foothold on the nearby Venezuelan mainland at Coro.

The French invasion of the Dutch Republic in 1795, and overthrow of the Orangist regime there, massively aggravated the already bitter rifts between the pro-British Orangists and anti-British democrats raging on all six Dutch Caribbean islands, as well as in the Guianas, most of which was then in Dutch possession. Curaçao became the focus of furious strife, and while neither side, Orangists or republican Patriots, favored emancipating the slaves, the latter, as French allies, could not prevent revolutionary papers and propaganda, or Guadeloupe privateers, from pervading the island. The major slave and free black revolts that subsequently erupted on Curaçao and at Coro in 1795 were among the biggest in the Caribbean arena during the revolutionary era and were clearly inspired in considerable part, as contemporary reports and correpondence indicate, by developments in Guadeloupe, the Guianas, Grenada, Saint-Domingue, and France.[52]

The Coro slave and free black revolt began on 10 May 1795 on a plantation in the sierra above Coro and spread rapidly to neighboring plantations. Besides blacks, local Indians joined in. Plantation houses were pillaged and some whites killed. On 12 May, a large force of rebels under their leader, José Leonardo Chirinos, a local *zambo* (son of a slave and an Indian woman), a free black married to a slave woman, descended on the town. Chirinos could read and write and while accompanying a Spanish merchant on several Caribbean business trips, had gathered information about both the French and Haitian Revolutions.[53] He was defeated by the armed militia assembled by the local white populace. During the subsequent pursuit of the rebels, a considerable number were caught and brutally executed.

The gains of the French and Dutch Patriots in the Caribbean in 1795 caused extraordinary apprehension in London and Madrid. So alarming did the combination of black slave emancipation and resurgent French and Dutch democratic-revolutionary arms, privateering, and rhetoric in the Caribbean seem to British ministers that it resulted in a major British counteroffensive that developed during 1796 into one of the largest military expeditions ever to cross the Atlantic, comprising nearly 100 ships and 30,000 troops. These joined the appreciable British force, already operating in the Caribbean, which was striving to overwhelm the Revolution in the islands, reverse the tide on Saint-Domingue, and halt black emancipation. Yet despite huge overall naval and military superiority and committing massive resources, this counteroffensive, apart from recovering Grenada and Saint Vincent and eventually occupying Curaçao (in 1800), proved broadly a failure. While the French dispatched far smaller expeditions to Guadeloupe and Saint-Domingue, these sufficed to hold the line. Yellow fever and malaria exacted an appalling toll. Altogether, it is estimated that approximately 40,000 British troops and sailors died or disappeared, through fighting, disease, and desertion, while combating the Revolution in the Lesser Antilles and Saint-Domingue from 1796 to 1800; many of the sick and wounded expired in Jamaica. In particular, the British offensive failed to recover Guadeloupe, the main focus of the French privateers and naval power, while draining off significant British (as well as French) resources from the struggle in Saint-Domingue, thereby enabling the black insurgents there to consolidate. Although black and mulatto representatives continued to sit in the French National Assembly from 1794 to 1799, by late 1797 Toussaint-Louverture had become virtually sole ruler of the French-speaking part of the island, the New World's first free black state.

Toussaint-Louverture's post-1795 isolationism and policy of disengaging from conflict with Spain and Britain eventually slowed the impetus of black emancipation. The Haitian revolutionary leadership in the colony's interior, keen to become independent, reassured the other colonial powers that Saint-Domingue's freed slaves did not intend to export revolution to other colonies, and would discontinue their collaboration of 1794–95 with the French revolutionaries. Sonthonax, saved by Thermidor, returned to Saint-Domingue and, in the coastal regions still held by the French, continued attempting to restore the Republic's grip, battling both Jacobins and white planters. Abandoned by Toussaint-Louverture, and with the area under French control steadily shrinking, Sonthonax was again captured by white colonists and dispatched to France shortly after the March 1797 French elections, which enabled the royalists briefly to dominate the French lower legislature and contemplate dismantling the Revolution. Sonthonax, ironically, was remitted to France to be tried for ruining the colonies for a second time, now by conservative monarchists. But again fortunate in his timing, he arrived just after the 1797 royalist resurgence was crushed by the coup of Fructidor. With militant republicans back in power, abolition of slavery was again resoundingly affirmed.[54]

The insurrections convulsing the greater Caribbean area in the 1790s, with their peak in 1795, represent a level of insurgency far larger than anything seen before 1790, or indeed again after 1800. Interaction between island revolt and the South American mainland was also more evident in these years than previously, or after 1815. Since the 1770s, disaffected Spanish American Creoles educated in Europe and imbued with radical enlightenment literature, men following in the wake of Francisco de Miranda, an enthusiast for the *Histoire philosophique* since the early 1770s, diffused subversive, radical ideas against the Spanish Crown and colonial system through the length of Spanish America.[55] In July 1797, Spanish authorities in Caracas uncovered a plot involving mulatto militiamen, *pardos*, *zambos*, poor whites, some regular soldiers, and also white officials and traders instigated by educated dissidents headed by a hacienda owner, Manuel Gual, a thirty-eight-year-old pardo barber of La Guaira, Narciso del Valle, and a veteran Spanish republican agitator and pamphleteer, Juan Bautista Picornell (1759–1825).[56] Although strictly defined, a pardo was someone of mixed race combining white, black, and Amerindian, the term by this time was often loosely applied to mulattoes. The barbershop of Narciso del Valle, where mulatto, black, and pardo artisans and soldiers congregated, served for many months as a veritable school of republican and egalitarian ideas and a recruiting center for revolution.[57]

Picornell had studied at Salamanca and, like Miranda, had become drawn to philosophical literature, especially the encyclopédistes. Sentenced to life imprisonment for involvement in a conspiracy in Madrid in May 1795, in 1796 he was deported to the Venezuelan fortress at La Guaira, near Caracas, where more than a hundred French prisoners captured in Saint-Domingue were being held and with whom he interacted, forming a new conspiracy.[58] Plotting revolution with discontented members of the garrison and residents of the nearby port, he held a series of clandestine meetings in his cell. Among the seditious manuscript pamphlets Picornell circulated in Caracas was a dialogue between two blacks, one French, that expressly propagated the French revolutionary idea of racial equality.[59] Gual, Picornell, and the Caracas conspirators aimed at creating a Venezuelan republic that included legal emancipation for the blacks.

If few blacks as yet were equipped to read revolutionary literature, Raimond, Toussaint-Louverture, and Belley were by no means the only ones who did. If black insurgents in the French colonies mostly preferred monarchism and Catholicism to revolution, some imbibed different views. General alarm at the overall situation in the Caribbean, prevalent among white planters and among the Dutch, Spanish, and British alike, reflected more than just alarmed, overwrought sensibility. Some Caribbean blacks espoused revolutionary ideas, and this plainly affected the character, frequency, and scale of the risings. In Curaçao, the presence of Guadeloupe privateers (with now predominantly black and mulatto crews), had a conspicuously destabilizing effect on the island's nonwhite population in the months preceding the 1795 rebellion, aggravating the rift between Orangists and Democrats. Repeated fights occurred between French sailors and Orangist members of the Curaçao military garrison. Blacks and mulattoes, often sailors from French ships, frequented gatherings in the popular district of Otrobanda where, reportedly, provocative songs were sung.[60] In all the islands, and on the mainland, existed a small fringe of literate blacks definitely susceptible to radical ideas. Charles Guillaume Castaing, like Belley and Raimond in Paris, assisted Sonthonax politically and ideologically. Other individual cases stood out. A defiant mulatto named Juan Bautista Olivares greatly perturbed the authorities and bishop of Caracas in 1795 by having reportedly read (and explained to another mulatto) a printed sermon discussing liberty and equality by a French constitutional priest. The bishop was horrified to learn that this black man possessed a whole library of books and knew all about the Rights of Man, which he was eager to expound to others. Arrested and sent to Spain, he was eventually released and returned to Caracas.[61]

The circumstances of the emancipation movement in the Caribbean in the 1790s proves those primarily instigating and exporting revolution in the islands and nearby South American mainland were usually white French republicans supported by blacks from the smaller French islands as well as Haiti. In Haiti, their main ally during the conflict of 1794–1800 was less Toussaint-Louverture, who increasingly detached himself from the French after 1795, than the mulatto leader André

Rigaud (1761–1811), a literate goldsmith born of a white father and black mother. A competent commander, from 1794, he militarily controlled the southern part of Saint-Domingue from where he pursued a more explicitly republican and pro-French agenda than Toussaint-Louverture.[62] The essential impulse behind revolutionary subversion in the Caribbean area in the 1790s, including Haiti, thus emanated from revolutionary France itself, as is demonstrated by the crucial roles of Sonthonax and Hugues. The principal agent of black emancipation in the Caribbean during the 1790s was unquestionably the philosophique tendency within the Revolution, that is, the Radical Enlightenment working through the Paris Amis des Noirs and the Brissotin faction.

CHAPTER 16

Robespierre's Putsch

(June 1793)

Dumouriez had to abandon his Dutch offensive, he informed the Convention on 12 March 1793 from Louvain, to prevent catastrophe overtaking the army. Six days later, the army of the north was crushed at Neerwinden. His shattered force fell back in a chaotic, headlong retreat, abandoning all Belgium, bereft of supplies, losing its equipment, and with many desertions. The defenses of Lille and the northeast's other key fortress towns were reportedly in a deplorable state. On 25 March, Britain and Russia signed their alliance against France. Over the next days, the Prussians overran most of the free Rhenish republic and, on 6 April, besieged Mainz. The Revolution stood on the verge of collapse.

Dumouriez chiefly blamed the war ministry's ineptitude, and especially Jean-Nicolas Pache (1746–1823), an official decried by him (and many others) as "vicieux et criminel," a scoundrel whose thieving and treachery aggravated the army's chronic lack of supplies and forced a chaotic retreat from Aachen where, disastrously, much of the French artillery was lost. With few exceptions, the political commissaires and fiscal agents posted in Belgium by Pache proved "rapacious tyrants," making every conceivable mistake and subjecting the local populace to vexations of every kind. Belgian religious feelings had been scandalously affronted, the country's holy cult objects brutally pillaged. Heading the war ministry since June 1792, Pache had been ousted in February by the honest Roland for gross dereliction of his responsibilities but been taken under his wing by Marat. Shortly after his dismissal, this corrupt "mannequin," so helpful to "Montagnard ambition," was triumphantly elected mayor of Paris, owing to powerful support, noted Fauchet, from Robespierristes employing their bullying and vote-rigging to secure "their candidate."[1]

With "our defeat," complained Dumouriez, Belgium's priesthood summoned the villagers "to take up arms against us," exploiting the revolutionaries' reputation for extortion earned by Pache. A war against aristocracy on behalf of the Belgian villager became a crusade of peasants allied to aristocrats to save religion. The Convention must halt the exactions and extirpate the rogues introduced by Pache. Dumouriez did not confine himself to berating opponents in Paris. The Convention's rule, he assured Danton while the latter was on inspection tour in Belgium, at the present rate would soon shrink to just the area around Paris. He was still more indiscreet with the three commissaires—Proly, Pereyra, and Dubuisson—accompanying the army. Whatever the Convention's 745 deputies called themselves, they were "regicides" and "tyrants"! Dumouriez alone could save France from their ineptitude. If the present performance continued, he would come to Paris and dissolve the Assembly, even if they called him "Caesar," "Cromwell," or "Monk." When Dubuisson asked whether he rejected the Constitution too, he called the projected new democratic Constitution excessively "stupid": Condorcet understood nothing.[2] Only restoring monarchy would save the Revolution, and he planned to use the army, he hinted, to restore the king.[3] Proly, Pereira, and Dubuisson were the first to warn the legislature of Dumouriez's pending treason.[4] The Montagne, holding off while he was successful, now demanded the general's arrest and trial as a covert royalist sacrificing "friendly peoples" to his vile ambition.[5]

Around France's borders and coasts, March and April 1793 were months of general humiliation and defeat aggravated by British naval action and blockade disrupting French shipping and seaborne supply routes. Provoked by mounting conscription and requisitioning, royalist-Catholic insurgency erupted on a massive scale during March in a largely rural region in the west, south of the Loire, the Vendée. Under local leaders, infuriated peasant bands fanned out in all directions, triumphantly decking themselves with crosses and white cockades, calling for the return of the clergy and monarchy. They stormed several small towns, the entire Vendée area quickly being lost to the Revolution. The so-called *armée catholique et royale* slaughtered numerous Patriots as they advanced. Farther north, again led by refractory clergy, much of rural Brittany also rose, fired up against taxes, requisitioning, and conscription.

Among prisoners taken by the revolutionary militias were several *réfractaire* priests, disguised as peasants, carrying metal boxes filled with hosts.[6] "Seditious" persons, actively fomenting resistance by disseminating circulars denouncing conscription and the Revolution, abounded also around Caen and Saint-Malo. A force of five to six thousand troops, reported the Revolution's commissaires from Rennes, would suffice to quell the Breton insurgency north of the Vendée if deployed quickly. The main revolt in Brittany *was* swiftly crushed but was followed by endemic guerilla war, the Chouannerie, which persisted in Brittany and coastal districts of western Normandy for years to come. Meanwhile, in addition to defeat in Belgium and the Rhineland, and the rebellions engulfing the Vendée, Brittany, and Normandy, much of Corsica also rose. On 2 April the Assembly ordered its commissaires to arrest Paoli for expressing "dangerous views," but their order to seize him arrived too late.[7] Paoli defected, assuming command of Corsica's counterrevolutionary insurgency and offering the island to Britain. French troops counterattacked. Paoli escaped to London. Later, in the summer of 1794, with British help, the Paolistes recovered most of Corsica, the island turning temporarily into a Catholic viceroyalty under the British Crown.[8]

Aghast at the shattering defeats, the Convention tried to sink their chronic differences. Danton rose to the occasion, determined to play a unifying role. The "Revolution cannot succeed, cannot be consolidated," he urged, in a furiously applauded speech on 27 March, "except through the people. The people are its instrument; it is for you to mobilize them en masse." Demanding a curtain be drawn over the wrangling of recent months, he passed over most of the latest unpleasantness. Vigorous measures were needed. Despite Brissotin hesitation, a special revolutionary tribunal with emergency powers, based in Paris and with branches in the provinces, was agreed upon and already functioning by 29 March. In departments where insurrection had broken out, those inciting counterrevolution were declared "hors de la loi" (outside the law), and were to be executed without trial.[9] The Assembly appointed a supreme Comité de Défense Générale, comprising twenty-five prominent deputies of both factions, headed by Brissot, Robespierre, Pétion, Gensonné, Danton, Sieyès, Condorcet, Buzot, Desmoulins, Barbaroux, Vergniaud, and Fabre.[10] But unlike Danton, Robespierre redoubled rather than ceased his attacks.

The show of unity, in fact, collapsed almost at once. In furious speeches at the Convention and Jacobins on 3, 10, and 18 April, Robespierre launched his culminating general denunciation of the "Girondins," vilifying "Vergniaud, Guadet, Brissot, Gensonné and all the friends of Prussia and Austria," and of Dumouriez.[11] It was necessary to finish with the "conspirators" in all the Paris sections where a fierce struggle was now in progress to disarm "all those who have given proofs of their *incivisme*," to chase away "impitoyablement" all "citoyens douteux" tarred with modérantisme.[12] The Revolution's misfortunes stemmed from defects of public spirit, lack of proper commitment, and excessive liberty of the press. The reverses stemmed from a blind eye being turned to "aristocratic intrigue" and painful indifference to persecution of everyone genuinely supporting liberty and the sansculottes. With the enemy at the door, within France "the people" were being "insulted." The "veritables traîtres" were not being dealt with.[13] Masters of the government and all the administrative bodies, the agents of the *coalition hypocrite* headed by Brissot, Guadet, Vergniaux, and Gensonné, had devoted all their might to undermine the esprit public, revive royalisme, and resurrect aristocracy, rewarding incivisme and perfidy.[14] The Revolution could not prosper without government, laws, and a public spirit becoming populaire.[15] Only when the people rose en masse against their foes without and within would the Revolution triumph, something possible only when the people found leaders fully possessing their confidence.[16]

Pressure exerted by the Paris sections for closer supervision of the army, and eradication of treason, intensified. The Republic was in direst danger, petitioned the Tuileries section, and yet, the Tribunal Révolutionnaire specially created to deal with the peril twenty days before still had not cut off any heads. Pouring vitriol on Dumouriez and Miranda, the Paris section Finistère demanded that the troops now elect their own commanders. On 28 March, section bosses sent a joint delegation to the Convention from all forty-eight Paris sections exhorting measures to alleviate the distress of the capital's poor, including reform of poor relief commissioned two years earlier but subsequently shelved, and accelerate eradication of "traitors."[17] With the enemy at the gates, the foe within was fomenting civil war—even in Paris. "Kings are loathsome," but no king had harmed France, averred Hébert's *Père Duchesne* on 8 April 1793, as much as "the villanous Brissotins." This "infernal clique" would deliver France to Austria and England unless all true Patriots rose as one to annihilate them. Arrogantly disdaining the sansculottes of the Faubourg Saint-Antoine, the Brissotins daily arranged for bread supplies to be bought up and hoarded by their valets in order to plunge the sansculottes deeper into misery. For unmasking their perfidy, Marat was pursued as if he, the people's friend, was the people's enemy! Marat—who sacrificed himself selflessly for the public good![18]

Denouncing Left republicans as traitors escalated as the situation on all war fronts deteriorated further, causing their very defense of the Rights of Man to count against them. Brissotin traitors were especially despicable since they had once been true patriots. Brissot, earlier the people's hero, defending their rights, was now a proven impostor deceiving countless gullible "imbeciles" (who according to Hébert abounded everywhere and were the Revolution's chief vulnerability), filling their heads with absurdities. Pétion, once venerated by ordinary Parisians as their "father," wallowed in baseness and treachery; his being "the people's implacable foe" was clearly proved by his backing Brissot "against the best citizens" during the 10 August insurrection and his perfidiously opposing Robespierre, the people's "best friend"![19] On 5 April Danton asked the Convention to empower the new special Tribunal to arrest and try suspects without prior formal indictment by the Convention. The Montagne wanted the Tribunal Révolutionnaire to have sweeping powers over the lives of individuals. The Brissotins demurred. Barbaroux, implacably opposed to Marat and Robespierre, urged his colleagues to stand firm against counterrevolution and royalism but not be executioners: "soyez législateurs, mais ne soyez pas assassins."[20] Such a measure, contended Lanjuinais, would violate "all the principles" of the Revolution. The Convention majority agreed, ruling that the *tribunal extraordinaire* could judge crimes of conspiracy and treason only after formal accusations were submitted to the Convention. The Brissotins had their way but at a cost, opponents styling them as waverers and prevaricators who were endangering the Revolution.

Dumouriez, having failed to persuade his men to march on Paris, on 5 April defected to the enemy instead. His departure unsettled Paris further, with exaggerated reports of the scale of the treachery, some ill-wishers estimating the number of deserters as high as twelve thousand. Only on 24 April did the Convention receive reliable news indicating that a mere handful of officers and men, six or seven hundred at the most, far less than defected with Lafayette, had betrayed the tricolor. This was greeted with rapturous applause in the Convention.[21] But there was little else to cheer: Valenciennes and Condé, where the garrisons had patriotically trampled Dumouriez's manifesto underfoot, famously vowing to conquer or die for liberty, were now tightly besieged by the Austrians. Dumouriez's defection, a severe setback for the Republic, was particularly disastrous for the Brissotins. When word reached Paris, uproar seized both Convention and the sections, the two sides heaping every insult on each other. Robespierre adroitly exploited the opportunity further to tar Brissot and other opponents as "Dumouriez's accomplices," a witheringly effective smear, as it was the Brissotins who had chosen him and extolled the general while he was winning. Accusing the Brissotins of betraying France and liberty formed the basis of the charges in the proceedings initiated in the Paris sections at this point, at Robespierre's fervent urging, and the surrounding publicity.[22] A general indictment was drawn up against twenty-two leading Brissotin deputies, and on 15 April, barely three weeks after Danton's speech of reconciliation, Pache delivered it in person to the Convention on behalf of the sections.

Amid the dismal catalog of reverses, Robespierre's and the sections' campaign to indict the Brissotins electrified Paris. Assuredly, not all Paris sections, much less all Parisians, backed the moves to bring the "traîtres" to trial. In around twenty sections, including Butte-des-Moulins, Mail, Lombards, Halle-aux-Bleds, Quatre-Nations, Champs-Élysées, Tuileries, Fraternité, Mont Blanc, Fontaine-Grenelle, Bon-Conseil, and Bonne-Nouvelle, local opinion predominantly condemned Montagnard "despotisme populaire,"[23] withstanding the arm-twisting and chicanery. Still, some of these were among the thirty-five Paris sections eventually herded into backing the Montagne's denunciation of the Brissotins, chiefly swayed by the ceaseless denunciation of the Brissotins as "enemies of Paris" and those principally responsible for the military setbacks, malignant men seeking to introduce all the horrors of *fédéralisme*.[24] How long, protested the *Patriote français*, were Brissotins unjustly to be labeled "calomniateurs de Paris," the city the Montagne dishonored? The real *calomniateurs* were those who ascribed the September massacres, February pillaging of grocery stores, and March "conspiracy" to the Parisian populace. Paris's true friends were those who attributed these "crimes" to "brigands," regarded with abhorrence by all decent Parisians.[25]

On 15 April, Pache and Hébert led a Commune general council deputation before the Convention on behalf of "a majority of the Paris sections," accusing twenty-two Brissotin deputies of conspiring with Dumouriez to "federalize" France by granting excessive autonomy to departments. The traitors included Brissot, Guadet, Gorsas, Pétion, Gensonné, Vergniaud, Lanjuinais, Buzot, Salles, Lanthenas, Barbaroux, and Fauchet.[26] Jean-Baptiste Salles (1760–94), a Third Estate deputy for Nancy in 1789, was a young physician, earlier a liberal monarchist and supporter of Lafayette, prominent among those who had called for Louis XVI's fate to be decided by popular referendum. Earlier a

Feuillant, Salles was useful to the Montagne as a means of linking the other traitors with Lafayette, as well as Dumouriez. Pache's presentation provoked uproar; the public galleries, packed with Montagnard supporters, wildly applauded the recital of charges, shouting "à la guillotine!"[27] But nothing further resulted since the Convention contained only around fifty or sixty deputies, sufficiently inept, gullible, or dishonest to espouse such glaring untruths. Ominously, though, despite knowing this rigmarole was totally false, Danton made no move to disassociate his group from the charges.

Most of the Assembly indignantly rejected the absurd petition. There was "a conspiracy" sure enough, granted Buzot, over the yelling, but it was the Montagne not the Brissot circle that was conspiring. He would not rest, declared Pétion, until the villainous Robespierre either proved the ridiculous calumnies he "daily vomited forth" or was dragged to the guillotine as he deserved.[28] Undaunted by the rebuff, the Commune printed the petition in twelve thousand copies and circulated it across France. Montagnard propaganda ceaselessly reiterated that if France was to be saved, "the Twenty-Two" must be arrested and punished. The drive to overthrow them was coordinated outside Paris by a five-member *comité de correspondance* of the Commune's general council, which ensured copies of Pache's indictment reached municipalities all across the country. "Twenty-Two" became a ritualized figure, carefully retained in subsequent petitions, despite changes in the actual names listed, some being removed to create room for others subsequently still more reviled.

Amid the general military collapse in March, the Montagne perceptibly gained ground, but Parisian opinion cannot be said to have run strongly in their favor. Robespierristes and Dantonistes enjoyed less support among Parisians than their own faction, both Louvet and Pétion maintained.[29] Fauchet also judged Paris's inhabitants "excellents" in their "immense majorité," meaning unswayed by the Montagne, if too passive in resisting the "brigands and rascals" manipulating the inner sections through the Jacobins and Cordeliers.[30] The Brissotins tried to counter Pache by filing formal charges against his obstreperous patron, Marat, their goal in pursuing Marat, according to Robespierre, being to provoke a movement that would furnish them with a pretext to "crush liberty."[31] Marat's arrest, along with that of the other calomniateurs destabilizing the Republic, was moved by Gensonné on 20 April, creating another huge tumult in the Convention. Of around 780 deputies, barely half were present for the ensuing Convention vote, the rest being absent or away *en mission* (a level neither higher nor lower than usual at this critical time). Of those present, 222 deputies voted in favor of Marat's impeachment, ninety-eight against, and fifty-five abstained.[32] The Brissotins undeniably remained the larger bloc in the Convention itself, as well as in France (and even probably Paris). The Convention majority resolved that Marat should be detained in the Abbaye pending trial, but all efforts to find him failed. The Commune retorted by placing Marat under its protection.

The reliably committed Montagne was indeed strikingly small. In January 1793, the elder Marc-Antoine Jullien remarked that the true "spartans of the Mountain, or should I say those that fought at Thermopilae," the deputies of "straightforward purpose and truly republican souls," that is, hard-core Montagnards, were only "about twenty."[33] He was referring to the genuine egalitarians. Dependable, regular Montagnard support in the Convention at this time amounted, as in the Marat vote, to well over ninety in normal circumstances. Authoritarian populists backing Robespierre, despite their grip on the Paris Commune and most sections, nevertheless clearly remained the voice of a minority, lacking broad-based support across France. Their formidable strength derived, in Paris as in some provincial cities, from the crowds of militant but erratic sansculottes sporadically willing to support them en masse under direction of the committees of the inner-city sections. But the sansculottes, though a decisive force in the Revolution down to the summer of 1795, were also an anarchic, inconsistent ebbing and flowing element, with little cognizance of the general scenario, much under the thumb of their trusted local *dominateurs*, forceful men with scant concern for, or knowledge of, the overall political situation. This means the Montagne, as a force in the Revolution, were good at bludgeoning but poor at persuading, and not just considerably less representative of France as a whole than the Brissotins but also ideologically precarious, constituting in reality a loose coalition of highly unstable, centrifugal groups intermittently rallying behind Marat and Robespierre but mostly decidedly confused and readily led in divergent directions.[34]

The Austrians and Prussians advanced while the Vendéean revolt grew in strength and extent, culminating during the very month of the Brissotin overthrow, June 1793, with the capture of Saumur and Angers (24 June). Returning from Corsica in late February 1793, Volney was among the "commissaires observateurs" dispatched westward as the Vendéean insurgency escalated. Appalled by the embattled state of the country, he strove with undiminished zeal to support the Brissotin executive, including his friend Garat, interior minister since 19 March. Reporting a catastrophe of major proportions from Nantes, he tried to analyze what had gone wrong in relations between the Revolution and the zone of chronic unrest, now provoked into a religious rebellion of astounding ferocity.[35] He could not help being afraid, he admitted to a friend, writing in June, lest "I, who have cursed the Koran" be captured by the "musulmans" (Vendéean insurgents).[36] Simultaneously, he was menaced from Paris by Marat's circle, who denounced him too as a traitor linked to Dumouriez. The fall of strongly defended Saumur, after a fierce battle, was yet another a shattering blow to the Revolution, the rebels capturing thousands of muskets, vast stores of munitions, eighty cannon, and eleven thousand prisoners.

The Vendéean uprising hugely encouraged the émigrés and exiled réfractaires abroad. By April, whole groups of refractory priests and monks converged on Western France from neighboring countries, making their way to the rebel areas, fomenting the flames of rebellion. Priests and monks reportedly labored to "fanaticize" the people by assuring them that heaven wished them to rise and fight the "impious horde" they proclaimed enemies of God, priests, and kings. It was decreed on 22 April 1793 that priests who had been deported, or who had voluntarily gone into exile and were already under the Convention's ban, if caught in France would receive the same penalty as insurgent aristocratic émigrés (i.e., execution). Refractory priests not previously proscribed but testified against by six registered citizens for inciting rebellion faced deportation to Guiana.[37] A few counterrevolutionaries began to be summarily sentenced to death by revolutionary courts for the first time in the Revolution. On 21 April, two men—one of Dumouriez's colonels and the former prior of the Abbey of the Trinity at Clisson, André-Jean Saint-André—were publicly guillotined in Paris, the latter for penning a brochure that summoned the people to revolt and to restore royalty, the manuscript of which he had delivered personally to the wife of a Paris bookseller with payment for its printing.[38]

The Convention's Comité de Sûreté Générale meanwhile received numerous warnings from commissaires in the provinces about the growing obstruction to army recruitment and to requisitioning, as well as a wave of royalist propaganda exhorting Frenchmen to rise and deliver the "young monarch and his august family from captivity." Paris allegedly teemed with subversives diffusing brochures and sowing sedition in public places, "principally the cafés."[39] Copies of some thirty different monarchist publications were seized from two clandestine Paris book-stores raided in late March. Royalist publications had a thoroughly undesirable impact even on republicans, it was believed, by grossly exaggerating the scale of the insurgency and exulting over military defeats. On 29 March, the Convention passed a draconian press-restraining decree aimed ostensibly just at the royalist press.[40] Anyone printing texts "calling for the re-establishment of royalty" or any other authority detracting from the people's sovereignty, or demanding the Convention's dissolution, would be brought before the Tribunal Révolutionnaire and sentenced to death. Distributors, street-vendors, and colporteurs selling such texts faced three months' imprisonment if willing to confess the names of the authors, printers, and persons from whom they received them, and two years if not.[41]

Thus ended, after four years, the virtually complete press freedom introduced by the Revolution. *Liberté de la presse* was replaced, observed the *Journal de Perlet* on 31 March, by a system of prohibition, limits, and license. Freedom of expression in engraving and political prints was likewise ended to prevent affixing to walls of portrait prints of royalty (and dissemination of pornography). It was forbidden to exhibit portraits of "Louis Capet" and his family, or offer erotic prints for sale.[42] But royalist publications, it soon emerged, were only one target of the efforts to muzzle the press. Furious at the Brissotin papers' disparagement of Marat and Robespierre, Montagnard deputies began using the new emergency decrees to curb the democratic Left republican press as well, where they could.[43] In rural areas and small towns, the press war was often the Revolution's central political arena, journals being the sole means of garnering details about political developments outside the immediate locality. Even the smallest local popular societies received at least one national paper regularly, and large ones sometimes more than twenty. The societies' reading and debating rooms, where the papers were digested, formed a projection of the wider battle. With the vicissitudes of the power struggle, papers were continually added to, or struck off, subscription lists.

In late April, a furor flared in Indre-et-Loire department, carved from parts of the former province of Touraine in the Loire valley. The representative on mission there, Jean-Lambert Tallien (1769–1820), backing Robespierre, and the departmental conseil général at Tours, controlled by Montagnards, set out to quash both the royalist papers and the Brissotin press. The town of Loches complained to the Convention that the local Montagne had banned no fewer than fifteen newspapers in the department, including the *Patriote français* and Gorsas's *Courrier des 85 departements*. Tallien was apparently also trying to ban Carra's *Annales patriotiques*, the *Courrier de l'Égalité*, the *Gazette nationale, ou le Moniteur universel*, and the *Journal des débats et des décrets*.[44] A similar fight erupted in the Loiret department with Orléans as its center, local Montagnards endeavoring to suppress every anti-Montagnard paper they could. If freedom of thought is "the most sacred of all the rights of most sacred liberty," commented the *Journal de Perlet*, only enemies of enlightenment and allies of intellectual blindness stifle this primary freedom. But it was exactly this that the Robespierriste bloc strove its utmost to accomplish.[45]

The theater remained a key arena of struggle. Latest in the sensational series of theater scandals to shake the capital during the Revolution was that of late March, at the Théâtre Montansier, a playhouse with a Bayonne-born female director, Marguerite Brunet (1730–1820). A former high-class courtisane, later entrusted with organizing entertainments at Versailles from October 1789, Brunet, now called Mlle. Montansier, emerged as one of Paris's leading pro-Revolution theater directors. Over the winter of 1792–93, authorized by Lebrun-Tondu and helped by a grant from the Republic's treasury, she introduced republican theater to French-occupied Brussels, performing Chénier's *Charles IX* and Voltaire's *Brutus* there through January and February 1793. The performances were, apparently, watched mainly by off-duty French soldiers since locals displayed only indifference or overt aversion. With the March military debacle, she returned to Paris and prepared a fresh staging of Voltaire's *Mérope* (1743), a play set in antiquity but topically concerned with tyranny, oppression, and civil war. Whether or not her views were influenced by Vonckist democrat and libertarian Lebrun (one of the Montagne's chief targets), she fell foul of a Commune directive of 31 March that added theater restrictions to the curbs on press freedom. As theater performances had "a powerful influence on the morale of peoples, they needed to be incorporated into the scheme of public instruction," that is, be more strictly controlled. Only plays promoting Montagnard virtue were henceforth permissible. Kings could no longer be represented except as loathsome tyrants. Among the first plays forbidden as "harmful," were Laya's *L'Amis des Lois* and Voltaire's *Mérope*. Voltaire's *Mérope*, explained the Montagnard deputy Charles-François Génissieux (1740–1804), needed banning because audiences would inevitably discover in it allusions relevant to current circumstances, thereby harming l'esprit public. The Convention could no longer obstruct the Commune's efforts to ban plays.[46]

Few if any, we have seen, among the better informed were likely to believe the Montagne's accusations against the Left democrats. Practically none of the highly motivated ex-patriot republicans in Paris did. Paine, Helen Maria Williams, David Williams, Mary Wollstonecraft, Barlow, Forster, and Lux all loathed the Montagne. The foremost Greek enlightener of the age, Adamantios Korais (1748–1833), who lived in Paris through the entire Revolution and witnessed the fall of the Bastille, Mirabeau's funeral, and much besides, keeping careful notes, considered Robespierre a "monster" and Marat the worst of men.[47] A bizarre incident, occurring in the spring, only deepened the gloom enveloping the ex-patriot community—the attempted "suicide" of one of Paine's circle, a young surgeon from Derby named Johnson. In mid-April, Johnson stabbed himself with a knife in the apartment block where Paine lodged, and announced he was dying, entrusting his will, papers, and watch to Paine. His will contained the stirring words, "I came to France to enjoy liberty, but Marat has murdered it. I cannot endure the grievous spectacle of the triumph of imbecility and inhumanity over talent and virtue." Paine passed the text to Brissot for publication in the *Patriote français* before, however, checking that Johnson was actually dead. When it was found that Johnson was wounded but alive, the whole business was converted by the Montagne into yet another example of Brissotin "fraud" and "perfidy."[48]

Paine wrote to Danton on 6 May, expressing profound dismay at the situation:

> When I left America in the year 1787, it was my intention to return the year following, but the French Revolution, and the prospect it afforded of extending the principles of liberty and fraternity through the greater part of Europe ... induced me to prolong my stay upwards of six years. I now despair of seeing the great object of European liberty accomplished, and my despair arises not from the combined foreign powers, nor from the intrigues of aristocracy and priestcraft, but from the tumultuous misconduct with which the internal affairs of the present Revolution are conducted.[49]

Danton, Paine realized, pursued a difficult, risky course, attempting to ease the Brissotin-Montagnard rift and check Marat and Robespierre, while simultaneously finessing the sansculottes and sympathizing with their economic woes. Even so, Paine believed, he was doing too little too late to save the Revolution.

On 24 April, Marat's trial began at nine in the morning; Marat himself, recently in hiding, suddenly resurfaced to answer the charges. The hearings, in which Paine and the *Patriote français*'s managing editor since October 1791, Girey-Dupré, figured among those attesting his unscrupulous activities, proved distressingly short.[50] No less than thirty-three Paris sections sprang vigorously to Marat's defense, calling for the extirpation of Brissot and his allies. So overwhelming and uncompromising was the sansculotte chorus that the divided tribunal judged it politic in the circumstances to terminate the proceedings briskly. After only six hours, at three in the afternoon, Marat was acquitted to tumultuous applause. His head crowned in a wreath of roses, the people's hero "was carried in triumph from the courtroom" by crowds of ecstatic sansculottes yelling, "Vive Marat! Vive la Montagne!" The euphoria was boundless. Returning to the Convention, Marat delivered a jubilant victory speech before being carried through the streets to the Jacobins, where such a throng surged in to cheer that the galleries collapsed, injuring five.

To help boost the public's adulation, a play entitled *Le triomphe de Marat, ou les Conspirateurs* was staged at the Théâtre de l'Estrapade two weeks later.[51] The Marat personality cult reached such dimensions, becoming so adulatory and aggressively *populaire*, it bothered others besides the Brissotins. To preclude automatic transfer of his body, after his death, to the Panthéon, as many were proposing, Danton (who had long distrusted Marat), joined with the Brissotins in early May to pass a resolution declaring that no Frenchman, whatever "services" he had rendered, could be buried in the Panthéon until minimally twenty years after death. Psychologically and politically, Marat's acquittal proved a turning point, decisively bolstering authoritarian populism. Not only had the Montagne consolidated their grip over most Paris sections, but they appeared to be extending it on all sides, aborting freedom of the press and suppressing basic human rights wherever they seized control, most flagrantly thus far in Marseille and Lyon but increasingly also in smaller towns.

Defeated militarily, the Revolution also faced a grim economic crisis. Conscripting vast numbers of men from the countryside, requisitioning supplies in the northeast and southeast for the war fronts, and serious disruption in the west, as well as the steadily falling value of printed money (*assignats*), combined to create chronic shortages. In Lyon, bread

Figure 11. Louis-Léopold Boilly (1761–1845), *The Triumph of Marat, 24 April 1793*, oil on paper mounted on canvas. Musée des Beaux-Arts, Lille, France / Giraudon / The Bridgeman Art Library.

prices, as in other southeastern cities, broke records exceeding—by over a third—those in Paris. At Grenoble, by early April 1793, bread prices had more than doubled compared to the previous year's levels.[52] At Montauban, bread prices rose by a quarter during the spring of 1793.[53] Everywhere, profiteering became a serious problem, making it easy for the uninformed to embrace Robespierre's accusation that the Brissotins were encouraging hoarding and deliberately supporting the interests of the rich against the poor.[54] Government efforts to restrain bread prices while upholding free trade policies, combined with assistance to those most deserving support, proved unavailing. In Paris, sansculotte indignation boiled over.

Impoverishment and unemployment blighted every aspect of plebeian life also in Marseille. Even so, in the great cities of southern France, the Montagne's authoritarianism, coercive methods, and obsession with surveillance antagonized not only republican democrats and conservatives but also distressed plebeians. The Marseille sections witnessed a vigorous upsurge of resistance to the vindictive, dictatorial methods of local Montagnards emulating their Parisian counterparts. Indeed, by the end of April the Montagne appeared to have already passed their zenith and begun to lose ground as more and more people saw through the charade. Earlier, in November 1792, Jacobin militants, led by Marie-Joseph Chalier (1747–93), a local manufacturer, destined to become one of the Montagne's supreme national heroes, the so-called Marat Lyonnais, triumphantly captured control of the Lyon city government. Lyon's Jacobins experienced no difficulty in converting their city into a redoubt for Marat and Robespierre, supported by the unemployed and poor. But it proved harder to keep the allegiance of sansculottes who had been promised cheaper food, especially as Chalier's clique, unrivaled at invective, proved highly deficient, not only in respect for human rights but general competence.

Montagnards, whatever they promised, could do little to limit the impact of recruiting and requisitioning, or boost the flow of supplies to the city, anymore than they could prevent the drop in output during dry periods caused by slowing watermills. They could not control flour and bread prices. What they did instead was supress criticism and intimidate opponents. Chalier showed the Lyon public what Montagnard virtue really meant, leaving the young lawyer Claude Bazire (1764–94), agent of the Paris Comité de Sûreté Générale, and his fellow commissaires, to help prop up what by April 1793 had become a thoroughly unpopular as well as ruthless local despotism.[55] The local democratic republican press, as everywhere in France, favored the Brissotins, not Chalier. The *Journal de Lyon* was owned by a certain Carrier who, from late 1792 onward had unceasingly satirized the *horde maratique*, lording it over Lyon. When they could, Chalier and Bazire decided to shut the paper down, seizing its archives and lists of subscribers, and arrested its editor, Fain. Carrier, then in Paris, was declared "dangerous" and his journal a cause of instability. He was only "dangerous," protested Carrier to the Convention on 22 April, to ill-intentioned intriguers, royalists, and "all those" of whatever faction "attempting to usurp the power of the people" and replace it with dictatorship.[56]

Striving to fortify their ascendancy in Marseille following the arrival of Moise Bayle and Pierre Baille as representatives on mission in late March, the Robespierristes launched a sweep against their rivals there. The mayor, Mourraille, and other allies of Barbaroux, were arrested on 11 April. The Marseille Robespierristes seized their leading opponents, but, as in Lyon, encountered increasing difficulties in the sections where populist intimidation failed to sway most working people. The Montagne's problem in Marseille was that the sections took popular sovereignty seriously and refused to bow to Jacobin arm-twisting.[57] On 25 April, twenty-two of the city's twenty-four sections repudiated the Montagnard municipality, confronting Bayle with an ultimatum: the people demanded restoration of order, union, and their rights. Two days later, Bayle himself was arrested, followed by the overthrow of the entire "joug tyrannique du club" in Marseille. Little blood was spilled at the time, though thirty-six arrested Montagnards were executed later.[58] On the night of the *sectionnaires*'s triumph over the Montagne, all Marseille celebrated, lit up with illuminations. The Brissotin *tribunal populaire* was restored to run the city. Democratic republicans boycotted the Marseille Jacobins. A few weeks later, on the same day as Robespierre's putsch in Paris, 2 June, the Marseille Jacobin club was closed.[59]

At Nîmes, the Montagnard société populaire, denouncing the Société Républicaine as aristocrats and crypto-counterrevolutionaries, likewise lost their grip and were overthrown. Spurred by the city's twelve sections, the municipality curtailed the société populaire's activities. Robespierre supporters were likewise toppled at Aix-en-Provence. By 27 May, in the whole southeast, only Lyon, Toulon, Arles, and also Avignon, where the royalist and papalist underground were strong, remained in populist hands. By late April, Paris seethed with reports of the "revolution d'opinion" in the Midi and of other successful coups against the Montagne. According to Louvet, the Montagne sensed that they must launch their coup quickly or it would be too late. Robespierristes denounced the Marseille and Lyon insurrectionists as aristocratic, royalist, and counterrevolutionary, and from then on it became a routine Montagnard accusation that Marseille and Lyon had been taken over by "whites," "royalists," and clergy, even though, on 6 May, commissaires sent by the Marseille sections expressly denied this, and while at Lyon too royalists were undoubtedly a minority among the Montagne's opponents.[60] If Robespierre's supporters were to succeed in aborting the Revolution of the republican democrats and Rights of Man, time indeed appeared to be running out.[61]

In Paris, the Montagne's chief difficulty was that of how to engineer much bigger turnouts in the streets than they had been able to achieve in February or March. For the Paris sections and Commune, it was easy to arrange small mobs of demonstrators. But that would not bring them to power. How could the Montagne martial large sansculotte crowds big enough to mount huge demonstrations? Their best chance lay in a further savage surge in food prices, such as occurred in the later spring. Montagnards substantially widened their appeal at this critical juncture by aggressively backing calls to halt the rise in bread prices. Marat's popularity in the Paris sansculotte quarters had grown in February through his openly inciting attacks on grocery stores and bakeries, criminal activity featuring in the formal charges against him in April.[62] On 1 May, the outlook improved for the Montagne: several thousand peaceful demonstrators from the three poor Paris sections of the Faubourg Saint-Antoine besieged the Convention, demanding strict price controls on bread and asking that property-owners possessing incomes over 2,000 livres annually be required to pay half that surplus toward the cost of the war. Approved by eight to nine thousand protesters in their sections, this petition rebuked the Convention for promising much but delivering nothing, not even the promised Constitution. Prices of basic foodstuffs must be fixed below a maximum. The crowds threatened armed insurrection if the emergency measures demanded were not adopted. The Convention, far from intimidated, argued over this for four hours, some deputies urging that the leading petitioners be arrested for menacing the legislature and calling for its dissolution.

The sanculottes could be mobilized with talk of punitive measures against hoarders and the rich.[63] On 2 and 3 May, while the Convention debated an emergency law fixing bread prices, food riots erupted in Rouen with sanscoulottes scouring the streets with knives and sticks. Many deputies sympathized with the hungry and cared about food prices, but they also saw the risk in attempting to impose prices at below market levels of driving supplies away and aggravating the shortages. Most were persuaded, not least by another powerful speech from Danton, to yield on this question nevertheless, to assuage popular anger. Exhorted by Couthon and other Robespierristes, on 4 May the Assembly fixed the Revolution's first "maximum," an emergency law stipulating limits on bread prices and obliging producers and grain merchants to declare their grain stocks and municipal authorities to verify the quantities declared, as well as impose the controversial forced war "loan." To enforce these measures, the law conceded wide new powers of search and requisition to municipal authorities, in particular in Paris.[64] A supplementary proposal by the Dantoniste Philippaux to compel bakers to bake only one kind of bread for all citizens, irrespective of whether they could pay for better-quality bread, was shelved for the moment.

The tussle in the Paris sections was crucial, these being the mainspring of Montagnard power. Trying to counteract the force of Marat's,

Hébert's, and Chabot's torrent of rhetorical violence and Robespierre's machinations, Pétion, as a former mayor, figured prominently along- side Louvet, Gorsas, Carra, and Prudhomme in local publicity clashes. Among anti-Montagnard pamphlets published on Gorsas's presses dur- ing May was an open letter of Pétion to the Parisians. He still loved Paris, he reminded them, imploring the majority to rise from their leth- argy and fight the repulsive bullies, capturing their city before it was too late. "How long will you put up with being governed by such a bunch? Have you overthrown royalty merely to place your necks under a still more loathsome tyranny? I observe Paris and I recognize her no lon- ger." How could ordinary Parisians let paid calomniateurs and the most contemptible types continually repeat the crassest impostures and lies, trampling on his and many other previously outstanding political repu- tations?[65] To defend liberty and justice, Parisians must show the same resolve and courage they did in 1789, and again in August 1792.

Hébert, Chabot, and Marat doubtless had some success in persuad- ing poor Parisians that Pétion had become an "enemy of the people." But it is a mistake to label the Montagnards as the people's representa- tives or a Left bourgeois faction aligning with the people. Most poor and unemployed, indeed most people generally, especially in provin- cial France but also Paris, undoubtedly preferred either one or the other form of anti-Montagnard politics, Brissotin, constitutional monarchist, or royalist. Only some of the most illiterate were attracted by Montag- nard tactics, propaganda, and suppression of freedom of expression, and there were enough of these to topple the Brissotins. Montag- nards appealing to the sansculottes were in most cases, including obvi- ously Chabot and Hébert, less genuine proletarian leaders than zealots for violent language and managers of aggressive intolerance and crush- ing dissent promoting dictatorship. There were, of course, also some authentic proletarian leaders more in tune with what is known of sans- culotte political culture, which especially stressed what has been called the "continuous, direct exercise of popular sovereignty," with the legis- lature's deputies conceived as *mandataires* subject to prompt recall and dismissal for failing to carry out the people's will.[66] Their political cul- ture was also much given to expressing hostility to the rich.[67] Political leaders, sincere in championing this sansculotte political culture, were undoubtedly striving to improve conditions for the poor. Furthermore, public "preachings" of the capital's Enragé street agitators, men like Jacques Roux and Jean Varlet, who denounced poverty and the oppres- sion of the poor by the rich, were not expurgated from Montagnard populist papers like Chabot's *Journal populaire* and Hébert's *Père Duchesne* until a later stage.

Varlet, a former postal worker among the capital's most effective populist street orators, was a genuine exponent of direct democracy who regularly complained of the Convention's "tyrannie législative."[68] Dismissed by Marat as a blockhead, he harangued sizable crowds of eager listeners in the streets for hours, denouncing speculation, engrossment, and hoarding. He possessed real empathy for the deprived experience of life among sansculottes in Bordeaux, Lyon, and Marseille, besides Paris, and firmly believed the sansculottes alone truly constituted "the people." He ranged shopkeepers among their enemies. An extremist Enragé, he wanted to see all nobles in France purged from public and military positions. The problem for the Montagne was that he and his comrades were honest idealists at odds with Marat and Robespierre.[69] Strongly motivated proletarian leaders, men like Roux, Varlet, Fournier, and Guzman, could be counted on to resist Robespierre and Marat. But they also blamed the Brissotins for the high food prices, and offered only a very narrowly framed political and social program. They were neither democrats nor republicans in any broad sense, but did speak for the sansculottes, showing that, in their majority, these were not under the thumb of the Montagne.

In Paris, tension rose, as food shortages and stepped-up recruiting for the Vendée and Belgium frayed tempers further. Marat poured invective on the Brissotin leaders as Robespierre sporadically joined in the rhetorical assault on the rich, assuring listeners "the people" needed to fight the criminal intentions of the bankers, financiers, and wealthy bourgeois—a rhetoric he adhered to, though only briefly and opportunistically, during these weeks, while his main point remained the need, as he saw it, to crush every variety of contre-révolutionnaire. The (Brissotin) "conspirators," who invaded the sections and covered their evil intentions with the mask of patriotisme, had to be unmasked and eradicated without delay.[70] Clashes between pro-Montagne sansculottes and often better-dressed "Muscadins," emanating from the more affluent quarters of town—street rowdies and activists encouraged by Pétion and other Brissotin leaders to form gangs and chase off the Montagnards—lent a distinct hint of class warfare to the stuggle, as did talk of forced loans from the rich. Pétion strove to mobilize the "honnêtes gens" against those willing to believe Montagnard propaganda. Like Lafayette, a vile "jean-foutre," according to *Le Père Duchesne*, Pétion was more "dangerous" than anyone: the Feuillants loathed him when he defended the sansculottes, but allegedly now sang his praises, realizing Pétion was really a tartuffe defending "royalty." A new Saint Bartholomew Day massacre loomed, and it was liberty's "best friends," Robespierre and Marat, who would be martyred if these "traitors" triumphed. If the plotters succeeded in engineering a contre-révolution, they would surely render the sansculottes more wretched than the lowest beasts of burden. *Le Père Duchesne* would fight to the last, undaunted by the prospect of death at the hands of such scum as Pétion.

What chiefly dismayed Hébert (and there is no reason to doubt Hébert's sincerity here) was the "indifference of most *sans-culottes*" who in their majority unaccountably failed to discern the "betrayal" all around. To defeat la contre-révolution, the sansculottes must rush to arms and annihilate all the *fripons* and traitors, but they were not doing so.[71] According to Pétion, only around five or six hundred hard-core militants staffed Robespierre's well-honed intrigue, propaganda, and vote-rigging machine, a mechanism that had conquered Paris superficially but did not represent local opinion. Chabot actually admitted that most young men in Paris were what he called Brissotin *contre-révolutionnaires.*"[72] The secret of the Montagne's success, held Pétion, was the gullibility and simplicity of a few honest citizens, aided by the deplorable lethargy of the great majority. The essence of the new populist tyranny was its use of professional hacks to dragoon the least aware, and then claim the section assemblies and officials were implementing what the people wanted. The people mostly failed to understand what the section bosses' real intentions were.[73] But they were still not easily dragooned in large numbers.

How vastly, complained Pétion, the Paris Jacobin Club had degenerated from its original character! No longer deeply divided, they had drastically narrowed and ceased being an arena for debate and free expression. Formerly, the Jacobins had been an association of enlightened men actively shaping the "public spirit" of the nation, burning with love of liberty, propagating only enlightenment and "les bons principes."[74] Captured by a despotic leadership, they had become something never known previously—"a school of lies and calumny." Open daily, regularly attended by some two thousand listeners, the Paris Jacobins had refined the art of mass deception, developing a method of deluding ordinary folk that even the most corrupt royal courts had never dreamed of. Untruth and misinformation endlessly repeated, they had discovered, is what most effectively mobilizes an ignorant public. False and improbable "facts" were broadcast with the utmost audacity. Paradoxically, the "ignorance and credulity of the people" was equally the explanation offered by Chabot's *Journal populaire* for how Pétion could have been so applauded in Paris earlier, and remained popular now despite his "vile" fédéralisme and continually betraying "the people."[75]

The Paris sections were split with six or seven adamantly resisting Montagnard bullying, creating a rift so bitter many momentarily forgot the emergencies in the northeast, the Vendée, and on the Rhine.[76] When Buzot rebuked the Commune for treating protesters from section Champs-Élysées, like Lafayette had treated the Champs de Mars petitioners, a furious chorus erupted from the Convention galleries of "à l'Abbaye" (to prison with him). "Yes," retorted Buzot ominously, "we must crush 'the new tyranny' or die: oppressed citizens of Paris, unite behind the Convention in resisting the yoke of these *despotes* calling themselves *patriotes* and republicans!"[77] In sections Champs-Élysées, Mail, De la Butte des Moulins, Lombards, and De la Fraternité, anti-Montagne public petitions were drawn up, swearing to maintain liberty and defend the Convention from the looming threat of Montagnard insurrection and warning of the perfidy of those who turned Liberty into "a goddess fed on blood." The section assemblies, complained the Commune, were being invaded by Brissotin aristocrats and *modérés*. More vigorous purges and arrests were needed to stop the counteroffensive. Surveillance of citizens and seizure of suspects were stepped up, but so were the protests. On 10 May, a Lombards section deputation asked the Convention to order the release of a "republican citizen" and "excellent patriot" imprisoned at the Conciergerie merely for complaining at a section meeting about the arbitrary arrests.[78] Testimonies were presented vouching for this citizen's civisme, causing an irate Robespierre to berate the delegation as a "batch of merchants" allied to nobles and privilégiés bent on contre-révolution. The petitioners should be behind bars beside the culprit. It astonished him that they had "protectors" in the Convention.

Almost every day during the nine months the Brissotins dominated the Convention (August 1792–May 1793), Levasseur recalled later, they accused Robespierre's and Danton's supporters of betraying the Revolution and obstructing finalization of the Constitution.[79] Condorcet and his colleagues, deeply dispirited by May, tried one last time to secure acceptance of their so laboriously wrought constitution. He resubmitted his draft constitution on 13 May in one of his last appearances at the Convention rostrum, trying, together with five other members of the Comité de Constitution, to counter the obstructionism of the Montagne. Again his constitution was dismissed, rightly Levasseur thought, as too "academic" and suffused with "questions métaphysiques." If the deputies had still failed to adopt a constitution by November 1793, Condorcet urged the Convention to agree, they should at least authorize new elections so that a fresh Convention could be chosen.[80]

Economic distress fed the impulse to insurrection during late spring 1793. But how long would the added boost continue? Conscious of their reverses in Marseille, Nîmes, Aix, and Lyon, and their difficulties in rallying genuinely broad mass support against the Convention, Montagnard bosses from twenty-six Paris sections could not afford to play for time. They had to concert their efforts swiftly and vigorously. Section delegates had in fact been convening secretly, from late March, at the Evêché, a hall adjoining Notre Dame cathedral, where they planned the use of especially vigorous crowd mobilization and propaganda techniques to escalate street support sufficiently to "save the country and liberty."[81] Facing an obvious emergency, the Convention considered proposals to temporarily move the Assembly from Paris to Bourges or some other town. On 18 May, over fierce Montagnard objections, with Danton also disapproving, a Convention majority adopted Guadet's motion to establish a Commission of Twelve (Commission de Douze), consisting of a mix of neutrals and Brissotins—but no Montagnards—to investigate insurrectionary conspiracy in Paris and examine the Paris Commune's records. The commission was to recommend countermeasures against the rampant misconduct, vote-rigging, and manipulation. The denouement could not be far off.[82] *Machinateurs* manipulating opinion in the inner sections, according to rumors, were scheming to engineer a massive insurrection far bigger than the February and March demonstrations. If most Parisians impassively scorned the "brigands," commented Fauchet, the most ignorant had been sufficiently "fanaticized" to make such plans for action practicable. Women, he predicted, would start the disturbances by clamoring for bread, and prearranged gangs of men would then rush to their aid.[83]

The commission set to work gathering incriminating evidence and, on 24 May, ordered the arrest of Hébert, Varlet, Claude-Emmanuel Dobsen (1743–1811), president of the section La Cité, and other known "conspirators," or as the Montagnard press preferred to call them, "brave heroes" of 14 July 1789 and 10 August 1792.[84] Sixteen Paris sections reacted indignantly, petitioning for the prisoners' release and immediate suppression of the "duodecimvirate." This became the populists' new war cry.[85] On 26 May, seeing there was now no turning back, Robespierre delivered one of the most decisive speeches of his career at the Jacobins, openly calling on the Paris populace to rise up against the "corrupt deputies" in the Convention and stop the Commission de Douze. For the first time in the Revolution, Robespierre directly instigated armed insurrection. Some sections supported him with alacrity, their revolutionary committees immediately setting to work to arrest individuals known for making critical remarks about Robespierre, Marat, and the revolutionary committees, but others, including Arsenal, where bitter internecine strife erupted, did not.[86] Hoping to bring out the citizenry in impressive force, Pache and the Commune leadership ordered the sounding of the tocsin and tambour that same day, and crowds, especially of women, gathered, clamoring for Hébert's release.[87]

Yet the size of the crowds on 26 May was not very impressive. Robespierre, Marat, Pache, and their supporters faced a serious dilemma. On 27 May, a day supposedly entirely devoted to discussing the Constitution in the Assembly, the Montagne tried to do better and did mobilize a significant ferment around the Convention. As spokesmen, a deputation from section De la Cité, carrying a banner inscribed "The Rights of Man and the Citizen Violated," surmounted by a red liberty bonnet, demanded release of their "president." The presiding deputy, Maximin Isnard (1755–1825), a Provençal known for advocating harsh action against émigrés and refractory clergy, was outraged. One of the few Brissotins who had voted against the appel au public, Isnard berated the rioters to their faces, telling them that "tyranny," whether dressed up with golden frills or sansculotte rags, is still tyranny. He was pushed aside, though, and a motion to suppress the Commission of Twelve was successfully carried at a moment of low attendance in the Assembly. Hébert, Varlet, and the others were released, to the great jubilation of the crowds, and escorted through the streets. But the Montagnard leadership was unable to build on their initial success because the crowds dispersed too quickly, and deputy attendance at the Convention increased later in the day. The Brissotins then secured a Convention majority vote (279 to 239 votes), reversing the earlier resolution and reinstating the Commission of Twelve.[88]

Robespierre, Marat, and their supporters could not overthrow their opponents without bringing out larger sansculotte crowds, applying heavier pressure, and intimidating the Convention more vigorously. This, they realized, could be done only by deploying carefully planned, organized force. On 28 May, a circular reached the section secretaries, summoning the pro-Montagne sections each to send two representatives with unlimited powers to an emergency meeting at the Evêché to concert measures massively to boost street support. On 29 May, sixty-six delegates, mostly professionals and merchants but with a sprinkling of artisans, including the Enragé leaders Varlet and Leclerc,[89] duly agreed the details entrusting direction of the rising to their Comité Central Révolutionnaire, twenty-five insurrectionary managers including Dobsen, Varlet, and the lawyer Jean-Baptiste Loys, the last termed by his fellow Marseillais, Barberoux, a "madman" thirsting for dictatorship.[90]

The supposedly sansculotte rising proper commenced at three in the morning on 31 May, with Varlet ordering the ringing of the bells of Notre Dame, followed by general bell-ringing and thunderous drum-beating, the veteran crowd managers pulling out all the stops, the whole operation directed, observed Fréron (no friend of the Brissotins), by just these few dozen section bosses, among them Andrés Maria Guzmán, a Frenchman of Andalusian extraction nicknamed Don Tocsinos after the alarm bell he constantly plied, and François Hanriot (1761–94), a former minor official born of a Nanterre peasant family, now appointed commander of the Paris National Guard by Dobsen, who acted with other Robespierre agents in the name of the Commune. As before, once gathered in the streets, the multitude, though larger this time, had not the slightest idea, Fréron and Mercier both emphasized, why their section leaders had summoned them, what they were meant to do, or where to go. Every step was orchestrated by the crowd managers, with nothing spontaneous or genuinely transacted by the people. Thus, the subsequently much-vaunted "popular insurrection" of 31 May, like that of 2 June, was really a preposterous charade. A crucial ploy was the cry—a flagrant fiction—that a "royalist insurrection" had broken out under the white cockade and royalist flags in the Butte des Moulins and fifteen other sections defying the Montagne.[91]

The first objective was to crush support in the Paris sections for the modérés and contre-révolutionnaires, as the Montagnards called their foes. A full-scale battle erupted in the Place du Carrousel outside the Convention where some two thousand pro-Brissotins fought the insurrectionists for a time. Groups of armed men roamed the streets. Once the streets were under Montagnard control, a purge of the Commune ensued to remove all residual dissent. One of the most effective measures taken by the planners of the uprising was the cutting of all communication between the Convention and the outside world so as to prevent letters reaching towns and departments around the capital and sounding the alarm. The insurgents' strategy was to prevent help from arriving before the Convention's resistance could be broken by the misled crowds. By late morning, the Convention, in session from 6:00 AM until 10:00 that evening, found itself cut off and completely surrounded by the multitude, headed by section assembly delegations. What "the people" demanded, the Convention was told, was for Marat and Robespierre to be empowered to lead the Revolution. However, for many hours, most centrist and Brissotin deputies refused to be intimidated.

The Brissotins' frightful "crimes" were intoned to the crowds and the Convention by the section spokesmen: they were the true authors of the Vendée rebellion. For too long these "traitors flattering our enemies' hopes and denouncing imaginary plots" in order to promote real ones had maligned "Paris" and maliciously deprived "the people" of the Constitution they so longed for.[92] "Législateurs," one orator, furiously applauded from the galleries, exhorted the floating center, "we must crush the designs of these vile plotters continually betraying the people." "The people" refuse any longer to tolerate resistance to "their will." Having overcome *le despotisme* on the immortal 10 August, "we shall fight the tyrants scheming to re-establish it to the last breath." Hour after hour, the Convention deputies sat tight as Montagne deputies underscored this chorus, denouncing the "great conspiracy." The Revolution, they insisted, could be saved only by the brave sansculottes guided by Robespierre, some speakers adding that workers "sacrificing their time for the Republic," "defending" the Revolution so heroically, should be paid at the rate of 40 sous daily.[93] As Michelet pointed out long ago,[94] every one of the insurgents' charges against the Gironde were as groundless and absurd as Hébert's accusing the Brissotins of removing bread stocks from the bakeries at night, and deceitful as Marat's claiming Pétion and Brissot were the true authors of the September atrocities. They had got just one word wrong in their script, retorted Guadet to the *petitionnaires*, against booing and yells of "calmoniateur!" from the galleries: instead of "*discovering* a great conspiracy," they should say that they had come to "*implement* a great conspiracy." It was plain enough who the conspirators were.[95]

The coup almost succeeded on 31 May. National Guard contingents appeared under Hanriot to tighten the siege of the Convention. A notorious ruffian with great personal prestige among the toughs of the Faubourg Saint-Marceau, and soon among Robespierre's most crucial aides, Hanriot played a pivotal part in directing the insurrection and menacing the Assembly.[96] Whether they wished to or not, the Convention must arrest the twenty-five traitors. All the Brissotin traitors threatening Paris with devastation must be detained. All were guilty of obstructing the Constitution. Their removal would be followed by the long-delayed Constitution swiftly being adopted.[97] But the intimidation of 31 May failed in the end because the conspirators were unable to sustain the distinctly lukewarm sansculotte pressure long enough. By the time Robespierre rose to follow up on Hanriot and bring everything to a conclusion, demanding compliance with the section delegations' demands, most of the crowd, thoroughly baffled and uninterested in Robespierre's designs, were already drifting away.[98]

The 31 May rising failed after all, due to tepid sansculotte support. In Lyon, meanwhile, Chalier had silenced individual opponents but encountered serious trouble in the streets. Crisis erupted on 24 May when a crowd of hungry women ransacked a warehouse containing requisitioned army supplies. The Convention's representatives on mission ordered troops from the southeastern front to Lyon, provoking the sections to rise against the Jacobin municipality. The Montagne tried to retain power in their usual manner, through brusque repression. The Lyon section assemblies were forbidden to convene, reported the Convention's commissaires on 28 May, having been infiltrated by "suspect persons."[99] But on 29 May, as the Paris section managers plotted their uprising, a full-scale insurrection engulfed Lyon, and Chalier was overthrown, arrested, and imprisoned. (He was subsequently guillotined on 16 July.) Left republicans took over the municipality, while the Jacobins denounced as a "federalist" rising what in fact was a variegated, broad-based, anti-Montagnard movement of Brissotins, monarchists of various stripes, and the generally just disgruntled. The common thread was rejection of Chalier and populist tyranny.

Simultaneously, a genuinely "Catholic and royal army" of eight thousand, reportedly headed by fifty refractory priests inspired by the Vendée rebellion and commanded by the lawyer Marie-André Charrier (d. 1793), who in 1789 had been a deputy in the Estates-General, gathered in the countryside north of Montpellier. By 27 May, Charrier's force had captured Mende, Randon, and Marvejols, everywhere tearing up tricolor flags, cutting down liberty trees, hauling up the white banner of royalism, restoring nuns to their convents, burning archives, and pointedly releasing political prisoners and replacing them with patriots.[100] Charrier issued his orders in the name of "Louis-Stanislaw Xavier de France, regent of the kingdom" (the future Louis XVIII).

With both Lyon and Marseille lost to the Montagne, Robespierre and Marat, and their chief agents, as well as Hébert, Danton, Chaumette, and the Enragé leaders supporting them, were boxed in a tight corner: they had to try again without delay or risk losing all chance of exploiting popular discontent to break the Convention. With France in an uproar, over the next few days Robespierre's cause was aided by news of further setbacks in the Vendée, the so-called royalist rising in Lyon, and the real royalist-Catholic insurgency in La Lozère and Ardèche. Yet again, Pache, Hanriot's officers, and the section bosses pulled out all stops, launching their culminating effort on 2 June. Huge crowds, some said more than eighty thousand strong, poured into the streets, furious, but again, according to Picqué, Mme. Roland, Louvet, Fréron, and Mercier, only the poorest, most illiterate, and unaware fed the most self-contradictory nonsense with little grasp of what was happening, or how they were being used to gag the Convention and install a Montagnard dictatorship.[101] Marat, Hanriot, Guzman, and the rest worked up the crowds, as did the butcher Louis Legendre, promising to annihilate "all the scoundrels."[102] As long as the *conspirateurs* controlled the Assembly, "we shall never have a free, republican Constitution." This time, Hanriot brought up more of the National Guard and, for good measure, a battery of cannon, which enabled Robespierre finally to exert ruthless, undeviating, irresistible pressure.

Besieged for many hours, the Convention was eventually bludgeoned into submission, but not without a spirited, prolonged defiance. Most of the Convention staunchly resisted. Lanjuinais delivered a fiery speech denouncing the Commune as the *autorité usurpatrice* that planned and organized "the conspiracy." To compel the Convention to surrender its authority, the Commune had systematically mobilized and deceived the *ignorants* of Paris. To stop him, Legendre threatened him physically, at which Lanjuinais defied his assailant to throw him off the podium. He and his colleagues were accused of calumniating Paris but this was utterly false: "Paris is good, only Paris is oppressed by tyrants thirsting for blood and domination." Lanjuinais's speech was finally drowned out by yells from the galleries, and Robespierre's younger brother, Augustin Robespierre (1763–94), Drouet, Jullien, and other Robespierristes helping Legendre push him off the podium. An ultimatum from the Commune was read out: for four days the people of Paris had been in arms to rescue the flame of liberty and equality; for the last time the people's delegates stood before the Assembly demanding immediate seizure of the Twenty-Two *factieux*. The people refused to see "its happiness" thwarted by the "conspirators." "The people" would stand for it no longer.[103]

Orator after orator demanded the immediate arrest of the Twenty-Two, the "treacherous" heads of France's fédéralistes, modérés, aristocrates, royalistes, Rolandistes, and *liberticides* "betraying the Revolution." Those to be detained (actually exceeding twenty-two) were "Gensonné, Guadet, Brissot, Gorsas, Pétion, Vergniaud, Salles, Barbaroux, Chambon, Buzot, Birotteau, Ducos, Isnard, Lanjuinais, Lidon, Rabaut, Lasource, Louvet, Boyer-Fonfrède, Lanthenas, Dusaulx, Fauchet, Grangeneuve, Lehardy [and] Lesage."[104] Tense hours passed. Deputies attempting to leave the building were forced back into the hall at gunpoint.[105] Finally, exhausted, the Assembly majority, first with François Mallarmé, a Montagnard (with reservations about Robespierre), as "president" and afterward the more pliant Hérault de Séchelles replacing him, reluctantly submitted. The Convention's motion to accept "the people's demands" was proposed by Robespierre's brother and seconded by Bazire and Couthon. Center deputies suggested that proscription of "the guilty" should begin by inviting the accused to resign voluntarily. This Isnard, Fauchet, and Lanthenas agreed to do, with Fauchet vowing to sacrifice himself "as a Christian" to save the Republic (though Lanjuinais objected to the term "sacrifice" to describe surrender to blackmail backed by cannon). With only three "voluntary" resignations forthcoming, the Assembly then ordered the arrest of the remaining "culprits" on the Montagnard list.

With Marat presiding, the Twenty-Two were seized one by one after some juggling with names, along with those members of the Commission of Twelve who were not among the Twenty-Two (including Kervélégan). Boyer-Fonfrède's name was removed due to his having voted several times against the rest of the Commission de Douze. Jean-Joseph Dusaulx (1728–99), a radical enlightener for thirty years, translator of Juvenal, Mably admirer, and member of the Académie des Inscriptions, long a passionate revolutionary (praised by Diderot as the most truthful of men), was also crossed off. Now sixty-five, Dusaulx nevertheless volunteered for the "honor" of inclusion among those arrested, to which Marat angrily retorted that he was an "old imbecile incapable of leading anybody."[106] Lanthenas and Ducos were likewise exempted.[107] The final total of Convention deputies detained by the coup leaders on 2 June, among them the foreign affairs minister Lebrun, actually came to thirty-four. But this number did not include several leading Left republicans the group dictatorship intended to seize, including Roland,

Carra, Manuel, Daunou, and Condorcet, who was absent. Roland's arrest had been ordered by the Commune the day before, but he had already fled Paris. Mme. Roland, though, *had* now been arrested and locked up at the Abbaye.

By late evening of 2 June, Robespierre's putsch was almost complete, except that even now, the official record reveals, "a large number of deputies" courageously stayed put in the Assembly hall, refusing to sign the Convention "edict" ordering the arrests.[108] The coup d'état, even if not spontaneous or rooted in any impulse, was certainly "popular" in the sense that the common people—or at any rate the least educated—made it possible. Ordinary men's ignorance, commented Picqué, enabled "this new Cromwell" to achieve as much as any Cromwell could by way of overthrowing all legality and the legislature, and eliminating the Convention's leading deputies.[109] The journée of 2 June, reported Toulouse's deputies to their municipal council, hinged entirely on the "excessive credulity of a people easy to mislead." Marat, Pache, Hanriot, and other leaders of the Paris city council, all men of consummate dishonesty, had gained the people's confidence. They pronounced Legendre "even more of a butcher in character than by profession." Robespierre they designated "the most unscrupulous schemer revolutionary upheaval has ever brought forth on the world stage."[110]

For the less unscrupulous Jacobin element, men like Levasseur, Jullien, and Romme, so much arm-twisting and deception needed justifying. Various theories were concocted. "A people is not truly regenerated," explained Jean-Baptiste Lecarpentier (1759–1829) in January 1794, an avowed foe of féderalisme and the *réprésentant* who later purged Saint-Malo, "a people is not truly free, until its thinking is regenerated." This necessarily involved expunging the Brissotins, "dangerous elements" who, after supporting the Revolution "of which they were, in truth, one of the motors, but not an integral or necessary component," tried to preserve "some of the vices of the *ancien régime* in the new body politic." Regenerating society is like the casting of metal: any alien alloy debases the outcome. Reason and "error" cannot subsist together; hence, "error" must be extirpated by "truth." True popular republicanism, contended Lecarpentier, means rejection of the atheism, materialism, and determinism championed by the philosophes, men who disdained ordinary folk—the backbone of true Jacobinism—and overthrew every religious concept. He called their atheistic ideas "ce delire du philosophisme" (this madness of philosophisme), an edifice of philosophy, perfidy, and aversion to the common man.[111]

But if the foundations were laid, the dictatorship was not yet built. Robespierre's putsch, after all, was the labor of four different factions—Robespierristes, Dantonistes, Hébertistes, and Enragés. Unsurprisingly, this coalition immediately began to unravel. The alliance between Robespierristes and authentic egalitarian sansculotte leaders, the Enragés, who did as much as anyone to unseat the Girondins, proved especially unsustainable, even for a few days,[112] for what the Montagne called the "revolution of 31 May" was devoid not only of legality, coherence, popular support, and any connection with the Revolution's core values but also—and this is crucial—of a genuine commitment to working people or the poor. Authentic sansculottes championing the proletarian masses, like Varlet, Roux, and Jean Leclerc (1771, after 1804), son of a Protestant road engineer, were at once elbowed aside by Robespierre, who knew perfectly well they commanded a popular following in the streets of a kind he did not. Belatedly grasping the real character of the looming dictatorship and the vastness of Robespierre's megalomania, paranoia, and vindictiveness, the Enragés rapidly became alienated.

CHAPTER 17

The Summer of 1793

Overturning the Revolution's

Core Values

It took time for the victors to consolidate their dictatorship. There could be no immediate imposition of repressive measures. At first, rather, there was widespread confusion. On 2 June, the Convention majority supported the democratic Left, not the Montagne.[1] Most of France and even, the evidence suggests, most of Paris, opposed Robespierre. Many eyewitnesses agreed with Gensonné, whose manifesto, dashed off in haste prior to his arrest, dated three in the afternoon of 2 June, held that after "seducing a few," the Montagne had captured the capital's *comités révolutionnaires* by employing every variety of intimidation, manipulation, and bullying to cajole the sections.[2] Treated respectfully, and initially only loosely guarded, many "so-called friends of the laws [*amis des lois*]," as the Montagnards derisively termed the impeached deputies, contrived to escape. Brissot, Pétion, Barbaroux, Louvet, Gorsas, Buzot, Lanjuinais, and Guadet all slipped away from house arrest. Manuel, not indicted on 2 June but arrested shortly afterward, likewise eluded his captors but was caught at Fontainebleau and returned to Paris in early August, as were Pétion's wife and children, seized at Honfleur.[3]

Most of the Convention's deputies had opposed the coup and actively or passively continued to do so. All nine Somme department deputies, including the fugitive Louvet, signed a manifesto, dated 5 June, in the *Mercure universel*, declaring 31 May and 2 June days of "mourning for all friends of liberty and the Republic." The Convention, besieged by a huge but drastically manipulated crowd and surrounded with bayonets and cannon, had been harried and abused at gunpoint. The only really "guilty deputies" were those orchestrating the plot. For seven hours, while the Assembly resisted proscription of the Twenty-Two and the Twelve, no deputy could leave the Convention hall unless escorted by armed conspirators, not even to satisfy the demands of nature, a truly humiliating indignity. The legislature had been violated "not by citizens or the Paris sections but certain men," paid or misled.[4] Several of the signatories, including Louvet, survived the Terror and later resumed their efforts, from late 1794, to forge a democratic republic.

The municipal authorities at Marseille, Lyon, Bordeaux, Toulouse, Nantes, Toulon, Bayonne, and Montpellier all condemned the coup, as did much of provincial France outside the main cities. Many small towns also formally repudiated it. Pont-Audemer's citizens, gathering in their main church, drew up a protest petition dated 4 June, indignantly deploring seizure of the Twenty-Two, whose only "crime" was to propose the appel au peuple, rendering "homage to the principle of sovereignty of the people."[5] Saint-Quentin initially reacted similarly: one would need to be very blind not to see the perfidy of those who had usurped power by dissolving the Commission of Twelve and arresting the Twenty-Two without the slightest evidence to support their accusations. Power has been seized by an "impious faction supported by all that is most vile and corrupt in Paris." "True republicans" were summoned to help restore genuine national representation, purge the "oppressors of the people and establish a fully republican constitution."[6]

An address from the conseil général of the Aisne department, centered on Saint-Quentin condemning the coup, was dated 4 June. Altogether, around forty-nine—more than half of all departments—officially declared against Robespierre and the Montagne after 2 June, with only thirty-two to thirty-four endorsing the Montagne's seizure of power.[7] A general summons was issued for representatives from opposition departments to gather in Bourges to save the Republic, urging all France to join the struggle "against our new tyrants." Brissotin leaders urging armed rebellion against the coup also joined Condorcet in condemning the June Constitution as a travesty of the more democratic February Constitution. To cap "their crimes," declared the physician Salles, Robespierre's acolytes devised a so-called constitution that was "a bundle of impracticable rules useless for impeding tyranny," just a "ceaseless violation of principles" and "new method of spreading disorder, particularly harmful in organizing anarchy constitutionally."[8] But the tally of departments officially opposed signified relatively little in itself, as most remained deeply divided. Vienne, for instance, a department concocted from fragments of Poitou, Touraine, and Berry, sided with the Left republicans at departmental level but the société populaire of Poitiers, the only sizable city, backed the Montagne. More relevantly, relatively few large towns followed Poitiers and Dijon in proclaiming the Brissotins "aristocrates" plotting "un république anti-démocratique," and in declaring for Robespierre, Danton, and Marat.[9]

Tenacious opposition persisted also on the Convention floor it-self, despite the detention or flight of most of the Brissotin leadership. There too, opponents tried to counter the enveloping tyranny with courageous speeches. On 4 June, the Abbé Grégoire and several others protested outright,[10] as did, on 5 June, the legal theorist and chemist Charles Dufrêche-Valazé (1751–93) and the Bordeaux deputy Jean-Baptiste Boyer-Fonfrède (1765–93), removed from the listed Twenty-Two at the last moment. Boyer-Fonfrède, a merchant and free press advocate, demanded the Committee of Public Safety's report on the arrested deputies. Was the Montagne not afraid of provoking a gen-eral insurrection in the country?[11] He was shouted down as an enemy of "la tranquilité publique." On 6 June, the Calvados deputy Gustave Deulcet-Pontcoulent (1764–1853), once an aristocrat, asked for evi-dence of the guilt of the arrested deputies. He and several others joining him were shouted down.[12] Petitions composed shortly before 31 May were still being read to the Convention over the next few days, helping the backlash in the Convention. A missive from Angers, dated 30 May, endorsed by all the town's section assemblies, accused the Montagne of suppressing the public's "true voice" with acts of tyranny scarcely imag-inable even under monarchy. If the "audacieuse et criminelle faction" blocking the Constitution did not desist, Angers would rise to arms. Its authors were duly dismissed as royalist calomniateurs maligning Paris. When Louis de La Réveillère-Lépeaux (1753–1824), a deputy from Angers and vocal anti-Montagnard, rose to contradict this, he too was brutally quelled.[13]

But if most of France resisted Robespierre's coup, coordinated oppo-sition nationally lacked cohesion, direction, and unity. A joint meeting of Saint-Quentin's three sections in the town's main church on 9 June revealed a deep split, not between "true republicans" and Montagnards, for practically no one supported the coup, but between those calling for armed insurrection and those preferring to hold back and await the outcome rather than ignite civil war.[14] The next day the town sections reassembled in the main church and applauded the Angers address of 30 May, voting to print three thousand copies and circulate that rous-ing manifesto around the north. The société populaire of Saint-Omer, addressing the Convention on 27 June after receiving contradictory accounts of the events of 31 May and 2 June, confessed that they hardly knew what to think or how to sift truth from lies.[15] It was the news, several weeks later, that the Convention had completed the Constitution that tilted the balance in favor of acquiescence in the coup. Across France, reaction to the June Constitution was predominantly positive. Finally, the Constitution had been achieved! A letter acquiescing in the coup from the "republicans of Reims," dated 23 June, expressly cited "this divine Constitution so long awaited" as the factor deciding the city's stance.[16]

Gradually, the tyranny's grip tightened. Fleeing via Chartres, Brissot was caught on 10 June while attempting to reach Caen, the focus of republican resistance in Normandy, where Barbaroux, Gorsas, Buzot, Guadet, and Louvet were organizing what became the headquarters of armed resistance to the Montagne in the north. From Caen, the Left democratic leadership strove to sway opinion by dispatching "commissaires" to neighboring departments and convening town meetings, urging "true republicans" and defenders of liberty to join their insurrection. Reaching Caen, Salles published his declaration decrying those "*factieux* dominating France today who had brought their crimes to a culminating point," destroying the National Assembly, usurping the people's sovereignty, and pillaging the public purse. Other opposition centers likewise dispatched commissaires to spread the armed revolt, the departmental council of Côte d'Or, for instance, to Haute-Vienne, l'Aisne, and La Sarthe.[17] In Paris, the Comité de Salut Public eventually answered with a publicity counteroffensive, issuing an address from the Convention, dated 26 June, denouncing the group of "conspirators" inciting the people to revolt and to march on Paris. The "traitors" misleading the *citoyens* amounted to just a tiny clique, only around thirty, wickedly beguiling the good, pure common folk with "their idolatry" of eminent persons and reputations, and prestige of their opinions. Brissotins pretend to abhor royalty and fédéralisme but their real goal was to divide France, encourage defiance of the (purged) Convention, and disseminate royalisme. How perfidious! Worryingly, the common man is all too easily misled. Fortunately, though, Robespierre assured his following, the "people is good everywhere," the ordinary person always pure and honest, so that once it is clearly pointed out to them, all ordinary people shun "Brissotin depravity and error."[18]

In repelling the Left republican challenge, Robespierre's chief assets were the prevailing confusion, and especially the universal desire for the

Constitution and fear of ruining the Revolution and ensuring defeat at enemy hands through internecine strife. The resulting vacillation produced frequent early shifts of position. Evreux's citizenry, summoned by proclamation shouted out in the town's public places and by ringing the cathedral bells, convened in emergency session on 14 June in the packed town cathedral. The people yelled their willingness to take up arms against the "bloody faction" of "tyrants" and "anarchistes" who bludgeoned the Convention into submission.[19] But only ten days later, this Norman town's two sections withdrew their bellicose resolutions after being comprehensively assured they had been misled and "deceived."[20]

With the armed rebellion spreading, the Comité de Sûreté Générale, through one of its most ruthless and unprincipled members (since 16 June), the Grenoble lawyer Amar, friend of the Caribbean slave-owners, requested the Convention, on 24 June, to impose emergency measures and, in particular, imprison under heavy guard those deputies thus far only under house arrest guarded by just one gendarme each. This vote passed amid a furious commotion, over the bitter protests of Ducos, Boyer-Fonfrède, and other republican stalwarts, but to thunderous applause from packed galleries.[21] Brissot, consequently, was now incarcerated along with a number of others, including the idealistic young educationalist Claude-Louis Mazuyer (1760–94), representative for Saône-et-Loire, who had been arrested for helping Pétion and Lanjuinais escape, and Vergniaud, who nevertheless managed to send a remarkable letter, dated 28 June, to two of Robespierre's prime henchmen, Barère and Robert Lindet, reproaching them as "*imposteurs* and assassins" preferring popularity to their consciences.[22]

Even formal imprisonment of a large part of the Brissotin leadership failed to halt protest in the Convention. How scandalous, declared Ducos, on 24 June, that more than three weeks after the arrests, no formal indictment detailing "the crimes" of the arrested deputies had emerged. He was heaped with opprobrium from both Montagne and galleries. Robespierre himself rose to answer. What! Are there still deputies feigning not to know what all France knows? With uprisings everywhere, the Vendée rebellion tearing France asunder, Ducos demands a report on the misdeeds of the Brissotin leaders! Ducos implies a bunch of "conspirators" represent the will of the Convention! This is the language of the Vendée and rebel departments! Inveighing against Ducos, Robespierre was interrupted by several opposition deputies, prompting the brutal Legendre to jump up and threaten the first "rebel to interrupt the orator again" with detention in the Abbaye. Ducos defends Brissot, sneered Robespierre, "Brissot," a former police spy, a miscreant "the people" had seized and denounced for his misdeeds. "Someone here pretends we need a report as if the crimes of the detained were not known! Besides conspiring with all the 'tyrants of Europe' and causing our setbacks, these men obstructed the Constitution, our holy Constitution now finished in the time since they are gone. The Constitution will rally all France around us despite the clamours of the malicious 'factieux.' Make no mistake! It is to the Constitution [he was shortly to suspend] that the French will rally to and not Brissot or Gensonné."[23]

No speech better illustrates Robespierre's adroitness and basic ideology—and dishonesty. The key to defeating the Brissotin insurgency, he knew, was to finalize the Constitution and convoke the nation's primary assemblies to endorse it. Having discharged "its most sacred responsibility," the Convention could label the schism splitting Convention and Republic as treasonable resistance to the people's most sacred interests. It was not whole departments who resisted, he maintained, but only some departmental officials, obvious "conspirators." What chiefly mattered, anyhow, was that "the people" supported the Montagne, "the people!" This was untrue like nearly everything else in his speech but could be made to look true. If more Frenchmen opposed than supported the coup, most proved too disconcerted and hesitant to make a stand. Could the accusations against the Brissotins conceivably be true? Was there really undisclosed evidence of treachery? If Brissotins charged the Montagne with deceiving the country, Robespierre's supporters accused the rebel leadership of precisely the same. Undeniably, France did seethe with royalists, contre-révolutionnaires, and other conspirators exploiting the turmoil by first joining the "Brissotins" but eventually donning the white cockade.[24] More and more suspects were rounded up. Over the summer, the numbers detained in Paris prisons climbed steadily to 1,347 by 24 June, including 319 in the Conciergerie and 295 in La Grande-Force, the two largest prisons, and no less than 2,300 by late September.[25]

Carefully crafted declarations and manifestos played a crucial role wherever serious opposition crystalized, for this was above all an ideological struggle. Toulouse's sections rebuffed Robespierre at their general assembly of 17 June, their declaration, sent to all France's departments, demanding Robespierre's arrest, dissolution of the Paris Commune, abrogation of the 2 June decree against "the 28 members of the Convention," and annulment of every Convention "decree" passed since 2 June, since all were illicit.[26] According to Marc-Antoine Baudot (1765–1837), Dantoniste deputy "en mission" in the Toulouse area together with Chabot, not only the southwest region's hardened anti-Montagnards but practically everyone, including the bons citoyens, opposed the Montagne. The Montagne was ousted in Toulouse, reported Baudot, because "many citizens were deceived" by the torrent of Brissotin printed propaganda, Toulouse printers reissuing several well-known anti-Montagnard tracts, including "the discourse of Lanjuinais."[27] No sooner had news of the 31 May insurrection arrived than mayor and municipality, backed by the Toulouse section assemblies, repudiated the Montagne, circulating more printed manifestos among neighboring communes.

At Lyon and Marseille, the newly victorious democratic republican leadership, backed by the city's artisan sections, raised their own departmental armed forces. On 7 June, Bordeaux proclaimed armed insurrection against the Convention (until the thirty-two proscribed deputies were reinstated) and formed a Bordeaux commission of public safety, or *commission populaire*, to organize the resistance. An army would be assembled to march on Paris and restore the Convention. Bordeaux's National Club was suppressed. Despite being assaulted by the Vendéean rebels at the end of June, Nantes too resisted the Montagne. Stubbornly anti-Vendéean and antiroyalist, as well as anti-Montagnard, Nantes withstood the Vendéean attack, the Revolution's first military success for many months. At Toulon, Maratiste populists retained control, but for all their incessant talk of "the people," refused to convene the section assemblies, knowing perfectly well most Toulon workingmen, like those of Lyon, Marseille, Montpellier, and Bordeaux, disliked Jacobin authoritarianism. In fact, Toulon's six thousand dockworkers, hungry and bitter at the exceptionally high price of bread, divided broadly between Brissotins and royalists, with hardly anybody backing the Montagne. To prevent their municipality from endorsing Robespierre, Toulon's artisans and laborers rose on 12–13 July, led by the section assemblies, and on 16 July, their general committee dissolved the municipality and suppressed the Jacobin Club.[28] As at Bordeaux, Marseilles, and Lyon, a people's tribunal was created and the militia purged; dozens of Robespierriste Jacobins were interned and death sentences passed on several Montagnard activists. Until late August, Toulon remained staunchly republican. Only when caught between surrendering to Robespierre or the British navy did the Toulonnais choose the latter and, hence, reimposition of monarchy and aristocracy.

Montpellier's response was concerted by the city's first democrati-cally elected mayor, Jean-Jacques Durand (1760–94), a firm republican and founder of the local revolutionary club and National Guard, re-elected mayor three times since January 1790. Durand moved to silence Robespierriste agitators already on 31 May, rallying the bons citoyens to purge the Jacobin Club and reorganize the militia. The departmental council, renamed the Comité Central de Salut Public of Hérault, con-vened in Montepellier on 11 June. Elected "president," Durand urged the raising of an armed force to join Bordeaux, Lyon, Toulouse, and Marseille, not against Paris but against the usurping clique. Besides dis-seminating the manifestos of Gensonné and Roland, Durand issued other "incendiary" tracts, one denouncing "the appalling Chabot." On 13 June, Montpellier issued a general call for national resistance to the "vile *conspirateurs*" who were subverting France and clapping "all talent and virtue in irons." The Montagne were a foe more ferocious than the Prussians, "nourished on our blood and gold," hiding rapacious hands "under Diogenes's mantle," subverting the Revolution and reducing the people to abject submission. The people must save the Constitution and repel "the monsters dishonouring it" by resorting to arms.[29] Del-egates were dispatched to Caen to align with the insurrectionary north and measures taken against neighboring towns—Béziers, Avignon, and Arles—backing the Paris Jacobins.

Montpellier's manifestos promised the people genuine equality, the equality of the new Declaration of Rights rather than just the equality of status before the law and freedom from oppression by courtiers, nobles, priests, magistrates, and parlementaires gained in 1789. The Republic's purpose was to advance the people's happiness by political means, se-curing the bonheur of all. According to (the affluent) Durand, the "hap-piness" of the people consists in economic well-being, education, and public esteem, together with eligibility for office. Under the democratic republicans, economic well-being (*l'aisance*) would, he maintained, be-come "general" by raising wages, promotion of industry, and via a more just relationship between the labor performed by some and produce of others, and a more just repartition of taxation, from which the poor will be exempt. The citizen with slight means will pay little, the main burden falling on those whose incomes can best sustain it. Well-being could also be spread more equally by ensuring equal inheritances among children and using laws to prevent fortunes from being bequeathed to collaterals intact. Education elevates human reason, as reason elevates man. Education would become universal. The children of every family were the Republic's children—all equal in its eyes. Education would teach the children their rights and how to exercise them, knowledge needed to participate in public affairs. Thus, men would increasingly become equalized in terms of legal status, economic standing, education, and public esteem.[30]

Montagnards accused Brissotin republicans of everywhere posting up anti-Montagnard manifestos, even in the tiniest villages, fomenting "treason," armed resistance, and civil war.[31] Pont l'Évêque was among the towns that summoned adjoining rural districts to rise against the dictatorship of those who had arrested "the most ardent defenders of true liberty."[32] One of the more awkward points the Montagne had to deal with was the constant citing of the September massacres. The directoire of the Pont l'Évêque district of Calvados, vowing to combat the "immoral faction seducing Parisians and assuming the mask of *patriotisme*," claimed the people were being duped by those responsible for the "September massacres," men who converted "crime into virtue and virtue into crime."[33] Allegedly, it typified the perfidy of those preaching "rebellion" against the "Convention" to harp on about the September massacres, which Manuel, Brissot, Condorcet, and Pétion, complained the Monagnard papers, did nothing to stop, and Gorsas basely first praised and then condemned. "For them, the bloody days of 2 and 3 September 1792" were just a pretext to "dishonour France in the eyes of other peoples."[34]

The armed rebellion, insisted the populist press, was a vile plot against the people, concocted by a handful of traitors mascarading as patriots on what Montagnards called "the Right." It was hard to explain, though, on this construction how, despite imprisoning or outlawing nearly forty Convention deputies, unyielding opposition continued even in the Convention, let alone the provinces. Chabot's *Journal Populaire*, cast in dialogue form to be read aloud at meetings of sociétés populaires, lambasted Brissotin doggedness as the "revolting audacity" of the Convention's "right wing" persisting even after removal of the Twenty-Two. Chabot explained such tenacious perversity in terms of corrupt morals. The Assembly had betrayed the people before August 1792, corrupted by the royal court. Later, many deputies continued betraying the people on behalf of the aristocracy. In fact, most of the new legislature elected in September 1792 had soon been corrupted by cash and opportunities, and sought to crush "Paris." "Cupidity and the desire to dominate" inspired "the rebels." Without the 31 May insurrection, "the brave Montagne" could not have saved "the people."[35]

The armed "revolt" provided the grounds for putting the Brissotins on trial for their lives. Robespierre's closest ally, Saint-Just, recently voted onto the Committee of Public Safety, was assigned the crucial task (for the Robespierristes) of drawing up the indictment against the arrested deputies. Since there were no crimes or "betrayal" prior to 2 June, and no "conspiracy," Saint-Just had to focus on the rebellion itself, despite the snag that this failed to justify the risings of 31 May and 2 June. He read his indictment to the Convention on 8 July. The prisoners were being tried not for their opinions but "treason," especially the heinous crime of "féderalisme"—seeking to divide the people, mobilizing feeling against Paris, and initiating civil war under the pretext of repressing "anarchy," for pretending to be republicans while really being covert "royalists." Buzot, Barbaroux, Gorsas, Lanjuinais, Salles, Louvet, and Pétion were "rebels" directly complicit in armed revolt, including even the Corsican rising. Gensonné, Guadet, Vergniaud, and several others were guilty more indirectly.[36]

By July the most heinous crime conceivable among the illiterate, ignorant, and unaware was "federalism," something previously unknown but suddenly appalling beyond measure. Wherever Montagnard control was undisputed, often the case in small towns, the story that the Brissotins were "federalist traitors" was swallowed without question. Cognac, addressing the Convention on 25 June, warmly acclaimed "the glorious 31 May" for saving the people. Cambrai professed the deepest sentiments of horror at the upsurge of fédéralisme throughout the surrounding northeast. Happily, federalist "leprosy," like that blighting nearby Saint Quentin, would "not infect our walls, we guarantee you that!" Only one viewpoint was permitted in loyal Jacobin Cambrai. Nobody was allowed to disagree. To make absolutely sure dissent was extirpated, the municipality had opened a register requiring citizens to sign within a fortnight, attesting their loyalty to the people and readiness to fight fédéralistes. "The names of those inscribed will constitute the list of all this town's good citizens." By ascertaining "those missing[,] we shall know who holds different opinions and is not a good citizen."[37]

Crushing dissent was the quintessence of Robespierriste dictatorship. Robespierre's coup was swiftly followed by suppression of every newspaper and publication rejecting the Montagne's version of events. For without annihilating press freedom, disinformation and manipulation could achieve no generally firm grip. Press, art, debating, and theater freedom had prevailed more or less intact since mid-1789, until brutally assaulted in March 1793. Within days of 2 June, freedom of expression ended abruptly and completely, the Committee of Public Safety, at Robespierre's behest, eliminating, on the grounds of rebellion, royalism, federalism, and sedition, all journalists and orators hostile to the regime.[38] Gorsas's *Le Courrier de Paris* and *Le Patriote français* had ceased already on 1 June 1793. The courageous twenty-four-year-old Girey-Dupré, head of the Bibliothèque Nationale's manuscript division and chief editor of the *Patriote français* since late 1791, was in hiding.[39] Louvet's *Sentinelle* lapsed as its editor fled. Fauchet's *Journal des Amis* ceased in mid-June, the *Chronique de Paris* in August.[40]

Joseph-François Michaud (1767–1839), editor of the last major royalist paper *La Quotidienne,* condemned to death for royalism, vanished too.[41] Prudhomme, among the few journalists actively supporting the feminist cause, was seized following the arrest of the Twenty-Two but amid the confusion released, then rearrested, then rereleased, all within days. His second release, opposed by the Paris section Unité, where local bosses greatly resented his paper, was extracted from the Commune by Chaumette and Hébert. Profoundly shaken, Prudhomme too fell silent. Freedom of the theater likewise ended as municipal supervision of the theater repertory intensified. Paris theaters, decreed the Comité de Salut Public in early August, must now provide weekly performances of republican tragedies like *Brutus, Guillaume Tell,* and *Caius Gracchus,* glorifying revolutionary zeal and "the virtues of the defenders of liberty." Theaters staging the wrong kind of plays, debasing the pubic spirit or encouraging the "shameful superstition of royalism," would be closed and their directors arrested.[42]

As the struggle developed, a principal drawback for the Left was thus the loss of their former press dominance, combined with the general silencing of the reading societies, academies, and theaters. The sweeping Law of Suspects promulgated on 17 September 1793, subseqently the main legal basis of the Terror, ensured all opposition papers stayed out of existence. This soon-notorious law authorized the arrest of anyone "who by their writings have shown themselves partisans of tyranny and fédéralisme, and enemies of liberty," code words for Left republicans championing revolutionary core values and radical thought.[43] After 2 June, Paris printers were too scared to risk producing opposition literature, while Brissotin provincial centers mostly lacked the means to distribute widely. Hard-hitting manifestos nevertheless continued appearing in provincial opposition centers and at Geneva. Addressing all the "republicans of France," Gensonné's declaration was distributed via Bordeaux and reprinted at Montpellier. Louvet's manifesto, published in Normandy, similarly urged solidarity with Paris and unremitting war on the guilty—the Montagne, Cordeliers, and the Paris Commune.[44]

Brissotin "revolt," contrary to what Montagnards implied by calling them fédéralistes, was nowhere an expression of local or regional feeling. Rather, Brissotins always indignantly rejected the thoroughly spurious charge of fédéralisme. They were not fighting Paris, or the people, but only the "imposteurs." Nowhere was regional particularism a factor except in Jacobin propaganda, which invariably possessed only the slenderest relation to the truth. Brissotins protested not that Paris tyrannized over the rest but that popular sovereignty had been violated by "brigands" and the Convention's authority usurped. The Republic was corrupted, the nation dishonored by the September massacres, the Convention and the law subverted by the "conspiracies" of 10 March, 31 May, and 2 June.[45] Calvados's printed manifesto, pronouncing the purged Convention's authority illicit, blamed not Paris but the Commune, a conspiratorial organization "gorged on blood," despotically holding "our representatives" captive. According to Gensonné, who professed never to have nurtured any goal as a deputy except the people's happiness under a republican constitution, the Paris sections had been deceived into denouncing as "traitors," the "most patriotic deputies," the true republicans genuinely devoted to the people's interests, but no one should "impute to the majority of Paris's inhabitants excesses that in our present unfortunate circumstances" the capital could not prevent. All Frenchmen must remember Paris's past services to the Revolution and "reserve all their indignation for the scoundrels who planned and executed this infamous scheme."[46] Gensonné would die a republican worthy of the confidence electors had placed in him. Barbaroux's manifesto, dated 18 June, circulating in Marseille, summoned Frenchmen to march on Paris, not to fight Paris but to fraternize with the Parisians, delivering them from "the new tyranny" while upholding the Republic's unity and indivisibility. "Marseillais, le rendez-vous est à Paris!"[47]

Driven from Paris, the republican leadership had to organize disjointedly in widely separated departments and, consequently, remained unable to concert or propagandize effectively. Lacking a central organ to issue edicts and coordinate their movements, resistance proved hard to organize outside the major provincial cities. Scant support flowed consistently from either small towns or the countryside. Of 559 communes in the Gironde region, only 130, under one-quarter, even nominally followed Bordeaux into armed rebellion.[48] Of those that did, most joined the revolt only half-heartedly and fleetingly. Vacillating like much of the southwest, the conseil général of the department of Lot withdrew its opposition only three weeks after the Paris coup, claiming to have been misled by a decree of the Côte d'Or department.[49] In Calvados most small towns vacillated and before long abandoned the revolt.[50]

After a month, Montpellier too lost its appetite for armed struggle, opting instead for a middle course. The comité central of the *assemblées primaires* of Hérault, meeting on 5 and 6 July, did not abandon their previous diagnosis of France's predicament: Montagnard malevolence and villainy, and that alone, had undermined the Convention. France had been consigned to pillage, its currency ruined and government usurped by *ignorants* with "narrow and limited views." Regenerating the national legislature and rescuing France would mean detaching the former from a capital deeply but not irretrievably corrupted and slavishly subjected to tyranny. However, given how destructive and uncertain a civil war would be, and the difficulty of mobilizing the departments for combat, Montpellier now preferred a nonviolent solution. Scorning the charge of fédéralisme, the comité central summoned all "true republicans" to endorse the Constitution and, in orderly fashion, elect representatives to gather in Paris by 10 August, when the French people's acceptance of the Constitution would be proclaimed.[51] Like their counterparts in Caen, Nantes, Marseille, Lyon, Bordeaux, Toulouse, Bayonne, and Toulon, Montpellier republicans still hoped to prevent France from succumbing to Robespierriste lies, barbarism, and terror, but imagined this could be best accomplished peacefully, by embracing and utilizing the Constitution.

The Constitution thus became the illusive mirage disarming the "true republican" rising. Though many "true republicans" would have preferred to allow a choice between the February Constitution and the version finalized in June, amid the crisis Montepellier recommended immediate acceptance of the June Constitution with elections to follow promptly, each deputy elected representing a constituency of forty thousand people. Electing a new legislature in a fair and orderly fashion created the opportunity, or so it seemed, to use the Constitution itself to halt the illegality, repression, and violence, and to many this appeared the preferable, conciliatory, and orderly way for the "friends of the laws" to win the struggle. To ensure the Constitution's proper implementation, Montepellier wanted the capital provisionally transferred to somewhere in central France, at least forty leagues from Paris. Before the capital's elected deputies to the legislature could be acknowledged, new magistrates, legitimately chosen, must be installed. If Paris needed confronting, this could occur without resorting to arms via the proposed provisional *comité républicain*, supposedly soon to convene at Bourges, representing the entire country.

Instructions for Montepellier's commissaires at Bourges were actually drawn up. Montpellier insisted on immediate annulment of the arrest of "the thirty-two" Convention deputies seized (the decree authorizing their arrest having been extracted by force). France's primary assemblies must be summoned, full recognition of popular sovereignty under the 1793 Declaration of Rights secured, the existing Paris municipality and National Guard disbanded, and the Commission de Douze's damning report on the Paris Commune submitted to all primary assemblies. Convention decrees contrary to free expression must be canceled and citizens arrested since the illegal edicts of 31 May must be released.[52] A special military force of twelve thousand men, directly under the new Assembly's control, was required to guard the national legislature. Composed of twenty men from every electoral cantonment in France, its commander and senior officers must be appointed by the legislature alone. No citizen could be admitted to serve in it without a certificate of republican civisme, issued by his commune's conseil général. Finally, a new national high court, a Tribunal de Justice Nationale, comprising one member for every department and meeting at Clermont-Ferrand or another town in central France, and at least twenty leagues from the legislature, should be instituted to try conspirators against the Republic, commencing with "the conspiracies" of 10 March, 31 May, and 2 June.[53]

The Montagnard leadership rightly calculated that the newly finalized Constitution would disarm "the people's enemies everywhere," clinching the Montagne's victory in every town, village, société populaire, and army battalion, securing even the remotest areas and every frontier. The entire outcome of the struggle in France, predicted Barère in a speech to the Convention on 27 June, hinged on convoking the primary assemblies to endorse the Constitution. Every electoral district would convene simultaneously all across France, promised the Comité, with vast quantities of printed copies diffusing the Constitution in every department, especially those "dishonoured by revolt and devastated by brigands." The Constitution would reunite France's citizens, forging a single common interest, "destroying the atrocious plans of our internal enemies." Each primary assembly, registering citizens present, would record how many voted (verbally) for and how many against.

Once popularly endorsed, the Constitution should be ceremonially inducted as if by one gigantic act of national will. The Comité proposed using the 14 July celebrations: "it is then that the sacred hymns of liberty will prepare all hearts," uniting "all interests in deliberation of the greatest project that could concern free men," followed by the 10 August celebrations commemorating the Republic's birth. The Comité d'Instruction Publique was directed to prepare an especially magnificent *fête nationale,* making 10 August (a date projected to replace 14 July as the Revolution's principal summer celebration) a splendid "patriotic altar" on which the Constitution would be confirmed.[54]

The national referendum on the 1793 Constitution was an impressive first example of modern direct democracy in action. Approximately 4,800 primary assemblies participated in a referendum that, by and large, was fairly conducted. In France as a whole there was virtual unanimity in favor of the Constitution.[55] Proclaiming the Constitution to the southwestern departments of Gironde, Lot, and Garonne, at Périgueux on 7 July, the Montagne's representatives on mission in the region, Jean-Baptiste Mathieu and Jean-Baptiste Treilhard, former head of the Assembly's ecclesiastical committee, highlighted the expanded Declaration of Rights and vital importance of reestablishing the rule of law. By a cruel irony, they declared, "internal disturbances were seemingly increasing in parts of the Republic" just as the Convention "presents the people a constitution so long awaited, a constitution ending anarchy," to be defended at all costs, abasing "for ever monarchism and the aristocracy," the Vendéean rebels, fédéraliste revolt, and France's foreign enemies.[56] At Périgueux, the Constitution was read out in all the town's public places amid artillery salvoes before being voted on in the section primary assemblies, and celebrated afterward in the streets with a civic repast to which everyone was invited.[57]

Adopting the Constitution amid general acclaim was brilliant political theater, parading the Republic's Constitution with its unparalleled *démocratisme* as the Montagne's work, whereas, in fact, it was the Montagne that had obstructed its introduction over so many months. The projected legislature, with its large size designed to minimize the risk of representatives being captured by vested interests, alluringly held out the prospect of a lawful, peaceful end to France's internal plight. It was less the Constitution's affinities to Brissotin radical principles that impressed voters than the irony of the Montagne's obtaining in days what the Girondins with all their *principes philosophiques* and "belles phrases constitutionelles" could not accomplish in many months.[58]

Montagnard boasts that their (drastically purged) Convention accomplished more in fifteen days than the Girondin Convention in eight months seemed amply justified to most Frenchmen.[59]

The 1793 Constitution remained a model, an ideal, for the rest of the Revolution, and continued to inspire democrats and remind everyone of the Revolution's essential principles. Brissotin deputies still active in the chamber and not (yet) arrested, a remnant including La Révellière-Lépeaux, Claude-Romain Duperret (1747–93; until July), Carra (until August), Ducos (until October), and Boyer-Fonfrède (until October), accepted the Constitution and even wrought concrete amendments rendering certain clauses more democratic. Providing a crucial fig leaf of legitimacy, and the outward appearance of good faith, the Constitution reassured the public by encouraging sincere revolutionaries to acquiesce in the coup in good conscience. Deft handling of the festivities not only impressed the "troupe of dupes" deceived by Robespierre's assurances, as Brissotins expressed it, but heavily sapped the main thrust of the anti-Montagnard offensive.[60] The spectacle of the Constitution hailed everywhere, including in rebel cities and embraced by Brissotin deputies in Paris, even if many still preferred Condorcet's February version, was heartening news indeed for Montagnards.

Yet the very success of the June Constitution in the summer of 1793 soon also thoroughly unnerved the Montagnard leadership. Embraced by the Convention on 24 June, and endorsed by general referendum amid great jubilation in August, the Constitution was bound to worry the Jacobin leadership as soon as talk started about the projected elections and composition of the new legislature. Brissotins, an anxious Chabot admonished the Jacobins in early August, spoke as if they would fill the new legislature with their supporters. If Lyon aristocrats and contre-révolutionnaires welcomed the Constitution, this could only mean they viewed it as a device to further divide and "federalize" the nation.[61] The fact that the Constitution was enthusiastically embraced by their critics meant the Montagne could no longer support it, for should it take effect, the Constitution would end the emerging dictatorship. Robespierre needed to act quickly to suppress it to reassure his own following and secure his goals. In the two months since the Constitution's inception, the anti-Montagnard risings had been successfully contained. He could now afford to announce—but not to delay—cancellation of the scheduled elections and suspension of the Constitution. He acted immediately following the 10 August celebrations. "Nothing can save the Republic," he assured the Jacobins on

11 August, if the motion before the Club to dissolve the Convention and hold democratic elections for a new legislature was put into effect.[62] Elections could only help the Brissotins. The Jacobins backed him unreservedly: democracy and the Constitution for the moment had to be replaced by dictatorial *gouvernement révolutionnaire*.

Thus, no sooner had much of the armed resistance folded than the Constitution was shelved indefinitely.[63] Canceling the Constitution was followed by more arrests of Convention deputies and a ruthless assault on the last remnants of a free press. On 2 August, in a thunderously applauded Convention speech, Robespierre inveighed against Carra as a "conspirateur" and disguised royalist.[64] Attempting to answer, Carra was shouted down, hounded from the Assembly, and, at the Jacobins, further denounced as a perpetrator of "*fédéraliste* conspiracy, a deputy and journalist *rolandisé, girondisé* and *brissotisé*."[65] He was arrested and imprisoned. Three days after suspending the Constitution, again speaking at the Jacobins, Robespierre delivered the coup de grâce to press liberty, mounting a devastating tirade against the "journalistes" whose "mercenary and murderous pens every day spew out the most seductive poison" and devote their existence to undermining the esprit public and calumniating patriots. He demanded a general clampdown on Carra, Louvet, Girey, and Gorsas, and all the "laches calomniateurs" of the people.[66]

Voted onto the Committee for Public Safety on 26 July, alongside Barère and other dependable supporters, Robespierre was close to consolidating his dictatorship. But still he had some distance to cover and, anyhow, never fully controlled this body on which several members remained unsympathetic toward him, including Lazare Carnot (1753–1823), a ruthless but competent officer elected to the committee for his military expertise soon after Robespierre, on 4 August. Robespierre's position was chiefly complicated, though, by the fact that 2 June was a victory as much for Dantonistes, Hébertistes, and Enragés as his own immediate acolytes. The coalition that overthrew the Brissotins comprised four diverse factions highly unlikely to cooperate or tolerate one another once the Brissotin challenge receded. If Robespierre's circle had no close bond with Danton's, the Danton and Hébert groups were on still worse terms with each other. Ardent Jacobins and exponents of sansculottism, Hébert and his ally François-Nicolas Vincent (1767–94) specialized in deploying pressure from below to exert control, through the Jacobins and Cordeliers, over appointments to executive committees, ministries, and the government apparatus. As part of this, Vincent especially began sniping at Danton and his friends. By late August, Hébert and Vincent were openly accusing Danton of corruption, which led to sharp exchanges between the two groups.[67]

Those marshaling support in the streets and poor quarters of Paris divided into two seriously divergent streams, one backing Marat, Hébert, and Vincent, closely tied to the Montagne and allied with Robespierre for the moment, and a much more independent, radical, and genuinely plebeian bloc, the Enragés supporting Roux, Leclerc, Fournier, and Varlet, whose chief forms of political expression were mass meetings and street agitation. On 5 August, Robespierre spoke at the Jacobins, defending Danton against Vincent while simultaneously inveighing against the fiery populist Jacques Roux (1752–94). The Enragés had emerged strongly in the February food riots, and since June had been vying for a bigger role in the political arena, challenging the Montagne and the Convention as a whole. A manifesto known as the *Manifeste des Enragés,* drawn up six weeks before on 21 June at the Cordeliers, with Roux and Varlet presiding, spelled out the Enragé aims. Despite Robespierre trying to prevent it, the manifesto was presented to the Convention on 25 June, in the name of the Gravilliers and Bonne Nouvelle sections, and the Cordeliers by a crowd of sansculottes with Roux as spokesman, and showed all too plainly that the hard-core sansculottes were no lackeys of the Montagne.[68]

Numerous petitions denouncing the heartless exactions of the "financier and merchant aristocracy" and requesting price controls on basic foodstuffs had been submitted previously, protested Roux, and a hundred times the deputies had promised to punish the bloodsuckers of the people. But what had the Convention actually done? "You have just finalized a new constitution. But has speculation in foodstuffs been prohibited? No! Has the Assembly imposed the death penalty on monopolists and hoarders? No!"[69] Hence, the Convention failed to do what it should to promote the people's happiness. Liberty is just a phantom when one class of men can with impunity starve another. Legality is just a figment when the rich man exercises the power of life and death over his equal by engrossing and monopolizing supplies. Roux demanded immediate relief for the people. The Montagne should take care. Friends of equality would not be the dupes of charlatans seeking to break them through hunger. Only by putting food on the table could the sansculottes be tied to the Revolution, and only when the government regulated trade, stopping the brigandage of big merchants, could there be truly free commerce.

The merchant "aristocracy" had proved even more rapacious than the old noble and priestly aristocracies. Instead of pampering the rich, the Convention should consider those outraged by the paper currency's debasement. Workers' wages, claimed advocates of free commerce, rise with food price increases and other basic costs. But while some workers' wages had risen, many had fallen since the beginning of the Revolution.[70] It was perhaps not always in the Montagne's power "to do the good that was in its heart," but now that the legislature was no longer hampered by Gorsas, Brissot, Pétion, and other partisans of the appel au peuple, traitors who "to escape the guillotine" now hid their "infamy in the departments they have fanaticized," no excuse remained for the Convention not to curtail speculation and hoarding, and stop the ruining and starving of the citizenry. After four years of Revolution, it was an outrage that only the rich had gained any advantages. "Oh, shame of the century," who would believe, persisted Roux, despite rising indignation on Montagnard faces and noisy interruptions, that the people's representatives, declaring war on external tyrants, could be so base as not to crush those within? Roux was stopped from reading out the rest of his address.[71]

Robespierre was not prepared to tolerate anything like this. The sansculottes were clearly the Montagne's weak point as much as their strength. High food prices from July onward meant the likelihood of serious social disorder persisted throughout the fraught summer.[72] On 27 June, further disturbances shook Paris, starting with rumors that river barges leaving for Rouen formed part of a plot to empty the capital of provisions. The rioters were women, especially washerwomen who besides cheaper food demanded detergent at prices lower than storekeepers were selling it for. The *blanchisseuses* (laundresses) mostly neither knew nor cared about the main political struggle gripping the country: they wanted bread, candles, and soap. A delegation sent to the Convention complained of speculation and high prices. The deputies began discussing whether the thesis of the économistes, that basic commodity prices cannot be fixed by government, was actually correct. The Montagnard François Mallarmé from Lorraine (loathed by the Abbé Grégoire as a "brigand" and, later, architect of the Terror) affirmed, against the économistes, that basic commodity prices "can and should be fixed." But the Montagne found themselves deeply and inconveniently divided over this issue. The Convention asked the Comité de Salut Public to consider whether the principle of imposed maxima, introduced by the 4 May law, fixing maximum prices for grain and bread, could be extended to other basic commodities and to confer over this with Mallarmé.

To hinder speculation in soap, candles, textiles, and other commodities, the Bourse (in the Rue Vivienne) was temporarily closed.[73] Other measures adopted at this time included a draconian law making food hoarding a capital offense. However, Couthon and other hard-core Robespierristes were also gravely concerned lest pillaging of shops and barges be cited as evidence of "the anarchy" gripping Paris, and thus help the Brissotins and royalists. The latest Paris riots, some Montagnards suggested, formed part of a plot to obstruct the constitutional referendum on which hinged the entire Robespierriste strategy. Paris was the fortress of the Revolution, and it was necessary to use every means, argued Couthon, to "maintain order and tranquility there." At Couthon's and Billaud-Varenne's urging, the Convention agreed to pursue the ringleaders behind the riots with unremitting severity.[74]

The Enragés had a good case, but seemed unable to distinguish between large-scale capitalist speculators and small shopkeepers who should be protected, not targeted. Roux and Varlet had connived at violence against small shopkeepers in the February riots and, more generally, seemed unwilling to acknowledge that war and disruption of transatlantic trade, rather than freedom of commerce, were the chief cause of the high prices, factors no government could do much to alleviate. Roux was uninterested in most of the Revolution's goals. He and his allies were not primarily concerned with liquidating opponents and gaining power, though he too lambasted the Brissotins as "royalists wanting to save the tyrant [Louis XVI]" and as "accomplices of Dumouriez," plotting civil war.[75] He was not actually a freedom fighter. But in one respect this fiery Jacobin priest (and former seminary science teacher) represented a genuinely Leftist position against Robespierrisme: he really aspired to defend the poor from capitalist exactions, bankers, and big merchants, denouncing exploitation and failure to aid the poor.

To Robespierre and the Montagne, Roux and Varlet were basically just a nuisance, as they were mobilizing sansculottes for completely different purposes than theirs. The Jacobin response was to savage Roux in the populist press and every other way. Marat (despite the fact it was Roux who hid him in his lodgings when Lafayette's men pursued him in 1791) denounced him in *L'Ami du peuple* as a fraud, liar, and immoral priest, monster of cupidity, and in his hometown, Angoulême, notorious as a criminal. Jacobins must expel him from their midst.[76] Note, admonished Robespierre, resuming the attack in the Convention, how Roux attempts to wrest the people's trust away from the true patriots, especially Robespierre himself, by perfidiously casting an implied semblance of modérantisme over the Montagne![77] On 28 June Robespierre again lambasted Roux and the Enragés. Roux was unceremoniously ejected from the Jacobins and deprived of his job as a supervisor of street posters. Under Jacobin pressure, on 30 June, the Cordeliers too expelled him.[78]

Marginalizing independent-minded sansculottes was essential to Montagnard strategy, but appropriating the world's first democratic constitution, securing its endorsement by the people amid great fanfares, and then immediately suspending it, was unquestionably Robespierre's masterstroke. From late June, opinion in the rebel zones increasingly divided between those for and those against a military offensive against Paris. Despite some defections, the army remained solid for the Montagne, while the columns of Normans, Bordelais, Marseillais, and Lyonnais, supposedly converging on the Convention, never materialized. Such disarray guaranteed steady erosion of the armed revolt over the ensuing weeks. In late July, Caen's patriotic societies, followed by the rest in Calvados, repudiated the Brissotin revolt submitting to the Convention, claiming to have been misled.[79] The Caen rising collapsed, partly through the lack of support in rural Normandy and partly through the leadership's error in entrusting their armed force, around five thousand men, to General Felix Wimpfen and his deputy, the marquis de Puysaie, a former émigré commander soon suspected of royalism. (Puysaie afterward joined the Chouans in the West.) After remaining inactive for weeks, Wimpfen's army simply melted away, obliging Barbaroux, Pétion, Buzot, Salles, and Girey-Dupré to flee as best they could toward Brittany. By August, the Brissotin revolt was visibly crumbling. The Convention summoned all Frenchmen to rally behind the nation. Anyone who had signed protests against the 2 June coup but retracted during these weeks could avoid being declared a traitor to the patrie.

Montpellier, having declined to resort to arms, was occupied and Durand and his comité central arrested. Accused of being among the "principaux moteurs et cooperateurs" of the Southern French "mouvements contre-révolutionnaires fédéralistes," and becoming "dictator" of Montepellier, Durand was brought to Paris and incarcerated at La Force.[80] If the Constitution, before its cancellation, did much of the work of undoing republican resistance, the main factor from August was the obvious truth of the Montagne's claim that the rebellion was everywhere encouraging royalist resurgence. In Brittany, Calvados, and the south, armed opposition was evidently driven by royalism and religion as much as republican rejection of Montagnard revolutionary ideology.[81] Royalist reaction, vigorous in many regions, thus sapped the Brissotins and assisted the pro-Montagnard backlash, leaving the Brissotin movement pulverized between the Montagne and royalism. Many localities had little choice but to submit. Professing to be overcome with remorse, the Société des Amis de la République of Saint-Yrieix-la-Perche, a small commune in rural Limousin, gateway to the southwest, abjectly apologized (for rejecting the regime's authority since June) in an address read on 12 September. "Perfidious writings" had seduced them into adopting "des sentiments contraires" to the people's.[82]

The Brissotin offensive disintegrated. But a single woman struck a resounding blow for the Revolution's true conscience against Montagnard authoritarian populism. Setting out from Caen on 13 July, Charlotte Corday (1768–93), posing as a Jacobine, secured access to Marat, promising lists of prominent insurgents supporting the Normandy rebellion. She stabbed the "friend of the people" to death in his bath with a kitchen knife. The evil of the 2 June insurrection could perhaps somehow be partly expunged, she believed, by eradicating the perpetrator most responsible for verbally violating the Convention, Rights of Man, and democratic Revolution. Marat's last vitriolic sally, savaging Carra, appeared in *L'Ami du peuple* that very day. Those aware knew, as well as Charlotte Corday, Adam Lux, or Tom Paine, that the murdered Jacobin was odious and despicable. Privately, even Robespierre scorned him. Yet, somehow, this shrill, unlovable militant came to be venerated by regime and people to an extent practically nobody else in history ever had. It was the world's first example of an organized mass political cult transforming a nonentity worthy of nobody's respect into a colossal "hero of the people," infinitely beloved by the masses.

The Marat cult drew adoration bordering on fanaticism, but only in certain districts like the sections Droits-de-l'Homme, Sans-culottes, Théâtre-Français, and Fraternité. Within hours of the assassination, Hébert delivered a glowing eulogy demanding the "great hero's apotheosization" by the Convention, a proposal warmly seconded by several sansculotte section assemblies. Marat was infinitely great, insisted Chabot, a mighty prophet who saved the people, recognizing before anyone else the perverse mischief of Mirabeau, Brissot, and other "traitors." The Cordeliers district with its fifteen thousand inhabitants, chief focus of Dantonistes and Hébertistes alike, successively renamed the section Théâtre-Français, and then Marseille was redesignated "Marat."[83] Marat's body, embalmed and on public display in the Cordeliers church near his home from 15 July, lay in state for weeks on a special bed covered in flowers surrounded by candles, attired by the Revolution's greatest artist, David, half uncovered to reveal his stab wounds and bloodied shirt, head topped with a crown of oak leaves. Vast crowds, predominantly women, effused inconsolable grief over the loss of their "martyr."[84]

Many Montagnards had reservations about the Panthéon and installing Marat's tomb there, but there was boundless enthusiasm for erecting a public obelisk in Paris honoring "the people's friend," to be paid for by public subscription. Raising the money was principally undertaken by the still active society of republican revolutionary women.[85] David was commissioned to immortalize Marat's "martyrdom," converting his demise into an unforgettable national icon. Besides the famous painting (finished later), David organized the magnificent funeral procession, which followed further public exposure of the corpse for four days on a pedestal in the Place des Piques (Place Vendôme; until recently called the Place Louis-le-Grand and occupied by the equestrian statue of Louis XIV). The Paris Jacobins engaged six of their leadership— Robespierre, Desmoulins, and four others (one a brother of the murdered Lepeletier)—to compose an "Address to the French," to be declaimed at the Club on 26 July, and afterward printed in immense quantity. Marat tirelessly served the people, intoned this address, always championing their rights. The woman who murdered him was the fanatical tool of the "Calvados conspirators," an "impious faction basely calling the true patriots *désorganisateurs, anarchistes, septembriseurs.*"[86] The new Marat section wanted him entombed in their section in an impressive shrine inscribed: "Here lies the friend of the people, assassinated by an enemy of the people." Busts of Marat proliferated in section assembly halls and clubs across France. Once Paris had sufficiently mourned, one of Marat's leading acolytes proposed to the Convention that the corpse should be displayed in all the departments of France. Indeed, the whole world should contemplate the remains of this "great man, this true republican."[87]

Conveyed to the guillotine four days later, Charlotte went calmly to her death amid indescribable execration but with some of the crowd silently witnessing her last moments admiringly, among them Adam Lux (1765–93), the twenty-eight-year-old tutor who venerated democracy, freedom, and the Revolution even more than his mentor, Forster. Like Paine, Helen Maria Williams, and Mary Wollstonecraft, the principal emissary of the Rheinisch-Germanischer Nationalkonvent, Forster, stranded in Paris by the siege of Mainz, had become deeply depressed.

Though refraining from publicly condemning the Montagne (and later the Terror), by July Forster privately likened the Montagne to a "severe illness" of the body, struggling to expel an extraneous substance that poisons it. Demoralized, aggravated by a recurrent fever contracted in the Pacific decades before, he died in Paris in January 1794.[88] With him in Paris since March 1793, Lux had spent his time in the Convention galleries and at the Jacobins, listening, obsessed and appalled. After the 2 June coup, he sank into despair, contemplating public suicide in central Paris, perhaps in the Convention assembly hall, as a means of displaying his despair to the world. His friends vainly tried to rouse him from his despondency: he had suffered "terriblement" since 31 May, he explained, and remained convinced his suicide would serve mankind more than his life.

He would first deliver a *Discours* before the Convention, he fantasized, a text he actually composed, denouncing the coup that blighted the hopes of millions and ignited civil war. His imagined farewell to the ruined Revolution, dated 6 June, ends with the "orator" requesting burial beside Jean-Jacques's tomb under the Ermenonville oak overshadowing the "Temple of *la philosophie*," marking Rousseau's favorite spot.[89] On 13 July, the day of Marat's assassination, he clandestinely published an alternative pamphlet, *Avis aux citoyens français*, signed "Adam Lux, citoyen français," denouncing the Montagne as the Revolution's wreckers, criminal "septembriseurs," and anarchistes, polluting everything valuable in it, even the names of the greatest men, "Rousseau, Brutus and other foes of oppression," all of whom would be promptly guillotined were they so unfortunate as to fall into the Montagne's abominable hands.[90] Two days after Charlotte's demise, Lux clandestinely issued a second pamphlet, this time recounting her execution, which he witnessed in person. From Germany he had come seeking "true liberty" but found only lies, crassness, and oppression, "le triomphe de l'ignorance et du crime." Never did anyone display greater *courage extraordinaire* than this courageous lady, assassin of one of the worst of men; he would never forget her beautiful comportment—a woman of immortal memory, lovely eyes, gentle enough to move the rocks! He dreamed of raising a statue to her, inscribed, "plus grande que Brutus."[91] Searching for him, the police seized him four days later, incarcerating him at La Force.

Marat's "martyrdom" and unparalleled "greatness" were trumpeted unremittingly for months. Nothing expressed the people's "sublimity" more wonderfully, held enthusiasts, or was more truly "populaire."

Figure 12. Louis-Léopold Boilly (1761–1845), *The Arrest of Charlotte Corday, Paris, 14 July 1793*, pen & ink and w/c on paper. Musée des Beaux Arts, Bordeaux, France / Giraudon / The Bridgeman Art Library.

During 1793–94, the Marat cult lent both unity and momentum to the Montagnard cause at a certain level. Ironically, the company printing mass-produced engravings of France's greatest heroes, having latterly added Buffon, Helvétius, Raynal, and Montesquieu, in August brought out Diderot as its sixth hero, which meant that Diderot had to be followed closely by Marat.[92] But the cult suffered an insuperable vulnerability. However "populaire," none but the simplest could take it seriously. Like the June 1793 coup itself, the Marat cult fed principally on public gullibility. Even the Montagnard leadership, let alone his enemies, knew Marat was a murderous charlatan, so dishonest and criminal he blamed the September massacres on "aristocrates" after himself signing orders for the massacre of imprisoned *gens suspects*. Marat was "un grand homme," insisted Robespierre and his colleagues, but this "mix of falsity and stupidity," as one observer put it, was too blatant to be sustainable for long.[93]

From August 1793, the hopes of the entire democratic republican Left withered. The tyranny's consolidation dejected virtually all the foreign revolutionaries congregating in Paris. As the Brissotin challenge crumbled, the regime tightened the pressure on remaining centers of resistance. Besieged from 8 August, Lyon was subjected to a relentless bombardment. Nevertheless, local sentiment in the main southern cities remained stubbornly anti-Montagnard. In early September, the mood in Bordeaux, complained Robespierre's adherents, still remained "very bad" with only the three or four poorest sections controlled by sansculottes supporting the Montagne, and these all blockaded by fédéralistes, modérés, royalistes, émigrés, and refractory priests.[94] Bordeaux itself, however, was ringed by Jacobin societies in numerous places elsewhere in the southwest from where the city obtained its essential supplies. A missive dated 28 August from the Société des Amis de la Liberté of Bergerac, a major grain and wine depot upriver in the Dordogne, rebuked Bordeaux for defying the people and being dupes of "perfidious men." Noting the growing food shortages, Bergerac's Jacobins urged Bordeaux's sansculottes to rise and overpower the city's Brissotin "membres grangénés." Bergerac's Jacobins wanted Bordeaux's resistance to end soon and Bordeaux's poor sansculotte sections Franklin, De la Liberté, and Rousseau to be the model for the future. Until the Brissotins *were* overthrown "all the granaries of the departments obeying the laws will remain closed to you."[95]

Some Bordelais openly admitted preferring to surrender to the British than to the Montagne. Committed by treaties to crush every manifestation of republicanism and democracy, aristocratic Britain waged unrelenting war on the Republic. Wherever the British appeared, as afterward in Toulon and Corsica, republicanism and democracy were outlawed and royalty reinstated. On 27 August, the British fleet, carrying many émigrés, seized Toulon in collusion with local elements. Toulon's populace duly acclaimed Louis XVII France's rightful monarch and reverted to the old order. As hunger gripped Bordeaux, the artisans and small shopkeepers of the city's National Club increasingly rallied behind the Montagne. Finally, on 17 September, huge sansculotte crowds gathered and assailed Bordeaux's city hall, overthrowing the Brissotin municipality. On 28 September, Héraut de Sechelles, speaking for the Comité de Salut Public, informed the Convention that all resistance had now ended in Bordeaux.[96]

The twenty-five Bordeaux sections opposing the Montagne, their population disarmed, had been reunited with the four supporting the "true Jacobins." The *commission populaire* was suppressed, the Commune fully purged. More than three hundred local leading Brissotins,

Figure 13. *The Contrast, 1793; Which is Best?* Contrasting "British" loyalty, religion, and morality with "French" atheism, perjury, and rebellion. Print made by Thomas Rowlandson, 1792. © The Trustees of the British Museum. All rights reserved.

the Convention heard, were already behind bars. The Jacobins being the only club still permitted, all the rest including the crypto-royalist Club of the Young Men, had been suppressed.[97] A forced subvention would be levied on the rich to indemnify wounded sansculotte victims. On 27 September, public obsequies for Marat were held with dozens of musicians converging from surrounding churches on Bordeaux's magnificent church of Saint-Dominique, where a requiem mass was performed and a rousing oration (sent from Paris) read to the multitude. The people's virtue was infinitely extolled, the "Marseillaise" sung, and the manifestos and edicts of the Brissotin *commission populaire* burned.[98] Prostitutes and ladies too elegantly dressed began to be harassed in the streets.

As it emerged that the Montagne would triumph, it became equally manifest that repression would intensify. Those likeliest to be targeted were in the first place intellectuals, journalists, and *hommes de lettres*. Aristocrats and priests followed and, after them, at a lower level of persecution, bakers, grocers, and prostitutes. Much as affluence and finery were now suspect, so "education above the ordinary level" came to be viewed as redolent of aristocratic attitudes and disdain for the artisan. The kind of virtue that honors humanity, proclaimed the new regime, was that of the ordinary person whose principles are presented "with the simplicity appropriate to them, and without adornment."[99] For Robespierre and the Committee of Public Safety, it was never a priority to target aristocrats as such. But during the summer of 1793, elimination of nobles from public service and the military became a recurrent demand of those surrounding Hébert.[100] Calls to eliminate nobles from civil and military posts, already heard in July before Toulon surrendered, were heightened by allegations that Toulon's artisan sections yielded to the British after being *brissotisé* by aristocratic naval captains.[101] The cry went up: "Remove all nobles, proscribe this impious race." Had not Marat urged the liquidation of "all the *coquins*"? Spurred on by Hébert, now among the club's most active speakers, the campaign fired up much of the Jacobin rank and file. On 26 November, the Jacobins authorized a general scrutiny of their own membership to eradicate ex-nobles (and Jacobin priests like Coupé resisting de-Christianization), the commission entrusted with conducting this purge headed by Hébert and Robespierre.

Montagnard Rousseauiste anti-intellectualism surged so strongly it sometimes approached total repudiation of reading, learning, and higher instruction. At one point, the Convention found it necessary to remind the Comité de l'Instruction Publique that newspapers were still needed, and that certain section bosses were carrying anti-intellectualism too far, construing Rousseau to mean that the people "should be ignorant in order to be happy," even urging them to burn books. Chaumette, chief procurator of the Paris Commune since August 1792 and, from 31 October, president of the Commune, emerged as a key figure in the ideological push of late 1793 to inculcate into the citizenry love for, and practice of, the virtues. An uncompromising pursuer of Brissotins, royalists, and modérés, and a fervent de-Christianizer, as well as persecutor of prostitutes, he shared Rousseau's view that woman's place is in the home. Persuaded the Revolution had encouraged excessive individual freedom, Chaumette agreed with Robespierre that virtue is less a matter of reason than something society imposes uncompromisingly. Enforcing the "ordinary," he explained, requires continual efforts to unmask feigned ordinariness. He had a method for spotting "men to whom certificates of *civisme* should be refused."[102] "Suspicious" individuals were identified by small signs. Besides those associating with known former nobles and priests, it was essential to guard against harder-to-spot dubious types adjusting their language and behavior to circumstances, often spreading bad news with a faked show of displeasure. Reprehensible types were especially given away, he stressed, by their opposing the common view: anyone criticizing the common opinion in popular assemblies was automatically suspect.[103] Every town received instructions as to how to ferret out such "suspects." The société populaire of Louhans in the department of Saône-et-Loire, in an address to the Convention of early September, pledged to wage unremitting war on "l'égoisme, le modérantisme et le fédéralisme," code words for democratic republicans. Not enough "foes of the people" were being captured and executed. Chalon-sur-Saône's sansculottes were continually alert, the Convention was assured, to detect modérantisme and knew how to spot the Revolution's concealed enemies. They wanted a roving revolutionary militia in their area, headed by a popular tribune, to help liquidate "all the vampires and serpents in human form."[104]

If no political party in the modern sense, the Brissotins represented more than a mere faction pursuing power or personal goals. Montagnard rhetoric has often led modern historians to suppose they really adhered to modérantisme or fédéralisme. They have sometimes been styled "the Revolution's right wing," the "party of the businessmen and merchants."[105] But if more tolerant of different views than their Montagnard opponents, and defenders of economic and personal freedom, they were not liberals or moderates. Rather, they were the first to envisage tackling economic inequality and attempting to create a fairer society by constitutional, legal, and nonviolent means, especially tax and inheritance laws combined with financial assistance for society's weakest. The Revolution's first republicans, they were also far more genuine republicans and democrats than the Montagne, and the real framers of both versions of the Declaration of Rights of 1789 and 1793. They were, in fact, the founders of the modern human rights tradition, black emancipation, women's rights, and modern representative democracy, though some Montagards, it must be remembered, like Desmoulins, Romme, and Cloots, were sincere democratic republicans too. Prime defenders of the Revolution's core values, Brissotins and Dantonists formed the essential link connecting the Revolution to the Enlightenment in both its eighteenth-century and modern contemporary sense, especially Enlightenment in its radical, secular, democratic form, and thus the first organized champions of democratic, rights-based, secular modernity.

CHAPTER 18

De-Christianization

(1793–94)

Reducing and marginalizing religious authority and the public role of religion and religious values was always central to the outlook and writings of the radical philosophes. Equally, curtailing religious authority was in every way central to the Revolution of Mirabeau, Sieyès, Barnave, Condorcet, and Brissot. But was a gradual process of diminishing and degrading ecclesiastical sway in politics, education, culture, daily life, and the economy without stoking civil strife a feasible goal? By the time the Republic was proclaimed in September 1792, relations between church and state in France had hugely deteriorated since 1789. Even so, as yet there were no physical attacks on churches, active persecution of clergy, or organized destruction of images and cult objects, nothing resembling a drive to expunge every reminder of traditional worship and extirpate from sight Christian piety and the routines of daily life.

Following the pope's public repudiation of the Rights of Man and the Revolution, many French priests who had earlier sworn their loyalty to the Constitution of 1791 formally retracted. Retractions, frequent during the winter of 1791–92, began seriously to alarm the revolutionary leadership. The trend added to the ideological and political strife plaguing France by reinforcing and emboldening the refractory clergy and émigrés, and further embittering the quarrel between the two warring halves of the French Church.[1] By denouncing the constitutional clergy as "rebels" and "schismatics," and disposing many people in towns and villages throughout France against them, the ultraroyalist press and refractory priests both widened the ecclesiastical rift and aggravated the Revolution's and the country's inherent instability. Ultraroyalist opinion, buoyed by Catholic insurgency in the west and parts of the south, Alsace, and Belgium, clashed directly and relentlessly with Feuillant constitutional monarchism, and the constitutional Church scarcely less than with democratic republicanism and populist authoritarian Jacobinism.

By mid-1791, the Legislative Assembly was dangerously trapped between freedom of conscience and cult on one side and containing the growing anger, divisiveness, and ferocity of religious conflict, as well as the stern admonitions of religious authority opposing the Revolution, on the other.[2] Growing antagonism between legislature and religious tradition fomented a battle of loyalties from which there was no easy exit. More and more deputies, including not just veteran anticlericals but also zealous constitutional priests like Fauchet, Grégoire, and the austere egalitarian disciple of Mably, Jacques-Marie Coupé, demanded ever tougher measures against opposition-minded, obstreperous refractory clergy, while yet professing to safeguard the Revolution's ceaselessly avowed commitments to toleration, religious liberty, and freedom of expression. In June 1791, the unbending Coupé personally supervised closure of the Catholic seminary at Noyon because it remained a hotbed of refractory obstructionism.[3] This campaign of intensifying pressure against obdurate réfractoires provoked loud complaints of "fanaticism" and hypocrisy from the French royalist-Catholic press. Voltaire, Montesquieu, Rousseau, and Raynal, admonished L'Ami du Roi in October 1791, had called the Church "fanatical" and intolerant, a persecutor of religious and nonreligious minorities. Yet, now the minority being persecuted was the refractory clergy itself, those the "party of philosophy" called "fanatics." Since turning their own doctrine into "a kind of religion," and conquering France, the philosophes and their disciples had themselves become France's persécuteurs. "What a paradox!"[4] Much of France was indeed appalled and outraged. Yet, for all the refractory clergy's loud protests over the alleged "persecution," real persecution and oppression were yet to begin.

During the years 1788–91, the conflict between Revolution and Christianity, then, remained largely a political struggle that elements among both revolutionaries and constitutional clergy made some effort to confine to the institutional and economic issues dividing Church and state, essentially a contest about the size, power, and wealth of the Church that some revolutionary leaders had no wish to see become a wider ideological, doctrinal, and spiritual clash. But in early 1792, a prolonged intermediate phase began, lasting until mid-1793, in which the spiraling antagonism between Christianity and the Revolution did indeed gradually develop into a broader conflict over religious authority, values, and doctrine. The impulse to repression and coercion, and threat to freedom of expression and cult, grew and became more obvious. Even so, until June 1793 the fight remained basically a war of words and symbols, a nonviolent cultural struggle. On Easter Day, the day of the Passion, 6 April 1792, the Assembly forbade the wearing of ecclesiastical dress of any kind, *costume sacerdotal*, in the streets or anywhere outside churches, a landmark change and signal blow to traditional culture, plainly aimed at curbing the clergy's participation and presence, as clergy, in society and everyday life.[5]

Relentless deterioration in relations and intensification of conflict stemmed from the fact that the early campaign to restructure the Church and regenerate it on a new basis had by early 1792 completely stalled. What had not stalled was the revolutionary regime's determination to weaken religious authority, and especially the role of religion in politics, education, and daily life. Reflecting increasing frustration with the Civil Constitution of the Clergy of 1791, Feuillants and Brissotins alike added to the mounting impatience and verbal violence typical of this period, albeit still paying fulsome lip service to toleration, individual liberty, and freedom of expression. By voting on 27 May 1792 to banish the most intransigent refractory priests from the country, the Assembly took a step further down the road to open conflict with Christianity and away from the principles of toleration, religious freedom, and peaceful secularization. Additional pressure to further curtail the Church's power and status during this intermediate phase arose among those charged with directing revolutionary France's financial and educational policies. In November 1792, Joseph Cambon (1754–1820), a prominent Brissotin deputy from Montpellier and former textile merchant, head of the Comité des Finances, urged the legislature to agree that the costs of maintaining the constitutional clergy (salaries and pensions) should no longer be met by society but rather become the exclusive responsibility of the Catholic congregations themselves, thereby placing Catholics on the same basis as the other religious cults. Expecting society at large to maintain the clergy, after all, infringed the rights of nonbelievers, Protestants, Jews, and other non-Catholics. Why should society maintain the constitutional anymore than the Protestant or refractory clergy? His advice, shelved for the moment, implied the complete overturning of the church settlement of 1790.

This intermediary phase, preceding the turn to de-Christianization proper, still operated on a level that was purely symbolic and verbal. Complaints about the inappropriate public cost of the Church to society, laced with denunciation of priestly royalist subversion of the Revolution, were loudly voiced by some Brissotin leaders. Denunciation of the priesthood and their influence was still more strident and vituperative in the rhetoric of many Montagnard populists—albeit not Robespierre, who always remained personally antagonistic to the philosophes' irreligion. In this way, the mounting strife during these months introduced the language of violent suppression and coercion that from mid-1793 was destined to be translated into action. The mathematician Jacob-Louis Dupont (d. 1813), deputy for a Loire constituency in the Legislative Assembly and the Convention, and, like Cambon, among the Convention's chief financial experts, on 14 December 1792 appealed for a greater effort to overthrow "the altars and idols," replacing religious education in France with a wholly secular education based on the projected publicly funded and directed primary schools.

In late December 1792, the Paris Commune, now dominated by Pétion and the Brissotins, forbade the "superstitious" practice of midnight mass. On 24 December, Christmas Eve 1792, the Commune announced that the Paris churches would be closed from 6:00 PM to 6:00 AM, which provoked outraged groups of the devout to gather at midnight around several main Parisian churches to ensure their curés did open up for midnight mass.[6] As this symbolic and verbal strife between militant secularists and Catholic pious intensified in early 1793, not least due to the Vendéean revolt and the Revolution's military collapse in Belgium, warning signs that in worsening circumstances an active persecution instigated by a pending aggressive de-Christianization campaign could begin became more frequent. Throughout 1792 and early 1793, nevertheless, the Brissotin democratic republican ascendancy continued to rein in anticlercial intolerance, kept the churches open, and broadly conserved religious freedom, respect for "liberty of cult," and the status of the constitutional priesthood. De-Christianization as such had not yet begun.

Only after the coup of 2 June 1793 and the overthrow of the Revolution's core values could a violently persecuting, fanatical offensive ensue, and this is precisely what occurred beginning in the late summer of 1793. The turn from a verbal and symbolic war between the Revolution and Christianity to a campaign of violent, coercive suppression was thus very closely and integrally linked, politically and ideologically, to the coup of June 1793 and the ousting of the democratic republicans, for it was this that removed the constitutional and legal barriers that had so far broadly held anticlerical exasperation, hostility, and intolerance in check. In the late summer of 1793, de-Christianization rapidly evolved into a repressive, vandalistic, inquisitorial movement, albeit essentially local and fragmented, and lacking central direction. In fact, de-Christianization in the French Revolution, though it became systematic in many places, was never a coordinated, nationwide campaign. Its momentum derived mainly from particular Montagnard leaders and political factions. It evolved unevenly, varying considerably in character from area to area, developing at the local level rather than from any comprehensive legislation or concerted initiative authorized by the Convention or revolutionary executive committees.[7]

De-Christianization as such emanated neither from the top of the group dictatorship nor the sansculotte social base of the new power pyramid, but rather from the revolutionary vanguard beneath Robespierre and Danton orchestrating the sociétés populaires.[8] Though strictly a minority movement, de-Christianization was nevertheless part of the urban populist authoritarian upsurge and hence enjoyed sporadic mass support, this aggressive ideology thriving mainly among the hard-liners and political bosses controlling France's local Jacobin societies and some Paris sections. Among the chief figures of this harsh and violent anti-Christian repression were Chaumette, Hébert, Chabot, Lequinio, Fouché, Desmoulins, Bourdon, Dupont, Fabre d'Églantine, Momoro, Dumont, and Cloots, all declared zealots of atheism. The leading de-Christianizer in Tarbes and the Basque Country, where he provoked bitter local opposition, was Benoît Monestier, himself a former priest and one of the most violent foes of the Brissotins. Chaumette, son of an artisan and former medical student, originally a protégé of Desmoulins later prominent in the Cordeliers (where he had exchanged his Christian first names for "Anaxagoras"), figured among the campaign's principal activists in Paris where the movement began. Dogmatically intolerant, neither he nor Hébert, claimed the atheist librarian Maréchal later, were genuine philosophique atheists. To Maréchal they were merely unscrupulous, power-hungry "tartuffes révolutionnaires."[9] In the early autumn of 1793, Chaumette, now a leading member of the Paris Commune, accompanied the fiercely anti-Christian zealot Joseph Fouché (1759–1820), a former Oratorian priest and among the Montagne's best orators, on one of the first large-scale de-Christianizing sweeps in the provinces, in the La Nièvre region of north-central France, while another Montagnard representative on mission, the lawyer André Dumont (1765–1836), initiated systematic persecution of curates and the devout in Abbeville and Lequinio at Rochefort.

Cloots and Maréchal were more serious ideologues than the rest. Chosen president of the Paris Jacobins for the period 11 to 29 November 1793, Cloots delivered an address to the Convention on 17 November (27 Brumaire) that marked the high tide of the de-Christianization movement and the militant atheistic-philosophique cult of reason and nature so detested by Robespierre. On that occasion, Cloots adamantly denounced revealed religion's "absurdity," citing the many clashes with religious faith in which he had engaged in the past. "L'explosion philosophique" transforming France was the fruit of fifty years of dogged perseverance in the face of persecution. Conversion of a great people to the "revelation du bon sens" proved the philosophes had not sown in vain. He heavily stressed the ties between the "révolution philosophique" prior to 1789 and the "la révolution politique" commencing in 1789. Early in the Revolution, he had tried to dedicate a new edition of his pre-Revolution, anti-Christian diatribe, *La Certitude des preuves du Mahométanisme* ("Londres" [i.e., Amsterdam], 1780), to the Legislative Assembly, only to find his motion blocked by Fauchet.[10] But times had changed. Full recognition could now be bestowed on the Revolution's first great "adversaries of religion." He proposed the public honoring of Jean Meslier (1664–1729), the intrepid curé of Étrépigny in Champagne whose *Testament philosophique* (composed in the 1720s) insisting on the need to rescue the peasantry from churchmen as part of a more general effort to redeem them from their misery and ignorance was the first summons for a general, unremitting war on religion, as well as on the nobility and clergy. A statue of Meslier erected in the Jacobin Club, he suggested, would fittingly commemorate that writer's achievement.[11]

Heralds of Jacobin persecution of religion claimed to be eradicating "superstition." They did so by combining vandalism aimed at the symbols and ritual objects of organized religion with harassing clergy and the devout psychologically and physically, and preaching an austere new secular *moralisme*. Fouché, keenly conscious of the refractory clergy's inciting peasants to violence against revolutionaries (having himself narrowly avoided assassination by insurgents in the Vendée), vehemently condemned "false religion" in La Nièvre department in September 1793, calling for its extirpation in favor of a deistic civic cult. The Revolution proclaimed freedom of conscience, he conceded in a manifesto of 10 October 1793, but authorized no faith other than that of universal morality. Catholicism should be stripped of its special status, and immediately. Crosses and other religious symbols should no longer be used in funerary rites. This edict initiated a campaign to erase crosses from cemeteries and country roads throughout the department, which soon took hold over large stretches of countryside. Fouché's fanaticism extended to ordering local cemetery gates to bear the rubric, "death is but an eternal sleep."[12]

During late 1793, constitutional clergy strongly committed to the Revolution, such as Grégoire, Fauchet, Coupé, and Lamourette, were still courageously proclaiming the inner compatibility of the Revolution with Catholicism, but found themselves in an increasingly marginalized and untenable position. The egalitarian, tolerant, and democratic principles of the Revolution of 1788–93 were perfectly defensible, they contended, without espousing irreligion, materialism, and anticlerical militancy. These men, eminent and brave, embodied a Catholic Radical Enlightenment that now verged on extinction. Until the late summer of 1793, they backed the revolutionary government as best they could, but they could not avoid publicly waging war on the philosophique roots of the anti-Christian tendency, which eventually pitted them too against the legislature and much of the Montagnard leadership. Having broken with the Cercle Social in the spring of 1791, Fauchet, like Grégoire, ended up becoming hopelessly isolated. Lamourette delivered an address at his episcopal seat of Lyon on 29 April 1793 publicly denouncing what he called the harmful dominance of philosophy in shaping the Revolution. The advance of "cette tenebreuse philosophie," materialist and atheist (in the style of Diderot, d'Holbach, Condorcet, Volney, and Cloots), was a deadly threat, he admonished, that would blight liberty itself and the Revolution's promised universal social regeneration, brutalizing the people and extinguishing all principles. In fact, he suggested, this was the real goal behind the verbal attacks on Christianity; the ambitious schemers driving it were deliberately aggravating division and factionalism within the Revolution for their own nefarious purposes.[13]

Constitutional clergy and those aspiring to synthesize Revolution and Christianity were a fast dwindling force in a fraught context that prevented them from developing a coherent political strategy. In the Rhone Valley, some constitutionals aligned with Chalier's hard-line Jacobins or remained neutral, but most sided unhesitatingly with the Brissotins. Although more likely than Robespierristes to be philosophical materialists, atheists, and radical secularists, Brissotins were also more genuinely committed to freedom of conscience and basic human rights. The latter included no leading active persecutors. Aggressive persecution of religion and vandalism was entirely a Montagnard prerogative. This explains the remarkable paradox that Left republicans, Christianity's main intellectual enemies through the years 1788–93 until eliminated during the autumn of 1793, nevertheless emerged as the main protectors of Christian conscience and freedom of cult. After the toppling of Chalier's Jacobin despotism at Lyon on 29 May 1793, for example, Lamourette unhesitatingly preached on behalf of the Brissotin faction, battling to save Lyon from the Jacobins. As strife between the Montagne and the Lyonnais escalated, the bishop issued a pastoral letter, dated 14 July, addressing the entire department, denouncing not just Chalier but also the "anarchist brigands" manipulating the Paris sansculottes as a pernicious subversive group knowingly or unknowingly assisting France's royalists and aristocrats.[14] The fact that leading constitutional prelates vigorously supported the Left republicans against the Montagne, however, only rendered Brissotins and constitutionals more vulnerable to persecution during the murderous strife soon engulfing the country.

The fanaticism and vandalism of organized de-Christianization collided head-on with the fervent religious zealotry everywhere driving France's rebel Counter-Enlightenment, and together the unstoppable force and unmovable object pulverized the openness and liberty of cult prevailing earlier, during the years 1788–93. Once de-Christianization set in, it rapidly gained traction in Paris and the northern and central provinces, followed by the southwest. Within weeks of the June 1793 coup, the Parisian section assemblies had closed down most of the capital's churches, and by December all, including the university chapels,[15] albeit in this respect the capital preceded the rest of France. In Bordeaux, by December 1793, only four churches remained open for Christian worship, the rest having been closed or put to alternative uses, among them the cathedral of Saint-André, now converted into a storage depot (with the surrounding Place Saint-André renamed the Place de la Montagne). In much of the country, closing churches was slower and more sporadic. In Marseille and most of the south, few churches were closed before January or February 1794, and even after that many remained open. Even so, by Easter 1794, the great majority of France's roughly forty thousand churches had been closed for Christian worship.[16] Wherever churches were shut, major and minor edifices alike were allocated new names and functions and were being used as public stores, workshops, meeting halls, barracks, and stables. Often, former Catholic sanctuaries, tombs, and chapels became mausoleums and commemorative temples.[17] The vast premises of the Abbey de Saint-Germain-des-Près in Paris, now renamed the Maison de l'Unité, became one of the capital's main prisons, with part of it becoming a salt-peter works. In August 1794, fire broke out in this refinery, consuming much of the abbey's priceless library, though the irreplaceable medieval manuscripts were largely saved thanks to volunteers rushing to fight the flames.[18]

Despite restricted popular support, de-Christianization proved perfectly capable of recruiting street gangs and orchestrating group vandalism. During late summer and autumn 1793 in the Paris sections and other main cities, and eventually in smaller places, demolition committees and teams set to work erasing religious symbols and images from everyday life. Effigies and names of saints disappeared from streets and church buildings, numerous Christ figures were decapitated, and the Virgin Mary was everywhere disfigured. Bells and belfries were pulled down, religious paintings trampled to shreds. In Notre Dame and Saint-Germain in Paris, anti-Christianizers risked their lives climbing makeshift scaffolding to smash saints, angels, and popes carved in upper niches, sometimes scarcely visible at all from below.[19] Religious images were then frequently replaced by busts of the Revolution's chief "saint" Marat, or that of his only near rival in popularity, Louis-Michel Lepeletier. A wealthy magistrate among the first Estates-General nobles, joining the Third in 1789, on the very evening of 20 January 1793 after he voted for Louis XVI's death sentence, Lepeletier was stabbed to death by a former royal guard while dining in a Palais-Royal restaurant.[20] David depicted this in a painting, just as he had Marat's death. Both paintings were then hung in the entryway to the Convention's meeting hall.

In timing, motivation, and context, de-Christianization was integrally linked to the violence, mass intimidation, and repression of the Terror.[21] On 6 November 1793, Lequinio presided over a ceremony before the entire population of Rochefort, gathered in the main parish church—now renamed the Temple de la Vérité—to watch eight Catholic priests and one Protestant pastor renounce their vows and holy orders in the name of philosophy.[22] On 7 November 1793, the elected constitutional bishop of Paris, Jean-Baptiste Joseph Gobel (1727–94), pressured by Chaumette, Cloots, and Léonard Bourdon, appeared with eleven renouncing priests before the Convention and ceremonially resigned his see and priestly status. This occurred four days after Bourdon, a fierce pursuer of the Brissotins, close to Hébert but at odds with both the Énrages and with Robespierre (who greatly scorned him), had delivered a long tirade at the Jacobins, demanding that the priesthood be compelled to admit that they were all either "imbeciles or deceivers": "oui, let us call them before the tribunal of the truth!"[23] During the ceremony, Gobel, stripping off his episcopal garb and insignia, donned a red cap of liberty, proclaiming the only true religion to be that of liberty and equality, confessing his previous life of faith one of "imposture."[24] Before long, the Paris Commune attempted to replace Christianity with "le culte de la Raison sans prêtres" throughout the capital, replacing Christian rites with republican ceremonies at which public authorities assumed the lead and republican hymns were sung.

This deistic public cult was formally inaugurated, with Chaumette presiding, on 10 November 1793 (20 Brumaire) with a grandiose public ceremony at Notre Dame, now renamed the Paris "Temple of Reason." Republican hymns, specially composed by Marie-Joseph Chénier, were recited by a girls' choir. The goddess "Reason," descending from her temple, lit by the flame of truth, to receive the congregation's homage, was represented by a leading opera singer, Mademoiselle Maillard. Numerous "temples of reason" displaced Christian churches in both Paris and, more sporadically, provincial centers, and soon also in villages. Street parades and "festivals of reason" created an elaborate new quasi-religious festival culture with Reason invariably represented as a female deity, mostly by a young woman from among the sansculotte leadership. Mme. Candeille, for example, wife of the Cordeliers orator Momoro, prominently performed this role, surrounded by dancers, musical fanfares, and entourages of priests and priestesses of Reason. Wine and feasting invaded the churches, and amid this strange mix of fanaticism, idolatry, intolerant deism, and carousing also occurred, reportedly, much erotic coupling in darkened chapels and niches.

The fast dwindling remnant of priests still frequenting the Convention in late 1793, including Alexandre-Marie Thibault (d. 1812), bishop and deputy of the Cantal, mostly followed Gobel's example and resigned from the priesthood by the end of the year. Before long, the Abbé Grégoire, constitutional bishop of Blois, found himself the last remaining deputy wearing ecclesiastical dress in the Convention. He too came under pressure to renounce but resisted, stubbornly affirming the oneness of Christianity and the Revolution.[25] The same could not be said for the Loire town of Blois, of which he was nominally bishop, since he was forced to boycott his own diocese. The ironic assurance of the local société populaire that "the saints" of Blois were coming to the defense of the patrie, signified that the town's numerous relics, crucifixes, and church bells were being removed for melting down and recasting into cannons, its large crosses replaced with liberty trees, and confessionals turned into sentry boxes. Blois cathedral, the société assured the Convention in late November, had been replaced with a temple dedicated to reason, while la philosophie was progressing triumphantly even in the countryside, where everything savoring of "superstition" was being eradicated. Blois Jacobins requested the Convention to appoint "patriotic and enlightened" commissaires to carry "the light" throughout their department and on to the Vendée.[26]

Resignation from the priesthood under, and sometimes not under, pressure became an established revolutionary ritual, involving a formal certificate of demission termed an "acte de déprêtrise." In November, and through December 1793, thousands of former Catholic priests, some addressing the Convention, renounced their vows, profession, and salaries, declaring before "all France they no longer wished to acknowledge any cult except that of reason and liberty, a cult destined to conquer the globe and break the chains of all peoples."[27] Paul Roland, sixty-year-old curé of Binos in the remote district of Saint-Gaudens (now renamed Mont-Unité) in the Haute-Garonne, village priest for forty years, resigned the priesthood forever in the name of reason, in a missive read to the legislature on 10 November. Justice is the "only true religion" and no other cult is required on earth "but that of virtue": "I believe also that Heaven is nothing other than the happiness of having been virtuous." Repudiating priest's garb and pension, Roland pledged himself henceforth exclusively to "la triomphe de la philosophie."[28] Public staging of forced priestly resignations and forced marriages of former ecclesiastics became favorite devices of many representatives on mission.[29]

Pressured by Fouché, the curé Pascal-Antoine Grimaud (1736–99) renounced the Church on 14 November and resigned, hoping he had never misused priestly authority to "arrest the progress of liberty, equality, philosophy or democratic government."[30] The société populaire of Moncontour in Vienne department assured the Convention on 29 December that their village, scorning aristocratic prejudices and "tired of the charlatanisme of priests," had informed their curé he was now just a simple citizen and must renounce the clerical state. The village church was immediately stripped of its plate and objects "used to feed superstition and fanaticism."[31] Constitutional priests in and around Saint-Malo mostly abjured their faith in December, among them Charles

Caron, curé of an outlying locality who had already been married two months when publicly renouncing. Caron had ardently supported the Revolution since 1789 with "all his heart," in the name of la philosophie and public peace. Such sentiments were decidedly not those of the town more generally. The Saint-Malo area was more distant from Paris than geography would suggest, complained Jean-Baptiste Lecarpentier (1759–1829), the people's représentant, especially in its "rapports philosophiques." Lecarpentier, who "republicanized" Saint-Malo by installing busts of Marat and Lepeletier everywhere he went, regretted that religion and tradition still retained an unfortunately strong hold on its inhabitants.[32]

By summer 1794, more than 20,000 constitutional priests, the great majority of the Church's priesthood, had formally resigned—and more than 6,000 had also married.[33] In the southeastern part of the Paris Basin around Auxerre and Sens (department of Yonne), where support for the Revolution remained solid (as throughout the Paris Basin) and more than 90 percent of clergy swore the 1791 constitutional oath, outward harmony between Revolution and faith persisted promisingly until late 1792. The middle stage of growing verbal violence was characterized here by increasing refractory influence and numerous retractions of the constitutional oath, a defiant attitude "incivique et contre-révolutionnaire," which, however, only seriously stirred the laity against the Revolution when the department's army recruiting drive intensified following the Republic's disastrous military defeats of March 1793.[34] In April, the revolutionary regime reacted to this growing, religiously sanctioned obstruction by arresting forty-eight clergy at Sens and thirty-six at Auxerre. Yet, however drastic such action, this was primarily still retaliation for disobedience to the civil authority rather than systematic persecution as such. The intermediate period, though one of sharply deteriorating relations between clergy and regime, still differed markedly from the post-June 1793 de-Christianization proper.[35] Organized, systematic de-Christianization gripped the Yonne department from late 1793 to summer 1794, spurred chiefly by the sociétés populaires. Images of saints toppled in the hundreds. Churches were closed. The nonbelieving departmental bishop, Loménie de Brienne, was arrested in November 1793. The constitutional clergy, even in small villages, were bullied into renouncing the priesthood and some into marrying. Fights erupted in several places between villagers and missionaries of militant anti-Christianity known as "apostles of reason." Finally, in February 1794, Auxerre and Sens cathedrals were closed.

Leaders of the de-Christianization movement depicted Christianity and its advocates as an additional layer of tyranny to be stripped away. Announcing the approaching triumph of la raison universelle over religion and the "fédéralisme des sectes politiques," Cloots assured the Paris Jacobins that "every idol overthrown by *la philosophie* is a victory gained over tyrants."[36] France had groaned under tyrants for centuries, claimed an address delivered by commissaires from the department of Charente before the Convention on 20 December 1793, until "la philosophie et la raison," reviving man's "natural energy, enabled him finally to understand his power and rights, break his chains" and initiate "une grande révolution . . . Vainly do creatures of the imbecile Pius VI threaten us with a terrible God in whom they themselves do not believe."[37] Small communes, no less than major cities, suffered such systematic stripping away of spiritual and physical "tyranny." "Regeneration" of Gagny, a municipality of the Seine-et-Oise department, was supervised by a member named Sarrette, of the Comité de Surveillance, of the Paris section Brutus, sent by the Comité de Sûreté Générale with a group of sansculottes to "take the measures necessary for the regeneration of the commune." He was instructed to lend assistance to oppressed patriots, extend *la Terreur révolutionnaire* to the ill-intentioned and "aristocrats," and "bring the light of truth to those misled." Convening Gagny's primary assembly in the town's main church on 28 Frimaire (19 December 1793), Sarette converted the church, now abandoned by its curate, into a "temple of reason," instituting a public festival venerating "the martyrs of liberty," Marat and Lepeletier, whose busts he installed. Amid cheers of "Vive la République!," the people, in a "spontaneous movement," stripped all the "relics, images and books from their church, heaped them up in front of the town's Liberty Tree, and burnt them." The church plate was remitted to their district's chief commune for melting down.[38]

De-Christianization, promoted by representatives on mission and local "popular societies" during the Terror, was linked also to the rapid spread of the "popular societies," which reflected the fact that de-Christianization was integral to the penetration and extension of the new system of Montagnard despotic power. In Yonne department, the number of sociétés populaires rose from thirty-seven to more than fifty during the winter of 1793–94.[39] Overt support for revolutionary authority, and participation in the societies and hence in de-Christianizing activities, became a means to promote oneself and one's family. Purported instruments of the "people's" cause, actually the popular societies, were levers of local authority and influence. De-Christianization and politicization of areas that had often been only slightly touched by the Revolution thus far proceeded together. The sansculottes of Avenay, near Épernay in the Marne department, established their société populaire in December 1793 and promised to promote patriotism, safeguard "liberty," propagate the sacred principles of equality, and wage war on "superstition." Removing ritual objects and plate, they closed their church. "The sacred principles of nature," announced their address to the Convention of 4 January 1794, were acquiring deep roots in the Avenay countryside, crushing all fédéralistes, modérés, and égoistes. "The tocsin of reason sounds among all peoples": they have slept too long, but their awakening will be "terrible." Liberty and Equality were the sole divinities acknowledged by Avenay's société populaire, although to them these principles chiefly meant proclaiming "the holy Montagne the only rampart of liberty" and reviling the "infamous" Brissotin deputies recently arrested for treason.[40]

At the little town of Saint-Fargeau, in a forested, thinly populated part of the Paris Basin where the Revolution had so far intruded only lightly, introducing revolutionary authority, crushing dissent, erasing the past's legal legacy, changing local place-names, and dismantling Christianity were all fused into a single ceremony on 1 December 1793. This occurred not through local initiative but when a gang of activists arrived from nearby Auxerre to overawe local resistance and purge the local Jacobin club. New leaders assumed control, Saint-Fargeau's name was changed to "Lepeletier," the church was vandalized, and a vast pile of legal documents were collected by the société populaire; certificates recognizing judges, notaries, and advocates active in the Commune (those until 1792 bearing royal seals), were ceremonially burned on a public bonfire in the town square while the townsfolk sang hymns of liberty. The singing was less than inspiring, apparently, as the société populaire complained to the Convention about the lack in places like Lepeletier of trained musicians to enhance public ceremonies and hymn-singing where new festivities, patriotic poetry, and "leçons philosophiques" needed to be supplemented by singing and music. Republican sentiment among country folk, the Convention was told, could best be inculcated by replacing superstitious old ceremonies with attractive new ones enhanced by music to help laborers relax from exhausting work.[41]

The campaign to change village, district, and street names, meanwhile, rapidly accelerated. The autumn *rage révoluionnaire* of 1793, besides destroying an immense quantity of sacred images, purged the word "saint" from thousands of street names in capital and provinces alike, rendering the process general and obligatory. In Gard department, in the south, a quarter of all communes changed their names to erase Christian allusion, Saint-Raphael becoming Baraston and Saint-Tropez, Héraclée, while another quarter substituted "Mont" or "Font" for "Saint," a procedure called *débaptisation*.[42] As more towns and villages divested themselves of Christian-sounding names, the pressure on those not yet debaptized increased. Saint-Omer since 1792 was officially called Morin-la-Montagne. This rendered it harder to resist changing Saint-Malo's name too, though the Commune there reluctantly agreed only to switch to "Port Malo," lest a totally unrecognizable, new name blight their overseas trade ties.[43]

A visitation of *réprésentants en mission* in October 1793 to Indre department in west-central France, formerly part of Berry province, was the signal for town and village name-changing throughout the department. Châteauroux, the chief town, swapped its ancient name for "Indreville" (and from March 1794 until March 1795, to "Indrelibre"), while the surrounding villages labeled "Saint" adopted alternatives, Saint-Gaultier becoming Roche-libre, and Saint-Genou Indreval.[44] Speeches delivered throughout the department proclaimed "the inutility and menace of the sect of men whose egoism and passions had so often exploited talk of the divinity to introduce conflict among peoples." Sunday observance and churchgoing ceased. "Docile to the voice of nature and religion, town and village inhabitants of Indre," the Convention was informed, "gathered in the very temples so recently consecrated to error," to celebrate "le triomphe de la philosophie" with patriotic songs. "The time is not far off," predicted de-Christianizers, "when reason will secure the suppression of all religious cults." An earlier order of 20 November 1793 required all the department's municipalities to remove silver plate and other "useful metals," supporting the "domination de la secte sacerdotale," from the churches. Objects formerly serving the "pride of priests" now afforded resources for weapons to "disperse the servile subordinates of the monsters called kings."[45]

Church closures and establishing the "festival of reason" in Angoulême (now renamed Montagne-Charente) were directed by représentant Jean-Baptiste Harmand (1751–1816). The citizens, he assured the Convention on 1 December 1793, had joyfully celebrated the triumph of la philosophie and dissipation of the darkness "in which the priests had immersed us the better to keep us under their yoke." This transpired in "the temple," until recently the cathedral of Saint-Pierre, until now a "stronghold of superstition, prejudice, error, and lies" where priests continually admonished the credulous that their hidden God would wreak terrible punishment on revolutionaries. The God of the priests, Harmand assured the townsfolk, is a divinity of cruelty and vengeance, the true God of nature and the Revolution a God of justice and reason, whose desire was the people's welfare. "The priests could deceive us because we had our eyes closed; let us now open them and the priests shall flee even more swiftly than our political tyrants." Let them join their "imbecile chief at Rome" (the pope), like the émigrés joined "the tigers of Germany [i.e., the German princes]. Soon we shall have salutary laws, expressing the *volonté générale*."[46]

Harmand's reports are significant because this former lawyer remained strictly neutral between Brissotins and Montagnards (while privately reviling Robespierre). Having opposed Louis XVI's death sentence, he deferred to the Montagne but only outwardly. Between speeches, fanfares, and hymns recounting how la philosophie liberated Angoulême from ignorance and superstition, the Rights of Man were intoned. If his assessment was a relatively independent one, he flavored it with language the Montagne wished to hear. Angoulême had not expected a representative sent by those disparaged by Brissotin calominateurs as "monsters thirsting for blood," anarchists without principles, to purify the city and eulogize virtue. Local people now grasped that toppling tyranny meant overthrowing "the lies of the ministers of the altars," that the Revolution truly wished to establish a morality applying to all, "la morale universelle," proclaiming men free and equal. Gladly they rejected the "vertus abstractives" propagated by Brissotins, substituting "one aristocracy for another." The only genuine religious dogmas are liberty and equality. Women, so often profaned by priestly impostors to further their criminal projects, must learn not to be the "passive instrument of imposture." Women receive Nature's precious gifts for the happiness of men, not to make them feel culpable. Society needs virtuous wives and tender mothers who are aware there are no mysteries other than those arising from the limits of our rational understanding. There is no other divinity than the truth and the laws. The "martyrs de cette sainte Révolution" (meaning Marat and Lepeletier) were true men of the people venerated by everyone.[47]

De-Christianization inspired a massive wave of iconoclasm across France, as well as Belgium and the Rhineland, and a new kind of "preaching." Integral to the process was liquidating celebrated local relics to prove, notwithstanding centuries of adoration, these possessed no miraculous powers. At Montagne-sur-mer—the new name of the old fortress town of Montreuil-sur-mer—where the local société républicaine's previous membership of two hundred was now savagely purged to thirty, the church was thoroughly vandalized and all the images removed. The liberation of Toulon (now renamed Port-la-Montagne) from the British, on 19 December 1793, an event celebrated across France (frequently in an explicitly anti-Christian manner), was marked in Montagne-sur-mer by the public incineration of a whole collection of male and female saints in the town square.[48] The representative on mission purging the Pas-de-Calais in the autumn of 1793, André Dumont, a brutal functionary esteemed by Robespierre, who assured the Convention he was a "missionaire républicain," celebrated the defeat of the Brissotins with a public banquet in Boulogne for the six thousand townspeople, organized by the local société populaire in the main square. Some wished to rename Boulogne "Port-de-l'Union." Planting a "Tree of Union," and hailing the Brissotins' destruction, Dumont assured Boulogne's inhabitants the city was being purged and "purified." As part of this, the "célèbre et très incompréhensible" black Holy Virgin known as "Notre Dame des Anges," which, according to local legend, the "English" had repeatedly tried but failed to burn during the Hundred Years' War due, the superstitious believed, to miraculous divine intervention, would now publicly be burned. "Vive la Montagne!" cried the crowds as this hallowed Madonna was consumed in flames without any miracle occurring.[49]

Another renowned "Black Virgin," at Sainte Claire at Le Puy-en-Velay (Haute-Loire), retrieved by Saint Louis on crusade from Egypt— probably ancient Coptic in origin, but locally reputed to have been crafted by Jeremiah himself—was hauled down by réprésentant Louis Guyardin (1758–1816) on 8 June 1794, Pentecost Day. Seated on her throne blindfolded, the Madonna was placed in a cart, conveyed into the town square, and guillotined before the people. The head and headless corpse were then ceremonially burned.[50] Discrediting popular relics and the locales of popular cults involved some truly astounding vandalistic outbreaks. At Sainte-Marie Madeleine at Vézelay (Burgundy), a venerable pilgrimage site and outstanding monument of Romanesque art, the entire elaborately sculptured facade of the abbey church was destroyed save for a few fragments, as were the attached Benedictine buildings, gems of early medieval architecture. Inevitably, both the vandalism and antirelic fervor elicited a strongly emotional reaction and the frequent incidence of yet more "miracles." Devout women strove desperately to save holy relics. Another Black Virgin retrieved by Crusaders, preserved at Mende cathedral in Lozère department, was hidden by a woman under her clothes and rescued while revolutionaries were distracted wrecking the altar and neighboring chapels. At Cusset, a tenth-century Virgin, among the most venerated miracle-working images of the Auvergne, was incinerated on a public funeral pyre in the town square on 5 December 1793, but not before a baker's wife salvaged its hands, remnants lavishly adorned with precious stones after the Revolution, and venerated until today.

Another de-Christianizing initiative affecting daily life was the adoption, on 5 October 1793, of the new republican calendar. This innovation, long demanded by Maréchal, Gorsas, Manuel, and other anti-Christian theorists, at once rational and poetic, was composed by Danton's secretary, Fabre d'Églantine, and the mathematician Romme, the deputy who later curbed the excesses of the Terror at Angoulême, an idealistic, ardently egalitarian philosophe, from June 1793 among the most active of the Comité de l'Instruction Publique supervising the change in the nation's calendar.[51] Under the new dispensation, years were no longer counted from Christ's birth but instead from the advent of the Republic. Sunday observance was forbidden, officially, though it lingered widely despite the authorities' efforts to enforce cessation. Every month now had the same length, thirty days, comprising three ten-day "weeks," ending in an official rest day (*décadi*), albeit no one was prohibited from working that day if desired. All public holidays were changed and Christian festivities and saint's days deleted. To replace the old holidays, five extra days termed "sans-culottides" fell outside the regular cycle of twelve months of thirty days each. These were dedicated to the new national festivals of "Genius," "Work," "Virtue," "Opinion," and "Recompense." Every first day of the new "decade," decreed the Paris Commune's conseil-général in early December 1793, the mayor and municipal officials had to appear in the "Temple of Reason," intone the Rights of Man, report the latest war news, and explain new laws introduced over the previous ten days. Afterward, a magistrate would deliver a discourse on republican virtue.[52] Similarly, mayors and municipal officers throughout France were expected to appear every *décadi* in a main church to deliver a patriotic discourse and conduct singing of patriotic hymns. These public ceremonies, led by civic officials, could no longer include clergy or religious rites of any kind. Under the rules adopted in the Channel departments of La Manche and Ille-et-Vilaine

(Saint-Malo), the only symbols to be publicly displayed were the tricolor flag and a pick with a liberty bonnet.[53]

Déchristianisateurs regularly employed the rhetoric of la philosophie without being genuine adherents of its message and while carrying it to vituperative and coercive extremes wholly contrary to the tolerance and human rights of the early Revolution. The philosophisme pervading the fanaticism of the Hébertistes and prominent ideologues, like the ex-Capuchin monk Chabot, Chaumette, Cloots, Lequinio, and Harmand, was hence a highly dogmatic as well as disfigured and debased creed designed to cajole women and the illiterate more than others. At the Paris Jacobins on 1 November, Chaumette deplored that French women were mostly still devout, raising their children to believe socially and morally "harmful" doctrines. But de-Christianization was incapable of becoming popular and provoked great opposition, aggravating local resistance in towns and villages throughout France, and introduced a profound split within the Montagnard coalition itself.

After liquidation of the leading Brissotins, the rift deepened and became, along with the suspension of the Constitution and the break with Roux and Varlet, the most divisive issue among the regime's supporters. On 8 November 1793, Hébert complained that the Jacobins' periodical, the *Journal de la Montagne*, carried articles about religion and God, "an unknown being," reaffirming "ces vieilles sottises," criticism aimed at Robespierre as well as the journal editor now forced to resign, Jean-Charles Laveaux (1749–1827), an eminent Germanist and historian of Frederick the Great. Refusing to apologize, Laveaux declared "atheism" inherently dangerous to republics. Robespierre defended Laveaux against Hébert at the Jacobins on 10 November, weaving his remarks into a general assault on the philosophes as a group, pronouncing them "ennemis du peuple" and hypocrites seeking to divide the Jacobins and undermine the unity of "the people's will." If Hébert, Cloots, and Chaumette intended to continue championing philosophes and la philosophie, there was going to be big trouble.[54]

Numerous nonjuring and constitutional clergy were incarcerated during the de-Christianization phase, with some being guillotined. But fanaticism and vandalism came at a high price. Hébert sensationalized the Gobel episode and defection of other Parisian priests in *Le Père Duchesne*, proclaiming a virulent antireligious fervor. But according to Desmoulins's *Vieux Cordelier*, his railing against religion proved in every way counterproductive and alienated "a hundred thousand imbeciles" from the Revolution, providing hordes of new recruits for royalism and priestcraft in Normandy, the Vendée, and elsewhere.[55] The "constitutional Church" was decimated through its clergy being forced to resign, imprisoned, or expelled, opening the door more than ever to ultraroyalist rejectionist clergy who eagerly filled the gap, mobilizing religious feeling against the Revolution and against what Desmoulins called "truth and the Rights of Man."[56] Consequently, the ascendancy of the déchristianisateurs proved brief. Robespierre's personal intervention first slowed and eventually halted both de-Christianization and militant, intolerant philosophisme.

Robespierre, though intermittently inclined to anticlerical views,[57] opposed de-Christianization from the outset. He considered it politically ill-advised and wrongly conceived in principle, repression bound to damage the people's moral fiber. A true disciple of Rousseau, religion to him was the pedestal of the social contract, to be assiduously conserved. Robespierre and Saint-Just opposed the déchristianisateurs, and disagreement about the place of religion became integral to the subsequent strife in particular between Robespierristes and Hébertistes. Professing "profound respect for religion," and especially popular piety, Robespierre spoke often of "God and Providence," noted Condorcet, a tendency that supported his claim of being the "friend of the poor and weak" and explained, suggested the philosophe, much of his success in attracting "women and the *faibles d'esprit*" (intellectually feeble minds) to his cause.[58] Robespierre remained convinced of the necessity of belief in the divinity and immortality of the soul for upholding the kind of antiphilosophique moral fervor he championed. Danton too showed little enthusiasm for persecuting clergy or Church. That the foremost Jacobins opposed the movement while most Frenchmen remained Catholic (or pious Protestants or Jews) confirms that the Jacobin dictatorship, consolidated in the summer of 1793, rested on a narrow and precarious coalition formed of strikingly disparate elements.

Robespierre first presented his critique in a major speech at the Jacobins on 21 November (1 Frimaire), one of the Revolution's notable turning points. It was a stinging rebuff to the déchristianisateurs that left Cloots (long detested by Robespierre) squirming in the president's chair. "Fanaticism" was not the main threat facing the Revolution, averred Robespierre, since Catholic zeal was "expiring." Catholicism was effectively "dead," he contended, a claim manifestly untrue given the Catholic revolts raging all over France. By turning "all our attention" against Catholic fervor, theology, and the clergy, "are we not being distracted from the true danger?" Priests were not the menace to the

Revolution Cloots and others claimed. Even the Vendée revolt, contended Robespierre (who had never traveled outside northeast France), fanaticism's "last asylum," did not prove traditional faith opposed the Revolution. Rather, the Vendée was a rebellion rapidly collapsing, and with it would subside fanaticism's last vestiges. Ambitious schemers who insinuated themselves to the forefront of the Revolution, seeking false popularity by distracting true patriots onto entirely the wrong path, were the real danger. Misguided philosophes were sowing discord among the people, disrupting freedom of religion in the name of liberty, and attacking "le fanatisme par un fanatisme nouveau."

It was imperative the Jacobins stop such types from deriding the simplicity and dignity of ordinary people. Placing everything under the "scepter of philosophy" had to stop. The Revolution must punish those disrupting freedom of religion and attempting to dishonor the Revolution, in the service of foreign courts, by falsely presenting it as "opposed to religion." Under the pretext of wanting to erase "superstition," these subversives were making a cult out of atheism when it would be madness to adopt the projects of the materialist philosophers and de-Christianizers in their midst. The Convention, held Robespierre, is not a writer of books or an author of metaphysical systems but a political body representing ordinary people charged with defending the rights and "the character" of the nation. Not for nothing had the Declaration of Rights been proclaimed in the name of the Supreme Being. Some might disparage him as a man of narrow horizons, and call him "un homme à préjugés," a "fanatic." (According to Cloots, Robespierre was a total fanatic, and to Mercier, "l'ignorance personifiée.")[59] But, never mind, he refused to expatiate like a *philosophe systématique*. He would speak only as a representative of the people.

"L'athéisme est aristocratique," intoned Robespierre to furious applause, and so is la philosophie. In the Revolution, what is "tout populaire" alone is legitimate, and what the people believe is that a Supreme Being watches over oppressed innocence and punishes crime.[60] Ordinary people embrace the idea of an incomprehensible being they can venerate and who rewards virtue. If God did not exist, it would be necessary to invent him. "The common people applaud me" as their defender. The hateful philosophisme abasing ordinary folk was seeking to persuade men the Republic's founders were mere "valets" of tyranny. In fact, a thorough investigation, "un scrutin épuratoire," was needed to purge the agents of the philosophisme undermining French society.[61] Virtue must conquer philosophy and override everything else! In this way a divide opened within the Jacobin camp in November 1793 that persisted unresolved until April 1794, and around which a remarkable ideological struggle developed. It was a split that could not readily be papered over. Robespierre, who personally instigated the drive against aristocratic atheists within the Revolution, later established his Cult of the Supreme Being as an antidote to both de-Christianization and philosophisme, and a bridge between religion and Rousseauism.

Robespierre's intervention was echoed by Desmoulins in the *Vieux Cordelier* on 11 December in an article praising Robespierre for his stand. Desmoulins (rather hypocritically) berated the "former baron" Cloots and "his cousin" Proly for their militant "atheism," as well as proximity to Roland and views about waging war abroad, scarcely distinguishable from Brissot's.[62] The "Incorruptible" delivered another attack on the de-Christianizers at the Jacobins with Cloots still in the president's seat on 8 Frimaire of Year II (28 November 1793), deploring the perfidious contre-révolutionnaires masking perfidy with an exaggerated display of antireligious zeal. "Traitors" disseminating reports of persecution and despoliation of churches were undermining the Revolution by helping the émigrés portray it in the eyes of all Europe, Protestant and Catholic, as "irreligious." "Aristocrats" joined in the attacks on churches, alleged Robespierre, to discredit the Jacobins as "atheists and foes of religion." The Revolution belongs to the people, emanates from the people, "et ne veut server que le peuple."[63] The attack gained momentum in December when the Convention, prompted by Robespierrre, forbade using force and menaces "contrary to the liberty of cults" to fight religion, urging Frenchmen to abstain "from all theological dispute" and focus on fighting the common foe.[64]

On 9 December, Robespierre delivered an extraordinarily violent attack on modérantisme for hampering the Convention and enabling foreigners to undermine the Revolution. A key part of this address resumed his assault on philosophique universalism. He deliberately sought to mobilize ordinary people's anti-intellectualism, xenophobia, and chauvinism against his targets. The next day, in his *Vieux Cordelier*, Desmoulins assailed Cloots as a particularly insidious déchristianisateur and "hypocrite de patriotisme," an assault astounding in that Desmoulins had earlier been an admirer and propagator of Cloots's ardent philosophisme and *République universelle*.[65] Cloots led a troop of betrayers whose "farces indécentes" presented the French to all Europe "comme un peuple d'athées." This so-called *ami des hommes* was hardly a friend to the blacks, moreover, since he had supported Barnave against Brissot in the struggle over the slave trade and emancipating the free blacks. In subsequent weeks, posted up in all the squares of Paris, appeared Robespierre's famous rubric, "le Peuple français reconnait l'existence de l'Être Suprême et l'immortalité de l'âme," signs that frequently remained in position long after his execution.[66]

Until late March 1794, Hébert and Chaumette remained within the ruling coalition, which meant de-Christianization retained some momentum in the Paris sections and many localities beyond, notably now also Marseille. However, in other places, including several departments where representatives close to Robespierre exercised authority, such as the southeastern departments of Var and Alpes Martimes, where his younger brother, Augustin Robespierre, presided, forced resignations of priests ceased already considerably earlier.[67] Moreover, while the elimination of Hébert, Momoro, and Chaumette in April 1794 stripped de-Christianization of much of its impetus, it did not completely grind to a halt until shortly before Robespierre's overthrow. Only in the last weeks before Thermidor, hence very briefly, could Robespierre and Saint-Just fully entrench their ideology of the ordinary man, virtue, and the "tout populaire." Robespierre eventually halted the organized preaching of atheism and direct attacks on churches. But he did little to curb persecution, imprisonment, and deportation of Catholic clergy. The total number of priests victimized under the Terror was in fact huge. In the district of Auxerre, in the Paris Basin, by July 1794, more than three-quarters of the originally 147 priests had abjured, been imprisoned, deported, or driven to emigrate.[68]

While de-Christianization continued, it remained impossible to decouple Jacobinism from the core values of Left republicanism and the Revolution altogether. For there was no rationale for attacking "superstition" and "fanaticism" without enlisting la philosophie. Montagnard representatives on mission leading the anti-Christian offensive, like Chaumette, Lequinio, Dupont, Fouché, Harmand, and Lecarpentier, always recited philosophique arguments to explain what to them was its necessity. As Armand Sabourain, a young philosophe and professor at Poitiers and a disciple of Condillac in epistemology, writing to the Convention, in December 1793, pointed out, it was impossible to explain to country folk how and why a religion they had unquestioningly embraced for centuries is false and harmful, needing to be eradicated urgently, without first undermining the hallowed authority of theology. To prove there is no legitimate criterion of what is true except philosophical reason, one must proclaim that theology contains no truth and that religious authority is a form of deceit; thus, the people had to be instructed in basic philosophy.[69]

The masterpiece of la philosophie is the Rights of Man, contended Sabourain, the most beautiful monument reason has erected to humanity. Hence, Robespierrisme—in religious policy just as in education, in its views on women, black emancipation, constitutional theory, press freedom, and individual rights—everywhere clashed fundamentally with the Revolution's essential principles and, above all, the Rights of Man. Robespierre invariably and uncompromisingly repudiated la philosophie moderne, both in its authentic, tolerant format, projected by Condorcet, the Brissotins, and the Dantonistes, and in its bastardized, militantly de-Christianizing guise favored by Hébert, Chabot, Chaumette, and Cloots.

CHAPTER 19

"The Terror"

(SEPTEMBER 1793–MARCH 1794)

Suppressing Freedom of Expression

By August 1793, with the Brissotin challenge faltering and the Constitution indefinitely suspended, revolutionary France had become a dictatorship. All genuine political debate was suppressed. Ending freedom of expression and initiating the trials and executions of the Brissotins effectively stripped the Convention and its thirty committees of all real participation in government, reducing the legislature to a mere cipher approving decisions of the Comité de Salut Publique. This committee, overseeing also the Comité de Sûreté Générale, was dominated by Robespierre (helped by Saint-Just and Barère), its eight other members more often seeming like Robespierre's "secretaries" than colleagues.[1] With this, the essential principles of the Revolution were aborted. Robespierre, the stubbornly reluctant republican of 1791–93, became the great antirepublican of 1793–94.

By late 1793, Robespierre wielded increasingly dictatorial power assisted by close aides, among whom Saint-Just, Couthon, Barère, Hanriot, and his brother figured prominently. But his circle was not yet the sole locus of power. A harsh tyranny subjecting all classes of the population to its sway, Montagnard rule proved extremely repressive and ruthless from the outset but for the moment remained a group dictatorship politically and institutionally fragile due to its dependence on several vying constituent factions. Considerable leverage, consequently, remained vested in the Jacobins and Cordeliers where, until April 1794, Robespierre had little choice but to share the stage with the competing populist groupings around Hébert and Danton.

As the summer of 1793 wore on, pressure for a vigorous crackdown on every category of critic and dissenter criticizing Montagnard repression grew intense. The Dantonistes, the only Montagnard faction disturbed by the September massacres, worried by the repression and inclined to defend the Revolution's core values, were to an extent marginalized at the outset. Too conciliatory toward the Brissotins, Danton was voted off the Committee of Public Safety on 10 July, shortly before Robespierre's elevation, marking a significant shift of power within the Jacobins. From July 1793, Danton found himself indeed in a distinctly awkward position, needing to flatter the sansculottes and keep up his pleas for unity, which left little scope for criticizing his rivals. Suspected of trying to soften the assault on the Brissotins, he could not do much to shield them and soon himself became a target. Hébert attacked him with well-founded accusations of graft and corruption. Rebutting Hébert's charges, on 26 August, first at the Jacobins and then the Convention, Danton effusively lauded the people for their revolutionary élan, proposing a revolutionary army to eliminate internal enemies, repress hoarders, and improve security.[2] His proposal that Jacobin workingmen be paid to attend sectional assemblies went down especially well.

Hébert launched his hue and cry against former nobles entrenched in the military and civil administration at the Cordeliers on 21 July, beginning with a ferocious attack on Adam Philippe, Comte de Custine (1740–93), the commander who overran the Rhineland for the Revolution in November 1792 but who had recently lost Mainz and allegedly "conspired" against the Republic.[3] Tried for "treason," Custine was executed on 27 August. Through August and September, however, executions remained sparse. A refrain continually heard in the clubs and populist press during these months was that liquidation of "suspect persons" was, as Chaumette expressed it at the Jacobins on 23 August, deplorably *insuffisante*.[4] The call for "more Terror" and tougher methods emanated especially from the tightly controlled "revolutionary committees" of the poorer Paris sections, spurred by Marat's acolytes, the Hébertistes, *who* continually incited popular indignation against fédéralistes, modérés, Brissotins, ministers, deputies, generals, hoarders, counterrevolutionaries, aristocrats, and other traitors of every description. Besides Hébert, Chaumette, and Chabot, among the most vocal insisting on "more Terror," were Collot d'Herbois, Amar, Bazire, and Billaud-Varenne, who was particularly keen on enforcing the death penalty for hoarding (with scant success).

Conspirateurs endangering "liberty" supposedly needed to be dealt with much faster.[5] An additional factor driving the onset of the Terror in the autumn of 1793 was chronic food shortage. By 3 September, several voices in the Convention, Danton's especially, warned of the immediate danger of massive insurrection in the capital against shopkeepers and the rich, apt to be exploited by undesirable elements if the *maximum* for bread was not more stringently imposed.[6] He was well informed. Early in the morning of 4 September, a massive demonstration began by disaffected construction workers and other sansculottes unsettled by surging food prices and increased recruitment for the army. Mobs, including many munitions workers demanding cheaper bread and the *maximum*, filled the streets, the unrest emboldening Roux, Varlet, and Théophile Leclerc (1771–?), who led the only group in Paris still strong enough to criticize the tyranny openly to try to channel sansculotte dissatisfaction into a sustained, organized political force.[7] On 4 September, Roux, Varlet, and their following, including Claire Lacombe, leader of the Société des Femmes Révolutionaires,[8] organized a raucous mass workingmen's and women's march of protest on the Convention, demanding action against "the rich," that was effectively a challenge to the Montagne. The deputies received the crowds cordially enough, seemingly acquiescing in their demands, but once the demonstrations dispersed, the leadership moved decisively to dismantle sansculottism as an active force within the Revolution.[9]

The Montagnard coup not only lacked broad support in the country, it plainly lacked the steady and consistent backing of the sansculottes. Danton urged the Assembly "to profit from the energy of the people" and tackle the shortages, punish hoarders, and suppress counterrevolutionaries by establishing an internal roving *armée révolutionnaire* directed against internal subversives and contre-révolutionnaires. Proposals to expand the revolutionary armies for internal as well as external use and boost arms production to equip them with muskets, moved by Billaud-Varenne and Danton, were adopted but were chiefly aimed at reinforcing the regime by curbing sansculotte unruliness, independent-mindedness, and sporadic anti-Montagnard street activity. Among measures aired in the Convention in response to the recent disturbances was a plan, advocated by Billaud-Varenne, Bazire, Léonard Bourdon, and, doubtless, Robespierre, to purge the section assemblies as soon as practicable, weakening them to dampen sansculotte energies, activities, and fervor.[10]

Leaders of the Paris sansculottes divided at this point between those focused principally on stirring agitation for better conditions, the authentic Enragés, and those headed by Hébert and Ronsin, more authoritarian, inquisitorial, and politically motivated, aligning (for the moment) with Robespierre. Briefly arrested in late August, Roux was rearrested on 5 September. He was condemned at the Jacobins, Cordeliers, and Commune alike as a "rebel" against the Revolution, barely less perfidious than the rebel priests of the Vendée. Purges of section committees began. The Convention issued a decree restricting the Paris section assemblies to a maximum of two meetings weekly. From early October, meetings were further restricted to two every ten days, on the fifth and tenth of each decade.[11] The sansculotte sections vociferously protested, organizing a delegation, headed by Varlet, to the Convention on 17 September. They denounced the decree that curtailed their independence and right to meet and the attempt to prevent the common people from exercising a proper surveillance over the regime. What conceivable justification had the Convention for limiting the rights of "the sovereign," subordinating the people's assemblies, and determining when they could meet? Did anyone doubt their patriotism? The edict, complained the sections (with every justification), violated both the Constitution and Rights of Man. Varlet, chief spokesman of *section-naire* autonomy and direct democracy, was arrested with other Enragé leaders the next day.[12]

The dictatorship's strategy, it emerged, was to stifle all dissent, relegate the campaign to curb food prices and punish hoarders to largely symbolic status, suppress the Constitution (that some Jacobins and Enragés greatly prized), and transfer effective power from the sections and sociétés populaires, now placed under the surveillance of the *comités révolutionnaires*, to the executive apparatus.[13] Enemies of the Republic, insisted the Montagne, were plotting behind a duplicitous mask of ultrapatriotism to undermine the Convention's authority. After the Brissotin overthrow, the main social and political force powering the insurrections of 31 May and 2 June, sansculottism, was thus the very first social and political category shackled by the Robespierre regime, the very agent that had overwhelmed the Brissotins and, from June to September 1793, had remained the sole force in the capital still capable of offsetting the committees of Public Safety and General Security. For the present, imprisoning the Enragé leaders ended the authentic sansculotte movement organized in and by sociétés populaires.

The regime sporadically attempted to ease discontent, chronic poverty, and food shortage by denouncing hoarding and forcing subventions from the rich. In late November, the Paris Commune decreed that sick, elderly, orphaned, and other impoverished citizens unable to maintain themselves should be housed, fed, and clothed at the expense "of the rich" of their respective sections. Pressure on the bakers increased, and the proposal discarded in the spring, to allow only one kind of bread in main cities, was taken up again. Since "wealth and poverty were equally disappearing under the regime of equality," declared the November edict on bread, bakers must no longer offer different categories—one kind of bread from wheat for "the rich" and another, from rough outer cereal husks, for the poor. Paris bakers and those of Nantes and other cities, under pain of imprisonment, could now sell only one type of bread, dubbed "le pain d'égalité."[14] While the regime's sympathy for plebeian economic distress did not, in general, stretch far, the Montagne included an energetic, idealistic segment who took the social crusade, the task of redistributing wealth, more seriously. Zealots for social egalitarianism included Romme and those "spartans of the Montagne," the Julliens, father and son. "I preach everywhere," reported Marc-Antoine Jullien to Robespierre from Saint-Malo on 1 October 1793, that the popular societies should "occupy themselves with the people's instruction, surveillance of the people's foes, the merchants, Muscadins and rich people, priesthood and notables favoring aristocracy. I work to raise up the people, show the Revolution is made for them, that it is time for the poor and the *sans-culottes* to prevail as they are the majority on this earth and the majority should dominate; that the general will is the exclusive source of law, and the good of the greatest number the purpose of the social contract." Deliberate "misleading of the public spirit," added Jullien, accounted for the troublingly conspicuous lack of support for the Montagne in Norman towns like Caen, and was "the primary and almost sole cause of resistance."[15]

With its slender support base outside Paris, the Robespierriste leadership needed the Terror to retain its grip on power. There was no other way such a tyranny, obsessively antimonarchist, antirepublican (without admitting it), and in practice even antisansculotte, could survive. Equally, the dictatorship required its powerfully leveling ideology of equality to provide a rationale for the Terror and ferocious crackdown on all opposition and dissent. New "revolutionary committees" in the sections and sociétés populaires emerged as watchdogs—often less over food prices than the activities of the sections' citizenry and shopkeepers—imposing "patriotic" values with an unrelenting hand. The Société Populaire et Républicaine of the Paris section Droits-de-l'Homme, for example, inaugurated by some thirty activists on 20 September with the installation of a bust of Marat in its hall, met daily to review matters of local concern and make sure no one in the area stepped out of line. It met in the same hall used by the section assembly (now only twice monthly) and was handpicked. While its meetings were open to the public, including women, it carefully vetted candidates for membership; those accepted had to pass scrutiny by a committee of seven, the Comité de Présentation. Through a system of instruction and denunciation backed by hearings, it rigidly imposed "patriotic" behavior and "correct" attitudes, enforcing "patriotic" values throughout the quarter. "Patriotic" became a code word for popular, anti-élitist, antiphilosophique, and committed to a highly intolerant conception of virtue. Everyone denounced received a hearing before the full body of members.

The popular societies' watchdog committees looked out for and strove to repress "monarchists," "aristocrats," "moderates," and "fédérés" while keeping an unfriendly eye on grocery and bakers' stores, cafés, theaters, possible gambling locales, independent-minded women, and courtesans. The drive to lock up prostitutes and suppress prostitution commenced in earnest in late summer 1793 and soon extended to other great cities as the Montagne suppressed the Revolution's essential principles there too. At Bordeaux, "les filles publiques," remarked a local diarist after the Brissotin defeat there, were treated in the most outrageous fashion, as if the Montagnards wished to establish "spartan morals" throughout the whole of France. Once the Brissotins were beaten, a parallel crackdown occurred in Lyon. Though partly a reaction to the conspicuous increase in prostitution due to economic distress, Jacobin surveillance seemed anxious to strip away every pastime and pleasure, terrorize the girls, and proscribe the erotic and immorality itself. Prostitutes were deemed a corrupt vestige of the ancien régime, an affront to virtue, a symbol of everything virtue sought to eradicate, the very antithesis of the Rousseauiste ideal of womanhood.[16] On 9 October, the publicly puritanical Chaumette—privately a highly active homosexual—assured the Convention that moral stringency was being imposed in Paris. He had just led a police swoop around the former Palais-Royal (now called the Palais Égalité) catching seven "girls." In Paris, open soliciting had now been largely driven from sight. The police were learning how to deal with more concealed whoring, too, "and soon Paris will be purged."[17]

The Convention endorsed his suggestion that girls caught soliciting should be shut up in public hospices and put to useful work. So obsessed was Chaumette with the alleged threat posed by prostitutes that by November he listed street whores among the chief agents and recruiting grounds for contre-révolutionnaires, along with *devôt* women and priests.[18] Two prostitutes, Catherine Alboury and Claire Servin, arrested in December in the Tuileries section for counterrevolutionary remarks, were afterward condemned and executed along with several other courtesans.[19] Mostly, though, prostitutes were merely imprisoned. Not just sexual forwardness but indications of republican militancy and (as with Mme. Roland) learning and erudition were frowned on as unmistakable signs of a woman forgetting the "virtues pertaining to her sex," in Jacobin parlance, something tied to being suspect and "whores."[20] There was no place for intellectually, politically, or sexually emancipated women in Robespierre's France. Olympe de Gouges, vilified in the populist press as an immoral "virago" by Chaumette, was arrested on 23 July for violating the 20 March 1793 edict forbidding counterrevolutionary writings. Among other protests, she had posted up an affiche around Paris urging a general referendum enabling the people to choose between republican, federal, and constitutional monarchical government.[21] Republican laws promised no illegal authority would oppress the citizenry, she berated her judges, "yet an arbitrary law worthy of the Inquisition, that even the *ancien régime* would have blushed to implement, imprisons the *esprit humain* and has wrested my liberty from me in the midst of a free people. Is not liberty of opinion and the press consecrated as the most precious patrimony of man in Article VII of the Constitution? Your [the regime's] arbitrary acts and atrocities must be condemned before the whole world. Where Rome burned under only one Nero, *la France libre* today languishes under a hundred."[22] This was far too close to the mark. Besides, she had insulted Robespierre. Sentenced to death for "counterrevolutionary writings," Gouges, guillotined on 3 November, reportedly met her end with impressive calmness.[23]

Olympe de Gouges, Mme. Roland, and Sophie Condorcet were not the only outstanding revolutionary women defying Montagnard tyranny. On 31 July 1793, Claire Lacombe, "president" of the Société des Femmes Révolutionaires, the activist society formed in May by her and Pauline Léon, the two legendary pike-bearing women's leaders of the 10 August rising, acted as spokeswoman before the Convention for a female delegation from all forty-eight Paris sections, complaining about the Convention's tardiness in erecting the obelisk commemorating Marat. Close to the Enragés, Lacombe aligned particularly with Jean-Théophile Leclerc, one of the Patriots expelled from Martinique by white monarchists in 1791, a revolutionary who vigorously championed women's, blacks', and sansculotte rights, while loudly denouncing the shelving of the Constitution and muzzling of the section assemblies. Hostile to the Montagne, both he and his partner, Lacombe, spurred other sansculotte women to demonstrate while copiously pouring scorn on Chabot and Bazire as worthless hypocrites "oppressing the people." On 16 September 1793, Chabot, Amar, and Claude Bazire (1761–94), key promoters of the Terror,[24] initiated a wider Montagnard campaign against the republican women's society, especially Lacombe herself, in the Jacobins. She and her circle were condemned outright and unreservedly since "these ladies spoke contemptuously of M. Robespierre" (after he called them contre-révolutionnaires). Following a scuffle in which she attempted to address the Jacobins from the galleries, Lacombe was overpowered and removed by women yelling "Down with the new Corday!"[25]

The Jacobins urged the Comité de Sûreté Générale to instruct the society of revolutionary women to purge their leadership and membership. The Convention decided to go even further. After a speech denouncing women's influence in politics by the increasingly influential Amar—now one of Robespierre's closest aides—the Convention dissolved all women's associations "under whatever name they may exist" on 31 October. A wealthy, surpassingly unprincipled Grenoble lawyer co-opted onto the Comité de Sûreté Générale following the coup in June, a fiercely anti-intellectual Montagnard later to become a devout mystic, Amar was an unabashed misogynist as well as ally of Caribbean slave-owners.[26] Republican women could henceforth only attend meetings of male sociétés populaires, though these too were now all tightly bridled to prevent expression of views like those of Lacombe, Leclerc, Roux, and Varlet.[27] The mounting restrictions placed even the male sociétés populaires under unrelenting pressure to become ever more dependable watchdogs of society. In January 1794, Robespierre, still dissatisfied, criticized them for being insufficiently "patriotic," too easily penetrated by undesirable elements, and unwitting tools of Brissotins and aristocrats.[28]

Executions were just the tip of the iceberg. In essence, the Terror was a general suppression of all the Revolution's essential principles and philosophy, especially freedom to criticize and liberty of thought and expression generally. While Montagnard bridling of debate and opinion affected all of society, curbing protest in proletarian sections featuring among its chief concerns, the principal target always remained the main exponents of revolutionary core values: the radical gens de lettres, philosophes, journalists, librarians, and intellectuals directing the Revolution. The intellectuals and philosophes had indeed initiated the Revolution, Robespierre admitted, but, according to him, they had afterward "dishonored themselves during the Revolution." His denouncing the gens de lettres was in fact a "glorious compliment for all French writers," suggested a Brissotin fugitive in a pamphlet appearing at Geneva in late August, since "not one was tarnished by having flattered this foe of the human race, a fact unparalleled in the history of conspiracy."[29] Indeed, no philosophes or significant publicists or writers did support Robespierre, although several prominent intellectual spokesmen for the Revolution, like Cloots, Romme, and Desmoulins, backed the Montagne despite despising Robespierre, believing alignment with sansculotte elements the only practicable way to salvage the Revolution.[30]

In major cities, arrests of "suspect persons" under the 17 September Law of Suspects, the main legal basis of the Terror that empowered local revolutionary committees to arrest any "enemy of liberty," accelerated markedly during the autumn, as did compiling lists of dénoncés—and dénonciateurs.[31] Suspects were arrested in their homes and on the streets merely because someone had informed local revolutionary committees that their speech or conduct suggested they were "unpatriotic," "partisans of fédéralisme and enemies of liberty." On 25 September, Robespierre delivered a key speech condemning political dissent and criticism, especially Convention resistance to suppressing Brissotins, justifying this and every further strengthening of the Committee of Public Security's authority uncompromisingly. Nothing any longer stood between the regime and imprisonment and trial of opponents, critics, and dissenters of every description—whether Left republicans defending the Revolution, artisans deploring shortages, Catholics resisting Jacobin iconoclasm, or aristocrats. Without a certificate of civisme, issued by district surveillance committees, it became hard to travel, conduct business, or attend meetings.[32] Anyone suspected of criticizing the regime, even the most eminent foreign visitors, were denounced and imprisoned. On 9 October, Helen Maria Williams, her mother, and her sister were arrested, as were Hurford Stone, president of the British Club in Paris, and his wife soon afterward.[33]

In the stunned atmosphere pervading France, everybody had to conform. Even lukewarmness in using the right phrases generated suspicion. Paris prisons, officially holding 1,640 prisoners on 4 September,[34] and 1,860 by 10 September, contained no less than 2,365 prisoners by

3 October, 529 in La Force and 364 at the Conciergerie.[35] The total reached 3,181 by 31 October and 4,603 by 29 December, with eighty more added in the next three days, bringing the total to 4,687 by 1 January 1794, held in twenty-one prisons.[36] Of these, 579 were crowded into La Force, on the Right Bank, and 531 into the ancient Conciergerie, the central prison on the Seine, in the former medieval royal palace neighboring the Sainte-Chapelle. Other main prisons were the Abbaye and the Luxembourg on the Left Bank. While fugitive nobles and their wives, former officeholders, and refractory and constitutional priests figured prominently among those arrested—tried and executed during the Terror—the principal targets initially were not aristocrats, hoarders, ancien regime officeholders, or priests, but Left republicans and gens de lettres (writers), the enlightened intellectuals who made the Revolution.

The Trial and Execution of the Brissotin Leadership

Every critic and exponent of revolutionary core principles was in dire peril. The indictment facing the leading Brissotins was finally produced on 3 October when Amar, the Comité de Sûreté Générale's spokesman, having ensured the Assembly's doors were closed to prevent anyone leaving, submitted the charges to the Convention. Twenty deputies were already "outlawed" and under sentence of automatic execution on capture. These included Buzot, Barbaroux, Gorsas, Lanjuinais, Louvet, Pétion, Guadet, and Kervélégan, author of the inflammatory 1788 pamphlet *Reflexions d'un philosophe Breton* (discussed in chapter 2) who had been arrested in June but had escaped and was in hiding. Forty-one more Brissotin deputies were indicted at this point, together with Brissot. These "conspirators" were accused of subverting the Convention, conspiring against the Republic's unity and indivisibility, assisting Lafayette, causing the Champ de Mars massacre, "ruining our colonies," embroiling France with all the European powers to stifle French liberty, and plotting with Dumouriez to "conserve royalty."[37] Clavière and Lebrun, denounced by Billaud-Varenne in the Convention on 5 September, had also been arrested and tried for helping Brissot enbroil France with the European powers.[38] Pétion was additionally charged with obstructing the 10 August 1792 insurrection. Those deputies who protested against the "tyranny" on 6 and 19 June, totaling another seventy-four deputies, were also purged from the Convention and stripped of their representative status, but only their leaders, headed by Daunou, Dusaulx, Blaviel, Ferroux, and Mercier, were imprisoned. Encompassing practically all of the more articulate and enlightened deputies of the Convention, the complete list of deputies removed from the Convention for opposing Robespierre totaled 135, leaving the Convention completely emasculated.

The press was brutally silenced, the "tyrant" knowing his tyranny could not function while newspapers refusing to flatter him remained free.[39] Gorsas in his *Courrier*, Brissot in his *Patriote français*, Condorcet in his *Chronique*, Rabaut in the *Moniteur*, and Louvet in his *Sentinelle* had all "perverted" l'esprit public. With searches for him proceeding in Normandy, Brittany, and at Bordeaux, his best chance of survival, Louvet surmised, lay in returning disguised to Paris; later he hid likewise under an assumed name in the Jura. Gorsas, on the run since June, also returned to Paris from Rennes by mail-coach, hoping to reach his hometown Limoges. Caught at the Palais-Royal on 6 October while attempting to escape through a back window of his mistress's bookshop, he tried to speak out in the courtroom but was prevented. Already "outlawed," he went to the guillotine the next day. Before the blade fell, surrounded by a large crowd jeering him for his "treachery," he was again stopped from speaking or making any gesture.[40] All he could do in his last moments was display impressive sangfroid, though even this contributed to an order from the Tribunal Révolutionnaire to the prison concierges (accustomed to selling liquor to the inmates) not to supply alcohol to prisoners less than twenty-four hours prior to execution, to prevent wine and brandy from causing "that apparent firmness and insolent air seemingly rendering condemned men insensible to their deaths."[41]

Crushing the Convention democrats produced no sign of disaffection in the capital. Rather, with the section assemblies firmly muzzled, these draconian measures were "generally applauded," people either expressing gratitude that they had been rescued from the horrors of fédéralisme or remaining sullenly silent.[42] In recently subdued Marseille, the situation on 6 October was likewise reported entirely quiet.[43] Documentary "proof" of the deputies' "treason" was circulated to all France's municipalities. The principal men accused and behind bars, but not yet "outlawed"—many remained at large—were transferred on 6 October from the Luxembourg, La Force, the Abbaye, and other Paris prisons to the Conciergerie, the central prison where the Tribunal Révolutionnaire sat in judgment. Brissot, lacking funds to purchase better accommodation, was packed into an ordinary, overcrowded cell. Hearing of this, his colleagues collected between themselves the thirty-three livres needed for a more dignified confinement where he could be alone.

The show trials themselves began on 15 October. Presented as a monster of betrayal, Brissot had wanted Louis XVI held in the Luxembourg after 10 August instead of the Temple where the Montagne confined him, as part of his alleged plot to help the royal family escape.[44] Equally solid evidence "proved" he had "prostituted" his following to Lafayette; led the people into a trap, enabling Lafayette to massacre them at the Champ de Mars; plotted against the sociétés populaires; incited the Vendée and Marseille to revolt; engineered Lyon's disaffection; ruined the French colonies under guise of promoting black emancipation; and betrayed Toulon to the British (besides helping arrange Marat's assassination).[45] Conspiring with Condorcet and the Convention Girondins, Brissot had provoked war with all Europe so as to stifle national liberty.[46] The key "witnesses" produced by Amar attesting to all this—Pache, Hébert, Chabot, and Chaumette—comprised the régime's choicest scoundrels and fanatics. More honest Montagnards like Baudot, in his *Notes historiques,* afterward recognized that Brissot was actually an unusually "honest man" "horriblement calomnié par Robespierre."[47]

To begin with, the "evidence" was "examined" and the defendants allowed to reply, a procedure that dragged the hearings out for two weeks,[48] but soon prompted the regime, following complaints at the Jacobins, to curtail the proceedings. All pretense of a defense ceased.[49] The "trial" ended on 30 October. All the indicted were pronounced guilty of conspiring against liberty and sentenced to death. Among the principal defendants was Carra, deputy for Saône-et-Loire, designated in the Tribunal Révolutionnaire's judgment as an "homme de lettres" and Bibliothèque Nationale employee.[50] Ducos, removed from the original list of Twenty-Two by Marat on 2 June, but later put back in the condemned group for leading the courageous June protests in the Convention hall, was likewise designated by the Tribunal Révolutionnaire as an "homme de lettres." On being sentenced, all the accused proclaimed their innocence, shouting "Vive la République!" Much to the court's consternation, Charles Valazé (1751–93), legal theorist and agriculturalist, then melodramatically stabbed himself through the heart with a concealed knife, expiring on the spot, blood spurting on all sides.

The night before their execution, the condemned, headed by Brissot, Gensonné, Vergniaud, Ducos, Fauchet, Boyer-Fonfrède, Carra, and the physician Pierre Lehardy, participated in a last supper together in the prison chapel. The next morning, 31 October, they were conveyed by the now usual route, in three *charettes*, to the guillotine. Hampered by vast crowds, the procession took two hours to reach the Place de la Révolution. Only Fauchet and the former noble, (the Comte de) Sillery, desiring confessors, affirmed religious faith in the last cart, all the rest preferring to sing the "Marseillaise," altering some words to mention the "bloody blade" of tyranny and shouting "Vive la République!" Facing the crowd's jeering, they reportedly displayed stirring courage, Ducos (singing) and Vergniaud showing particular defiance. It took forty minutes to guillotine the twenty victims plus Valazé's corpse; Brissot was seventh or eighth in line. Missives read out to the Convention over the next days from provincial Jacobin societies fervently congratulated the Convention, urging it to remain undeviating in implementing the promised "Terror" and crushing the "enemies of liberty."[51] It was the first time ever, noted several observers, that an entire batch of any major nation's most eminent and distinguished men was publicly executed together as a group.

Danton would have wished to curb the Terror but, boxed in, was powerless to deflect the widening repression. Distressed at seeing he could do nothing to save the Brissotins, before long he was being continually assailed himself in the Jacobins and in Hébert's *Père Duchesne*.[52] Two days before the executions of the Brissot circle, Hébert delivered a key speech at the Jacobins, reminding the Montagne that those facing execution represented only a fraction of the "conspiracy." Why was retribution proceeding so slowly? Brissot, Ducos, and many of the worst were being liquidated, but what of the remaining "conspirators" "Bailly, Barnave, Manuel, Lafayette, etc. etc." and the despicable Mme. Roland, who "had directed everything"?[53] Were all these "enemies" of the Revolution to escape retribution? "No, no," yelled the Jacobins and the galleries! Crushing the Revolution's "enemies" must proceed and accelerate!

Mme. Roland, after five months of imprisonment, was moved to the Conciergerie shortly after the execution of Brissot and his colleagues. A true *femme d'état*, about whom Marat, Hébert, and others had made so many ungentlemanly allusions, and yet so superior to them in mind, the lady whose crime was "directing" others, her salon uniting the Brissotin faction, was intensively interrogated. No one said anything on her behalf. Condemned, she was guillotined on 8 November, aged only thirty-eight, without a single paper, a friend noted, uttering one word of criticism. Rather, in recent days the worthy Tribunal Révolutionnaire, commented *Le Moniteur* afterward, had given "un grand example" to

(a)

(b)

(c)

(d)

Figure 14. (a) Olympe de Gouges, (b) Madame Roland, (c) Helen Maria Williams, (d) Charlotte Corday.

(a) Pierre Vidal, portrait of Olympe de Gouges, engraving, 1760. © Roger-Viollet / The Image Works. (b) Adélaïde Labille-Guiard (ca. 1749–1803), *Portrait of a Woman*, ca. 1787, oil on canvas. Musée des Beaux Arts, Quimper, France / The Bridgeman Art Library. (c) Helen Maria Williams published by Dean & Munday, after unknown artist. © National Portrait Gallery, London. (d) Jean-Jacques Hauer (1751–1829), portrait of Charlotte Corday, painting preserved in the Museum of Versailles and Trianon, ca. 1920–1930. © Alinari Archives / The Image Works.

women that they should not forget—the execution in rapid succession of Olympe de Gouges, Marie Antoinette, and that contemptible *monstre* and "queen of a moment" surrounded by mercenary writers to whom she fed sumptuous suppers, Mme. Roland, France's "philosophe à petits billets."[54] Later that month, Roland himself, hiding in rural Normandy, hearing of his wife's execution, committed suicide. (His brother was guillotined in Lyon in December.)

Theater and the Arts under the Terror

The Terror, eliminating all dissent, every publication diffusing democratic republican principles, concomitantly suppressed the free French theater and sought to discipline artists. While the Jacobins promoted the arts, after June their leadership politicized and popularized painting, architecture, and the theater, disallowing, unlike the Brissotin Jacobins earlier, every discordant note.[55] For the Montagne, the arts were primarily mechanisms of political propaganda and discipline. From the autumn of 1793, undesirable themes and attitudes were ruthlessly expunged. Following denunciation by Collot d'Herbois, the entire Comédie-Française theater troupe was arrested on 2 September for performing an adaptation of Goldoni's *Pamela*, written by the noted deputy, writer, agronomist, and former Caribbean official François de Neufchâteau: they had pronounced lines about persecution that could readily be construed as criticism of the regime. Neufchâteau was imprisoned with the actors; he remained behind bars until after Thermidor.[56] On 27 September, Pierre-Yves Barré, one of those responsible for staging *La Chaste Suzanne* at the Vaudeville, and several leading actors at that theater, were imprisoned for staging plays filled with "perfidious allusions."[57] Likewise at Bordeaux and other major regional centers, strict surveillance now became the rule, not just regarding content but equally audiences' and the actors' behavior.[58] Robespierre's foremost detractor in the theater world, Laya, was unremittingly hunted but survived in hiding.

Theater censorship in Robespierriste France was not just a matter of banning plays and selecting others. It enforced a pervasive self-censorship of guarded comment, manipulative editing, audience submission, and altering the text of plays. On 5 October, under pressure from Chaumette, the now aged Palissot, a playwright celebrated for the furor over *The Philosophes*, a satirical comedy first performed amid much controversy in 1760 and often since, found himself obliged to issue a public denial in the Paris journals that the contemptible valet it featured was not "Rousseau" as theatergoers assumed (even though he plainly *was* "Rousseau"). This wretch "is no more Rousseau," he announced, "than a monkey is a man."[59] The theater becomes "every day more a school for *patriotisme*," commented the *Journal de Perlet* on 28 November, reporting that Voltaire's *La Mort de César* (1733), revived at the Théâtre de la République two evenings before, now had a different ending—not that written by Voltaire but "a better one" by citizen Louis-Jérôme Gohier (1746–1830), the Breton deputy who replaced Garat as justice minister and a staunch proponent of Terror. The changes were not ones the original author would have repudiated, the journal assured readers: the worthy Gohier (a lawyer known for pursuing Brissotins), besides other "happy alterations," had "improved" Voltaire by deleting completely Anthony's long "and servile" closing harangue.[60]

Throughout France, repertoires changed abruptly during the autumn of 1793, and the theaters assumed new names. Every theater now had to be uniformly "populaire" and noncritical. Running at a loss, but thanks to the theater-loving Danton receiving government aid since September 1792, the Paris Théâtre Molière became the Théâtre des Sans-Culottes; the Théâtre-Français, after refurbishment, reopened under the Commune's supervision renamed (by the Comité de Salut Public) Théâtre du Peuple. At Rouen, the two main theaters—the Théâtre de Rouen now renamed the Théâtre de la Montagne—were sternly supervised by a civic cultural commission that both controlled the repertoire and distributed thousands of free tickets to workers, the infirm, and the elderly.[61] At Bordeaux, classical republican and de-Christianizing plays became the rule. Tours, reported the representatives on mission there on 22 November, contained numerous suspect types, several of whom had provoked an incident in the town's theater, shouting "à bas le bonnet rouge," compelling two worthy republicans wearing the republican bonnet to remove this "symbol so dear to all good Frenchmen." To teach Tours theatergoers a lesson, the theater was shut down for a time and the actors dispersed.[62]

Racine and Corneille, observed the newly established and for the moment extremely cautious thrice-monthly journal *La Décade philosophique*, were still considered "great dramatists" but were also officially faulted for promoting gallantry, royalty, and nobility in excessively "beautiful verse." Voltaire had avoided "these great defects," putting la philosophie onstage and teaching audiences to scorn credulity and fanaticism. But where, until 1793, the revolutionary theater accommodated divergent styles, points of view, and frivolity, now everyone had to defer to Rousseau's strictures.[63] Playwrights must promote virtue, principally offering tragedies representing tyranny overthrown by popular heroes, themes supposedly best presented draped in classical styles and themes.[64]

The "tout populaire" remained the sole criterion in theory, but increasingly the regime alone spoke for "the people's collective and indivisible will." During the Laya affair, early in 1793, the Montagne had found that censuring the theater by authority from above in a revolutionary context creates a constant friction between audience preference and political direction by the leadership. Control over the theaters tightened inexorably but continued, if more subtly now, to clash with the public. On 23 November, when Gilbert Romme urged the Convention to direct the Comité d'Instruction Publique more closely to vet plays proposed for staging, choosing those "most worthy for performance," another deputy, Antoine-Christophe Merlin de Thionville (1762–1833), objected that it was "the people," surely, who had made the Revolution and "who should judge what was staged." Was Merlin, retorted Romme, then willing to see plays like Laya's *Amis des Lois* and *Pamela* performed simply because audiences desired to see them? Of course not, hastily retracted Merlin.[65] After the premiere of *La Veuve du républicain* (Widow of the republican) at the Paris Théâtre of the Rue Favart, the next day, various citizens recommended it for "all the theatres of the Republic." This prompted the Convention to ask the Comité d'Instruction Publique to investigate whether it was actually "suitable."[66] On 21 November 1793, Robespierre himself assured the Jacobins he had no sympathy for the theater's leading ladies, "princesses" lately fallen foul of Pache's and Hébert's cleanup of the Paris theaters. He backed the drive to stop actresses from representing anything frivolous or erotically suggestive.[67] From autumn 1793, the entire French theater world became geared to instilling the values of Montagnard virtue, revolving around work and family, including woman's awareness of her subordinate place.[68] All the Paris theater troupes, the Comité de Salut Public ruled, must consult and together draw up the capital's repertoire of plays, with final decisions endorsed by the Commune.[69] The gradual shift to mandatory prior submission of scripts for censorship was not completed by the Comité d'Instruction Publique until mid-March 1794. After that, so uniformly did the theater present only officially sanctioned values, affirmed one commentator with apparent pride in June 1794, that "could Rousseau return and watch our revolutionary plays," exalting only virtue, filial piety, and hard labor, he "would not have complained of the immorality of our theatres" as he did of those in his time. Pre-1789 playwrights had been "vains, vils esclaves des grands," corrupting audiences by converting the stage into theater "en boudoir." All that was now replaced with unyielding Spartan austerity, Cato, Brutus, and "heroic deaths of martyrs of liberty" setting the tone. Under the Montagne, even the austerest matron could bring unmarried daughters to the theater without the least apprehension.[70]

Jacobin ideology and culture under Robespierre was an obsessive Rousseauiste moral puritanism steeped in authoritarianism, anti-intellectualism, and xenophobia. Repudiating free expression and basic human rights and democracy, Robespierristes replaced core revolutionary values with an unrelenting emphasis on the need to purify and equalize the people's *mœurs* (morals and customs). Everyone remaining in public life had to bend to this. Lanthenas, a publicist earlier prominent in the campaign for unrestricted press freedom, democracy, and equality in education, having narrowly escaped imprisonment in June, publicly reversed his own former plea for unrestricted liberty of expression of 1791 in his *Bases fondmentales de l'instruction publique* (1793). Society would be "perpetually unhappy," he now contended, if it did not establish effective means for protecting citizens "from libels and calumny." Imposing virtue thorough discipline and policing morals matters more than freedom of expression. Under the new dispensation, the Convention must have the power to suppress writings and censure everyone in any way compromising true republican attitudes or proper morals.[71]

Thus, while the stage came increasingly under what *La Décade philosophique* called "active surveillance," supposedly emanating from below, from the people, in reality, control emanated from above but sometimes rather inconsistently. In a group tyranny operated by a precarious coalition, occasional disarray among the censoring agents was inevitable. A comic opera written by Léonard Bourdon ridiculing Catholic rites, entitled *Le Tombeau des Imposteurs et l'inauguration du temple de la vérité*, about to be performed in Paris, was banned by executive order signed by Robespierre personally on 22 December, along with other productions apt to encourage abuse of the "theatre in favor of the Revolution's enemies," despite both Hébertistes and Commune wanting it performed. Ideologically Hébertiste in tone, Robespierre banned it chiefly owing to the opera's fiercely irreligious content but also its unfortunate title, *Le*

Tombeau des Imposteurs, which could readily be construed by "the malicious" as alluding to himself and the Montagne.[72]

In October 1793, David, principal organizer of the new regime in the arts, completed his famous painting of "the murdered Marat" on his deathbed, commissioned by the Convention in whose assembly hall the painting was to hang alongside his painting of the assassinated Lepeletier. This is the most memorable of the republican paintings painted during the Terror (today in Brussels); David first displayed it in his rooms at the Palais National (i.e., the Louvre). Even before 1789, David and other artists had been lodged in the palace together with the royal art collection. Subsequently, David seems to have lent it to his section assembly, the Museum, to feature it in a "fête patriotique" venerating Marat that all the Paris sections planned to participate in on 25 October.[73] In the autumn of 1793, everywhere in revolutionary France, "patriotic" festivities commemorated France's supposedly greatest man amid great pomp and rousing music, with elaborate flower arrangements and garlands surrounding the numerous busts of Marat. Splendid festivities were also held honoring the murdered Lepeletier, Lazowski, and Marie-Joseph Chalier, the "Marat of Lyon," likewise now venerated in Paris "with the greatest pomp." All sections participated in a grand cortege on 20 December that wound its way from the Place de la Bastille to the Convention, with contingents from the sociétés populaires singing hymns, glorifying the "great" Chalier, including (with consummate unconscious irony) the line "Jurons de purger la terre de la liberté de tous les scélerats" (Let us swear to purge the land of liberty of all its rascals).[74]

To eliminate aristocratic elitism from the fine arts and bring public artistic expression more firmly under "popular control," the Convention replaced the suppressed Royal Academy of Painting, Sculpture, and Architecture with the Commune Générale des Arts, based on equality and patriotism. Any artist could belong provided he passed scrutiny designed to sift "all the old aristocratic *levain*" from the nation's art community. Under elaborate rules established in November 1793, the new steering body, the Société Populaire et Républicaine des Arts, presided with a firm hand over painting, sculpture, and architecture, educating the public and administering the nation's prize competitions. Organized as an assembly of equals, the Société convened from February 1794 in the Louvre where, since the first anniversary of the 10 August insurrection, the former royal art collection was now open as a public museum, displaying paintings from the past (often religious paintings) but excluding works by living artists.[75]

The Société's meetings, held three times every ten days, were open to the public. Reports of its meetings and prize contests appeared in its *Journal de la Société Populaire et Républicaine des Arts séante au Louvre*, edited by the classicizing architect Athanse Détournelle. Fixing the themes and judging exhibits, the Société's decisions were reached by a grand jury of fifty exercising general oversight over the nation's art and connoisseurship, a body of artists and critics, presided over by Barère, that included discriminating "art lovers" from the Comité d'Instruction Publique such as Hébert, Ronsin, and Pache.

Art for the people meant new themes publicly projected in ideological terms, scrupulously replacing aristocratic, erotic, and overly decorative topics with sober, classicizing, revolutionary earnestness. Besides shaping young careers and choosing themes for artistic endeavor, the new procedures aimed at replacing the personal influence and patronage typical of the ancien régime with a new collective artistic culture. Large commissions became public events. Works submitted for national prizes, after five days of public display in the Louvre, were assigned to small, specialized juries, drawn from the fifty, that delivered their verdicts at public gatherings, and awarded the prizes. The first grand theme chosen for the annual painting competition was the corpse of Caesar's assassin, Brutus, carried back to Rome after his death in combat. No entry was judged good enough for first prize, but a pupil of David's, Hariette, received the *prix d'encouragement* or second prize. David, a leading protagonist of the Republic's cult of Brutus, ensured that both the art scene and the great public parades he was entrusted with organizing regularly featured Roman republican themes, insignia, emblems, and medallions. The first annual architecture prize, awarded for designing a barracks for six hundred cavalry troopers, was conferred on the architect Protin. After the société's first collective annual prize-giving ceremony, held on 10 February 1794, the prizewinners, carrying their designs, appeared together with the grand jury before the Convention to loud acclaim.[76]

Among the artists disciplined during the Terror for focusing on amorous instead of republican topics was Louis-Léopold Boilly (1761–1845). He was denounced before the Société Populaire et Républicaine des Arts in April 1794, shortly before the Société announced a painting competition to commemorate the triumph of Marat, which had taken place exactly a year before. Boilly entered the competition, it appears, as a way of making amends with the regime. The result was his painting *The Triumph of Marat* (figure 11), today in Lille, one of the best-known pictures painted in France during the Terror. Painting was expected to present an imposing backdrop to the revolutionary public sphere. But in this regard sculpture carried still greater prestige. The most grandiose planned undertaking in the world of art projected during these months was extensively debated but never materialized. The Convention had decided, in August 1793, to erect four major triumphal public statues in bronze and marble representing key revolutionary themes at strategic points in the capital.

The four projected monuments were *Nature Regenerated*, symbolizing Rousseau's doctrines, intended to stand on the Bastille's ruins; an Arc de Triomphe, commemorating 6 October 1789, for the Boulevard des Italiens; the figure of La Liberté to replace the smashed equestrian statue of Louis XV inaugurated in 1763, demolished by the mob on 11 August 1792 to stand near the guillotine on the Place de la Révolution; and a vast monument impressively commemorating the crushing of fédéralisme. Repeatedly delayed until finally halted by Thermidor, the competition for the commissions for the triumphal statues was scheduled to last three months, with an extra *décade* for artists dwelling outside Paris, but only commenced on 30 April 1794. Models were to be exhibited in the Convention hall and then displayed in the Hall of Laocoön for judgment by the *jury des arts*. Besides the four prizewinners, three sculptors coming highest below them were also expected to be publicly honored and subsequently chosen by the Société's committee for lesser commissions for public monuments.[77]

The Terror in the Provinces

In Paris, until late in the Terror nearly all executions took place in the Place de la Révolution where the king was guillotined. Only Bailly's execution on 12 November occurred on the Champ de Mars, the site of the massacre he had perpetrated. During the Terror's last weeks, by contrast, much of the slaughter shifted to Paris's East End. As the Terror intensified, it also extended its grip over several (but not most) provincial centers. "Representative of the people" Joseph Lebon (1765–95), a pathological ex-Oratorian and former constitutional parish priest who renounced the priesthood after the 1792 August revolution, presided at Arras. First mayor and then Convention deputy for the town, he was a particular friend of Robespierre.[78] Filling the prisons with traitors, Lebon erected his guillotine in the main square, opposite the town theater, a spot plainly visible from the Robespierre family house. A fanatical de-Christianizer, he had a total of 298 men and ninety-three women guillotined in Arras, besides others executed in Lille and neighboring towns.[79] At Marseille, the dreaded Tribunal Révolutionnaire, headed by Fréron and the notoriously corrupt officer Paul-François Barras (1755–1829), tried 975 suspects between August 1793 and April 1794, convicting 500 traitors, of whom 289 were executed.[80] The landowner and former lawyer Marie-Joseph Lequinio, fresh from vandalizing the royal tombs at Saint-Denis, presided at Rochefort. Lequinio's local Terror dispatched naval officers and officials, besides dozens of Vendéean rebels and priests, and a Brissotin Convention deputy for Lower Charente, Gustave Duchazeu, guillotined for publishing writings against the "unity and indivisibility of the Republic."[81] It was "the rich class," reported Lequinio, that furnished all the royalists, modérantistes, and the fédéralistes imprisoned at Rochefort, and the sansculottes alone on whom the regime could count to fight "counterrevolutionary" influence, albeit the people needed to be continually "enlightened regarding their true interests" by Jacobins like himself.[82]

The Terror's worst atrocities occurred at Lyon, Toulon, and Nantes. On 12 October the Committee of Public Safety voted to make an unforgettable example of the "rebellious city" that had defied the Montagne, executed Chalier, and resisted the people for five months. Renamed Ville-Affranchie by the Convention, old Lyon would be "effaced and demolished." Over its ruins would tower a national monument, dated the 18th of the first month of Year II of the Republic, inscribed: "Lyon fit la guerre à la Liberté, Lyon n'est plus" (Lyon made war on Liberty, Lyon is no more). Demolition would be unsparing. Residences of the rich were to be torn down, with only those of the poor, whom the Montagne hoped to win over, left standing. Once the city fell in early October, more than four hundred "chefs conspirateurs" were executed within a month. But this was too few, complained the fresh commissaires, Collot d'Herbois and the ex-Oratorian Fouché, who arrived in November. A seven-member *commission révolutionnaire* was formed to dispatch the "guilty" faster. From November, men were slaughtered in batches, mowed down by cannon filled with grapeshot, those still breathing finished off with muskets and sabers. To avoid delays caused by grieving daughters, sisters, and wives, the commission kept the womenfolk well back from the butchery.

Henceforth, only Montagne supporters would be tolerated in positions of responsibility, and the Montagne would permit no dissent.[83] But in Lyon this presented an insuperable difficulty, since practically

Figure 15. The siege and bombardment of Lyon (9 August to 9 October 1793). Image courtesy Bibliothèque nationale de France.

nobody there supported the Montagne, a fact attested by the Jacobin commissaires themselves. Couthon and the first commission stated in their initial postvictory report to Paris dated 13 October that Montagnard supporters were "such a frighteningly small minority" in Lyon "that we despair of being able to revive it." The only practicable way to mobilize support among Lyon's large artisan class was to transplant "a colony of *patriotes*," sturdy sansculottes (including at least "forty experienced administrators") from elsewhere to direct and manage them.[84] Collot d'Herbois (hissed off the stage in Lyon, only six years before) supervised most of the city's demolition. But to Couthon belonged the honor of commencing destruction of the patrician residences around the Place Bellecour, "the sumptuous edifices belonging to the Lyonnais rebels," and urging the watching crowds of Lyon's poor (not very successfully) to assist. A partly paralyzed lawyer, close to Robespierre (since breaking with Roland in November 1792), Couthon was so anti-intellectual, remarked Mercier, that when one spoke to him about Rousseau's ideas, he would just shrug his shoulders, saying he understood nothing about it.[85] Collot improved on Couthon by using troops, gunpowder explosions, and flames instead.

Only by blowing up and burning buildings, explained Collot on 23 November, could Lyon's thoroughly merited chastisement be accomplished.[86] While in Paris Jacobins debated whether the "glorious Chalier" should be entombed in the Panthéon, at Lyon, executions, numerous in October, accelerated, culminating in December.[87] A petition from Ville-Affranchie, presented by a delegation of Lyon women, came before the Comité de Sûreté Générale in mid-December. Lyon *had* erred by opposing the 2 June coup, the women abjectly confessed, and deserved "the French people's indignation," but since the "traitors who misled us" were overthrown, Lyonnais repentence was "true, profound and unanimous." Had the people understood the character of the Brissotins, "never, never would they have been instruments of their scheming." In October the Montagne had assured the people that if they submitted, all would be "as peaceful and majestic as the law." "Why has this beautiful spectacle not been realized?" Vengeance was due, but vengeance cannot continue unceasingly without destroying its own salutary effect. "Whoever is an *ultra-révolutionnaire*," proclaimed the Montagne, "is as dangerous as a *contre-révolutionnaire*." "*Législateurs*, you command us to abide by the sacred principles of 'virtue,' prevent republican vengeance from becoming a low and ferocious atrocity."[88] The petition was ignored.

Collot d'Herbois's repression was relentless. By April 1794, 1,880 people had been executed in Lyon, and virtually all the city's churches and better residences, around 1,600 stone houses, lay in ruins.[89] His brutality was vigorously seconded by Charles-Philippe Ronsin (1751–94), artisan son of a barrel-maker, an unscrupulous, corrupt, and wealthy protégé of Pache who was merciless toward all fédérés and modérés, and deaf to all protests. Whispering critics dared accuse Collot and Ronsin of excessive harshness, of being men of blood, "anthropophages! Who are those who insolently slander us, crying over the corpses of liberty's enemies?" It might appear on the surface, Collot warned the Convention on 24 December 1793, that unremitting Terror had crushed all resistance. Yet, in Lyon, as throughout the entire Midi, unrepentant counterrevolution seethed in the populace's hearts and minds. Grieving womenfolk were a particular nuisance, the troops occupying the city being continually deflected from their duty by misplaced sympathy. Lyon's despicable women "are all contre-révolutionnaires," all admirers of Charlotte Corday. Amid the ruins of the city, these whores practiced adultery unceasingly, luring Montagnard soldiers using all the attractions of their sex, married and unmarried women alike continually seducing the men.[90]

After securing Lyon, the army commanded by Barras undertook the three-and-a-half-month siege of Toulon. On 27 August, Toulon's republicans had surrendered to the British, despite the announcement of Admiral Hood, the British commander, that he would protect only those "clearly and frankly pronouncing in favour of monarchy and raising the French royal standard."[91] After Captain Napoleon Bonaparte, one of the officers to whom Barras entrusted the siege, expelled the British and Spanish contingents from the heights surrounding the town, in mid-December, however, Hood's fleet was forced to evacuate under heavy fire. During the three-day evacuation, thousands of refugees departed with the British, but numerous others implicated in the four-month British-backed regime remained behind. Local Jacobins, released from prison, soon "identified" these "rebels" to Barras and his revolutionary commission, which included also Fréron, Salicetti, and Robespierre's younger brother, Augustin. Within days, virtually without trial, 800 suspects were executed, mostly shot. Between December and March 1794, another 282 traitors went to the guillotine. Toulon, renamed now Port-la-Montagne, abounded in poor workingmen, yet, much as in Lyon, Barras and his team could find only an embarrasingly "small number of Patriots ready to support the Montagne."[92]

Abominable excesses occurred likewise at Nantes and Rennes, as well as nearby places recaptured from the Vendéean royalists. After defeat at rebel hands in two battles in September, regular troops supplemented by sansculotte volunteers from Paris, crushed the royalists in the *bocage* around Cholet on 17 October. Recovering Saumur and Angers, the Montagne drove the "whites" deep into the Vendéean heartland. Large numbers of rural women were raped by republican soldiery, noted Lequinio, and often then bayoneted with their children afterward. By late October 1793, Nantes overflowed with prisoners. The rebel remnant crossed the Loire and, joining local Chouans, marched on Granville, on the Cotentin Peninsula opposite Jersey, hoping to link up with the British, but were forced back southward. The final battle in the west resounded on 12 December at night, in pouring rain in the picturesque ancient town of Le Mans. Hundreds of the Catholic royal army were slaughtered in the streets. Those who escaped, including many women and priests, were cut down during their retreat toward Brittany. After a last stand at Sauvenay, the Catholic-royalist army was wiped out.[93]

In Nantes, the probably mentally unstable representative on mission, Jean-Baptiste Carrier (1756–94), outdid Lebon in brutality and sadism, unleashing a ferocious repression. Entrusted with sweeping authority, having earlier ruthlessly purged the Cherbourg coast of Brissotins, this fanatical Montagnard found Nantes' prisons crammed to overflowing. Eager to enforce the bread price maximum, and advance de-Christianization, he also faced severe food shortages and, as elsewhere, a divided, hesitant workforce. After guillotining dozens, he pronounced the guillotine too slow. To reduce the "rebels" on his hands, on 19 November 1793, he introduced his soon notorious *noyades*, commencing with ninety priests executed by drowning in the Loire estuary, bound together in a holed barge intended to sink quickly. Six other batches of victims, many refractory priests accused of inciting peasant fanaticism, were similarly dispatched over the next weeks. Around 1,800 rebels perished in these *noyades* and thousands more in massed shootings. Estimates put the total of Carrier's victims at around 10,000. From the townspeople came little protest as the captured "whites," they assumed, would have perpetrated frightful massacres had they seized Nantes or Rennes. Carrier, who liked indulging in nighttime orgies with female prisoners, was recalled in disgrace to Paris in February 1794, after Jullien denounced his excesses directly to Robespierre. He subsequently aligned with the Hébertistes.[94]

Compared to Lyon, Toulon, and Nantes, or Arras and Marseille, at Toulouse, Montpellier, and Bordeaux, as at Strasbourg and Nancy, the Terror proved comparatively mild. At Toulouse, once people's representatives Marc-Antoine Rodeau and Chambon-Roux established their control, more than fifteen hundred suspects were imprisoned and several dozen sent to Paris where they were executed. But, as at Montpellier, few executions took place at Toulouse itself. Also at Bordeaux and most of the southwest, apart from the Basque Country, where there was a severe repression along the border with Spain, relative leniency prevailed initially. Most citizens' attitudes were "excellent, pure and révolutionnaire," reported envoy on mission Alexandre-Clément Ysabeau (1754–1831) on 12 March 1794. Ysabeau directed the repression there together with Tallien until shortly before Thermidor. The *beaux-esprits*, *orateurs*, and writers who had misled the local populace had all disappeared.[95] Hymn-singing at the Temple of Reason the day before had been well attended. No former noble would be released even if he could prove his patriotisme. A constitutional priest, convicted of royalism, had been guillotined two days before, and that very day a nun would be executed. In all, 104 victims were guillotined at Bordeaux between October 1793 and June 1794, a figure sufficiently modest to prompt high-level complaints. A final flurry of repression concluded the Bordeaux Terror in June and July 1794 after Robespierre's acolyte, Marc-Antoine Jullien, was sent to repair the "negligence" of Tallien and Ysabeau; while there, he condemned 198 more victims to the guillotine.

Crushing Intellectual Dissent

On 3 October, on a motion of Billaud-Varenne, the Convention directed the Tribunal Révolutionnaire to try the "widow Capet."[96] Interrogated interminably, Marie Antoinette was accused of ordering the Swiss Guards to open fire on 10 August and much else. After a concluding all-night session on 16 October, the Tribunal pronounced her death sentence at five in the morning; she showed little emotion. Humbly attired all in white and followed by an immense crowd, at 11:00 AM on the twenty-fifth day of the first month of Year II, the "new Agrippina" began her last journey (during which David made a sketch of her), her *charette* proceeding from the Conciergerie through a vast throng, her calm demeanor reportedly displaying neither regal pride nor *abattement*. After the blade fell, her head was presented to the crowds, which responded for "many minutes," yelling, "Vive la nation! Vive la République!"[97]

Those witnessing the scene, however, were by no means all jubilant. So obvious was the disapproval of some that Hébert harangued the Jacobins the next day, demanding the arrest of journalists who reported her trial unenthusiastically or, as he expressed it, in "a false and perverse manner."[98] Despite the intensity of the repression, the press was still not entirely cowed. Addressing the Jacobins on 1 November, Chabot publicly discoursed on the sharp contrast between the Revolution's basic values prior to June 1793 and the entirely different ideology championed by the Montagne. Between 1788 and 1793, the Revolution had embraced comprehensive individual liberty and freedom of the press; such liberty was essential to the Revolution then, because press freedom "was necessary against tyranny and at that time the people applauded such liberty."

But now, with France under a "popular" regime, everything had changed. The press would never again be permitted to diverge from the proper path or fail to "respect" the people. Anyone criticizing the Montagne would be severely dealt with. Had not the sansculotte crowds, the former friar Chabot reminded the club, applauded the smashing of the printing presses of "Gorsas and the other counterrevolutionary journalists" in March? Everyone with correct ideas backed the smashing of dissident printing presses. "La liberté de la presse," needed before, could be discarded now the nation's press existed only for the "défense de la liberté; voilà ses limites."[99]

Nor were unsubmissive journalists the only section of the intelligentsia specially targeted. The Montagne, observed François de Neufchâteau, later a leading revolutionary himself, set out to silence all criticism.[100] Victims of the Terror in Lyon, Marseille, Toulon, Nantes, Bordeaux, and the Vendée alike were, in the great majority, ordinary people, often artisans and laborers suspected of opposing the Montagne. Among more prominent victims, though, the chief targets were undeviatingly the Left republican intellectuals, writers, and journalists who had forged the Revolution. The point of the Terror, noted Ysabeau at Bordeaux, was to eliminate Brissotins and the *beaux-esprits, orateurs,* and writers "with eloquent pens" who had misled the people. Robepierre and his colleagues," one observer summed the matter up, "pursued the *gens de lettres.*"[101]

One after the other, the Montagne liquidated its democratic republican critics and other resolute detractors. Adam Lux, perfectly calm, even embracing his executioners, was guillotined on 4 November. Two days later, it was the turn of Louis XVI's ambitious cousin, Louis-Philippe, Duc d'Orléans, known since the declaration of the Republic as "Philippe Égalité." Imprisoned since June, on 14 November Louis-Pierre Manuel, whose last book *Lettres sur la Révolution receuillies par un ami de la Constitution* had appeared the year before, faced the blade. Girey-Dupré, caught in Bordeaux and brought to Paris, appeared before the Tribunal Révolutionnaire, where he was denounced as Brissot's helper and disciple. He replied by eulogizing his mentor as "a second Sidney," a true republican and freedom fighter whose fate, he told an unsmiling court, he was content to share. Aged only twenty-four, he rapidly did so, conveyed through the streets on 20 November shouting, as he passed Robespierre's lodgings, "À bas les tyrants et les dictateurs!"[102] Also seized in November was France's most celebrated scientist, a prominent and enthusiastic supporter of the Revolution throughout 1789–93, Antoine-Laurent Lavoisier (1743–94), arrested not as a leading académicien opposing suppression of the academies but among twenty-four former royal tax "farmers-general" deemed "oppressors of the people."[103]

After hiding briefly in the now-abolished Académie des Sciences, Lavoisier gave himself up, being unwilling to endanger those who tried to save him. Scientific colleagues submitted petitions, explaining the signal importance of his research. But as he himself stressed in one of his last letters, even a record of outstanding contribution to the Revolution, major contributions to the arts, and surpassing scientific work put together could not save a critic from the Montagne.[104] Before being guillotined, he languished for several months in the former Jansenist convent of Port-Royal where several other prominent intellectuals were also incarcerated, a dreaded place now renamed (with unintended irony) Port-Libre.

The Paris suburb of Auteuil, key redoubt of la philosophie, underwent repeated searches by revolutionary committees hunting especially for Condorcet. Garat, linked to the radical philosophes Diderot, Helvétius, and Condorcet since 1774, forced to resign his post as justice minister in favor of Gohier on 20 August, was denounced by Collot d'Herbois and imprisoned on 27 September (but survived). Antoine Destutt de Tracy, materialist philosophe, herald of black emancipation and among the first nobles to join the Third in 1789, earlier an officer under Lafayette, was arrested on 19 October after Hébertistes led by Ronsin surrounded his house at Auteuil. Subsequently released, he was rearrested and imprisoned on 2 November. He used the eleven months of his second incarceration for a close study of Locke's and Condillac's epistemology.[105] The circle's other foremost philosophe, Volney, was arrested on the Comité de Sûreté Générale's orders, while emerging from the Ministry of Foreign Affairs on 16 November.[106] Another of the Helvétius circle, La Roche, former confessor to the Comte d'Artois, was arrested over the town council's protest for delaying removal of Mirabeau's bust from the town hall, publicly denigrating Marat, and on suspicion of aiding Condorcet's escape.[107] Cabanis, guardian of the elderly Mme. Helvétius and her Auteuil villa, purged from the town council in November, remained indoors in Mme. Helvétius's house, scarcely venturing out until after Thermidor.

Shortly before his seizure, Volney published his popularizing tract *La Loi naturelle, ou Catéchisme du Citoyen français*. Like the *Bon-Sens* of d'Holbach, directed at the masses in simple terms, it was a vigorously argued plea for a philosophical transformation of all human values on the basis of freedom and individual fulfillment in diversity. Celebrated for large works, Volney, noted the *Moniteur*, had now published a slim but remarkable volume aimed at everyone, even the barely literate. An overriding ethical law exists, irrespective of religion, constituting the common rule for all, guiding men whether they know it or not without distinction of sect or faith toward human happiness—the natural law deriving directly from God. This alone, observed the paper, sufficiently refuted rumors spread by Corsican counterrevolutionaries accusing Volney of "atheism." (In reality, Volney, a full-blown exponent of radical ideas, was a d'Holbachian materialist who wholly rejected divine Providence.) Morality's foundations, "good" and "bad," contended Volney (like Diderot, d'Holbach, Helvétius, and Condorcet), are purely social values unconnected to revelations and theology. He defined "good" as whatever helps conserve and improve human society; "bad" is the opposite.

Morality, for Volney, was an immediate, universal, invariable, and evident science derived from the particular character and needs of men, a political discipline pivoting on the principles of equity, justice, charity, and toleration, entrusting all with the collective common fight against ignorance, superstition, and intolerance and demanding the most perfect indifference to all organized cults and priests. This *loi naturelle*, held Volney, stigmatized senseless violence and shedding of blood.[108] Especially contrary to Robespierre's ideology was Volney's contention that ignorance is the worst of human failings because it damages and prejudices everyone and directly harms society, liberty, and the Republic.[109] Rejecting Rousseau's praise of the savage state, *La Loi naturelle* claims that man in *l'état sauvage* is brutish, ignorant, and ill-intentioned, and that universal "natural law" grounded on reason and experience not only intends man for life in a free society but is the only path to morality, order, and a decent life for all.[110] Volney had throughout been among the most eloquent and fervent advocates of the Revolution's democratic principles: incarcerated at La Force, he remained confined for ten months.

Yet another literary-philosophical foe silenced was Chamfort. Appointed codirector of the Bibliothèque Nationale by Roland in 1792, by late 1793 he was principal director in practice. A convinced republican long before his Montagnard opponents, he created the first truly national European library open daily to the public, rather than a few specialists for a few hours weekly. He vastly expanded the library's holdings, saving many works from destruction. After the 2 June coup, Pache ordered the slogan "Liberty, Equality, Fraternity or Death" inscribed on the front of the library; Chamfort's suggesting this be replaced with "Be my Brother or I will kill you" and other sarcasms were hardly

appreciated. He was an obvious "suspect" who loathed Marat and venerated Charlotte Corday. Under pressure from Robespierre, he and the
rest of the library's staff had been sacked on 16 August and replaced by
"patriots" of the approved variety. Arrested on the anniversary of the
great prison atrocity, 2 September, Chamfort was released after publicly
disavowing the Brissotins. But in mid-November, in a fit of despair on
hearing he would be rearrested, he cut his throat with a razor and shot
himself. Lying grievously wounded for weeks, he died early in 1794.[111]
Although his friend Ginguené, gathering up those of his aphorisms
and anecdotes as he could find, many scrawled on scraps deposited in
boxes scattered around his rooms, published these after Thermidor in
four volumes, dated "L'An Trois de la République," much of his literary
legacy was permanently lost. For this partial literary rescue, Ginguené
just had time before he too was arrested. He was incarcerated in Saint-
Lazare (where the poet André Chénier also languished).

High priority for the regime was Condorcet's liquidation. Sentenced to death as an outlaw on 2 October 1793, he asked his wife to
divorce him to protect her and save his assets for their daughter. Despite repeated searches, he eluded his foes and during many months
successfully hid with Cabanis's help, alternately at Mme. Helvétius's
residence and Garat's. Later he transferred to another hiding place in
Paris's southern fringe, remaining concealed until March 1794. Fend-
ing off their depression, Sophie—who according to Hébert had had an
affair with Ducos—labored at translating Smith's *Wealth of Nations*,
Condorcet at his *Tableau historique des progrès de l'esprit humain*. As
the Terror engulfed them in his last months, he refused to give up the
courageous optimism infusing his efforts throughout the revolutionary
years. If anyone persevered indomitably under Robespierre's menace, it
was Condorcet.

> Shall we believe the opinion interpreting equality not as equal access
> to enlightenment, or equal development of moral sentiments puri-
> fied and perfected by reason, but instead as equality of ignorance,
> corruption and ferocity, can permanently degrade a nation? Shall
> we believe these men [Marat and Robespierre] fostering this stupid
> opinion, whose ambitious and jealous mediocrity renders enlighten-
> ment odious and virtue suspect, can maintain a durable illusion? No,
> they can make humanity weep over the loss of some rare and precious
> men that are entirely worthy of her, they can make their country sigh
> over the irreparable injustices they wreak, but they will not prevent

the Enlightenment's advance, even if it is checked temporarily; it will resume and accelerate. Certainly it is possible to deceive peoples and mislead them—but not permanently brutalize and corrupt them.[112]

Such a valiant profession of faith required great inner resolve at a time when elimination of the intellectual bloc who forged the Revolution was unrelenting, and paralleled by stringent measures emasculating all political debate, the city sections, clubs, and departmental administrations. A Convention decree of 4 December 1793 abolished the departments' general councils, presidents, and *procureurs-généraux* to ensure departments became wholly submissive political entities.[113] Every week, the oppression grew more and more terrible. Much of the surviving republican intelligensia sank into deep dejection. Yet Mary Wollstonecraft, however shocked and appalled, was another who refused to abandon hope. She trusted still in the Revolution's ultimate promise. Resolving not to follow Helen Maria Williams's advice and burn letters and manuscripts that could be deemed incriminating (Williams had burned everything she had from Mme. Roland), in February 1794, Wollstonecraft withdrew from Paris to Le Havre. "Though death and misery, in every shape of terrour" haunt France, she wrote on 10 March 1794, still she was glad "that I came to France, because I never could have had else a just opinion of the most extraordinary event [the Revolution] that has ever been recorded."[114]

Depressed, closeted with Barlow and a few others, Paine fitfully composed *The Age of Reason*, seeking consolation in cognac and Spinoza.[115] On 25 December, reversing every republican revolutionary principle, including Brissotin commitment to cosmopolitanism, the Convention decreed that no foreigner could represent the French people in the legislature. Foreigners were henceforth excluded "from every public function during the war."[116] The credentials of the two foreign deputies, Paine and Cloots, were canceled that very day. Cloots, after being harassed for weeks, was arrested three days later.[117] The police seized Paine and his papers, invading his rooms at the Hotel de Philadelphie (where Barlow also lodged), and conducted him to the Luxembourg, though not before he managed to slip Barlow the still-unprinted sections of part 1 of *The Age of Reason*, a work leaning heavily on Spinoza's Bible criticism, ready for Stone's printing press.[118] Appeals for Paine's release, signed by Barlow and seventeen other Americans in Paris, testifying that he had labored heroically for American liberty and that of France, were ignored, with the connivance of the United States ambassador,

Morris, who detested Paine, Barlow, and their democratic republican-ism.[119] Barlow visited Paine in prison frequently over the next months but, from March 1794, was denied further access.

Fissures within the Montagne

At Paris, executions ensued daily over the winter of 1793–94, the vic-tims an increasingly bizarre mix of supposedly scheming "aristocrats," counterrevolutionary priests, Brissotins, Feuillants, and associates of Mirabeau. The trial of Barnave, imprisoned in Grenoble since three days after the 10 August 1792 rising, but brought to Paris only in early November 1793, and Marguerite-Louis Duport-Dutertre (1754–93), Roland's Feuillant predecessor as justice minister, concluded at mid-night on 28 November. Complicit in the Champs de Mars and 10 Au-gust massacres, both went to the guillotine the next day—Barnave still only thirty-two—dispatched together with a condemned curé and the latter's devout sister.[120] On 4 December followed Convention deputy Armand Guy, Comte de Kersaint (1741–93), who had courageously opposed both the king's execution and Montagnard tyranny. The next day it was the turn of Rabaut Saint-Étienne of the Commission of Twelve, recently found hiding in a friend's house. Hearing he had been guillotined, his wife shot herself. On 8 December, the Genevan repub-lican Clavière, seized in September, committed suicide, the day before he was to appear before the Tribunal Révolutionnaire, by plunging a dagger into his heart. Learning he was dead, his wife too shot herself.

On 26 December, a naval officer, Charles-August Prévost Lacroix, born at Louisbourg, in Nova Scotia, met his end for treading the tri-color cockade underfoot, together with a baker, Nicolas Gomot, exe-cuted for uttering counterrevolutionary remarks while selling bread of different qualities in defiance of the bread equality decree. Yet, overall, strikingly few bakers, grocers, shopkeepers, food retailers, or other busi-nessmen accused of hoarding figured among those guillotined. Montag-nard, and especially sansculotte rhetoric, loudly condemned hoarding of and profiteering in bread and other basic food supplies, and these were much resented by the populace,[121] but the Terror never seriously concerned itself with retailers or merchants, or bankers or any variety of businessmen. In every French city, action against food hoarders and merchants remained strictly secondary. The principal target was not the rich, corrupt, financially active, or highborn, but always rather those opposing or criticizing the dictatorship. On 29 December the former Strasbourg mayor, Pierre-Frédéric Dietrich (1748–93), a Feuillant considered by Robespierre an "homme dangereux," the ex-noble in whose Strasbourg apartments in April 1792, with Mme. Dietrich accompanying at the harpsichord, the "Marseillaise" was first performed, was executed. With him was guillotined one of the the Revolution's most outstanding republican democrats, Pierre Lebrun-Tondu (1754–93), former foreign minister, Belgian radical deputy, and editor of the *Journal général de l'Europe*. Arrested on 2 June 1793, he had escaped and gone into hiding. Recaptured and tried, he was condemned for "conspiring against liberty." Lebrun reportedly strode to the guillotine with "assez de sang froid."[122]

A new phase commenced in December with the onset of a bitter feud within the Jacobins and the Convention, with Robespierre mediating, between the populist faction around Hébert and the Cordeliers grouping behind Danton. According to Garat later, Danton tried to restrain the Terror and check Robespierre, Collot d'Herbois, and Billaud-Varenne, and outmaneuver the Hébertistes by building a majority against them in the Convention and Comité de Salut Public. He was backed by Desmoulins, who held no important post in the government but remained a famed revolutionary orator, journalist, and figurehead, and, prompted by Danton, at this point established *Le Vieux Cordelier*, a new revolutionary journal focusing attention on the contradiction between revolutionary core values—freedom of the press especially—and those of the regime. The title of Desmoulins's paper implied that the Revolution's authentic veterans were reawakening and mobilizing against usurpers and impostors, which was indeed the effect he tried to achieve. "La liberté politique," he emphasized in the first issue, has no finer weapon than the press. He asked whether France should be allowed to fall behind England in this respect: "Should reason fear a duel with stupidity"? Philosophique reason and populist crassness, he reminded readers, were irreconcilable enemies, and press freedom the crux of the struggle.[123]

By mid-December, the rift within the revolutionary leadership could no longer be papered over. Only traitors and counterrevolutionaries, suggested Desmoulins, sought to constrain liberty of expression. A fierce public quarrel erupted at the Jacobins over the *Vieux Cordelier*'s third issue, where Desmoulins almost openly denounced the Terror, criticizing the Committee of Public Safety, and in particular Marat's protégé François-Nicolas Vincent (1767–94), secretary-general of the

War Office, a Cordeliers firebrand at daggers drawn with another of Danton's adherents, Pierre-Nicolas Philippeaux (1756–94), a judge from Le Mans and Convention deputy highly critical of the conduct of the Vendéean campaign. Desmoulins assailed Hébert's allies Vincent, Ronsin, and Stanislas-Marie Maillard (1763–94), a leader of the movements of 5 October 1789 and 10 August 1792, a notorious bully, drunkard, and perpetrator of the September massacres.[124] In a stormy Convention session on 17 December, Philippeaux and Fabre d'Églantine (defending himself, being mired in financial scandal, more than helping Desmoulins), joined in denouncing Vincent, Ronsin, and Maillard for "terrorist" excesses and excessive harshness in the Vendée. Hébert retaliated, accusing Fabre d'Églantine of publishing counterrevolutionary writings and being "a flatterer of the great." The Dantonistes gained ground briefly, persuading the Assembly to detain Vincent and Ronsin in the Luxembourg.[125]

Appealing to the rump Convention, publicly declaring Desmoulins, Fabre, and Philippeaux ripe for liquidation, Hébert paid lavish tribute to Danton as well as Robespierre as the "two pillars of the Revolution."[126] Was it conceivable the Terror could be directed against true patriotes? "No—it is against aristocrats and perfidious agents alone that it is justly aimed." The Hébertistes specifically denounced the Dantonistes criticizing the Terror as concealed allies of "the defeated faction" (the Brissotins), men sowing division in the Republic and maligning the best patriotes.[127] The Brissotin leadership had deservedly suffered for "their crimes," but "their agents and accomplices breathed still." Death to the "modérés, comme celle des royalistes et des aristocrates," intoned Hébert's *Père Duchesne*, denouncing Desmoulins as a vile *intrigueur* who should be dragged to the guillotine without delay. Hébert, retorted Desmoulins in the *Vieux Cordelier*, was a total scoundrel, employing "ignorance" and "stupidity" as his tools.[128] Returning from Lyon, Collot d'Herbois joined Hébert in accusing Desmoulins of "Brissotin" tendencies. Ronsin's arrest, he complained, had ruinously discouraged the few "true Jacobins" fighting modérantisme in Lyon. The "new Brissotins" were trying to besmirch "the brave Ronsin," known in Lyon only for unbending severity. By so doing, the Dantonists were giving comfort to all the Brissotins, modérés, and aristocrates dominating Lyonnais sentiment.[129]

Robespierre hesitated for many weeks to turn on those Hébert labeled "conspirators," preferring to play the mediator, shielding them from expulsion from the Jacobins while continually issuing ominous warnings. The clash ended for the moment in deadlock. Robespierre called for unity. Vincent and Ronsin were released. But on Christmas Day, in a speech in which he plied the Convention with some of his choicest maxims, Robespierre also set the scene for the soon-resumed internecine struggle that was to tear the Montagnard leadership to shreds. "The [correct] theory of revolutionary government" was as new as the Revolution itself, and it was useless searching for it, like Desmoulins, in books of political writers "who had not predicted this Revolution."[130] If the Revolution must choose between "an excess of patriotic fervour" and the "nothingness" of incivisme, there could be no hesitation: le modérantisme was the great enemy, le modérantisme "is to the Revolution what impotence is to chastity." If vice served their enemies, he and his supporters had virtue on their side. The Revolution must liquidate all "enemies of the people." Who they were was for him to specify.[131]

Robespierre at this point enunciated a doctrine as bizarre as any formulated during the Revolution: the Revolution was simultaneously menaced by *two* concealed enemies donning cunning masks: modérantisme and "fanaticism." Superficially, these might appear quite different but actually were one and the same thing. When he and the comité attacked "fanatics," critics complained they embraced modérantisme; when they assailed modérantisme, they were accused of "l'exagération" (extremism). Nothing more closely resembled an apostle of modérantisme than a republican extremist. Strangely enough, Robespierristes, Hébertistes, and Dantonistes all seemed convinced by early 1794 that insidious extremism was closely connected to modérantisme. Hérault de Sechelles, having supervised the Terror in Alsace from Strasbourg during the autumn, after reporting on his mission on 29 December before the Convention, came under Hébertiste criticism in connection with his ties with the Convention's former commissaires in Belgium— Proly, Pereyra, and Dubuisson. These three eminently illustrated the new logic. Close to Danton, they were accused by Hébert's faction of complicity in Dumouriez's monarchist conspiracy while, rather paradoxically, simultaneously being ultra-révolutionnaires trying to split the Montagne by promoting democratic ideas too energetically.[132] The Republic, agreed Desmoulins, *was* now caught in a perilous crosswind between modérantisme on one side, and, on the other, the heinous "error" of extremism; everything depended on applying these labels with undeviating precision.[133]

Furthermore, for Robespierre, the fact that modérantisme was linked to extremism proved it was tied also to la philosophie. The perfidious "moderate," Robespierre continuously assured both Convention and Jacobins, had everything in common with the materialist philosophe. Moderates and extremists understood each other only too well. What a diabolical strategy! All the *fanatiques* urging strict adherence to the Constitution, accusing the leadership of being "arbitrary or tyrannical," were "sophistes stupides ou pervers," obstructing the people's will.[134] The Convention must use only the most discriminating judgment. In early January 1794, with Hébert and Collot piling on their accusations—and the fifth issue of the *Vieux Cordelier* on 5 January mounting a further blistering attack on Hébert—Robespierre became increasingly suspicious of Danton's motives, while the fiery Desmoulins, though aware he was losing Robespierre's support, got into increasingly hot water. Fabre, denying contributing to Desmoulins's recent writings, as his foes claimed, was publicly disgraced for financial corruption. At the Jacobins on 6 January, Collot d'Herbois also demanded Philippeaux's expulsion. Finally, on 7 January, Robespierre himself denounced *Le Vieux Cordelier* at the Jacobins as a paper "for aristrocrates."

Previously, the "Incorruptible" had defended his old friend Desmoulins but now changed his language. Camille had undertaken to abjure his "hérésies politiques," the "errors" pervading his journal, but had lamentably failed to do so. A spoiled child, admiring Philippeaux like Demosthenes and Cicero, his writings were ill-advised and "dangerous." In fact, the issues of the *Vieux Cordelier*, being undoubted "heresy," should be burned on the floor of the Jacobins. "Well said, Robespierre," answered Desmoulins, "but I reply like Rousseau: to burn is not to answer."[135] Desmoulins was perilously close to breaking with the only personage who could save him. On 8 January, *Le Vieux Cordelier*'s third and fourth issues were read out to the indignant Jacobins, after which Robespierre pronounced it "useless" to read out the (electrifyingly critical) fifth issue. In Desmoulins's writings, he concluded, one finds pure revolutionary principles mixed with pernicious modérantisme. Desmoulins upheld patriotisme on the one hand and "aristocracy" on the other. What was Desmoulins's true standpoint? Plainly, under the "torn banners" of Brissotisme, a new and insidious faction had arisen that was reviving Brissot's principles. At bottom, the people's new enemies were the same as before; the actors had changed and assumed a new mask, but the performance was still that of the Gironde.[136] Absurdly illogical and paranoid on one level, there was nevertheless some logic to the new categorization and terminology: both Hébertistes and Dantonistes resented the excessive centralization of power in the two executive committees, and complaints about this echoed in the Jacobins, Cordeliers, and Convention alike. Philippeaux, Fabre, and Desmoulins, voted the Cordeliers on 11 January, had "lost the society's confidence," a declaration read out at the Jacobins by Momoro the next day; Desmoulins, however, was a special case who could regain that confidence by disavowing all his "héresies révolutionnaires."[137]

"Heresy," as in Inquisition times, was now firmly established. "Liberty" was menaced from both wings, one group of conspirateurs plotted counterrevolution under the mask of modérantisme tainted with Girondisme, the other feigned to be more patriotic than everyone else, promoting extremism again to subvert liberty.[138] These warring factions were really the same thing, argued Robespierre, and were obviously manipulated by foreign powers. The strife between populist militants controlling the Cordeliers—Hébert, Ronsin, Vincent, and Momoro forming one leg of the regime and Dantonistes trying to rescue the revolutionary values of 1789–93—was clearly irresolvable and threatened to capsize the Committee of Public Safety, shattering Robespierre's always fragile group *dictature*. On 10 January 1794, Robespierre spoke at the Jacobins in a manner hinting that he now counted Philippeaux and Desmoulins among his innumerable detractors. But he remained unpredictable and could turn on the Hébertistes at any moment.

What chiefly mattered to Robespierre was his own dominance and standing. Had not the vile Louvet labeled him, Robespierre, a "dictator"? Now, others too called him a "dictateur." Well, he *was* a dictator, but a dictator for "the people." "My dictatorship," he exclaimed to frantic, thunderous applause, "is that of Lepeletier and Marat." He, Robespierre, embodied Marat's "dictatorship." The true "martyr of the Revolution," it was only he who was genuinely under threat, because he was the one thrusting the dagger at the throat of "tyrants."[139] Still, Robespierre hesitated. While Danton, Philippeaux, and Desmoulins pondered how to save themselves by countering the militant populists orchestrating the Cordeliers, from late December 1793 to March 1794, France's self-confessed dictator brooded long and hard over whether to silence the threat from the streets first, the flatterers of the sansculottes, before crushing the Terror's critics, or proceed vice versa. Despite a show of unity to mark the anniversary of Louis XVI's execution, on 21 January, when the entire Convention marched to the Place de la Révolution singing republican hymns, murderous tension fed the underlying fratricidal struggle.

The Terror, meanwhile, ground on inexorably, bearing little apparent relation to the current tussle for power. Early in the new year, Lamourette, another leading democrat, and, in particular, leader with

Figure 16. French School, portrait of Camille Desmoulins, 18th century, oil on canvas. Musée Carnavalet, Paris. © BeBa / Iberfoto / The Image Works.

Grégoire and Fauchet of "la démocratie chrétienne," followed Fauchet onto the scaffold. Where other condemned constitutional bishops, like Charles Benoît Roux, moderate royalist constitutional bishop of Bouches-du-Rhône, imprisoned at Marseille and liquidated there in April 1794, were tried in the provinces, and Loménie de Brienne, arrested in November, committed suicide at the seat of his bishopric, Sens, five days after Lamourette's demise, the latter was sent from Lyon to face the Paris Tribunal Révolutionnaire. During his weeks at the Conciergerie, Lamourette behaved with exemplary dignity.[140] His trial on 10 January pivoted on a celebrated address delivered in Lyon cathedral on 12 June 1793, ten days after the Robespierriste coup in Paris, eulogizing those who died in the anti-Montagnard Lyon insurrection of 29 May. In that discourse, he publicly condemned the Montagne, glorifying the Lyon rebellion and extolling "the Twenty-Two [Brisso-tin] *conspirateurs*" as upholders of the "true and wise liberty," the soul of the Revolution, claiming that the people were being "grossly misled."[141] This guaranteed his death sentence. He went to the guillotine the next day. Most of the democratic Revolution's principal men were now dead or behind bars. But reputations lived on and Brissot, Condorcet, Pé-tion, and Mirabeau continued to dominate the trials and terroriste rhetoric, remaining the key category-markers for repression through the rest of the Terror.

If less than two hundred people had thus far been guillotined in Paris, arrests of opponents, especially with Brissotin, Feuillant, or roy-alist connections, accelerated over the winter. The total of political prisoners cramming Paris prisons rose spectacularly by 19 January to 5,073—a staggering figure compared with four months earlier. In late January, Jacobins implicated in the financial scandal surrounding Fabre joined the prison population. Yet the destabilizing deadlock paralyz-ing the Jacobins dragged on.[142] Still no reckoning occurred with either rival coalition wing. Tense relations between the executive and socié-tés populaires, between Robespierre and the streets, continued, as did wrangling over price controls, which again surged to the fore in late Jan-uary under renewed pressure of rising prices, reinforced by Hébertiste complaints. Before anything else, the regime felt it needed to more fully bridle independent populism, vesting power in the sociétés populai-res and sansculottes, and hence directly in the streets, though, as Dan-ton agreed, this could not be done explicitly or too overtly. The masses cared little or nothing for the regime's ideological obsessions and were only really concerned about bread supplies, price controls, and their vendetta against hoarders. Jacques Roux, apostle of economic equality, now an isolated figure whose influence was much reduced but still rep-resented a residual threat from the streets, was hauled before the Tri-bunal Révolutionnaire on 25 January. He had publicly disparaged the Montagnard leadership, which meant he stood no chance of evading the death sentence, but his judges were prevented from implementing it: Roux ended his life sensationally, stabbing himself five times before his accusers, expiring on the spot amid torrents of blood.[143]

Frightful and appalling though the Terror was, until March 1794 its victims in Paris remained relatively few by the standards of Lyon, Nantes, Toulon, or the Vendée. A total of 177 were executed in the capi-tal between October and the end of 1793. Overall, the Terror thus far was less a catalog of show trials and executions than a wave of general repression, searches, imprisonment, xenophobia, and militant populism aimed at intimidating everyone from the sansculottes, shopkeepers, bakers, and prostitutes—and local Jacobin clubs—to artists' salons, cafés, theaters, and opera houses. Execrable atrocities were committed in many places. But even if the true figure for victims who died in France during the Terror surpassed the official estimate of around thirty thousand deaths in ten months, the catastrophe must be considered in the light of the age's other great atrocities.[144] Compared with the numbers slaughtered in Frederick the Great's battles, or the brutal suppression of the 1798 Irish rebellion (despite Ireland having barely one-sixth of France's population), the mortality caused by the Terror remained comparatively modest.

Terror wielded by virtue, according to Robesierre, was the very pillar of liberty. Despite it all, remnants of the republican vanguard managed to survive precariously either in the Convention, in hiding, or in prison, including Bonneville (who had failed to get elected to the Convention but remained a prominent critic of Marat and Robespierre), Louvet, Isnard, Lanjuinais, Lanthenas, Boissy d'Anglas, Kervélégan, Paine, Roederer (who long disappeared from view), and the historian-archivist Pierre-Claude Daunou, constitutional priest and philosophy professor, deputy for the Pas-de-Calais, among the seventy-two protesters of June 1793, among the chief framers of the Constitution of 1795. After Thermidor, these men, battered and deeply traumatized though they were, slowly reemerged and, with growing resolution from early 1795, strove to piece together again the principles and the decimated but not altogether destroyed remnant of the democratic republican Left.

CHAPTER 20

The Terror's Last Months

(MARCH–JULY 1794)

Eliminating the Hébertistes

The Terror pervaded every aspect and dimension of society and life. "It was a real sickness," recalled Roederer, who survived it in hiding, in which the "moral and physical constantly interacted; an extreme case suspending use of reason, and almost reason's aberration. It concentrated everyone within himself, detaching him from everything but preservation, from the most important affairs, most intimate affections and most sacred duties, paralyzing arm and soul simultaneously."[1] The irrational and criminal character of the Terror seemed so obvious to so many that appalled onlookers in France, like the Bordeaux diarist Brochon, tended to assume that Jacobin conspirateurs deliberately sought to "deshonorer la Révolution" with slaughter and crime,[2] not realizing its aim was not to besmirch the Revolution in the interest of royalty and reaction but to reject the essential principles of the Revolution of 1788–93 in the name of a very different and antagonistic ideology.

The numbers alone prove the Terror affected all classes of the population, not only intellectuals, nobles, army officers, and clergy. Officially, under the Terror, the government's Revolutionary Tribunals executed a total of 16,594 victims in France, without counting the thousands extrajudicially shot or drowned by Montagnard forces in Lyon, Toulon, Nantes, the Basque Country, and the Vendée. The approximately 17,000 judicially signed executions were certainly exceeded by the unauthorized killings, which amounted to perhaps around 23,000. Some estimates put the total of imprisoned *and* killed at more than 300,000. But all such estimates other than those for official executions are very vague. Some estimates for the number of people slaughtered during the repression in the Vendée go as high as 4 percent of the population—or

190,000—just for that region.[3] Of the approximately 17,000 officially executed, around 31 percent were artisans (democrats and royalists), and 28 percent peasants (often royalists). By contrast, smaller groups, 1,158, just over 8 percent, were nobles, counting both noblesse "of the sword" and "the robe" (parlementaires), and around 2 percent were priests. In Paris, 9,249 people were imprisoned for political reasons between August 1792 and July 1794, of whom 766, or well under a tenth, were nobles, male and female.[4]

The psychological impact was vast and incalculable. Around 29,000 émigrés, a considerable but not immense number, had departed France down to January 1793. But under the Terror, the pace of emigration quickened dramatically. By July 1794, around 145,000 émigrés nobles, priests, and commoners had fled the country. The Terror of 1793–94, it is safe to say, was by far the chief cause of flight from the country during the Revolution, accounting for more than four-fifths of the total. The number of ex-patriot French nobles rose to 16,431, eventually reaching more than 12 percent of the entire French noblesse. Even so, the French clergy in exile became twice as numerous, representing a quarter of all French émigrés.[5] In proportionate terms, these privileged social strata could perhaps be said to have been especially targeted.

The paralyzing political crisis gripping France from December 1793 to mid-March 1794 was aggravated by Robespierre's psychological sickness and his vacillation as to how to control the rival cliques underpinning the Montagnard tyranny. Both tendencies gravely threatened his position. Suffering from an acute form of nervous collapse, he remained physically absent from both Jacobins and the Convention throughout the critical period from 10 February to 13 March. Even to Danton, Hébert, Barère, and other prominent political insiders, it was far from obvious when Robespierre's hand was firmly on the levers of power and when not. Compulsively suspicious and neurotically wary, he increasingly kept his distance from colleagues as well as the people. "The people" for him had always been an abstraction, not something that he had widely experienced or knew. First of the great modern populist dictators, he never received the sort of mass adulation Marat did and eventually grew remote and aloof. Until February 1794, he had kept his distance but without being actually enclosed and out of touch, showing himself around Paris frequently, fastidiously dressed, with elegant silk embroidered clothes and linen, hair dressed in neat, scrupulous fashion, all the time observing, cultivating contacts, and regularly conversing with other main figures, taking meticulous notes.[6] Now, more powerful and autocratic than ever, but under intensifying nervous strain, he (like Danton), grew increasingly withdrawn.

His absence enabled Saint-Just, Barère, and Hanriot, to expand their power as Robespierre's immediate subordinates and active proxies, certainly, but also encouraged other advocates of Terror to extend and fortify their spheres. An able administrator and military commissaire, Saint-Just was also absent for much of December and January, at the front, supervising the military effort together with other Convention representatives in the field. Unbending dogmatist of virtue, he flexibly adjusted to every shift in Robespierre's stance, always promptly and efficiently seconding and reinforcing his every move. In Alsace, Saint-Just had offered no objection to the de-Christianization process there. But once Robespierre began assailing de-Christianizers as "conspirators," aiming to provoke a popular backlash against the Montagne, he immediately adopted this line too, denouncing de-Christianizers as counter-revolutionaries in disguise. Like Robespierre, Saint-Just urged the most inflexible harshness toward critics and dissenters as the surest way to Montagnard goals. He was acutely conscious that those criticizing the Terror were endeavoring to undermine the regime.

While the public saw only the steady expansion of the Terror, a swelling stream of arrests and executions through spring and summer 1794, the country's leadership remained locked, unperceived by most, in murderous fratricidal strife. Sporadic relaxation of Robespierre's personal grip only aggravated the pent-up accumulation of tension within ruling Montagnard circles, and further fragmented the precarious tyranny's political base. Eventually, Robespierre was compelled to act decisively by the spiraling ferment in the Cordeliers, a series of rowdy gatherings presided over by Hébert, Momoro, Vincent, and Carrier, the "butcher" of Nantes. Since his recall by Robespierre in February, Carrier had become an undeclared opponent. At a packed meeting at the Cordeliers on 4 March 1794, the tablet of the Rights of Man was ceremonially veiled, and Vincent and Carrier loudly criticized prominent figures who pretended to sit with the Montagne while actually, in their view, undermining "liberty"—namely, Desmoulins, Fabre, Philippeaux, and also Chabot (arrested on 17 November with his friend Bazire and charged with corruption). These personages, allegedly, were the new standard-bearers of Brissot's principles, of the modérantisme menacing France. At the Cordeliers, Vincent and Hébert called for the remaining "Brissotins" in detention to be swiftly liquidated, along with the other pernicious modérés (the Dantonistes).[7] Emboldened by massive applause, the Hébertistes began to speak openly of the need for a fresh sansculotte insurrection.

Collot d'Herbois, deploring these raucous proceedings, responded on 6 March at the Jacobins, urging the sister club to purge itself of those who were irresponsibly stirring the sansculottes. There was no immediate threat of a new insurrection, replied Momoro and Carrier, but the threat to the patriotes and true revolutionary virtue, they insisted, was extreme. At issue were not the sansculottes or anyone stirring their anger, but modérantisme, irresponsible negligence, and counterrevolutionary scheming. On 7 March, Collot d'Herbois headed a Jacobin delegation to the Cordeliers, demanding union and harmony between the two mother political clubs. Hébert and Momoro agreed that solidarity was essential. They spoke reassuringly and unveiled the table of rights; many present loudly cheered. But some frustrated and disgruntled sansculottes at the club ventured to publicly rebuke Robespierre for being too soft on "Brissotins" and modérantisme. In closing, Vincent even dared to publicly criticize Robespierre, if only obliquely, decrying (Robespierre's) usage of the term "ultra-révolutionnaire" as a sinister ploy for disabling the avant-guarde and allowing modérés to oppress loyal Patriots.[8] The deadlock continued unresolved until mid-March. As tension mounted, the Jacobins mostly rallied to Robespierre and the executive committees, while the Hébert-Vincent bloc turned to the sansculottes, redoubling their efforts to subvert Robespierre's standing in the streets.[9]

The gravity of the crisis could no longer be papered over. Even abroad, discerning observers noticed a massive new eruption brewing. Observing from Berne, the exiled royalist journalist Mallet du Pan confidently predicted a fresh "revolution" at Paris. Among the émigrés, morale rose as word spread that the Montagne was publicly split. Only with Robespierre's visible personal return to the helm on 13 March could the dictatorship fully coordinate and concentrate its energies to face the double Hébertiste-Dantoniste challenge. Whether or not the strategy Robespierre and Saint-Just followed was consciously devised as the best way to outmaneuver both rival factions, it proved devastatingly effective. Saint-Just initiated the new coup a few days before Robespierre's return, strongly denouncing modérantisme but for the moment ignoring what Robespierre had termed the *ultra-révolutionaire* threat. The Revolution's most uncompromising adversary of Left democratic republicanism, aside from Robespierre himself, he was no street agitator but a populist administrator and ideologue, propagating simplistic Rousseauist notions of the sort favored by Marat. He ardently extolled

Marat and, unlike Robespierre (personally always jealous of others), remained a tireless enthusiast for the Marat cult.

As devoted to Spartan austerity as Robespierre or Chaumette, Saint-Just helped bring the obsession with revolutionary virtue to its peak, tying Jacobin intolerance to fresh laws aimed at alleviation of hardship and enforcing price controls. While announcing in the Convention that trials of modérés were to be sharply stepped up, at the same time he introduced a set of measures known as the Ventôse decrees (of 26 February and 3 March) that looked harshly punitive and consonant with the demands of the Hébertistes. These initiated the mass expropriation of property belonging to the now well over 100,000 émigrés, and required the country's communes to draw up lists of deserving poor to whom payments from the confiscated assets should be distributed.[10] For some months the poorer Paris sections had been debating the feasibility of assigning annuities to the poor from a public domain consisting of the confiscated property of conspirators. Hence, the proposals looked like a shift of policy in the direction of the sansculottes and Hébertistes.

On the night of 10 March, the Comité de Sûreté Public, acting through Saint-Just (presumably, on Robespierre's orders, though this is unclear), secretly instructed the Revolutionary Tribunal's public prosecutor, Antoine-Quentin Fouquier-Tinville (1746–95)—a minor official promoted to his key position in August 1792 by Danton and Desmoulins—to prepare general indictments against Hébert, Vincent, Ronsin, Carrier, Momoro, and the other Cordeliers leaders for "conspiracy" and incitement to insurrection. Romme, a prominent voice on the Comité d'Instruction Publique, and another leader of the drive against food hoarders, despite having joined the Hébertistes in combating Desmoulins in December, and no friend of Robespierre, was left aside. Immediately after Robespierre's return, to the stupefaction of all Paris (including the victims, who had no inkling of what was to happen and had taken no prior precautions), on the evening of 14 March, Hébert and his Cordeliers colleagues were suddenly dramatically denounced by Saint-Just in the Convention as conspirateurs, arrested on the spot, and escorted to the Conciergerie.

At an emergency session of the Jacobins that same evening, Billaud-Varenne explained to his stunned audience that it had been discovered just in time that Hébert, Vincent, Ronsin, and Momoro were "agents of foreign powers" who were betraying France. They had forged an "atrocious conspiracy" aimed at massacring the worthy Jacobins and the Convention's deputies and sowing anarchy in the country, and to this end had plotted to arm the worst cutthroats from the prisons.[11] Rising after Billaud to elaborate, Robespierre suddenly felt ill, "his physical strength," states the Jacobins' record, "not allowing him to continue."[12] Collot concluded for him. Most Jacobins backed the regime and turned on the Cordeliers, though it remained doubtful whether this sufficed to silence Hébert's real stronghold, the outraged sections, and keep the sansculottes' heroes behind bars. That evening, the Cordeliers Club, convening leaderless and dazed, failed to react with any vigor.[13]

The prospect of a mass sansculotte uprising lingered for days. Copies of a recent defiant speech by Ronsin appeared posted up across the city while, at the Cordeliers, orators spoke openly of the need for an insurrection to liquidate "the traitors," "dominateurs," and "Cromwellistes." Opposition to Robespierre's dictatorship in the sections was undoubtedly widespread and overt. The feuding within the section assemblies turned ferocious. More of Hébert's allies were arrested, especially section commissaires and artisans from his own section, Bonne-Nouvelle, where the police reported more than three thousand loyal Hébertiste adherents. Rumors that Hébert had been corruptly profiteering in pork were deliberately spread to dampen sansculotte sympathy for the arrested men. By 20 March, sections Lombards, Contrat Social, Champs-Élysées, Guillaume Tell, Fraternité, and Chalier had all rallied to Robespierre. Finally, the demonstrations subsided, the summons to topple the "dominateurs," who were blind to the people's needs, petered out, though some sections—République and, as usual, Marat (Momoro's section)—remained sullen and restless.[14]

Incarcerated together in the Conciergerie, Hébert and eighteen co-defendants were charged with being "ultra-révolutionnaires," which, according to Saint-Just and Robespierre, was the same as being covert royalistes. Their plan was to dissolve the Convention and murder the "true Patriots." Briefly, their arrests seemed to relieve the pressure on Danton, Phillipeaux, and Desmoulins. The latter could now proclaim they had been right all along. Had they not been the first to warn the Jacobins of the peril of insidious "extremism" masquerading as patriotism?[15] But there was also worrying news for the Danton circle. On 18 March, Amar finally produced his "evidence" against Chabot, Bazire, and also Fabre, the last one of Danton's closest associates. Mired in financial corruption, with ties to the Alsatian Jewish Frey brothers, arrested earlier as suspected Austrian spies, Chabot had now languished behind bars, denying all charges against him, for four months. A leading Jacobin and advocate of the Terror, Chabot lacked close ties to any main clique apart from Bazire. Even if in Vienna they had had their assets confiscated as "Jacobins" and were being "burnt in effigy," his Frey brothers-in-law had profiteered and had, he admitted, given their sister, Leopoldine, to him in marriage (sweetened with a handsome dowry) only to gain a "reputation for patriotism."[16]

A new massive state show trial was prepared in which Saint-Just, Barère, and Amar were especially instrumental. Their elaborate spectacle ingeniously combined charges of insurrection with fiercely xenophobic denunciations of foreigners, corrupt paymasters, and spies, all linked by revelations of corruption at the war ministry. In this way, a group of key sansculotte leaders, the Hébertistes, long voicing sansculotte discontent and demanding justice for the poor, were tried for "treason" shoulder to shoulder with the wealthy Baron Cloots, against whom a whole batch of absurd charges were leveled; the Dutch Patriot financier Johannes Conradus de Kock (1756–94), a thirty-eight-year-old from Heusden, close to Dumouriez; Pereyra, the Jewish tobacco manufacturer and supplier of war materials; Pierre-Ulric Dubuisson, a Belgian radical democrat; and another Belgian, Pierre-Joseph Proly (1752–94). The tangle of conspiracy charges sounded plausible enough to some, as they had already been previously suggested by Fabre and had appeared in Desmoulins's *Le Vieux Cordelier*.

As an accomplished journal editor and exponent of representative democracy, connected with the war ministry and technically a "subordinate" of Vincent,[17] from the standpoint of Robespierre, Saint-Just, Barère, and Amar, Proly was the choicest of targets. A native of the Austrian Netherlands based in Paris, descended from an Antwerp financial dynasty of Italian origin who had aligned with the democratic Vonckists during the Brabant Revolution, and a sophisticated economic theorist, outside France he, like Cloots, ranked socially as a "baron." He had founded his Paris journal, *Le Cosmopolite*, in December 1791, using its pages to criticize the rival ideals of cosmopolitanism and universalism propagated by Cloots, reject the belligerent policies of the Brissotins, urge peace not war with Austria, and condemn the annexation of Belgium as a disastrous, reprehensible blunder. He had drawn some Frenchmen and many Belgian and Dutch revolutionists in France into his vehemently anti-Catholic, democratic circle, detested by Robespierre for its undisguised philosophisme, cosmopolitanism, and atheism. Proly's death sentence was a foregone conclusion, for he had criticized Robespierre. Specifically denounced by Robespierre, Proly's condemnation cemented the regime's "case" against the Hébertistes and the discrediting of the déchristianisateurs.[18]

De Kock, leader of the Dutch revolutionary committee in Paris, renowned for revolutionary gestures and financial contributions, including one for the Vendée campaign, was also a choice target. A long-standing intimate of Dumouriez, he was close to Hébert and the latter's wife, and in addition, according to *Le Vieux Cordelier*, was an agent of the British premier, Pitt. Hébert had stayed repeatedly at De Kock's residence at Passy where he and his wife drank "le vin de Pitt," allegedly toasting the ruin of the "fondateurs de la liberté."[19] Proly, Pereyra, and several others incarcerated with Hébert, ominously for Hérault de Séchelles, happened also to be intimate friends of his.[20] Cloots was accused with the others of scheming to slaughter the Jacobins, beginning with Robespierre, as part of his plan to establish "une république universelle." But really only Hébert, Vincent, and Ronsin, among those on trial, interested opinion in the streets.

This show trial lasted four days (21–24 March 1794) during which the court interrogated more than two hundred witnesses. Excited discussion of the event pervaded nearby cafés and corners throughout that time, with dissidents openly voicing their hopes that another "trial of Marat" would occur, ending in triumphant acquittal and popular acclaim. But though disgruntled, and unwilling to credit the treason charges against Hébert (who did believe them?), the sansculottes were too cowed to demonstrate even remotely as much as the fervor displayed in support of Marat.[21] Ten days after their arrest, the Hébertiste leaders, sentenced to death and confiscation of their property, were brought together by charette to the Place de la Révolution and guillotined. Three months and five days before Thermidor, Hébert, Vincent, Ronsin, De Kock, Proly, and Cloots, Hébert last, came under the blade. The large crowd of sansculotte onlookers was sullen, according to the subsequent police report, but caused no disturbance.[22] All France was made aware of the dire "conspiracy" from which the Jacobins had saved the country, the Convention's public proclamation "explaining" the affair, signed by Barère, being printed and circulated in 100,000 copies.

Eliminating the Dantonistes

Elimination of the Hébertistes left the way clear to finish with the weaker recalcitrant faction—Danton, Desmoulins, Philippeaux, Hérault, and Fabre. The Dantonistes, imagining they had triumphed, reminded the *Vieux Cordelier*'s readership that they had led the way in organizing insurrection and building the Revolution. Loyal throughout to liberty and the Rights of Man, Danton's bloc, had unremittingly combated "les Royalistes, les Feuillants, les Brissotins, [and] les Fédéralistes," and now helped crush the Hébertistes.[23] Foreign monarchs, perusing Hébert's *Père Duchesne*, Desmoulins had pointed out, could claim Paris had become the world capital of barbarism and crassness. Proper Jacobins knew the sansculottes were not really so blind, unaware, and ignorant as Hébert wanted foreign observers to infer.[24] Besides, Desmoulins had ferreted out treason unerringly long before it was officially "confirmed." Time and again, his journalism had foreshadowed what then became official proceedings against "Bailly, Lafayette, Malouet, Mirabeau, les Lameth, Pétion, d'Orléans, Sillery, Brissot, and Dumouriez."[25]

Furthermore, the Dantonistes had a stirring message: only with democracy and free expression can "the good citizen" expect to see baseness, intrigue, and crime cease, "et pour cela le peuple n'a besoin que d'être éclairé [and for that the people need only to become enlightened]." Without Enlightenment, there could be no democracy; and without democracy no cleansing of crime and insecurity. Danton, who helped shape Desmoulins's last sallies in the *Vieux Cordelier*, was a true republican and democrat. Nothing could be less compatible with Robespierre's and Saint-Just's ideology. To affirm people are brought to embrace democracy and become free and happy through enlightenment and philosophy, as Desmoulins regularly did, was to contradict Robespierrisme in its essence. It was this tendency in Danton and Desmoulins that Saint-Just complained of most in his denunciation of them—conciliatoriness toward the Brissotins, stress on revolutionary unity, their opposition to 31 May journée. Desmoulins proclaimed the Rights of Man the cornerstone of republican liberty and the masterpiece of la philosophie. He and Danton had tirelessly reaffirmed the core values of republican freedom, rejecting Robespierriste views that equated equality and liberty with Spartan austerity, and refused individuals a reasonable degree of economic freedom. (Remarkably, Desmoulins included Brissot among revolutionary theorists advocating an excessively leveling, Spartan conception of economic equality.)[26] Compared to Robespierre, the Dantonists *were* honest and enlightened.[27]

Danton once famously said that for making revolution, what is needed is "l'audace, de l'audace, et encore de l'audace."[28] Yet, this key Jacobin faction never really challenged Robespierre and his perversion of the Revolution's ideals head-on at the Jacobins and in the Convention. Rather, little by little they crumbled. On Robespierre's orders,

Hérault, chief codifier of the Jacobin Constitution of 1793, and friend of Proly and Danton, was incarcerated in the Luxembourg for betraying state secrets "to foreign powers" shortly after Hébert's downfall on 15 March. Chaumette, in Robespierre's eyes an atheist fanatic and tool of Cloots, was arrested on 17 March. Robespierre still hesitated to break finally with Danton, as Collot d'Herbois, Billaud-Varenne, and other Montagnard stalwarts were urging. He had at least two final meetings with Danton before making up his mind and throwing his weight behind the calls for his arrest and indictment.[29] But, finally, two and a half weeks after the downfall of the Hébertistes, having disastrously failed to gather support or slow the Terror, Danton, Desmoulins, Philippeaux, and another leading deputy and friend of Danton, Jean-François Delacroix (1753–94), accused of conspiring with Dumouriez and enriching himself in Belgium, were arrested on Robespierre's orders on 31 March. For whatever reason, the fervent Belgian republican François Robert, earlier Danton's secretary and a loyal Dantoniste, was spared.[30]

Their arrests occurred three days after Condorcet was finally caught in disguise, under a false name, still hoping the Revolution could be saved, at a restaurant eating an omelet in a southern Paris suburb. His arrest was certain to entail his prompt execution as an "outlaw." Condorcet forestalled this outcome by poisoning himself on 29 March in his cell. Although his remains were buried in an unknown place, many realized at the time that his demise signally contributed to what Mme. de Staël called the "decimation of the glory of France."[31] Assessments of the great philosophe's contribution to the Revolution varied widely but none was more negative than Robespierre's, delivered in a speech a few weeks later. Robespierre both hated and scorned him. Rural laborers, spreading the "true light of philosophy" in the countryside possessed more sense than the supposedly "great mathematician" Condorcet, a figure "despised by all factions," who worked indefatigably to obscure the light of philosophy with the trash of "ses rapsodies mercenaires."[32]

Two days later, 31 March, Claire Lacombe, rescued from imprisonment in October 1793 by the Hébertistes, was rearrested. That same day, Robespierre came in person to the Jacobins to "explain" the latest "conspiracy" overshadowing the Revolution: devious factions plotting against the people had formed two separate but connected conspiracies. Where the Hébertistes sought to overthrow everything, the second bloc cunningly schemed to inculcate "principles of aristocracy and modérantisme." Since the crushing of the Hébertistes, the modérés had stepped up their efforts and were now insidiously attempting to smear "pure Patriots" (i.e., Robespierre and Saint-Just) as "Hébertistes." Typical of their malevolence was their striving to discredit the "glorious" and upright Chalier (who had been guillotined by the Brissotins in Lyon three days after Marat's assassination in Paris). "Pure Patriots" always venerated Chalier, just as they did Marat.[33] About Danton himself Robespierre said little; but he denounced him too, soon after, as a "conspirator." Danton, he disclosed, had tried to sabotage the 31 May rising by opposing the worthy Hanriot, and had even rebuked the latter and his armed force for "saving" the Convention from its foes.[34]

Saint-Just indicted Hérault before the Convention on 1 April, demanding his execution. Hérault was an accomplice of Dumouriez, Mirabeau, Brissot, and Hébert, who had behaved duplicitously during the 31 May and 2 June insurrections. He also denied divine Providence and had sought to forge "atheism into a cult more intolerant than superstition," publicly denying immortality of the soul, "which consoled Socrates when he was dying."[35] Such views could not be tolerated. During the last months of his life, Saint-Just became almost as morbidly dogmatic about belief in the Supreme Being, immortality of the soul, and evils of atheism as Robespierre himself.[36] On 2 April, in the Convention, Saint-Just assailed Danton, using notes supplied by Robespierre, accusing him of subservience to Mirabeau early in the Revolution and covert royalism and Brissotin sympathies later.[37] Besides maintaining treasonable links with Dumouriez and trying to get the "worthy" Hanriot arrested, Danton had eyed the "revolution of 31 May" with distaste and been guilty of serious misconduct in Belgium.[38]

During the four-day trial of the Dantonistes, the regime introduced a new element to their judicial procedure: four members of the Comité de Sûrété Générale sat in the trial room supervising the proceedings, among them one of the committee's most ruthless figures, an implacable foe of the Brissotins, Marc-Guillaume Vadier (1736–1828), son of a church tax collector and former army officer. One of those behind the story about a plot to recruit assassins in the prisons, brutal and thoroughly dishonest, Vadier detested Danton, whose downfall he called "gutting the fat stuffed turbot." Reusing the technique deployed so adroitly against the Hébertistes, Danton's circle was arraigned alongside foreigners and wealthy speculators—the semi-Spaniard Guzmán, the Abbé Espagnac, and the brothers Siegmund (Junius) and Emanuel Frey, the Moravian Jewish army suppliers based earlier in Strasbourg (and linked to Fabre as well as Chabot), now formally charged with corruption.[39] Marc René, Abbé Espagnac (1752–94), a professed disciple of Voltaire accustomed long before 1789 to make outrageously irreligious remarks in public, was a wealthy, somewhat disreputable ex-churchman, already notorious at Versailles in the early 1780s. Failing to win a seat in the 1789 Estates-General, he made his mark during 1790–91 as an antiecclesiastical agitator, vociferously proposing seizure of church property in the Jacobins. Like Fabre, a prominent speculator in French East India Company shares, he suited the prosecution perfectly, having corrupt ties with several of the accused, besides links, through providing horses and other supplies to the army, with Dumouriez.

The atmosphere at the public hearings was electric. Hérault uttered ironic witticisms. Asked his name and age, Desmoulins replied that he was thirty-three (actually thirty-four) like the "sans-culotte Jesus." A furious Danton delivered a powerful speech, ridiculing the notion they were "conspirators," insulting Robespierre and reaffirming his atheism, exerting such an impact within and outside the trial chamber that the committee became worried about the effect in the streets. Renewed murmuring against Robespierre's "dictature" were heard. To forestall possible trouble, the proceedings were aborted in a scandalously arbitrary manner. Unreasoning arbitrariness, as Roederer stressed, was indeed the very quintessence of the Robespierre regime. Unsettled by signs of public sympathy for Danton, the Tribunal rushed its guilty verdict through, ordering immediate execution that very day, 5 April (24 Germinal).[40] Desmoulins, Fabre, and Hérault were conveyed to the Place de la Révolution in the same charette as Danton. Danton towered over the crowds impassively. Desmoulins was forcibly dragged to the guillotine in a tragic, highly emotional scene. Bazire was guillotined with them, but Chabot had evaded the blade by committing suicide earlier, like Condorcet and the latter's younger republican acolyte, Achille du Chastellet, using poison.[41] Last but one under the guillotine, Hérault displayed his usual aristocratic poise. That evening, the Opéra performed a rousing sans-culottide entitled La réunion de 10 aout ou l'Inauguration de la République française.

A week later, on 13 April 1794, Chaumette, denounced for links with the Hébertistes, was guillotined together with Bishop Gobel, Hébert's widow, and Desmoulins's famously beautiful, brokenhearted wife. The two major political purges of March and April 1794, elimination of the Hébertistes silencing the Paris sections, and liquidation of Danton, Desmoulins, Hérault, and Philippeaux, extinguished the last vestiges of Jacobin adherence to both principle and the sansculottes. The purges were followed by a marked further concentration of power in the hands of the Committee of Public Safety and Robespierre himself. Suppression of *Le Vieux Cordelier* put the seal on a scene of near total press and theater repression. "Tyranny cannot allow the justice of the courts to compete with arbitrariness," commented Roederer later, "and neither can it allow public opinion any sway. If it did not completely crush freedom of the press and speech, this freedom would overthrow it."[42] The number of pamphlets published in France in 1792 had stood at 1,286. In 1793, that number had dropped to 663; in 1794, it fell to 601, under half the 1792 figure and under one-fifth of the level for 1789–90.[43] Prudhomme had ceased publishing the *Révolutions de Paris* in February 1794 under plea of illness; he and his family left Paris.[44] The last main royalist paper, *Quotidienne*, started in late 1792 with Alphonse Coutely as editor, was suppressed in October 1793 but was later resumed as the *Trois Décades*. After reprinting extracts from Demoulins's *Vieux Cordelier*, it finally ceased in March 1794.[45]

At every level, arbitrariness and intolerance infused the Robespierriste dictatorship—dishonest, hypocritical, and Cromwelliste to the core. But even ruthless tyranny requires a seemingly coherent ideological and legal mask, providing ostensible justification for its acts. Experience showed, Desmoulins had remarked, the uneducated mass will believe anything, but even this "anything" cannot be too inconsistent with itelf. The regime directing the Terror had to reaffirm its ideology of virtue, the ordinary, and Rousseausime with greater insistence than ever. It was on 15 April 1794 that Saint-Just delivered the last major speech of his career, and perhaps the most astounding—a complete review of the "conspiracies" aiming to "destroy" the Revolution from the outset down to the crushing of the Brissotins, considered by him the Revolution's climax. He discerned a recurring plot to utilize famine and high food prices to spread distress sufficiently to prevent liberty from consolidating itself. What the successive purges revealed was "the moral corruption" of the false révolutionnaires undermining virtue. The lesson for everyone was that the true révolutionnaire evinces the unbending severity of a Cato, is always inflexible and austere, "like Marat" detests all affectation, and never censures the Revolution but is merciless to its enemies. Gentle in his household, the true Jacobin, like the sublime J. J. Rousseau, is unforgiving toward all "traitors." Like Rousseau, every true revolutionary venerates the ordinary and reflects the common view, adopting the common opinion unreservedly. The Revolution must be ruthless with "suspect persons," especially anyone lamenting the liquidation of Hébert and Danton.[46] The principal remaining danger, contended Saint-Just, was that aristocracy was continually attempting to divide France by implying the revolutionary government was a "tyrannical dictatorship." A new, sweepingly repressive law was needed to counter such subversion and finally bridle "the aristocracy."

A resumed offensive against "the aristocracy" was indeed a central theme of the spring and summer of 1794. From late April, the proportion of nobles among those arrested and executed under the now rapidly escalating Terror rose steeply. "Former nobles" were, like foreigners, henceforth expressly excluded from the sociétés populaires and comités de surveillance, as well as section assemblies and town councils. No former noble or foreigner from any country with which the Republic was at war could reside in Paris or any fortress town. Any noble lacking a special pass issued by the authorities, found in fortress towns after ten days, would be declared an "outlaw." Municipalites had to send the Committees of Public Security and Sûreté Générale lists of all former nobles and foreigners, resident or staying within their jurisdictions. Couthon clarified on 29 April that under the rubric "nobles," the executive included anyone who, though not a noble under ancien régime criteria, had obtained or fabricated false titles prior to 1792 to affect noble status.[47]

Also on 15 April 1794, and not coincidentally, a deputation appeared before the Convention from the republican society of the township of Saint-Denis (now renamed Franciade). Saint-Denis, site of the famous abbey where France's kings and queens were buried, was an ancient focus of devotion that had been looted and ransacked in October 1793. The remains of monarchs had been removed and thrown into a common pit in a cemetery north of the church. This deputation, accompanied by Rousseau's widow, pleaded for the remains of the author of *Émile* and the *Social Contract* at last to be transferred to the Panthéon. Who had a greater right to be buried there than this great apostle of equality and liberty? Replying, the Assembly president stressed how much Rousseau's name meant to the Convention and how resonant his renown and glory were in the hall of their deliberations. Transfer to the Panthéon, it was agreed, should finally now take place.[48] During the closing weeks of the Terror, the revolutionary cult of Rousseau reached its climax. Renewing the long-shelved decree to commission a statue of Rousseau for Paris, the Comité de Salut Public announced in April a new competition for a major public monument cast in bronze, to be erected on the Champs-Élysées. Designs were invited for 30 May from all wishing to compete.[49] Models entered would be displayed for five days in the Convention hall and then brought to the Louvre's Salle de Laocoön where the jury des arts would pronounce judgment the following *décade*.[50] An enterprising publisher, Defer de Maisonneuve, published several hundred sets of an octavo album of ten of the best engravings selected from illustrated editions of Rousseau's political works published in recent years, including much-prized designs by Charles-Nicolas Cochin, François-André Vincent (an older contemporary and long-standing rival of David), Jean-Baptiste Regnault, and David's follower, Nicolas-André Monsiau.[51]

The cult of Rousseau was surpassed only by the cult of the "common man" and the exaltation of "Nature." On 28 April, the Convention was reminded by Joseph Lakanal (1762–1845), deputy for the Ariège, speaking for the Committee of Public Instruction, of its earlier decision to provide financial aid to citizens mutilated or wounded during 10 August 1792. Ancient Rome, declared Lakanal, inscribed signal services rendered to the patrie in marble, where the citizen reads better than in books his duties and the virtues on which republics rest. A column of marble would be erected in the Panthéon, the Convention duly decreed, on which would be carved in gold letters the names of those who perished "for equality" on 10 August. As with the other major art commissions, the Comité de Salut Public invited the Republic's artists to compete for the commission, allowing three weeks (two *décades*) for submission of their designs, with an extra *décade* for those residing outside Paris. Models would be publicly displayed in the Convention's debating hall for five days before being laid before the jury des arts for their decision.[52]

An interesting further manifestation of the deistic cult of nature in the Terror's last phase was the project, again promoted by Lakanal, to establish a National Museum of Natural History, installed in the former Royal (renamed National) Botanical Gardens, today the Jardin des Plantes. Lakanal, fomerly a professor of philosophy, was the indefatigable enlightened educationalist who masterminded most of the major cultural projects of importance during the Robespierre dictatorship and was the foremost survivor in the Convention of the philosophique tendency of the pre-June 1793 Revolution. Although for the moment his revised version of Condorcet's educational plans were blocked by Robespierre, he had several notable successes. At his suggestion, the Convention agreed to establish a national collection of physical, fossil, mineral, anatomical, and botanical specimens and rarities, bringing together cabinets previously dispersed around the country. It was declared

Figure 17. "The Triumph of the Montagne." Image courtesy Bibliothèque nationale de France.

worthy of a great nation to organize its education system around Nature, creating a new kind of "temple" where everyone could come, to "consult nature" and be inspired by its riches.

Completing Robespierre's Dictatorship

Only with the elimination of the Hébertistes and Dantonistes was the full maturing of Robespierre's power and of his and Saint-Just's ideology possible. The Jacobins were now drastically further purged and narrowed, the Cordeliers reduced to a state of intimidated impotence, the Paris Commune subservient, and the Convention more of a cipher than ever. Loudly denouncing ultra-révolutionnaire deviationism (Hébertistes) and modérantisme (Dantonistes), the dictatorship now launched its culminating assault on freedom of thought, philosophisme, and atheism. Virtue was now elevated to the level of a state cult, into a civil religion of Robespierre's own devising. Shrewdly conceived, the new cult did appeal to some with its relentless attacks on materialism and philosophisme, insistence on belief in God, and immortality of the soul. Bizarre and wholly alien to the Revolution's core values, Robespierre's and Saint-Just's obsession with nature and "the ordinary" became an all-crushing colossus. On 18 Floréal (7 May), following one of Robespierre's longest and most important speeches to the legislature, explaining the new ideology and its relationship to previous thought and ideas, the Convention endorsed his new creed, ordering the main churches in all towns and villages of France to be rededicated to the Cult of the Supreme Being. The principal public festivals of the French Revolution were declared to be those of 14 July 1789, 10 August 1792, 21 January 1793 (the execution of Louis XVI), and 31 May 1793; these would in future be celebrated as part of the proclaimed state cult, continually reminding citizens of the dignity of the Supreme Being.[53]

Robespierre's most extended speech on basic principles, explaining his ideology on behalf of the Comité de Salut Public, delivered to the Convention on 7 May (18 Floréal), was couched in astonishingly turgid, paranoid, and personal terms, and widely reprinted in the papers. Continually echoing Rousseau, including the lines about man being born free but everywhere in chains, Robespierre, as so often, especially emphasized the need to promote and cultivate virtue. Man's "rights" are "written on his heart" and "his humiliation" in history. Sparta, nurturing the warlike, disciplined virtue, beloved by disciples of Rousseau (and Mably), shone "like a star" amid the surrounding darkness, but alas, all too briefly. Despite progress in the arts and sciences, mankind had long remained sunk in darkness, especially regarding "la morale publique." Thus far, men had practically always been corrupt. Only in the land now liberty's special domain, among "this people proud and truly born for glory and virtue," had men rediscovered their rights and duties. Astoundingly, Robespierre accused all the revolutionary legislatures of 1789–92 of betraying and trying to efface from men's hearts "the eternal principles" they had outwardly professed. In its successive stages, the entire Revolution down to June 1793 was, in Robespierre's eyes, a "conspiracy" disguised under the banner of perfidious modérantisme. Blighting virtue, it had led the French via an oblique path to renewed tyranny.[54] During 1791–92, the Jacobins had thwarted the initial "betrayal" and successfully forged the true revolutionary ideal. But new methods of corrupting men's hearts, new forms of modérantisme and perfidy, had arisen, enabling most ostensible revolutionary leaders to ply fresh "subversion," stifling the Republic at birth, producing a show of democracy "pour le déshonorer" (to dishonor it). Monarchism and Brissotin "democrats" clashed superficially, but were really close allies. With public opinion polluted, national representation debased, and the common people marginalized, the Brissotin hypocrites emerged as the vilest of all the conspirateurs, invoking "sovereignty of the people" to save royalty and foment civil war.

Brissotins preached "equality" allegedly to render this principle hateful while actually arming "the rich" against the poor. "Liberty" to them was just license for crime, "the people" an instrument, the patrie prey. Brissotins denounced tyranny to serve "tyrants." These destroyers of democracy had erected immorality "non seulement en système, mais en religion."[55] They appealed to popular sovereignty to abase the Convention, professing hatred of "superstition" only to foment strife and spread the "poison of atheism." What was the true goal of these "fanatical missionaries of atheism" who in the midst of the political conspiracies engulfing France attacked every religious cult? Was it hatred of priests? Priests were their friends. Loathing of fanaticism? Fanaticism was what they cultivated. Zeal to accelerate Reason's triumph? They aspired to relegate Reason to the temples, to banish it from the Republic. The conspirators aimed to deceive the French and destroy their liberty; the Convention's task was to reunite the people and establish liberty sustained by virtue. What advantage do the corrupters of virtue see in persuading men that a blind force presides over their destiny and that there is no supernatural being punishing crime and rewarding virtue? Will philosophique ideas inspire greater devotion to the patrie, boldness in defying tyranny, contempt for death and pleasure? Wretched sophistes! By what right do the philosophes seek to wrest the scepter of reason from innocence, to transfer it to crime, throwing a dark veil over Nature, reducing the wretched to despair, exalting vice, repressing virtue, degrading humanity?[56] Robespierre did not question the virtue of particular philosophes—the personal qualities of Diderot, d'Holbach, and Helvétius. What he execrated was atheism and la philosophie as a political and moral culture, labeling these "immorality" linked to conspiracy against the Republic. Why should legislators concern themselves that certain philosophes (i.e., Diderot, d'Holbach, and Helvétius) embraced certain hypotheses to explain nature (i.e., materialism)? Free men, being neither metaphysicians nor theologians, should leave the philosophes to their eternal disputes: in the legislator's eyes everything useful to society and good "dans la pratique est la vérité." The idea of a Supreme Being ordaining the soul's immortality is "sociale et républicaine." Great legislators like Lycurgus and Solon always invoked oracles and mixed appropriate "fictions" with "truth" to impress ordinary people and better connect them to public institutions. True legislators seek not to enlighten but, as Rousseau maintained, by laws and institutions to call men back to "nature and truth." The déchristianisateurs had nothing with which to replace the popular piety they pilloried. Instead of genuinely enlightening the people, déchristianisateurs strove to deprave.

The Revolution, by permitting philosophy to attack an ancient cult long established among the people, risked great harm to morality. Corruption and crime had always fed on atheism. Robespierre here strikingly elevated the ancient Stoics above the Epicureans, claiming Cato never hesitated between Epicurus and Zeno (the Stoic), because Epicurus's philosophy, as construed by the corrupt, had deplorable consequences that all antiquity denounced. As "the human heart is the same at all times," the political effects Cato discerned applied also now. The "Epicurean sect" was pernicious. The women of France should take the women of Sparta as their model and become chaste, austere, disciplined, dedicated in rearing young heroes to serve the patrie, self-sacrificing, relentless, and unbending.

Robespierre's culminating assault on philosophisme, Brissotin republicanism, and the Revolution's core values, was combined with his decrying churchmen as false friends of morality and truth who allied with despotism, slavery, and lies. How different is "la religion universelle de la nature" from ecclesiastical, confessional faith, how remote the God of nature from "the God of our priesthood." He accused priests of being to virtue what common charlatans are to medicine. They had fashioned God after their own image, projecting a capricious, jealous, vengeful, cruel divinity. Nature was the true priest of the Supreme Being and the universe his temple, his cult being virtue itself.[57]

Robespierre conceded that before the Revolution, the philosophes had gained a hold on opinion, and before 1789 "les observateurs éclairés" foresaw and foretold the Revolution itself. Famous intellectuals (*les hommes de lettres renommés*) acquired a powerful influence on thought and affairs. Ambitious writers and literary men formed a coalition that extended their ascendancy. The philosophes had divided into two "sects," one obdurately defending despotism, the other, it turned out, stronger and more insidious, the encyclopédistes, including some "hommes estimables" but chiefly comprising scheming charlatans. Whoever is unaware of this group's influence on developments, granted Robespierrre, has no adequate idea of what created "our Revolution." Whoever is ignorant of the influence of Turgot, d'Alembert, and other leading intellectual figures well connected and influential in the 1770s and 1780s, "des personnages considérables" in the state, lacks understanding of the prelude to "our Revolution." But this vicious philosophique sect entirely undermined the rights of the people, uttering tirades against despotism while (like d'Alembert and Diderot) accepting pensions from despots, producing books attacking the court while providing discourses for courtiers. Defiant in their writings, they were rampant "dans les antichambres," erotically, financially, and politically, and hence tied to the aristocracy. They forged the doctrine of materialism prevailing among aristocrats and *beaux esprits*.[58]

Prior to the Revolution, only one thinker (Rousseau) evinced true grandeur of soul and true purity of doctrine, presenting virtue and the Divinity as drawn from nature in opposition to la philosophie. Humanity's true teacher, Rousseau assailed tyranny in every way, spoke of the Divinity with enthusiasm, and defended immortality of the soul and reward and punishment in the hereafter. Rousseau's "invincible" contempt for "les sophistes intrigants," usurping the name of philosophes, provoked the lasting hatred of his despicable rivals (Diderot, d'Holbach, and Helvétius). Had Rousseau witnessed this Revolution of which he was the chief precursor, his generous soul would ecstatically embrace the cause of justice and equality. But what had Rousseau's philosophique adversaries done for the Revolution? They fought the Revolution from the moment they feared it would raise up the people. Some questioned republican principles, prostituting themselves to the political factions, especially the Orléanist clique; others withdrew into cowardly neutrality (Raynal, Naigeon). Overall, the intellectual elite "dishonoured themselves in the Revolution" and left the "reason of the people" to carry the burden to the eternal disgrace of the philosophique sect. These rascals should blush with shame, the achievements of the Revolution being accomplished without and in spite of them. Good sense, without education or intrigue, brought France to perfection, arousing their disdain and revealing their nullity.[59]

Philosophes were the people's enemies. How vastly preferable was the common artisan with robust understanding of the Rights of Man to philosophes. There was an urgent need to purge all doctrines, as well as persons detrimental to the quick, sure instinct of the ordinary person. Certainly, the philosophes were republicans before others and predominantly republicans before the Revolution in 1788 (Robespierre correctly reminded his audience, alluding to Condorcet, Brissot, Mirabeau, and the radical philosophes). But afterward, in 1793, they had "stupidly defended" the royal cause (resisting execution of Louis without an appel au public). A culminating restatement of Robespierre's ideological standpoint, this was a landmark speech (following a long, mysterious, nearly three-week absence from the Convention and public view since 19 April, again resulting from nervous strain). The philosophes cultivated "loathsome" views he was resolved to combat. Guadet rebuked a citizen at a société populaire meeting for invoking divine Providence. Vergniaud and Gensonné delivered speeches in the Convention, urging deletion of all reference to God in the preface to the new Constitution![60] Whoever seeks to extinguish the people's sublime enthusiasm for virtue with desolate philosophical doctrines opposes the Revolution and must be crushed.[61]

Above all, this speech was a defense of the great purges of March and April, attributing the *perfide modérantisme* sullying the Revolution's opening years to the corruption of the political sphere and destruction of virtue, which he saw as the prime obstacle to implementing republican principles. The common thread infusing all the cunning factions controlling the Revolution prior to himself was their criminal hypocrisy. Lafayette invoked Constitution and popular sovereignty to reaffirm royal power, Dumouriez to incite Brissotins against the Convention, Brissotins to save monarchy and "arm the rich against the people," and Hébertistes to liquidate the Convention. Danton promised many a rogue his protection. All the betrayers of the Revolution invoked la philosophie to elevate immorality into a system and attacked religion, which they termed "superstition," to propagate atheism and civil war.[62] In short, Robespierre comprehensively abjured every component of the Revolution apart from Rousseau and himself.

The new Cult of the Supreme Being pleased villagers because it returned to churchgoing something of its former collective character and centrality in their lives, and also better linked the Revolution's personality cults with the churches. During the Robespierriste regime's final weeks, multiple addresses poured in from across France to the Convention, acclaiming the new state cult. Public expressions of thanks, rejoicing that the "schemes of atheism are undone," arrived on 23 May from Chantilly, Senlis, and Melun.[63] On 9 July was read out the address of Port-Louis, a picturesque walled port in Southern Brittany, in the department of Morbihan, long besieged by royalists, renamed Port-Liberté in 1792 by order of the Convention: the town rejoiced that the Supreme Being and immortality of the soul were now officially proclaimed. Saint-Marcellin (renamed Thermopyles) in Isère and Le Donjon in Allier (renamed Val-Libre), likewise celebrated. Pauillac, in the department of Bec-d'Ambès, warmly welcomed the 18 Floréal decree, remarking that its people were simple country souls previously filled with consternation by the "idées extravagantes" of the Hébertistes and "scandalous madness of materialism"; they now joyfully rededicated their church to the Supreme Being.[64] The société populaire of Lausargues, department of Hérault, rejoiced in the elimination of the "Cloots, Héberts, and Dantons," along with their plans to replace the community's traditional virtues with "degrading atheism."[65]

From the dictatorship's viewpoint, a decided benefit of the new state cult was that for many people it provided persuasive grounds for destroying the Brissotins, Hébertistes, and Dantonistes while restoring simple veneration of the sacred. With atheism, the Libourne district administrators agreed, the Revolution's foes had sought to wreck the Republic's unity and overthrow all principles of public morality.[66] The Revolution's enemies tried to "banish the moral and religious ideas dictated by nature," affirmed the société populaire of Langogne (department of La Lozère), but thankfully were annihilated: "the existence of a Supreme Being and immortality of the soul which you proclaim has reassured virtuous souls."[67] Noireau, in Calvados, installed the "precious images of the martyrs of liberty," Marat, Brutus, and Lepeletier, in their

Temple of the Supreme Being, inaugurating their busts with a "touching ceremony."[68] No community regretted the demise of atheism or materialism, but one or two, like Saint-Maximin (renamed Marathon), in Var department, dared request the shelved 1793 "democratic Constitution," a "work worthy of immortality."[69]

The new cult adroitly merged politics and religion. Celebrating the 31 May insurrection on 31 May 1794, Blaye, in the department of Bec d'Ambès, began by ringing the town's bells, summoning everyone, including a nearby military garrison, to attend. The citizenry converged on the Temple of the Supreme Being, streaming through village streets now shorn of saints' names and renamed Rue des Sans-Culottes and Rue de la Montagne. The celebration combined prayers and hymns to the Supreme Being with denunciations of fédéralisme and atheism. "Our enemies," affirmed the société populaire of Jouvence, "preached atheism and plunged us into the horrors of anarchy." The Revolution's foes, concurred the société populaire of Entrevaux, department of Basses-Alpes, denied God's existence and claimed the soul was a piece of matter that perishes like other matter. *Petits philosophes* extolled atheism while lacking the sense to see this created a trap fatal to the Revolution. Until 2 June 1793, the Revolution was no "model of liberty" but a chimera like Plato's Republic, admired only by savants, philosophes, and sophistes. The Revolution's greatness since June 1793 lay in rejection of the philosophes by the "friends of virtue and sound morality."[70]

The culminating public celebration of Robespierrisme as an ideology and set of values was the first Festival of the Supreme Being, on 20 Prairial (8 June 1794). The festivities were designed and supervised by David, with musical arrangements composed by "the father of the French symphony," François-Joseph Gossec (1734–1829), who often led instrumental bands at the Revolution's principal public ceremonies.[71] Gossec also composed the final culminating hymn, consecrated by the Comité de Salut Public, and simple enough for everyone to participate in. The celebrations, arranged on a massive scale, were attended by probably most of Paris's population and many from outside. Smaller celebrations took place in every other town, all twenty-six million Frenchmen from one end of the land to the other being simultaneously summoned to adore the Supreme Being. In the speeches, the stress was overwhelmingly on virtue, discipline, sobriety, and uncompromising repudiation of atheism, Epicureanism, and materialism. Before men could duly honor the virtues, they must acknowledge him who had sown the seed of moral sense in their hearts.

The windows and doors of Paris were decorated with flowers and branches on the morning of 20 Prairial. Drums summoned vast crowds from the sections, the women and girls mostly dressed in white, crowns of vine leaves on their heads, roses in their hands. Every section was independently represented by delegations in the Jardin National (the Tuileries), the entire surface of which was covered by the multitude. All eyes turned on Robespierre, who stood alone, apart from the other leading figures of the regime, in a heightened state of nervous anxiety, partly because this event possessed a special emotional significance for him, but also due to two recent actual (or perhaps staged?) attempts to assassinate him. Obsessed with his role as the supreme "martyr to virtue," Robespierre had long brooded on the topic of assassination. "Everyone admired the purity of the crowd's emotion," according to the paper *Décade philosophique*, though practically every important personage there, apart from his immediate entourage, according to the Dantonist Baudot, who was standing behind Robespierre on the podium, whispered complaints behind his back both about the ridiculous ceremony and the insufferable "dictatorship" of the "monster" Robespierre.[72] Seeing the people, noted the *Décade*, one grasped more accurately that the pernicious "system of atheism" had made few proselytes. While deviant, ill-advised authorities were trying to impose atheism by force, Paris's persecuted deists had been driven to seek refuge in silence. Now the Cult of the Supreme Being reigned, "all hearts seemed to recover hope." The people were one vast family to which their Father was restored. After trumpet fanfares, the entire Convention appeared on a special platform.

Robespierre first delivered a short discourse, assuring the crowd that God had purposely created the perfidy of kings and priests, just as he required the honest to hate malefactors and respect justice. It was God who created female modesty, maternal feeling, and filial piety. Everything natural is God's work; everything evil the fault of depravity, the unnaturalness of those who oppress. After this, accompanied by hymns to the Supreme Being, Robespierre carried a torch symbolizing the light of deism up steps to the "hideous visage of atheism," which was then consumed by the flames, revealing behind it a statue of "true philosophical wisdom."[73] Robespierre then delivered a second discourse, assuring the crowds the atheistic creed they sought to destroy was a "monster" the cunning of kings "had vomited on France." With atheism's final extirpation, all the crimes and maladies of the world would disappear. Materialism, armed with the twin daggers of religious fanaticism and philosophical atheism, the weapons with which kings "conspired to assassinate humanity," was toppled. Everyone was summoned to attune their lives to the pursuit of virtue in the sight of God and knowledge of their soul's immortality. After Robespierre's second discourse, more hymns to the Supreme Being were sung, exhorting the people to virtue, denouncing those "vils professeurs de l'athéisme" who under the false guise of civisme and la philosophie ventured to efface veneration of God from the human heart.[74] Robespierre harvested from what was supposedly his greatest triumph, recorded Baudot later, only the hatred of some and the contempt of others.[75]

In the Terror's final weeks, repression both escalated dramatically in scale and became increasingly diffuse as the daily toll of executions in Paris rose to more than twice that of the spring. The prisons burst to the seams despite the accelerating execution rate. The prisoner total in Paris increased from 6,984 on 23 May to 7,528 by 10 July and 7,765 by 18 July.[76] As against 1,251 persons executed in the capital between 1 March and 10 June, around a dozen a day, during the Terror's last forty-seven days, from 10 June to 27 July, 1,376 were guillotined around thirty per day. In June 1794, 659 death sentences were passed in Paris, a record so far, though even more were passed, more than 900, in July.[77] In a paroxysm of paranoia, surrounded by Brissotin conspiracy, extremism, modérantisme, corruption, aristocracy, atheistic philosophie, and assassination plots, Robespierre and the Comité de Sûreté Public introduced in the Convention the notorious law of 10 June (22 Prairial) "reforming" the Revolutionary Tribunal. Streamlining its procedures, insisted Couthon, was essential, as the "enemies of the people" were not being dealt with fast enough. The Revolutionary Tribunal should now consist of six benches of judges and juries functioning simultaneously. (Only one additional tribunal actually became operative.) Anyone charged with spreading false news, slandering patriotism, or echoing Brissotin, Hébertiste, or Dantoniste notions, could, with royalist conspirators, be sent directly before the Revolutionary Tribunal by the executive committees without preliminary hearings or even notifying the Convention.[78]

Material evidence of guilt was no longer needed: "moral proofs" sufficed. Denied legal counsel, defendants could be arraigned, tried, sentenced, and executed literally within hours. The law of 22 Prairial helped generate the Terror's final dramatic spurt. This targeted no particular social class in the way historians, Marxist and non-Marxist, once believed, though ex-nobles became highly vulnerable. Many diverse groups were now targeted—army officers, wives of earlier victims,

ex-nobles, constitutional as well as refractory priests, former officeholders, alleged speculators, and former legal officers of the parlements.
Targeted especially were individuals connected with those previously
declared "enemies of the people," an ideological catchall applied to just
about anyone of prominence or standing. Logic, other than the twisted
logic of the populist dictatorship, had little to do with it. On 22 April
1794, Le Chapelier, a pillar of Feuillant modérantisme, discovered in
Rennes, was guillotined in Paris. The great chemist Levoisier was guillotined on 8 May. On 7 July, twenty-two former councillors of the
Parlement of Toulouse, charged with colluding in the parlement's defiance of 25 and 27 September 1790, were dispatched as "enemies of the
people."[79] "My blood runs cold," wrote Mary Wollstonecraft to Ruth
Barlow the following day from Le Havre, "and I sicken at thoughts of
a Revolution which costs so much blood and bitter tears."[80] Alexandre
Beauharnais, the passionately pro-Revolution anticlerical republican
noble (Josephine's first husband), was guillotined in Paris on 23 July
1794, the poet André Chénier (1762–94) on 25 July, two days before
Robespierre's overthrow, for disparaging Marat and publishing constitutional monarchist articles in the *Journal de Paris*.

Unreasoning arbitrariness ruled. "The Terror was imposed by and for
proletarians," affirmed Roederer, "it affected all who were not such, and
the higher the proportion of proletarians to property-owners within the
same commune the more heavily their power bore down."[81] But the social categories targeted were scarcely at all defined by economic roles and
status. The "people's enemies" the regime attacked were those diverging
from the ordinary, especially anyone suspected of voicing criticism of
the tyranny. Immediately prior to Robespierre's downfall, the famous
playwright émigré Beaumarchais, author of the *Marriage of Figaro*, and
early in the Revolution a national hero, as well as chief promotor of Voltaire's reputation, found himself proscribed on "moral" grounds following Danton's liquidation. Danton had signed papers authorizing him to
be abroad on government business. In exile, at Hamburg, he received
news that his wife, daughter, and sister had been taken to Paris's Port-
Libre prison, awaiting trial for their lives owing to their association with
him. They were among the lucky ones not yet dispatched on 9 Thermidor (27 July).

After their destruction in October, the dead Brissotin leadership still
played a key role in the Revolution, their shadow everywhere permeating the final speeches of Robespierre and Saint-Just. These weeks also
witnessed the liquidation of much of the Brissotin leadership's remnants. After the Caen rising's collapse, Pétion, Buzot, Barbaroux, Salles,

and Guadet had fled first to Quimper in Brittany, where they hid for a time, and then to the environs of Bordeaux. Guadet survived in hiding in his hometown, Saint-Émilion, together with Salles, until betrayed in mid-June. They were executed in Bordeaux on 17 June 1794, along with six members of Guadet's family accused of hiding them. Pétion and Mme. Roland's lover, Buzot, concealed in the same town, fled disguised into the fields on hearing of the arrests, but on finding all avenues of escape cut off by the Montagnard squad sent by the young Marc Jullien to hunt them down, on 17 June they shot themselves; their bodies, half-eaten by wolves, were found soon afterward.[82] Barbaroux, hiding nearby, attempted suicide too but was found wounded and taken to Bordeaux, where he was guillotined on 25 June 1794.

Even during these last indiscriminate weeks of mass repression and slaughter, the special focus of Robespierre on eliminating critics and the revolutionary *hommes de lettres* continued. Besides André Chénier, among the last writer victims in early July were Coutouly, J. B. Duplain, and Antoine Tournon. On 13 July, it was the turn of Roch Marcandier (1767–94), among the Revolution's most heroic journalists, guillotined together with his wife, more army officers (including the Scottish colonel C.E.F.H. Macdonat), a Protestant minister, and a member of the conseil-général of the department of Doubs. The twenty-seven-year-old Roch Marcandier (1767–94), Cordeliers member and former assistant (and friend) of Desmoulins, after 10 August 1792 had been an agent for Roland's police, spying on the Cordeliers. He was among the few journalists valiant enough to continue denouncing the Montagne, and Robespierre and Danton in particular, through the summer of 1793. Between May and July 1793, he edited an anti-Maratiste paper, provocatively entitled the *Véritable Ami du Peuple*, satirizing Marat's and Hébert's denunciatory style, and lambasting them and Robespierre, the supreme hypocrite, the "cunning fox," now "king" of the Jacobins. Marcandier persisted after 2 June 1793 clandestinely, hidden in an attic, posting up his newssheets in the streets at night, his underground paper labeling the Convention "a place of sedition, "conciliabule d'anarchistes," a "monstrous assembly of men without character." Malfunctioning machinery finally forced him to stop printing in July, but he remained concealed for nearly a year, trying to encourage resistance and exchanging letters with Desmoulins, until betrayed by Legendre, arrested, tried, and guillotined.[83]

Shortly before the crisis that toppled Robespierre, an intensified drive against the remnants of the Hébert circle seemed about to occur. Fresh evidence of conspiracy had been uncovered, announced a Jacobin deputation to the Convention on 26 July. In his last issues Hébert had frequently remarked on what he saw as the need for a new 31 May 1793 insurrection to eliminate the remaining "enemies of the people." What this meant, "explained" Barère, one of those on whom Robespierre now relied most, was that he planned to eliminate the "true friends of the people." The sansculottes of several Paris sections, Barère also reminded everyone, seemed ready for a renewed upsurge of Hébertiste agitation. Hébert's partisans abounded and his maxims echoed![84] Immediately after the Law of 10 June ensued a sudden resurgence of bitter friction and personal rivalries on both executive committees—and a rise in background opposition to the dictator—that left Robespierre and Saint-Just increasingly isolated. Ideologically, the Montagne had always been a minority faction, and within the ruling Montagnard coalition, Robespierre and Saint-Just represented a minority within a minority. Their values were directly antithetical to those of the Revolution in a way the rival ideologies of the Dantonistes and Hébertistes were not to the same degree. After April, most of the Comité de Sûreté Public remained hostile or ironic about the Cult of the Supreme Being, which (like Danton) most considered absurd, like Robespierre's and Saint-Just's endless rhetoric of virtue and natural right.

The festivities surrounding the 14 July Bastille commemoration were doubtless more subdued than in earlier years. Even so, claimed one reporter, Paris was uplifted by a sight entirely satisfying for "true republicans": all the inhabitants of particular quarters gathered in the evening with their families sitting at tables laid in the streets, each bringing their own suppers and all joining in the patriotic songs and toasts, all partaking of roughly the same sort of fare and acting truly as equals. These *repas civiques* were characterized by quiet, modest enjoyment of the kind the regime approved, entirely without drunkenness or misconduct. Everywhere, virtue was the theme of an evening capped by music and singing in the splendidly illumined gardens of the Tuileries. The music continued until late at night and included, sung by a huge choir, the "Hymne à l'Être Suprême," "The Taking of the Bastille," the "Marseillaise," and the two most famous songs of the Revolution, "Ça Ira," first sung in 1790, and "La Carmagnole," besides other revolutionary anthems and marches.[85]

After Hébert's and Danton's elimination, it seemed clear that veteran Montagnards and Cordeliers were as much at risk as anyone else. This rendered the Robespierriste clique ever more isolated.[86] The Law of 22 Prairial, unsurprisingly, shocked and frightened numerous members of the executive committees. Although Robespierre denied it, a strong suspicion arose that Convention deputies could be seized and tried without the Assembly even being notified beforehand.[87] A devastating mix of aversion, fear, and ridicule sapped the prestige and reputation of the "incorruptible." When their authority within the Montagne was finally challenged in late July, comparatively few came to their defense. In its final hours, apart from Hanriot and a few directly self-interested National Guardsmen, nobody rushed to arms to support the collapsing dictatorship. Unlike the cult of Marat, Hébertisme, demand for the 1793 Constitution, or the legacy of the Enragés, by the summer of 1794 Robespierrisme proved practically inert and moribund. In ideological terms, nothing Robespierre stood for was subsequently exalted as something lost or valuable for the Revolution. His ideology was simply too threadbare and remote from the essential principles of the Revolution. Immediately after his downfall, neither the sansculottes nor anyone else seemed to regret his demise.[88]

CHAPTER 21

Thermidor

Robespierre's Downfall

Increasingly irritable and in bad health, by late June Robespierre was manifestly losing his grip. The weeks immediately preceding the overthrow of his authoritarian, populist tyranny witnessed a receding of both his physical presence and prestige. He and Saint-Just sensed the growing hostility of several executive committee members. Yet another nervous breakdown kept Robespierre from executive meetings and the Convention for three crucial weeks, from 1 to 22 July, a critical absence that marked the beginning of the end.

Vadier, threatened by recent remarks of Robespierre relating to him, created a peculiarly unpleasant scene, with a Voltairean eye for the ridiculous, at a Comité de Sûreté Générale meeting on 15 June. The ruthless Vadier was literally a Voltairean as well as an atheist and materialist who posed as a friend of the poor; he talked a lot about philosophy, liked deriding religious belief, and was emphatically anti-Rousseauiste.[1] On that occasion, he ridiculed Robespierre's Supreme Being cult, which he thoroughly scorned by expatiating on the case of Catherine Théot (1716–94), an old woman known for her visions and a former nunnery domestic considered by her followers a prophetess, who was incarcerated in the Bastille before the Revolution for claiming to be the Holy Virgin reincarnate. She had been rearrested by the police in May 1794 for again professing to be the "mother of God," pregnant with "the new messiah" who this time, she claimed, was "Robespierre." She inspired mystic gatherings, presided over by her and the revolutionary priest Dom Gerle, who had caused such a stir in the National Assembly in April 1790, and who had also been arrested, imprisoned, and interrogated. According to reports used by Vadier and Amar, Dom Gerle—who was on excellent terms with Robespierre—embraced Catherine's vision that Robespierre was the long-awaited messiah.[2] Their imprisonment and Vadier's use of the affair placed the dictator, never deft in handling ridicule, in a highly embarrassing position.

The sudden collapse in late July of a regime that had eliminated all organized opposition and saturated France with its ideology had its causes chiefly in the distinctly abstract character of, and reliance on, "the people." Although it had overwhelming police, military, and bureaucratic force at its disposal, and had virtually liquidated all organized challenges, the group dictatorship was chronically lacking in genuine support in the cities and countryside. Despite eliminating Hébertistes and Dantonistes, the regime's grip on the Jacobins, Cordeliers, and Paris sections became ever more precarious. Although substantial numbers of civic and police officials stayed loyal to Robespierre, committed backers and accomplices with a stake in the dictatorship's survival proved too scarce in the clubs, Convention, National Guard, section assemblies, and army command to survive even a modest buffeting. The leadership had removed itself so far from the Revolution's essential principles and Rights of Man that once directly challenged in a concerted way, and its chief men confronted, it collapsed precipitately and completely. Nothing proved flimsier than Robespierre's rhetoric of "the people."

Robespierre's third prolonged withdrawal enabled his detractors on the executive committees to organize. They were headed by Vadier, Lazare Carnot (widely credited with the Republic's recent military victories), Billaud-Varenne, Collot d'Herbois, Barras, and Jean-Lambert Tallien (who had presided over the Terror in Bordeaux). By the time Robespierre returned, at Saint-Just's pleading, to reaffirm his authority, the regime found itself in deep trouble, with Billaud-Varenne, Collot d'Herbois, Vadier, and others actively conspiring to bring him down.[3] Robespierre's counteroffensive, beginning with a long, rambling speech on 8 Thermidor (26 July) at the Convention, where he had made no appearance for over a month, was a disaster. A bitter, paranoid complaint against those conspiring against "the Revolution," it especially stressed the "malicious" innuendo labeling the regime "dictators ruling by Terror." Robespierre's detractors were trying to render him and *le gouvernement révolutionnaire* odious. Hidden opponents were calling the Tribunal Révolutionnaire a "tribunal of blood operated by Robespierre." Who were these vile calomniateurs "who question immortality of the soul and call me a tyrant?" Undoubtedly those attacking "truth and the people" were preachers of "atheism and vice." According to these malefactors, his "dictatorship" threatened liberty. "Who am I these perverse men accuse?" A selfless slave of liberty, the living martyr of the Republic.[4]

Little had changed, Robespierre complained, since "the crimes" of Danton, Fabre, and Desmoulins, who had sought clemency for "the people's enemies." Hébert, Chaumette, and Ronsin had slighted and disparaged the revolutionary government, while Desmoulins assailed it with satirical writings and Danton conspired to defend him. The same pattern of subversion was recurring now. Danton's and Hébert's adherents, cowardly wretches styling him "a tyrant," abounded on all sides. How perfidiously they abused his good faith! Praising him to his face "for the virtues of Cato," behind his back they spoke of "a new Cataline"! Counterrevolutionaries instigating famine deliberately resorted to the methods of Hébert and Chabot. Others used Brissot's strategems to stifle truth. Scoundrels in the Convention plotted with *deputés perfides* on the Comité de Sûreté Générale. The factions opposing virtue and the Revolution needed to be exterminated without delay.[5]

Robespierre defined the "seditious factions" accused of menacing the Revolution's purity as the heirs of Danton, Desmoulins, Hébert, Chabot, and Chaumette. The conspirators combined the systems of Hébertisme and the Dantonistes, purposely obstructing and ridiculing his Festival of the Supreme Being. But he denounced his foes only in the vaguest terms, without actually naming anyone, so that the speech placed everybody in the Convention with whom he had reason for dissatisfaction at immediate risk, thereby unnecessarily panicking some frightened deputies who had no other reason for opposing him into the arms of Billaud-Varenne, Collot d'Herbois, and Vadier. His real foes had been served notice that they must strike now or never. Robespierre's rambling, vigorously applauded speech was, of course, unanimously approved. But when it was proposed that it be printed and circulated among all the communes of France, murmuring and then objections surfaced. Billaud-Varenne, Cambon, and some others advised against publication, and Étienne-Jean Panis (1757–1833), a Paris deputy prominent in the 20 June and 10 August risings, went so far as to remark that Robespierre had had worthy men expelled from the Jacobins merely for refusing to bend to his wishes, and even referred to "his dictatorship." The scene was set for a murderous showdown.

That evening, a sharp tussle erupted at the Jacobins in which Collot d'Herbois, Billaud-Varenne, and Robespierre all fought to speak first. Robespierre won the podium and repeated essentially the same paranoid tirade as in the Convention, lambasting his enemies, continually invoking his struggle against atheism and his defense of the immortality of the soul, and being a "martyr to virtue." Momentarily, he succeeded in cornering the "prédicateurs de l'athéisme et du vice," supposedly emulating Brissot and following the path of Hébert, Desmoulins, Danton, and all his other predecessors. In principle, the Revolution was the first ever "founded on the theory of the rights of humanity and the principles of justice," but in practice, all the Revolution's leaders prior to him had without exception been worthless *fripons*. All betrayed the Revolution while their followers continually accused him—Robespierre!—the "martyr to virtue," of being "a new Cataline," of "dictatorship"![6] The Jacobins voted to expel everyone opposing publication of Robespierre's speech.

Robespierre assumed too quickly that he had won the fight. Billaud-Varenne and Collot d'Herbois, knowing they would be denounced in the Convention the next day, had only hours to save themselves. Their backs to the wall, they spent the night appealing to every conceivable ally on the two executive committees, including the so far always-subservient Barère. Aghast at remarks indicating that Robespierre was dissatisfied with him too, Barère reluctantly turned against him at the last moment, while Carnot, Vadier, and Tallien secured all possible support among the terrified deputies.[7] The culminating drama in the Convention began on the morning of 9 Thermidor (27 July 1794), with Collot d'Herbois presiding. Saint-Just had just begun his report on the "factions" imperiling the Revolution, remarking that on the executive committees "Collot d'Herbois and Billaud-Varenne have taken little part for some time," appearing to "have abandoned themselves to particular interests and views," when uproar ensued. In the fight to strengthen the Revolution and its moral conscience, Saint-Just was about to say, Collot d'Herbois and Billaud-Varenne insinuated that it was best not to highlight the Supreme Being and immortality of the soul. Opposing the proper shaping of the esprit public, they disdained talk of divine Providence, "the sole hope of the ordinary man who, surrounded by *sophismes*, implores Heaven for the wisdom and courage to fight for truth."[8] But just when Saint-Just began complaining that "traitors" were reviving philosophique attitudes, he was brusquely interrupted by Tallien calling out that a dangerous "conspiracy" had been unmasked that needed the Convention's immediate attention.[9] "The men who talk ceaselessly about virtue," interjected Billaud-Varenne, "are the ones who trample it underfoot." He then announced, with the concurrence of the chairman, Collot d'Herbois, that "conspirators" had summoned an armed force commanded by Hanriot to implement their treachery.[10]

Demanding Hanriot's immediate arrest and seizure of his principal National Guard officers, Billaud-Varenne and Collot d'Herbois further proposed that another of Robespierre's principal aides, the implacable lawyer René-François Dumas (1757–94), ruthless president of the Tribunal Révolutionnaire, be arrested too. When the uproar subsided sufficiently, the Convention ordered the arrests of Dumas, Hanriot, and two of Hanriot's key officers, Boulanger and Lavalette. Several deputies then yelled that Robespierre headed "the conspiracy." Leaping to the podium, Robespierre was shouted down: "à bas le roi, à bas le tyran, ce nouveau Cataline!" Tallien and Vadier fiercely denounced "the tyranny of this ambitious hypocrite," this "nouveau Cromwell," Tallien swearing he would personally stab in the chest any deputy lacking the courage to endorse "the tyrant's arrest." On Collot d'Herbois's motion, amid swelling applause, Robespierre's arrest was decreed, immediately followed by those of Couthon, Saint-Just, Augustin Robespierre, and Pierre Lebas (1765–94), another of the most despotic of the Comité de Sûreté Générale, a pitiless lawyer who had behaved abominably in Alsace and other regions, an intimate friend of both Robespierre and Saint-Just.

Thus began the coup of Thermidor—arising directly from a split among the most complicit in repression and the Terror.[11] A principal charge, entirely characteristic of the ruthlessness of those who brought down the tyrant, was that over the winter of 1793–94, Robespierre had insidiously endeavored to save Chabot, Desmoulins, Bazire, and Lavalette from the guillotine.[12] On being taken away, Robespierre had only moments to insult Collot d'Herbois, the president, and the entire legislature. But he was not finished yet. That afternoon, while the Convention drew up and printed their proclamation announcing the "dangerous conspiracy" and dispatched it to the Paris sections, communes, and armies of France, Robespierre's supporters fought to raise the Commune, National Guard, Jacobins, and Paris sections, at first, with some success. The prisoners, instead of being secured in the Luxembourg, were wrested from their guards and brought under the Commune's protection to the town hall, as was Augustin Robespierre, separately sent to Saint Lazaire. Pro-Robespierre elements retained the upper hand initially at the Jacobins, and decreed the expulsion of those deputies supporting Robespierre's arrest.[13] The tocsin was sounded to raise the sections and bring out the sansculottes.[14] Hanriot, on horseback, at the head of his partisans, galloped through the streets yelling that the

Convention was trying to assassinate "the best Patriots" and mobilized some National Guard contingents.[15] The Convention replied that evening by outlawing Hanriot, the mayor of Paris, and all members of the Commune's general council joining the insurrection.[16] A commission of twelve was appointed to oversee suppression of the revolt, and Paul-François Barras, a deputy for Var, veteran terroriste and leading Jacobin, and one of the few Thermidorians not to lose his nerve at this decisive moment, was named to command the Convention's armed force. Measures were taken to fortify the Convention hall in the hope of repelling mobs raised against the deputies by the Commune.

Gathering in emergency session, the Paris section assemblies immediately split. This marked the climax of the struggle. The essence of Robespierrisme was the dragooning of misinformed artisans by manipulated section assemblies. Precisely this key mechanism of popular Jacobinism now fractured. Not enough of the least aware could be produced when it mattered most. After hours of wrangling, the revolutionary committees of eighteen sections refused to back Robespierre, sending deputations to the Convention, promising the deputies their support. The sansculottes of the Paris faubourgs were lukewarm even for Hanriot, previously a great favorite among them, and largely unwilling to back Robespierre.[17] The Jacobins too divided, some aligning with Robespierre, others, eventually the majority, backing the Convention and insisting those opposing Hanriot's insurrection were the "true Jacobins." The supporters rallying to Robespierre proved less than fervent, moreover, and after a few critical hours the crowds that briefly rallied to the regime drifted away. By late evening of 9 Thermidor, the town hall square was reportedly empty. When, at two in the morning, Barras appeared with armed men loyal to the Convention, the town hall was found undefended and the indicted within wholly abandoned by their lukewarm adherents. There was a brief affray with pistols: Augustin Robespierre jumped from a window, severely injuring himself; Lebas shot himself; Hanriot escaped, but was captured later; the others, mostly wounded, were seized.[18]

Botching his effort to shoot himself, Robespierre was captured, bleeding profusely from the jaw. The following (beautifully sunny) day, 10 Thermidor, the Convention sat throughout the day, hearing numerous speakers condemning the "immorality and baseness of the modern Cromwell and his brother," the latter charged with pilfering public funds. With indecorous haste, sentenced after a brief appearance before the Tribunal Révolutionnaire, Robespierre and twenty-two principal supporters, including Saint-Just, Hanriot, Couthon, Augustin Robespierre, Payan, and Fleuriot-Lescot, were conveyed in carts to the Place de la Révolution, where crowds of women performed a joyous dance, yelling their delight at the prospect of the abominable tyrant's pending descent into the "depths of Hell."

Among the condemned figured a dozen Commune officials headed by the new mayor of Paris, Jean-Baptiste Fleuriot-Lescot (1761–94), and Claude-François Payan (1766–94), head of the correspondence office of the Comité de Salut Public and later, despite being a Dauphiné ex-noble, *agent national* of the Paris Commune, one of Robespierre's principal spies on his colleagues, a ruthless member of the Tribunal Révolutionnaire handpicked by Robespierre. Fleuriot-Lescot was a Belgian member of the Tribunal Révolutionnaire and friend of Robespierre who (despite being a native of Brussels) had replaced Pache as mayor in the spring, due to the latter's reluctance to proceed against Hébert. After Hanriot, Fleuriot-Lescot had been the most energetic backer mobilizing support against "the new conspirators" the previous afternoon. The executions took several hours before a largely enthusiastic crowd. When it came to his turn, the executioner first ripped off Robespierre's bandages, eliciting a howl of rage from a horribly contorted face pouring blood. As the guillotine blade fell, thunderous mass applause erupted that, according to Mercier, lasted more than fifteen minutes.[19]

When word arrived that "the tyrant" was dead, there was great jubilation in the Convention too. The next day, seventy more hard-core Robespierristes, mostly municipal and National Guard officers, were guillotined. On 12 Thermidor (30 July), a third batch, police administrators and Commune officials, including the vice president of the conseil-général, followed.[20] At no point was there any popular protest. Fouquier-Tinville, the notorious chief public prosecutor, proved as coldly methodical and cynical in dispatching Robespierre and his entourage as he had Marie Antoinette and the Brissotins.

A Stunned Nation

Over the next days and weeks large numbers of club leaders, officeholders, and army officers associated or reputedly associated with Robespierre were arrested all over France, some briefly, some for longer spells. To his shocked amazement, Fouquier-Tinville himself was arrested and imprisoned on 1 August; the rest of the Tribunal Révolutionnaire was purged on 10 August. Many arrests were motivated at least partly by thirst for personal vengeance. Jullien the Younger, gaoled on returning to Paris from Bordeaux two weeks after Thermidor in early August, had indeed been close to Robespierre but was imprisoned mainly owing to fierce denunciation by his Jacobin rivals and detractors Tallien and Carrier; like many others, Jullien remained behind bars until October 1795.[21] A leader of the Metz Jacobins, J. B. Trotebas, a music teacher falsely reported to be a Robespierre underling, was locked up and remained behind bars until August 1795.[22] Napoleon, close to Robespierre's brother while at Toulon and Nice, figured among those incarcerated briefly (at Nice), though he subsequently also suffered temporary demotion.[23]

Also gaoled, along with his brushes and easel, was Jacques-Louis David who had reportedly embraced Robespierre after his last speech at the Paris Jacobins, saying, "if you drink the hemlock, I will drink it too."[24] David might well have been guillotined with the hard-core Robespierristes were he not so esteemed as an artist. Arrested too, following Robespierre's downfall, were Louis-Julien Héron (1746–96) and Joseph Lebon (the "butcher of Arras"); after many weeks of imprisonment, Lebon was eventually guillotined at Arras on 16 October 1795.[25] Héron, the Comité de Sûreté Générale's executive agent, was a Jacobin leader, wounded during the journée of 10 August 1792, who had assisted Marat's triumph in April 1793. Exempted by Robespierre from the purge of Hébertistes in March 1794, he had later become one of the most brutal Paris police chiefs, employed, among other things, in keeping the tyrant's executive committee colleagues under surveillance. As hundreds of fresh prisoners were hauled into the prisons, they switched places with other hundreds being released.

Once Robespierre fell, virtually nobody resisted or protested, so begrudged was "the new Cataline's" person, and tyranny.[26] More than eight hundred addresses acclaiming the tyrant's overthrow poured in congratulating the Convention from communities all across France. Ironically, a simultaneous stream of pre-Thermidor petitions were still arriving, expressing fury that Robespierre's "sacred" person and leadership were under dire threat. Popularity in politics, commented François Noël "Gracchus" Babeuf (1760–97), one of the Revolution's most ardent egalitarians, in late September 1794, is "a sort of nothingness." Of 100, 000 Parisians yelling "Vive Robespierre!" before 9 Thermidor, none would admit to having done so a day or two later. Of the

100,000 Frenchmen stamping on busts of Marat in autumn 1794, most had venerated him fervently when he was "canonized." In 1790, had not vast crowds adored Lafayette posing on his white horse on the Champ de Mars, while nobody praised him following his defection? More than 30,000 furious Parisians had yelled "Pétion or death," before deserting their once-popular mayor just months later. Since the common people possessed little understanding of what was happening, how could the Jacobin Revolution be saved and consolidated? In September 1794, painfully few declared themselves publicly, like Fréron and Babeuf, demanding freedom of thought and the press. The task now, urged Babeuf, an ardent disciple of the "honest and unfortunate Camille Desmoulins," was to restore Jacobinism's reputation by mobilizing all the lethargic and diffident citizens of France, silently appalled by the great miscreant, for a much wider and more energetic sweep against Robespierrisme.[27]

Numerous victims, facing execution, owed their survival to Robespierre's overthrow. Volney, missed by officers sent to fetch him shortly before Thermidor, outlived the tyrant only due to a Commune official (subsequently himself guillotined) transferring him to another prison just before his scheduled execution. Destutt de Tracy, detained at the Abbaye for eight months, survived by a two-day margin, only because his trial was fixed for 11 Thermidor. However, narrowly escaping the guillotine was not the same as regaining one's liberty. If hundreds, including Garat, Sonthonax, Antonelle, Mme. Helvétius, Sophie de Condorcet, Helen Maria Williams, Ginguiné, and others of the Condorcet and Mme. Roland circles were released within days, hundreds more stayed in prison for many more weeks and months. By the time Volney was relased on 16 September, he had been held (in three different prisons) for ten months.[28] Destutt de Tracy was released and allowed to return to Auteil only on 5 October, ten weeks after Thermidor, and he was among the lucky ones.[29] Paine and many others languished behind bars much longer. Though seriously ill, Paine was held until, belatedly, the new United States envoy, James Monroe, effected his release on 6 November, by which time Paine too had been detained for more than ten months. The mulatto fighter for the civil rights of free blacks, Julien Raimond, imprisoned on 26 September 1793, was also released on 6 November.[30] Lafayette's wife, Adrienne, remained incarcerated until January 1795, Claire Lacombe until August 1795.

But in place of the ruthless men Robespierre had selected with an eye to their usefulness to himself, the Thermidorians substituted only other proven terroristes scarcely less tyrannical, dishonest, and demagogic. Their sole qualification for replacing their predecessors was having had less proximity to Robespierre. Ideologically, and in terms of revolutionary ideals and principles, this left everything unresolved. If the repressive Law of 10 June was abrogated the day following Robespierre's overthrow, most Montagnards had disliked it anyway. The Law of Suspects of 17 September 1793, the true legal basis of the Terror, for the moment remained firmly in place.[31] Following noisy scenes in the Paris sections, the first major clash in the Convention after Thermidor occurred on 13 August, the day James Monroe was received as United States ambassador. The Convention agreed to place the United States flag in the Assembly hall beside the tricolor, signaling an "eternal alliance" between the world's two premier republics, and Geneva's alongside those of France and the United States, in recognition of Geneva's new democratic constitution and being Rousseau's birthplace—but not on much else. While numerous speakers denounced Robespierre, the prolonged debate about the new situation provoked a bitter row over whether to continue the repression or drastically curtail the executive committees' powers and more comprehensively denounce the Terror. Many deputies were more troubled by resurgent monarchism, aristocracy, and counterrevolution than the travesty of justice burying the Revolution's basic principles. Consequently, the Montagne contrived precariously to retain power for more than six months more. The so-called Thermidorian reaction focused only on eradicating Robespierre's following, the Thermidorians being helped in this by the fact that most genuine libertarians and democratic republicans prominent earlier in the Revolution were now either dead, in hiding, or, like Daunou, Garat, Volney, and Paine, still in prison. During August, Daunou, the distinguished constitutional and educational reformer and Pas-de-Calais deputy, while still behind bars, composed a text proclaiming a reformed education system, the sole effective antidote to Montagnard repression and authoritarianism.[32]

Thermidor, accordingly, ushered in only a very limited restoration of suppressed liberties. In the autumn of 1794, there seemed little likelihood of soon restoring the Revolution's core values. In and outside Paris, assiduous care was taken not to step beyond a cautious easing of the repression. If many hard-core Robespierristes had been eliminated or imprisoned, thousands of other active agents of the Terror—deputies, officials, and police officers—remained in post. By linking the Terror to just Robespierre's accomplices, provincial agents of the Terror sought to cover their tracks and reemerge, despite their crimes, as re-spected representatives of a wronged people.

The sociétés populaires congratulated the Convention, therefore, not on halting the repression or Terror, or demolishing the ideology of virtue vitiating the Revolution, but merely for removing the "nouveau Cromwell," the would-be "king," "the monster" perverting the Conven-tion. Certainly, a real change ensued in the country's power structure. The Thermidorians moved quickly to suspend the Tribunal Révolution-naire, reorganize the National Guard, purge the executive committees, and replace key military and administrative officials. On 24 August, the Committee of Public Safety had its powers drastically clipped, subse-quently being largely confined to military and foreign affairs. On 1 Sep-tember, Vadier, who was being increasingly denounced as a hypocrite who in 1790–91 had supported Bailly and Lafayette, and with hav-ing rejected and reviled "le systeme républicain" even more than had Robespierre,[33] was purged from the Comité de Sûreté Générale. Even if limping excruciatingly slowly psychologically, emotionally, and intel-lectually from the terrible trauma, a change in atmosphere quickly be-came palpable. The shadow of Terror itself ended. The Convention was back in charge. Within weeks, several papers, muzzled or suppressed during the Terror, reappeared, all now vehemently condemning the ex-cesses of Robespierre's tyranny, notably Tallien's *L'Ami du citoyen*, the *Décade philosophique,* and Fréron's *L'Orateur du peuple*, the last from 12 September.

The press could now attack Robespierre's tyranny without inhibi-tion, but not the Montagne or Thermidorians. Authors venturing fur-ther still risked paying a stiff price. Jean Varlet, "orator" of the poor faubourgs, a sansculotte leader execrating not just Robespierre but the entire clique now ensconced in power, published an incisive pamphlet, *L'explosion*, dated 1 October 1794, condemning in particular Barère, Vadier, Billaud-Varenne, Collot d'Herbois, Amar, Carrier, and the phy-sician Pierre-Joseph Duhem (1769–1807), a Montagnard stalwart from Lille. In June 1793, Varlet reminded readers, he had been pushed aside almost immediately after the Brissotin overthrow by individuals he had only belatedly recognized as scoundrels betraying the sanscu-lottes and the Revolution, those who engineered the Montagne's "hor-rible dictature." He had refused to have any further truck with what struck him as the gross deceit perpetrated by the Montagne. Arrested in the autumn of 1793, he had then been released shortly afterward. In his pamphlet of September 1794, Varlet claimed the only way to save the

Revolution was to eradicate abuse of power and return to the Revolution's core principles, which in his eyes meant restoring an ample share of direct democracy to the sections. "Républicains! Vous dormez! La République est dans les fers" (Republicans! You are asleep! The Republic is in chains).[34] He was perfectly correct: the Thermidorian regime now rearrested him. He remained behind bars until October 1795.

The press remained partly shackled. Protest remained muted. Thermidor thus marked a total rejection of Robespierre's person and dictatorship, liquidating and imprisoning hundreds, yet a purge carried out by many of the worst and most unscrupulous terroristes on a totally bogus premise. They created a wholly false and artificial wall between themselves and Robespierre's accomplices, pursuing former colleagues on grounds without any moral or ideological force whatever. At Marseille, where Granet and Moise Bayle took charge, and other principal cities, the same tyrannical scene prevailed as in Paris.[35] At Metz, Merlin de Thionville, whose dishonesty had so shocked Forster at Mainz, combined continuing gross financial corruption with particularly malevolent pursuit of his former Jacobin allies. Denouncing Robespierre after Thermidor—a chorus in which David emphatically joined—was hence not remotely a wholehearted disavowal of the Montagne, debased Rousseauisme, authoritarianism, or the Terror. While the Terror slowed drastically, the ascendancy of Barras, Collot d'Herbois, Billaud-Varenne, Vadier, Amar, Merlin de Thionville, and other leading terroristes ensured that for the moment power remained not just in Montagnard hands but hands no less compromised and unscrupulous than those responsible before Thermidor.[36] The new Montagnard leaders controlling the executive committees included, besides those already named, Treilhard, Dumont, and Jacques-Alexandre Thuriot (d. 1829), former member of the Comité de Sûreté Générale, once a Brissotin, later a Montagnard leader of the Terror, but one who broke with Robespierre shortly before Thermidor, having been expelled from the Jacobins as a concealed "moderate" and "Brissotin." André Dumont (1764–1836), by any reckoning a veteran terroriste, had been among the most fanatical persecutors of priests in Northern France. After Thermidor, these men joined Collot d'Herbois, Billaud-Varenne, Amar, and Barère in resisting more fundamental changes and denouncing modérantisme as the chief "passport" of counterrevolutionaries.

The time was not far off, suggested Babeuf, when it would be an insult to say to anyone, "you are a Jacobin."[37] But who were "the Jacobins" after Thermidor? The real Jacobins had mostly been guillotined or expelled. The club still included some "true patriots," granted Fréron and Babeuf, but these secretly groaned under the continuing yoke of the tyranny imposed by a discredited leadership, consisting, according to Fréron, of only around fifteen unscrupulous men attempting the impossible task of prolonging the repression in a less overtly ruthless fashion than had Robespierre, while still upholding a threadbare ideology. Fréron voiced the feelings of many aggrieved by the limited scope of Thermidor, and yet his own record was far from unsullied. If he loathed Robespierre and "Barèrisme," he still venerated Marat (who considered him his most cherished disciple).[38] The difficulty with the wall the Thermidorians so assiduously erected between themselves and Robespierre's tyranny was that it was completely fictitious. There was no clear dividing-line separating them from Robespierre's despotism. Robespierre's demise was thus followed by a crushing public discrediting of his character and what *La Décade philosophique* called the "perfides agents" he had everywhere introduced, vile, unscrupulous men deliberately employed "to corrupt republican principles."[39] But nothing more.

In fact, a whole new political mythology was being created. By ceaselessly vilifying Robespierre, Couthon, and Saint-Just, the myth that the Jacobins themselves were pure and upright but had been betrayed gained currency. The Paris Commune, armed forces, tribunals of justice, public opinion itself, had supposedly been directed by a single monstrously corrupt individual. That single tyrant had held every citizen's life and death in his hand. Unquenchable egoism, suggested the *Décade philosophique*, the journal founded shortly before his death in April 1794 by Chamfort, together with Ginguené (shortly before he was imprisoned) and the young économiste, Jean-Baptiste Say (1767–1832), was Robespierre's distinctive trait: with all his rhetoric of "virtue" and "patrie," he considered only himself.[40] In one way, the "Incorruptible" had not been at all corrupt: after his execution, little money and few valuables were found among his possessions. Politically, though, nobody could be more corrupt, cast-iron proof of this being his deliberately choosing as trusted agents only the basest, most ignorant, and immoral "satellites hors de toute instruction et de toute morale," as the Dantonist doctor Baudot expressed it, and his employing only the most abominable types—such as Pache, Hanriot, Lebon, Fleuriot-Lescot, Héron, and Payan—which enabled the tyrant both to tyrannize over colleagues and eliminate subordinates whenever he chose.[41]

The transition from denouncing Robespierre's personal dictatorship to acknowledging group dictatorship, to a serious analysis of a severely blighted system, of those responsible for wrecking the Revolution and perpetrating tyranny beyond Thermidor, proved hard, long, and fraught. Amid the stream of denunciation and sensational press revelations, a pamphlet of particular impact, *La Queue de Robespierre* (Robespierre's tail), punning on the word for tail (i.e., following), appeared a month after the dictator's overthrow on 9 Fructidor (27 August 1794), with a vast print-run amounting to tens of thousands. Its author was Jean-Claude Méhée (1760–1826), an unscrupulous double agent and ally of Tallien, implicated in the 2 September massacres, who afterward became the Paris Commune's deputy registrar. While Robespierre had been overthrown, insisted Méhée, his most callous subordinates had not. In particular, he denounced three of the leading Thermidorians—Collot d'Herbois, Billaud-Varenne, and Barère.[42] Two days after his pamphlet appeared, and not coincidentally, Laurent Lecointre (1744–1805), a Versailles businessman and energetic adversary of the Jacobins, delivered a withering indictment, under twenty-six headings, of the agents of Terror in the Convention. He accused seven leading Jacobins—Collot d'Herbois, Billaud-Varenne, Barère, Amar, Vadier, Jean-Henri Voulland (1751–1801), and also David—of complicity with Robespierre and Saint-Just in the most appalling atrocities. They had liquidated or imprisoned tens of thousands, afflicting all France with fear and despair, and also deliberately hindered or slowed the subsequent release of captives and freeing the Convention and other government institutions from the Terror.[43]

For the moment, the attack was successfully deflected. If no one spoke in Robespierre's defense, many championed the Montagne. Those Lecointre denounced accused him of casting the net irresponsibly widely, slurring the honest and dishonoring the Convention. The public interest, held Thuriot, required the Assembly to repudiate Lecointre's charges unreservedly. As the debate developed, more than fifty speakers intervened, most pointing out that were Billaud-Varenne and Collot d'Herbois to fall, not just the executive committees but the entire Convention would stand charged with horrific crimes mixed with supine complicity in Robespierre's villainy. "It is the Convention that is accused," exclaimed one leading deputy, "it is against the French people that the action is brought, because they have acquiesced in the tyranny of the infamous Robespierre."[44] By a comfortable margin, the deputies rebuffed Lecointre's denunciation as "false and slanderous."[45] Tallien, Fréron, and Lecointre were all expelled from the Jacobins, and Lecointre also from the Convention, but not otherwise molested.

Not everyone seeking to minimize Jacobin as distinct from *terroriste* responsibility was dishonest. Many, including Babeuf, Fréron, Varlet, Jullien, and Antonelle, remained convinced that the 31 May 1793 coup d'état was justified and that Robespierre had become a vengeful "Nero" only afterward, during the summer of 1793. There must be two different Robespierres, suggested the first issue of Babeuf's *Journal de la Liberté de la Presse*, in September 1794. Until early 1793, Robespierre had been a true Jacobin, pure and upright, heroically defending the Revolution's essential principles; the contemptible dictator emerged only later.[46] In this way, Babeuf's journal too contributed to manufacturing the myth that the "Old Jacobins" were true heroes of the people until early 1793, while the New Jacobins, from June 1793, were unmitigated culprits. The veritable Jacobins, claimed Babeuf, Fréron, and Antonelle, were "diametrically opposed" to the New Jacobins, the former upholding the Rights of Man as vigorously as the latter demolished them.[47] New Jacobins betrayed the people; Old Jacobins promoted the truth. Babeuf deplored the Thermidorians' unwillingness to purge all the *terroristes*: Robespierre had been dealt with, but genuine Jacobinism needed to be preserved intact. Yet, Babeuf, like Fréron, remained strangely blind to Marat's vitiating influence, as well as Robespierre's, already long before May 1793.

True republicans upholding the Rights of Man today, suggested Babeuf's journal, are first expelled from the Jacobins, then imprisoned, then murdered. If press freedom was being gradually recouped, this was despite, not thanks to, the Thermidorians. Liberty was being clawed back by only a very few courageous opponents, like Fréron and himself.[48] On 5 October, Fréron's paper witheringly denounced Barère as someone who had first been a royalist, then a supporter of the Lameths, then a Feuillant, and finally among the most dishonest "terrorists."[49] Babeuf, who, like Jullien later, aspired to become a revolutionary leader like Desmoulins before him via the press, sought to set an example as a true "philosophe républicain."[50] Above all, more revolutionary backbone was needed! Genuine philosophical *démocratisme* could be revived through building on freedom of the press. But for the moment the Revolution remained an arena sharply divided between an oppositional bloc aiming to reestablish government based on the "eternal rights of man," part old Jacobin and part Brissotin, and a corrupt remnant actually in power continuing Robespierre's methods.[51]

Before long, the campaign to unseat the ex-Montagnards resumed. Those the *Orateur du peuple* termed "the ferocious beasts" were never

able fully to deflect the slowly growing outcry or stifle "the few courageous writers seeking to unmask their crimes." Inexorably, if gradually,
the trauma, horror, and indignation stemming from Robespierre's dishonesty and despotism grew into loud calls for a genuine, broad-ranging
analysis of what had gone wrong, for a full disclosure of Montagnard
moral and ideological perversity.[52] Many sansculottes, like Varlet, willingly confessed they had been appallingly misled. The rhetoric of the
"people's will," it was now plain to all but the most obtuse, was all deception. Tallien, backed by Fréron and his *L'Orateur du peuple*, began
demanding a definitive end to the Terror and restoration of probity.
"Let us unmask all the traitors, all the rascals, all the conspirators, all of
Robespierre's emulators." "Let us establish the empire of virtue"—but
this time *la vertu véritable,* not Robespierre's false virtue.[53] Fréron, in
his post-Thermidor articles, invoked Desmoulins as his chief inspiration, providing guidance still "from the next world." Too much blame
was being heaped on Robespierre personally. Was it not while Robespierre absented himself from the executive committees, in the summer
of 1794, Fréron pointed out, that the guillotining of innocent victims reached its peak? Nothing could hide the complicity of Billaud-
Varenne, Collot d'Herbois, Barère, Amar, and Vadier in the Terror's
worst excesses.[54] During Robespierre's forty-five-day absence from the
Committee of Public Safety from 12 June to 27 July, 1,285 condemned
were executed in Paris, estimated Fréron, as against 577 in the previous
forty-five days.[55] Here was indictment enough of the currently ruling
clique.

Yet, the "voice of *patriotisme,*" lamented Fréron, in his paper *L'Orateur
du peuple* in September, still remained muted and *la tyrannie* dominant.
Throwing out the oppressors, eradicating *le Machiavelisme, Barèrisme,*
and *le Néronisme,* and reinstating the eternal principles of justice and
liberty, was proving no simple or easy undertaking. Only through an arduous, painful process could the Revolution find its way back to its true
republican ideals—the Rights of Man, liberty, equality, freedom of expression, and a new order seeking the benefit of society as a whole. Fortunately, the current Montagnard leadership, observed Fréron, enjoyed
no respect or popularity whatsoever, not even the minimal popularity
"the modern Nero" enjoyed after six years of "diverting to his own account" the credit of those who really engineered the Revolution. Most
of the new despots—he cited in particular Duhem, Levasseur, Audouin,
and Amar—were complete mediocrities.[56] (Payan had warned Robespierre of Amar's incompetence in a secret report of June 1794.)[57]

Meanwhile, the entire country was deeply unsettled. Even if precariously, the New Jacobins still dominated the arena. Understandably, the sansculottes remained resentful and discontented. Deputations from various Paris sections denounced the "revolutionary committees" as tools of despotism.[58] Twelve to fifteen Paris sections now sympathized with defenders of the Rights of Man against the New Jacobins, estimated Babeuf in September, but the rest stubbornly acquiesced in the New Jacobin ascendancy.[59] The "aristocracy," contended the regime's spokesmen, aimed to exploit the instability and overthrow the Revolution by putting subversive talk in the mouths of patriotes. Throughout the autumn, the political initiative remained predominantly if not solidly in ex-Montagnard hands. Numerous warnings were uttered against relaxing *la justice révolutionnaire,* which alone, supposedly, could save France. Veteran Montagnards adamantly asserted the need to stick to the previous course and bolster the executive committees—or the Counter-Revolution would triumph.[60]

What Montagnards termed the "system of modérantisme and weakness" could only produce "terrible disturbances."[61] Brissotin deputies purged from the Convention in the summer of 1793, those still surviving numbering more than seventy deputies, among them Louvet, Garat, Paine, and Daunou, were prevented from being rehabilitated and from returning to the Assembly for as long as possible. Those who had survived in hiding or been released needed to watch their step. Roederer resumed writing but kept a low profile, using a pseudonym until late 1794.[62] Volney, released in October, fled the capital, retreating to Marseille, where he had left belongings and manuscripts after returning from Corsica in February 1793, and then Nice. Paine, though eventually reinstated in December by a unanimous vote in the Convention, along with the other Brissotins proscribed in June 1793, and receiving some back pay, remained silent for months. His long imprisonment had left him ill and despondent, and he did not think it prudent to state his views openly as yet. Generally, he remained dejected about the Revolution's prospects.[63] Not until 8 July 1795 did he rise to speak in the Convention, encouraged by his ally, Lanthenas.[64] Comte Louis-Philippe de Ségur (1753–1830), a liberal noble, writer, and historian, among the more talented of Louis XVI's courtiers at Versailles, later one of Napoleon's eulogists, having survived in hiding, did not think it safe to return to Paris with his family until spring 1795.[65]

At the heart of the quarrel in Assembly and country lay the question of how far to reestablish freedom of opinion and liberty of the press. Fear of aiding the Brissotin recovery, as well as the royalist resurgence, doubtless explains why other committed Jacobins victimized by the Robespierre regime, like Robert and Antonelle, recently released from prison, preferred to remain silent under the Thermidorians rather than echo Fréron and Babeuf.[66] And from their perspective, they had a point: How could press freedom and the "eternal principles of the Rights of Man be restored without handing back hegemony over the Revolution to the Brissotins whom Fréron, an ally of Desmoulins and Philippeaux, had always opposed?

A vigorous neo-Brissotin opposition was already emerging among the handful of deputies, who for one reason or another had survived the 1793 purges and remained in the Convention. Among them was Jean Debry (1760–1834), a friend of Roland whose daughter he had protected during the Terror,[67] now a member of the Comité de Sûreté Générale and a vehement critic of the authoritarian populists' "Néronisme." Another was the anti-Catholic republican Jacques-Antoine Creuzé-Latouche (1750–1800), a supporter of the appel au public during Louis XVI's trial, voted onto the Comité de Salut Public after Robespierre's demise. Another was Paine's translator, the physician Lanthenas, removed by Marat from the original list of the Twenty-Two as a "poor harmless fellow" (Lanthenas believed Marat to be mad). Also among them was François-Antoine de Boissy d'Anglas (1756–1828), an anticlerical of Protestant background who had backed the appel au public and denounced the arrests of the Brissotin leadership. As a stutterer, Boissy had subsequently been left a silent presence in the Convention; but now he also came onto the Comité de Salut Public. These men constituted a formidable bloc.

Although "liberty's" defenders were already coming under mounting assault from Brissotin sympathizers, complained the Jacobin press, most prominent Brissotins who survived still remained in hiding or in prison. Behind demands to reinstate the seventy-four surviving, expelled "Girondin" deputies, the regime professed to detect a menacing horde of modérés and royalistes.[68] But no call for a return to liberty, justice, and probity could be in any way genuine as long as the Left republicans remained proscribed. Pressure to free them gradually built up until, more than four months after Thermidor, they had to be reinstated as Convention deputies in mid-December 1794. The released Brissotins lost no time in denouncing the Thermidorians as "partisans of Robespierre," an effective strategy since nothing could be more dangerous to ex-Montagnards in late 1794 than this accusation. The Montagne, whether for or against Robespierre, were indiscriminately condemned together en bloc by disciples of Brissot, Gensonné, Barbaroux, and Louvet. The political arena heated up once again. Were the Brissotins, having failed to prosecute Marat and having been overthrown in June 1793, now about to topple the Montagne and win the struggle for the soul of the Revolution after all?[69]

CHAPTER 22

Post-Thermidor

(1795–97)

A Democratic Republic?

Slowly but surely power slipped from the hands of the Thermidorians. Given the circumstances, it could hardly have been otherwise. But could the Revolution's reputation, integrity, and principles be restored? Among the Revolution's originally ardent supporters, a great many had become so disillusioned under the Montagnard tyranny—and its perverse Thermidorian aftermath—they were scarcely disposed to think so. Diderot's disciple, Naigeon, loathing the Montagne and the Terror with every fiber of his being, did not abandon his earlier revolutionary ideals to the extent La Harpe did but also now believed it would have been better to suffer "the abuses of the *ancien régime*" indefinitely rather "than experience all the evils" of Robespierre's tyranny. The very word *révolutionnaire* had changed its meaning since June 1793, he lamented, from defender of human liberty and dignity to a political and moral "monster." Was the Revolution worth such a price?[1]

Yet, society could not go back. All intelligent men of goodwill "who have reflected on the matter" at all deeply, added Naigeon, must rally to the Revolution's true principles, acknowledging that the rights anyone has by nature are reciprocal and shared by all.[2] Other survivors of the libertarian, republican Revolution of 1789–93, however traumatized, wounded, and sullen, equally vowed to try to reverse the collapse of the "real Revolution" and rebuild a republicanism truly infused with Enlightenment, anti-Rousseauiste, and geared to enlightening and ameliorating society. Rescuing the Revolution, to them, meant above all comprehensively eradicating Montagnard despotism and the miscreants who had perverted the Republic and restoring the Revolution of democracy, equality, and human rights. To this end, surviving Brissotins could, at least in theory, clasp hands with reemerging Old Jacobins and Vieux Cordeliers like Fréron, Babeuf, Jullien, Réal, and Antonelle, who cherished the legacy of Danton and Desmoulins and were seemingly equally eager to uncouple the Revolution from the likes of Robespierre, Saint-Just, and the Thermidorians. Pierre-François Réal (1757–1834) was a legal official who became a leading democratic republican journalist in 1795.[3] Opposing the Brissotins, he had nevertheless deplored the April 1794 purges and, after Danton's arrest, been imprisoned in the Luxembourg. These distinct streams, Old Cordeliers, Old Jacobins, and ex-Brissotins, potentially reconcilable perhaps, were supplemented by a fresh influx of idealistic republicans from abroad, including Benjamin Constant (1767–1830), the "father of modern liberalism," who at this time, however, was no "liberal" or "moderate" but a committed (he changed later) democratic republican.

Yet the perverse logic of the Montagne was far from altogether eclipsed. When the twelve proscribed deputies, arrested on 3 October 1793, still behind bars at Port-Libre, headed by Daunou and the classicist scholar Jean-Joseph Dusaulx (1728–99), collectively published a manifesto on 9 October 1794, appealing to the public, the response was a resumption of the old feuding. An eminent scholar and member of several academies, later in 1799 among the republican deputies sent to Rome to help organize the new revolutionary republic also there, Boulogne-born Pierre-Claude Daunou had been among the courageous deputies imprisoned in the summer of 1793 for contesting proscription of Brissot and his colleages. Like other republican intellectuals returning to the fray in 1795, he was an ardent disciple, in particular, of Condorcet. A member of the Commission of Eleven who drafted the Constitution, and of the Committee of Public Instruction, he was to figure among the legislature's principal figures under the Directoire and became first "president" of the Council of Five Hundred.

Summoning their Convention colleagues to acknowledge their contribution to the 1793 Constitution and accept that the journées of 31 May and 2 June, though enacted by the people, were wrought by a people misled, they encountered stubborn resistance. The 2 June 1793 coup lacked all legitimacy. Why were they still in prison? "Fédéralisme was plainly a trumped up, nonsensical accusation."[4] But the charge was not fictitious, answered the Old Jacobins and Dantonists, and the coup not illicit. Even if Robespierre's suspending of the June 1793 Constitution *was* illicit, how could the Convention absolve the Twelve without rehabilitating all seventy-one surviving Brissotin deputies? And how could the seventy-one be reinstated without admitting that 31 May and 2 June 1793 was a gross crime against both Revolution and nation, that the charge of fédéralisme was utterly absurd? Such a shift would mean conceding the Montagne were wrong all along, and the Brissotins in the right. Jacobins could not repudiate the journée of 2 June 1793. To do so would suggest the people had wrecked their own Revolution through ignorance, gullibility, and unawareness.

For Old Jacobins fédéralisme was neither fictitious nor irrelevant. How strange that even after Thermidor, remarked Babeuf's paper, these Brissotins still exerted so great an influence over the Revolution! Revolutionaries like Babeuf, Fréron, and Antonelle, recoiling from granting moral victory to the Gironde, preferred to deride the tracts of Daunou, Roederer, Jollivet, and others that were urging the release of the seventy-one. Besides, there also remained concrete differences in principle that authentic Old Jacobins could highlight. Where they sympathized with sansculotte direct street action, Brissotins did not, or at least, after their recent experiences, did so no longer. Then there was the June 1793 Constitution. When alive, had not Gorsas joined Condorcet in "insolently" dismissing the June 1793 Constitution as grotesque, a "deformed carcass"? Remarking that several neo-Brissotin tracts were being printed on the widow Gorsas's press, Babeuf sarcastically inquired whether Gorsas had now become a holy being remitting oracles to the people from Elyseum?[5]

Gracchus Babeuf, revolutionary survivor and ardent advocate of social justice, active earlier at Amiens, where he had edited a noted local democratic journal, *Le Correspondant Picard*, had, like so many editors, been silenced during the Terror and spent many months in prison. It was through reading "philosophy," he explained, that he had become an ardent republican, democrat, and advocate of "equality." From late 1794, he emerged as the Revolution's most uncompromising egalitarian and guardian of that strand of revolutionary tradition emphasizing equality. After Thermidor, in late 1794, he clamored loudly for press freedom and the Constitution of 1793. Denouncing the Terror, his *Journal de la liberté de la presse*, launched in September 1794, complained—like Fréron and Varlet—that "the monster" had gone, but too little was being done to extirpate Robespierrisme more broadly.[6] However, Babeuf loudly regretted the Terror's excesses only briefly,[7] shifting his ground during 1795, realizing that the egalitarian crusade he had embarked on inevitably led him up against a legislature dominated by foes of the now-suppressed militant Jacobins, his only likely allies.

Babeuf's brief rejection of the Terror and Robespierre in late 1794 did not prevent his viewing Brissotins with resentful hostility, much like his future ally and fellow egalitarian Pierre-Antoine, Marquis d'Antonelle (1747–1817). The first democratically elected mayor of Arles, Antonelle figured among the Revolution's most remarkable personalities. Renouncing his aristocratic background, he had become a militant Jacobin. Appointed to the Montagnard Tribunal Révolution-naire, he was directly complicit in the October 1793 show trials and condemnation of Brissot and his colleagues. Later, though, in March 1794, clashing with Fouquier-Tinville, he was arrested himself on the Comité de Salut Public's orders and incarcerated in the Luxembourg. Released after Thermidor, Antonelle remained silent for a whole year before reemerging as a leading advocate of neo-Jacobin egalitarianism, especially in the influential *Journal des hommes libres*, on which he worked with the able young René Vatar (1773–1842), another key figure in providing an element of cohesion on an ideological level to France's surviving, adapting, and reemerging neo-Jacobinism.[8]

Antonelle and Vatar, like Babeuf, believed a revival of Brissotin fortunes would be disastrous for the Revolution by renewing old divisions and leaving the Jacobins and common people looking as if they had been systematically duped ever since August 1792.[9] To their minds, and they were right, there remained a real tension between militant egalitarianism and la philosophie, with its stress on intellect and knowledge, between Rousseausime and Enlightenment, between *principes populaires* and the secte philosophique. Likewise, the veteran Montagnard Marc-Antoine Baudot (1765–1837) abhorred Robespierre and despised Marat but also remained convinced the masses were the Revolution's true motor, that the Terror had been necessary, and that the Girondins were an ambitious, power-hungry clique designing *une ré-publique oligarchique*.[10] The Revolution's great men in Baudot's opinion were not the philosophe-révolutionnaires of 1788–93 but Danton, Desmoulins, and Romme. Hence, one republican bloc aimed to restore the "real Revolution" and its true principles by reviving the Brissotin legacy and reinvigorating the Convention, its rivals by appealing to the Paris sections and reviving Jacobin esprit public. Brissotins, such men remained convinced, were not true "republicans" or "friends of liberty" and disdained the sansculottes.[11]

Because forming an anti-Montagnard alliance of Old Jacobins and Brissotins seemed distasteful, and illegitimate to many Montagnard veterans of the May 31 rising, once the Thermidorians faded during

1795–96, Dantonists and other Old Jacobins and Old Cordeliers confronted several decisive, unpalatable, and, for them, often excruciating choices. Since neo-Brissotin republicanism rapidly reemerged during early 1795 as the real backbone of enlightened, libertarian, democratic republicanism, and hence of the Revolution, the situation ultimately forced anti-Brissotin Old Jacobins to divide: either they embraced Daunou, Debry, Lanjuinais, Guyomar, Lanthenas, and Boissy d'Anglas or else became outright opponents of the legislature, swallowing their criticism of Thermidorians, Robespierre, and the Terror. Babeuf adopted the latter strategy: he dropped press freedom from among his major concerns, and by early 1796, his new paper, *Le Tribun du peuple,* was already making excuses for the Terror and even the September massacres. More press freedom, he realized, would merely aid the right-wing monarchist-Catholic revival, as well as the Brissotins, who, to him, were the "grave-diggers of democracy," and thereby aggravate the Republic's political instability. Shouldering what he saw as a genuinely revolutionary task, he aimed to restore Robespierre's, the Terror's, and even Joseph Lebon's reputation, thus justifying the annihilation of the Hébertists and Dantonists.[12]

The Thermidorians, meanwhile, clung to power tenaciously for as long as they could. Every possible ploy was utilized to shore up their sagging prestige. Minimizing their role in the Terror, they delayed Fouquier-Tinville's trial for months. Trying to recoup sansculotte support, on 7 September 1794, they renewed the Law of the General Maximum on prices and wages for another year, signaling their intention to hold food prices steady. The measure was enforced, though in a hesitant, vacillating manner, without wielding the harsh penalties sporadically imposed before Thermidor until, on 23 December 1794, the Maximum lapsed altogether. In an effort to breathe new life into Montagnard ideology and values, they devised several grand publicity coups designed to impress the public: the Convention voted to deposit Marat's remains in the Panthéon,[13] and finally install Rousseau there, while simultaneously removing Mirabeau. Robespierre had planned to alter the Panthéon's character, aiming to dephilosophize the sanctuary and firmly associate it instead with populist cult figures like Lepeletier and Chalier, who meant more to ordinary folk. Briefly, the Thermidorians persisted with this policy. Amid great fanfares, Marat was entombed in the Panthéon on 21 September 1794.

However, pantheonizing Marat and negating the Panthéon's philosophique character offended not only Brissotins but also libertarian

Rousseauistes, who refused to see Marat as a genuine standard-bearer of Rousseau. Mercier, who had joined the Convention protests against the 2 June 1793 coup and been imprisoned with other Brissotins in October 1793, and who believed that dismantling Montagnard authoritarianism was proceeding too slowly, fiercely condemned Marat's pantheonization. A republican long before 1789, like Brissot, Bonneville, Guyomar, and Dusaulx, Mercier loathed Marat and Robespierre but nevertheless shared the latter's aversion to interring Rousseau among philosophes. Like other Rousseauistes, he was less drawn to pantheonizing Rousseau than depantheonizing Voltaire. How can anyone reconcile Voltaire's writings with republican maxims?[14] Mercier also scorned the Convention's decree of 2 October 1793 (never implemented), envisioning the transfer of Descartes's remains to the Panthéon. Whatever Descartes's merits as a philosopher, he meant nothing to ordinary folk, a point Mercier loudly affirmed in a discourse to the Council of Five Hundred on 8 February 1796. Mercier, in fact, disliked the whole idea of the Panthéon.[15] The project had resulted in a sumptuous building full of magnificent decor costing vast sums better spent, in his view, on charitable institutions aiding the poor.

Still, the people's hopes had to be kept alive. Installing Rousseau in the Panthéon on 20 Vendémiaire (11 October 1794), a beautiful day, counted among the outstanding commemorative events of that fraught and gloomy post-Thermidor autumn. The cortege was accompanied by the legislature, bands of musicians, and crowds of young people singing hymns, including one especially composed by Marie-Joseph Chénier for the occasion, beginning, "O Rousseau! modèle des sages," benefactor of humanity, "accept the homage of a people proud and free, and from the depths of your tomb support equality!"[16] A rousing occasion staged by the Thermidorians and some Brissotins to restore the Republic's wilting reputation, the event was designed to create a reassuring tableau of union, harmony, and reconciliation.

Montagnard recovery, however, was wholly out of the question. There was an insuperable contradiction in the Thermidorian logic. Once the Terror ceased and a partial freedom of expression returned, there was no way the people's pent-up indignation and revulsion, or thirst for revenge, could be withstood. "They write now with great freedom and truth," reported Mary Wollstonecraft from Paris on 24 September 1794, predicting even this partially revived liberty of the press and expression "will overthrow the Jacobins."[17] She was right. Pressure to bring the terroristes and *vandalistes* (cultural vandals) to book mounted, while provincial Jacobin clubs, long repressed, began to grasp that responsibility for the Terror, repression, vandalism, and Robespierre's despotism extended far beyond Robespierre's own immediate circle. When Robespierre betrayed the Revolution, asked one pamphlet expressing this deepening trauma, "what were you doing, mother?" The Paris Jacobins, answered this tract, had continually bolstered Robespierre's image among the sansculottes. In fact, they were equally guilty, the "foyer of the conspiracy," the true "arsenal" of "the subversion" that engineered the 2 June 1793 coup, wrecking the Revolution and the people's hopes. Even now, in the autumn of 1794, Paris Jacobins still defended Collot d'Herbois, Billaud-Varenne, and Barère while harassing the shopkeepers.[18] "Oh mother, how perverse you are!" Ludicrous pretexts were being adduced to justify still keeping the proscribed Brissotin deputies behind bars. The ridiculous claim that they were really "royalists" just repeated the flagrant lies used by Collot d'Herbois on 31 May 1793 in mobilizing the poor faubourgs against Brissotin republican democrats accused of donning the white cockade.[19]

There was no way the Thermidorians and New Jacobins could halt the erosion of their position. At the level of the provincial Jacobin clubs, the return of ousted Brissotins, and counterpurges reversing the Montagnard ideological purges of June 1793, proceeded through the autumn. At Caen, Cherbourg, Falaise, and Le Mans, the Brissotin sympathizers ejected fifteen months earlier were rehabilitated toward the end of October.[20] By late October, anti-Jacobin revulsion seethed in the Paris streets, the resurgence of the Muscadins, or so-called Gilded Youth, featuring considerable numbers of rightists and sons of nobles. France grew more and more divided but with much of the populace boiling with fury against the terroristes, expessing a *revanchisme* rhetorical, political, and cultural. Elegantly clad Muscadins began attacking the wearers of typical Jacobin attire in the streets, drowning out the "Marseillaise" and smashing the symbols of the Marat cult. To soften this vindictive fury, the Convention felt driven to adopt more and more measures against those responsible for the Terror, distancing themselves increasingly from the now discredited Jacobins. Whatever the reservations of a Babeuf, Varlet, or Antonelle, in reality there was no alternative, if the Revolution was to be rescued, but to revert to a neo-Brissotin logic and strategy, repudiating not just Robespierre but also Marat and all the rest. On 9 November, a Muscadin mob stormed and ransacked the Jacobins' meeting hall, smashing windows and beating up everyone present. The club, declared a source of serious public disorder by the

Convention, was closed on 11 November 1794, three and half months after Robespierre's overthrow. This was a massive symbolic setback for populism and the Montagne, but an unavoidable, necessary symbolic step toward renewing the Revolution of 1788–93.

By December, the anti-Montagnard offensive had acquired unstoppable momentum. More traumatized survivors reemerged from the shadows and began asserting themselves, among them Louvet, who suddenly resurfaced and reminded the deputies that he had been the first to publicly defy Robespierre and denounce his tyranny and crimes. Robespierre, whom even the painter David now deemed "repulsive,"[21] had gone, but many of the vilest malefactors who had betrayed the Revolution had still not been disgraced and punished. If Hébert, Hanriot, Couthon, Saint-Just, and Fleuriot-Lescot had, happily for mankind, all been guillotined, why were Amar and Barère still sitting in the Convention? Louvet demanded his own readmittance to the legislature, specifically to confront these perpetrators of atrocities.[22] Such voices could no longer be ignored. Carrier, responsible for shooting, guillotining, and drowning thousands, was now arrested and brought to trial. Guillotined to general applause on 15 December, his demise helped dampen the continuing endemic conflict in the Vendée and Brittany, where many former armed rebels laid down their arms under the provisional amnesty of September 1794 and the Republic's general amnesty of January 1795.[23]

Little of this helped stabilize the Revolution, however, since chronic shortages and high food prices again rendered the winter of 1794–95 dreadfully harsh for the needy, helping revive sansculottism as a powerful destabilizing threat to the Convention and the Republic. Royalism gained ground. Lack of bread at affordable prices renewed the basis for violent protest and insurrection, enabling disgruntled, committed revolutionaries appealing to the sansculottes to again fuse dissatisfaction in the streets with orchestrated pressure for popular sovereignty, price controls, and renewed Jacobin control. Calls for implementation of the 1793 Constitution resounded in section assemblies and cafés. Protest posters appeared in the streets; subversive meetings convened in many places. Prominent among those inciting popular unrest against the vacillating Convention, and propagating talk of insurrection, were Babeuf and Antonelle. On 29 January 1795, the Convention ordered Babeuf's arrest, the police tracking him down in February. He was imprisoned this time at Arras for seven months until amnestied in October 1795.

Among pamphlets maintaining that the 31 May and 2 June

insurrections were not the popular triumphs they had been projected as, but a charade perverting the Revolution and destroying those who had made it, was *De l'Intérêt des Comités de la Convention Nationale*, by Roederer. Having survived in hiding, he only fully reemerged in January 1795, denouncing the Terror and Robespierre in the *Journal de Paris* and elsewhere, and demanding immediate rehabilitation of the seventy-one.[24] Another powerful anti-Jacobin reproach was *Rappellez vos collègues* by Jean-Baptiste-Moise Jollivet (1753–1815), printed on Mme. Gorsas's press. The Revolution would be saved, claimed Jollivet, congratulating the Convention on guillotining Carrier, only when the pernicious rift dividing "les républicains les plus sincères," that is, the genuine Old Jacobins and the Brissotins, was healed. Restoring the Convention's shattered integrity and saving the Revolution meant disavowing the wrong turn of 31 May and 2 June 1793. For this, the Convention must rehabilitate the imprisoned and other surviving Brissotin deputies illegally suspended from the Convention for a year and half. First to unmask Robespierre's betrayal, they had been amply justified. One needed only to meet honest sansculottes from Paris's poorest sections to know that they sincerely regretted having been duped by Robespierre's lies and the scoundrels and hypocrites he had recruited: "as much as they were the dupes of these men eighteen months ago, they detest them now."[25]

Another pamphlet proclaiming 31 May and 2 June a "great crime" that violated the people's sovereignty was the work of the fervent Rousseauiste anti-enlightener Michel-Edme Petit. Petit deplored the systematic deceit plied by the insurgent leaders in Paris on 31 May and 2 June, and their constant abuse of language, the perversion of the terms "people" and "liberty" so characteristic of Robespierre, his employing the term "the people" exclusively to mean himself. The 1793 democratic Constitution, Petit reminded readers, was not the work of the Montagne but the democratic republicans whom they so basely supplanted. Among those Petit assailed was the pro-Montagne lawyer Robert Lindet (1746–1825), even if he was among the least compromised of the Committee of Public Safety under the Terror. Did Lindet not still maintain that the 2 June rising represented the people's aspirations and that the 1792 September massacres were "the work of the people"?[26]

As the myth of Marat, the journée of 31 May, and Jacobin uprightness disintegrated, throughout France plaster busts of Marat, the false *L'Ami du peuple*, were smashed by the hundreds. On 8 February 1795, only five months after his entombment, Marat had to be ceremonially *dépanthéonisé* amid rapturous applause. It was an event truly signaling the resuscitation of the Revolution. Before long, it was usual to insult or stamp on images of Marat and Lepeletier in provincial towns. Indeed, early 1795 witnessed an overwhelming psychological and cultural reaction against Maratisme, Montagnard sansculottism, Terror, and intolerant egalitarianism, a generalized revulsion against Robespierre's "tout populaire" that rapidly turned into a feverish craze, replacing Jacobin "virtue" with antiausterity, a blaze of finery, elegant fashion, fine food, and drink. Fashionable restaurants proliferated as never before. Women's fashions, not least in official circles, changed dramatically. Overt elegance and frivolity with an erotic allure powerfully revived, as did prostitution.[27]

Josephine Beauharnais, released from prison after Thermidor, Juliette Récamier, and Térésa Tallien (1773–1835) emerged as the most glamorous of the fashionable Parisian ladies leading the triumphant new trend in fashion—Greek Revival–style flimsy dresses with astoundingly low necklines flaunting the female bosom, plus jewelry.[28] Térésa, a famous beauty, daughter of a Madrid banker and courtier of French origin, as the divorced former wife of a noble émigré, the last marquis of Fontenay, had been imprisoned at Bordeaux in October 1793 under the Law of Suspects. Struck by her beauty, Tallien, then *réprésentant en mission* at Bordeaux, freed her and made her his mistress. Her moderating influence on him, and overtly anti-Jacobin style, caused Robespierre to have her rearrested in Paris through the Comité de Salut Public. Her imprisonment at La Force contributed to Tallien's breaking with Robespierre in July 1794. Among the first freed after Robespierre's overthrow, she then helped free others, earning her nickname "Notre Dame de Thermidor." In December 1794, she and Tallien married amid general acclaim. "Une grande dame, célèbre par sa beauté, son esprit, et ses grâces," her elegance, flimsy dresses, many love affairs, and reputation as one of the Terror's fiercest opponents, made her a constant focus of attention.[29] Barras was among her lovers.

The frantic partying of the winter of 1794–95, though, was just a palliative, not a sign of forgetting. The deep rift in the country and the chronic political difficulties it generated persisted unresolved. Rank-and-file republicans found it far easier to renounce Robespierriste austerity and Marat than to rehabilitate Brissotins or reject the Montagne's view of the September massacres and the sansculottes' role in 31 May and 2 June 1793. Only hesitantly and tentatively did the Old Jacobins, struggling to come to terms with the catastrophe, especially surviving

Dantonistes and Hébertistes, join with outcast Brissotins, apportioning blame, punishing the guilty, and ascertaining how far the Convention had erred. On 6 February erupted a particularly "violent discussion" in the Assembly over the case of the editor of the *Spectateur français*, Pierre-Firmin de Lacroix (1743–ca. 1827), a professor of public law who was considered a covert royalist and counterrevolutionary. Certain deputies wished to send the arrested man before the department of Paris's "criminal tribunal" for trial as a counterrevolutionary, but this, objected others, contradicted "all principles of justice and legislation." Press liberty must be restored. A war of words ensued. "Do you [the Thermidorians] think we are still at 22nd Prairial (10 June 1794)," demanded Jean Pelet de la Lozère (d. 1842), one day to be a leader of the Revolution of 1830, "when Robespierre labeled us 'royalistes' simply because we were not criminals? Royalists are insurgents aspiring to seize power, willing to murder, pillage, and lie. The people have been ceaselessly perplexed for five years [i.e., since the split between liberal monarchists and republicans in 1790] by denominations like *Fayettiste, clubiste, modéré, fédéraliste, Feuillant, royaliste*." The people should hear the truth.[30]

Duhem, a leading member of the Comité de Sûreté Générale and implacable antagonist of libertarian journalists (and priests), led those defending Jacobin authoritarianism on this occasion. Under present laws a mandatory death sentence applied to anyone publicly propagating royalism, the grounds on which Lacroix was remanded. "Do you not understand," Duhem urged the chamber, "that those demanding freedom of expression nurtured perfidious designs? Do you not know that rascals frequenting the Palais-Royal, the Gilded Youth, persecute and attack Patriotes? The *peuple doré*, the *brillante jeunesse* following Fréron make war on the Jacobins and *sans-culottes*. Royalism and aristocracy gain ground on all sides while the Convention stands idly by!" His unreformed Montagnard Jacobinism was greeted with cries of indignation, yells of "lock him up in the Abbaye!" The Assembly did actually vote for Duhem to cool off in the Abbaye for three days, despite another veteran Montagnard, Choudieu, protesting that he had not insulted the Convention but merely stated the truth. Choudieu was shouted down by members reminding him that he had been the accuser of the "virtuous Philippeaux," whose reputation, along with those of Desmoulins and Danton, was now fully restored.

By February 1795, the Thermidorians had lost their grip, but it remained unclear what had replaced it.[31] A besieged, discredited regime struggled to check the inevitable, growing surge of disorderly opposition. A new revolutionary rationale was needed. Parisians witnessing the scandalous scene provoked by Duhem, affirmed Barras, will not again be the "dupes of villains" plotting civil strife: "we must make unremitting war on both *royalistes* and *terroristes*," a summons loudly applauded. Lawyer Jean-François Reubell (1747–1807) heartily agreed, repeatedly equating "aristocracy" and *terrorisme* as the twin dangers facing the Revolution, justifying "putting them on the same line" because their aspirations and goals were similar—both vilifying and seeking to dissolve the Convention. Besides needing to confront resurgent monarchism and terrorisme simultaneously, the Convention felt bound to dismantle Robespierre's Cult of the Supreme Being while also curbing any remaining impulse behind coercive de-Christianization. Religion had been a chronic problem for the Revolution throughout. Most of the Convention deputies were deists, or at least deism was the creed most often admitted to in discussion among them.[32] But few now doubted that the Republic had to jettison Robespierre's much-ridiculed Cult of the Supreme Being without either embracing the decimated and discarded constitutional church or relaxing proscription of the refractory clergy.

Accordingly, the Convention entered upon an entirely new path, edging further toward secularization and democratic modernity. In September 1794, a degree of legal separation of religion and state was introduced, permitting the Catholic mass in private halls, apartments, and some monastic chapels, while large churches remained out of bounds to the pious. Complete separation ensued after a remarkable clash in the Convention on 21 February, initiated by the irreligious ex-Protestant Boissy d'Anglas. He loudly rejected both Catholic dominance of society and the de-Christianizing intolerance and dogmatism of Hébert and Chaumette. This momentous debate ended with the Convention dismantling whatever remained of the Montagne's antireligious oppression and restoring full liberty of conscience and religious practice. But rather than revert to the 1790–93 pattern with the constitutional clergy maintained by state and society, formal separation of church and state—legally, financially, and ceremonially—followed. Under the decree of 21 February 1795, no one could be hindered from practicing the religion of his or her choice, nor compelled to contribute to any cult; the Republic would not pay the salaries of any clergy of whatever denomination.[33] During March 1795, some larger churches were allowed to reopen for Catholic worship, albeit strictly on the basis that state and church were now wholly distinct and public displays of priestly vestments, ceremonies in the streets and squares, and ringing church bells remained forbidden. Much of what remained of the constitutional clergy at this point abandoned the Abbé Grégoire and his colleagues, making their peace with orthodoxy.

A clear solution to the religious conflict was found. But how was the Convention to deal with its other difficulties? As the subsistence crisis deepened and the sansculotte mood grew uglier, the Convention adopted a riot-control act, proposed by Sieyès, on 21 March. On the 27 and 28 March 1795, fresh bread riots erupted in Paris, followed by attempts to march on the Convention, though this was nothing more than a prelude to major further unrest, culminating in the journée of 12 Germinal (1 April). This began with crowds mobbing the bakeries and with women fighting over loaves of bread but turned into an immense mass demonstration that besieged the Convention hall for many hours. Crowds of many thousands demanded bread, renewal of the Maximum, and the democratic Constitution of 1793. Section leaders used the opportunity to harangue the deputies for the release of hard-line Montagnards imprisoned after Thermidor, which placed the Convention's Jacobin remnant in a peculiarly awkward position, caught between their agreement with sansculotte demands and their needing not to be seen fomenting a new wave of populist authoritarianism. Fobbed off with vague promises, the marchers were eventually persuaded to leave empty-handed. National Guard reinforcements under General Jean-Charles Pichegru (1761–1804), once a simple soldier, later president of the Jacobin society of Besançon and conqueror of Holland, energetically restored order.

Germinal, a rising widely attributed to neo-Jacobin intrigue, if not in its economic origins then in its direction and demands,[34] had the opposite effect to that envisaged by the section organizers as far as the Montagne's faltering grip on the Convention, and the imprisoned Montagnards, were concerned. Billaud-Varenne, Collot d'Herbois, Barère, and Vadier had already been detained pending trial on 2 March, following investigations by a special commission into their activities on the Robespierriste executive committees. Boosted by Germinal, proceedings against the terroristes accelerated. The Convention's leadership, now decisively weighted against the Thermidorians, ordered a much broader crackdown on authoritarian populists. Amar, Duhem, Choudieu, Lecointre, Levasseur, Cambon, and Léonard Bourdon figured among protagonists of the Terror now arrested in Paris, and Bayle and Granet in Marseille. Numerous sansculotte activists were interned, and the National Guard was reorganized to create a firmer barrier against popular insurrection.[35]

It was grimly ironic that Billaud-Varenne, Collot d'Herbois, Barère, and Vadier, tyrants who had massacred thousands, were now tried according to the strict letter of the law, under scrupulous new rules of procedure. All were pronounced guilty, but they were sentenced not to execution but deportation to the Guianas, causing immense chagrin to surviving widows and relatives intent on revenge, though deportation to Devil's Island, off Cayenne, was supposedly a virtual death sentence, slow and uncomfortable. The four were transported to the Atlantic coast for embarkation, but Barére managed to get left behind, causing a Convention wit to remark that "it was the first time Barère had missed the wind"; in October, he escaped and subsequently remained in hiding at Bordeaux for the next four years. Vadier too escaped and successfully hid.[36] Billaud-Varenne reached Cayenne but eventually also escaped, reaching Mexico under a false name where he joined a Dominican monastery; he later embarked on a new career as an official in Saint-Domingue, surviving until 1819. Only Collot d'Herbois obligingly expired in Cayenne in January 1796.

Fouquier-Tinville, on the other hand, following a thirty-nine-day meticulously correct trial for gross perversion of justice, *was* publicly executed in Paris, dispatched on 7 May, coldly arrogant to the last, answering jeers with defiant scowls, guillotined with fifteen other Tribunal Révolutionnaire judges to the joy of the crowds. From April 1795, a new large-scale, and now more general, roundup of former Montagnards implicated in the Terror proceeded throughout France (and also Belgium).[37] In Toulon, the authorities arrested "partisans of Robespierre" while simultaneously also imprisoning royalists. In a huge sweep across France, many thousands of suspects were interned, though most were afterward released under the October amnesty. A minority were deported or sentenced to longer terms of imprisonment. In the southeast, reaction against the Thermidorians was particularly *revanchiste* and violent. Psychologically, Lyon, of course, represented a special case, owing to the city's still severely traumatized condition and the unparalleled barbarity of the repression there during autumn 1793.

By April 1795, Joseph de Boisset (1748–1813), the Convention *réprésentant* sent to Lyon to stabilize the city, faced an unruly, explosive situation permeated by revulsion against everything and everyone associated with Robespierre and the Terror. Republican, anti-Catholic, and antiroyalist, Boisset was one of the honest Montagnards and detractors of Marat who found himself boxed more and more into an awkward corner the more conscious he became of the need to restore justice and make amends. The more he acknowledged the misdeeds of the Montagne, the more he exposed himself to accusations of encouraging overt anti-Jacobinism and royalist resurgence. His biggest problem was the secret "companies of Jesus" that began exacting vengeance on known Jacobins, initially with small bands pouncing on terroristes individually in the streets. Before long, Boisset faced a full-scale "White Terror" perpetrated by roaming "murder gangs" he proved powerless to halt. On 4 May 1795, major rioting erupted, with insurgents attacking the Lyon prisons to exact vengeance on the Montagnard internees. More than a hundred former terroristes were hacked to death.[38] Amid the paroxysm of anti-Jacobin fervor, playing the "Marseillaise" ceased in Lyon for a time. Comparable outbreaks occurred at Marseille, Nîmes, and Aix-en-Provence. Many southeastern rural areas also suffered the sporadic violence of the White Terror, marauding gangs knifing or lynching victims, who besides known Jacobins, in several areas included Protestants and, around Carpentras, also Jews.[39] But the violence provoked counterrisings by Jacobins deeming themselves victims of a vicious aristocratic-royalist crusade. Toulon's arsenal workers rose in insurrection on 17 May, seized the arsenals and weapons supply, and marched on Marseille, intent on releasing the imprisoned Montagnards there, shouting "Vive la Montagne!" It required a week of operations by a force of regular troops and National Guard to disperse the insurgents. When this rising was suppressed, fifty-two insurgents were tried and guillotined by a special commission set up to identify those behind it.[40]

During 1795, the Convention pursued ex-Montagnards but liberalized and especially democratized too hesitantly and slowly for many committed republicans. How could the Republic be stabilized, the Convention's authority bolstered, and the principle of representative democracy restored? Constitutionally, as modified in 1795–96, the Republic by no means adjusted as conservatively as is usually claimed. Vacillating over whether to reinstate the 1793 Constitution or not, the Assembly voted on 18 April to establish an eleven-man commission—headed by Sieyès, Daunou, Boissy d'Anglas, the deist ideologue La Révellière-Lépeaux, and the Breton jurist Lanjuinais, who had only just resumed his seat in the Convention, having been one of the chief Brissotin detractors of the Montagne during the months preceding the 2 June 1793 coup. This Commission des Onze, replacing a prior, smaller Comité de Constitution, was charged with considering whether the 1793

Constitution (which in essence was not a "Jacobin" constitution at all but a Brissotin one modified) should be readopted, and, if so, preparing the ground. Between 3 April and 22 August 1795, the commission closely examined and debated the 1793 Constitution. But to resolve disagreements among themselves and counter the resurgent sansculottism of Germinal, the commission eventually opted to replace the 1793 text with a completely new constitution, a project easier once the unbending Sieyès withdrew from the process. The emerging consensus to replace the 1793 text, shaped by the growing impulse to curb sansculottism, further converted the June 1793 Constitution into the rallying cry of Jacobin opposition and sansculotte insurrection.[41]

The 1795 Constitution was hammered out against a background of escalating political and social turmoil. On 20 May, and especially 21 May 1795 (3 Prairial), after days of disturbances, the biggest popular outbreak in Paris of the entire Revolution since 1792 occurred. Erupting shortly after the Toulon insurrection, this upheaval completed the discrediting of direct democracy in the Convention's eyes. Some rioters were swayed by an anonymous pamphlet, *Insurrection du peuple pour obtenir du pain et réconquerir ses droits*, that appeared a day or two before, which fused demand for bread and price controls with an exhortation to rise for the Rights of Man and the 1793 Constitution. The huge crowds that mobilized on 21 May for the march on the Convention following the sounding of the tocsin in the Faubourg Saint-Antoine, and other artisan eastern suburbs where the section assemblies had lately revived, yelled "Vive la Montagne!" and demanded bread and the 1793 Constitution. The slogan "Bread and the Constitution of 1793" was also worn by many pinned to or tucked into their hats. The Paris sections aimed to capture the government and the National Guard for the people. Some of the National Guard did defect and join the rioters.[42]

Once again, sansculottes surrounded and invaded the Convention. Space being limited, most of the multitude stayed outside in the Place du Carrousel. One of the younger neo-Brissotin deputies, Jean-Bertrand Ferraud (1764–95), attempting to stop the vanguard breaking down the doors, was shot and finished off with knives. Cries of "Cut off his head!" resulted in decapitation of his corpse. The Convention's "president," Boissy d'Anglas, detested by sansculottes as a Brissotin opponent of the Maximum (his nickname was Boissy-Famine), when threatened with pikes, on one of which was affixed the bloodied head of Ferraud, showed commendable sangfroid, calmly saluting the head but refusing to budge. The sansculottes yelled their demands; most of the Assembly listened, unswayed. Several Montagnard deputies, headed by the mathematician Romme, Jean-Michel Duroy (1753–95), and Pierre Soubrany (1752–95)—a friend of Romme's and a noble army officer and mayor of Riom whom some Prairial demonstrators wanted as their military leader—however, openly sided with the crowds. Regular troops and loyal National Guards massed nearby. A bloody conflict was avoided though, and, at length, after no less than eleven hours of nerve-wracking confrontation and, according to Louvet, frightening menaces, the demonstrators drifted away again with nothing concrete accomplished. There was in fact considerable sympathy in the Convention regarding deprivation and the bread price, but less and less for popular insurrection, direct democracy, and the 1793 Constitution.[43]

News of the Paris mass uprising thrilled militant egalitarians and Jacobins around the country, among them Antonelle, Jullien, and Babeuf, the last still in jail at Arras. When the armed rebellion revived the next day, announced by ringing the tocsin, immense crowds gathered and yet again converged on the Convention. Troops and gendarmes surrounding the Convention hall wavered, and then dispersed, many defecting to the insurgents. Crowds burst into the hall, once more intimidating the deputies and wresting resolutions and empty promises. Fortunately for the neo-Brissotin legislature, no populist leader emerged with the prestige and skill to channel and direct the popular pressure sufficiently to gain power. The mob was again eventually persuaded to depart with nothing tangible accomplished. By 23 May the Faubourg Saint-Antoine was ringed by troops and armed men from other sections. The concrete outcome of Prairial, as of Germinal, was a further forceful reaction against the menaces of Jacobin populism. Montagnard intransigence, combined with the unruliness of the sansculottes, had by now convinced most deputies that the common people were just too ignorant, unpredictable, and easily manipulated to receive the right to directly elect the National Assembly. The uprising reinforced the arguments of Daunou, Boissy d'Anglas, and the constitutional commission that the representative principle needed strengthening, the principle of universal suffrage qualifying, and "the people" prevented from directly intimidating the legislature.[44]

A vigorous crackdown followed. The sections were scoured for the "men of blood" who had supported Robespierre. At least three thousand agitators and suspects of one sort or another were detained in Paris over the next week, Antonelle among them, although most were released shortly afterward. By 10 Prairial, forty-seven insurgents had been arrested in the Droits-de-l'Homme section alone. The specific grounds for their detention were usually less involvement in the Germinal and Prairial insurrections than a longer record of Jacobin activism in the sections under Robespierre's ascendancy or else as *septembriseurs* implicated in the 1792 prison massacres.[45] A special commission erected to deal with unrest in the capital tried the murderers of Ferraud, who were sent to the guillotine along with thirty-six others. At the same time, a further sixty-one Montagnard deputies were purged from the Assembly, eleven dubbed "agents of tyranny" and accused of condoning the insurrection in the hope of recovering power for the Jacobins. The ten most implicated were tried for treason during June; six, including Romme, were found guilty and sentenced to death. Romme, worthy egalitarian to the last (he had regularly donated part of his salary as a deputy to the poor), Soubrany, and two others eluded the guillotine by stabbing themselves beforehand in an act of final Montagnard defiance. With their deaths, a grand total of no less than eighty-six Convention deputies of all stripes had died violent deaths linked to the Revolution since the summer of 1793, by execution, assassination, or suicide.[46]

Prairial eliminated all prospect of a straightforward reversion to the 1793 Constitution.[47] Painstakingly, over the summer of 1795, the commission compiled an exceptionally detailed new constitutional text, couched in 377 articles (as against 208 for the 1791 monarchist Constitution and 124 articles for that of June 1793).[48] But though the strategy now was to replace the 1793 Constitution, this does not mean that Boissy d'Anglas, Daunou, Lanjuinais, Guyomar, and the other anti-Montagnards of Brissotin background now assuming the lead turned their back on democracy, or were abandoning revolutionary principles, or reverting to constitutional monarchy (as many in France desired). Theirs was not an unprincipled retreat. Rather, the revolutionary leadership of the summer of 1795 believed democracy had to be restrained and qualified due to the overwhelming need to check popular unruliness, counter the anarchistes' abuse of the term "people," stabilize the Revolution, and conserve its essential principles. Otherwise, they feared (with considerable justification) a descent either into a new Montagnard despotism or else a new monarchism violently reimposed by what they saw as the turbulent, unreasoning plebs. "If the people make bad choices," as Boissy d'Anglas put it in a speech to the Convention on 23 June 1795, "and opt for monarchism, *terrorisme* or *fanaticisme*, the Republic will be lost!"[49]

A lively debate followed. Paine, backed by Lanthenas, joined in the July discussion about the new Constitution by attacking "aristocracy," expounding what became his *Dissertation on First Principles of Government*. Paine termed the right of voting for representatives as "the primary right by which other rights are protected," and therefore the basis of any true democratic republic. Though Pierre Guyomar and other democrats agreed, the Convention's anti-Montagnard majority saw little real alternative but to refashion representative democracy, this time with the representative body's supremacy carefully safeguarded and Rousseauiste direct democracy precluded.[50] Montesquieu's separation of powers, it was felt, should be adopted as an additional safeguard against populist intimidation and violent suborning of the legislature. No other course of action looked plausible after Germinal, especially following the demise of the ten-year-old Louis XVII on 6 June 1795, and the proclaiming among the émigré diaspora of Louis XVI's younger brother, the count of Provence, as "Louis XVIII" king of France. The pretender's announcement of his plans, issued from Austrian Verona, pledged to restore monarchy, ancien régime social hierarchy, and ecclesiastical authority as uncompromisingly as could be conceived. The Convention, consequently, felt equally menaced by revived sansculottism and resurgent royalism. The only way forward, it was agreed, was a fresh constitution designed to fortify the Revolution's core values— representative democracy, republicanism, freedom of expression, minimal religious authority, legal equality, and human rights against both populism and royalism.

During the summer of 1795, the Convention moved to entrench constitutional checks and balances, and lessen the sway of direct democracy.[51] The new Constitution was prefaced by a fresh Declaration of the Rights and Duties of Man and the Citizen, comprising this time twenty-two as against thirty-five articles in 1793. Where both the Condorcet draft of February 1793 and the Hérault constitution affirmed sovereignty to reside "in the whole people," that of September 1795 avoided invoking "the people,"[52] declaring that "the universality of French citizens is the sovereign."[53] Where all three earlier declarations of rights proclaimed la volonté générale without mentioning division of powers, the 1795 text redefined volonté générale as "the law as approved by the majority of citizens or their representatives," while simultaneously embracing division of powers. Where the earlier constitutions provided for a single-chamber legislature, the new Constitution provided for two chambers. Where the Condorcet declaration omits supernatural presence, that of August 1795, like the Hérault declaration of June 1793, invokes "the presence of the Supreme Being." Critics of the new Constitution abounded; most republicans and democrats, though, rallied behind it.

After a three-week debate, with only one deputy, Diderot's old comrade Alexandre Deleyre, holding out for a single chamber, the new Constitution was approved by the Convention on 22 August. As in the summer of 1793, approval by the legislature needed prompt, popular endorsement, and this soon followed (6 September 1795).[54] A retreat from the democratic provisions of Condorcet or Hérault in some respects, the 1795 Constitution nevertheless remained unparalleled and impressively democratic compared with everything else then available in the world, including the then British or United States constitutions. As an embodiment of modern democratic and egalitarian principles, it assuredly had no rival at all outside France. Every male older than twenty-one who paid taxes was declared a citizen, together with every man who had fought for the Republic, whether paying taxes or not. Most adult males retained the right to vote in the first stage of elections for the legislature. The 1795 Constitution was less democratic than that of 1793 principally in that the legislature's deputies were now appointed not directly, as under the 1793 Constitution by the electorate through the primary assemblies, but by assemblies of electeurs. The 1793 Constitution grouped the primary assemblies in batches of fifteen or sixteen so that each deputy was elected by securing a majority vote among roughly 7,500 adult male voters representing around 40,000 people.[55] Now the voters chose only electeurs empowered to choose the deputies in each department, each elector representing 200 citizens. To qualify as an elector one needed to be older than twenty-five and possess property assessed at 200 days of work (or rent a house, or have income status at an equivalent level), property qualifications proposed by Boissy d'Anglas, Sieyès, and other leading figures. In communities of less than 6,000 inhabitants, property qualifications were adjusted one-quarter lower.[56]

Under the Constitution endorsed by the Convention on 22 August 1795, elections replacing one-third of the Assembly's deputies were to be held each year. The lower chamber, or Council of Five Hundred, remained the sole body empowered to initiate legislation. The upper chamber, or Conseil des Anciens, comprising 250 older legislators, was charged with scrutinizing, and approving or rejecting, legislative proposals. Executive power was invested in a Directoire of Five elected by the Conseil des Anciens from a list compiled by the Five Hundred. One director would be replaced each year. The directors were not ministers entrusted with separate departments and spheres of activity, but supposed to act collectively, albeit each had his particular specialism. A widely appreciated feature was that the new Constitution guaranteed all accused individuals the right to unfettered defending counsel, as already prefigured in the trials of Barère, Collot d'Herbois, and Billaud-Varenne.

Devised to repel Jacobin populism and riotous pressuring of the legislature, as well as all forms of monarchism, aristocracy, and reviving religious authority, the new Constitution espoused representative democracy against popular, direct democracy. With most adult males possessing the vote, the Constitution possessed a more democratic character than has often been suggested and did command widespread respect. One proof of this was that France's now huge and steadily expanding army operated efficiently under its control while remaining steadfastly subordinate to this newly reconstituted republican authority until 1799. "The best generals in Europe," commented Madame de Staël later, "obeyed five directors, three of whom were only lawyers." Love of country and freedom still sufficed to make the troops "grant more respect to the law than to their general, should he wish to place himself above it."

Had Britain, Prussia, and Austria desired peace, the Revolution could in fact have stabilized on the basis of the 1795 semidemocratic Constitution, or so at any rate she believed.[57] This seemed and was perhaps a conceivable outcome, though the 1795 Constitution did also dangerously split the republican Left committed to the Revolution. Militant egalitarians loyal to the legacy of Romme vocally resisted in the name of the 1793 Constitution, convinced (with reason) that the motive for displacing it with the new Constitution was to weaken the voice of—if not wholly disenfranchise—the poor. Babeuf pronounced the new Constitution "atrocious," a travesty compared to its predecessor, a fresh set of chains.[58]

While the 1795 Constitution was rejected in militant neo-Jacobin populist circles and bracketed with the 1791 Constitution as an "aristocratic charter" intended to tighten the people's fetters, that of 1793 continued to be venerated by some as a preferable framework and "a great step towards true equality."[59] Overall, there was indeed much to criticize in the new situation of the Republic. In theory, the 1795 Constitution guaranteed full freedom of expression and the press. If properly respected, it would ensure legislative supremacy, genuinely free primary assemblies, and freedom to debate locally in clubs.[60] But press freedom revived in 1795–96 only tentatively, remaining in practice more than half blocked. Force of circumstance and practical difficulties persuaded the legislature that restrictions adopted earlier could not be either quickly or easily dispensed with. There were numerous compromises, some rather unedifying. Marie-Joseph Chénier, now again an influential deputy backed by Louvet, defended restrictions aimed against royalism but plainly also against authoritarian populism, demanding exile for life for those publicly defaming Convention deputies in writing or at meetings. This measure passed on 1 May 1795 (12 Floreal, Year III).[61] The Abbé Morellet, a veteran foe of the Revolution but nevertheless a fervent advocate of press freedom, accused Chénier in a pamphlet of dragging the press back under a *despotisme* like that of Robespierre. The number of pamphlets published in France dwindled further, from 601 in 1794 to 569 in 1795 and only 182 in 1796, though this was now predominently due to fatigue and disillusionment with revolutionary politics.[62] Yet, despite these shortcomings, most democratic republican Left sentiment did rally behind the 1795 Constitution, intent on fighting the immediate twin challenges of revived Jacobin populism and resurgent monarchism, encouraged to adopt this stance by the continuing external pressure.

Britain and the European powers showed little inclination to moderate their insistence on restoring monarchism, aristocracy, and ecclesiastical authority. Except in recently conquered Holland, there was no official foreign approval or support whatsoever for the 1795 Constitution, or the Republic's proclaimed goal of orderly representative democracy. The British remained in occupation of Corsica. In March 1795, an attempt planned by Napoleon to invade Corsica from Toulon was thwarted by the British navy.[63] In late June 1795, the British landed a French royalist expeditionary force of 3,000 armed rebels, a mixture of émigrés and recruits levied from among captured French seamen and fishermen, at Quiberon Bay, in Brittany with the aim of rekindling major royalist-Catholic insurgency in the West. Their arrival indeed evoked great jubilation and fervor and some 10,000 Breton Chouans joyfully joined the invasion, unsettling a wide territory. They had only days, though, to celebrate the restoration of religion and the old order. On 3 July, the republican commander in Brittany, Louis-Lazare Hoche (1768–97), once an ordinary soldier in king's army, routed the insurgent army, capturing 6,000 men. Under the draconian laws in force, no less than 640 returning émigrés found in arms were shot by firing squads, along with 108 Chouans. The commander of the Whites in the Vendée, François Charette (1763–96), retaliated by shooting hundreds of republican prisoners. A second expedition, under the French pretender's younger brother, the Comte d'Artois, embarked at Portsmouth for the Vendée in early September. This second émigré invasion captured an island off the coast, the Île d'Yeu, but Hoche lined the opposite coast in sufficient strength to prevent any linkup with Charette's men, obliging the British, in mid-November, to ship the remnants back to England. In March 1796, Hoche captured and executed Charette, extinguishing organized counterrevolution in the West for the moment.

Radical Enlightenment Revived

The struggle within the Revolution, the fight for the Revolution's soul during the period from Thermidor to the neo-Jacobin defeats of 1797, was a struggle for political control couched in an ideological struggle steeped in polemics and recrimination. Neo-Brissotins aimed to reconnect the Revolution to its radically enlightened roots, neo-Jacobins to the common people. The Terror was a repression of opinion, free expression, religion, and the individual. Opposition neo-Jacobins increasingly sought to justify this, stressing virtue and republican purity, as opposed to selfish individualism, echoing Rousseau; unlike those defending the 1795 Constitution and the conduct of the regime, they unstintingly eulogized the uprightness and purity of the masses.[64] The nub of the quarrel between pro-regime republicans and opposition democrats during 1795–97 was over how far the 1795 Constitution secured the Revolution's authentic goals and how far correcting the Revolution's course and reinstating the "real" Revolution's principles involved rehabilitating the Brissotins. The quarrel was heavily embedded in intellectual controversy throughout.

Only five weeks after Thermidor, the Abbé Grégoire delivered the first of several reports in the Convention highlighting the destruction caused by the antireligious and cultural vandalism of the Montagnard tyranny.[65] Besides destruction of art, images, and churches, encompassed within the "vandalism" Grégoire passionately denounced was the antiintellectualism, attack on libraries, and rejection of the Enlightenment itself. He expressly pointed to Robespierre's frequently repeated and insistent sallies against the men of learning and intellect. He directly linked this pervasive intellectual and cultural vandalism to the political oppression Robespierre and Robespierrisme had instigated. Aside from Babeuf, Antonelle, Maréchal, and Buonarroti, now already ceasing their earlier disparagement of the tyrant, practically everyone in France roundly denounced Robespierre's crimes and betrayal of the Revolution. Like the Convention itself, during the years 1795–99, nearly all France's pro-Revolution editors, publicists, and ideologues committed themselves to combating Jacobin appeals to the masses, unconstitutionality and populist authoritarianism, fed by sansculotte dissatisfaction.

If Babeuf's ally, Buonarroti, had already begun what later became an unapologetic campaign to revive Robespierre's prestige and reputation,[66] it was clear to most that there could be no stabilization of the Republic or consolidation of republican freedoms without a sustained, nationally concerted effort—political, military, organizational, educational, cultural, and ideological—to disavow and discredit Montagnard authoritarianism comprehensively. Yet wholly extirpating Robespierre's legacy while any vestiges of the Thermidorian regime persisted was impeded at every step. Rehabilitation of the Left republicans, pursued and decimated by Robespierre, ensued only sporadically over many months. Not until the spring of 1795 did full, unqualified rehabilitation of the values of Left republicans become even a plausible goal. Yet, without a Brissotin resurgence, no revival of the Revolution's core values could attain logical cogency, sincerity, or much substance. Only with Maratisme and the Montagne, as well as Robespierre's doctrines altogether rejected in practice and theory, could constitutionalism, human rights, religious toleration, and freedom of expression (albeit within limitations) be restored—and, equally, reaffirmation of Radical Enlightenment, the source of the Revolution's ideology of human rights and democratic freedoms, again direct the main flow of official thought and culture.

Official rehabilitation of Condorcet, Helvétius, and the secte philosophique was hence a vital, indispensable step toward relaunching the Revolution of individual liberty, democracy, and freedom of thought. If Montesquieu's separation of powers now also played a part, the prime intellectual inspiration remained that of the radical stream. Condorcet not only provided the "real Revolution," reviving in 1795 with its best and most systematic philosophical defense, but afforded the reviving secte philosophique with their essential vision of education and the social sciences as their primary tools for furthering the quest for universal human happiness and the common welfare buttressed by individual human rights.[67] Radical ideas reemerged in 1795–97, fomented and encouraged not just by the new Constitution and legislature but also by partial restoration of freedom of the press, the resumption of orderly, properly grounded juridical procedures, and the Republic's now rapidly expanding education system, as well as the revived culture of republican festivals and theater.

From early 1795, a whole new intellectual climate prevailed in France, characterized by la philosophie's reversion to the special, privileged status it possessed in the Revolution's formative years until June 1793. Several major new reforms introduced during Year III underlined the fact that, besides politics, public ceremonies, and education, daily life in the democratic Republic itself was being reorganized and rationalized on the basis of la philosophie. Among the most notable changes was the official, nationwide introduction of the metric system of weights and measurements adopted after five years of study and preparation on 7 April 1795, less than a week after the journée of 1 Germinal.[68] This was not just a new standard for France but was intended, as it had been since the commencement of the research, in 1790 to constitute a unified, universal, and invariable decimal system, designed to replace the chaotically disparate existing European and global patchwork of measurement systems. The new metric system was one that Condorcet, Talleyrand, and others had conceived as being for all people and for all future time.

That a major text of Condorcet had survived him, an unfinished masterpiece, the *Tableau historique des progrès de l'esprit humain*, expounding the progress of the human spirit, was announced in December 1794. This work, first sketched in 1772, was greatly expanded while Condorcet was in hiding in 1793–94. On 2 April 1795, the Convention accepted Daunou's proposal to publish Condorcet's final book as an official text, at the Republic's expense, in three thousand copies. Afterward, many more were printed, and Garat had large quantities of copies distributed free. For Daunou, this was merely part of his unremitting campaign to persuade the public that social and political wisdom stem from such philosophy and science and decidedly not from Robespierre's cult of the ordinary and Rousseauism.[69] Condorcet's *Tableau* appeared in the spring of 1795, to be followed by five other editions down to 1798. Stendhal, then a radical young officer with Napoleon's army of Italy, later recorded reading it through enthusiastically, two or three times. Editing this text and plans for a complete edition of Condorcet's work, supervised by his widow, Sophie de Grouchy, were entrusted to a group of Condorcet's disciples headed by Cabanis and Garat.[70]

Signs of the Radical Enlightenment's rehabilitation proliferated during late 1794 and 1795. Among the most important was the renewed primary and secondary school plan presented to the Convention on behalf of the education committee on 3 Brumaire of the Year III (25 October 1794) by Lakanal. Approved a week later, it was adopted together with the commission's major reform program for higher education. The plans to accord an automatic right of access to primary education free of charge, provided by teachers paid by the Republic, with a state primary school established for every thousand inhabitants throughout the country, and boys and girls studying the same curriculum, originally devised in 1792–93, were refurbished in their pre-Montagnard format.[71] The Rousseauiste dimension to the educational changes introduced by the Montagne was discarded and the original philosophique inspiration restored at all levels, in the secondary schools with a typically materialist approach to philosophy and study of the human mind.[72]

Implementation was speeded up. A key objective was that the Republic should employ teachers trained and paid by the state. Garat, appointed chairman of the Convention's commission for public education, was entrusted, among other tasks, with supervising the team composing the new textbooks to be used by the state's teachers in the secondary schools. Garat wrote the textbook for history himself; Diderot's former aide, Daubenton, that for natural history, and Volney, back from the Midi, the civics textbook, a work emphasizing liberty, the Rights of Man, and the Constitution.[73]

The Assembly enactments of 1794–95 adopting these educational reforms, later referred to collectively as "the Daunou law," covered everything from primary schools to national festivals. Like Condorcet before him, Daunou urged a symbiotic relationship between public instruction and republican institutions, deeming each structurally dependent on the other.[74] The package exerted a long, profound influence on the subsequent development of French republican education and tradition. Lakanal and Deleyre, among the most philosophique deputies, were appointed to oversee what was intended to be a crucial component, the Paris École Normale. Garat's commission in effect revived Condorcet's plan to establish a higher-learning education institute in Paris as the apex of an integrated national network of écoles centrales immediately under his projected national institute of sciences and arts and pivotal to the new system of primary, secondary, and tertiary education. This École Normale, established on the grounds of the Paris Jardin des Plantes, was for training schoolmasters, not least in secularism

Figure 18. (a) Volney, (b) Daunou.
(a) J. Boilly, portrait of Constantin François Chassebœuf, Count of Volney, lithograph. Paris, Musée Carnavalet, Paris. © Roger-Viollet / The Image Works. (b) *Pierre Claude François Daunou*, engraving. Château de Versailles et de Trianon, Versailles, France. © RMN–Grand Palais / Art Resource, NY.

and republican awareness, and for laying the ground plan for what would eventually become the world's first comprehensive system of state-organized and funded universal education. At the École Normale, students who were at least twenty-one years old, with appropriate educational qualifications and proven civic consciousness and moral caliber, would converge from every part of French society.[75]

The inaugural ceremony of the École Normale, dedicated to teaching civics and secular values as well as the academic disciplines, took place amid high hopes on 20 January 1795 in the amphitheater of the Botanical Gardens with Garat, Volney, La Harpe, Lagrange, Laplace, Monge, Daubenton, and the celebrated chemist, Claude-Louis Berthollet (1748–1822), all delivering celebratory lectures that amply reflected the fact that France now led all Europe in social science, chemistry, and several branches of mathematics. Regular lectures commenced at once with Volney teaching history in the manner introduced by Condorcet, based on the idea of *histoire universelle* and the progress of the human mind, encompassing not only Europe but the Islamic world, China, Japan, and the pre-Muslim Persians, all supposedly progressing toward liberty, human rights, democracy, and republicanism. Condorcet's outright refusal to make "national history," nation-building, and patriotism the core of historical studies infused the new philosophical conception of history and historiography, as did the underlying commitment to metaphysical monism and one-substance philosophy.

Plagued by financial difficulties, the École Normale closed down after a few months, though it was revived again by Napoleon in 1808 (and then again closed by the Restoration monarchy in 1822). But the écoles centrales and the Institut de France in Paris soon figured among the post-Thermidor Revolution's foremost successes. The Institut de France, established by decree in October 1795, was the apex of the whole new system. This national institute for the sciences and arts was intended to replace the old royal academies, suppressed in 1793, and to organize and supervise the whole education system, together with scientific and scholarly research and debate. For the first time in human history, proclaimed Lakanal, the most eminent researchers in the social and natural sciences would, as Condorcet had urged, become the educators of a people. It gathered the most eminent savants and scholars into a single organization at the Republic's heart, dividing them into three classes: (1) mathematical and physical sciences, (2) moral and political sciences, and (3) literature and fine arts. The second class in particular came to embody a revolutionary new approach to research, knowledge, social sciences, and education rooted in the philosophies of Diderot, Helvétius, Beccaria, d'Holbach, and Condorcet.

The Institut was publicly inaugurated on 4 April 1796 with a glittering ceremony held in the newly refurbished exhibition hall of the Musée Nationale des Arts, attended by the entire Directoire and more than fifteen hundred invited guests. A speech by Daunou underlined the necessity for full freedom of thought and independence of research within the Institut and for performing the Institut's public role. The Brissotin director, Letourneur, rejoiced that the philosophes who had made the Revolution "by attacking tyranny and superstition" now finally enjoyed that formal primacy over France's official culture, public instruction, and education that was rightfully theirs.[76] The Institut, hoped the Directoire, would assist the Republic politically and socially by instilling confidence in its laws and institutions, helping revive commerce, agriculture, and industry, promoting medicine and hygiene, advancing military and naval technology, and stimulating urban and architectural improvements.

The philosophe-révolutionnaires viewed the Institut as a kind of National Assembly of the world republic of science and letters, precisely the reason that Marat and Robespierre so abhorred the concept. The nomination in November 1795 of forty-eight principal philosophes, scientists, and scholars to constitute the "electing third," responsible for choosing the other ninety-six members, institutionalized the philosophique ideal that society's leading minds should choose the academic senate and inevitably encouraged rivalry and intrigue as well as lively discussion. Brissot, Condorcet, Desmoulins, Pétion, Cérutti, Volney, Lanjuinais, Lakanal, and the men who had made the democratic Revolution had always maintained that only philosophical reason and its dissemination through society could defeat ignorance, error, and the ingrained popular prejudices nourishing tyranny that rendered society and politics hostages to villainy and inherently irrational, unstable, and repressive. Enlightenment in their eyes was above all a process of eradicating prejudices, ignorance, and mistaken traditional views. Social harmony and stability depended, they believed, on forging rational laws, securing basic freedoms, and ensuring a viable constitution, besides laying an adequate basis in morality, social harmony, and civics to enable society to accomplish its goals, all of which were unattainable, they insisted, without extirpating credulity, intolerance, and religious authority.

Social science conceived as applied moral philosophy based on monism and one-substance philosophy, and the key to constitutional,

political, and social stability within a democratic republican framework, saturated the thinking of the Institut's intellectual leadership,
the group known as the "Idéologues." This group, including Daunou,
Volney, Destutt de Tracy, Ginguené, Lakanal, Deleyre, Roederer, Garat,
Sieyès, Cambacérès, and La Révellière-Lépeaux, had their headquarters
in the Institut's second class, that of moral and political sciences. An
astounding total of no less than twenty-eight of the leading intellectuals elected to the Institut's second class had figured in the revolutionary
legislatures and on their committees, mostly but not entirely among the
Brissotins. Other prominent materialists, atheists, and anti-Christian
deists among their number were Naigeon and Cabanis. Several were associated with the economist Say's *Décade philosophique*, the journal that
virtually became the house review of the Idéologues, a group nurtured
in the circle around Mirabeau and drawn from the salons of Mesdames
Helvétius, Condorcet, and Roland that most explicitly sought to revive
the legacy of the revolutionary parti de philosophie of 1788–93.[77]

The Idéologues, in effect, reconstituted the Radical Enlightenment
in its post-Thermidor aspect. No less than thirty-four members of
the Institut's second class, a strikingly high percentage, had been imprisoned or forced to emigrate during the Terror, including Daunou,
Ginguené, Destutt de Tracy, Volney, and the former Benedictine monk,
the Abbé Martin Lefebvre La Roche, friend and secretary of Helvétius,
the man entrusted by him, and later, Mme. Helvétius, with editing
the first complete and freely edited posthumous edition of Helvétius's
works. Tied by friendship to several others of the group, Jean-Baptiste
Say, an ex-Protestant habitué of Mme. Helvétius's salon and also that of
Helen Maria Williams,[78] acolyte of Clavière and Roederer and warm
admirer of Diderot, whom he regarded as the "best antidote against the
reactionary poison of superstition and servitude," emerged among the
foremost propagators of this revived Brissotin ideology of Idéologie.[79]

Idéologues neither sought nor achieved a monopoly over the Institut's proceedings, prize competitions, or policies, but were the men
who chiefly gave expression to the philosophique standpoint underpinning the Revolution's values, aims, and ideology.[80] A crucial part of the
Institut's activities was the presentation of its work to the public each
trimester via announced days of public readings, debate, and lectures.
On 3 July 1797, for example, a day devoted to the Classe des Sciences
Morales et Politiques, the Institut offered public lectures on future international collaboration and peace in a world of republics committed

to the pursuit of the *bonheur général* (by the philosophe Delisle de Sales), a discourse on economics and colonies by Dupont du Nemours, three mémoires by Roederer, one of the Institut's most active speakers, on public finances, a mémoire by La Révellière-Lépeaux on civil religion and national festivals, a lecture on the medieval maps in Venice's Saint Mark's Library, and reports of Volney's impressions of the United States.[81] The cultural milieu fomented by the Institut's public meetings and prize competitions pitted two rival currents represented within the Institut against each other. Ardent republicans predominated, but not exclusively. They remained at odds with a rival group of crypto-royalists (strong among the historians) who scorned the militant deists and especially the materialism, atheism, and democratic doctrines of the Idéologues.

Another of Condorcet's projects energetically revived in the later 1790s was the society of the Amis des Noirs, which had lapsed under the Montagnard tyranny in 1793–94. The second Society of Friends of the Blacks "and of the colonies," again featuring the Abbé Grégoire, was essentially a Parisian intellectual salon—albeit including a number of blacks, among them several former slaves. Expressly embodying the legacy of Condorcet and Brissot—and while he was in Paris often chaired by Sonthonax—it was a group of a few dozen intellectuals but one with a specific political agenda. Martinique and and other French islands, under British occupation, remained bastions of slavery, while Haiti had largely broken free of the Republic's control, but all of these might soon be regained by the French so that there were hopes both of extending abolition and helping to build new approaches to the social integration of blacks into republican society. Volney believed that educating the blacks was the only ultimate solution; when he visited Jefferson in Virginia for three weeks in June 1796, he was deeply shocked both by the sight of slavery itself and the justifications for black abasement that he constantly encountered.[82]

At the same time the revived Amis des Noirs had to fight the resurgent colonial interest within France. Under the Directoire, especially during the elections of 1797, powerful conservative longings and prejudices surged once again and this backlash demanding religion and monarchy included many voices seeking to reintroduce slavery in the colonies. As the second Amis des Noirs saw it, slavery, oppression of blacks, and the pretexts for it needed to be vigorously rebuffed. Among their arguments was that of Say, who became an active member in 1798 and sought to demonstrate theoretically that paid free-black labor could as a general rule produce sugar at a lower cost than slave labor. The most detailed analysis of the troubles in Haiti was drawn up in the years 1797–99 by Garran-Coulon, an admirer of Toussaint-Louverture and forthright defender of "the principles of the Declaration of Rights."[83]

A restrictive liberal tendency to discard Condorcet's and Brissot's concern for countering economic inequality undoubtedly flourished in the social science of several of these leading figures, notably Cabanis and Roederer, and in several cases involved a definite retreat from the goal of reducing economic inequality and Condorcet's preoccupation with women's equality. A particularly mean streak pervaded the thought of Cabanis, who certainly exemplified the Idéologues' preoccupation, in the tradition of Diderot and d'Holbach, with materialist philosophy and their emphasis on the unity of nature, but reacted to the horrors of the Montagnard tyranny by heavily stressing the need for social stability and order and seeking to minimize public assistance to the poor, though he did not reject the principle of subsidizing the unemployed.[84] Cabanis's strong preoccupation with physiology, emotional states, and the sex drive became linked to a tendency to differentiate male and female intellect based on bodily functions and women's role in childbirth and child-rearing. Especially remote from the stance of Condorcet was Cabanis's conviction that while women have more sensitivity and awareness of emotions, the female mind was unsuited for "long and profound meditations" and ultimately subordinate to that of men intellectually and politically.[85]

Crypto-royalists viewed the Idéologues' d'Holbachian refusal to conceive morality as something divinely installed in the human heart to be deeply damaging to the social order. But this endemic strife lingered mostly below the surface until after the triumph of Bonaparte's authoritarianism in 1799–1800, a development that encouraged expression of more forthrightly antimaterialist and Christian positions. La Révellière-Lépeaux, though also promoting a new public morality, found himself in a category of his own as a militant Rousseauist, anti-Robespierriste, and ardent enthusiast for an organized public cult of deism. For his part, Mercier agreed with the Idéologues that Robespierre had declared war on both the Enlightenment and the Revolution, and that the Institut's task was to obliterate every vestige of Montagnard thinking and ideology, and restore the (nonreligious) Enlightenment to its proper place as the veritable guide of a humanity bolstered by democracy, human rights, and the world revolution. But he nevertheless went his own way, rejecting the irreligious radicalism, atheism, and d'Holbachian materialism of the Idéologues, still preferring Rousseau and the moderation of the new Kantian philosophy.

Institutions and government, held Condorcet, generally lag well behind "la marche de la philosophie," the progress men make in their ideas. To a lesser extent, institutions also lag behind public opinion. "There exists at every instance a great distance between the point to which the philosophes have brought enlightenment" and the way of thinking generally accepted by educated opinion.[86] This doctrine lay at the heart of the ideology motivating the Institut de France: by fostering the moral and political sciences, institutionalization of beneficial ideas can be accelerated especially when the most enlightened philosophes are placed at the head of the educational and public instruction system. Attendances at the combined public sessions of the three Institut classes were commonly impressive, as many as fifteen hundred listeners filling the Louvre's Salle des Antiques. The Idéologues tried to integrate the exact sciences with social science and morality, employing the arts and literature as amplifiers and elucidators of social and moral reality. Idéologie, for its adherents, was the true science of ideas and institutions, a category standing in outright opposition to every variety of traditional thought and metaphysics, a philosophical methodology enabling men to establish social science and politics on a basis of moral truth, science, and indisputable facts.

Robespierre and the Montagne, they contended, had introduced a wholly false, despotic, and unenlightened conception of equality, wreaking untold havoc. Inequality, being a phenomenon of nature rooted in inequality of talents, diligence, and intelligence, cannot be erased altogether. Nevertheless, economic inequality perennially threatens justice and social well-being. Hence, the duty of a properly constituted government, that is, of republican representative democracy—other forms of government being by definition illicit and predatory—is to combat the three prime causes and factors of inequality. First, legislators must eradicate institutionalized inequality of status, every sort of privilege or hereditary, or caste distinction, producing inequality of power and influence being pernicious. Second, legislators must counteract inequality of wealth by using the fiscal system to enforce progressive taxation and regulations governing trade and industry designed to curb exploitation and maximize wealth dispersal, especially by fighting commercial engrossing and imposing rules on marriage settlements and inheritance to dismantle wealth consolidation.

Third, legitimate government combats inequality in education and access to skills. Democracy must assist the poor not with a view to fighting class wars or pillaging the rich but to even the balance, in conformity, as Destutt de Tracy put it, with reason and the "general interest."[87]

Vendémiaire (October 1795): An Unstable Republic

Reaffirming the Revolution's core principles and introducing a new Constitution, however, hardly sufficed either to realize the Idéologue program or stabilize the Republic. Generating more support and robust progams of sweeping reform were needed. To bolster the neo-Brissotins' revived primacy, and ensure neither royalisme nor populism triumphed in the new elections, as well as afford continuity, on 30 August 1795 the Convention passed a highly controversial and soon bitterly contested "two-thirds law." This stipulated that two-thirds, or 500, of the new legislature's 750 deputies should be drawn from the existing Assembly.[88] It was an arbitrary, unconstitutional decree opposed by several departments and most Paris sections, where rigorous purging of terroristes had transferred control in many instances into the hands of out-and-out conservatives. The decree undoubtedly was irregular and unconstitutional, but at the time it seemed an indispensable emergency safeguard to many. To democratic republicans, ensuring that royalism and authoritarian populism were kept at bay appeared more immediately vital than any niceties of democratic theory. Limiting the electorate's choice beforehand appealed to most outgoing deputies and also many external observers alarmed by the mounting triple threat of reactionary monarchism, rebellious populism, and the population's mounting fatigue with the Revolution's endless travails and difficulties.

In Septmber 1795, the new Constitution was approved by a democratic national referendum in which more than a million people cast their votes, and more than 900,000 endorsed the Constitution, even though many people angrily denounced the two-thirds rule shoring up the republican majority in the new Assembly (which, apart from anything else, facilitated participation of former terroristes).[89] Royalist reaction, supplemented by continuing sansculotte exasperation, generated a powerful resurgence of resentment against this unsteady republican, neo-Brissotin, and anti-Catholic regime, which nevertheless also refused to combat *terroristes* unreservedly (indeed, had released many Jacobin suspects). Opposition and protest welled up in particular in Paris. The intensity of royalist-Catholic *revanchisme* became fully apparent only ten days after inauguration of the Constitution of the Year III, setting up the Directoire and the new two-chamber legislature on 25 September 1795. On 4 and 5 October 1795 (10 and 11 Vendémiaire), and especially on 6 October (13 Vendémiaire), three of the most traumatic days of the Revolution, erupted one of the Revolution's largest, unruliest, most frightening, and most confused popular convulsions.

On 4 October 1795 (12 Vendémiaire), a formidable mass of royalists, Catholics, populists, and furious sansculottes, drawing support from around thirty of the capital's sections, demanded revenge on terrorists, repudiation of the two-thirds law, and fresh elections. Seven sections, Lepeletier, Théâtre-Français, Place-Vendôme, and other both working- and middle-class districts, rose in mass armed revolt, mobilizing their units of the National Guard against the regime. Opposition to the republican regime was strongest in the Lepeletier section, where finance and investment were concentrated and where, in its primary assembly sessions of 7 and 12 September, counterrevolutionary sentiment boiled over. Despite being partly or predominantly royalist, this new insurrection strikingly embraced the rhetoric of direct sovereignty employed earlier by the sections under Robespierre and included a strong element of sansculotte protest, only now channeling popular hostility directly against representative democracy and the Convention.[90]

On 5 October, some 25,000 insurgents marched on the Convention from south of the river. Against them, republican activists, including many ex-Montagnards, Antonelle among them, calling themselves the "Patriotes de 1789," formed up at the Tuileries. The "rebels" were also opposed by a small, hastily summoned military force of 4,000 men under Barras (accompanied by several army officers, most notably Napoleon, who seized the opportunity to restore their political reputations), sent to occupy the bridges. Despite a long standoff lasting most of the afternoon, negotiation failed and the Convention's artillery opened fire on the mass of insurgents, amounting to some 7,000 armed sansculottes, precipitating a pitched battle on the Quai de Voltaire and neighboring streets during the night of 5/6 October that turned into one of the longest journées (lasting seven hours), and second bloodiest (after 10 August 1792), in Paris of the Revolution. The two armed forces, roughly equal in size, fought on the Seine's banks, in the streets and squares, and around the massive Baroque church of Saint-Roch, the battle intently followed not least in the prisons, where still-imprisoned Montagnards, Jullien among them, made ready to kill themselves rather than be slaughtered by royalist revenge seekers should the latter manage to overwhelm the republicans and reenact the September 1792 prison massacres in reverse. In the end, though, the government's artillery, Napoleon's military professionalism, and the resolve of the 1,500 armed Jacobins won the day.

When the battle ended, hundreds lay dead.[91] Many besides royalists were appalled by the violence and the soldiery's heavy-handed resort to force. Lanjuinais termed it a "massacre."[92] Afterward, the National Guard in the capital was disarmed; regular troops remained on hand; hundreds more suspects were arrested in the sections. But most of these, the Comité de Sûreté Générale wisely recognized, were merely "gens égarés," "misled people" with little grasp of what was happening. Nearly everyone was released within a few days. Forty-nine populists were condemned to death by the courts but only two executions were actually carried out—those of two rebel section presidents, Lebond and Lebois. With the new Constitution only just introduced, the Convention wisely preferred to exhort reconciliation and constitutionality rather than impose a new round of severity and executions, risking the very stability the Directoire so desperately sought. Only nine days after the revolt's suppression, on 4 Brumaire of the Year III (26 October 1795), the Convention—approaching its conclusion—voted to release all those earlier imprisoned as "Jacobins or Feuillants, terrorists or *modérés*," a general political amnesty under which a whole army of Jacobins and militant dissidents, including Jullien, Babeuf, and Augustin Darthé (1769–97), besides the Marseille Jacobin leaders Bayle and Granet, were released.[93]

The way to stabilize the Revolution in the autumn of 1795, contended Marie-Joseph Chénier, was to liberate the press, rehabilitate the Brissotins, and definitively release most political prisoners while severely punishing the worst "revolutionary murderers."[94] At first, the Directoire followed precisely this course and, among other signs of republican rectitude, proved willing to ease restrictions on pro-Jacobin journalism, enabling Babeuf to establish his *Tribun du peuple* and Jullien his radical but progovernment *L'Orateur plébéien*. Hard-line egalitarians, for their part, found themselves in a quandary. Economic distress, plainly, was just as likely, or more likely, to propel the monarchist-Catholic Right to power as direct democracy and sansculottism. Plainly, there was simply no such thing as a coherent sansculotte tendency or ideology; rather, the volatility and incoherence of populist sentiment, whether Enragé, Hébertiste, royalist, or Robespierriste, was indisputable. Not the least of the contradictions inherent in this chronic situation, as both Babeuf and Jullien acknowledged, was that the sansculottes had undeniably been economically better off under the ancien régime than they were in the Republic's present context. "Royalism," commented Babeuf, "lies in wait at the doors of this sanctuary."[95] He urged all democrats to consider what would happen should the royalists sway more of the poor and gain the upper hand: "throughout the length and breadth of France death and outlawry will be decreed for republicans." Nothing whatever could be achieved, stressed his *Tribun du peuple*, unless the Revolution weaned "the masses from their royalist sympathies."[96]

Appalled by the strength of populism, royalism, and reactionary Catholicism, on 10 October, the new legislature abolished the section assemblies altogether, along with sectional control of National Guard units, thereby demolishing, many hoped for good, the chief tools of direct sovereignty in the Revolution and fundamentally altering the Republic's character. The new legislature boasted notably more Brissotins than its predecessor and shunned terrorists, populists, and royalists with equal fervor. Among its leading figures were Daunou, Boissy d'Anglas, Lanthenas, Lakanal, Debry, Lanjuinais, Guyomar, Marie-Joseph Chénier, and, until both died in 1797, Louvet and Diderot's old companion, Deleyre. The Council of Five Hundred and Conseil des Anciens that convened with the inauguration of the Constitution and the Year III in late October strove to uphold the Constitution and the law. Sieyès was elected one of the five directors but refused to serve. The elected directors installed in office—Barras, Carnot, La Révellière-Lépeaux, Reubell, and Letourneur—were from the middle ground, all proven anti-Robespierristes professing to be committed republicans, equally vigilant against Robespierrisme and royalism. Lazare Carnot, credited with being the architect of the victory at Fleurus (26 June 1794) and a main contributor to Robespierre's downfall, remained for the next three years at the forefront of the Revolution, dominating military affairs, with Barras policing Paris, La Révellière-Lépeaux supervising the interior, and Reubell foreign affairs.[97] But thoroughly alarmed by populist monarchism, the Directoire consistently preferred rallying former Montagnards, and countering those involved in the October 1795 rising, than rooting out former terrorists. To begin with, the new regime also encouraged the reemergence of anti-Robespierre provincial neo-Jacobin clubs, like those of Toulouse and Metz, where the Jacobins triumphed in the municipal elections of November 1795.[98]

If the hunger riots in Paris in the spring of 1795 represented a dangerous "paroxysm" of sansculottism,[99] Vendémiaire was the failed uprising of a still broader populism lurching violently to the right. But monarchist or republican, populists and populism of whatever variety were utterly unable to steer the Revolution as a system of general emancipation, democracy, freedom of expression, and enlightenment. Direct democracy was never less the motor of the Revolution's democratic and libertarian impulses than during 1795–97. If stability was to be achieved and the Revolution consolidated, republican intellectuals saw little alternative but to steadfastly support the Constitution and Directoire. Among leading editors, publicists, and ideologues participating in the constitutional debate of 1795, most unreservedly endorsed the Constitution and supported the democratic Republic.

However, some did not, notably Babeuf, Antonelle, Maréchal, and Buonarroti (who, expelled from Corsica with Salicetti and Volney in early 1793, had now joined the Paris Jacobins while remaining among the Revolution's chief publicists in Italian). Refusing to abandon direct democracy and the 1793 Constitution, and defending the Terror, September massacres, and Robespierre, these men persevered in trying to mobilize fresh popular insurrections. Jullien, who felt some sympathy for both sides in this unceasing contest, did not doubt that the latter, the militant democrats, were a smaller movement than the main republican bloc. His conclusion was that the republican Revolution's survival depended on the larger entity, constitutional reform rather than revolutionary direct action, and hence required the defeat of the militant egalitarians. In contrast to Babeuf, Maréchal, and Buonarroti, Jullien saw no alternative but for all democrats, whether militant egalitarians, such as he had hitherto always been, Dantonistes, or neo-Brissotin republicans, to coalesce and work together.[100]

Given the fraught circumstances, there could be no return to unrestricted press freedom; urging restoration of the monarchy remained illegal. But a wide range of opinion was allowed and various important papers reappeared or were founded in these months.[101] Even a partial return of freedom of expression, Mary Wollstonecraft had predicted, would reinvigorate politics, the arts, and theater, bring outstanding women back to the fore, and encourage vigorous intellectual salons and political clubs to reemerge. She was right. Among the liveliest salons

from summer 1795 were those of Juliette Récamier and Germaine de
Staël, newly returned to Paris in May 1795 from Switzerland, where she
had fled in September 1792. Staël, daughter of Necker and lover of Benjamin Constant (who accompanied her to Paris), was an intellectually
outstanding thirty-year-old, and like her father, a convinced moderate
distinctly wary of radical ideas, but she was also devoted to defending
basic human rights and building true political freedom. Although her
salon exuded more than a hint of aristocratic allure, she was more inclined than her father to endorse the 1795 Constitution and support
the neo-Brissotin republicanism, purged of Robespierrisme, which
shaped the surviving French Revolution of the later 1790s. She openly
admired Boissy d'Anglas, Daunou, and Lanjuinais, and respected Louvet, "a sincere republican," even if his experience of the Terror had left
him too paranoid and suspicious. The neo-Brissotins, it seemed clear to
her, had saved and redeemed the Revolution. Like the beautiful Mme.
Récamier, she aimed to encourage broad debate, making a point of welcoming to her salon a varied spectrum of opinion—not just supporters
of the Directoire, like Constant and herself, but also royalists of different hues and ex- and neo-Jacobins, together with some of the capital's
brash nouveaux riches.[102]

Distinctly less elegant was the club Réunion des Amis de la République, called "the Panthéon," meeting from 16 November 1795 in a dis-
used convent near the Panthéon. Endorsed by papers like the *Journal des
hommes libres* and the *L'Orateur plébéien*, this club became the gathering place of republican democrats and ex-Montagnards such as Babeuf,
Felix Lepeletier, Darthé, Drouet, Jullien, Buonarroti, and Antonelle.[103]
The Club de Panthéon's talks and meetings apparently drew substantial crowds but, before long, inevitably, it too became an arena split between republicans acquiescing in the Constitution of the Year III and
hard-line rejectionist militants.[104] Through the pages of his Paris paper,
the *Tribun du peuple*, published from November 1795, Babeuf figured
among those who denounced the Directoire. He did so while plotting
with sansculotte friends and veteran Montagnards sympathetic to direct democracy and sansculottism, including Vadier and Jean-Baptiste
Drouet (1763–1824), the man who recognized Louis XVI, preventing
his flight, in 1791, later among the most violent foes of the Brissotins.
Drouet was now a deputy for the Marne. Another prominent conspirator was Felix Lepeletier (1767–1837), who had delivered the funerary
eulogy over the body of his assassinated brother at the Panthéon.

By early 1796, the Directoire, and especially Carnot, the director responsible for interior security, had reverted to viewing neo-Jacobinism and the neo-Montagnard clubs as the chief threat to the regime. Carnot, the regime's strong man, had initially been the most resolute of the directors in steering an evenhanded middle course, pursuing former terroristes (despite having been one himself), while holding royalism at bay. Respectful of constitutionality initially, later it became obvious that he cared much less for republican values than administering the army to consolidate his own authority. His opportunism rendered him a target for both former Montagnards and Louvet and the neo-Brissotins.[105] Before long, Carnot saw the meetings at the Panthéon Club as especially menacing to stability and himself. On 27 February 1796, after a speech at the club in which Darthé read out incendiary remarks extracted from the *Tribun du peuple* denouncing the Directoire and the 1795 Constitution as "tyrannical," the Directoire ordered the club closed, sending Bonaparte to expel its members and bar its doors.[106] Four other clubs and a theater were likewise closed at this point. Several neo-Jacobin papers, including the *Tribun du peuple*, were proscribed. These measures shook the confidence of a wide variety of republicans loyal to the ideals of the Revolution, some of whom began asking themselves whether perhaps the likes of Babeuf, Darthé, and Buonarroti were right after all.

By early 1796, the positive, widely applauded early phase of post-Thermidor and the new Constitution was over. Driven underground, both Panthéonistes and the *Tribun* henceforth led a shadowy, clandestine existence. Their message, that those in power were hypocrites and false republicans and those who conspired against them were justified, came to be widely shared. It was at this point that Babeuf began actively to conspire. Before long, a secret directorate of the "conspiracy for equality," a heterogeneous group organized by Lepeletier, Maréchal, and Buonarroti, meeting regularly in the home of Amar, clandestinely plotted, nurturing plans for another 21 May–style mass popular insurrection, hoping this time for more lasting and concrete results.[107] Under a law of 27 Germinal Year IV (16 April 1796), freedom of expression was further restricted and the death penalty for summoning citizens to insurrection introduced. Inciting the people to dissolve the legislature or Directoire, reestablish monarchy, murder deputies, or reinstate the Constitutions of 1791 or 1793 were all declared capital crimes.[108]

The Babeuf movement's agents appeared in cafés and taverns across Paris, affixing posters, distributing pamphlets, and propagating egalitarian anti-Directoire propaganda, especially the message that artisans were being enslaved by the greed of the rich. During 1796, theirs grew into a full-scale nationwide conspiracy with cells in several provincial towns. The conspirators endeavored to win over several of the most committed republican journalists to their stance, notably Antonelle and Vatar, current editors of the *Journal des hommes libres*. Many of the movement's proposals—land redistribution on a fairer basis, progressive taxation, and universal public education—were not as such incompatible with the goals of the former Cercle Social of Bonneville and Condorcet, and radical ideas more generally, but they were with the current Directoire. However, it was the plotters' uncompromisingly leveling philosophy much indebted to Mably and Morelly, Babeuf's and Buonarroti's neo-Robespierrisme—and especially their tactics and methods, their reliance on violent mass insurrection, and plans to reestablish a neo-Montagnard dictatorship to push through their reforms[109]—that set them firmly apart from the main republican bloc at a time when the Convention's grip and the Revolution's gains looked in every way unstable and precarious.

After the Terror and Vendémiaire, Left republicans generally, including militant democrats and egalitarians like Jullien and Antonelle, were principally concerned with reconquering individual liberties and freedom of expression while keeping the sansculottes at arm's length. In explaining his concept of virtue in October 1795, Jullien expressly cited Helvétius and d'Holbach's thesis in the *Système social*, holding that private virtue is formed and defined by the "esprit public" and depends on education inculcating a "habitual disposition to do what contributes to the happiness of the beings of our species."[110] Brissotins and former Old Jacobins rejecting Babeuf's clandestine subversion agreed that the Revolution was not over, that the revolutionary regime had much still to accomplish in the economic as well as in the legislative, educational, cultural, and international spheres. They were far from blind to questions of social amelioration. But they did not agree that pursuit of greater economic equality possessed the urgency or degree of primacy Babeuf and Maréchal insisted on. Most rejected the proposition that the Republic's existing Constitution and institutions needed to be overthrown by popular insurrection to clear the way for redistribution of wealth by force.[111]

By May 1796 France had descended further into instability and drift with widespread discontent evident, and even more inertia. The Directoire and Council of Five Hundred, besieged from right and left, simply lacked a sufficiently sturdy support base in society, and this in large part due to the spring repression of basic freedoms. If mainstream republicans rejected Babeuf's incitement to insurrection, they spurned the new repressive instincts of the Directoire no less. Of around fifty-four more-or-less national newspapers in France, by autumn 1796 most almost daily attacked the Directoire and, to a lesser degree, the legislature itself for inconsistency, timidity, hypocrisy, and failure to honestly uphold the Constitution.[112] "Will we escape from the crisis we now face?," demanded the *Journal des hommes libres* in October 1796. The resurgence of royalism and Catholicism was undeniable, as was the waning enthusiasm for the 1795 Constitution on the left.

The 1795 Constitution, there was every indication, was being disparaged and subverted by the press (and by *royalisme*) as mercilessly as had that of 1791 by the Brissotin press during 1791–92.[113] Yet despite everything, so menacing for the Revolution's values and future were the efforts of the Republic's enemies, the *Journal des hommes libres* admonished its readers in late 1796, that there was really no viable alternative for true republicans and democrats but to work together and rally behind this disappointing and defective government. Republicans and democrats must help rescue the Directoire and legislature, because every available alternative would prove immeasurably worse.[114]

CHAPTER 23

The "General Revolution"

(1795–1800) HOLLAND, ITALY, AND THE LEVANT

The Batavian Revolution

The General Revolution's brief but dramatic foray into Western Europe in 1792–93 immensely alarmed Europe's rulers, nobles, and churchmen. The Revolution totally denied their validity and wherever it broke through set furiously to work to break their power, abolish their authority, and confiscate their possessions. A particularly worrying feature of the situation for defenders of the old order was that the well-drilled and attired armies of Prussia and Austria showed unsuspected signs of weakness in confronting the ragged, poorly trained and supplied, and badly equipped revolutionary armies. If the French could win astounding victories under such disadvantages, hampered by a partly still noble officer class rife with disloyalty and betrayal, what would happen when their armies became larger, better trained, and better supplied? Princely and ecclesiastical anxiety was assuaged briefly from March 1793 until June 1794, a period when it was realistic to expect the Revolution to disintegrate under the strain of its internal splits and the Vendée revolt. During 1793–94, Europe's rulers could relax in the hope that the Republic would falter from within.

But the Revolution failed to disintegrate and from late 1794 its resilience posed a growing threat to the established order. Even a precarious, modest degree of political stabilization, as was achieved after Thermidor, sufficed to renew the menace along the lines posed in 1792. The dramatic expansion of the revolutionary armies achieved in 1793–94, thanks to Danton's call for mobilizing the masses and rigorous conscription, along with the purging of the disloyal element and forging a new revolutionary army officer corps, and the huge expansion in the supply of weapons and munitions, raised the level of threat exponentially. In fact, by 1795 ancien régime Europe faced not just a threat but the looming likelihood of extinction. Even standing resolutely all together, it could be predicted that Britain and the European great powers would not be able to withstand the Revolution militarily.

If the chances of Britain being successfully invaded were slim, Ireland looked vulnerable and the likelihood of England losing much of her global power and influence very real. If the catastrophic losses Britain suffered in the Caribbean during the years 1795–99 occurred only because the French were aided there by free blacks and emancipated (or hoping-to-be emancipated) slaves, in India and Europe too, large segments of society could be expected to ally with the French. If no other power had been remotely as successful as Britain in stripping France of prestige and her choicest colonies in the eighteenth century, the balance of power and resources appeared to be reversing itself. Thus, the British ruling classes shared in the anxieties gripping Prussia, Austria, Russia, Italy, and Spain; their leading position in European affairs and the country's maritime and commercial primacy in the rest of the world appeared to be seriously threatened.

Nowhere were Prussian, Austrian, and British interests more immediately menaced than in the Low Countries. Republicanism had a long tradition in the Netherlands, and the democratic opposition to the nobility, churches, and stadtholderate, firmly anti-British and anti-Prussian in outlook, had already become a formidable if not very coherent force in the 1780s, before the French Revolution. By 1787, the Dutch democratic movement had virtually gained control of the United Provinces and was vigorously promoting democratic ideas. It had been halted and suppressed only by massive Prussian military intervention backed by Britain. Thousands of Dutch Patriots had been compelled to flee their homeland and seek refuge in Belgium and France. Thus far, stadtholder and Estates-General had experienced little difficulty in maintaining their grip. But what if the repressive apparatus of the Dutch ancien régime was challenged by a French follow-up invasion repeating the brief but successful incursion of 1793, only this time in greater force?

A month before Thermidor, on 26 June 1794, the Austrian army in the Low Countries, despite being reinforced by Dutch Orangist contingents and exceptionally large, suffered crushing defeat at Fleurus, just inside Belgium. Though well-equipped, the Austrian army was unable to withstand the size (80,000 men), élan, and massive artillery resources organized by Carnot and Saint-Just. To add insult to injury, the French commander, Jean-Baptiste Jourdan (1762–1833), was the son of a common surgeon, a veteran of the American war, in which he had enrolled and fought as a common soldier. Like Hoche and Jean-Baptiste Bernadotte (1763–1844)—later one of Napoleon's key generals and from 1810 hereditary prince of Sweden—he was one of the new breed of non-noble officers selected from the ranks for high command by Carnot. Before long, the revolutionaries recaptured Brussels.

Hardly was Robespierre overthrown than the General Revolution recaptured Liège and Antwerp. Two months later, on 24 September, the French set siege to the principal Dutch fortress in North Brabant, 's-Hertogenbosch, a vast stronghold taken after a three-week siege in which Daendels and De Winter, the commanders of the Dutch revolutionary legion, figured prominently. 's-Hertogenbosch became a strategic base and propaganda center from where revolutionary incitement, newsletters, and pamphlets infiltrated the not-yet-liberated territory to the north.[1] By October 1794, Jourdan had overrun not only much of Dutch Brabant but also Cologne, Coblenz, and Düsseldorf. How were Britain, Prussia, and Austria going to halt the democratic General Revolution?

The successful advance triggered a buildup of prorevolutionary fervor in Holland's main cities. The country's numerous reading societies revived their former Patriot zeal and again openly propagated anti-Orangist sentiment and republican-democratic ideas. Enthusiasm for the Dutch democrat ex-patriots was openly displayed. The commander of the Dutch legion fighting with the French, Herman Willem Daendels, and his secretary, Gerrit Paape (1752–1803), a leading exponent of radical thought in the Low Countries, heartily loathed Robespierre and publicly rejoiced over his downfall, but were also strongly motivated republicans. Detailed information about the military and political situation in the Dutch Republic poured onto their desks from sympathizers, militant anti-Orangists, in Amsterdam, The Hague, and Utrecht, not least from Willem van Irhoven van Dam (1760–1802),[2] the Dutch Legion's principal contact within Holland, a preeminent intellectual and radical enlightener, as well as editor of the Amsterdam *Coerier*.

Irhoven had been warning of the "unruliness of an unlimited and incorrectly constructed democracy that we must avoid" for years, at least since 1783, insisting that what he (and Gerrit Paape) called "philosophical republicanism" was the only right path to republican liberty, equality, and stability.[3] Citing Raynal, Diderot, Mably, Priestley, and Price, Irhoven employed the term "onweesgerige" (unphilosophical) to mean anything undemocratic, intolerant, monarchical, and allied to aristocracy. One might object that he and Paape belonged to a tiny, unrepresentative fringe, and this is true. But it was precisely these men, believing philosophy alone could lead men to "love of man and the people's liberty," who were the active fringe at the forefront of revolutionary subversion in Holland. They led the group that initiated and steered the Batavian Revolution of 1795–1800.[4]

In fact, the collapse of aristocracy, court culture, conservatism, and Anglo-Prussian influence in the Northern Netherlands proved spectacularly swift. If mostly quiescent and sullen until the late summer of 1794, opposition to the stadtholderate became widespread and intense from August, active opposition in close contact with Daendels and Paape, and hence with the French commanders and executive committees in Paris. On 31 July 1794, thirty-six delegates from local clubs in Groningen, Overijssel, Utrecht, and Holland gathered in a tavern in Amsterdam, under Irhoven van Dam's chairmanship, to coordinate plans with the advancing French.[5] In Utrecht, where there were at least a dozen reading societies meeting in private homes, hundreds of former Free Corps democrat militiamen with guns in their houses were reportedly ready to come out and fight the Orangists as soon as the French appeared—information that proved correct. By late September Amsterdam was flooded with posters and pamphlets produced by the secret committee for the Patriot Revolution. In October, armed disturbances broke out, which the Orangist regime crushed, but with difficulty and only with the help of the Prussian and British contingents stationed in the country.

When the great rivers had frozen up sufficiently for cavalry to cross, in January 1795, the French revolutionary armies swept forward. If the allies' military defeat, rather predictably, was crushing and extremely swift, the psychological and symbolic defeat was even more galling. Franco-Dutch republican entry into the core of the Republic in January 1795, British observers felt obliged to admit, resembled a carnival procession "happily conducted" more than a military campaign, with the towns bedecked with tricolor flags and revolutionary posters, as well as the black cockades of the Dutch democrats.[6] Thoroughly humiliated, the stadtholder and his family fled to England on 18 January. On entering Utrecht, the French found the city festooned in tricolor pendants and the insignia of the Revolution, and packed with jubilant crowds. Three days before French troops entered Amsterdam, the local Comité Revolutionair had already overwhelmed the Orangist opposition and

Figure 19. Champions of the "General Revolution": (a) Georg Forster, (b) Tom Paine.
(a) J.H.W. Tischbein (1751–1829), portrait of Georg Forster, painting. © TopFoto / The Image Works. (b) John Wesley Jarvis (ca. 1781–1839), portrait of Thomas Paine, ca. 1805, oil on canvas. © Atlas Archive / The Image Works.

taken over Holland's principal city.[7] Strikingly, there was little violence against—or pilfering the property of—the many thousands of fleeing Orangists.

The 1795 Batavian Revolution was thus a genuine liberation that swept away princely, Anglo-Prussian, and aristocratic control, aided by the relatively disciplined, tactful conduct of the French troops, which, on this occasion, contrasted strikingly with the conspicuous indiscipline of the retreating Prussians and British, who reportedly angrily pillaged whole towns and villages as they departed. Everywhere, revolutionary committees and their militias assumed control, removing Orangist officals and replacing them with Patriots. All the town oligarchies of the Northern Netherlands were thus purged. Those who took over were mostly the democratic Patriots of 1787. In the town of Deventer in Overijssel, for example, the first municipal elections after the Revolution in March 1795 resulted in no fewer than seven of the ten most popular candidates being anti-Orangist former members of the Patriot city council that had been suppressed following the Prussian invasion of 1787.[8] This sense of the Batavian Revolution of 1795 being a restoration of democratic gains lost in 1787—as much or more than a new beginning based on French example—was reflected in the innumerable victory parades, thanksgiving ceremonies, banquets, and special theatrical performances that greeted its inception.

Leaving the Dutch to shape their own republican future, with a minimum of interference from Paris, had many advantages from the French standpoint, but also presented difficulties. How exactly the Dutch past could be reconciled with the demands of democratic republicanism and radical ideas remained unclear. The new Batavian Republic was bound to diverge from the French Republic in important respects. For one thing, religion continued to exert a strong hold on both the Protestant and Catholic Dutch, who evinced little sympathy either for French "atheism" or the comprehensive freedom from religious authority the French Revolution had introduced. There remained much resistance to according equal rights to Catholics, Jews, and Anabaptists, and a good deal of support also for the traditional federal structure of the Republic, which meant retaining many inequitable "privileges," "rights," and procedures from the past. Also, there was practically no discussion of black emancipation despite the fact that the General Revolution was now also engulfing all the Dutch colonies in the Caribbean and the Guianas. But there was no resisting the upsurge of feverish discussion in Holland's clubs and revolutionary committees, which was about to reshape Dutch politics and institutions. In December 1795, the purged but otherwise still unreformed oligarchic Estates-General yielded to demands for the convening of a National Assembly to reform the Republic's Constitution along democratic lines. For the first time in Dutch history, this would be an assembly not of delegates of town oligarchies but representatives elected by the people, one delegate for every 15,000 inhabitants.

In the first Dutch democratic elections in early 1796, a great landmark in Dutch and world history, all male citizens older than twenty not receiving poor relief were entitled to vote. The first Dutch National Assembly duly convened on 1 March 1796. Amid the sunshine, applause, artillery salvos, and the hoisting of the new Dutch tricolor flag, and much cheering of "Vivat de Republiek!," the 126 representatives of the Dutch National Assembly solemnly began their proceedings. Pieter Paulus (1754–96), a leader of the democratic movement of the 1780s, was elected chairman. Before anything else, he announced "in the name of the Dutch people which we here represent that this Assembly is the representative body of the Dutch people!" A great public festival in The Hague followed on 3 March. Among the Dutch National Assembly's first acts was a decision to appoint a commission of twenty-one to study the Dutch constitutional debates of the 1780s, as well as the Unites States Constitution and the various French constitutions since 1791, and draw up proposals for the new Dutch constitution.[9]

Radiating from France, the Low Countries, the Rhineland, and Switzerland, by 1795 unrelenting ideological warfare penetrated most urbanized and literate parts of Europe, unnerving the authorities and stirring the populace. Fear lest French and Franco-Dutch democratic republicanism should prove contagious thus pervaded the Western world in a more urgent and immediate form from 1795 than it had in the early 1790s. The speed and ease with which the Austrian Netherlands and Dutch ancien régime had disintegrated under the impact of the General Revolution was bound to encourage republican democratic elements elsewhere, including in Ireland and Britain itself. In Britain, democratic radicalism was undoubtedly a small but also a highly motivated fringe, widely viewed as a threat to Crown, aristocracy, and Church, and not to be underestimated, even if the British radicals, continually denounced by the government and press, remained highly unpopular with most of society. For they nevertheless had some support in England and Scotland, and still more in Ireland, all of which greatly alarmed the government.

The main radical organization in London, the London Corresponding Society, was closely linked to intellectual circles around Godwin,
the atheist Thomas Holcroft, and the ousted Cambridge ex-don, William Frend, and, by dispatching delegates and handbills to the provinces, showed some capacity to foment agitation. Among other
demonstrations, they secretly organized a public mass rally and petition to Parliament, demanding universal suffrage, annual parliaments,
comprehensive parliamentary reform, and an end to Britain's "unjust
war" against the French Republic, to take place in London in July 1797.
When the authorities discovered the details of the projected rally, all
police leave was canceled. A crowd of some three thousand duly converged on a vacant space at Saint Pancras to endorse a mass petition to
be laid before the king, demanding parliamentary reform, universal suffrage, and the other radical desiderata, none of which were in the slightest degree acceptable to conservative opinion. Scarcely had the rally
commenced than justices of the peace appeared, declaring the gathering
illegal under the Seditious Meetings Act. Royal cavalry appeared and
began making arrests. The demonstrators dispersed but only slowly and
raucously, booing and hissing, to which the troops replied by heaping
abuse on the protesters.[10]

Outside the zones conquered by the French, European writers courageous enough to applaud the Revolution—Godwin, Holcroft, Fichte,
Hölderlin, Cramer, Forster, Wedekind, Thorild, and the Irish republicans Wolfe Tone and Edward Fitzgerald among them—were virulently
assailed in the press as dissidents and traitors to Crown and religion.[11]
By 1796, Italian exiles and revolutionaries had for several years proclaimed the Revolution's immanent spread to Italy. Giuseppe Gorani
(1740–1819), in his *Lettres aux souverains sur la Révolution française*
(1792), held that all enlightened men should embrace the Revolution
and help overthrow the princely courts and destroy their power, and
he was far from alone. Before 1795, though, in Italy the revolutionary
challenge, however disturbing to princes and Church, remained distant and theoretical. From 1795 it became real and immanent rather
suddenly when the newly formed "army of Italy," placed under Napoleon's command by Barras and Carnot, began advancing from Nice.
It won a much-trumpeted victory over the Austrians at Lodi on 10
May 1796—the same day as Babeuf's and Buonarroti's arrest in Paris.
Though a relatively small battle in itself, the success opened the road to
Milan, placing Lombardy at Napoleon's feet. Suddenly, the clarion call
of Gorani, Salicetti, and Buonarroti assumed a spellbinding, immediate
resonance.

Revolution in Italy (1796–1800)

The year 1796 proved the most decisive in the Italian Peninsula for centuries. In that year, the Italy of the ancien régime simply disintegrated. During the spring, panic gripped the Italian princely courts. On 15 May, the French entered Milan in triumph; on the same day, Piedmontese envoys in Paris signed Piedmont's surrender, formally ceding Nice and Savoy to France. Napoleon entered Milan accompanied by Salicetti and the new Milanese National Guard in green uniforms with tricolor cockades on their hats, alongside the French troops. The size and enthusiasm of the crowds and the splendor of the triumphal entry were doubtless much exaggerated in subsequent revolutionary propaganda, but this only added to the unnerving of the Italian courts, public, and Church. Within days of Milan's fall, Italian Patriots set up a local branch of the Jacobins there complete with a local newspaper, the *Giornale della Società degli amici della libertà e dell'uguaglianza*, edited by a young Pavia professor of medical pathology, Giovanni Rasori (1766–1837). On 16 May 1796, a new era was proclaimed, Napoleon ordering all the Lombard communes to submit to revolutionary principles and his enactments unreservedly. As in Holland in 1795, the French tried to avoid their errors in Belgium in 1792 by minimizing organized pillage (except from princely art museums and churches) and leaving political and legal direction as far as possible in local hands. In both respects, they had some success. Pavia resisted; the town was occupied and looted, but mostly the army of Italy, like Jourdan's in the Low Countries, did its best to curb rapine and pillage. Liberty trees were erected, religious authority drastically curtailed, the universities reformed, aristocracy and privilege abolished, and the important local Jewish communities emancipated from stifling ghetto and papal restrictions, along with numerous other changes, many immediate, fundamental, and deeply symbolic.

A subversive press became operative in Milan in the hands of anticlerical, especially Neapolitan, refugees who by 1797 did not scruple to publish d'Holbach, Volney, and other atheistic authors deemed heinous and sacrilegious by the clergy and ancien régime authorities. A pervasive *Catechismo repubblicano* addressed to "free workers and artisans" by the republican professor Girolamo Rostagni, published at Milan in 1797 (and subsequently reprinted in various Italian regional capitals), was partly a summary of d'Holbach's *La Politique naturelle*.[12] No one could any longer prevent overt displays of irreligion or the influx of revolutionary writings from France, or the return of a motley collection of Italian revolutionary exiles, and their setting up base in the Milanese.

Napoleon distributed his forces to overawe Venetian as well as Austrian Lombardy and also the Austrian border areas. On 1 June, Verona, in the Venetian Republic, was occupied. On 12 June 1796, French troops entered the Papal States, seizing Ferrara and Bologna and obliging the papacy to sign the "armistice of Bologna." Among the humiliating terms was a clause providing for the punitive transfer of hundreds of artworks to France to be selected by the Republic's commissaires—a provision that deeply affronted many Italian artists and authors, including Europe's greatest sculptor at the time, Antonio Canova.[13] On 27 June the port of Livorno in Tuscany, Italy's preeminent commercial entrepot, was seized.

The Revolution had no intention of making war on the people, Napoleon's Italian decrees proclaimed, only on tyrants.[14] All who conducted themselves peacefully would be treated "fraternally" and have their property and persons respected, but resistance would be repressed harshly. Yet, despite the troops' relatively disciplined conduct, the occupation undoubtedly shocked much or most of the population. Little respect was shown for princes, nobility, or the Church, and none for customs or local authorities. The formal neutrality of Venice, Tuscany, and the papacy was disregarded. Historians often stress that, in Italy, the Revolution enjoyed hardly any support among the people, and that there was considerable resistance. This is true. Nevertheless, there was crucial support from certain groups. Everywhere, local clubs of Giacobini came into existence. These represented the views of only a tiny segment of the general population, but a large proportion of the most educated, literary-minded, and aware, especially professors, lecturers, poets, and students of recently reformed universities like Pavia where Enlightenment ideas prevailed since the 1780s. As in France and Germany, hard-core democratic republicans were predominantly savants, academics, students, tutors, journalists, librarians, book dealers, and medical or legal professionals, especially those bearing grudges against the ruling privileged elites. Prominent among these men were the revolutionary poet Ugo Foscolo (1778–1827), the poet Giovanni Fantoni (1755–1807), the chemist, agriculturalist, and drainage expert Vincenzo Dandolo (1758–1819), and the writer of democratic odes and historical tragedies Giovanni Pindemonte (1751–1812).

The key supporters, then, as in France in 1789, were intellectuals and not least ambitious journalists, like Rasori and Melchiorre Gioia (1767–1829). Gioia, in whose eyes loyalty to monarchy signified only ignorance and stupidity,[15] was a democratic publicist who had renounced the priesthood and was steeped in Montesquieu, Helvétius, Diderot, and Rousseau. He had been imprisoned by the Austrians in Milan just before Napoleon's triumphal entry for publishing a text calling for Italy to be "free, republican and provided with democratic institutions."[16] He hoped for "one single indivisible republic in all Italy." Released by the French, Gioia initiated a campaign in the revolutionized Milan papers, including the paper *Il Monitore italiano*, which between January and April 1798 he edited jointly with Foscolo to explain the meaning of a "costituzione democratica." Declaring monarchs and aristocrats "the most formidable enemies of Italian liberty," these prorevolutionary journalists eulogized the French Constitution of 1795.[17] Gioia also echoed economic ideas rooted in French radical thought, clashing with Adam Smith's free trade doctrines, contending that "philosophy had declared war on inequality." A just and democratic society, held Goioa, necessarily requires scrupulous state regulation, especially of industry and commerce. But he was also at pains to emphasize that philosophy's conception of "equality" did not mean, as many Italians indignantly assumed, that everyone must be rendered exactly equal in wealth and influence.[18]

Undoubtedly, Italy's foremost writers and intellects, like those of the Dutch Republic, were appalled by the Terror, and some were irreversibly disillusioned with the Revolution, even before Napoleon's arrival. The great investigator into the properties of electricity, Alessandro Volta, resident in Como, though a materialist and atheist, remained politically conservative and pro-Austrian. The greatest Italian dramatist and poet of the age, the Piedmontese Vittorio Alfieri (1749–1803), following conversion to radical ideas in 1777–78 under the impact of Diderot, d'Holbach, Helvétius, and Raynal, initially supported the Revolution but then underwent a remarkable volte-face. Before 1789, he had been a fierce critic of absolutism and princely courts, both in Italy and generally.[19] Greeting the Revolution of 1789 enthusiastically, he lived in exile in Paris during 1791–92 but became increasingly estranged, especially from the sansculottes and populist militancy. A proud aristocrat at bottom, he was outraged by the journée of August 1792, which jolted him and his mistress into fleeing France, abandoning their books and possessions, and returning to Italy, now avowed foes of the Revolution.[20]

Whether or not particular Italians supported the General Revolution usually had less to do with national sentiment than education, background, and views about religion. The more educated, and the less religious, the more likely Italians were to join the Revolution, unless they had a large economic stake in the prevailing system. In the Milanese, so many professors embraced the Revolution, acclaiming Napoleon and the Republic, that when the Austrians briefly recovered Lombardy in 1800, not only were Gioia and some others put back in prison but the entire University of Pavia was closed and all the professors dismissed, some permanently deprived of their chairs and salaries. In Italy, then, just as in Germany, France, and Britain, the solid support for democracy, equality, radical ideas, and what Gioia called "la libertà italiana" was to be found in academic, scientific, literary, and intellectual circles.

The Paris legislature wanted extensive delegation of power to local officials, personalities, and groups, and encouraged Italians to form their own revolutionary institutions, like the Dutch. Napoleon concurred. The new municipalities and *amministrazione generale* in Lombardy became essentially locally staffed bodies.[21] By the autumn of 1796, the French-style National Guard, partly consisting of Italian volunteers from outside the Milanese, was widely operative, entrusted, for example, with guarding, without French supervision, many of the thousands of Austrian prisoners captured in recent battles.[22] With the French urging the establishment of local republics, one of the Lombard *amministrazione*'s first acts in 1796 was to hold a prize competition for political writers to ascertain "which of the free forms of government is most conducive to the happiness of Italy?"[23] Gioia's vehemently antimonarchist thesis was proclaimed the winner. In the occupied northern part of the Papal States, similar procedures were adopted. A republican "senate" was established at Bologna and revolutionary political forms adopted, the first point on the reformers' agenda being to abolish papal Italy's old forms of address; the only permissible form of address in future was "citizen."[24]

This so-called Cispadane Republic (Repubblica Cispadana) was the first of the Italian sister republics officially inaugurated. It was proclaimed by a congress of 116 representatives from Modena, Bologna, Ferrara, and Reggio Emilia that convened on 16 October 1796. Partly spontaneously but encouraged by the French, the Repubblica Cispadana comprising the northern areas of the Papal States, Emilia and Romagna, took over adjacent areas, including the former duchy of Modena—wholly supplanting the fleeing duke and court of that principality—and formed its own armed force. A constituent assembly convened at Modena in March 1797 to inaugurate the first (partly) democratic Italian republican constitution. Modeled largely on the French Constitution of 1795, the constitution established two chambers: a council of sixty and a smaller body of thirty. The Repubblica Cispadana acquired its own separate National Guard, embellished with red, white, and green republican cockades and tricolor banners, the ancestor of the modern Italian flag. The deputy who proposed its tricolor banner, Giuseppe Compagnoni (1754–1833), a native of Lugo, was one of Italy's most prominent revolutionaries and a typical representative of the emerging new republican leadership. A professional intellectual deeply infused with Enlightenment reading, in the 1780s, he had coedited the Bolognese *Memorie Enciclopediche* with special responsibility for philosophy. Fiercely anticlerical well before 1789, he became a leading historian of the American Revolution. Appointed general secretary of the Cisalpine Republic (Repubblica Cisalpina), Compagnoni, besides his political role, was appointed in 1797 to Europe's first chair in constitutional law at the newly revolutionized University of Ferrara.

Enlightenment, not popular opinion or class friction, was the chief spur to the Revolution in Italy. The French Republic's policies acknowledged this by treating Italy's savants, academics, and intellectuals as a distinct social group, especially favored over others, particularly over the old nobility, courtiers, churchmen, and lawyers presiding over society in the past. In this respect, if in few others, Napoleon later, after capturing control of the French Republic in 1800, continued the General Revolution in Italy. It was a tendency that combined Enlightenment with overturning the ancien régime elites, an impulse strengthened by the form of the new Italian constitutions themselves with their two-stage elections prioritizing the new republican elites of merit and accomplishment over others.

The French interfered mainly to force the old town oligarchies to make way for the new democratic administrations, initiating a vigorous program of municipal "democratisations" designed to eradicate the old elites controlling the Northern Italian cities for centuries and replace them with local Giacobini allied to France. The process began in Milan and extended steadily over the next year across Lombardy. Wherever this purging process succeeded, a fairly robust, new, reformed legal and professional elite emerged. The old town council of Brescia was replaced by local Giacobini in March 1797. By April, "democratization" had reached Verona, and the counterrevolutionary revolt there in April 1797 was in large part a direct reaction to its *democrazione*. Italians were offered autonomous liberty under French protection, but the common people did not view matters in the same light as the revolutionary leadership, preferring instead the summons of religious authority and tradition. Resistance escalated, leading to a serious rebellion at Lugo in the Romagna in late June 1796, and antirevolutionary revolts at Genoa, Carrara, and Bergamo, besides the Verona revolt, or Pasque Veronesi, of late April 1797.

The Pasque Veronesi insurrection occurred over Easter, following a summons from the local bishop and clergy to rise against the "Jacobins" and slaughter the French garrison. Some dozens were killed. The resistance was widespread but promptly suppressed by French reinforcements. Rather remarkably, these restored order without any looting. Only eight rebel ringleaders were executed, with another fifty or so sent to France for dispatch to Guiana. Napoleon, consulting Barras and the Directoire in Paris, treated this uprising as subversion incited by the Venetian oligarchy. A major international imbroglio resulted, followed by a brief state of war. As the French army advanced to within sight of Venice, however, the Venetian Great Council voted by 537 to 20 to surrender without a fight rather than risk devastating the city. French troops entered Venice on 15 May 1797 and at once began erasing the symbols of patrician rule, dismantling the thousand-year-old noble republic, dismissed by Napoleon (who still had the reputation of being a radical republican at this time) as an obsolete relic. The sculptor Canova, a conservative loyal to the Serenissima and its traditions, like many others, bitterly lamented its passing.[25] Most of the Veneto remained under the new Venice, but the republic was now a French dependency, obliged to suppress the nobility, ceremonially burn the famous *Libro d'oro*, which listed Venice's old ruling patriciate, cede civil equality, transform its universities, and emancipate Jews and Protestants.[26]

Another major uprising occurred on 23 and 24 May 1797 at Genoa. When this subsided, the ancient, aristocratic Republic of Genoa was also suppressed, and, on 14 June 1797, its democratic successor, the Ligurian Republic, proclaimed. France amnestied those involved in the counterrevolutionary outbreaks under the Convention of Montebello (6 June 1797), but the Genoese had to acknowledge sovereignty to reside in the entire Ligurian people and abolish all forms of oligarchy, "distinction," aristocracy, and privilege.[27] Every Ligurian town received a democratically elected municipality. The only institutions retained intact were the Catholic Church and the ancient Bank of San Giorgio. Liguria's new constitution was drafted, put to a referendum, and endorsed by more than 100,000 votes to 17,000 against,[28] bringing the Ligurian

Republic into existence on 2 December 1797. Liguria's new constitution failed to provide freedom of conscience and freedom of thought—bowing to popular loyalty to the Church—but was otherwise modeled on the 1795 French Constitution with two legislative chambers and a directory.[29] Only later, after Napoleon made himself emperor, did the new antiaristocratic, egalitarian procedures in Liguria lapse and reversion to formal oligarchy occur.

During the summer of 1797, virtually on his own authority, Napoleon merged the Cispadane into the Cisalpine Republic, now covering much of the northern half of Italy, with its capital at Milan. The new republic comprised the Milanese, Mantua, Venetian Lombardy, and the Valteline area (which in October 1797 broke away from the Swiss federation). The Cisalpine Republic's constitution, proclaimed on 8 July 1797, again provided for two separate legislative chambers and a five-member Directoire, largely based, like its administration, on the current French model. Its territory was duly divided into departments, creating districts of equal population, with local assemblies of electors each representing, as in France, approximately two hundred people. The two chambers were called the Gran Consiglio, with around eighty members, and a smaller Consiglio dei Seniori. The "people's representatives" were mostly co-opted, comprising partly Italian revolutionaries with reputations acquired abroad, partly local academics, and partly progressive local notables, including several former friends and disciples of Beccaria, and occasionally also French supervisors. Alfonso Longo (1738–1804), one of Beccaria's and Pietro Verri's collaborators on the Milan journal *Il Caffè* in the 1760s, was among ten notables who signed the new constitution alongside Napoleon. "It is not without interest," observed Roederer, that it is the remaining friends and collaborators of Beccaria—Verri, Lambertenghi, and Longo—who "today occupy the chief places in the new republic, which indeed augurs well for its future."[30] To maintain the revolutionary ardor of the army of Italy, Napoleon established a regular paper in French published every two days, at Milan, the *Courrier de l'armée d'Italie ou le Patriote français à Milan*, which appeared in 248 issues between July 1797 and December 1798, edited in Milan by Jullien.[31] The paper's chief tasks were to help foster discipline and morale and present the commander, Napoleon, to his troops and to all Italy as a paragon of republican probity.

Among the new Italian republics, only the Cisalpine and Ligurian Republics transformed their legal and institutional structures in the later 1790s in anything like a throrough and comprehensive fashion.[32]

Elsewhere, in Piedmont, Tuscany, Venice, and the Romagna, as well as afterward in Naples, reform of law and institutions was fragmentary and sporadic. Yet, not only Northern but also all Southern Italy was profoundly affected by the changes. By mid-1796, the papacy and Neapolitan court found themselves caught in a severe dilemma. Although almost defenseless against Napoleon, for ideological reasons it was impossible for them to fully make peace with a Revolution they abhorred and dreaded and that would, should it advance further, inevitably despoil them of their authority, power, territory, and wealth. Both courts negotiated but in a prevaricating, halfhearted manner, continuing their ideological-cultural counteroffensive against Enlightenment and democratic values, albeit in a lower key, advisedly toning down their anti-French rhetoric for fear of reprisal. The Vatican also associated less than before with exiled French royalty and aristocracy. Increasingly uncomfortable, as earlier in the Swiss oligarchies, the émigrés were perhaps even deliberately encouraged to leave Rome. In October 1796, Louis XVI's two aunts, residing there since 1791, transferred to Naples, the French royal coats of arms and insignia being erased from the facade of their Rome residence behind them.[33]

Naples was widely considered one of the most backward and decayed realms of Western Europe. The admiration of foreigners under the Greeks, "Naples today," observed Gioia, "is degraded, one might say destroyed."[34] Around one-third of the land, taking mainland Naples and Sicily together, belonged to the Church and provided splendid revenues for the realm's twenty-two archbishops and 116 bishops, as well as its many baronial abbots, but left most peasants deprived and destitute. What was not owned by the Church belonged to large or medium landowners called "the baronage." Between them, ecclesiastical and noble landlords possessed practically all the olive oil presses in the kingdom. So entangled were baronial and ecclesiastical ownership, "rights" and tenures with non-noble tenure peasant occupancy, and sharecropping arrangements that the princely administration was unable to determine even how far the elites' "rights" and fiscal immunities extended, let alone reduce them. Sicily, remarked Gioia in 1797, though once termed the "granary of Italy" enjoyed "not even one third of the prosperity which her soil and climate should provide."[35]

The Neapolitan countryside seethed with disputes about land tenure and property rights serviced by an army of lawyers sworn to uphold justice but who mostly, Gorani noted, found it in their interest to support the landowners and Church against both townsmen and peasants.[36]

The peasantry was practically entirely illiterate; the dominance of the Church went unquestioned. In Naples and Sicily there simply existed no social class or group capable of mounting a revolutionary challenge. Nevertheless, at court, in the administration, and at Naples University, one encountered a highly motivated, enlightened fringe, deeply inspired by Vico, Giannone, Genovesi, and Filangieri. Owing to the many obstacles impeding more moderate reform programs, this group, taking their cue from the great Neapolitan legal reformer, Gaetano Filangieri (1752–88), an admirer of Raynal and Diderot, had become radicalized in recent years and profoundly antagonistic to the baronage and lawyers, and potentially to the bishops and the court.

Desperate to solve its acute economic and fiscal difficulties, for a time the Neapolitan court tried to compromise with the Enlightenment and accommodate Filangieri and the reformers by displaying some willingness to moderate aristocratic and ecclesiastical power, privilege, and revenues. But after 1789, and especially the first French revolutionary offensive in Western Europe in 1792–93, the Neapolitan court, like those of Tuscany, Modena, and the Rhenish ecclesiastical princes, reversed direction, repudiating reform and the reformers and aligning with Austria, Britain, and the papacy. By 1794, the Neapolitan court had broken completely with enlightened reform and thrown itself especially into the arms of the British.[37] This left the reformers, men like Francesco Mario Pagano (1748–99), Vincenzo Russo, and the eminent botanist, Domenico Cirillo (1739–99)—the deceased Filangieri's friends and followers—marginalized, repudiated, and in some cases stripped of their administrative and university positions with nowhere to turn except Paris, and nothing to invest their hopes in but the Revolution. Thus, Pagano and his friends became subversives and conspirators.[38] Pagano's *Saggi politici* of 1783, reissued in a more republican, radical version in 1791, proclaimed all humanity a single "universal society" mostly so backward and superstitious (and nowhere more so than in Naples), that human salvation is achievable only through vigorous advancement of enlightened thinking. This, in turn, would become possible only through the intensified efforts of academies, theaters, and societies, the sole effective instruments of dissemination of enlightened ideas in Southern Italy.

Following the murder of a French general in Rome in January 1798, the Directoire opted to occupy the papal city and expel the pope (who was escorted into exile at Florence). The French commander was instructed to work with a local group of Giacobini and two special emissaries, constitutional experts sent from Paris, Daunou and the mathematician Gaspard Monge, to forge a republic also there. On 15 February, the new Roman Republic was proclaimed. But popular resistance remained fiercer and more resolute in Central and Southern than in Northern Italy, and in November 1798, Ferdinand IV of Naples, in alliance with Austria and Britain, invaded the Roman Republic, resulting in a second French expedition to secure Rome, which then also invaded the Neapolitan realm. A French force under General Championnet captured Naples itself in January 1799. The Revolution in Italy continued with the occupation of Florence in March 1799 and the flight abroad of the grand duke of Tuscany. A liberty tree was erected in Florence in front of the Palazzo Vecchio, and the main square (hitherto the Piazza del Granduca, today the Piazza della Signoria) was renamed the Piazza Nazionale. All Florence's ducal academies were converted into "patriotic societies."

With the French troops in Naples, the ill-fated Repubblica Partenopea or Parthenopean (Neapolitan) Republic—named after the ancient Greek colony on which Naples was founded—was proclaimed. Its government was staffed by what was perhaps the most distinguished of the various local teams of Giacobini installed by the French in Italian regional capitals. This Neapolitan task group worked in concert with Marc-Antoine Jullien who had joined Championnet's staff and was assigned by him to serve as secretary-general of the new Parthenopean Republic. Headed by Pagano, Russo, Cuoco, and other disciples of Filangieri, it was a small but impressive coterie, the Republic's main newspaper being edited by a woman, the Rome-born poetess of Portuguese noble descent, Eleonora Fonseca Pimentel (1752–99). Like their colleagues in the other republics, the Neapolitan revolutionaries set out to abolish aristocracy, privilege, and feudal lordship, and establish an elected representative assembly while attempting to transform the local press, reading public, and the theater. A bill was introduced to confiscate the lands and property of the king's supporters and those courtiers who had fled with him to Sicily. Francesco Mario Pagano, best known and most distinguished of the Neapolitan revolutionary intellectual leadership, took the lead in formulating such measures and drawing up the constitution.[39]

Unlike their colleagues in Northern Italy, the Neapolitan Giacobini failed to achieve any real progress toward equality, individual liberty, or democracy. The Neapolitan population was simply too antagonistic, illiterate, and tradition-bound, and as it seemed to the Giacobini, too tied to the Church and credulity. At Pagano's insistence, the new draft Neapolitan constitution (that was never implemented) included both educational and financial qualifications for the right to vote. Pagano championed an undiluted, pure representative republicanism based on a selective franchise as the most appropriate for the Neapolitan context where it seemed impossible, at this stage, to accord the peasantry citizenship rights. Some of his colleagues, Russo and Cuoco, more taken with Rousseau and Mably, and in the latter case with the French democratic Constitution of 1793,[40] felt Pagano should have moved significantly further toward democracy, especially direct democracy.

The supreme error of the Neapolitan revolutionaries in 1799, Cuoco argued later, was to imagine constitutions can be devised from purely abstract principles without regard to local history, customs, and tradition. Pagano's edifice accommodated too little that was specifically Neapolitan. From an early stage, Cuoco expressed anxiety, as they all did, at the almost total lack of local support beyond a tiny intellectual fringe.[41] In reality, the Parthenopean Republic was doomed. Already in February, agents sent from Sicily began mobilizing a rural peasant army of resistance in the southernmost provinces of the kingdom, men sworn to fight to the death for monarchy and faith. These *sanfedisti*, religious zealots vowing to obliterate the Jacobin Republic, incited what rapidly developed into a massive rising. Pro-French democrats and anticlericals caught in the countryside were simply butchered. Occurring at a time when French troop strength in Italy was much reduced, the Neapolitan rising set off a peninsula-wide general revolt against the Revolution that turned ferocious in many areas of Central and Northern, as well as Southern, Italy and deeply shocked the temporarily retreating French.[42]

Mostly a rural and small-town phenomenon, Italian counterrevolutionary revolt in 1796–99 was centered in the poorest, remotest, and most illiterate areas, like the Neapolitan interior and Tuscan Apennine valleys. According to both French and Patriots, hard-core rebels were illiterate peasants incited by clergy, landowners, and foreign agents. But in places, urban artisans joined in, responding to a range of economic pressures.[43] In June 1799, a bloody battle erupted in the streets of Naples itself as enraged mobs of artisans, fishermen, and peasants drove the Giacobini back. The outcome was decided when Admiral Nelson and the British fleet sailed into the bay. The remaining revolutionary fighters besieged in Naples's almost impregnable inner fortress were promised that they could leave with honors of war if they surrendered. They surrendered, but were then promptly all seized at Nelson's insistence, and

dozens of them were afterward shot or hanged, those executed including most of the revolutionary leadership—Pagano, Russo, Fonseca Pimentel (who was hanged), and Cirillo.

Only Vincenzo Cuoco was imprisoned and later got away. In 1800,
he composed his *Saggio storico sulla rivoluzione napoletana del 1799*,
claiming "liberty is not established except by moulding free men." Too
much abstract thinking, he contended, had had ruinous consequences:
"imagining a republican constitution is not the same thing as founding
a republic." The Revolution collapsed, he urged with hindsight, owing
to its leaders' overestimation of the power of reason and philosophy.
The outcome was a tragedy that deeply affected the subsequent history
of Italy, a tragedy caused, insisted Gioia, by the "the moral, political and
religious prejudices that debase the Italian mind."[44] The revolutionary press in Milan defiantly replied to the royalist triumph in Naples
in 1800 by republishing Pagano's *Saggi politici* and the *Pensieri politici*
(1799) of Vincenzio Russo.[45]

Greece and the "Enterprise of Egypt" (1797–1800)

In the Italian Peninsula, between 1796 and 1800, the Revolution's impact was culturally, intellectually, and politically profound, and nowhere more so than in Venice. Besides losing her nobility and ancient
constitution, and being despoiled of parts of the Veneto, Venice lost
what remained of her empire in Greece. On 27 June 1797, a French
fleet under the Corsican general, Enselm Gentili, arrived in Corfu and
ended Venetian control there. Oligarchic, traditional, and Catholic
government in the Ionian Islands abruptly ceased. During elaborate
republican celebrations held in Corfu on 5 and 6 July, a liberty tree
was erected in the main square, the old Corfu oligarchy dismissed, the
Catholic Church stripped of its special privileges, and the Jews declared
free citizens. The Venetian *Libro d'Oro* was ceremonially burned, along
with a mass of aristocratic and ecclesiastical documents affirming feudal
rights and lordship.

No other major enterprise of the Western Enlightenment came to be
more inflated by overwrought expectations, excessive conjecture, arrogant presumption, and vivid imagination than the enterprise of the Levant, commencing with the conquest of Corfu and the Ionian Islands.
Before 1789, the French had dominated Europe's Levant trade for
more than a century. In 1797, carried away by a revolutionary mirage, a

number of leading figures, Napoleon among them, came to believe they could conquer and fundamentally remold Egypt, Palestine, and Syria, as a prelude to liberating India from the British. Some French revolutionaries imagined they could preside over the Near East as they did the Low Countries and Italy. If the world's peoples, wrote one French revolutionary propagandist, had every reason to dread an imperial power that knows only how to wreak vengeance and punish (i.e., Britain), the universe would surely admire a republic that purges the earth, like Hercules, and employs its "invincible arm to open up new sources of opulence accessible to all nations without imposing its yoke on any, appreciatively returning the sciences and arts to lands which transmitted them to us but where their flame is now extinguished [Egypt, Syria, and the Near East]."[46]

The reform-minded Ottoman sultan, Selim III (r. 1789–1807), intrigued by the Enlightenment but thus far knowing little of Jacobins and their activities, reportedly turned pale with shock on hearing, in January 1793, that Louis XVI's own subjects proposed to behead him. He began to reconsider his previously positive assessment of the Enlightenment and the large French community resident in Ottoman and other Levantine ports. In January and February 1793, Europeans in Ottoman ports, including many French, felt the guillotined French monarch should be extravagantly mourned. So outraged by Louis's execution were some French merchants that they then and there disavowed the Revolution, hurling down their tricolor cockades in protest before France's ambassador to the Porte, the Comte de Choiseul-Gouffier (1752–1817). When the French occupied Corfu five years later in 1797, the Revolution had for various reasons, and especially its divisive effect on the European merchant colonies scattered throughout the Ottoman Empire and Egypt, become a substantial factor in the politics and culture of the Near East. Revolutionary politics had become a weapon in European rivalry for the Levant trade. Observing the intrusion of French forces, reforms, and ideas into Greece, the Ottoman authorities grew apprehensive.

Choiseul-Gouffier, active in Constantinople since 1784, was rather more than just an ambassador in the normal sense. A cultivated nobleman and enlightener who researched ancient Greek history and possessed an Ottoman firman, like Lord Elgin later, authorizing him to remove antiquities from Athens, he encouraged French *érudits* to come to Turkish lands and also supervised the French military mission established there earlier in 1774. This French military academy

included officers expert in artillery, fortifications, and naval construction who advised the Ottoman court on a range of projected military and naval reforms while surreptitiously, at times almost openly,
extending French influence in the Levant, much as the Germans did
a century later.[47] Among other projects, Choiseul-Gouffier and his
staff helped establish the first Turkish school of fortifications, the
Muhendishane-i Barr-i Humayun, founded in October 1784. By February 1793, though, the count had become distinctly perplexed and
embarrassed by the liberty tree gracing his courtyard in Constantinople. After the Montagne captured the Revolution, he fled to Saint
Petersburg, where he became director of the Russian Imperial Public
Library.[48]

With the French in the Eastern Mediterranean increasingly divided,
a Jacobin popular society—with its membership strictly confined to
Frenchmen—was established at Constantinople in August 1793. It secured formal affiliation with the Jacobin Club in Paris, for a time at-
taining a membership of around twenty. Its leadership took care that
neither the big merchants (with one exception) nor the diplomats traditionally dominating the French Levantine community figured among
its membership, which comprised small business people, jewelers, and
intellectuals. The last included Brugières and Olivier, medical men and
naturalistes sent out at the Republic's expense by Roland and the Brissotin foreign minister, Lebrun, from whom they held commissions to research the region's natural history. Another member was citizen Amic,
brother-in-law of Olivier, likewise in Turkey at the Republic's expense,
sent to study oriental languages.[49] From such beginnings, anchored in
the minds of a few ambitious men in the embassy, military mission,
and Constantinople Jacobin club, and also in Paris, did the Revolution's *philosophique* leadership conceive, debate, and plan the *expedition d'Égypte*.

Contemporary Islamic society, held Diderot and the team that compiled the *Histoire philosophique*, was a world steeped in oppression,
ignorance, and misery, due not to any innate deficiency of the Arab people or their religion but rather their institutions, laws, and structures of
authority. It is governments and institutions, contended Diderot and
Raynal, that shape moral dispositions and attitudes, a reversal of Montesquieu's doctrine that moral and climactic contexts form the world's
different moral and legal codes. A crucial difference between Montesquieu's doctrine and the opposite radical approach was that the latter
set of relations was in principle reversible by men whereas the former

was fixed by the cosmos and irreversible. There was nothing innate for Volney and the radical philosophes about the current degradation of Arab lands: if ever Egypt emerged from the anarchy, argued Diderot, under an enlightened government where "la nouvelle constitution" is founded "sur des loix sages," this region of the world would reemerge among the most flourishing, industrious, and fertile existing.[50] Diderot's argument about Egypt and Syria was powerfully restated by the *Décade philosophique* in April 1798, while Napoleon prepared his military expedition at Toulon.[51]

Diderot's and d'Holbach's ideas about the Islamic world, widely diffused by the *Histoire philosophique*, were reproduced in a more erudite, sophisticated form by Volney in his *Voyage en Syrie et en Égypte, pendant les années 1783, 1784, et 1785* (2 vols., Paris, 1787), a work also appearing in German at Jena in 1788.[52] Political tyranny blights every society over which it gains control, contended Volney, like Diderot earlier, devastating its moral fiber and rendering men oppressed, exploited, ignorant, and poor. Egypt and Syria had been morally depleted centuries before by despotism and religious authority. However, according to Volney (like the Marquis d'Argens before him), only sedentary Muslims dwelling in cities or toiling in Egypt's irrigated fields, the mass of town and village life, were trapped in this moral degradation forged by tyranny and religious authority. Outside this abject sphere flourished an autonomous fringe of nomadic groups, especially Bedouin and Kurds, but also Druze, Turkmen, and other nomads, who preserved their natural freedom and equality. These peoples formed a potentially vital counterweight that could be mobilized against oppression.[53]

Admirably free men, untroubled by seriously destructive disputes, the Bedouin, argued d'Argens already much earlier in his *Lettres Juives* (1738), dwelt so far beyond the yoke of the despotic system "disfiguring" sedentary Arab society that they wholly lacked disputes about religion, and hence possessed, as it is put in the English translation, "no wrangling doctors and divines."[54] By contrast, in sedentary Islamic society, everything had degenerated since the dynamic early period. Despotism flourished, the sciences and philosophy had withered, and religious authority and popular credulity had rendered "the Egyptians . . . even more superstitious than the Turks leaving the Spaniards scarce a match for them." Moral and intellectual decay had debased Muslims to the point that they scorned science and philosophy and "do not much care for the Arabian doctors [i.e., Avicenna and Averroes], as the latter are enemies to miracles and superstition."[55]

Volney followed d'Argens in insisting on a vital difference between sedentary Arabs and those of the desert. The first lived under the double yoke of political and religious despotism in agricultural villages even more wretched than the towns that were supposedly all dismally abject: "even in Cairo the newly arrived foreigner is struck by an 'aspect général de ruine et de misère.'"[56] Bedouin, Turkmen, and the Kurds, very differently, were entirely free men, forming a social context altogether superior to that of the Arab towns and villages.[57] Though technically also Muslims, Kurds "ne s'occupent ni de dogmes ni de rites."[58] The same uprightness and autonomy characterized Marionites and the "Arabes de Daher." "The moral outlook of peoples," like that of individuals, concluded Volney, rebuking Montesquieu for his "errors," "depends above all on the social state in which they live."[59] Neither climate nor natural context had caused Egypt's misery and degradation. "Barbarism" prevailed in Syria and Egypt without either soil or climate being in the least responsible for the people's abasement and poverty.[60] Like Diderot and d'Holbach, Volney attributed the people's misery exclusively to the social institutions "called government and religion."[61] He pronounced the common people of the Near East the prey of those wielding religious authority, the victims of the credulity and ignorance sustaining *la barberie générale* in place of the philosophy and sciences that had once constituted the Levant's greatness but had long since been trampled under and become "entièrement inconnues," replaced by despotism and misery.[62]

Muslims can escape from their abasement and wretchedness only through enlightenment and revolution. These considerations hardened Volney's strange but then influential conviction that nothing is easier than to cause "une grande révolution politique et religieuse dans l'Asie" (a great political and religious revolution in Asia). He believed that such a "grande révolution" was not just immanent but urgently required and "easy" to accomplish. Muslim society's defects were structural and deep-rooted but readily curable, not innate. Arabs can read, contended Volney, as intelligently as Europeans but are prevented by cultural and religious prohibitions and their political institutions. The general ignorance enslaving the Arab mind was rooted in what he called the universal "difficulté des moyens de s'instruire," especially scarcity of books.[63] In all Syria, only two libraries were worth mentioning, those of Djezzar at Acre and the Marhanna at Aleppo; and even the second, the larger, possessed only around three hundred books. Why are books so exceedingly rare in Ottoman lands? Because nearly all books appear there only in manuscript, printing being practically nonexistent owing to the despotic whims of government and religious authority. Without printing (which Volney afterward tried to establish in Corsica) humanity cannot advance. Volney predicted that a Near Eastern version of the General Revolution would commence among the Bedouin and other nomads but that it would be ultimately driven by the resentment and a profound anger, he predicted, of the downtrodden remainder of the population.[64]

Robespierristes evinced markedly less interest in spreading the revolutionary creed abroad than Volney, Cloots, Proly, Lebrun, Paine, or the Brissotins. Following the Montagnard victory of June 1793, the Jacobin club at Constantinople hastened to reassure the parent society that it in no way wished to spread their revolutionary ideology among the Turks, Greeks, Armenians, or Jews, as the Brissotins had done. They confined their activities, they explained, to observing republican festivals and nurturing a republican spirit among the French community itself. Nevertheless, the Paris Jacobins remained suspicious because the Republic's experts and diplomatic staff in Turkey mostly had ties with Roland and Lebrun (and because the wealthier French merchants in the Ottoman Empire opposed the Revolution). Frowned on, because their very existence could readily be exploited by the British and French émigrés to alienate the Turks from France,[65] the Constantinople Jacobins, now reduced to just ten members, disbanded in March 1794.

Yet the views and attitudes of Volney and other Brissotin sympathizers had become diffused among the French community in the Ottoman Empire, and in Marseille and Toulon, and this foundation expanded once the Thermidorians gave way to a neo-Brissotin regime in 1795. By the time the new French ambassador, General Aubert du Bayet, settled in at Constantinople in late 1796, Brissotin revolutionary concerns were again fully in the ascendant. The General Revolution needed to be promoted vigorously. Aubert du Bayet (who had been imprisoned during the Terror) brought with him an astoundingly large staff, including no less than seventy artists and architects, besides military experts and naturalists, assigned to all manner of research projects in diverse parts of the empire on behalf of the Republic. But this only fueled Ottoman fears of French activity in the Ionic Islands and the Balkans where the French were directly appealing to Greek national feeling. Napoleon's treaty of Campo Formio (17 October 1797), partitioning the Venetian Empire between France and Austria, established France as a power in the Levant through her acquisition of the Ionian Islands. By this time

Napoleon, conferring with now foreign minister Talleyrand, was already thinking of breaking with the Turks and seizing Egypt.[66] The Ottoman Porte sensed the danger. Since the death of the Turkish Empire's chief enemy, Catherine II, in November 1796, the Turks were less fearful of having to fight Russia without French aid. The sultan decided to reconsider his close ties with France.[67] By the time Bonaparte's expedition to Egypt set sail some months later, the considerable body of French advisers and experts in Turkey, Greece, Syria, and neighboring lands were already under orders to pack their bags and leave.

The strategic and psychological, as well as propaganda, bridge between Napoleon's Italy and the Levant were the Ionian Islands. The ascendancy of *il democratico governo* there, though brief, is significant in French Revolution history due to its intensely ideological character and its bearing on the wider French vision for the Near East. The French lost no time in suppressing Venetian ways and procedures in Corfu, or attempting to win over Greek Orthodox sentiment by according equal status and more advantages to their clergy than to the Catholics favored by Venice. The Revolution appealed not to rulers or the past but to peoples, urging the Greeks to consider the benefits of allying with France. While church property belonging to the Islands' eleven Catholic churches and monasteries was immediately confiscated by the revolutionary state, Greek church property was deliberately left untouched. In July 1797, an "anti-aristocracy decree" was published in Greek and Italian, condemning all "aristocracy" as evil and declaring that the peasants throughout the islands were now entirely free of all "feudal" exactions and obligations.[68] Outraged by the loss of his revenues, prestige, and authority, and the pilfering of silver crucifixes and plate, the vociferously protesting Latin bishop of the Islands was expelled for inciting the Catholic faithful against the Revolution.

All official letters circulating in the islands, whether in Italian, French, or Greek, were headed "freedom" and "equality." Citizens were expected to appear in the streets bearing revolutionary cockades, and no one was permitted to disregard the changes the Revolution introduced. The first modern Greek public library was founded in Corfu in May 1798, dedicated to Greek national reawakening, liberty, and enlightenment. In August the first Greek publishing house followed, dedicated to publishing for the Greek people, which, among other items, produced revolutionary calendars in Greek, and soon reports of French victories in Egypt. The Islands' forts and redoubts were renamed after great revolutionary events or victories in Italy. One of Corfu town's quarters was renamed the Quartier du 10 Aoust, another, the Quartier de Mars, where an "altar to liberty" was erected and revolutionary public celebrations were held. The Venetian Fort Salvador became Fort Lodi, and Fort Abram, Fort Rivoli.[69] The revolutionaries also replaced some discarded Venetian nomenclature with Greek names, the Gate of the Hospital becoming the Gate of Epirus.[70] The local Jewish community received equal rights and freedom of expression alongside Catholics and Greeks. Eager to revolutionize and modernize, the French intro- duced street lighting, ballet, and printed bulletins (mainly in French and Italian) concerning local affairs.

As elsewhere, the theater became a key resource for reeducating the populace. The first anniversary of the French occupation of Corfu, coin- ciding with the 10 Messidor (29 June) festival of agriculture, prompted a special effort to impress the inhabitants with what the French termed this "era of the liberty of Greece."[71] It was not easy to impress them. The new rhetoric and freedom of expression provoked various incidents in the theater, where "malicious" individuals hissed and stamped at scenes they were supposed to applaud.[72] To ensure better order in the town's theater, S. Giacomo, Corfu's police commissaire, in October 1797, published disciplinary rules in Greek, French, and Italian, forbidding swearing, smoking, and bringing arms into the theater.[73] Early signs of friction between French and Greeks soon grew into a serious problem. The frequent instances of Corfu inhabitants insulting the revolution- ary cockade or other revolutionary symbols provoked arrests. With the ghetto restrictions imposed by the Venetian government dismantled, Corfu's Greeks now had to rub shoulders with the Jews in public spaces, law courts, and theater, and address Jews in the same way as they ad- dressed each other—as "citizen." Before long, the thorniest problem in policing revolutionary Corfu, reported the commissaire, was the increasingly "bad humour of the Christian citizens toward the Jewish citizens," antipathy responsible for numerous ugly incidents that the French commandant repeatedly took up with both Greeks and local Italian Catholics.[74]

The sultan did not need to be told, even before Napoleon's invasion armada took shape in Toulon, that sweeping plans for a wider revolu- tionary intervention in the Near East were evolving in Paris. Before Au- bert du Bayet left Paris for Turkey in 1796, he discussed a scheme to overrun Crete, an island closely inspected earlier by an officer attached to the Constantinople military mission. Officers posted in Constanti- nople regularly spoke of the Ottoman Empire's military weakness, as did Napoleon, encouraging the deliberations that led to the Directoire's decision to invade Egypt. Between the coup of 18 Fructidor (4 September 1797) and 11 May 1798, the early phase of the second Directoire, vigorous measures were taken against royalists, émigrés, and refractory priests, and there was a brief revival in Jacobin fortunes. The mood was emphatically republican and the army more saturated than ever with republican ideology. It was in this context, steeped in philosophique ideas and plans, that the Egyptian expedition was conceived and launched. The Directoire's final decision to invade was made on 5 March 1798. Within two months, the expedition was prepared amid great secrecy to avoid arousing suspicion in London and Constantinople. The revolutionary armada comprised thirteen ships of the line, forty-two lesser warships, 280 transports, 38,000 troops, and 16,000 seamen.[75] Leaving Toulon on 19 May, it reached Malta (the seizure of which Napoleon had been advocating for some time) on 9 June, the grand master surrendering without a fight.

The French occupation of Malta continued until September 1800 when the British gained possession of the island (which they were to keep for a century and a half). On Malta, the French abolished nobility and canceled the Church's power, confiscating a great quantity of silverware and other items from churches and monasteries that was sent back to Paris. Jews, Greek Orthodox, and others were granted religious freedom and equal status to Catholics; the British by contrast afterward restored the privileges of both Church and nobles. Only after departing from Malta did the main expedition's officers and men learn their true destination. The army was admonished to respect Islam, and especially their muftis and imams, and collaborate with them "as we have done with the Jews and Italians."[76] Accompanying them were 160 savants and scientists (some accounts put the number as high as 187) who were recruited and commissioned by the Directoire and equipped with a wealth of books and scientific instruments.[77] While crossing the Mediterranean, not only the scholars but also Napoleon's officers were required to read Volney, Niebuhr, and other recent accounts of the Near East. Among its aims, the scholarly, scientific section of the expedition intended to carry out a thorough study of the region's topography, flora, and fauna, and impart new momentum to the disciplines of archaeology, Egyptology, Arabic studies, and deciphering ancient scripts, all then still in their infancy. Science, enlightenment, and emancipation, as well as strategic concerns, thoroughly infused the expedition, the ultimate goal of which was to threaten Britain's hold on India and topple Britain's world hegemony.

French Enlightenment ambition in the Near East extended much further than simply a desire to carry out research. Montesquieu was mistaken, held Volney, like Diderot, d'Holbach, and Raynal, to classify Asia and the Middle East as unalterably "despotic." These were undoubtedly lands of oppression and despotism, but their people were unnecessarily downtrodden, poor, and wretched. Their wretchedness could be ended swiftly via an ambitious program of enlightenment and emancipation, a general revolution transforming the legal, institutional, and political format of society. By replacing despotism with democratic republicanism based on the Rights of Man, Egypt could be emancipated, the people made happier, and France and Egypt be rendered firm friends and allies. Military and strategic expansionism fused in this way with the Revolution's Left democratic republican ideology.[78]

Arriving in the Nile Delta on 1 July 1798, the French were exhorted by their commander not to rape or pillage and to respect Islam for the benefit of their country and the Revolution. They stormed Alexandria, where they lost no time in obliging local inhabitants, records the Egyptian chronicler Abd al-Rahman al-Jabarti (1754–1825), "to sew their emblem [tricolor cockade] on their breasts."[79] The Muslim religious authorities were assured that the revolutionaries were ardent friends of Islam, as was proved by their measures against the papacy, their ending the centuries-long drive of the Knights of Malta against Muslims, and their having "destroyed" the Knights.[80] With the Delta secured, the French advanced on Cairo. During the advance, printed proclamations in Arabic denouncing the Turkish Mamluk elite governing Egypt were dispatched ahead, records Al-Jabarti, to many places. For centuries, the Mamluks had exploited the merchants and generally oppressed the people "in the fairest land on the face of the globe," as well as insulted the French. Cairenes would doubtless be assured by the Revolution's enemies that the French had come to abolish "your religion." But this was "pure falsehood" and the Cairenes must not believe it. Slanderers should be told that Napoleon had come solely to restore the people's rights. Napoleon "served God—may he be praised and exalted—and revered his prophet Muhammed and the glorious Koran" more than did the Mamluks. Egyptians were urged to "tell the slanderers" that "all people are equal in the eyes of God and that the only qualities distinguishing one man from another are reason, virtue and knowledge."[81] Any village resisting the army's passage would be burned down.

Barely had he crushed the Mamluks at the Battle of the Pyramids (21 July) and captured Cairo than Napoleon, on 22 August 1798, set up the Egyptian Institut pour les Sciences et les Arts in a former Mamluk palace. It was based on the model of the Institute at Paris, of which Napoleon was a keen supporter. Condorcet, Volney, Daunou, and the Idéologues had conceived the Paris Institute as the pivot linking Enlightenment and social and political reform. The Cairo Institute, presided over by the mathematician Monge, its secretary, another mathematician, Jean-Baptiste Fourrier (1768–1830), and especially Claude-Louis Berthollet (1748–1822), a famous chemist and electrical expert, renowned for introducing new techniques of bleaching and dyeing textiles in France (and, with Monge, devising new explosives), was conceived in the same spirit. The new foundation, under its constitution, was directed to spread enlightenment, bring Egypt into a new era, conduct systematic research, and advise the government and army on specific issues where required. The Cairo Institute was divided into four sections (not three, as in Paris)—mathematics with twelve savants, physics with ten, political economy with six, and arts and literature with nine.

The Institute swiftly set up its own printing press, as well as acquiring a library, laboratory, and garden, its impressive rooms and quarters being well suited to treating local Cairo Muslim dignitaries to guided tours.[82] The laboratory and library in particular attracted visiting Egyptian notables. The printing press published the Institute's reports and also Egypt's first newspapers, *Le Courier de l'Égypte* and *La Décade Égyptienne*.[83] The Institute and the papers took the lead in Napoleon's effort to introduce the republican ten-day weeks, the *décade*, and to steer Egypt away from religious observance toward celebrating instead the revolutionary festivals adorned with all the characteristic republican trappings—tricolor flags, cockades, sashes, fireworks, and liberty trees.

Napoleon, having studied the Koran, was convinced that he could work with Islam. The French invaders had arrived with what they considered an all-encompassing regenerative ideology, and this conviction helped guide their entire approach in Egypt throughout. But any illusions the savants harbored that they could pursue science and learning on the banks of the Nile as freely and systematically as on the Seine, propagating new ideas among the public and effecting improvements in education and in the civil and criminal code as Napoleon urged,[84] were rudely shattered from the outset. The British destroyed the French fleet in Aboukir Bay on 1 August, cutting off the army in Egypt from all contact with France, Italy, and the Ionian Islands, and hence from supplies, reinforcements, publications, and scientific instruments. Egyptians, much to their disappointment, seemed entirely unimpressed with their assurances that they immensely respected Islam and medieval Arab achievements. Religion was the main cause of the embittering of relations in almost every way, Egyptians abhorring many aspects of French daily conduct, especially their treatment of women, drinking, permitting non-Muslims of every description to ride horses (forbidden under sharia), and preference for dealing with local Christians. Before long, Muslim Egyptians turned distinctly hostile and confronted the Institute and its savants with all manner of difficulties, especially during and after the Cairenes' violent uprising against the French occupation in October 1798.

A powerful wave of disillusionment and exasperation soon darkened the Enlightenment in Egypt but did not entirely extinguish the sense of adventure and enthusiasm attending its inception. Efforts were made to achieve rapid, visible amelioration in the conditions of life. As Al-Jabarti notes, the French "announced that lamps should be lit all night in the streets and markets. Each house was required to have a lamp as well as every third shop. The people were to sweep, splash water, and clean the streets of the rubbish, filth and dead cats." The French also set up a new court, or diwan, for Cairo, to handle commercial and civil disputes, though in doing so they further antagonized local opinion by appointing as many Copts as Muslims as judges, and by according Christians and Jews equal status.[85] This diwan became the pivot of French efforts at public reeducation.

On one occasion, all the sheikhs and grandees of Cairo were summoned to a general meeting and assured the "sciences, arts and reading and writing which people in the world have knowledge of at present were learnt from the forefathers of the ancient Egyptians." The French had come to deliver "Egypt from its sad state and to relieve its people from the Ottomans who dominated it in ignorance and stupidity." They planned to set the country's affairs in order and "make the canals which had fallen into oblivion flow with water. For then Egypt would enjoy access both to the Mediterranean and the Red Sea, with a resulting massive increase in fertility and income."[86] Contact with India would be restored. All this was grandiose and overly ambitious, but not cynical. Having carefully studied the Koran, Napoleon sincerely nurtured plans for harmonious friendship, as well social, economic, and technological improvements, rendering Egypt a showcase of enlightened amelioration.[87]

All manner of expeditions were dispatched into the desert, to the south, and the Delta, over ensuing months. A vast amount of scientific and other research, and numerous topographical, architectural, and archaeological drawings, accumulated. The expedition caused a stir in France from the outset in 1798, and gradually built a wider platform of interest for the project among readers at home. Volney's *Voyage en Syrie et en Égypte*, observed the *Décade philosophique* when announcing the third edition in April 1799, was a work that had grown in stature and attracted wide interest due to recent developments in the Near East.[88] The major scientific and scholarly encyclopedia later to emerge from the efforts of the French enlighteners in Egypt, the *Description de l'Égypte*, one of the most impressive of all monuments to the Enlightenment, a venture commencing already in 1798, was indeed massively impressive, but it was also slow, the first volume appearing only in 1802. The discovery in July 1799 of the Rosetta stone with its three columns of identical text in hieroglyphics, Coptic, and Greek, and the exciting possibility this afforded for deciphering ancient Egyptian hieroglyphics, was reported to the Institute in Paris, recounts the *Décade philosophique*, already at a meeting on 27 October 1799, by Napoleon himself after his return from Egypt. The projected canal linking the Mediterranean to the Red Sea, the scheme that would one day become the Suez Canal, Napoleon assured the Paris Institute's professors, had actually once existed, dug by the Pharaohs, and he did not doubt it was possible to reestablish it.[89]

Napoleon had often conversed with Volney in Corsica in 1791–92, when he first contemplated waging war for the Revolution against the Counter-Enlightenment (in Corsica).[90] He took a keen interest in the Cairo Institute and generally in the idea of spreading Enlightenment in the Near East, being especially eager to show the Egyptians the superiority of Western science and technology. Several meetings attended by elite members of the Cairo community, Al-Jabarti among them, were intended to impress Egyptians with scientific equipment and experiments, including spectacular electrical and chemistry displays put on by Berthollet. But Egyptians construed these proceedings differently from the French, more as magic than science, obdurately refusing to be impressed or interested.[91] Their stubborn indifference to science surprised and annoyed the French, not least Napoleon, as he records in his correspondence. Their indifference he deemed yet another instance of the dismal and deleterious effects of religion that the French seemed totally unable to erase.

The Cairo Idéologues remained obsessed with the contradiction between the astounding misery and destitution of Egypt's population and the imposing fertility and wealth of the land where irrigated. They hoped to resolve this contradiction through the power of ideas, science, and technology. The Cairo Institute savants may have been part of a military occupation, convinced of their own superiority and scornful of ordinary Egyptians, but they also deliberated on how Egyptian, Palestinian, and Syrian agriculture could be revived, commerce and industry stimulated, Nile hydraulics improved, and how all this should be combined with a general emancipation, commencing with the Greeks, Copts, Armenians, Kurds, Syriac Christians, and Jews. Lectures in French were provided for all wishing to hear them. In all, the Institute held sixty-two lecture and discussion meetings that were mostly well attended, mainly by French officers and savants but also by a few Christian, Jewish, and Muslim Cairene notables.[92] Monge and Berthollet, savants with enviable international reputations, whom Napoleon knew from Italy, were the star lecturers, but both returned to France with Bonaparte after a year, in August 1799. Among the Institute's more topical debates was that concerned with how best to deal with the plague outbreak gripping Alexandria since December 1798. Institute deliberations resulted in a raft of measures and sanitary rules requiring Egyptian city dwellers to fumigate their houses to disperse putrescence, hang out their clothing and bedding for several days on their roofs, and desist from burying their dead in cemeteries close to dwellings.[93]

The revolutionary Enlightenment brought to Egypt by Napoleon failed entirely with the Muslims. During the Cairo insurrection of October 1798, the rioters pillaged the house occupied by one of Napoleon's commanders where most of the stock of telescopes, astronomical equipment, and mathematical instruments was stored; everything was destroyed. Yet, there was a sense in which the Cairo Institute and the savants participating in its work succeeded in advancing the Enlightenment in the Near East, even if not along the lines originally intended. Some Egyptian non-Muslims were interested in republican ideas and in the Enlightenment. Greeks living in Egypt, reported the *Décade philosophique* in Paris in January 1799, warmly welcomed the French, as did the large Coptic community (which some Western savants thought larger than it actually was), despite its abject condition and backwardness due to centuries of servile subjection. Armenians were also interested and, as in Corfu, the Jews too stood to gain from the spread of French power and Enlightenment in Egypt and, in fact, everywhere in the Near and Middle East. Besides, added Joachim Le Breton (1760–1819), an art historian much swayed by Volney, there were the Bedouin, men quite different from other Arabs, and, as d'Argens and Volney stressed, less enslaved to religious authority.[94]

All this seemingly offered possibilities for expanding French influence and activity. At this point Volney published an article, reiterating his view that reliance on Bedouin, Druze, Kurds, Turkomans, Armenians, and Marionites offered good prospects for consolidating France's presence in Egypt, Syria, and the Near East generally.[95] Le Breton, a defrocked former monk who had entirely rejected his Christian background, also proposed, rather remarkably, encouraging the colonization of persecuted Jews from Central and Eastern European lands in Syria, Palestine, and Egypt as a way of stimulating commerce and industry in the region.[96] "There is an assured means to give especially Syria an active, affluent and numerous population—namely, to call in the Jews. We know how much they love their ancient land [i.e., Judaea] and the city of Jerusalem!"[97] This, he argued, would be an effective way to permanently entrench French influence. Le Breton devoted several pages to elaborating on how revival of the Near East under French auspices could be advanced by summoning the Jews. The universal hatred and prejudices against the Jews was a problem, but "la philosophie" teaches and urges everyone who is not ignorant to utterly discard all of that, as indeed had Napoleon while the French armada was on its way from Malta.[98]

Having overrun Egypt, and in December 1798 having occupied the ancient port of Suez on the Red Sea, the main French military expedition set out for Syria in early 1799. The army totalled 12,945 effectives. Napoleon's partial conquest of Palestine in early 1799 gave rise to speculation that he would proclaim the deliverance of Jerusalem and recall the dispersed Jews of the earth back to "their ancient homeland."[99] In Palestine, then part of Turkish Syria, Napoleon proved victorious at first, capturing Jaffa on 7 March (where an appalling massacre of the inhabitants was perpetrated by the troops over whom their officers lost control) but was defeated eventually, partly by British naval power, partly Turkish tenacity, and partly disease. Marching up the Palestinian coastal plain, Napoleon was halted at the old Crusader stronghold of Acre, a formidable Ottoman base the French besieged in vain for two months in the spring of 1799. Acre, once the last surviving Crusader stronghold in Arab lands, in Turkish hands withstood no less than thirteen French assaults, resulting in 2,000 wounded and 550 dead. Another 600 men died from the plague, many in the French hospital on Mount Carmel, in what is today Haifa, others at Jaffa. By the time the army extricated itself and marched back from Palestine across the Sinai Desert to Egypt, another 400 had expired from disease, heat, and exhaustion.

But this was not the end of the Near Eastern adventure. To the revolutionaries, the French occupation of Egypt had an important purpose. It continued for another two years, until the army finally surrendered to the British on 27 September 1801. The philosophe and économiste Jean-Baptiste Say, an enthusiast for revolutionary festivals, Diderot, Helvétius's utilitarianism, and (following Helvétius and Condorcet) advocate of social amelioration through progressive taxation forcing diffusion of wealth away from the richest,[100] enthused in the *Décade philosophique* issue of October 1798 over the alluring prospect of once again turning Egypt into a fulcrum of commerce between Asia and Europe. That land would be for a second time "la patrie" of the sciences and the "séjour le plus délicieux de la terre."[101] The notion that Bonaparte came to liberate Egyptians, Syrians, Jews, and Palestinians sounded not just benevolent but like eminently good sense in 1798–1800. As the Idéologues understood it, the French sought to emancipate Egypt from her enslavement to tyranny, religion, ignorance, and the Turk, and improve the lives, economy, and society of the Egyptians and their neighbors; and this they resolutely strove to accomplish.[102]

CHAPTER 24

The Failed Revolution

(1797–99)

Unbridgeable Fissures

During 1795–96, support for the regime among the French electorate remained decidedly tepid. Republicans pointing to the mounting royalist threat had, since Thermidor, been continually denounced by conservative opponents as *terroristes* and *anarchistes*.[1] Heavily burdened with war, requisitioning, and recruiting, the country was trapped in a ceaseless three-way internecine struggle between royalists, neo-Brissotin democrats often allied to Dantonistes, and Montagnards, in part allied to followers of Babeuf (Babouvistes). This ensured an unbreakable deadlock that continually fed the mounting fatigue, frustration, and sense of drift: everything was suffused with ideological struggle, daily life, religion, the press, and the theaters, while at the same time, the popular mood, volatile and unpredictable, lurched toward the right. A key part of this battle was the constant polemics over the question of the Terror, its real nature, and meaning.

To further add to the Republic's predicament, the Directoire's rightward shift during 1796–97 eventually became obvious enough to seriously split the republican mainstream, disillusioning many principled supporters and causing some to be sucked into clandestine conspiracy against the Directoire. A major factor sapping support for the Republic was certainly the still furiously contested legacy of the Thermidorian regime. Numerous posts remained in the hands of supposedly reformed Montagnard ex-Jacobins often of highly dubious character; among the most detested were Barras, Joseph Fouché, and François-Louis Bourdon (1758–98), who "combines," Robespierre once observed, "perfidy with fanaticism."[2] Quarreling with Robespierre and isolated in the Jacobins after having already been expelled from the Cordeliers in early 1794, Bourdon had emerged after Thermidor among the most implacable pursuers of his former terroriste colleagues. Brutal, corrupt, and utterly unprincipled, such men kept assiduously to one particular principle: they must hang on to power, come what may, for if royalists once laid hands on them, they would indubitably be executed as regicides and terroristes.

Driven underground, Panthéonistes and the *Tribun* carried on a shadowy existence, meeting at private addresses in Paris. The movement was organized, from March 1796, by a secret directorate, including Maréchal, Buonarroti, Darthé, Babeuf, and Lepeletier, who plied subversion in cafés, prisons, and gardens, disseminated clandestinely printed tracts and posters, and formed cells in Arras, Cambrai, Rennes, Nantes, Reims, and Lyon.[3] Establishing "revolutionary agents" in the capital's poorer sections, gradually the "conspiracy for equality" matured its plans for another, and this time decisive, 21 May–style mass popular insurrection. As the conspiratorial underground movement grew, it was joined by many widely loathed veterans of the Terror, Amar, Vadier, and Pache among them, and amid the frequent debates in these subversive circles about philosophes and the great revolutionary personalities arose a movement to revive the reputation of Robespierre to which, according to Buonarroti, even Amar, one of the leading Thermidorians, adjusted (years afterward, Amar converted to Swedenborg's mysticism). "Robespierre" was thus resurrected among this conspiratorial underground as a heroic champion of economic equality, Babeuf himself actively participating in this attempt to rehabilitate the lawyer from Arras and condemn the Thermidorians.

The conspirators saw their task as to achieve the overthrow of the Five Hundred and the Directoire by revolutionary action, to restore the 1793 Constitution, and ultimately to achieve a general equality (*l'égalité sans restrictions*), resuming the project supposedly shattered by 9 Thermidor.[4] Tension between the ex-Montagnards and authentic Babouvists or egalitarian democrats, however, created an irresolvable tension within the body of the underground movement. In February 1796, the *Journal des hommes libres* of Vatar published statements by Babeuf—now an unabashed apologist for Robespierre—Lepeletier, Antonelle, and Buonarroti, denying that they had captured the Panthéon Club, or that they were calling for dictatorship.[5] Yet the conspirators remained divided as to how to attain equality and democracy once the Directoire was overthrown by the destitute of Paris. Some of the leadership, notably Darthé, certainly urged the need for a dictator, arguing that a *dictature* was essential to forcibly imposing equality. Amar and a second group wanted the previous Montagnard Convention recalled, albeit without firmly opposing dictatorship. Most of the conspiracy's leadership, however, deterred both by the prospect of a new dictator and reservations about Amar and his friends, appear to have preferred a different approach: once the people of Paris triumphed, the secret leadership would convene the victorious people in the vast Place de la Révolution, explain their aims and strategy to the crowds—stressing the primacy of economic equality in their plans—and ask the people then and there to create an "autorité provisoire" to supervise the Revolution and govern France until the 1793 Constitution could be rendered operative.[6]

Before long, though, the Directoire infiltrated, and, in early May 1796, arrested the leadership. Babeuf and Buonarroti were seized on 10 May 1796, along with several sansculotte agitators and a cache of incriminating documents. Drouet, Lindet, Maréchal, Vatar, Darthé, and Antonelle were arrested soon afterward. Altogether more than fifty conspirators were detained; their imprisonment sent tremors through all the networks and clubs with ex-Jacobin sympaties around the country.[7] The Babeuf conspiracy and the thinking it embodied with its summons to the French to found "the republic of equals," was soon to attract a vast amount of attention. Like the republican bloc as a whole, its leadership consisted partly of intellectuals steeped in Radical Enlightenment philosophy who vehemently repudiated repression and tyranny. Yet these men aspired to make a different kind of revolution from that which France had achieved in 1789–93, rejecting not just the pragmatic, authoritarian format offered by the Directoire but also the more democratic, libertarian vision proclaimed by the neo-Brissotins and Idéologues. The author of the Babouvistes' manifesto, Pierre-Sylvain Maréchal, former deputy librarian of the Collège Mazarin, had been an atheist and materialist philosophe long before 1789, and typically of those who forged the Revolution was a man steeped in radical philosophical literature. Before aligning with Babeuf, he had been a prominent revolutionary journalist collaborating with Prudhomme and Chaumette. While the Revolution had achieved equality before the law, argued his *Manifeste des égaux*, what the people really needed was genuine "equality," a community of goods and property.

The French Revolution of 1788–93, contended Maréchal, like Babeuf, was merely the herald of another revolution "bien plus grande, bien plus solennelle" that will be the last revolution: "We declare that we can no longer accept that the great majority of men work solely at the service and for the good pleasure of a small minority. For far too long less than a million individuals dispose of what belongs to more than twenty million of their fellow men, the possessions of their equals."[8] Maréchal's Bavouiste ideology, unlike the populism of Robespierre and Saint-Just, or of Chabot or Hébert, was an authentic social reformism and a real offshoot of Radical Enlightenment and the Revolution, but, equally, and divergently, it was a militant protosocialism with strong dictatorial tendencies, albeit sometimes sharing the Ideologues' preoccupation— here in sharp contrast to the royalists and the neo-Jacobins—with uncovering the real nature of the Terror and Montagnard repression. Even so, this philosophique element became fatally diluted by Babeuf's neo-Robespierrisme and the alliance with hard-line militants like Darthé and Buonarroti, as well as thoroughly unprincipled types like Vadier and Amar.

Most Frenchmen and most voters, meanwhile, inclined more to the Catholic and royaliste side than to any sort of republicanism, whether democratic or Babouvist, and monarchist leaders, convening their followers at the Clichy Club, and the royalist press, sensed that among the directeurs Carnot too now supported them, indeed lent them virtually a free hand. Admittedly, the Right too remained hopelessly divided. Ultraroyalists detested constitutional monarchists while right constitutional monarchists admiring Mounier loathed the watered-down "moderation" of liberal monarchists adhering to the memory of Barnave and the Feuillants. Monarchists were then further divided between constitutional monarchists loyal to the rigidly conservative Louis XVIII, legitimate heir to the throne, and those aligning with the royal family's junior but more liberal Orléanist branch. Louis XVIII further complicated matters for the Right by releasing a curtly blunt manifesto on 10 March 1797 in Germany, urging Frenchmen to reject constitutionalism and republicanism unreservedly. Louis seemed unwilling to make any concession to constitutionalism let alone embrace major reforms. Yet, despite these ultimately unbridgeable divisions, the country's tenacious royalists and militant Catholics eagerly anticipated sweeping gains in the forthcoming elections of 1797. With most people seemingly won back for royalism and Catholicism, noted the *Journal de Perlet* in late March 1797, many were now openly predicting a new legislature that would be predominantly conservative. To republican stalwarts, France appeared to be on the verge of a new "explosion terrible."[9]

The *Journal des hommes libres*, earlier hostile to Babeuf's neo-Jacobinism and apologetics for Robespierre, shifted its ground during the course of 1796, becoming increasingly worried by the threat of royalism. The *contre-revolution*, warned the *Journal des hommes libres* in early February 1797, seemed already to have invaded most of the press and theaters. Much as republicans had subverted monarchy in 1789–92 by steadily infusing republican attitudes and ideas into society at every point, royalists were now repeating the procedure in reverse.[10] In fact, the run-up to the national elections of the Year V in March and April 1797 generated hugely renewed tension throughout France. No less than 234 former members of the Convention were due to retire, and the results would, for the first time since 1792, decisively shape the legislature, executive, and future of the Revolution. Together with the democratic republican press, most of the Council of Five Hundred and the Directoire hoped for the return of a constitutional republican majority that rejected both royalism and *la tyrannie révolutionnaire* of the Montagne, choosing representatives committed to a stable, democratic outcome. Deputies like Daunou, Boissy d'Anglas, Lanjuinais, Camus, and Pierre Durand-Maillane (1729–1814), another former Brissotin returned to the forefront, aspired to win over the public and build a predominant bloc in the legislature.[11] Jacques-Antoine Creuzé-Latouche (1749–1800), who had endorsed the appel au public and indictment of Marat, was another of this group now returned to prominence. But the democratic republican Left proved too lacking in popular support, and the public too apathetic and weary of revolutionary politics, as Bonneville's new paper, *Le Vieux Tribun et sa Bouche de Fer,* sadly observed,[12] for anything like the hoped-for breakthrough to transpire. During the run-up to the elections, the *assemblées primaires* were frequently manipulated and occasionally violently interrupted; vote-rigging flourished once again.[13]

As feared, the elections resulted in a crushing defeat for the Directoire, Republic, secularism, and the Revolution itself, greatly dismaying both the Left and authoritarian populists. One of the defeated republican candidates, the naturalized Swiss Benjamin Constant, described the outcome as "abominable."[14] The unpalatable but undeniable truth was that ordinary people were no longer interested in revolutionary politics and spurned democratic rhetoric; most wanted the return of the old order, monarchy and religion. No less than 182 of the 234 newly elected deputies were committed royalist-Catholics of one hue or another. This "disaster," declared the *Décade philosophique*, was due to the corruption of public opinion through the "poison spread by a hundred venomous journals." According to the *Décade philosophique*, a majority of the Five Hundred was now bent on abandoning revolutionary principles, the lower legislature having become a sink of "prejudice, traditional notions, bigotry, royalism and Catholic fanaticism."[15] By July 1797, the now predominantly conservative Council of Five Hundred began debating a draft edict to recall réfractaires in exile on favorable terms, release those still being held, and restore to all refractory priests rights of citizenship and confiscated personal possessions. Boissy d'Anglas and the much-diminished band of republicans resisted as best they could, maintaining that such a decree would be a license for clergy to undermine "republican principles" in all hearts as much as they wished. But the new majority of the legislature was adamant and the lower chamber—albeit opposed by the upper chamber—passed the relevant motion by 210 to 204 votes. This outcome convinced at least some republicans that in a world of free elections, an upper chamber, as Montesquieu recommended, can (as Condorcet had also suggested) prove an invaluable check on the elected body. But the growing confrontation between the two chambers and between the lower chamber and some of the Directoire only heightened the sense of paralysis and drift in the country.

The Revolution's prospects deteriorated further with the Dutch summer referendum to approve the Dutch Republic's new constitution, a referendum orderly and well conducted but which ended in voters rejecting the proposed republican constitution. Orangists and supporters of monarchy everywhere were jubilant. Evidently, even under French occupation, the common people, if given a clear choice, would reliably refuse republics, equality, and democracy. Most people preferred tradition, dynasticism, and religion, and were encouraged in this by their clergy. This weariness with republican politics and estrangement from the Revolution was the most important result of the Terror and the continuing war. To anti-Robespierre Jacobins inspired by Desmoulins and la philosophie moderne, like Pierre-François Réal, now a leading newspaper editor, the Terror represented the supreme abomination, an "atrocious" blot, "unrestrained tyranny," utterly ruinous to the Revolution's image. To commentators like Réal, Bonneville, Jullien, and the Décade philosophique, in August 1797, the Terror was a catastrophe, contradicting everything the authentic Revolution stood for, paving the way for the royalist resurgence now triumphantly advancing in and outside of France, a resurgence continually citing the Terror to tar the Revolution as a whole.[16]

Democratic republicanism stood seemingly on the verge of extinction. It was against this fraught and paradoxical background that the Babeuf hearings approached their conclusion. Facing a barrage of denunciation of the Terror among the public and abroad, the Directoire took every care not to appear to be reverting to its methods. Justice, constitutionality, and legality were the order of the day. The scrupulous procedures of the trial formed a reassuring contrast, even Babeuf himself admitted, to the methods of the Robespierriste regime. The well-guarded court consisted of a presiding judge, four lesser judges, and a sixteen-man jury chosen by electoral assemblies in several departments. To remove the exceptionally large number of defendants from Paris so as to minimize risk of interference and disturbance, the directors arranged a specially constituted court to try them at Vendôme in the Loire valley. When the long-delayed, massively documented trial finally opened on 20 February 1797, no less than sixty-five defendants were formally indicted, eighteen of whom, including Lepeletier and Drouet (who had escaped to the Canaries), had eluded the authorities and were tried in absentia. Babeuf and his codefendants were charged with conspiracy against the Constitution and legislature, and with intent to massacre innocent citizens and organize "looting of private property."[17]

Babeuf conducted his own defense, and his right to speak unhindered was scrupulously respected. "The aim of the Revolution," he contended, "can only be to establish the happiness of the majority." Legitimate government must express the "general will": "No one may be permitted to monopolize society's cultural resources or deprive others of the education needed for their well-being." Education is a universal right, he insisted, alluding to the success of the écoles centrales benefiting a few and the relative failure of the plans for universal free primary education. He eulogized d'Holbach, Helvétius, and especially Diderot, while mistakenly assuming, as was widely thought at the time, that Diderot was the author of the *Code de la Nature*, actually by Morelly, and one of the main sources of his militant egalitarianism.[18] Babeuf especially diverged from the Radical Enlightenment legacy in the crude dogmatism of his views on property and straightforward embrace of Mably's and Morelly's idea that abolishing property ensures everyone's happiness and puts an end to crime. This and his seeming blindness to the unpredictability and xenophobia of the sansculottes, and to the nature of the alliance he had formed with men like Buonarroti, Darthé, Lindet, and Amar, undermined the logic of his position. Early nineteenth-century liberals, betraying the entire spirit of the republican Revolution of 1788–93, lost their social conscience while the Babouvistes erred equally by mistaking Spartan austerity for an uplifting morality and detaching the question of how to secure an adequate subsistence from philosophy and understanding.[19] Babeuf's radical ideology was thus only coherent up to a point and, at his trial, tended to degenerate into fanatical tirades against the existing Constitution and private property. "All the evils of society," he claimed, flow from private property so that society must organize a "communal regime that will suppress private property"; he failed to see the danger inherent in his trumpeted "people's sacred, inalienable right to make the laws" or grasp the evident difficulty of declaring the "rich who refuse to give up their superfluous wealth for the benefit of the poor, enemies of the people."

In France, insisted Maréchal, "fewer than a million persons dispose of wealth that rightfully belongs to twenty millions of their fellow men, their fellow citizens."[20] "We need not only the equality stipulated in the Declaration of the Rights of Man," he continued, "we [also] need equality in life, in our very midst, in our homes. For the true and living equality we will give up everything."[21] On Maréchal's and Babeuf's premises, "there must be an end to this outrage!" But did it follow that the people must establish the "republic of equality" by overthrowing established authority, that the common good was just a matter of imposing community of goods or that it would be easy "to end civil strife and the sufferings of the masses"?[22] This was Maréchal's and Babeuf's delusion. In the Spartan egalitarianism of Mably's, Morelly's, Babeuf's, and Maréchal's communism, one could surely detect a philistinism rooted in unreality, a forbidding bleakness and austerity. Maréchal resembled Babeuf in being a product of radical thought with a dose of outright fanaticism added. "Maréchal's manifesto includes the chilling sentence, "Equality or death: that is what we want. And that is what we shall have, no matter what the price to be paid." To this he added, "Let the arts perish, if need be! But let us have real equality [Périssent, s'il le faut, tous les arts, pourvu qu'il nous reste l'égalité réelle!]."[23]

At the session on 30 Ventose, Babeuf became quite carried away, not only denouncing the 1795 Constitution as an abomination but labeling judges and jury as "*royalistes*, rascals and imbeciles." After this, he was forbidden to add anything further that was not strictly relevant to his defense.[24] But the Directoire faced a dilemma. The republican press showed considerable sympathy for the Babouvistes despite rejecting their call to overthrow the Constitution by insurrection, for royalism and revived Catholicism was what chiefly menaced republican France, not Babeuf. Moreover, Babeuf's ties ramified so widely throughout the republican and democratic community that any suggestion of harsh sentences for those accused risked permanently fragmenting and antagonizing prospective allies (against royalism) that the Directoire could ill afford to lose. Much to the satisfaction of the *Journal des hommes libres* and other republican papers, the judges finally opted for wide-ranging leniency—acquitting Maréchal, Antonelle, Amar, and most other defendents.[25] Only a handful, including Babeuf and Darthé, were found guilty of conspiring to overthrow the government and reintro-ducing the 1793 Constitution by force. On 24 May, Babeuf and Darthé were condemned to death, Buonarroti and six others to deportation. The rest were freed.

Babeuf and Darthé went to the guillotine on 27 May 1797, but their legacy lived on. Maréchal's manifesto is the first explicitly revolution-ary communist manifesto of modern times and the legend forged by Babeuf, Buonarroti, and Maréchal was the only precursor of their own communism that was truly respected later by Marx and Engels. It was a legacy that directly fed into the birth of Marxism and the modern Communist movement in the 1840s, a transference of inspiration engi-neered, in particular, by Buonarroti, who was imprisoned after the trial but survived, emerging later as the historian of the movement he had helped forge. His *Histoire de la conspiration pour l'égalité, dite de Babeuf,* published in 1828, and subsequently reappearing in various editions and translations, had a lasting impact, tying memories of Babeuf to the birth of modern Communism.[26]

The Second Directoire

March 1797, with the Babeuf trial still unresolved, plunged the repub-lican Left into defeat, dejection, and turmoil. Many deputies, journal-ists, and other leading figures in French society regarded the upsurge of rightist support in the Assembly during early 1797 not just with repug-nance but acute apprehension; to them this was an immediate crisis, and they were ready to embrace a violent subversion of the Constitu-tion to resolve it.

Fear of royalism, conservatism, and counterrevolution, confirmed Madame de Staël later, was at that moment far greater than any wor-ries about Babeuf, sansculotte insurgency, the fate of liberty, or neo-Jacobins.[27] Using the pretext that certain members of the two chambers had been meeting secretly at the Tuileries and elsewhere, illegally, form-ing a clandestine network of known "fanatiques et anti-républicains," as the *Décade philosophique* put it,[28] and conspiring with known foes of the Directoire, the more emphatically republican element in the regime organized their counterstroke. When the republican coup of 18 Fructidor (4 September 1797) finally ensued, it was eagerly supported by nearly all France's republicans, including most of the foreign theorists and journalists in France. Sieyès sided with the many, insisting that at this point desperate measures were unavoidable to prevent the triumph of royalism and ecclesiastical authority.[29] The Idéologues Cabanis, Destutt de Tracy, and Say welcomed the coup, as did Benjamin Constant. The resurgence of royalism and Catholicism in society and the Council of Five Hundred was judged so dangerous by Constant and the editors of the *Décade philosophique* that without a violent coup to purge the legislature, the outcome in their opinion would almost certainly be civil war.[30] Republicans viewed the coup as indispensable surgery, a momentary violation of the Constitution essential to save freedom and constitutionalism itself.

Unwilling to risk a popular insurrection aided by Jacobin militants, the three "triumvirs," as the right-wing press called them, Barras, La Révellière-Lépeaux, and Reubell, chief organizers of the virtually bloodless coup, surreptitiously concentrated troops in the Paris area and then used them to seize strongpoints in the city, surround the legislature with bayonets and cannon, and invade the Assembly hall. The election results in forty-nine departments were annulled and 177 deputies declared purged. Arrested at bayonet point was one of the two directors who refused to support the coup, though the most important, Carnot, long somewhat to the right of most Montagnard deputies, eluded his pursuers, escaping to Switzerland where he remained until after the coup of 18 Brumaire. Fifty-three deputies were physically removed from the legislature by the grenadiers, including General Pichegru, who had evinced blatant royalist sympathies since late 1795, and placed himself at the head of the monarchist faction. Pichegru was actually chairing at the moment the troops burst in. Despite efforts of a few royalist deputies who slipped through the net to ignite a popular insurrection, initial reaction was confused, with no forceful demonstrations either for or against the republican coup. Once the republicans had the upper hand, panic on the right led to many of the royalist deputies who were still at large attempting to flee the capital.

Some hours later, the remaining 320 deputies of the Council of Five Hundred resumed their seats amid shouts of "Vive la République!" and continued with their proceedings. Only afterward did posters go up around Paris explaining what had happened, denouncing royalist intrigues, and presenting documentary proof of Pichegru's treason, posters approvingly read by republicans of all hues. Many believed the coup had indeed saved the Revolution, liberty, and the Rights of Man. If so, one thing was certain: the people had played no part in saving or perpetuating the Revolution. The coup d'état of 17 and 18 Fructidor (3 and 4 September 1797) of the Year V was the work of a clique and was followed by a major revolutionary purge, but one impelled wholly from above. Besides two directors and dozens of deputies of both chambers, numerous other officials and administrators were dismissed from the departmental and civic administrations and replaced. The 177 rightist deputies purged were afterward replaced, not by election but co-option. Sixty-five prominent conservatives were sentenced to deportation to Cayenne, though in the end only seventeen were actually sent. Of these, eight died there while several others, including Pichegru, escaped. Besides sentencing the guilty to deportation rather than execution—and then not deporting most of them—Fructidor further demonstrated its desire to avoid harshness and pointedly distance itself from the Terror by sentencing the deportees to deportation but not confiscation of their possessions, hence avoiding ruin for their families.[31]

Royalists lost no time in accusing the Fructidorians of emulating the sinister style and illegalities of the 31 May 1793 insurrection. What, constitutionally, is the difference between using populist mass insurrection to eliminate "Girondins" sitting in the legislature and using troops to remove royalists from the legislature? The Fructidorians were plain Montagnards and terroristes. The pro-Revolution press roundly rejected this as absurd. To republicans it seemed self-evident that genuine foes of the Revolution were being justifiably deported because they menaced the Revolution, whereas on 2 June 1793, and subsequently, innocent men were arbitrarily removed, imprisoned, or guillotined on the flimsiest grounds, or no grounds at all. In September 1797, the country faced a dire emergency. In the circumstances, it seemed vital to halt the audacious subversion in progress and "make *la philosophie* and enlightenment," as the *Décade philosophique* expressed it, "which these men continually insult triumph," curtailing their conservatism and "fanatisme" and consoling the "true friends of liberty, morality and principles," whom royalists subsumed under the odious title of terroristes and brigands. What dishonesty and bad faith it betrays to compare 18 Fructidor with the 31 May 1793, to compare the present regime with the reign of Terror![32]

Fructidor marked a considerable rupture with the France of the first Directoire, as it was a decisive repudiation of royalisme, Carnot-style pragmatism, and Robespierriste populism alike. The so-called second Directoire reorganized the government, the triumvirs filling the two vacant Directoire seats with committed republicans, the anticlerical François de Neufchâteau (1750–1821), a poet, voluminous writer, and tireless propagandist for agrarian reform,[33] and the Montagnard jurist, Merlin de Douai (1754–1838).[34] If the Thermidorian Republic of 1794–97 was an unstable attempt to steer between Jacobin egalitarianism and resurgent royalisme, the Republic of 1797–99 was of a definitely sturdier republican stamp but also more authoritarian in character.[35] Its professed aim was to reimpose core republican values from above by firmly repressing both royalisme and populist authoritarianism. Punitive measures were reintroduced against the aristocratic émigrés, many of whom had returned with the reviving royalist expectations of spring 1797—and against the refractory clergy. Returned noble émigrés were given two weeks to depart and threatened with execution if they disobeyed. Over the next months 160 nobles were actually executed under this decree, or earlier laws against the émigrés, prompting the tag "Fructidorian Terror." Reaffirmation of republican values in the France of 1797, however, turned out to be more a question of reassuming the war on Catholicism and the battle of symbols than restoring freedom of the press, the political clubs, the right to petition, or the integrity of the electoral process.[36] It again became de rigueur at public meetings to address other speakers as "Citoyen," not as "Monsieur."

The Catholic revival had made steady progress since the first Directoire conceded it partial legitimacy in the spring of 1795, and with the royalist recovery of the Year V, many refractory priests in exile had returned. They had found congregations eager to receive them and provide livings, and everywhere vigorously rallied Catholic and royalist sentiment against republicans and republicanism. This process was now vigorously reversed. A decree passed the very day after the coup required a civic oath affirming outright rejection and detestation of royalty from all preachers. Under a law of 25 October 1797, refractory priests refusing the new oath were given two weeks to leave France or face imprisonment, deportation, or execution, and hundreds departed or were expelled over the coming months. Those failing to depart quickly were rounded up and faced with the choice of swearing the required oath or severe punishment.[37] Crucifixes in the streets, crosses in cemeteries, and ringing church bells were again officially suppressed.

Around 1,400 such nonjurors were interned on the west coast islands of Ré and Oberon prior to deportation to Guiana, though only
around 230 were actually deported there. Altogether, from Fructidor to
the coup of Prairial (18 June 1799), the Directoire deported approximately 9,000 ecclesiastics, though the vast majority, some 7,500, were
driven from Belgium rather than France.[38] Those targeted were recalcitrant priests refusing to repudiate monarchy or swear allegiance to the
Republic. On 29 September, the regime issued a long edict summariz-
ing all previous restrictions on the churches and forbidding manifesta-
tions of religious cults in the streets, such as processions, the wearing of
ecclesiastical dress, images, and crucifixes. Likewise forbidden was ringing church bells to summon the faithful, whether in town or country.
Equally, the regime renewed Condorcet's efforts to combat "superstition" in the classroom by insisting teachers use more explicitly republican and anti-Christian materials in teaching. An emphatic form of
deism was everywhere preferred to atheism but this did not prevent
republican teachers from being widely boycotted by parents in favor
of private Catholic teachers readier to promote what the new regime
called "les prejugés et la superstition."

Reaffirming the Revolution's essentially philosophique character,
Fructidor revived its universalism and determination to reeducate everyone, representing a decisive rebuff for Montesquieu, the British
model, and all forms of liberalism focusing solely on individual rights
and freedoms without stressing the duty of legitimate governments to
promote the common interest and guard the collective good against
vested interests, elites, and religious authority, as well as monarchy.
The second Directoire also acted promptly to bridle royalist journalists. At the same time, the new regime tried in various ways to revive
the distinctly flagging revolutionary enthusiasm of the masses. Louis La
Révellière-Lépeaux, prime mover of the coup, deeply fearful of moral
and social anarchy, and a long-standing opponent of Robespierre and
his "Cromwellisme," placed a particular stress on reviving republican
practices and festivals. Orders were issued for revolutionary songs to
again be sung in all the theaters (though in some there was resistance
to this). La Révellière-Lépeaux was especially keen on huge mass ceremonies featuring enormous choruses singing revolutionary hymns
intended to renew the people's emotional attachment to the Revolution.[39] He also promoted Théophilanthropie, a new organized deist
cult established in Paris earlier in April, though most kept their distance
from this peculiar and short-lived new church.

Fructidor acclaimed and revived the Revolution and showed that it still overshadowed all Europe. Fructidorians, republicans, and the philosophique Left still faced a formidable double threat, though, which some conceived of as two parts of the same menace. Surely royalism and Robespierrisme were really twin evils, sharing a common basis! Do not religious fanaticism and *le fanatisme politique*, as the *Décade philosophique* expressed it, equally find both their appeal and their support among that class of the population devoid of education and hence "ignorant et crédule"? Reversing Catholic resurgence and populist authoritarianism, royalism and Montagnard principles, traditional notions of schooling and Rousseauist education was hence considered by democratic republicans as parts of the same process. Countering Robespierrisme and the Terror went together with fighting sansculottisme, ignorance, and religion. To defeat its enemies, the Revolution required a more systematic cultural and propaganda countermovement of which the hallmark was the campaign to firmly establish the écoles centrales, the large, secular, publicly supported secondary schools organized on uncompromisingly philosophique principles and set up in all the departmental capitals, which now gained a decisive impetus throughout France and also Belgium and the conquered Rhineland.

The vehemently anticlerical new minister of the interior, François de Neufchâteau, lost not a moment in sending out government instructions and questionnaires to all the departments and public schools, requiring details about the content of courses being taught, so that he could advise the Directoire on the general state of enlightenment, teaching, and social mores. Teachers were reminded of the need to use only approved textbooks, adhere to the revolutionary calendar, and celebrate republican festivals. The questionnaires sought simultaneously to gather information and goad teachers toward more explicitly Enlightenment, republican, and anti-Catholic attitudes. The school agenda, teachers were reminded, must include the recommended course on "morals and legislation" aimed at turning children into worthy citizens and teaching enlightened values, the Rights of Man, and republican legislation.[40] Only through Enlightenment, by attacking ordinary men's ignorance and lack of education, and men's unfortunate upbringing amid prejudice and credulity, could the people be rescued from the two seemingly connected forms of fanaticism: reactionary Catholicism and Robespierrisme.

This was the ideology of Fructidor and the leading pro-Revolution journals of the late 1790s. Yet of the major new educational tools forged by the Revolution—universal primary and secondary schools, the departmental écoles centrales for higher study, and the Institute—the écoles centrales, each of which was supposed to have thirteen professors and teach the whole range of requisite disciplines, were only just beginning to gain real momentum, and only the last, "the one that was perhaps least urgent," stressed the *Décade philosophique*, approached being fully realized. In the department of the Seine, centering on Paris, only two of the projected five écoles centrales were functioning in the autumn of 1797, Sainte-Geneviève, next to the Panthéon, and that in the Quatre-Nations section.[41] At both, Institute professors regularly assisted with the teaching. Most French communes still either had no public schools or else schools remaining in the hands of teachers deemed ignorant and antirepublican. The schools' deficiencies could nearly all be blamed, it was assumed by republicans, on negligent officials, Catholics, and royalists.

Fructidor endeavored to tighten, energize, and accelerate the educational reforms initiated by the Daunou law of October 1795. Vetting what was taught, and eliminating the priesthood and Catholic doctrine from public education, accompanied resumed efforts to halt the ringing of church bells and the wearing of clerical dress in the streets. Ending the partial autonomy introduced by the law of October 1795, the Republic began to interfere extensively in the activities of the private schools, subjecting them to state supervision while insisting on the use of secularizing, anti-Catholic texts in public schools. Under a law of 5 February 1798, municipal councils were obliged to make regular surprise visits to private schools to ensure that teachers were employing secular and republican texts, and not religious texts, in their instruction and teaching children the Constitution. Where they were not, municipalities were supposed to shut them down. Sporadic and uneven though the pressure was, hundreds of recalcitrant teachers were dismissed and traditional Catholic teaching vigorously curtailed. Especially useful for unmasking concealed opponents of the Republic, it was judged, was the requirement that teachers accompany their pupils to the major public republican festivities.[42] The reforms eventually led to the establishment of an executive council of public instruction charged with regulating publicly supported schools, an eight-member commission functioning for two years from late 1798 until October 1800, including Ginguené, Garat, and Destutt de Tracy.[43]

If the inevitable result was a heightening of tension between much of the urban and rural population and the republican authorities, and further alienation of much of the population, the Fructidorians did not flinch from their course. Education and enlightenment, held Ginguené, Say, and the other journalists of the *Décade philosophique*, like Réal's paper and Bonneville's *Le Vieux Tribun*, were what would render the Revolution firm and republican values irreversible, just as printing had made the Enlightenment itself irreversible. These men considered the abusive denunciations of *réfractaires*, royalists, and counterrevolutionaries as "a title of glory," and urged all lovers of Enlightenment and la philosophie to take heart. The Republic would survive and their enemies would be beaten.[44] Where Robespierre made war on the Enlightenment, as the veteran republican Bonneville expressed it, the écoles centrales robustly defended the sciences and arts and would repel all superstition and *le vandalisme*, thereby strengthening the Republic.[45] What was needed to direct and energize the schools was to impart more resolve from the top. One useful publicizing mechanism was the school prize-giving ceremonies, which in the écoles centrales were presided over by senior departmental officials and Institute professors, events accompanied by fanfare and much applause. In the Paris écoles centrales, school prizes were awarded in 1797 for mathematics, natural history, grammar, ancient languages, writing, and drawing, with first and second prizes followed by honorable mentions. A Directoire exhortation to the legislature on 24 October 1798 proposed to set teachers' salaries and tighten further exclusion of priests from public schools, laying down that "*philosophique*, universal morality must be the exclusive basis of republican education" and that priests were "unfit" to educate youth in the principles of "purified virtue" and republican awareness.[46]

The Revolution reaffirmed by Fructidor showed both important continuities and differences with the Left republicanism of the Brissotin era, both in terms of values and personalities. If the Republic's commitment to secularism, universal education, and equality of opportunity remained unbending, the new anti-Montagnard republicanism was far less democratic than that of 1792–93, and also diverged from the early Revolution's core ideals in refusing to continue even the restricted degree of freedom of the press prevailing in 1797. So scared was the second Directoire of resurgent royalism, Catholicism, and Robespierrisme, and apprehensive about militant egalitarianism, that it preferred to systematically suppress this whole dimension of basic rights. At least forty-two newspapers were aborted in the wake of Fructidor, with another twenty being closed down over the next two years. Around forty royalist journalists were proscribed and condemned to deportation, including Jean-Baptiste Suard, a former member of d'Holbach's dinner club who had consistently opposed the Revolution since 1789 and now fled abroad.[47] Of remaining papers, several were co-opted by the regime while others were officially discouraged. Here, as in its policing activities and authoritarianism more generally, the Fructidorian Directoire was a clear precursor to the consulate of Brumaire and Napoleon's authoritarianism.

The revolutionary government during 1797–98 was emphatically antiroyalist, anticlerical, and antiaristocratic. The two main public pillars of revived republican ideology in 1797–98, all the more vital to the regime given its blatant departure from freedom of expression, constitutionalism, and democracy, were a new emphasis on republican festivals and unyielding concern with imposing the republican calendar's ten-day week—a point on which La Révellière-Lépeaux and Merlin de Douai, despite the latter's private Catholic belief (and lack of genuine philosophique sympathies), were especially insistent.[48] Government efforts to close churches on Sundays, and town and village markets on the *décadi*, developed into an arduous, rather unrewarding struggle driven by a Directoire that manifested uncompromising support for secularism, toleration of other religions, deism, universal education, and irreligion, along with the *culte théophilanthropique*.

The efforts to persuade the French to think more *philosophiquement* were aimed against royalism, Catholicism, and tradition, and no less against the cult of the populaire, Maratisme, sansculottism, and Robespierre's authoritarian egalitariansim. To achieve its goals the Directoire also abandoned much of the early Revolution's stress on equality, aiming instead to forge a new social elite trained by the state to occupy the professions, administration, and higher positions of society. This meant abandoning the blanket egalitarianism of 1793–94 and encouraging a new educational elitism. The families of boys sent to the écoles centrales paid fees, which hence became the path to securing social position and affluence. Nevertheless, the hardening, republican culture of the late 1790s still firmly advocated a comprehensively antiaristocratic, merit-based social elite that functioned on the basis of knowledge and training rather than inherited position, family ties, and privilege. Radical enlighteners like Helvétius, Condorcet, and Volney had always emphasized "experience" and knowledge rather than authority or Rousseauiste visions of nature as the basis of civic consciousness and morality. Besides teaching the principles of morality, human rights, and legislation, the interior ministry, like the 1798 school board, required a new focus on history and classics as the path for understanding society, politics, and republican attitudes. If Robespierristes infused with Rousseauiste visions of nature and virtue scorned history as distinct from nature and feeling, radical enlighteners commanding the revolutionary educational apparatus in the late 1790s believed all true philosophy and understanding builds on science and a proper grasp of world history. "Philosophy" in their sense was the exclusive foundation for a broad understanding of society, politics, and the human condition.[49] This involved rejecting all traditional philosophy and political science, as well as religion and Rousseauiste populism.

Besides promoting public festivals and reforming education, Fructidorians disseminated the writings of the radical philosophes. Neufchâteau, whose appointment to the Directoire was intended to stimulate republican "public instruction" in France, dispatched copies of d'Holbach's *Contagion sacrée* to the departmental prefects to frighten them out of complacency regarding the social and political implications of the Catholic resurgence.[50] Meanwhile, the pro-Revolution press, especially the *Décade philosophique*, warmly congratulated the teams of editors, including Naigeon (still busily sorting out Diderot's papers), who were producing more complete, accurate, and better edited versions of the works of the radical philosophes who, more than ever, were acknowledged as having laid the Revolution's foundations. Condorcet, Naigeon, and Cérutti had begun to promote D'Holbach's reputation back in 1789–90 when Naigeon had published a résumé of *La Morale universelle* (1776), which was the first edition to appear under d'Holbach's own name.

These efforts resumed in 1795. Among those active in this recovery and propagation of the Revolution's radical philosophique foundations was the Abbé Martin Lefebvre de la Roche, whom Helvétius had sent to Holland prior to his death in December 1771 to arrange publication of *De l'Homme* (1773). Far surpassing the five-volume edition of Helvétius's *Œuvres complèttes* [sic] that appeared in 1795, when complete, in the summer of 1797, La Roche's fourteen-volume edition of Helvétius was definitive, including for the first time extensive unedited notes, correspondence, and Helvétius's thus far unpublished *Réflexions*. Celebrated as "a great service to letters and to philosophy," its publication prompted the *Décade philosophique* to remind readers that Helvétius figured among the Revolution's foremost precursors. First to place moral philosophy on a fully materialist, utilitarian, self-interested basis, Helvétius dissipated vacuities that had long burdened moral philosophy and hidden the true meaning of virtue.[51] "No one had better shown on what principles it is necessary to establish a government" and the "inconveniences of every political constitution where the advantages of a small minority are preferred to the happiness of the great number." No one contributed more to the present advances in Western Europe (i.e., including Belgium, Holland, and Italy), "where it is for the happiness of the great number that the Constitution is made."[52]

Texts by, or inspired by, the radical philosophes proliferated during 1796–97, among them the previously unpublished *Jacques le fataliste*, *The Nun*, and the *Supplement to Bougainville's Voyage*, all by Diderot,[53] and a subsequently published Institute public lecture by Jacques-Antoine Creuzé-Latouche (1749–1800), one of the chief framers of the 1795 Constitution. A deputy of the lower legislature, Creuzé-Latouche designed his *De l'intolérance philosophique et de l'intolérance religieuse* to combat the efforts of Catholic apologists to pin the charge of intolerance onto the Enlightenment. Originally leveled by the radical philosophes against the Catholic priesthood and Protestant ministry, Catholic apologists claimed it was the philosophes who were the real "fanatics," that no fanaticism was worse than *fanatisme philosophique*. No one possessing any knowledge or intelligence could possibly take such an absurd calumny seriously, countered Creuzé-Latouche, expounding the philosophique doctrine of toleration and individual freedom of thought, and citing Marmontel's powerful lines in his play *The Incas*, which depicted religious zealotry as an exterminating angel that believes itself in accord with God's will while actually wreaking only death and destruction. Disastrously, this Catholic calumny, "repeated a hundred times from Nonnotte down to La Harpe," lamented the *Décade philosophique*, derived some superficial plausibility precisely from the revolting excesses of the Terror.

Despicable characters like Hanriot and Chaumette *had* invoked la philosophie when persecuting Christians. But to claim la philosophie was therefore responsible for the 1793–94 persecution of the clergy was flagrant calumny. "La philosophie," recalled Creuzé-Latouche, "was among the first targets of the fury propagated by Robespierre's *gouvernement révolutionnaire*." Reminding his audience of Robespierre's trampling of Helvétius's bust underfoot and the hounding of Malesherbes, Lavoisier, and Bailly, besides Condorcet, he recounted also the scandalous incident when Robespierre championed manipulation of the sansculotte section deliberations in Paris to exclude "le célèbre Priestley" from election to the Convention, on behalf of the loathsome Marat. Robespierre spoke directly against the philosophes on that occasion. The Jacobins had established a tyranny in which it was a mark of infamy to be labeled a savant, man of letters, or author.[54]

As part of its wider strategy, the Fructidorian Directoire actively promoted journals expounding radical philosophique views, especially the *Décade philosophique*, *Journal de Perlet*, and a new journal, *Le Conservateur* (1797–98), established by Garat, Daunou, and Chénier. The Directoire regularly took two thousand copies of the last journal to distribute among the revolutionary armies and the administration, its objective being to encourage that part of society deemed "friends of liberty, of la philosophie, and of letters," willing to conserve and uphold the Revolution's basic standpoint.[55] The authentic principles of the Revolution, contended these journals, provided the best available basis for France's future while also projecting a revolutionary universalism and cosmopolitanism that reached out to neighboring countries and strengthened their commitment to republican liberty, science, learning, and the Revolution. The Idéologues and republicans of 1795–99, consequently, were not therefore forerunners of nineteenth-century liberalism, primarily focused on individual rights and freedoms alone, men unconcerned with or actively opposed to molding society into a different shape and reinforcing the power of the state to protect, guide, and curb inequality.[56] Rather, they consciously and unconstrainedly sought social amelioration across the board, but strictly within a framework of orderly republican government, semidemocracy, and human rights. Their project included fairer and better economic arrangements but refused to concede primacy to the goal of economic equality alone.

The second Directoire's measures against the émigrés and refractory priests were applauded in both republican and democratic circles. After Fructidor, Jacobin and other republican clubs were temporarily permitted to reopen. But there remained a nagging contradiction at the heart of the Directoire's stance: anxious to encourage a watered-down, tame republicanism and antiroyalism, as well as anticlericalism, the new leadership before long began to repress democratic pressures, such as those emanating from the Parisian left-bank Rue du Bac Club, which attempted to promote electoral reform with a view to widening the franchise and redemocratizing the political process. The Directoire made a fateful and, according to some, rather inept choice: it opted to oppose broadening the electorate and to base its authority on the country's propertied elite. Eventually, this meant losing the backing of the democratic wing, the Left republicans as well as the neo-Jacobins, and retrospectively lending some degree of rectitude and legitimacy to the clandestine movement of Babeuf, Maréchal, and Buonarroti.

The Directoire began to face opposition from the Left in the republican press, republican clubs, and also the legislature itself, not least owing to the fact that most deputies passively acquiesced in the executive's increasingly heavy-handed control, permitting the Assembly's supposed sovereignty to lapse to a largely theoretical status. What began promisingly as the Fructidorian regime became gradually more unresponsive, repressive, and antidemocratic in character. Democratic republican opposition was expressed through the semiclandestine democratic neo-Babouviste and neo-Jacobin press, most impressively, the *Journal des hommes libres*, edited by Félix Lepeletier, Antonelle, and Vatar. Like Babeuf, Antonelle was steeped in Mably, Diderot, Morelly, and Helvétius, and sought restoration of the democratic 1793 Constitution, but unlike Babeuf, he, like Jullien and Réal, refused to assign the drive for economic equality priority over the drive for civil equality and democracy.[57] Vatar, a journalist from Rennes, was also a brave and resolute republican democrat (later deported to Cayenne by Napoleon from whence he escaped to the United States). But little by little their efforts to rekindle the ardor of 1789–93 were stifled. On 11 April 1798, the Directoire closed down the *Journal des hommes libres*, now the foremost democratic paper. Vatar kept the paper alive briefly in a reduced format, under different titles, but was finally reduced to silence.[58]

As the April 1798 elections approached, the Directoire revealed all too clearly that it was as anxious to curb the democratic tendency, and suppress the democratic clubs and Jacobin journals, as to prevent another royalist success at the polls.[59] To most this seemed a blatant betrayal. Confronted by a growing royalist prevalence in many French regions among the propertied and the poor, and unable to widen its support base, the Directoire tried, disasterously, to resolve its central dilemma—how to impose its authority without the help of the democrats—by rigging the elections. With 437 seats, including those left vacant after Fructidor, needing to be filled, the executive interfered on a massive scale in the electoral process, albeit with more success in blocking royalism than Left republicanism. In many departments, the Directoire failed to prevent the clubs from overawing the primary assemblies and securing the election of republican democrats rather than government supporters. Directorial candidates triumphed in only forty-three departments, barely over half. A remarkable 162 former members of the old Convention reappeared, including no less than seventy-one regicides.

Refusing to give ground to the growing democratic republican opposition, the Directoire encouraged the filing of all manner of objections and complaints, finding pretexts to cancel the election results in nearly forty departments. Many initially successful democratic candidates, around eighty-six, were subsequently debarred from taking their seats. A special law, the Law of 22 Floreal (11 May 1798), a kind of supplementary coup, was introduced to further strengthen the authoritarian executive's hand, though at the cost of further discrediting the electoral system and alienating the regime's rapidly dwindling republican support. Many departmental and judicial officials and a total of 127 deputies, or more than a quarter, were purged. At this point, Neufchâteau retired and was replaced by Jean-Baptiste Treilhard, a member of the Comité de Salut Public from April to June 1793 and later an energetic Thermidorian who in 1794–95 had proven his willingness to participate in rigid, unprincipled government.

The elections of March 1799 (Germinal of the Year VII) were once more heavily rigged but again resulted in a substantial group of democrats being elected and the divisions within the Directoire becoming deeper. The clash between the democratic tendency, the principles of the Revolution, and the narrow, bureaucratic, authoritarian vision of the Directoire intensified. Despite the escalating military and ideological struggle in Italy, Germany, Egypt, and in fact everywhere between the Revolution and the monarchies, during June 1799 a full-blown political crisis ensued at home, culminating in what became known as the coup of Prairial. The Five Hundred, encouraged and partly concerted by Sieyès after his return as French envoy from Berlin, the figurehead who now replaced Reubell as one of the five directors, rebelled and confronted the executive, accusing it of corruption and incompetence. La Révellière-Lépeaux and Merlin were forced to resign and, on 30 Prairial of the Year VII (18 June 1799), were replaced with Ducos and a sympathetic military figure, General Moulin. A fresh purge of officials from the departmental and civic administrations began.

Prairial, a noteworthy landmark in revolutionary history, was the only time the legislature purged the Directoire rather than vice versa. It represented a fateful, rather tragic last chance. Momentarily, Prairial ushered in a republicanism characterized, for the first time since 1795, by the legislature ruling the executive.[60] It marked the last point at which the Revolution's core values were loudly and powerfully reaffirmed. For a few months during 1799, the latest coup seemingly revived the failed promise of Fructidor. With between sixty and ninety democratic republicans in the Assembly affirming revolutionary principles, freedom of expression, and the Rights of Man, a last flurry of optimism arose. After being broadly suppressed for a year, freedom of the press was officially reinstated on 1 August 1799; democratic journals triumphantly reappeared during the summer of 1799, the most significant being *Le Démocrate* and the *Journal des hommes libres*. Though its circulation never recovered to the high levels of 1794, from June to September 1799, the *Journal des hommes libres*, now edited chiefly by Antonelle, enjoyed a vigorous revival and helped promote what turned out to be the Revolution's last call for liberty, equality, and democracy.[61]

The promise was undermined by Prairial's inner contradictions. A new, openly neo-Jacobin club called the Manège Club was established in a hall in the heart of Paris, detailed reports of whose meetings were published in the *Journal des hommes libres*.[62] Its inaugural ceremony on 6 July was attended by eight hundred enthusiastic supporters. Yet, the coup simultaneously reinforced the authoritarian, antidemocratic middle bloc around Sieyès and Barras who were attempting to steer a constitutional and anticlerical course under a strong executive, resisting democracy and legislative control. When the Manège Club's original meeting hall was closed by the police in late July, it moved its premises to the Rue de Bac, where it continued disseminating democratic republican ideology, still claiming its views were in no way incompatible with the Constitution. The Directoire disagreed. On 13 August, the police closed its new premises, which ended its public role and forced the remaining rump to continue meeting clandestinely. The democratic papers were suppressed in September. The Revolution as a democratic tendency was driven underground.

Sieyès had accepted elevation to the Directoire as a means to an end. Long convinced that the democratic, republican tendency had to be countered by a stronger executive, he now also believed the Constitution in its present form was unworkable, mired by an inherent instability and dispersal of power. He now made his fateful decision to try to concert yet another coup to redirect the Revolution into a securer, more orderly course, betraying by doing so the very legislature and Directoire to which he had been elected and of which, on 18 June 1799, he became president. This late 1799 coup, orchestrated by Sieyès, effectively marks the Revolution's end. This time the coup d'état was initiated neither by

Figure 20. The unity and indivisibility of the Republic, 1793. Image courtesy Bibliothèque nationale de France.

the legislature nor the Directoire but was the outcome rather of a conspiracy planned by a disaffected group of would-be political, legal, and constitutional reformers, the Brumairians, a clique led by Sieyès and backed by several liberal-minded, sophisticated men, including the best liberal theorists and journalists in the legislature and the Institute. Volney, Cabanis, Daunou, Marie-Joseph Chénier, Destutt de Tracy, Garat, and Constant (who greatly admired Sieyès), the *Décade philosophique*'s editors, all believed that if the Republic continued much longer on its present path of division, weakness, and instability, it must collapse into humiliation and ruin.[63] They had a clear political-philosophical vision. They sought to establish their new order of liberty, human rights, freedom of expression, secularism, and representative constitutionalism.

They hoped to emasculate royalism, Catholicism, and Jacobin Terror for good by authoritarian and extralegal means, but their project failed.[64]

Plotting his coup, Sieyès needed the assistance of a general to put the plan into effect. Bonaparte happened to return unexpectedly from Egypt in mid-October, receiving a hero's welcome and apparently scarcely embarrassed at all by the question of why he had returned from Egypt without his army. It was then that Sieyès made his decisive error of enlisting his collaboration in overthrowing the legislature, Directoire, and Constitution. On 18 and 19 Brumaire, Bonaparte deployed his men: power was transferred from the legislature at bayonette point to a provisional consulate of three comprised of Sieyès, Ducos, and Bonaparte, albeit not without hours of outraged opposition. The usual brochures and posters appeared across Paris explaining what had transpired. Sieyès set to work as head of a commission of twelve, including Daunou, charged with drawing up a new constitution—however, with crucial alterations insisted on by Bonaparte. This Constitution of the Year VIII was promulgated toward the end of 1799. It did not take long for Bonaparte to succeed in wholly outmaneuvering Sieyès, Ducos, Daunou, and the constitutional commission: the consulate was formalized with Napoleon at its unchallenged head. Sieyès withdrew humiliated into permanent retirement.[65]

Insofar as anything did, the coup of Brumaire of the Year VIII (November 1799), and the new Constitution of 13 December 1799, ended the Revolution. There were now three chambers with the most senior and powerful—consisting of eighty nonelected, nonremovable members co-opted by the senators themselves from a short-list presented by the first consul—charged with overseeing the legality and constitutionality of the legislature's actions. To round off the first consul's overweening authority, Cambacérès and Lebrun, the second and third consuls, possessed only an advisory role, not only in initiating legislation but also in appointing ministers, generals, and ambassadors. The 1799 Constitution, in short, effectively suspended the Rights of Man, press freedom, and individual liberty, as well as democracy and the primacy of the legislature, wholly transferring power to initiate legislation from the legislature to the executive, that is, the consulate, making Bonaparte not just the central but the all-powerful figure in the government. The Declaration of the Rights of Man was removed from its *preambule*.

CHAPTER 25

Conclusion

THE REVOLUTION AS THE OUTCOME OF THE
RADICAL ENLIGHTENMENT

The French Revolution, we may conclude was really three revolutions —a democratic republican revolution, a moderate Enlightenment constitutional monarchism invoking Montesquieu and the British model as its criteria of legitimacy, and an authoritarian populism prefiguring modern fascism. These distinct impulses proved entirely incompatible politically and culturally, as well as ideologically, and remained locked in often ferocious conflict throughout. It is true that two other social movements largely unconnected with these—the peasant risings and the by no means wholly inchoate sansculotte street movement preoccupied with subsistence—had a massive impact on society and the political scene in one way or another at nearly every stage of the Revolution. But however essential these elements in the picture they were not revolutionary movements in the sense that they attempted to transform the whole of society and its laws and institutions, they did not represent comprehensive plans for change in the same sense as the three main ideological tendencies.

In shaping the basic values of the Revolution and the Revolution's legacy, the first, the democratic republican revolution, was from 1788 onward always the most important, the "real revolution," despite its successive defeats. Obviously, the causes of the French Revolution are very numerous and include many economic, financial, and cultural as well as social and political factors. But all of these can fairly be said to be essentially secondary compared with the one major, overriding cause driving the democratic republican impulse—the Radical Enlightenment. This is the factor that needs to be placed at center stage.

By 1799, Napoleon was master of France; the Revolution was at an end. Yet, in a crucial sense, it did not end. The Idéologues primarily supported the coup of Brumaire, believing, like Sieyès, that a stronger executive had become necessary to saving the Republic. But at no stage did they want the authoritarian regime they got, and they never endorsed or condoned the onset of the Napoleonic dictatorship that was resisted by them and also by many other prominent committed republicans, including Sieyès, Daunou, Jullien, Guyomar, Sonthonax, Bonneville, Say, Constant, and Vatar. Eventually enforcing a whole series of basic compromises with the past—with the aristocracy, Church, colonial planters, and the principle of monarchy—Napoleon in effect used authoritarian methods to impose a more efficient version of the moderate Enlightenment. What the Idéologues sought was a healthy balance between a vigorous legislature, holding the initiative in forging legislation and free to criticize the executive, and an executive committed to maintaining the Revolution's secular ideals, especially individual liberty, legal equality, universal education, and freedom of expression, criticism, and the press. They did not abandon these ideals, and from his authoritarian perspective, Napoleon had ample reason to always distrust Sieyès, the Idéologues, and all who shared in the making of the Revolution.[1]

The French Revolution was qualitatively different from all known previous revolutions and also remains more fundamental for us than subsequent revolutions thus far, more fundamental, for example, than the Russian Revolution. The reason consists in the Revolution's special relationship to the Enlightenment, and especially to the Enlightenment's republican, democratic, and secularizing radical wing. It was especially foundational in that it fed into all later revolutions in Europe, Latin America, and Asia, fixing both the contours and dilemmas of modern republicanism, constitutional monarchy, and democracy, and introducing the social and constitutional principles that defined the modern political world. The only democratic revolution thus far that conceived democracy as the pursuit of the majority's welfare, assigning government the duty to promote the welfare of all as a society and combat economic inequality rather than just maintain order and defend property, it was the first sustained attempt to establish a secular, educated, welfare-orientated, human rights–based modernity. It sought maximization of "social freedom" combined with equal opportunities for all. All this affords the French Revolution a unique centrality in modern history and relevance to the challenges of our own time.

In 1796, the young Swiss political thinker and commentator Benjamin Constant (1767–1830), settling in Paris after Thermidor, published his first major political pamphlet, *De la force du gouvernement actuel*. Sincere, committed republicans and democrats, he asserted, should and must support the Revolution's core principles and vigorously rebut both the royalist resurgence then commencing in France and the militant egalitarianism of Babeuf, Buonarroti, and Maréchal seeking to overthrow the revolutionary republic in the name of a more rigorous economic equality (while simultaneously attempting to rehabilitate and eulogize "Robespierre"). The repression and stifling of basic freedoms instigated by the Montagne, and the horrors of the Terror, contended Constant, did not stem from the Revolution's essential principles and values and were not a logical consequence of the efforts and groups that generated it. Not yet the "moderate" or liberal he became later, Constant argued that the catastrophe of Robespierre and the Terror sprang rather from the illiberal, anti-Enlightenment reaction permeating Montagnard Jacobinism. Much like Roederer in a pamphlet of 1796 on la philosophie moderne, Constant rightly considered Robespierre's and Saint-Just's rejection of the Revolution's core values as the wrecking of the Revolution and a virulent form of Counter-Enlightenment and anti-intellectualism, hostile to freedom of thought, individual liberty, erudition, and the right to criticize. In terms of principles, Robespierre was the Revolution's contradiction, the Enlightenment's very antithesis.[2]

Constant's denunciation of the Terror triggered a historical quarrel that has continued to this day. Where counterrevolutionary and Counter-Enlightenment writers like Antoine de Rivarol declared the Terror the fruit of la philosophie moderne, adamantly claiming Condorcet had been forced to take poison by "his brothers in philosophy," Constant, Roederer, Creuze-Latouche, Say, Louvet, Naigeon, and many others proclaimed Robespierre "le chef" of the Terror, contending that he was neither a republican nor an adept of la philosophie moderne but, on the contrary, the Enlightenment's foremost enemy.[3] If Rivarol scorned republicanism and remained loyal to the ancien régime throughout, by the mid-1790s many disillusioned revolutionaries, like La Harpe and Gorani, and some Catholic and Protestant apologists likewise preferred to view the Montagne as the quintessence of the revolutionary spirit and the Terror as both the Revolution's and la philosophie's logical culmination.

In effect, only commentators championing the Rights of Man, press freedom, universal education, and democracy, like Constant, Daunou, Louvet, Guyomar, Say, and Roederer, firmly denied that the Montagne was the Revolution's climax and correctly identified the trajectory set by Sieyès, Mirabeau, Condorcet, Brissot, and Pétion as the Revolution's veritable course. The valid conclusion to draw from Robespierre and the Terror, they maintained, was that a democratic republican revolution is impossible without first enlightening and preparing the population. Equally, these were the views of Tom Paine, Mary Wollstonecraft, Helen Maria Williams, Joel Barlow, Georg Forster, Gerrit Paape, Irhoven van Dam, Wedekind, and the great mass of foreign republicans and democrats of the time, besides the first great feminists, Sophie de Condorcet, Olympe de Gouges, Etta Palm, and other leaders of the revolutionary movement for women's rights. By January 1794, even the prominent Swedish radical and Spinozist, Thomas Thorild, slowest and most reluctant of the leading foreign republican democrats to repudiate the Montagne, publicly proclaimed his previous misreading of the situation, designating the Terror a catastrophic betrayal and Robespierre himself "an all-consuming crocodile."[4]

The Terror, averred Roederer in 1796, was a *véritable contre-revolution*, directly antagonistic to the Enlightenment.[5] For Robespierre, in direct contrast, the radical philosophes, who he admitted had originally led the way in rejecting monarchy, aristocracy, and religious authority, were mere "charlatans ambitieux." This fundamental disagreement continued after 1794. Precariously, the democratic republicans regained the upper hand after the Terror and again became the guiding force within the Revolution from early 1795 until the summer of 1799, while the Montagne's and Robespierre's legacy, if not entirely forgotten, was driven underground and marginalized. Even so, the wrangling over whether Robespierre and the Terror were or were not the outcome of la philosophie moderne, and hence were or were not inherent in the Revolution, came to overshadow not just the later 1790s but much of the nineteenth century. After Thermidor, constitutional monarchists, in the tradition of Necker, Mounier, Lally-Tollendal, Maury, and Malouet, revived the cause of moderation and rejected the democratic, republican libertarian path in the name of Montesquieu and the British model. But the liberal monarchists subsequently always remained vulnerable to the charge that they were concealed, or not-so-concealed, opponents of equality, democracy, universal education, and freedom of expression. Republican democrats, Idéologues, and neo-Brissotins during the late 1790s maintained, like Constant earlier, that constitutional monarchists were in reality defending aristocracy, privilege, and religious authority, and were unjustifiably restricted in their goals.

Only Brissotins and the Danton-Desmoulins faction, argued Constant in 1796, were authentic democratic republicans, and these "republicans" had courageously resisted Robespierre, Saint-Just, repression, and the Terror in every way possible and were in fact the Terror's primary victims. Because they promoted the Revolution's core values, most democratic republican leaders and newspaper editors were annihilated by the Montagne between September 1793 and July 1794. The Terror began with the Brissotins' defeat in June 1793, and matured, as Constant expressed it, "on their tombs." He dismissed Robespierre's ideology as a system attractive and useful to nobody except fanatical levelers seeking to resurrect Montagnard dictatorship or else royalist-Catholic conservatives rejecting and vilifying the Revolution so as to restore religious authority and the sway of theology. Apart from Montagnards, only monarchist and ecclesiastical (Protestant as well as Catholic) exponents of counterrevolution depicted the Jacobins, terrroristes, and "followers of Robespierre" as the "républicains véritables." No error would be more catastrophic, held Constant, than to suppose modern society can coherently and justly be based on either militant, dogmatic egalitarianism or the primacy of religious authority and tradition. A society based specifically on economic equality is surely as utopian and impossible in the modern context as a society of social hierarchy and religious authority. No valid arguments but only ignorance, bigotry, and unawareness, maintained Constant, Roederer, and the rest, could inspire rejection and condemnation of the legacy of Condorcet, Brissot, and the democrats.[6] Their democratic constitutionalism was the Revolution's true motor and message to humanity, the only outcome of the Revolution offering a rational and just resolution of the dilemmas and predicaments of modern society.

Among those opposing Constant's, Roederer's, and Daunou's standpoint was a young Counter-Enlightenment theorist, Joseph de Maistre (1751–1821), who retorted with his *Considérations sur la France* (1796), published in Switzerland. A Savoyard count and magistrate who had once venerated Voltaire but had turned against both Enlightenment and Revolution after the annexation of Savoy, Maistre became the leading intellectual foil to the Revolution's reviving Left republicanism. The royalist and religious reaction which he believed most Frenchmen ardently longed for was not the misguided, bigoted, reactionary

Figure 21. Nicolas-Henri Jeaurat de Bertry (1728–1796), Allegory of the Revolution featuring a portrait of Rousseau, triangular monument to Equality, the tricolor, and a column of arms topped by a red Liberty cap, 1794, oil on canvas. Musée de la Ville de Paris, Musée Carnavalet, Paris, France / The Bridgeman Art Library.

obscurantism Constant depicted, and would, he insisted, by no means involve the bloody "contrary revolution" the republicans of 1796–97 warned against, but would be the peaceful, harmonious "opposite of revolution."[7] While Counter-Enlightenment ideology by this time already boasted a long and formidable tradition, reaching back to the 1750s, post-Thermidor Counter-Enlightenment like Maistre's contained a new central feature: it highlighted Robespierre, the Terror, and Montagnard ideology justifying atrocities, depicting Robespierre's legacy as the authentic, as well as horrific, outcome of the Revolution.[8] In the Terror, the Montagne and Robespierrisme enemies of the Enlightenment recognized not the aberration, perversion, and betrayal Constant and Roederer identified but the philosophique core principles of 1789 and of post-Thermidor that the democratic republicans championed and that practically everyone agreed had engineered the Revolution from the outset.

Catholic-royalist reaction in France during the later 1790s, held the *Décade philosophique*, like Jullien's and Réal's journals, drew its nationwide, formidable vigor invariably from the most ignorant part of the population, the illiterate and semi-illiterate. In the eyes of the editors of the main post-1794 republican journals, the Counter-Revolution's success stemmed precisely from the Counter-Enlightenment and the Enlightenment's limitations. The appeal of reactionary loyalism, maintained democrats, fed on ignorance and credulity spiced with xenophobia, anti-intellectualism, and bigotry. If Catholic royalism proved an immensely powerful opponent to modern republican-democratic ideology, it was one they judged a simplistic as well as pernicious rival, blending religious authority and politics in ways that blinded its own adherents, whether artisans, peasants, or bourgeois, "to their true interests." If today Constant, Réal, and Jullien, like Volney and Cabanis, can be seen to have been historically more accurate than Maistre and the Counter-Enlightenment in their evaluation of the Revolution and its ideology, and philosophically more discerning, Restoration conservatism and the Counter-Enlightenment succeeded in persuading most nineteenth- and twentieth-century readers and commentators that Robespierre and the Montagne were indeed the leading representatives and not the perversion and reversal of the Revolution.

This outcome seemingly contributed to the strange willingness of modern historians to view Robespierre's role as a well-meaning and relatively positive and benign one, at least prior to June 1793,[9] whereas at the time the democratic republican Left more correctly judged his role nonrepublican, undemocratic, and insidious, even as early as the summer of 1791. In any case, conservative interpretations propagated by Maistre, Rivarol, Feller, La Harpe, and many others during the mid- and later 1790s, presenting Robespierre and the Montagne as the true face of the Revolution, not only proved more convincing for most readers and more lastingly influential but grew into a wider construction, vilifying both the Revolution and Enlightenment together. This became the common view but one that in its philosophical, cultural, and political implications and resonance is surely as unfortunate as it is questionable, and fragile as a historical interpretation.

The strange persistence of the view that Robespierre and the Terror marked the culmination of the Revolution, a view that utterly distorts our historical and philosophical understanding of the Revolution's meaning as well as of the actual course of events, cannot hide the fact, in any case, that conflating Robespierre and the democratic Enlightenment was originally linked to a furious intellectual reaction against the Enlightenment, a reaction that began precisely in the mid-1790s. As Réal observed in his *Journal de l'Opposition*, Counter-Enlightenment thinking in France massively surged at that point (as it already had in Britain and Central Europe earlier) and subsequently spread even to the United States. It became "the fashion and the ordinary way of thinking," as Réal put it, to scorn the very thinkers and inspirers of the Revolution, the philosophes, who ten years before had been generally considered the public's teachers, "leurs oracles, leurs dieux."[10]

Among the factors militating against democracy and the Revolution in the years 1795–99, then, and paving the way to Napoleon's authoritarianism, was the public discrediting of la philosophie moderne, the principal ground of equality, human rights, and republican democracy. The irony was that the public turned against the Enlightenment because it was correctly identified by most commentators as the chief cause of the Revolution, which, thanks to the Montagne, had now acquired a universally bad name. The fact that radical thought had caused and shaped the Revolution seemed to a great many to be incontestable proof that the Enlightenment was the prime generator of Robespierre's tyranny and the Terror. In this way, popular political culture, alleged Constant, Roederer, and Réal, became contaminated with a wholly erroneous interpretation of the Revolution, which became (and remains) a formidable political device in the conservative arsenal. Misuse and misappropriation of the fact that the Enlightenment *was* the major shaping cause of the Revolution thus helped open the gate wide to the prevailing royalist-aristocratic-ecclesiastical reaction of the early nineteenth century and dismal catalog of Counter-Enlightenment ideologies plaguing and decrying modern democracy and republicanism ever since.

Part of the historiographical obscurantism impeding a proper view of the Revolution has been the unfortunate consensus prevailing until today that early revolutionary France down to June 1791 was overwhelmingly monarchist and traditional. Historians have assumed this because the vast majority of society thought in traditional terms. But among the writers and reformers responsible for the most incisive and noticed revolutionary pamphlets of 1788–89, as well as for the leading pro-Revolution journals and papers, and the great enactments and political developments of 1789 (as opposed to the rural unrest), the dominant tendency consistently, from 1788 onward, was not monarchist but democratic republican. Officially, the Revolution became republican only in September 1792. But the political thought of the chief authors of the authentic Revolution of human rights, equality, and free expression—Brissot, Desmoulins, Condorcet, Cérutti, Pétion, Carra, Gorsas, Robert, Kersaint, Mercier, Bonneville, Prudhomme, Lanthenas, Roederer, Guyomar, Marie-Joseph Chénier, and Jean-Joseph Dusaulx, as well as, if less overtly, Mirabeau and Sieyès, those laying the foundations of democratic modernity, as distinct from Marat's and Robespierre's authoritarian populism—was uninterruptedly and uniformly republican throughout.

Democratic republicanism was, in turn, linked to secularism, rejection of religious authority, and the adoption of one-substance philosophy. Radical Enlightenment is indeed best defined as the linking of one-substance monism with democracy and sweeping egalitarian social reform. There had always existed a close connection between the anti-scripturalism, *tolérantisme*, and critique of ecclesiastical authority dominating radical freethinking in its pre-1750 stages, and the comprehensive egalitarianism, antimonarchism, and preoccupation with basic human rights of the post-1750 period. In early modern times, social hierarchy and monarchy, as well as church hegemony in education, censorship, and social theory, were predominantly justified in terms of revelation, divine creation, and divine ordering and governance of the world. Most people at all social levels in the late eighteenth-century transatlantic world accepted, as they had earlier, the legitimacy and rightness of the existing order. It was what they were used to and what was sanctioned by religion and the churches. Without overturning this trust in a divine Providence that had supposedly fixed human society's forms and norms as they ought to be, and without undermining the belief that traditional, conventionally accepted morality had been divinely revealed, it was impossible to champion the far-reaching reforms needed for a worldwide emancipation, secularization, and rationalization of society and culture. Despite the passionate but misplaced protestations of Fauchet and Grégoire, without first weakening faith in a knowing, benevolent divine governance of the world, and in religious authority generally, there existed no path to a revolutionary consciousness equipped to build a new moral order, to replace the ancien régime with reforms fundamentally redirecting the pursuit of happiness—individual and collective—and the essential goals of the state.

The radical philosophes viewed the societies of their time as inherently oppressive and corrupt. At the same time, they sought to discredit and delegitimize existing constitutions and legal systems on the ground that they depended on authority rooted in religion, tradition, received thinking, and aristocratic values. Radical enlighteners and democratic revolutionaries rejected the whole edifice of their society's laws, precedents, charters, and institutionalized inequality unequivocally, and this inevitably involved rejecting all religious authority as well. By the 1780s, the kind of reform radical thinkers envisaged had become a potent, massive factor of disturbance and renewal in European politics, not just in France but also Holland, Switzerland, Italy, Ireland, Germany, and Britain. Their undertaking spread the doctrines of universal enlightenment, human rights, freedom of expression, and democracy everywhere, including the world beyond Europe and North America, vilifying the ancien régime colonial empires, seeking to emancipate the black, brown, and yellow peoples of the world, and changing the relationship between Europe and the rest fundamentally.

Paine's exhortation, "lay then the axe to the root, and teach governments humanity," implied a totalizing approach to reform, envisaging it as a universal need prevalent throughout the globe, something neither conceivable nor realizable without the arguments provided by radical Enlightenment thought.[11] The chief tools for remaking human society, as befits the Enlightenment, were to be education and reeducation. What antidote can there be, asked d'Holbach in 1773, to the "dépravation générale des sociétés" where so many powerful interests conspire to perpetuate the prevailing oppression, corruption, disorder, and human misery? There is only one way to transform such an edifice of wrong notions, exploitation, and repression: abolish the whole corrupt system of religious prejudice and superstition allied to rank, privilege, and nobility. Only thus could oppression and exploitation be replaced with a more equitable society, and "error" replaced with "the truth." If ignorance and error are the exclusive origin of all the world's corrupt laws, institutions, and political systems, if men are vicious, intolerant, oppressed, and poor only because they have wrong ideas about society and their "happiness," held d'Holbach, then it is only by combating error, teaching men their true interests, and instilling "des idées saines" that society's ills can be corrected.

As Desmoulins affirms in his *La France Libre* (1789), rejection of divine Providence and divine governance of the world was and is closely connected to the genesis of revolutionary democratic republicanism. The universe, replied Voltaire and Rousseau, is governed by divine Providence and God is just. But if God had really created the cosmos, objected Diderot, d'Holbach, and Helvétius, not only would the order of the universe be due to divine Providence but so would all the disorder, violence, and oppression, rendering all worldly existence precarious and frequently wretched and miserable.[12] If the order of the universe proves the omnipotence and intelligence of a divine Creator, then the disorder and the world's ubiquitous tyrannical political systems prove that Creator's inconstancy and unreasonableness. If Voltaire and Rousseau were right about the divinity, divine Providence, and Creation, then the fact that "human institutions are one mass of folly and contradiction," as Rousseau expressed it in *Émile* in 1762,[13] and as Diderot's veritable disciples all accepted, was a mystery as obscure as those of the theologians whose "mystères" the deists themselves constantly ridiculed. Deists, without saying so, make the "God" who is the foundation of their natural religion himself the greatest of mysteries. What are his powers and wherein resides his justice? How does he direct the world and rule over humanity?

The cruel, unjust way most people have been governed, held Diderot, d'Holbach, and Condorcet, proves that fear of divine punishment does not curb the perverse, either in social life or politics. Do not monsters like Tiberius, Caligula, and Nero demonstrate clearly enough the nonexistence of a Providence "qui s'intéresse au sort de la race humaine"?[14] Rousseau and the radical philosophes disagreed about many things, but there were two basic political doctrines where they converged: first, the entire institutional structure of contemporary society was corrupt, reprehensible, and despotic, and needed replacing; second, transforming the entire structure of laws, institutions, and politics has the capacity to make men happier and better. They were agreed also on the need of an educational revolution to change how men think as an essential element in the political revolution of which they dreamed. But the radical philosophes were much more insistent than Rousseau on the need for an educational revolution that transformed the people's religious and moral ideas and sapped the power of religious authority. They deemed this necessary for a true democratic republicanism. They were also more insistent than Rousseau on the need for political revolution to engineer moral change: "c'est à la politique," wrote d'Holbach, reversing Montesquieu (as the other radical philosophes also did), to form the outlook and attitudes of people, to inspire "les dispositions nécessaires à leur maintien, à leur sureté, à leur prosperité [the dispositions necessary for their maintenance, security and prosperity]."[15] Condorcet, Volney, and, in Egypt, also Napoleon all followed this principle.

Against this argument, it has been objected that "surviving members of d'Holbach's salon, including figures such as the Abbé Raynal ... opposed the French Revolution from its very outset."[16] But this contention, though again widely subscribed to, also turns out to be part of the misleading historiography. Some of d'Holbach's dining circle, including Raynal (albeit not before 1790), Grimm, Suard, Morellet, and Marmontel, did oppose the Revolution. But these men had long since abandoned key aspects of the social and political thought of Diderot, Helvétius, and d'Holbach. The estrangement of Grimm from Diderot, for example, began with their quarrel over whether or not Catherine the Great was an oppressive tyrant, already early in the 1780s. When turning against the Revolution in 1790–91, Raynal expressly declared in the National Assembly that he was now repudiating the very principles he had proclaimed together with Diderot in the 1770s and early 1780s, and he willingly acknowledged, as we have seen, that precisely an unyielding promotion of the principles expounded in the *Histoire philosophique des Deux Indes* was what generated and molded the Revolution. Those more loyal to the legacy of Diderot, d'Holbach, and Helvétius, adhering to it through the 1780s and early 1790s, like Condorcet, Naigeon, Deleyre, the young Volney (who formed an attachment to d'Holbach in his last years), Garat, Say, Cabanis, and Mme. Helvétius, all ardently championed the Revolution of republicanism, equality, and democracy prior to and even (if in some cases more hesitantly) after the Terror.[17]

Neither classical republicanism, then, nor Rousseau's deism underpinned the democratic thrust behind the most comprehensively radical and revolutionary writings of the late eighteenth century. The true underpinning was the confident secularism pronouncing philosophical reason the engine of universal human emancipation, deriving from the encyclopédistes and, earlier still, from the radical thinkers of the late seventeenth-century Enlightenment. The major textual sources that shaped this democratic republican political culture after 1750 were Diderot's political articles and exposition of la volonté génerale in the *Encyclopédie*, Rousseau's *Discourses* and *Contrat Social* (1762), the *Histoire philosophique* (1770), d'Holbach's *La Politique naturelle* (1773), d'Holbach's *Système social* (1773), Helvétius's *De L'Homme* (1773), and Paine's *Rights of Man* (1791) and *Age of Reason* (1793), along with Condorcet's political writings and Volney's *Les Ruines* (1791). The conviction that there is a true moral order and that that moral order is the creation of man and based on equality and reciprocity, and not on nature or God, drove the revolutionary impulse.

"The Enlightenment project failed," it has been wrongly claimed, "because the radical empiricism of modern science, when applied to the history and sociology of morals, revealed no human consensus but instead an ultimate diversity of moral perspectives."[18] This is the postmodernist cry. But in fact, radical Enlightenment critique provided logical, convincing grounds for discarding all religious and traditional perspectives and basing the claim to universal emancipation on a systematic monism and materialism that alone matched and fitted the criteria of the critique of existing politics, moral systems, and conditions. Mirabeau, Condorcet, Volney, Roederer, and the Brissotin revolutionaries followed Diderot, d'Holbach, and Helvétius in maintaining that true morality is one, cosmopolitan, and identical "pour tous les habitants de notre globe," and should everywhere underpin the system of laws because there exists only one exclusive code of universal human rights and one logic treating everybody's interests as equal.[19]

Spreading genuine republicanism on all sides, creating only governments that sincerely promote the interests of the majority, the democratic republican revolutionaries maintained, also directs us on the path to universal peace. Their substituting a new moral code for that upheld by the theologians (and for the deism of Voltaire and Rousseau) was what made equality of the races, religions, and of men and women, as well as of individuals, and universal education, freedom of expression, and individual freedom, the philosophical foundation of democratic republicanism, the lynchpin of what d'Holbach dubbed the true *système social*.

For all these reasons, Radical Enlightenment was incontrovertibly the one "big" cause of the French Revolution. It was the sole fundamental cause because politically, philosophically, and logically it inspired and equipped the leadership of the authentic Revolution. It could do so because the Radical Enlightenment alone offered a package of values sufficiently universal, secular, and egalitarian to set in motion the forces of a broad, general emancipation based on reason, freedom of thought, and democracy.

Cast of Main Participants

Amar, Jean-Pierre-André (1755–1816), Grenoble financial official and magistrate before the Revolution, among the most corrupt leading Montagnards. An implacable pursuer of Brissotins, worked closely with the Caribbean slave-owners. Led the Montagne's autumn 1793 campaign to suppress the women's clubs, joined the Thermidorian coup against Robespierre, and, later, Babeuf's conspiracy against the Directory. Ended as a devout mystic.

Antonelle, Pierre Antoine (1747–1817), Provençal nobleman and fervent Jacobin. Elected mayor of Arles and then to the National Assembly, collaborated in the 1793 anti-Brissotin repression until his independent-mindedness led to his imprisonment. Released after Thermidor, figured among the foremost revolutionary journalists of the later 1790s, especially as an editor of Vatar's *Journal des Hommes Libres*. Implicated in the Conspiracy of Equals, was imprisoned again in 1797. In 1814 publicly converted to royalism and Catholicism.

Artois, Charles-Philippe comte d' (1757–1836), younger brother of Louis XVI and of Louis Stanislas, count of Provence (Louis XVIII). Eventually, on Louis XVIII's death, became king of France as Charles X (reigned 1824–30). Vain, superficial, and reactionary; before 1789 chiefly hunted, practiced sports, and collected horses and mistresses. Fled France in July 1789 and with his older brother, Louis Stanislas, commanded the ultra-royalist counter-revolution based in Germany. In 1805, underwent a personal conversion from libertinism to extreme Catholic piety.

Babeuf, François Noël (called "Gracchus") (1760–1797), revolutionary journalist and fervent champion of equality, inspired by Morelly and Diderot. Among the forerunners of militant socialism, consistently placed the social question and issues of land distribution before other issues. Imprisoned during the Terror, released after Thermidor, and imprisoned again in 1795. Released in March 1796, organized the Conspiracy of Equals, the foremost underground opposition movement opposing the early Directory together with Antonelle, Maréchal, and Felix Lepeletier. Arrested and tried for treason, guillotined by the Directory on 27 May 1797.

Bailly, Jean Sylvain (1736–1793), astronomer and member of all three royal academies in Paris, leading figure in the Estates-General of 1789. Chosen as mayor of Paris by the assembly of electors following the Bastille's fall, prominent among the temporarily dominant liberal monarchist faction headed by Barnave and the Brothers de Lameth during 1790–91. Withdrew defeated from revolutionary politics in the autumn of 1791, settling in Nantes; imprisoned during the Terror. Guillotined in Paris on 12 November 1793.

Barbaroux, Charles Jean-Marie (1767–1794), affluent devotee of the sciences, and gifted orator. Won considerable popularity as a revolutionary leader in Marseille.

After serving as secretary to the Marseille city government was elected to the national legislature where he sided with Brissot. Among Mme. Roland's admirers, inspired the sending of the column of Marseillais to Paris in June 1792, and led the Marseillais in Paris during the rising of 10 August. Outlawed following the June 1793 Montagnard coup, was captured, wounded, a year later. Guillotined at Bordeaux on 25 June 1794.

Barlow, Joel (1754–1812), Connecticut-born, Yale-educated American poet and democratic republican veteran of the American Revolution. Active in France from 1788, adhered to the Brissotins' democratic cosmopolitanism and played a leading part in republicanizing Savoy when the area was annexed by the French in 1792. Assisted Paine in getting the first part of The *Age of Reason* published while Paine was incarcerated during the Terror, and made repeated attempts to get him released.

Barère, Bertrand (1755–1841), leading Montagnard, from Tarbes. A magistrate of the Toulouse *parlement* before the Revolution, elected to the Third in the 1789 Estates-General. A royalist moderate during 1789–92, was brought onto the Committee of Public Safety, in April 1793, for his administrative and "legal" competence. Doggedly loyal to Robespierre until July 1794, joined the Thermodorians at the last moment. Escaped prior to deportation to Cayenne as a principal agent of the Terror during the 1795 neo-Brissotin resurgence and successfully hid in Bordeaux. Reemerged in 1799, proclaiming support for Napoleon. Banished from France in 1815.

Barnave, Antoine Joseph (1761–1793), Grenoble lawyer active in the revolutionary movement in the Dauphiné from 1788. Elected to the Third in the Estates-General of 1789, emerging among the early Revolution's most brilliant orators. A leading centrist after the Revolution's first phase, advocated constitutional monarchy and a protected autonomy for the white slave-owners of the Caribbean. An eminent and fiercely anticlerical theorist, perceiving the centrist bid had failed, retired from revolutionary politics in early 1792. Guillotined in Paris on 29 November 1793.

Barras, Paul, vicomte de (1755–1829), Provençal noble elected to the Convention in 1792 by his native Var department, in March 1793 was sent as a representative-on-mission to southern France. A competent military organizer, directed the siege of Toulon, where he became the patron of the young Bonaparte. A dissipated opportunist among the initiators of the Thermidorian conspiracy, commanded the Thermidorian armed force in Paris during Robespierre's overthrow. Under the 1795 Constitution, served for five years among the Directory's directors, adopting an opulent, princely life-style. Among his numerous mistresses were Thérèse Tallien and Bonarparte's future wife, Josephine Beauharnais. Welcomed Napoleon's coup of Brumaire in 1799.

Basire, Claude (or, as here, Bazire) (1761–1794), former archivist renowned for the virulence of his speeches in the Jacobins, among the most unscrupulous Montagnard leaders. A close ally of Chabot, like him became mired in corruption scandals and clashes with Marat. Denounced for modérantisme at the Jacobins, was imprisoned in September 1793. Guillotined in Paris on 4 April 1794.

Bayle, Moïse (1755–1812), an ex-Protestant leading revolutionary of Marseille. Initially a republican ally of Barbaroux, broke with him after being elected to the Convention in 1792 and sided with Marat. A member of the Committee of General

Security, joined the coup of Thermidor against Robespierre but was afterwards imprisoned as a principal agent of the Terror. An incorrigible opportunist, died disgraced and destitute.

Beauharnais, Alexandre, vicomte de (1760–1794), army officer from Martinique and husband of Josephine, Napoleon's future wife, served in the American Revolution under Rochambeau. Elected to the Estates-General of 1789 for the noblesse of Blois, among the first nobles to defect to the Third. Prominent in the 1791 legislature, unsuccessfully commanded the revolutionary army defending the Rhenish Republic during the summer of 1793. Guillotined in Paris four days before Thermidor (27 July 1794), on 23 July 1794.

Beaumarchais, Pierre-Augustin Caron de (1732–1799), former music teacher at the court of Louis XV and leading French dramatist. Author of the *Barber of Seville* (1775) and the *Marriage of Figaro* (1784). Was also a prominent arms supplier to the republicans during both the American and French Revolutions. Making a fortune from business enterprises and plays, in 1779 bought the rights to Voltaire's manuscripts; edited and published the first complete edition, in seventy volumes, of Voltaire's works (1783–90). An Enlightenment standard-bearer and among the principal organizers of the Voltaire revival during the early Revolution. Fled to Germany in late 1792, returning to France in 1796.

Bergasse, Nicolas (1750–1832), Lyon lawyer, among the prominent pamphleteers of 1788, elected to the Third in the Estates-General of 1789. Adhering to the *parti monarchien*, the center-right, withdrew in disgust from the National Assembly after Mounier's defeat in October 1789. Hid from late 1792, but was caught and imprisoned in December 1793. Behind bars at Tarbes and Paris until released in January 1795.

Billaud-Varenne, Jacques Nicolas (1756–1819), failed teacher and thwarted author from La Rochelle, a principal agent of the Terror. In 1791 expelled for republicanism from the Jacobins while the club was still moderate and joined the Cordeliers. Emerged as a central figure in the radicalized Jacobins after the centrist monarchists seceded. Prominent in the Paris city government from August 1792, figured among Robespierre's principal adherents until July 1794, when he joined the Thermidorian coup. Deported to Cayenne in 1795 for his role in the Terror, escaped from there in 1816 to evade Louis XVIII's reach, to Haiti.

Boissy d'Anglas, François Antoine (1756–1826), son of a Protestant physician who, despite a stammer and being a poor speaker, was elected a deputy of the Third to the Estates-General of 1789, consistently adhered to moderate positions. Flattered Robespierre during the Terror. Voted onto the Committee of Public Safety after Thermidor, among the most strident critics of the Terror. Considered a royalist at heart and too centrist to reliably oppose the monarchist resurgence of 1796–97, went into hiding after the republican coup of Fructidor (4 September 1797). Amnestied by Napoleon, became a member of the Napoleonic senate in 1804 and "count of the empire" in 1808. Pardoned and made a peer of France under the Restoration monarchy.

Bonaparte, Napoleon (1769–1821), member of the Corsican lower nobility, rose through the army and brilliant generalship to become emperor of France. In September 1789 and May 1792 active in Corsica supporting Paoli and Volney in rallying the island behind the Revolution, breaking with Paoli in 1793 when the latter turned against the Revolution. Distinguished himself in the 1793–94 siege of Toulon, became linked with Augustin Robespierre resulting, after Thermidor, in his arrest at Nice as a Robespierriste, brief imprisonment and, in September 1794, deletion from the Committee of Public Safety's list of reliable generals. Barras and his role in suppressing the Vendémiaire rising (5 October 1795) secured his rehabilitation. Conquering northern Italy in 1796–97, won renown as an exemplary republican as well as outstanding general. Discarded his republican posture only in 1799.

Bonneville, Nicolas de (1760–1828), revolutionary journalist, idealist, and professional translator from English and German. In 1782, published a twelve-volume collection of German drama. In Germany in 1787, established ties with the Illuminati. A leader of the 1789 march on the Bastille, subsequently launched *Le Tribunal du peuple* and, in October 1790, with Fauchet formed the Cercle Social, the early Revolution's foremost radical reform movement. From October 1790, edited the Cercle's paper, *La Bouche de fer*, until late 1791. Imprisoned during the Terror, released after Thermidor. Paine boarded with the Bonnevilles, friends since his arrival in Paris, during his final five years in France (1797–1802).

Boyer-Fonfrède, Jean-Baptiste (1765–1793), son of a wealthy Bordeaux merchant family and brother-in-law of Ducos, lived in Holland during 1785–89, prominent in the revolutionary ferment in Bordeaux after the Bastille's fall. With Ducos led the remaining opposition to the Montagnard coup-d'état in the Convention during the summer of 1793 until formally proscribed as an ally of the Brissotins. Guillotined with Brissot on 31 October 1793.

Brissot (de Warville), Jacques-Pierre (1754–93), prolific author, revolutionary publicist, and champion of freedom of expression, leader of the democratic republican faction often misleadingly termed the "Gironde." Drawn to the democratic revolutions of Geneva (1782) and Holland (1780–87) which he studied firsthand, toured the United States in 1788, investigating the revolutionary outcome there. Devotee of *la philosophie nouvelle*, became a prominent revolutionary journalist in 1789, emerging among the Revolution's chief architects and earliest principled republicans. Among the Revolution's foremost advocates of human rights, internationalism, and black emancipation. After 10 August 1792, worked closely with Condorcet, unsuccessfully striving to use the Brissotin majority in the Convention to consolidate the democratic republic. Loathed by Marat and Robespierre, was imprisoned in June 1793. Guillotined in Paris on 31 October 1793.

Buonarotti, Philippe (1761–1837), Florentine nobleman and conspirator among the leading revolutionary republicans in Corsica in 1791–93. Imprisoned after Thermidor for his role in the Terror, amnestied in 1795. Implicated in Babeuf's Conspiracy of Equals in Paris, was again imprisoned on its collapse but later acquitted. His history of the Babeuf conspiracy, eventually published in 1828, led to his reputation, including among Marxists, as the first historian of the origins of modern socialism.

Buzot, François-Nicolas (1760–1794), Evreux lawyer and passionate Rousseauist, elected to the Third in the Estates-General 1789. Among the 1792 Convention's leading republicans, in December 1792 urged expulsion from France of all the Bourbons, including Philippe-Égalité, which, like all his proposals, antagonized the Montagne. Close to Brissot, and lover of Mme. Roland, early in 1793 worked against the concentration of power in the executive committees and for Marat's expulsion from the Convention. Detested by Robespierre, was hunted down by the Montagne during the Terror, committing suicide on 18 June 1794.

Cabanis, Pierre-Jean (1757–1808), physician and man of letters, prominent in the Auteuil circle around Mme. Helvétius with ties to Condorcet, Franklin, Mirabeau, Garat, and Volney. Provided the poison capsules for fugitive Brissotins, enabling several, including Condorcet, to commit suicide when caught. A leading Idéologue and, from 1796, a professor of the Institut de France, was elected to the Five Hundred in 1797 where he allied with Sieyès. Despite supporting the 1799 Brumaire coup, was, like all the Idéologues, regarded with suspicion by Napoleon.

Calonne, Charles Alexandre (1734–1802), senior magistrate and intendant under Louis XV and Louis XVI. As royal controller-general of the finances, in 1786, presented the general plan for the reform of the French tax system that led to the summoning of the Assembly of Notables and sequence of events precipitating the Revolution. Disgraced and exiled to England in April 1787. During 1790–92, proclaiming the Revolution a menace to kings, aristocracy, and the privileged everywhere, served as principal adviser to Artois and the émigré command in Germany. Ruined himself financially in the émigré princes' service.

Cambacérès, Jean-Jacques de (1753–1824), nobleman from the Montpellier region, elected to the 1792 Convention where he paid lip-service to the republican Revolution but remained aloof from doctrinal disputes, remaining neutral in the struggle between Brissotins and the Montagne while emerging as a principal law reformer. With the 1799 coup of Brumaire, became Second Consul under Napoleon. Instrumental in negotiating the 1801 Concordat with the papacy and drafting the Napoleonic Civil Code.

Camus, Armand Gaston (1749–1804), before 1789 *avocat* of the clergy of France and in earlier life an ardent Jansenist and Gallican, during the Revolution became an equally ardent republican detested by most churchmen as a principal architect of the Civil Constitution of the Clergy. Presided over the reform of the French pension system in 1790–91, applying stringently antiaristocratic, republican principles. Hugely erudite, served as the archivist and librarian of the National Assembly. Handed over to the Austrians by Dumouriez in April 1793, refused to take his hat off to any princes or aristocrats, and remained imprisoned for nearly three years in Germany.

Carnot, Lazare (1753–1823), son of a notary, trained before the Revolution in military engineering and forts, joined the Committee of Public Safety in August 1793, becoming the Montagne's preeminent military organizer. Architect of the victory of Fleurus (1794) over the Austrians and a leading Thermidorian, rose after Robespierre's downfall becoming one of the five directors (1795–97). But increasingly royalist in sympathy, ended his revolutionary career as a target of the September 1797 coup of Fructidor. Escaping to Switzerland, remained outside France until the advent of Napoleon's dictatorship; exiled again at the Restoration in 1814, died in Prussia.

Carra, Jean-Louis (1742–1793), among the Revolution's principal republican journalists and electorally most popular deputies; published several books before the Revolution. An adventurous autodidact, in the 1770s spent several years in

England, Russia, and in Rumanian Wallachia (as secretary of the hospodar). From the summer of 1789, his *Annales politiques* figured among the foremost revolutionary papers, always backing, like his numerous speeches in the Jacobins, the democratic, antiaristocratic tendency and general emancipation. A key organizer of the 10 August 1792 rising and adversary of Robespierre, subsequently with Chamfort, became a director of the Bibliothèque nationale. Guillotined in Paris on 31 October 1793.

Carrier, Jean-Baptiste (1756–1794), a taciturn alcoholic, among the most sadistic, mentally unbalanced, and brutal Montagnard leaders. Sent to supervise the war against the Brissotin fédéralistes in Normandy in the summer of 1793, in August was appointed to direct the suppression of the royalist revolt of the Vendée. His atrocities in and around Nantes, his slaughtering thousands, and noyades and nighttime orgies, resulted in his recall, in February 1794, and falling out with Robespierre. Subsequently aligned with Hébert but was not seized in the April 1794 purge. Arrested by the Thermidorians, guillotined in Paris on 16 December 1794.

Cazalès, Jacques-Antoine (1758–1805), among the nobles championing voting by separate orders in the Estates-General of 1789, emerged from October 1789 as a leader of the National Assembly's center-right faction striving to defend royalty, aristocracy, and the clergy against the Revolution's increasingly radical course. Withdrawing from revolutionary politics after the flight to Varennes, with the fall of the monarchy, fled to Germany to join the émigré princes.

Cérutti, Giuseppe (Joseph Antoine) (1738–1792), Piedmontese ex-Jesuit philosophy teacher and revolutionary orator whose *Mémoire pour le peuple françois* was among the leading political pamphlets of 1788. Ally of Mirabeau, Cérutti figured prominently in the Cercle Social and was among the first to defend the reputation of d'Holbach in print against Rousseau. Founder and editor of *La Feuille villageoise* (1790–94), the only important revolutionary paper addressed primarily to rural society, turned it into a highly successful paper with a wide circulation.

Chabot, Francois (1756–1794), renegade Capuchin monk turned revolutionary. In the Convention and his paper, the *Journal populaire*, projected himself as a zealous champion of sanculottisme. No-one more vociferously denounced Lafayette, Brissot, Condorcet, and many others. Active in the de-Christianization movement and in promoting the Terror, lack of powerful friends as well as love of money and women hastened his downfall. Mired in corruption scandals, was imprisoned in November 1793 and guillotined in Paris on 4 April 1794.

Chalier, Joseph (1747–1793), the so-called Marat of Lyon, main organizer of the coup of 6 February 1793 that brought the Montagne to power in Lyon. Earlier elected president of the local tribunal of commerce, was for a time the idol of the Lyon silk-workers and unemployed. But so ruthlessly despotic was his regime, Lyon's population soon became deeply alienated. The Brissotin rising of 29 May 1793 overthrew the local Montagne, imprisoning Chalier. Guillotined in Lyon on 15 July 1793.

Chamfort, Nicolas (1741–1794), renowned aphorist and man of letters, a prominent revolutionary publicist and leading foe of the royal academies. In 1789, joined the entourage of Mirabeau for whom he wrote speeches and became a prominent journalist contributing to several revolutionary papers. Appointed a director of the Bibliothèque Nationale in 1792, was driven to suicide during the Terror.

Chaumette, Pierre Gaspard (1763–1794), failed medical student and leading member of the Montagnard Paris city government after 10 August 1792. City procurator from December 1792, in the autumn of 1793 played a prominent part in both the Terror and the de-Chistianization campagne. A homosexual, he also led the Montagnard campaign against prostitutes for whom he nurtured a fanatical hatred. Servile toward Robespierre, the latter nevertheless loathed him, his friends, and his overt atheism. Guillotined in Paris on 13 April 1794.

Chénier, Marie-Joseph (1764–1811), younger brother of the poet André Chénier, became (aside from Voltaire) the Revolution's leading playwright with his drama *Charles IX* first staged in 1789. Foremost spokesman for full freedom of the theater, played a key role both in the Jacobins and the direction of the Revolution's general republican propaganda. His plays were generally banned during the Montagnard ascendancy. A member of the Council of Five Hundred from 1795, was stripped of all public functions in 1802 for opposing Napoleon's dictatorship.

Clavière, Étienne (1735–1793), Genevan financier and democratic republican, prominent in the Genevan Revolution of 1782 and ally of Mirabeau and Brissot in Paris in 1789. Subsequently among Brissot's closest political associates. Arrested on 2 June 1793, stabbed himself to death in his cell on 8 December 1793 to avoid the guillotine.

Cloots, Jean-Baptiste "Anacharsis" (1755–1794), wealthy Dutch-born Prussian baron resident in Paris. A leading journalist and publicist publishing widely both before and during the Revolution, was an avowed atheist and de-Christianizer, and the Revolution's most dogmatic cosmopolitan. Despite his estrangement from the Brissotins, Robespierre procured his downfall, maligning him as a foreign agent. Guillotined in Paris, 24 March 1794.

Collot d'Herbois, Jean-Marie (1749–1796), failed actor prominent in the insurrectionary Montagnard Paris city government from 10 August 1792. Voted onto the Committee of Public Safety in September 1793, with Fouché directed the atrocities of the Terror in Lyon. Joined the conspiracy of Thermidor. Tried for his crimes in 1795, was banished to Cayenne where he died.

Condorcet, Jean-Antoine Nicolas de Caritat, marquis de (1743–1794), leading philosophe, republican ideologue, theorist of elections, and champion of democracy, black emancipation, and women's rights. Planner of the Republic's education reform program in 1791–93, was the primary author of the world's first democratic republican constitution (February 1793). Loathed by Robespierre, was outlawed in June 1793. Imprisoned on 28 March 1794, committed suicide the next day using poison to avoid the guillotine. Rehabilitated by the National Convention as one of the Revolution's foremost architects in April 1795.

Condorcet, Sophie de (Grouchy), Mme. de (1758–1822), Condorcet's wife, author, and leading exponent of women's rights. A declared atheist, presided over one of the principal and most philosophique revolutionary salons. Imprisoned during the Terror, released after Thermidor.

Constant, Benjamin (1767–1830), Swiss political theorist who settled in Paris with Mme. de Staël in 1795. In later years a moderate and a liberal, in 1795–1800 figured among the foremost critics of Robespierre and the Terror and republican apologists of the democratic Brissotin Revolution and of the Directory.

Corday, Charlotte (1768–1793), from a pious royalist family but converted to Brissotin sympathies, assassinated Marat on 13 July 1793 for having, in her view, "killed" the law on 2 June 1793. Became a Europe-wide symbol of resistance to Montagnard populism and despotism. Guillotined in Paris 17 July 1793.

Couthon, Georges (1755–1794), famously anti-intellectual lawyer suffering from rheumatic paralysis, among Robespierre's principal and most loyal aides. From November 1792, an implacable foe of the Brissotins in the legislature and a main author of the removal of legal safeguards for the individual. Helped direct the Terror. Guillotined with Robespierre on 28 July 1794.

Danton, Georges (1759–1794), among the principal leaders of the Revolution. A lawyer of modest educational attainments but a brilliant orator, dominated the Cordeliers Club in 1789–92 and was prominent in all the more radical initiatives up to and including the rising of 10 August 1792. When dominance of the Cordeliers passed to Hébert and Vincent following the 2 June 1793 coup, was in a weakened position, his efforts to curb the Terror only weakening him further. Joined Robespierre and Couthon in slowing the de-Christianization but was precariously placed from December 1793. After Robespierre finally broke with him, imprisoned on 30 March 1794; guillotined in Paris 5 April 1794.

Daunou, Pierre Claude (1761–1840), philosophy and theology professor elected to the Convention. Imprisoned under the Terror, after Thermidor was voted onto the Committee of Public Safety, becoming a leader of the neo-Brissotin revival. Continued Condorcet's educational reforms but was less democratic in his approach to education as well as in his republican constitutional theory. Appointed to help organize the Roman Republic of 1798–99, was too republican for Napoleon, ending his career by serving for many years as director of the National Archives.

David, Jacques-Louis (1748–1825), the Revolution's greatest artist; organizer of many of the major revolutionary ceremonies and fêtes, including the public cult of Marat after the latter's assassination. A loyal adherent of Robespierre up to and including Thermidor, he afterwards publicly repudiated his legacy. After Brumaire, adhered to Napoleon as deferentially as he had to Robespierre, becoming peintre de l'empereur. At the Restoration, went into exile in Brussels.

Debry, Jean-Antoine (1760–1834), Picard lawyer and ardent republican political theorist, a prominent member of the revolutionary legislature from 1791 until 1799 and a member of the Committee of General Security from January to June 1793. Among the leaders of the neo-Brissotin revival in 1795, supported Napoleon's dictatorship in 1799. Banished from France as a regicide with the Restoration.

Démeunier, Jean Nicolas (1751–1814), member of the National Assembly's constitutional committee (1789–91), a leading French expert on the American federal and state constitutions. Though too influenced by Raynal for Jefferson's taste, became chief translator and popularizer of the texts of the American Revolution and American republicanism within the French and Belgian revolutions.

Desmoulins, Camille (1760–1794), café intellectual and Cordelier firebrand, became a leading revolutionary journalist and orator in 1789 and Danton's closest ally. Broke with Robespierre in December 1794. Attempted through his last paper, *Le Vieux Cordelier*, to discredit the Terror and those responsible for it in the name of the "authentic" Revolution. Guillotined with Danton on 5 April 1794.

Destutt de Tracy, Antoine-Louis (1754–1836), philosophe among the first nobles to join the Third in the 1789 Estates-General. A keen supporter in the National Assembly of the initiatives to abolish feudalism and for measures of black emancipation. Imprisoned under the Terror. Published widely as a leading Idéologue in the late 1790s and read until far into the nineteenth century.

Dobsen, Claude Emanuel (1743–1811), lawyer and close accomplice of Robespierre. Among the principal organizers of the Paris disturbances of February and March 1793, and of the 31 May and 2 June 1793 coups d'état. Worked with Hanriot whom he helped make commander of the Paris National Guard. A judge of the Paris Tribunal Révolutionnaire during the Terror, was removed in May 1794 for being insufficiently ruthless. His siding with Robespierre at Thermidor left him without prospects. In 1796, joined Babeuf's Conspiracy of Equals.

Ducos, Jean-François (1765–1793), ardent propagator of the new philosophique ideas and, from 1791, of democratic republicanism, a leading representative for Bordeaux in the legislature among the inner, policy-making circle of the Brissotins. Arrested in October 1793, at the instigation of Billaud-Varenne and Amar, guillotined with Brissot on 31 October 1793.

Dumas, René-François (1757–1794), ex-priest, lawyer, and small-town Montagnard mayor specially selected by Robespierre in September 1793 as vice-president of the Paris Tribunal Révolutionnaire and, from April 1794, its president. Ruthlessly presided over the trials of the Hébertistes and Dantonistes. Guillotined with Robespiere on 28 July 1794.

Dumouriez, Charles François (1739–1823), army officer and purported ally of Brissot, minister of Foreign Affair from March to June 1792. Subsequently appointed commander of the Army of the North, won great prestige with his victories at Valmy (September 1792) and Jemappes (November 1792). Increasingly at odds with the Convention, and in sentiment privately antirepublican, unsuccessfully attempted a coup against the Brissotin revolutionary government in April 1793. Defected to the Austrians when his men refused to follow him.

Fabre d'Églantine, Philippe François (1750–1794), actor, playwright, and notorious womanizer, from late 1789, prominent in the Cordeliers (where he backed Danton) and the Jacobins. Mired in financial scandal linked to his activities on various Convention committees, became useful to Montagnard opponents denouncing him as Danton's corrupt evil genius. Guillotined with Danton on 6 April 1794.

Fauchet, Claude (1744–1793), democratic republican revolutionary priest who led the efforts to combine la philosophie with Catholicism. Among the founders and best speakers of the Cercle Social, was a passionate egalitarian and disciple of Rousseau. Accepted most of the 1790–91 sweeping church reforms but not the 1792 divorce law, or marriage of priests. Guillotined with Brissot on 31 October 1793.

Fleuriot-Lescot, Jean-Baptiste (1761–1794), obscure Belgian revolutionary fled from Brussels, made deputy to Fouquier-Tinville on the Paris Tribunal Révolutionnaire in March 1793 by Robespierre who, on 10 May 1794, also arranged his election as Paris mayor in succession to the equally unscrupulous but less ruthless Pache. At Thermidor, led the pro-Robespierre forces together with Hanriot. Guillotined with Robespierre on 28 July 1794.

Forster, Georg (1754–1794), Mainz university librarian, professor, and Jacobin leader. Among the principal writers of the later radical *Aufklärung*, and Germany's foremost eighteenth-century ethnographer. Represented the Rhenish democratic republic of 1792–93 in Paris where he died naturally in 1794. Among the foremost editors and propagators of democratic republicanism in Germany.

Fouché, Joseph (1759–1820), former priest and zealous Montagnard, among the chief initiators of the de-Christianization movement. Jointly responsible with Collot d'Herbois for the atrocities at Lyon in November 1793. After quarreling with Robespierre, sided with the Thermidorians. Although thoroughly dishonest, in July 1799 Barras appointed him the Republic's police minister. Only months later, betrayed Barras to aid Napoleon's quest for dictatorship, becoming Napoleon's chief of police. In 1814–15, betrayed Napoleon to become Louis XVIII's chief of police.

Fouquier-Tinville, Antoine (1746–1795), obscure lawyer appointed to head the Tribunal Révolutionnaire in Paris in March 1793, by Danton, then minister of justice. Ruthlessly methodical, presided over most major trials in Paris under the Terror, issuing hundreds of political death sentences including that of Robespierre on 10 Thermidor. Guillotined in Paris with fifteen other unscrupulous judges and lawyers of the tribunal on 7 May 1795.

Fournier, Claude, "l'Américain" (1745–1825), former Saint-Domingue plantation owner, slave-owner and rhum producer of unruly temperament who, from the storming of the Bastille onward, emerged as a leading populist agitator and champion of sansculottisme around the Palais-Royal. In 1793, after breaking with Marat and the Montagne was expelled from the Cordeliers and imprisoned several times. At the Restoration in 1814, claimed to have always been a royalist.

François de Neufchâteau, Nicolas Louis (1750–1828), poet, playwright, agronomist, and legal theorist, imprisoned under the Terror after the banning of one of his plays deemed subversive by the Montagne. Elected one of the five directors after Fructidor (September 1797), further stiffened the Republic's republican anticlerical educational reforms, using his ministry to propagate Radical Enlightenment texts.

Fréron, Stanislas Louis (1754–1802), disciple of Marat, and leading journalist and member of the Convention who with Barras and Augustin Robespierre served the Montagne as a key "missionary of Terror" in Provence in late 1793. After Thermidor, became prominent (despite his own atrocities) in denouncing the crimes, corruption, and hypocrisy of the Montagne.

Garat, Dominque Joseph (1749–1833), member of the circles of Diderot, Helvétius, and Condorcet since the mid-1770s, selected by Brissot to succeed Danton as the Republic's minister of justice in October 1792. Investigated the September 1792 Paris massacres but was deterred from punishing its instigators. Proscribed and imprisoned during the Terror, a leading Idéologue from 1796 and professor of the Institut de France who supported the 1799 coup of Brumaire.

Gensonné, Armand (1758–1793), Bordeaux lawyer, leading Brissotin close to Dumouriez, played a prominent role in drawing up the decrees outlawing the king's brothers and the émigré nobility. As the second most active member of the Convention's constitutional committee after Condorcet, contributed to formulating and presenting the world's first democratic constitution (February 1793). Arrested 2 June 1793; guillotined with Brissot 31 October 1793.

Ginguené, Pierre-Louis (1748–1816), man of letters, author of a literary history of Italy, and an editor of *La Feuille villageoise*, headed the 1791 petitioning movement for pantheonizing Rousseau. Imprisoned under the Terror, afterwards headed the Thermidorians' Commission for Public Instruction. Opposed Napoleon's dictatorship.

Gioia, Melchiorre (1767–1829), Italian Radical Enlightenment publicist and Utilitarian philosopher from Piacenza. Influenced by Bentham, one of the architects of the Italian republican revolutions of 1796–97 and, in July 1796, a founder of the Milanese paper *Giornale degli amici della libertà e dell' uguaglianza*. Appealed to his compatriots to form authentic democratic republics that would not be merely subservient to the French Directory.

Girey-Duprey, Jean-Marie (1769–1793), ardent republican, keeper of manuscripts at the Bibliothèque Nationale, and ally of Brissot, especially as editor of *Le Patriote françois* from October 1791. Denouncing Marat and the Montagne, forced to cease publication on 2 June 1793. Outlawed, escaped and hid in Bordeaux but was caught a few months later. Guillotined in Paris on 20 November 1793.

Gobel, Jean-Baptiste (1727–1794), ex-Jesuit, in March 1791 the National Assembly's first bishop deputy to swear the oath of allegiance to the Civil Constitution of the Clergy. Became the first popularly "elected" bishop of Paris, obtaining far more votes than Fauchet, Grégoire, or Sieyès. Publicly renounced Christianity and his bishopric for la philosophie on 7 November 1793. Guillotined in Paris, on 13 April 1794.

Gorsas, Antoine Joseph (1752–1793), before 1789 a tutor, founded the *Courrier de Versailles à Paris* in July 1789, and became one of the Revolution's principal republican journalists. Among the Montagne's sharpest critics and an organizer of the 20 June and 10 August 1792 risings, was denounced by Robespierre in the Jacobins from April 1792 onwards. Guillotined in Paris on 7 October 1793.

Gouges, Olympe de (1748–1793), renowned female dramatist, admirer of Mirabeau, and radical publicist for women's rights, black emancipation, and freedom of expression. Among the most prominent female participants in the Revolution. Vehemently denounced and derided Robespierre. Guillotined in Paris on 3 November 1793.

Grégoire, Henri, Abbé (1750–1831), priest but also a leading champion of toleration through love of l'esprit philosophique and reverence for Voltaire and Rousseau. Following his 1788 essay on Jewish emancipation, became a leading promoter of the rights of Jews and blacks. Supported most of the Revolution's ecclesiastical reforms. An architect of the February 1795 separation of state and church.

Guadet, Marguerite Elie (1758–1794), leading Brissotin deputy and advocate of a philosophique stance, repudiating populist Rousseauism and deriding all invoking of divine providence. A vigorous orator, in the Convention prominent in denouncing Marat and Robespierre. Escaped after the coup of 2 June 1793. Guillotined in Bordeaux, 17 June 1794.

Guyomar, Pierre (1757–1826), mayor of a small town of Lower Brittany, elected to the Convention on September 1792. Played a prominent part in the constitutional debate over the winter of 1792–93. Among the most ardent advocates of women's equality and right to participate in politics. Prudently quiescent under the Montagnard dictatorship, after Thermidor was instrumental in getting the surviving Brissotins restored to the Convention and organizing the neo-Brissotin resurgence.

Guzman, Andres Maria de (1752–1794), naturalized Frenchman of Andalusian origin, among the foremost Parisian crowd agitators. Initially allied to Marat and Hébert, a key sansculotte mobilizer on 31 May and 2 June 1793. Resenting his sansculotte popularity, Robespierre had him publicly denounced. Guillotined with Danton, on 5 April 1794.

Hanriot, François (1759–1794), notorious ruffian enjoying great prestige in the sansculotte quarters of Paris, made commander of the Paris Nation Guard by Robespierre on 31 May 1793. Played the leading role in overpowering the Convention during the coup of 2 June 1793. At Thermidor, headed the efforts to rescue Robespierre. Guillotined with Robespierre on 28 July 1794.

Hébert, Jacque René (1757–1794), middle-class disciple of Marat and editor of the most overtly populist revolutionary paper, *Le Père Duchesne*, gained great prestige among the sansculottes and in the Jacobins. Headed the Montagnard faction that was most amenable to compromise with sansculotte demands. Denounced in the Jacobins by Saint-Just on 14 March, guillotined in Paris on 24 March 1794.

Hérault de Séchelles, Marie-Jean (1759–1794) *avocat-général* of the Paris parlement at the young age of twenty-six in 1785, a sophisticated, wealthy, cynical aristocrat and political trimmer deftly steering between Feuillants, Brissotins, and the Montagne. Headed the commission that finalized the Montagnard constitution of June 1793. Loathed by Robespierre and Saint-Just, guillotined with Danton on 5 April 1794.

Houdon, Jean-Antoine (1741–1828), chief sculptor of the Enlightenment, renowned for his busts of Diderot, Mirabeau, Lafayette, Turgot, Gluck, Jefferson, Barnave, Marie-Joseph Chénier, and Barlow, as well as of the Rousseau bust gracing the National Assembly and the famous statue of Voltaire seated. Also sculpted Washington during his visit to the United States (1785) and Catherine the Great in Petersburg. In difficulties under the Montagnard despotism, clashed with David, narrowly escaping imprisonment.

Irhoven van Dam, Willem van (1760–1802), radical egalitarian and republican journalist in Amsterdam and editor of the *De Courier van Europa* (1783–85). In 1794–95, headed the underground committee in Amsterdam planning the failed rising of October 1794 and, more successfully, preparing the way for the French invasion of Holland and Batavian Revolution of early 1795.

Isnard, Maximilien (1755–1825), Grasse *parfumeur*, converted to philosophique ideas and an aggressive republicanism, during the Convention in 1792–93 was among the leaders of the Brissotin ascendancy. Hid during the Terror, reemerged after Thermidor, restored to the Convention in February 1795. After 1800, converted to ultra-royalism and mystical Catholicism.

Jullien, Marc Antoine (1775–1848), ardent egalitarian among Robespierre's most youthful and trusted agents, directed the stepped-up Terror at Bordeaux in the summer of 1794. After Thermidor, imprisoned as a Robespierriste until October 1795. During 1796, edited the republican French-language newspaper of Napoleon's army in Italy. Among the organizers of the Neapolitan republic of 1799.

Kersaint, Armand Guy, comte de (1742–1793), Breton republican naval officer chairing the Paris assembly of electors in 1789. In January 1793, led the Convention deputies demanding Louis XVI's life imprisonment rather than execution, resigning in protest shortly before the execution. Vehement foe of the Montagne. Arrested on 2 October, guillotined on 4 December 1793.

Kervélégan, Augustin Bernard de (1748–1825), republican pamphleteer in 1788, opposing royal despotism, aristocracy, and ecclesiastical authority. A member of the Brissotin Commission de Douze of May 1793 set up to investigate the Montagnard Commune, outlawed during the Terror, survived in hiding. Reappeared in the Convention in March 1795, remaining prominent in republican politics until the Brumaire coup. Submitted without protest to Napoleon's dictatorship.

Klopstock, Friedrich Gottlieb (1724–1803), poet and enlightener among the leading German apologists for the American and French revolutions. A constitutional monarchist rather than democrat, horrified by the September massacres and Robespierre, resigned his honorary French citizenship during the Terror.

Lacombe, Claire (1765–?), actress and prominent female organizer of the 10 August 1792 rising, presided over the Parisian republican women's section organizations and women's Marat cult after his assassination. Associated with several Enragé petitions for food price regulation. Criticized Robespierre, arrested on 3 April 1794, and imprisoned for thirteen months until released in August 1795.

Lafayette, Marie-Joseph Paul, marquis de (1757–1834), general in the American Revolution from June 1777, appointed commander of the Paris National Guard after the Bastille's fall. Gained control of the 5 October 1789 march on Versailles when he escorted the royal family back to Paris. Committed to constitutional monarchy, participated in the Feuillant ascendancy of 1791–92. Fled Paris during the rising of 10 August 1792, defecting to the Austrians.

La Harpe, Jean-François de (1739–1803), playwright, man of letters, and ardent disciple of Voltaire. Originally an enthusiastic revolutionary, was imprisoned by the Montagne in April 1794. Released after Thermidor, became an implacable foe of the Revolution and the "philosophy" that caused it. Punished for constantly denouncing the Republic, was prevented from teaching after the coup of Fructidor.

Lakanal, Joseph (1762–1845), philosophy professor, directing many of the Republic's educational and cultural initiatives during the Montagnard ascendancy, including establishment of the Paris Natural History Museum (June 1793) while deferring to Montagnard school policy. After Thermidor, reversed Robespierre's education priorities as president of the legislature's education committee, among other undertakings founding the écoles centrales secondary school system.

Lalande, Jérôme (1732–1807), renowned astronomer, atheist, and philosophe, doyen of French astronomy in the late eighteenth century and together with Romme the main theorist and designer of the new republican calendar presented to the Convention in November 1792.

Lally-Tollendal, Trophime Gérard, marquis de (1751–1830), with Mounier headed the monarchiens in the National Assembly from August to October 1789, striving for mixed government on the British model, including bicameralism and a permanent royal veto. Briefly imprisoned after the 10 August 1792 rising, fled to England on his release. At the Restoration, Louis XVIII made him a peer of France and member of the royal privy council.

Lameth, Alexandre de (1760–1829), an Artois noble and leader of the Feuillant faction. A cavalry colonel and veteran officer of the American war, defected from the nobility to the Third in the Estates-General of 1789 and opposed the constitutional monarchy retaining any significant powers. A left-centrist anticlerical opposed both to Mounier's monarchism and to democratic republicanism, he defected to the Austrians with Lafayette after 10 August 1792.

Lameth, Charles de (1757–1832), an Artois noble and, like his brother, a prominent Feuillant faction leader. Veteran of the American Revolution, wounded at the siege of Yorktown, defected from the nobility to the Third in the Estates-General of 1789. After 10 August 1792 resided in Hamburg. Adhered to Napoleon, the Restoration, and the 1830 revolution.

Lamourette, Antoine Adrien (1742–1794), prominent Catholic democratic republican popularly "elected" constitutional bishop of Lyon in February 1791. Long urging reconciliation of the Brissotins and Montagne, from June 1793 opposed the Montagne in Lyon. Guillotined in Paris on 11 January 1794.

Lanjuinais, Jean Denis (1753–1827), Rennes university professor and founder of the Club Breton, the antecedent of the Jacobins. Opposed the trial of Louis XVI and the Montagnard ascendancy. After surviving in hiding, concealed for eighteen months in Rennes, reappeared in the Convention in 1795 and participated in drafting the 1795 constitution. Opposed the coup of Fructidor, Napoleon, and Louis XVIII.

Lanthenas, François Xavier (1754–1799), physician, educationalist, and translator of Tom Paine, a protegé of Roland prominent among the Brissotin faction. After Thermidor, secretary of the Convention and until 1797 a leading critic of the Directory.

La Revellière-Lépeaux, Louis-Marie de (1753–1824), fervent anti-Catholic republican and egalitarian idealist from Angers. A Commission de Douze member forced to hide during the Terror, reappeared in the Convention in March 1795. Among the drafters of the 1795 constitution, was afterwards elected one of the five directors. Backed the coup of Fructidor (1797), patronized the deistic sect of the Théophilanthropes.

Lavoisier, Antoine Laurent (1743–1794), the eighteenth century's greatest chemist, also an agronomist and among the weights and measures reformers during the Revolution who introduced the kilogram. A keen supporter of the "real" Revolution, was guillotined in Paris on 8 May 1794. From 1795, became the object of the republican cult of the "martyred" scientist.

Le Bon, Joseph (1765–1795), Oratorian priest who renounced the priesthood after 10 August 1792 and became mayor of Arras. A friend of Robespierre, uninterested in revolutionary issues and ideas, directed the Terror in Arras and the Pas-de-Calais with pathological ferocity. Guillotined in Amiens for his crimes, 16 October 1795.

Lebrun-Tondu, Pierre (1754–1793), journalist, leader of the Liège revolution of 1789, and vigorous critic of Belgian conservatism. Exiled in Paris and close to Brissot and Roland, he became the Republic's Foreign Affairs minister in August 1792. A prominent internationalist republican and critic of Marat and Robespierre, guillotined in Paris on 27 December 1793.

Le Chapelier, Isaac René (1754–1794), participated in drafting many of the National Assembly's legislative enactments in 1789–91. Prominent in the Feuillant defection from the Jacobins. Denounced for modérantisme, guillotined in Paris 22 April 1794.

Lepeletier (de Saint-Fargeau), Ferdinand (1767–1837), younger brother of Louis-Michel, fervent Jacobin nobleman and participant in Babeuf's Conspiracy of Equals. An active opponent of Napoleon's dictatorship, was expelled from France first by Napoleon and then by Louis XVIII.

Lepeletier, Louis-Michel (1760–1793), leading magistrate of the Paris parlement before 1789, defected from the nobility in the 1789 Estates-General and vociferously supported abolition of noble titles in June 1790. After voting for the king's execution, was assassinated in a Paris restaurant a few days before Louis was guillotined, becoming the object of an extravagant Montagnard heroic martyr cult.

Lequinio, Marie-Joseph (1755–1814), lawyer, landowner, and promoter of peasant adult education, a leaders of Jacobin de-Christianization on the French west coast in 1793–94 and a rapacious director of the Terror in La Rochelle and Rochefort. After Thermidor, escaped punishment in hiding. Under Napoleon, spent several years as French vice-consul in Newport, Rhode Island.

Levasseur, René (1747–1834), Jacobin surgeon and Marat disciple, among the Convention's fiercest anti-Brissotins. Loyal to Robespierre, the latter considered him insufficiently ruthless. After Thermidor, a leading Jacobin critic of the Thermidorian reaction. Implicated in the Germinal rising (April 1795), was imprisoned for some months in 1795.

Lindet, Robert (1746–1825), lawyer and mayor of Bernay, elected to the Convention, voted onto the Committee of Public Safety in April 1793. A Jacobin leader discreetly hostile to Robespierre, tried to save Danton in April 1794. Imprisoned after Thermidor, following his release joined Babeuf's Conspiracy of Equals.

Louis XVII (1785–1795), France's dauphin after his older brother's demise in June 1789 until Louis XVI's execution, subsequently deemed king of France by royalists. Held at the Temple prison in Paris from 10 August 1792, died of tuberculosis after three years' confinement, at the age of ten.

Louvet (de Couvret), Jean-Baptiste (1760–1797), book-seller's agent and man of letters turned journalist, editor of *La Sentinelle*. Led the republican denunciation of Robespierre in the Convention in late 1792. Concealed during the Terror, reentered the Convention in March 1795, remaining a stalwart antiroyalist and anti-Robespierriste republican.

Lux, Adam (1766–1793), Mainz University philosophy lecturer and representative of the Rhenish democratic republic of 1792–93 in Paris. Published stirring anonymous pamphlets defending the Brissotins and Charlotte Corday. Guillotined in Paris 25 November 1793.

Mallet du Pan, Jacques (1749–1800), Genevan patrician and disciple of Voltaire based in Paris who propagandized against democracy and republicanism. Edited the royalist paper *Mercure de France* (1789–92), and was a secret intermediary between Louis XVI and the émigré princes at Coblenz.

Malouet, Pierre Victor (1740–1814), royal official and intendant of Toulon before 1789, a leader of the National Assembly's right-center monarchists in 1790–91, closely aligned also with the Saint-Domingue white planters. Fled to England after the 10 August 1792 rising. From there, with other émigrés he plotted a British takeover of the French Caribbean colonies (where his main income derived).

Manuel, Louis Pierre (1751–1793), tutor, book-seller's agent, and author, elected *procureur* of the Paris Commune in December 1791. Among the organizers of the 10 August 1792 rising. Aligning with Brissot, loudly condemned the September massacres, including in the Jacobins. Arrested during the Montagnard coup d'état, guillotined in Paris on 14 November 1793.

Marat, Jean-Paul (1743–1793), Swiss physician and anti-philosophe, and the greatest populist hero of the Revolution. Editor of *L'Ami du peuple*, the most chauvinistic and blood-thirsty of the revolutionary papers, consistently called for Robespierre's dictatorship. Among the main instigators of the February, March, and May 1793 risings in Paris, was a principal organizer of the coup of 2 June 1793. Assassinated by Charlotte Corday on 13 July 1793, becoming the chief cult figure and "martyr" of the authoritarian populist anti-intellectuals.

Maréchal, Pierre-Sylvain (1750–1803), librarian, poet, and materialist philosophe among the regular journalists of Prudhomme's *Revolutions de Paris*. A leader of Babeuf's Conspiracy of Equals in 1796–97, he composed its manifesto, the *Manifeste des Égaux*.

Marie Antoinette (1755–93), France's queen from 1774, whose indiscreet behavior and inadvisable choice of companions generated torrents of scurrilous scandal concerning the royal marriage bed seriously depleting the monarchy's ebbing prestige in the 1780s. Rightly suspected of exercising undue influence over her husband, opposed the principle of constitutional monarchy and Louis's reconciling himself with Lafayette, preferring an underhand counter-revolutionary strategy allied to her native Austria. Guillotined on 16 October 1793.

Maury, Jean Siffrein, Abbé (1746–1817), brilliant court preacher and staunch defender during 1789–91 of the royal prerogatives in the National Assembly. With Malhouet headed the center-right monarchist bloc. In 1792 fled France, transferring to Rome, becoming a cardinal in 1795. Following reconciliation with Napoleon became archbishop of Paris in 1810 in defiance of the pope. At the Restoration, expelled from France by Louis XVIII and imprisoned in Rome by the pope.

Mercier, Louis Sebastien (1740–1814), prolific author famous for his *Tableau de Paris* (1781–88), journalist, and utopian. A key promoter of Rousseau's standing during the Revolution, at first tried to steer between the Brissotins and Montagne, but signed the Convention deputies' protest against the coup d'état of 2 June 1793 and, in October 1793, was imprisoned. After Thermidor, resumed his place in the Convention, loudly denouncing the Montagne and the "sanguinocrat" Robespierre.

Merlin de Thionville, Antoine Christophe (1762–1833), corrupt Metz lawyer and Montagnard Convention deputy allied to Chabot and Basire, appointed main French representative to the Rhenish democratic republic of 1792–93 (to the disgust of Forster). Joined the Thermidorians and subsequently lived peacefully, enjoying the riches extorted from his numerous victims.

Merlin de Douai, Philippe-Antoine (1754–1838), lawyer prominent on the National Assembly's committees drawing up the decrees abolishing feudalism in 1789–90. Later, a Montagnard and prime author of the Law of Suspects (17 September 1793), in September 1797 was among the chief organizers of the coup of Fructidor, after which he was elected one of the five directors.

Mirabeau, Honoré Gabriel Riquetti, comte de (1749–1791), dissolute philosophe, internationally renowned before 1788 as a radical critic of enlightened despotism and ancien regime legal systems. A leader of the revolutionary ferment in Provence in 1788, dominated the National Assembly in 1789–90 through force of oratory and a large retinue of aides, speech writers, and researchers. A key promoter of all the major Radical Enlightenment reforms of the early Revolution, he did not, however, seek to eliminate royal authority completely, preferring a limited veto and continuing role for the monarch.

Miranda, Francisco de (1756–1816), Spanish army officer from Venezuela converted to radical ideas in the 1770s through reading Raynal. After 1783, circulated among the radical networks in Europe, forming an alliance with Brissot and Pétion and becoming deputy commander of the revolutionary army of the north in 1792–93 under Dumouriez. From around 1800, first major instigator of the early nineteenth-century South American rebellions against the Spanish crown.

Momoro, Antoine-François (1756–1794), Parisian printer and book-seller, among the principal printers of the revolutionary Commune and a powerful orator of the Cordeliers. Invented the device "Liberté, Égalité, Fraternité" and persuaded the Paris mayor, Pache, to have it inscribed on all the capital's public buildings. A prominent de-Christianizer and vociferous egalitarian frowned on by Robespierre, guillotined in Paris, on 4 March 1794.

Monge, Gaspard (1746–1818), professor of mathematics, protégé of Condorcet and the Revolution's navy minister from August 1792 to March 1793 reorganizing the Republic's naval bases and fleet. Sent with Daunou to Rome in 1797–98, helped establish the new Roman Republic. Accompanied the expedition to Egypt in 1798, where he participated in founding the French Institut d'Égypte.

Moreau de Saint-Méry, Louis (1750–1819), lawyer, deputy for Martinique in the National Assembly, and member of the white planters' Conseil supérieur on Saint-Domingue, a leading spokesman of the French Caribbean royalists and slave-owners. Published extensively on the French Caribbean colonies, using Montesquieu to justify institutionalized slavery. After the 10 August 1792, fled to Philadelphia and prospered as a book-seller before returning as a minor official under Napoleon.

Mounier, Jean-Joseph (1758–1806), Grenoble lawyer and admirer of Montesquieu, espoused the British model and English empiricism against the radical tendency. Principal leader of conservative constitutional monarchism in the National Assembly until October 1789, seeking an absolute veto, royal primacy, and an aristocratic upper house in the new constitution.

Necker, Jacques (1732–1804), Genevan banker and reformer established in Paris who as controller-general of the royal finances induced Louis XVI to convoke the Estates-General of 1789. An admirer of the British model, aimed for a harmonious collaboration of court and National assembly. His dismissal by Louis on 11 July 1789 precipitated the Revolution's first major crisis. Withdrawing to Switzerland, continued to defend "moderation" and centrist policies.

Orléans, Louis-Philippe, duke of (1747–1793), descended from a younger brother of Louis XIV, this prince, among the wealthiest men in France, ambitiously espoused the cause of the Revolution and equality. Suspected of complicity in the Bastille's storming and the 5 October march on Versailles, many assumed that he aspired to supplant Louis XVI as king. Under the name "Philippe Égalité" joined the Jacobins, and the Montagne faction in the Convention, supporting the death penalty for his royal cousin. Discredited from April 1793, guillotined in Paris on 6 November 1793.

Paape, Gerrit (1752–1803), of humble Delft origin, Dutch Patriot leader and prominent writer and journalist of the Dutch liberation movement in exile between 1787 and 1795. Author of numerous books and articles praising French revolutionary values and scorning Belgian conservatism, was secretary of the commander of the Dutch legions accompanying the French revolutionary army that overran the Netherlands in 1794–95.

Pache, Jean-Nicolas (1746–1823), minor official before 1789, joined Roland's entourage early in the Revolution becoming minister of war (from October 1792 to February 1793). Famously corrupt and colluding with Marat, broke with Roland, defecting to the Montagne. Elected mayor of Paris on 15 February, was a principal organizer of the Montagnard coup of June 1793, but lost his standing with Robespierre by declining to direct the trial of Hébert. Replaced as mayor by Fleuriot-Lescot, involved in the risings of Germinal and Prairial, and imprisoned after the latter.

Paine, Thomas (1737–1809), emerged as the preeminent radical publicist of the American Revolution with his *Common Sense* (1776). His *Rights of Man* (1791) launched the radical counter-offensive in English against Burke's conservatism. Immersed in French revolutionary politics from 1791, Paine formed a democratic republican alliance with Condorcet and Brissot. Elected to the Convention in September 1792, was imprisoned by the Montagne from December 1793 to November 1794. In early 1795, resumed his place in the Convention evincing fierce antagonism to the Montagne, George Washington, and the British government alike.

Palm d'Aelders, Etta (1743–1799), Dutch feminist, resident in Paris as a high-class courtesan at the Palais-Royal from 1773, in 1790–92 set up the network of women's groups affiliated with the Cercle Social, agitating for equal rights within marriage for women, and equal rights of divorce, consistently urging the right of women to participate in politics. A heroine of the Revolution, was at the same time (rightly) suspected of being an Orangist agent aiming to discredit Dutch Patriot refugees in France and their clubs at Dunkirk, Béthune, and Lille. Sent to Holland by Lebrun-Tondu to spy on French émigrés resident there, was judged suspect by the Batavian Revolution in 1795 and imprisoned for three years (1795–98) at Woerden.

Paoli, Pascal (1725–1807), leader of the 1755 Corsican rebellion against Genoa and the 1769 uprising against French rule, spent many years in exile in England. Returning in 1790, collaborated with and dominated the Revolution in Corsica until 1793, but then changed sides, expelling the French and bringing Corsica into a short-lived political union with Britain.

Pétion (de Villeneuve), Jérôme (1756–1794), crypto-republican pamphleteer and deputy during the early Revolution, in 1790–92 joined Robespierre in opposing the centrist constitutional monarchists and Feuillants. Elected mayor of Paris after Bailly in November 1791, achieved great temporary popularity. Complicit in the 20 June 1792 rising against the court and the *journée* of 10 August 1792, broke with Robespierre and the Montagne from mid-1792. Arrested on 2 June 1793, but escaped. Committed suicide on 18 June 1794 to escape the guillotine.

Philippeaux, Pierre Nicolas (1756–1794), revolutionary judge and journalist from Le Mans, ally of Danton in the Convention. Highly critical of the conduct of the war in the Vendée during 1793, incurred numerous enemies within the Montagne, including Robespierre. Arrested, tried, and declared a traitor, was guillotined with Danton on 5 April 1794.

Pichegru, Jean-Charles (1761–1804), rose from private to general in the revolutionary army. Commander of the Army of the North, overran Holland in 1794–95. Led the repression in Paris after Germinal (April 1795), emerging as leader of the monarchist faction in the legislature of 1797. Arrested during Fructidor, was deported to Cayenne, but escaped to London in 1798 and later returned secretly to Paris. Imprisoned again, was found dead in his cell in April 1804.

Proly, Pierre Joseph Berthold (1752–1794), Belgian baron, financier, agitator, and journalist, a natural son of the Austrian minister, Kaunitz. In 1791 established in Paris a democratic republican and internationalist journal, *Le Cosmopolite*. A declared atheist and supporter of de-Christianization, incurred Robespierre's displeasure. Guillotined in Paris, 24 March 1794.

Rabaut Saint-Étienne, Jean-Paul (1743–1793), Nîmes Protestant preacher, champion of toleration and freedom of the press, historian of the early Revolution, and man of letters prominent in the National Assembly in securing many of the great enactments of 1789. A member of the Commission de Douze in May 1793, was outlawed by the Montagne following the coup of 2 June 1793. Discovered at his hiding place, was guillotined in Paris on 5 December 1793.

Reubell, Jean-François (1747–1807), Alsatian lawyer opposing emancipation of the Jews in 1789, and a leading Montagnard until Thermidor. Subsequently, a vehement anti-Jacobin demanding closure of the Club. Among the five directors chosen under the 1795 Constitution, helped organize the coup of Fructidor.

Robert, Pierre François Joseph (1762–1826), Belgian republican and journalist, married to the journalist Louise Robert-Keralio, editor of *Le Mercure national* and an early propagator of republican ideas. Close to Danton and a Cordelier leader in 1791, he allowed women to participate at meetings. In the late 1790s, charged with hoarding groceries and rhum, became unpopular in Paris; his stores were pillaged during the Prairial rising, royalists and many sansculottes dubbing him "Robert Rhum."

Robespierre, Augustin (1763–1794), Arras lawyer, Maximilien's younger brother and a Convention deputy for Paris from September 1792. Sent as representative-on-mission to Provence in early 1794, participated in directing the Terror there and organized the army of Italy's operations together with Napoleon at Nice. Standing by his brother during the coup of Thermidor, was guillotined with him on 28 July 1794.

Robespiere, Maximilien (1758–1794), Arras lawyer, fervent disciple of Rousseau, head of the populist authoritarian group dictatorship from June 1793 until Thermidor. Spoke frequently and with great effect until the end of 1793 both in the legislature and the Jacobins, adroitly outmaneuvering opponents, organizing a joint political program for the diverse Montagnard factions, and for a time strengthening the Montagne's support. In his speeches often railed against the Enlightenment philosophes and men of letters, denouncing them as "atheists," friends of kings and aristocrats, enemies of his idol Rousseau, and betrayers of the people. Showed little regard for republican principles and none for basic human rights. From June 1793 to July 1794 exerted his authority mainly through the Republic's executive committees. A principal director of the Terror.

Roederer, Pierre Louis (1754–1835), before 1789 a leading light of the Academy of Metz, author of books on political representation and economic affairs. During 1789–90, a prominent National Assembly speaker supporting Sieyès and Mirabeau, helped extricate the royal family from the Tuileries on 10 August 1792. Survived in hiding during the Terror, subsequently participating in the neo-Brissotin resurgence.

Roland, Manon Jeanne Philipon, Mme. (1754–1793), wife of Roland and much admired head of the foremost Parisian revolutionary salon from June 1791 to May 1793. A passionate disciple of Rousseau and major influence among the Brissotin leadership, she seriously misread both Robespierre and Danton. Imprisoned in the Abbaye at the end of May 1793, guillotined in Paris on 8 November 1793.

Roland (de la Platière), Jean-Marie (1734–1793), a local inspector-general of commerce and manufactures in Rouen and Amiens before the Revolution, twenty years older than his famous wife, served as royal minister of the interior from March to June 1792 and the Republic's interior minister from August 1792 to late January 1793. Fled Paris in late May 1793, committed suicide in Normandy on 15 November 1793.

Romme, Gilbert (1750–1795), mathematician and tutor, spent five years in Russia in the early 1780s, elected to the legislature in 1791, served prominently on the educational and constitutional committees. Main architect of the revolutionary calendar presented to the Convention on 17 September 1793, an egalitarian idealist aligned with the Montagne who disliked both Robespierre and the Thermidorian reaction. Implicated in the Prairial rising in Paris, committed suicide on 16 June 1795.

Ronsin, Charles Philippe (1751–1794), soldier, playwright, and leading light of the Cordeliers, appointed by Pache executive commissaire of the army of Belgium in late 1792 where he presided through ineptitude, unruly temper, and corruption over a singularly disorderly military administration. Directed the repression at Lyon in the autumn of 1793 with Collot d'Herbois. Allied with Hébert, was arrested on 14 March and guillotined with him on 24 March 1794.

Roux, Jacques (1752–1794), priest and seminary teacher, a passionate prophet of economic equality and formidable crowd agitator, among the leading Enragés. Allied early in the Revolution with Marat, the two later quarreled. Despised by Robespierre, was imprisoned in August 1793. Stabbed himself to death before the Tribunal Révolutionnaire on 15 January 1794.

Royou, Thomas Marie, Abbé (1743–1792), philosophy professor and royalist journalist, editor of the foremost royalist paper, *L'Ami du roi* (1790–92). Calling on loyal Frenchmen to oppose the Revolution, his paper circulated widely in Paris and the provinces until suppressed in May 1792, shortly before his death.

Saint-Just, Louis Antoine (1767–1794), served as Robespierre's right-hand man in managing the Convention during 1793–94 and stepping up the Terror. A National Guard officer, dogmatic Rousseauist, and mediocre but prolific political theorist, was the youngest of the deputies elected to the Convention. A competent organizer with a ruthless authoritarian streak, expert in intimidation, was instrumental in outmaneuvering and destroying the rival Hébertiste and Dantoniste Montagnard factions. Guillotined with Robespierre on 28 July 1794.

Salicetti, Christophe (1757–1809), deputy at the 1789 Estates-General for Corsica, arranged the return of Paoli from England in 1790, fought Paoli for control of the island in 1793–94. Accompanied the army of Italy as political supervisor, one of the architects of the 1796–97 Italian revolutions.

Sieyès, Emmanuel Joseph (1748–1836), a priest with no priestly vocation, the most effective political pamphleteer of 1788–89. Played a leading part in securing the great enactments of 1789, but subsequently moved to a more centrist position in the legislature. Prominent on the constitutional committees through much of the Revolution, but often stood rather isolated. Renounced the priesthood during the de-Christianization, kept silent under the Terror. With Napoleon, organized the 1799 coup of Brumaire.

Sonthonax, Léger-Félicité (1763–1813), idealistic follower of la philosophie and Brissotin chief commissaire of the Revolution on Haiti (Saint-Domingue) in 1792–93, the revolutionary leader who first began enforcing equal rights for free blacks and mulattoes on Haiti against the wishes of the white planters, decreeing the end of slavery there in 1793. An ally of Tousaint-Louverture in 1793–94, and for a time after his return to Haiti following his imprisonment in France during the last part of the Terror. Toussaint-Louverture expelled him from Haiti in 1797.

Staël, Anne-Louise, Mme. de (1766–1817), daughter of Necker, Swiss writer and commentator on the Revolution. Returning to Paris in 1795, presided over one of the principal revolutionary salons under the Directory; opposed Napoleon's dictatorship.

Talleyrand, Charles Maurice de (1754–1838), aristocrat made bishop of Autun in 1788. Betrayed the French clergy in October 1789 by joining Mirabeau in seeking nationalization of the Church's property, the Republic in December 1792 by fleeing to London and offering his services to the royal family, and the émigrés by seeking reconciliation with the Revolution. Returned to Paris in September 1796. Welcomed Napoleon's dictatorship, later betrayed Napoleon in favor of Louis XVIII and the Bourbons (yet again) during the Revolution of 1830.

Tallien, Jean Lambert (1767–1820), corrupt Montagnard leader, directed the Terror at Bordeaux until March 1794 when, being less ruthless than other representatives-on-mission, was denounced for modérantisme. A leader of the coup of Thermidor and subsequent Thermidorian reaction, systematically betrayed first the Jacobins, then the Republic, then Napoleon, then Louis XVIII, dying in disgrace, sickness, and misery.

Toussaint-Louverture, François Dominique (1743–1803), black slave born on Saint-Domingue who obtained his freedom and some education before the Revolution. A military leader of the black rising on Haiti from September 1791, allied first with royalist Spain but then, from 1793, with Sonthonax and the French Revolution. Helping to end slavery in Haiti, succeeded in 1796–97 in driving back the British and Spanish royalist invasions. By 1799, was virtual master of Haiti and subsequently introduced a constitution with himself as governor-general for life. In 1802, Napoleon sent an army to reconquer Haiti and reintroduce slavery (initially successful), capturing Toussaint who died a prisoner in France, in 1803.

Treilhard, Jean-Baptiste (1742–1810), lawyer elected to the Estates-General of 1789, played a leading part in the National Assembly as head of the committee for ecclesiastical affairs, in confiscating the Church's property and the Civil Constitution of the Clergy. Uninvolved in the Terror, was prominent in the Thermidorian reaction as a firm republican, replacing François de Neufchâteau among the five directors in May 1798. After Brumaire, abandoned republicanism for Napoleon.

Vadier, Marc Guillaume (1736–1828), corrupt Montagnard leader, son of an ecclesiastical tithe collector, voted onto the Committee of General Security by the Convention in September 1793. Instrumental in Danton's downfall and the coup of Thermidor. Evaded deportation to Cayenne for promoting the Terror, in 1795, by managing to hide. Joined Babeuf's Conspiracy of Equals.

Varlet, Jean (1764–1837), postal employee who became a prominent Enragé leader. Detested by Marat and Robespierre, was popular among the sansculottes of the faubourgs, haranguing crowds in the streets from his stand. Among the main crowd organizers of the coups d'état of 31 May and 2 June. Publicly criticized Robespierre, defended the rights of the section assemblies to gather and petition, and urged the mandating of deputies by their electors. Briefly imprisoned under the Terror, was held for much longer by the Thermidorians (from September 1794 to October 1795). Avoided Babeuf's conspiracy; after Brumaire, became a staunch Bonapartiste.

Vatar, René (1773–1842), Breton printer, journalist, and owner of the *Journal des Hommes Libres de tous les pays, ou le Républicain* (1796–97), a democrat and prominent opponent of the Directory associated with the Babeuf conspiracy. Acquitted in 1797, was later banished to Cayenne for opposing Napoleon's dictatorship, but escaped and stayed some years in the United States.

Vergniaud, Pierre-Victurnien (1753–1793), prominent in the legislature from October 1791 as a republican orator, delivered powerful radical speeches denouncing émigré aristocrats and refractory priests. Allied to Brissot, among the leaders of the 20 June and 10 August 1792 risings and main advocates of political rights for free blacks and mulattoes. Refused to flee from Paris after the coup of 2 June. Guillotined with Brissot on 31 October 1793.

Villette, Charles, marquis de (1736–1793), protégé of Voltaire, leading promoter of Voltaire's reputation during the Revolution, and renowned antagonist of priests and parlementaires. Advocated admitting women, married and unmarried, to the primary assemblies and was publicly ridiculed for championing what today would be called gay rights, as well as those of the illegitimate. Vehement opponent of the Montagne in Paris, died before the Terror; his famously beautiful wife remained imprisoned throughout the Terror and Thermidorian reaction.

Vincent, François-Nicolas (1767–1794), son of a Paris jailer, a lawyer's clerk before the Revolution, among the Cordeliers' leading orators and a principal ally of Hébert, Momoro, and Ronsin. Appointed general secretary of the war ministry, turned the ministry into a bastion of Hébertisme during 1792–93. A vigorous advocate of de-Christianization. Guillotined with Hébert on 24 March 1794.

Volney, Constantin François de Chasseboeuf, comte de (1757–1820), atheist, materialist and philosophe, a leader of the antiaristocratic agitation in Brittany in 1788–89, and the antiaristocratic offensive in the Estates-General in 1789. His *Les Ruines* (1791) figured among the chief Radical Enlightenment philosophical works written during and about the Revolution. Director-general of commerce and agriculture in Corsica in 1792–93, was imprisoned under the Terror. Among the leading Idéologues during the late 1790s.

Wedekind, Georg Christian (1761–1831), court physician of the Elector of Mainz, leading German republican and revolutionary journalist, a founder of the Mainz Jacobins and of the 1792–93 Rhenish Republic. Prominently contributed to the propagation of revolutionary values, among the first outspoken advocates of democracy and general emancipation in Germany.

Notes

PROLOGUE

1. Roe, *Wordsworth and Coleridge*, 81–82; Erdman, *Commerce des Lumières*, 305.
2. Buel, *Joel Barlow*, 177–81.
3. The account of the toasts in Girey-Dupré, *Patriote français* 1199 (21 Nov. 1792), 588, and Alger, "British Colony," 673, 678, is incomplete; for a fuller account, see *Journal de Perlet* 2, no. 61 (21 Nov. 1792), 485–87.
4. Grenby, *Anti-Jacobin Novel*, 30–32; Bindman, *Shadow of the Guillotine*, 173; Erdman, *Commerce des Lumières*, 230, 305.
5. *Journal de Perlet* 2, no. 61 (21 Nov. 1792), 486–87.
6. Ibid.
7. Volney, *Œuvres complètes,* 1:267–75; Israel, *Democratic Enlightenment*, 30, 749–50.

CHAPTER 1

Introduction

1. Campbell, introduction to *Origins of the French Revolution*, 9.
2. Stone, *Genesis of the French Revolution*, 86–88, 93–95; Colin Jones, *Great Nation*, 324–33.
3. Spang, "Paradigms and Paranoia," 122.
4. Goldstone, "Social Origins," 70–72.
5. Kaiser and Van Kley, *From Deficit to Deluge*, 5.
6. P. Jones, *Peasantry*, 1–2, 15–16, 31, 33, 40–41; C. Jones, *Great Nation*, 404–5.
7. Doyle, *Oxford History*, 5–6.
8. Ibid., 18–28; Goldstone, "Social Origins," 73–76; Doyle, *Officers, Nobles*, 101–3.
9. Campbell, introduction to *Origins of the French Revolution*, 18; Goldstone, "Social Origins," 84.
10. Doyle, *Origins of the French Revolution*, 133–34.
11. Ibid.; Goldstone, "Social Origins," 90–91.
12. Hunt, *Politics, Culture*, 178; Tackett, *Becoming a Revolutionary*, 7; Desan, "What's after Political Culture," 164.
13. Goldstone, "Social Origins," 93.
14. Desmoulins, *France Libre*, 10.
15. Cobb, *The French*, 33; Van Kley, "From the Lessons," 76; Kaiser, "From Fiscal Crisis," 140, 162–64; Hunt, "Global Financial Origins," 32–33, 42–43.
16. Kaiser and Van Kley, *From Deficit to Deluge*, 5.

17. Applewhite, *Political Alignment*, 4–5; C. Jones, *Great Nation*, 377.
18. Fajn, "Attitude," 232.
19. Tackett, *Becoming a Revolutionary*, 6–7; Spang, "Paradigms and Paranoia," 120–21.
20. Heuer, "Family Bonds," 53–54, 61, 68.
21. Swenson, *On Jean-Jacques Rousseau*, 16.
22. Necker, *Révolution française*, 1:14; Linton, *Politics of Virtue*, 199–200.
23. E. Badinter and R. Badinter, *Condorcet, 1743–1794*, 258–62.
24. Bailly, *Mémoires de Bailly*, 1:51–53; Roland, *Memoirs*, 250; Tackett, *Becoming a Revolutionary*, 50.
25. Roederer, *Spirit of the Revolution*, 5.
26. Garat, *Mémoires historiques*, 2:230, 2:315.
27. Desmoulins, *France libre*, 10.
28. Brissot, *Examen*, 127.
29. Desmoulins, *France libre*, 11; Lachappelle, *Considérations philosophiques*, 109.
30. Ginguené, *Lettres*, 64–65.
31. Ravitch, "Abbé Fauchet," 254; Swenson, *On Jean-Jacques Rousseau*, 9.
32. Feller, *Journal historique et littéraire* (1792), 22–23.
33. Portalis, *De l'usage*, 15:119–21, 15:124–25, 15:130–31, 15:361; Barnave, *Power, Property*, 123-4.
34. Ibid., 226–27; Mallet du Pan, *Considérations*, 6–7.
35. Ibid., 277.
36. La Harpe, *Philosophie du dix-huitième siècle*, 1:3 and 2:192–95, 2:268; Strugnell, *Diderot's Politics*, 207, 228.
37. Brissot, *Le Patriote français*, 145 (31 Dec. 1789), 4; Rasmussen, "Burning Laws," 90–91.
38. Roederer, *De la philosophie moderne, et de la part qu'elle a eue à la Révolution française*. Paris, 1799, 24; [Prudhomme], *Les Révolutions de Paris*, 1:35.
39. Ibid.; Mounier, *De l'influence*, 125.
40. La Harpe, *Philosophie du dix-huitième siècle*, 1:107–8; La Harpe, *Réfutation du livre*, 156.
41. La Harpe, *Réfutation du livre*, 158.
42. La Harpe, *Philosophie du dix-huitième siècle*, 1:126.
43. Swenson, *On Jean-Jacques Rousseau*, 172.
44. Mirabeau, *Courrier* 20 (14/27 July 1789), 20.
45. Ibid., 28 (17/18 Aug. 1789), 1–2; Brissot, *Le Patriote français* 1 (28 July 1789), 382.
46. Brissot, *De la vérité*, 109–12, 178, 185, 196–97, 212, 216–17.
47. Ibid., 253, 257–58; Mercier, *De J. J. Rousseau considéré*, 1:60–61 and 2:12, 2:32–34, 2:173; Furet, "Rousseau," 173–75; Swenson, *On Jean-Jacques Rousseau*, 173, 175, 180, 191–92; Villaverde, "Spinoza, Rousseau," 96, 100; Israel, *Democratic Enlightenment*, 645–47.
48. Cobb, *The French*, 178–79.
49. Culoma, *Religion civile*, 189–93.
50. Desmoulins, *France libre*, 23–25, 31–41.
51. Ibid., 43–46.

52. Ibid., 13, 16, 20; Volney, *Œuvres complètes,* 1:255, 1:273–74 .

53. Israel, *Democratic Enlightenment,* 633–47.

54. Thouret, *Vérités philosophiques,* 16–17; Tackett, *Becoming a Revolutionary,* 112.

55. Bredin, *Sieyès,* 163, 542–43; Baker, "Political Languages," 630; Bates, *Enlightenment Aberrations,* 116–20.

56. Desmoulins, *France libre,* 28, 30–31.

57. Ibid., 62.

58. Brissot, *De la vérité,* 225, 258.

59. Kervélégan, *Réflexions d'un philosophe breton,* 1, 36.

60. Ibid., 67–69; Ozouf, "La Révolution française," 216–18.

61. Kervélégan, *Réflexions d'un philosophe breton,* 67–71.

62. Ibid., 72.

63. Roederer, *De la philosophie,* 2–3; Forsyth, *Reason and Revolution,* 10, 18–19; Pasquino, *Sièyes et l'invention,* 17–19, 169.

64. Marmontel, *Mémoires,* 3:296; Condorcet, "Essai sur la constitution," in *Œuvres complètes,* 8:187–88, 8:230–31, and "Sentiments d'un républicain," in *Œuvres complètes,* 9:130–31, 9:132–33, 9:135–36.

65. Roederer, *De la philosophie,* 6–7.

66. Ibid., 7.

67. Ibid., 23; Roederer, *Spirit of the Revolution,* 9–13, 18.

68. [Prudhomme], *Les Révolutions de Paris,* introduction to vol. 1, 1–3, 6, 17, 35, 47.

69. Ibid., 17; Baker, *Inventing the French Revolution,* 219.

70. [Prudhomme], *Les Révolutions de Paris* 5 (9/15 Aug. 1789), 12–14 and 6 (16/22 Aug. 1789), 1–4.

71. Ibid., 3 (26 July/1 Aug. 1789), 14.

72. Aston, *Religion and Revolution,* xii; Van Kley, "Christianity," 1088.

73. See Jennings, "Reason's Revenge," 4.

74. BL pamphlets 103 2/3 no. 8: *Réponse de J. L. Carra deputé à la Convention Nationale,* 14; Lachapelle, *Considérations philosophiques,* 81–82, 98.

CHAPTER 2

Revolution of the Press (1788–90)

1. Gorani, *Recherches sur la science,* 2:176; La Harpe, *Réfutation du livre,* 152; Israel, "Failed Enlightenment," 36–42.

2. Mounier, *De l'influence,* 27.

3. Campbell, introduction to *Origins of the French Revolution,* 23–24; Mounier, *De l'influence,* 153, 309–10; Martin, *Violence et révolution,* 49; Doyle, *Origins of the French Revolution,* 184.

4. Campbell, introduction to *Origins of the French Revolution,* 17; Tlili-Sellaouti, "Pouvoir local," 120–21; Goyhenetche, *Histoire générale du Pays Basque,* 4:149, 4:160, 4:162–63.

5. Gruder, *Notables and the Nation,* 168–79; De Baecque, "Pamphlets," 165.

6. Goyhenetche, *Histoire générale du Pays Basque,* 128–29.

7. Lachapelle, *Considérations philosophiques,* supplement, 73.

8. Marmontel, *Mémoires,* 3:185; Arnaud, *Chamfort,* 151–52; Doyle, *Origins of the French Revolution,* 185.

9. Mallet du Pan, *Considérations*, 11; Kates, *Cercle Social*, 77; Bertaud, *Les Amis du roi*, 22; Garrioch, *Making of Revolutionary Paris*, 244–46.

10. Jones, *Great Nation*, 395–97, 401; Campbell, introduction to *Origins of the French Revolution*, 24–26.

11. Applewhite, *Political Alignment*, 30–33; Campbell, introduction to *Origins of the French Revolution*, 24–26.

12. Rabaut Sainte-Étienne, *Précis historique*, 24, 56–57; Stone, *Genesis of the French Revolution*, 214–16.

13. Sinéty, "Réflexions importantes," in *Archives Parlementaires*, 26:661–62, 26:664 (31 May 1791).

14. Cérutti, *Mémoire pour le peuple françois*, 65–66.

15. Sieyès, *Manuscrits, 1773–1799*, 99, 361; Sewell, *Rhetoric of Bourgeois Revolution*, 67–71.

16. Linguet, *Annales politiques* 15 (1788–89), 431–34, 436, and 16 (1789–90), 272.

17. Volney, *Œuvres complètes*, 1:32, 1:35, 1:41, 1:46, 1:57, 1:64–65; Gruder, *Notables and the Nation*, 281; Dupuy, *Aux origines idéologiques*, 13–15.

18. Volney, *La Sentinelle du peuple*, no. 1, 6–7; no. 3, 16, 18; no. 4, 7; Eisenstein, "Le Publiciste comme démagogue," 189; Doyle, *Aristocracy and Its Enemies*, 173.

19. BL 911 c. 3/5, Lettre de M. C. F. de Volney à M. le Come de S., 14, 17.

20. Marmontel, *Mémoires*, 3:188; Arnaud, *Chamfort*, 155.

21. Baker, *Condorcet*, 248–60, 266; D. Williams, *Condorcet and Modernity*, 252.

22. Gruder, *Notables and the Nation*, 282–84.

23. Ibid., 295–97; E. Kennedy, *Cultural History*, 35, 41.

24. Sewell, *Rhetoric of Bourgeois Revolution*, 63–64.

25. Garrone, *Gilbert Romme*, 249–50.

26. Sabatier, *Journal Politique* 1 (1790), 41–42.

27. Burke, *Reflections on the Revolution*, 36–40; Marmontel, *Mémoires*, 3:178–79.

28. Mounier, *De l'influence*, 69–70.

29. Brissot, *Mémoire aux États-généraux*, 46; Tortarolo, *L'Invenzione*, 137, 148.

30. Ibid., 71; Villette, *Lettres choisies*, 11; Hampson, *Will and Circumstance*, 84–85; Lüsebrink et al., *The Bastille*, 30.

31. Brissot, *Mémoire aux États-généraux*, 22; Gueniffey, "Brissot," 447.

32. Ibid., 5; Brissot, *Mémoires (1734–1793)*, 2:185–86; Hampson, *Will and Circumstance*, 86–88.

33. Brissot, *Mémoire aux États-généraux*, 9.

34. Ibid., 10; Gueniffey, "Brissot," 447–48; Popkin, "Journals," 145.

35. [Prudhomme], *Les Révolutions de Paris* 8 (29 Aug./4 Sept. 1789), 26; De Luna, "Dean Street," 172, 176.

36. Tocqueville, *L'Ancien régime*, 157.

37. Brissot, *Mémoire aux Etats-généraux*, 68; Tortarolo, *L'Invenzione*, 136–37, 148.

38. Brissot, *Mémoire aux États-généraux*, 38; Labrosse and Rétat, *Naissance du journal révolutionnaire*, 177–78.

39. Brissot, *Mémoire aux États-généraux*, 29; Pétion, *Avis*, 70; Labrosse and Rétat, *Naissance du journal révolutionnaire*, 279; Halévi, "Les Girondins," 148–49.

40. Brissot, *Mémoire aux États-généraux*, 27.

41. Ibid., 34.
42. Ibid., 40; Labrosse and Rétat, *Naissance du journal révolutionnaire*, 176; Halévi, "Les Girondins," 148.
43. Brissot, *Le Patriote français* 1 (28 July 1789), 1; Granié, *De l'Assemblée*, 61; Andries, "Les imprimeurs-libraires parisiens," 248; Labrosse and Rétat, *Naissance du journal révolutionnaire*, 22–23, 89; Hesse, "Economic Upheavals," 72–73.
44. Gorsas, *Courrier* 1, no. 9 (15 July 1789), 129; Mortier, *Anacharsis Cloots*, 114; Wauters, "La naissance," 111.
45. Censer, *Prelude to Power*, 22; Dommanget, *Sylvain Maréchal*, 169–73; Gough, *Newspaper Press*, 24, 163.
46. Labrosse and Rétat, *Naissance du journal révolutionnaire*, 169–71.
47. Gorsas, *Courrier* 1, no. 86 (1 Oct. 1789), 1, 19, 22; Badinter, *Libres et égaux*, 109–10, 115.
48. Girard, *La Révolution française*, 74–91; Mortier, *Anacharsis Cloots*, 67–69; Badinter, *Libres et égaux*, 72–74.
49. Thierry, *Dissertation sur cette question*, 29, 37–38.
50. Ibid., 79–82; Girard, *La Révolution française*, 80–81, 84.
51. M. L. Kennedy, "Development of a Political Radical," 144.
52. Censer, *Prelude to Power*, 17; Gough, *Newspaper Press*, 24, 56.
53. BHP pamphl. 958555, *Aux Génies de France*, 4–5, 17–18; M. L. Kennedy, "Development of a Political Radical," 144.
54. Murray, *Right-Wing Press*, 272; Gough, *Newspaper Press*, 64; Popkin, "Journals," 150; Wauters, "La naissance," 110.
55. Acomb, *Mallet du Pan (1749–1800)*, 230–31.
56. *Assemblée Nationale, Commune de Paris*, no. 468 (16 Nov.1790), 6–7; Acomb, *Mallet du Pan (1749–1800)*, 4–5, 12–19, 24.
57. Acomb, *Mallet du Pan (1749–1800)*, 58, 62–63, 66–73.
58. Chisick, *Production, Distribution*, 222–26.
59. Ibid., 34–35; Israel, *Democratic Enlightenment*, 62–64, 648.
60. Chisick, *Production, Distribution*, 37; Popkin, "Journals," 148.
61. Bergasse, *Lettre de M. Bergasse*, 28, 32–33.
62. Sabatier, *Journal politique* 1 (1790), 119–20.
63. Ibid., 121.
64. Ibid., 120–22.
65. D. Bertrand, *Lettre à Monsieur Raynal*, 22–23.
66. Sabatier, *Journal politique* 1 (1790), 121; Israel, *Democratic Enlightenment*, 773.
67. Desmoulins, *France libre*, 9.
68. [Carra], *La Raison*, 21–22, 29n.
69. Ibid., 45.
70. [Carra], *L'Orateur*, 19, 21, 202; Whaley, *Radicals*, 23.
71. [Carra], *L'Orateur*, 23–25; Labrosse and Rétat, *Naissance du journal révolutionnaire*, 183.
72. [Carra], *La Raison*, 50.
73. Ibid., 1–3, 6, 21–22.
74. Ibid., 182–83, 202; Lüsebrink et al., *The Bastille*, 82–83.
75. Rabaut Sainte-Étienne, *Précis historique*, 19–20; Cottebrune, *Mythe et réalité*, 133.

76. Rabaut Saint-Étienne, *Précis historique*, 21.
77. Ibid., 22–23.
78. Rabaut Saint-Étienne, *Précis historique*, 23–24; Mounier, *De l'influence*, 100–103.
79. Naigeon, *Adresse à l'Assemblée Nationale*, 81–83, 86.
80. Ibid., 9.
81. Ibid., 41–42, 53, 71, 77.
82. Naigeon, *Adresse à l'Assemblée Nationale*, 113, 122.
83. Brissot, *Mémoire aux États-généraux*, 4.
84. Ibid., 55–57; Tortarolo, *L'Invenzione*, 165.
85. Israel, *Democratic Republic*, 398–99, 646; Dorigny, "L'émergence d'un 'parti républicain,'" 111.
86. Desmoulins, *Vieux Cordelier*, 74–76, 80, 90, 96, 119.

CHAPTER 3

From Estates-General to National Assembly (April–June 1789)

1. Morellet to Bentham, Paris, 8 May 1789, in Morellet, *Lettres*, 2:128–30; Petit-fils, *Louis XVI*, 2:161–69.
2. Volney, *Discours prononcé dans la Chambre* (8 May 1789), 2, 4; Baker, "Political Languages," 631.
3. Brissot, *Plan de conduite*, 104–5.
4. Ibid., vii–viii.
5. Ibid., 224, 229–30.
6. Baker, "Political Languages," 631; Tackett, *Becoming a Revolutionary*, 23; Fitzsimmons, *Remaking of France*, 42.
7. Jefferson, *Papers of Thomas Jefferson*, 15:196.
8. Jefferson to Jay, Paris, 24 June 1789, in ibid., 15:205.
9. *Archives Parlementaires*, 8:144–45 (23 June 1789).
10. Ibid., 8:145; Fitzsimmons, *Remaking of France*, 43.
11. *Archives Parlementaires*, 8:143 (23 June 1789).
12. Ibid., 8:145–47.
13. Jefferson to Jay, Paris, 29 June 1789, in Jefferson, *Papers of Thomas Jefferson*, 15:221–22.
14. *Archives Parlementaires*, 8:165–66 (27 June 1789).
15. Ibid., 8:171–72 (30 June 1789).
16. Slavin, *French Revolution*, 62; Lemny, *Jean-Louis Carra*, 158–59; E. Badinter and R. Badinter, *Condorcet, 1743–1794*, 267.
17. Tønnesson, "La démocratie directe," 298.
18. Slavin, *French Revolution*, 57–58.
19. Jefferson to Paine, Paris, 11 July 1789, in Jefferson, *Papers of Thomas Jefferson*, 15:268–69.
20. Ibid., 15:230–32.
21. Sabatier, *Journal politique* 1 (1790), 47; McMahon, *Enemies of the Enlightenment*, 65.
22. Jefferson to Jay, Paris, 19 July 1789, in Jefferson, *Papers of Thomas Jefferson*, 15:285.

23. *Archives Parlementaires*, 8:208–10 (8 July 1789).

24. "Réponse du roi," 10 July 1789, in Gorsas, *Courrier* 1, no. 3, 108; Mirabeau, *Collection complète*, 1:317–19.

25. Gorsas, *Courrier* 1, no. 9 (15 July 1789), 131.

26. Jefferson to Paine, Paris, 273, in Jefferson, *Papers of Thomas Jefferson*, 15:273.

27. Gorsas, *Courrier* 1, no. 11 (17 July 1789), 161.

28. Desmoulins, *Vieux Cordelier*, 115; Malouet, *Mémoires*, 1:326.

29. Hammersley, *French Revolutionaries*, 36–37, 60; Ozouf, "La Révolution française," 213.

30. Gorsas, *Courrier* 1, no. 9 (15 July 1789), 142.

31. *Archives Parlementaires*, 8:223, 8:229 (8 July 1789).

32. Lucas, "Crowd and Politics," 264.

33. Villette, *Lettres*, 4.

34. *Lettre à M. le Marquis de Luchet*, 60, 101.

35. Gaulmier, *Un grand témoin*, 89–90; Peterson, *Thomas Jefferson*, 379.

36. Marmontel, *Mémoires*, 3:185, 3:187; Staum, *Cabanis*, 122–23; Arnaud, *Chamfort*, 151–52, 162–63, 166–75.

37. Morellet, *Mémoires*, 1:381; Mortier, *Le Cœur et la raison*, 458.

38. Naigeon, *Lettre du Citoyen*, 2, 7.

39. Garat, *Mémoires historiques*, 2:315, 2:354, 365–66; Pellerin, "Naigeon," 32; Mortier, "Les héritiers," 457–59.

40. Morellet, *Mémoires*, 1:387–88; Guillois, *Salon de Madame Helvétius*, 71–72; Rials, *La Déclaration des droits*, 125.

41. Lawday, *Giant of the French Revolution*, 49–52.

42. Monnier, "L'Évolution," 50–51; Geffroy, "Louise de Kéralio-Robert," 6; Hammersley, *French Revolutionaries*, 18–19.

43. Lucas, "Crowd and Politics," 274.

44. "Vie de Sylvain Bailly," in Bailly, *Œuvres posthumes*, xii–xiii, xxxi, xlii–xliii.; Mounier, *De l'influence*, 103–4; Lortholary, *Le mirage russe*, 259.

45. Bergasse, *Considérations sur la liberté*, 19, 27.

46. Tønnesson, "La démocratie directe," 298; Hampson, *Will and Circumstance*, 174–76.

47. Kates, *Cercle Social*, 34–36, 41; Hammersley, *French Revolutionaries*, 24–27.

48. *Actes, Commune de Paris*, Lacroix (ed.), ser. 1, introduction, 1:xvii–xviii; Hammersley, *French Revolutionaries*, 18, 22–24.

49. *Actes, Commune de Paris*, Lacroix (ed.), ser. 1, introduction, 2:ix; [Carra], *La Raison*, 198–99.

50. Villette, *Lettres choisies*, 6.

51. Hardman, *Louis XVI*, 105–8; Lüsebrink et al., *The Bastille*, 39, 46.

52. Herding and Reichardt, *Die Bildpublistik*, 76.

53. Doyle, *Parlement of Bordeaux*, 304–5; Auerbach, "Politics, Protest," 151–52; Forrest, *Revolution in Provincial France*, 64–65, 67–68.

54. Fontana et al., *Venise et la Révolution*, 320; Martin, *Violence et révolution*, 67–69.

55. Dumont, *Mémoires de Mirabeau*, 94–95.

56. Furet, *Revolutionary France*, 69; Martin, *Violence et révolution*, 61–62.

57. Chénier, *De la Liberté du théâtre*, 13, 45; Schama, *Citizens: A Chronicle*, 495; Friedland, *Political Actors*, 260–69.

58. Chénier, *Dénonciation des Inquisiteurs*, 45–46; Brown, "Le Débat sur la liberté," 45.
59. Chénier, *Dénonciation des Inquisiteurs*, 41; Chénier, *Discours prononcé à la Convention*, 20–23.
60. Chénier, *Dénonciation des Inquisiteurs*, 30–31; *Chronique de Paris* 1, 28 (20 Sept. 1789), 110; Birn, "Religious Toleration," 280.
61. Maslan, *Revolutionary Acts*, 30–31.
62. *Mercure national* 24 (10 May 1791), 384.
63. Ibid., 33.
64. Chénier, *De la Liberté*, 22, 43.
65. Ibid., 28; Marsan, *Revolutionary Acts*, 38.
66. Chénier, *De la Liberté*, 38–39; Friedland, *Political Actors*, 266.
67. Marsan, *Revolutionary Acts*, 49–50.
68. [Prudhomme], *Révolutions* 6 (16/22 Aug.), 26; Brissot, *Le Patriote français* 19 (18 Aug. 1789), 1; Lichtenberg, *Schriften und Briefe*, 1:700; Graczyk, "Le théâtre de la Révolution française," 399.
69. Thompson, *French Revolution*, 29; Quiviger, "Sieyès," 128–29, 134.
70. Sieyès, *Manuscrits, 1773–1799*, 214, 256, 259.
71. Quiviger, "Sieyès," 141–42; Sewell, *Rhetoric of Bourgeois Revolution*, 53–54.
72. Thompson, *French Revolution*, 29; Forsyth, *Reason and Revolution*, 38.
73. Price to Jefferson, Hackney, 3 Aug. 1789, in Jefferson, *Papers of Thomas Jefferson*, 15:329.

CHAPTER 4

The Rights of Man: Summer and Autumn 1789

1. Hardman, *Louis XVI*, 110.
2. Sieyès, *Essai*, 5; Sieyès, *Quest-ce que le Tiers*, 175–76, 179–80; Sewell, *Rhetoric of Bourgeois Revolution*, 28.
3. Sieyès, *Essai*, 3, 9–10; Forsyth, *Reason and Revolution*, 86–88.
4. [Prudhomme and Tournon], *Les Révolutions de Paris* 5 (9/15 Aug. 1789), 27–29; Marmontel, *Mémoires*, 3:195; La Gorce, *Histoire religieuse*, 1:215–16; Whaley, *Radicals*, 22.
5. Rabaut de Saint-Étienne, *Précis historique*, 58, 62–64; Doyle, *Origins of the French Revolution*, 146.
6. Sieyès, *Essai*, 5; Forsyth, *Reason and Revolution*, 64–68, 72–78.
7. Mirabeau, *Courrier* 23 (3/5 Aug. 1789), 24–28.
8. Mackrell, *Attack on "Feudalism,"* 173–74; Sonenscher, *Sans-Culottes*, 305.
9. Bailly, *Mémoires de Bailly*, 2:266; Marmontel, *Mémoires*, 3:308; Fontana et al., *Venise et la Révolution*, 320.
10. Bailly, *Mémoires de Bailly*, 2:216.
11. Chaudon, *Dictionnaire anti-philosophique*, 1:324.
12. Brissot, *Le Patriote français* 10 (7 Aug. 1789), 3; Loft, *Passion, Politics*, 177–79.
13. Sieyès, *Qu'est-ce que le Tiers*, 32; Baker, "Reason and Revolution," 87; Sewell, *Rhetoric of Bourgeois Revolution*, 58–63.
14. Baudot, *Notes historiques*, 7, 220, 225; Bailly, *Mémoires de Bailly*, 2:255–56, 2:275; Sewell, *Rhetoric of Bourgeois Revolution*, 131–36.

15. Loft, *Passion, Politics*, 9–13.
16. Doyle, *Aristocracy and Its Enemies*, 122–30.
17. Luttrell, *Mirabeau*, 116–17, 174–76; Staum, *Cabanis*, 125–27; Gaulmier, *Un grand témoin*, 85, 96, 106–7; Israel, *Democratic Enlightenment*, 900–901.
18. *Archives Parlementaires*, 8:434 (13 Aug. 1789); *Journal des décrets* 5, 10 (1789), 26; Brissot, *Le Patriote français* 17 (15 Aug. 1789), 2, 5 and 18 (17 Aug. 1789), 1–3.
19. *Actes, Commune de Paris*, Lacroix (ed.), ser. 1, 1:xvii–xviii and introduction, 2:v–vi, ix.
20. Mirabeau, *Courrier* 22 (1/3 Aug. 1789), 13; [Prudhomme and Tournon], *Les Révolutions de Paris* 6 (16/22 Aug. 1789), 36–37 and 7 (22/27 Aug. 1789), 38–41.
21. Guilhaumou, *L'Avènement*, 120–22.
22. Brissot, *Mémoires (1734–1793)*, 2:105.
23. Bailly, *Mémoires de Bailly*, 2:211; Dumont, *Mémoires de Mirabeau*, 96–97; D. Williams, *Condorcet and Modernity*, 28–29; Baker, *Condorcet*, 265–68.
24. [Carra], *La Raison*, 205; [Carra], *L'Orateur*, 2:7–11.
25. Baker, *Condorcet*, 265; Rials, *La Déclaration des droits*, 118.
26. Rials, *La Déclaration des droits*, 123–24.
27. *Archives Parlementaires*, 8:462 (20 Aug. 1789); Gaulmier, *Un grand témoin*, 93; Rials, *La Déclaration des droits*, 219.
28. Bailly, *Mémoires de Bailly*, 2:211; Dumont, *Mémoires de Mirabeau*, 15–16; Baker, *Inventing the French Revolution*, 263–64.
29. Baker, *Condorcet*, 265–68; D. Williams, *Condorcet and Modernity*, 28–29.
30. Sieyès, *Préliminaire de la constitution*, 6–8; Baker, "Idea of a Declaration," 193–95; Wright, "National Sovereignty," 224.
31. Sieyès, *Préliminaire de la constitution*, 15; *Archives Parlementaires*, 8:462 (20 Aug. 1789); [Prudhomme and Tournon], *Révolutions de Paris* 6 (16/22 Aug. 1789), 36.
32. *Archives Parlementaires*, 8:453 (18 Aug. 1789).
33. Ibid., 8:438–39 (17 Aug. 1789); Rials, *La Déclaration des droits*, 206.
34. Sieyès, *Préliminaire de la constitution*, 20, article no. 26.
35. Brissot, *Le Patriote français* 21 (20 Aug. 1789), 1; Rabaut Saint-Étienne, *Projet*, iv–v.
36. *Archives Parlementaires*, 8:424–25 (12 Aug. 1789); Rials, *La Déclaration des droits*, 179–81.
37. Baker, "Idea of a Declaration," 165–69; Loft, *Passion, Politics*, 225–27, 232–33.
38. Rials, *La Déclaration des droits*, 156–59.
39. Marat, *L'Ami du peuple* 1, 1; Malouet, *Mémoires*, 1:338; Rials, *La Déclaration des droits*, 121–23, 189–90; Thomann, "Origines et sources doctrinales," 68.
40. Wright, "National Sovereignty," 225; Rials, *La Déclaration des droits*, 134–55.
41. Dumont, *Mémoires de Mirabeau*, 108; Villette, *Lettres choisies*, 9–10; Barnave, *De la Révolution*, 164; Baker, "Political Languages," 631–32, 635; Wright, "National Sovereignty," 221–23.
42. Mirabeau, *Courrier* 29 (18/19 Aug. 1789), 7–8; Gauchet, *Révolution des droits*, 49; Robespierre, *Le Défenseur*, 6:267–68; Edelstein, *Terror*, 194.
43. Rials, *La Déclaration des droits*, 197–98.

44. *Archives Parlementaires*, 8:438 (17 Aug. 1789); Rials, *La Déclaration des droits*, 197–202; Baker, "Idea of a Declaration," 184–86.

45. *Archives Parlementaires*, 8:438 (17 Aug. 1789).

46. Rials, *La Déclaration des droits*, 220–24, 236–39.

47. *Archives Parlementaires*, 8:473, 8:478; [Prudhomme and Tournon], *Révolutions de Paris* 7 (23/27 Aug.1789), 38–41; Mirabeau, *Mirabeau à la tribune*, 1:44–46.

48. Mirabeau, *Courrier* 31 (22/23 Aug. 1789), 1, 40–45; Aston, *Religion and Revolution*, 128; Walton, *Policing Public Opinion*, 90–92, 97.

49. Mirabeau, *Courrier* 31 (22/23 Aug. 1789), 44, 46; ibid., 32 (24/25 August 1789), 3; Forst, *Toleranz*, 452; Birn, "Religious Toleration," 271–72.

50. Mirabeau, *Collection complète*, 2:70–72; Aston, *Religion and Revolution*, 128; Birn, "Religious Toleration," 272–73.

51. Mirabeau, *Courrier* 30 (20/21 Aug. 1789), 16; Hunt, *Inventing Human Rights*, 221.

52. *Archives Parlementaires*, 8:439 (19 Aug. 1789); Mirabeau, *Courrier* 22 (21 Aug. 1789), 2; Hunt, *Inventing Human Rights*, 16, 21, 220.

53. Dumont, *Mémoires de Mirabeau*, 97; Baker, *Inventing the French Revolution*, 263–64, 272–73; Blamires, *French Revolution*, 144.

54. Mirabeau, *Courrier* 32 (24/25 August 1789), 1–3; Condorcet, *Œuvres complètes*, 9:166–68.

55. [Carra], *L'Orateur*, 2:32–33.

56. Ibid., 2:37–39, 2:73.

57. Rials, *La Déclaration des droits*, 21–26; Taylor, *Secular Age*, 413–14, 570.

58. Portalis, *De l'usage*, 2:387.

59. Möser, "Ueber das Recht des Menschheit," in *Berlinische Monatschrift* 18 (July–Dec. 1790), 396–401, 499–506; Knudsen, *Justus Möser*, 168–71; Peters, *Altes Reich*, 389.

60. Eberhard, *Philosophisches Magazin* 3 (1790/1), 377–96; Dippel, *Germany*, 166.

61. Knoblauch, "Gibt es wirklich Rechte der Menschheit?," *Philosophisches Magazin* 4 (1791/2), 424–46.

62. Ibid., 441–42.

63. Gibbon, *Memoirs of My Life*, 237.

64. Bergasse, *Considérations sur la liberté*, 19; Mortier, *Anacharsis Cloots*, 157, 186; Pasquino, "Nicolas Bergasse," 81–82.

65. *La Chronique de Paris* 9 (1 Sept. 1789), 33; *Lettre à Monsieur Raynal* (March 1789), 4, 11.

66. Mounier, *Considérations sur les gouvernements*, 44–46; Craiutu, *A Virtue*, 93–95; Schama, *Citizens: A Chronicle*, 443.

67. Mounier, *Considérations sur les gouvernements*, 42; Baker, *Inventing the French Revolution*, 260, 281–82.

68. Mounier, *Considérations sur les gouvernements*, 23, 28; Mounier, *De l'influence*, 5; Ozouf, "La Révolution française," 217.

69. Sieyès, *Qu'est-ce que le Tiers*, 96; Furet, *Revolutionary France*, 76; Pasquino, *Sieyès et l'invention*, 27.

70. Van Horn Melton, "Enlightenment to Revolution," 121–22.

71. Sieyès, *Qu'est-ce que le Tiers*, 96–97; Quiviger, "Sieyès," 134; Forsyth, *Reason and Revolution*, 21; Doyle, *Aristocracy and Its Enemies*, 219.
72. *La Chronique de Paris* 10 (2 Sept. 1789): 37–38.
73. Ibid., 19 (11 Sept. 1789), 75; another count states by 490 to 89, Applewhite, *Political Alignment*, 99.
74. Jefferson, *Papers of Thomas Jefferson*, 15:354; Bates, *Enlightenment Aberrations*, 128–29, 133–34, 141; Craiutu, *A Virtue*, 95, 107.
75. Villette to Cérutti, 10 Sept. 1789, in Villette, *Lettres choisies*, 8; Doyle, *Oxford History*, 120–21.
76. Dumont, *Souvenirs de Mirabeau*, 101, 104; Bailly, *Mémoires de Bailly*, 2:326–27, 345; Baker, "Enlightenment Idioms," 190–91.
77. [Prudhomme], *Révolutions de Paris* 8 (29 Aug./4 Sept. 1789), 25–26; [Carra], *L'Orateur*, 2:20–24; Popkin, "Journals," 160–61.
78. *La Chronique de Paris* 1, 30 (22 Sept. 1789), 117–19.
79. Ibid.; Mounier, *De l'influence*, 123.
80. *La Chronique de Paris* 1, 46 (8 Oct. 1789), 181.
81. Ibid., 29 (21 Sept. 1789), 113; Dawson, *Gods of Revolution*, 57, 68.
82. Marat, *L'Ami du peuple* 12 (22 Sept. 1789), 107–8 and 13 (23 Sept. 1789): 114–15; Sa'adah, *Shaping*, 119.
83. Marat, *L'Ami du peuple*, 13:114; Baczko, "The Terror," 24.
84. Marat, *L'Ami du peuple* 20 (28 Sept. 1789), 170–71.
85. Ibid., 20 (29 Sept. 1789): 174; Dawson, *Gods of Revolution*, 64–65.
86. Marat, *L'Ami du peuple* 19 (28 Sept. 1789): 165–66; Baczko, "The Terror," 31–32; Guilhaumou, *L'Avènement*, 135–36; Andries, "Les imprimeurs-libraires parisiens," 252.
87. Staël, *Considerations*, 194; Walton, *Policing Public Opinion*, 5–6; Whaley, *Radicals*, 28.
88. Chisick, "Intellectual Profile," 122–24.
89. Marat, *De l'Homme*, preface, 1:xiv–xv, 1:xix, and 1:174, 1:207–8, 1:310; 2:256, 2:378–79.
90. Forsyth, *Reason and Revolution*, 59–63; Sewell, *Rhetoric of Bourgeois Revolution*, 47–8, 68; Furet, "Rousseau," 173; Pasquino, *Sieyès et l'invention*, 45, 78–79.
91. Mortier, *Combats*, 336; Baker, *Condorcet*, 316.
92. Marat, *De l'Homme*, 1:251, 1:310.
93. Gorsas, *Courrier* 1, no. 88 (3 October 1789); Petitfils, *Louis XVI*, 2:242–44.
94. Lapied, "Une absence de révolution," 306–7; Kramer, *Lafayette*, 40–41.
95. Petitfils, *Louis XVI*, 2:263–65.
96. Malouet, *Mémoires*, 1:383; Petitfils, *Louis XVI*, 2:264–65; May, *Elisabeth Vigée Le Brun*, 71–72, 74.
97. Gibbon, *Memoirs of My Life*, 236.
98. Doyle, *Oxford History*, 123.
99. *La Chronique de Paris* 1, 45 (7 Oct. 1789), 177–79; Hunt, *Politics, Culture*, 58–59.
100. Fontana et al., *Venise et la Révolution*, 405.
101. *Actes de la Commune de Paris*, ser. 1, 2 (10 Oct. 1789), 245–48.
102. Elyada, "L'appel aux faubourgs," 192–93.

103. Elyada, "La Mère Duchesne," 3–5; Elyada, "L'Appel aux faubourgs," 185–89.

104. Elayda, *Lettres bougrement patriotiques*, 5–9; Goldberg Moses, "Equality," 235.

105. Elyada, *Lettres bougrement patriotiques*, 9–10; Elyada, "La Mère Duchesne," 10–13.

106. Granié, *De l'Assemblée*, 87; Arnaud, *Chamfort*, 169–70; Aston, *Religion and Revolution*, 132.

107. Griffiths, *Le Centre perdu*, 114–15; Pasquino, "Nicolas Bergasse," 81.

108. *La Chronique de Paris* 2, 67 (9 March 1790), 269; Griffiths, *Le Centre perdu*, 112.

109. Short to Jefferson, Paris, 19 Nov. 1789; Jefferson, *Papers of Thomas Jefferson*, 15:547; Malouet, *Mémoires*, 1:348.

110. Mounier, *Considérations sur les gouvernements*, 18, 32, 35; Craiutu, *A Virtue*, 72–3.

111. Mounier, *Considérations sur les gouvernements*, 51; Baker, *Inventing the French Revolution*, 258–61.

112. *La Chronique de Paris* 2, 201 (20 July 1790), 802.

113. Ibid., 2, 87 (28 March 1790), 345.

114. Griffiths, *Le Centre perdu*, 142–45.

115. Barnave, *De la Révolution*, 190–91.

116. Jefferson, *Papers of Thomas Jefferson*, 15:329, 15:458.

117. [Prudhomme], *Révolutions de Paris* 5 (9/15 Aug. 1789), 27–29; Marmontel, *Mémoires*, 3:195; La Gorce, *Histoire religieuse*, 1:215–16; Griffiths, *Le Centre perdu*, 155–57.

118. Godineau, *Women of Paris*, 99–100; Mortier, *Anacharsis Cloots*, 186.

119. *La Chronique de Paris* 1, 65 (27 Oct. 1789).

120. Thouret, *Discours*, 2–4, 9–10; Baker, *Condorcet*, 214, 267–68.

121. Bailly, *Mémoires de Bailly*, 3:252; *La Chronique de Paris* 1, 86 (17 November 1789), 341–42, 352; Condorcet, *Œuvres complètes*, 9:363, 9:395–97.

122. Bailly, *Mémoires de Bailly*, 3:253, entry for 12 Nov. 1789.

123. Cited in E. Badinter and R. Badinter, *Condorcet, 1743–1794*, 284.

124. *La Chronique de Paris* 1, 105 (11 Dec, 1789), 437.

125. Naigeon, *Encyclopédie méthodique*, 2:224–25; *Journal des décrets* 5, 3:7–8; Doyle, *Parlement of Bordeaux*, 308.

126. Barlow, *Advice to the Privileged Orders*, 6.

127. Israel, *Democratic Enlightenment*, 923.

128. Bailly, *Mémoires de Bailly*, 3:285–86, 294, 298, entries for 16 and 17 Nov. 1789.

129. *La Feuille villageoise*, 1:42–43.

130. *La Chronique de Paris* 1, 91 (22 Nov. 1789), 361–63; and 2, 1 (1 Jan. 1790), 3.

131. *Assemblée Nationale et Commune de Paris* 104 (16 Nov. 1789), 1–2; and no. 146 (28 Dec. 1789), 8.

132. Roederer, *Spirit of the Revolution*, 133–34; Bailly, *Mémoires de Bailly*, 3:298–99.

133. Baudot, *Notes historiques*, 130–31, 156; Guilhaumou and Monnier, "Cordeliers," 201–2.

134. Bertaud, *Camille et Lucile Desmoulins*, 98–100.

135. *Journal du Club des Cordeliers*, 31–33; Hammersley, *French Revolutionaries*, 56, 62.

136. Bailly, *Mémoires de Bailly*, 3:299; Hampson, *Will and Circumstance*, 175–76.

CHAPTER 5

Democratizing the Revolution

1. Desmoulins, *Révolutions de France et de Brabant*, no. 65, 575.
2. Necker, *De la Révolution française*, 2:47–55.
3. Durozoy, *La Gazette de Paris*, 19 June 1790, 1–3; Buonarroti, *Giornale Patriottico di Corsica* 16 (24 July 1790), 139.
4. Durozoy, *La Gazette de Paris*, 10 Oct. 1791, 1–3.
5. Feller, *Journal historique et littéraire* (1 Jan. 1792), 21.
6. Sieyès, *Préliminaire*, 15; Pasquino, *Sieyès et l'invention*, 55–56, 65.
7. Sieyès, *Préliminaire*, 36–37; Furet, "Rousseau," 173; Forsyth, *Reason and Revolution*, 170–80; Urbinati, *Representative Democracy*, 167.
8. Sieyès, *Préliminaire*, 15–16, Jennings, *Revolution*, 32–33.
9. Baker, *Condorcet*, 281–83; E. Kennedy, "Aux origines," 12.
10. Malouet, *Mémoires*, 1:374–81.
11. *Archives Parlementaires*, 13:113 (19 April 1790).
12. Ibid., 13:111 (19 April 1790); Griffiths, *Le Centre perdu*, 155–56; Elyada, "La mise au pilori," 3.
13. *Archives Parlementaires*, 13:112 (19 April 1790); Rousseau, *Social Contract*, 114.
14. *La Chronique de Paris* 2, 223 (11 Aug. 1790), 889.
15. Gorsas, *Le Courrier de Paris*, 20 Dec. 1790, 1; Gorsas, *Courrier des LXXXIII* 23, 14 (14 April 1791), 220; Fréron, *L'Orateur du peuple* 4, no. 3, 19–20; Griffiths, *Le Centre perdu*, 119–21.
16. BHP pamph. 953463, *l'Anti Carra-co-Gorsas* (31 Dec. 1790), 2–3; BHP pamph. 953466, *Pour quoi Mesdames sont elles parties?*," 3.
17. Elyada, "La représentation," 535; Doyle, *Aristocracy and Its Enemies*, 208, 249–50, 253; Higonnet, *Class, Ideology*, 58–59, 84; Klooster, *Revolutions*, 56–57.
18. *Archives Parlementaires*, 17:449 (31 July 1790).
19. *La Chronique du mois* 1 (1791), 47.
20. Raynal, *Histoire philosophique*, 1:124.
21. Sieyès, *Préliminaire*, 32; Gross, *Fair Shares*, 5–6, 9.
22. Applewhite, *Political Alignment*, 99.
23. PFL Pamphlets 1509 178 999, vol. 35, no. 2, 5–6; Tackett, *Religion, Revolution*, 210–11; Aston, *Religion and Revolution*, 137–38.
24. Durozoy, *La Gazette de Paris*, 1 Jan. 1791, 1–2.
25. [Ferrand], *État actuel*, 4–6; Mallet du Pan, *Considérations*, 33–34.
26. [Ferrand], *État actuel*, 4–7, 28–29.
27. *Archives Parlementaires*, 17:448–49 (31 July 1790).
28. Durozoy, *La Gazette de Paris*, 8 Oct. 1791, 3.
29. Darrow, *Revolution in the House*, 40–44; Aston, *Religion and Revolution*, 246–48.
30. Prudhomme, *Histoire générale*, 3:195–96; La Gorce, *Histoire religieuse*, 1:232–44.
31. *Assemblée Nationale, Corps administatifs*, no. 319 (19 June 1790), 2–3.

32. PFL Pamphlets 1509 178 999, vol. 35, no. 18.
33. Doyle, *Aristocracy and Its Enemies*, 213; P. Jones, *Peasantry*, 86–89; Conchon, *Le Péage*, 440–41.
34. *La Feuille villageoise* 1, no. 17 (20 Jan. 1791), 307.
35. Ibid., 306.
36. *Archives Parlementaires*, 11:685–89 (24 Feb. 1790).
37. Ibid., 11:689 (25 Feb. 1790).
38. BHP pamph. 953466, *Pour quoi Mesdames sont elles parties?*, 5.
39. *Actes de la Commune*, 2:359, 2:367, 2:377 (31 Jan. and 14 Feb. 1791).
40. Ibid., 2:208–9, 357 (27 and 31 Jan. 1791).
41. *Archives Parlementaires*, 22:490–92 (25 Jan. 1791); Malouet, *Mémoires*, 1:328.
42. *Archives Parlementaires*, 27:135–38 (16 July 1790).
43. Speech of La Réveillère de Lépeaux, in *Archives Parlementaires*, 17:444 (31 July 1790).
44. Ibid., 17:444–45 (31 July 1790).
45. Ibid., 17:446 (31 July 1790).
46. *La Chronique de Paris* 2, 74 (15 March 1790), 293; Fontana et al., *Venise et la Révolution*, 410.
47. Condorcet, "Lettre VIII to the Assemblée Nationale," *La Bouche de fer*, l:57–61; E. Badinter and R. Badinter, *Condorcet, 1743–1794*, 278.
48. Kates, *Cercle Social*, 21; Monnier, "Républicanisme," 99.
49. Halévi, "Les Girondins," 151–52.
50. *La Chronique du mois* 2 (February, 1792), 117.
51. May, *Madame Roland*, 171–72; Whaley, *Radicals*, 31–32.
52. Lanthenas, *Liberté indéfinie*, 4.
53. *La Chronique de Paris* 46 (Oct. 1789), 181.
54. Ibid., 2, 46 (25 Feb. 1790), 222; *La Feuille villageoise* 1, no. 22 (27 Feb. 1791), 410.
55. Cloots, *Œuvres*, 3:6, 3:20, 3:27–28.
56. Bouissounouse, *Condorcet*, 113; Staum, *Cabanis*, 293, 298–99.
57. D'Abrantès, *Salons révolutionnaires*, 44–45, 51, 61–62; E. Badinter and R. Badinter, *Condorcet, 1743–1794*, 385; Pagden, *The Enlightenment*, 22–23.
58. Rothschild, *Economic Sentiments*, 216–17.
59. Démeunier, *L'Esprit des usages*, 1:77–133.
60. Ibid., 1:229; Brissot, *Lettres philosophiques*, 116, 119–21.
61. Portalis, *De l'usage*, 226.
62. *La Chronique de Paris* 2, 35 (4 Feb. 1790), 137; Corno, "La loi révolution-naire," 62, 65.
63. *La Chronique du mois* 2 (March, 1792), 86.
64. *La Chronique de Paris,* no. 22 (22 January1792), 86–87.
65. Ibid., 2, 5 (5 Jan. 1790), 17–18.
66. D. Williams, *Condorcet and Modernity*, 168.
67. See *Lettre XI* (Feb. 1790), "de Marseille" au Cercle Social, *La Bouche de fer*, 1:107–12.
68. *La Chronique de Paris* 6 (6 Jan. 1791), 21.
69. Royou, *L'Ami du Roi*, 16 Oct. 1791, 1; Norberg, "Love," 40–41.
70. Royou, *L'Ami du Roi*, 28 Feb. 1792, 1.

71. Condorcet, *Tableau historique*, 898–901; Condorcet, *Political Writngs*, xxix.
72. *La Chronique de Paris* 2, 206 (25 July 1790), 822.
73. Palm d'Aelders, *Appel aux françoises*, 1–3.
74. Ibid., 9–12.
75. Bonneville, *La Bouche de fer*, no. 39 (6 April 1791), 43.
76. Ibid., no. 36 (29 March 1791), 572, 575.
77. Palm d'Aelders, *Appel aux françoises*, 25–28.
78. Ibid., 38–40, 46.
79. *La Chronique de Paris*, no. 201 (20 July 1791), 813.
80. Bonneville, *La Bouche de fer*, no. 39 (6 April 1791), 43.
81. Ginguené, *Lettres*, 55, 61–62.
82. Palm d'Aelders, *Appel aux françoises*, 34; Geffroy, "Louise de Kéralio-Robert," 18; Censer, *Prelude to Power*, 16.
83. Hunt, *Inventing Human Rights*, 63; Kates, *Cercle Social*, 120–24; Scott, *Only Paradoxes*, 40–50.
84. Feller, *Journal historique et littéraire* (1 Jan. 1792), 23.
85. Proly, *Le Cosmopolite*, no. 123 (16 April 1792), 394.
86. Blanc, "Une humaniste," 31, 33–34.
87. *La Chronique du mois* 2 (May 1792), 33; Godineau, *Women of Paris*, 278.
88. *La Chronique de Paris* 2, 230 (18 Aug. 1790), 918; Bonneville, *La Bouche de fer*, no. 42 (14 April 1791), 118.
89. Bonneville, *La Bouche de fer*, 2:5.
90. Ibid., 1:14; Kates, *Cercle Social*, 56–57.
91. Elyada, "La mise au pilori," 6–8, 14–15; Bertaud, *Camille et Lucile Desmoulins*, 104–7.
92. Sieyès, *Manuscrits, 1773–1799*, 344.
93. *Archives Parlementaires*, 17:480, 17:484 (31 July 1790); Elyada, "La mise au pilori," 3–6, 11.
94. *Assemblée National, Commune de Paris*, no. 170 (21 Jan. 1790), 4; *La Chronique de Paris* 2, 238 (26 Aug. 1790), 949; Forsyth, *Reason and Revolution*, 208–9; Lawday, *Giant of the French Revolution*, 66–68.
95. Marat, *L'Ami du peuple*, no. 163 (16 July 1790), 2–3.
96. *La Chronique de Paris* 2, 192 (11 July 1790), 767; Marat, *L'Ami du peuple*, no. 162 (15 July 1790), 1058.
97. *La Chronique de Paris* 2, 205 (24 July 1790), 817–18; Trousson, *Jean-Jacques Rousseau*, 748; Fitzsimmons, *Remaking of France*, 109.
98. *Assemblée Nationale, Commune de Paris*, no. 344 (14 July 1790), 3 and no. 345 (16 July 1790), 3–4; Bindman, *Shadow of the Guillotine*, 93–94.
99. Gorsas, *Le Courrier de Paris*, 20 Dec. 1790, 12–13; Walton, *Policing Public Opinion*, 107–8.
100. *Archives Parlementaires*, 17:458 (31 July 1790); *Assemblée Nationale, Commune de Paris*, no. 362 (2 Aug. 1790), 2–3.
101. *La Chronique de Paris* 2, 183 (2 July 1790), 731; Lanthenas, *Liberté indéfinie*, 8.
102. Audouin, *Journal universel*, no. 272 (21 Aug. 1790), 2173–74.
103. Lanthenas, *Liberté indéfinie*, 9; Walton, *Policing Public Opinion*, 110–11.
104. Lanthenas, *Liberté indéfinie*, 15–21.

105. Ibid., 31; Walton, *Policing Public Opinion*, 111.

106. Lanthenas, *Liberté indéfinie*, 34–35.

107. Robespierre, *Le Défenseur*, 6:284; Lüsebrink et al., *The Bastille*, 119–25; Bell, *Cult of the Nation*, 169–70.

108. *La Chronique de Paris* 2, 214 (2 Aug. 1790), 853; Aaslestad, *Place and Politics*, 117–18; Engels, "Freye Deutsche!," 248, 251–52.

109. [Palissot], *Considérations importantes*, 6; La Harpe, *Discours sur la liberté*, 6.

110. *La Chronique de Paris* 2, 182 (1 July 1790), 725–27; Friedland, *Political Actors*, 263–66.

111. [Palissot], *Considérations importantes*, 10–13; *La Chronique de Paris* 2, 223 (11 Aug. 1790), 890.

112. Fréron, *L'Orateur du peuple* 4, no. 18 (Dec. 170), 140–41 and no. 19, 161.

113. Ibid., 3, no. 65 (Dec. 1790), 526.

114. PFL Pamphlets 178 999, vol. 35, no. 3; Maslan, *Revolutionary Acts*, 51.

115. *Journal de Paris*, no. 322 (18 Nov. 1790), 1310.

116. Ibid., no. 353 (19 Dec. 1790), 1433–34.

117. *La Chronique de Paris* 2, 216 (4 Aug. 1790), 863.

118. *Archives Parlementaires,* 17:460 (31 July 1790).

119. Fréron, *L'Orateur du peuple,* no. 14 (June 1790), 439 and no. 54 (July), 105–7.

120. Labbé, *Anacharsis Cloots*, 100.

121. *Archives Parlementaires*, 17:178–79 (17 July 1790).

122. *La Chronique de Paris* 2, 234 (21 July 1790), 933; *La Feuille villageoise* 1, no. 10 (2 Dec. 1790), 187; E. Badinter and R. Badinter, *Condorcet, 1743–1794*, 337; Vincent, "Les Américains," 483–86.

123. Bonneville, *La Bouche de fer,* 1 (1790), 110–11.

124. Whaley, *Radicals*, 33.

125. Censer, *Prelude to Power*, 21; Whaley, *Radicals*, 35.

126. Ravitch, "Abbé Fauchet," 247–62; Sorkin, *Religious Enlightenment*, 273–74, 283.

127. Fauchet, *Sermon sur l'accord*, 24; Bonneville, *La Bouche de fer,* no. 36 (29 March 1791), 578–80 and no. 42 (14 April), 104.

128. Bonneville, *La Bouche de fer,* no. 36 (29 March 1791), 581; Mortier, *Anacharsis Cloots*, 196–97; Shovlin, *Political Economy*, 193.

129. Popkin, "Journals," 158.

130. *La Feuille villageoise* 1, no. 10 (2 Dec. 1790), 1–3, 5; Bell, *Cult of the Nation*, 165.

131. *La Feuille villageoise* 1, no. 12 (16 Dec. 1790), 221; *La Chronique de Paris* 2, 234 (21 July 1790), 933.

132. *La Feuille villageoise* 1, no. 7 (11 Nov. 1790), 115–16.

133. Ibid., no. 7 (11 Nov. 1790), 122–23.

134. Ibid., no. 19 (3 Feb. 1791), 351.

CHAPTER 6

Deadlock (November 1790–July 1791)

1. Bates, *Enlightenment Aberrations*, 133–35.

2. Letter of Pétion, 24 April 1791, in Robert and Keralio, *Mercure national* 9, 135–36; Baudot, *Notes historiques*, 28.

3. Letter of Pétion, 24 April 1791, in Robert and Keralio, *Mercure national* 9, 137.
4. Manuel, *Lettres sur la Révolution,* 1–4, 7, 15, 20.
5. *La Chronique de Paris,* prospectus for 1791, no. 1 (1 Jan. 1791).
6. Ibid.; and *La Chronique de Paris,* prospectus for 1792.
7. Robert and Keralio, *Mercure national* 17 (2 May 1791), 260; Tackett, *Becoming a Revolutionary,* 279–80.
8. *Assemblée Nationale, Commune de Paris,* no. 319 (19 June 1790), 2–3.
9. Durozoy, *La Gazette de Paris,* 12 April 1791.
10. Fréron, *L'Orateur du peuple* 2, no. 57, 452–53.
11. *Assemblée Nationale, Commune de Paris,* no. 398 (7 Sept. 1790), 2–5; no. 430 (9 Oct. 1790), 4; no. 431 (10 Oct. 1790), 2–3; and no. 432 (11 Oct. 1790), 2.
12. Elyada, "Les récits," 281.
13. Gorsas, *Le Courrier de Paris,* 20 Dec. 1790, 11; Hanson, *Provincial Politics,* 36, 42, 68.
14. PFL Pamph. 109, 178 999, vol. 35, no. 2, *Déjeuner de Vaugirard* (n.p. 1790), 3–6.
15. *Archives Parlementaires,* 17:486 (30 July 1790).
16. *Assemblée Nationale, Commune de Paris,* no. 347 (18 July 1790).
17. Gorsas, *Le Courrier de Paris,* 20 Dec. 1790, 4–5, 16.
18. Fréron, *L'Orateur du peuple* 3, no. 65, 523–24.
19. Johnson, *Midi in Revolution,* 85, 97.
20. Proly, *Le Cosmopolite,* no. 356 (12 March 1792).
21. Gorsas, *Le Courrier de Paris,* 20 Dec. 1790, 2.
22. Johnson, *Midi in Revolution,* 72, 74, 92, 133, 137; *Journal de Paris,* no. 354 (20 Dec.1790), 1436.
23. Gorsas, *Le Courrier de Paris,* 20 Dec.1790, 4; Fréron, *L'Orateur du peuple* 3, no. 66, 528, 531–32.
24. Marat, *L'Ami du peuple,* no. 320 (24 Dec. 1790), 1954–56.
25. Scurr, *Fatal Purity,* 136–39; McPhee, *Robespierre,* 79–86.
26. *La Feuille villageoise* 1, no. 21 (17 Feb. 1791), 391; Bessy, "Le parti Jacobin," 28–29.
27. Roland, *Memoirs,* 75, 80; D'Abrantès, *Salons révolutionnaires,* 65–66, 84–85; May, *Madame Roland,* 186–87.
28. *Journal de Paris,* no. 93 (3 April 1791), 376.
29. *Archives Parlementaires,* 24:537 (4 April 1791).
30. Ibid., 24:558–59 (4 April 1791); *Journal de Paris,* no. 95 (5 April 1791), 381–82; Fréron, *L'Orateur du peuple* 5, no. 35 (April 1791), 293–94.
31. Durozoy, *La Gazette de Paris,* 6 April 1791, 2–3.
32. Gorsas, *Courrier des LXXXIII,* no. 23, 21 (21 April 1791), 322.
33. Ibid., no. 23, 4 and 5 (4 and 5 April 1791), 51–52, 56.
34. Ibid., no. 23, 17 (17 April 1791), 263; Trousson, *Jean-Jacques Rousseau,* 747; Robisco, *Jean-Jacques Rousseau,* 200.
35. Gorsas, *Courrier des LXXXIII,* no. 23, 17 (17 April 1791), 263.
36. Barber, "Financial History," 165–67.
37. *Journal de Paris,* no. 151 (31 May 1791), 605–6.
38. Robert and Keralio, *Mercure national* 24 (10 May 1791), 377–79; Fréron, *L'Orateur du peuple* 5, no. 46 (April 171), 382–83.

39. Gorsas, *Courrier des LXXXIII* 23, no. 19 (19 April 1791) and 84 (20 April 1791), 292–93, 295, 313; Fréron, *L'Orateur du peuple* 5 (April 171), 365; Petit-fils, *Louis XVI*, 2:311–13; Burstin, *Révolution*, 249–52.

40. Robert and Keralio, *Mercure national* 24 (10 May 1791), 383 and 29 (25 May 1791), 617–18.

41. Ibid., 23 (9 May 1791), 377.

42. Marat, *L'Ami du peuple* 455 (11 May 1791), 3–5; Monnier, "Démocratie représentative," 7.

43. Sewell, *Work and Revolution*, 87–91.

44. *Journal du Club des Cordeliers* 7 (10 July 1791), 63.

45. Monnier, "Démocratie représentative," 7.

46. Robert and Keralio, *Mercure national* 35 (21 May 1791), 555–58.

47. Kates, *Cercle Social*, 147.

48. Ibid., 149–50.

49. Brissot, *Le Patriote français* 676 (15 June 1791); Hampson, *Will and Circumstance*, 186–87; Gross, *Fair Shares*, 124–26.

50. Brissot, *Le Patriote français* 676 (15 June 1791); Edelstein, "Feuille villageoise," 190–93.

51. See, for instance, Dorigny, *Les Girondins*, 569–83.

52. Hampson, *Social History*, 183.

53. BL 910.c.16/7, "Lettre d'un citoyen de Marseille . . . , sur M. de Mirabeau et l'Abbé Raynal," 1–2, 45–46.

54. Manuel, *Lettres sur la Révolution*, 91, 178; *Conversation entre Messieurs Raynal et Linguet*, 3, 11, 31, 40; De Luna, "Dean Street Style," 179.

55. Manuel, *Lettres sur la Révolution*, 46, 50.

56. Maréchal and Lalande, *Dictionnaire des Athées*, 260.

57. *La Chronique de Paris* 2, 30 (30 Jan. 1790), 117; Brissot, *Le Patriote français* 152 (7 Jan. 1790), 3–4.

58. *Assemblée Nationale, Commune de Paris*, no. 398 (7 Sept. 1790), 8.

59. Malouet, *Mémoires*, 2:36–50; Pagden, *The Enlightenment*, 168–69.

60. Raynal, *Adresse* (31 May 1791), 6–7, 15; *Journal de Paris*, no. 152 (1 June 1791), 611–12 and no. 153 (2 June 1791), 613–14.

61. *Archives Parlementaires*, 26:650–53 (31 May 1791).

62. Sinéty, "Réflexions importantes," in *Archives Parlementaires*, 26:661–62 (31 May 1791).

63. Brissot, *Mémoires (1734–1793)*, 2:85–86; Audouin, *Journal universel*, no. 560 (5 June 1791), 8075–7.

64. Audouin, *Journal universel*, no. 559 (4 June 1791), 8069; Labbé, *Anacharsis Cloots*, 165.

65. *T. G. Raynal démasqué*, 6; Mortier, *Anacharsis Cloots*, 212–13; Israel, *Democratic Enlightenment*, 936.

66. Brissot, *Le Patriote français* 665 (4 June 1791), 619–20 and 667 (6 June 1791), 626–27.

67. BN pamph. étampes, no. G162323 and 10978.

68. BL R 643/6, *Lettre du Citoyen Naigeon, 6 Germianl An V*, 2, 4; Israel, *Democratic Enlightenment*, 947.

69. Naigeon, *Encyclopédie méthodique*, 2:viii, xxiii–xxv.

70. Naigeon, *Adresse à l'Assemblée Nationale*, 100–102; Pellerin, "Naigeon," 30, 32.
71. Staum, *Cabanis*, 29, 91.
72. Naigeon, *Encyclopédie méthodique*, 2:221–22.
73. Elyada, "Les récits," 283–85.
74. Bonneville, *La Bouche de fer,* no. 42 (14 April 1791), 116.
75. Ibid., no. 42 (14 April 1791), 104–7; Mortier, *Anacharsis Cloots*, 200–202.
76. [Bonneville], *La Bouche de fer* no. 37 (1 April 1791), 20; Sorkin, *Religious Enlightenment*, 302.
77. [Bonneville], *La Bouche de fer*, no. 42 (14 April 1791), 108–14.
78. Ibid., no. 43 (16 April 1791), 122, 129.
79. Fauchet, *Journal des Amis* 1, prospectus, 4–5.
80. [Bonneville], *La Bouche de fer*, no. 42 (14 April 1791), 101.
81. Chopelin-Banc, *De l'Apologétique*, 296–305; Mortier, *Anacharsis Cloots*, 204.
82. Elyada, "Le représentation," 532–37.
83. *Archives Parlementaires*, 27:378–83 (21 June 1791); Hardman, *Louis XVI*, 115; Hampson, *Will and Circumstance*, 155.
84. Elyada, "Les récits," 286 –88.
85. Ibid., 288–89; Elyada, "La représentation," 528.
86. Marat, *L'Ami du peuple*, no. 497 (22 June 1791), 3068–69; Dingli, *Robespierre*, 135, 183–84; Barnave, *De la Révolution*, 144.
87. *Archives Parlementaires*, 27:364, 27:366, 27:372 (21 June 1791); *Journal de Paris*, no. 177 (26 June 1791), 709.
88. *Journal du Club des Cordeliers* 10 (4 Aug.1791), 86–87.
89. Ibid., 1 (28 June 1791), 1–2.
90. Audouin, *Journal universel*, no. 580 (25 June 1791), 10034–35; Bertaud, *Les Amis du roi*, 209.
91. Carra, *Annales patriotiques* 638 (2 July 1791), 1625; Durozoy, *La Gazette de Paris*, 22 June 1791, 1–2.
92. Fontana et al., *Venise et la Révolution*, 584; Levasseur, *Mémoires de R. Levasseur*, 1:40; Prudhomme, *Histoire générale*, 1:11.
93. *Journal du Club des Cordeliers* 1 (28 June 1791), 3.
94. Ibid., 2–3; Antheunis, *Le conventionnel belge*, 23–25.
95. *La Chronique de Paris* 207 (26 July 1791), 835.
96. Carra, *Annales patriotiques* 642 (6 July 1791), 1643 and 663 (7 July 1791), 1651.
97. Ibid., 645 (9 July 1791), 1656 and 666 (10 July 1791), 1661.
98. Ibid., 649 (13 July 1791), 1673; Monnier, "Républicanisme," 104.
99. Roland, *Memoirs*, 82; D'Abrantès, *Salons révolutionnaires*, 90–91; Gueniffey, "Brissot," 440, 450; Dingli, *Robespierre*, 163.
100. Kates, *Cercle Social*, 161; Hampson, *Life and Opinions*, 78–79; Nelson, *Thomas Paine*, 212–13.
101. Carra, *Annales patriotiques* 645 (9 July 1791), 1655.
102. Ibid., 643 (7 July 1791), 1648, 1651; Lemny, *Jean-Louis Carra*, 208.
103. M. L. Kennedy, *Jacobin Clubs*, 280.
104. *Journal du Club des Cordeliers*, no. 7 (10 July 1791), 60; Whaley, *Radicals*, 41.
105. Doyle, *Oxford History*, 152–53; M. L. Kennedy, *Jacobin Clubs*, 282; Monnier, "Démocratie représentative," 8.

106. Jordan, *Revolutionary Career*, 72.
107. Whaley, *Radicals*, 42.
108. Hébert, *Le Père Duchesne* 59 (June 1791), 1 and no. 60, 2; Elyada, "La représentation," 533, 537, 541, 544.
109. Carra, *Annales patriotiques* 638 (2 July 1792), 1623; Desmoulins, *Révolutions de France et de Brabant* 86 (July 1791), 5–6; *Journal du Club des Cordeliers* 1 (28 June 1791), 7–8.
110. *Journal du Club des Cordeliers* 1 (28 June 1791), 7; Fontana et al., *Venise et la Révolution*, 586–87.
111. *Journal du Club des Cordeliers* 7 (10 July 1792), 62, 64.
112. Brissot, *Discours sur la question*, 2–4.
113. Fréron, *L'Orateur du peuple* 7, no. 2 (July 1791), 9.
114. Carra, *Annales Patriotiques* 647 (11 July 1791), 1655; *La Chronique de Paris* 193 (12 July 1791), 779, 781.
115. Bouissounouse, *Condorcet*, 233; Jones, *Great Nation*, 530; Jourdan, "Le culte de Rousseau," 60–61.
116. Fontana et al., *Venise et la Révolution*, 538; Staël, *Considerations*, 267; Scurr, *Fatal Purity*, 130–31.
117. *La Chronique de Paris*, no. 193 (12 July 1791), 781; ibid., no. 262 (20 September), 1061.
118. Ibid., no. 192 (11 July 1791), 773 and 781–83; Carra, *Annales patriotiques* 647 (11 July 1791), 1664.
119. Feller, *Journal historique et littéraire* (1792), 149.
120. *Archives Parlementaires*, 29:736–37 (27 Aug, 1791).
121. Ginguené, *Petition to Assemblée nationale*, 27 Aug. 1791, 2; Ginguené, *Lettres*, 63–65.
122. Ginguené, *Petition to Assemblée nationale*, 5.
123. *Archives Parlementaires*, 29:756 (27 Aug. 1791); Miller, *Rousseau*, 139, 241; Swenson, *On Jean-Jacques Rousseau*, 10.
124. *Archives Parlementaires*, 29:755–56 (27 Aug. 1791); Jourdan, "Le culte de Rousseau," 62–63.
125. Ginguené, *Lettres*, 30, 53.
126. Ibid., 80–82.
127. Ibid., 87–88, 131–45.
128. Ibid., 132.
129. Ginguené, *Petition to Assemblée nationale*, 3–4; *Archives Parlementaires*, 29:756 (27 Aug. 1791).
130. *Archives Parlementaires*, 29:760–61 (27 Aug. 1791).
131. Ibid., 29:191 (4 Sept. 1791).
132. *La Chronique de Paris,* no. 211 (30 July 1791), 851.
133. Ibid., no. 195 (14 July 1791), 788, 790, and no. 196 (15 July 1791), 793.
134. Ibid., no. 207 (26 July 1791), 835–36.
135. *Archives Parlementaires*, 28:325–26 (15 July 1791); Fitzsimmons, *Remaking of France*, 124–25.
136. Barnave, *Power, Property and History*, 27, 29, 33, 38.
137. Ibid., 101, 141.
138. *Archives Parlementaires*, 28:330–31 (15 July 1791); Barnave, *Power, Property and History*, 19–20, 27; Furet, "Les Girondins," 197.

139. Feller, *Journal historique et littéraire* (19 Aug. 1792), 148.

140. *La Chronique de Paris*, no. 197 (16 July 1791), 798.

141. Doyle, *Oxford History*, 153.

142. *La Chronique de Paris*, no. 197 (16 July 1791), 796, and no. 207 (26 July 1791), 836; Roederer, *Spirit of the Revolution*, 37.

143. *La Chronique de Paris*, no. 207 (26 July 1791), 836; Burstin, *Révolution*, 256.

144. *Grande Petition presentée . . . par quarante mille citoyens* (15 July), 2.

145. *La Chronique de Paris*, no. 197 (16 July 1791), 796–97.

146. *Grande Petition presentée . . . par quarante mille citoyens* (15 July).

147. *La Chronique de Paris*, no. 208 (27 July 1791), 839.

148. Ibid., no. 199 (18 July 1791), 805; Applewhite, *Political Alignment*, 124–25.

149. *La Chronique de Paris*, no. 200 (19 July 1791), 809, and no. 202 (21 July 1791), 816.

150. Fontana et al., *Venise et la Révolution*, 596–97; Barnave, *De la Révolution*, 146.

151. *La Chronique de Paris*, no. 200 (19 July 1791), 809 and no. 207 (26 July 1791), 837.

152. *Journal du Club des Cordeliers* 8 (19 July 1791), 68–69.

CHAPTER 7

War with the Church (1788–1792)

1. Ravitch, "Abbé Fauchet," 251; Desan, *Reclaiming the Sacred*, 3; Petitfils, *Louis XVI*, 2:288.

2. Cérutti, *Mémoire pour le peuple françois*, 20–22.

3. McManners, *Church and Society*, 1:210–12, 215, 249, 287.

4. Forsyth, *Reason and Revolution*, 195.

5. Durozoy, *La Gazette de Paris*, 1 Jan. 1791, 1 and 15 Jan. 1791, 1–2.

6. Volney, *Les Ruines*, in Volney, *Œuvres complètes*, 1:268.

7. Tocqueville, *L'Ancien régime*, 202–4; Aston, *Religion and Revolution*, 3.

8. McPhee, *Robespierre*, 41, 83, 135, 174.

9. Quoted in Aston, *Religion and Revolution*, 132.

10. Royou, *L'Ami du Roi*, 23 Oct. 1791, 2.

11. Mirabeau, *Collection complète*, 3:42–44.

12. *La Chronique de Paris* 2, 25 (25 Jan. 1790), 98; Fontana et al., *Venise et la Révolution*, 158–59, 372.

13. Hertzberg, *French Enlightenment*, 351; Schlechter, *Obstinate Hebrews*, 55.

14. *Archives Parlementaires*, 10:756–58 (23 Dec. 1789), speeches of Maury and de Lafarre; Jaher, *The Jews*, 69–70; Schechter, *Obstinate Hebrews*, 157; Girard, *La Révolution française*, 125–27.

15. *Journal des décrets* 5, no. 10, 12–14; Fontana et al., *Venise et la Révolution*, 371–72.

16. *Archives Parlementaires*, 11:364–65 (28 Jan. 1790); Jaher, *The Jews*, 72.

17. Fontana et al., *Venise et la Révolution*, 392.

18. Doyle, *Oxford History*, 411; Aston, *Religion and Revolution*, 252–54.

19. Michaud, *La Quotidienne*, no. 333 (9 Aug. 1793), 703.

20. E. Kennedy, *Cultural History*, 146.

21. Castelot, *Talleyrand*, 63–64.

22. *Archives Parlementaires*, 11:590 (13 Feb. 1790).
23. See chapter 2, note 20.
24. Gaulmier, *Un grand témoin*, 102–3, 118–19.
25. Arnaud, *Chamfort*, 179–81.
26. Ravitch, "Abbé Fauchet," 255–56; Sorkin, *Religious Enlightenment*, 286–87.
27. Fontana et al., *Venise et la Révolution*, 350.
28. Bailly, *Mémoires de Bailly*, 3:238–40, entries for 30 and 31 October 1789; Culoma, *Religion civile*, 82.
29. Bailly, *Mémoires de Bailly,* vol. 3, entry for 2 Nov. 1789; Van Kley, *Religious Origins*, 355; Applewhite, *Political Alignment*, 99.
30. Bailly, *Mémoires de Bailly*, vol. 3, entry for 2 Nov. 1789.
31. *Archives Parlementaires*, 11:438 (5 Feb. 1790).
32. Hampson, *Social History*, 90–91.
33. E. Badinter and R. Badinter, *Condorcet, 1743–1794*, 271.
34. Mirabeau, *Courrier* 47 (28/30 Sept. 1789), 5–6.
35. *La Chronique de Paris*, 2, nos. 44–45 (13 and 14 Feb. 1790), 175, 179; McMahon, *Enemies*, 71; Aston, *Religion and Revolution*, 134–35.
36. La Gorce, *Histoire religieuse*, 1:200.
37. Ibid., 1:155–56.
38. *Archives Parlementaires*, 11:580 (12 Feb. 1790).
39. *La Chronique de Paris* 2 (13 and 14 Feb. 1790), 175 and 179; Burstin, *Révolution*, 190–91.
40. *La Chronique de Paris* 2, 5 (5 Jan. 1790), 17; Fontana et al., *Venise et la Révolution*, 392, 394.
41. *Archives Parlementaires*, 11:591 (13 Feb. 1790).
42. Aston, *Religion and Revolution*, 134.
43. Dommanget, *Sylvain Maréchal*, 163–64; Israel, *Enlightenment Contested*, 725–28.
44. Camus, *Observations*, 10–11; Malouet, *Mémoires*, 1:304; Van Kley, *Religious Origins*, 335, 355.
45. E. Badinter and R. Badinter, *Condorcet, 1743–1794*, 301; Tackett, *Religion, Revolution*, 7, 59; Forsyth, *Reason and Revolution*, 201; Doyle, *Aristocracy and Its Enemies*, 257–58.
46. *Lettre d'un curé de l'Assemblée Nationale à un de ses confrères de province* (Paris, 1791), BL R-155/1, 2, 5, 8; Sorkin, *Religious Enlightenment*, 289.
47. Fauchet, *Sermon sur l'accord*, 5–6, 23; Tackett, *Religion, Revolution*, 12; Chopelin-Blanc, *De l'Apologétique*, 346–57.
48. Camus, *Opinion*, 2.
49. Fréron, *L'Orateur du peuple*, no. 8 (May 1790), 63; Buonarroti, *Giornale Patriottico di Corsica* 16 (24 July 1790), 141–42; La Gorce, *Histoire religieuse*, 1:213.
50. La Gorce, *Histoire religieuse*, 1:210; Kennedy, *Cultural History*, 150.
51. *Actes de la Commune* 2, 119 (12 Jan. 1791).
52. Rocher, "Aspects," 304; McPhee, *Robespierre*, 104.
53. Fauchet, *Sermon sur l'accord*, 24; Taggett, *Religion*, 15.
54. Mirabeau, *Courrier,* no. 186 (3/5 1790), 145–47.
55. Tackett, *Religion, Revolution*, 10–11, 15.

56. Mongrédien, *French Music*, 161.

57. Van Kley, *Religious Origins*, 354–56; Sorkin, *Religious Enlightenment*, 273.

58. Mirabeau, *Courrier* 192 (15/17 Sept. 1790), 293–94.

59. *La Chronique de Paris*, no. 205 (24 July 1790), 817–18.

60. *Archives Parlementaires*, 17:184 (17 July 1790).

61. Ibid., 17:179 (17 July 1790).

62. Aston, *Religion and Revolution*, 153.

63. Marat, *L'Ami du peuple*, no. 311 (15 Dec. 1790), 1907.

64. Durozoy, *La Gazette de Paris*, 2 Jan. 1791, 2, and 24 Jan. 1791, 1.

65. *Journal de Paris*, no. 322 (18 Nov. 1790), 1310.

66. Malouet, *Mémoires*, 2:127; Margairaz, *François de Neufchâteau*, 212, 214.

67. *Journal de Paris*, no. 333 (29 Nov. 1790), 1353; Marat, *L'Ami du peuple*, no. 305 (9 Dec. 1790), 1879; Barnave, *De la Révolution*, 210.

68. *Journal de Perlet*, no. 510 (28 Dec. 1790), 2.

69. Ibid., no. 517 (4 Jan. 1790), 3; Tackett, *Religion, Revolution*, 20, 25.

70. Morellet, *Lettres*, 2:170; La Gorce, *Histoire religieuse*, 1:362; Sewell, "Ideologies and Social Revolutions," 80–81.

71. Kennedy, *Cultural History*, 151; Aston, *Religion and Revolution*, 110, 201.

72. Rutledge, *Le Creuset* 6 (20 Jan. 1791) and 7 (24 Jan. 1791).

73. *La Chronique de Paris*, no. 12 (12 Jan. 1791), 46.

74. Ibid., no. 10 (10 Jan. 1791), 38; Fréron, *L'Orateur du peuple* 4, no. 21 (Jan. 1791), 170 and 26, 205–6.

75. *Actes de la Commune* 2 (22 Jan. 1791), 199.

76. *Archives Parlementaires,* 28:893 (17 July 1791).

77. Aston, *Religion and Revolution*, 175; Jones, *Peasantry*, 197–98; E. Kennedy, *Cultural History*, 151.

78. Auerbach, "Politics, Protest," 156; Hanson, *Provincial Politics*, 58.

79. Rocher, "Aspects," 304.

80. Royou, *L'Ami du Roi*, 21 Dec. 1791, 3–4.

81. Tackett, *Religion, Revolution*, 109; Aston, *Religion and Revolution*, 151–52.

82. *La Feuille villageoise* 1, no. 21 (17 Feb. 1791), 392.

83. Ibid., no. 20 (10 Feb. 1791), 365–66.

84. Hermon-Belot, *L'Abbé Grégoire*, 109–11; Chopelin-Blanc, *De l'apologétique*, 376–77.

85. Royou, *L'Ami du Roi*, 3 Oct. 1791, 2–3; Gorsas, *Courrier des LXXXIII* 23, nos. 19 and 22 (19 and 22 April 1791), 321, 343.

86. Gorsas, *Courrier des LXXXIII* 23, no. 23 (23 April 1791), 355.

87. Aston, *Religion and Revolution*, 202; Sorkin, *Religious Enlightenment*, 286–89; Bourdin, *Le noir et le rouge*, 233.

88. Forrest, *Revolution in Provincial France*, 166–67.

89. Cousin, "Religion et Révolution," 141.

90. Casta, "Réorganisation," 55; Martin, *Violence et révolution*, 105.

91. *La Chronique de Paris*, no. 199 (18 July 1791), 804.

92. Ibid., no. 12 (12 Jan. 1791), 46; Tackett, *Religion, Revolution*, 221–22.

93. Brissot, *Le Patriote français* 553 (12 Feb. 1791), 171–72; Dard, *Hérault de Sechelles*, 138.

94. McManners, *Church and Society*, 1:407–8, 413.

95. *La Chronique de Paris*, no. 200 (19 July 1791), 809; Aston, *Religion and Revolution*, 15–16, 224; Tackett, *Religion, Revolution*, 294.
96. Tackett, *Religion, Revolution*, 76–77.
97. *Archives Parlementaires*, 24:548–51 (4 April 1791).
98. Ibid., 26:595 (25 May 1791).
99. *La Feuille villageoise* 1, no. 20 (10 Feb. 1791), 360–61.
100. Tackett, *Religion, Revolution*, 113–15.
101. *La Chronique de Paris*, no. 10 (10 Jan. 1791), 37.
102. Audouin, *Journal universel*, no. 561 (6 June 1791), 8087.
103. *Archives Parlementaires*, 36:277 (20 Dec. 1791).
104. Chopelin-Blanc, *De l'Apologétique*, 382–83; Tackett, *Religion, Revolution*, 32–34; Sorkin, *Religious Enlightenment*, 300.
105. *La Feuille villageoise* 1, no. 22 (24 Feb. 1791), 410; Tackett, *Religion, Revolution*, 110.
106. *Archives Parlementaires*, 82:684.
107. Tackett, *Religion, Revolution*, 173–75.
108. *La Feuille villageoise* 1, no. 20 (10 Feb. 1791), 365–66.
109. Ibid., no. 18 (27 Jan. 1791), 336.
110. *Assemblée Nationale, Corps administatifs* 4, 308 (8 June 1791), 3.
111. Culoma, *Religion civile*, 90; Forsyth, *Reason and Revolution*, 201.
112. Camus, *Observations*, 55; Royou, *L'Ami du Roi*, 23 Oct. 1791, 2; Tackett, *Religion, Revolution*, 27.
113. *Archives Parlementaires*, 28: 894 (17 July 1791).
114. Camus, *Observations*, 35, 51–52, 54, 57; Camus, *Opinion de M. Camus*, 2.
115. Ibid., 6; Auerbach, "Politics, Protest," 154.

CHAPTER 8

The Feuillant Revolution (July 1791–April 1792)

1. Fréron, *L'Orateur du peuple* 7, no. 7, 50–51; Roederer, *Spirit of the Revolution*, 37; Scurr, *Fatal Purity*, 152–53; Sonenscher, *Sans-Culottes*, 338.
2. *Archives Parlementaires*, 28:399–401 (18 July 1791); Burstin, *Révolution*, 254–56.
3. *Journal du Club des Cordeliers* 8 (21 July 1791), 69–71; Desmoulins, *Révolutions de France et de Brabant* 86 (July 1791), 6; Bailly, *Mémoires de Bailly*, 3:392; Martin, *Violence et révolution*, 116–17.
4. *Journal du Club des Cordeliers* 9 (25 July 1791), 75; Malouet, *Mémoires*, 2: 118–19; Scurr, *Fatal Purity*, 156, 183.
5. Fréron, *L'Orateur du peuple* 7, no. 2 (July 1791), 12–13; M. L. Kennedy, *Jacobin Clubs*, 239.
6. Žižek (ed.), *Robespierre*, 108; Scurr, *Fatal Purity*, 182; McPhee, *Robespierre*, 92.
7. *Journal du Club des Cordeliers* 9 (25 July 1791), 75.
8. Desmoulins, *Révolutions de France et de Brabant* 86 (July 1791), 27.
9. Ibid., 85 (July 1791), 292, 331; Paine, *Rights*, 151.
10. *La Chronique de Paris*, no. 201 (20 July 1791), 812.
11. Kates, *Cercle*, 170–71; Lawday, *Giant of the French Revolution*, 98–99.
12. *La Chronique de Paris*, no. 201 (20 July 1791), 812–13.

13. Desmoulins, *Révolutions de France et de Brabant* 86 (July 1791), 20–21; Lagrave, "Thomas Paine," 60.
14. Desmoulins, *Révolutions de France et de Brabant* 88 (August, 1791), 35.
15. Ibid. (July 1791), lxviii, 15; Audouin, *Journal universel*, no. 606 (21 July 1791), 120–48.
16. Desmoulins, *Révolutions de France et de Brabant* 67 (July 1791), 1–2.
17. *La Chronique du mois* 2 (April, 1792), 84.
18. Desmoulins, *Révolutions de France et de Brabant* 67 (July 1791), 10, and 88 (August 1791), 6; Pasquino, *Sieyès et l'invention*, 83.
19. Desmoulins, *Révolutions de France et de Brabant* 86 (July 1791), 27; Hermon-Belot, *L'Abbé Grégoire*, 178–79.
20. Desmoulins, *Révolutions de France et de Brabant* 67 (July 1791), 4.
21. *La Chronique de Paris*, no. 211 (30 July 1791), 853; M. L. Kennedy, *Jacobin Clubs*, 4, 221.
22. *La Chronique de Paris*, no. 248 (6 September 1791), 1003.
23. Fréron, *L'Orateur du peuple* 7, no. 6 (July 1791), 45.
24. Carra, *Annales patriotiques* 639 (3 July 1791), 1628.
25. Chisick, *Production, Distribution*, 56–59; Bertaud, *Les Amis du roi*, 44.
26. Marat, *L'Ami du peuple,* no. 529 (10 Aug. 1791), 3324–26.
27. Condorcet and Paine, *Le Républicain* 1:3–4; E. Badinter and R. Badinter, *Condorcet, 1743–1794*, 333–34.
28. "Lettre de Thomas Paine à M. l'Abbe Sieyès, Paris, 8 July 1791," in Condorcet and Paine, *Le Républicain* 3:52–56; Carra, *Annales Patriotiques* 650 (14 July 1791), 1681; Nelson, *Thomas Paine*, 212; D. Williams, *Condorcet and Modernity*, 31, 33.
29. Pasquino, *Sieyès et l'invention*, 80–86; Gauchet, *La Revolution*, 80–85.
30. Sieyès, *Manuscrits, 1773–1799*, 445; Forsyth, *Reason and Revolution*, 176–78; E. Badinter and R. Badinter, *Condorcet, 1743–1794*, 335–36.
31. Condorcet and Paine, *Le Républicain*, 2:17, 2:22.
32. *La Chronique de Paris*, no. 248 (6 Sept. 1791), 1003.
33. Ibid., no. 228 (16 August 1791), 921; Gueniffey, "Brissot," 437; Bates, "Political Pathologies," 446.
34. Carra, *Annales patriotiques* 639 (3 July 1791), 1628.
35. *La Chronique de Paris*, no. 207 (26 July 1791), 835–36.
36. Ibid., no. 211 (30 July 1791), 852 and no. 230 (18 August 1791), 927.
37. Ibid., no. 218 (6 August 1791), 879 and no. 220 (8 August 1791), 887.
38. Ibid., no. 220 (8 August 1791), 887; Hunt, *Family Romance*, 110, 114, 121; Whaley, *Radicals*, 53.
39. *La Chronique de Paris*, no. 211 (30 July 1791), 852.
40. *La Chronique du mois* 1 (1791), 28.
41. [Leger], *L'Auteur*, 16.
42. Ibid., 18, 34–35; Maslan, *Revolutionary Acts*, 58–60.
43. *Archives Parlementaires*, 29:151 (2 Sept. 1791).
44. Ibid., 29:189–90 (3 Sept. 1791).
45. Ibid., 29:633–35 (14 Sept. 1791); *La Chronique de Paris*, no. 256 (14 Sept. 1791), 1038.
46. *La Chronique de Paris*, no. 262 (20 Sept. 1791), 1060.

47. Williams, *Letters from France*, 2:2–3.

48. *La Chronique de Paris*, no. 248 (6 Sept. 1791), 1004.

49. Louvet, *Mémoires*, 1:26; Dard, *Hérault de Sechelles*, 148.

50. Royou, *L'Ami du Roi*, 31 Oct. 1791, 1.

51. Dickinson, "Counter-Revolution in Britain," 358–63.

52. Fréron, *L'Orateur du peuple* 6, no. 2 (July 1791), 11–13.

53. *La Chronique de Paris*, no. 218 (6 August 1791), 879; Royou, *L'Ami du Roi*, 13 Oct. 1791, 3–4.

54. Kennedy, *Jacobin Clubs*, 5–8, 366; Serna, *Antontelle, Aristocrate révolutionnaire*, 179–80; Monnier, "Républicanisme," 101.

55. Louvet, *Mémoires*, 1:37; Hampson, *Life and Opinions*, 99–100.

56. Constant, *De la Terreur*, 353–54; Lefebvre, *French Revolution*, 208.

57. Rousseau, *Social Contract*, 138–40; Miller, *Rousseau*, 205.

58. Royou, *L'Ami du Roi*, 27 Oct. 1791, 1.

59. Mortier, *Anacharsis Cloots*, 348.

60. Maslan, *Revolutionary Acts*, 55.

61. M. L. Kennedy, *Jacobin Clubs*, 56.

62. Ibid., 51–52, 358; Pineau-Defois, "Une élite," 110–11, 114, 117–18.

63. Mitchell, *French Legislative*, 208–9.

64. Royou, *L'Ami du Roi*, 5 Oct. 1791, 1; Mitchell, *French Legislative*, 15, 19–20, 22.

65. *La Chronique de Paris*, no. 257 (15 September 1791), 1041.

66. Tackett, "Conspiracy Obsession," 709; Mitchell, *French Legislative*, 19–20, 24, 274.

67. Mitchell, *French Legislative*, 29, 299.

68. M. L. Kennedy, *Jacobin Clubs*, 7–8.

69. *La Chronique de Paris*, no. 260 (18 September 1791), 1047–52.

70. Raynal, *Histoire philosophique*, 10: 66–67.

71. *La Chronique du mois* 2 (March, 1792), 3–6.

72. *Assemblée Nationale, Corps administratifs* 4, no. 295 (22 July 1792), 414–16; Dorigny, "Condorcet," 337.

73. Popkin, "From Dutch Republican," 543; Israel, *Democratic Enlightenment*, 273–74, 524–26.

74. *Assemblée Nationale, Corps administratifs* 4, no. 216 (4 May 1792), 267–69.

75. *La Chronique de Paris*, no. 257 (15 Sept. 1791), 1039; P. Jones, *Peasantry*, 87–88.

76. Royou, *L'Ami du Roi*, 26 Feb. 1792, 3.

77. *Archives Parlementaires*, 41:470 (11 April 1792).

78. Ibid., 41:485 (11 April 1792); P. Jones, *Peasantry*, 91–92, 120.

79. P. Jones, *Peasantry*, 92–93.

80. Royou, *L'Ami du Roi*, 3 Oct. 1791, 1–2.

81. Ibid., 26 Feb. 1792, 3–4; Bertaud, *Les Amis du roi*, 229.

82. *La Chronique du mois* 2 (April 1792), 87.

83. Ibid., 71–73.

84. *Archives Parlementaires*, 34:309–17 (20 Oct. 1791); Mitchell, *French Legislative*, 43.

85. C. Jones, *Great Nation*, 446–48, 456; Bates, "Political Pathologies," 451–52; Davidson, *How Revolutionary Were the Bourgeois Revolutions?*, 66–67.

86. *Archives Parlementaires*, 44:273–78 (29 May 1792); Louvet, *La Sentinelle*, no. 9 (1792), 1.

87. E. Badinter and R. Badinter, *Condorcet, 1743–1794*, 423–25; Whaley, *Radicals*, 60; May, *Madame Roland*, 217–19.

88. Roland, *Lettre écrite au Roi*, 11–12; Bertrand de Molleville, *Mémoires secrets*, 2:220–21, 231–32.

89. Mitchell, *French Legislative*, 3, 171–72, 212.

CHAPTER 9

The "General Revolution" Begins (1791–92)

1. Grüner, "Deutschland," 378.

2. Wedekind, "Einleitung und Kommentar," 37–38.

3. Rehberg, *Untersuchungen*, 1:98–99.

4. Ibid., 1:87; Pagden, *The Enlightenment*, 316.

5. *Journal de Paris*, no. 322 (18 Nov. 1790), 1307–8.

6. Malouet, *Mémoires*, 2:132; C. Jones, *Great Nation*, 456.

7. Popkin, *News*, 219; McPhee, *Robespierre*, 113–16.

8. Carra, *Annales patriotiques* 642 (6 July), 1643, and 643 (7 July), 1651.

9. Furet, *Interpreting the French Revolution*, 65–66; Doyle, *Oxford History*, 176; Doyle, *Aristocracy and Its Enemies*, 263–64.

10. Mallet du Pan, *Considérations*, 41.

11. Royou, *L'Ami du Roi*, 15 Oct. 1791, 1.

12. Furet, *Interpreting the French Revolution*, 126; Lawday, *Giant of the French Revolution*, 112–13.

13. *Relation exacte de ce qui s'est passé à Bruxelles* (March 1790), 4–7.

14. Dhont, "Conservatieve Brabantse omwenteling," 433–44; Van den Bossche, *Enlightened Innovation*, 44–46.

15. Feller, *Journal historique et littéraire* 1 (15 April 1793), 175–78; Van den Bossche, *Enlightened Innovation*, 177–80.

16. *La Feuille villageoise* 1, no. 10 (2 Dec. 1790), 183–84.

17. Weber, *Georg Christian Gottlieb Wedekind*, 156–57.

18. Blanning, *Reform and Revolution*, 273.

19. Rehberg, *Untersuchungen*, 2:117.

20. Ibid., 1:126–27, 1:150–52.

21. Ibid., 1:178–79, 1:210.

22. Losfeld, *Philanthropisme*, 3-4.

23. Ibid., 214–15, 225–26, 229–30, 233.

24. Blanning, *Reform and Revolution*, 272–73; Voss, "Die Kurpfalz im Zeichen," 16.

25. Ruiz, "Deutsche Jakobiner," 135.

26. Pestalozzi, *Sämtliche Briefe*, 3:280.

27. Hölderlin, *Sämtliche Werke*, 670–71.

28. Weber, *Georg Christian Gottlieb Wedekind*, 165.

29. Gaulmier, *Un grand témoin*, 130–31.

30. Hardman, *Louis XVI*, 139, 142–45; C. Jones, *Great Nation*, 454–55.

31. Malouet, *Mémoires*, 2:128–29.

32. Hardman, *Louis XVI*, 147; E. Badinter and R. Badinter, *Condorcet, 1743–1794*, 361.

33. Malouet, *Mémoires*, 2:132; Hamspon, *Life*, 95–96.

34. Malouet, *Mémoires*, 2:133; E. Badinter and R. Badinter, *Condorcet, 1743–1794*, 372–75.

35. *Archives Parlementaires*, 36:606 (29 Dec. 1791).

36. Doyle, *Oxford History*, 178–79; C. Jones, *Great Nation*, 455–56.

37. *Archives Parlementaires*, 36:607 (29 Dec. 1791).

38. Pestalozzi, *Sämtliche Briefe*, 3:287.

39. Jaume, *Le discours Jacobin*, 196–98.

40. Robespierre, "Sur la guerre (2 Jan. 1792), in Žižek (ed.), *Robespierre*, 115, 118–19.

41. *La Chronique du mois* 2 (May 1792), 24–25; Baker, *Condorcet*, 307–9.

42. *Archives Parlementaires*, 36:616–17 (29 Dec. 1791); Bouissounouse, *Condorcet*, 205–6.

43. *La Chronique du mois* 2 (May 1792), 123–24.

44. Ibid., 123, 125; Louvet, *Mémoires*, 1:44–45; Hampson, *Life and Opinions*, 99–100.

45. Hansen, *Quellen zur Geschichte*, 2:168–69.

46. Dumouriez, *Mémoires*, 1:2, 1:8.

47. Mallet du Pan, *Considérations*, 40.

48. *La Chronique du mois* 2 (May 1792), 38–39.

49. Baker, *Condorcet*, 307–8; Bell, *First Total War*, 114–17.

50. *La Chronique du mois* 2 (April 1792), 58–66.

51. Ibid. (May 1792), 62–63.

52. Rosendaal, *Bataven!*, 305–8.

53. Marat, *L'Ami du peuple*, no. 648 (3 May 1792), 3961–62; E. Badinter and R. Badinter, *Condorcet, 1743–1794*, 407.

54. E. Badinter and R. Badinter, *Condorcet, 1743–1794*; Tarin, *Diderot*, 60.

55. Marat, *L'Ami du peuple*, no. 648 (3 May 1792), 3963–64.

56. Ibid., no. 649 (6 May 1792), 3966–67.

57. E. Badinter and R. Badinter, *Condorcet, 1743–1794*, 409–10; Tarin, *Diderot*, 60.

58. Marat, *L'Ami du peuple*, no. 648 (3 May 1792), 3959.

59. Losfeld, *Philanthropisme*, 3–4, 184.

CHAPTER 10

The Revolutionary Summer of 1792

1. *Archives Parlementaires*, 75:523 (3 Oct. 1793); Mitchell, *French Legislative*, 134–39.

2. Louvet, *La Sentinelle*, no. 20 (1792), 1; Chaumette, *Mémoires*, 7; Baker, *Condorcet*, 309.

3. Burstin, *Révolution*, 369–72.

4. Louvet, *La Sentinelle*, no. 20 (1792), 1–2; Chaumette, *Mémoires*, 15.

5. Durozoy, *La Gazette de Paris*, 9 Aug 1792, 1.

6. Malouet, *Mémoires*, 2:138–39; Carra, *Annales patriotiques* 183 (1 July 1792), 806–7.

7. Brissot, *Opinion de J. P. Brissot*, 1–4.

8. Levasseur, *Mémoires*, 1:262.

9. May, *Madame Roland*, 215; E. Badinter and R. Badinter, *Condorcet, 1743–1794*, 384–86; Whatmore, *Republicanism*, 78–80.

10. Louvet, *La Sentinelle* 21 (1792), 1–5, and 23 (1792), 1; Furet, *Revolutionary France*, 110; Scurr, *Fatal Purity*, 191.

11. Robespierre, *Le Défenseur*, 5:215, 5:217, 5:225–26, 5:240.

12. Ibid., 1:1–2; Roederer, *De la philosophie moderne*, 29; E. Badinter and R. Badinter, *Condorcet, 1743–1794*, 410.

13. Robespierre, *Le Défenseur* 11 (July 1792), 538.

14. Ibid., 1; Scurr, *Fatal Purity*, 182, 184; McPhee, *Robespierre*, 91, 123.

15. Robespierre, *Le Défenseur*, 1:45 and 4:174–77.

16. Ibid., 4:184–86; McPhee, *Robespierre*, 107–8.

17. Robespierre, *Le Défenseur*, 4:186.

18. Ibid., 1:38–41; Scurr, *Fatal Purity*, 182.

19. Louvet, *La Sentinelle*, no. 1 (1792), 1.

20. Carra, *Annales patriotiques* 190 (8 July 1792), 838.

21. *La Chronique de Paris*, 26 June 1792, 711–12.

22. Burstin, *Révolution*, 378–79.

23. Chaumette, *Mémoires*, 33–34.

24. Baker, *Condorcet*, 313–14; E. Badinter and R. Badinter, *Condorcet, 1743–1794*, 391–93.

25. Chaumette, *Mémoires*, 37–38; Mandar, *Des Insurrections*, 189; Bertaud, *Les Amis du roi*, 244.

26. Pétion, *Les Vœux*, 8; Princeton UL Pamphlets 1509 178999, vol. 35, no. 10; Pétion, *Discours*, 1.

27. Carra, *Annales patriotiques*, 194 (12 July 1792), 856; Mongrédien, *French Music*, 44; Scurr, *Fatal Purity*, 202.

28. Durozoy, *La Gazette de Paris*, 7 Aug. 1792, 1 and 9 Aug. 1792, 1.

29. Bertaud, *Les Amis du roi*, 235.

30. *Extrait des Registres . . . Mauconseil*, 1–4; Carra, *Annales patriotiques*, 219 (6 Aug. 1792), 965, 968; Louvet, *La Sentinelle,* no. 47, 1–2.

31. Bayle, *De l'Inutilité*, 5, 7, 16, 28.

32. *Archives Parlementaires*, 47:627–28 (session: 9/10 August 1792).

33. Quoted in Baker, *Condorcet*, 313.

34. Slavin, *French Revolution*, 110–11.

35. Louvet, *Mémoires*, 2:142; Baker, *Condorcet*, 315.

36. Whaley, *Radicals*, 68–74.

37. Louvet, *Mémoires*, 2:244; Burstin, *Révolution*, 403–6.

38. Robespierre, *Le Défenseur* 12 (August), 570.

39. Robespierre, *Œuvres complètes*, 8:427; Rocques, *État de France*, 10; McPhee, *Robespierre*, 125–26; Ansart-Dourlen, *L'Action politique*, 152.

40. Durozoy, *La Gazette de Paris*, 10 Aug. 1792, 1; Martin, *Violence et révolution*, 135–39.

41. Gough, *Newspaper Press*, 87; Bertaud, *Les Amis du roi*, 247.

42. Louvet, *La Sentinelle*, no. 47 (12 Aug. 1792), 3–4; Chaumette, *Memoires*, 58–61; Mercier, *Paris,* 1:144–47; Slavin, *French Revolution*, 112–13.

43. *Archives Parlementaires*, 47:611 (session: 10 Aug. 1792); Boroumand, *La Guerre*, 304–5.
44. *Archives Parlementaires*, 47:692 (session: 10 Aug. 1792); Louvet, *La Sentinelle*, no. 47 (12 Aug. 1792), 6.
45. *Archives Parlementaires*, 47:691 (session: 10 Aug. 1792); Buonarroti, *Conspiration pour l'égalité*, 15; Woloch, "Contraction," 311.
46. *Archives Parlementaires*, 47:647–48 (session: 10 Aug. 1792).
47. E. Badinter and R. Badinter, *Condorcet, 1743–1794*, 457.
48. Whaley, *Radicals*, 76–77.
49. *Archives Parlementaires*, 48:151 (15 Aug. 1792); Robespierre, *Œuvres complètes*, 8:438.
50. Scott, *Terror and Repression*, 35–38; Johnson, *Midi in Revolution*, 204, 211.
51. Scott, *Terror and Repression*, 35–36.
52. Lanthenas, *Motifs*, 9–10.
53. Prudhomme, *Histoire générale*, 1:28.
54. Furet, *Revolutionary France*, 110.
55. *Archives Parlementaires*, 47:660 (session: 10 Aug. 1792).
56. Gorsas, *Courrier* 15 (15 Aug. 1792), 230; Robespierre, *Œuvres complètes*, 8:432.
57. Rocques, *État de France*, 2:26, 2:44, 2:75.
58. Gorsas, *Courrier* 14 (14 Aug. 1792), 215; Slavin, *French Revolution*, 120.
59. Carra, *Annales patriotiques*, no. 229 (16 Aug. 1792), 1011; Louvet, *La Sentinelle* 48 (15 Aug. 1792).
60. *Gazette nationale,* 3rd ser., 2, no. 20 (20 Jan. 1793), 178.
61. Girey-Dupré, *Patriote français* 1196 (18 Nov. 1792), "Discours de Jerome Pétion"; Buonarroti, *Conspiration pour l'égalité*, 20.
62. Mandar, *Des insurrections*, 6.
63. Hesse, "La Logique culturelle," 926–27.
64. Monnier, "L'Évolution," 61–62.
65. Wahnich, *L'impossible citoyen*, 175–77; Desan, "Foreigners," 89–91.
66. On Bolts, see Israel, *Democratic Enlightenment*, 590, 592–93.
67. Chénier, *Pétition*, 2.
68. Losfeld, *Philanthropisme*, 3–4, 177, 192–96; Desan, "Foreigners," 91.
69. Chénier, *Pétition*, 3–4; Schüttler, *Mitglieder*, 33; Hermann, *Knigge*, 148.
70. Klopstock, *Werke* 8, 1:272–74. Klopstock to Roland, Hamburg, 19 Nov. 1792.
71. *Archives Parlementaires*, 48:180–81 (15 Aug. 1792); Baker, *Condorcet*, 315; E. Badinter and R. Badinter, *Condorcet, 1743–1794*, 459–60.
72. Gueniffey, "L'election," 66–67.
73. Bertaud, *Les Amis du roi*, 250.
74. Robespierre, *Œuvres complètes*, 8:444–45.
75. *Archives Parlementaires*, 49:118 (30 Aug. 1792); Girey-Dupré, *Patriote français* 1118 (1 Sept. 1792), 249–52; Bluche, *Septembre 1792*, 42.
76. Robespierre, *Le Défenseur*, 1:48–49.
77. Louvet, *Mémoires*, 2:159–60; M. L. Kennedy, *Jacobin Clubs*, 182–83; Scott, *Terror and Repression*, 62.
78. Louvet, *La Sentinelle*, no. 52 (21 Aug. 1792), 1.
79. Ibid., no. 55 (29 Aug. 1792), 1.

80. Louvet, *Mémoires*, 2:150–51, 2:154–56; Baker, *Condorcet*, 315.
81. Robespierre, *Œuvres complètes*, 8:457–58.
82. Ibid., 8:459.
83. Ibid., 8:458.
84. Louvet, *Mémoires*, 2:195.
85. Ibid., 2:196–97; Coquard, *Jean-Paul Marat*, 360; Baker, *Condorcet*, 315.
86. Bluche, *Septembre 1792*, 38–39.
87. Levasseur, *Mémoires*, 1:540; Buzot, *Lettres*, 5, 8; Prudhomme, *Histoire générale*, 1:vii–viii; Cottebrune, *Mythe et réalité*, 166–70.
88. Mercier, *Paris*, 1:77; Necker, *De la Révolution*, 2:220.
89. Bluche, *Septembre 1792*, 99, 101; Martin, *Violence et révolution*, 141; Dupuy, *La république jacobine*, 24.
90. Aston, *Religion and Revolution*, 183.
91. Bluche, *Septembre 1792*, 122–33; Prudhomme, *Histoire générale*, 1:viii.
92. Mandar, *Des Insurrections*, 29; Girey-Dupré, *Patriote français* 1300 (4 March 1793), 262.
93. Ibid., 152–53; Guilhaumou, *L'Avènement*, 236; D'Espinchal, *Journal*, 368–69; Dupuy, *La république jacobine*, 22.
94. Necker, *De la Révolution*, 2:222, 2:228; Walter, *Marat*, 245–48.
95. Lawday, *Giant of the French Revolution*, 137–39; Bluche, *Septembre 1792*, 264–65.
96. Scurr, *Fatal Purity*, 200; McPhee, *Robespierre*, 129–30.
97. Levasseur, *Mémoires*, 1:379, 1:383; Guilhaumou, *L'Avènement*, 237–38; Whaley, *Radicals*, 84.
98. Girey-Dupré, *Patriote français* 1120 (2 Sept. 1792), 258 and 1121 (4 Sept. 1792), 263 and no. 1125 (8 Sept. 1792), 279; Bluche, *Septembre 1792*, 255.
99. Zizek, "Plume de fer," 639.
100. BL Pamphlets 645 a 38/6: Robert, *À ses comettans*, 5.
101. Louvet, *Mémoires*, 2:163–64; Bluche, *Septembre 1792*, 259; Guilhaumou, *L'Avènement*, 239.
102. Robespierre, *Œuvres complètes*, 8:461; Patrick, *The Men*, 183.
103. Louvert, *La Sentinelle,* no. 59 (14 Sept. 1792); McPhee, *Robespierre*, 131.
104. Louvet, *La Sentinelle,* no. 56 (31 Aug. 1792), 1; Slavin, *French Revolution*, 120–21.
105. Aulard, *La Société des jacobins*, 4:261.
106. Louvet, *Mémoires*, 2:151–53; Bredin, *Sieyès*, 235.
107. Louvet, *La Sentinelle,* no. 59 (14 Sept. 1792), 1.
108. Girey-Dupré, *Patriote français* 1125 (8 Sept. 1792), 279–80.
109. Levasseur, *Mémoires*, 1:54; Prudhomme, *Histoire générale*, 1:ix–xii, xxxiii; Louvet, *Mémoires*, 1:56–57 and 2:149–51; Gershoy, *Betrand Barère*, 126.
110. BL F664/5/no. 15: *Réponse du corps électoral de Paris*, 3; Louvet, *Mémoires*, 1:56.
111. Louvet, *La Sentinelle*, no. 58 (8 Sept. 1792); Bredin, *Sieyès*, 228–29.
112. Kennedy, "Development," 142; Patrick, *The Men*, 178.
113. Norberg, "Love," 40; Whaley, *Radicals*, 86–87.
114. Louvet, *Mémoires*, 2:93.
115. Levasseur, *Mémoires*, 1:51–52, 55.

CHAPTER 11

Republicans Divided (September 1792–March 1793)

1. *Journal de Perlet* 7, no. 385 (13 Oct. 1793), 96.
2. *La Quotidienne* 2 (23 Sept.), 2; La Harpe, *Réfutation*, 160.
3. Mercier, *Paris*, 2:362.
4. Gross, *Fair Shares*, 98; Shovlin, *Political Economy*, 201–2.
5. Lanthenas, *Motifs*, 9.
6. Dorigny, "Condorcet," 337.
7. Levasseur, *Mémoires*, 1:54; Mercier, *Paris*, 1:224–26.
8. Mercier, *Paris*, 1:93–94.
9. Ibid., 1:153–55; Levasseur, *Mémoires*, 1:62–63.
10. Bouissounouse, *Condorcet*, 241.
11. *La Quotidienne* 27 (18 Oct. 1792), 2.
12. Ibid., 8 (30 Sept. 1792), 2 and 25 (16 Oct.), 2.
13. Linton, *Conspiracies Real and Imagined*, 133.
14. BL FR 366/31: Brissot, *À tous les républicains*, 14–15, 21–22, 27; Dorigny, "Les Girondins," 576.
15. Lemny, *Jean-Louis Carra*, 289; Hanson, *Provincial Politics*, 50–51; Walton, *Policing Public Opinion*, 207.
16. Louvet, *Mémoires*, 2:125, 2:141.
17. Robespierre, *Œuvres complètes*, 9:45, 9:58.
18. Louvet, *Mémoires*, 1:65; Albouys, *Principes constitutionelles*, 77; Walton, *Policing Public Opinion*, 207.
19. Louvet, *Mémoires*, 2:126–27.
20. *La Quotidienne* 1 (22 Sept. 1792), 2.
21. Levasseur, *Mémoires*, 1:59.
22. Fauchet, *Journal des Amis*, 1:29–32.
23. Mercier, *Paris*, 1:93–94.
24. Palmer, *From Jacobin to Liberal*, 24.
25. Buonarroti, *Conspiration pour l'égalité*, 16–17.
26. Mercier, *Paris*, 1:229.
27. Mercier, *Mémoires*, 1:223.
28. Desmoulins, *Vieux Cordelier*, 114, 117, 134–35.
29. *La Chronique du mois* 2 (May 1792), 27; Proly, *Le Cosmopolite*, 394 (26 March 1792); Mercier, *Paris*, 1:184–85; May, *Madame Roland*, 233–36.
30. Louvet, *La Sentinelle*, no. 61 (29 Sept. 1792).
31. Ibid., no. 62 (4 Oct. 1792), 1.
32. M. L. Kennedy, *Jacobin Clubs*, 297.
33. Mandar quoting Diderot and Raynal, Mandar, *Des Insurrections*, 76.
34. Mandar, *Des Insurrections*, 18–21, 45.
35. Ibid., 113.
36. Ibid., 76.
37. Ibid., 57–64.
38. Ibid., 136.
39. Courtenay was a British MP who visited Paris in 1789 and who often spoke in Parliament and ridiculed Burke; see Locke, *Edmund Burke*, 2:146n, 2:245; Mandar, *Des Insurrections*, 122.

40. Rousseau, *Discourses*, 115–16.
41. Mandar, *Des Insurrections*, 202–3.
42. Ibid., 245.
43. Ibid., 255.
44. *Archives Parlementaires*, 53, 50–51 (29 Oct. 1792); Lawday, *Giant of the French Revolution*, 201–3, 229–31.
45. *Archives Parlementaires*, 53 (29 Oct. 1792), 52–58; Louvet, *Mémoires*, 1:59–60 and 2:91; Levasseur, *Mémoires*, 1:80–82, 1:535–37; Hampson, *Life and Opinions*, 132; Scurr, *Fatal Purity*, 213–14.
46. Robespierre, *Œuvres complètes*, 9:63; Louvet, "Accusation contre Maximilien Robespierre," in Louvet, *Mémoires*, 2:106; Gershoy, *Betrand Barère*, 133; Dingli, *Robespierre*, 286–88.
47. Louvet, *Mémoires*, 1:60–61.
48. Labbé, *Anacharsis Cloots*, 160.
49. Cloots, *Ni Marat, ni Roland*, 1–4; Gouges, *Pronostic*, in Gouges, *Œuvres*, 338–39.
50. Mortier, *Anacharsis Cloots*, 345.
51. May, *Madame Roland*, 235–36; Mortier, *Anacharsis Cloots*, 334.
52. Prudhomme, *Révolutions de Paris*, no. 176 (week 17/24 November 1792), 407–9; Mortier, *Anacharsis Cloots*, 341–42.
53. Mortier, *Anacharsis Cloots*, 346.
54. *Archives Parlementaires,* 57:32 (session: 13 Jan. 1793); Buzot, *Lettres*, 6.
55. *Journal de Perlet* 1, no. 70 (30 Nov. 1792), 559.
56. Villette to the mayor of Paris in *Gazette nationale*, no. 1 (1 Jan. 1793), 3.
57. *Gazette nationale*, 3rd ser., no. 1 (1 Jan. 1793), 8.
58. *Archives Parlementaires*, 55:33–34 (13 Jan. 1793).
59. Marat, *L'Ami du peuple*, no. 92 (3 Jan. 1793), 5416; no. 93 (9 Jan. 1793), 5443; and no. 96 (12 Jan. 1793), 5462; Mortier, *Anacharsis Cloots*, 432.
60. Marat, *L'Ami du peuple*, no. 97 (13 Jan. 1793), 5468.
61. Hébert, *Père Duchesne* 201 (1792), 6; Marat, *L'Ami du peuple* 93 (9 Jan. 1793), 5443, 5446.
62. Hébert, *Père Duchesne* 201 (1792), 7.
63. Ibid., 4; Hunt, *Family Romance*, 120.
64. Hébert, *Père Duchesne* 201 (1792), 5.
65. Ibid., 1–2; *Père Duchesne* 206, 7 and 211, 2.
66. *Journal de Perlet* 2, no. 100 (30 Dec. 1792), 237.
67. Ibid., 4, no. 216 (25 April 1793), 197.
68. Ibid., 2, no. 104 (3 Jan. 1793), 268; Bell, *Cult of the Nation*, 114, 116, 121, 134.
69. *Journal de Perlet* 2, no. 108 (7 Jan. 1793), 298.
70. *Gazette nationale*, 3rd ser., 2, no. 4 (4 Jan. 1793.), 29–30; Hébert, *Père Duchesne*, 208, 3; Darlow, *Staging the French Revolution*, 151–52.
71. *Journal de Perlet* 2, no. 113 (12 Jan. 1793), 343.
72. Ibid., no. 112 (12 Jan. 1793), 332; *Gazette nationale,* 3rd ser., 2, no. 13 (13 Jan.); Welschinger, *Le Théâtre*, 388–90.
73. *Archives Parlementaires*, 55:12 (session: 12 Jan. 1793); *Gazette nationale*, 3rd ser., 2, no. 14 (14 Jan.), 124.
74. Hébert, *Père Duchesne* 208, 3–4.
75. *Archives Parlementaires*, 52:331 (16–17 Jan. 1793).

76. Ibid., 52:331–33, 52:339 (1–17 Jan. 1793); *Gazette nationale,* 3rd ser., 2, no. 15 (15 Jan.), 125–26; Maslan, *Revolutionary Acts,* 63.

77. *Journal de Perlet* 2, no. 113 (12 Jan. 1793), 343, and no. 116 (15 Jan. 1793), 366.

78. *Archives Parlementaires,* 67:333 (1–17 Jan. 1793); *Journal de Perlet* 2, no. 118 (17 Jan. 1793) 377–79.

79. Maslan, *Revolutionary Acts,* 186–91, 205–7.

80. Hébert, *Père Duchesne,* 208, 4.

81. Ibid., 7–8.

82. Lemny, *Jean-Louis Carra,* 290.

83. *Journal de Perlet* 2, no. 102 (1 Jan. 1793), 255.

84. Desmoulins, *Vieux Cordelier,* 75.

85. *Archives Parlementaires,* 82:684 (4 Jan. 1794).

86. M. L. Kennedy, *Jacobin Clubs,* 183–84.

87. Louvet, *Mémoires,* 1:43–44.

88. May, *Madame Roland,* 224–25; Dorigny, "Condorcet," 338.

89. Roland, *Memoirs,* 81–84; May, *Madame Roland,* 192, 197.

90. Garat, "Jugement sur Mirabeau," xi.

91. Brissot, *Mémoires (1734–1793),* 2:113–14.

92. Scurr, *Fatal Purity,* 218; Culoma, *Religion civile,* 191.

93. Feller, *Journal historique et littéraire* (Maastricht, 15 Jan., 1793), 148; Hampson, *Will and Circumstance,* 173.

94. Gouges, *Pronostic,* in Gouges, *Œuvres,* 122; Scott, *Only Paradoxes,* 51.

95. Hampson, *Life and Opinions,* 82–83, 98, 108, 240; McPhee, *Robespierre,* 94.

96. *Journal de Perlet* 2, no. 108 (7 Jan. 1793), 300; *Gazette nationale,* 3rd ser., no. 11 (11 Jan. 1793), 95–96.

97. Levasseur, *Mémoires,* 1:102–3.

98. *Archives Parlementaires,* 56:34–36 (13 Jan. 1793).

99. *Adresse de la section Gravilliers* (4 Aug. 1792), 4–6.

100. BN pamph. Lb 41 2728, *Lettre de Jerome Pétion aux Parisiens,* 12.

101. Walzer, *Regicide,* 125–27; Hampson, *Saint-Just,* 84–85.

102. *Gazette nationale,* 3rd ser., no. 19 (19 Jan. 1793), 171.

103. *Archives Parlementaires,* 55:93 (15 Jan. 1793).

104. *Gazette nationale,* 3rd ser., no. 4 (4 Jan. 1793), 34.

105. Ibid., no. 2 (2 Jan. 1793), 11–13; Marat, *L'Ami du peuple* 96 (12 Jan. 1793), 5457–59.

106. *Archives Parlementaires,* 52:87 (18 Jan. 1793).

107. Bredin, *Sieyès,* 247.

108. *Gazette nationale,* 3rd ser., no. 19 (19 Jan. 1793), 168.

109. *Journal de Perlet* 2, no. 118 (17 Jan. 1793), 377–78 and 119 (18 Jan. 1793), 385, 389.

110. *Gazette nationale,* 3rd ser., no. 19 (19 Jan. 1793), 173; *Journal de Perlet* 2, no. 118 (17 Jan. 1793), 377–78; Patrick, *The Men,* 96–97.

111. Lemny, *Jean-Louis Carra,* 298.

112. *Gazette nationale,* 3rd ser., no. 20 (20 Jan. 1793), 191.

113. Hébert, *Père Duchesne* 210, 2; Mortier, *Anacharsis Cloots,* 368–69.

114. Mercier, *Paris*, 2:205; Walzer, *Regicide*, 49–60; Bredin, *Sieyès*, 247.

115. *Archives Parlementaires*, 57 (16 Jan. 1793).

116. Hébert, *Père Duchesne* 215 (early February 1793), 2.

117. *Gazette nationale*, 3rd ser., no. 1 (1 Jan. 1793), 3–4.

118. *Archives Parlementaires*, 61:14 (31 March 1793); Rose, *Gracchus Babeuf*, 129; Slavin, *French Revolution*, 129n8 and 130–32.

119. *Archives Parlementaires*, 61:14–15 (31 March 1793); Girey-Dupré, *Patriote français*, 1327 (2 April 1793), 367.

120. Marat, *L'Ami du peuple*, no. 142 (March 1793), 5812–16; Marat, *L'Ami du peuple*, no. 143 (11 March 1793), 5817–21.

121. Quoted in Boursier, "L'émeute parisienne," 211; Burstin, *Révolution*, 536–37.

122. Girey-Dupré, *Patriote français* 1307 (11 March 1793), 288–89; Louvet, *Mémoires*, 1:76–78 and 2:227–31, 239–40; Bellanger, *Histoire generale*, 1:506 Boursier, "L'émeute parisienne," 215.

123. Auerbach, "Politics, Protest," 158–59.

124. Slavin, *French Revolution*, 132; Whaley, *Radicals*, 125.

125. Girey-Dupré, *Patriote français* 1308 (13 March 1793), 297; Louvet, *Mémoires*, 2:244; Boursier, "L'émeute parisienne," 229–30.

126. Sonenscher, *Sans-Culottes*, 273; Whaley, *Radicals*, 124–25.

127. BL Pamphlets 645 a 38/6 dated Paris, 14 March 1793, 4–6; Walter, *Marat*, 340, 344; Rose, *Gracchus Babeuf*, 132–33.

128. Marat, *L'Ami du peuple* 145 (15 March 1793), 5862; Burstin, *Révolution*, 362–63, 549–52.

129. Robespierre, *Œuvres complètes*, 9:323; Girey-Dupré, *Patriote français* 1356 (30 April 1793), 479–80; Levasseur, *Mémoires*, 1:116 and 2:263; Ozouf, *Festivals*, 148–49; Slavin, *Making*, 15.

130. Louvet, *Mémoires*, 2:239–40; Boursier, "L'émeute parisienne," 207, 210, 213, 216.

131. M. L. Kennedy, *Jacobin Clubs*, 341–42.

CHAPTER 12

The "General Revolution" from Valmy to the Fall of Mainz (1792–93)

1. Goethe to Herder, 27 Sept. 1792, in Herder, *Briefe*, 13:338.

2. Mortier, *Anacharsis Cloots*, 379–81; Labbé, *Anacharsis Cloots*; Pagden, *The Enlightenment*, 127.

3. Dumouriez, *Mémoires*, 1:5.

4. Mortier, *Anacharsis Cloots*, 324.

5. Ibid., 333; Bell, *First Total War*, 114, 116.

6. Cloots, *Ni Marat, ni Roland*, 3–4; *Journal de Perlet* 3, no. 181 (21 March 1793), 385; Buel, *Joel Barlow*, 158–59.

7. *La Chronique de Paris*, no. 216 (4 Aug. 1791), 871.

8. Mortier, *Anacharsis Cloots*, 360; Rosendaal, *Bataven!*, 358–66; Rosendaal, *Nederlandse Revolutie*, 83–93; Cottebrune, *Mythe et réalité*, 130–61.

9. Forster, *Werke, Sämtliche Schriften*, 17:213–14, 216; Blanning, *Reform and Revolution*, 276; Wegert, *German Radicals*, 19–21.

10. Voss, "Die Kurpfalz im Zeichen," 16–19.
11. Klopstock, *Werke* 8, no. 2, 970–71.
12. *Journal de Perlet* 2, no. 72 (2 Dec. 1792), 9–10; Mathy, "Anton Joseph Dorsch," 18–20.
13. Forster, *Werke, Sämtliche Schriften,* 17:284–85, 308–10.
14. Wedekind, *Der Patriot*, vol. 1/A, 3; Blanning, *Reform and Revolution*, 276–77.
15. Wedekind, *Der Patriot*, vol. 1/A, 12–14.
16. Ibid., 5–20.
17. Wedekind, *Der Patriot*, vol. 1/C, 2–3.
18. Blanning, *Reform and Revolution*, 277–78.
19. BL 643/4 Revolution Tracts: Condorcet, "Aux Germains," 6, 23–24.
20. Ibid., "Adresse aux Bataves," 4–5.
21. Ibid., "Avis aux espagnols," 9–10, 16–17.
22. *Journal de Perlet* 1, no. 63 (23 Nov. 1792), 504; Kossmann, *Low Countries*, 68.
23. Feller, *Journal historique et littéraire* 1 (1 Jan. 1793), 77–79.
24. Ibid. (15 Jan. 1793), 154.
25. Ibid. (1 March 1793), 396–97.
26. *Gazette nationale*, 3rd ser., 1 (1 Jan. 1793), 1.
27. Ibid., 2, no. 20 (20 Jan. 1793), 177.
28. Ibid., 2, no. 15 (15 Jan. 1793), 125–26.
29. Ibid., 2, no. 6 (6 Jan. 1793).
30. Feller, *Journal historique et littéraire* 1 (1 April 1793), 552.
31. *Journal de Perlet*, no. 79 (9 Dec. 1792), 71; Dumouriez, *Mémoires*, 1:22–23; Godechot, *Counter-Revolution*, 167–68.
32. Feller, *Journal historique et littéraire* 1 (15 March 1793), 466–67.
33. *Neue Mainzer Zeitung*, no. 24 (24 Feb. 1793), in Forster, *Werke, Sämtliche Schriften*, 10:345.
34. Hansen, *Quellen zur Geschichte*, 2:63.
35. Ibid., 2:277–78, 313–14.
36. Losfeld, *Philanthropisme*, 147–48.
37. Hansen, *Quellen zur Geschichte*, 2:710–11.
38. Ibid., 2:694–96, 710.
39. Weber, *Georg Christian Gottlieb Wedekind*, 65–67.
40. Hansen, *Quellen zur Geschichte*, 2:713–14.
41. Ibid., 2:743–45.
42. Dupuy, "Le Roi," 198.
43. Feller, *Journal historique et littéraire* 1 (15 Jan. 1793), 152.
44. Ibid., 151.
45. Ibid. (15 March 1793), 407–15.
46. Gibbon, *Memoirs of My Life*, 283, 289; Spurr, "Gibbon et la révolution," 272.
47. Gibbon, *Memoirs of My Life*, 266, 270, 275.
48. Ibid., 286–88.
49. *Gazette nationale,* 3rd ser., 2, no. 18 (18 Jan. 1793), 154; *Journal de Perlet* 2, no. 92 (22 Dec. 1792), 176, and no. 96 (26 Dec. 1792), 205; *Neue Mainzer Zeitung* 13 (29 Jan. 1793), in Forster, *Werke, Sämtliche Schriften*, 10:263.
50. Gibbon, *Memoirs of My Life*, 286–87; Spurr, "Gibbon et la révolution," 272–73.

51. Gibbon, *Memoirs of My Life*, 292; Spurr, "Gibbon et la révolution," 273.

52. Gibbon, *Memoirs of My Life*, 292.

53. Cottebrune, *Mythe et réalité*, 186, 188, 194.

54. Beretti, *Pascal Paoli*, 24.

55. *La Chronique de Paris* 2, no. 218 (6 Aug. 1790), 870.

56. "Extrait d'une lettres de Bastia en Corse," in *La Chronique de Paris* 2, no. 218 (6 Aug. 1790), 870.

57. Beretti, *Pascal Paoli*, 247.

58. Casta, "Clergé corse," 17–18.

59. Volney, *Œuvres*, 1:631–32, 634; Gaulmier, *Un grand témoin*, 137–38.

60. Michaud, *La Quotidienne*, no. 298 (5 July 1793), 726.

61. Girey-Dupré, *Patriote français* 1328 (2 April 1793), 370.

62. Knigge, *Ausgewählte Werke*, 10:107.

63. Ibid., 10:108; *Journal de Perlet* 2, no. 100 (30 Dec. 1792), 238.

64. Mühlpfordt, "Deutsche Union," 356, 386–87; Losfeld, *Philanthropisme*, 10–11; Israel, *Democratic Enlightenment*, 832–40.

65. Constantine, *Hölderlin*, 18–22.

66. Pinkard, *Hegel*, 50–51; Constantine, *Hölderlin*, 26–27.

67. Mühlpfordt, "Deutsche Union," 357–58, 368.

68. Klopstock, *Werke*, 8:1062, 8:1069; Weber, *Georg Christian Gottlieb Wedekind*, 196–98.

69. Schütt, "Von Kiel nach Paris," 36–37; Israel, *Democratic Enlightenment*, 846–56.

70. Knigge to Campe, 9 July 1792, in Knigge, *Ausgewählte Werke*, 10:96.

71. Fichte, *Schriften*, 17, 28; Sauter, *Visions*, 107, 120–21.

72. Fichte, *Schriften*, 64, 66, 70, 91.

73. Cramer to Klopstock, Kiel, 22 Feb. 1793, in Klopstock, *Werke* 8:1; Åhlén et al., *Censur och tryckfrihet*, 93, 100, 104.

74. Girey-Dupré, *Patriote français* 1269 (1 Feb. 1793), 129; [Feller], *Journal historique et littéraire* 1 (1 Feb. 1793), 195–96, and 1 (15 Feb. 1793), 281–82; Forster, *Werke, Sämtliche Schriften*, 10:289, 10:388.

75. Rosendaal, *Bataven!*, 385–86.

76. [Feller], *Journal historique* 1 (1 March 1793), 395.

77. Ibid., 1 (1 April 1793), 544.

78. Dumouriez, *Mémoires*, 1:125–26 and 2:5, 32.

79. Ibid., 2:32; Rosendaal, *Bataven!*, 312–18, 383.

80. Dumouriez, *Mémoires*, 2:42; Rosendaal, *Bataven!*, 193–96.

81. Hansen, *Quellen zur Geschichte*, 2:751–52, 755; Forster, *Werke, Sämtliche Schriften*, 10:142.

82. [Feller], *Journal historique* 1 (15 March 1793), 541; Uhlig, *Georg Forster*, 205.

83. Hansen, *Quellen zur Geschichte*, 2:758–60.

84. [Feller], *Journal historique* 1 (1 April 1793), 563.

85. *Archives Parlementaires*, 60:560, 60:584–85 (20 and 26 March 1793).

86. [Feller], *Journal historique* 1 (1 April 1793), 562; *Journal de Perlet* 4, 193 (2 April 1793), 14–15.

87. [Feller], *Journal historique* 1 (1 April 1793), 566–67.

88. *Journal de Perlet* 4 (12 April 1793), 94.

89. Dumouriez, *Mémoires*, 2:142, 2:147–50.

90. *Archives Parlementaires,* 10:729–30 (30 March 1793); Girey-Dupré, *Patriote français* 1326 (31 March 1793), 361; Wegert, *German Radicals,* 43–45, 47–48.

91. Forster *Werke, Sämtliche Schriften,* 10:555.

92. Ibid., 17:310; Mathy, "Anton Joseph Dorsch," 21.

93. Forster, *Werke, Sämtliche Schriften,* 17:314.

94. Hansen, *Quellen zur Geschichte,* 2:814–15.

95. Cottebrune, *Mythe et réalité,* 397.

96. Ibid., 162–72.

97. Uhlig, *Georg Forster,* 204–7.

98. Locke, *Edmund Burke,* 2:434.

99. Roe, *Wordsworth and Coleridge,* 98–103.

100. [Feller], *Journal historique* 1 (15 April 1793), 627–28.

101. Dumouriez, *Mémoires,* 2:16.

102. Girey-Dupré, *Patriote français* 1372 (17 May 1793), 548; Buel, *Joel Barlow,* 168; Blanc, *La Corruption,* 85–86, 89.

103. Herder to Klopstock, Weimar, 12 May 1793, in Herder, *Briefe,* 7:42–43.

CHAPTER 13

The World's First Democratic Constitution (1793)

1. Charles Pottier, deputy for Indre-et-Loire, see *Archives Parlementaires,* 67:376 (24 June 1793).

2. Aberdam, "Délibérations," 17.

3. Girey-Dupré, *Patriote français* 1291 (22 Feb. 1793), 222; E. Badinter and R. Badinter, *Condorcet,* 1743–1794, 513–14; Favreau, "Gensonné," 424.

4. Sieyès, *Manuscrits, 1773–1799,* 456–59, 464–66; Baudot, *Notes historiques,* 220; Forsyth, *Reason and Revolution,* 180; Bredin, *Sieyès,* 257.

5. Sieyès, *Manuscrits, 1773–1799,* 470; Baudot, *Notes historiques,* 225.

6. Buonarroti, *Conspiration pour l'égalité,* 17; Gershoy, *Betrand Barère,* 168.

7. Sonenscher, *Sans-Culottes,* 219; Urbinati, *Representative Democracy,* 176–87.

8. Bates, *Enlightenment Aberrations,* 81–89.

9. E. Badinter and R. Badinter, *Condorcet, 1743–1794,* 514.

10. *Archives Parlementaires,* 67:365 (24 June 1793).

11. *Archives Parlementaires,* 57:604–5 (15 Feb. 1793).

12. Dard, *Hérault de Sechelles,* 229; Gueniffey, "Les Assemblées," 247.

13. Albouys, *Principes constitutionnels,* 179.

14. Articles XI and XII of the 1793 Constitution, *Archives Parlementaires,* 67:145; Baker, *Condorcet,* 321–22.

15. *Archives Parlementaires,* 67:289 (24 June 1793).

16. Poultier Delmotte, in *Archives Parlementaires,* 67:383 (24 June 1793).

17. Ibid., 67:382 (24 June 1793).

18. *Archives Parlementaires,* 67:366 (24 June 1793); Baker, *Condorcet,* 323.

19. Urbinati, *Representative Democracy,* 174–75.

20. *Archives Parlementaires,* 67:364 (24 June 1793).

21. Ibid., 67:325 (24 June 1793).

22. Ibid., 67:327 (24 June 1793).

23. Rutledge, *Le Creuset* 18 (3 March 1791), 350.
24. *La Chronique du mois* 5 (Feb. 1793), 39; Gauchet, *Révolution*, 114.
25. D. Williams, *Observations sur la dernière Constitution*, 583–86, 589; Sonenscher, *Sans-Culottes*, 42–44.
26. Condorcet, *Tableau historique*, 857.
27. Picqué, *Au peuple*, 372.
28. Ibid., 370–71.
29. Condorcet, *Tableau historique*, 858.
30. Montgilbert, *Avis au peuple*, 341–42; Edelstein, *Terror*, 192–93.
31. Montgilbert, *Avis au peuple*, 348–49; D. Williams, *Condorcet and Modernity*, 275.
32. Condorcet, *Tableau historique*, 785.
33. Billaud-Varenne, "Elements," extracts, in *Archives Parlementaires*, 67:222 (21 June 1793).
34. Marat, *L'Ami du peuple,* no. 123 (15 Feb. 1793), 5677–78.
35. Brissot in *La Chronique du mois* 5 (Feb. 1793), 28.
36. Ibid., 5 (Feb. 1793), 28–29, 33–34.
37. Condorcet, "Rapport," in *Archives Parlementaires*, 58:583 (15 Feb. 1793); Boroumand, "Girondins," 245.
38. Condorcet, "Rapport," in *Archives Parlementaires*, 58:590 (15 Feb. 1793); Jaume, "Individu et souveraineté," 300.
39. Condorcet, "Rapport," in *Archives Parlementaires*, 58:591–92 (15 Feb. 1793).
40. Draft Declaration of the Rights of Man, *Archives Parlementaires*, 53:601–2; Marat, *L'Ami du peuple*, no. 126 (18 Feb. 1793), 5692; Bredin, *Sieyès*, 258.
41. *Journal de Perlet* 4, no. 215 (24 April 1793), 188–89.
42. Tulard, *Histoire,* 94; Culoma, *Religion civile,*146
43. Gross, *Fair Shares*, 45.
44. Favreau, "Gensonné," 424.
45. *Archives Parlementaires*, 58:604–5 (15 Feb. 1793); Jaume, "Individu et souveraineté," 301.
46. Pertué, "Les projets constitutionnels de 1793," 183.
47. Salle , *Examen critique*, 394–95; Furet, " Roussseau," 177.
48. Marat, *L'Ami du peuple*, no. 126 (18 Feb. 1793), 5693.
49. *Archives Parlementaires*, 58:624 (16 Feb. 1793); Marat, *L'Ami du peuple*, no. 126 (18 Feb. 1793), 5693.
50. Marat, *L'Ami du peuple*, no. 126 (18 Feb. 1793), 5694; Pertué, "Les projets," 174.
51. Quoted in Gueniffey, "Les Assemblées," 247.
52. Condorcet, "Sur la necessité," 24.
53. Ibid., 25; Miller, *Rousseau*, 157–58; Boroumand, *La Guerre*, 176.
54. Condorcet, "Sur la necessité," 26.
55. *Archives Parlementaires*, 59:41 (20 Feb. 1793).
56. Girey-Dupré, *Patriote français*, 1304 (8 March 1793), 276–77 and 1306 (10 March 1793), 283–85; Garrone, *Gilbert Romme*, 359–60.
57. Girey-Dupré, *Patriote français*, 1325 (30 March 1793), 357.
58. *Archives Parlementaires*, 58:43–44 (20 Feb. 1793); Marat, *L'Ami du peuple* 126 (18 Feb. 1793), 5694.

59. *Archives Parlementaires*, 58:625 (16 Feb. 1793); Bredin, *Sieyès*, 259.
60. Marat, *L'Ami du peuple* 126 (18 Feb. 1793), 5694.
61. Saint-Just, "Discours sur la constitution" (24 April 1793), in Saint-Just, *Œuvres complètes*, 543; Urbinati, *Representative Democracy*, 163.
62. Saint-Just, "Discours sur la constitution" (24 April 1793), in Saint-Just, *Œuvres complètes*, 546.
63. Ibid., 544.
64. Ibid., 547.
65. *Journal de Perlet* 4, no. 216 (25 April 1793), 196; Hampson, *Saint-Just*, 101–4.
66. Saint-Just, *Œuvres completes*, 555; Hampson, *Saint-Just*, 102–3.
67. Hampson, *Saint-Just*, 102–3; Bredin, *Sieyès*, 259–60; Boroumand, "Girondins," 250–51.
68. Gueniffey, "Les Assemblées," 250–51.
69. Albouys, *Principes constitutionnels*, in *Archives Parlementaires*, 67:178.
70. Guyomar, *Partisan de l'égalité*, 592; Sophie de Condorcet, *Lettres*, 34; Gainot, "Pierre Guyomar," 261–62, 267–70.
71. *Archives Parlementaires*, 67:186 (24 June 1793).
72. Ibid., 67:415; Culoma, *Religion civile*, 159–61; Aston, *Religion and Revolution*, 97.
73. Boroumand, "Girondins," 244–46; Garrone, *Gilbert Romme*, 361–62, 398.
74. *Archives Parlementaires*, 63:241 (24 April 1793).
75. Ibid., 63:561–67 (29 April 1793).
76. Bohan, *Observations*, 251.
77. Ibid., 252.
78. Bonguyod, *Reflexions,* in *Archives Parlementaires*, 67:253–54.
79. Baraillon, "Projet de constitution," in *Archives Parlementaires*, 67:187–89.
80. *Archives Parlementaires*, 60:562 (29 April 1793) and 67:285–86 (24 June 1793); Welch, *Liberty and Utility*, 26–27; Jennings, *Revolution*, 49–50.
81. Daunou, "Remarques," in *Archives Parlementaires*, 67:283.
82. *Archives Parlementaires*, 62:263 (24 June 1793).
83. Ibid., 62:266 (24 June 1793).
84. Boroumand, "Girondins," 247–48.
85. Coupé, *Idées simples de Constitution,* in *Archives Parlementaires*, 67:266–67; Gross, *Fair Shares*, 96, 182.
86. Coupé, *Idées simples de Constitution,* in *Archives Parlementaires*, 67:268; Girey-Dupré, *Patriote français* 1310 (15 March 1793) 304–5; Ikni, "Jacques-Marie Coupé," 345–46, 348; Edelstein, *Terror*, 192n73.
87. *Archives Parlementaires*, 67:403–7 (24 June 1793); Hampson, *Life and Opinions*, 168.
88. *Archives Parlementaires*, 64:428-33 (10 May 1793); Robespierre, *Œuvres complètes*, 9:495–500.
89. Condorcet, *Political Writings*, 185; Wokler, *Rousseau*, 202.
90. Billaud-Varenne, *Les Élements du republicanisme*, 224.
91. Montgilbert, *Advis au peuple*, 330–31, 333, 337.
92. Billaud-Varenne, *Les Éléments du républicanisme*, 232; Billaud-Varenne, *Principes*, 83, 85, 87, 95.

93. Billaud-Varenne, *Les Éléments du républicanisme*, 236; Edelstein, *Terror*, 215.
94. Billaud-Varenne, *Les Éléments du républicanisme*, 235.
95. Harmand, *Observations*, 320–24; Gross, *Fair Shares*, 43, 64.
96. Herault's "Declaration of Rights and Constitution," in *Archives Parlementaires*, 66:259–64 (10 June 1793).
97. Tulard, *Histoire et dictionnaire*, 694; *Archives Parlementaires*, 58:601 (15 Feb. 1793).
98. Salles, *Examen critique*, 392–93; *Archives Parlementaires*, 66:262 (10 June 1793).
99. Salles, *Examen critique*, 395.
100. *Archives Parlementaires*, 66:257–58, 66:263 (10 June 1793); Dard, *Hérault de Sechelles*, 229–30.
101. *Archives Parlementaires*, 67:138 (24 June 1793).
102. Robespierre's intervention, *Archives Parlementaires*, 66:530 (14 June 1793); Pertué, "Les Projets," 184–85; Aberdam, "Délibérations," 18–19.
103. Dard, *Hérault de Sechelles*, 229; Bouissounouse, *Condorcet*, 269; Pertué, " Les Projets," 183.
104. *Archives Parlementaires*, 66:510–11 (15 June 1793).
105. Ibid., 67:440 (25 June 1793).
106. Condorcet, *Reflexions sur la revolution de 1688*; Pasquino, *Sieyès et l'invention*, 144.
107. *Archives Parlementaires*, 67:145 (24 June 1793).
108. Ibid., 67:150 (24 June 1793).
109. Vovelle, *Découverte*, 200–201, 205; Baczko, *Politiques*, 283.
110. E. Badinter and R. Badinter, *Condorcet, 1743–1794*, 578–79; Bouissounouse, *Condorcet*, 276–77; D. Williams, *Condorcet and Modernity*, 276.

CHAPTER 14

Education: Securing the Revolution

1. Forsyth, *Reason and Revolution*, 117, 162–63; Sewell, *Rhetoric of Bourgeois Revolution*, 155–57.
2. E. Kennedy, *Cultural History*, 35–40.
3. Rousseau, *Émile*, 43, 65, 73, 81–86, 116, 189–90.
4. McEachern, "La Révolution française et les editions," 304–6; Bloch, "*Émile*," 339.
5. Granderoute, "Rousseau," 326; Israel, "Natural Virtue," 10–13.
6. Forsyth, *Reason and Revolution*, 117.
7. Mirabeau, "Travail sur l'éducation publique," 79; Baczko, *Éducation*, 13, 70.
8. Mirabeau, "Travail sur l'éducation publique," 82–86.
9. Ibid., 78, 88–91; Grevet, *L'Avènement*, 20–21.
10. Condorcet, *Nature et objet*, 37–39, 51; Loft, *Passion, Politics*, 91–92.
11. Condorcet, *Nature et objet*, 51; Baker, *Condorcet*, 296–97.
12. *La Chronique du mois* (April 1792), 72.
13. Ibid., 77; Granderroute, "Rousseau," 326–37.
14. Daunou, *Essai sur l'Instruction Publique*, 309–10.
15. Condorcet, *Nature et objet*, 64.

16. Ibid., 67; Sophie de Condorcet, *Lettres*, 33; E. Badinter and R. Badinter, *Condorcet, 1743–1794*, 397; D. Williams, *Condorcet and Modernity*, 166.

17. Condorcet, *Rapport* (April 1792), 212; Baczko, *Éducation*, 178.

18. Condorcet, *Nature et objet*, 70.

19. Kates, *Cercle Social*, 107–8.

20. *La Feuille villageoise* 1, no. 3 (14 Oct. 1790), 43.

21. Bouissounouse, *Condorcet*, 190–91; Forsyth, *Reason and Revolution*, 205.

22. Condorcet, *Rapport* (April 1792), 183,

23. Ibid., 186–88; E. Badinter and R. Badinter, *Condorcet, 1743–1794*, 397–98; Loft, *Passion, Politics*, 144–45.

24. Baker, *Condorcet*, 298; E. Kennedy, *Cultural History*, 156–57.

25. Condorcet, *Rapport* (April 1792), 184–87.

26. Ibid., 195.

27. Draft of Declaration of the Rights of Man of 1793, in *Archives Parlementaires*, 58:602.

28. La Gorce, *Histoire religieuse*, 2:236; Bouissounouse, *Condorcet*, 191; Grevet, *L'Avènement*, 131.

29. Montgilbert, *Avis au peuple*, 361.

30. Baker, *Condorcet*, 297; Chappey, "Les Écoles," 333.

31. Condorcet, *Œuvres complètes*, 7:419.

32. Furet and Ozouf, *Dictionnaitre critique*, 240.

33. Proly, *Le Cosmopolite*, no. 128 (21 April 1792), 497; Levasseur, *Mémoires*, 1:93–94.

34. E. Kennedy, *Cultural History*, 160; Gross, *Fair Shares*, 22–23, 134–35, 137, 140–41.

35. Forsyth, *Reason and Revolution*, 205; Edelstein, *Terror*, 218.

36. Bensaude-Vincent, *Lavoisier*, 113–14; E. Kennedy, *Cultural History*, 192; Staum, *Minerva's Message*, 13.

37. Grevet, *L'Avènement*, 32–33.

38. E. Kennedy, *Cultural History*, 188–89; Chappey, "Les Écoles," 333.

39. Bensaude-Vincent, *Lavoisier*, 345.

40. Hampson, *Life and Opinions*, 176–77; McPhee, *Robespierre*, 162–63.

41. Hampson, *Saint-Just*, 233; Bell, *Cult of the Nation*, 162–63; C. Jones, *Great Nation*, 533.

42. Billaud-Varenne, *Principes*, 90–91; Granderoute, "Rousseau," 332–34.

43. Mercier, *De J. J. Rousseau considéré*, 1:35–36.

44. Hampson, *Life and Opinions*, 176–78; E. Kennedy, *Cultural History*, 354–55; McPhee, *Robespierre*, 162.

45. Kates, *Cercle Social*, 107–8, 261–62.

46. Petit, *Opinion*, 3, 24.

47. Ibid., 4; Bloch, "*Émile*," 349–50; Culoma, *Religion civile*, 122.

48. Petit, *Opinion*, 4–5; Grevet, *L'Avènement*, 36–37; Culoma, *Religion civile*, 196–97, 242.

49. Petit, *Opinion*, 32.

50. Forrest, *Revolution in Provincial France*, 229, 274, Gross, *Fair Shares*, 22, 33, 183–84.

51. Hunt, *Family Romance*, 67; E. Kennedy, *Cultural History*, 355–56.

52. Scott, *Terror and Repression*, 246.
53. Woloch, "La République directoriale," 313.
54. Livesey, *Making Democracy*, 178–82.
55. Grevet, *L'Avènement*, 30, 64–5, 136; Margairaz, *François de Neufchâteau*, 364.
56. Daunou, *Essai*, 331; Baczko, *Éducation*, 344; Livesey, *Making Democracy*, 170–71.
57. Grevet, *L'Avènement*, 136–42, 145.
58. Isaac and Sorgeloos, *L'École centrale*, 47.
59. Ibid., 148, 173, 179; Williams, *Condorcet*, 32; Jainchill, *Reimagining Politics*, 82–84.
60. Isaac and Sorgeloos, *L'École centrale*, 148, 258, 277, 298; Margairaz, *François de Neufchâteau*, 392–96.
61. Isaac and Sorgeloos, *L'École centrale*, 517; Staum, *Minerva's Message*, 57.

CHAPTER 15

Black Emancipation

1. Condorcet, *Political Writings*, 154.
2. Brissot, *Mémoires (1734–1793)*, 2:1; Curran, *Anatomy*, 204–6; Hampson, *Will and Circumstance*, 103; Piquet, *L'Émancipation*, 48–49.
3. Lagrave, *Fleury Mesplet*, 350–52.
4. Condorcet, *Political Writings*, 153; Brissot, *Le Patriote français* 24 (24 Aug. 1789), 4; Thomas, *Slave Trade*, 520.
5. *La Feuille villageoise* 1, no. 16 (13 Jan. 1791), 298.
6. Blackburn, *Overthrow*, 163.
7. Popkin, *You Are All Free*, 39–40.
8. *La Chronique de Paris* 2, 69 (10 March 1790), 274.
9. Ibid., 1, 48 (10 Oct. 1789), 234.
10. Ibid., 2, 15 (15 Jan. 1790), 57.
11. Griffiths, *Le Centre perdu*, 200–202; Piquet, *L'Émancipation*, 53–55.
12. Gouges, *Œuvres*, 83–87; Verdier, "From Reform," 190.
13. BL Pamphlet collection R-328/7, 1–2.
14. Brissot, *Le Patriote français* 115 (1 Dec. 1789), 4, and 117 (3 Dec. 1789), 2.
15. Destutt de Tracy, *Premiers écrits*, 32–33; Granié, *De l'Assemblée*, 120; Régent, *La France*, 215.
16. Piquet, *L'Émancipation*, 59.
17. Bertrand de Molleville, *Mémoires secrets*, 2:244.
18. *Découverte d'une conspiration* (BL R-328/10), 3–17.
19. *Il est encore des Aristocrates* (BL R-328/ 11), 5.
20. Ibid., 6–7.
21. Brissot, *Mémoires (1734–1793)*, 2:96–97; Garrigus, "Opportunist," 11; Hunt, *Inventing Human Rights*, 163.
22. Destutt de Tracy, *Premiers écrits*, 72.
23. Montesquieu, *De L'Esprit des Lois*, vol. 3, book 7, in *Œuvres complètes*, 620; Ghachem, "Montesquieu," 12–14; Ehrard, "Audace," 35–38; Piquet, *L'Émancipation*, 32–35; Israel, *Democratic Enlightenment*, 423–24.
24. Régent, *La France*, 219.

25. Brissot, *Mémoires (1734–1793)*, 2:96–99; Benot, *La révolution*, 67, 77–78; Garrigus, "Vincent Ogé," 37, 49, 52, 61.
26. Brissot, *Patriote français* 531 (21 Jan. 1791), 84.
27. See J. Garran de Coulon's essay in *La Chronique du mois* (Jan. 1792), 88–108; Griffiths, *Le Centre perdu*, 202–3; Chill, *Power*, 7–8.
28. Popkin, *You Are All Free*, 78.
29. Garrigus, "Opportunist," 7; Klooster, *Revolutions*, 98–99.
30. Hunt, *Inventing Human Rights*, 160, 163–64; Popkin, *You Are All Free*, 45–46.
31. Benot, *La révolution*, 126–27; Régent, *La France*, 242–43; Piquet, *L'Émancipation*, 206–7; Curran, *Anatomy*, 206.
32. Raimond, *Réflexions*, 35–36.
33. Malouet, *Mémoires*, 2:195.
34. Girey-Duré, *Patriote français* 1278 (10 Feb. 1793), 164–65.
35. Blackburn, *Overthrow*, 197–99, 228–29; Régent, *La France*, 243–45.
36. Popkin, *You Are All Free*, 210–11; 234–35, 248–49; Garrigus, "Opportunist," 11; Hunt, *Inventing Human Rights*, 165.
37. Popkin, *You Are All Free*, 250–51.
38. Raimond, *Réflexions*, 8, 10.
39. Popkin, *You Are All Free*, 338, 344.
40. BL R-328/12. [Momoro?], *Coup d'œil sur la question*, 5.
41. Ibid., 4–5, 12.
42. Ibid., 8.
43. Benot, *La révolution*, 172, 174; Piquet, *L'Émancipation*, 391–98; McPhee, *Robespierre*, 173.
44. Crow, *Emulation*, 160–1.
45. Doyle, *Oxford History*, 412; Lawday, *Giant of the French Revolution*, 240; Popkin, *You Are All Free*, 356.
46. Toussaint Louverture, *Lettres*, 155–58; Klooster, *Revolutions*, 106.
47. Toussaint Louverture, *Lettres*, 165, 172; Régent, *La France*, 249–50.
48. Baggio, "Toussaint Louverture," 98–99.
49. Régent, *La France*, 252; Spieler, "Abolition and Reenslavement," 136–37, 145–46.
50. Spieler, "Abolition and Reenslavement," 137, 146–48.
51. Blackburn, *Overthrow*, 230–32.
52. Klooster, "Rising Expectations," 66–67.
53. Aizpurua, "Revolution," 99.
54. Toussaint Louverture, *Lettres*, 369–70; Blackburn, *Overthrow*, 238.
55. Israel, *Democratic Enlightenment*, 504–33.
56. Jordaan, "Patriots, privateers," 101–3; Fulgencio López, *Juan Bautista Picornell*, 75, 80–81, 85, 88, 135.
57. Fulgencio López, *Juan Bautista Picornell*, 91–92.
58. Ibid., 73, 75.
59. Ibid., 35, 80, 89.
60. Jordaan, "Patriots, privateers," 154–55.
61. Klooster, "Rising Expectations," 59–60.
62. Klooster, *Revolution*, 105, 107.

CHAPTER 16

Robespierre's Putsch (June 1793)

1. Dumouriez to the Convention, Louvain, 12 March 1793, in *Archives Parlementaires*, 61:40–41 (1 April 1793).
2. *Archives Parlementaires*, 61:44 (1 April 1793).
3. Ibid., 61:45 (1 April 1793).
4. Girey-Dupré, *Patriote français* 1334 (8 April 1793), 391.
5. *Archives Parlementaires*, 61:16 (31 March 1793).
6. *Journal de Perlet* 3, no. 186 (26 March), 426.
7. [Saint Martin], *Journal des décrets* 2 (1793), 7; *Journal de Perlet* 4, no. 194 (3 April 1793), 18–19.
8. *La Décade philosophique* 2 (20 Fructidor), 303–4.
9. *Archives Parlementaires*, 60:603 (27 March 1793); *Journal de Perlet* 3, no. 188 (28 March 1793), 443–45.
10. *Journal de Perlet* 3, no. 187 (27 March), 435.
11. Robespierre, *Œuvres complètes*, 9:421.
12. Ibid., 9:359; Slavin, *Making*, 26–45.
13. *Archives Parlementaires*, 60:606–8 (27 March 1793).
14. Robespierre, *Œuvres complètes*, 9:378–79, 9:410–16.
15. *Archives Parlementaires*, 60:608 (27 March 1793).
16. Ibid.; Lawday, *Giant of the French Revolution*, 203.
17. *Archives Parlementaires*, 60:668–69 (28 March 1793).
18. Hébert, *Père Duchesne* 229 (8 April 1793), 1–4.
19. Ibid., 232 (11 April 1793), 1–3, 6–7.
20. Wahnich, *L'impossible citoyen* 17–18; Whaley, *Radicals*, 2–3.
21. *Journal de Perlet* 4, no. 215 (24 April 1793), 188, and 216 (25 April), 199.
22. Robespierre, *Œuvres complètes*, 9:415–16, 421.
23. Ibid., 9:478, 9:526; Slavin, *Making*, 25.
24. Robespierre, *Œuvres complètes*, 9:359, 9:406, 9:526; BHP pamph. 957082, *Anecdotes curieuses*, 19–20; Fréron, *L'Orateur du peuple* 7, no. 89 (21 Ventose Year II), 715–16; Michelet, *Histoire*, 7:218.
25. Girey-Dupré, *Patriote français* 1356 (30 April 1793), 479–80.
26. *Journal de Perlet* 4, no. 207 (16 April 1793), 125; Mercier, *Paris*, 1:158–59; Slavin, *Making*, 14–15.
27. *Journal de Perlet* 4, no. 206 (15 April 1793), 113.
28. Robespierre, *Œuvres complètes*, 9:418; *Journal de Perlet* 4 (13 April 1793); [Ferrand] *État actuel*, 4–7 (April), 98–102.
29. Louvet, *Mémoires*, 1:60–61, 85; Slavin, "Robespierre," 145–46.
30. Fauchet, *Journal des Amis*, 1:33.
31. Robespierre, *Œuvres complètes*, 9:420.
32. *Journal de Perlet* 4, no. 212 (21 April 1793) and no. 213 (22 April 1793), 163–66, 170–71; Patrick, *The Men*, 111.
33. Palmer, *From Jacobin to Liberal*, 26.
34. Lewis-Beck, "Was There a Girondist Faction?," 526; Cobb, *The French*, 238–44; Dupuy, *La république jacobine*, 38–39; Sonenscher, *Sans-Culottes*, 2, 7–8, 57.

35. Gaulmier, *Un grand témoin*, 147–48.
36. Ibid., 149.
37. *Journal de Perlet* 4, no. 213 (22 April 1793), 173.
38. Ibid., 175.
39. *Journal de Perlet* 3, no. 188 (28 March 1793), 447.
40. Bellanger, *Histoire générale*, 1:503–4.
41. *Archives Parlementaires*, 60:700 (29 March 1793); *Journal de Perlet* 3, no. 190 (30 March 1793), 459–60.
42. *Journal de Perlet* 3, no. 191 (31 March 1793), 470.
43. Marat, *Œuvres politiques*, 10:1611; *Journal de Perlet* 3, no. 182 (22 March 1793), 393.
44. *Journal de Perlet* 4, no. 221 (30 April 1793) and 222 (1 May 1793), 235, 246; M. L. Kennedy, *Jacobin Clubs*, 184.
45. *Journal de Perlet* 4, no. 243 (22 May 1793), 413.
46. Ibid., no. 192 (1 April 1793), 4 and 193 (2 April 1793), 15; Friedland, *Political Actors*, 189–96; Darlow, *Staging the French Revolution*, 95, 117.
47. Kitromilides, "Itineraries," 9–10.
48. Alger, "British Colony," 679–80; Foner, *Tom Paine*, 242.
49. Nelson, *Thomas Paine*, 251–52.
50. Ibid.
51. *Journal de Perlet* 4, no. 230 (9 May 1793), 312.
52. Ibid., no. 203 (12 April 1793); Gross, *Fair Shares*, 72–73.
53. Darrow, "Economic Terror," 513.
54. Robespierre, *Œuvres complètes*, 9:378.
55. Carra, *Annales patriotiques,* no. 144 (24 May 1793), 661.
56. Girey-Dupré, *Patriote français* 1326 (31 March 1793), 361; Gough, *Newpaper Press*, 93, 96.
57. Guilhaumou, *Marseille*, 182–89; Scott, *Terror and Repression*, 110–15.
58. Girey-Dupré, *Patriote français* 1357 (2 May 1793), 488; *Journal de Perlet* 4, no. 242 (21 May 1793), 407.
59. Carra, *Annales patriotiques* 139 (19 May 1793), 642; Guilhaumou, *Marseille*, 191–92; Johnson, *Midi in Revolution*, 234; Hanson, *Jacobin Republic*, 81–90.
60. Benoit, "Lyon rouge," 188–89.
61. Fauchet, *Journal des Amis* 2, 154; *Journal de Perlet* 4, no. 228 (7 May 1793), 290–91; Johnson, *Midi in Revolution*, 214–15; Slavin, *Making*, 154.
62. Fauchet, *Journal des Amis* 9, 464 (2 March 1793).
63. Sewell, *Work and Revolution*, 105–6.
64. *Journal de Perlet* 4, no. 222 (1 May 1793), no. 223 (2 May 1793), and no. 226 (5 May 1793), 253–55, 265, 274.
65. BHP pamph. 602672/5; Gorsas, *Précis rapide des evenemens*, 5–6; *Journal de Perlet* 4, nos. 245 (24 May 1793) and no. 246 (25 May), 429, 438–39; Dorigny, "Les Girondins," 572.
66. Sewell, *Work and Revolution*, 102–3; Slavin, "Robespierre," 143–44.
67. Sewell, *Work and Revolution*, 105–6.
68. Varlet, "Projet," 56–57; Slavin, "Robespierre," 146–47.
69. Marat, *L'Ami du peuple* 233 (4 July 1793), 1; Guillon, *Notre Patience*, 95.
70. *Journal de Perlet* 4, no. 230 (9 May 1793), 307.

71. Hébert, *Père Duchesne* 237, 1–2, 7.
72. Chabot, *Journal populaire* 12 (1793), 305–6.
73. BN pamph. Lb 41 2728, *Lettre de Jerôme Pétion*, 8, 15.
74. Ibid., 2–4.
75. Chabot, *Journal populaire* 7 (1793), 25.
76. Levasseur, *Mémoires*, 1:211–12, 220; Slavin, "Robespierre," 144–46.
77. *Journal de Perlet* 4, no. 230 (9 May 1793), 310.
78. Girey-Dupré, *Patriote français* 1365 (10 May 1793), 519–20.
79. Levasseur, *Mémoires*, 1:271.
80. Ibid., 1:257–58; *Journal de Perlet* 4, 235 (14 May 1793), 349.
81. Doyle, *Oxford History*, 233.
82. Slavin, *Making*, 19–21.
83. Fauchet, *Journal des Amis* 2 (25 May 1793), 103–5.
84. Audouin, *Journal universel,* no. 14115 (9 Oct. 1793), 5902; Levasseur, *Mémoires*, 1:216, 1:218, 1:220; Gershoy, *Betrand Barère*, 160–62; Slavin, *French Revolution*, 144–45.
85. Carra, *Annales patriotiques,* no. 148 (28 May 1793), 681.
86. Ibid.; Slavin, "Robespierre," 143.
87. *Journal de Perlet* 4, 249 (28 May 1793), 462; Slavin, *French Revolution*, 145–46; McPhee, *Robespierre*, 154.
88. *Archives Parlementaires*, 67:168 (24 June 1793); *Journal de Perlet* 4, no. 250 (29 May 1793), 470; Levasseur, *Mémoires*, 1:221–22.
89. Guillon, *Notre patience*, 157.
90. Slavin, *Making*, 76–80, 87–88; Fehér, *Frozen Revolution*, 73–76; Dingli, *Robespierre*, 337–39.
91. Mercier, *Paris*, 1:335; Slavin, *French Revolution*, 145; Slavin *Making*, 90–98, 112–13.
92. *Archives Parlementaires*, 65:653.
93. Ibid., 65:646.
94. Michelet, *Histoire*, 7:191–92.
95. *Archives Parlementaires*, 65:646–47.
96. Burstin, *Révolution*, 572–73; Slavin, *Making*, 99.
97. *Archives Parlementaires*, 65:654; Slavin, "Robespierre," 150; Burstin, *Révolution*, 425–26.
98. *Archives Parlementaires*, 65:655.
99. Ibid., 66:22; Martin, *Violence et révolution*, 168.
100. *Archives Parlementaires*, 66:7.
101. BHP pamph. 957082, *Anecdotes curieuses*, 31; Picqué, *Au peuple*, 374; Roland, *Memoirs*, 30–37.
102. *Archives Parlementaires*, 65:689.
103. Ibid., 65:699–700.
104. *Archives Parlementaires*, 65:688; Favreau, "Gensonné," 426; Walton, *Policing Public Opinion*, 219.
105. *Archives Parlementaires*, 65:706–7; Dard, *Hérault de Sechelles*, 218–21.
106. Trousson, *Diderot*, 615; Sonenscher, *Sans-Culottes*, 399–402.
107. *Archives Parlementaires*, 65:698, 65:706.
108. Ibid., 65:708.

109. Picqué, *Au peuple*, 374.
110. *Archives Parlementaires*, 67:170 (24 June 1793).
111. Ibid., 80:531 (1 Jan. 1794).
112. Levasseur, *Mémoires*, 240–41; Friedland, *Political Actors*, 288.

CHAPTER 17

The Summer of 1793: Overturning the Revolution's Core Values

1. Baczko, *Politiques*, 252.
2. "Declaration du citoyen Gensonné" (2 June 1793), in *Archives Parlementaires*, 82:680.
3. Audouin, *Journal universel*, no.1352 (6 Aug, 1793), 5397–98; *Journal de Perlet* 6, no. 317 (4 Aug. 1793), 29.
4. *Archives Parlementaires*, 66:530–31 (14 June 1793).
5. Ibid., 67:129–30 (24 June 1793).
6. Ibid., 67:521–23 (26 June 1793).
7. Forrest, "Federalism," 314; Hanson, *Jacobin Republic*, 64–65.
8. Salle, *Examen critique*, 391.
9. *Archives Parlementaires*, 67:535, 67:562 (27 June 1793).
10. Hermon-Belot, *L'Abbé Grégoire*, 281.
11. *Archives Parlementaires*, 66:60, 66:68.
12. Ibid., 66:96.
13. Ibid., 66:94–96.
14. Ibid., 67:523–24 (26 June 1793).
15. Ibid., 67:525 (27 June 1793).
16. Ibid., 67:528–29 (27 June 1793).
17. Ibid., 67:562 (27 June 1793).
18. Ibid., 67:513–17 (26 June 1793); Jaume, *Discours*, 121–22.
19. *Archives Parlementaires*, 67:130–31 (24 June 1793).
20. Ibid., 67:131 (24 June 1793); Hanson, *Provincial Politics*, 166,168.
21. *Archives Parlementaires*, 67:136 (24 June 1793).
22. Wallon, *Histoire*, 1:358–59.
23. *Archives Parlementaires*, 67:136–37 (24 June 1793).
24. Louvet, *Mémoires*, 1:103–4; Forrest, "Federalism," 315–16.
25. *Archives Parlementaires*, 67:433 (25 June 1793); *Journal de Perlet* 6, no. 368 (25 Sept. 1793), 439.
26. *Archives Parlementaires*, 67:160 (24 June 1793).
27. Ibid., 67:159 (24 June 1793).
28. Crook, *Toulon*, 126–27, 129–31.
29. Edict of the Montpellier *assemblées primaires*, 13 June 1793, *Archives Parlementaires*, 82:679.
30. *Archives Parlementaires*, 82:682.
31. Audouin, *Journal universel*, no. 1351 (5 Aug. 1793), 5389; Serna, *Antontelle, Aristocrate révolutionnaire*, 204–5.
32. *Archives Parlementaires*, 68:91.
33. Ibid., 68:89–91.
34. Audouin, *Journal universel*, no. 1351 (5 Aug. 1793), 5390–91.

35. Chabot, *Journal populaire* 7 (1793), 10–17 and 8 (1793), 308.
36. Levasseur, *Mémoires*, 1:314–15; Hampson, *Saint-Just*, 117–21.
37. *Archives Parlementaires*, 68:75–78.
38. Gough, *Newspaper Press*, 98–99; Walton, *Policing Public Opinion*, 109–12, 133–34.
39. Gough, *Newspaper Press*, 61, 89, 95; Zizek, "Plume de fer," 628; Andress, *The Terror*, 179.
40. Gough, *Newspaper Press*, 95; Bellanger, *Histoire générale*, 1:507–8.
41. Murray, *Right-Wing Press*, 207, 268n.
42. Audoin, *Journal universel,* no. 1350 (4 Aug. 1793), 5380; Darlow, *Staging the French Revolution*, 152.
43. Prudhomme, *Histoire générale*, 1:xxiii–iv; Baczko, "L'expérience thermidori-enne," 347; Walton, *Policing Public Opinion*, 133–35.
44. Open letter of Barbaroux, Caen, 18 June 1793, in *Archives Parlementaires*, 67:468–70.
45. *Archives Parlementaires*, 82:681.
46. "Declaration du citoyen Gensonné" (2 June 1793), in *Archives Parlementaires*, 82:680
47. BHP pamph. 602672/2, *La Patrie outragée nous appelle*, 1–2.
48. Forrest, "Federalism," 313.
49. *Archives Parlementaires*, 68:123; Forrest, *Revolution in Provincial France*, 202–5.
50. Ibid., 68:89.
51. Ibid., 82:685 (4 Jan. 1794); Johnson, *Midi in Revolution*, 235–36; Dupuy, *La république jacobine*, 121.
52. Decree of *comité central* of Hérault, 6 July 1793, in *Archives Parlementaires*, 82:677–78, 681–83; Forrest, "Federalism," 315.
53. "Instruction pour les commmissaires du departement de l'Hérault" (5 July 1793), in *Archives Parlmentaires*, 82:678–79, 681.
54. *Archives Parlementaires*, 67:554–58 (27 June 1793).
55. Buonarroti, *Conspiration pour l'égalité*, 32–33; Audouin, *Journal universel*, no. 1352 (6 Aug. 1793), 5397–98.
56. *Compte de la mission*, 43, 45–46, 68–69.
57. Ibid., 64, 66; Forrest, *Revolution in Provincial France*, 209–10.
58. Levasseur, *Mémoires*, 1:271–72, 286.
59. Chabot, *Journal populaire* 7 (1793), 21–26; *Journal de Perlet* 4, 276 (25 June 1793), 188.
60. BHP pamph. 957082, *Anecdotes curieuses*, 18–19.
61. Aulard, *La Société de Jacobins*, 5:327–28 (4 Aug. 1793).
62. Ibid., 5:343 (11 Aug. 1793) and 5:373 (23 Aug. 1793).
63. Ibid., 5:241; Buonarroti, *Conspiration pour l'égalité*, 34; Woloch, "Contraction," 311–12.
64. Lemny, *Jean-Louis Carra*, 334–35.
65. BL Pamphlets 1031 2/3 no. 8, *Réponse de J. L. Carra deputé*, 1–2; Lemny, *Jean-Louis Carra*, 325, 327.
66. Aulard, *La Société de Jacobins*, 5:35 (14 Aug. 1793); Gough, "Robespierre," 121.

67. Aulard, *La Société de Jacobins*, 5:378–80 (26 Aug. 1793).

68. Hampson, *Life and Opinions*, 15–16; Sewell, *Work and Revolution*, 106; Guillon, *Notre Patience*, 163.

69. *Archives Parlementaires*, 67:455 (25 June 1793).

70. Guillon, *Notre Patience*, 101.

71. *Archives Parlementaires*, 67:455–58 (25 June 1793); Sewell, "Sans-culotte Rhetoric," 255–56; Jaume, *Discours*, 142, 214, 435.

72. Darrow, "Economic Terror," 507, 513–14.

73. *Archives Parlementaires*, 67:544–45 (27 June 1793).

74. Ibid., 67:543–44 (27 June 1793); Hampson, *Saint-Just*, 126.

75. Guillon, *Notre Patience*, 97–98.

76. Marat, *L'Ami du peuple*, no. 233, 1–3 (4 July 1793); Cobb, *The French*, 222.

77. *Archives Parlementaires*, 67:459 (25 June 1793); Boroumand, *La Guerre*, 149.

78. Guillon, *Notre Patience*, 163.

79. Audouin, *Journal universel* 1350 (4 Aug. 1793), 5381; *Journal de Perlet* 6, no. 315 (2 Aug. 1793), 315; Hanson, *Provincal Politics*, 154–57.

80. *Archives Parlementaires*, 82:674 (4 Jan. 1794).

81. Levasseur, *Mémoires*, 1:262–63; Dupuy, *La république jacobine*, 120.

82. *Archives Parlementaires*, 74:7.

83. Chabot, *Journal populaire* 11 (1793), 312; Slavin, *French Revolution*, 345–46; Monnier, "L'Évolution," 51.

84. Godineau, *Women of Paris*, 143; Roessler, *Out of the Shadows*, 136–39.

85. Aulard, *La Société de Jacobins*, 5:314 (26 July 1793) and 5:356 (15 Aug. 1793).

86. Ibid., 5:313, 5:315–16 (26 July 1793).

87. *Journal de Perlet* 4, 298 (16 July 1793), 366, and 4, 299 (17 July), 369–70; Kennedy, *Cultural History*, 336.

88. Lüsebrink, "Georg Forster," 469; Cottebrune, *Mythe et réalité*, 210–14.

89. Trousson and Eigeldinger, *Dictionnaire de Jean-Jacques Rousseau*, 306.

90. Lüsebrink, "Georg Forster," 474; Cottebrune, *Mythe et réalité*, 242–44.

91. Lüsebrink, "Georg Forster," 476.

92. *Journal de Perlet* 7, no. 385 (12 Oct. 1793), 96.

93. BHP pamph. 957082, *Anecdotes curieuses*, 41–42, 45.

94. Brochon, *Mémoires*, 38–42; *Journal de Perlet* 6, 368 (25 Sept. 1793), 434.

95. *Archives Parlementaires*, 74:8–9; Hanson, *Jacobin Republic*, 125–29.

96. *Journal de Perlet* 6, no. 370 (27 Sept. 1793), 453 and no. 371 (28 Sept. 1793), 459–60.

97. Aulard, *La Société des Jacobins*, 5:418; Brochon, *Mémoires*, 42; Auerbach, "Politics, Protest," 160.

98. *Journal de Perlet* 7, no. 380 (7 Oct. 1793), 55, report from Bordeaux (28 Sept.).

99. Chabot, *Journal populaire* 8 (1793), 103–4, 306.

100. Aulard, *La Société des Jacobins*, 5:309 (21 July) and 5:325–26 (2 Aug.); Serna, *Antontelle, Aristocrate révolutionnaire*, 223; Doyle, *Aristocrats*, 288.

101. Crook, *Toulon*, 126–39.

102. *Journal de Perlet* 6, no. 369 (26 Sept. 1793), 442.

103. Ibid., no. 372 (29 Sept. 1793), 468; Bell, *Cult of the Nation*, 162–63.

104. *Archives Parlementaires*, 74:6–7.

105. See Foot, *Red Shelley*, 140.

CHAPTER 18
De-Christianization (1793–94)

1. Royou, *L'Ami du Roi*, 21 Dec. 1791, 3; Proly, *Le Cosmopolite*, no. 378 (22 March 1792).
2. Culoma, *Religion civile*, 100–101.
3. Ikni, "Jean-Marie Coupé," 343.
4. Royou, *L'Ami du Roi*, 26 Oct. 1791, 1–2.
5. *La Chronique du mois* 2 (May 1792), 31.
6. *Journal de Perlet*, no. 96 (26 Dec. 1792), 205.
7. Vovelle, *La Découverte*, 167.
8. Mercier, *Paris*, 2:92–98.
9. Lachapelle, *Considérations philosophiques*, 225–26; Dommanget, *Sylvain Maréchal*, 294.
10. Mortier, *Anacharsis Cloots*, 421.
11. Ibid., 421–22.
12. Andress, *The Terror*, 203; Bourdin, *Le noir et le rouge*, 316, 320, 386–87; Vovelle, *1793: La Révolution*, 25–26, 93.
13. Chopelin-Blanc, *De l'apologétique*, 505.
14. Ibid., 511–12.
15. Burstin, *Révolution*, 673–76.
16. Vovelle, *1793: La Révolution*, 78–79; Tallett, "Dechristianizing France," 10; Forrest, *Revolution in Provincial France,* 226.
17. Mercier, *Paris*, 2:102.
18. *La Décade philosophique* 2 (10 Fructidor), 247–48.
19. *Journal de Perlet* 8, no. 435 (1 Dec. 1793), 1; Bourdin, *Le noir et le rouge*, 319; Vovelle, *1793: La Révolution*, 88–92.
20. Rocques, *État de France*, 2:41–42; Spang, *Invention*, 133–36.
21. Hermon-Belot, *L'Abbé Grégoire*, 293–95; Burstin, *Révolution*, 670, 673, 677.
22. Forrest, *Revolution in Provincial France*, 227.
23. Aulard, *La Société des Jacobins*, 5:497–98.
24. Hermon-Belot, *L'Abbé Grégoire*, 294; Rocher, "Aspects de l'histoire religieuse," 312; Bourdin, *Le noir et le rouge*, 332.
25. Hermon-Belot, *L'Abbé Grégoire*, 293–95.
26. Ibid., 301.
27. *Journal de Perlet* 7, no. 432 (28 Nov. 1793), 466; Bourdin, *Le noir et le rouge*, 333.
28. Audouin, *Journal universel*, no. 1448 (21 Brumaire, II), 6164.
29. Forrest, *Revolution in Provincial France*, 223, 227; Vovelle, *1793: La Révolution*, 57, 120, 134.
30. Bourin, *Le noir et le rouge*, 332.
31. *Archives Parlementaires*, 82:443–44 (29 Dec. 1793).
32. Ibid., 82:530, 82:532 (1 Jan. 1794).
33. Tallett, "Dechristianizing France," 10.
34. Rocher, "Aspects de l'histoire religieuse," 307.
35. Ibid., 308–11.
36. Mortier, *Anacharsis Cloots*, 421–22.

37. *Archives Parlementaires*, 82:23 (20 Dec. 1793).

38. Ibid., 82:664 (4 Jan. 1794).

39. Hohl, "Les sociétés politiques," 211.

40. *Archives Parlementaires*, 82:646–47 (4 Jan. 1794).

41. Ibid., 82:477 (29 Dec. 1793); Hohl, "Les sociétés politiques," 213, 217, 221.

42. Vovelle, *1793: La Révolution*, 75; Tallett, "Dechristianizing France," 5.

43. *Archives Parlementaires*, 82:530 (1 Jan. 1794).

44. Aston, *Religion and Revolution*, 266.

45. *Archives Parlementaires*, 82:9 (20 Dec. 1793).

46. Ibid., 82:21–23 (20 Dec. 1793); Tulard, *Histoire et dictionnaire*, 870.

47. *Archives Parlementaires*, 82:21–23 (20 Dec. 1793).

48. Ibid., 82:529 (1 Jan. 1794).

49. Ibid.; Vovelle, *1793: La Révolution*, 91, 201; Biard, *Missionaires de le République*, 496.

50. Aston, *Religion and Revolution*, 193; Bourdin, *Le noir et le rouge*, 320.

51. Garrone, *Gilbert Romme*, 405–9, 430; Gross, *Fair Shares*, 19–20, 22.

52. *Journal de Perlet* 8, no. 438 (4 Dec. 1793), 28.

53. *Archives Parlementaires*, 82:532 (1 Jan. 1794); Hunt, *Politics, Culture*, 98–99.

54. Aulard, *La Société des Jacobins*, 5:500–1 (8 Nov. 1793); Gough, *Newspaper Press*, 97, 104.

55. Desmoulins, *Vieux Cordelier*, 113.

56. Rocher, "Aspects de l'histoire religieuse," 314–15.

57. Scurr, *Fatal Purity*, 111–13.

58. McPhee, *Robespierre*, 40–41, 65, 138.

59. Mercier, *Paris*, 2:105.

60. Robespierre, "Contre le philosophisme," 49; Aulard, *La Société des Jacobins*, 5:527–28 (21 Nov. 1793).

61. Robespierre, *Discours*, 45–52; Aulard, *La Société des Jacobins*, 5:529; Tarin, *Diderot*, 51–52.

62. Desmoulins, *Vieux Cordelier*, 54–55.

63. Mortier, *Anacharsis Cloots*, 426.

64. *Journal de Perlet* 8, no. 441 (7 Dec. 1793), 52.

65. Mortier, *Anacharsis Cloots*, 435.

66. Mercier, *Paris*, 2:105–6.

67. Vovelle, *1793: La Révolution*, 205.

68. Desan, *Reclaiming the Sacred*, 84.

69. *Archives Parlementaires*, 82:647–53 (4 Jan. 1794).

CHAPTER 19

"The Terror" (September 1793–March 1794)

1. Rocques, *État de France*, 1:2–8.

2. Aulard, *La Société de Jacobins*, 5:378–80 (26 Aug. 1793).

3. Guilhaumou, "Le Discours," 51–53; Doyle, *Aristocracy and Its Enemies*, 287.

4. Aulard, *La Société de Jacobins*, 5:373 (23 Aug. 1793).

5. Ibid., 5:386–87 (2 Sept.) and 394 (9 Sept. 1793).

6. *Archives Parlementaires*, 72:367–68 (3 Sept. 1793); Sewell, "Sans-culotte Rhetoric," 257.

7. *Archives Parlementaires*, 72:395, 72:408–9, 72:413–14, 72:5–17 (4 Sept. 1793).
8. *Journal de Perlet* 6, no. 368 (25 Sept. 1793), 439; Singham, "Betwixt Cattle," 147; Lapied, "Une absence de révolution," 309.
9. *Archives Parlementaires*, 72:429 (5 Sept. 1793); Higonnet, *Sister Republics*, 256; Burstin, *Révolution*, 619, 637.
10. *Archives Parlementaires*, 72:417 (5 Sept. 1793).
11. Audouin, *Journal universel*, no. 1415 (9 Oct. 1793), 5900.
12. Jaume, *Discours*, 140, 435; Guillon, *Notre Patience*, 53, 70, 166; Boroumand, *La Guerre*, 163–64.
13. Rocques, *État de France*, 22–24, 58.
14. *Journal de Perlet* 8, no. 429 (25 Nov. 1793), 447; Guicheteau, "La Terreur sociale," 314.
15. Palmer, *From Jacobin to Liberal*, 35; Manevy, *La Révolution et la liberté*, 68.
16. Brochon, *Un Bordelais*, 36; W. Scott, *Terror and Repression*, 131; Cobb, *The French*, 105; Hunt, *Family Romance*, 159.
17. *Journal de Perlet* 7, no. 382 (9 Oct. 1793), 71; Lachapelle, *Considérations philosophiques*, supplement, lxx; Higonnet, *Goodness beyond Virtue*, 200–201.
18. *Journal de Perlet* 7, no. 429 (25 Nov. 1793), 448.
19. Ibid., 8, no. 449 (15 Dec. 1793), 117.
20. Godineau, *Women of Paris*, 275.
21. Blanc, "Une humaniste au XVIIIe siècle," 30–31.
22. Gouges, *Œuvres*, 126; McPhee, *Robespierre*, 138.
23. *Journal de Perlet* 7, no. 408 (4 Nov. 1793), 276, and no. 409 (5 Nov. 1793), 284.
24. Aulard, *La Société des Jacobins*, 5:506 (11 Nov. 1793); Lapied, "Une absence de révolution," 309.
25. Aulard, *La Société des Jacobins*, 5:406–7 (16 Sept. 1793); Applewhite and Levy, *Women and Politics*, 92; Roessler, *Out of the Shadows*, 151–53, 163; Guillon, *Notre patience*, 154–55.
26. Roessler, *Out of the Shadows*, 156–61.
27. *Journal de Perlet* 7, no. 243 (31 Oct. 1793), 404; Godineau, *Women of Paris*, 165–70; Hunt, *Family Romance*, 153; Slavin, *French Revolution*, 326–27.
28. Slavin, *French Revolution*, 334–37.
29. BHP pamph. 957082, *Anecdotes curieuses*, 4; Baczko, "Tournant culturel," 27–28.
30. Garrone, *Gilbert Romme*, 342–43, 347.
31. *Journal de Perlet* 6, no. 368 (25 Sept. 1793), 437; Gross, *Fair Shares*, 56–57; Andress, *The Terror*, 211–13.
32. Rocques, *État de France*, 5.
33. Bindman, *Shadow of the Guillotine*, 160; Buel, *Joel Barlow*, 177.
34. *Archives Parlementaires*, 72:371 (4 Sept. 1793).
35. Ibid., 72:618 (10 Sept. 1793) and 75:489 (3 Oct. 1793).
36. Ibid., 77:105 (31 Oct. 1793), 82:442 (29 Dec. 1793), and 82:541 (1 Jan. 1794); *Journal de Perlet* 6, no. 368 (25 Sept. 1793), 439 and 7, no. 424 (20 Nov. 1793), 406.
37. *Archives Parlementaires*, 75:520–22 (3 Oct. 1793); Linton, *Conspiracies Real and Imagined*, 135.

38. *Archives Parlementaires*, 73:428 (5 Sept. 1793).

39. BHP pamph. 957082, *Anecdotes curieuses*, 3–4; Manevy, *La Révolution et la liberté*, 63–69; McPhee, *Robespierre*, 169–70.

40. *Journal de Perlet* 7, no. 381 (8 Oct. 1793), 60, and 382 (9 Oct. 1793), 70; Wallon, *Histoire*, 1:375.

41. *Journal de Perlet* 7, no. 382 (9 Oct. 1793), 70–71.

42. Ibid., no. 379 (6 Oct. 1793), 45.

43. Ibid., 46.

44. *Archives Parlementaires*, 75:520–21 (3 Oct. 1793), 523.

45. Ibid., 75:521 (3 Oct. 1793); *Journal de Perlet* 7, no. 377 (4 Oct. 1793), 27–29.

46. BN Lib 41/3447, *Jugement du Tribunal revolutionnaire*, 1.

47. Tulard, *Histoire et dictionnaire*, 603.

48. Levasseur, *Mémoires*, 2:189; Serna, *Antontelle, Aristocrate révolutionnaire*, 211.

49. Aulard, *La Société des Jacobins*, 5:481–82 (28 Oct. 1793) and 5:488 (30 Oct. 1793); Serna, *Antontelle, Aristocrate révolutionnaire*, 212.

50. BHP pamph. 602672/1, "Proces de J. P. Brissot et complices," 1; Wallon, *Histoire*, 1:367, 1:376–80, 1:383–84.

51. *Journal de Perlet* 7, no. 382 (9 Oct. 1793), 65.

52. Aulard, *La Société des Jacobins*, 5:473 (30 Oct. 1793).

53. Ibid., 5:481–83 (28 Oct. 1793).

54. Clemenceau-Jacquemaire, *Vie de Madame Roland*, 2:252; Lapied, "Une absence de révolution," 308.

55. Higonnet, *Goodness beyond Virtue*, 224.

56. Darlow, *Staging the French Revolution*, 142, 155, 165; Friedland, *Political Actors*, 254, 336.

57. *Journal de Perlet* 6, no. 370 (27 Sept. 1793), 453; Maslan, *Revolutionary Acts*, 248n29.

58. Forrest, *Revolution in Provincial France*, 231–32.

59. *Journal de Perlet* 6, no. 378 (5 Oct. 1793), 40.

60. Ibid., 7, no. 432 (28 Nov. 1793), 466–67.

61. Le Bozec, "Théâtre à Rouen," 184–85.

62. *Journal de Perlet* 7, no. 426 (22 Nov. 1793), 418–19.

63. *La Décade philosophique* 1 (30 Floreal), 143.

64. Ibid., 139–43.

65. *Journal de Perlet* 7, no. 429 (25 Nov. 1793), 443–44; E. Kennedy, *Cultural History*, 179.

66. *Journal de Perlet* 7, no. 429 (25 Nov. 1793), 445.

67. Aulard, *La Société des Jacobins*, 5:530 (21 Nov., 1793).

68. *La Décade philosophique* 2 (10 Thermidor), 64.

69. *Gazette nationale*, no. 178 (18 March 1794), 719; Friedland, *Political Actors*, 176–77.

70. *La Décade philosophique* 1 (30 Prairial), 353.

71. Walton, *Policing Public Opinion*, 218–20.

72. Darlow, *Staging the French Revolution*, 165.

73. *Journal de Perlet* 7, no. 388 (15 Oct. 1793), 114, and no. 397 (24 Oct. 1789), 190.

74. Ibid., 8, no. 455 (21 Dec. 1793), 163–64.

75. E. Kennedy, *Cultural History*, 221–25.
76. *La Décade philosophique* 1 (10 Floreal), 10–11; E. Kennedy, *Cultural History*, 190, 382.
77. *La Décade philosophique* 1 (20 Floreal), 76–77.
78. Biard, *Missionaires de la République*, 363, 537; McPhee, *Robespierre*, 105, 161.
79. McPhee, *Robespierre*, 195; Hampson, *Life and Opinions*, 282–83.
80. W. Scott, *Terror and Repression*, 147–49; Andress, *The Terror*, 288.
81. *Journal de Perlet* 7, no. 425 (21 Nov. 1793), 411.
82. Ibid., no. 382 (9 Oct. 1793), 66; Andress, *The Terror*, 250.
83. *Journal de Perlet* 7, no. 386 (13 Oct. 1793), 101; Prudhomme, *Histoire générale*, 1:18.
84. Aulard, *La Société des Jacobins*, 5:464–46 (17 Oct. 1793); Hanson, *Jacobin Republic*, 220, 243.
85. Mercier, *Paris*, 2:201.
86. *Journal de Perlet* 7, no. 427 (23 Nov. 1793), 427; Andress, *The Terror*, 210–11, 236–37.
87. Aulard, *La Société des Jacobins*, 5:467 (17 Oct. 1793); Biard, *Missionnaires de la République*, 334.
88. *Archives Parlementaires*, 82:34–35 (20 Dec. 1793).
89. Andress, *The Terror*, 210–11; Dupuy, *La république jacobine*, 131; Biard, *Missionnaires de la République*, 220–21.
90. *Gazette nationale* 94 (24 Dec. 1793), 26; Friedland, *Political Actors*, 291–94.
91. *Archives Parlementaires*, 73:389 (4 Sept. 1793).
92. Prudhomme, *Histoire générale*, 1:xlix; Crook, *Toulon*, 150–52; Dwyer, *Napoleon*, 143.
93. Andress, *The Terror*, 250.
94. Martin, *Violence et révolution*, 203–5; Baczko, *Ending the Terror*, 148–57; Guicheteau, "La Terreur sociale," 312–14, 318–19.
95. *Gazette nationale* 176 (16 March 1794), 702; Biard, *Missionnaires de la République*, 246.
96. *Archives Parlementaires*, 75:522 (3 Oct. 1793).
97. Audouin, *Journal universel* 1423 (26 First, Year II), 5967; *Journal de Perlet* 7, no. 390 (17 Oct. 1793), 133.
98. Aulard, *La Société des Jacobins*, 5:479 (27 Oct. 1793).
99. Ibid., 5:492 (1 Nov. 1793).
100. Margairaz, *François de Neufchâteau*, 369.
101. Prudhomme, *Histoire générale*, 1:lxi.
102. Louvet, *Mémoires*, 2:47–48; *Journal de Perlet* 7, no. 427 (23 Nov. 1793), 429.
103. *Journal de Perlet* 7, no. 429 (25 Nov. 1793), 445, 462.
104. Bensaude-Vincent, *Lavoisier*, 345–47.
105. Joly, introduction to Destutt de Tracy, *Premiers écrits*, 42–43; Harris, *Antoine d'Estutt de Tracy*, 21.
106. Gaulmier, *Un grand témoin*, 155.
107. Staum, *Cabanis: Enlightenment*, 50.
108. Volney, *La Loi naturelle,* in Volney, *Œuvres complètes*, 1:461–63; Gaulmier, *Un grand témoin*, 151–53.
109. Volney, *La Loi naturelle,* in Volney, *Œuvres complètes*, 1:466–67.

110. Ibid., 1:458–59; Gaulmier, *Un grand témoin*, 154–57.
111. Arnaud, *Chamfort*, 242–43, 248–49; Destain, "Chamfort et Rousseau," 88–89.
112. Condorcet, *Tableau historique*, 865; Staël, *Considérations*, 360; Condorcet, *Political Writings*, xii; Pagden, *The Enlightenment*, 3.
113. Hanson, *Provincial Politics*, 60–61.
114. Wollstonecraft, *Collected Letters*, 249.
115. Belissa, "Les Leçons de républicanisme," 64–66.
116. Wahnich, *L'impossible citoyen*, 160–61; Doyle, *Aristocracy and Its Enemies*, 290.
117. Mortier, *Anacharsis Cloots*, 453.
118. Wahnich, *L'impossible citoyen*, 185; Buel, *Joel Barlow*, 179.
119. Buel, *Joel Barlow*, 179–80.
120. *Journal de Perlet* 7, no. 434 (30 Nov. 1793), 485–86.
121. Sewell, "Sans-Culotte Rhetoric," 257–61.
122. *Journal de Perlet* 8, no. 461 (27 Dec. 1793), 214, no. 463 (29 Dec. 1793), 229–30, and no. 464 (30 Dec. 1793), 238.
123. Desmoulins, *Vieux Cordelier*, 46, 148–49,181–83; Robisco, *Jean-Jacques Rousseau*, 233.
124. Audouin, *Journal universel*, no. 1492 (5 Nivose, Year II), 6516; Guilhaumou and Monnier, "Cordeliers," 207.
125. Hampson, *Saint-Just*, 162–63.
126. *Gazette nationale*, no. 94 (24 Dec. 1793), 27; *Journal de Perlet* 8, no. 459 (25 Dec. 1793), 198–200 and no. 460 (26 Dec. 1793), 208; Hampson, *Life and Opinions*, 218–19.
127. Audouin, *Journal universel*, no. 1492 (5 Novise, Year II), 6517–18; *Journal de Perlet* 8, no. 456 (22 Dec. 1793), 171.
128. Desmoulins, *Vieux Cordelier*, 108–9.
129. *Gazette nationale*, no. 94 (24 Dec. 1793), 26–27; *Journal de Perlet* 8, no. 461 (27 Dec. 1793), 214–15.
130. *Journal de Perlet* 8, no. 465 (31 Dec. 1793), 241.
131. Ibid., no. 460 (26 Dec. 1793), 204–5; Dupuy, *La république jacobine*, 242–43.
132. *Archives Parlementaires*, 82:464 (29 Dec. 1793); Moore, *Moral Purity*, 69–76.
133. Desmoulins, *Vieux Cordelier*, 89, 115; Sa'adah, *Shaping*, 182.
134. *Journal de Perlet* 8, no. 45 (31 Dec. 1793), 241–43.
135. Aulard, *La Société des Jacobins*, 5:598–99 (7 Jan. 1794); Audouin, *Journal universel*, no. 1509 (22 Nivose, Year II), 6652–53; Gershoy, *Betrand Barère*, 206.
136. Aulard, *La Société des Jacobins*, 5:601 (8 Jan. 1794); Hampson, *Saint-Just*, 163–64, 179; Sonenscher, *Sans-Culottes*, 405.
137. Aulard, *La Société des Jacobins*, 5:610 (12 Jan. 1794); *Journal de Perlet* 8, no. 480 (15 Jan. 1794), 35.
138. Aulard, *La Société des Jacobins*, 5:605 (10 Jan. 1794); Moore, *Moral Purity*, 131.
139. Aulard, *La Société des Jacobins*, 5:605 (10 Jan. 1794).
140. *Journal de Perlet* 8, no. 477 (12 Jan. 1794), 340; Chopelin-Blanc, *De l'apologétique*, 520–21, 534–37.
141. *Journal de Perlet* 8, no. 478 (13 Jan. 1794), 348–49; Chopelin-Blanc, *De l'apologétique*, 510–11.
142. *Journal de Perlet* 8, no. 483 (18 Jan. 1794), 388.

143. Ibid., no. 481 (26 Jan. 1794); Hampson, *Life and Opinions*, 194–95.
144. Doyle, *Oxford History*, 258.

CHAPTER 20

The Terror's Last Months (March–July 1794)

1. Roederer, *Spirit of the Revolution*, 82.
2. Becamps, *Un Bordelais*, 74–75.
3. E. Kennedy, *Cultural History*, 405; Popkin, "Not Over After All," 814.
4. Tulard, *Histoire et dictionnaire*, 1114; Doyle, *Aristocracy and Its Enemies*, 293; Andress, *The Terror*, 212–13.
5. Tulard, *Histoire et dictionnaire*, 798; Doyle, *Aristocracy and Its Enemies*, 293.
6. D'Abrantès, *Salons révolutionnaires*, 105.
7. Aulard, *La Société des Jacobins*, 5:674 (6 March 1794); Jacob, *Hébert*, 317; Mortier, *Anacharsis Cloots*, 460.
8. Audouin, *Journal universel* no. 1556 (9 Ventose, Year II), 7052; Jacob, *Hébert*, 317, 319.
9. Audouin, *Journal universel*, no. 1573 (26 Ventose, Year II), 7161–62.
10. Hampson, *Saint-Just*, 176–80.
11. Aulard, *La Société des Jacobins*, 5:683–84 (14 March 1794); Mortier, *Anacharsis Cloots*, 462–63.
12. Aulard, *La Société des Jacobins*, 5:686–87 (14 March 1794).
13. Jacob, *Hébert*, 333; Antheunis, *Le conventionnel belge*, 64–65; Tulard, *Histoire et dictionnaire*, 1075.
14. Audouin, *Journal universel*, no. 1577 (30 Ventose, Year II), 7194; Dupuy, *La république jacobine*, 252–53; Scurr, *Fatal Purity*, 277; Jacob, *Hébert*, 336.
15. Saint-Just, *Œuvres complètes*, 713; Desmoulins, *Vieux Cordelier*, 90–91; *Gazette nationale* 176 (16 March 1794), 706.
16. Linton, *Conspiracies Real and Imagined*, 138.
17. Aulard, *La Société des Jacobins*, 6:11–12 (21 March 1794).
18. Hampson, *Life and Opinions*, 202, 211; McPhee, *Robespierre*, 189; Linton, *Conspiracies Real and Imagined*, 137–41.
19. Desmoulins, *Vieux Cordelier*, 110; Saint-Just, *Œuvres complètes*, 713; Wallon, *Histoire*, 1:37, 1:49, 1:53; Rosendaal, *Bataven!*, 413.
20. Andress, *The Terror*, 268; Rosendaal, *Bataven!*, 414–15; Klein, *Patriots republikanisme*, 249.
21. Jacob, *Hébert*, 350–51.
22. Ibid., 353; Gershoy, *Betrand Barère*, 213–14; Mortier, *Anacharsis Cloots*, 469, 481.
23. Desmoulins, *Vieux Cordelier*, 96.
24. Ibid., 113; Sa'adah, *Shaping*, 181–82.
25. Desmoulins, *Vieux Cordelier*, 96–97.
26. Ibid., 134–37.
27. Baudot, *Notes historiques*, 102, 130, 150, 156; Desmoulins, *Vieux Cordelier*, 61; Gueniffey, *La politique de la Terreur*, 30–31, 271–72.
28. Baudot, *Notes historiques*, 205.
29. Hampson, *Life and Opinions*, 221–23; McPhee, *Robespierre*, 190–91.

30. Baudot, *Notes historiques*, 215, 231; Antheunis, *Le conventionnel belge*, 67–68.
31. Staël, *Considerations*, 362; Guillois, *Salon de Madame Helvétius*, 83–84.
32. Robespierre, *Discours du 8 Thermidor*, 32.
33. Aulard, *La Société des Jacobins*, 6:36–37 (31 March 1794).
34. Ibid., 6:51 (5 April 1794).
35. Dard, *Hérault de Sechelles*, 357.
36. Vinot, *Saint-Just*, 277–79.
37. Saint-Just, *Œuvres complètes*, 718–25; Hampson, *Saint-Just*, 193, 195–96; Godineau, *Women of Paris*, 187–88.
38. Aulard, *La Société des Jacobins*, 6:43–52 (5 April 1794).
39. Wahnich, *L'Impossible citoyen*, 202.
40. Roederer, *Spirit of the Revolution*, 81–88.
41. Audouin, *Journal universel* 1576 (29 Ventose, Year II), 7186, 7190.
42. Roederer, *Spirit of the Revolution*, 84.
43. De Baecque, "Pamphlets," 166.
44. Zizek, "Plume de fer," 627–28.
45. Popkin, *Right-Wing Press*, 17, 19.
46. Saint-Just, *Œuvres complètes*, 748; *La Décade philosophique* 1 (10 Floreal), 35–37; Hampson, *Saint-Just*, 199.
47. Saint-Just, *Œuvres complètes*, 756–62; *La Décade philosophique* 1 (10 Floreal), 39–40, 42; Doyle, *Aristocracy and Its Enemies*, 291.
48. *La Décade philosophique* 1 (10 Floreal), 33.
49. Ibid., 76.
50. Ibid.
51. Ibid., 73–74.
52. Ibid., 77.
53. *Archives Parlementaires*, 90:137 (7 May 1794); Ozouf, *Festivals*, 108–9.
54. Robespierre, *Discours du 18 Floreal*, 16.
55. Ibid., 20.
56. Ibid., 21.
57. Ibid., 36; E. Badinter and R. Badinter, *Condorcet, 1743–1794*, 575.
58. Robespierre, *Discours du 8 Thermidor*, 30; Saint-Just, *Œuvres complètes*, 716; Roederer, *De la philosophie*, 36.
59. Robespierre, *Discours du 8 Thermidor*, 31–32; Crow, *Emulation*, 175–76, 178.
60. Robespierre, *Discours du 8 Thermidor*, 33; *La Décade philosophique* 1 (30 Floreal), 190.
61. Robespierre, *Discours du 8 Thermidor*, 43–44; Ozouf, *Festivals*, 108; Edelstein, *Terror*, 232–34.
62. Robespierre, *Discours du 8 Thermidor*, 20–21; Hampson, *Life and Opinions*, 273; Scurr, *Fatal Purity*, 289–92.
63. *Archives Parlementaires*, 90:567–68 (23 May).
64. Ibid., 93:8–9, 13, 39 (9 July 1794).
65. Ibid., 90:576 (13 June).
66. Ibid., 93:37 (10 July 1794).
67. Ibid., 93:122 (13 July 1794).
68. Ibid., 91:302 (4 June 1794).
69. Ibid., 91:228 (2 June 1794).

70. Ibid., 93:301, 310–11 (19 July 1794).

71. Mongrédien, *French Music*, 39–40, 266; Gueniffey, *La politique de la Terreur*, 275, 301, 315.

72. *La Décade philosophique* 1 (30 Prairial), 339–40; Baudot, *Notes historiques*, 4–5.

73. *La Décade philosophique* 1 (30 Prairial), 341–42; Kitchin, *Journal*, 6, 17, 30–31, 34.

74. *La Décade philosophique* 1 (30 Prairial), 342–46; Tallett, "Robespierre and Religion," 102–6.

75. Baudot, *Notes historiques*, 4–5.

76. *Archives Parlementaires*, 90:569 (23 May 1794), 93:59 (10 July1794), and 93:284 (18 July 1794).

77. Dupuy, *La république jacobine*, 264; Andress, *The Terror*, 311, 325, 330.

78. Gueniffey, *La politique de la Terreur*, 277–84.

79. *Annales Patriotiques*, no. 552 (7 July 1794), 2420.

80. Wollstonecraft, *Collected Letters*, 255.

81. Roederer, *Spirit of the Revolution*, 82.

82. Hanson, *Jacobin Republic*, 243.

83. *Annales patriotiques,* no. 558 (13 July 1794), 2444–45; Girey-Dupré, *Patriote français* 1372 (17 May 1793), 548; Prudhomme, *Histoire générale*, 2:153; Gough, *Newspaper Press*, 102; Mathiez, *Fall of Robespierre*, 173–83.

84. *Annales patriotiques*, no. 571 (26 July 1794), 2496.

85. Ibid., no. 561 (16 July 1794), 2456; Mongrédien, *French Music*, 42–43; Gross, *Fair Shares*, 196–97.

86. Hampson, *Life and Opinions*, 290–92; Baczko, *Ending the Terror*, 36; Sa'adah, *Shaping*, 177,183–84; Dupuy, *La république jacobine*, 275–77.

87. Dupuy, *La république jacobine*, 262–24; Edelstein, *Terror*, 249–50, 254.

88. Cobb, *The French*, 233; Baczko, "L'expérience thermidorienne," 344–45.

CHAPTER 21

Thermidor

1. Mathiez, *Fall of Robespierre*, 116, 226–27; Tackett, *Becoming a Revolutionary*, 88.

2. Hampson, *Life and Opinions*, 204, 296; Hampson, *Saint-Just*, 217–18; Scurr, *Fatal Purity*, 303–4; McPhee, *Robespierre*, 205.

3. Baudot, *Notes historiques*, 152.

4. Robespierre, *Discours du 8 Thermidor*, in Žižek, *Robespierre*, 256.

5. Aulard, *Jacobins*, 6:257–69 (26 July 1794); Robespierre, *Discours du 8 Thermidor*, in Žižek, *Robespierre,* 266, 270.

6. Aulard, *La Société des Jacobins*, 6:246, 6:257–60, 6:269–81 (26 July 1794).

7. Roux, *Relation*, 9; Aulard, *La Société des Jacobins*, 6:282 (26 July 1784); Gershoy, *Betrand Barère*, 252–53.

8. Saint-Just, *Œuvres complètes*, 780–82.

9. *Archives Parlementaires*, 93:541, 93:551 (27 July 1794).

10. Saint-Just, *Œuvres complètes*, 773–74; *La Décade philosophique* 2 (20 Thermidor), 116–17.

11. *Annales patriotiques* 572 (27 July 1794), 573 (28 July), and 574 (29 July), 2503, 2508, 2510.
12. *Archives Parlementaires*, 93:553 (27 July 1794).
13. Ibid., 93:564–65, 93:575.
14. *Annales patriotiques* 575 (30 July 1794), 2511–12.
15. Ibid., 574 (29 July 1794), 2512; Roux, *Relation de l'Évènement*, 8.
16. *Archives Parlementaires*, 93:564 (27 July 1794).
17. Fréron, *L'Orateur du peuple* 7, no. 5 (1794), 34; Gershoy, *Betrand Barère*, 256–57; Miller, *Rousseau*, 158; Burstin, *Révolution*, 835–45.
18. *La Décade philosophique* 2 (20 Thermidor), 119.
19. *Annales patriotiques* 574 (29 July 1794), 2513–14; Mercier, *Paris*, 2:376; Baczko, *Politiques*, 134–35.
20. *Annales patriotiques,* no. 576 (13 July 1794), 2516.
21. Palmer, *From Jacobin to Liberal*, 60–61, 71.
22. Woloch, "Revival of Jacobinism," 15; Mastroberti, *Pierre Joseph Briot*, 38–39; Peyrard, *Jacobins de l'Ouest*, 264.
23. Dwyer, *Napoleon*, 154–55.
24. *La Décade philosophique* 2 (20 Thermidor), 121, and 2 (10 Fructidor), 242; Lefevre, *French Revolution*, 138.
25. Biard, *Missionaires de la République*, 364.
26. Baudot, *Notes historiques*, 3–4, 41, 244–46.
27. Babeuf, *Journal de la Liberté*, no. 16 (4 Vendémiaire, Year III), 5–6 and no. 17 (5 Vendémiaire, Year III), 1–3.
28. Gaulmier, *Un grand témoin*, 163–64.
29. Destutt de Tracy, *Premiers écrits*, 58–59; Joly, introduction to Destutt de Tracy, *Premiers écrits*, 47.
30. Garrigus, "Opportunist or Patriot?," 11.
31. Baczko, "L'expérience thermidorienne," 347.
32. Dauteribes, "Daunou et le modèle," 132–33; E. Kennedy, "Aux origines," 13.
33. Fréron, *L'Orateur du peuple* 7, no. 4 (30 Fructidor, Year II), 29–30.
34. Varlet, *L'Explosion*, 5–7, 14.
35. Fréron, *L'Orateur du peuple* 7, no. 4 (30 Fructidor, Year II), 27–28.
36. Necker, *De la Révolution*, 3:68–69; Woloch, "Revival of Jacobinism," 16; Baczko, *Ending the Terror*, 32–34.
37. Babeuf, *Journal de la Liberté*, no. 16 (4 Vendémiaire, Year III), 5.
38. Fréron, *L'Orateur du peuple* 7, no. 1 (23 Fructidor, Year II), 2.
39. Hampson, *Life and Opinions*, 163, 286; McPhee, *Robespierre*, 192, 218.
40. *La Décade philosophique* 2 (20 Thermidor), 112–13; Baudot, *Notes historiques*, 3, 215.
41. Baudot, *Notes historiques*, 41; *La Décade philosophique* 2 (20 Thermidor), 112–15; Kitchin, *Un journal "philosophique,"* 35–36.
42. Baczko, *Ending the Terror*, 53; Baczko, *Politiques*, 186.
43. *La Décade philosophique* 2 (20 Fructidor), 315–16; Gershoy, *Betrand Barère*, 266–67.
44. Baczko, *Ending the Terror*, 57.
45. *La Décade philosophique* 2 (20 Fructidor), 317–23.
46. Babeuf, *Journal de la Liberté* 1 (17 Fructidor, Year II), 3.

47. Ibid., 6 (27 Fructidor, Year II), 2.
48. Ibid., 10 (30 Fructidor, Year II), 2.
49. Gershoy, *Betrand Barère*, 270–71.
50. Babeuf, *Tribunal du Peuple* 23 (14 Vendémiaire, Year III), 4–6; Jullien, *L'Orateur plébéien*, prospectus, 4.
51. Babeuf, *Journal de la Liberté*, no. 13 (1 Vendémiaire, Year III), 1–4.
52. Andress, *The Terror*, 239–40; Baczko, "L'expérience thermidorienne," 345.
53. Fréron, *L'Orateur du peuple* 7, no. 11 (12 Vendémiaire, Year II), 83.
54. Ibid., 85 and 7, no. 13 (16 Vendémiaire, Year II), 101.
55. Ibid., 101; Dupuy, *La république jacobine*, 264.
56. Fréron, *L'Orateur du peuple* 7, no. 1 (23 Fructidor, Year II), 4–5.
57. Hampson, *Life and Opinions*, 286.
58. Audouin, *Journal universel*, no. 1725 (28 Thermidor, Year II), 8378–79.
59. Babeuf, *Journal de la Liberté*, no. 13 (1 Vendémiaire, Year III), 2.
60. *La Décade philosophique* 2 (10 Fructidor), 242–44; *Journal de Perlet* 14, no. 480; Baczko, *Ending the Terror*, 68–69.
61. Audouin, *Journal universel*, no. 1725 (28 Thermidor, Year II), 8382; Serna, *Antontelle, Aristocrate révolutionnaire*, 247–50.
62. Forsyth, introduction to Roederer, *The Spirit of the Revolution*, xxv.
63. Nelson, *Thomas Paine*, 286.
64. Gauchet, *La Révolution des droits*, 299–300.
65. Apt, *Louis-Philippe de Ségur*, 90–91.
66. Serna, *Antontelle, Aristocrate révolutionnaire*, 246–47.
67. Mathiez, *La Théophilanthropie*, 114–15.
68. BN pamph. LB41-1451, *Abjuration des petites filles jacobites*, 1–2.
69. Audouin, *Journal universel*, no. 1725 (28 Thermidor, Year II), 8381.

CHAPTER 22

Post-Thermidor (1795–97)

1. BL 643/6, *Lettre Du Citoyen Naigeon, habitant de Sedan*, 2, 4.
2. Ibid., 7.
3. Woloch, *Jacobin Legacy*, 53, 330, 338.
4. BL 843-4, 5/3, 17, *Les Douze Représentants du Peuple détenus à Port-Libre*, 2, 5–6, 27.
5. Babeuf, *Tribun du peuple*, no. 28 (28 Frimaire, Year III), 246.
6. Monseignat, *Un chapitre de la Révolution française*, 217; Baczko, *Ending the Terror*, 84, 87; Mason, "Never Was a Plot So Holy," 186–88.
7. Rose, *Gracchus Babeuf*, 214.
8. Woloch, *Jacobin Legacy*, 146–47.
9. Babeuf, *Tribun du peuple*, no. 28 (28 Frimaire, Year III), 244–45; Jullien, *L'Orateur plébéien* 2 (Frimaire Year IV), 3; Serna, *Antonelle*, 213.
10. Baudot, *Notes historiques*, 98, 113, 139, 155.
11. Buonarroti, *Conspiration pour l'égalité*, 1:21; Peyrard, *Jacobins de l'Ouest*, 291–92.
12. Buonarroti, *Conspiration pour l'égalité*, 1:22; Rose, *Gracchus Babeuf*, 214–15.
13. Mathiez, *La réaction thermidorienne*, 176–77; Burstin, *Révolution*, 870–71.

14. Mercier, *Paris*, 2:387–405.
15. Jourdan, "Le culte de Rousseau," 68–69.
16. Mercier, *Paris*, 2:21–22.
17. Wollstonecraft, *Collected letters*, 266.
18. BN pamph. LB41-1451, *Abjuration des petites filles jacobites*, 3–4.
19. Ibid., 8–11.
20. Peyrard, *Jacobins*, 265–66.
21. Lajer-Burcharth, *Necklines*, 24–55, 49, 52.
22. Louvet, *Mémoires*, 2:77–78.
23. Mathiez, *La réaction thermidorienne*, 217, 221–23.
24. Roederer, *De l'interet*, 8–10; Roederer, *Spirit of the Revolution*, xxv; Mathiez, *La réaction thermidorienne*, 186–87.
25. Jollivet, *Rappellez vos collègues*, 8–9, 17, 26–27; Mathiez, *La réaction thermidorienne*, 187.
26. Petit, *Procès des 31 Mai*, 9–12, 16, 30–31; Ozouf, "Terror after the Terror," 8–10.
27. Peyrard, *Jacobins de l'Ouest*, 292; Spang, *Invention of the Restaurant*, 138–39, 143–44; Lajer-Burcharth, *Necklines*, 191.
28. Apt, *Louis-Phillipe de Ségur*, 91; Lajer-Burcharth, *Necklines*, 259.
29. Baudot, *Notes historiques*, 139; Tulard, *Histoire et dictionnaire*, 1111.
30. *Journal de Perlet* 14, no. 857, 18 Pluviose (7 Feb. 1795), 479.
31. Ibid., 474–80.
32. Baudot, *Notes historiques*, 159.
33. Lalouette, *Séparation des églises*, 47–50.
34. *Journal de Perlet*, no. 33 (30 Nov. 1795, Year III), 262.
35. Woronoff, *Thermidorean Regime*, 15–16; W. Scott, *Terror and Repression*, 333; Slavin, *French Revolution*, 367–68; Peyrard, *Jacobins de l'Ouest*, 293–94.
36. *Journal de Perlet* 7 (22 Dec. 1796), 413; Gershoy, *Betrand Barère*, 285, 292.
37. Woronoff, *Thermidorean Regime*, 16; Crook, *Toulon*, 167.
38. Jullien, *L'Orateur plébéien* 1 (21 Brumaire Year IV), 3, 5; Fuoc, *La réaction thermidorienne*, 95–131.
39. Cobb, *The French*, 191–93; Doyle, *Oxford History*, 291–92, 327.
40. Crook, *Toulon*, 166–67; Scott, *Terror and Repression*, 333.
41. Conac, "La Convention thermidorienne," 221–22; Nicolle, "Lanjuinais," 94–95.
42. Woronoff, *Thermidorean Regime*, 17–19; Slavin, *French Revolution*, 369.
43. Baudot, *Notes historiques*, 108; Baczko, *Ending the Terror*, 236–40; Lebozec, "Les idées politiques," 150.
44. Lebozec, "Les idées politiques," 148–49.
45. Slavin, *French Revolution*, 376–77; Serna, *Antonelle*, 254–55.
46. Baudot, *Notes historiques*, 202–3; Gross, *Fair Shares*, 25, 163.
47. Conac, "La Convention thermidorienne," 224.
48. Woronoff, *Thermidorean Regime*, 29; Guachet, *Révolution des pouvoirs*, 159–71.
49. Luchaire, "Boissy d'Anglas," 45; Nicolle, "Lanjuinais," 109; Lebozec, "Boissy d'Anglas," 85.

50. Gainot, "Pierre Guyomar," 264–66; Conac, "La Convention thermidorienne," 227–30.

51. Luchaire, "Boissy d'Anglas," 44–46; Conac, "La Convention thermidorienne," 223–30.

52. *Archives Parlementaires*, 58:602 (15 Feb. 1793); Tulard, *Histoire et dictionnaire*, 696.

53. Tulard, *Histoire et dictionnaire*, 702; Jainchill, *Reimagining Politics*, 18–19.

54. Baczko, *Politiques*, 237; Jainchill, *Reimagining Politics*, 40; Lebozec, "Boissy d'Anglas," 89.

55. Tulard, *Histoire et dictionnaire*, 696–97.

56. Gauchet, *Revolution des droits*, 206.

57. Staël, *Considerations*, 386.

58. Babeuf, *Tribun du peuple,* no. 43, 299.

59. Maréchal, *Manifeste des égaux*, 89; Buonarroti, *Conspiration pour l'égalité*, 1:56–58.

60. Tulard, *Histoire et dictionnaire*, 722; Andries, "Les imprimeurs-libraires parisiens," 256; Woloch, *Jacobin Legacy*, 396–97.

61. Bellanger, *Histoire générale*, 1:521; Walton, *Policing Public Opinion*, 228.

62. De Baecque, "Pamphlets," 166.

63. Dwyer, *Napoleon*, 157.

64. Woloch, *Jacobin Legacy*, 150–54.

65. Hermon-Belot, *L'Abbé Grégoire*, 361–66; Baczko, "Tournant culturel," 22–23.

66. Buonarroti, *Conspiration pour l'égalité*, 1:24, 1:37–45.

67. Staum, "Individual Rights," 411–12.

68. Baczko, "Tournant culturel," 17.

69. Schandeler and Crepel, "Introduction génerale," 1, 9–10, 24, 45; E. Kennedy, "Aux origins," 13–14.

70. Condorcet, *Tableau historique*, 46–47; Whatmore, *Republicanism*, 111.

71. Baczko, "Tournant culturel," 33.

72. Livesey, *Making Democracy*, 172–73.

73. Gaulmier, *Un grand témoin*, 165–66; Staum, *Cabanis*, 129, 164–65.

74. Dauteribes, "Daunou," 118, 128–33; Jainchill, *Reimagining Politics*, 76–77.

75. Gaulmier, *Un grand témoin*, 168–69; Staum, "Individual Rights," 413–17; Chappey, "Les Écoles," 337.

76. Staum, *Minerva's Message*, 13; Wokler, *Rousseau*, 194; Whatmore, *Republicanism*, 111–12.

77. Dauteribes, "Daunou et le modèle," 117, 132–33; Jennings, *Revolution*, 310, 325.

78. Whatmore, *Republicanism*, 122; Schoorl, *Jean-Baptiste Say*, 18.

79. Ibid.

80. Welch, *Liberty and Utility*, 5, 10–11, 27–29; Staum, *Minerva's Message*, 46–47.

81. *La Décade philosophique*, no. 30, Year V, (4th trimestre), 18 July 1797, 129–33.

82. Gaulmier, *Un grand témoin*, 207–12.

83. Gainot, "Pierre Guyomar," 263; Staum, "Individual Rights," 418; Schoorl, *Jean-Baptiste Say*, 19–20.

84. Staum, *Cabanis*, 142–44, 205.

85. Ibid., 215.

86. Condorcet, *Tableau historique*, 374–75.
87. Goetz, "Destutt de Tracy," 70–71; Whatmore, *Republicanism*, 128.
88. Baczko, *Politiques*, 239–40.
89. Baudot, *Notes historiques*, 23.
90. Baczko, *Politiques*, 279–82, 287–89; Slavin, *French Revolution*, 387–89.
91. Palmer, *From Jacobin to Liberal*, 71; Baczko, *Politiques*, 293–96.
92. Baczko, *Politiques*, 296.
93. Ibid., 308–9; Woronoff, *Thermidorian Regime*, 31–33; Serna, *Antonelle*, 261; Mastroberti, *Pierre Joseph Briot*, 40.
94. Baczko, *Politiques*, 312–15.
95. Babeuf, *Défense*, 24; Jullien, *L'Orateur plébéien* 2 (1 Frimaire, Year IV), 5.
96. Babeuf, *Défense*, 46.
97. *Journal de Perlet*, Year IV, no. 46 (13 Dec. 1795), 361.
98. Beyssi, "Parti Jacobin," 31.
99. H. G. Brown, "Search for Stability," 23.
100. Palmer, *From Jacobin to Liberal*, 73; Woloch, *Jacobin Legacy*, 163–65.
101. Vovelle, *Révolution française*, 77.
102. Staël, *Considerations*, 379–80; Baczko, *Politiques*, 389, 391; Craiutu, *Virtue for Courageous Minds*, 175–78; Lajer-Burchardt, *Necklines*, 257, 275.
103. Palmer, *From Jacobin to Liberal*, 71; Serna, *Antonelle*, 300–301.
104. Buonarroti, *Conspiration pour l'égalité*, 1:101–2.
105. *Journal de Perlet*, Year VII, no. 406 (22 Dec. 1796), 412; Staël, *Considerations*, 384, 398; J. A. Scott, "François Noël Babeuf," 7.
106. Buonarroti, *Conspiration pour l'égalité*, 1:107.
107. Dommanget, *Babeuf*, 30; Scott, "François Noël Babeuf," 7; Rose, *Gracchus Babeuf*, 226–27.
108. Bellanger, *Histoire générale*, 1:523.
109. Rose, *Gracchus Babeuf*, 215–16; Mason, "Never Was a Plot So Holy," 179–81.
110. D'Holbach, *Système social*, 75–78; Jullien, *L'Orateur plébéien* 12 (23 Frimaire, Year IV), 3–4.
111. Jullien, *L'Orateur plébéien* 4 (5 Frimaire, Year IV), 4; Palmer, *From Jacobin to Liberal*, 72–75; Serna, *Antonelle*, 263–64.
112. *Journal des hommes libres*, no. 5 (20 Vendémiaire, Year V), 20 and no. 7 (22 Vendémiaire, Year V), 27.
113. Ibid., 19.
114. Ibid., no. 59 (14 Frimaire, Year V), 235.

CHAPTER 23

The "General Revolution" (1795–1800): Holland, Italy,
and the Levant

1. Altena, *Gerrit Paape*, 360–71.
2. Rosendaal, *Nederlandse Revolutie,* 92–93; Altena, *Gerrit Paape*, 347–64.
3. Israel, *Democratic Enlightenment*, 885.
4. Ibid., 890.
5. Rosendaal, *Bataven!*, 446.
6. Schama, *Patriots and Liberators*, 179–212; Jourdaan, "Politieke en culturele transfers," 561–64.

7. Rosendaal, *Bataven!*, 3.

8. Te Brake, *Regents and Rebels*, 170.

9. Rosendaal, *Bataven!*, 99

10. Wells, *Insurrection*, 69, 110.

11. *Décade philosophique*, no. 33, Year V (4th Trimestre), 17 Aug. 1797, 373.

12. Cremona, *Catalogo*, 62–63, 274, 325–26.

13. Johns, *Antonio Canova*, 47.

14. Gioia, *Dissertazione*, 195.

15. Ibid., 28–29.

16. Ibid., preface, 3 and 156–61; Capra, *I progressi*, 571–72.

17. Gioia, *Dissertazione*, 162.

18. Ibid., 37–39.

19. Israel, *Democratic Enlightenment*, 46, 271, 274, 278, 350, 363.

20. Pancaldi, *Volta*, 8, 160, 175; Ferrone, *Società giusta*, 219; Symcox, "Of Princes, Poets," 515–16, 534–35.

21. Gioia, *Dissertazione*, preface, 4 and 195; Capra, *I progressi*, 588–92.

22. *Journal des hommes libres*, no. 5 (20 Vendémiaire, Year V), 17.

23. Ghibaudi, *La fortuna*, 230; Capra, *I progressi*, 590.

24. *Journal des hommes libres*, no. 11 (26 Vendémiare, Year V), 41.

25. Johns, *Antonio Canova*, 46–47, 56.

26. *La Décade philosophique*, no. 29, Year V (4th Trimestre), 118.

27. Ibid., 119–20.

28. Da Passsano, "Dalla democrazia," 288–91.

29. Ibid., 289.

30. Venturi, *Illuministi italiani* 3 (Milan-Naples, 1958), 220.

31. Dwyer, *Napoleon*, 306–7.

32. Broers, *Napoleonic Empire*, 32–34.

33. *Journal des hommes libres*, no. 3 (18 Vendémiaire, Year V), 11.

34. Gioia, *Dissertazione*, 153.

35. Ibid., 155–56.

36. Gorani, *Mémoires secrets*, 1:54–55; Palmieri, *Riflessioni*, 28; Israel, *Democratic Enlightenment*.

37. Rao, *Regno di Napoli*, 128–29.

38. Ferrone, *Società giusta*, 217, 230–36.

39. Jacobitti, *Revolutionary Humanism*, 24; Ferrone, *Società giusta*, 232–33; De Francesco, "How Not to Finish," 172.

40. De Francesco, "How Not to Finish," 175.

41. Jacobitti, *Revolutionary Humanism*, 25.

42. Broers, *Napoleonic Empire*, 41–44.

43. Ibid., 44–45.

44. Gioia, *Dissertazione,* 253, 262–63, 267; Jacobitti, *Revolutionary Humanism,* 26; De Francesco, "How Not to Finish," 170–71.

45. De Francesco, "How Not to Finish," 168.

46. Le Breton, "Considérations sur l'Egypte," in *La Décade philosophique*, no. 20 (20 Germinal, Year VII), 78.

47. Hitzel, "La France," 10–11.

48. [Feller], *Journal historique*, 1:433 (15 March 1793) and 1:601–2 (15 April 1793).

49. *Gazette Nationale,* no. 180 (20 March 1794), 742.
50. Raynal, *Histoire philosophique* 6:20 (1780).
51. Le Breton, "Considérations sur l'Egypte," in *La Décade philosophique,* no. 20 (20 Germinal, Year VII), 79–81.
52. Fromm, *Bibliographie,* 6:261.
53. Raynal, *Histoire philosophique,* 4:110, 4:112 (1770).
54. D'Argens, *The Jewish Spy,* 2:104, 2:155–56.
55. Ibid., 2:158.
56. Volney, *Voyage en Syrie,* 1:173.
57. Ibid., 1:379, 1:382–83.
58. Ibid., 1:342.
59. Ibid., 1:436.
60. Ibid., 2:405.
61. Ibid., 2:432.
62. Ibid.
63. Ibid., 2:410.
64. Ibid., 1:186, 1:381–82; Israel, *Revolution of the Mind,* 222–23.
65. Israel, *Revolution of the Mind,* 743.
66. Dwyer, *Napoleon,* 338–39; Lawday, *Napoleon's Master,* 92, 108.
67. Hitzel, "La France," 15.
68. GSAC GD (1797–98) 2, section 2, fols. 7, 8, and 21.
69. Bartolini to Commandant Gentili, Corfu, 22 March 1798, GSAC Allilografia diaphoros (1797–98) 1, fol. 87.
70. Report, "Isles de Levant" (8 Feb. 1798), in Anoyatis-Pele, *Six rapports,* 21–24.
71. GSAC GD (1797–98) 2, section 5, 17, fol. 47, edict Corfu, 26 Prairial, Year VI.
72. Ibid., 1, section 2, fol. 78.
73. Ibid., 1, section 2, fols. 132, 144.
74. Ibid., 1, fols. 444–46.
75. Lefebvre, *French Revolution,* 219.
76. Cherfils, *Napoleon and Islam,* 5.
77. Bourguet, "Des Savants," 21.
78. Bourguet, "Science and Memory," 96–97.
79. Al-Jabarti, *History,* 22; Cherfils, *Napoleon and Islam,* 5–8.
80. Cherfils, *Napoleon and Islam,* 6–7.
81. Al-Jabarti, *History,* 25–26; Bell, *First Total War,* 209.
82. Laissus, "Commission," 39–40; Dentz, *Napoleon Bonaparte,* 83; Raymond, "Les Egyptiens," 105–6, 108.
83. Coller, "Egypt," 127.
84. Cherfils, *Napoleon and Islam,* 11–12.
85. Al-Jabarti, *History,* 67, 71, 75, 81, 117; Dentz, *Napoleon Bonaparte,* 62, 64.
86. Al-Jabarti, *History,* 75–76.
87. Dwyer, *Napoleon,* 341, 343–47; Dentz, *Napoleon Bonaparte,* 35, 82–83.
88. *La Décade philosophique,* no. 30 (20 Germinal, Year VII), 119–20; Régent, "L'Égypte," 85.
89. Régent, "L'Égypte," 90–91.
90. Gaulmier, *Un grand témoin,* 235.

91. Ortega, "La régénération," 97, 99.
92. Laissus, "Commission," 39–40; Raymond, "Les Égyptiens," 108–9.
93. Al-Jabarti, *History*, 71; Dwyer, *Napoleon Bonaparte*, 390–91.
94. Le Breton, "Considérations sur l'Egypte," in *La Décade philosophique*, no. 20 (20 Germinal, Year VII); Régent, "L'Égypte," 84; Coller,"Egypt," 129.
95. Gaulmier, *Un grand témoin*, 232–33.
96. Kitchin, *Journal*, 14–15; Régent, "L'Égypte," 86–87.
97. Le Breton, "Considérations sur l'Egypte," in *La Décade philosophique*, no. 20 (20 Germinal, Year VII), 149.
98. Le Breton, "Considérations sur l'Egypte," in *La Décade philosophique*, no. 20 (20 Germinal, Year VII), 149–54.
99. Régent, "L'Égypte," 88.
100. Staum, *Minerva's Message*, 134; Sonenscher, *Before the Deluge*, 334–36, 338–46.
101. Régent, "L'Égypte," 87.
102. Régent, "L'Égypte," 89; Raymond, "Les Egyptiens," 104.

CHAPTER 24

The Failed Revolution (1797–99)

1. Jullien, *L'Orateur plébéien* 1 (21 Brumaire, Year IV), 10; *Journal des hommes libres,* no. 119 (14 Pluviose, Year V), 482–83.
2. *Journal des hommes libres,* no. 5 (20 Vendémiaire, Year V), 20 and no. 7 (22 Vendémiaire, Year V), 27.
3. Buonarroti, *Conspiration pour l'égalité*, 1:53, 1:70–72, 1:81–82, 1:113–14; Scott, "François Noël Babeuf," 7.
4. Buonarroti, *Conspiration pour l'égalité*, 1:88–89; Mathiez, *Fall of Robespierre*, 224–26; Fajn, "Attitude of the *Journal des hommes libres*," 233.
5. Rose, *Gracchus Babeuf*, 214–15; Fajn, "Attitude of the *Journal des hommes libres*," 234.
6. Buonarroti, *Conspiration pour l'égalité*, 1:134–40, 1:154, 1:156, 1:198.
7. Ibid., 1:24; Vovelle, *Les Jacobins*, 32.
8. Maréchal, *Manifeste des égaux*, 86.
9. Ibid.
10. *Journal des hommes libres*, no. 119 (3 Feb. 1797), 482.
11. *Journal de Perlet*, no. 497 (23 March 1797), 177, 180.
12. Bonneville, *Vieux Tribun*, 115, 126–27.
13. *Journal de Perlet,* no. 500 (26 March 1797), 198.
14. Gueniffey, *Dix-huit Brumaire*, 113.
15. *La Décade philosophique*, no. 31 (4th trimeste, 20 Thermidor, Year V), 249–51 and no. 32 (4th Trimester, Year V, 7 Aug. 1797), 313.
16. *La Décade philosophique* no. 32 (4th Trimestre, Year V, 7 Aug. 1797), 311.
17. Babeuf, *Defense*, 23; Buonarroti, *Conspiration pour l'égalité*, 2:22–27.
18. Tarin, *Diderot et la Révolution*, 110–15.
19. Kouvelakis, *Philosophy and Revolution*, 79.
20. Ibid.
21. Maréchal, *Manifeste des égaux*, 92.

22. Ibid., 94.
23. Ibid., 86–87; Kouvelakis, *Philosophy and Revolution*, 81.
24. *Journal de Perlet*, no. 500 (26 March 1797), 200.
25. Buonarroti, *Conspiration pour l'égalité*, 2:59–61; Fajn, "Attitude of the *Journal des hommes libres*," 238–39.
26. Dommanget, *Babeuf*, 80–81; Kouvelakis, *Philosophy and Revolution*, 52.
27. *La Décade philosophique*, no. 31 (4th trimestre, 20 Thermidor, Year V), 247–56; Staël, *Considerations*, 399–400.
28. *La Décade philosophique*, no. 36 (4th Trimestre, Year V, 16 Sept., 1797), 563.
29. Forsyth, *Reason and Revolution*, 8; Craiutu, *Virtue for Courageous Minds*, 184; Welch, *Liberty and Utility*, 36–37.
30. Staum, *Cabanis*, 282; Wood, "Benjamin Constant," 7–8.
31. *La Décade philosophique*, no. 36 (4th Trimestre, Year V, 16 Sept., 1797), 566.
32. Ibid., 567.
33. Chopelin-Blanc, *De l'apologétique*, 104–5.
34. Leuwers, *Un Juriste en politique*, 194–96.
35. H. G. Brown, "Search for Stability," 24–25.
36. Woloch, "La République directoriale," 312.
37. Desan, *Reclaiming the Sacred*, 12, 162; Leuwers, *Un Juriste en politique*, 197–98.
38. H. G. Brown, "Search for Stability," 25; Aston, *Religion and Revolution*, 281.
39. Mathiez, *La Théophilanthropie*, 132–33.
40. Woloch, "La République directoriale," 315–17.
41. *La Décade philosophique*, no. 36 (4th Trimstre, Year V, 16 Sept. 1797), 536.
42. Woloch, "La République directoriale," 317–18.
43. Ibid., 315–17; Staum, *Cabanis*, 274; Jainchill, *Reimagining Politics*, 80–81.
44. *La Décade philosophique*, no. 32 (4th Trimestre, Year V, 7 Aug. 1797), 317.
45. Bonneville, *Vieux Tribun*, 1:120.
46. Staum, *Cabanis*, 274.
47. *La Décade philosophique*, no. 36 (4th Trimestre, Year V, 16 Sept. 1797), 565; Bertaud, *Les Amis du roi*, 251.
48. Leuwers, *Un Juriste en politique*, 109–10, 193–96.
49. Jainchill, *Reimagining Politics*, 82–83.
50. Wickwar, *Baron d'Holbach*, 112.
51. *La Décade philosophique*, no. 32 (4th Trimestre, Year V, 7 Aug. 1797), 283–86; Helvétius, *Réflexions*, 32n; Smith, *Bibliography*, 292–93.
52. *La Décade philosophique*, no. 32 (4th Trimestre, Year V, 7 Aug. 1797), 284.
53. Rasmussen, "Burning Laws," 82.
54. *La Décade philosophique*, no. 35 (4th Trimestre, Year V, 6 Sept. 1791), 461–66.
55. Ibid., 498.
56. Spitz, "Républicanisme," 36–37, 41.
57. Martin, *Violence et révolution*, 253–54; Serna, *Antonelle*, 308–10.
58. Gainot, *1799, un nouveau Jacobinisme?*, 249.
59. Ibid., 30.
60. Ibid., 31–32.
61. Fajn, "Attitude of the *Journal des hommes libres*," 229–30.
62. Gainot, *1799, un nouveau Jacobinisme?*, 235–37, 455–56.

63. Welch, *Liberty and Utility*, 37–38 Bredin, *Sieyès*, 463–64.
64. Gaulmier, *Un grand témoin*, 234–6; Forsyth, *Reason and Revolution*, 8–9; Harris, *Antoine d'Estutt de Tracy*, 28; Jainchill, *Reimagining Politics*, 198–200; Wood, "Benjamin Constant," 8.
65. Bredin, *Sieyès*, 454, 459, 461, 466.

CHAPTER 25

Conclusion: The Revolution as the Outcome of the Radical Enlightenment

1. Welch, *Liberty and Utility*, 38–41.
2. Constant, *De la terreur*, 349–50; Spitz, "Républicanisme," 29–30, 44; Craiutu, *Virtue for Courageous Minds*, 216–17.
3. Rivarol, *De la philosophie*, 68–72, 75; Roederer, *De la philosophie*, 29; McMahon, *Enemies of the Enlightenment*, 95–99.
4. Muschik, "Die Ideen der Französischen Revolution," 173–74.
5. Roederer, *De la philosophie*, 29, 36.
6. Constant, *De la terreur*, 347; Baczko, *Ending the Terror*, 245–7; Wokler, *Rousseau*, 195–202.
7. De Luca, "Benjamin Constant," 97.
8. McMahon, *Enemies of the Enlightenment*, 98–108.
9. Popkin, "Not Over," 814.
10. Réal, *Journal de l'Opposition* 7, 33; Jullien, *L'Orateur plébéien* 1 (21 Brumaire, Year IV), 10–13; *La Décade philosophique*, no. 32 (4th Trimestre, Year V, 7 Aug. 1797), 312; Jullien, *L'Orateur plébéien* 1 (21 Brumaire, Year IV), 10–13.
11. Paine, *Rights of Man*, 58.
12. [D'Holbach], *Le Bon-Sens*, 31–32, 36–37; Dupré, *Enlightenment*, 265–67.
13. Rousseau, *Émile*, 46.
14. [D'Holbach], *Le Bon-Sens*, 79, 92, 159.
15. D'Holbach, *Politique naturelle*, 330.
16. Kors, *D'Holbach's coterie*, 309; Mortier, "Les héritiers," 456–58; De Dijn, "Politics of Enlightenment," 800.
17. Naville, *Paul Thiry d'Holbach*, 41–43, 97, 126–27; Staum, *Cabanis*, 24, 28; Israel, *Democratic Enlightenment*, 776–77, 900, 931.
18. Gray, *Enlightenment's Wake*, 163.
19. D'Holbach, *Système social*, 71; Diderot, *Supplément*, 178.

Bibliography

ABBREVIATIONS

Journals

AHR: *American Historical Review*
AHRF: *Annales historiques de la Révolution française*
FHS: *French Historical Studies*
JMH: *The Journal of Modern History*

Archive and Library Collections

BHP pamph.: Bibiliothèque historique de la ville de Paris, collection of revolutionary pamphlets
BL: British Library, London, collection of revolutionary pamphlets
BN pamph.: Bibliothèque Nationale, Paris, collection of revolutionary pamphlets
GSAC: General State Archives, Corfu, Old Fort
PFL pamph.: Princeton, Firestone Library, revolutionary pamphlets

PRIMARY SOURCES

Actes de la Commune de Paris pendant la Révolution. Ed. Sigismond Lacroix. Series 1 (7 vols., Paris, 1894–99) and series 2 (7 vols., Paris, 1900–1909).

Albouys, Barthélemy. *Principes constitutionnels, présentés à la Convention nationale.* Paris, 1793.

Al-Jabarti, Abd al-Rahman. *History of the French Occupation of Egypt, 1798.* Trans. Shmuel Moreh. Princeton, 1993.

Anecdotes curieuses et peu connues sur différentes personnages qui ont joué un rôle dans la Révolution. BHP pamph. 957082. Geneva, 1793.

Archives Parlementaires. Series 1 (1787–94). Ed. M. J. Mavidal et al. 102 vols. thus far. Paris, 1879–2005.

Argens, Jean-Baptiste de Boyer [Marquis d']. *The Jewish Spy: Being a Philosophical, Historical and Critical Correspondence, by Letters which lately pass'd between certain Jews in Turkey, Italy, France, etc.* 4 vols. Dublin, 1753.

Assemblée Nationale, Commune de Paris, et Corps Administratifs. Journal, Paris, 1790.

Assemblée Nationale, Corps administratifs et Nouvelles politiques et littéraires de l'Europe. Continuation of the above. Journal, Paris, 1791–92.

Audouin, Pierre-Jean (ed.). *Journal universel.* Journal, Paris, 1789–95.

Aulard, François Vicor Alphonse (ed.). *La Société des Jacobins: Recueil de documents sur l'histoire du Club de Jacobins de Paris.* 6 vols. Paris, 1889–97.

Babeuf, Gracchus. *Defense*. In Scott (ed.), *Defense of Gracchus Babeuf*, 19–90.

———. *Journal de la Liberté de la Presse*. Journal, Paris, 1794–95.

———. *Tribun du peuple, ou Le défenseur des droits de l'homme*. Journal, Paris, 1795–96.

Bailly, Jean-Sylvain. *Mémoires de Bailly, avec un notice sur sa vie*. 3 vols. Paris, 1821–22.

———. *Œuvres posthumes*. Paris, 1810.

Barlow, Joel. *Advice to the Privileged Orders in the Several States of Europe*. 2 vols. New York, 1792–94.

Barnave, Antoine-Pierre-Joseph-Marie. *De la Révolution et de la Constitution*. Ed. P. Gueniffey. Grenoble, 1988.

———. *Power, Property and History: Joseph Barnave's Introduction to the French Revolution*. Ed. E. Chill. New York, 1971.

Baudot, Marc-Antoine. *Notes historiques sur la Convention Nationale, Le Directoire, l'Empire et l'Exil des Votants*. Paris, 1893.

Bayle, Moise. *De l'inutilité et du danger d'un roi dans un gouvernement libre et représentatif*. Marseille, 1792.

Bécamps, Pierre. *Un Bordelais sous la Terreur: Mémoires de Jean-Baptiste Brochon*. Bordeaux, 1989.

[Bergasse, Nicolas]. *Considérations sur la liberté du commerce*. Londres, 1788.

———. *Lettre de M. Bergasse sur les États-Généraux*. Paris, 1789.

Bertrand de Molleville, Antoine-François. *Mémoires secrets pour servir à l'histoire de la dernière année du règne de Louis XVI*. 3 vols. Londres, 1797.

Bertrand, Dominique. *Lettre à Monsieur l'abbé Raynal*. Marseille, 1789.

Billaud-Varenne, Jacques-Nicolas. *Les Élémens du Républicanisme*. Paris, 1793.

———. *Principes régénérateurs du système social*. Ed. F. Brunel. Paris, 1992.

Bohan, Alain. *Observations sur la Constitution du peuple français*. Paris, 1793.

Bonneville, Nicolas de. *La Bouche de fer*. Journal, Paris, 1790–91.

———. *Le Vieux tribun et sa Bouche de fer*. Journal, Paris, 1797.

Brissot de Warville, Jacques-Pierre. *À tous les républicains de France sur la Société des Jacobins de Paris*. Paris, 1792.

———. *Bibliothèque philosophique du législateur*. 10 vols. "Berlin," 1782.

———. *Correspondance universelle sur ce qui intéresse Le Bonheur de l'Homme et de la société*. "Londres" [Neuchâtel], 1783.

———. *De la vérité, ou Méditations sur les moyens de parvenir à la verité dans toutes les connaisances humaines*. Neuchâtel, 1782.

———. *Discours sur la question de savoir si le roi peut être jugé prononcé à l'Assemblée des Amis de la Constitution*. 10 July 1791.

———. *Examen critique des voyages dans l'Amérique septentrionale de M. le marquis de Chatellux*. "Londres" [Paris], 1786.

——— (ed.). *Le Patriote françois: Journal libre, impartial et national*. Journal, Paris, 1789–93.

———. *Le Philadelphien à Genève, ou Lettres d'un Américain sur la dernière Révolution de Genève*. "Dublin" [Amsterdam?], 1783.

———. *Lettres philosophiques sur Saint Paul, sur sa doctrine, politique, morale et religieuse, et sur plusieurs points de la religion chrétienne, considérés politiquement*. Neuchâtel, 1783.

———. *Mémoire aux Etats-généraux sur la nécessité de rendre, dès ce moment, la presse libre et surtout pour les journaux politiques*. Paris, 1789.

———. *Mémoires (1734–1793)*. Ed. Claude Perroud. 2 vols. Paris, 1910.

———. *Opinion de J. P. Brissot député du département de Paris . . . prononcée le 26 Juillet 1792*. Paris, 1792.

———. *Plan de conduite pour les députés du peuple aux Etats-Généraux de 1789*. Paris, 1789.

———. *Recherches philosophiques sur le droit de propriété considéré dans la nature*. N.p., 1780; repr., Paris, n.d.

———. *Tableau de la situation actuelle des Anglois dans les Indes Orientales*. Paris, 1784.

Buonarroti, Philippe. *Conspiration pour l'égalité dite de Babeuf*. Bruxelles, 1828.

———. *Giornale Patriottico di Corsica*. Journal, Bastia, 1790.

Burke, Edmund. *Reflections on the Revolution in France, and on the proceedings in certain societies in London relative to that event*. London, 1790.

Buzot, François. *Lettres de F.N.L. Buzot, député du département de l'Eure, à ses commétans*. Paris, 1793.

Camus, Armand-Gaston. *Observations sur deux brefs du pape*. Paris, 1791.

———. *Opinion de M. Camus, dans la séance du 31 Mai 1790, sur le plan de constitution de clergé*. Paris, 1790.

[Carra, Jean-Louis]. *Annales patriotiques et littéraires de France*. Journal, Paris, 1789–93.

———. *La Raison, ou le prophète philosophe*. "Londres," 1782.

———. *L'Orateur des États-Généraux sur 1789*. 2 parts. Paris, 1789.

Cérutti, Giuseppe. *Mémoire pour le peuple françois*. N.p., 1788.

Chabot, François. *Journal populaire, ou le Catéchisme des sans-culottes*. Journal, Paris, 1792–93.

Chaudon, L. M. *Dictionnaire anti-philosophique: Pour servir de commentaire & de correctif au Dictionnaire philosophique, & aux autres livres qui ont paru de nos jours contre le Christianisme*. Avignon, 1769.

Chaumette, Pierre-Gaspard. *Mémoires de Chaumette sur la Révolution de 10 août 1792*. Ed. F. A. Aulard. Paris, 1893.

Chénier, Marie-Joseph de. *De la Liberté du théâtre en France*. Paris, 1789.

———. *Dénonciation des Inquisiteurs de la pensée* (25 Aug. 1789). Paris, 1789.

———. "Discours préliminaire" in *Charles IX, ou l'École des rois, tragédie*. Paris, 1790.

———. *Discours prononcé à la Convention nationale, dans la séance du 10 Germinal, l'an III*. Paris, 1795.

———. *Pétition à l'assemblée National du 24 Août 1792 l'an de la liberté*. BL RF 790-1, 2 no. 21.

Cloots, Anacharsis. *De Algemeene Republiek of aanspraak aan de ombrengers der dwingelanden*. Dunkirk, 1792.

———. *La Certitude des preuves du mahométisme*. "Londres," 1780.

———. *Ni Marat, ni Roland*. Paris, 1792.

———. *Œuvres*. 3 vols. Repr., Munich, 1980.

Compte de la mission des représentants du peuple, Treilhard et Mathieu, délégués dans les départemens de la Gironde, Lot et Garonne. Paris, 1793.

Condorcet, Marquis de, Jean-Antoine-Nicolas de Caritat. *Ce que les citoyens ont droit d'attendre de leurs représentans*. Speech of 7 Aug. 1791. Paris, 1791.

———. *Nature et objet de l'instruction publique* (1790). Ed. B. Jolibert. Paris, 1989.

———. *Œuvres complètes*. Ed. L. S. Caritat et al. 21 vols. Brunswick and Paris, 1804.

Condorcet, Marquis de, Jean-Antoine-Nicolas de Caritat. *Political Writings*. Ed. Steven Lukes and N. Urbinati. Cambridge, 2012.

———. "Rapport sur l'organization générale de l'instruction publique" (April 1792). In Baczko, *Éducation pour la démocratie*, 177–261.

———. *Réflexions sur la Révolution de 1688, et celle du 10 août 1792*. N.p., n.d. Paris, 1792.

———. *Tableau historique des progrès de l'esprit humain: Projets, Esquisse, Fragments et Notes (1772–1794)*. Ed. J. P. Schandeler and P. Crépel. Paris, 2004.

Constant, Benjamin. *De la terreur* (1796). In B. Constant, *Œuvres politiques,* ed. Ch. Louandre, 337–60. Paris, 1874.

———. *Political Writings*. Ed. B. Fontana. Cambridge, 1988.

D'Abrantès, Laure. *Salons révolutionnaires*. Ed. L. Chotard. Paris, 1989.

Daunou, Pierre-Claude-François. *Essai sur l'Instruction Publique* (July 1793). In Baczko, *Éducation pour la démocratie*, 303–44.

Démeunier, Jean-Nicolas. *L'Esprit des usages et des coutumes des différents peuples*. 3 vols. Paris, 1776.

Desmoulins, Camille. *La France libre*. 4th ed. Paris, 1789.

———. *Le Vieux Cordelier*. Ed. P. Pachet. Journal, 1793–94. Paris, 2010.

———. *Œuvres*. Ed. Jules Clarette. 2 vols. Paris, 1874.

———. *Révolutions de France et de Brabant*. Journal, Paris, 1789–91.

D'Espinchal, Joseph Tomas. *Journal*. Ed. E. Hauterive, trans. R. Stawall. London, 1912.

Destutt de Tracy, Antoine. *Premiers écrits*. Ed. Claude Joly. Paris, 2011.

D'Holbach, Paul-Henri Thiry. *Le Bon-Sens du Curé Jean Meslier suivie de son Testament*. "Londres" [Amsterdam], 1772.

———. *La Politique naturelle, ou Discours sur les vrais principes du gouvernement*. 1773; repr., Paris,1998.

———. *Système social, ou principes naturels de la morale et de la politique*. "Londres" [i.e., Amsterdam], 1773; repr., Paris, 1994.

Diderot, Denis. *Supplément au voyage de Bougainville*. Ed. A. Adam. Paris, 1972.

Dumont, Étienne. *Souvenirs sur Mirabeau*. Ed. J. Benetruy. Paris, 1951.

Dumouriez, Charles-François. *Mémoires écrits par lui-même*. 2nd ed. Frankfurt-Leipzig, 1794.

Durozoy, Barnabé. *La Gazette de Paris*. Journal, Paris, 1789–92.

Eberhard, J. A. *Philosophisches Magazin*. Journal, Halle, 1788–92.

Extrait des Registres de la Section Mauconseil à tous les citoyens du Département de Paris. 1792.

Fabre d'Églantine, Philippe-François. *Portrait de Marat*. Paris, 1793.

Fauchet, Claude. *Journal des Amis*. Journal, Paris, 1792–93.

———. *Lettre Pastorale de Claude Fauchet, Evêque du Calvados aux pasteurs et aux fidèles du Diocèse*. N.p., 1792.

———. *Sermon sur l'accord de la religion et de la liberté prononcé dans la métropole de Paris, le 4 Fevrier 1791*. Paris, 1791.

Feller, François-Xavier de. *Journal historique et littéraire*. Journal, Liège-Brussels-Maastricht, 1773–94.

[Ferrand, Antoine-François-Claude]. *État Actuel de La France*. Paris [Janvier], 1790.

Fichte, Johann Gottlieb. *Schriften zur Revolution*. Köln, 1967.

Fontana, A., et al. (eds.). *Venise et la Révolution française: Les 470 dépêches des ambassadeurs de Venise au Doge, 1786–1795*. Paris, 1997.

Forster, G. *Werke, Sämtliche Schriften, Tagebücher, Briefe*. Ed. K. G. Popp et al. 18 vols. Berlin, 1968–82.

Fréron, Louis-Stanislas. *L'Orateur du peuple*. Journal, Paris, 1790–92 and 1794–95.

Garat, Dominique-Joseph. *Jugement sur Mirabeau*. Paris, 1820.

———. *Mémoires historiques sur la vie de M. Suard, sur ses écrits et sur le XVIIIe siècle*. 2 vols. Paris, 1820.

Gazette nationale, ou le Moniteur universel. Ed. Charles Panckoucke et al. Journal, Paris, 1789–95.

Gibbon, Edward. *Memoirs of My Life and Writings*. Ed. A.O.J. Cockshut. Keele, England, 1994.

Ginguené, Pierre-Louis. *Lettres sur les Confessions de J. J. Rousseau*. Paris, 1791.

Gioia, Melchiorre. *Dissertazione sul problema Quale dei governi liberi meglio convenga alla felicità dell'Italia*. Milan, 1797.

Gorani, Giuseppe. *Mémoires secrets et critiques des cours, des gouvernemens, et des mœurs des principaux états de l'Italie*. 3 vols. Paris, 1793.

———. *Recherches sur la science du gouvernement*. Paris, 1792.

Gorsas, Antoine-Joseph. *Le Courrier de Paris dans les 83 départemens* (later entitled just *Le Courrier des LXXXIII départemens*). Journal, Paris, 1790–91.

———. *Précis rapide des évènemens qui ont eu lieu à Paris dans les journées de 30 et 31 mai, premier et 3 juin 1793*. Paris, 1793.

Gouges, Olympe de. *Œuvres*. Ed. Benoîte Groult. Paris, 1986.

Grande Pétition présentée ce matin à l'Assemblée Nationale, par quarante mille Citoyens de Paris, rassemblées au Champ de Mars. 15 July 1791. Paris, 1791.

Granié, Pierre. *Histoire de l'Assemblée constituante de France: Écrite pour un citoyen des États-Unis de l'Amérique septentrionale*. Paris, 1797.

Grouchy [Condorcet], Sophie de. *Lettres sur la sympathie, suivies des lettres d'amour*. Montréal, 1994.

Guyomar, Pierre. *Le Partisan de l'égalité politique entre les individus, ou problème très important de l'égalité en droits et de l'inégalité en fait*. April 1793. In *Archives Parlementaires*, 60:591–99.

Hansen, Joseph (ed.). *Quellen zur Geschichte des Rheinlandes im Zeitalter der französischen Revolution*. 4 vols. Bonn, 1931–33.

Harmand, Jean-Baptise. *Observations sur le nouveau projet de constitution*. In *Archives Parlementaires*, 67:320–24.

Hébert, Jacques-René. *Le Père Duchesne*. Journal, Paris, 1790–94.

Helvétius, Claude Adrien. *Réflexions sur l'homme et autres textes*. Paris, 2006.

Herder, Johann Gottfried. *Briefe: Gesamtausgabe*. Ed. G. Arnold et al. 14 vols. Weimar-Tübingen, 1977–2009.

Hölderlin, Friedrich. *Sämtliche Werke*. Ed. F. Beissner et al. 8 vols. Stutgart, 1946–85.

Jefferson, Thomas. *The Papers of Thomas Jefferson*. Vol. 15 (March–November 1789) and vol. 16 (November 1789–July 1790). Ed. Ch. Cullen and J. P. Boyd. Princeton, 1958, 1961.

Jollivet, Jean-Baptiste-Moise. *Rappellez vos collègues*. Paris, 1794.

Journal des hommes libres de tous les pays. Ed. R. Vatar and Ch. Duval. Journal, Paris, 1792–1800.

Journal du Club des Cordeliers. Ed. Antoine-François Momoro et al. Journal, Paris, 1791.

Journal de Paris. Journal, Paris, 1777–1811.

Journal de Perlet: Convention National, corps administratifs et Nouvelles politiques et littéraires de l'Europe. Journal, Paris, 1789–97.

Jullien, Marc-Antoine. *L'Orateur plébéien, ou le défenseur de la République.* Journal, Paris, 1795–96.

Kervélégan, Augustin le Goazre. *Réflexions d'un philosophe Breton sur les affaires présentes.* N.p., 1788.

Klopstock, Friedrich Gottlieb. *Werke und Briefe: Historisch-kritische Ausgabe.* Ed. H. Riege et al. 24 vols. Berlin, 1998–2013.

Knigge, Adolph Freiherr. *Ausgewählte Werke in zehn Bänden.* Ed. W. Fenner. 10 vols. Hanover, 1991–96.

Lachapelle, J. *Considérations philosophiques sur la révolution française.* Paris, 1797.

La Chronique de Paris. Ed. L. P. Manuel, Rabaut, Cloots, et al. Journal, Paris, 1789–93.

La Chronique du mois, ou les cahiers patriotiques. Ed. J. Oswald, L. S. Mercier, et al. Journal, Paris, 1791–93.

La Décade philosophique. Ed. Pierre-Louis Ginguené, Jean-Baptiste Say, et al. Journal, Paris, 1794–1807.

La Feuille villageoise. Ed. Joseph-Antoine Cérutti et al. Journal, Paris, 1790–94.

La Harpe, J. F. de. *Discours sur la liberté du théâtre.* 17 Dec. 1790. Paris, 1790.

———. *Philosophie du dix-huitième siècle.* 2 vols. Paris, 1818.

———. *Réfutation du livre "de l'Esprit."* Paris, 1797.

Lanthenas, François. *De la liberté indéfinie de la presse.* Paris, 1791.

———. *Motifs de faire du 10 août un jubilé fraternel.* Paris, 1793.

L'Anti-Carra-Co-Gorsas: Les Secrets révélés. BHP pamphlet 953463. Paris, 1790.

Léger, François. *L'Auteur d'un moment: Comédie.* Paris, 1792.

Les Douze Représentants du Peuple détenus à Port-Libre à leurs collegues. Paris, 1794.

Lettre à M. le Marquis de Luchet contenant la Quinzaine Mémorable, ou le précis des évènemens qui ont eu lieu à Paris, depuis le 12 de Juillet (1789). Leuven, n.d.

Lettres bougrement partiotiques de La Mère Duchêne. Ed. O. Elyada. Paris, 1989.

Levasseur, René. *Mémoires de R. Levasseur (de la Sarthe) ex-conventionnel.* 4 vols. Paris, 1829.

Lichtenberg, Georg Christoph. *Schriften und Briefe.* Ed. Wolfgang Promies. 4 vols. München, 1959.

Linguet, Simon Nicolas Henri. *Annales politiques, civiles, et littéraires du dix-huitième siècle.* Journal, Brussels, 1777–92.

Louvet, Jean-Baptiste. *La Sentinelle.* Journal affiche, Paris, 1792–93.

———. *Mémoires de Louvet de Couvrai sur la Révolution française.* Ed. F. A. Aulard. 2 vols. Paris, 1889.

Mably, Gabriel Bonnot de. *Collection complète des œuvres de l'Abbé de Mably.* 15 vols. Paris, Year III (1794/95).

Mallet du Pan, Jacques. *Considérations sur la nature de la Révolution de France.* "Londres," 1793.

Malouet, Pierre-Victor. *Mémoires.* 2 vols. Paris, 1868.

Mandar, Théophile. *Des Insurrections: Ouvrage philosophique et politique.* Paris, 1793.

Manuel, Louis-Pierre. *Lettres sur la Révolution.* Paris, 1792.

Marat, Jean-Paul. *De l'Homme, ou, des principes des loix de l'influence de l'âme sur le corps, et du corps sur l'âme.* 3 vols. N.p., 1775.

———. *L'Ami du peuple.* Journal, Paris 1789–93.

Maréchal, Sylvain, and Jerome Lalande (eds.). *Dictionnaire des Athées* (1800). Ed. J. P. Jackson. Paris, 2008.

————. *Manifeste des égaux*. In Dommanget, *Babeuf,* 86–90.

Marmontel, Jean-François. *Mémoires*. Ed. M. Tourneaux. 3 vols. Paris, 1891.

Mercier, Louis-Sebastien. *De J. J. Rousseau considéré comme un des premiers auteurs de la Révolution.* 2 vols. Paris, 1791.

————. *Paris pendant la Révolution ou le Nouveau Paris.* 2 vols. 1862.

Michaud, Joseph-François. *La Quotidienne, ou Nouvelle Gazette Universelle, par une société de gens de lettres.* Journal, Paris, 1792–93.

Mirabeau, Honoré Gabriel Riquetti. *Collection complète des travaux de M. Mirabeau l'Aîné, à l'assemblée Nationale.* Ed. E. Mejan. 5 vols. Paris, 1791–92.

————. *De la réforme des Juifs et sur Moses Mendelssohn.* N.p., 1787.

————. *Essai sur le despotisme* (1775). 3rd ed. N.p. 1792.

————. *Le Courrier de Provence.* Journal, Paris, 1789–91.

————. *Mirabeau à la tribune, ou Choix des meilleurs discours de cet orateur.* 2 vols. Paris, 1796.

————. "Travail sur l'éducation publique." In Baczko, *Éducation pour la démocratie,* 9–105.

Montesquieu, [Baron de] Charles de Secondat. *Œuvres complètes.* Ed. D. Oster. Paris, 1964.

Montgilbert, François. *Avis au peuple sur la liberté et l'exercise de ses droits contenu dans un projet de constitution républicaine.* Paris, 1793.

Morellet, André. *Lettres.* Ed. D. Medlin. 3 vols. Oxford, 1991–94.

————. *Mémoires sur le dix-huitième siècle et sur la révolution française.* 2 vols. Paris, 1822.

Möser, Justus. "Ueber das Recht des Menschheit." In *Berlinische Monatschrift* 18 (July–Dec. 1790), 396–401 and 499–506.

Mounier, Jean-Joseph. *Considérations sur les gouvernements et principalement sur celui qui convient à la France.* Versailles, 1789.

————. *De l'influence attribuée aux philosophes, aux franc-maçons et aux Illuminés sur la Révolution de la France.* Tübingen, 1801.

Naigeon, Jacques-André. *Adresse à l'Assemblée Nationale sur la liberté des opinions.* Paris, 1790.

————. *Encyclopédie méthodique: Philosophie ancienne et moderne.* 3 vols. Paris, 1791.

————. *Lettre du Citoyen Naigeon habitant de Sedan, à ses concitoyens.* Sedan, 1797. BL Pamphl. R 6436.

Necker, Jacques. *De la Révolution françoise.* 4 vols. N.p., 1796.

————. *De l'importance des opinions religieuses.* "Londres" [Paris], 1788.

Paape, Gerrit. *De Hollandsche wijsgeer in Vrankrijk.* Dordrecht, 1790.

————. *De onverbloemde geschiedenis van het Bataafsch Patriottismus.* Delft, 1798.

Pagano, Francesco. *Saggi politici de' principi, progressi e decadenza della società.* Naples, 1791–92.

Paine, Thomas. *The Age of Reason, Part the First.* London, 1796.

————. *Rights of Man* (1790). Ed. E. Foner. New York, 1985.

[Palissot, Charles]. *Considérations importantes sur ce qui passe, depuis quelque tems, au prétendu Théâtre de la Nation.* Paris, 1790.

Palm d'Aelders, Etta. *Appel aux françoises et necessité de l'influence des femmes dans un gouvernement libre.* Paris, 1791.

Palmieri, Giuseppe. *Riflessioni sulla pubblica felicità relativamente al regno di Napoli.* Naples, 1787.

Paulus, Pieter. *In welken zin kunnen de menschen gezegd worden gelyk te zyn?* (1793). 4th ed. Haarlem, 1794.

Pétion, Jerôme. *Avis aux François sur le salut de la Patrie.* Paris, 1788.

———. *Discours prononcé dans l'Assemblée de la Société des Amis de la Constitution de Paris, séante aux Jacobins.* Paris, 1791.

———. *Les Vœux du véritable souverain exprimés à l'Assemblée Nationale.* 3 August 1792.

Petit, Michel-Edme. *Le Procès des 31 Mai, 1r et 2 Juin, ou, la défense des 71 représentants du peuple.* N.p., n.d. Paris, 1794.

———. *Opinion sur l'éducation publique prononcé le premier octobre 1793.* Paris, 1793.

Picqué, Jean-Pierre. *Au peuple, sur la Constitution qui va lui être présentée par la Convention nationale* (1793). In *Archives Parlementaires,* 67:369–76.

Portalis, J.E.M. *De l'usage et de l'abus de l'esprit philosophique durant le XVIIIe siècle.* 1798; repr., Paris, 2007.

Price, Richard. *Political Writings.* Ed. D. O. Thomas. Cambridge, 1991.

Proly, Pierre-Joseph-Berthold. *Le Cosmopolite.* Journal, Paris, 1791–93.

Prudhomme, Louis-Marie. *Histoire générale et impartiale des erreurs, des fautes et des crimes commis pendant la Révolution française.* 6 vols. Paris, 1797.

———. *Les Révolutions de Paris.* Journal, Paris, 1789–94.

Rabaut de Saint-Étienne, J. P. *Précis historique de la Révolution française.* Paris, 1807.

———. *Projet du Préliminaire de la Constitution françoise.* Paris, 1789.

Raymond, Julien. *Réflexions sur les véritables causes des troubles et des désastres de nos colonies, notamment sur ceux de Saint-Domingue.* Paris, 1793.

Raynal, Abbé Guillaume-Thomas-François (ed.). *Adresse de Guillame Thomas Raynal remise par lui-même à M. le Président, le 31 mai 1791, et lue à l'Assemblée nationale le même jour.* Paris, 1791.

———. *Histoire philosophique et politique des établissemens et du commerce des Européens dans les Deux Indes.* 10 vols. Geneva, 1780.

Réal, Pierre-François. *Journal de l'Opposition par une société de républicains.* Journal, Paris, 1797.

Rehberg, Wilhelm August. *Untersuchungen über die französische Revolution.* 2 vols. Hanover, 1793.

Relation exacte de ce qui s'est passé à Bruxelles, dans la journée du 16 et 17 Mars 1790. Brussels, 1790.

Riffard de Saint Martin, François-Jerôme. *Journal des décrets de l'Assemblée Nationale.* 5 vols. Paris, 1789–91.

Rivarol, Antoine de. *De la philosophie moderne.* Hamburg, 1797. 2nd ed. N.p., 1799.

Robert, Pierre-François, and Louise-Félicité de Keralio (eds.). *Mercure national et étranger, ou Journal politique de l'Europe.* Journal, Paris, 1790–91.

Robespierre, Maximilien. *Discours du 8 Thermidor an II* (26 July 1794). In Žižek (ed.), *Robespierre,* 248–47.

———. *Le Défenseur de la Constitution.* Journal, Paris, 1792–93.

———. *Œuvres complètes.* Ed. E. Hamel. 10 vols. Paris, 1910–67.

———. *Réponse à l'accusation de J. B. Louvet* (5 Nov. 1792). In Žižek (ed.), *Robespierre*, 127–40.

———. *Sur les principes de morale politique* (5 Feb. 1794). In Žižek (ed.), *Robespierre*, 222–47.

Rocques, Jean Gabriel Maurice [Comte de Montguillard]. *État de France au mois de Mai 1794.* 2 vols. Londres, 1794.

Roederer, Pierre-Louis. *De la philosophie moderne, et de la part qu'elle a eue à la Révolution française.* Paris. 1799.

———. *The Spirit of the Revolution of 1789.* Ed. M. Forsyth. Aldershot, 1989.

Roland, Jean-Marie, and Mme. Roland. *Lettre écrite au Roi par le ministre de l'Intérieur.* Paris, 1792.

Roland, [Madame] Marie-Jeanne [Manon]. *Memoirs.* Ed. E. Shuckburgh. Wakefield, RI, 1986.

Rousseau, J. J. *The Discourses and Other Early Political Writings.* Ed. V. Gourevitch. Cambridge, 1997.

———. *Discours sur l'origine et les fondemens de l'inégalité parmi les hommes* (1755). Trans. and ed. Heinrich Meier. 5th ed. Paderborn, 2001.

———. *Émile.* Trans. W. H. Payne. New York, 2003.

———. *The Social Contract and Other Later Political Writings.* Ed. V. Gourevitch. Cambridge, 1997.

Roux, Louis. *Relation de l'Événement des 8, 9, et 10 Thermidor sur la conspiration des triumvirs Robespierre, Couthon et St.-Just.* Paris, 1794.

Royou, Abbé Thomas-Marie. *L'Ami du Roi.* Journal, Paris, 1789–92.

Russo, Vincenzo. *Pensieri politici e altri scritti.* Naples, 1999.

Rutledge, James. *Le Creuset.* Journal, Paris, 1791.

Sabatier de Castres, M. *Journal politique national des États-Généraux et de la Révolution de 1789.* Journal, Paris, 1789.

Saint-Just, Antoine-Louis de. *Œuvres complètes.* Ed. A. Kupiec and M. Abensour. Paris, 2004.

Salle [Salles], Jean-Baptiste. *Examen critique de la Constitution.* Paris, 1793.

Sieyès, Abbé Emmanuel-Joseph. *Écrits politiques* (ed.). Roberto Zapperi. Paris, 2009.

———. *Essai sur les privilèges.* Paris, 1788.

———. *Manuscrits, 1773–1799.* Ed. Chr. Fauré. Paris, 1999.

———. *Préliminaire de la Constitution française.* Paris, 1789.

———. "Qu'est-ce que le Tiers État?" In Zapperi (ed.), *Écrits politiques*, 115–88.

Sinéty, André Louis Esprit de. *Réflexions importantes sur l'Adresse présentée à l'Assemblée nationale le 31 mai par Guillaume-Thomas Raynal.* Paris, 1791.

Staël, Germaine de. *Considerations on the Principal Events of the French Revolution.* Ed. A. Craiutu. Indianapolis, 2008.

T. G. Raynal démasqué, ou Lettres sur la vie et les ouvrages de cet écrivain. Paris, 1791.

Thierry, M. *Dissertation sur cette question: "Est-il des moyens de rendre les Juifs plus heureux et plus utiles en France?"* Paris, 1788.

Thouret, Jacques-Guillaume. *Discours Fait à l'Assemblée Nationales sur la Nouvelle Division territoriale du royaume.* Paris, 1789.

———. *Vérités philosophiques et patriotiques sur les affaires presents.* N.p., 1788.

Tocqueville, Alexis de. *L'Ancien régime et la Révolution.* Ed. F. Mélonio. Paris, 1988.

Tone, Theobald Wolfe. *An Address to the People of Ireland*. Belfast, 1796.

Toussaint-Louverture, François-Dominique. *Lettres à la France (1794–1798)*. Ed. M. Baggio and R. Augustin. Bruyères-le-Châtel, 2011.

Varlet, Jean. *L'Explosion* (1 Oct. 1794). BN: LB41-4090.

———. "Projet d'un mandat special et impératif" (1792). In Guillon, *Notre Patience*, 54–65.

Villette, Charles. *Lettres choisies sur les principaux évènemens de la Révolution*. Paris, 1792.

Volney, Constantin-François. *Discours prononcé dans la chambre du tiers état*. Paris, 1789.

———. *La Sentinelle du peuple*. Journal, Rennes, 1788.

———. *Œuvres complètes*. 2 vols. Paris, 1821.

———. *Ruins of Empires and the Laws of Nature*. New York, 1950.

———. *Voyage en Syrie et en Egypte, pendant les années 1783, 1784, et 1785*. 2 vols. Paris, 1787.

Walzer, Michael (ed.). *Regicide and Revolution: Speeches at the Trial of Louis XVI*. New York, 1992.

Wedekind, Georg Christian. "Einleitung und Kommentar zu den Rechten des Menschen und Bürgers" (1793). In J. Garber (ed.), *Revolutionäre Vernunft: Texte zur jakobinischen und liberalen Revolutions Rezeption in Deutschland, 1789–1810*. Kronberg Taunus, 1974.

———et al. (eds.). *Der Patriot eine Wochenschrift*. Journal, Mainz, 1792–93.

Williams, David. *Observations sur la dernière Constitution de la France avec des vues pour la formation de la nouvelle Constitution* (April 1793). In *Archives Parlementaires*, 60:583–91.

Williams, Helen Maria. *Letters from France*. Ed. J. M. Todd. Delmar, 1975.

Wollstonecraft, Mary. *The Collected Letters*. Ed. Janet Todd. London, 2003.

Žižek, Slavoj (ed.). *Robespierre: Entre vertu et terreur*. Paris, 2007.

SECONDARY SOURCES

Aaslestad, Katherine. *Place and Politics: Local Identity, Civic Culture, and German Nationalism in North Germany during the Revolutionary Era*. Leiden, 2005.

Aberdam, Serge. "Délibérations en assemblées de citoyens et portions de souveraineté en 1793." In Michel Pertué (ed.), *Suffrage, citoyenneté et révolutions, 1789–1848: Journée d'études du 10 mars au lycée Henri IV*, 9–32. Paris, 2002.

Acomb, Frances. *Mallet du Pan (1749–1800): A Career in Political Journalism*. Durham, NC, 1973.

Åhlén, Bengt, Agneta Åhlén, and Lillemor Widgren. *Censur och tryckfrihet: Farliga skrifter i Sverige, 1522–1954*. Oslo, 2003.

Aizpurua, Ramón. "Revolution and Politics in Venezuela and Curaçao, 1795–1800." In Klooster and Oostindie (eds.), *Curaçao*, 97–122.

Alger, J. G. "The British Colony in Paris, 1792–93." *English Historical Review* 13 (1898), 672–94.

Altena, Peter. *Gerrit Paape (1752–1803): Levens en werken*. Nijmegen, 2011.

Andress, David. *The Terror: Civil War in the French Revolution*. London, 2005.

Andries, Lise. "Les imprimeurs-libraires parisiens et la liberté de la presse (1789–95)." *Dix-Huitieme Siecle* 21 (1989), 247–61.

Anoyatis-Pele, Dimitris (ed.). *Six rapports français concernant les Îles Ioniennes et le continent voisin (1798–1809)*. Corfu, 1993.

Ansart-Dourlen, Michèle. *L'Action politique des personnalités et l'idéologie Jacobine: Rationalisme et passions révolutionnaires*. Paris, 1998.

Antheunis, L. *Le conventionnel belge François Robert (1763–1826) et sa femme Louise de Kéralio (1758–1822)*. Wetteren, 1955.

Applewhite, Harriet Branson. *Political Alignment in the French National Assembly, 1789–1791*. Baton Rouge, 1993.

Applewhite, Harriet Branson, and D. G. Levy (eds). *Women and Politics in the Age of Democratic Revolution*, 61–80. Ann Arbor, MI, 1993.

Apt, Leon. *Louis-Philippe de Ségur: An Intellectual in a Revolutionary Age*. The Hague, 1969.

Arnaud, Claude. *Chamfort: A Biography*. Chicago, 1992.

Aston, Nigel. *Religion and Revolution in France, 1780–1804*. Washington, DC, 2000.

Auerbach, Stephen. "Politics, Protest and Violence in Revolutionary Bordeaux, 1789–1794." *Proceedings of the Western Society for French History* 37 (2009), 149–61.

Baczko, Bronislaw. *Ending the Terror: The French Revolution after Robespierre*. Cambridge, 1994.

———. "Le tournant culturel de l'an III." In Dupuy and Morabito (eds.), *1795 Pour une République*, 17–37.

———. "L'expérience thermidorienne." In Lucas (ed.), *Political Culture*, 341–70.

———. *Politiques de la Révolution française*. Paris, 2008.

———. "The Terror before the Terror?" In Baker (ed.), vol. 4 of *The French Revolution and the Creation of Modern Political Culture*, 19–38. Oxford, 1994.

———. *Une Éducation pour la démocratie*. Geneva, 2000

Badinter, Elisabeth, and Robert Badinter. *Condorcet, 1743–1794: Un intellectuel en politique*. Paris, 1988.

Badinter, Robert. *Libres et égaux: L'Emancipation des Juifs (1789–1791)*. Paris, 1989.

Baecque, Antoine de. "Pamphlets." In Darnton and Roche (eds.), *Revolution in Print*, 165–76.

Baggio, A. M. "Toussaint Louverture et l'existence politique du peuple noir." In Toussaint Louverture, *Lettres*, 9–141.

Baker, Keith Michael. *Condorcet: From Natural Philosophy to Social Mathematics*. Chicago, 1975.

———. "Enlightenment Idioms, Old Regime Discourses, and Revolutionary Improvisation." In Kaiser and Van Kley (eds.), *From Deficit to Deluge*, 165–69.

———. "The Idea of a Declaration of Rights." In Van Kley (ed.), *French Idea*, 154–96.

———. *Inventing the French Revolution*. Cambridge, 1990.

———. "Political Languages of the French Revolution." In Mark Goldie and Robert Wokler (eds.), *The Cambridge History of Eighteenth-Century Political Thought*. Cambridge, 2006.

———. "A Script for the French Revolution: The Political Consciousness of the Abbé Mably." *Eighteenth-Century Studies* 14 (1981), 235–63.

———. (ed.). *The Terror*. Vol. 4 of *The French Revolution and the Creation of Modern Political Culture*. 4 vols. Oxford, 1994.

Ballard, R. *A New Dictionary of the French Revolution*. London, 2012.

Barber, G. "The Financial History of the Kehl Voltaire." In W. H. Barber et al. (eds.), *The Age of Enlightenment: Studies Presented to Theodore Besterman*, 152–70. London, 1967.

Bates, David. *Enlightenment Aberrations: Error and Revolution in France*. Ithaca, NY, 2002.

———. "Political Pathologies: Barnave and the Question of National Identity in Revolutionary France." *Canadian Journal of History* 36 (2001), 427–52.

Belissa, M. "Les leçons de républicanisme de Thomas Paine (1802–1807)." *AHRF* 363 (2011), 59–84.

Bell, David. *The Cult of the Nation in France*. Cambridge, MA, 2001.

———. *The First Total War: Napoleon's Europe and the Birth of Warfare as We Know It*. Boston, 2007.

Bellanger, Claude, et al. *Histoire générale de la presse française*. 3 vols. Paris, 1969.

Benoit, Bruno. "Lyon rouge ou/et blanche, 1789–1799." In Peyrard (ed.), *Minorités politiques*, 181–94.

Benot, Yves. *La révolution française et la fin des colonies, 1789–1794*. 1987; new ed., Paris, 2004.

Bensaude-Vincent, B. *Lavoisier: Mémoires d'une révolution*. Paris, 1993.

Beretti, F. *Pascal Paoli et l'image de la Corse au dix-huitième siècle*. Oxford, 1988.

Bertaud, Jean-Paul. *Camille et Lucile Desmoulins: Un couple dans la tourmente*. Paris, 1986.

———. *Les Amis du roi: Journaux et journalistes royalistes en France de 1789 à 1792*. Paris, 1984.

Bessy, J. "Le parti jacobin à Toulouse sous le Directoire." *AHRF* 22 (1950), 28–54.

Bianchi, Serge. *Des révoltes aux révolutions (1770–1802)*. Rennes, 2004.

———. "Les Curés rouges dans la Révolution française." *AHRF* 262 (1985), 447–79.

Biard, M. (ed.). *La Revolution française: Une histoire toujours vivante*. Paris, 2010.

———. *Les politiques de la terreur*. Rennes, 2008.

———. *Missionaires de la République: Les représentants du peuple en mission (1793–1795)*. Paris, 2002.

Bindman, David. *The Shadow of the Guillotine*. London, 1989.

Birn, Raymond. "Religious Toleration and Freedom of Expression." In Van Kley (ed.), *French Idea*, 265–99.

Blackburn, R. *The Overthrow of Colonial Slavery (1776–1848)*. New York, 1998.

Blamires, C. *The French Revolution and the Creation of Benthamism*. Basingstoke, 2008.

Blanc, Olivier. "Cercles politiques et 'salons' du début de la Révolution (1789–1793)." *AHRF* 344 (2006), 63–92.

———. *La corruption sous la Terreur (1792–1794)*. Paris, 1992.

———. "Une humaniste au XVIIIe siècle: Olympe de Gouges." In E. Morin-Rotureau (ed.), *1789–1799: Combats des femmes*, 15–34. Paris, 2003.

Blanning, T.C.W. *Reform and Revolution in Mainz, 1743–1803*. Cambridge, 1974.

Bloch, Jean. "*Émile* et le débat révolutionnaire sur l'éducation publique." In Thiéry (ed.), *Rousseau, l'Émile et la Révolution*, 339–53.

Bluche, Frédéric. *Septembre 1792, logiques d'un massacre*. Paris, 1986.

Bonacina, G. *Eretici e riformatori d'Arabia: I wahhabiti in prospettiva europea, 1772–1830*. Naples, 2011.

Boroumand, L. *La Guerre des principes. Les assemblées révolutionnaires face aux droits de l'homme et à la souveraineté de la nation (1789–94)*. Paris, 1999.

———. "Les Girondins et l'Idée de République." In Furet and Ozouf (eds.), *La Gironde*, 233–64.

Bosc, Y. "Thomas Paine et les constitutions de 1793 et 1795." In Vincent (ed.), *Thomas Paine*, 79–86.

Bosc, Y., and F. Gauthier. Introduction to Mathiez, *La réaction thermidorienne*, 7–52.

Bouissounouse, J. *Condorcet, Le philosophe dans la Révolution*. Paris, 1962.

Bourdin, Philippe. *Le noir et le rouge*. Maringues, 2000.

———. *Le Puy-de-Dôme sous le Directoire: Vie politique et esprit public*. Clermont-Ferrand, 1990.

Bourdin, Philippe, and G. Loubinoux (eds.). *Les Arts de la Scène et la Révolution française*. Vizille, 2004.

Bourguet, M. N. "Des savants à la conquête de l'Égypte." In Bret (ed.), *L'Expédition d'Égypte*, 21–36.

———. "Science and Memory: The Stakes of the Expedition to Egypt." In Brown and Miller (eds.), *Taking Liberties*, 92–109.

Boursier, A. M. "L'émeute parisienne du 10 mars 1793." *AHRF* 44 (1972), 204–30.

Bredin, Jean-Denis. *Sieyès: La clé de la Révolution française*. Paris, 1988.

Bret, Patrice (ed.). *L'Expédition d'Égypte, une entreprise des Lumières, 1798–1801*. Paris, 1999.

Broers, Michael. *The Napoleonic Empire in Italy, 1796–1814*. Basingstoke, 2005.

Brown, Gregory S. "Le Débat sur la liberté des théâtres en France, 1789–1790." In *Les Arts*, ed. Bourdin and Loubinoux, 39–53.

Brown, Howard G. "The Search for Stability." In Brown and Miller (eds.), *Taking Liberties*, 20–50.

Brown, Howard G., and Judith A. Miller (eds.). *Taking Liberties: Problems of a New Order from the French Revolution to Napoleon*. Manchester, 2002.

Brunel, Françoise. *Thermidor: La chute de Robespierre*. Brussels, 1989.

Buel, Richard. *Joel Barlow: American Citizen in a Revolutionary World*. Baltimore, 2011.

Burney, J. M. "The Fear of the Executive and the Threat of Conspiracy: Billaud-Varenne's Terrorist Rhetoric in the French Revolution, 1788–1794." *French History* 5 (1991), 143–63.

Burstin, Haim. *Une Révolution à l'œuvre: Le Faubourg Saint-Marcel (1789–1794)*. Paris, 2005.

Campbell, Peter. Introduction to *The Origins of the French Revolution*. In Peter Campbell (ed.), *The Origins of the French Revolution*. Basingstoke, 2006.

———. "Redefining the French Revolution, 1989–2009." *H-France Salon* 1 (2009), 7–23.

Campbell, Peter, Thomas E. Kaiser, and Marisa Linton (eds.). *Conspiracy in the French Revolution*. Manchester, 2007.

Capra, Carlo. *I progressi della ragione: Vita di Pietro Verri*. Bologna, 2002.

Casta, François J. "Le clergé corse et les serments constitutionels pendant la Révolution française." *Corse historique*, Year XI, no. 33 (1969), 5–35.

Casta, François J. "La réorganisation religieuse en Corse au lendemain de la Révolution française." In Paul Arrighi (ed.), *Mélanges d'Études corses*. Aix, 1971.

Castelot, André. *Talleyrand, ou le cynisme*. Paris, 1980.

Censer, Jack Richard. *Prelude to Power: The Parisian Radical Press, 1789–1791*. Baltimore, 1976.

Chappey, Jean-Luc. "Les Écoles de la Révolution: Pour en finir avec la thèse de la *table rase*." In Biard (ed.), *La Révolution française*, 331–44.

Cherfils, Christian. *Napoleon and Islam*. Kuala Lumpur, 1999.

Chisick, Harvey. "An Intellectual Profile of a Jacobin Activist: The Morality and Politics of Dufourny de Villiers (1789–1796)." In Christine Adams et al., *Visions and Revisions of Eighteenth-Century France*, 105–33. University Park, PA, 1997.

———. "Politics and Journalism in the French Revolution." *French History* 5 (1991), 345–72.

———. *The Production, Distribution and Readership of a Conservative Journal of the Early French Revolution: The "Ami du Roi" of the Abbé Royou*. Philadelphia, 1992.

Chopelin-Blanc, C. *De l'apologétique à l'Église constitutionelle: Adrien Lamourette (1742–1794)*. Paris, 2009.

Clemenceau-Jacquemaire, M. *Vie de Madame Roland*. 2 vols. Paris, 1929.

Cobb, Richard. *The French and Their Revolution*. London, 1998.

Coller, Ian. "Egypt in the French Revolution." In Desan, Hunt, and Nelson (eds.), *French Revolution*, 115–31.

Conac, Gérard. "La Convention thermidorienne." In Conac and Machelon (eds.), *La Constitution*, 201–86.

Conac, Gérard, and Jean-Pierre Machelon. *La Constitution de l'an III*. Paris, 1999.

Conchon, Anne. *Le Péage en France au XVIIIe siècle*. Paris, 2002.

Coquard, Olivier. *Jean-Paul Marat*. Paris, 1993.

Corno, Philippe. "La Loi révolutionnaire du divorce et ses représentations théâtrales." *Dix-Huitième Siècle* 41 (2009), 61–78.

Cottebrune, Anne. *Mythe et réalité du "jacobinisme allemande."* Lille, 2001

Cousin, Bernard. "Religion et Révolution dans le département du Var." In Jean-Clément Martin, *Religion et Révolution*, 141–48. Paris, 1994.

Craiutu, Aurelian. *Liberalism under Siege: The Political Thought of the French Doctrinaires*. Lanham, MD, 2003.

———. *A Virtue for Courageous Minds: Moderation in French Political Thought, 1748–1830*. Princeton, 2012.

Crépel P., and Chr. Gilain (eds.). *Condorcet, mathématicien, économiste, philosophe, homme politique*. Paris, 1989.

Crook, M. *Toulon in War and Revolution*. Manchester, 1991.

Crow, Thomas. *Emulation: Making Artists for Revolutionary France*. New Haven, CT, 1995.

Culoma, M. *La religion civile de Rousseau à Robespierre*. Paris, 2010.

Curran, Andrew S. *The Anatomy of Blackness: Science and Slavery in an Age of Enlightenment*. Baltimore, 2011.

Daline, V. "Robespierre et Danton vus par Babeuf." *AHRF* 32 (1960), 388–410.

Da Passano, Mario. "Dalla democrazia dirretoriale all'olgarchia senatoria: Le vicende costituzionali della Repubblica Ligurie (1797–1805)." *Studi Settecenteschi* 17 (1997), 287–334.

Dard, Émile. *Hérault de Sechelles (1759–1794): Un Épucurien sous La Terreur*. Paris, 1907.

Darlow, Mark. *Staging the French Revolution: Cultural Politics and the Paris Opéra, 1789–1794*. Oxford, 2012.

Darnton, Robert, and Daniel Roche (eds.). *The Revolution in Print: The Press in France, 1775–1800*. Berkeley, 1989.

Darrow, M. H. "Economic Terror in the City: The General Maximum in Montauban." *FHS* 17 (1991), 498–525.

———. *Revolution in the House*. Princeton, 1989.

Dauteribes, André. "Daunou et le modèle du régime représentatif." In G. Conac et al. (eds.), *La Constitution de l'An III*, 111–38. Paris, 1999.

Davidson, Neil. *How Revolutionary Were the Bourgeois Revolutions?* Chicago, 2012.

Dawson, Christopher. *The Gods of Revolution*. New York, 1972.

De Dijn, A. "The Politics of Enlightenment from Peter Gay to Jonathan Israel." *Historical Journal* 55 (2012), 785–805.

De Francesco, Antonino. "How Not to Finish a Revolution." In G. Imbruglia (ed.), *Naples in the Eighteenth Century*, 167–82. Cambridge, 2000.

De Luca, Stefano. "Benjamin Constant and the Terror." In Rosenblatt, *Cambridge Companion to Constant*, 92–114.

De Luna, Frederick A. "The Dean Street Style of Revolution: J.-P. Brissot, Jeune Philosophe." *FHS* 17.1 (Spring 1991), 159–90.

De Martino, G. "Metamorfosi dell'illuminismo." In Russo, *Pensieri Politici*, 11–44.

Dentz, Paul. *Napoleon Bonaparte in Egypte*. Soesterberg, 2011.

Desan, Suzanne. "Foreigners, Cosmopolitanism, and French Revolutionary Universalism." In Desan, Hunt, and Nelson (eds.), *French Revolution*, 86–100.

———. *Reclaiming the Sacred*. Ithaca, NY, 1990.

———. "What's after Political Culture? Recent French Revolutionary Historiography." *FHS* 23.1 (2000), 163–96.

Desan, S., Lynn Hunt, and W. M. Nelson (eds.). *The French Revolution in Global Perspective*. Ithaca, NY, 2013.

Destain, Christian. "Chamfort et Rousseau: De l'individualité littéraire à la réflexion politique." In L'Aminot (ed.), *Politique et révolution*, 79–89.

Dhombres, Jean. "Enseignement moderne ou enseignement révolutionnaire des sciences." *Histoire de l'éducation* 42 (1989), 55–78.

Dhondt, Luc. "De conservatieve Brabantse ontwenteling van 1789 en het proces van revolutie en contrarevolutie in de Zuidelijke Nederlanden tussen 1780 en 1830." *Tijdschrift voor Geschiedenis* 102 (1989), 422–50.

Dingli, Laurent. *Robespierre*. Paris, 2004.

Dippel, Horst. *Germany and the American Revolution, 1770–1800: A Sociohistorical Investigation of Late Eighteenth-Century Political Thinking*. Chapel Hill, NC, 1977.

Dommanget, Maurice. *Babeuf et la conjuration des égaux*. 1922; repr., Paris, 2009.

———. *Sylvain Maréchal, l'égalitaire, "l'homme sans Dieu," sa vie, son œuvre, 1750–1803*. Paris, 1950.

Dorigny, Marcel. "Condorcet, libéral et girondin." In Crépel (ed.), *Condorcet*, 333–40.

———. "L'émergence d'un 'parti républicain.' " In Vovelle (ed.), *Révolution*, 109–19.

———. "Les Girondins et Jean-Jacques Rousseau." *AHRF* 1 (1978), 569–83.

Doyle, William. *Aristocracy and Its Enemies in the Age of Revolution.* Oxford, 2009.

————. *Officers, Nobles and Revolutionaries: Essays on Eighteenth-Century France.* London, 1995.

————. *Origins of the French Revolution.* 1980; 2nd ed., 1988.

————. *The Oxford History of the French Revolution.* Oxford, 1989.

————. *The Parlement of Bordeaux and the End of the Old Regime, 1771–1790.* London, 1974.

Dupuy, Roger. *Aux origines idéologiques de la Révolution: Journaux et pamphlets à Rennes (1788–89).* Rennes, 2000.

————. *La république jacobine: Terreur, guerre et gouvernement révolutionnaire, 1792–1794.* Paris, 2005.

————. "Le Roi de la Contre-Révolution." In Lucas (ed.), *Political Culture,* 193–211.

Dupuy, Roger, and Marcel Morabito (eds.). *1795: Pour une République sans Révolution.* Rennes, 1996.

Dwyer, Philip. *Napoleon: The Path to Power.* New Haven, CT, 2007.

Edelstein, D. *The Terror of Natural Right: Republicanism, the Cult of Nature, and the French Revolution.* Chicago, 2009.

Edelstein, M. "*La Feulle villageoise,* the Revolutionary Press and the Question of Rural Political Participation." *FHS* 7 (1971), 175–203.

Ehrard, Jean. "Audace théorique, prudence pratique: Montesquieu et l'esclavage colonial." In Olivier Petre-Grenouilleau, *Abolir l'esclavage: Un réformisme à l'épreuve (France, Portugal, Suisse, XVIIIe-XIXe siècles),* 27–40. Rennes, 2008.

Eisenstein, E. L. "Le Publiciste comme démagogue: *La Sentinelle du Peuple* de Volney." In Pierre Rétat (ed.), *La Révolution du Journal, 1788–1794,* 189–95. Paris, 1989.

Elliott, Marianne. "Ireland and the French Revolution." In H. T. Dickinson (ed.), *Britain and the French Revolution, 1789–1815,* 83–101. Basingstoke, 1989.

Elyada, Ouzi. "La Mère Duchesne: Masques populaires et guerre pamphlétaire, 1789–1791." *AHRF* 1 (1988), 1–16.

————. "La mise au pilori de l'Abbé Maury: Imaginaire comique et mythe de l'antihéros pendant la révolution française." *AHRF* 3 (2005), 1–24.

————. "L'appel aux faubourgs: Pamphlets populaires et propagande à Paris, 1789–1791." In M. Vovelle (ed.), *Paris et la Révolution,* 185–200.

————. "La représentation populaire de l'image royale avant Varennes." *AHRF* 3 (1994), 527–46.

————. "Les récits de complot dans la presse populaire parisienne (1790–1791)." *Studies on Voltaire and the Eighteenth Century* 287 (1991), 281–92.

————. "L'usage des personnages imaginaires dans la presse et le pamphlet populaires pendant la Révolution française." *Revue de l'histoire moderne et contemporaine* 44–43 (July–Sept., 1997), 484–503.

————. Preface and notes to *Lettres bougrement patriotiques de "La Mère Duchêne";* suivi du *"Journal des Femmes."* Paris, 1989.

Engels, Hans-Werner. "Freye Deutsche! Singt die Stunde . . ." In R. Schütt (ed.), "Ein Mann von Feuer und Talenten," in *Leben und Werk von Carl Friedrich Cramer,* 245–70. Gottingen, 2005.

Erdman, David V. *Commerce des Lumières: John Oswald and the British in Paris, 1790–93.* Columbia, MI, 1986.

Fajn, Max. "The Attitude of the *Journal des hommes libres* toward the *Babouvists.*" *International Review of Social History* 19 (1974), 228–44.

Favreau, B. "Gensonné ou la fatalité de la Gironde." In Furet and Ozouf (eds.), *La Gironde*, 409–35.

Fehér, Ferenc. *The Frozen Revolution: An Essay on Jacobinism*. Cambridge, 1987.

Ferrone, Vincenzo. *La società giusta ed equa: Repubblicanesimo e diritti dell' uomo in Gaetano Filangieri*. Rome-Bari, 2003.

Fitzsimmons, M. P. *The Remaking of France: The National Assembly and the Constitution of 1791*. Cambridge, 1994.

Fletcher, Loraine. *Charlotte Smith: A Critical Biography*. New York, 1998.

Foner, Eric. *Tom Paine and Revolutionary America*. 1976; rev. ed., New York, 2005.

Foot, Paul. *Red Shelley*. London, 2004

Forrest, Alan. "Federalism." In Lucas (ed.), *Political Culture*, 309–25.

———. *The French Revolution and the Poor*. Oxford, 1981.

———. *The Revolution in Provincial France: Aquitaine, 1789–1799*. Oxford, 1996.

Forst, Rainer. *Toleranz im Konflikt*. Berlin, 2003.

Forsyth, Murray. *Reason and Revolution: The Political Thought of the Abbé Sieyès*. Leicester, 1987.

Friedland, Paul. *Political Actors: Representative Bodies and Theatricality in the Age of the French Revolution*. Ithaca, NY, 2002.

Frijhoff, W.Th.M. "De triomf van burger en burgerdeugd?" In S. W. Couwenberg (ed.), *Opstand der burgers: De Franse Revolutie na 200 jaar*, 67–82. Kampen, 1988.

Fromm, H. *Bibliographie deutscher Übersetzungen aus dem Französischen, 1700–1948*. 6 vols. Baden-Baden, 1950–53.

Fulgencio López, C. *Juan Bautista Picornell y la conspiración de Gual y España*. Caracas, 1955.

Fuoc, Renée. *La réaction thermidorienne à Lyon*. Lyon, 1957.

Furet, François. *Interpreting the French Revolution*. Cambridge, 1981.

———. "Les Girondins et la guerre." In Furet and Ozouf (eds.), *La Gironde*, 189–205.

———. *Revolutionary France, 1770–1880*. Oxford, 1992.

———. "Rousseau and the French Revolution." In C. Orwin and N. Tarcov (eds.), *The Legacy of Rousseau*, 168–82. Chicago, 1997.

Furet, François, and Mona Ozouf (eds.). *Dictionnaire critique de la Révolution française*. Paris, 1988.

———. *La Gironde et les Girondins*. Paris, 1991.

Gainot, Bernard. *1799, Un nouveau Jacobinisme? La démocratie représentative, une alternative à Brumaire*. Paris, 2001.

Garrigus, J. D. "Opportunist or Patriot? Julien Raimond (1744–1801) and the Haitian Revolution." *Slavery and Abolition* 28 (2007), 1–21.

———. "Vincent Ogé jeune (1757–91)." *Americas* 68 (2011), 33–62.

Garrioch, David. *The Making of Revolutionary Paris*. Berkeley and Los Angeles, 2002.

Garrone, Alessandro Galante. *Gilbert Romme, storia di un rivoluzionario*. Turin, 1959.

Gauchet, Marcel. *La Révolution des droits de l'homme*. Paris, 1989.

———. *La Révolution des pouvoirs*. Paris, 1995.

Gaulmier, Jean. *Un grand témoin de la Révolution et de l'empire, Volney*. Paris, 1959.

Gauthier, Florence. *Triomphe et mort du droit naturel en Révolution: 1789–1795–1892*. Paris, 1992.

Geffroy, A. "Louise de Kéralio-Robert, pionnère du républicanisme sexiste." *AHRF* 344 (2006), 107–24.

Ghachem, Malick W. "Montesquieu in the Caribbean: The Colonial Enlightenment between 'Code Noir' and 'Code Civil.'" *Historical Reflections/Reflexions Historiques* 25.2 (1999), 183–210.

Ghibaudi, S. R. *La fortuna di Rousseau in Italia (1750–1815)*. Turin, 1961.

Gibbs, F. W. *Joseph Priestley, Adventurer in Science and Champion of Truth*. London, 1965.

Gillion, Anne. "La mémoire de Robespierre à Arras." *Revue du Nord* 71 (1989), 1037–50.

Girard, Patrick. *La révolution française et les Juifs*. Paris, 1989.

Godechot, Jacques. *The Counter-Revolution: Doctrine and Action, 1789–1804*. Princeton, 1981.

Godineau, Dominique. "Masculine and Feminine Political Practice during the French Revolution, 1793–Year III." In H. B. Applewhite and D. G. Levy (eds.), *Women and Politics in the Age of Democratic Revolution*, 61–80. Ann Arbor, MI, 1993.

———. *The Women of Paris and Their French Revolution*. Berkeley and Los Angeles, 1988.

Goetz, R. "Destutt de Tracy et le problème de la liberté." *Corpus, Revue de philosophie* 26, no. 17 (1994), 57–74.

Goldberg Moses, Claire. "'Equality' and 'Difference' in Historical Perspective: A Comparative Examination of the Feminisms of French Revolutionaries and Utopian Socialists." In Melzer and Rabine (eds.), *Rebel Daughters*, 231–54.

Goldstone, Jack A. "The Social Origins of the French Revolution Revisited." In Kaiser and Van Kley (eds.), *From Deficit to Deluge*, 67–103.

Gough, Hugh. *The Newspaper Press in the French Revolution*. London, 1988.

———. "Robespierre and the Press." In Haydon and Doyle (eds.), *Robespierre*, 111–26.

Goyhenetche, M. *Histoire générale du Pays Basque*. Vol. 4, *La Révolution de 1789*. Bayonne, 2002.

Graczyk, Anette. "Le théâtre de la Révolution française: Média de masse entre 1789 et 1794." *Dix-Huitième Siècle* 21 (1989), 395–410.

Granderoute, Robert. "Rousseau et les plans et les projets d'éducation, 1789–1795." In Thiéry (ed.), *Rousseau, l'Émile et la Révolution*, 325–38.

Gray, John. *Enlightenment's Wake: Politics and Culture at the Close of the Modern Age*. New York, 1995.

Greenlaw, R. W. "Pamphlet Literature in France during the Period of the Aristocratic Revolt (1787–1788)." *JMH* 29 (1957), 349–54.

Grenby, M. O. *The Anti-Jacobin Novel: British Conservatism and the French Revolution*. Cambridge, 2001.

Grevet, René. *L'Avènement de l'école contemporaine en France (1789–1835)*. Paris, 2001.

Griffiths, R. *Le Centre perdu: Malouet et les "monarchiens" dans la Révolution française*. Grenoble, 1988.

Gross, Jean-Pierre. *Fair Shares for All: Jacobin Egalitarianism in Practice*. Cambridge, 1997.

Gruder, Vivian R. *The Notables and the Nation*. Cambridge, MA, 2007.

Grüner, W. D. "Deutschland zwischen Revolution, Reform und Restauration, 1770–1830." *Tijdschrift voor Geschiedenis* 102 (1989), 368–400.

Gueniffey, Patrice. "Brissot." In Furet and Ozouf (eds.), *La Gironde*, 437–64.

———. *La politique de la Terreur*. Paris, 2000.

———. *Le Dix-huit Brumaire: L'Épilogue de la Révolution française*. Paris, 2008.

———. "L'élection des députés de l'Yonne a la Convention (1792)." In Hamon, *Révolution*, 61–92.

———. "Les Assemblées et la représentation." In Lucas (ed.), *Political Culture*, 233–57.

Guerci, Luciano. "Incredulità e rigenerazione nella Lombardia del triennio repubblicano." *Rivista storica italiana* 109 (1997), 49–120.

Guibert-Sledziewski, E. *Idéaux et conflits dans la Révolution française*. Paris, 1986.

Guicheteau, S. "La Terreur sociale à Nantes." In M. Biard (ed.), *Les Politiques de la Terreur, 1793–1794*, 307–19. Rennes, 2008.

Guilhaumou, Jacques. *L'Avènement des porte-parole de la République (1789–1792)*. Paris, 1998.

———. "Le Discours de salut public d'Hébert au Club des Jacobins le 21 juillet 1793." In Chr. Peyrard (ed.), *Minorités politiques en Révolution*, 43–59. Aix-en-Provence, 2007.

———. *Marseille républicaine (1791–1793)*. Paris, 1992.

Guilhaumou, Jacques, and R. Monnier. "Les Cordeliers et la République de 1793." In Vovelle (ed.), *Révolution et République: L'Exception française*. Paris, 1994.

Guillois, Antoine. *Le Salon de Madame Helvétius: Cabanis et les Idéologues*. New York, 1894.

Guillon, Claude. *Notre patience est à bout: Les écrits des Enragé(e)s 1792–93*. Paris, 2009.

Guitton, Edouard. *Ginguené: Idéolgue et médiateur*. Rennes, 1995.

Halévi, Ran. "La révolution constituante." In Lucas (ed.), *Political Culture*, 69–85.

———. "Les Girondins avant la Gironde." In Furet and Ozouf (eds.), *La Gironde*, 137–68.

Hammersley, Rachel. *French Revolutionaries and English Republicans: The Cordeliers Club, 1790–1794*. Rochester, NY, 2005.

Hamon, Léo (ed.). *La Révolution à travers un departement* (Yonne). Paris, 1990.

Hampson, Norman. *The Life and Opinions of Maximilien Robespierre*. London, 1974.

———. *Saint-Just*. Oxford, 1991.

———. *A Social History of the French Revolution*. London, 1963.

———. *Will and Circumstance: Montesquieu, Rousseau and the French Revolution*. Norman, OK, 1983.

Hanson, P. R. *The Jacobin Republic under Fire: The Federalist Revolt in the French Revolution*. University Park, PA, 2003.

———. *Provincial Politics in the French Revolution*. Baton Rouge, LA, 1989.

Hardman, John. *Louis XVI, the Silent King*. London, 2000.

Harris, Jean-Pierre. *Antoine d'Estutt de Tracy: L'éblouissement des Lumières*. Précy-sous-Thil, 2008.

Haydon, C., and William Doyle (eds.). *Robespierre*. Cambridge, 1999.

Herding, Klaus, and Rolf Reichardt. *Die Bildpublistik der Französischen Revolution*. Frankfurt, 1989.

Hermann, Ingo. *Knigge: Die Biografie*. Berlin, 2007.

Hermon-Belot, R. *L'Abbé Grégoire: La Politique et la vérité*. Paris, 2000.

Hesse, Carla. "Economic Upheavals in Publishing." In Darnton and Roche (eds.), *Revolution in Print*, 69–97.

Hesse, Carla. "La Logique culturelle de la loi révolutionnaire." *Annales: Histoire, Sciences Sociales* 57 (2002), 915–33.

Heuer, Jennifer. "Family Bonds and Female Citizenship: Émigré Women under the Directory." In *Taking Liberties: Problems of a New Order from the French Revolution to Napoleon*, ed. Howard Brown and Judith Miller, 51–69. Manchester, 2002.

Higonnet, P. *Class, Ideology and the Rights of the Nobles during the French Revolution.* Oxford, 1981.

———. *Goodness beyond Virtue: Jacobins during the French Revolution.* Cambridge, MA, 1998.

———. *Sister Republics: The Origins of French and American Republicanism.* Cambridge, MA, 1988.

Hitzel, F. "La France et la modernization de l'Égypte." In Bret (ed.), *L'Expédition d'Égypte*, 9–20.

Hohl, Claude. "Les sociétés politiques dans l'Yonne durant la Révolution." In Hamon (ed.), *La Révolution*, 203–24.

Hunt, Lynn. *The Family Romance of the French Revolution.* Berkeley, 1992.

———. "The Global Financial Origins of 1789." In Desan, Hunt, and Nelson (eds.), *French Revolution*, 32–43.

———. *Inventing Human Rights: A History.* New York, 2007.

———. *Politics, Culture and Class in the French Revolution.* Berkeley, 1984.

Ikni, G. R. "Jacques-Marie Coupé, curé Jacobin." *AHRF* 56 (1984), 339–65.

Isaac, Marie-Thérèse, and Claude Sorgeloos. *L'École centrale du département de Jemappes, 1797–1802: Enseignement, livres et Lumières à Mons.* Brussels, 2004.

Israel, Jonathan, I. *Democratic Enlightenment: Philosophy, Revolution and Human Rights, 1750–1790.* Oxford, 2011.

———. *Enlightenment Contested: Philosophy, Modernity and the Emancipation of Man, 1670–1752.* Oxford, 2006.

———. "Failed Enlightenment: Spinoza's Legacy and the Netherlands (1670–1800)." Netherlands Institute for Advanced Study, Wassenaar, Netherlands, June 21, 2007.

———. "Natural Virtue versus Book Learning: Rousseau and the Great Enlightenment Battle over Education." *European Journal of Developmental Psychology*, 2012. Special Supplement (Jean Jacques Rousseau 300th Birthday Anniversary Commemoration), 6–17.

———. *Radical Enlightenment: Philosophy and the Making of Modernity, 1650–1750.* Oxford, 2001.

———. *A Revolution of the Mind: Radical Enlightenment and the Intellectual Origins of Modern Democracy.* Princeton, 2010.

Jacob, Louis. *Hébert: Le Père Duchesne, Chef des sans-culottes.* Paris, 1960.

Jaher, F. C. *The Jews and the Nation: Revolution, Emancipation, State Formation and the Liberal Paradigm in America and France.* Princeton, 2002.

Jainchill, A. *Reimagining Politics after the Terror.* Ithaca, NY, 2008.

Jaume, Lucien. "Individu et souveraineté chez Condorcet." In P. Crépel and Chr. Gilain (eds.), *Condorcet, mathématicien, économiste, philosophe, homme politique*, 297–304. Paris, 1989.

———. *Le discours Jacobin et la démocratie.* Paris, 1989.

Jennings, Jeremy. "Reason's Revenge." In the *Times Literary Supplement*, no. 5695 (25 May 2012), 4.

———. *Revolution and the Republic.* Oxford, 2011.

Johns, Christopher. *Antonio Canova and the Politics of Patronage in Revolutionary and Napoleonic Europe.* Berkeley and Los Angeles, 1998.

Johnson, H. C. *The Midi in Revolution: A Study of Regional Political Diversity, 1789–1793.* Princeton, 1986.

Joly, Claude. Introduction to Destutt de Tracy, *Premiers écrits*, 9–49.

Jones, Colin. *The Great Nation: France from Louis XV to Napoleon, 1715–99.* New York, 2002.

Jones, Peter. *The Peasantry in the French Revolution.* Cambridge, 1988.

Jordaan, H. "Patriots, Privateers, and Inernational Politics." In Klooster and Oostindie (eds.), *Curaçao*, 141–69.

Jordan, D. P. *The Revolutionary Career of Maximilien Robespierre.* New York, 1985.

Jourdan, Annie. "Le culte de Rousseau sous la Révolution: La statue et la panthéonisation du Citoyen de Genève." In L'Aminot (ed.), *Politique et révolution*, 57–77.

———. "Politieke en culturele transfers in een tijd van revolutie: Nederland, 1795–1805." *Bijdragen en Mededelingen betreffende de Geschiedenis der Nederlanden*, no. 124 (2009), 559–79.

Kaiser, Thomas E. "From Fiscal Crisis to Revolution." In Kaiser and Van Kley (eds.), *From Deficit to Deluge*, 139–64.

Kaiser, Thomas E., and D. K. Van Kley (eds.). *From Deficit to Deluge: The Origins of the French Revolution.* Stanford, CA, 2011.

Kates, G. *The Cercle Social, the Girondins, and the French Revolution.* Princeton, 1985.

Kennedy, Emmet. "Aux origines de l'idéologie." *Corpus, Revue de philosophie* 26/27 (1994), 11–36.

———. *A Cultural History of the French Revolution.* New Haven, CT, 1989.

Kennedy, M. L. "The Development of a Political Radical, Jean-Louis Carra, 1742–1787." *Proceedings of the Western Society for French History* (1974), 142–50.

———. *The Jacobin Clubs in the French Revolution: The Middle Years.* Princeton, 1988.

Kitchin, Joanna. *Un journal "philosophique": La Décade (1794–1807).* Paris, 1965.

Kitromilides, P. M. "Itineraries in the World of the Enlightenment." In P. Kitromilides (ed.), *Adamantios Korais and the European Enlightenment*, 1–33. Oxford, 2010.

Klein, S.R.E. *Patriots republikanisme: Politieke cultuur in Nederland (1766–1787).* Amsterdam, 1995.

Klooster, Wim. *Revolutions in the Atlantic World: A Comparative History.* New York, 2009.

———. "The Rising Expectations of Free and Enslaved Blacks in the Greater Caribbean." In Klooster and Oostindie (eds.), *Curaçao*, 57–74.

Klooster, Wim, and G. Oostindie (eds.). *Curaçao in the Age of Revolutions, 1795–1800.* Leiden, 2011.

Knudsen, J. B. *Justus Möser and the German Enlightenment.* Cambridge, 1986.

Kouvelakis, Stathis. *Philosophy and Revolution from Kant to Marx.* London, 2003.

Kramer, Lloyd S. *Lafayette in Two Worlds: Public Cultures and Personal Identities in an Age of Revolutions.* Chapel Hill, NC, 1996.

Labbé, François. *Anacharsis Cloots le prussien francophile*. Paris, 1999.

Labrosse, Claude, and Pierre Rétat. *Naissance du journal révolutionnaire, 1789*. Lyon, 1989.

Ladjouzi, Diane. "Les journées des 4 et 5 septembre 1793 à Paris: Un mouvement d'union entre le peuple, la commune de Paris et la convention pour un exécutif révolutionnaire." *AHRF* 321 (2000), 27–44.

La Gorce, Pierre de. *Histoire religieuse de la Révolution française*. Paris, 1909.

Lagrave, Jean-Paul de. *Fleury Mesplet: the Enlightenment Comes to Canada*. Montréal, 1992.

———. "Thomas Paine et les Condorcet." In Vincent (ed.), *Thomas Paine*, 57–64.

Laissus, Yves. "La Commission des sciences et des arts et l'Institut d'Égypte." In Bret (ed.), *L'Expédition d'Égypte*, 37–41.

Lajer-Burcharth, E. *Necklines: The Art of Jacques-Louis David after the Terror*. New Haven, CT, 1999.

Lalouette, J. *La Séparation des églises et de l'état: Genèse d'une idée (1789–1905)*. Paris, 2005.

L'Aminot, Tanguy (ed.). *Politique et révolution chez Jean-Jacques Rousseau*. Oxford, 1994.

Lapied, Martine. "Une absence de révolution pour les femmes?" In Michel Biard (ed.), *La Révolution française: Une histoire toujours vivante*, 303–16. Paris, 2010.

Lawday, David. *The Giant of the French Revolution: Danton*. New York, 2009.

———. *Napoleon's Master: A Life of Prince Talleyrand*. 2006; new ed., New York, 2007.

Lebozec, Chr. "Boissy d'Anglas et la constitution de l'an III." In Dupu and Morabito (eds.), *1795 Pour une République*, 81–90.

———. "Les idées politiques de Boissy d'Anglas." In Conac and Machelon (eds.), *Constitution*, 141–52.

———. "Le Théâtre à Rouen pendant la Révolution française." In Bourdin and Loubinou (eds.), *Les Arts*, 181–88.

Lefebvre, Georges. *The French Revolution from 1793 to 1799*. London, 1964.

Leith, James A. "The Terror: Adding the Cultural Dimension." *Canadian Journal of History* 32 (1997), 315–37.

Lemny, Stefan. *Jean-Louis Carra (1742–1793), parcours d'un révolutionnaire*. Paris-Montreal, 2000.

Leuwers, Herve. *Un Juriste en politique: Merlin de Douai (1754–1838)*. Arras, 1996.

Lewis-Beck, M. S., A. Hildreth, and A. Spitzer. "Was There a Girondist Faction in the National Convention, 1792–1793?" *FHS* 15 (1988), 519–36.

Linton, Marisa. "'Do you believe that we're conspirators?': Conspiracies Real and Imagined in Jacobin Politics, 1793–94." In Campbell, Kaiser, and Linton (eds.), *Conspiracy*, 127–49.

———. *The Politics of Virtue in Enlightenment France*. New York, 2001.

Livesey, J. *Making Democracy in the French Revolution*. Cambridge, MA, 2001.

Loft, Leonore. *Passion, Politics, and Philosophie: Rediscovering J.-P. Brissot*. Westport, CT, 2002.

Lortholary, Albert. *Le mirage russe en France au XVIIIe siècle*. Paris, 1951.

Losfeld, Christophe. *Philanthropisme, Libéralisme et Révolution: Le "Braunschweigisches Journal" et le "Schleswigsches Journal" (1788–1793)*. Tübingen, 2002.

Lucas, Colin. "The Crowd and Politics." In Lucas (ed.), *Political Culture*, 259–85.

———(ed.). *The Political Culture of the French Revolution*. Vol. 2 of *The French Revolution and Modern Political Culture*. Oxford, 1988.

Luchaire, François. "Boissy d'Anglas et la Constitution de l'an III." In Conac and Machelon (eds.), *Constitution*, 43–50.

Lüsebrink, Hans-Jürgen. "Georg Forster et Adam Lux dans la France révolutionnaire de 1793." *Revue de Littérature comparée*, no. 251 (1989), 463–78.

Lüsebrink, Hans-Jürgen, Rolf Reichardt, and Norbert Schürer (eds.). *The Bastille: A History of a Symbol of Despotism and Freedom*. Durham, NC, 1997.

Luttrell, Barbara. *Mirabeau*. New York, 1990.

Mackrell, J.Q.C. *The Attack on "Feudalism" in Eighteenth-Century France*. London, 1973.

Manevy, Raymond. *La Révolution et la liberté de la presse*. Paris, 1965.

Margairaz, Dominique. *François de Neufchâteau: Biographie intellectuelle*. Paris, 2005.

Martin, Jean-Clément. *Violence et révolution: Essai sur la naissance d'un mythe national*. Paris, 2006.

Maslan, Susan. "Resisting Representation: Theater and Democracy in Revolutionary France." *Representations* 52 (1995), 27–51.

———. *Revolutionary Acts: Theater, Democracy, and the French Revolution*. Baltimore, 2005.

Mason, Laura. "Never Was a Plot So Holy: Gracchus Babeuf and the End of the French Revolution." In Campbell, Kaiser, and Linton (eds.), *Conspiracy*, 172–88.

Mastroberti, Francesco. *Pierre Joseph Briot: Un giacobino tra amministrazione e politica (1771–1827)*. Naples, 1998.

Mathiez, Albert. *The Fall of Robespierre and Other Essays*. New York, 1968.

———. *La réaction thermidorienne*. 1928; new ed., Paris, 2010.

———. *La Théophilanthropie et la culte décadaire (1796–1801)*. Paris, 1904.

Mathy, Helmut. "Anton Joseph Dorsch (1758–1819): Leben und Werk eines rheinischen Jakobiners." *Mainzer Zeitschrift* 62 (1967), 1–55.

May, Gita. *Elisabeth Vigée Le Brun: The Odyssey of an Artist in an Age of Revolution*. New Haven, CT, 2005.

———. *Madame Roland and the Age of Revolution*. New York, 1970.

Mazzanti Pepe, Fernanda. *Il nuovo mondo di Brissot: Libertà e istituzioni tra antico regime e rivoluzione*. Turin, 1996.

McEachern, J.A.E. "Le Révolution française et les éditions de l'*Émile* en France et à l'étranger." In Thiéry (ed.), *Rousseau, l'*Émile *et la Révolution*, 301–8.

McMahon, Darrin M. *Enemies of the Enlightenment: The French Counter-Enlightenment and the Making of Modernity*. New York, 2001.

McManners, John. *Church and Society in Eighteenth-Century France*. 2 vols. Oxford, 1998.

McPhee, Peter. *Robespierre: A Revolutionary Life*. New Haven, CT, 2012.

Meier, Heinrich. "'Einführender Essay" and Critical Notes to Rousseau." In *Essai sur l'inegalité*, xxi–xci.

Mellor, Anne. "English Women Writers and the French Revolution." In S. E. Melzer and W. Rabine (eds.), *Rebel Daughters: Women and the French Revolution*, 255–72. New York, 1992.

Melzer, S. E., and L. W. Rabine (eds.). *Rebel Daughters: Women and the French Revolution*. New York, 1992.

Michelet, J. *Histoire de la Revolution*. 9 vols. Paris, 1888.

Miller, James. *Rousseau: Dreamer of Democracy*. New Haven, CT, 1984.

Mitchell, C. J. *The French Legislative Assembly of 1791*. Leiden, 1988.

Mongrédien, Jean. *French Music from the Enlightement to Romanticism, 1789–1830*. Portland, OR, 1986.

Monnier, R. "Démocratie représentative" ou "république démocratique": De la querelle des mots (république) à la querelle des anciens et des modernes." *AHRF* 325 (2001), 1–21.

———. "L'Evolution du personnel politique de la section Marat." *AHRF* 263 (1986), 50–73.

———. "Républicanisme et révolution française." *FHS* 26 (2003), 87–118.

Monseignat, Ch. de. *Un chapitre de la Révolution française ou histoire des journaux en France de 1789 à 1799*. Paris, 1853.

Moore, Barrington. *Moral Purity and Persecution in History*. Princeton, 2000.

Moravia, Sergio. *Il tramonto dell'Illuminismo: Filosofia e politica nella società francese (1770–1810)*. Rome, 1986.

Mortier, Roland. *Anacharsis Cloots ou l'utopie foudroyée*. Paris, 1995.

———. *Le Cœur et la raison*, 454–66. Oxford-Paris, 1990.

———. *Les Combats des Lumières*. Ferney-Voltaire, 2000.

———. "Les héritiers des 'philosophes' devant l'expérience révolutionnaire." In R. Mortier, *Le Cœur et la Raison*, 454–66. Oxford-Paris, 1990.

Mortier, Roland, and Hervé Hasquin (eds.). *Idéologies de la noblesse*. Brussels, 1984.

Murray, W. J. *The Right-Wing Press in the French Revolution: 1789–92*. Woodbridge, Suffolk, 1986.

Muschik, Alexander. "Die Ideen der Französischen Revolution in Schwedisch-Vorpommern." *Baltische Studien N.F.* 93 (2007), 163–84.

Naville, Pierre. *Paul Thiry d'Holbach et la philosophie scientifique au XVIIIe siècle*. 5th ed. Paris, 1943.

Nelson, Craig. *Thomas Paine: His Life, His Time and the Birth of Modern Nations*. London, 2006.

Nesbitt, Nick. *Universal Emancipation: The Haitian Revolution and the Radical Enlightenment*. Charlottesville, VA, 2008.

Nicolle, Bruno."Lanjuinais et la constitution de l'an III." In Dupuy and Morabito (eds.), *1795: Pour une République*, 91–113.

Norberg, K. "'Love and Patriotism': Gender and Politics in the Life and Work of Louvet de Couvrai." In Melzer and Rabine (eds.), *Rebel Daughters*, 38–53.

O'Hagan, Timothy. *Rousseau*. London, 1999.

Olsen, Mark. "A Failure of Enlightened Politics in the French Revolution: The Société de 1789." *French History* 6, no. 3 (1992), 303–34.

Ortega, Maria Luisa. "La 'régéneration' de l'Égypte." In Bret (ed.), *L'Expédition d'Égypte*, 93–101.

Ozouf, Mona. *Festivals and the French Revolution*. Cambridge, MA, 1988.

———. "La Révolution française et l'idée de l'homme nouveau." In Lucas (ed.), *Political Culture of the French Revolution*. Vol. 2 of *The French Revolution and the Creation of Modern Political Culture*, 213–32. Oxford, 1988.

———. "L'Opinion publique." In Baker (ed.), *Political Culture*, 419–34.

———. "Madame Roland." In Furet and Ozouf (eds.), *La Gironde*, 307–28.

———. "Massacres de septembre, qui est responsable ?" *Histoire* 342 (2009), 52–55.

———. "The Terror after the Terror." In Baker (ed.), *The Terror*, 3–38.

Paganella, M. *Alle origini dell'unità d'Italia*. Milan, 1999.

Pagden, Anthony. *The Enlightenment and Why It Still Matters*. Oxford, 2013.

Palmer, R. R. *From Jacobin to Liberal: Marc-Antoine Jullien, 1775–1848*. Princeton, 1993.

———. *Twelve Who Ruled: The Years of the Terror in the French Revolution*. 1941; repr., Princeton, 1989.

Pasquino, Pasquale. *Sieyès et l'invention de la constitution en France*. Paris, 1998.

Patrick, Alison. *The Men of the First French Republic: Political Alignments in the National Convention of 1792*. Baltimore, 1972.

Pellerin, Pascale. "Naigeon: Une certaine image de Diderot sous la Révolution." *Recherches sur Diderot et sur l'Encyclopédie* 29 (2000), 25–44.

Pertué, Michel. "Les projets constitutionnels de 1793." In Vovelle (ed.), *Révolution*, 174–99.

Peters, Martin. *Altes Reich und Europa: Der Historiker, Statistiker un Publizist August Ludwig Schlözer (1735–1809)*. Münster, 2005.

Peterson, Merrill D. *Thomas Jefferson and the New Nation: A Biography*. New York, 1970.

Petitfils, Jean-Christian. *Louis XVI*. Vol. 2 (1786–1793). Paris, 2005.

Peyrard, Christine. *Les Jacobins de l'Ouest: Sociabilité révolutionnaire et formes de politisation dans le Maine et la Basse-Normandie (1789–1799)*. Paris, 1996.

——— (ed.). *Minorités politiques en revolution, 1789–1799*. Aix-en-Provence, 2007.

Pineau-Defois, Laure. "Une élite d'*Ancien régime*: Les grands négociants nantais (1780–1793)." *AHRF* 359 (2010), 97–118.

Piquet, Jean-Daniel. *L'émancipation des Noirs dans la Révolution française (1789–1795)*. Paris, 2002.

Polasky, Janet. "Women in Revolutionary Brussels." In Applewhite and Levy, *Women and Politics*, 81–107.

Popkin, Jeremy. "Journals: The New Face of News." In Darnton and Roche (eds.), *Revolution in Print*, 141–64.

———. "Not Over After All: The French Revolution's Third Century." *JMH* 74 (2002), 801–21.

———. *The Right-Wing Press in France, 1792–1800*. Chapel Hill, NC, 1980.

———. *You Are All Free: The Haitian Revolution and the Abolition of Slavery*. Cambridge, 2010.

Quastana, François. *La pensée politique de Mirabeau (1771–1789)*. Aix-en-Provence, 2007.

Quiviger, Pierre-Yves. "Sieyès as a Reader of John Locke." In C. Miqieu and M. Chamie (eds.), *Locke's Political Liberty*, 127–42. Oxford, 2009.

Rao, A. M. *Il regno di Napoli nel Settecento*. Naples, 1983.

Rasmussen, D. C. "Burning Laws and Strangling Kings? Voltaire and Diderot on the Perils of Rationalism in Politics." *Review of Politics* 73 (2011), 77–104.

Ravitch, N. "The Abbé Fauchet: Romantic Religion during the French Revolution." *Journal of the American Academy of Religion* 42 (1974), 247–62.

Raymond, André. "Les Égyptiens pendant l'expédition française." In Bret (ed.), *L'Expédition d'Égypte*, 103–20.

Régent, Frédéric. *La France et ses esclaves*. Paris, 2007.

Régent, Frédéric. "L'Égypte des idéolgues: Le regard de la *Décade philosophique* sur l'expédition de Bonarparte." In Bret, *L'Expédition d'Égypte*, 81–102.

Rials, Stéphane. *La Déclaration des droits de l'homme et du citoyen.* Paris, 1988.

Robisco, Nathalie-Barbara. *Jean-Jacques Rousseau et la Révolution française.* Paris, 1998.

Rocher, J. P. "Aspects de l'histoire religieuse du département de l'Yonne pendant la Révolution." In Hamon (ed.), *La Révolution*, 299–339.

Roe, Nicholas. *Wordsworth and Coleridge: The Radical Years.* Oxford, 1988.

Roessler, S. E. *Out of the Shadows: Women and Politics in the French Revolution, 1789–95.* New York, 1996.

Rose, R. B. *Gracchus Babeuf: The First Revolutionary Communist.* Stanford, CA, 1978.

Rosenblatt, Helena (ed.). *The Cambridge Companion to Constant.* Cambridge, 2009.

Rosendaal, Joost. *Bataven! Nederlandse vluchtelingen in Frankrijk, 1787–1795.* Nijmegen, 2003.

Rothschild, Emma. *Economic Sentiments: Adam Smith, Condorcet, and the Enlightenment.* Cambridge, MA, 2001.

Sa'adah, Anne. *The Shaping of Liberal Politics in Revolutionary France.* Princeton, 1990.

Sauter, M. J. *Visions of the Enlightenment: The Edict of Religion of 1788 and the Politics of the Public Sphere in Eighteenth-Century Prussia.* Leiden, 2009.

Schama, Simon. *Citizens: A Chronicle of the French Revolution.* London, 1989.

———. *Patriots and Liberators: Revolution in the Netherlands, 1780–1813.* London. 1977.

Schechter, R. *Obstinate Hebrews: Representations of Jews in France, 1715–1815.* Berkeley, CA, 2003.

Schoorl, E. *Jean-Baptiste Say: Revolutionary, Entrepreneur, Economist.* London, 2013.

Schütt, R. (ed.). "Ein Mann von Feuer und Talenten." In *Leben und Werk von Carl Friedrich Cramer*, 245–70. Gottingen, 2005.

Scott, J. A. "François Noël Babeuf and the Conspiration des Égaux." In J. A. Scott (ed.), *The Defense of Gracchus Babeuf.* Boston, 1967.

Scott, Joan. "A Woman Who Has Only Paradoxes to Offer: Olympe de Gouges Claims Rights for Women." In Melzer and Rabine (eds.), *Rebel Daughters*, 102–20.

Scott, William. *Terror and Repression in Revolutionary Marseilles.* London, 1973.

Scurr, Ruth. *Fatal Purity: Robespierre and the French Revolution.* London, 2006.

Serna, Pierre. *Antonelle, Aristocrate révolutionnaire (1747–1817).* Paris, 1997.

Sewell, William H. "Ideologies and Social Revolutions: Reflections on the French Case." *Journal of Modern History* 57 (1985), 57–85.

———. *A Rhetoric of Bourgeois Revolution.* Durham, NC, 1994.

———. "The Sans-Culotte Rhetoric of Subsistence." In K. M. Baker (ed.), *The Terror,* vol. 4, 249–70. Oxford, 1994.

———. *Work and Revolution in France.* Cambridge, 1980.

Shovlin, John. *The Political Economy of Virtue.* Ithaca, NY, 2006.

Shulman, A. *The Secular Contract: The Politics of Enlightenment.* New York, 2011.

Singham, S. M. "Betwixt Cattle and Men: Jews, Blacks and Women, and the Declaration of the Rights of Man." In Van Kley, *French Idea,* 114–53.

Slavin, M. *The French Revolution in Miniature: Section Droits-de-l'Homme, 1789–1795.* Princeton, 1984.

————. *The Making of an Insurrection*. Cambridge, MA, 1986.

Smith, David. *Bibliography of the Writings of Helvétius*. Ferney-Voltaire, 2001.

Sonenscher, M. *Before the Deluge: Public Debt, Inequality, and the Intellectual Origins of the French Revolution*. Princeton, 2007.

————. *Sans-Culottes: An Eighteenth-Century Emblem in the French Revolution*. Princeton, 2008.

Sorkin, David. *The Religious Enlightenment*. Princeton, 2008.

Spurr, David. "Gibbon et la révolution génevoise de 1792." In V. Cossy et al. (eds.), *Genève, lieu d'Angleterre, 1725–1814*, 269–79. Geneva, 2009.

Spang, R. *The Invention of the Restaurant*. Cambridge, MA, 2000.

————. "Paradigms and Paranoia: How Modern Is the French Revolution?" *AHR* 108 (2003), 119–47.

Spitz, Jean-Fabian. "Républicanisme et libéralisme dans le moment révolutionnaire." *AHRF* 358 (2009), 19–45.

Staum, Martin S. *Cabanis: Enlightenment and Medical Philosophy in the French Revolution*. Princeton, 1980.

————. "Individual Rights and Social Control: Political Science in the French Institute." *Journal of the History of Ideas* 48, no. 3 (July–Sept., 1987), 411–30.

————. *Minerva's Message: Stabilizing the French Revolution*. Montreal, 1996.

————. "Robespierre and the Insurrection of 31 May–2 June 1793." In Haydon and Doyle, *Robespierre*, 141–54.

Stone, Bailey. *The Genesis of the French Revolution*. Cambridge, 1994.

Strugnell, A. *Diderot's Politics: A Study of the Evolution of Diderot's Political Thought after the Encyclopédie*. The Hague, 1973.

Swenson, James. *On Jean-Jacques Rousseau Considered as One of the First Authors of the Revolution*. Stanford, CA, 2000.

Symcox, G. "Of Princes, Poets and the People: Alfieri's Critique of Absolute Monarchy." In D. Balani et al. (eds.), *Dall'origine dei Lumi all Rivoluzione: Scritti in onore di Luciano Guerci e Giuseppe Ricuperati*, 513–35. Rome, 2008.

Tackett, Timothy. *Becoming a Revolutionary: The Deputies of the French National Assembly and the Emergence of a Revolutionary Culture (1789–1790)*. Princeton, 1996.

————. "Conspiracy Obsession in a Time of Revolution." *AHR* 105 (2000), 691–713.

————. *Religion, Revolution, and Regional Culture in Eighteenth-Century France: The Ecclesiastical Oath of 1791*. Princeton, 1986.

Tallett, Frank. "Dechristianizing France." In F. Tallett and N. Atkin (eds.), *Religion, Society and Politics in France since 1789*, 1–28. London, 1991.

————. "Robespierre and Religion." In Hayden and Doyle (eds.), *Robespierre*, 92–108.

Tarin, René. *Diderot et la Révolution française*. Paris, 2001.

Taylor, Charles. *A Secular Age*. Cambridge, MA, 2007.

Te Brake, W. Ph. *Regents and Rebels*. Cambridge, MA, 1989.

Thiery, Robert, ed. *Rousseau, l'Émile et la Révolution: Actes du colloque international du Montmorency, 27 Septembre–4 Octobre 1989*. Paris, 1992.

Thomann, M. "Origines et sources doctrinales de la Déclaration des Droits." *Droits* 8 (1988), 55–70.

Thomas, Hugh. *The Slave Trade: The Story of the Atlantic Slave Trade, 1440–1870*. London, 1997.

Thompson, J. M. *The French Revolution*. New York, 1945.

Tlili-Sellaouti, R. "Pouvoir local et révolution." In R. Dupuy (ed.), *Pouvoir local et Révolution: La frontière intérieure,*117–33. Rennes, 1995.

Tønnesson, Kare D. "La démocratie directe sous la Révolution française: Le cas des districts et sections de Paris." In Colin Lucas, *The French Revolution and the Creation of Modern Political Culture.* Vol. 2. Oxford, 1988.

Tortarolo, Eduardo. *L'Invenzione della libertà di stampa.* Rome, 2011.

Trousson, Raymond. *Denis Diderot ou le vrai Prométhée.* Paris, 2005.

———. *Jean-Jacques Rousseau.* Paris, 2003.

Trousson, R., and S. Eigeldinger (eds.). *Dictionnaire de Jean-Jacques Rousseau.* Paris, 2006.

Tulard, Jean. *Histoire et dictionnaire de la Révolution française: 1789–1799.* Paris, 1987.

Uhlig, Ludwig. *Georg Forster.* Tübingen, 1965.

Urbinati, Nadia. *Representative Democracy: Principles and Genealogy.* 2006; new ed., Chicago, 2008.

Van den Bossche, G. *Enlightened Innovation and the Ancient Constitution (1787–1790).* Brussels, 2001.

Van Horn Melton, James. "From Enlightenment to Revolution: Hertzberg, Schlözer, and the Problem of Despotism in the Late *Aufklärung.*" *Central European History* 12 (1979), 103–23.

Van Kley, Dale. "Christianity as Casualty and Chrysalis of Modernity: The Problem of Dechristianization in the French Revolution." *American Historical Review* 108, no. 4 (October 2003): 1081–1104.

———. "From the Lessons of History to the Truths of All Time and All People." In Van Kley (ed.), *French Idea,* 72–113.

———. *The Religious Origins of the French Revolution.* New Haven, CT, 1996.

Van Kley, Dale (ed.). *The French Idea of Freedom: The Old Regime and the Declaration of Rights of 1789.* Stanford, CA, 1994.

Venturi, Franco. *Illuministi italiani.* Vol. 3. Milan, 1958.

Verdier, G. "From Reform to Revolution: The Social Theater of Olympe de Gouges." In C. R. Montfort, *Literate Women and the French Revolution.* Birmingham, AL, 1994.

Villaverde, Maria José. *La illusión republicana: Ideales y mitos.* Madrid, 2008.

———. "Spinoza, Rousseau: Dos concepciones de democracia." *Revista de estudios políticos,* 116 (2002), 85–106.

Vincent, Bernard. "Les Américains à Paris et leur image sous la Révolution." *Revue de Littérature Comparée,* no. 251 (1989), 479–95.

———(ed.). *Thomas Paine ou La République sans frontières.* Nancy, 1993.

Vinot, Bernard. *Saint-Just.* Paris, 1985.

Voss, Jürgen. "Die Kurpfalz im Zeichen der Französischen Revolution." In V. Rödel (ed.), *Die Französische Revolution und die Oberrheinlande (1789–1798),* 9–31. Sigmaringen, 1991.

Vovelle, Michel. *La découverte de la politique.* Paris, 1993.

———. *Les Jacobins de Robespierre à Chevènement.* Paris, 1999.

———(ed.). *Révolution et république: L'Exception française.* Paris, 1994.

———. *1793: La Révolution contre l'Église.* Paris, 1998.

———. *Théodore Desorgues ou la désorganisation.* Paris, 1985.

——. "Une Troisième voie pour la lecture de la Conspiration des Égaux?" *AHRF* 312 (1998), 217–27.

Wahnich, S. *L'impossible citoyen: L'étranger dans le discours de la Révolution française.* Paris, 1997.

Wallon, H. *Histoire du Tribunal Révolutionnaire de Paris.* 5 vols. Paris, 1880.

Walton, Charles. *Policing Public Opinion in the French Revolution.* New York, 2009.

Wauters, Eric. "La naissance d'un 'quatrième pouvoir'?" In Michel Biard (ed.), *La Révolution française: Une histoire toujours vivante,* 109–22. Paris, 2010.

Weber, Martin. *Georg Christian Gottlieb Wedekind, 1761–1831.* Stuttgart, 1988.

Wegert, K. H. *German Radicals Confront the Common People: Revolutionary Politics and Popular Politics, 1789–1849.* Mainz, 1992.

Welch, Cheryl. *Liberty and Utility: The French Idéologues and the Transformation of Liberalism.* New York, 1984.

Wells, Roger. *Insurrection: The British Experience, 1795–1803.* Gloucester, 1983.

Welschinger, Henri. *Le Théâtre de la Révolution, 1789–1799.* Paris, 1880.

Whaley, Leigh. *Radicals: Politics and Republicanism in the French Revolution.* Stroud, 2000.

Whatmore, Richard. *Republicanism and the French Revolution: An Intellectual History of Jean-Baptiste Say's Political Economy.* Oxford, 2000.

Williams, David. *Condorcet and Modernity.* Cambridge, 2004.

——. "The Influence of Rousseau on Political Opinion, 1760–95." *English Historical Review* 17 (1993), 414–30.

Wokler, R. *Rousseau, the Age of Enlightenment and Their Legacies.* Princeton, 2012.

Woloch, Isser. "The Contraction and Expansion of Democratic Space during the Period of the Terror." In Baker, *The Terror,* 309–25.

——. *Jacobin Legacy: The Democratic Movement under the Directory.* Princeton, 1970.

——. "La République directoriale et l'enseignement primaire." In Vovelle (ed.), *Révolution,* 312–23.

——. "The Revival of Jacobinism in Metz during the Directory." *JMH* 39 (1966), 13–37.

Wood, Dennis. "Benjamin Constant: Life and Work." In Rosenblatt, *Cambridge Companion to Constant,* 3–19.

Woronoff, Denis. *The Thermidorean Regime and the Directory, 1794–1799.* Cambridge, 1984.

Wright, J. K. *A Classical Republican in Eighteenth-Century France.* Stanford, CA, 1997.

——. "National Sovereignty and the General Will." In Van Kley (ed.), *French Idea,* 199–233.

Zamoyski, Adam. *Holy Madness: Romantics, Patriots and Revolutionaries, 1776–1871.* London, 1999.

Zizek, Joseph. "'Plume de fer': Louis-Marie Prudhomme writes the French Revolution." *FHS* 26 (2003), 619–60.

Index

Montgilbert, François de (1747–ca. 1814), Montagnard Convention deputy, 353, 383

Montpellier (Herault department), 111, 301, 385, 451, 457–58, 460–63, 470

Montreil (Pas-de-Calais department), 495

Moreau de Saint-Méry, Louis (1750–1819), Club Massiac apologist for slavery, 400, 403, 725

Morellet, Abbé André (1727–1819), "moderate" encyclopédiste, 62–63, 387, 614, 706

Morelly, Étienne Gabriel (ca. 1715–ca. 1755), radical philosophe, 633, 676–77; *Code de la nature*, 676

Möser, Justus (1720–94), conservative *Aufklärer*, 85

Mounier, Jean-Joseph (1758–1806), conservative constitutional monarchist leader, 48, 50, 54, 59, 77, 82, 86, 95, 673, 698, 725; and Anglophilia, 95–96; rejects "popular sovereignty," 95, 698–99; as theorist of "moderation," 82, 95–96; *Considérations sur les gouvernements et principalement sur celui qui convient à la France* (1789), 95–96, 114

Mouraille, Jean-Raymond (1721–1808), mathematician and mayor of Marseille (Nov. 1791–April 1793), 230, 434, municipal government reform, 65, 67, 76, 103

Muscadins, 438, 507, 599

Naigeon, Jacques André (1738–1810), radical philosophe, 22, 51, 63, 98, 158–60, 593, 622, 687, 697; allegiance to the Revolution, 63, 593, 706

Nancy (Lorraine; department of Meurthe-et-Moselle), 183, 425

Nantes (Loire-Atlantique department), 11, 201, 399, 451, 456, 671; and clergy, 191, 201; and Club Mirabeau, 220, 283; and merchants, 220; and *noyades*, 529; and Terror, 525, 528–29

Naples, kingdom of, 238, 288, 342, 650–54; and bishops and archbishops, 650; and nobility, 650–52; and peasantry, 650–51, 653. *See also* Italian revolutionary republics

Napoleon Bonaparte (1769–1821), 12–13, 123, 203, 395, 528, 624, 627, 642, 644, 646–47, 650, 655, 659–64, 686, 694, 696, 702; blacklisted after Thermidor, 581; in Corsica, 331, 666; and Islam, 662–66; and Life Consulate, 12; and republicanism (1792–99), 643–47, 649, 662–64, 666; restores slavery in the French Caribbean (1802), 414

National Assembly (1789–91), 10–11, 15, 25, 55–61, 73–76, 84–87, 105–7, 110–12, 148, 155, 157, 163, 169, 177, 193, 204–5, 396–99; allegedly dominated by Protestants and unbelievers, 182, 186, 202; and clergy, 188–89, 191, 194–95; and Comité de Pensions, 118; and Comité des colonies, 403; and Comité ecclésiastique, 186–87, 189–90, 194, 202; main factions of, 95–96, 107–8, 136–37, 175–76, 191, 207–8; and ultra-royalist rump, 208, 215

National Convention (Sept. 1792–1795): deadlocked (spring 1793), 281, 290, 298–99, 310–15, 358–59, 369, 425–27, 440–42, 464–65; elections for (Aug. and Sept. 1792), 264, 273–76, 316; purged and silenced (from June 1793), 503, 511, 513, 537, 572–73, 587; and Montagnard faction, 276, 282, 308, 315, 429, 505; proclaims the end of monarchy, 276–77; stifled from 2 June 1793, 452–56, 594

National Guard, 60, 63, 67, 91, 93, 130–31, 150, 165, 195–96, 204–5, 238, 463; bias of, in favour of liberal monarchy (1789–92), 153, 174, 204–5, 207; complicity of, in "September massacres," 273; democratized (July 1792), 238, 251–52, 313; under Hanriot (1793–94), 578–79, 584; after Thermidor, 605–6, 608, 627–29

national holidays. See *fêtes nationales*

natural right theories (Rousseauist), 77–78, 364, 366, 410